CULT FICTION

UNIVERSITY OF
GLOUCESTERSHIRE
at Cheltenham and Gloucester

**FRANCIS CLOSE HALL
LEARNING CENTRE**
Swindon Road Cheltenham
Gloucestershire GL50 4AZ
Telephone: 01242 714600

NORMAL LOAN

The Queen of Cheese descends . . . Betty Page, top pin-up model and
the original Sweater-Girl, 6 September 1954 (Range/Bettmann/UPI)

Cult Fiction

Popular Reading and Pulp Theory

Clive Bloom

First published 1996 by
MACMILLAN PRESS LTD
Houndmills, Basingstoke, Hampshire RG21 6XS
and London
Companies and representatives
throughout the world

ISBN 0–333–62301–0 hardcover
ISBN 0–333–62302–9 paperback

A catalogue record for this book is available
from the British Library.

10	9	8	7	6	5	4	3	2	1
05	04	03	02	01	00	99	98	97	96

Printed and bound in Great Britain by
Antony Rowe Ltd, Chippenham, Wiltshire

Published in the United States of America 1996 by
ST. MARTIN'S PRESS, INC.,
Scholarly and Reference Division
175 Fifth Avenue, New York, N.Y. 10010

ISBN 0–312–16194–8

For James and Jonathan, Natasha and Kirsty, Zack and Charlie

Contents

Acknowledgements

I would like to thank Alan Durant, Michael Walters and Middlesex University for a sustained study leave in which much of this book was written; Charmian Hearne for her editorial support; Gary Day, Greg McCue, David Pringle and Helena Blakemore for ideas over the years; Vivien Miller for research on US Census Records; Kelly A. Cornelis for her research on Mills & Boon; Steve Holland for his help in making various contacts; Lionel Fanthorpe for his inside knowledge; Antony Smith for his help in tracking down the names of certain authors; John Wolf of the Open University, Judith Champ of Kings College, London; Eleanor Wordsworth at *Reader's Digest*; Maurice Flanagan for his supreme ability to supply rare paperback material; Steve Chibnall, chair of the British Association of Paperback Collectors; finally Lesley Bloom and Susan Tourick for getting my disordered notes into proper typographic order and Anne Rafique for her editorial assistance.

The chapter on Jack the Ripper originally appeared in slightly different form in *Nineteenth-Century Suspense* edited by Clive Bloom, Brian Docherty, Jane Gibb and Keith Shand (1988); the chapter on H.P. Lovecraft appeared in *American Horror Fiction* edited by Brian Docherty (1990); the chapter on Sax Rohmer appeared in *Twentieth-Century Suspense* edited by Clive Bloom (1990); the chapter on Harry Price appeared in slightly different form in *Creepers* edited by Clive Bloom (1993). The author wishes to thank Lumiere Co-operative Press, Macmillan and Pluto Press for permission to reprint.

Part I
Et In Arcadia Ego

1
'Scuse me Mr H'officer:
An Introduction

Cult Fiction is an exploration of pulp literature and pulp mentalities: an investigation into the nature and theory of the contemporary mind in art and in life. Here the violent, erotic and sentimental excesses of contemporary life signify different facets of the modern experience played out in the gaudy pages of sensational and kitsch literature: novels, comic books, tabloid newspapers.

This book offers the reader a chance to investigate the underworld of literary production and from it find a new set of co-ordinates for questions regarding publishing and reading practices; ideas of genre; theories of commercial production; concerns regarding high and low culture, the canon and censorship; and the nature of the theories we use to explore the above areas. Concentrating on many disregarded and forgotten authors the book provides a theory of kitsch art that radically alters our perception both of literature and literary values while providing a panorama of an almost forgotten history: the history of pulp.

Pulp is not only a descriptive term for certain forms of publishing produced on poor quality paper, but it is also indicative of certain attitudes, reading habits and social concerns. For the aficionado, this literature is exemplified by those forms of magazine and paperback publication which flourished between the 1920s and 1950s in America and which should be distinguished from both dime novels, paperbacks per se and comic books. For academics, the term vaguely expresses a field of popular publishing neglected through the overemphasis placed upon canonic texts, while for cultural critics it often has meant the exemplary instance of mass culture's propensity to debase everything and exalt the lowest common denominator.

This study attempts to explore all these concerns and definitions, traverse them, broaden them and deepen them. It is axiomatic of this study that artistic movements and aesthetic concerns are intimately involved with social, commercial and perceptual history and that the formal questions we might ask cannot be asked without

3

some sense of *location* in questions necessarily not formal. As such, the study does not overemphasize the definition of genre nor that of production, nor that of social history but attempts to negotiate through these toward an opening out of the question beyond such narrow definitions of the subject.

I do, however, want to provide a dynamic model of cult fiction and of pulp – an aesthetic as well as a history of trash art which acknowledges its vibrancy and excitement and its own mores of taste, hierarchy and validity. In this way, trash art speaks for itself, but within those constituting frameworks of commercial necessity and ephemerality that mark all trash out for what it is.

One can see this book as attempting to outline a different literary history and provide a different set of aesthetic criteria in order to investigate the complexities of print as both entertainment and provider of information. Within this history of *information* I delineate a second tale of cultural and social negotiation and of Anglo-American reading habits in which the *suppression* of one form of literacy becomes a marked theme. Lastly I must stress my attempt to tease out the complex negotiations that occur within the publishing market, within literary forms and within class structures and human relationships that an investigation of this kind must take into account. Evidence for ephemeral enjoyments, including reading for pleasure (as against utility), is often thin and its assessment problematical, nevertheless I have conjectured only where a link is not available in evidence so much as in logic and where problems of structure required a paradigm offered by the evidence but ignored by other writers.

Literary history of the type found in these pages is a discipline which needs to remind itself constantly that literature is not merely historical evidence (far from it), but is of course, always itself and yet *in* history. Yet literature is a kind of historical evidence not merely for its own evolution but also for attitudes of mind. This is, therefore, a history of perception using literature as a highly specialized, highly attenuated and usually distanced evidence. Literature 'represents' only in a curiously non-imitative and non-representational manner. Thus it is itself and yet indicative of those wider movements it mediates and metamorphoses through the printed page. I have been conscientious to see literature both in and for itself and as a social force representing conditions of cultural change.

I have divided the following pages into three parts. The first part offers the work's central argument and deals with questions of taste, publishing history and definitions; the second offers examples across a limited range of texts and genres in an effort to suggest both pulp's aesthetic concerns and pulp's attitudinal concerns. Part III is a requiem not only for pulp but also for a certain theoretical adventure. As readers will see, I delineate not just a history of that underclass of literary production usually known as pulp but I also give some hints as to the wider context of pulp aesthetics or trash art with examples from further afield. Although a history of print, this also gives an opening into other areas which are related.

More ambitiously, so most problematically, I have attempted to suggest a model which incorporates Anglo-American history and reading habits to show how intimately both sides of the Atlantic have shared (and been divided by) a common language. Too many studies ignore the basic importance of this linguistic relationship in their concern for one country's literary heritage. This book is about another as yet unsung heritage and consists of a history, a general theory and a series of examples. The examples are drawn from as many areas as possible but it is inevitable that certain areas, favoured by particular readers, may be less well covered than those readers might desire. For this I excuse myself on grounds that the book is designed as an argument, not a compendium. Books and authors are referred to for their illustrative value, their significance for the argument and their intrinsic interest, and inevitably they can only act as a sample. My terms neither include nor exclude bestsellers and blockbusters but where these are better dealt with in other studies I have ignored them, unless to dispute a point or take forward an argument. 'Popular' here does not mean merely common and much of my argument is taken up with writers and books neither commonly read nor bestsellers, but nevertheless determinedly popular by definitions concerned with market forces, mass reading habits and education, class divisions and attitudes at once political, social, cultural and always aesthetic.

The reader of this book will be well aware by the time they reach the last page that it has been about the context and history of popular reading habits, but it has been more than that and I have tried to explore the hidden byways of a literary history rarely taught in academia, hidden in second-hand bookstores and often only collected by a small band of enthusiastic 'amateurs' or left even by them to be finally bought by someone like me to whom the eccentric connection may just be the right one.

In one sense these pages contain an unseen map of bookshop visits in and around London as well as phone calls to mail order dealers and an occasional trip to a convention (both as a participant and as a spectator). I am not a dedicated fanatic but a fascinated by-stander who is perhaps too ready to pick and choose, too *disengaged* ever to join the ranks of those whose life is measured in checklists, nevertheless my life too has been measured by popular fiction.

My life as an academic has divided itself between esoteric liter-ary theory and esoteric literary 'trash' – a term I use in the same way that the gay community returned to the word 'queer'. Critical essays on spy novels, thrillers, comic books and horror stories and a continued interest in the popular and ephemeral has kept me returning to the well, a loyalty I cannot shake. Years in dusty book-shops tells one, as nothing else can, that all art dies eventually and that it is indeed no less mortal than the ephemera that surrounds it and no less vulnerable to being passed over in silence by the casual browser. Only seek and you will find! Every second-hand bookshop and junk shop with its shelf of decaying and musty paperbacks is a catacomb of the undead. A visit is a type of Gray's 'Elegy', an archaeological trip into the past of the ordinary, a re-minder of one's mortality. In rereading or refinding long-forgotten and half-remembered writers one does a service not only to history but to a communal memory which is different from 'history' and which is shot through with an affection history does not feel.

But you need not get too mushy: there are huge numbers of books printed each year that are simply unreadable, some deserve forgetting and no longer exist as art but merely as history. In this book I have made choices, finding certain books either too dull or too empty for discussion; there is good and bad in everything and every pulp fan has his or her 'list' not only of the significant and worthy but also of those which keep their affection. I doubt if we can ever make the dead live again but we can give them a good send-off and perhaps in doing so learn something of the true place of the living in the schemes of social and literary culture.

I have not dealt with children's literature as a specific subcategory, indeed to do so would have been against the principles behind some of the ideas in this book. Instead, such literature is mentioned where it falls naturally within the argument in general or forms a bridge upon which adult and adolescent readers meet. It is a fact that all the arguments here rehearsed regarding adult reading matter can be applied to, or have already been applied to children's reading matter; debates over quality, taste, the canon, morality and ethical acceptability as well as questions of content and style mirror such debates elsewhere regarding literature, its cultural significance and social importance.

It is ironic that, as with publishing for adults, there has long been a tradition of wilfully refusing to acknowledge why children read certain things, in effect to rescue books from both their readers and their authors. This tradition of *denial* still prevalent today, but especially so from the 1950s to late 1970s, was in its most virulent form an unconscious equation between the reading interests of foolish middle-class boys and girls and those of the inarticulate, semi-literate adult proletarian, such imaginary creatures represented by Enid Blyton and Mickey Spillane. How else could one such critic make such an equation: '...I would as soon consider including [Enid Blyton] in a study of children's literature as I would consider including say Mickey Spillane in a literature degree course.'[1] One is inclined to ask, despite changes in current university curricula how much has, or would change?

A word must be said, given some of my later arguments, about the omission of detailed information concerning the unstamped radical press of the early eighteen-hundreds. After 1815 newspapers carried a stamp or tax duty of 4d. (four pence) which meant working people could not afford to buy them. This effectively removed the chance of such people, the working middle classes, also joining in any real political debate. From the 1830s onwards, due to internal political pressures and inspired by the July Revolution in France there appeared a new wave of illegally printed and distributed unstamped newspapers selling for 1d. (one penny). By 1836 such papers had far exceeded sales of the legitimate press, were read right across the country in both town and countryside and were driven by a dissident movement of printers, booksellers, authors and illegal distribution centres. Many hundreds of people were fined or imprisoned or both but the 'tax on knowledge' was repealed and reduced to a general rate of one penny. Thus finally ended this highly popular form of subversive publishing.

Effective as popular means of radicalizing the unenfranchised 'the Unstamped ... were [also] a colourful and strident step towards cheap journalism and cheap literature'.[2] They were designed by such means to bring their readers to 'political and economic self-awareness' of, on the one hand, the oppressions of aristocracy and monopoly, or on the other the newer oppressions of exploitation

and property.³ In each case the attempt was to elevate the reader
and to provide self-improvement and education.

While these productions could be considered an abortive attempt
to create a *national* politicized consciousness among working people they were nevertheless a highly prophetic precursor of cost-
effective production – ironically the very system they opposed.
Reading was widened and encouraged if not elevated or overtly
politicized. The reading public of the middle nineteenth century
were still parochial in their political affiliations and it was only the
monopolizing of ownership in the later years of the century that
flattened out local divergence and nationalized the political attitudes of working people now able to participate, through reading,
in a commonality of attitudes.

This commonality of attitudes, which allowed working people to
participate in national affairs, occurred later in the century in the
United States where from the 1870s a virtual state of anarchy existed
between workers and their bosses. If the presses of Hearst and
Pulitzer provided one sort of news, packed with 'personality' and
'sensation-mongering' as Matthew Arnold sourly remarked in his
essays of the 1880s (collected 1888), then the growth of populism
and radicalism during the same period also provided ground for
cheap socialist and anti-capitalist newspapers, pamphlets and
broadsheets aimed at uniting working people. Where Arnold found
'a community singularly free from the distinction of classes [and]
singularly homogeneous', as well he might having been 'sponsored'
by Andrew Carnegie, there was, in fact, a country divided on class
and ethnic lines – divisions which proved irresolvable. Blacks and
Whites read in their newspapers of suppressions and violence,
reports reaching their climax in the collapse of 1893. Such reports
and the obvious hardship of workers and their families made
socialists of such as Eugene Debs and populists of Henry Vincent
who started a journal in 1886 called *The American Non-Conformist
and Kansas Industrial Liberator*, which aimed to 'tend to the education of the labouring classes'.⁴ The *National Economist* found 100 000
readers among working people and in the South newspapers appeared with names such as *The Comrade, the Toiler's Friend* and
Revolution.⁵ Lectures were organized and books and pamphlets provided at a prodigious rate:

One gathers from yellowed pamphlets that the agrarian ideolo-
gists undertook to re-educate their countrymen from the ground

up. Dismissing 'history as taught in our schools' as 'practically valueless', they undertook to write it over – formidable columns of it, from the Greek down. With no more compunction they turned all hands to the revision of economics, political theory, law, and government.[6]

All in all, these attempts paralleled and finally blended into the Democratic Party platform, if they were not already suppressed by other means.

The legacy of the early radical press in Britain was a public able to afford nationally disseminated ideas provided, ironically, by the monopolistic ownership of press 'barons', a situation paralleled later in America. It is therefore entirely to miss the point to argue that press ownership is merely conservative, manipulative and degraded.[7] While ownership was monopolized, consumption was always a matter of *local* negotiation – readers of popular papers were and are a peculiar mixture of gullibility and shrewd refusal (what Richard Hoggart might have called 'common sense'). The radical penny press did not simply vanish but rather it went underground, absorbed into the very sensibility of British reading habits. Opposed by temperament to the very nature of pulp, the cheap radical publisher's subversive nature modified into the illicit pleasures of gaudy literature – hardly, perhaps, educational or morally elevating, but effectively democratic for all that.[8]

Finally, the reader should be warned that I do not include a specific chapter on women's romantic fiction. This area has been a 'cause' among feminist critics and social historians for sufficient time for much of the argument to have become stale and commonplace. Such publishers as Mills & Boon are also self-reflexive in their attitudes and their promotional material itself has provided a wealth of information as to their aesthetic concerns. Thus, although some areas (the cheapest women's story magazines and film-story magazines) have been less explored by critics, I have let their testimony stand except where I take issue with their findings or believe they have insufficiently credited certain evidence.

Rarely is research work, even in the humanities, carried out in isolation. During the 1980s a number of significant studies emerged from the radical left which clearly showed the complexity inherent in working with 'popular' culture and the problematic discontinuities which emerge in such work.[9] The links between culture, politics, class, gender, race and economic realities found themselves plotted in a more sophisticated way than had previously been offered by many earlier liberal or left-wing thinkers. Ultimately, nearly all these writers went on a diversionary search for a supposedly authentic lost proletarian voice, at once both popular and radical. Through generalizations regarding the linked nature of capitalist publishing and patriarchy (a history of suppression and manipulation) and a consistent refusal to really get to grips with the specific nature of such publishing, its readers and the nature of capital's internal history, the Marxist studies which emerged against the background of Thatcherism upheld a project that ultimately fell back on the old clichés of an earlier leftism.

My admiration for their exploratory abilities is offset by my inability to accept such general statements as make simplistic equations without either theoretical or carefully tested empirical evidence. While these are still important books one cannot help but think that the writers were trying hard to understand lowbrow writing but could not rid themselves of the belief that there is a *conspiracy* behind mass culture which must be *resisted*. Like the penny press of old these writers still wanted serious licit reading, in a word, legitimation. They risked – so obvious in their examples of unread proletarian print (however interesting) – losing the very notion of the popular they wished to save, itself vulgar, intractable, Technicolor and consistently resistant to the patronage of such theory.

My own study is primarily an analysis of literature determined in its outlook by concerns which are both aesthetic, sociological and to a lesser, though significant extent economic. In using this mixture of approaches I have tried to 'get inside' certain literary problems which are seen either as unproblematic or which have, in my opinion, been prematurely closed off. Withal, this is not merely a study of literature and history for it is informed by Marxist debate on the relationships between structure and agency and class and community. My own work is Marxian rather than Marxist and my conclusions are far more determined by ideas concerning popular *accommodations* than popular revolution. I have seen the capitalist mentality in a kinder light than Marxist critics.

If it is true that explanations concerning production and class are necessarily central to the debate conducted here, nevertheless they are not sufficient in themselves as explanations of the complex range of perceptual nuances which may be encountered; what answers for humankind in the aggregate may not correspond at all to the peculiar circumstances of men and women individually and what has significance statistically may not signify for any one person (whose relation to the statistical norm will always be aberrant). The residue left after all else is exhausted by the discussion of production and class must give us a lived experience which cannot simply be reabsorbed into either of the two categories. Equally, Marx's jaundiced comments on the 'nightmare on the brain' of 'the tradition of all the dead generations' fails to recognize the positive significance of the plurality of traditions between individuals, families, communities and even nations and the constant remaking of history by the present generation in its own image and no longer in 'borrowed language' able, in a word, to liberate itself from the dead hand of the past. Yet to step into the absolute present is not a liberation but a futile attempt to step out of history itself and thereby into the real nightmare of a continuous contemporaneity where human destiny would be once and for all out of the hands of humankind and history itself cancelled. Curiously this is the dream of a rapacious capitalism and revolutionary Marxism. This book narrates one aspect of the tale of the continuous present.

My own claims and comments I hope add to the debate above, especially in terms of sectional groupings and with regard to urban and rural fantasies inter- and *intra*-class. If such grand claims are at all valid then they are only so in relation to the debate they may open rather than to any definitive answers they might give.

I am only too aware of the debt I owe to enthusiastic workers both academic and amateur upon whose efforts this book draws. In this regard I am conscious of the warning recently issued by Brian Stableford in his introduction to a work by one of Britain's best 'amateur' pulp literary investigators:

> The Mushroom Jungle – or, more likely, a semi-sanitised, semi-plagiarism by some academic hack who specialises in repackaging the research of better men – will take its place on university reading lists.[10]

Suitably chastened, I hope this effort will be neither a semi-plagiarism nor a mere repackaging. The comments on academic authors I leave to the reader to judge.

2

Throwing Rice at Brad and Janet:
Illicit, Delinquent Pleasures

This is a book about popular fictions and pulp fantasies. At one level this is also a book which attempts to redirect a certain critical attention toward 'trash' art, situate it *within* popular culture generally and consider its aesthetic. On another level this is a book about taste and popular perception in a social as well as artistic history determined by commercialism and urbanization but lived in the sphere of the acutely personal and private. Just as with all popular arts, pulp is a moveable feast since it can be appropriated by and on behalf of the hierarchists of taste at any particular time and thus taken out of its pulp status. Pulp is both a desire for respectability and a refusal. As I argue later, its legitimacy as pulp is correlative with its illegitimacy as 'serious' art. Hence it is both forced into illicitness and is always illicit.[1] But the delights of trash art are always contrary – at once risqué and conformist – always out of the grasp of legitimation. When you have defined them, then, like street talk, they slip away to appear elsewhere in their own secret language of seduction.

If what is explored here is only partial the nature of the task is to some extent overwhelming, for a vast archaeological programme would have to be undertaken if the consequences of pulp and all its many contributing factors, not to say biographies of its mainly ignored and anonymous producers were to be fully explored and put into some sort of order. Such an exploration is one in which trash art is not seen as a mere sociological symptom nor is it reduced to a dull and inconsequential set of formal problems but is rather understood as vibrantly alive both socially and aesthetically. It also emerges as the aesthetic context within which much that is of consequence politically and otherwise is played out on a flickering and evanescent stage of ghostly ephemeral objects. If it doesn't live up to carnival, it does, at least make a spectacular parade. Pulp, like 'rock 'n' roll works as a common experience and private obsession', as Greil Marcus, citing critic Jim Miller has pointed out.[2]

Any good critic of such ephemeral and fleeting material must be alive to its nature and not try to redeem or rehabilitate; the canon can take care of itself and is sufficient to itself. I do not wish to widen the canon. I want the canon to define my own interests as specific, different, and enjoyably *illicit*. We may again talk of pleasure and about the vulgar (in its original sense) something alive because crude and because totally contemporary. As such I am the complete fan and the ironic spectator and I fully comprehend the disjunction needed to uphold the aesthetic of temporality (the aesthetic of immediacy and the ephemeral) and the inquiry of the historical (finding continuities and moments of breakage and rupture). Every fan knows this: that the cult following preserves the ephemeral traces of the newly forgotten. The cult is religiosity after the fact, recognition almost too late – almost but not quite. At this point, the cult itself re-enacts in itself the drift of that which it hopes to preserve at its shrine. Which is only to say that pleasures that are fleeting are hard to recall. If Betty Page is the queen of trash art then she will return speaking Klingon.

Doubling back upon itself, the cult obsession provides for the ever-present reinvoking of capitalism as personal destiny. Hence QVC, the worldwide telesales channel, sells teach yourself Klingon tapes to those whose personal destinies and most intimate expressions are fully integrated into the anarchic capitalist loop. Nor does this produce a bliss so moronic that it cannot also be self-reflexive. As Nick Hornby has pointed out in a recent book about English soccer, obsessives have no choice: they have to lie on occasions like this.

> If we told the truth every time, then we would be unable to maintain relationships with anyone from the real world. We would be left to rot with our Arsenal programmes or our collection of original blue-label Stax records or our King Charles spaniels, and our two-minute daydreams would become longer and longer and longer until we lost our jobs and stopped bathing and shaving and eating, and we would lie on the floor in our filth rewinding the video again and again in an attempt to memorise by heart the *whole* of the commentary, including David Pleat's expert analysis, for the night of 26th of May 1989. (You think I had to look the date up? Ha!) The truth is this: *for alarmingly large chunks of an average day, I am a moron.*[3]

Few critics, as will be seen in these pages, are able to maintain that ability to be both simultaneously inside and outside this trash art/popular aesthetic and also able to see the gradations within the popular itself. It is a difficult job to recognize pulp for what it may be (but so many incarnations) and to balance celebration with cerebration – to want to explore what to many is at best repetitive and at worst abject – and to find instead consequence in the fleeting and a sympathy for the mundane. It is banality which is in some ways most surreal, and pulp takes us into the most bizarre corners of the most banal worlds – freakishness, the irrational, morbid eroticism, pathological conditions of all sorts, Martians, crop circles, spiritualism, UFOs, vampires, costumed superheroes, love at first sight; money, success, revenge – in short a whole other universe which is at once commonsensical and crackpot. Readers are alive to the fantasies of money and sexuality in an S and F fantasy of the modern world and yet they are prepared to accept Fortean explanations for almost any natural or physical phenomenon. If the high priestess is the late clairvoyant Doris Stokes, then the age is forever Edwardian, the war always the first but the goal the glitz and razzmatazz of Hollywood consumer goods, *Hello* magazine, houses in the country and a wild promiscuity lived only and happily in the head. Pulp is essentially a benevolent, conservative and godless form determined by chance and luck.

Pulp is public expression lived out privately. If human nature is at once private and historical (that is, subject to change) pulp may have more than art to tell us about ourselves. Pulp is the child of capitalism and is tied to the appearance of the masses and the urban, mediums of the nineteenth and twentieth centuries. As such it is the embodiment of capitalism aestheticized, consumerized and *internalized*. Hence it is both oppressive and liberating, both mass manipulation and anarchic individualistic destiny. Pulp is our daily, natural heightened experience: a product and a channel for a moment in human self-consciousness and its aspirations lived in the banal and in the now.

Real pulp is a refusal of bourgeois consciousness and bourgeois forms of realism. It is capitalistic, anarchic, entrepreneurial and individualist and it found expression not only in the gaudy covers of pulp magazines, cheap paperbacks and comic books with their aliens, gangsters and silk-stockinged floozies in our century, but also in the flimsy chapbooks and ballad sheets of years before which celebrated the adventures of Jack Sheppard, Dick Turpin or Jack the

Ripper. Here fiction and fact are both fantasy. Here the *Police Gazette* meets the *National Enquirer* and neither fact nor fiction can any longer be trusted.

Here also, authors become entrepreneurial producers, as this characteristic but possibly apocryphal anecdote from the life of Jeffrey Archer illustrates.

> 'I've tried property', Jeffrey went on, 'and that didn't work. I've tried shares and that didn't work. I've tried all the things that everyone else has tried and they didn't work'. . . .
>
> 'The only thing I can think of is to write a bestseller'. . . .
>
> 'A bestseller', Jeffrey went on, 'which turns into a movie. That's the only way of making enough money to sort out my problems.'
>
> 'Jeffrey', said [Adrian] Metcalfe, 'you can't write!'
>
> 'Don't be ridiculous, Adrian. It's nothing to do with writing, I'll *produce* a bestseller. I can tell a good story. I'm convinced of it.'[4]

If authors become producers and readers become consumers this is neither a mindless slavery to the market nor a revolution in advanced taste. Rather it marks a style of negotiation and rapprochement in *democratic* mass experience. For instance, for Greil Marcus popular music offered both commercial opportunity and personal freedom within a mass consensus:

> The Beatles and their fans played out an image of utopia, of a good life, and the image was that one could join a group and by doing so not lose one's identity as an individual but find it: find one's own voice.[5]

No really authoritarian states can stand pulp culture – it reeks of anarchy and nonconformity and subversion. Thus authoritarian states ban such corruption and condemn rock 'n' roll alongside comic books, erotic literature, fast food, Levi jeans, James Bond, US soap operas and Coca Cola. No authoritarian state has produced a quarter decent rock group – anarchic, uncontrollable, open to cult status (a challenge to the ruling oligarchy), sexually explosive and ever youthful. For Marxist-Leninism, spiritualism and rock 'n' roll were one and the same thing, not surprising that authoritarians can find themselves in Shakespeare and Dante but cannot tolerate Batman comics read by the lightning flashes of rock technology.

Such accommodation as can be made with great Western art in authoritarian regimes leads them to overvalue realist, and by implication bourgeois, fictions – ones that can be incorporated into the body of the authoritarian aesthetic. Part of the internal contradiction of modern authoritarian regimes is that their artistic taste is abysmal, hierarchist and propagandist: the populace must be educated, moralized, always sit bolt upright. The result is bad art and bad faith against which pulp seems (and is) liberating and terrifyingly complex (bewildering to newly 'enfranchised' peoples released from subservience). Pulp acts as a corrosive and subversive force in totalitarian countries for it represents democracy and capitalism and individualism redefined within a new loose and anarchic collective. In democratic culture it has an essentially longer and uninterrupted history in which subversion is now an illicit behaviour always seeking accommodation within a progressively decentred consumerism. When it seeks bourgeois status (a rare event) it does so only by proxy and then only temporarily.

It is an interesting irony that pulp thrives on the fantasy *representation* of authoritarian, fascistic figures and situations, situations simplified into violence and erotica. Pulp never was the apparently totalitarian brainwashing that George Orwell warned against in his reading of James Hadley Chase's *No Orchids for Miss Blandish*. Quite to the contrary, pulp represents an anarchic edge on the margin of bourgeois propriety and at the centre of modern consumerist multiplicity. This, if anything, is the totalitarianism of an unrealized and groundless space of endless choices of *no consequence*.[6]

High art has since the beginning of this century attempted to assimilate pulp culture into its regime. T.S. Eliot's 'Fragment of An Agon' was, originally less pretentiously entitled 'Wanna go home Baby'.[7] In the field of the visual arts the work of Marcel Duchamp and Stuart Davis gave birth to those 1960s pop artists whose aim was to make pulp over in their image. They made themselves respectable but did nothing for pulp. Marcel Duchamp's found objects – the flotsam of pulp culture, were always irreducible, always 'wrong' – a continual refusal to assimilate into mainstream art consciousness, that same consciousness that Stuart Davis's *Lucky Strike* and *Odol* of 1921 and 1924 would attempt to bind to serious art and Western iconography.

It may not be surprising that Davis's successors, whether pastiching benday dots as with Roy Lichtenstein, or satirizing painting by numbers as in Andy Warhol, distanced themselves further from the *irreducibily* popular, ending up as superior commentators for bourgeois gallery visitors. The pulp psychedelia of 1960s London (of which the Beatles shop sported a considerable amount) was irretrievably lost under layers of white paint. Andy Warhol's work remained – a collector of pulp freakdom, but only an occasional participant. Warhol's factory was art *refusing* its subject matter, a true élitism from which all but the in crowd were excluded, the public works acting merely to sanitize and control pulp and its own internal aesthetic in order to repackage it as decoration and as safe simulation.

In the realm of cinema and television, director/producer David Lynch has endlessly explored the bizarre nature of smalltown American banality. From the crazy schlock of *Erasurehead* to the opening sequence of *Blue Velvet* where a man aimlessly waves to us from his fire engine, to the television series *Twin Peaks* to *Fire Walk with Me*, Lynch is determined to find the pattern in the Formica of the roadside diner. For Lynch, pulp culture is essentially both familiar and totally alien and in the complex mixture of these two emerges an innocence of the banal, a type of transcendent goodness. Despite the evil that lurks in the angles of Lynch's imagination, innocence is continually proclaimed. At the end of *Fire Walk with Me*, Lynch's prequel to *Twin Peaks*, Laura Palmer meets the angel of love helped by 'spirit' guide Dale Cooper in the Black Lodge: smalltown USA is returned to its innocence and each particular dark history rewritten or erased in love and salvation. The last scene of *Fire Walk with Me* is itself schlock, sentimental and pulp – Lynch stops being a commentator and joins in.

Like Divine, (but also obviously quite unlike Divine!) La Cicciolina is pure pulp fantasy – an exotic and unlikely latin Betty Page (see Chapter 7). But now Betty Page has married the foremost pop artist of the *fin de siècle*. Jeff Koons is his own consumer durable. Koons (and La Cicciolina no doubt – and Betty Page) understands the relationship between art and the market. He knows that late twentieth-century art cannot *be art* without the market. The subject of such art cannot therefore be otherwise than the market itself – consumer culture at its most vulnerable and effective:

> I have always used cleanliness and a form of order to maintain for the viewer a belief in the essence of the eternal, so that the viewer does not feel threatened economically. When under economic pressure you start to see disintegration around you. Things

do not remain orderly. So I have always placed order in my work not out of a respect for minimalism, but to give the viewer a sense of economic security. [. . .] Where I see art going, its exchange value, its economic substructure, will be removed: it will function solely as a means of support and security. From this point of view, my work has strong biological implications: the encasement of the vacuum cleaners with the ideas of removal and protection, and the equilibrium tanks with water suspending basketballs – these are all very womblike.[8]

Such a configuration creates not tension but an essential innocence – the artist again speaks of spirituality, innocence and love *because* of market forces. Such consumer theology for Koons is essentially televangelism with Koons the Messiah of the ordinary.[9] 'Everybody grew up surrounded by this material. I try not to use it in any cynical manner. I use it to penetrate mass consciousness – to communicate to people.'[10]

Yet whether creating *Popples* (1988) or *Poodle* (1991) Koons's work in its heart is a refusal – a sleight of hand which, like all fakes, cannot sustain (oh, yes, pulp is always genuine – its fans are never fooled). The use of hard materials and shiny surfaces which reflect the viewer's helplessness deny the very claims Koons makes for universality and connection. Koons's works contain, indeed proclaim the pure surface of pop culture in the same way as Baudrillard's proclamation of seduction or Guy Debord's society of the spectacle where everything is shiny, surface, depthless and meaningless: a society for the mindless lost in a Disneyworld run by ad agencies and fuelled by Sprites. Yet pulp culture, when *lived*, is all depth, passion, erotics. If it is innocent, its innocence is that of the damned who don't yet know it, not of the saved who have been rescued by consumer artefacts in upmarket galleries. That's what makes Koons so sterile compared to, say the early graffiti of Keith Haring. When Koons declares 'Embrace your past' he knows there is only the present.[11] But all pulp cultures know their past – its lineage is preserved, protected and cherished but only for the initiated. All pulp has history – only complacent artists miss the point through the violence of benevolent pastiche. Pulp is all depth and depth as style – as that very surface drawn down into itself.

In *Manet* one of a serious of works completed in 1991 of the artist and his wife copulating, Koons is shown licking La Cicciolina's open thighs – Koons acts the outrageous artist but La Cicciolina, dressed in lace and white high heels, her pubis air-brushed clean, pouts the pout of the pulp queen she is – she alone understands the pulp impulse, its trash art aesthetic. Koons wishes to save pop culture and the pulp erotic by making it into safe, married love – innocent, spiritual, homely. His later work has puppies, children and kittens. Yet his work breaks the very respectability pulp craves (its own irony) – this is not pulp because it is too *crude* and too explicit. In La Cicciolina's fake orgasm and airbrushed nudity she alone understands the heart of trash art – (Think of the real eroticism and humour and innocence of the still available poster of a tennis player scratching her naked bottom). La Cicciolina is a symbol of the illicitness of pulp, while Koons is the benevolent authoritarian restoring order to his wife's tease. La Cicciolina is authentic cheesecake, whilst Koons is anarchic – entrepreneurial pop promoter. In their alliance is the very accommodation and refusal at the heart of pop culture and trash art.

It is this accommodation and uneasiness between commercial interest and aesthetic or ethical goal which marks literary works in a way that other forms avoid. The printed medium since the seventeenth century and certainly since the eighteenth has maintained the closest and most necessary links between entrepreneurial activity and cultural definition. The entrepreneurial act links the printer-publisher of the eighteenth century to the author-producer of the twentieth. It is no coincidence that Max Weber in his search for the spirit of capitalism found it in America during the eighteenth century and in the figure of Benjamin Franklin whose life was that of a printer-publisher (as was that of his brother) and who was responsible for the first major popular work of American literature *Poor Richard's Almanack* which was at once cheaply produced and widely consumed by a growing population. It was not a work of spontaneous folk art but of commercial, calculated material distributed for profit and determined by print. This was predicated on the *primacy* of reading and literacy and only secondarily on oral repetition. It is America's first work of mass literature for a large and largely heterogeneous society held together by printed news and factual information. It is therefore no coincidence that Franklin's autobiography moves medieval hagiography into the realm of personal anecdote and democratic remembrance. Franklin represents the movement from the craftsman-artisan to the individualist-entrepreneur and can be seen to be unaware of either monopoly capital or corporate capital in the modern sense. The individualist-entrepreneur could equally be a gentleman. Thus Franklin closes the gap between individual endeavour and mass aspiration – the personal and public spheres – through the matter of print.

The links between mass literacy and personal aspiration, eccentric desires and public requirements always proved unbridgeable when the medium was print – public duty being abandoned in favour of craftsmanship and inspiration. This was in no little part due to the essential intervention of capitalist activity in the realm of printed aesthetics. It should not be forgotten how many respectable publishers and proprietors began their lives in the underworld of publishing for a mass or 'semi-literate' readership. Rupert Murdoch, after all, financed *The Times* from profits earned at *The Sun*. A previous entrepreneurial newsman, Alfred Harmsworth, the future Lord Northcliffe, proprieter of *The Times* from 1908 and one of Britain's greatest media magnates, began as a journalist who dealt in anecdote and trivia and was the founder of *Answers to Correspondents on Every Subject Under the Sun* which specialized in sensationalist competitions and sold at a penny an issue. Nor should it be forgotten that his bedside reading was *The Newgate Calendar*, nor that his career began with George Newnes proprietor of both *Tit Bits* and the *Strand*.[12]

Through such publications the new reading public satisfied its curiosity about the world and itself; curiosity about self now competed with public duty. During the age of criminalization the world of Newgate already represented a sentimental nostalgia for a history determined by hero robbers and larger-than-life thief takers. Harmsworth's personality was already sentimentalized in parallel with and no less than his readers'. Where Marx and Engels saw the masses, Harmsworth and his brother saw also the individual. It was Marx, not Harmsworth, who opposed the popular – the two attitudes forged in the reading room of the British Library and in Fleet Street marked out the contest for the medium of print.

This contest, marked out by growing ethical and social qualms, can be seen enacted in the most unexpected places. Owners of middlebrow or even 'society' magazines might go downmarket to earn quick money. Even H.L. Mencken who was co-owner of *The Smart Set* was not indifferent to the mass-market sales enjoyed by *Detective Story Magazine* which had benefited from social trends after World War I.

The disillusionment that followed the war, the frustration over the mushrooming gangster control of the cities affected the detective story as much as it did mainstream fiction. And the 1920s occupation with the American language, the dissatisfaction with the Victorian rhetoric and polite exposition was nowhere more strongly felt than among the writers of private eye stories.[13]

Attempting to compensate for uneven sales Mencken began *Black Mask* in 1920. Highly successful and hugely influential, the magazine proved an embarrassment for Mencken who referred to it as 'our new louse'. He finally sold the enterprise and returned to defending culture.

This two-tiered publishing and reading system was repeated on both sides of the Atlantic. However, by the middle twentieth century even though many entrepreneurial and opportunistic Victorian publishers had consolidated their position and become large corporate enterprises they gave rise to a flourishing subsystem of pulp publishers which existed alongside them. Such publishers included Thorpe & Porter and E.H. and Irene Turney in Britain who between them ran a stable of extraordinarily named pulp authors who enjoyed universal success in the aftermath of World War II and the early years of the welfare state – years in which American imports were restricted.

Even the Booker Prize, established in 1968 in Britain to ratify the art of the novel was the consequence of a shrewd move made to establish a public profile and respectability for a long-time food business. The prize grew out of an idea by Tom Maschler and Graham C. Greene of Jonathan Cape. Cape had bought Ian Fleming's *Casino Royale* and Fleming had created a company called Glidrose to protect potential profits. Booker chairman Jock Campbell who was a friend of Fleming, bought the company and put Booker into the publishing business. Originally named Artists Services, Booker Books already represented a number of authors by 1968 and had also acquired 51 per cent of the rights to Agatha Christie. The entire sequence of events had been determined as much by commercial interest as by aesthetic concern.[14]

If significant authors were accorded the privilege of such prizes others had this recognition refused both by working practice and by social and cultural expectation. What recognition, and by what hierarchy of definitions can one begin to bring to visibility the writers who were refused canonic status and whose style was demoted to mere technical skill? Such writers, even those who are popular classics (a bizarre status), are refused a meaningful place within the fluctuations of literary culture. At best, they become sociologically interesting, at worst they become pathological cases.

If Robert Louis Stevenson, John Buchan and Arthur Conan Doyle, Agatha Christie and Ian Fleming are second-league popular classics, what becomes of Sidney Horler, Guy Thorne, William Le Queux or Sax Rohmer who are remembered but rarely read, or Barbara Cartland, Catherine Cookson or (from a quite different direction) horror writer Shaun Hutson, who are all read but certainly not recognized, or the likes of early Mills & Boon authors Joyce Dingwall and Kathryn Blair who are totally forgotten alongside so many others who nevertheless made a living out of print. Indeed, how does one deal in any real sense with writers such as 'Bartimeus', 'Taffrail', 'Seamark'*, 'Seaforth' and 'Dam Buster' or the anonymous authors of *The Man who Killed Hitler* of 1939?† Moreover, unless we are driven to sociology or matters of taste it is only with difficulty that we are able to speak 'academically' about such authors as 'Hank Janson', 'Ben Sarto' and 'Paul Renin' (all pseudonyms), or the multiple authorial enterprise of Nick Carter, or of 'Desmond Reid', the name given to all stories needing editing for the *Sexton Blake Library* and which linked a large number of writers including Michael Moorcock.[15] Moreover, how does one approach those well-written novelizations of the 1920s to 1950s, published by Dell among others and based on successful plays and films or even those more recent novels based on *Star Trek, Dr Who* or the Warhammer gamesworld? Is 'bastardization' all we can speak of? And in such a light doesn't the work of Ernest Hemingway or Nathanael West seem to have more in common with Dashiell Hammett, W.R. Burnett, Cornell Woolrich and the movies than with Henry James or Jane Austen. And isn't it this which precisely locates their power and place as literature?

What emerges is a fluctuating field, a set of possibilities rather than a set of results: a network as well as a hierarchy.

---

* 'Seamark' was actually Austin J. Small. He was a bestselling Hodder & Stoughton author until the 1950s, yet he has not enjoyed any bibliographic attention even by compilers of encyclopaedias on popular fiction. He wrote thrillers and romances and contributed to the *Strand Magazine*. For information about 'Seamark' see the article by J.E. Miller, 'Mystery Maker' in *Million* (Nov–Dec 1991) pp. 28–9.
† The actual authors of this book were Dean Southern Jennings, Ruth Landshoff and David Malcolmson. It was published by T. Werner Laurie in London and sported a swastika on its title page. This book should not be confused with one of the same name by Robert Page Jones published in 1980.

After all Dashiell Hammett himself wrote the syndicated comic strip 'Secret Agent X-9' and (partially) the radio series 'The Adventures of Sam Spade,' while William Faulkner worked on the scripts of *The Road to Glory* and *Land of the Pharaohs* . . . It's easy for a critic to make a clean distinction between the accomplished art of *Red Harvest* and *Sanctuary* . . . and such expendable trash as 'Secret Agent X-9' or *Land of the Pharaohs*, but in the American cultural web they are interwoven densely and inextricably.

The paperbacks provide just such a stew of high and low, vigorous and decayed; . . . In short, they partake of the characteristic America. It is useless to speak of 'high art,' 'personal art,' 'folk art,' 'commercial art,' or 'exploitation'; in the living situation, they all float about in the same pond.[16]

We are then confronted with the question of why *serious* novels do not last. What life is left in Joyce Cary or Hugh Walpole?

Mackinley Kantor, a pulp writer turned respectable novelist, pointed out the nature of these pulp writers' lives and the immensely complex mixture of writing talents and temperaments that participated.

Of these, the first group is much the largest. These are professional pulp writers – men and women whose talents for simple story telling at a rapid pace are profound, and whose output is amazing. They write hundreds of thousands of words every year. Most of them never land in the big money, but average from two to ten thousand dollars a year. A very few, relying on dictaphones and batteries of stenographers, manage to make considerably more than that. But these are freaks – minor, unsung Edgar Wallaces, who work by graph and by chart, who manufacture stories at a sweat-shop pace.

In the second class come young writers on the way up: people whose capabilities do not as yet permit them entry to the better markets, and who regard the cheap magazine market solely as a means towards an end. They write with intent and ambitious gaze fixed upon the *Saturday Evening Post* and *Cosmopolitan* and the *American Magazine*. Even in their angry days of struggle and reluctant apprenticeship, they firmly believe that their stories are good enough for the more expensive magazines; unless they need a quick cheque for a few dollars in a great hurry, they will send their manuscripts around to all the better markets before they have any truck with the pulps. As their skill improves, more and more frequently these writers have their stories accepted by the better magazines and eventually the one-cent, two-cents-a-word crime and detective and adventure story magazines become stained little steps in the ladder beneath and behind them.

Then there's the dismal third group: a few unfortunates who may have achieved a certain popularity in slick paper at one time, or perhaps in the book world, but now – unable to continue meeting the excruciating demands of the 'class' editors and the 'class' public – are compelled to slide back into the pulp field from which they had once fondly imagined themselves forever emancipated.[17]

And then there are those entirely marginal writers who earned a living or a part living through writing, whose work sold regularly, who themselves were neither merely eccentric nor spurred on by simple vanity and who must be accounted for if a theory of literature is to have any meaning. In these writers can be found traits which may confirm or question the nature of the literary *per se*. By any account these writers need to be situated both in regard to the canonic and in regard to the *popularly* canonic. Excluded in *all* accounts of literature's history, disregarded by critics and usually unknown to academics such works and their authors belong to a twilit existence where their very act of writing and their publisher's commitment to market their work seem, as if by magic, to cancel by those acts their value either as books or even as products. Removed from the land of the living the readers of such books are ignored or spirited away as the 'masses'. Through such means a wider aesthetic, much cruder and racier at its margins but possibly more vigorous, is duly impoverished.

These 'invisible' writers and their forgotten publishers produced an imaginative space at once banal and luxuriant, naive and yet oddly complex. Somewhere between the written culture of the nineteenth century and the visual culture of the late twentieth, these writers act as an historical link which is also and at the same time an aesthetic link in its appeal to readers sophisticated in the media of film and television and perhaps only merely competent in the realm of the written. In the marginal world of the pulp magazine and the throwaway paperback is the essence of the imagination of our times. Far more than in the stylistic contrivances of the modernists here exists, warts and all, the core of the modern sensorium – our imaginative life lived in the instant and the contemporary as well as the moral and the conservative.

the pulp-created genres – science fiction, horror, private eye, Western, superhero – now dominate not only popular literature but every sort of mass entertainment, from movies and television to comic books. This legacy will remain long after the last of the pulp magazines themselves – haphazardly saved and physically unsuited for preservation – have all turned to dust.[18]

One genre above all others exists to explore the contemporary and the futuristic and here too in the interstices of the mainstream popular the marginalized writer can be found. Two such are Robert Lionel Fanthorpe and H(orace) B(owne) Fyfe and their respective books *Phenomena X* (*sic*) and *D-99* which may stand as examples both of the work of these authors and as indices of some of the issues suggested in this brief discussion.

Lionel Fanthorpe turned 60 in 1995. A resident of Cardiff, but born in Norfolk, Fanthorpe's writing career began when he was only 17 with the publication of his first novel in 1952. Contracted to publisher John Spenser, Fanthorpe was to produce considerably more than a hundred books on science fiction, fantasy and the supernatural using 17 house 'names' including John E. Muller (the name may be a corruption of Johnny Weissmuller), the one under which *Phenomena X* appeared. Indeed, most of his output appeared between 1957 and 1966 with book titles being generated by the publisher or the author, the tape machine replacing the typewriter, speed dictation (which sometimes saw a book produced within days) and a total disregard for proof-reading or professional checking. Fanthorpe's career coincides with and is an integral part of the pulp fiction publishing world in Britain in the late 1940s and early 1950s in which small-scale publishers (the 'mushroom' publishers) flourished. With an astonishing ability to produce exciting and readable ephemeral literature, Fanthorpe's works appealed to a broad, (probably young male and often working-class) readership, although they also would have appealed to more literate middle-class school boys. Stocked regularly at Smith's Station Book Stalls, such literature also sold well at seaside resorts in Britain especially as holiday or escapist reading as a recent novel by Gordon Burn, *Alma Cogan* recreates, and as the central character comments:

Books, like churches and classical music, have always made me feel turned in on myself and involuntarily gloomy. It gives me no pleasure at all to say it, but there's hardly a book that I've started at the beginning and read all the way through.

The only exceptions are the American pulps, the paperback shockers which circulated on ... long train journeys ... in the fifties. They completed my education.

Like violets, and small saucers of prawns and whelks, they were sold by men with trays around the pubs in Soho and the equivalent areas of the bigger towns, and this contributed to the sense of illicitness I always felt about them. 'Any health mags, love stories?'

I always picked them up from where they were lying in a studiedly casual way and read them with a growing feeling of guilt and a packed hotness behind the eyes. . . .

Sin Circus, Shame Slave – She knew the little tricks that fan lust in men and women. *One Hell of a Dame* – The naked story of lusty-bodied Sheila whose uncontrollable desire put her name in lights. *Resort Girl. Diamond Doll. She Had To Be Loved. Gay Scene* – Every time a man had her it was rape. But with other women it was love. Gutters of lust ran wild in this *Sex Town*.

Along with the American magazines you found on sale at some station bookstalls – *Zipp, Abandon, Caress, Hollywood Frolics* – these were titles which struck me then as a kind of concentrate of eroticism. (And recalling them now, I have to say, still give me a certain frisson.)

(chapter 4)

It comes as a surprise to find that many print runs of these cheap paperbacks were often in excess of 10 000 copies (although returns are not accounted for), such figures far exceeding the print run of 'respectable' novel-writers unless they were lucky enough to have become bestsellers. High publishing runs were normal within the pulp industry regardless of the author's name, indeed house names acted as substitutes for author's names, replacing them with *brand names* – markers of product identity, clues to a book's contents and guarantors of excitement and escape. Here the author's name is a controlled trade mark, the name of the actual author effaced in order to give them a house identity which would repay them by prolonging their writing life.

By 1966 when Fanthorpe had finished with John Spenser he had produced, under a series of names, most of their fantasy and science fiction list and he has produced to date almost 200 novels, technical works, studies of unsolved mysteries, Celtic mythology and ecclesiastical studies (Fanthorpe is an ordained priest in the Church of Wales). Much of his vast output was produced part-time when he was a teacher.

Horace Bowne Fyfe was born in Jersey City in 1918 and began his career as a pulp writer in 1940 with the publication of his first short science fiction tale for *Astounding Science-Fiction*. Thereafter he produced 60 tales, many about the 'Bureau of Slick Tricks', a terrestrial secret organization set up to defeat alien plots. The only novel he produced, *D-99* (1962) continued these tales in a light-hearted manner in which 'a host of confused, outsmarted, and frantic aliens' prove no match for human ingenuity.[19] In *D-99* aliens are all referred to as 'BEMS', shorthand for bug-eyed monsters. Unlike Fanthorpe, Fyfe produced no more stories and seems to have stopped writing soon after.

In many ways it would have been impossible for Fanthorpe to flourish without the foundations having been laid a decade previously by Fyfe and the pulp science fiction produced in the United States. Fanthorpe and others 'translated' this work into an English setting. The fascination with alien civilizations, BEMS, ray guns, technological innovation and futurology (for good or ill), flying saucers and distant galaxies was a product of and a stimulus to the notion and nature of modernity in the 1930s to 1950s: The future was engineered, technological, progressive and *endless*, tempered only during the late 1940s and 1950s by a Cold War mentality. (Could it not also be said that the propaganda of dehumanization aimed at the Soviet Union during the Cold War was at its foundation a replotting of the alien empire pulp magazine stories of the 1930s and 1940s, a re-coordination of the popular imagination?)

Behind such writers as Fyfe stood figures like John W. Campbell Jr. Technologically educated, although an unsuccessful scientist, Campbell was an enthusiast of modernity, a technocrat and a futurist. As editor of *Astounding Science-Fiction* he discouraged the 'gothic' and promoted tales in which scientific prediction had a logical imaginative setting within tales of electronic innovation, social engineering and the exploration of the possibilities of a harnessed physics. Nevertheless Campbell was intelligent enough to recognize the potential of Fritz Lieber Jr.'s satiric rethinking of the Conan tales of R.E. Howard. It is to Lieber we owe the term 'sword and sorcery'. Among Campbell's other authors could be numbered Isaac Asimov, Arthur C. Clarke, Theodore Sturgeon and A.E. Van Vogt and it is no coincidence that L. Ron Hubbard, then a successful pulp author, should first publish his ideas on *Dianetics* (space-age therapy) in the pages of Campbell's magazine.

By the mid-1950s, during the heyday of both British pulp writing and science fiction and as Lionel Fanthorpe and H.B. Fyfe were respectively pursuing their careers as authors, the very nature of the genre and its broad inclusiveness were being questioned. 'Serious' science fiction as a type of 'white' propaganda for technological change (an educational tool) would now be separated from the pulp dreams of *Phenomena X* or the Bureau of Slick Tricks: The debate reached international proportions, as Patrick Parrinder has pointed out:

> Typical of the time was a paper by the astronomer Patrick Moore which inspired a lengthy debate at the 1955 UNESCO conference on the dissemination of scientific knowledge. Moore argued that each country should set up a science fiction selection board, so that novels distinguished by 'scientific soundness' (together with a category of scientifically unsound novels thought to possess 'wholesome' qualities of literary merit) could be given a stamp of approval. If this were done, science fiction could play a useful part in the propagation of knowledge, thanks to its ability to reach readers in urgent need of instruction who seldom if ever read a factual work.[20]

By the time C.P. Snow came to give his lecture on 'the Two Cultures' writers like Fanthorpe and Fyfe had already joined the aesthetically unmentionable even within their own chosen genre: the fictionalized dreams of scientific progress. By a twist of fate the exclusion of such writers did little to promote science *within* the genre, indeed by the late 1980s: 'the aspiring science fiction writer, a contributor to *Fantasy and Science Fiction, Interzone* or *Isaac Asimov's*, is more likely to be an English teacher than a research student in physics.'[21]

Phenomena X is a ripping yarn concerning Dolores (yes, Dolores!) Foster who works in an electronics laboratory as a computer operator with her bespectacled colleague Garth (yes, Garth!) Hainforth. Walking along the road one day Dolores finds a mysterious brooch in the gutter. The brooch seems to contain within it myriad shifting patterns and she decides to wear it to a cocktail party thrown by the weirdly sinister Tony Delmont. A stranger with bizarrely translucent features takes a particular interest in the ornament and Dolores and Garth follow him home. Dolores gets too close and she and the stranger vanish through a wall. Garth finds himself arrested, convinces a government psychiatrist and a chief inspector he has not murdered Dolores and an adventure ensues in which it is shown that the mysterious stranger is an alien. Delmont and other humans, including a conniving politician, all have implants in their heads in order to obey the game rules of the 'Engineers' as they orbit (*sic*) the dark side of the moon. Discovered at their diabolical plans the aliens are threatened with destruction by earth missiles and agree to depart as Garth and Dolores are reunited. The story is foolishly overwritten and naive but it is also amusing and enjoyable, while if its style is unfortunate its metaphors are more satiric than incompetent, as this example suggests: 'the brooch inside her bag was as incapable of influencing her as the writings of an Oriental philosopher of the Ming dynasty whose work she had never seen.' (chapter 2)

Conversely *D-99* is a competently written but dull piece in which a number of short stories are poorly woven together through the simplistic device of having them all related to a secret earth ('terran') rescue organization. The tales include a woman sentenced on a puritan planet for being too sexy (she ends up having a weightless sex scene!), a man kidnapped by aliens and implanted with a control device, a couple of space explorers shipwrecked on a planet where it is illegal to crash and an underwater explorer on a distant planet imprisoned by alien crustaceans but befriended by a telepathic fish who relays messages to the terran rescuers. It is hardly surprising that the last story is never resolved. Back on earth, the rescue organization itself has suffered a power failure and fears run high that Lydman, the mad scientist and chief gadget-maker has gone crazy. Even here, in this foolish and boring tale you are aware of a satiric self-awareness: 'What did you say?' demanded Smith. 'Telepathic? A telepathic *fish*? . . . Don't ask us to – Well what I mean is . . . well, how do you know they're reliable?' (chapter 1) Isn't that unfinished sentence aimed at the reader? The universe of bug-eyed monsters and half-civilized galaxies peopled by 'crazy savages' (chapter 3) collapses into itself and marks the limits of its own fantasy with telepathic fish.

The definition of such books by reference to concepts of formula

or genre is itself often refuted by both the peculiarity of the contents and the strange direction of the narrative. Indeed, part of the
nature of these books is the bizarre direction 'genre' is forced in and
the unrestrained and yet clearly self-conscious and manipulative
way genre boundaries are crossed and so-called formulas mixed in
order to produce hybrid plots. Readers have expectations which
include a desire for consistency and an unspoken request for going
to the limit. Reference to formula can in these circumstances only
properly be applied as a crude starting-point or mythic origin in
order to explain what these books actually contain. Formula becomes for such authors a mythical point of reference in the game of
mix and match.

Far from acting as a limit or restraint, the idea of a formula is
merely the point of departure for the writer's imagination. While
John E. Muller's, *Phenomena X* seems (from internal evidence) to be
set in 1966 it makes no effort to be contemporary, rather, with its
electronics boffins, satiric cocktail host, kindly chief inspector and
alien humanoids it reminds the reader (and that's as strong as it
gets) of a mixture of 1920s English villains, 1940s pulp science
fantasy, 1950s British television police tales (especially Inspector
Lockhart), late 1950s English cinema (with its endless cocktail parties, smart addresses and sports car drivers) and the vogue for alien
tales (for instance *Quatermass* and *Dr Who*) – in short, it reminds but
does not copy and it mixes ingredients into a tale rather more suited
to Edgar Wallace or E. Phillips Oppenheim than Arthur C. Clarke
or Isaac Asimov despite the publishers listing the book as science
fiction.

Equally, Fyfe's *D-99* appears to have greater affinities with both
the pulp smart detective tales of the 1940s (especially in the description of the office secretaries who are *all* 'babes'), and the colonial
adventures of Edgar Rice Burroughs than the science fiction that is
its subject matter. In its confirmed emphasis on the secret department's office routines (despite the obligatory mad scientist) the story
comes closer to the contemporary (the book appeared in 1962)
Hollywood and television portrayal of the corporate man as hero.
Here is the world of Rock Hudson and Doris Day, *Bewitched* and
The Man from U.N.C.L.E. The inset series of tales about the problems
of interstellar travellers are sealed from this main narrative into a
series of self-contained colonial adventure stories, quite able to stand
outside the central narrative. But even here one is finally less reminded of Edgar Rice Burroughs than a prefiguring of a meeting

between Gerry Anderson's *Thunderbirds*, or *Planet of the Apes* and Steven Lucas's *Star Wars*: colonial space opera with humanoid enemies and instant rescue facilities provided by a fabulously rich and benevolent secret organization.

Here ideas of genre are simply meaningless. This is where a theory of popular literature based on generic explanations breaks down. The revisionist chant that *all* literature is simply genre based, a chant designed to challenge canonic views is as unhelpful here as its opposite, both avoid the question of what cannot be accounted for in actual texts. That such writing may be recognizable, and therefore in some sense consistent, is only to say that consistency is one necessary factor among others in fiction, such writing being no less consistent than that of the classics.

It is equally unhelpful to shift genre definitions. Both books are labelled science fiction but neither concerns itself with the truths of science fictionalized, as it were, in the style of Arthur C. Clarke, nor are they versions of that type of space opera so consistently satirized by L. Ron Hubbard, nor for that matter are they totally of the space serial style exemplified by Flash Gordon, although both have more in common with the last type than with the previous two. This qualifies neither book as space fantasy *per se*.

These books are themselves a type of sub-branch of one sub-branch of the science fiction community. This particular route would necessarily see an unbroken line of authors and editors stretching back through the pulp magazine tradition to Hugo Gernsback, founder of *Amazing Stories* – a man dedicated to putting science (that is technological progress) into fiction. Such a 'tradition' may be said to be characteristically American with an emphasis on technology, contemporaneity and future progress – a fiction bound for the 'final frontier' and one which had a resonance even for American defence policy in the 1980s. Gernsback was to popularize what Marconi, Edison and the Wright brothers had achieved, not directly, but through an attentuated literature in which the past was left behind and science fiction was freed to explore a fantastic extrapolation from the present. In so doing Gernsback and then Campbell moved away from an earlier European science fiction tradition which had predated the pulps by many years and which was essentially *literary* in nature. Thus disengaged, science fiction changed from a variation of romantic literature into a subcultural lifestyle based on 'the future'. When Isaac Asimov dedicated *I Robot* to Campbell, who, he said, 'god-fathered the robots', he did so by ignoring the rich vein containing European tales of automata that led to the coining of the term 'Robot' in the 1920s by the brothers Čapek.

The problem of definition and explication becomes even more acute when dealing with literature that has changed its genre and status over the years. This is the case with work that falls into other categories such as propaganda or pornography but which uses the rhetorical devices of fiction. A curious example of this concerns an anonymous Canadian tract of 1836, *The Awful Disclosures of Maria Monk* which began life as a dramatized piece of anti-Catholic propaganda following Emancipation in 1829 and continued to be reprinted in 1837, 1854, 1860, 1875, 1939, 1948/49, 1965 and 1971, not as propaganda but as pornography.

The story itself is easy to summarize. Maria Monk, having been given a rudimentary education by Protestants asks her mother if she can learn French which she is taught by nuns of a local order in Montreal. Despite the fact that the nuns appear uncouth and ill-educated our heroine joins their order and thus a Monk becomes a nun! Virtually held a prisoner, Maria is forced to endure the drudgery of a nun's life until she realizes the frequent visits of the local priests are motivated by the fact that the nunnery is being used as an official Catholic brothel run by a masculine and ugly mother superior cum madam. Infanticide is the usual means of contraception, the babies' bodies disposed of in a cellar/*oubliette*. Any nun causing problems is faced with or endures torture – two nuns being held in dungeon cells – and at least one nun is tortured to death in Maria Monk's presence. This routine of violence, superstitution, rape and drudgery is Monk's daily ordeal until she finally escapes to tell her tale. To relieve the dark and melodramatic atmosphere there is the character of Jane Ray, an eccentric, vulgar and violent madcap who is tolerated by the authorities for reasons never revealed.

By 1948, the Modern Fiction company's edition could boast that the book had been 'for over a hundred years . . . a bestseller', the cover of this particular edition being a four-colour picture of a nun in full habit whose large emerald green eyes, plucked eyebrows and voluptuous red painted lips suggest a book at once erotic and pruriently moral, in a word: *kinky*.

Of course, the potential for erotic and kinky violence in religious bigotry has always been a recognizable feature of its central theme. These can be found in attacks on Catholicism, where nunneries become bordellos, and priests perform satanic rites, on Judaism with its supposed 'white slavery' and ritual child murder, and on Islam with the emphasis on harems and decadence. By the 1948/9 edition we are also invited by the publishers to purchase *Lolita in Soho* by Scott Morley, 'the intimate story of what happened to a young girl who fell for the illusions of security offered by a married man'. The high cover price suggests less a hardback edition than a risqué read.

No information seems to exist as to the author or authors of 'Maria Monk' whose style nevertheless suggests professional or semi-professional writers of those broadsheets, melodramas or chapbooks so popular at the time among working people in both Britain and America (See Chapter 3). This book has the sensationalism of popular expression but puts it to the service of middle-class (that is, respectable) bigotry, combining as it does the vogue for tales of exotic mayhem and gothic horror. The title itself also suggests continuity with other older forms of ephemeral tractarian literature of which 'An *Awful* [emphasis mine] Memorial of the State of Francis Spina after he turned apostasy from the Protestant Church to Popery', printed in Falkirk in 1815 stands as one example. Even the heroine's name suggests reference to 'Monk' Lewis's bestselling work.

Purporting to be a *true* account and thereby utilizing the style of the universely popular 'confessional' literature of the time, 'Maria Monk' is nevertheless a blatant forgery – a clever fiction which declares both 'what I have written is true' and all characters in this novel are entirely fictitious' (1948/9 edition). The theme itself was not a new one and the equation nunnery equals brothel is an old literary theme. Moreover, the strange and eccentric character of Jane Ray seems modelled, borrowed or plagiarized from a now lost or forgotten fictional source known to the authors yet not known by readers of 1836. The exact meaning of the character 'Jane Ray' may indeed be lost to us entirely although she is suggestive of a cross between the later figures of Nellie Dean and Crazy Jane.

An assertion that the whole book was a plagiarism was hotly refuted though an open letter published in the *Protestant Vindicator* in March 1836.

We ... declare that the assertion, originally made in the Roman Catholic newspapers of Boston, that the book was copied from a work entitled 'The Gates of Hell Opened' is wholly destitute of foundation; it being wholly new and not copied from anything whatsoever.

The letter was signed by a number of Protestant activists: W.C. Browntree; John J. Slocum (of whom more later); A. Drew Bruce; D. Fanshaw; Amos Belden; David Werson; Thomas Hogen. These same signatories were convinced of the truthfulness of Maria Monk's tale, having met her *in person*. Who they met or what her fate was is lost to us.

Soon after the book's publication in New York it was circulating among gullible middle-class Protestant activists and ministers in both Canada and the United States. In New York it was taken up by those fearful of Irish immigration and a popish conspiracy while in Montreal it formed the basis for Anglo-Scottish fears of French superstition. By May 1836, *The Dublin Review* had refuted the book as a forgery but this did not prevent continual reprinting and trans-lation, a version in Dutch being printed in Newcastle, England, for export during 1836. The attack by the *Dublin Review* reveals the probable class of reader anticipated by the book's authors and publisher. Indeed, one can imagine the book as a basis for sermons on popish ways both in America and Britain throughout the early nineteenth century where other sensational tales of nunneries and debauchery similarly circulated (for example, the case of the Mercy Nuns of Hull in the 1850s).

The history of the book's reception is nowhere better shown than in the changes in its title. By 1948 the book was simply 'The Awful Disclosures of Maria Monk' but it had begun life as 'The Awful Disclosures of Maria Monk as exhibited in an narrative of her resi-dence of five years as a novice and two years as a Black Nun, in the Hotel Dieu Nunnery at Montreal'. In, 1837, an appendix had been added (suggestive of the original book's popularity) giving 'further disclosures of Maria Monk conerning her visit to Nun's Island' and a reply to *The Priest's Book* by J.J. Slocum who we previously met as John J. Slocum in the *Protestant Vindicator* from the spring of 1836. Re-emerging every ten years or so in new editions the book's title had been modified to 'A True Account' by 1860 but had been embellished with illustrations which were then omitted by the present century. A version printed in 1971 contained an account of the 'Ladière Case' as a further modification.

What all this suggests is that the work known as 'The Awful Disclosures of Maria Monk' was continuously subject to modifica-tion and embellishment for over a hundred years of publishing and that there is a *tradition* of reprinting and reading exemplified in this work which is undocumented and disregarded. By the twentieth century the book was read not as 'factual' Protestant propaganda but as pornographic fiction. Its own internal structure had aided this process of metamophosis. 'Maria Monk' shows us clearly that pulp fiction is a matter of *process* and that there is no clearly fixed text (although there is an *original* one) in which its essential nature can be described. Instead, the work develops, mutates and spawns over history, being both monstrous (in the nineteenth century) and almost homely (in the twentieth century).

In marked contrast to Shakespeare's work which moved from fluidity into fixity in the nineteenth century and became *the* signifier for cultural literacy for the middle classes thereafter (see Chapter 6 for the complex history and problematic status of Shakespeare), the anonymous 'Maria Monk' lost its respectability, became subject to flux and ended up acting as a signifier for a banal plebeian and titillatory eroticism. Pulp is literature as process: unfixed, illicit and 'anonymous'. Such work may thrive but will only have a half life (that is, as a form of recognized fiction) because of its unclassifiable nature.

'Maria Monk' is marketed as pornography or religious tract – it is all one, as the book is both these things simultaneously as well as being an 'autobiography' and a gothic novel. The book is hardly a candidate for critical applause and one need not treat it with respect either as good art (which it is not – except as a convincing tale) or good pulp (it is neither very erotic nor very exciting – the narrative is virtually non-existent). However, the book's presence and longevity does demand our attention because it has enjoyed longer continuous production than many popular classics and its aesthetic outlook acts as a bridge between respectable genres and disreputable genres – the gothic and the pornographic. It is these 'bridge' texts that rarely get attention and yet which force us again to reconsider concepts of a formal and aesthetic nature (style and genre) as well as resiting the nature of the literary.

Maria Monk was the nineteenth century equivalent of Linda Lovelace, her book is a pornographic adventure: what do you do with a problem like Maria? Adverts at the back of the 1948/9 edition offer for sale Edwin J. Henri's *Kiss of the Whip* which for 25s. (twenty-five shillings) presents: 'a veritable cavalcade of notorious methods of self-abasement and corporal punishment – particularly with the *whip*.' Alternatively there was *Erotic Love* by 'Sardi' a snip at 30s. (thirty shillings) in which, 'Individual orgies, such as those of the Marquis de Sade and Jack the Ripper, send a chill down one's spine, reminding one that many a man is but the victim of "a twisted nerve, a ganglion gone awry".' These two books could be purchased 'post free' alongside *Your Destiny* and *Astrology and Sex* or 'How the Stars Control your Sex Life'.

Steven Marcus has suggested the way nineteenth-century pornography operated and in so doing he is able to expose some of the rhetorical structures of 'Maria Monk'. Marcus tells us that: 'Pornography . . . typically undertakes to represent itself not as a story or fantasy but as something that "really" happened.'[22] He then continues:

> Pornography, as I have mentioned earlier, moves ideally away from language. In its own way, and like much modern literature, it tries to go beneath and behind language; it tries to reach what language cannot directly express but can only point toward, the primary processes of mental energy. This is a partial explanation of why pornography is also the home of the forbidden, tabooed words. These are the stubborn, primitive words of the language; . . . The very deadness of much of the language of pornography, even its clichés and meaninglessness in a verbal sense, demonstrate to us that its meaning is to be found in some other area. . . . Its intention is, rather, unmetaphoric and literal; its aim is to *de-elaborate* the verbal structure and the distinctions upon which it is built, to move back through language to that part of our minds where all metaphors are literal truths, where everything is possible.[23]

On one level this appears to pinpoint the pornographic nature of 'Maria Monk', it certainly catches the nature of the *culture* the book exists within, nevertheless, at the risk of becoming pedantic, these comments miss the essential *avoidances* of the text. At each and every point of erotic contact, the mechanics of such contact are replaced by either lacunae or by a secondary discourse of violence and incarceration. An example of such description is offered with regard to Jane Ray.

> I received a great shock one day when entering the room for the Examination of Conscience, for I saw a Nun hanging head downwards by a cord from a ring in the ceiling. Her clothes were kept in place by a leather strap tied around them, and her head was some distance from the floor. Her face was dark and swollen by

the rush of blood; her hands were tied and her mouth was stopped by a large gag. It was Jane Ray.

This is itself followed by a comment put in the mouth of Maria Monk but too knowledgeable to be something she could have known: 'I could not help noticing how similar this punishment was to those of the Inquisition.'

Such writing hovers *between* fiction and pornography and acts as a primitive bridge between the two: a type of pseudo-pornography born out of gothic prejudice. In this culturally ignored backwater all literature becomes anonymous, processed and fluid. Here the expected boundaries of fiction and of pornography are breached and the fixity of print disestablished.

Here, in these texts is displayed the essential instability in a system which is fluid and protean. The creation of a stable canon was a necessary component of this system, an attempt to codify and taxonomize an anarchic situation. Thus the canon was entirely artificial and entirely necessary – an attempt to retrieve the personal and communal from the social. The canon is *the* determinant in a system which allows the self-validation of hierarchy but at the same time provides an escape mechanism (the refusal of legitimation) for the vast majority of printed material. In the offensive against the canon, academics have not 'opened' the canon to fresh air but made the canon itself the mere product of socio-pathology. The needs of the canon (which are dealt with in detail later) defined an area for debate which gave a language to pulp while refusing it a voice. What we need to do now is retrieve pulp *without* reference to the canon and thereby avoid a debate in which definition is already decided. Pulp literature demarcates that fluidity, protean nature and simple abundance in language in which excess is key. The canon allows us to see clearly why pulp was historically excluded and made as 'other' but it also allows us through such grounding to comprehend pulp's social, cultural and *aesthetic* functions in *their own right* and conditioned by their own productive and consumptional complexity. Blinded by distaste for the canon, liberal- and left-wing critics have failed to assimilate the popular arts that they tend to distrust: pulp is inherently unstable and this is pulp's power and why it is feared.

The vast majority of writers who had to earn their living by writing, that is proletarianized writers, were, and are, part of that congruence of money, work and art and are always the victims of canonizing and exclusion. The voices of writers, mostly working class it should not be forgotten, thus doubly excluded, equals the denial of a real living history (messy, contradictory, problematic) represented by the world of publishing and authorship. Most critics simply recreate the canon in mirror form. This has nothing to do with retrieving the half-forgotten history of pulp and its aesthetic conditions. It again simplifies history and art and ignores the archeological recovery required if we are to do justice to real men and women who earned their livelihoods through printed artefacts and who contributed to a significant portion of the information media. To do so is simply to seal the coffin twice. To rediscover these voices is to find a scandal by scandalous methods.

The circumstances surrounding the creation of the modern canon were such that various interest groups – some establishment and others opposed to the establishment – were able to agree on the conversion of Arnoldian ethical propositions into Wildesque functional propositions. 'Is it right' was corrected into 'is it well done'. This movement, modernistic in temperament, led anti-establishment figures such as F.R. Leavis, for instance, in the 1930s, to look to a canon antithetical to upper-class interests. In separating the divisions of fiction, which he saw as the supremely democratic medium, he attacked the control of culture by upper middle-class interests at Cambridge, and especially those of Bloomsbury.

Whether defending or refusing democratic reading rights, canonic creation managed to turn political and ethical issues into aesthetic issues. The question of the canon is in essence an ethical question determined by moral right. Thus canonic texts could both widen and control access to Literature (*not* access to literacy or access to ordinary print forms which circulated regardless). Such control coincided with the progressive appearance of Great Books programmes in the United States and the origins of the Norton Anthology. Such programmes consolidated a certain history of America, as the widening of the educational programme in Great Britain coincided with the explosion of pulp literature but acted to suppress it or ignore it in favour of an undeclared great books 'Eng Lit' programme. In the United States this trajectory was activated by the influence of such factors as the movement of Blacks into Northern cities, mass peasant immigration from middle Europe and fear of White degeneration. In Britain it coincides rather with a widening franchise spearheaded by a consensus politics more and more in the moral and cultural hands of a lower middle class distrustful of other groups and anxious to claim the moral ground of culture. Corporate capitalism and welfare statism both helped create the grounds of cultural debate. Art's moral focus would now be the necessary depiction of the *real*: all else would be sacrificed, not only on moral, but on aesthetic grounds – bad art would be bad for your health – a point already being made in the 1920s on both sides of the Atlantic.

A later chapter on taste will detail some of the essential history and characteristics of canon-making and the cultural debate that followed. Now it is sufficient to note that the creation of a modern canon coincided with the appearance first of a protean new print medium based on industrial production, intensive capital investment and monopolistic practices (themselves parasitically preying on entrepreneurial inventiveness), which gave way to a further information explosion with the appearance of photography, cinema, radio and television vertically and horizontally integrated into the previous print culture. The result was cultural confusion and lost social coherence of a sort unexpected and unwelcome by many:

Our emergent world society, with its particular qualities of speed, mobility, mass production and consumption, rapidity of change and innovation, is the latest phase of an ongoing cultural and social revolution. It has few historical precedents as a cultural context. Industrial technologies, now approaching global scale, linked to an attendant multiplicity of new communication channels, are producing a planetary culture whose relation to earlier forms is as Vostok or Gemini to a wheeled cart. World communications, whose latest benchmark is Telstar. . . . This interpenetration, rapid diffusion and replication is most evident in the position of fine art in the new continuum. Transference through various modes changes both form and content – the new image can no longer be judged in the previous canon. The book, the film of the book, the book of the film, the musical of the film, the TV or comic strip version of the musical – or however the cycle may run – is, at each stage, a transmutation which alters subtly the original communication. These transformative changes and diffusions occur with increasing rapidity. Now, in the arts, an avant garde may only be 'avant' until the next TV news broadcast or issue of '*Time/Life/Espresso*'. Not only pop but op, camp and super-camp styles and 'sub-styles' have an increasingly immediate circulation, acceptance and 'usage' whose feedback directly influences their evolution. We might formally say that they become 'academic' almost as they emerge, but this notion of academy versus avant-garde élites is no longer tenable, and may take its place with the alienated artist and other myths.[24]

The denial of legitimacy to certain forms of publishing, authorship, subject matter and reading practice left reading habits little changed in reality – what changed was educational practice and *the allowable limits of debate*. The other of the canon was pulp and pulp was also its bastard offspring.

The pulp purchaser was now the same as the enthusiast of industrialized artefacts – mass men and women were transformed into *Kitsch-mensch*, the *Untermenschen* of urban life. The result was a denial both of the modern, of the manufactured and of the multiple – a point made explicit in Walter Benjamin's famous essay 'The Work of Art in the Age of Mechanical Reproduction' of 1936. Pulp, like kitsch, was the worst pandering to an infantilized, sentimentalized, blind consumption; narcissistic and vicious. For Harold Rosenberg 'There [was] no counterpart to kitsch. Its antagonist is not an idea [i.e. art] but reality'.[25]

For Herman Broch, kitsch lovers are born of Romantic extreme narcissism and industrial abundance – comfort and sentiment and conformity all become symptoms of individualism (rather ironically) and the neurotic. The religious impulse ends for Gillo Dorfles in the fetishism of empty objects. For Clement Greenberg, pulp as a form of kitsch is a 'rudimentary culture' which imitates in empty form the 'genuine' effects of high culture:

If the avant garde imitates the processes of art, kitsch, we now see, imitates its effects. The neatness of this antithesis is more than contrived; it corresponds to and defines the tremendous interval that separates from each other two such simultaneous cultural phenomena as the avant garde and kitsch. This interval, too great to be closed by all the infinite gradations of popularized 'modernism' and 'modernistic' kitsch, corresponds in turn to a social interval, a social interval that has always existed in formal culture, as elsewhere in civilized society, and whose two termini converge and diverge in fixed relation to the increasing or decreasing stability of the given society. There has always been on one side the minority of the powerful – and therefore the cultivated – and on the other the great mass of the exploited and poor – and therefore the ignorant. Formal culture has always belonged to the first, while the last have had to content themselves with the folk or rudimentary, culture or kitsch.[26]

This rudimentary culture is a second level reality but a reality which points away from the 'truth' towards an empty factuality – it coincides with journalism and conformity. If kitsch, and therefore, pulp fiction, equal falsehood, then it is because they aim at effect not reality. They aim to make beautiful not make more 'real'. Broch argues that, 'In science and art alike the important thing is the creation of new expressions of reality.'[27] Indeed, he goes further in arguing,

> Kitsch is certainly not 'bad art'; it forms its own closed system, which is lodged like a foreign body in the overall system of art, or which, if you prefer, appears alongside it. . . . The enemy within, however, is more dangerous than these attacks from outside: every system is dialectically capable of developing its own anti-system and is indeed compelled to do so.[28]

Kitsch is a cancer within the aesthetic appreciated by people who form themselves into cultural and social viruses. But bio-medical social analogies are thrust aside for quasi-theological ethical considerations.

> [A]n ethical system cannot do without conventions . . . Can the same be said of a life inspired by kitsch? The original convention which underlies it is exaltation, or rather hypocritical exaltation, since it tries to unite heaven and earth in an absolutely false relationship.[29]

From such musings Broch concludes pulp/kitsch to be a 'neurotic [i.e. unhealthy] work of art' and that one expression of it, radio, is 'a volcano vomiting a continuous spout of imitation music'.[30] His conclusion: universal neurosis and spiritual death.

What underlaid these fears, played out against totalitarianism in Europe, the Far East and elsewhere was that pulp was the cynical, conspiratorial link between corporate capitalism and state monopoly

capitalism. As in the paradoxes of Orwell's *1984*, slavery was freedom and escapism was true conformity. This concern was founded
on fears regarding the State's possible total control of information,
whether in the United States, Britain or Russia, and that this *exter-
nalization* of control was effected through the manipulation of *ephemera* constituted in an ever-elongated contemporaneity. Now, 'now'
lasted forever and history was at an end: Yet, as J.A. Sutherland has
pointed out with regard to modern publishing and reading habits,

> In fact culture would seem to be more resilient and resourceful
> than we habitually take it to be. Indices of production and con-
> sumption have all multiplied, rival media have installed them-
> selves, without the feared collapses. The reading public has not
> been reduced to the condition of denatured Epsilons; nor has it
> stratified as it should have done to fulfil pessimistic prophecies.
> These facts have lent strength to more recently fashionable theo-
> ries which oppose gloom and argue that the problem of the fu-
> ture will not be cultural regimentation in a consumer manipulating
> society, but the bewildering diversities and cultural opportuni-
> ties of a post-industrial, technocentric world.[31]

Such pluralism in reading habits needed not merely new packaging
but new ways of understanding print consumption.

In 1935, Allen Lane launched Penguin. Penguin Books continued
a tradition of good quality books at cheap prices: quality content
yet inexpensive packaging. As yet, in Britain, cheap was not exactly
nasty.

> Yet Penguins needed the most aggressive and Americanised of
> the multiple stores to break into the market. They needed mass
> sales, above the bestseller threshold (13,000–17,000 was the initial
> break-even range; Lane calculated that he would need an annual
> volume sale of 2 million. . . . And they exploited a new, techno-
> logically transformed kind of book.[32]

Pulp publication was in every sense except expectations based on
similar concepts of production (if not economies of scale) and newspapers and paperbacks of all sorts were the *sine qua non* of mass
reading habits.

The publishing revolution brought about by Allen Lane did not
occur spontaneously; other British companies had experimented with

limp-cover or paper-cover books of which Heinemann (challenging the monopoly held by Tauschnitz) and Hodder & Stoughton (who were producing a large format paperback series as early as 1905) were leading examples. 'Heinemann had even set up a separate company to do so with co-directors Bram Stoker (*Dracula*), Arthur Waugh (Evelyn's father) and W.L. Courtney (a leading journalist) and even this company had the precedent of Hutchinson's 6d. (six-penny) 'Blacks' of the previous century (in which such leading authors as Charles Garvice appeared) and limp or paper-cover books produced sporadically in the United States by publishers such as Arthur Westbrook in Cleveland.[33]

Lane's genius was one of *application* and American publishers were not slow to relearn the marketing and packaging techniques Lane borrowed. In 1939, Robert De Graff founded Pocket Books based on the Penguin concept, mixing popular and classic titles, soon others followed: Popular Library (1942); Dell (1943); Bantam (1945); Graphic (1948); Pyramid (1949); Lion (1949); Checker (1949); New American Library (1949) which was Penguin's own US imprint.[34]

From now on fiction and other human interest material would feed directly into paperback production, just as it had done previously with the pulp magazines which paperbacks had mainly replaced by the 1940s. Aggressive marketing, lurid covers, violent and erotic stories about money, drugs, the city, teenage delinquents, mobsters and action combined with a very low price gave these paperbacks as air of sleaze, and cheap soon stood for nasty. Many pulp authors transferred their loyalties to paperbacks and for a decade the paperback ambivalently represented good reading at cheap prices and 'cheap' reading at low prices.

The paperback author remained resolutely on the edge of that 'sensationalism' which had been so noticed by nineteenth-century commentators and which was the constant target of the censor's vilification. But the paperback pulp author also united the exposé of the earlier muckraking journalist with the exploitative fiction-alizing of the pulp-magazine writer. Just as the censorious were shocked by the revealing nature of the paperback so the paperback itself traded on shocking revelations; journalism and fictional authorship both rewrote and yet also reported the banality of 1940s and 1950s America. This introduction, for instance, to *The Man Who Rocked the Boat* (1956) (later renamed *Slaughter on 10th Avenue* (1961)), a book about New York assistant district attorney Bill Keating, begins,

I believe many readers will be *shocked* by the *revelations* in this book. It is an 'inside' story in every sense of the word, based on a remarkable man's experiences as an assistant district attorney and as counsel to the private, citizen-supported New York City Anti-Crime Committee. I find it *far more exciting than any fictional detective thriller* I have ever read, because it deals in reality. Bill Keating has resisted the temptation to romanticize or *sensationalize*. The facts of his career are *sensational* enough.

(Emphasis mine.)

This is the *ante* in the age of Spillane, in which Spillane competed with the revelation and the exposé.

Spillane's early novels, with their libido, violence and gangsterism were both a commentary and a pulp prophesy. When John Kennedy was assassinated by unknown gunmen it seemed to confirm the existence of a gigantic and hidden conspiracy involving gangsters ('The Mafia' now steps onto the stage), the red menace (Lee Harvey Oswald), union corruption (Jimmy Hoffa) and paranoid secret agencies (The CIA); Kennedy's death and the subsequent revelations about his libidinous adventures (especially with Marilyn Monroe) reconstituted the nature of the office of president and in so doing confirmed the growing cult of *celebrity*.

The older interest in the extraordinary nature of the banal had been noticed as early as the 1880s by Matthew Arnold in his comments on the American Press.

The Americans used to say to me that what they valued was news, and that this their newspapers gave them. I at last made the reply: 'Yes, news for the servants' hall!' I remember that a New York newspaper, one of the first I saw after landing in the country, had a long account, with the prominence we should give to the illness of the German Emperor or the arrest of the Lord Mayor of Dublin, of a young woman who had married a man who was a bag of bones, as we say, and who used to exhibit himself as a skeleton; of her growing horror in living with this man, and finally of her death. All this in the most minute detail, and described with all the writer's powers of rhetoric. This has always remained by me as a specimen of what the Americans call news.[35]

This interest in the bizarre nature of the ordinary, which had been the mainstay of mass publishing and had become enshrined in such papers as *The News of the World* and magazines such as *Reader's Digest* was now paralleled by a fascination with the bizarre nature of the celebrity, libidinous, wealthy and corrupt, connected with power (finance/politics) and with Hollywood, dead too soon, by violence either accidental (Jayne Mansfield's decapitation in a car crash; James Dean's 'haunted' Porsche); self-administered (Marilyn Monroe's nude suicide; Judy Garland's death in a toilet bowl); or by assassin (John Kennedy; Bobby Kennedy). Kennedy's death was history re-enacted as pulp fiction, a Technicolor world (remember the Zapruder tapes) of lasciviousness and violence in Camelot.

The world of the celebrity also narrowed the gap between the bizarre and the banal (the two extremes of reality). Whereas previously the interest had always focused on the revelation of weirdness just below the surface of normalcy (the banal as extraordinary – a type of transmogrification of the mundane), now the bizarre was merely ordinary. By the late twentieth century, New York had become its own pulp scenario, superseding Spillane, in a hyperreal displacement of the imagination. 'I've been doing crime work a while, and I've been doing it in New York a while, and New York stories are just so off the wall, so crazy – the mayhem is beyond belief.' Such were the thoughts of the Deputy City Editor on the New York *Daily News* in the late 1980s – the pulp fiction atmosphere duly brought out by the use of 'mayhem', recalling the machine-gun mayhem of 1920s Chicago.[36]

The market which provided a living for Spillane later buoyed up the work of Generoso Pope Jr. A graduate of MIT and a Cold-War warrior in the US psychological warfare programme, Pope bought the New York *Enquirer* in 1952.[37] With a change of name to the *National Enquirer*, circulation increased from 17 000 to one million on a diet of violence, gore and the bizarre. This was a paper devoted to an almost Fortean view of human nature and a presentation at once horror comic, Spillane novel and *Twilight Zone*. Fictional pulp which had dealt in the self-same subjects had now been replaced by reality *as* pulp: an endless carnival of the extreme.

> Pope based his appeal on the public's prurient interest in violence. [He combined] the world of bizarre and horrific tales of shark attacks, decapitation, white slavery, . . . lunatics, and the occasional . . . special.[38]

Nevertheless by 1967, 'the newspaper had passed reluctantly from the profitable "gore era" into a kind of schizoid phrase which incorporated a bit of the old tried-and-true horror with personal beauty tips, celebrity chit-chat and reader-oriented human interest stories'.[39]

With the market's obsession with television stars and the sales-stand in the supermarket guaranteeing a captive female audience, the *National Enquirer* soon took off, backed by the new tabloid style of British emigré journalists weaned on crime, sex and celebrity – a mixture intrinsically British since the founding of papers such as the *News of the World* in the previous century. By 1991, S.J. Taylor could point out:

> The only genuine profit centres left today in the American press are 'the supermarket tabloids' – bizarre hybrids which combine magazine layout and design with investigative news gathering techniques. To a large extent, they have been manned [*sic*] by Brits, imported either by the late Generoso Pope in Florida or by Rupert Murdoch operating out of New York. In unsynchronized movement, and with the full cooperation of Hollywood's 'hype' machine, the supermarket tabloids succeeded in inventing and exporting the cult of celebrity that encircles the globe today. It is the last outpost of the tabloid mentality in the US . . .[40]

Yet, for Taylor, the message is also positive, for her the tabloids prevent conformism, complacency and conformity, an attitude re-freshingly opposed to the orthodoxies one expects. 'The lesson from America is that, without the tabloids and their spirit of irreverence, the press becomes a bastion of conformity'.[41]

The gap between reality and fiction is closed and widened, a ploy successfully used again and again in both popular fiction and journalism and one in which the everyday is seen as both incon-sequentially dull and mind bendingly bizarre *all at once*, with the ephemerality of the paperback mirroring in its very form the tran-sience and also the essential nature of the society it serves.

What shocked in the paperback's form was the knowledge that printed material (of whatever nature) was now transient, ephem-eral, trivial, without history or a future, disposable, degradable, escapist and *anonymous*; neither Shakespeare nor Tolstoy was spared and Shakespeare was now as available and as disposable (because of the very form in which 'He' was packaged) as any 'hack' writer of science fantasy or crime fiction. What shocked was the very *lack* of hierarchy, the free-for-all refusal to differentiate through packaging, marketing or purchaser. Printed fiction had begun in a mercantile age and the age of mass reading had confirmed that literature from the eighteenth century onwards was always essentially a commodity at the heart of which lay an unresolvable ambivalence over the nature of creativity, authorship, imagination and genius.

The two, product and producer, could never be disentangled but they were always required to exist in mutual antagonism (many paperback authors stood for principals opposed to the very commodity they helped produce). What paperbacks did for a brief period between the 1940s and 1950s was to conflate this antagonism: authorship again became anonymous, quixotic – simple labour. The mystique was removed and it threatened every sector with its violence. Moral outrage and social concern recognized not a refertilizing of the literary imagination *from below*, nurtured in the pre-war pulp magazines but, rather, a decadence in which print was unrestrained and unclassifiable. The containment of paperbacks was in the final analysis not a cultural cauterizing but a type of quartering in which morality may have won a spurious victory but art and creativity were partially lobotomized, brought in line with an authoritarian but paranoid age.

It is ironic therefore that when George Orwell was finishing *1984* during the paper shortages and import bans on print of the post-war years, a whole new print industry had grown up in Britain, which forged the modern publishing of paperbacks and which, consumed by print-starved ordinary people, helped widen, cheapen and democratize reading habits in the UK, a fact which most standard histories of publishing elide or ignore. That the initial impulse for a new mass market was not the sudden withdrawal of American pulp offerings after the war but was, rather, the appearance of quality paperback printing before the war began is ironic. Far from being totalitarian such offerings as British post-war pulp and American pre-war pulp were anarcho-capitalist, anti-establishment and popular.

Pulp consensus was now at the heart of democratic culture-making and decision-taking.

3

Turning the World Round:
The Print Revolution

Raymond Chandler was a Victorian. To be exact, his youthful aspirations and ideals were formed in England, at Norwood in South London with his mother, grandmother and aunts in genteel middle-class surroundings and at Dulwich College for Boys, designed to prepare middle-class males for a professional and civil-service life serving the Empire. A.E.W. Mason, author of *The Four Feathers*, had taught at Dulwich College and its headmaster was A.H. Gilkes. Chandler began school there a year before Victoria's death, some forty years before his first novel. An aspiring poet and satirist he learnt those late Victorian verities and inherited those late Victorian doubts that later emerged in his fiction. Schooled in English history, passing the civil service Classics exams with extraordinary ability, Chandler was the model of an English gentleman, bred of the Edwardian rapprochement with its immediate past.[1]

When Chandler began writing it was this inheritance that returned in an American context. Marlowe, originally named Malory after the author of *Le Morte Darthur*, that quintessential influence on the image of the gentleman in the Victorian age (think of Tennyson or Morris) is an Arthurian knight (looking for Mrs *Grayle* and the *Lady in the Lake*) who smokes a pipe, wears pyjamas, acts graciously towards women, believes in honour, plays chess and looks nostalgically backward to a golden age. Like Chandler, Marlowe is reserved, fastidious and élitist.

A product of an English education and an American lifestyle, Chandler was a true product of the late nineteenth century and early twentieth – oilman and novelist, corporate executive and gentleman. In this sense, Chandler was the perfect late Victorian contradiction and his famous detective adventurer reworks that contradiction in print. Marlowe lives on the edge – he is a relic of the late Victorians' legacy to the Edwardians – a thoroughly modern character whose first-person narrative (itself reinvented in late

48

Victorian adventure fiction) echoes Matthew Arnold's worst fears about democracy: if not looking on Dover Beach, then on the worst of Los Angeles and Bay City, the 'remnant' could say with Chandler 'I have lived my life on the edge of nothing'.[2]

The crime novel seems an apt vehicle for someone for whom modern democratic man is either utterly alone or utterly criminal and the first-person narrative an appropriate vehicle for the doubting voice which both upholds old-fashioned certainties and knows that they have not merely passed but never really existed. This is the voice of the nineteenth century, a voice often both startling and unfamiliar – it is a voice without anchor: a voice on the edge.

This excursion into the work of Raymond Chandler should serve to remind us of the breadth of the term Victorianism and of its consequences. If the railway is at the centre of Victorian modernity then the aeroplane is a consequence of the restlessness of that century: much of the modern world having come into being in the last century is still around us and still part of our daily lives – refined perhaps, perhaps disguised. Indeed, it may be argued that the uprisings of 1968 were the last moment of a Victorian belief in radical change, psychological and existential longing and a socialist and Marxist dialectic based upon Germanic idealism and a belief in liberation through struggle. This takes us to the heart of the matter – the Victorian age was an age dominated by the radical disestablishment of an older sensibility and a continuing revolution in another and newer sensibility which lasted until 1968.

Through looking at Victorian literary publishing, purchasing and reading habits we can see the appearance of a new literary sensibility produced by, and a consequence of, market forces and commodity production. Here the book is both product and work of art, decided both by unit cost and critical taste, an object of purchase and a process of reading. Books were not new, fiction was not new, what was new was the emergence of new fictions, new types of books and a new reading public. The novel and short story (the tale), poem and journalistic essay were the creation and driving force behind new ways of perceiving in a literate democracy.

In this way, a new information industry emerged which coincided with the world of entertainment, bringing with it new forms of professionalism (authors and publishers), new distributive networks

(Smith and Mudie) and new forms of presentation (part publications, three-deckers, serials). The power of widening literacy and the emergent market-driven literary world created a demand for new forms of expression and therefore new forms of content – the woman's question and the demands of women readers created the content of many works whose structure was designed to optimize the potential sales from new areas of representation.

The field was volatile and expansive. A greatly expanded industry brought about a new meaning to representation. The forms of this new literature were created experimentally in the crucible of a market constantly testing its products until it could stabilize not merely the product's form but the ways such form could be consumed. Once established, these products were again quickly destabilized by the publishing demands of newly discovered publics whose reading habits and purchasing ability aided the pursuit of both publishing profits and product excellence but also led publishers to create different aesthetic forms and different artistic subjects. New readers were found as the forms developed to *make visible* otherwise invisible subject areas (the genres of horror, detective or science fiction). Forms and contents, authors and publishers, readers and markets emerged together to create the literature of the nineteenth century. As such this history is one not only of process and change, but above all one where there are moments of uncertainty in an alliance between profit and art, democracy and modernity. Victorian literature was conditioned by exploration and uncertainity.

Novelty dominated Victorian literature; the literary arts were firmly rooted in, indeed one *condition of*, the Victorian entrepreneurial business spirit. To talk of *Victorian literature* is, as the Victorians well knew, to fantasize about a stable entity and therein a set of fictitious stable values. Victorian literature was conditioned by doubt (the gamble of the market) and was determined by doubt (the moral dimension of the narrative). Furthermore, its shape was also determined by doubt. Victorian literary production and consumption owed its vitality to this doubt, this instability in the very conditions of its making. The growth of Victorian reading and the extraordinary momentum of the publishing machine were the uncontrollable virus of Victorian liberal democracy. The authority of the printed word was guaranteed by its ungrounded nature in democratic (and therefore unpredictable) mass reading habits. It was the triumph of Victorian reading and publishing that they were both eclectic and protean and it was the tragedy of Victorian literature that the authors, publishers, academics and critics who were made by this new world also sought to hierarchize it, restrict it, stabilize it and divide it: in a word, to tame the very forces that made Victorian literature come alive.

At the beginning of the nineteenth century the concept of a vast reading public and a publishing industry would have been little more than a dream to contemporaries: relatively few published books existed; fewer were published each year; fiction was rare and read by only a few; libraries were even rarer and expensive; distribution was virtually impossible while travel was dominated by poor roads; publishing houses were still mainly printers; authors, as yet mainly unrecognized, were undervalued and disorganized.

By the third quarter of the century this situation had completely changed. New printing techniques emerged as publishing houses grew in size and sloughed off their old printing associations while incorporating new business attitudes. Marketing and distribution became possible with the appearance of trains, railway bookshops, library purchase and the ubiquitous bagmen; passengers could now read in a train compartment whereas before the coach was simply too shaky. Added to this, the power of authorship had grown, allowing some to grow rich in the trade because of the vast increase in the consumption of fiction and newsprint encouraged by and part of a new mass literacy. This also spawned new markets especially in children's literature and magazines for adults. As markets grew they split and created specialist genres both in fiction and in the appearance of hobby or sport journals. Finally authorship became a professional business about to be protected by an author's union: the Society of Authors. If at worst it was a free-for-all, at its best this protean growth meant that the English-speaking world, both sides of the Atlantic and beyond was one that read and discussed the central issues of industrial democracy. As such the trade in information and in books (including piracies) was truly international.

Louisa May Alcott's *Little Women* stands as a perfect example of the evolution of the novel. Published in 1868 it was read by adults and children in England familiar with American prose since the success of *Uncle Tom's Cabin* which had arrived in 1852 and been bought by Mudies and others in such considerable quantities that it soon passed the million-seller mark. At the time, the question of abolition had been *the* moral issue for British readers of all ranks. Thus American political issues were already British moral conundrums.

Alcott's book is a veritable encyclopaedia of the evolution of the novel form from its early days in Walter Scott and Charlotte Yonge to its development by Dickens. Encased in chapter headings and moral reminders borrowed and adapted from Bunyan, Alcott manages to incorporate not only Shakespeare (*Hamlet* and *Macbeth*) but also Richard Brinsley Sheridan and Fanny Burney as well as *Undine and Sintram*, which so influenced Newman and the Oxford Movement; but here too are large numbers of contemporary authors central to the development of fiction. Into *Little Women* come the already mentioned Charlotte Yonge and her *Heir of Redclyffe* * (chapter 3); Sir Walter Scott's *Ivanhoe* (chapter 5); *Uncle Tom's Cabin* (chapter 4); *Vanity Fair* via both Thackeray and Bunyan (chapter 9); Dickens's *Pickwick Papers* (chapter 10) and *Great Expectations* (chapter 11) and Elizabeth Wetherell's *The Wide, Wide World* (chapter 11). To add to this, references are made to novel-reading, poems are written by the sisters and plays of a melodramtic and gothic nature produced. At the very end Alcott points to the contemporaneity of her chosen genre:

> So grouped, the curtain falls upon Meg, Jo, Beth, and Amy. Whether it ever rises again, depends upon the reception given to the first act of the *domestic drama* called
> LITTLE WOMEN
> (chapter 23; italics mine)

Far from being unaware, this writing is self-conscious and only too aware of the evolution, importance and development of the novel both as entertainment, art and moral instrument. Moreover, this is a work calling for a new market – young people's reading, and, as here, the domestic novel for young people was aimed at women. Thus central to the evolution and uncertainties of the nature of fiction was the equally uncertain moral education of a household of women, left to define themselves during the American Civil War.

---

* Accredited by some as being the first women's romance.

The definitions of women's roles and the fictional form in which their roles were dramatized and rehearsed were inexorably linked: the publishers answer to the first being the structural answer to the second. It is no coincidence that Jo wants to be a journalist and her frustrations as an emerging adult (which mirror her mother's) are as 'unresolved' as the 'clear' moral of this edifying Christian text. The irresolvable nature of the moral may be linked then to the required subject of the novel – the domestic setting. What is meant by a Christian moral and therefore a proper role for women is as unresolved as what is meant by a novel and its true subject – in moving from Bunyan through Charlotte Yonge and temperance tract to Dickens, Alcott's book, in its very structure, tends toward secular action: neither its subject matter nor its temperance roots can return it to Bunyanesque allegory. The novel refuses its allegorical role in the pursuit of the secular fact. From whence did this instability *and* power emerge?

Although publishers, printers and booksellers all existed before the turn of the century it was the new rationalisation of these areas plus the appearance of new forms of print enterprise and new methods of selling printed material to an expanded reading public that marked the emergence and domination of fiction and newsprint. The case of fiction is instructive. Without the monopolistic control of Mudie and his library system and W.H. Smith and his sales system working in alliance with the publishing houses of John Murray, George Routledge, Chapman & Hall and many others the very *shape* and form of fiction would have been different. The importance of the three-decker novel to the industry and to Mudie's, the appearance of the serial form through Chapman & Hall and the new reading matter (part work or short novel) aimed at train commuters and pioneered by Routledge (in order to avoid Mudie), made the imaginative space which determined the *art* of the novel. This cannot be ignored. The art of the novel, even that of George Eliot and especially that of Charles Dickens, was a product of a commercial alliance which was rarely other than productive.

Publishers had since the late eighteenth century been reorganizing their businesses in such a way that they may be taken as the first great appearance of the capitalistic method of production. It should not be forgotten that Benjamin Franklin, Max Weber's archetypical proto-capitalist, was both a publisher and a printer. Through legal, administrative and technological changes, the primitive proto-capitalist publisher/printers of the previous century had by the nineteenth transformed themselves into modern businesses, although it is also true that, until the 1870s, publishers that had not evolved could still flourish.

The new middle-class entrepreneurial (gentleman) publishers succeeded because of their willingness to learn from the older, more primitive popular printer/publisher entrepreneurs whose family businesses stretched back, at least in spirit, to Tudor times. It was from these crude presses that almost all working people gained their reading material in the form of broadsheets and chapbooks – a literature that died out only in the 1870s and which, as children's publishing, had a half-century of life longer.

Such businesses, although organized on a small scale in terms of management and productive functions, were able to pour out vast amounts of printed material: fiction, half-fiction and news, which covered the printing of popular 'folk' tales, confessional crime, reports of superstitions and the supernatural, of recent battles, of births, marriages and royal scandals, as well as reprinting jokes, anecdotes and comments on political questions. Many chapbooks (folded and cut to produce 24-page booklets) contained a mixture of topics, fillers and woodcuts. Stories were recycled, 'true' tales invented, true confessions made up; the emphasis almost always was to make stories *contemporary*; history, as the rural past, was never popular, the popular subjects being up-to-date sex, crime and murder.[3] The result was a thriving popular publishing industry in which there was no discernible difference either philosophically or commercially between fact and fiction.[4] Such publications flourished both sides of the Atlantic and if tales of Robin Hood were mutually enjoyed by Americans, so tales of Indians, scalpings and abduction also enjoyed popularity with the British working population.[5]

Fiction fed fact and both fed profits. Seduction and betrayal, a central theme of gothic and popular fiction, gave structure to the true crimes of men like William Corder whose murder of Maria Marten at the Red Barn in Suffolk and subsequent trial, confession and execution in 1828 led to a veritable orgy of fascinated reading. One broadsheet sold over a million copies, a figure not to be surpassed until 1897 when the circulation of *Pearson's Weekly* reached one and quarter million after it ran a competition.[6] This particular broadsheet, containing the murderer's confession (in quartrains), was penned by the sharp–eyed publisher, James Catnach, a man who gained great wealth from such writing and publishing. As one

street hawker said to Henry Mayhew 'there's nothing beats a stunning good murder after all'.[7]

Catnach is one of the better-remembered names among the scores
of anonymous penny-publishers, although others such as the Worrals
of Liverpool, Bebbington of Manchester, John Harkness of Preston
and John Pitts of London, James Kendrew of York, John Cheney
and J.G. Rusher of Banbury and Isaiah Thomas of Worcester,
Massachusetts, are recorded or gained posthumous fame through
biography.[8] The vast number of authors working in this industry
themselves remain biographically silent although some are known
because of later fame or because Henry Mayhew spoke to them:
one such was John Morgan who complained to Mayhew about
Catnach's unwillingness to pay up.

Catnach's works printed all sorts of ephemera from his premises
at Monmouth Court in London and it was here that street hawkers
would settle their accounts for wholesale broadsheets and chapbooks
and from here that they would travel the country selling their wares
in markets, at street corners or door-to-door in remote farming
communities. With a staff of only four, rapid turnover and the quick
reflexes of a later tabloid mentality, Catnach was able to command
considerable profits.

> Catnach almost cornered the market in a wide range of publica-
> tions for children that sold at a halfpenny or even a farthing and,
> as he was not over-particular concerning type or the choice of
> relevant illustrations, he was able to print rapidly and at small
> cost. He was also adept in putting out broadsides at the right
> moment on any crime or scandal that occupied the public's atten-
> tion, as well as historic occasions such as a battle or a royal event.
> In addition, there was a steady income to be gained from print-
> ing tradesmen's cards, posters, theatre programmes and other
> fugitive items; and there was a very brisk trade every Christmas
> in the sale of carols.[9]

Such a publisher/printer could die a rich man, as Catnach did in
1841.

John Pitts was the son of a Norfolk baker who made his way to
London and trained as a printer. He too became wealthy with the
publication of halfpenny ($\frac{1}{2}$d.) ballads. One historian has labelled
these men and their class 'rough, tough and uncouth opportun-
ists'.[10] Nevertheless,

there were no popular newspapers written at a level to suit [work-
ing people's] background and interests. The chapbooks and the
broadsides ... filled a gap. While they might have heard of a
criminal's being brought to trial, they might hear little of the
outcome, until the broadside arrived with the whole of the story.
This applied to historical events as well – the details of a naval
victory, a royal event or a political squabble must wait on the
arrival of the broadside, which not only reprinted the details in
the press but relayed it in ballad form as well. The latter point
was especially important: illiterate people often have remarkable
memories – aided by the recommended and familiar tune at the
head of the ballad, many a listener would effortlessly commit the
verses to memory after hearing them only two or three times.
The language was simple, the rhymes crude but memorable. To
a large mass of the population the chapbooks and the broadsides
filled a need that was not otherwise met until the introduction of
the popular press in the 1850s.[11]

Furthermore, the reading habits of the poor fed directly into those
of the richer classes. Crime, sex, royalty – in a word sensation –
filled respectable newspapers, and sentimentality and vulgarity
could feature in articles in *The Times*, without the readers of such
articles realizing the continuum of earthy vulgarity and language
that linked them to the poor.[12] Here was a true democracy of the
vulgar, latterly to be swallowed up in publications like *Tit Bits* and
in the juxtaposition of Sherlock Holmes stories in the *Strand
Magazine* with another regular feature: curiously shaped fruit and
vegetables, contained in illustrations of oddly distorted garden produce. Such juxtapositioning was the life blood of popular reading,
something quite lost when we anthologize literature by such as
Conan Doyle.
    Vulgarity filtered *upward* and hence it is far less instructive to
notice sources of influences in 'serious' or 'classic' literature than to
notice parallel developments and contemporaneous *cross-fertilization* (not to say plagiarism). *Sweeney Todd* stands between the modern serial and the archaic chapman and his wares just as Edgar
Allan Poe stands between the hack and the 'serious' fictionalist.[13] It
is not merely in terms of imagery that we can follow 'the continuing
process of cross-fertilization between the "highest" of high art and
popular genres', but also in terms of their forms as commodities

(that is structures within a market and a community of readers based on that market).[14] As such, productive techniques changed and modified subject matter as subject matter enlarged the possibilities of production. To cope with these changes popular 'serious' publishers rapidly modernized to take advantage of the sales potential exposed by the 'older' methods of broadsheet hackdom.

Changes incorporated capital-intense investment, partnership with banks, divisions in labour and production (i.e. Marx's 'means of production'), specialized management functions, new means of marketing, advertising, wholesaling and retailing; authors were treated as contracted professionals as books became commodities, essentially ephemeral and determined by a reading public (the market). Large-scale production was helped by new means of creating paper (first by the Fourdrinier machine) and mass printing (the steam press) even if other methods including modernized typesetting lagged behind. Thus with the book seen simultaneously as *moral vehicle* and *commodity* the publishing, lending and retailing empires progressed in mutual alliance.

The British book trade in the nineteenth century was a modern industry in every way. It took advantage of mechanised systems of production, developed highly efficient distribution arrangements based on the most up-to-date means of transport, and evolved a division of labour both between and within its various branches. Many firms were still family businesses, but they were large and well-organised, and many of their owners were employers of labour on a substantial scale. Millions of pounds of capital investment poured into the trade, much of it generated directly from profit. It was inevitable that attitudes within the industry also underwent a profound change. The parochialism of the battle for literary property and the restrictive practices of the congers and the trade sales vanished into history; the trade was in the marketplace, and the first consideration was economic success in the face of competition.[15]

Moreover, the three-decker novel, with its high price and stable form acted as the 'gold standard for an otherwise shaky market'.[16] This form acted to give depth to art and breadth to sales, indeed 'It is probable that the artificial maintenance of the thousand-page novel in this way made for greater as well as bigger fiction'.[17] Yet at the same time it acted to define other versions of fiction, in which the production techniques of penny-dreadful publishers were put to the service of middle-class reading, where 'huge figures were involved. In 1847, for example, Chapman & Hall printed 2 290 000 'parts' of Dickens's novels.[18] Thus was Charles Knight, the nineteenth-century printer, able to state with a considerable level of conviction that 'the penny magazine produced a revolution in popular art throughout the world'.[19]

Three further points need to be emphasized here. The first is obvious but little noticed, that the 'novel is the only literary genre to have been invented since the invention of printing, and its literary history is inseparable from the history of its publication'.[20] The second is that the continuing and lucrative trade in reprints of non-copyright work made older literature itself into an infinite resource for new literature of all kinds, and thus the content of such literature was a cheap and conveniently renewable resource both in its own right and as a prompt to new fiction using it as a basis. Lastly the new literatures slowly undermined the 'older' moralities (already worn thin in the eighteenth century).

The secularization of fiction (which meant it merely had to *represent* and *entertain*) was to form the backdrop for a slowly developing movement which led from the Christian moral tales of Charlotte Yonge and the tractarians to the sentimental, mystical Christianity of Marie Corelli and her populist and highly popular ideology to the growing body of literature in which the subject matter was society and the individual represented naturalistically. The moralism of Mudie, Smith, the Macmillan brothers and many publishers such as John Cassell had finally been defeated by their very success. Moreover, the centrally important need to lower both production costs and purchase price in order to widen ephemeral print's distribution, which had originally been intended to increase access to radical unstamped (i.e. untaxed) news, and revolutionary opinion was itself a highly moral crusade. That too was defeated by the very success of its technical and costing methods and the absorption of its politics into mainstream liberal debate.

is amusing to reflect that the dramatic increase in pub-
ght an equal rise in pornography during Queen Vic-

Such an alliance brought into being the new age of information without which the later industrial revolutions would not have succeeded. By the end of the nineteenth century almost all of Britain's workforce could read (see next chapter) and by the 1840s Britain was already a 'print-dependent society'.[21] It is no exaggeration to say that William Henry Smith and Charles Edward Mudie were the first information moguls whose monopoly on printed information was virtually impregnable in Britain and whose 'editorial' or purchasing decisions were decisive in the production and shape of British literature, especially fiction. When publishers were avoiding Mudie they had to devise new forms to do it, although until the decisive intervention of William Heinemann very late in the century these forms were often supportive rather than antagonistic towards Mudie's standardized form.

Serialisation by no means threatened the three-decker in which the majority of lesser novelists continued to appear. The *Publishers' Circular* listed six times as many in 1887 (184) as in 1837 (31). A prime factor in its survival, and increased prosperity, in the mid-century period was the dramatic growth in the circulating library business. In the 1840s and 50s Mudie's library in particular expanded to control a major section of the metroplitan market and a sizeable portion of that in the country and overseas. At his zenith, in the 1860s, he earned up to £40 000 a year in subscriptions. . . . Mudie's triumph was the outcome not of cautious whittling down of costs but of slashing them dramatically, so short circuiting the gap that existed between high book prices and low income. . . . One reason that fiction tends to gravitate towards the cheapest form of publishing is that in most cases it is read once only, and then quickly. In America this economic logic led to books of incredible cheapness, designed to be thrown away after use. In Britain it was not the book which was cheapened but the reading of it.[22]

The essential point here is that unless purchased as part works and then privately bound or purchased as serials and possibly lost or lent to friends, bound books were not bought in the nineteenth century by *any* class. They were *borrowed* and it is this habit which made reading what it was.[23] It was the library, the reprint and the

home-bound book which established the classics of the nineteenth
century.

The collapse of the firm Constable & Ballantyne in 1826 had
suggested that the publishing of inexpensive books could not succeed and yet the industry was soon joined by young entrepreneurs
who did not see money-making and morality as mutually incom-
patible and sought ways to enlarge the former while promoting the
latter.[24]

John Murray began his rise to fortune when, on coming of age,
he bought out his partner and left retailing to become a phenomenally
successful publisher. Dickens was only 24 when he began with
Pickwick Papers and still in his thirties when he began *Household
Words*. In the case of all these young men there was a felt need to
stabilize and control a changing market place – to find a common
currency from which all could prosper. To a large extent Mudie
provided such stability as well as upholding the inherent conservative moralism of most respectable publishers.

> Charles Edward Mudie's own career began, when in 1840 he
> opened a shop in King Street (now Southampton Street) in Lon-
> don to which students from the newly created London Univer-
> sity would go. Having realised the potential of *lending* rather
> than selling Mudie's career took off. Unlike other library/book-
> sellers Mudie soon professionalised his approach and taking as
> his mainstay the newly emerging novel helped create both a read-
> ing public in the middle class and the very form of their enjoy-
> ment: the three-decker novel which they borrowed in ever
> increasing numbers at affordable rental subscription. Such fiction
> at 31/6 was a luxury happily borrowed, rarely bought, 'it seemed
> to me in those days that the patronage of Mudie', recalled Mrs
> Oliphant, 'was a sort of recognition from heaven'.[25]

Mudie's vast purchasing power kept many publishers and novelists in comfort so no one needed to 'rock the boat'. However, even
Mudie outdid himself and had by 1864 relinquished some of the
shares in his business, although not control.

In 1861 it was estimated that the library included 800,000 books,
and that 10,000 passed in and out of its walls every day.

The cost of building the hall proved, however, too great for Mr. Mudie's resources, and in 1864 the library became a limited company. Half the shares were held by Mr. Mudie, and he retained the sole management, so that there was no change in the conduct of the business. He still bought freely all such books as seemed to him suited to the tastes . . . of his large public.[26]

Through this 'moral' control and his censorious conduct, Mudie created a middle-class, middle-brow readership which still exists and which later began to change its allegiance to public libraries, where fiction could be had with somewhat less, though not always much less, censorship.[27] It was in the Croydon Public Library in 1908 that D.H. Lawrence, that archetypical man of the masses, found a copy of Nietzsche and first formulated his thoughts on the destruction of the very class from which he had emerged.[28]

While fiction helped define the age it did so in the context of many other forms of literature. Of the taste for encyclopaedic knowledge and the search for facts nothing fitted better than the newspaper. The newspaper was central to the spreading of mass literacy as it predated both the educational reforms of the 1870s and the appearance of the 'modern' novel. For some, the thought of a public reading newspapers alongside the new literacy which followed the Education Act of 1870 was just too much, as George Bernard Shaw lamented, 'The Education Act of 1871 [sic] . . . was producing readers who had never before bought books, nor could have read them if they had. . . . I, as a belated intellectual, went under completely'.[29] Of course, this did not prevent him from indulging in a journalistic career. Yet a much more optimistic picture arises concerning the new mass literacy if we turn elsewhere.

The cheap newspaper and periodical cannot perhaps be defined strictly as educators. Yet for good or evil, and probably on the whole for good, they are very powerful ones. Notwithstanding the many sins and shortcomings of the newspaper press, the working man of today, with his broadsheet for a penny is by its aid a man of fuller information, better judgement and wider sympathies than the workman of thirty years back who had to content himself with gossip and rumour, and whose source of information as to public events was the well-thumbed weekly newspaper in the public house.[30]

It is significant that this was noted *before* the Education Act, by social commentators in 1867. It may therefore be assumed that a great many working people could read before the implementation of the Act; that they read news, sport and popular fiction is proved by the print runs of broadsheets, chapbooks, almanacs, newspapers, special journals, serials and part works aimed specifically at that market.

> One consequence of [the 1870 Act], however, was the creation of a myth about literacy in nineteenth-century Britain. The Act was supposedly to turn out hundreds of Board School literates. It was, therefore, easily assumed that the previous level and extent of literacy must have been very poor. The years before 1870 thus came to be seen as a dark age. Recent work has shown up the myth for what it is, but it is equally important to remember that for generations after 1870 it was a very widely accepted version of the past, and judgements and analyses of the relationship of education to the press were made in its light. By the 1890s at the latest it had become a cliché to link the large circulation of the popular press with the effects of Board School education.[31]

What might be said, is that the Act *redirected* literacy for the lower reading classes, created new patterns and provided a greater means of creating homogeneity in print and *controlling* print for certain sectional views. Shaw's claims against the new literacy were not on behalf of an old élite being pushed out but a new élite created in antipathy to current trends. Matthew Arnold's 'remnant' was a new 'faction' which defined its own role as one of opposition. Thus the ills at the end of the Victorian era could be blamed respectively on centralization, philistine taste, monopolistic interest and 'tabloid' journalism. Together, they spelled the end, for many commentators of the older liberalism of the early nineteenth century.

> W.J. Fisher, sometime editor of the *Daily Chronicle*, wrote in 1904, 'the provincial Liberal press has become feebler and feebler, and in the smaller towns has almost ceased to exist'. The young liberal historian G.M. Trevelyan wrote in 1901, 'the Philistines have

captured the Ark of the Covenant (the printing press), and have learnt to work their own miracles through its power'. L.T. Hobhouse, social philosopher and leading 'new liberal' journalist, wrote in 1909, 'the Press, more and more the monopoly of a few rich men, from being the organ of democracy has become rather the sounding-board for whatever ideas commend themselves to the great material interests'.[32]

The newspaper was in all respects the *sine qua non* of a modern print industry and a society defined by printed material. 'As early as the 1870s suburban trains were left strewn with the litter of thousands of newspapers every morning'.[33] Indeed, in the 1860s, noisy commuter trains had forced travellers into the privacy of reading – a situation credited with saving them time at their work.[34] Admittedly such habits were middle class in the 1860s but all literate workers spent time reading and Sunday became the day when such activity was especially sanctioned.

Like the publishing industry before it, the newspaper industry had, by the later nineteenth century tended toward a stabilized oligarchical structure. The protean world of the 1840s had become concentrated in the hands of newspaper 'magnates' by the 1900s. In 1910 the London Metropolitan press was controlled by Northcliffe, Pearson and the Morning Leader Group; the Sunday Press was divided by H.J. Dalziel, G. Riddell, F. Lloyd and again Northcliffe between whom 80 per cent of the market was distributed.[35]

Such concentration was cause for infinite doom-laden predictions from a disaffected intelligentsia and constant carping about the poverty of culture not just in the working people (who were disregarded anyway!) but in the real enemy: the philistine, suburban, middle class. If it was true that earlier patterns of local social life had been partially erased by this concentration of newspaper owners, and if the older local politics had been pushed out too, it was also true that the new journalism created a wider view of the world, thus uniting the British into a nation with common interests, common national politics and a homogeneity (in the 'ordinary') which gave the class system its definition and the classes their communal self-identity. There was no real or coherent industrial proletariat in Britain before there was a reading public aware of national affairs, and in this the middle class came to a consciousness of their role only with the appearance of print designed for them from the 1840s onwards. Self-definition learnt through the newspapers and educational processes of the latter part of the century was always a negotiation between the reader and the pressures exerted by school boards, library committees and editors. Print monopolies with their moral and political biases were not simply matters of evil but also causes of a thriving national culture capable of serious debate, as well as the creative forces behind the communal dreams of a literate consumer society. By 1957, Richard Hoggart could regret the passing of this world of industrial communities and urban villages which was based on the common pleasures and knowledge derived from the popular press of the later Victorian period.[36]

Print was intrinsically connected with the various strands of the concept of Victorian modernity. It was essential to educational, technological, and business change as it was also essential to the pursuit of knowledge, the demands of the daily news and the world of printed entertainment.

My argument, that the great perceptual movements of the nineteenth century were the result of a spreading and protean literacy, also suggests that any study of all *literatures* of the period must be aware that commercial demands and market forces were constantly creating and modifying literary forms, whether they be novels, text books, newspapers or even the smaller world of poetry. In mid-century the serialized works of Dickens were always 'works in progress'. Furthermore, the movement and growth of significantly Anglo-American reading publics led to constantly shifting forms. The publishing of fiction changed across the century to allow new forms to appear, the short story being the most notable, suited as it was to new consumer demands. Thus another group of writers got their chance to publish. Similarly subgenres were created which embraced spy thrillers, westerns, women's romance, imperial adventures and, of course, detective stories.

More than this the very nature of authorship changed. Writers became celebrities – toured America and thrilled packed houses. A long time before the end of the century a writer's name meant money, although many writers were keen to be known as 'the author of' rather than by their real names, the use of *noms de plume* being widespread (see Chapter 5). Author's names and styles were their fortune and their stock, part of the common ownership of readers.

Writers had finally become Carlylean heroes. To further this new heroism, a new technology was born. The typewriter allowed for rapid mechanical processing, and duplication of precious manuscripts came with the use of carbon paper: 'Mark Twain boasted of his willingness to use this curious new machine, and *The Adventures of Tom Sawyer* is reputed to be the first typewritten manuscript to be set into a book'.[37]

Forged on this metallic alphabet was something even more peculiar than this mechanical means of expression. Authors were now becoming aware that they owned a unique form of invisible goods – intellectual property. Copyright had for authors the same status as patents for inventors. Walter Besant's Society of Authors became, by the 1890s, their protective agency and it helped to create the proper atmosphere for those agreements which protected British authors from the piracies of foreigners (especially Americans).

Such changes encouraged both artistic creativity and popular entertainment and often the two happily combined, but tensions at the end of the period already revealed the neurotic nature of this continued expansion.[38] Yet, whilst Trollope and George Eliot and their publishers and readers were well aware of the distance between 'high seriousness' in fiction and simple entertainment their attitudes were not quite the same as those held by both the early and later Bloomsbury in defiance of popular literacy and antagonistic to its implications.

Daniel Boorstin has pointed out, in his monumental study of the rise of American modern consumer society that, 'Democracy required a new lexicon, a redefinition of what was excellent, of what was good, and – most significantly – of what was good enough.'[39] This new lexicon of good and 'good enough' (that cheap luxury of books offered by Mudie to the middle classes) was fought out in print and formed by print, especially advertising print and the language of consumption. This new lexicon more and more provided 'extravagant possibilities in the language of the commonplace'.[40]

The language of the commonplace was itself undergoing radical changes. This was especially so when new methods of transcription impinged upon the very sentiments transcribed. By the 1880s it had already become possible to mass produce steel pens, and once problems concerned with the corrosive effects of the old inks had been overcome with the production of new non-corrosive dyes, the steel nib was to become the standard instrument of transcription. Later in the century, this nib allied to an internal reservoir allowed for more rapid transcription using fountain pens filled with *synthetic* dyes such as nigrosine (patented in 1867).[41] The creation of the fully practical typewriter in 1874 (with continuous improvements from 1892) further aided rapid transcription, but it also marked a decisive break in the act of writing which now came closer to a form of rapid typesetting.

Authors were quickly organizing their expression to fit a new imaginative and structural space between the physicality of the fountain pen and the technological distance of the typeface of a typewriter. Rapidly changing the constituents of the old sentence structure such instruments created a substituted expressive form in the 'organic' paragraph.

In 1860 . . . the average English sentence had half the words of an Elizabethan sentence. [But] the penny press and tabloid journalism would further shorten . . . sentences. . . . No story longer than 250 words, guest editor Alfred Harmsworth demanded for the January 1, 1901, issue of Joseph Pulitzer's newspaper *The World*.[42]

The 'new' concept of the paragraph was a substitution inherently 'modern', combining a belief in technological integrity, organic fluidity and the psychosomatic correspondence of thought and gesture. In a word, here was a new harmonics.

A prime determinant of the pattern of gestures accompanying speeches read from written texts, . . . the paragraph . . . was generally ignored by rhetoricians until Alexander Bain's *English Composition and Rhetoric* of 1866. . . . Bain had developed a sophisticated associationalist psychology whose laws he applied to the structure of writing. . . . [He] drew from the Laws of Similarity, Contiguity, and Compound Association a systematic theory in which paragraph structure should be anticipatable from sentence structure (Similarity), thoughts within a paragraph should flow from one sentence to the next (Contiguity) and, together, the concordance of sentences should yield a powerful resultant (Compound Association). In other words, a paragraph truly expressive of one's thoughts should have Unity, Coherence and Mass (Emphasis).

In less than 40 years writers of American textbooks such as John S. Hart, author of *Manual of Composition and Rhetoric* (1870), had moved from an emphasis on the sentence to an insistence on the primacy of the paragraph. Charles Sears Baldwin, Assistant Professor of Rhetoric at Yale, had by 1902 produced his *A College Manual of Rhetoric*, which took the totality and unity of a composition as its starting point.

> By 1916, William D. Lewis, a high school principal, and James F. Hosic, instructor at Chicago Normal College, were explaining in their *Practical English for High Schools* that a paragraph is 'a unit of thought'.... Writing in paragraphs was at once the organic statement of coherent ideas and a training toward clear thought.
>
> This organic paragraph ... stood in trust of the link between mental activity and physical movement ... following not only the laws of associationalist psychology but also of psychophysiology.[43]

For popular fiction authors the combination of typewriter and dictation machine allowed for the creation of rapidly produced stories to feed the new reading public's tastes. Such innovation and demand became especially important for those professional authors who made their living as writers and had no other means of support, nor could afford to dally between titles. 'The popular storyteller, part of the working population, became the writer employed by the press owner – poised between the tastes and outlooks of employer on the one hand and customer on the other.'[44]

Working-class authors such as Edgar Wallace became intermediaries between two groups and two classes: to both they owed an allegiance and yet from both they remained separated. Wallace, himself the son of a Billingsgate porter, seemed to have little time for the 'working man', his targeted reader.

If Charlotte Yonge and Raymond Chandler have anything in common then it is that they and hundreds of other authors acted as witnesses and dramatists of the heroically mundane: the morality of spirit having become the necessity of ownership. By the late 1890s the Sears catalogue was the best-selling book of the nineteenth century.

Some have called the big mail-order catalogues the first characteristically American kind of book. Since colonial times, Americans had been more notable for their almanacs, newspapers,
magazines and how-to-do-it manuals than for their treatises: the
relevant, the topical, the ephemeral, had been more expressive of
American life than the systematic and the monumental. The Sears
Roebuck Catalogue was the Bible of the new rural consumption
communities.[45]

In such a bible was the morality of ownership – a book for democratic
peoples held together by a common language of consumption – peoples thinned by distance but joined by print. The Sears Roebuck catalogue is the quintessential book of the modern age. In its illustrated
pages the concept of object information and consumer anticipation
was heralded and advertising and print circulation came of age.

By the twentieth century, the very act of shopping itself was a fit
subject for Anglo-American fictional representation, Virginia Woolf,
Edna Ferber, O. Henry, Hugh Walpole, H.G. Wells and James Joyce
all understood that shopping was a crucial activity in the definition
of self in the modern world.[46] In the Sears catalogue people were
introduced to the universe of things and from their newspapers to
that of facts. What united these two areas was a curiosity about
neighbours who were also 'strangers'. Their needs and desires were
also the needs and desires of others in the community who also
looked to purchase the universe of things and consume the universe of facts.

Learning from the marketing methods of the Sears catalogue and
obsessed with the 'problem' of facts, DeWitt Wallace, founder of
the magazine *Reader's Digest*, proved himself the inheritor of a
tradition of popular publishing stretching back to *Poor Richard's
Almanack*.[47] Wallace had been a failure in his attempts to be a university lecturer and a copy writer, but it had been this very failure,
and his autodidactic beliefs that made him a successful publisher
when he combined the little magazine format with an approach
more reasonably associated with pulp presses.

Wallace's almost neurotic obsession with printed material, facts,
tabulation and memory coincided with a general concern for such
things and the growing popularity of that mind-training technique
called 'Pelmanism' which had become a major cult between the
wars. The new owner and editor of the *Reader's Digest* (which be-

gan publication in 1922) exemplified in his character the commonly held beliefs about modernity, change and business which he was able to commodify in his magazine of self-improvement and self-education: progressive in its contents, it proved populist in its attitudes. The central theme of the *Digest* became 'change itself'.[48] Here were factual articles condensed to their essentials for those who believed themselves to be too busy to spare too much time to read but who needed to be 'up to date' – the reader would be a practical person, business-orientated, mobile, domestic, conservative, family-centred, someone wanting 'knowledge of rather than knowledge about'.[49] Thus it was that *Reader's Digest* was at once middle-brow and plebeian, a product of America's belief both in endless progressive change and the conservative homely values of small-town communities.

The factual contents of the *Reader's Digest* and the pocket-book size of the format made it at once an 'essential' almanac and an escapist compendium, each condensed article being some titbit to store away in a moment of leisure and a possible clue to future business success to be remembered later when needed.

In 1950, a new departure led to the *Reader's Digest* Condensed Book Club in which new middle-brow literature was stripped of inessentials and reproduced in abridged form. The novel now was changed into its bizarre other: knowledge of rather than knowledge *about*. Stripped of its *style* (its nature as 'art') the novel became pure information as escapism, a practical guide to relaxation for the overworked. In retaining the 'essential' elements of character and narrative, the Condensed Book Club editors succeeded in losing the very 'writerliness' of the originals – that upon which the writers had worked longest, the very opposite impulse to that invoked by the enterprise of the avant garde. Popular fiction was thus proved a type of process of 'rewriting' within a framework of data converted into practical knowledge. The *utility* function of fiction was no longer in its moral trajectory but in its offering practical aid towards relaxation and escape.

While vilified by intellectuals, such escapism was embraced by the vast majority of popular writers. In the 1920s, for instance, writers like Ethel M. Dell catered for 'women with tiring and monotonous jobs; housekeepers, governesses, lady companions, maids [and] nurses' and this was certainly not due to incapacity or mere venality on the part of the writer.[50]

That Ethel [Dell] never aimed her cultural sights higher was not due to any lack of education, since, like her sister, she was well read and cultured. Her sympathies, however, were with those who were forced to work in uncongenial jobs; to them she set out to bring glamour and excitement.[51]

It is hardly surprising that in such a world the old certainities were redefined and that for some this meant a crisis in the very nature of meaning: the neuroses of high literary modernism were the neuroses of the age of print itself.

4

A River So Deep:
Literacy, Language

The massive social, economic and technological changes which allowed the new print industry to circulate and flourish could not have ocurred without a continuously increasing rate of literacy amongst the new democratic masses. While figures cannot prove particularly accurate in terms of how people read, why they read and at what level they understood the material, they offer a foundation for any further conjectures on the form and nature of literature *as is was consumed*.

Investigations into literacy have often taken the marriage signatures of men and women in parish registers as at least indicative of functional literacy. In 1867, one of the first British investigators, W.L. Sargant, found that 51 per cent of couples in England and Wales could sign the marriage register between 1754 and 1762 and that this had risen to 54 per cent by 1799–1804.[1] Nevertheless, this gradual rise took a dip while rural communities moved into towns and came to terms with factory life and urban communities. Despite regional variations and the fact that the universal literacy of all classes is not essential for industrial growth, literacy levels did continue to rise as did educational opportunity before 1870.[2] By 1851, the SPCK had 23 135 schools and approximately three quarters of all five to fifteen-year-olds were gaining some sort of organized education regardless of whether the institutions they attended were benevolent or coercive.[3]

Hobsbawm, in an interesting variation of literacy testing, has pointed out that if two letters were posted per person in the 1790s, then by the 1880s, 42 letters per head were being sent and that this may be taken as another indicator of growing literacy.[4] Whatever the case, by 1831 a quarter of the 14 million population of Britain now lived in towns and general literacy was increasing regardless of regional variation or industrial disruption to a point where 75 per cent of men and 50 per cent of women were literate.[5] By the end of the nineteenth century and with the institution of compulsory education literacy became almost universal. In 1891, 94 per cent of men and 93 per cent of women could read.[6] By 1910, only 5 per cent of the British population was considered illiterate and by 1914 that level had dramatically dropped to 0.8 per cent, measured by marriage registers signed by 'mark'.[7] It was only in the worst slums between the 1900s and 1940s that literacy could not be taken for granted and a call from the School Board Man could upset the precarious system of earnings and family structure of the very poorest. Even the British Labour Party would not court the illiterate and avoided recruiting them, in favour of literate *respectable* working voters.[8] Nevertheless the very poorest still read newspapers such as the *Daily Herald* or *Daily Chronicle* and retained a totemistic respect for books.[9] Katherine Mansfield tartly observed in 1914 when creating one of her lower-class characters that:

> Henry was a great fellow for books. He did not read many nor did he possess above half a dozen. He looked at all in the Charing Cross Road during lunch-time and at any odd time in London; the quantity with which he was on nodding terms was amazing. By his clean neat handling of them and by his nice choice of phrase when discussing them with one or another bookseller you would have thought that he had taken his pap with a tome propped before his nurse's bosom. But you would have been wrong.
>
> ('Something Childish But Very Natural')

Books played a part within a complex web of social and economic relations and ownership helped to define status amongst the humblest. Literacy was always literacy within a *context*, as one resident of a poor London street makes clear in talking of his father's concern for family repectability and the correct façade to adopt when cadging a charitable handout:

> And this is where my old man displayed both his contempt for the higher-ups – the *toffs* as he used to call them – and his natural con-artist's appreciation for the suitable stage-setting. . . . Shabby-genteel was my old man's *forte*: impoverished rather than hard-up. . . . [My] old man organised my mother to scrub and scour, to create the general image of poverty, hunger, and sparkling cleanliness – to show that Jack's little brood had no intention of

succumbing to the squalor and lethargic helplessness abounding on all sides of this little oasis of culture. To emphasise the cultural angle, Poppa had painstakingly cherished the dozen or so reminders of our former happy state of affluence before falling from grace in the shape of his library . . . Odd titles which the old villain had culled discriminately from totters' Sunday markets in which they displayed the gems and plums of their weekly gleanings from the totting with their barrows. They'd put them on the pavements outside their houses. Titles like *The Mill on the Floss* . . . *Cricket on the Hearth*, Marie Corelli's *The Sorrows of Satan*, Hall Caine's *The Christian*, *The Manxman* and *The Bondman*, etc. Predominance of place . . . was given to titles . . . with biblical connotations – *The Way of the Transgressor* would have been most appropriate. The book-case itself had been painstakingly crafted from an eggbox, lovingly finished in two pennorth of mahogony-stain varnish. . . . When old Goodrum [the Relieving Officer] knocked at the street door, two knocks for us on the first floor, not for him the bald invitation to 'Come on up!' No, the old man went down in person, to escort this distinguished visitor. . . . Short of pinning a poster with 'Down With Drink!' on the door, old Jack went through the card.[10]

The situation in the United States was somewhat different from that of Great Britain. Even from the earliest years a premium was set on literacy. John Adams, writing in 1765, could be proud of the fact that 'a native American who cannot read or write is as rare an appearance as a Jacobite or a Roman Catholic, that is as a comet or an earthquake', instead 80 per cent of men were literate in the colonies.[11] Women's literacy lagged behind but demands for cultural participation from 1790 onwards greatly improved the 40 per cent literacy rate of the 1760s.[12] By mid-century, literacy rates stood at 67 per cent for men and 51 per cent for women (accounting for immigration) and this was before compulsory elementary schooling was introduced in Massachussetts (1852), the District of Columbia (1864) and Vermont.[13]

Such an increase in literacy and education in mid-century America did not however have a direct relationship with industrial processes nor urbanization as in Britain. Indeed, while American technological practice was designed to *eliminate* expertise, generate consumer goods and spread general wealth, human management was generating a literate class of its own.

The scarcity of legal learning did not lead to a scarcity of laws or lawyers ([America] soon became the most lawyered and most legislated country in the world), but instead of a new kind of legal profession and a new concept of law; the scarcity of specialized medical learning soon led to a new kind of doctor and a new concept of medicine; and a scarcity of theological learning led to a new kind of minister and a new concept of religion. Similarly, the scarcity of craft skills set the stage for a new nearly craftless way of making things. And this prepared a new concept of material plentitude and of the use and expendability of things which would be called the American Standard of Living.[14]

Alexis de Tocqueville, that assiduous nation-watcher, found literacy well rooted in America when he visited in 1847. If an 'industrial spirit' had crept into the tastes of 'the industrial classes', nevertheless the democratic 'classes' of America showed a taste for literacy and a desire for reading matter.[15] 'The ever growing crowd of readers' were well catered for by numerous bookshops with 'American books crowding the shelves' even if few of those works were notable or their authors known to an educated public.[16] Thus, while Americans lacked a classical education, nevertheless one could still find plenty of books from England which were printed or plagiarized and de Tocqueville was happy to offer this encomium to the reading habits of ordinary Americans:

> The literary inspiration of Great Britain darts its beams into the depths of the forests of the New World. There is hardly a pioneer's hut which does not contain a few odd volumes of Shakespear. I remember reading the feudal drama of *Henry V* for the first time in a log cabin.[17]

If 'Americans [had] not yet . . . got any literature' of their own by which de Tocqueville meant poetry and drama, then they had found a voice in the political pamphlet and in journalism.[18] 'Only the journalists strike me as truly American', de Tocqueville wrote, sharing as they did an appetite for information as entertainment, a concentration on the individual and a new more fluid use of the English language.

Progress in eliminating illiteracy sped up as the century moved on.[19] The introduction of an eight-year compulsory education programme (delayed in the South to disenfranchise the Black population) had led by 1900 to 22 per cent of the population being in elementary schooling and by 1940, in a population of 132 million, 7 million were regularly attending high school.[20] Between 1870 and 1940 the population had trebled from 44 million to 132 million and high school attendance had now risen from 5 per cent of the total possible school population in 1900 to 42 per cent in 1940.[21] Equally, illiteracy had progressively fallen from 20 per cent in the 1840s to 11 per cent in 1900 and thence down to 4 per cent in 1930 and 2 per cent in 1950 (of the population over 10 years old).[22] This was against European rates of 15 per cent illiteracy in 1930 and 8 per cent in 1950. But if America's population was more literate it was also differently literate.

By 1941 in his preface to the revised *American Language*, H.L. Mencken could point to the appearance, rise and conquest of a new form of English language, similar to, but different from the English of the British Isles.

> [T]he pull of American has become so powerful that is has begun to drag English with it, and in consequence some of the differences once visible have tended to disappear. The two forms of the language, of course, are still distinct in more ways than one, and when an Englishman and an American meet they continue to be conscious that each speaks a tongue that is far from identical with the tongue spoken by the other. But the Englishman, of late, has yielded so much to American example, in vocabulary, in idiom, in spelling and even in pronunciation, that what he speaks promises to become, on some not too remote tomorrow, a kind of dialect of American, just as the language spoken by the American was once a dialect of English. The English writers who note this change lay it to the influence of the American movies and talkies, but it seems to me that there is also something more, and something deeper. The American people now constitute by far the largest fraction of the English-speaking race, and since the World War they have shown an increasing inclination to throw off their old subservience to English precept and example. If only by the force of numbers, they are bound to exert a dominant influence upon the course of the common language hereafter.[23]

It seemed to Mencken, as it did to the ancestors he cites, that the *experience* of America needed a new language, one more loose or fluid than the English of the English and as adaptable to circumstance as the language of the Elizabethans. By 1778, a Congressional Committee was demanding replies by foreigners be in the language of the United States and by the later eighteenth century, John Witherspoon, president of Princeton, could coin the term *Americanism* for the divergent language of the nation.[24] Witherspoon, writing as 'The Druid' (from 1781) contributed a series of articles to the *Pennsylvania Journal and Weekly Advertiser* on the nature of American speech and its need of *reform*.[25] To this end he noted:

1. Americanisms, or ways of speaking peculiar to this country.
2. Vulgarisms in England and America.
3. Vulgarisms in America only.
4. Local phrases or terms.
5. Common blunders arising from ignorance.
6. Cant phrases.
7. Personal blunders.
8. Technical terms introduced into the language.[26]

Happily *unreformed*, the American language continued to adapt to the experience of nation-making and it was Noah Webster in his *American Dictionary of the English Language* (1828) who began to provide a formal framework for the speech, spelling and grammar of the continent. In so doing he anticipated Mencken by a century.[27]

As an independent nation, our honor requires us to have a system of our own, in language as well as government. Great Britain, whose children we are, and whose language we speak, should no longer be *our* standard; for the taste of her writers is already corrupted, and her language on the decline. But if it were not so, she is at too great a distance to be our model, and to instruct us in the principles of our own tongue. . . . Several circumstances render a future separation of the American tongue from the English necessary and unavoidable. . . . Numerous local causes, such as a new country, new associations of people, new combinations of ideas in arts and sciences, and some intercourse with tribes wholly unknown in Europe, will introduce new words into the American tongue. These causes will produce, in a course of time, a language in North America as different from the future language of England as the modern Dutch, Danish and Swedish are from the German, or from one another: like remote branches of a tree springing from the same stock, or rays of light shot from

the same center, and diverging from each other in proportion to
their distance from the point of separation. . . . We have therefore
the fairest opportunity of establishing a national language and of
giving it uniformity and perspicuity, in North America, that ever
presented itself to mankind. Now is the time to begin the plan.

Alexis de Tocqueville also noted the appearance of 'American' as a
distinct branch of English.

Educated Englishmen, better able to appreciate these fine
nuances than I, have often told me that the language of well-
educated Americans is decidedly different from that spoken by
the same class in Great Britain.

Their complaint is not only that the Americans have introduced
a lot of new words (the difference between the two countries and
the distance between them would have been enough to account
for that), but that these new words are generally taken from the
jargon of parties, the mechanical arts, or trade. They also say that
the Americans have given new meanings to old English words.
Finally they maintain that the Americans often mix their styles in
an odd way, sometimes putting words together which, in the
mother tongue, are carefully kept apart.[28]

He put this change in usage down to the need in a democratic
country to respond to new things and relationships not covered in
a traditional, conservative and autocratic setting.[29]
    The changes in linguistic usage were the vital element in giving
national identity to the United States because they encapsulated
American political, legal and moral values and gave expression to
the contractual nature of participation. To these ends English was
adaptable, absorbing, as it could, the language usage of waves of
immigrants, whether Irish, Jewish, Polish, French, German or any
number of others, as well as being responsive to native American
words and place names, and open enough for the creation of a
lively vulgate, the slang of ordinary speech. New concerns demanded
new structures of expression. By the 1920s, the gangster novel
(curiously unlike the western) with its 'low' character and emphasis on speech over narrative placed the slang of the street in the
context of the literary. Slang was no longer a curiosity (as with Sam
Weller in Pickwick Papers) for middle-class readers – a la
a foreign race – but the very heart of literary expression.

William Fowler in 1850 could find in American words and usages from foreign languages reworked and jumbled together with new technical, professional, ecclesiastical, and legal words while nouns were turned into verbs, spelling was rationalized and different compound words had begun to appear.

The expansion of the language of Americans accompanied the increasing population and changes in industrial and agricultural practice. By 1851, the population of the United States exceeded that of Britain by over 2 million, by 1890–91 it had doubled the population of Britain with comparative figures of just over 33 million for the United Kingdom as compared with just over 63 million for America and by 1951 it was three times the size of Britain's population of 49 million.[30] The labour force also grew accordingly and although it did not exceed Britain's workforce until the 1880s it had exceeded it by 75 per cent during the 1930s.[31] Nevertheless, this hides the fact that until the 1860s the labour force available in the United States was approximately 2 million less than in Britain (i.e. at the height of Britain's prestige in the nineteenth century) and of the total population a much greater proportional movement into towns and industrial centres can be found between the 1850s and the 1950s for Britain than America.[32] America retains an agricultural base and culture throughout the history of the industrialization of the continent. Of the total workforce, by 1900, 27 per cent were in industry and that proportion has not shifted much in America.

Bagwell and Mingay in their comparative economic study of Britain and America between 1850 and 1939 point out:

> The relatively low proportion of the labour force engaged in American industry at the end of the nineteenth century reflected two important differences: the greater (but diminishing) role of agriculture in the American economy, and the already higher output per head of the American worker. It was only about 1890 that the absolute numbers employed in American industry passed those in British industry, but in the output of certain key products such as coal and steel, the United States had forged well ahead by 1900.

With industrialization came urbanization. In Britain, as early as 1841 only 39 per cent of the population was living in rural areas, and by 1911 this figure had fallen to 19 per cent. In the United States, in 1850 only some 3.5 million people (15 per cent of the population) lived in places having over 2500 inhabitants, and only 2m people (9 per cent) in places having over 25 000 inhabitants. As late as 1910 the rural population of the United States still outnumbered those living in urban areas, and it was only after that date that the urban population came to form the majority. But the tendency for large industrial centres to be created had been marked since the middle of the century, and by 1910 nearly 15.5m people (17 per cent of the total) lived in towns with a population of over a quarter of a million.[33]

Whereas in Britain writers tended to avoid or attack the twin concepts of business and technology, in America, writers embraced the conditions provided by both to explore and concentrate their language *as* writers. If Alexis de Tocqueville could notice as early as the 1830s that Americans were already obsessed with business and commerce, then Wallace Stevens could unapologetically write many years later that 'money was a kind of poetry',[34] and William Carlos Williams (attacking the Englishness of T.S. Eliot) could point out the industrial side of the American language, both its nature as raw material and its potential as representative of modern commercial exchange (that is as a mode of *communication* between people):

what we are trying to do is not only to disengage the elements of a measure but to seek (what we believe is there) a new measure or a new way of measuring that will be commensurate with the social, economic world in which we are living as contrasted with the past. . . .
It is as though for the moment we should be profuse, we Americans; we need to build up a mass, a conglomerate maybe.[35]

Williams continues, 'we [are], loose disassociated (linguistically), yawping speakers of a new language.'[36]

Both e.e. cummings and later Charles Olson found in the technology available to authors the definition and liberation of American 'speech'. The typewriter became both a form of convenience and a structuring device for the 'looseness' of the American tongue.

The irony is, from the machine has come one gain not yet sufficiently observed or used but which leads directly on toward projective verse and its consequences. It is the advantage of the typewriter that, due to its rigidity and its space precisions, it can, for a poet, indicate exactly the breath, the pauses, the suspensions

even of syllables, the juxtapositions even of parts of phrases, which
he intends. For the first time the poet has the stave and the bar
a musician has had. For the first time he can, without the convention of rime [sic] and meter, record the listening he has done to
his own speech and by that one act indicate how he would want
any reader, silently or otherwise, to voice his work.[37]

Later this machine would itself become an item of nostalgia, an icon
to the concept of real authorship and authentic inspiration in the
face of the increasing use of computerized typefaces (see Chapter
12).

    If poets were able to notice this configuration of commerce,
technology, language and *space* so too were popular novelists.
The American language became a kind of cartographical space to
be mapped over and over again by each new writer in order to
capture afresh an 'essence' forever evasive and forever mythically
distant. James M. Cain writing of his style could point out in his
preface to *Double Indemnity* that,

> I make no conscious effort to be tough, or hard-boiled, or grim,
> or any of the things I am usually called. I merely try to write as
> the character would write, and I never forget that the average
> man, from the fields, the streets, the bars, the offices and even the
> gutters of his country, has acquired a vividness of speech that
> goes beyond anything I could invent, and that if I stick to this
> heritage, this logos of the American countryside, I shall attain a
> maximum of effectiveness with very little effort.

What was at issue was the definitions of both a country and the
subjectivity of its citizens in whose individual identity the national
identity took shape. The American publishing industry was primarily engaged in a dialogue with speech patterns that print would
both conventionalize, define and liberate.

    Despite the fecundity of the American language and the gener-
ous inclusiveness and expressiveness of its nature, the English
spoken in the British Isles remained and still remains relatively untouched by Americanisms. If critics from both sides of the political
divide have deplored the influence of American culture they are
not supported by anything other than superficial and emotional
arguments. It can be shown that only relatively recently did American language usage make any real impression on spoken, written

or literary English. Richard Hoggart, for one, amply demonstrated the vitality of colloquial English in his *Uses of Literacy* and Orwell's 'Newspeak' is concerned less with the *expansion* of language in the American model than with the closing down of language suggested by 'Basic English'.

While it is true that American business practice had been noted early in Britain, it made little impact except in retailing, where F.W. Woolworth stores were thoroughly Anglicized from the 1930s onwards; Ford and Woolworths are as British as they are American. Ordinary language too has proved resistant to America and it cannot be claimed that English became either a dialect of America nor that, on the whole, Americans and Britons cannot understand each other perfectly well through both spoken and printed media. Even the advent of the 'talkies' did not immediately subvert ordinary English language patterning, the taste for Chicago slang was not reflected in English youth slang to any great extent and American authors play an insignificant part in the everday reading matter of most Britons between 1900 and the 1950s. Indeed, the attempt to capture slang idioms in such diverse works as Colin MacInness's *Absolute Beginners* (1959), Anthony Burgess's *Clockwork Orange* (1962) and *Richard Allen's* 'Skinhead' books remain obstinately *English* in tone and *literary* intention.

Of the top 130 bestselling authors read between 1900 and 1960 by British working people only 10 were actually Americans, although both James Hadley Chase and Stephen Frances ('Hank Janson') who were English assumed a voice to appear authentically American and 'tough'.* Equally, many authors in Britain included an American character in their work to gain greater sales both sides of the Atlantic. Arthur Conan Doyle has Jefferson Hope as the true central character in 'A Study in Scarlet' ostensibly a detective story but in actuality a cross genre mixing the western and the desert tale (where Mormons have 'harems'), while Bram Stoker, another transatlantic traveller like Conan Doyle has Quincey P. Morris help out in *Dracula*. Long before these writers, Dickens had added an American episode to *Martin Chuzzlewit*. In each case the American features were *reinvented* in acordance with English linguistic and conventional needs: America is Anglicized. This pattern holds good today even

---

* Compiled from various sources. By the latter half of the 1980s the figures for most-read authors (as opposed to most sold) had changed by only a few per cent in favour of American authors.

if many of our own authors have 'internationalized' themselves and chosen to live in America (such as Jackie Collins in Hollywood or Barbara Taylor Bradford in New York). On the whole, the English used in Britain has absorbed, changed and attuned American patterns to its own rhythms. America stood as icon for modernity, style, and the future. For the British reader America is a 'style' of *doing* and an imaginative stage. In this sense, it holds a meaning not too different to the meaning is has for American writers. The languages of the western and the gangster genres are, to that, extent, neither American *per se* nor English, but literary conventions acceptable both sides of the Atlantic.

A number of crucial points follow this survey of language and of levels of literacy. The first is simply that what is at stake is not literacy levels as such but levels sufficient for and widespread enough for the sustained growth of a viable industrialized print industry viewed as a whole, however small each individual unit may be. Only then can the conditions for a growth in literacy rates be created and a mutual dependence exist. Such sustained levels of growth were the products of continual negotiation, revision, expansion and attempted restraint of that which could be printed and read in the first place. Secondly, the industry tapped into a never ending *and* commerciable resource: the abstract space of language itself. The industrial revolution so demanding of raw material found its material even in the substance of human interaction, self-renewing and infuriatingly wasteful. Literacy in its necessary relationship with the various stages of the industrial revolution was the essential resource for transmitting information and for providing the worker with both the ability to follow orders *and* to question them. Social progress and democratic reading habits (for entertainment and instruction) go hand in hand as structural co-requisites of technological progress. The profusion of printed material denies ascendancy to any one ideology or platform. All viewpoints are provided for and none more or less applauded in terms of their mere existence as print. The dominance of one viewpoint would destroy the necessary circulation needed to maintain continuous consumption and growth.

Thirdly, the common language itself began to break up and come under the growing pressure for hierarchization and differentiation. Until the middle eighteenth century the vernacular and its written or printed form had been largely disregarded by polite society except for news, gossip, opinion and entertainment. Rules were few, spelling and grammar erratic. The printed languages of culture and science were often still the 'dead' classical tongues. The democratization of print (and therefore opinion) led to a demand (often unconsciously demonstrated) for a restratification of linguistic use *within* the vernacular. Serious literature was now carefully fenced off from mere entertainment or instruction. This hierarchization was a relatively slow process and is traceable across the nineteenth century and into the first half of our own. It accompanied a further division of the common language into that used respectively by the new professionals, technocrats and the 'lay person'. The appropriation of certain discourses cut across and excluded all not otherwise involved regardless of class or position. Theology was replaced by 'expertology'. And of all the professions to elicit an ambivalent response from the lay person none was so powerful as medicine, combining as it does intimacy, secrets, biology and technology with a moral and physical discourse regarding the healthy and the diseased. The very designation doctor comes to stand for expert and technocrat, possibly benevolent or evil. Again and again the 'doctor' becomes the focus of popular imaginings whether good like Dr Watson, Dr Petrie, Dr Kildare or Dr Finlay or evil like Dr Jekyll, Dr Fu Manchu or Dr No or ambivalent but 'mad' like Dr Strangelove or Abraham Van Helsing M.D.

Professionalized and hierarchized the common language was now irrevocably split against itself.

Fifthly, hierarchization and professionalization in the common language also cut deeply into the special language of literature. Those not wishing to compete in the marketplace or have their work viewed as mere entertainment created a recategorization of narratives in which serious fiction was differentiated from escapist literature by its thematics and truth-telling functions. Works of entertainment had for Henry James and the avant garde that followed,

> in common with many literary artistic compositions the fact that they presented an invented subject-matter. The term 'fiction' could thus be used as the lowest common denominator for two modes of discourse that were outwardly similar, but essentially different in purpose.[38]

A cordon sanitaire around serious fiction effectively turned an aesthetic question into a moral one: the question of the health of fiction (differentiated by them, and by their technique).

Sixthly, the new print industry and the appearance of universal literacy could be used as a political weapon. From the 1850s onwards first in Connecticut (1855), then in Massachusetts (1857), literacy tests could be used to exclude undesirable foreigners from full citizenship. Between 1889 and 1924, seventeen states adopted such rules to exclude Blacks against a background of rising White literacy levels. The tests consisted of the ability either to read a page of English prose or read such a page and discuss it. In Louisiana between 1896 and 1900 Black voters dropped from 130 000 to just over 5000. Illiterate Whites were helped by 'grandfather' clauses. Despite Woodrow Wilson's second use of his veto in 1917 against the Literacy Laws (which he saw as unconstitutional and against the democratic principles of the United States), the matter of literacy and enfranchisement remained a live issue.[39]

To write of the growth of a 'reading *public*' is a misleading shorthand, although just acceptable in its most generalized sense, but to use the term as a historical concept is genuinely misleading, except to show up the marked tendency toward aggregation (into class, mass, urban, etc.) that affected all social analysis from the early nineteenth century onwards. This tendency to aggregate blends and distorts the conclusions placed upon it. Questions of gender or class or ethnicity cannot adequately be dealt with as questions of the mass, nor indeed, must it be said, can the *eccentricity* of individual examples be disentangled from some attempt to view such activity as a social tendency. Between the two methods lies a delicate negotiation.

Instead of the term 'reading public', I shall substitute the idea of *constituencies of readers* not only determined by class, gender, ethnicity and economic grouping but also classed by reading habit. Altogether these constituencies make up reading *publics*, general entities incorporating specific activities and attitudes. Such a movement towards disaggregation allows us a unique view of different communities of readers determined by their specific interests and bound by their places in history. No continuous history of development emerges. Rather we are confronted with parallel and contiguous developments that often but not always overlap and that run to their own timetable and that rarely have any relationship with canonic taste.

5

Outlaws Against the Law Badge:
Readers Reading

What might constituencies of readers look like? The following examples may act as guides.

In the eighteenth century, a new and powerful group had arisen which would be central to the subsequent industrial revolutions in Britain and America. The men of the merchant marine represented a vast labour force of skilled workers, proletarians without machines, who plied the trade of the Atlantic ocean.[1] Conspicuous as figures in later seagoing narratives this group has a mystic, *anti-industrial* character for both British and American authors of the late nineteenth century. Yet these sailors were not merely mute exemplars for later fiction, for they were also, and more especially, the conveyors of ideas between the two countries: *international* in composition, metropolitan in nature, and articulate. What the signing of parish registers does not signify for these mariners was their literacy or their reading matter. Although such details are often consigned to mere speculation, it can be shown that at least some sailors approached or surpassed levels of literacy as high as the officer class they served and in conditions far more harsh. Henry Fielding's belief that all sailors were 'savages' ignored the fact that those like Isaac George and John Cross, though hanged as felons, were both educated enough to read.[2] One sailor, Olaudah Equino was conversant with *Paradise Lost* and had translated the Koran while in the American colonies.[3] What may come as a surprise is that all three were Black, part of a multiracial male nation sailing between Britain and the American colonies: a community in which reading was one of many methods of escaping the dullness of a voyage.

In the radical days of the unstamped penny press, soldiers regularly purchased and discussed seditious popular literature. In 1819, there were reports returned to Lord Sidmouth on all non-commissioned officers reading *Black Dwarf* and one man was apprehended for selling material to a private.[4] Soldiers were recorded being punished for reading radical material during 1832 and at least one newspaper seller was prosecuted for selling such material to soldiers in a public house.[5] The Police informer 'Popay' reported that one soldier in the Foot Guards read *The Guardian* regularly and freely discussed his views with other recruits.[6] Fearful of being caught reading such material, the probable result being flogging and a possible drumming out of the service, soldiers are recorded as 'tearing up such reading material and chewing it into actual pulp!'[7]

While in port or on home duty, these sailors and soldiers would have mixed with the city 'mob', a boisterous, articulate, anti-authoritarian and largely free community. Within this group literacy also seems to have been higher then the parish registers would suggest, with pamphlets and ballad sheets freely circulating until the mid-nineteenth century. These loosely affiliated metropolitan groups, especially in London, were avid readers of the personal lives and deaths of those who had risen above the community and for a brief time disturbed the sleep of the magistracy. Jack Sheppard quickly gained mystic status during his lifetime and two weeks after his death was the subject of a Drury Lane play, John Thurmond's *Harlequin Sheppard*.[8] Dick Turpin also became a legendary figure – a modern-day Robin Hood – and the legacy of both these figures passed into the subliteracy of pamphlet, 'blood' and penny dreadful. By the nineteenth century, Ned Kelly was being compared to Jack Sheppard and Frank and Jesse James signed the letters they sent to the *Kansas City Star* as 'Jack Sheppard'. Sheppard became part of the vernacular landscape for sailors who used his first name as a nickname, for gypsies who retold his 'story' and for the urban proletariat of industrial cities in the 1840s.[9] Dick Turpin's name, his famous horse and his equally famous ride to York captivated those in Australia, as well as the Alleghenies and Ozarks.[10]

Turpin's deeds inspired many episodes in cheaply produced mass literature throughout the nineteenth century and his name and heroic attributes rapidly became a resource for fiction itself.

There were scores of highwaymen stories, in both penny and halfpenny parts: *Dick Turpin, Tom Turpin, Captain MacHeath, Captain Midnight, Moonlight Jack, Gentleman Jack, Black Hawk, Black Wolf, Black Highwayman, Sixteen-string Jack, Turnpike Dick* and *Tyburn Dick*, to name but a few; and, on the distaff side, *May*

Turpin, Starlight Nell and *Nan Darrell*. Consistently the most favoured character was Dick Turpin. Any similarity between the facts of his life and the fancies of his chroniclers was purely coincidental; and the liberties the authors took with the facts of Turpin's career (even his schooldays became a theme for high-flown adventure) were as nothing compared with the liberties they took with time and space.[11]

Of all the tales of Dick Turpin, the first and most 'respectable' was W. Harrison Ainsworth's *Rookwood* of 1834, poured out at an extraordinary rate (the equivalent of one hundred printed pages in 24 hours!) in which Turpin's heroic ride to York was a major factor in promoting the legend.[12] By the 1870s, Turpin had gained in moral authority; if his deeds were illicit, he was still a true 'gentleman'. In *The Blue Dwarf*, the author clearly contrasts Turpin's lifestyle of highway robbery to that of mere commercial chicanery.

> The sum realized by some highwaymen in those days was something fabulous. The money spent in riot and debauchery in a week would often have provided for fifty families.
>
> 'Light come light go' had always been the motto of those whose money came to them in a nefarious way. But many modern ways of making money are infinitely more nefarious than taking it by force. . . .
>
> The cheating done by lawyers and brokers whose clients trust them, the hundred and one ways of levying blackmail by men in power and with influence in any place of trust, the disgraceful sweating exercised in professions where such mean tricks were never supposed to have been heard of, are infinitely more despicable than highway robbery.
>
> At all events, the man risked his neck, and was always amenable to the laws of his country. . . .
>
> But for the mean, crawling thieves we speak of there is no punishment – not even that of their consciences, for they have none.[13]

In the age of *criminalization* the romanticized bandit now stood for freedom, the individual, justice and, above all, honour.

The figures of Jack Sheppard and Dick Turpin, alongside lesser figures like Claude Duval were central to and developed by the growth of mass printing and mass urban reading habits long before such reading habits should have *statistically* existed! The newer popular presses printing millions of words and hundreds of thousands of part works and serials thrived on the legacy of eighteenth-century proletarian heroes, and were the descendants of the considerable circulation of popular ephemeral urban literature in the previous century, especially that concerned with the dying confessions of those going to Tyburn. In contrast, Jane Austen's lampoon of the gothic novel in *Northanger Abbey* was an attack on a limited, class-tied female readership. Quite another group, by far the larger, wanted tales from their *own* world, not that of the aristocracy or gentry, but human interest tales of unlawful doings and illicit heroes. It was these characters who gave that readership its thrills and its hopes and it was the taste for the *facts* in these characters' lives (as opposed to gothic fancies), that was the immediate ancestor of the fact-filled and personality-filled journalism of the nineteenth-century yellow press.

The reading population of London was large and cut across the classes. It was, perhaps the result of greater self-dependence and contractual relationships than elsewhere and those that moved to the city tended to be urban refugees from other cities (especially Dublin) and therefore themselves, literate. In cities generally it was found that some book ownership was not infrequent.

> In 1839 there were books in 73.2 per cent of the homes; Grays Inn, West Bromwich, Trevethin and Blaenavon in Monmouthshire, Kingston-upon-Hull and St. George's, Hanover Square in London produced findings of 78, 85, 86, 75, and 89 per cent. Of the twenty-three investigations of book ownership in a total of over twenty-five thousand working-class homes carried out in this period, only one, a Central Society for Education survey of an Irish slum in Marylebone, found more than half to be devoid of any literature.[14]

Thus only the very poorest were without access to books or unable to read them.

Literacy in the British countryside was lower than in London and disruption during the 1840s as people moved into provincial and northern cities may have lowered urban literacy rates. Whatever the case, recovery was swift. Nevertheless, the country labourer would have had less access to urban printed materials and may have felt less need to read. This can be examined through the reports of those sent among the rural poor (usually after some civil unrest) as agents of religious or other improving societies.

What these early nineteenth-century explorers of darkest rural England found were orderly homes and a keenness for education. Many homes had small collections of books which were treated with care and respect, and researchers were impressed with the number of rural homes with books, a figure that ranged between 50 and 75 per cent of all households visited.[15] They were equally impressed with the sober and religious nature of the books owned, with an overwhelming preponderance of religious works (unlike the reading habits of their urban fellows) and few of the new 'newspapers, cheap novels and penny magazines' were to be found.[16]

Modern historians have accepted this argument of reading habits both sober and self-improving among the literate urban poor, and their findings bear out the earlier comments by statistical and religious observers. We are told, for instance, by one modern commentator, that:

> it was still very unusual to find a working-class domestic library composed solely of secular items. Taken as a whole, the surveys bear striking witness to the comparative literariness of the traditional popular culture. The statistical societies had proved beyond question that the written word, most frequently in the form of the classic prose of the Bible and Prayer Book, was no stranger to the homes of the labouring poor.[17]

This type of continuity of Bible reading among working people can be traced to our own century where books like *The Pilgrim's Progress* and the anonymous *Hours with the Saints* were selling well before the First World War.[18] The rhythms of the *Book of Common Prayer* and chapel worship can also be detected in D.H. Lawrence's early work.

The movement away from overtly church-based reading for working people continued across the nineteenth century although the publishing of popular theological books was still strong before 1914 especially with publishers such as Hodder & Stoughton who otherwise were known for their adventure and thriller lists. Secularization of reading matter among working-class readers by the early twentieth century may be attributed not only to antagonism toward the recommended reading matter suggested by those who were seen as belonging to another class (teachers were a special case) but also to:

the deep disaffection from religious values shared by many working-class boys and girls in their early teens and derived from the
feeling that religion was unrelated to the daily struggle for survival, which demanded a practical and opportunistic code of
conduct that conflicted with the absolute moral dictates of the
Bible. This contradiction between esoteric Christian dogma and a
practical morality rooted in family and community relationships,
is often hinted at, yet rarely articulated.[19]

What all this disguises is what was read when the do-gooder had
no longer to be impressed by your piety. How many 'Bunyans' and
Saints came home later in the century as prizes and were never read
is again open to opinion. If the Bible was democratically read, then
school prizes from religious missionaries would be less likely as
popular reading. Indeed, the failure of Religious Tract Society publications was in direct proportion to the success of *novels* with a
Bible or religious theme.

The reasonable literacy rates of the rural poor (excluding the
poorest field labourers) and the growing provision of elementary
education in villages meant that reading was often the province of
the children of labouring families. It was hardly the Bible and Bunyan
alone that interested them.

At all times informal instruction by parents or friends or even
by unaided self-help must have been almost as important as systematic instruction in schools. Since Tudor times popular literature in the form of ballads, broadsides and pamphlets had formed
part of the stock-in-trade of the travelling bagman and furnished
means of self-instruction. In the eighteenth century there was a
great increase in the output of popular reading and didactic
material intended primarily for juveniles, though also for their
elders: spelling books, writing sheets, fairy stories, moral tales,
fables, histories. Hack-written, crudely printed and illustrated,
chapbooks of this kind were produced in great variety in
numerous towns, and peddled round the fairs, villages and farms
of the countryside by the 'travelling stationers'. The publisher
John Newbery, who died in 1767, was the father of the children's
book trade. Many intelligent but unschooled labourers and their
children must have learned to read by puzzling their way through
The History of Tom Hickathrift, Jack the Giant Killer or *Tommy Trip
and his Dog Jowler*, bought at the door for a few pence.[20]

As the representative of the statistical society stood on the doorstep perhaps the chapbook hawker hid behind a convenient hedge! It is necessary therefore to place Bible and self-improving reading within the context firstly of children's education and the fact that often it was they who read to their (non-reading) parents and secondly, that the adult reading matter that followed consisted of a diet of sensation, superstition and political agitation.

The polite middle-class visitor at the door of the agricultural worker who approved the *conservative* nature of their bookshelf nevertheless had less liking for the interest they may have taken in the work of Tom Paine or the interest taken in William Cobbett's *Weekly Political Register* read aloud or in groups at gatherings at local public houses and then, when available at prices workers could afford, in people's homes.[21] The damning relationship between political unrest and alcohol could hardly have been missed and was condemned on the one hand while praise was heaped on Bible ownership on the other. Yet the two were inexorably connected within English working-class political thought and found their expression in the programme of the emergent Labour Party. Furthermore, these political views found readers in both women and children.[22] As a further sidelight, it is interesting to note that where reading took place at home it was often the woman who read out loud for her either illiterate or too tired husband at a time when women's illiteracy rates were supposedly a third to a half higher than that of men.[23]

Bible, political and childhood reading can all be viewed as a continuum that included almanacs, horoscopes and superstitious leaflets and booklets. If, as E.P. Thompson has pointed out, Bunyan and Paine were the key texts of the emergent working class then the reading of the prophecies of Joanna Southcott mark a moment of crisis both in political and millenarial thought. The artisan readers of Southcott saw politically in their practical life and apocalyptically in their imagination.[24] With the tide water of revolutionary zeal flowing away under the oppressions of the 1800s to 1820s, the anti-establishment millenarial writings of latter-day prophets turned into the practical and *political* adjustments of the middle of the century. What remains of this millenarial desire is a landscape of images and a deep conservatism and distrust of change in a certain superstitiousness that political action could not fully shift.[25]

Moreover, the religious engagement of Joanna Southcott's writings marked a peculiar *dis*engagement with the everyday (even as

they suffused the everyday with magical portents). Existing only as
a half-hidden subliterature (Southcott's box was still a matter of
newspaper advertisements in 1994), this type of writing feeds into
the secular wish-fulfilment fantasy of a later age, in which the
engagement of otherworldliness is abandoned for the escapism *into*
otherworldliness of secular working-class fiction. While working-
class readers throughout the nineteenth century enjoyed reading
about the personal details of contemporaries from their own class
(especially from police reports) they also enjoyed indulging a parallel fascination with fate, spirits, freaks of nature, signs and portents, (and later in our own century) belief in Atlantis, reincarnation,
magical secret societies, telekinesis, UFOs and conspiracy theories.*
In the latter half of the nineteenth century these interests rapidly
spread across all classes to become a staple of many eccentric
societies, sectarian churches and the context of a great deal of
the emergent popular-fiction industry. A prey to residual forms of
atavism, the working rural poor were themselves a subject for the
urban sensational press of the 1850s; one tale of witchcraft, sexual
relations and abortion, for instance, showed that the poor still
believed in the power of local 'wizards' who could step in when
conventional doctors failed. Science and magic still complemented
each other for those poor agricultural workers who were migrating
from the countryside to the industrial cities or who had recently
arrived.[26] In the age of progress, the inate conservatism of the rural
poor was not confined to the reading of Bunyan and the family
Bible, but was darker, more political, more fantastical and more
complex.

These comments on the rural reading constituency suggest the
need to contextualize reading habits and sometimes to consider
prima facie evidence with reasonable scepticism. In so doing we find
a complex web of habits and beliefs and that, 'however difficult and
inadequate an experience, reading in the home came to be an essential element in the emergence of an independent working-class
culture.'[27]

The emergence of a reading public in the latter half of the nineteenth century had, by the middle of the twentieth become a given
fact. Investigator after investigator, from Wilkie Collins to George
Orwell, testified to the consolidation of a mass market for literatures
of the escapist kind read during leisure for mere entertainment.

---

* David Morris has coined the term techno-occultism for this phenomenon. See *The
Masks of Lucifer* (London: Batsford, 1992).

Needless to say this 'new' reading public consisted solely of the lower-middle classes and large chunks of an unidentifiable but philistine nouveau suburbia.

Recent work by Joseph McAleer has confirmed the research conducted, rather informally, by the likes of Wilkie Collins and George Orwell, and McAleer has provided much new information with regard to popular publishers.[28] What is entirely missed from McAleer's account is an analysis of reading constituencies that opens up a debate about the *heterogeneous* nature of the mass reading public.

That certain sections of the lower middle and working classes could read and did so for leisure and escape, that their reading was secular and formulaic was known prior to the use of mass publishing which simply widened and deepened reading opportunities. Moreover, the reading matter and reasons for reading adopted by the 'lower' classes had penetrated middle-class and upper middle-class reading by the twentieth century and any sharp differentiation between groups (something possibly visible up to the 1850s) had disappeared. Although a middle-class reader may have, and will still read other more 'literary' work, it is also likely that they will share a taste for tabloid newspapers, escapist literature and television game shows with economic and cultural groups they would not wish to mix with socially. Queenie Leavis pointed out as long ago as 1932 that there 'is no reason for supposing that novelettes are bought exclusively by the uneducated and poor' and Mills & Boon could refer to its success in the commercial lending library at Harrods just as much as to its success in the twopenny newsagent libraries of the industrial towns.[29]

Economic distance and snobbery do not change the simple facts that science fiction and detective stories appeal to all social groups and that a children's comic such as *The Beano* is read by children in both public and comprehensive schools as an adult comic such as *VIZ* is enjoyed by young white-collar male clerks from all walks of life. Fan clubs cross social boundaries. Thus, in one sense, a *mass* reading public of a homogenous nature does exist; nevertheless it is clear that within such aggregation reading consituencies provide patterns of *difference*.

Let us take two areas in which we can reconsider the reading public: literature by and for women and imperial adventure literature.

The importance of feminist thought throughout this century has been profound, as has that of feminist literary criticism which has recovered many a 'lost' or half-forgotten woman writer. Feminist literary theory has been concerned with a number of constraints put on women, firstly, but in no particular order, their oppression as writers who write against the grain, their enforced use of certain genres and styles of language in a 'patriarchal' society and lastly their subjection to pornographic and violent representation.

In order to examine these areas it is useful to turn to the production and the reading of women's literature and the literature enjoyed by women (something somewhat different). It is a truism that Shakespeare's Sister was somehow suppressed or refused a voice. There is little evidence for this (as there is little evidence for proof that Victorian men couldn't satisfy their wive's sexual needs and that they spent all their time with prostitutes or indeed that the Victorian women did not know how to reach orgasm!). It is true that certain writers changed their names or remained anonymous but the use of *noms de plume* and anonymity was often *de rigeur* for nineteenth-century writers and therefore this proves almost nothing. If Jane Austen chose anonymity so did Bulwer Lytton, who threatened to sue his publishers when they accidentally put his name in an advert for his latest novel. Jane Austen, George Eliot and even the Brontës were all recognized by F.R. Leavis as constituent authors in *The Great Tradition*; everyone knew throughout the last century who Eliot really was and that she was considered the century's greatest fiction writer. Where 'suppression' occurred it did so in the censorious atmosphere of those who feared libel, scandal or impropriety and as such women writers were treated no differently from men when dealt with by fearful publishers. It is the rare occasion which proves the rule that has as its subject the suppression of a woman's writing *because she is a woman* and the complaints of writers such as Mrs Oliphant seem merely to confirm the rule in the exceptional case.[30]*

---

* My argument is aimed at a certain dogmatic feminisn taken too often as merely reflecting a given (and never quite stated) 'reality'. Elaine Showalter asserts, for instance, that, 'the ongoing history of women's writing has been suppressed' by 'the dominant (male) group' and that (quoting Gilbert and Gubar) in the nineteenth century it was 'the antagonism of male readers' that suppressed the 'female artist'. This wilful reductionism is itself antagonistic to history and produces a creed at odds with the careful research needed to expose the complex web that produced women writers and women readers. The question of women's self-censorship and self-image is more intractable. The problem of self-perception is as much related to mere delusion as it is to any actual social circumstance and therefore should never be taken at face value – a point some critics seem to ignore.

Ouida, Mrs Henry Wood, Rhoda Broughton and Florence Barclay were all successful, independent and forceful businesswomen; James Catnach's mother continued his business when he was in prison and Geraldine Jewsbury was a highly influential publisher's reader. Mary Braddon combined magazine editing with bestselling novel writing; Madame Sarah Grand (Mrs Frances McFall) was a champion of women's rights and became mayor of Bath; Lady Emma (Caroline) Wood although dubbed too immoral was allowed on to Mudie's list, and sensationalism has done little to damage women writers from Elinor Glynn to Jackie Collins; Marie Corelli gained fame through her anonymous novel *The Silver Domino* and Ethel Lillia Voyrich made simple use of initials to gain fame with *The Gadfly*; it is true that *The Roadmender* was produced by *Margaret Fairless Barber** under the *nom de plume* 'Michael Fairless' but this was because the tale was told by a navvy; Agatha Christie is, perhaps, the most famous British novelist of our century if you exclude Barbara Cartland or Catherine Cookson.

Mrs Oliphant's complaints did not prevent her being published but from becoming financially comfortable and she herself acknowledged that perhaps she was not committed enough to her own characters to really excite the public. Finally there is the issue of anonymity which was so general and so enforced at the very lowest level of fiction that very few names either of men or women come down to us. Anonymity on the level of the middle-class novel seems never to have harmed writers of either sex and was often requested by the authors themselves; on the level of working-class fiction anonymity was a matter of common business practice and common sense, as it usually prolonged the writer's professional career.

Women writers flourished in the nineteenth century (as did women readers) and the domestic novel, family saga, detective genre, horror yarn, ghost story and children's tale as well as the more familiar romantic novel, historical drama and moral fable could not have existed without their input. Women writers were not confined to certain genres as has been suggested, but wrote across most, although the spy, adventure and western tale (with the exception of B.M. Bower) as well as science fiction tended to be male preserves.

---

* Serialized from 1900 in *The Pilot*, *The Roadmender* was published in book form in 1901 and was successful before the First World War. John Buchan may have used this book as inspiration for the roadmender episode in *The Thirty-Nine Steps*. Writing while convalescing, Buchan may have been given Barber's book.

Women writers flourished, as publishers catering for a mass market expanded. Whatever stereotypical images these authors are supposed to have peddled were eagerly sought by *all* women across the classes. At the very moment of their greatest patriarchal oppression (doubly so because the images were provided by other women), these readers were demanding political, health, economic and social equality. The two sides show that women were not mere dupes of circumstance but active participants in the reading process and quite able to make rational decisions despite reading the romantic 'novels' provided in women's twopenny reading. Few feminist critics notice the inherent contradiction in the fact that women were reading to *escape* the confines of their ordinary lives and that whatever propaganda their reading contained on behalf of patriarchal conformism it also offered an alternative *non-real* world where things were directed to the *control of fantasy* by women and for women.

If love and marriage were the only themes in twopenny sagas then at least they suggested happiness, harmony, equality and love, but of course they were not the only themes and death, detection, the supernatural, moneymaking, travel and the erotic were also available. The simple fact is that throughout this century women have overwhelmingly demanded stories from romance publishers that are 'moral' and ultimately conformist and where good (in the form of marriage and a family) defeats evil (the temptress, the blackguard). This may have less to do with patriarchal discourse than with an inherent need for order and harmony in complex and very unfictional lives; 'escapism had to be grounded in realism, not fantasy' and the important thing was to 'write it up in [a] homely way' not 'sensational'.[31]

A list of women writers popular in the twentieth century in Britain clearly shows the academic bias against the ordinary reading of ordinary women of all classes. This itself amounts to a massive suppression of the facts in which the enjoyments of millions of otherwise voiceless and faceless readers are denied validity because they don't participate in a struggle for linguistic or semantic liberation. Looked at in this way, *local* male or other forms of oppression can be shown to exist, but patriarchal discourse vanishes as a mere chimera of intellectualism.

This is why at least two feminist critics (we suspect middle class in origin) find women who read true crime fiction, with its violence, 'male' erotic bias and unpleasant authoritarian values incomprehensible:

Who are the actual, as opposed to the implied, readers of true-crime magazines? The British titles are not included in the National Readership Survey, but during 1984 a small survey was conducted via a questionnaire placed in all three magazines. Of the 1200 readers who responded, over 85 per cent were women and most respondents were aged between forty-four and fifty-four.

In so far as this survey accurately reflects the whole readership – and it is telling that our informant at Argus Publications said it confirmed her previous conviction that the typical reader was 'a C2DE woman aged 45+' – it seems to raise two rather puzzling questions. First, why do middle-aged women enjoy reading this kind of literature, against all the stereotypes? And secondly, given their awareness that the magazines are read mainly by women, why do the producers so consistently address their visual and verbal content to *men*? We put both these questions to the editor and to the publishers, but they were either unable or unwilling to give any opinion.[32]

In a book designed to show that men are psychologically predisposed to violence and sexual aggression ('dedicated . . . in the fight against male violence'), this point is never satisfactorily cleared up despite talk of women's fascination with 'transgression'.[33] What it does reveal is a *class* bias which needs to contextualize women's 'pleasure' in terms of patriachal discourse.

On the other hand, a great deal of transgressive male behaviour is frighteningly alien to women's experience – is directed against women, or contains misogynist elements – so that women's attraction to violent transgression cannot be unmixed with anxiety and distaste. It could be argued that true-crime literature offers a way of resolving this contradiction, or rather, a way of satisfying both sides. The woman consumer of *True Detective* can read about depraved and revolting behaviour, but in a framework which emphasizes moral condemnation and which make her appear as merely an eavesdropper on a dialogue really intended for men. This solution accommodates the desire for 'thrills' alongside the feeling that one ought not to desire them and it also allows for ambivalent feelings about the *kinds* of thrills which the magazines present.[34]

What is ignored is women's *own* pleasure in aggression, lust and violence regardless of male presence; thus moralized, working-class older women can be brought back into the sorority (of middle-class views).

Women's distaste for the oppression of pornography is also a staple of some feminist criticism. Instead, what is advocated is a female 'erotics' evident in the appearance of new popular novels under the general title 'Black Lace'. The inherent class bias of this approach is clearly seen by those creators of male pornography whom women are supposed to oppose. Headed, 'Not a made-up letter' is this recent ironic reply to feminist criticism by Stephen Bleach, publisher for Paul Raymond Publications, he says,

> It was refreshing to read about [the woman reviewer's] prefer-ence for honest 'pornography' over hypocritical 'erotica'. (I know what she's driving at, but both words have been subjected to so many different interpretations that they're all but meaningless now.) If our postbag is anything to go by, many other women share her view.
>
> Our magazines concentrate on photographs of naked women and written accounts of heterosexual sex. A good deal of the material comes from our readers, and nearly half of that comes from women – thousands of letters and photographs a year.
>
> These are certainly not coy, evasive or romantic. Most are di-rect, dirty and score minus 50 on the political correctness scale. The irony of this massive female response to magazines aimed at men isn't lost on us. But where else do women who unasham-edly enjoy their sexuality – women who read their pornography with the lights on – have to turn?
>
> Whoever wins the intellectual argument, I suspect our female readers are having a far better time than their middle-class, middle-brow, mediocre sisters at publishing houses like Black Lace.[35]

We might conclude therefore that while women and men popular writers may have been and may continue to be constrained by genre and by formula there is nothing *inherently* repressive in this at all and the fortunes of popular authors were not and are not *merely* allied to their sexual preferences or gendered bias but to the genre they chose to, or choose to work in. Moreover, the continued and often continually useful use of *noms de plume* meant that 'male' writers of westerns and 'female' writers of romances turn out not quite as expected, while Richmal Crompton could enjoy a career happily authorially ungendered with a hero equally clearly a little boy.[36]

David Trotter has described the complex mixing of genres that went toward the writing of popular fiction at the end of the nineteenth century.[37] Yet such structural complexity seems to hide only a rather monstrous, seamless and universal discourse of repression, both of gender, class and colonial peoples. This reductionism misses the highly involved negotiation between authors and publishers, and readers, their classes, genres and ethnic origins. In an otherwise interesting discussion of the difference between American and British 'frontier' literature, Trotter points out (in a study aimed at undergraduates and from a progressively sociological perspective) of one bestseller before the First World War that it was 'unflinchingly prurient not to mention racist and sexist' despite its 'exuberant' nature.[38] The book accused was *The Dop Doctor* by Richard Dehan, an imperial romance set in the Boer War.

Trotter's judgement is, to say the least, peremptory and his enthusiastic attack on racism and sexism in the book (I fully accept the book is both) nevertheless is a moral judgement not a literary one. The problem with Trotter's attack is that it *avoids* the very issues he accuses the book of including, and he avoids either defining his terms or of saying to what degree the book is therefore guilty. Here is a classic example of critical loss of nerve (in an otherwise excellent study) in the face of an (academically) intractable popular book. What substitutes for literary sociology is moral outrage or description by accusation. One suspects that for Trotter this is a 'safe' book, being ideal as (a) a 'sympton' of sociological interest, (b) an example of racial and sexual stereotyping in the heyday of imperialism (he nevertheless offers no quoted evidence) (c) it was obviously written by a dead white European male (DWEM) and, (d) it would be unlikely to be read by students who would take Trotter at face value. What this amounts to is an abdication of the critic's responsibility to history and social context, to the reading constituency who would have purchased or borrowed the book and finally to the biographical specificity of the author. We need to begin again. To do so I will very briefly re-examine some of the issues raised by Trotter and consider some of the questions we might ask regarding the contextual evidence available. The specific problems of racism and sexism are examined more clearly in the second half of this book.

To begin at the beginning: 'Richard Dehan' was the pen name of
Miss Clotilde Graves, a fifty-year-old woman with a bad heart who
always dressed in black and ended her days in a convent. It took
two years for her identity to come to light after the book was published in 1910.[39] Having already had success both in London and
New York as the author of 16 plays the redoubtable Miss Graves
required a *'nom de guerre'* to serve as [her] *mask* [my emphasis]
when the thoughts, reflections, experiences and griefs of a
lifetime . . . should be sent out into the world'.[40] And this despite
the fact that William Heinemann and Sydney Pawling his assistant
publisher wanted her to trade on her fame.
  The Dop Doctor was a huge success both sides of the Atlantic.

> There were eighteen reprints of the first 6s edition; eight reprints
> of a 2s edition first issued in 1913; five of the 3s 6d edition first
> issued in 1918; at least eight colonial (export) editions; and vari-
> ous others up to 1940, making a total of thirty-seven impressions
> and 229,877 copies sold.[41]

Moreover, the Press were generous in their praises, seeing a book
at once more complex and deep than Trotter's recent assessment,
for instance,

> The *Spectator*, [commented] 'A vividly interesting novel . . . Readers
> who do not mind having the horrors of war laid naked before
> their eyes will be intensely interested by Mr. [*sic*] Dehan's book,
> and will be unable to read without a thrill his accounts of the
> adventures and escapes of the heroic defenders of the historic
> little town.' *Observer*: 'A great novel. The author has written a
> fine and moving tale, wide in its range, deep in its sympathies,
> full of the pain and the suffering, the courage, and truth of life.'
> *Daily Express*: 'Pulsatingly real – gloomy, tragic, humorous, digni-
> fied, real. The cruelty of battle, the depth of disgusting villainy,
> the struggles of great souls, the irony of coincidence, are all in its
> pages. . . . Who touches this touches a man.'[42]

However overpraised the book may have been by its pre-Second
World War admirers it is revealed as a complexly 'racist' and 'sexist'
work as well as much more beside of clearly a more admirable
nature ('the horrors of war laid naked'). Trotter's attack on this
book is a veiled attack on the *generation* who read it, and thus

without care or interest taken over the question of the meaning of the Boer War and the issues raised by such a setting to the generations and classes and genders who avidly enjoyed the book (and others by 'Dehan') from 1910 to the 1940s. What Trotter's comments avoid are all the issues he needed to address, not the least of which was the gender of the author hidden as it was under a *nom de guerre*, a device used by so many others to disguise identity and cross genre borders otherwise closed.

The Dop Doctor now strikes us as inconsequential and overpraised, but unless we make some effort to understand popular literature *on its own terms* we can never come to understand anything of the continuum this book has with books more highly prized. It is essential that we understand all the determinants of a book if we are to see it both in its historical circumstances and as an enduring or ephemeral cultural artefact. The praise and interest lavished on Richard Dehan's work before 1940 is enough to require us to have some humility before the facts and to discuss less complacently the popular reading (and readership) of days gone by. What is crucially avoided by Trotter is the *specific* natures and contexts of the racisms and sexisms of *The Dop Doctor* if such exist and the nature of the 'mask' for genre authors of both sexes.

Much too has been made of the rise, late in the nineteenth century, of imperialist fiction and the wide currency it gained, especially among boys in all classes through the cheap publication of boy's own papers. The doctrine of imperialism could legitimately be seen as last-ditch attempt to replace religion as an enforcer of cultural values and certainly the muscular Christianity of duty, patriotism and honour informed writers from Sir Henry Newbolt to Rudyard Kipling, A.E.W. Mason to G(eorge) A(rthur) Henty. What emerged was religiosity or a secularized religious sense.

The supposed jingoism in the imperialist message has nevertheless to be placed in the context of the commonsense refusals of those to whom this literature was primarily addressed: the young. Working-class children could happily enjoy the pageantry and display, the street parties and Empire Day celebrations without accepting the easily decoded imperial message, a message which implied the inequality and exploitation of the very class from which such children sprang. Hence one woman recalled of her school days,

I loved poetry, and the school was assembled and they stood me on top of the headmistress's desk and I had a Union Jack draped round me. And I had to recite, 'Oh, where are you going to, all you big steamers? To fetch England's own grain up and down the great sea. I'm going to fetch you your bread and butter.' And somehow or other it stirred a bit of rebellion in me. I thought, where's my bread, where's my butter? And I think it sowed the first seeds of socialism in me, it really did.[43]

Such a love of literature but a refusal to accept its 'message' can be found in many youthful political conversion:

Now we 'ad a [teacher] . . . today you'd call 'im a communist, but looking back, he didn't tell us history out of the books. Now if you got hold of all those history books we had at the time, they was all a load of flannel, about Edward the Peacemaker, Queen Victoria and Elizabeth the First. When he did give us history the way he did give it, he did show us that they wasn't as glorious as what they made out, how we lost the American colonies and in India and places like that. He gave us a truer picture because all the books were glorifying the monarchy and I used to honestly think as a lad that there was nobody like the British. All the rest, if he was a foreigner, that was it, he was like a load of rubbish. Well, you can tell by the way they did call 'em 'Froggies' and 'Eyties' and 'Dagoes' and things like that. I mean, the only way you'd describe them was they were beneath you. But he started me on the trail, that bloke, that teacher. And later on, when I was getting on to fourteen, I started to read these historical books an' I took an interest in 'em. And I thought to myself at the time, well, what a load of rubbish we've been taught in the past.[44]

History emerges here as a type of lie or simply plain propaganda for the ruling classes (represented by teachers and 'them') but the reader is never confused into believing history is merely another form of story. As such, some history becomes a story which reinforces class control, a manipulation far more devious and brutal then mere fiction where escapism into the imperialist landscape is firmly understood as make-believe. The result is a distrust of history and an ambivalence towards fiction. Even the most overtly imperialist dogmatist needed to be aware of the necessary negotiations required to gain the reader's acceptance.

Even a cursory discussion of reading habits, reading levels and reading material reveals a highly intricate and complex set of equations. In each empirical instance the general nature of theory is tested, confirmed or rebuked, revealing the space between a 'uniform' manufactured culture and a differentiated consumption which is always personal, refuses simple historical categorization, is constantly reinvented in the 'name' of contemporaneity, either disregards or negotiates with establishment values and is finally defeated by chronological process – made ephemeral by time.[45]

6

Smart Like Us:
Culture and Kulcha

It is no coincidence that the years which witnessed the appearance of the modern corporate business were also the years which saw the fragmentation of culture and the appearance of the most acute form of the social class system. Just as the classes separated so taste was divided and redistributed among the deserving. In this new world the old categories were relentlessly broken down and replaced by professional interest groups whose powerful opinions determined market reaction. Just as surely as the older communities were moulded and reacted to the market so too came that now familiar stratification of economic groups into working-class, middle-class and upper-class *consumers* and with these came the new hierarchies of taste considered suitable for such a convenient taxonomic arrangement. Low-, middle- and high-brow tastes were born together out of economic, social and cultural desire for forms of recognizable stability in an age of inherent instability.

When money alone ruled, the cultural niceties were no longer paramount, perhaps no longer recognizable. Taste alone would make culture safe and would above all preserve civilization – for Matthew Arnold in the 1880s, as for Frank and Queenie Leavis in the twentieth century in Britain, this was the overriding obsession. The cultured person, not market forces, would now make the world civilized. But if the cultured person stood against the market place (and the very success of entrepreneurs was proof of their lack of culture) then it was a paradox that the world of literature was ultimately driven by market forces and a public whose taste for books was insatiable. To cope with this situation a whole viper's nest of reasons was paraded to justify distinctions in literary culture unknown to earlier generations. At the same time, major industrialists and corporations needed 'culture' to create the respectability which would then be recognized by the guardians of taste. Despite their pre-eminent positions as cultural arbiters both Matthew Arnold and the Leavises were essentially a self-styled 'remnant' of *amateurism* pitted against what was for them an alliance of corporate interests, professionalized literary journalism and a public taste hoodwinked by both of these former groups into accepting middle-brow literature as great art: the barbarians were not merely at the gates they were already in charge.

Two quotations give some sense of the cultural upheaval and dislocation felt by the emerging intelligentsia on both sides of the Atlantic brought about by the changes occuring in public taste in the nineteenth century.

When George Templeton Strong sat down with his diary to record his reactions to the death of Charles Dickens in 1870, he found no ready-made cultural category sufficient to sum up the novelist and was forced to deal with the kaleidoscopic, complex strands of Dickens's work and following: 'His genius was unquestionable; his art and method were often worthy of the lowest writer of serials for Sunday papers. . . . Few men since Shakespeare have enriched the language with so many phrases that are in everyone's mouth. . . . I feel Charles Dickens's death as that of a personal friend, though I never even saw him and though there was so much coarseness and flabbiness in his style of work.[1]

By 1899, William Dean Howells was one of a growing band of authors and thinkers determined to give status to the *modern* novel. In so doing it was essential to sift out those very elements that had made Dickens universally popular so few years before.

Not one great novelist, not a single one in any European language, in any country, has for the last twenty five years been a romanticistic [*sic*] novelist; while literature swarms with second-rate, third-rate romanticistic novelists. . . . If you wish to darken council by asking how it is that these inferior romanticists are still incomparably the most popular novelists, I can only whisper, in strict confidence, that by far the greatest number of people in the world, even the civilized world, are people of weak and childish imagination, pleased with gross fables, fond of prodigies, heroes, heroines, portents and improbabilities, without self-knowledge, and without the wish for it. . . . the novelist [however] has a grave duty.[2]

By 1898, the old definitions of culture hade begun to fade. No longer was culture a word associated primarily with husbandry and farming: rather now in pocket dictionaries aimed at ordinary readers, the word simply stood for refinement.

> *The People's Webster Pronouncing Dictionary and Spelling Guide*, a pocket dictionary of 23,000 words with single-word definitions, defined 'culture' simply as 'refinement'. By 1919 *Webster's Army and Navy Dictionary* and an elementary school edition of *Webster's New Standard Dictionary* armed American servicemen and school children with precisely the same succinct definition.[3]

The concept of taste as a synonym for refined sensibility was a device inherently conservative, anti-democratic and reactionary, it served to separate and sift non-economically separable groups on lines as invisible as those of the phrenologist or spiritualist (whose own habits of mind reinforced the methods by which critics determined taste in the first place). In such a way political order in unruly and industrialized mass democracies could be maintained by other means. Such means also created vast public recreational areas, parks and gardens in city centres, municipal museums and libraries open to all, often financed from the philanthropic bequests of dying entrepreneurs. Taste was democratized and withheld all at once.

The two great literary prizes in Britain, the Whitbread and the Booker, turn on the unresolved ambiguities between the undemocratic and democratic meanings of taste. These ceremonials are both dignified recognitions of worthiness and media circuses. The very success of both these events is predicated on the happily unresolved nature of the meaning of good public taste. There is considerable negotiation in the giving of these prizes between, on the one hand, a definition of culture as educational, literary, hierarchical and somehow withheld, and on the other hand the degraded spectacle provided by the need to award the prizes on television, the journalistic discussions, the quoting of odds at bookmakers and the potential provided by Hollywood for the winning book. Any ambivalence towards such prizes is haunted by the notion that literature is simply entertainment, commodified and ephemeral like any other form of entertainment.

Yet what marks the issue of these prizes is the valorization of the contemporary. From the later nineteenth century the issue of taste was bound up not merely with an adherence to a bygone, Latinate and classical culture, refined in the present time, but also to a sensibility able to recognize the *classic contemporary* work newly created and worthy of inclusion in the pantheon. Taste became a special concern for and ability to understand the important modern work, instantly historicized into the continuities of civilized taste and behaviour. This was the province of those experimentalists whose modernism was avidly collected by patrons with considerably educated palates. They were collecting, in their taste for the avant garde, the very nature of the future. This cultural investment (also, of course, an economic speculation) was a form of refusal of the past which was apostrophized more and more as mere cliché. Even T.S. Eliot whose 'Tradition and the Individual Talent' of 1921 made a plea for historical continuity was investing in the instant modern classic, the reception of *The Waste Land* in 1922 being the validation of this principle.

Equally, F.R. Leavis, whose attempt at stabilizing literary taste around a small select group of older novelists led to endless and fruitless debate among academics, was an early advocate of James Joyce at a time when Joyce was banned in Britain. The validation of the contemporary work of literature by reference to 'tradition' and the appearance of a so-called fiction canon, creations of Eliot and Leavis respectively (Leavis based his ideas on Eliot), was the neurotic outcome of this new entity, the instantly recognizable work of art.

Rules seemed now to have replaced the work of longevity and common recognition. Once learned, these rules could be used to measure the new literary work and place it in the canon or expel it into the abyss of popular taste. In such a way, the work of literature, the new great novel, was either eternal in an instant or ephemeral and irrelevant. Taste was a weapon which had an aesthetic power beyond mere aesthetics. It crept into all areas of personal life as a marker of self-respect and integrity. For some, such as I.A. Richards, a founding father of academic literary study, taste was the equivalent of health itself.

> For the critic is as closely occupied with the health of the mind as the doctor with the health of body. . . .
> The most important general condition is mental health, a high state of 'vigilance'; . . . None of the effects of art is more transferable than this balance or equilibrium.[4]

Taste had a psychological resonance and was a mark of character – the trace of gentlemanly behaviour, an outlook both liberal and élitist. As such, it marked the appearance of a politics internalized in the individual, now seen as self-sufficient and self-reliant because of *inherent* good taste. In effect, the notions of taste (as cultivation) and character (as personality) were interchangeable and tautological.

The guardian of the new culture of taste and refinement were always a small minority. T.S. Eliot's *Criterion* never had more than 800 subscribers and F.R. Leavis's supposedly influential *Scrutiny* never printed above 750 copies in the 1930s.[5] By the early years of this century the battle lines had been drawn and sharp boundaries were being marked across the cultural map. Even with the beginnings of full education after 1870 in Britain, indeed precisely because of this widening of the educational franchise,

> A revolution had taken place, and George Bernard Shaw assessed it with characteristic clarity. In 1879 his novel *Immaturity* was turned down by almost every London publisher. Looking back on this event, and working out the reasons for it, he realized that a radical change had occurred in the reading public. 'The Education Act of 1871' [sic], he explained, 'was producing readers who had never before bought books, nor could have read them if they had'. Publishers were finding that people wanted not George Eliot nor the 'excessively literary' Bernard Shaw, but adventure stories like Stevenson's *Treasure Island* and *Dr Jekyll and Mr Hyde*. In this situation Shaw concludes, 'I, as a belated intellectual, went under completely'.[6]

It may be no coincidence that these self-styled guardians were for the most part outsiders: George Bernard Shaw, an Irish socialist and failed novelist was forced into more lucrative journalism for readers he despaired of; T.S. Eliot was an expatriot American whose (classicist and monarchist) leanings were more extreme than even the snobbery of Bloomsbury; Frank Leavis, an outsider at Cambridge who came from that very class that would produce our only woman prime minister; D.H. Lawrence, self-appointed sex guru and world wanderer, who learned his contempt for the class he hailed from through his readings of Nietzsche in the public library, a free institution created precisely to enfranchise that class, to which he could not be reconciled.

Differences between the consumers of culture were emphasized by the confusion and hostility among the arbiters of taste. In *Crome*

Yellow, Aldous Huxley caustically satirized a James Joyce-like avant-garde novelist at the same time as he aspired to become one himself:

> 'Of course', Mr Scogan groaned. 'I'll describe the plot for you. Little Percy, the hero, was never good at games, but he was always clever. He passes through the usual public school and the usual university and comes to London, where he lives among the artists. He is bowed down with melancholy thought: he carries the whole weight of the universe upon his shoulders. He writes a novel of dazzling brilliance; he dabbles delicately in Amour and disappears, at the end of the book, into the luminous Future.'
>
> (chapter 3)

Graham Greene in his 'entertainment' detective novel *Brighton Rock* savagely lampooned the supposed heroine who comes from the lower middle-brow readership that Greene could not reconcile himself to writing for.

> Ida turned on the gas-fire and drew the old scarlet velvet curtains to shut out the grey sky and the chimney-pots. Then she patted the divan bed into shape and drew two chairs to the table. In a glass-fronted cupboard her life stared back at her – a good life: pieces of china bought at the seaside, a photograph of Tom, an Edgar Wallace, a Netta Syrett from a second-hand stall, some sheets of music, *The Good Companions*, her mother's picture, more china, a few jointed animals made of wood and elastic, trinkets given her by this, that and the other, *Sorrell and Son*.

It should be no surprise that Greene's ambivalence over his public came from the conflict that existed between his artistic ambitions and his journalistic income gained mainly from film reviewing: 'Furthermore, the popular newspaper presented a threat, because it created an alternative culture which bypassed the intellectual and made him redundant.'[7]

By 1945, this general ambivalence among the critics and aesthetic arbitrators gave rise to a never-ending speculation over the next great work or literary movement. Critics of all hues looked feverishly around for a new cultural flourish amid the wreckage of the austerity years. Ironically, the hunt itself was a creation of journalism's appetite. In an era on the brink of even greater uncertainities concerning the role of culture and the meaning that culture had as an oppositional force strong enough to fight Americanization, popular cinema, novelettes, journalism of the 'lower sort' and finally commercial television, this was both, an ameliorative measure and an act of faith in national identity and hierarchic continuity.

> As John Lehmann recollects in *The Ample Proposition* (1966), 1945 seemed a 'time . . . of hope and confidence' with the prospect of 'a great epoch' lying ahead for the arts, promising 'a magnificent harvest', but such hopes had been quickly dashed. In *Horizon's* editorial for April 1947 Cyril Connolly vividly described the effects of the aftermath of war and Stafford Cripps's austerity programme following an economically crippling winter: 'most of us are not men or women but members of a vast seedy, over-worked, over-legislated, neuter class, with our drab clothes, our ration books and murder stories, our envious, stricken, old-world apathies and resentments – a careworn people. It was self-evident to Connolly that new art could not be expected to flourish amid such drabness and privation: 'there is no deterrent to aesthetic adventure like a prolonged struggle with domestic difficulties, food shortages, cold, ill-health and money worries. Art is not a necessity but an indispensable luxury; those who produce it must be cosseted.'[8]

The new cultural enemy was not necessarily the working classes. Here was to be found a rich source of new talent and subject matter, whether it be John Braine's Joe Lampton, Shelagh Delaney's Helen and Josephine, John Osborne's Jimmy Porter, Richard Hoggart's hymn to working-class life or somewhat later the canonization of Liverpudlian working-class music. The working class were colourful, exotic and authentic. 'New Provincialism' was not a swing towards middle-brow taste, now conflated with misunderstood Leavisite attitudes, but rather an attempt to defend and recuperate the élite, hierarchical culture of pre-war modernism despite any other egalitarian or provincial bias that may have sometimes shown through.

No, the real enemy was the middle-class middlebrow vitriolically portrayed or simply ignored by writers such as Evelyn Waugh in *Brideshead Revisited* (1945), Kingsley Amis in *Lucky Jim* (1954) and John Osborne in *Look Back in Anger* (1956). Even a novelist such as Ian Fleming rarely showed interest or sympathy with the readership he aimed his novels at and who regularly took the papers that advocated purchasing or borrowing his books. This was a world of the heroic rich, the heroic poor, or the 'angry' intellectual, classless, disinherited and celebrated in Colin Wilson's *The Outsider* (1956).

Whatever vigour existed in this atmosphere was increasingly sought out and encouraged by (or recruited to) the needs of journalism, both that of the literary magazines and that of mainstream newspapers.

By the early fifties impatience with country house conventions was growing. The *Observer's* young theatre critic, Kenneth Tynan, embarked on a critical crusade against 'Loamshire' plays, and a handful of other writers began to show a similar reaction against the fiction of refined nostalgia. One of these was Angus Wilson, whose collections of short stories – *Such Darling Dodos* (1949) and *The Wrong Set* (1950) – were notable for depicting current social changes, particularly as they affected a section of the middle class, the 'nouveaux pauvres'. In his criticism Wilson began to attack the country house school and call for novelists to come to terms with the new realities of the Welfare State.[9]

Tynan's criticism was part of a wave of activities from the Third Programme's *New Soundings* (which ran from 1952 to 1953) to *First Reading* and *Encounter* edited by Stephen Spender and Irving Kristol. All went in search of elusive new talent. A war over the control of taste had begun guided by and organized around the newspaper and periodical journalist. Thus, *First Reading* encouraged,

a profound feeling that amounts almost to knowledge that a literary renaissance is about to take place, or is taking place now, in Britain. There is a great urge towards creative expression, an impatience with the verbose outpourings of sterile criticism. There is a belief that this creative drive will find new things to say; if not new things then at least old things worth saying again and important to the times in which we live.[10]

Yet such belief could also conveniently be used as a rallying cry for the *true* believers of *Encounter* to reject all those so praised. Hence Spender was able to define his journal's tastes by stating, as policy, his refusal to publish anyone praised or promoted in *First Reading*, detecting, as he did, the 'dark hand of F.R. Leavis' behind it all.[11] By the mid-1950s, 'provincial' and 'academic' were the new labels applied to fiction and poetry respectively.[12] Against these, and against the waves of popular culture, high art seemed helplessly doomed and Spender's attempts to recuperate an international, humanist avant garde out of date. For C.P. Snow the end of high modernism was to be warmly welcomed.

> On Boxing Day 1954 in the *Sunday Times* Snow applauded the 'quiet and effective counter-revolution' against the 'novel of total sensibility' and selected *Lucky Jim* as a welcome replacement for 'obsolete' works of 'mindless subjectivism' such as (almost inevitably) *Finnegans Wake*.... A *Spectator* article published on April Fool's Day 1955, supported the 'New Provincialism' [and the] rejection of 'Bloomsbury'.[13]

This search for the new work finally found itself a name – *the Movement* and came to the notice of a wider public during 1956 through the *Observer*, *Sunday Times* and *Evening Standard*. On the brink of political humiliation and international withdrawal the English had found a new cultural stability to restate and reinforce their identity. Taste was the recuperation of politics by other means. It was the rediscovery of a principal which led to the furious debate over C.P. Snow's 1959 lecture *The Two Cultures* – a debate into which F.R. Leavis waded axe in hand – over who should rule British culture and determine Britain's values.[14]

This was an essentially journalistic debate, even if its various advocates were primarily novelists or academics and, as such, it may be no wonder that central to the imagery of the era's most famous play, *Look Back in Anger*, is the reading and discussion of the Sunday papers, caustically dismissed but obsessively read.

> JIMMY: Why do I do this every Sunday? Even the book reviews seem to be the same as last week's. Different books – same reviews.
>
>   . . .
>
>   I've just read three whole columns on the English Novel. Half of it's in French. Do the Sunday papers make you feel ignorant?
> CLIFF: Not 'arf.
> JIMMY: Well, you *are* ignorant. You're just a peasant.
>
> (Act. 1)

Further irony is added when one realizes that these debates about the *rejection* of middle-brow liberalistic conformism were conducted in the name of independence of thought through publications determined by the policies of corporate publishing interests.

> [*Encounter*] appeared in October 1953, to be followed by the launch of the *London Magazine* in February 1954. Only now did it appear that English letters might recover from the epidemic of closures which had hit literary magazines in the late forties. The revival of the London literary scene was in fact being financed from two very unlikely sources – Daily Mirror Newspapers Ltd., whose chairman, Cecil King, sponsored the *London Magazine* as a 'useful piece of do-gooding' at the suggestion of Rosamond Lehmann (and appointed her brother John as editor), and the CIA, which funded *Encounter* under the cover of the 'Congress for Cultural Freedom'.[15]*

Middle-browism and middle-class taste generally became the victims of all the protagonists in the struggle for the high ground of culture during the 1950s but this was simply symptomatic of a much older struggle, stretching back across the previous century for the control of print itself – the parallel coming to being of modern taste and corporate control. The fear of corporatism, consumerism, middle-browism and a mass reading public has driven twentieth-century cultural hierarchists. A selection of views across the century confirms a growing mania, amounting to a neurotic drive, for a separation compelled by fear of cultural debasement and defilement. It is always a battle to the death.

In America the distaste for philistinism has extended from Thorstein Veblen's *The Theory of the Leisure Class* published as early as 1899 through to the work of Allan Bloom whose 1988 attack on the 1960s, *The Closing of the American Mind*, itself became a middle-brow bestseller and to Harold Bloom's *The Western Canon* (1995).[16] The 'death' of literature debate which to Allan Bloom signalled the end of refined and civilized values in a liberal (but not liberated) culture, was joined during the 1980s by E. Donald Hirsch Jr, Roger Kimball and William Bennett.

The death of the old literature in the grand sense, Shelley's unacknowledged legislation of the world, Arnold's timeless best

---

* Although they seemed unable to determine editional policy or curb intellectual independence.

that has been thought and written, Eliot's unchanging monuments of the European mind, from the rock drawings in Lascaux
to *The Magic Mountain*, has seemed to people who matured intellectually in the ancien regime of high culture nothing less than
the setting of the sun of the human imagination in the evening-
lands of Western civilization.[17]

Even Robert Hughes, expatriot Australian domiciled in the United
States and quite capable of logically and sensibly debunking both
P.C. rejectionism and neoconservative canonical revisionism, can-
not resist a swipe at that cultural *bête noir*, television.

> Those who complain about the Canon think it creates readers
> who will never read anything else.
> If only! What they don't want to admit, at least not publicly, is
> that most American students don't read much anyway and quite
> a few, left to their own devices, would not read at all.
> Their moronic national babysitter, the television set, took care
> of that. In 1991, the majority of American households (60 per
> cent, the same as in Spain) did not buy one single book. Before
> long, Americans will think of the time when people sat at home
> and read books for their own sake, discursively and sometimes
> even aloud to one another, as a lost era – the way we now see
> rural quilting-bees in the 1870s. No American university can *as-
> sume* that its first-year students are literate in a more than tech-
> nical sense. Perhaps they never could. But they certainly can't
> now. It is hard to exaggerate the narrowness of reference, the
> indifference to reading, the . . . cultural shallowness of many young
> products of American TV culture, even the privileged ones.[18]

However, in the latter half of the twentieth century more books are
being produced than ever before. For some critics this was itself
proof that 'real' or serious reading was in terminal decline. Statistics quoted by Alvin Kernan give some idea of the growth of print
in an age supposedly inimical to it.

> When the impact of television first began to be felt, 11,022 books
> were published in the United States. In 1970, when the impact
> of the computer began to reach major proportions, the number
> of books had risen to 36,071. In 1979, after almost thirty years of
> television and ten years of major computer use, 45,182 books

were published in the United States. Book publishing revenues in the United States in 1950 were less than $500 million; in 1970 they were more than $2.9 billion; in 1980, more than $7.0 billion. In new forms of computer printouts and desktop publishing, microfilm and microfiche, laser disks storing millions of words, computer databases containing masses of information in readable form, as well as in magazines, newspapers, and conventional books, the flood of print continues and grows.[19]

Yet, for guardians of culture this increase in reading material was of necessity simply the production of more corporate consumables merely dressed up as literature. One such social commentator, Herbert I. Schiller, argues that the publishing industry and the very idea of literacy (as the mark of a humanistic mentality) are opposed. For Schiller, literacy as defined a self-expression and self-emancipation is being underminded by a new and powerful culture industry.

> Another feature (mostly ignored) of the modern cultural industries is their deeply structured and pervasive ideological character. The heavy public consumption of cultural products and services and the contexts in which most of them are provided represent a daily, if not hourly, diet of systemic values, spooned out to whichever public happens to be engaged. 'The typical film from which investors anticipate a profit', writes film analyst Thomas Guback, 'may be art or non-art, but it is always a commodity.' The same can be said for Broadway musical comedies, best-selling novels, and top-of-the-chart records. They are commodities and ideological products, embodying the rules and values of the market system that produced them. Multi-million-dollar investments in film, theater, or publishing can be relied upon to contain systemic thinking. In the late twentieth century, those few spaces that have escaped incorporation into the market are being subjected to continuous pressure and, often, frontal attack.[20]

Such capitalistic totalitarianism is Orwell's *1984* nightmare written for a mass consumer public and Schiller's opposition can trace its heritage as much to the Thoreau of *Walden* as it can to the work of Theodor Adorno, Leo Lowenthal or Noam Chomsky.

The result of this corporatism is the fascism of a market organized to produce more but with less variety: to frame things and experience in the language of *Newspeak*. For Paul Fussell this amounts to 'the dumbing of America', in which culture most books are not read but shown, consumed or worn as labels; the corporate book is the new literature of corporate humanity, to be rewarded with corporate prizes and reworked into other more lucrative corporate activities (e.g. film and television).

[N]ow BIG BAD books – those immense, everlasting weighty novels that middle-class people like to be seen toting around – are specifically the commodities that keep numerous publishers from foundering, and only one per season, if it catches on, will be enough to do the trick.

For years the industry has puzzled over the question of why people acquire these wordy, overstuffed, great big thick novels promising a protracted read lasting from September ('the fall list') until June or July. The best answer: if you read only one book a year, and you're proud of it, you want that one *to look like a book* – thick, hardbound, serious, one to be seen with on bus, train, or plane, or on the street, and one so heavily advertised and well known that your owning a copy will proclaim your solid location in the main line of consumers.

. . . the expensive hardbound is not always the most important commodity being sold: the subsidiary rights (first and second serial, movie, stage, audiocassette, TV, T-shirt etc.) often bring in more money. Novelist and scriptwriter Larry McMurtry has had the wit to notice that 'it is really reductive to call what we have now a 'publishing industry', when it is a media complex, in which promotability, not literary merit, is the *sine qua non*.[21]

Culture in Britain, was and is, according to its own guardians, in little better state than in the USA and considerably worse *because* of the USA! Given the thoughts of these American commentators it is therefore doubly ironic that both George Orwell and Richard Hoggart blamed Americanization for the lowering of cultural standards in Britain. Here is Hoggart attacking the new consumerism.

Perhaps even more symptomatic of the general trend is the reading of juke-box boys, of those who spend their evening listening in harshly lighted milk-bars to the 'nickelodeons'. . . . [M]ost of the customers are boys aged between 15 and 20, with drape-suits, picture ties, and an American slouch. . . . [M]any of the customers

– their clothes, their hair-styles, their facial expressions all indicate – are living to a large extent in a myth-world compounded of a few simple elements which they take to be those of American life.

They form a depressing group. . . .

The hedonistic but passive barbarian who rides in a fifty-horse-power bus for threepence, to see a five-million dollar film for one-and-eightpence, is not simply a social oddity; he is a portent.[22]

Better public transport, easy access to libraries and those milk bars were all to blame for the philistinism of the young. For contrasting yet complementary views of youth one only has to compare Anthony Burgess's pessimistic *A Clockwork Orange* (1962) with Colin Mac-Innes's optimistic *Absolute Beginners* (1959). Notwithstanding, it was not youngsters who were the real enemies of taste – after all the doors of the citadel could be closed against them and, to be fair to Hoggart, youth was not beyond intelligent, educational redemption.

The real enemy, as Queenie Leavis, the other partner in that formidable Leavisian double-act pointed out during the 1930s was 'middle-brow' literature masquerading as high-brow art – this was the really fraudulent activity and she attacked it with a vengeance. Her target was Dorothy L. Sayers in a review printed in *Scrutiny* of *Gaudy Night* and *Busman's Holiday*.[23]

For Q.D. Leavis, Dorothy Sayers's books were not just bad, they were BAD, to use Paul Fussell's terminology· exhibiting 'elements of the pretentious, the overwrought, or the fraudulent' but mistaken by those *who should know better* for the authentic product.[24]

This odd conviction that she is in a different class from Edgar Wallace or Ethel M. Dell apparently depends on four factors in these novels. They have an appearance of literariness; they profess to treat profound emotions and to be concerned with values; they generally or incidentally affect to deal in large issues and general problems (e.g. *Gaudy Night*, in so far as it is anything but a bundle of best-selling old clothes, is supposed to answer the question whether academic life produces abnormality in women); and they appear to give an inside view of some modes of life that share the appeal of the unknown for many readers, particularly the life of the older universities.

Literature gets heavily drawn upon in Miss Sayers's writings, and her attitude to it is revealing. She displays knowingness about literature without any sensitiveness to it or any feeling for quality – i.e. she has an academic literary taste over and above having no general taste at all.[25]

How revealing that the academics themselves were the barbarians, middle-brow, semi-literates whose learned opinion merely sanctioned popular taste; how revealing that Sayers should have worked in advertising; how revealing that academia was, after all, merely another branch of business. 'In fact the more one investigates the academic world the more striking appears its resemblance to the business world.'[26]

For Mrs Leavis's husband in another *Scrutiny* article, entitled 'The Literary Racket', things could not be expected to be otherwise.

> But social pressure and the pressure of the Advertising Manager are, after all, symptoms rather than causes. The radical fact is the advance of civilization. The supply of literature has become an industry subject to the same conditions as the supply of any other commodity. For many firms publishing is a business like the manufacture of 50s [shillings] suits, and the methods of Big Business are accordingly adopted. The market is raked for authors – for potential profit-makers – the wares are boosted by the usual commercial methods. The gigantic advance in output that makes good reviewing more than ever necessary has been its destruction – by asphyxiation in various forms.[27]

In the 1980s, fate led avant-garde British and America academics to roundly and widely condemn the exclusive, canonical, Eurocentric attitudes of the Leavisites and New Critics who, for purposes of vilification, they rounded up together. Now, of all things, the Leavises were the barbarians, so it is hardly surprising that the reforms in education brought about by the Conservative governments of the 1980s were themselves understood by many liberal and left critics as the return of a virus formed around Leavisism. The government itself and the Secretaries of State for Education were now the targets of accusations of barbarism and while the government's policies (specifically over testing) may have been confused this hardly excused the reaction of left-centre liberal English professors who signed their names to an equally confused letter to the *Times Higher Education Supplement* and which took as its central concern the 'appropriation' of Shakespeare.

As University Professors of English, we view with dismay the Government's proposed reforms to the teaching of English in schools.

Like all academics, we expect sound grammar and spelling from our students; but the Government's doctrinaire preoccupation with these skills betrays a disastrously reductive, mechanistic understanding of English studies.

Similarly, its evident hostility to regional and working-class forms of speech in the classroom betrays a prejudice which has little or no intellectual basis, and which is seriously harmful to the well-being and self-esteem of many children.

We are all committed to the study of Shakespeare; but to make such *study compulsory* for 14-year-olds, as the minister intends, is to risk permanently alienating a large number of children from the pleasurable understanding of classical literary works.[28]

[italics mine]

The letter left unquestioned the relationship between Shakespeare and popular working-class forms of expression. What might these be?

The continuing centrality accorded Shakespeare on stage, in print and as a cultural and educational marker even in the 1990s is indicative of the more general trend towards culture's modern hierarchical nature and the necessary readjustments that accompanied that progress. In England, theatrical regulation prevented Shakespeare's plays from being seen in full by popular audiences who watched abbreviated versions heightened by the musical accompaniments and interludes that allowed 'unlicensed' theatres to pretend that Shakespeare was merely a display of rhetoric during an evening otherwise given over to a concert. In America, Shakespeare had little status on the East Coast and didn't start to become regularly played until the 1840s.

And yet, there is ample evidence to show that alongside Shakespeare's canonization there remained a thriving popular theatre for Shakespeare played quite possibly nearer to the playwright's intentions. In England there is evidence of a knowledge of Hamlet in melodramas such as *The Factory Lad* (1832) a play written by John Walker who wrote short plays for the popular theatre between 1825 and 1834, and in America by Louisa Hamblin's 1839 play of Robert

Montgomery Bird's novel *Nick of the Woods* (1837) in which there is an opening speech reminiscent of *Julius Caesar*.[29]

Of importance here is the shadowy presence of Shakespeare in these two popular melodramas which both echo his more extravagant character devices. Shakespeare then, had a clear presence in the popular theatre both in his own right and as an influence on plays where audiences may not have recognized his presence. Moreover, as academics like Harriett Hawkins have clearly demonstrated his language rhythms endure in films like *Snow White*, songs such as Michael Jackson's *Thriller* and even jazz lyrics, while his work has been continuously updated through Broadway shows, films and television plots. Hawkins convincingly demonstrates that Shakespeare first became a standard in the America mid-west and frontier not on the East Coast.

> It came from strolling players who followed the flatboats floating down the Allegheny and rode into the rowdier pioneer towns springing up around and across the Appalachians. . . . But where did these vagabonds get their knowledge of Shakespeare? The real infusion of Shakespeare's art into the American literary tradition began around 1835, when a schoolteacher named William Holmes McGuffey published two school readers designed to introduce children in rural schools to the best models of their own language.[30]

Ironically the pioneers who measured their lives through Bunyan, the Bible and Shakespeare first encountered him in a school book.

> They were bought in job lots and used as basic English textbooks in the very elementary schools of the empire of the Mississippi and the South. In the sixth edition there were 138 selections from over a hundred authors, and Shakespeare was the preferred author of choice with nine extracts. Time and time again the memoirs of pioneers across three thousand miles are studded with saws and instances from the Bible, *Pilgrim's Progress*, and Shakespeare. Children in log huts who could only imagine New York or London and who, unlike the divines of New England, had never heard of Rousseau or Goethe, could – unlike the divines of New England – yet quote Hamlet and recite the Fall of Wolsey. For the distribution of the McGuffey readers stopped short of New England. Everywhere else, the readers sold, at the last count, something like 200 million copies.[31]

It is not only the hierarchists of culture like Allan Bloom who misunderstand the role of Shakespeare in Anglo-American culture but also his opponents who fail to recognize that Shakespeare resonates in popular culture too and that there is no reason to fear the imposition of required reading if that required reading belongs to both ends of the cultural divide and signifies in a multiplicity of ways: imposition is not control, regulations are often honoured in the breach.

Lawrence W. Levine, in his excellent book *Highbrow, Lowbrow* has shown how it was the battle over the ownership of 'Shakespeare' that constituted the centre of the culture wars and that it was this battle that accelerated the cultural divide that marked the nineteenth century in America.

In 1992, as the letter to the *Times Higher Education Supplement* proved, the ownership of Shakespeare was again in dispute in both Britain and the United States ... *plus ça change*. The end of the Cold War, the fall of the Soviet bloc and the re-emergence of liberalism all suggest that the question of cultural values had not gone away, nor would it.

We have seen the considerable attention and continued fascination born of horror that popular culture and by implication mass-democratic modern society (both industrial and urban) continued to exert over 'disenfranchised' intellectuals. Often this attention was dismissive, sometimes it has been downright hysterical. For one critic even middle-brow prize-winning authors, can be 'gutter writers' providing 'pathetic garbage under disguise',

> Middlebrowism becomes truly offensive only when it veers into glaring pretentiousness, or takes on certain characteristics of gutter culture, a sinister phenomenon which is of extreme interest, but which has no connection with literature. It must be mentioned here only because it is beginning to take over middlebrow territory, which (as we have seen) does have literary features. ... Reviewers of the *Time Out* sort, and others, are beginning to fail to be able to distinguish between this kind of material and the seriously intended.[32]

thus 'D.M. Thomas's *The White Hotel*, one of the few successes of this sort to be treated as having literary quality, reads as though it

were the desperate plagiarism of a professional masturbator'.[33] Even
sympathetic commentators finally baulk at the *exuberant popularity*
of mass art. For Raymond Williams, fearful of the future at the end
of his life (in thoughts echoed better by Robert Hughes), television
was still the opium of the masses.[34]

Against such a tide of professional distaste there have been those
who have defended popular fiction (in its middle-brow/low-brow
and pulp incarnations) but in many cases this has been tempered
with disclaimers in order to placate those who feel anyone interested in popular culture (and therefore contemporary life) is a pathological case. Lawrence Levine, in a work I have already cited as
exemplary in showing the merely historical (rather than theoretically valid) divide that occurred in nineteenth-century culture is
still unable to avoid an apology to the unknown and, by implication, sceptical reader. He tells us, that '[his] own interest is not in
attacking the notion of cultural hierarchy per se' at the very moment he proves cultural hierarchy to be aesthetically unjustified
except by the ad hoc historical development of defensive rules.[35]
Peter Keating in an otherwise groundbreaking analysis of late nineteenth-century fiction, its consumption and formal development is
unable to make real sense of the popular forms that came into being
from the 1880s onwards.

> The imagery of exploration was clearly as important to the ro-
> mance as to the realistic novel and social documentary, and here
> also it functioned on both a literal and a metaphorical level, though
> its emphasis was totally different. The realist, the journalist and
> the sociologist employed exploration imagery to dramatise present
> social conditions, to draw the reader's attention to neglected ar-
> eas of contemporary life. In contrast, the writer of romance em-
> ployed the same imagery in order to escape from the present, or,
> if he had a point to make of direct contemporary relevance, to set
> up a process of extrapolation that the reader was expected to
> follow through. Of the four major kinds of late Victorian romance
> examined here – historical, scientific, supernatural, detective –
> only the writer of detective fiction shared the social explorers'
> preoccupation with present time and conditions. The other three
> were interested in the present only in so far as it could be placed
> within the huge vistas of space and time of which it was, if truly
> understood, merely an insignificant speck. In the process, they
> divided among themselves not merely types of fiction, but time

as well. The historical novelist took as his special province the whole of time past; the writer of science fiction took the whole of time future; while the writer of the supernatural and occult embraced or ignored both time future and time past in his exploration of states of consciousness which were beyond any concept of time available to human understanding. . . . Day-dream and adult play really had taken over.[36]

Thus popular fiction becomes again *simple* escapism designed to a formula: commercial and therefore of only historical interest. Geoffrey O'Brien in his semi-serious exploration of the 'Lurid years of Paperbacks' (to quote the book's subtitle) suggests:

The paperbacks were a microcosm of American fantasies about the real world. They took the ordinary streets, the dives, the tenements, the cheap hotels, and invested them with mystery – with poetry even – turning them into the stuff of mythology. Shamelessly exploitative, they made their points with a maximum of directness. No trace of subtlety was permitted to cloud the violent and erotic visions that were their essence, and that very lack of subtlety lifted them out of this world. The people they depicted seemed to exist in some impossibly energetic super-America parallel to the one we know. . . . They are, then, little monuments, frozen moments in the history of a culture.[37]

And yet O'Brien is also capable of seeing such escapism and parallelism as pointing to deep and disturbing social concerns, usually ignored or half realized in more respectable fiction.

The Thirties pulp imagery of secret societies bent on world domination, mad sadistic scientists, and bloody avengers is plainly fantastic, but by the late Forties these images are taken as utterly real, just as the rocket ships of *Flash Gordon* and *Buck Rogers* become actual cigar-shaped phenomena seen in the sky. . . . The Thirties pulp hero in mask and cape, battling the Purple Menace or the Green Menace, has by 1947 become a down-to-earth Mike Hammer battling the Red Menace.

In such an atmosphere, the pulp imagination can rise to new heights of glory. An L. Ron Hubbard can move from second-rate science fiction to the founding of a worldwide 'religion'. A hack thriller writer like Howard Hunt can end up acting out his fantasies as national policy at the Bay of Pigs and the Watergate.[38]

If such books are a neglected popular art form they are ultimately only *symptomatic* of historical change and social divergence. The vitality of these popular forms then becomes frigidified in a historical moment backdated and bankrupt if still amusing, a view substantially repeated by others.

> The essays . . . seek instead to weave together the text, the genre and the specific history of the period. And all these essays create specifically different 'histories' in order to answer the question why those books were a popular 'good read' in their own day.[39]

John G. Cawelti, as long ago as 1979, pointed out why academia should study popular arts forms as *art* but his argument was tautological at best and was itself unable to resolve the relationship between historical instance and aesthetic continuity. Here the patterns appear to be familial prior to their becoming cultural.

> Older children and adults continue to find a special delight in familiar stories, though in place of the child's pleasure in the identical tale, they substitute an interest in certain types of stories which have highly predictable structures that guarantee the fulfillment of conventional expectations: the detective story, the western, the romance, the spy story, and many other such types. For many persons such formulaic types make up by far the greater portion of the experience of literature. Even scholars and critics professionally dedicated to the serious study of artistic masterpieces often spend their off-hours following a detective's ritual pursuit of a murderer or watching one of television's spy teams carry through its dangerous mission. . . . In fact, they are examples of what some scholars have called archetypes or patterns that appeal in many different cultures.[40]

If 'older children and adults' are also sometimes 'scholars and critics' then a study of popular forms becomes a deep regressive psychotherapy in which the archetypes of popular literature take on a mythic deep structural form. For the critic of literature, a recognition of this mythic power is also a recognition of artistic value but only if the value is *formulaic*. Such an argument affirms in an ironic way the repeatable pattern so often attacked as debased by other critics, but it salvages popular forms only if they become eternal, deep, unconscious and historically continuous – in other words another version of serious literature. For Cawelti, historical continuity requires a mythic or 'archetypal' substratum more folk than pop, more Jung than Freud.

However, Cawelti's thorough treatment of such formulas, in the western, romance, detective story etc., did attempt 'to illustrate how the changing story patterns through which this mythology is dramatised relate to cultural changes'.[41] Nevertheless, Cawelti is stuck with the problem of relating myth to history. How can popular fiction be essentially modern and mythic? Thus it is that times change but the mythology remains timeless – taken up and 'dramatized' anew in each suceeding generation. History and the cultures that sustain it are, in the final analysis, simply gratuitously ephemeral expression of the archetypes behind popular fiction. The result of Cawelti's formal specificity is ultimately metaphysical vacuity.

Cawelti followed such British studies as Colin Watson's *Snobbery with Violence* and E.S. Turner's *Boys will be Boys* neither of which was aimed at an academic audience but both of which revealed a whole universe of attitudes and consumption in which detective fiction, thrillers, penny dreadfuls and boys-own adventures were once enjoyed but which has now passed.[42] Pieces for nostalgia only. It is these types of book however that bridge the gap between scholarly investigations and affectionate, often uncritical, but usually highly knowledgeable works by and for aficionados by writers such as Ron Goulart in the USA, Peter Haining in Britain and even such books as Stephen King's *Dance Macabre*, an intelligent narrative of King's own chosen genre.[43]

Leslie A. Fiedler in a book about contemporary mass entertainment leads an attack on the cultural mandarins which recognizes the aggressively 'defensive' attitude of the defenders of cultural standards (including Marx) but which at the same time is unable to see what makes popular art intrinsically different from highbrow creation and *indifferent* to highbrow demands. Thus,

What [he will] be discussing are the kinds of songs and stories which have tended, since the invention of moveable type, to be 'ghettoized', which is to say, excluded from classes in 'literature' and endured only as long as they clearly know their own place.[44]

And of one of the great nineteenth-century popular authors Eugene Sue:

But if Sue was falsified in his own self-consciousness by the theor-
izing of the *Phalange*, in the consciousness of his contemporaries
and ours, he was even more drastically falsified by Marx who
taught us first to regard him, and all like him, as purveyors of
junk, panderers to the misled masses.[45]

Yet his next thoughts suggest an overly literal view, itself paranoid,
about the meaning of popular forms:

> Clearly, what we consider 'serious novels' or 'art novels': works,
> say, by Henry James or Marcel Proust, Thomas Mann or James
> Joyce, are indistinguishable, *before the critical act*, from 'best-
> sellers' or 'popular novels' by Jacqueline Susann or John D.
> MacDonald, Conan Doyle or Bram Stoker. Despite peripheral
> attempts to sort them out before the fact by invidious binding or
> labelling, by and large, they are bound in the same boards and
> paper; edited, printed, distributed, advertised and peddled in quite
> the same way.[46]

It is not *after the fact* that the critical act becomes important but
throughout production and prior to any production in a complex
relationship between art and the many processes and factors in its
making and consumption. The aesthetic question is always a critical one and always *dynamic* – there can be no 'fact' to follow.

C.W.E. Bigsby, who edited the volume in which Fiedler appears,
reveals the ambiguity in the interested critic's attitude to popular
art forms. Again, we have an attack on the cultural hierarchists, in
this case, Matthew Arnold, Oswald Spengler, Ortega y Gasset, Karl
Jasper and F.R. Leavis, but this is itself followed by:

> But just as Spengler had seen the city, with its aggregated masses,
> as providing only a parody of community, so the communal
> modes suggested by the media are, perhaps, more apparent than
> real. Far from creating a global village with shared values ex-
> pressed in a common visual and verbal symbolisation, the city-
> world of today and the media with which it addresses itself may
> be seen as creating only the imagery and *not* [my italics] the
> substance of communication. Thus the film is the first mass art in
> which people are gathered together in communal buildings in
> which the communal element is unimportant. Television, simi-
> larly, groups the family in the posture of group contact only to

interdict the contact which that configuration implies. Symbol without content. When the teenager plugs the transistor into his ear, he necessarily unplugs from those around him; the juke box, in order to function, must make conversation ineffective. Progressively, society falls back on visual images, distrusts language, fills the air with Muzak to avoid silence, and plumbs the individual psyche in preference to chancing a human relationship which implies an avoidable vulnerability.[47]

Such comments, compounded by others, such as the commonplace that 'post-literate popular culture is very much a product of the machine age' and examples drawn almost exclusively from 'legitimate' forms show that Bigsby is unsure what should be said about popular forms and that any form of culture which utilizes electronics (television, transistor radios and juke boxes) is quite beyond his 'pre-electronic' understanding.[48] On the one hand he can point out (if rather weakly),

Yet the potential for social subversion which popular culture also clearly possesses (as in the comic book, pornography, the lyrics of acid-rock), explains the difficulty in defining a phenomenon which has been seen both as the cause and effect of social dislocation and the embodiment of a liberated democratic spirit.[49]

and on the other hand he can state (perhaps his deeper opinion) that,

The commonplaces of Hollywood, Broadway, the cartoon, the comic book, the Western, the detective story, are all concerned with offering assurance that things are under control, that ambiguity will be resolved, that violence is assimilable, that disorder will resolve into order, that sexuality is not anarchic, that death is not real, that injustice is a temporary state, that rebellion is a predictable phase which will be subsumed eventually in a necessary corporate stability.

Art and literature, on the other hand are rooted in a fundamental dissonance between appearance and reality, indeed express a basic conviction that reality is indefinable.[50]

This ambiguity is more pronounced elsewhere. In an extraordinarily old-fashioned and well-meaning text-book which seeks to celebrate and define popular literary style (published as late as 1990) Walter Nash, without a hint of irony can tell us that,

> Here in the airport lounge, how becalmed our voyagers are, all spellbound and dreambound! . . . We are all characters in enjoyable bad books, it seems. We are in the right place for Popular Fiction . . . to keep us happy and hypnotized in our confinement.[51]

The message ultimately is the same as Bigsby however,

> Pop fiction does have its merits, and they are by no means negligible. . . . Our deeper allegiance, nevertheless, is to a very special kind of 'merit', which we detect in the capacity of a book to illuminate our own experience, to enlarge our perceptions of human nature and conduct, and, without overt moralizing to establish and confirm in us the knowledge of a morality. The lessons of 'serious' literature are not quickly learned.[52]

By the late 1980s the study of popular fiction became theorized within the new post-structuralisms and thus began a short and profitless war over the canon and literary hierarchy, élitism in the academy etc., in which mass culture became the site of a political struggle for the ownership of English letters as we saw earlier in the debate over Shakespeare in British schools. The result was that 'newer' texts from outside the so-called 'canon' were admitted, *but* only if they displayed proof of 'contradictions'. Thus studies of Barbara Cartland novels concentrated on 'highlighting',

> a contradiction in the narrative, between the intended 'message' which focuses on the role of a woman as a transcendent, spiritual being, and the actual process of narration which concentrates on the more mundane reality of 'love and marriage'. The main narrative threatens to undermine the romantic message by highlighting the historical 'necessities' which lead women to pursue men and to turn love into an 'economically rational career'.[53]

Inevitably, such contradictions show up what plain common sense knew, namely,

> although Cartland's novels can be interpreted in a manner which renders them potentially subversive of the author's overt intentions, that does not mean that they generate an alternative view of female identity.[54]

Such approaches tell us only that Cartland is neither politically correct nor an academic. Cartland's work is criticized for what it is *not*, while ignoring what its own *voice* speaks and why such a voice is so successful – surely not because the poor women who *like* Cartland are all fools? Cartland's agenda, which in its belief in *seduction* is curiously close to some contemporary theory, does not fit well with a left-liberal feminist agenda. Ultimately, this approach does little to explain Cartland's texts or their specific cultural position – it is in fact a value judgement disguised as analysis. Popular women's fiction is only good *if* it is both feminist and subversive; a question of taste rather than history. Thus for one contemporary editor, in an otherwise well argued book, a contributor to a volume of women's writing, 'shows how [Jean] Rhys constructs a feminist anticolonialism. The novel subverts colonialism, the appropriation of what is different, other; it subverts colonial romance, and turns over then refertilizes the psychologically and socio-politically rich romantic fictional soil of *Jane Eyre*.'[55]

How curious that for Cawelti the fiction of the mass market deals in deep mythic constructions available only to formalists and anthropologists of contemporary life while to a latter-day feminist the only good popular fiction (admittedly middle-brow) is one that overturns mythic structures – thus it becomes self-consciously high, self-reflexive, subversive and radical (that is, feminist canonical). Not surprising then that some critics had to make 'feminist interventions' into SF (in order to produce remainder fodder which was good politics and bad art). In each case popular art required correction and academic therapy. Thus, popular fiction is lost amid the real row over academic Newspeak. One grovelling apology will suffice for a range of critics who are involved with the popular arts for reasons which suggest they are using this material as an *excuse* in the war over 'gender' definitions and control.

Following on from this, it is not the intention that the contributions by male writers to this collection should be seen as 'men doing feminist work'. Such a strategy is a contradiction in terms and one which frequently registers that characteristic masculine practice of appropriation and even in its more bizarre manifestations the most extraordinary arrogance of 'setting women right', 'correcting' the 'errors' of feminism. Rather, the objective is to begin to frame, describe and unearth the notion of 'men as readers' as a *project* rather than as the usual, unquestioned normative procedure. Clearly, this raises questions about self, sexuality and identity within specific social and historical formations. It should also be agreed that the readings and arguments set forth here are inflected by our generation (we are in the main of that generation who entered secondary and higher education in the 1960s) and by our ethnicity (all of the contributors are white English or American women and men).[56]

For some, such absurdities were left aside to be replaced by others so that,

> Those who read or scrutinize Dickens as a novelist secure within the canon (if not 'the great tradition'), and ignore his simultaneous appearance on TV at Sunday tea-time, are substituting a previously freeze-dried version of the past for the dynamics of historical process. A properly *historical* reading of Dickens, or any other writer, has to recognize these seismic shifts – movements which make any Richter-like measurement of 'popular' and 'classic' fiction futile or partisan.[57]

Setting aside the foolish snipe at F.R. Leavis who did *not* include Dickens in the canon and specifically made him a special case of great popular writing, we are confronted with the suggestion that Dickens is a 'text' (i.e. a nexus) rather than a mere text and that we can no longer see Dickens as a historical figure in an actual location – after all what does the writer mean when we cannot 'ignore his simultaneous appearance on TV', simultaneous with what? In all, this type of writing suggests, all protestations to the contrary, that these writers actually do not *like* popular fiction or art (so different from George Orwell or Richard Hoggart for example) and are far happier in the land of middlebrowism. Liking popular fiction and the popular arts is (as any fan knows) to create a hierarchy of taste and a popular set of canonical rules – an aesthetic of the popular which is at one and the same time a social negotiation – a *success*, not, in short, a failure of portrayal or of genre subversion or of not having politically correct views. Indeed, few writers will take the popular arts for what they are on their own terms. This is a shame, as only *The Modern Review* seemed willing to take on popular culture in a serious way. Cosmo Landesman, one of the *Review's* founders, pointed out in 1993,

The cultural studies movement wasn't really interested in popular culture in itself – for them it was means to a radical end. Never mind the merits of this or that film, what mattered was waging the war against the oppressive Eurocentric culture of Dead White Males. The movement enjoyed a monopoly on the subject of popular culture, until the appearance of *The Modern Review* in 1991. Under the banner of 'Low Culture for Highbrows', *The Modern Review* rejected the cultural studies notion that popular culture was only worth studying if it served a radical cause.[58]*

It may come as no surprise to the reader to find that the *Review* is essentially anarchic-entrepreneurial, overtly capitalistic-Thatcherite and at the same time peculiarly traditionalistic and conservative. When it came to it, only certain elements of the Right could take popular culture for what it was and is.

---

* Almost as these words were written *The Modern Review* closed due to falling circulation figures (below 10 000 readers) and an extremely public disagreement between the editor Toby Young and the owner, Julie Burchill. The failure of the enterprise is, however, equally indicative of the collapse of the category distinctions that I discuss in Chapter 12.

7

Living in Technicolor: The Rules of Pulp

Can there be an aesthetic of pulp? For those who would defend high culture the notion of an aesthetic of pulp would simply be a misuse of the term; for those who would defend low culture there would be an avoidance of the question as not relevant. Caught between antagonism and embarrassed approval it remains to create an aesthetic of pulp which acknowledges both social force and artistic taste. We have descended through highbrow culture to middlebrow culture but pulp is a rejection of both, a messy, sprawling, indefinite phenomenon with a vitality that is both exciting and terrifying.

Pulp may be popular (as the academic uses the term popular culture) but often it is not; it may deal in the commonplaces and stereotypes of everyday life, but again often it may not. Always pulp will be allied to the commercial but not necessarily determined purely by it. Thus, while *Star Trek* is popular culture, *Star Trek* novels and products are pulp and kitsch respectively, existing just as much as lifestyle as literature. *Betty Page in Bondage* was pulp but hardly popular, while *Coming of Age in Samoa* became pulp in the 1960s through its consumption by sexually curious teenagers, as did the life story of April Ashley, one of Britain's first sex-change cases which was designed as pulp, and *Lady Chatterley's Lover* which was not. Edward, Baron Russell of Liverpool's *Scourge of the Swastika* (1956), the horrendous retelling of Nazi war crimes, was read by many at the time of its publication in paperback with the same salacious interest as *Those about to Die* (1958), written about the excesses of the Roman Circus and produced by freak expert Daniel P. Mannix. And between both of these books stands Garry Hogg's *Cannibalism and Human Sacrifice* (1958), the opening line of which invites a salacious reading, thus, 'man is a carnivorous animal: he eats flesh'.

Popular canonic fiction can also fall into the illicit, both knowing and refusing to know what it is doing. Here, for instance, is Rider Haggard:

There, not more than forty or fifty miles from us, glittering like silver in the early rays of the morning sun, soared Sheba's Breasts; . . . I am impotent even at its memory. . . . Their bases swell gently from the plain, looking at that distance perfectly round and smooth; and upon the top of each is a vast hillock covered with snow, exactly corresponding to the nipple on the female breast.

(*King Solomon's Mines*, chapter 6)

'Impotent' indeed if the fetishized object of desire is a little lower on the female anatomy.

'She burned,' he went on in a meditative voice, 'even to the feet, but the feet I came back and saved, cutting the charred bone from them.' . . . he drew something forth which was caked in dust that he shook on to the floor. It was covered with the remains of a rotting rag, which he undid, and revealed to my astonished gaze a beautifully shaped and almost white woman's foot. . . . Poor little foot!

(*She*, chapter 9)

It is the last comment 'poor little foot' – so spuriously pious, so gloriously knowing, that disguises and yet makes the preceding passage into pulp and does not merely leave it as popular. Pulp too is what this comment by Stan Lee (creator of Spiderman) becomes by a slip of the tongue when refering to Rider Haggard.

I think people love things that are bigger than life, that are filled with fantasy, as long as they're done in such a way that they seem to be believable . . . H. Rider Haggard's *She, King Solomon's Mines*, movies [sic] like that.[1]

Pulp is what refuses respectability by its very craving for the respectable. Pulp is the illicit dressed up as the respectable, but it is not disguised, nor does it hide its true nature from the consumer. Thus it becomes a type of coded play: a seduction agreed in advance by both sides but *unspoken* by either. Pulp pleasure is illicit pleasure. Such pleasure comes from reading for the *wrong* reasons and knowing it. Pulp does not want to be respectable, it wants to pretend to be respectable – it is, to use a pulp-generated metaphor, transvestite in its enjoyments. Then pulp is not to be defended, nor

is it to be made more available for serious study at the academy –
pulp never went to school and hates the academy. Academic respect kills pulp with kindness. Pulp does not wish to be part of the
canon – what does it care for the canon except to plunder and
pastiche it (as the contemporary 'serious' artist now plunders and
pastiches pulp). Here pulp has its own language and rhythm which
only becomes pidgin when assimilated into or compared with 'respectable' language. It is essential for pulp to remain pulp and for
it to retain its *unassimilable* nature, thereby preserving the *frisson* of
its secret passion enacted among fans, coteries, cults and followings
– the secret handshakes of the initiated. What canonical work or
author ever aroused such inexplicable passion in the ordinary consumer except when it became a *lifestyle* lived beyond the actual
literature – a subculture for readers? Isn't this passion for the details of geographical location, personality and anecdote exactly a
pulp transformation in the followers of the Brontës or D.H. Lawrence? What difference is there here between academic and amateur? Literature lived as lifestyle is pulp. Pulp needs no defence,
indeed it has no defence in its refusal to be determined by cultural
rules.

Such as pulp is, it is always illicit, rarely controllable, maybe
actually illegal but only sometimes subversive. Some writers in their
exploration of working-class popular entertainment and its reor-
ganization by market and hierarchic social forces are keen to point
out that while church music, variety theatre and English football
were all *reorganized* by forces *opposed* to the spontaneous entertainment of the urban working class, nevertheless resistance was and is
a constant theme of ordinary life. Thus for these writers the thriving streetlife of the early nineteenth century was subverted and
indeed destroyed by capitalist manipulation. What was lost, it is
argued, was at least a subculture of artistry and skills in popular
recreation.[2]

Such an analysis, with its populist Marxist argument, seems naive and redundant. The dichotomy of worker and capitalist rarely
exists in such a simple form when looking at the question of cultural participation.[3] The working class embraced professional soccer and reworked their response to the game in a vital and usually
positive (and often rebellious and violent) manner. In other words
they were not manipulated. Rather an accommodation was reached
which came from negotiations both spoken and unspoken, allowing new rituals, social activities and traditional factors to play their

part. Pulp culture, like working-class culture, is a negotiation which is neither unthinking, nor spontaneously naive, but thought through at a level which seeks to gain everything from hierarchic culture while yielding as little as possible. The logic of pulp is not necessarily the logic of educated society nor may it even be the logic of working-class resistance. Sometimes it will revel in an unresolvable and irresolute illogicality – the knowing and not saying of pulp as *form*.

A word needs to be said about this accommodation between capitalistic producer and ordinary consumer. It is far too simplistic to argue that each time a woman reads a magazine advocating heterosexual marriage, or a Barbara Cartland novel, a rubber fetishist goes and buys a favourite magazine or a teenager buys a Batman comic that they are all equally vulnerable, equally exploited, equally duped. To patronize every reader of Harold Robbins and Jackie Collins is to grossly misjudge and diminish the subject.

Curiously, both hardline Marxist commentators and cultural élitists (sometimes one and the same) often seem blind to this fact and the fact of the essentially unpredictable nature not just of the market but of those who make the market work – authors, publishers and readers (consumers and producers). John G. Cawelti stated categorically in 1979:

> One cannot write a successful adventure story about a social character type that the culture cannot conceive in heroic terms; this is why we have so few adventure stories about plumbers, janitors, or streetsweepers.[4]

And Walter Nash, as late as 1990 and against the evidence of commercial and technological history, could echo 'can we imagine a romantic tale in which the leading man is an obese plumber?[5] It hardly needs pointing out that two such fat, ugly plumbers, Italians from New York, incarnated as Super Mario Brothers have adventures and save romantic princesses. Popular culture is not without its own sense of irony.

Vance Packard had this to say on the market and the forces that dominate it in his bestselling populist work of the 1950s *The Hidden Persuaders*. He pointed out that,

> In the early fifties, with over-production threatening on many fronts, a fundamental shift occurred in the preoccupation of people

in executive suites. Production now became a relatively secondary concern. Executive planners changed from being maker-
minded to market-minded. The president of the National Sales
Executives in fact exclaimed: 'Capitalism is dead – consumerism
is King!'[6]

Yet consumerism seemed the result of manipulative, totalitarian
psychological warfare:

> As early as 1951 [experts were] exhorting ad agencies to recog-
> nize themselves for what they actually were – 'one of the most
> advanced laboratories in psychology'. [They] said the successful
> ad agency 'manipulates human motivations and desires and de-
> velops a need for goods with which the public has at one time
> been unfamiliar – perhaps even undesirous of purchasing'. The
> following year *Advertising Agency* carried an ad man's statement
> that psychology not only holds promise for understanding peo-
> ple but 'ultimately for controlling their behaviour'.[7]

The consumer was king only if the consumer was a fool! The paradox escaped all but a very few. If the end result was the creation of
the age of the 'image' then what that image came to represent was
the negotiation necessary to create a market and commercial success.[8] Commercial success, i.e. the ownership and successful exploitation of the means of distribution (rather than production), through
networks and marketing, was no guarantee of controlling consumers only of controlling sales.

The simple fact was that Packard was witnessing the fragmentation of capitalism (euphemistically now called consumerism)
where *no* predictive methods could adequately foretell, organize or
manipulate groups of purchasers. The desire to manipulate public
opinion and thus purchasing by creative packaging was never so
strong as to programme anarchic choice out of ordinary people.
Indeed, there is no simple correlation between the desired directed
meanings of the ownership of production in the mass arts and any
equivalence to their consumption.

This can be shown through a consideration of the comic book
industry in the United States: an activity bound to the commercial
world but *consumed* privately, illicitly and sometimes subversively.

The comic strip is as old as the twentieth century, now a venerable age, and comic books themselves have been with us for over

half a century, gaining a respectability nowadays that was neither expected nor desired. This special art form, which until recently was recognized only by its antithesis to both art and form, is the product of a creativity at once industrial and commercial as well as aesthetic. The world of comic books is no less related to that of advertising and Hollywood than it is to the more 'legitimate' realm of literary publishing. Indeed, it is only recently that comic-book producers have seen themselves as working within mainstream publishing and have found acceptance, through the appearance of graphic novels, within that world.

Comic book production is a hybrid activity: an *industrial* artistic activity which has created an imaginative and imaginary space for itself out of the popular cultural forms of American urban, commercial life. From this world emerge two of the greatest iconic figures of the century: Batman and Superman, and with these the evolution of a pantheon of villains including Lex Luthor and the psychotic presiding genius known as Joker. These creatures belong to a universe uniquely its own.

The external pressures on the industry that brought 'the Comic Code' into existence in the 1950s have, in the 1990s, given way to internal pressures within an industry bifurcating into both children's publishing and adult publishing and which has once again – but this time not innocently – to confront the adult themes of violence, sexuality and obsession. The comic-book medium has now reached a level of sophistication that combines Hollywood effects at pocket-money prices; even graphic novels printed on good quality papers and handsomely bound sell at a reasonable price. The world of the pop art collector and the museum curator has finally come together with the world of the pulp fan and the fanzine. The last few years have made respectable the realm of commercial artefacts, throwaway ephemera and popular consumables: the postmodern age is the age of popular art become high art, commercial comics transformed into icons for a literate and visually and semiologically sophisticated audience.

Yet, as comic books have gained respect, their artists have discovered their own artistic roots before the 'rules' were learned and codified, before practice became mechanical and conservative. The medium is still dominated by the genre of the superhero and supervillain – a titanic and never-ending struggle, not just between good and evil but between authority and anarchy, between a benevolent authoritarianism and a demonic and chaotic outer cosmos where temporal life is constantly upset, inverted and demolished. Comic books are about irruption and control and, as comics gain a kind of reverence, these themes paradoxically reoccur in more extreme and pathological form.

Dark heroes, little differentiated from villains in their obsessions, stalk work read by serious and approving adult, literate collectors. *The Killing Joke* transformed old Batman material into a shocking remodelling of classic and conservative Batman themes. The highly controlled and aesthetically exacting artwork released the violence and horror within the psyche obsessed with crime. Batman meets Joker in the Asylum at last. This 'shocking' irreverence again returns comic-book literature to its rightful place: a truly popular culture, anarchic and gaudy, mythic and protean, anonymous and 'naive'. Such violence in adult comics may again herald certain innocencies.

The current acclaim heaped upon 'star' artists may be little more than a retrograde step. Only time will tell. What is of consequence is that comic-book artists' work is no longer available to 'great' artists to rework for museums. Thus, Roy Lichtenstein's 1960s reworking of comic themes for the purpose of producing great art has been displaced by comic book artists' work *itself* being recognized as art in its own right. Such art is, however, already commercial, industrial and 'anonymous'. For art collectors of comics, the question is one of style not content. In the world of comics, authenticity in artistic creation is gained by reworking those themes, costumes and scenarios first thought out by others, often as long as 50 years ago. Batman, Superman, Green Lantern or Spiderman are reworked and remoulded generationally by an industry that is both conservative and recuperative about its commercial properties. Both Batman and Superman are commercial properties, before or perhaps because they are cultural and artistic icons. In this the comic-book artist is an 'anonymous' craftsman despite any individual wealth or fame – superheroes will continue without him and (if his creatures do not revert to him by copyright) they will be drawn and narrated by others. That Batman and Superman were the property of their companies was the saving grace and the personal disaster of their creators.

Pre-eminent among our modern icons stand Monroe and Batman, both in their own ways a focus for the differing and multiple messages of modernity. In either case – the one screen goddess, the other comic-book graphics – the image is infinitely reworkable, renewable, commercial and consumable. The image is convertible (through franchising of goods and through other media) and open to historical accretions (malleable to an age and a demand, in which such demands are added without removing other older dimensions which themselves signify as 'nostalgia'). Consequently, the image of Batman becomes not just that of a character but a resource for modern cultural messages – a place for an inexhaustible supply of meanings. Such reworking of meaning links the world of the superhero and the world of Batman specifically to the conditions governing urban, *contemporary* myth. Batman as image, and as an accretion of tales and meanings, has passed into modern consciousness: violent mean-streets detective in the 1940s; cold war conservative in the 1950s; camp satiric figure of the 1960s and brooding, psychotic authoritarian of the 1980s and 1990s. Yet always there is the urban modernist landscape, the metropolitan alienation and disturbance of Gotham City aka New York – iconic city of the modern imagination.

In this respect Bruce Wayne belongs to another universe in his rural mansion, where he is sequestered with his butler and his smoking jacket – image of a 1920s and 1930s hero who began his activities in public school and ended them as a gentleman adventurer and amateur detective. Bruce Wayne was outdated as a character at his inception – already the adolescent literature (sub-British in origin) from which he took his cue preferred the world of criminality and urban chaos to the world of gentleman-millionaires. But Richie Rich went native: not Tarzan but the Batman – a dark vampiric figure driven by his strange and insatiable appetite for consuming crime. Batman is a heroic figure from capitalism's evolution, a New Dealer born out of the Depression into a Death Wish vigilante.

The obsessional appetite of Batman gives rise to the *doppelgänger*, the Joker: the true 'objective correlative' for Batman's impulse to punish. We recognize in Batman and Joker the anarchic impulse of capitalism, an entrepreneurial spirit removed from the laws of time, space and 'reality'.

The poisoned chemical-loaded water that turned Joker's hair green and his lips red and his face white is the original ecological disaster from which the spirit of demonic appetite could be released: a true creature of the urban, industrial, western world. The demons of appetite grapple on the rooftops of Manhattan, and middle-class propriety and sobriety find themselves threatened and protected by authoritarian mania and anarchic psychosis. Such figures pass into our consciousness without our necessarily having read or even seen much actual comic-book work – the images are ubiquitous.

It was the ubiquity of these images that frightened the cultural guardians in the 1940s just as previously cultural guardians had been frightened in the 1840s by the rise of popular (that is, uncontrolled) literature. At once, it seemed, comic books had established themselves as legitimate news-stand magazines *and* also become illegitimate cultural products – subversive *because* commercially successful. As a new medium, comic books were becoming more violent, erotic and horrific, money spinning 'non conformity', 'perversions' and brand loyalty. By the late 1940s, comic-book covers sported lurid and violent scenes. On the cover of *Crime Does Not Pay* for May 1943, a half-dead man is being thrown into an apartment incinerator as the police burst in with tommy guns. The artist writer and publisher was Charles Biro.[9] *True Crime Comics*, created by artist and writer Jack Cole, was by 1947 already producing stories with titles such as 'Murder, Morphine and Me' which aficionado Ron Goulart has called 'sexy, fevered and violent in the extreme'.[10]

At the same time, that is from the 1940s onwards, there had begun a noisy wave of protest against comic culture from alarmed cultural guardians.

> In May of 1940, for example, an editorial in the *Chicago Daily News* labeled comic books a 'national disgrace'. Written by Sterling North, the piece was not a critique but a call to arms. Charged North, 'Badly drawn, badly written and badly printed – a strain on young eyes and young nervous systems – the effect of these pulp-paper nightmares is that of a violent stimulant. Their crude blacks and reds spoil the child's natural sense of color; their hypodermic injection of sex and murder make the child impatient with better, though quieter, stories. Unless we want a coming generation even more ferocious than the present one, parents and teachers throughout America must band together to break the "comic magazine."' North's recommended cure for this blight was good books. 'There is nothing dull about *Westward Ho or Treasure Island*,' he declared optimistically. North concluded, 'The shame lies largely with parents who don't know and don't care what their children are reading. It lies with unimaginative teachers who force stupid twaddle down eager young throats, and, of course, it lies with the completely immoral publishers of the comic'

– guilty of a cultural slaughter of the innocents. But the antidote to the "comic" magazine poison can be found in any library or good book store. The parent who does not acquire that antidote for his child is guilty of criminal negligence.[11]

PTAs, teachers organizations and library associations added their voice to what became by the middle 1950s a McCarthyite witch-hunt for moral criminals, subversives, deviates and crypto-fascist-communists. By 1948, radio shows were airing programmes such as 'What's wrong with the Comics?' and in the same year the Association for the Advancement of Psychotherapy held a symposium on the 'Psychotherapy of Comic Books'.[12]

The speaker whose voice emerged most clearly from that 1948 symposium was Dr Frederic Wertham, a senior psychiatrist from the New York Department of Hospitals. Features and newspaper articles with titles such as 'What Parents don't know about Comic Books' from *The Ladies Home Journal* of 1953 kept Wertham's name before the public until in 1954 he published *Seduction of the Innocent* in which he,

connected comic books with every kind of social and moral perversion imaginable including sadism, drug abuse, theft, murder and rape. Some of his allegations burst at the seams with evil: 'Homosexual childhood prostitution, especially in boys, is often connected with stealing and with violence. For all these activities children are softened up by comic books'. While focusing on the crime and horror comics, Wertham had a special distaste for superheroes.

'What is the social meaning of these supermen, superwomen, super-lovers, superboys, supergirls, super-ducks, super-mice, super-magicians, super-safe crackers? How did Nietzsche get into the nursery? . . . Superheroes undermine respect for the law and hard working, decent citizens'.[13]

In an attempt to defend their now overly visible industry, publishers formed first into the Association of Comics Magazine Publishers and then appointed an attorney to head their lobby. Henry Schultz, however, was not able to fend off a Senate Subcommittee hearing in which, just as with the later 'Lady Chatterley' trial in England, there was the usual level of foolishness displayed by the authorities. The results however went contrary to the spirit of that later 'trial'. In order to stave off regulation and backruptcy, the comic publishers reformed as the Comics Magazine Association of America and instituted their own Hays Code under the Comics Code Authority.[14] From now on comics would carry a code-approved seal indicating that the work was wholesome, entertaining and educational.

The Comics Code, in its comprehensiveness and in its authoritarian attitudinizing proved to be, and remains, a classic guide to the nature of pulp: the mirror image and antidote to pulp's Technicolor dreaming. Among such rules as those which banned attacks on religious or ethnic ('racial') groups and required women to be portrayed 'realistically' and 'without exaggeration of any physical qualities', rules apparently sane and reasonable, were a far larger group which demanded certain 'general standards' which would tend towards 'good taste' 'decency' and good grammar. Thus, for example,

- Illicit sex relations are neither to be hinted at or [*sic*] portrayed. Violent love scenes as well as sexual abnormalities are unacceptable.
- Respect for parents, the moral code, and for honorable behavior shall be fostered. A sympathetic understanding of the problems of love is not a license for morbid distortion.
- The treatment of love-romance stories shall emphasize the value of the home and the sanctity of marriage.
- Passion or romantic interest shall never be treated in such a way as to stimulate the lower and baser emotions.
- Seduction and rape shall never be shown or suggested.
- Sex perversion or any inference to same is strictly forbidden.

Anti-authoritarian ideas, represented exclusively as 'criminal' acts were also to be banned from now on, hence,

- Policemen, judges, government officials and respected institutions shall never be presented in such a way as to create disrespect for established authority.

Moreover, if erotic tales were to be curbed so too were their accompanying genres, crime . . .

- Crimes shall never be presented in such a way as to create sympathy for the criminal, to promote distrust of the forces of law and justice, or to inspire others with a desire to imitate criminals.

• If crime is depicted it shall be as a sordid and unpleasant activity.
• Criminals shall not be presented so as to be rendered glamorous or to occupy a position which creates a desire for emulation.
• In every instance good shall triumph over evil and the criminal punished for his misdeeds.
• Scenes of excessive violence shall be prohibited. Scenes of brutal torture, excessive and unnecessary knife and gun play, physical agony, gory and gruesome crime shall be eliminated.

and horror . . . .

• No comic magazine shall use the word horror or terror in its title.
• All scenes of horror, excessive bloodshed, gory or gruesome crimes, depravity, lust, sadism, masochism shall not be permitted.
• All lurid, unsavory, gruesome illustrations shall be eliminated.
• Scenes dealing with, or instruments associated with walking dead, torture, vampires and vampirism, ghouls, cannibalism and werewolfism are prohibited.

In all cases, either of sex, violence or horror, the reader was to have the reinforcing message of moral condemnation, the very language used subject to control and manipulation: made safe, made wholesome.

• Profanity, obscenity, smut, vulgarity, or words or symbols which have acquired undesirable meanings are forbidden.
• Although slang and colloquialisms are acceptable, excessive use should be discouraged.

Moreover, this was *intended* to be an intrusion into the privacy of the consumer and, if advertising was required to tell the truth, it would only do so wholesomely, avoiding the very issues (salacious, vulgar) that urgently exercised the minds of adolescent readers.

• Advertisement of medical, health, or toiletry products of questionable nature are to be rejected.

In the seeds of such benevolent authoritariarism, the tendrils of political correctness begin to flex.

William Gaines, who had been a flourishing publisher prior to the Senate Hearings and whose testimony was much remembered, initially refused to join the new Association. Blackballed, he ironically salvaged his career by founding MAD Magazine with Harvey Kurtzman, a satirical refusal as well as an ironic testimony to the leftover paranoia of 1940s America and the Cold War mania of the early 1950s.

When all is said and done, satire may be seen merely as revenge after the fact. For many Americans forced out of their jobs in publishing and journalism, Britain must have appeared a liberal haven. Yet Britain was also suffering a wave of official hysterics in the form of book prosecutions aimed at closing down the pulp paperback trade that had grown up by the end of the Second World War. Unlike America, the attack tended to be piecemeal and undirected. Unfortunately its effects were nevertheless largely the same.

The most important prosecution was that brought against the publishers and printers of the 'Hank Janson' novels and the subsequent trial of Stephen (Steve) Frances, Janson's creator. Janson was the creation of the shortage of American pulp crime fiction during and after the war and the ability of small author/producers to cash in on trends or, as in this case, gaps in the market: by 'mid 1953 over eight million copies (of Janson novels) had been sold in five years'.[15] This huge success was based on a mixture of violence and erotica, a disregard for pre-war values and a fascination with 'modern' concerns which were Americanized, youthful and consumerist as well as inimical to rigid class boundaries. It was also based on the opposite of all these categories: a literature aimed at a 'working class' or a 'proletarianized' readership craving imaginary freedoms in a more authoritarian Britain now defined by its welfare state, national military service, continued rationing, utility and deepening austerity. Janson looked forward to the sixties while alleviating the fifties. Whatever the case, 'Janson' was a huge success, and seemed, with its values and cover art, an attack on conformist establishment values, the sort of book that Raymond Hoggart later vilified in *The Uses of Literacy*.[16]

Steve Frances wrote as Janson, the books based on fake autobiographical details. Indeed, Frances had never even been to America, rather getting his ideas from Hollywood gangster movies, novels, guides and *Inside America*.[17] Furthermore, when interviewed

on David Farson's television programme *Success Story*, Frances chose
to heighten the Janson character by wearing a mask! By the late
1940s and early 1950s, Frances was successful enough to live mod-
estly in Spain, and like Edgar Wallace and Barbara Cartland made
use of a dictaphone and secretaries to create his stories. Frances also
used other names: Ace Capelli; Johnny Greco; Steve Markham; Tex
Ryland; Link Shelton; Max Clinten.[18] Finally, perhaps exhausted
with watching over every aspect of his one-man business, Frances
sold the rights to the name Janson to publisher Reginald Carter in
1952.[19]

Increasingly under the notice of the Director of Public Prosecutions, Carter was himself brought to trial for publishing obscene
material, having been previously raided by Scotland Yard. Seven
Janson novels were brought as evidence.[20] Opening on 14 January
1954 at the Guildhall, the trial paved the way for the successful
prosecution of other publishing houses and was only halted by the
more famous Lady Chatterley trial in 1960. In the eyes of the prosecution it did not matter if it was Hank Janson or D.H. Lawrence
in the dock – both became equal in the face of prosecution and
censorship. Even the concept of 'intention' to corrupt and deprave
was dubiously dropped in the first trial so keenly was a successful
conviction sought. Badgered by the prosecution the defendants were
finally found guilty by a jury little inclined to persecute them. Sum-
ming up, Recorder Gerald Dodson made it clear that it was modernity itself that was on trial.

> No doubt you are quite aware that you are being asked to slide,
> to let yourselves slide into the degeneracy of modern times as
> depicted in these books which have been produced on behalf of
> the defence. . . . contributing to the general slide downwards of
> this type of modern literature.[21]

Mervyn Griffiths-Jones who led the prosecution was to reappear
some years later when he unsuccessfully prosecuted *Lady Chatterley's
Lover*: ironically, respectable Penguin were the publishers. Times
were indeed changing.

The sentence in the spring of 1954 ruined the publisher and the
printer and an appeal was quashed.[22] Yet this was not the end of
the story. Having returned to Britain, Stephen Frances was arrested
for authoring obscene books. Frances defended himself with the
equivocation so typical of this period. He claimed the books had

been 'written' by Geoffrey Pardoe (probably a pseudonym for his secretary who took dictation and therefore had actually *typed* the books!).[23] By 1954, Janson was selling more copies than ever and even the NAAFI was proved to have purchased the books for national servicemen.[24] In 1955, The Horror Comics Bill was brought before Parliament and by the late 1950s it was clear that a new ruling on obscenity was needed. The Obscene Publications Act of 1959 attempted to fulfil that requirement.

The results of this continued assault by the establishment coupled with overproduction, undercapitalization and a national printers' strike finally destroyed the success of the 'mushroom' publishers and their pulp production, but one cannot help thinking that what actually occurred was the suppression of a whole class of literature and a whole class of reader and, perhaps, readers *from* a certain class. Modernity was indeed under siege. Much later these episodes of actual British book-burning and suppression were little documented and almost forgotten. Even a recent book recording the trial of *Lady Chatterley's Lover* which was edited by H. Montgomery Hyde and has an introduction by him blatantly ignores the immediate post-war cultural determinants of the prosecution and the trials for obscenity which led up to Penguin finding themselves in the dock of the Old Bailey. Instead, Hyde chooses to document 'worthy' books irresponsibly prosecuted.

> During the thirty years following the case of *The Well of Loneliness*, several prosecutions for obscenity in England aroused public interest. They included *Sleeveless Errand*, a novel by Norah James in 1929 (condemned); Count Potocki de Montalk's poems in 1932 (condemned); *Boy*, a novel by James Hanley in 1934 (condemned); *Bessie Cotter*, a novel by Wallace Smith in 1935 (condemned); *The Sexual Impulse*, a medical manual of sex instruction for lay readers in 1935 (condemned); *Love Without Fear*, a similar work by Dr Eustace Chesser in 1942 (acquitted); also five prosecutions of novels in 1954 – *The Image and the Search*, by Walter Baxter (formally acquitted after the jury had twice disagreed); *September in Quinze*, by Vivian Connell (condemned); *The Man in Control*, by Charles McGraw (acquitted); *Julia* by Nargo Bland (condemned); and *The Philanderer* by Stanley Kauffman (acquitted). In all these cases except the second, where the poems were not printed, the publishers were also convicted. Several classics were also ordered to be destroyed, such as the *Satyricon* of Petronius and the *Decameron* of Boccaccio.[25]

What collectively is forgotten is the far greater attempted suppression of popular reading before the 1960s.

Equivocation seemed the only defence on both sides of the Atlantic as the following dialogue, reminiscent of Stephen Frances's statement, suggests. This time it is John O'Connor of Bantam Books introducing evidence to the 1952 House Select Committee on Current Pornographic Materials. When questioned by Edward Rees of Kansas, the hearing turns into a trial.

MR. O'CONNOR. Let's see. I have read *Don't Touch Me* [a thencontroversial novel by MacKinlay Kantor], and perhaps that is a good one for your purpose.

MR. REES. You say that is a good one?

MR. O'CONNOR. I thought it might be a good one.

MR. BURTON. For our purpose.

MR. REES. What do you say about it? Is it good for the public?

MR. O'CONNOR. Am I being questioned now on the contents of the book?

MR. REES. Yes. You said it was good for us, and I am asking you.

MR. O'CONNOR. I sensed from what I read of the earlier hearings, that the committee is searching for books which, in its opinion, tend toward the pornographic side, but that does not by any means mean that I agree with the committee.

MR. REES. What I want to know is, do you approve that book for reading?

MR. O'CONNOR. I can't answer the question, that question, 'yes' or 'no,' because that is a question –

MR. REES. Do you think it is a good book for the public to read?

MR. O'CONNOR. I do; yes.

MR. REES. And you approve that sort of stuff?

MR. O'CONNOR. May I expand my answer?

MR. REES. Well, I just asked you if you said that is good; that is the end of it. It is either good or bad.

MR. O'CONNOR. I believe, if this book is not pornographic, if it is not pornographic –

MR. REES. Do you think the material is good, the reading of it is good?[26]

The inconclusive nature of this 'trial' by other means led, as in Britain, to a clean-up campaign by the industry. Malevolently attacked in America and lamentably also repeatedly attacked in Britain,

paperbacks seemed to their persecutors to represent modern life –
their suppression the reinstatement of an old-fashioned moral order.

> Some of the most offensive infractions of the moral code were
> found to be contained in the low-cost, paper-bound publications
> known as 'pocket-size books.' . . . The so-called pocket-size books,
> which originally started out as cheap reprints of standard works,
> have largely degenerated into media for the dissemination of artful
> appeals to sensuality, immorality, filth, perversion, and degen-
> eracy. The exaltation of passion above principle and the identifi-
> cation of lust with love are so prevalent that the casual reader of
> such 'literature' might easily conclude that all married persons
> are habitually adulterous and all teen-agers completely devoid of
> any sex inhibitions.[27]

In none of this, of course, could any one, prosecutors and prosecuted alike, quite put their finger on what was so subversive. At
its best, it was simply an unstated threat of something decayed and
of changing times. Hierarchized moral authority, vested in an established oligarchy, could just as easily be supported as questioned
by this material. Perhaps what pulp highlighted was an unspoken
fragility in the system in which collectivism, either of the right or
of the left was now under threat from a protean literature at once
individualistic, erotic, violent, consumerist and youthful – like the
urban environment in which it flourished. Such literature was a
direct consequence of modern American urban history, but it was
never founded on a political programme. Rather it was illicit by
being made illicit, ironically and supposedly subversive of the very
values that allowed it to succeed and which provided its usually
conformist readership with the values and attitudes we label 'American'. In Britain, perhaps 'modern' was a code word for American,
as some years before New York had, for Henry James, been synonymous with Jewish values.[28]

The impulse to ban, seize and burn books during the 1950s as
well as the parallel hounding of publishers, printers and authors,
was in the first instance a moral crusade. Yet this moral crusade,
conducted to protect the public good and mobilized through the
use of legislation almost a hundred years old was also a 'political'
campaign waged by other means. The origination for such an impulse is graphically demonstrated by a prosecution in the 1850s
brought against Robert Martin, a minor pornographer who brought
out a penny weekly entitled *Paul Pry* during 1856. The journal itself

provided a veneer of morality for a large dose of harmless pruri-
ence, including letters to the editor asking sexual questions and
anecdotes about London's sexual haunts. His tales included the
adventures of one Rt. Hon. Filthy Lucre which came to the notice
of the authorities and led to Martin's prosecution for immorality
(then classed as a misdemeanour). The comments of Lord Campbell,
Lord Chief Justice of England, suggest a growing authoritarism and
intolerance.

> His Honour, after reading the account of the Rt. Hon. Filthy
> Lucre's gallantries, expressed 'astonishment and horror', particu-
> larly at the low price at which it was sold. Hitherto, he said, there
> had been some check to these publications, arising from the high
> price which was extracted for them. . . . But to sell them for one
> penny was a state of things which his Lordship, with great feel-
> ing, pronounced a disgrace to the country. It was no excuse, he
> said, that the defendant had also sold the *Household Words* and
> other publications of most interesting moral, instructive and beau-
> tiful character, for which the country was indebted to Mr. Charles
> Dickens. The jury agreed that these cheap publications had 'a far
> greater tendency to demoralize' than more costly ones.[29]

Here is the key to the suppression of pulp material – its inexpensive
nature and ready availability. Economic liberty equalled moral
laxity – at least, it seemed, for the lower orders – while expensive
pornography was presumably less likely to corrupt those with a
classical education (that is, the upper class). It was indeed the rich
'wot got the pleasure'.

The issue did not rest there. Lord Campbell then presented a bill
to Parliament in order to strengthen the current law on obscenity.
Violently opposed for attacking civil liberty, it remained for
Campbell's successor, Lord Chief Justice Cockburn, in 1868 to pronounce (again during a judgment on a Robert Martin publication)
that the test must be the 'tendency' to 'deprave and corrupt'.[30] The
die was cast both sides of the Atlantic which led to so much mischief in the 1950s and the necessary equivocation of authors such as
Stephen Frances and publishers such as John O'Connor. At least in
part, the suppression of pulp was motivated by economic and class
concerns (covertly political) which were simultaneously moral and
ethical attitudes. One should not forget that many respectable
ordinary people would have seen such prosecutions as a triumph
of common sense and civil decency.

Having come thus far in our argument it should be possible to talk of the aesthetic of trash without the nature of this amalgamation (trash *and* art) becoming a contradiction in terms and without those same terms simply recreating it as the inversion (perversion) of serious art. Of course, trash art is always connected to serious art by those who would judge one by the other – like high art, trash is itself and always reflects its 'other'.

In this equation one need only reverse terms: art is serious and permanent, trash is ephemeral and light; art reveals and trash conceals; art is a new reality and trash is an old reality repackaged; art is unique and authentic while trash is formulaic and mechanical; art is history and trash is nostalgia; art is truth but trash is lies; art emancipates as surely as trash incarcerates. Such an equation will always put trash art down, and it will always be *correct* for the simple reason that the terms of the equation were written by those to whom it falls to 'defend' serious art. I do not wish to challenge those terms, determined as they usually are by those ethical considerations (masquerading as aesthetical) of interest groups whose standpoints are irreducibly there to defend an interest. The canon is a necessary and logical (though not *natural*) determinant of modern cultural and hierarchical social division: it defines as it excludes. Trash art and pulp visions get their definition through exclusion and thus gain the strength primarily to be what they are and not something other.

Trash art, loved to destruction and always one step ahead of its analysis will, of necessity, always incorporate a *hierarchy* of pulp values, the creation of fans, each of whom knows what comes where and in what order of acceptableness. A pulp aesthetic then emerges. Aesthetic and commercial, pulp speaks its own language and has its own grammar, both of which must be learnt. Thus will be created cults, fans, aficionados, desperadoes and addicts, fanzines and conventions – lives determined by reference to potent fictions with genres as organizing principles for people's lives. Pulp knows its audience and that audience determines its life, which is purely ephemeral, the product of mass production and cheap materials, and because ephemeral eventually carefully collected and preserved (usually by those in search of a substitute for their own lost past). Thus does commercial entertainment end as personal destiny. Speaking a secret language of desires unfulfilled, pulp is truly a type of embarrassing perversity negotiated between producers and consumers – a guarantee of order and yet anarchically sub-cultural.

To destroy the canon by opening it up to trash (now, of course horribly respectable) would simply be to remove one set of criteria of judgement for another, this time a hierarchy of reading practices (theory) as rigid as the previous pattern. One way or another, legitimation would be imposed on the actual anarchy of printed material. Thus in one guise or another, trash would merely play the canonic game and the fantasy escapism of pulp become simply a secondary reality parallel to that of an established avant garde; another reality in which common sense and madness are partners. As the benchmark by which high culture knows itself in its reflection, pulp remains gloriously bad taste. Pulp is an ethical division in society made into an aesthetic question of culture.

Trash art is the ever illicit enjoyment of contemporaneity. It is a refusal *without* consequence, a resistance which is also an accommodation. In this way it differs from subversive literature, which is resistant *with* consequences, although unintended consequences may be imposed upon pulp by others. Pulp celebrates the *now*, the industrial and the metropolitan in history: nature and human progress are rewritten in these terms. Pulp is the eternalized moment of the now lived irrationally in the overtly sentimental, nostalgic, sensational, erotic, romantic, violent and fantastic. Without an encumbering *authenticity*, trash art is liberated into a space of pure effect and style. But if pulp escapes authenticity altogether (and therefore bourgeois realism) it does not fall into the anti-humanism of avant-gardism. Pulp is not a pursuit of structure for its own sake (although pulp has many structures). Whereas for the modernist, structure was meaning (not just a carrier for it), for pulp, meaning precedes structure in the conditions needed to tell a story or create a character. If avant-gardism is determined by the subordinate clause, pulp is determined by the single imperative clause: it is a case of being versus doing as determinant of character and culture – the psychological against the social. And the peopling of this narrative, preceding and defining it is already determined by a framework of author/reader networks: doctors and nurses, space travellers and aliens, criminals and detectives, cowboys and Indians, super-heroes and supervillains.

All these characters had emerged or were developing as fictional figures when the intellectual avant garde tacitly agreed that psychology and sociology (and therefore alienation, immobility and impotence) were the determining factors in the making of the metropolitan ego. Popular genres and their fictional inhabitants however,

consistently denied the onslaught of the psychological and the
social. Nevertheless, they were not merely recuperations of older,
heroic ideas of the self but rather contemporary attempts to locate
the self in character and determine character by *action*. The choice
of hero and heroine was played out in the professional and technological spaces of new careers and, in the case of cowboys or space
travel, current frontiers of knowledge.

Because read and understood by millions, these narratives act for
us as fictional realms of social possibility. If Anglo-American avant-
gardism was about self, then pulp, even or especially in its extrem-
ist forms (superheroes, etc.) was about *society* and the constraints
on action. Yet it must be firmly stated that pulp is always
deterministically individualist and personal in its interpretation of
social action. In the act of portraying social factors, pulp converts
these factors into traits of *character* lived in the public sphere as acts.
Indeed, popular fiction emphasizes personality within a structure
different from that of much avant-garde art. It emphasizes episodic
narrative (good for serialization), teleological and purposive movement (the unveiling of secrets and the unmasking of villains), outward appearance and the avoidance of psychology and an elevation
of character over plot. All this is provided within a bland (or heightened) accessible language which reinforces the values of society.
While many 'serious' novels written in this manner emphasize science, social determinism, class confrontation and sexual warfare,
the less serious convert these issues into personalized battles: the
spy novel, cowboy novelette, romantic love story and detective novel
predominate – in a phrase, works of fantasy which reduce or re-
make the social into the personal.[31]

Urban, 'proletarian' and fantastical, pulp is also loud, brash, sexy,
violent, passionate and unlikely. Protean in its forms, although
constrained by a limited number of scenarios and plots, it is both
predictable (on the level of genre) and unpredictable (on the level
of manipulation of reader expectation). Creating its own reader
patterns and stealing from any cultural area to form new channels
of communication, pulp is happiest when it traverses the media
and uses each medium as an infinitely transferable resource.

Pulp is the first to give content to new media: film, radio, television. These then give back to pulp its vibrancy and life. Pulp is not
one medium but a *transferable condition* of the medium's content
and structure. Disrespectful of boundaries, pulp as form is anarchic,

capitalistic, market-led: its characteristic heroes and heroines are individualists – larger than society or outside of social constraint, their fate demonically personal. Nevertheless, these characters are always fated (chosen) to be superheros, or else fall in love, by forces greater than themselves – if a man's gotta do what a man's gotta do, if creatures from a dying planet choose earth to conquer, if the boy from the back street becomes a mobster, then it is fortune makes it so. The circumstances of constraint are at once also the circumstances and possibilities of anarchic individualism. In this paradox, pulp content is both individualistic and socially decided. For those producing pulp, their task will be aesthetic *and* industrial, determined by a commercial context. For readers, their act will be a communal, conformist activity and a *private*, escapist, secret passion (like making love or going to the cinema). Thus pulp acts to confirm control in the realm of the imagination and escapes from such control by use of the same mechanism.

Pulp is an infinite attempt to put back the 'lost' security of the 'I' of self in its battle with time. Thus it becomes, unexpectedly a nostalgia for self. But now this self is only recoverable in its weird reflection as gangster, alien, superhero or cop. In pulp, we recognize ourselves as strangers: contradictions of escapism and conformism, banality made strange. Through such a formulation (that is, the banal made strange) we can relate pulp art to the folkloristic urban legends collected under such titles as 'The Hook', 'The Phantom Hitchhiker' or 'Poodle in the Oven'.[32] Such semi-oral tales circulate among adolescents and adults in all metropolitan areas. While many of these tales can be traced into the last century, *none* can really be shown to exist outside a modern, industrial, urbanized and technologized environment. These are truly tales of the city and of the automobile, and they express erotic, demonic and violent fantasies surrounding our relationship with cars, ovens and microwaves, fast food, modern hairstyles, drug addiction, canned drinks, television, telephones and sexual freedom. Clearly such tales make the banal strange and turn the technological into the magical: all are *parables of the contemporary* (they are never related as just legends), continuously updated to conform to present conditions, feeding off new consumer goods and mass interests. In this way they obviously relate to the governing principles of pulp art, but while pulp and urban legends (sophisticated oral anecdotes of the 'stranger than fiction' type) have common ground, the former is not merely myth for modern mentalities. Rather, urban legends are parallel, non-literary excursions into the pulp arena, secondarily using pulp material within a pulp context. Such an explanation allows us to see how readers and audiences situate their identities both communally and individually within such forms of reworked banality – the ordinary as the weird and the weird as determinant of a self both outside social constraint (in the world of anecdotal demonic phenomena) and accepting of social constraint (the reinforcing of a collective metropolitan imagination). Such is the folklore of the literate and the intelligent.

Thus pulp may be, and will probably be, the central formation process of an individual's cultural and personal aspirations – freedom, power, love, success, security, happy endings; abandoned and also authoritarian, paranoid and traditionalistic. Such displacements make pulp fully aware of what it is formally and technically but also tell of what it cannot be and cannot know (need not know), of itself and its social and historical place. Craving respectability through such illegitimate means may leave pulp sometimes illegal or subversive but it will always leave it *illicit*.

And what of Betty Page left 'in bondage' at the beginning of this chapter, that other Marilyn, the dark one? These are my Betty pages dedicated to another history and another glamour.

After one early broken marriage Norma Jean became Marilyn Monroe and married a baseball star and a world renowned playwright; after an early broken marriage, Betty Page moved to New York and found Irving Klaw, small-time pin-up photographer and cheesecake pornographer; Marilyn starred in *Bus Stop* and *The Misfits*, Betty starred in *Teaserama* and magazines such as *Eyeful*. Marilyn – Monroe – icon and goddess, died the mistress of a president, Betty Page simply vanished after a *Playboy* centrefold one day in 1957. RIP Monroe, long live Betty.

Betty Page is the raven-haired double, the illicit *Doppelgänger*; in her oversize, badly fitted bondage gear she appears a cut-price Marilyn whose own couture was body-clinging, sprayed on, sequins and all. But Betty is no cut-price Marilyn, rather she is the respectable girl who acts out the disreputable with her body-to-die-for and her sham innocence, her wide eyes and kinky accessories: harem-girl, Tarzan-girl, girl-next-door. For a time Betty Page was a teacher of English; the theory of pulp is written on her body, she takes it with her, displays it in the curves of her stomach and the rise of her breasts. Here is the nice-naughty girl, whose body is the icon of pulp, pulp in action – pulp consciousness. There is no theory of pulp from *within*. Betty Page is that theory lived as action – herself the Queen of Trash and the Muse of this book.[33]

Part II
Ars Gratia Artis

8

The Ripper Writing:
A Cream of a Nightmare Dream

Jack of Hearts, Jack O'Lantern, Jack the Giant-Killer, Jack the Lad, Jack Sheppard and Springheeled Jack; 'Jack', a common name that represents ubiquity: the nomenclature of the ordinary. In the late nineteenth century as for us in the late twentieth there was only one Jack – *the Ripper*; of the famous nineteenth-century criminals this one alone has endured into legend. Of Charlie Peace, Neill Cream or Israel Lipski little is remembered; of other famous murders only the victim is recalled: Maria Marten offering herself to melodrama and Fanny Adams to a coarse joke. Jack survives, but not merely because he was not caught.

This chapter is an attempt to consider the determinants and the progress of the Ripper legend as both text and history and to consider the constellation of historico-psychological notions that have gathered around the name of the Ripper.

Jack, it seems, timed his murders at a correct psychological moment, for almost immediately, not least for their ferocity, his deeds became the stuff of legend. He instantly became both a particular and a general threat, a focus for numerous related fears among metropolitan dwellers across Europe and America. One newspaper late in 1888 declared,

> The Whitechapel murderer, having been arrested all over the metropolis and in several provincial towns, is now putting in an appearance in various foreign countries, and also in the United States of America. . . . [he is] a Russian with a religious mania . . . murdering Magdalens in order that their souls may go to heaven, or [on New York advice] . . . [He is] a butcher, whose mind is affected by changes of the moon.
>
> (*The Times*, 3 Dec 1888)

Already, only one month after the murders had ceased, Jack has an international 'appeal'. His ubiquitous nature allows him appearances

159

on both sides of the Atlantic and he is claimed by or accused of being a variety of nationalities. The article is already in light-hearted mood and Jack has taken on the serio-comic aspects of Sweeney Todd, himself a type of 'butcher'. Not only may he be both a Russian religious and sexual fanatic, but he may also be a New Yorker under biblical delusions (which the paper places under the 'Ezekiel Theory'). The Russian is not merely a religious fanatic but also a 'nihilist' and a member of a 'secret society' – Russia (the paper tells its readers) being notorious for secret societies. Thus, Jack becomes the focal point for an attack on foreigners (in particular Russians) and especially foreigners who are bent on undermining society in secret via covertly ritualized murder.

This mixture of grim charnel humour, political and religious fear, xenophobia and sexual innuendo (those journalistic 'Magdalens') partook of the atmosphere during the murders. At one end of the spectrum *Punch* (13 October 1888) dedicated a doggerel verse to the Ripper around a cartoon of Jack as a Mephistopheles bill-posting London with his latest exploits. This lampoon of the recent 'penny-dreadfuls' and 'Ripperana' was matched more seriously by the upsurge of anti-foreign agitation fanned by phantom messages (supposedly by the Ripper) accusing 'the Juwes', and by the Assistant Metropolitan Police Commissioner's claim that 'in stating that he [Jack] was a Polish Jew [he was] merely stating a definitely established fact' (which nearly started a pogrom in the East End).

On 13 February 1894 the *Sun*, a sensationalist newspaper, began printing a piece of popular investigative journalism about the 'real' Ripper, traced by 'WK', one of the staff reporters, to Broadmoor, 'a living tomb of a lunatic asylum' (17 February 1894) where the 'greatest murder mystery of the nineteenth century' was about to be solved by Jack the Ripper's 'confession'. This further accretion to the legend attempted to locate Jack in the world of 'debased' humanity in Broadmoor where inmates (and especially Jack) showed no moral awareness of the import of their deeds. In linking his home life to 'Camden Town' and his criminal insanity to Broadmoor the paper ably accused middle-class prudery of responsibility for Jack's upbringing. Nevertheless, the paper absolved that same class from blame by accepting that, in contrast to Jack, the paper's readers obviously possessed moral awareness. Curiosity was thus legitimized by a veneer of morality.

Unlike the clippings of the 1880s, this series put together insanity and the middle class. The murders were already thought of as the work of a depraved doctor. Nevertheless, the linking of 'the greatest murder mystery' and a 'living tomb' put together mysteriousness and living death in a way guaranteed *not* to reveal the killer's identity and guaranteed to increase sales of the *Sun* for the duration of the series. Moreover, the paper could congratulate itself and its readers on tracking down the perpetrator without undoing the 'edge' of fear they wished to create – for, as the paper clearly stated, this lunatic had *escaped* in order to kill. So horrible was he, so morally unaware, that armed guards stood about his bed. Jack's ubiquity is therefore reinforced by his unnamed status (he is identified only by initials) and by the hints of his origins and his ability to vanish from the lunatic asylum at will if not guarded. The lunatic asylum was represented by the paper as a type of purgatorial doom from which the 'living dead' returned to reap vengeance on the twilight world of the living (twilight, precisely because the victims were prostitutes). One mysterious world preys on another. Indeed, by returning from Broadmoor the journalist literally returns from the dead to tell his tale.

Medical and criminological science are used in this series to reinforce secrecy and threat; commercialism dictates the possibility of other (and) endless articles on the Ripper.

However, even during the season of the killings in the autumn of 1888, papers quickly realized the value of Jack's exploits, conducting their own post-mortems and reporting coroner's verdicts at length. *The Times*, for instance, ran articles in its *Weekly Edition* from September 1888 to November 1888. On 28 September 1888 it gave a full page to the social background of Spitalfields and the poverty endured there by Annie Chapman, the Ripper's first victim. *The Times* was quick to guess the direction in which police might look. They thought a post-mortem surgeon's assistant might be the culprit because of 'his' specialized knowledge of the uterus, which was removed from the victim's body.

The Times further noted the curious circumstance of an American surgeon who wished to include real uteri with a journal he was mailing to clients! Could this bizarre surgeon, whose name was not known, have prompted the killer to get 'a uterus for the £20 reward?' asked the paper. In a later issue, next to the report of other Ripper murders (26 October 1888), a clergyman protested in a long letter at the condemnation of the destitute by the middle classes, at their hypocrisy over prostitution and at their ignorance of the conditions prevailing in the East End. He concluded that this had 'blotted the pages of our Christianity'.

The freakish, of which the nineteenth century was inordinately fond, found itself beside the missionary, which in its guise as Mayhew, Engels or Booth consistently restated the ordinariness of the 'freak' (the destitute, the prostitute, the opium addict, the derelict). 'Body snatching' (and the notion of a uterus as a 'free gift' with a new journal) then weirdly allies itself with murder for greed (the reward offered of £20) and murder as the act of the desperately destitute. Jack becomes the focus for the bizarre in the ordinary misery of everyday life in the metropolitan slums. Jack the murderer becomes Jack *the missionary* who focused on problems other investigators were unable to bring to such a wide audience. Murder allowed for social reform. The newspapers, by keeping Jack the centre of attention, ironically kept the slum problems central too.

After reports covering three months by *The Times* and *The Times Weekly Edition*, the newspaper concluded that 'the murderer seems to have vanished, leaving no trace of his identity ... with even greater mystery' (*The Times*, 10 November 1888). Jack the Ripper, given his *nom de guerre* by Fleet Street, was the first major figure to offer himself to, and to become, a creation of journalism. By the 1880s newspapers commanded audiences large enough to make Jack a major figure of international interest rather than a local folktale figure for the East End of London.[1] The power of journalism and the crowded warrens of the central city of the Empire together provided ground for the dissemination of the legend, a legend based upon both fear *and* curiosity – a terrible ambivalence. The possibilities for the dissemination of *rumour* could never be more fortuitous, and letters from 'Jack' fed interest and added to the atmosphere of uncertainty.

Indeed, Jack's letters themselves may have been the work of an entrepreneurial journalist providing 'copy' for himself. These letters, conveying a black humour and a certain 'bravado' (*Stratford Express*, 7 May 1965), may be read not merely as the realization of the power (for the first time) of the mass media but, whether authentic or fake, yet another accretion to the fictionalizing of the Ripper and the self-advertising and self-confidence of an entrepreneurial murderer (acquiring kudos by self-advertisement).

These letters convey a music-hall atmosphere and a self-important theatricality through which the Ripper's letters create an imaginary persona for the perpetrator. Addressed to 'the Old Boss', and signed (at least once) 'from Hell', Jack goes into his music-hall act for the bewildered audience – appalled, amazed (and applauding) the virtuoso performance. 'He' tells us that

> I was goin' to hopperate again close to your ospitle – just as i was goin to drop my nife along at er bloomin throte them curses of coppers spoilt the game but i guess i will be on the job soon and will send you another bitt of innerd.

In another letter he finds the search for his identity a source of amusement: 'They say I am a doctor now. Ha! Ha!'

Each letter becomes a performance put on by an actor assuming a part. The letter-writing gives a self-importance to the writer and a grandeur and status which is uncompromised by capture and identification. Hence, this letter activity becomes, for the legend at least, as important as the deeds themselves just as Davy Crockett or P.T. Barnum were to make legends of their own lives by writing their 'autobiographies' and adventures.

The Ripper letters are a form of *true life confession* heightened to the level of a fiction which embraces a 'cockney' persona, a sense of black humour, a melodramatic villain ('them curses of coppers') and a ghoul (sending 'innerds'), and mixes it with a sense of the dramatic and a feeling for a rhetorical climax. In these letters life and popular theatre come together to act upon the popular imagination. The Ripper (now possibly many 'Rippers' all reporting their acts) autographs his work as a famous artist (death as creativity) – anonymous and yet totally well known. Here, confession only adds to confusion (even Neill Cream claimed to be the Ripper). Jack's letter 'from Hell' concludes 'catch me when you can', adding a sense of challenge and a stronger sense of a 'hint' to the frustration of authority in its quest for an actual identity to the murderer.[2]

By the time of these letters Jack has ceased to be one killer but has become a multiplicity of performing personas for the popular imagination. The possibility of copycat crimes (although finally dismissed from at least two other 'torso' cases) lent to Jack the amorphous ability to inhabit more than one physical body (a point which I shall develop later).

Consequently, for the late nineteenth century, the Ripper became a type of 'folk' character whose exploits spilled into the twentieth century via cinema, theatre and fiction. In our own century the

Ripper has been tracked and traced by numerous writers after a positive identity. Writers have named a Russian doctor called Konovalov (Donald McCormick), the Duke of Clarence (Thomas Stowell), William Gull (Stephen Knight), Montague Druitt (Daniel Farson) and J.K. Stephen (Michael Harrison) as possible candidates. Each, in his turn, has been refuted – the 'royal theory' being denied by Walter Sickert's son Joseph, who dismissed it as a hoax that he had played on an over-receptive author. The 'debate' heats up every few years with new flushes of theory and further refutations, while works such as Stephen Knight's *Jack the Ripper: The Final Solution* added to the growing heap of books searching for scandal in suburbia or in the freemasons, in highest government or the royal family.[3] Knight, himself a journalist, stated in the *East London Advertiser* (7 December 1973) that 'the evil presence of Jack the Ripper still seems to haunt . . . the imagination of crime investigators', and he noted that in the 1970s letters were still arriving from people claiming knowledge of or claiming actually to be 'the Ripper'. In the twentieth century Jack has become the centre of a conspiracy debate. Indeed, so vast is the volume of literature to date that Alexander Kelly was able to write an article for *The Assistant Librarian* about his compilation of a bibliography of 'Ripperana and Ripperature'.[4]

The Ripper literature however is far from confined to the work of amateur sleuths (and they are a study in themselves) but extends to both fiction and film. Such fictionalization began almost immediately in 1889 with J.F. Brewer's *The Curse upon Mitre Square* and has continued in a steady stream of writers including Frank Wedekind (1895), Marie Belloc-Lowndes (1911), Robert Bloch (1943) and many others, and the Ripper has also made appearances in science fiction and fantasy tales, has been a staple of thriller movies and has appeared in opera (Alban Berg's *Lulu*) and pop music (a single by 'Lord Sutch').[5] As Kim Newman points out 'The Ripper' is a type of *given* of a certain landscape – a required designation or focus for a number of traits.[6] Jack the Ripper is a name for both a necessary fiction and a fact missing its history. Here fiction and history meet and mutate so that the Ripper can be searched for by 'historians' of crime at the very same moment that he can appear in a Batman comic. Separable from his origins, the Ripper is a strange historicized fiction, a designation for a type of murderer and his scenario (for the game is to give 'Jack' his real name and collapse fiction into biography), while also being a structural necessity for a type of fictional genre: the author of the 'Dear Boss' letter, etc. The Ripper is never quite the same person as the slayer of several prostitutes.

> Whereas popular heroes . . . usually have their origins in a particular work or body of fiction, they break free from the originating textual conditions of their existence to achieve a semi-independent existence, functioning as an established point of cultural reference that is capable of working – of producing meanings – even for those who are not directly familiar with the original texts in which they first made their appearance.[7]

This dual movement and reciprocity can be seen clearly in the parallel claims made on the Ripper by the latest 'biographer' and by the artists and scriptwriters of Batman. As has been said of Adolf Hitler, that other bogy man of our own century, the figure overshadows the circumstances and as with Hitler so the Ripper acts as 'a dark mirror held up to Mankind'.[8] It was indeed the appearance and exposure of the Hitler diaries that were uppermost in researchers' minds when the 'Diary' of the Ripper was itself published in 1993.[9] Apart from the simple matter of authentication, the 'Hitler' and 'Ripper' diaries are curious mirror images: the Hitler diaries represent a scandal of celebrity while the Ripper diaries represent a scandal in the ordinary; the Hitler diaries were needed as proof of innocence (of the persecution of the Jews and of warmongering) while the Ripper diaries were needed as proof of guilt (of a psychopathic personality); both sets of diaries purported to be major documents authenticating the narrative and nature of historical process. Whatever the two sets of documents actually represent they both attempt to put a *face* and fix a character on to two historical figures whose evil actions are at once ambivalently symbolic and legendary and yet specific and located. This ambivalence seems irreconcilable with the nature of the facts of either case as the facts are themselves transmogrified into symbolic co-ordinates for the transmission of the two legends; in this way authentication acts as a means of refictionalizing the subjects under scrutiny. Each stage is simply more authentic (less fictional) than the last in a chain of never-ending speculation.

In chasing the identity of the Ripper and in placing his personality upon numerous more or less well-known historical characters (the latest being James Maybrick) investigators acknowledge the

bizarre silence at the heart of the tale, a place where history has
closed in upon itself and refused its *fact*. History becomes an abyss
antagonistic to its own determinants and played upon by conspiracy
in the fiction of the secret of Jack's identity. Scanning the grim,
grainy, obscure picture taken of Mary Kelly's eviscerated body as
if in search of clues we become dabblers in the oracular and the
occult. In her photo the Ripper steps out of Victorian history
to become the *epitome* of Victorian history, its embodiment and
spokesman.

It is hardly surprising that Jack the Ripper has passed so easily
into the world of fiction. Jack's most recent incarnation has been
in the pages of DC Comics' *Gotham by Gaslight* as the opponent
of Batman himself.[10] Dedicated to 'Elsa Lanchester, the Bride of
Frankenstein' and with an Introduction by Robert Bloch, Jack the
Ripper travels across the Atlantic to Gotham City for his final
showdown. The comic treats Batman with the same seriousness as
the Ripper and Bruce Wayne's own biography is rewritten and
reauthenticated during the story (indeed is integral to the Ripper's
identity). In such a context, Batman is as 'real' as the Ripper and
using a 'what if' scenario he is placed not in 1940s or 1950s America
but back in time – the 1880s. Who else would the greatest comic
crime fighter confront in a steam-driven Gotham but the Ripper,
only worthy opponent of the Bat. (Just as Sherlock Holmes had
been pitted against the Ripper in the film *The Seven Per Cent Solution*.) Both Batman and Jack the Ripper become designationary loci
for a scene and a moment. As such, Batman is every bit as real as
the Ripper, inhabiting a location every bit as real and as distant as
the foggy streets of London. New York/Gotham City or Victorian
London, Jack the Ripper and Batman are the locations and the
inhabitants of a certain modernity. As Robert Bloch points out
(writing as the Ripper), 'Batman? Yes I know the name'.[11] Batman's
authenticity (*the* Batman as he has now become) and the status of
his myth are reaffirmed in our ability to accept the migration of his
character into a historical past. That Jack the Ripper awaits him is
confirmation of his status, that there is parallel publication of
Ripperological works and comic books only heightens the reciprocity between the production methods of two different yet dependant
forms of publishing.

As Geoffrey Fletcher in the *Daily Telegraph* (9 October 1974) commented, 'hence it is that Jack belongs not only to the criminologist,
but also to folklore'.

The first part of this chapter dealt with the rapid dissemination of the Ripper legend and its endurance in popular publishing. I now wish to turn to the constellation of possibilities around which this publishing industry revolved and upon which the legend was built.

It is obvious that any legend requires a small and possibly spectacular fact to unleash a great deal of 'fiction'. Before turning to the legend as a type of 'fictional' genre it is necessary to consider the Ripper legend as revolving around (a) a series of bizarre and ferocious crimes, (b) an impotent and mocked authority (the Criminal Investigation Department being left totally in the dark and being criticized from Windsor), (c) a mysterious and unapprehended felon, and (d) the power of fiction and the use of the human sciences.[12]

The murders of autumn 1888 allowed for the appearance of a new urban dweller, a dweller on the limits of society and yet fully integrated into it – the homicidal maniac, *the psychopathic killer*. Unlike de Sade, the psychopath is always *in disguise*; his intentions and his secret actions are on another plain from his social responsibilities. Consequently, the psychopath delineates that absolute psychological and mental 'deterioration' that Kraepelin had considered as a form of dementia praecox and that was not defined as schizophrenia until 1911. The Ripper, however, was seen as split not merely in personality but in *morality* as well. The case of the psychopath is a case not of deterioration of mental power but of a demonic engulfing of the egotistic soul by a monstrous and sensuous will. Here the psychopath unites theology and science, unites the lowest and the highest impulses in his society. The psychopath is ill and yet suffers only from an overwhelming need to impose his will on his surroundings. The psychopath 'lets go' only in order to secrete his lost personality more fully in those daylight hours of responsibility. The demonic had not yet lost its force in the 1880s, reinforced as it was by scientific research.

In order to explore the paradox of the psychopath more fully we can turn to the popular fiction of the 1880s. Robert Louis Stevenson's *Dr Jekyll and Mr Hyde* was published in 1886, two years before 'Jack' made his own spectacular appearance.

Stevenson's story deals specifically with split personality – split between the sensual and the socially and morally responsible. Jekyll is the epitome of middle-class propriety, living in a street described as having houses with 'freshly painted shutters well polished brasses and general cleanliness', while Hyde is a monstrous and 'ape-like' maniac who lives amid the sexual depravity of Soho: 'that dismal

quarter of Soho seen under these changing glimpses, with its muddy
ways, and slatternly passengers, and its lamps, which had never
been extinguished or had been kindled afresh to combat this mournful reinvasion of darkness, seemed, in the lawyer's eyes, like a district of some city in a nightmare'.

This duality of personality and class (the more working-class the
more depraved) is considerably complicated by Stevenson's own
mixing of Darwinism and pseudo-science. Degeneracy for Stevenson
(as for Edgar Allan Poe in 'The Murders in the Rue Morgue') is a
decline into an animal state – the noble savage has become the sex-
crazed ape. However, this motif (repeated by Rider Haggard in *She*)
is interrupted by a 'psychological' study of Jekyll from whose dark
side Hyde is generated. Jekyll has always been aware of his dual
nature:

> Hence it came about that I concealed my pleasures; and . . . I stood
> already committed to a profound duplicity of life . . . that made
> me what I was and, with even a deeper trench than in the major-
> ity of men, severed in me those provinces of good and ill which
> divide and compound man's dual nature. In this case, I was driven
> to reflect deeply and inveterately on that hard law of life which
> lies at the root of religion, and is one of the most plentiful springs
> of distress. Though so profound a double-dealer, I was in no
> sense a hypocrite; both sides of me were in dead earnest; I was
> no more myself when I laid aside restraint and plunged in shame,
> than when I laboured, in the eye of day, at the furtherance of
> knowledge or the relief of sorrow and suffering. And it chanced
> that the direction of my scientific studies . . . led wholly towards
> the mystic and the transcendental.

Indeed, it is Jekyll's very aspirations toward the ideal that have
caused his degeneracy. Such a duality makes Jekyll tell his friend
that 'if [he is] the chief of sinners [he is] the chief of sufferers too'.

Highlighted here is not schizophrenia as illness but Jekyll's schizoid nature as showing signs of *moral* degeneracy. Mental decay is
seen as a consequence of original sin lurking in the hearts of all
men of whatever class – the more denied (by the respectable) the
more virulent its final outburst. Stevenson makes this quite plain in
his description of Hyde's manic progress during the opening narrative. He lets his narrator tell us that 'then came the horrible part
of the thing; for the man trampled calmly over the child's body and

left her screaming on the ground. It sounds nothing to hear, but it was hellish to see. It wasn't like a man; it was like some damned Juggernaut'.

Hyde becomes an abominable *it*, a desecration of the sanity of the human causing revulsion even in the doctor who witnesses the deed. Equally this combines with fear at the bizarre and freakish appearance of the culprit: 'There is something wrong with his appearance; something displeasing, something downright detestable. I never saw [a man] I so disliked, and yet I scarce know why. He must be deformed somewhere; he gives a strong feeling of deformity'. Hyde combines animality and the terror of the 'troglodytic' with fear of evil, for he has 'a kind of black sneering coolness . . . really like Satan'.

This mixture of the animal and the devilish comes from the perverse idealism of Jekyll, a scientist and pillar of society who is bent on unlocking *his own* potential for experiencing the limits of perception through the power of his own will. His science is therefore put to the cause of metaphysical speculation. He tells us that, 'it chanced that the direction of his scientific studies . . . led wholly toward the mystic and transcendental'. Here, then, the scientist manipulates the soul in order to reorganize the nature of the body, for, in destroying the 'fortress of identity' Jekyll employs science as if it were magic: 'man is not truly one, but truly two'.

Stevenson's short story became a massive popular hit when published. In it he summed up the pseudo-science of the popular imagination as well as the confused state of the emergent psychological sciences which were 'treating' schizophrenic patients. The psychopath (Mr Hyde is such through his maniacal killing for killing's sake and the enjoyment he gains) crosses the border of scientific discourse and acts as its limit, beyond the rational explanations of form and natural function. Instead, the psychopath takes us beyond science and before it into theology, into the analysis of *sin*.

In picking upon this duality, Stevenson made repeated statements about the nature of evil and its relationship with insanity. He tells us,

The pleasures which I made haste to seek in my disguise were, as I have said, undignified; I would scarce use a harder term. But in the hands of Edward Hyde they soon began to turn towards the monstrous. When I would come back from these excursions, I was often plunged into a kind of wonder at my vicarious

depravity. This familiar that I called out of my own soul, and
sent forth alone to do his good pleasure, was a being inherently
malign and villainous; his every act and thought centred on
self. . . . The situation was apart from ordinary laws, and insidi-
ously relaxed the grasp of conscience. It was Hyde, after all, and
Hyde alone, that was guilty. Jekyll was no worse; he woke again
to his good qualities seemingly unimpaired; he would even make
haste, where it was possible, to undo the evil done by Hyde. And
thus his conscience slumbered.

Here the 'monstrous' connects with meta-laws that organize consciousness but cannot escape from it, for *will* (according to Jekyll's
philosophy) and the drive to power dominate the consciousness of
mankind. According to Stevenson, from the socially responsible,
the morally restrained and the intellectually ideal come anarchy,
moral degeneracy and perversity dominated by a Calvinistic notion
of predestined sin.

As with Jekyll and Hyde so Jack the Ripper too was seen as
an inhuman, if not non-human, monster who combined possible
middle-class respectability (a doctor or a surgeon) with lower-
working-class savagery (an immigrant, 'Leather-Apron', a mad
butcher). The Ripper united both classes inasmuch as he was excluded by his acts from both (just as were his victims). The Ripper
was both a technician (a post-mortem surgeon, a doctor, a butcher)
and an insane lunatic (incapable of finesse). He was supposedly at
once able to focus his aggression in anatomical detail and yet unable to curb its force. Thus, the forensic nature of the Ripper's 'work'
(his 'job') provided a focal point for popular fears and prejudices
against those professions dealing in the limits of the 'decent' (psychologists, doctors, post-mortem surgeons, forensic experts). The
Ripper's supposed anatomical expertise suggested all sorts of horrible possibilities about the life of the 'expert' and the specialist. His
ability with a knife united him to the very professionals paid to
track him down!

Like Hyde, he was the *alter ego* of the police force and the letters
clearly demonstrate him showing off his expertise to them and the
vigilante forces operating in Whitechapel. Later his dual nature as
criminal and enforcer-of-law became explicit when reports of his
deerstalker gave one attribute to the occupier of 221b Baker Street,
whose business was forensic science, whose other real-life model
was a surgeon and whose friend was a doctor.

Thus the Ripper was not merely a murderer but the catalyst for a series of psychological and social reactions. He combined the supposed popular idea of the expert as well as the darker side of the madman, lunatic, animal degenerate. As a median point between middle-class respectability and a debased Darwinian proletariat, the Ripper became the invisible man; like Jekyll he might well have said that 'for him in his impenetrable mantle, the safety was complete. Think of it – he did not exist!' The Ripper's letters acknowledge the pretence of cockney patois while pointing directly toward a middle-class author – but the author of what: a letter or the murders? The Ripper is both murderer and social 'reformer', both scientist and magician.

In the previous section of this chapter we have seen that the combination of popular prejudice and fiction produced a character and a rationale for the Ripper *qua* murderer *and* respectable member of society. His split nature (if such it was or presumably had to be) was completed by a hypocrisy concerning the very people he killed (the 'Magdalens'). For these people were themselves invisible, acting as a certain outlet *and* limit to urban society. The psychopath and the prostitute were two ends of a society that refused to acknowledge their presence. Invisibly, they provided their services on the edge of the rational, morally degenerate as both supposedly were.

Yet Jack the Ripper's threat is one that spills back into 'ordinary' society and threatens that society. In the period when the legend of 'the Ripper' begins, the psychopath becomes an urban reality but as a character-type is not quite part of a mental spectrum and yet is not fully freed from being a theological problem either. Jack combines notions of evil, insanity and moral justice at the moment when the nineteenth century saw itself as the century of progress, enlightenment and escape from 'moral' prejudice. The Ripper's name denotes a certain consequent frontier for the human sciences at this time.

At the culminating point of the human sciences came the science of legitimized 'murder'. James Berry, the public executioner at the time of the 'Ripper' murders, wrote his autobiography in the 1890s and in it we see combined Jack's role as breaker *and* upholder of the law and of natural justice.[13] Berry, who became an abolitionist (he decapitated one of his clients because of an incorrect 'drop'), viewed his work as 'a job like any other'[14] and H. Snowden Ward in his appraisal called Berry 'tender-hearted'.[15] This businesslike and tender-hearted man carried out public executions and gave his rope to Madame Tussaud's. His contribution to the human sciences was to calculate the proportion of rope needed relative to body weight, in order to cause death without mutilation of the victim. He also endeavoured to 'understand' the mind of a murderer, whom, unlike the general public, he viewed as neither a 'fiend' nor a 'monster'.[16] He commented that he hoped he could 'advise his readers to consider that a murderer has as much right to judge the state as the state has to judge him',[17] which is an oddly radical comment for the ultimate enforcer of the state's law! Indeed, Berry saw quite clearly the anomaly of his position.[18] Hence he becomes both killer and killed, both culprit and revenger, both state appointee and state victim. Within Berry's own person these ambiguities were traced.

James Berry and Jack the Ripper are joined by the technology of death. This unites and yet ultimately separates their purposes, for Berry participates in the oddly humanitarian enterprise that Michel Foucault sees as a movement from torture to the timetable in dealing with miscreants. Berry, working in secret, takes on the onus of the executioner's task as a duty as well as a job. His book portrays a deep ambivalence as well as pride in work well done. The business of death puts professionalism at a premium. Berry's expertise is, however, the expertise of an almost defunct craftsman, for, although hanging remained for another eighty years, its power was severely limited and its function debilitated by secrecy and humanitarian concern. The acknowledged schizoid nature of the executioner begins to crack open in James Berry and his autobiography in his constant justifications and special pleading. The Ripper takes pride in his particular executions, for Jack belongs to another *older* tradition of execution.

Michel Foucault, quoting eighteenth-century sources, gives the grisly details of the form of public execution then required in France:

> The executioner, who had an iron bludgeon of the kind used in slaughter houses, delivered a blow with all his might on the temple of the wretch, who fell dead: the *mortis exactor*, who had a large knife, then cut his throat, which spattered him with blood; it was horrible sight to see; he severed the sinews near the two heels, and then opened up the belly from which he drew the heart, liver, spleen and lungs, which he stuck on an iron hook,

and cut and dissected into pieces, which he then stuck on the other hooks as he cut them, as one does with an animal.[19]

We may compare this to Jack's own 'private' (but very public) methods. His last victim, 'Mary Kelly ... was lying on her back on a bed, where she had been placed after the murderer cut her throat ... he set to work mutilating the body, which was stabbed, slashed, skinned, gutted and ripped apart. Her nose and breast were cut off; her entrails were extracted: some were removed.'[20]

In the eighteenth century executions became a ritual in which the 'main character was the people, whose ... presence was required for the performance'.[21] By Jack's time public execution was long since over, but Jack took on the symbolic weight of a 'higher' justice operating beyond the arm of the law, exposing and cutting out the cancer of sexual commerce. His role was acknowledged in his instant fame and his ferocity in his attack on the condemned: the prostitute class. It appears that Jack represented the return of a social memory of the proximity of death (by violence, cholera, starvation) now distanced by the work of social and medical reformers.

In that latter half of the industrialized nineteenth century ceremonies about the integration of death had long ceased to be necessary. In a sense the body had gained utility value but lost its 'sacred' humanness (its 'mystery' that early Christians feared). Jack represents the unconscious of that society – a repression not yet exorcized; he forcibly reminded society (unable to speak of bodies without blushing) of the crudest function of that mass of organs. Jack clearly unites ideas about the mortification of the flesh and the technology that manipulates the body (the human sciences: biology, psychology, forensic science, medicine). One end of the spectrum acknowledges desire for and the power of the flesh while the other denies both and reduces the body to a mass of functions and utilities: an automaton. The body hence becomes ironically 'sacred' (as an object in religious devotion to be escaped *from*) and yet also machinic.

Yet the savagery of Jack's attacks suggests more. As the attacks became more savage, so the mutilation of the victim became more complete. Finally it took pathologists six hours to piece together the empty shell of Mary Kelly scattered around the room in which she died. For Jack this final attack meant more than an attempt to punish womankind for its sins and its tempting flesh. Here the body is emptied, turned into a shell into which the murderer could plunge his knife and hands. The emptying assumes the form of an attempt to 'go beyond' the boundaries of flesh in a 'new' and horrific way. This violence demolishes and liquefies the body, which flows away and takes with it its ego boundaries. The body is opened, penetrated, dissected, made totally possessable.

As the bodily boundaries vanish we are reminded of the search for the auguries at Rome, a desperate search for a stable and knowable destiny. As the uterus determines the growing foetus, so the 'innerds' of the female body offer themselves for decoding. But what do they signify? Nothing, or more properly, an absence, for the place of origin is missing. The quest carried out by the probing knife reveals only a mess of tangled 'innerds'. Jack's attack signifies a going beyond toward an otherness that is totally non-human. The object and the possessor mesh into one critical quest.

What did Jack search for? Inside the body, finally opened, the culprit used the technique of a manic autopsy in order to find the non-body: the beyond and yet absolute of his own existence – his soul perhaps? In finding this origin Jack may have been able to find his own significance unhindered by the body which forced him to kill. For Jack as for his public, these killings, graphically illustrated and documented in the popular press, may have signified, as they still may do, the final frenzied acknowledgement of the coming of the age of materialism.

The body of the 'Magdalen' signifies the absence of purity and the presence of sin; but what does each weigh – what atomic weight can be assigned to the soul? Can the significance of the Ripper's violence, which has fascinated readers and researchers for so long, be explained in this way – that his quest was for a lost and discarded origin and that his method was a repressed and supposedly outdated one? The object of Jack's killing is not to take on the power of 'the other' but to bypass 'the other' altogether in order to confront otherness itself.

This may be borne out perhaps in the nature and morbid (perhaps healthy?) interest of generations of readers. Jack's killing partakes of a deep sub-stratum of cultural knowledge, a cultural awareness of the nature of sacrifice. If this appears far-fetched we can turn to René Girard's *Violence and the Sacred*, an anthropological work which appeared in 1972.[22]

First, though, let me briefly recapitulate the ideas outlined above. I have drawn attention to the dual nature of the popular notion of alienation – both demonic and machinic, with its consequent ambiguities over the relationship of victim to killer: social pillar and social pariah. At this juncture the psychotic killer, a product of urban life at the end of the nineteenth century, appears as both mentally defective and metaphysically gifted – both cancer and purgative. I have further suggested the possibilities and limits of Jack's 'quest' and the disturbance to identity that that caused. To further this inquiry let us now return to Girard's work on sacrifice.

Girard tells us that initially 'the sacrificial act assumes two opposing aspects, appearing at times a sacred obligation . . . at others a sort of criminal activity'. He notes the 'ambivalent' nature of sacrifice but says this does not fully account for its 'value'.[23] In his view, 'sacrifice contains an element of mystery',[24] and it is this mystery that he wishes to penetrate. Quoting Joseph de Maistre, he adds, 'the sacrificial animals were always those most prized for their gentleness, most innocent creatures, whose habits . . . brought them most closely into harmony with man'.[25] Indeed, we are told that 'sacrificial victims are almost always animals'.[26]

Here then we see that Jack the Ripper and James Berry share both a criminal and a 'sacred' (legitimized by the state) obligation. Berry acknowledged the ambivalence in his role. Moreover, in both cases, secrecy adds an air of mystery to the proceedings. The 'Magdalens' fit the role of sacrificial 'animals' through their own ambiguous position: both gentle, and aggressive in selling their wares; innocent and sexually aware; *and* in harmony with 'man' while in competition with and engaged in commercial transactions with him.

We may go further, for Girard points out that the very lowest (slaves) and the very highest (sacrificial kings) are the ends of the sacrifice spectrum.[27] But he concludes that 'in many cultures women are never, or rarely, selected as sacrificial victims',[28] because of the feuds this would cause between husbands and children and the class that claims them. However, these points can be easily met, for prostitutes are both 'animals' and 'Magdalens'; both subhuman and sacred. Moreover, in the culture of which we speak these women are precisely those that were forced (therefore to the popular mentality *chose*) to break all their ties with husbands, children, class. They became the sacrificial victims for that culture, without ties or kinsfolk to gain revenge on their behalf. At one end of our spectrum Jack does nothing illegitimate – but his act is illegal for he kills outside the *context* of the sacrificial system (long since forgotten, of course, in the nineteenth century). His act is both sacred and lunatic, bestial and totally 'sane'.

Moreover, Jack's acts of sacrifice/murder appeal to a deeply archaic level of human response – a response long since channelled
elsewhere into 'humane' destruction for sane offenders and lunatic
asylums for 'morally degenerate' offenders. In the 1880s these two
conditions partook of a peculiar mixture of demonic ability and
psychological disintegration neither properly disentangled from the
other in either the popular imagination, literature or the human
sciences.

Yet we must go deeper to fathom the legendary power of Jack
(for structuralist approaches consider the action of legend and myth
in too formalistic a way). We have seen the specific historico-
psychological aspects of the Ripper's enduring fame. But we must
return to Girard for our final formulation of his power over our
imaginations.

Girard considers sacrifice an attempt by society to 'deflect upon
a relatively indifferent victim . . . the violence that would otherwise
be vented on its own members, the people it most desires to protect'.[29] Consequently 'the sacrifice serves to protect the entire community from its own violence.'[30]

Let us return to *Dr Jekyll and Mr Hyde*. Jekyll *generates* from *his
own* personality the characteristics of the psychopath. His dual nature
partakes not of a ghostly *Doppelgänger* but of aspects from *within*
himself. His violence is a hatred of his own class and its expectation
of restraint and decorum – its understanding of order. Girard comments on the Bible story of Cain and Abel that 'Cain's "jealousy" of
his brother is only another term for his own characteristic trait: his
lack of sacrificial outlet'.[31] Right at the beginning of *Dr Jekyll and Mr
Hyde* we are introduced to Mr Utterson the lawyer, the ultimate
figure of respectability, who 'was austere with himself' and who
says of himself, 'I incline to Cain's heresy.' As with Jekyll, it is more
than a psychological problem; it is 'deeper'. Like Jack, Jekyll crosses
a profound border, a border that disturbed 'anthropologists' and
theologians alike in the nineteenth century.[32]

Thus we see the truly ritualistic and 'psychological' nexus of Jack's
violence, for his work dissolves boundaries, acts as a gaping maw
into which perception of order and rightness are sucked. Jack's
name as well as his deeds and the deeds in his name disturb our
order, trangress boundaries, translate legitimacy into illegitimacy
and the sacred into the bestial and translate them back again. For
Jack there is no 'other', only a gaping hole within self that is beyond
reconciliation with laws of man or God.

Jack, like any legendary figure, represents this effectively because he steps out of historical circumstance and into the imagination of the future. As such, like King Arthur or Robin Hood or Count Dracula, he is the undead. Jack, however, bypasses the criminal underworld, for he does not belong to it. He is outside that underworld, which is itself defined within the comprehension of the living (the non-animal). Jack is demon/animal and therefore totally other, therefore unrecognizable (invisible), therefore the perfect criminal. He disturbs the human only to reinforce it. Indeed, this monstrosity embeds himself in the imagination of each generation that needs his presence. For that reason alone there is a smile on the face of the Ripper.

The historical details of the Whitechapel Murders are nothing less than the facets of a scenario for a script about modernity itself. Reworked in fiction and film as well as the focus for true crime books (of the solve-it-yourself variety), the Ripper's deeds are ever reworked to remain forever contemporary, and thus curiously emphasized by layers of nostalgia. The Ripper's script has violence, eroticism, sentimentality and the supernatural: a text to live out the sensationalism of the modern.[33]

9

West is East:
Nayland Smith's Sinophobia
and Sax Rohmer's Bank Balance

It is commonplace nowadays to note the inherent racism of English fiction at the beginning of the twentieth century. Sapper, Dornford Yates, John Buchan, Edgar Wallace and many others are targeted as the promulgators of a fearsome and totally irrational hatred of all things foreign. For them the Black, the Chinese, the Argentinian, the Levantine and the Jew become sinister 'niggers', 'chinks', 'dagos', 'greasy levantines' and 'oily Jews'. The race hatred of these authors employs a feverish conjunctivity, with oily Jews who are both capitalists and 'bolsheviks', or Chinese who are mandarin warlords and opium den keepers in Limehouse. Moreover, when not acting themselves these essentially cowardly folk employ peculiarly simian dacoits or things of a polyglot and nauseous origin.

That such feverish racism could become so popular and that the overt racism carried along in that popularity was so rarely noticed by the consumers of such hatred needs some explaining. Although such disgust at foreign things was general and central to much fiction of the time it was also used in a gratuitous and quite unnecessary way to 'fill-in' when the action dulled. Such targeting of minority races is important not merely because we nowadays consider it loathsome, but because it was the result of the imaginative processes of creativity and life-enhancement claimed by novel writers. Furthermore, it was not the result of racial contact, but of an unknowing racial quarantine, and where not of quarantine of double-think. John Buchan often had despicable Jews in his work while openly supporting the ideals of Zionism and admiring its advocates. The question, therefore, remains to be answered as to why there is such race hatred and why such unconscious acceptance of its message?

The novelist Sax Rohmer was one such pedlar of racial hatred and it is especially toward an understanding of his work and its

178

own particular and peculiar racial resonances that this chapter is dedicated. D.J. Enright in his introduction to the reissued *The Mystery of Dr Fu Manchu* tells us:

Arthur Henry (later Sarsfield) Ward was born in 1886 [actually, 1883], of Irish parents living in Birmingham. He worked very briefly as a bank clerk in Threadneedle Street, and then as a journalist. At 20 he had two stories accepted, at last, by *Pearson's Magazine and Chamber's Journal*, and adopted the pen-name Sax Rohmer, later explaining that 'sax' was Saxon for 'blade' and 'rohmer' meant 'roamer'. Some years afterwards (so the story goes) he and his young wife consulted a ouija board as to how he could best make a living. 'C-H-I-N-A-M-A-N' came the enigmatic answer. Before long, and after ghosting an autobiography by the comedian Little Tich, Rohmer wrote his first story about the Chinaman Dr Fu-Manchu (the hyphen was dropped after the third novel). *The Mystery of Dr Fu Manchu* (1913) and subsequent books sold in their millions, notably in the 1920s and 30s, were translated into many languages, and adapted for radio, television and comic strips.[1]

And this great success, we are told was due to the fact that '[he] made [his] name on Fu Manchu because [he knew] nothing about the Chinese!'[2]

It is worth lingering over Fu Manchu's cultural origins. Born in the decade of the publication of *Dr Jekyll and Mr Hyde*, just prior to the first Sherlock Holmes tale and only five years away from the doings of Jack the Ripper, Arthur Henry Ward was to spend his childhood as one of the urban lower middle class who fed off the new popular scandal press which had come into existence during the 1880s and 1890s. Surrounded by growing class dissension the new journalism would particularize the threat posed by unions and by the labour movement as one by particularly wicked individuals whose conspiratorial natures threatened the very peace of the people on behalf of whom they fought. Thus a paradoxical situation arose in which people instinctively took the news from newspaper moghuls whose entrepreneurial interests were inherently opposed to the collective interests of their lower-middle-class and working-class readership. The reader's desire for a conservative stability in their own lives contrasted with the emergent moneyed working and lower-middle class to which they themselves belonged bent willy nilly on rising to middle-class sobriety. Hence, individual desire for a stable status quo was threatened by the class movement of those very individuals.

To cope with such changes, which seemed inexplicable in class terms and deeply disturbing in personal terms, the readership of the new journalism and of the popular thriller were treated to externalized threats that could 'easily' be accommodated to the new serried front parlours of the numerous lower-middle-class suburbs which went sprawling out into the countryside around urban centres and which were serviced by the suburban railway lines; on every platform a W.H. Smith bookstand and in every third-class compartment a thriller to equal those read, perhaps, in the first-class carriages. Moreover, the new enforcedly *leisured* mobility of the train service could be put to use by the publishing fraternity, and in so doing the taxonomic and conservative dimension of the suburban stopping train could unite the various carriage classes in their daily rehearsal of the class system.

Having been a journalist who serviced this commuter trade, Arthur Ward then wrote thrillers for the same audience. This commuter mentality which, combined with a mentality used to standardization and repetition, allowed the work of Sax Rohmer to translate easily into the technological world of the radio and cinema. The repetitiveness of the form of the Fu Manchu tales was part of the internalized need of people whose daily routine was itself *formally* repetitive, the expected *escapism* of the tales being a blind for the formula repetition of the genre's conformity to stock patterns which were easily reproduced and duplicated. Hence, even though the diabolical doctor's methods are amusingly antiquated they are reproduced on an exotic production line of indivisible thrills.

But the biggest chink in Fu Manchu's armour consists in his peculiarly elaborate and roundabout techniques of assassination and his use of highly eccentric accomplices. They include, a scorpion attracted by the perfume in which a preliminary letter to the victim has been soaked, an army of zombies (*The Island of Dr Fu Manchu*, 1941, set in the Caribbean), a lethal gas, the device of pulling people out of windows with a silken cord once they have been drawn there by a strange cry ('the Call of Siva'), and a hollow can containing a live adder. Fu Manchu speaks of his 'partiality for dumb allies': among them, a cat whose claws are coated with deadly poison, a hamadryad, black spiders, an insect which crosses a tsetse fly with a plague flea, a venomous giant centipede from Burma, an Abyssinian sacred baboon, mice who run around with tiny bells attached to their tails and thus frighten people to death, and ('the most ravenous in the world') Cantonese rats.[3]

This exoticism of content, therefore, was used exclusively to reinforce the mundane and ordinary through the episodic repetitive form of the tales. Readers escaped only to look up from their book in half relieved fear: seeing their pipe racks; wearing their slippers. This desire for a type of conformity can be seen in Ward's choice of a *nom de plume*. In a period hell-bent on recovering a Celtic past Ward denied his Irish ethnic origins by choosing a supposedly exotic name. 'Sax' might mean blade but it sounds like Saxon, that is, a *true* Englishman. Sax Rohmer, with its hint of danger (Rohmer–Roamer–Rover – a man of mystery) nevertheless also tells of a straightforward need to be *within* a community of interest. Such a community required an outsider to threaten it in order to bring mutual antagonisms to the surface the more easily to dissipate them harmlessly in anti-outsider and anti-foreign hatred.

By all accounts Sax Rohmer, as author and as Arthur Ward, happily married family man, had found his particular niche. He had 'the good fortune to have been born to authorship at just the right moment to reap the benefit of cheap printing, big-scale serialization . . . and the direct marketing and wide distribution made possible by the growth of the railways.'[4]

He also started writing at the moment when 'Literature had joined the list of human products that the industrial revolution brought within the field of organized exploitation. It had become a commodity.'[5] Moreover, he wrote for and, despite wealth, belonged to a class that:

> nursed no hopes of climbing into the seats of power, but their contentment always was tinged with the fear of falling. They prayed for a three-fold stability: the stability of the country in relation to the rest of the world, political stability – the continued prevalence of those rules of behaviour which they had been brought up to revere.[6]

So why was it that such a man wrote novels whose only message, according to Colin Watson in *Snobbery with Violence*, was 'one of

racial hatred'?[7] And why is it that 'So vehement and repetitive were
Sax Rohmer's references to Asiatic plotting against "white" civilization that they cannot be explained simply as the frills of melodramatic narration. The man clearly was possessed by some sort of
private dread'?[8]

To answer these questions we must turn to the novels themselves. Ward, as Sax Rohmer, was one of many lesser authors who
owed a debt of gratitude to Conan Doyle for the basic relationship
at the centre of their narratives. Petrie, with his love of authorship,
is a straight copy of Watson (even to his MD), although his knowledge of psychology only runs to pseudo-expert pronouncements on
Fu Manchu's mentality which he diagnoses as 'symptomatic of dangerous mania' (*The Return of Dr Fu Manchu*, chapter 13). Yet the
relationship between Petrie, Nayland Smith and the narrative itself
borders on a pastiche of Conan Doyle. It is a reified 'commodity'
solidified around certain stock characters.

> I had jumped to my feet, for a tall, lean man, with his square-cut,
> clean-shaven face sun-baked to the hue of coffee, entered and
> extended both hands with a cry:
>   'Good old Petrie! Didn't expect me, I'll swear!'
>   It was Nayland Smith – whom I had thought to be in Burma! . . .
>   'Mysterious enough for you?' he laughed, and glanced at my
> unfinished MS. 'A story, eh? From which I gather that the district
> is beastly healthy – what, Petrie? Well, I can put some material in
> your way that, if sheer uncanny mystery is a marketable com-
> modity . . .'
>   (*The Mystery of Dr Fu Manchu*, chapter 1)

Yet with all his old-boy exuberance Nayland Smith is no Sherlock
Holmes. He is unable to prevent the diabolical machinations of his
foe Fu Manchu, rarely solves a crime, never gets his man and is
forever being helped out of horrible cliff-hanger situations by the
mysterious slave-girl Kâramanèh. Withal, that his authority is maintained at a laughable level of magnitude.

> 'My name is Nayland Smith,' he said rapidly – 'Burmese Com-
> missioner.' He snatched a letter from his pocket and thrust it
> into the hands of the bewildered man. 'Read that. It is signed
> by another Commissioner – the Commissioner of Police.' With

amazement written all over him, the other obeyed. 'You see,' continued my friend, tersely – 'it is *carte blanche*, I wish to commandeer your car, sir, on a matter of life and death!'
(*The Return of Dr Fu Manchu*, chapter 2)

It is by now not an authority based on ability, but simply on class lines made invisible by a false textual authority centred on commanding (and upper-middle-class *sporting*) individuality. 'It was an insect, full six inches long. . . . These things I realized in one breathless instant; in the next – Smith had dashed the thing's poisonous life out with one straight, *true blow of the golf club*' (*The Mystery of Dr Fu Manchu*, chapter 3; my italics). Nevertheless, within the tales individuality is defeated at every turn by circumstances dictated by deadly commodities – gas, orchids, centipedes, trap-doors and booby-trapped boxes.

Unlike Sherlock Holmes, Nayland Smith is a roving representative of the West, acting on behalf of the 'interests of the entire white race' (*The Mystery of Dr Fu Manchu*, chapter 1). But now that representation is paralysed and inescapably doomed merely to holding back the floodtide of the *invisible* 'Yellow Peril' (*The Mystery of Dr Fu Manchu*, chapter 6), a peril only ever present in its representatives. The character of Nayland Smith is one caught between his own designated role as the representative of Western white culture (the 'golf club') and his war with the never-to-be-pinned-down Si Fan, a secret organization, in a secret place in China, plotting unspecified horrors against the West. In this way Nayland Smith becomes just another victim of the repetitive machinations of the dread Chinese doctor and his dacoits, thus representing not Western action but a more deadly form of fictional inertia bogged down, as Nayland Smith is, in the formal standardizations of Rohmer's own plotting. For, despite Rohmer's extravagant episodic style, which was a consequence of serialization, his work lacks the usual sequential and teleological narrative technique of most novels.

Quite different from Sherlock Holmes, Nayland Smith is never greater than the sum total of Rohmer's bit-part tales. Ultimately, of course, he is dispensable, for he is merely an oppositional usher of Fu Manchu himself.

Dr Petrie, who bubbles with repressed, and often not so repressed, hysteria throughout is the real conduit to the heart of each tale. His exotic obsession with Kâramanèh, the slave of Fu Manchu, allows for innumerable escapes from impossible corners (paradoxically, the male reader's mundane existence) and an exotic and erotic awareness that brings Edwardian latent obsessions with middle-eastern women to the fore.

> Kâramanèh was a closed book to my shortsighted Western eyes. But the body of Kâramanèh was exquisite; her beauty of a kind that was a key to the most extravagant rhapsodies of Eastern poets. Her eyes held a challenge wholly Oriental in its appeal; her lips, even in repose, were a taunt. And, herein, East is West and West is East.
>
> (*The Mystery of Dr Fu Manchu*, chapter 27)

However, Kâramanèh is no liberated woman, despite her deadly ability with a gun. She is a triple victim: of slavery, of Petrie's daydreams and of Western erotic sadism: '"Throw me into prison, kill me if you like, for what I have done!" . . . She twisted around so that the white skin was but inches removed from me. . . . I clenched my teeth. Insane thoughts flooded my mind. For that creamy skin was red with the marks of the lash!' (*The Return of Dr Fu Manchu*, chapter 5). Indeed, the extreme of this attitude occurs when Nayland Smith tells Petrie that he should 'seize her by the hair, drag her to some cellar, hurl her down, and stand over her with a whip' (*The Mystery of Dr Fu Manchu*, chapter 12).

Petrie, a victim of his own worst wet-dream-girl nightmares is, however, the direct line to Dr Fu Manchu, who mistakenly considers him his equal in scientific knowledge. Thus, Petrie's overt upholding of Western racism is joined *textually* to the Chinese menace. Indeed, the most vehement racial invective comes not from Nayland Smith but from Petrie's own overly imaginative pen.

> I found myself bound along Whitechapel Road. . . .
> Jewish hawkers, many of them in their shirtsleeves, acclaimed the rarity of the bargains which they had to offer; and, allowing for the difference of costume, these tireless Israelites, heedless of climactic conditions, sweating at their mongery, might well have stood, not in a squalid London thoroughfare, but in an equally squalid market street of the Orient. . . .
> Poles, Russians, Serbs, Roumanians, Jews of Hungary, and Italians of Whitechapel mingled in the throng. Near East and Far East rubbed shoulders. Pidgin English contested with Yiddish for

the ownership of some tawdry article offered by an auctioneer whose nationality defied conjecture. . . .

North, South, East, and West mingled their cries. . . . Sometimes a yellow face showed close to one of the streaming windows; sometimes a black-eyed, pallid face, but never a face wholly sane and healthy. This was an underworld where squalor and vice went hand in hand through the beautiless streets, a melting-pot of the world's outcasts; this was the shadowland, which last night had swallowed up Nayland Smith.

(The Return of Dr Fu Manchu, chapter 11)

Clearly divided into West End and East End, London became the microcosmic battlefield of Imperial neuroses. In 1913 (yet already in the 1880s when Ward was born) London *was* the Empire for fictionalists, in novels and in journalism – the East End became the Dark Continent, not Africa but South East Asia, an inscrutable land beyond the comprehension of the white race of the West End. But what was most important was that the West End was *also* inscrutable to Rohmer's readers in their suburban solitude. Nayland Smith might belong to a clubland to which few could aspire, but his *real* battlefield was *suburban* London – 'the quiet suburban avenue' at the heart of his readers' domestic world (*The Return of Dr Fu Manchu*, chapter 8). Such suburban danger was constantly repeated and follows Conan Doyle's own interest in dangers lurking in the newly built villas of South London's Upper Norwood (Rohmer lived in Herne Hill, South London) and North London's Finchley 'You ought to see his house in Finchley. A low, squat place. . . . Damp as a swamp; smells like a jungle. . . . The rest of the house is half a menagerie and half a circus. He has a Bedouin groom, a Chinese body-servant, and heaven only knows what other strange people!' (*The Mystery of Dr Fu Manchu*, chapters 10 and 11). Wapping, Shadwell and the 'notorious' Ratcliffe Highway (*The Return of Dr Fu Manchu*, chapter 10) crawled out to the suburbs and mysteriously called charabanc loads of suburban dwellers on trips to Limehouse in search of non-existent opium dens and sinister aristocratic cocaine addicts (see Sir Crichton Davey in *The Mystery of Dr Fu Manchu*, chapter 1).

But if these Sunday afternoon trippers came in search of the titillation of having pointed out to them the 'real' life origins of dubious opium dens such as 'John Ki's [junky] Joy Shop' (*The Hand of Fu Manchu*, chapter 5) or Shen Yan's (*The Mystery of Dr Fu Manchu*,

chapter 6), which in all probability were no more than the dwellings of poor seamen, then what greater thrill than to imagine that
each pig-tailed Lascar was a potential enemy, each malignant look
(of hatred or contempt at the gawping tourists) was the disguised
Dr Fu Manchu himself. These gawping tourists in their own land,
in their own city, the heart of Empire, were not Sinophobes bent on
holding back the waves of alien ships' workers but idly curious
Sunday afternoon tourists whose ignorance fed Sax Rohmer's bank
balance. And nowhere was that bank balance better served than
with the invention of Rohmer's great monster, for like all thriller
writers Rohmer knew that the real centre of such a genre was a
monumental villain against whom the ordinary decent folk pitted
their limited wits.

Rohmer's descriptions of Dr Fu Manchu are highly instructive.

This man . . . is, unquestionably, the most malign and formidable
personality existing in the known world today. He is a linguist
who speaks with almost equal facility in any of the civilized languages, and in most of the barbaric. He is an adept in all the arts
and sciences which a great university could teach him. He also is
an adept in certain obscure arts and sciences which no university
of today can teach. He has the brains of any three men of genius.
Petrie, he is a mental giant. . . .

Imagine a person, tall, lean and feline, high shouldered, with a
brow like Shakespeare and a face like Satan, a close-shaven skull,
and long, magnetic eyes of the true cat-green. Invest him with all
the cruel cunning of an entire Eastern race, accumulated in one
giant intellect, with all the resources of science past and present,
with all the resources, if you will, of a wealthy government –
which, however, already has denied all knowledge of his existence. Imagine that awful being, and you have a mental picture of
Dr Fu Manchu, the yellow peril incarnate in one man. . . .

Of his face, as it looked out at me over the dirty table, I despair
of writing convincingly. It was that of an archangel of evil, and
it was wholly dominated by the most uncanny eyes that ever
reflected a human soul, for they were narrow and long, very
slightly oblique, and a brilliant green. But their unique horror lay
in a certain filminess (it made me think of the *membrana nicitans*
in a bird) which, obscuring them as I threw awide the door,
seemed to lift as I actually passed the threshold, revealing the
eyes in all their brilliant viridescence.

(*The Mystery of Dr Fu Manchu*, chapters 2 and 6)

Set within a jewel of purple prose and hyperbolical nonsense, Dr Fu Manchu rises upon the stage of world villany the most complete of terrors. Rohmer repeated the description, like an intoned ritual, in book after book. But if Dr Fu Manchu is the *beyond* of all imagination he is also, paradoxically, within the cognizance of the 'partly' literate public who clammered for more of him – he signified for that public who knew Shakespeare stood for genius (although his plays may have been unread) and that Satan was a genius (or more properly Milton's Satan was a genius, as we may consider Arthur Ward's literary knowledge would have found this Satan simply by association with Milton).

But, if Fu Manchu's origins are directly and commonplacedly English literary, then from whence the Chinese connection? In this it is noteworthy that Rohmer said that '[he] made [his] name on Fu Manchu because [he knew] nothing about the Chinese!' and that he found his 'Chinaman' through the use of a 'ouija board'. If, for the moment, we dismiss the ouija board comment as hokum then the Chinese connection still needs to be made. So where did the dread doctor originate from? One origin may be the mysterious Chinese Tong boss 'Mr King', who Rohmer tried to find during a series of journalistic forays into Limehouse in 1911.[9]

Yet, if one looks for a possible original model for Dr Fu Manchu one need look no further than the famous music hall 'Chinese' magician Chung Ling Soo. Chung Ling Soo was in reality William Ellsworth Robinson, a New Yorker born in 1861. Formerly an illusion builder he was invited, in imitation of the original real Chinese magician Chung Ling Soo, to perform at the Paris *Folies Bergère*. Changing his stage name to Hop Sing Loo, Robinson finally decided to plagiarize the name Chung Ling Soo. By skilful publicity, Robinson, the fake Chung Ling Soo, was able to oust the real Chung Ling Soo and take his place. The authentic and original Chinese magician was now irrevocably replaced by a white man in costume who had shaved off his Victorian moustache and donned a Mandarin costume and pigtail. Indeed, Robinson's whole life was a way of

acknowledging the greatest illusion he ever performed, namely the skilful way in which he lived up to the identity of his *alter ego* from the moment he shaved his head to don his first pigtail on 17 May 1900.

A master of the art of mime, Soo never spoke on stage, even though he often gave marathon performances of two hours duration. Off-stage in public he would continue to wear his Chinese

make-up and spoke only 'Chinese', accommodating reporters
through the 'interpretations' of his stage manager, Frank
Kametaro. In 1908 he did allow the first edition of the *Liverpool
Theatrical News* to publish a story regarding his true identity,
mainly as a ploy to clear his name from any accusations that
might be levelled against a member of the race that had committed the atrocities of the Boxer Rebellion. The story went unnoticed. The public did not want to know, probably dismissing it all
as a hoax. In the eyes of the public Soo continued to live up to
his publicity as 'A Gift from the Gods to Mortals on Earth to
Amuse and Mystify', while in retrospect Robinson sedately earned
his title as the all-time Emperor of inscrutability.[10]

This vivid and extraordinary performer was almost certainly one
major influence on the character of Dr Fu Manchu. Indeed, the
bullet-catching trick that in 1918 led to Soo's death may account for
at least one episode in which Fu Manchu is 'fatally' wounded only
to recover for the next adventure.

Given that Sax Rohmer's wife was a music-hall juggler, given he
wrote sketches and theatrical songs, given his friendship with George
Robey and given his ghosting of the autobiography of Little Tich
we can surmise that he may well have been personally acquainted
with Chung Ling Soo.[11] If not, at least he would have been familiar
with the latter's role as a performer. The message of the ouija board
may well simply have been the auto suggestion of a man who had
recently visited the music hall and seen a 'Chinaman' perform.

We have seen the coincidence between various forms of 'popular'
culture and the commodification of fictional 'types'. In this respect
two forms of commodification, that of fiction and that of 'the Orient', allowed for a marketable package that could be sold in the
same interchangeable way. Hence, Rohmer's writing career which
happily embraced commercial fiction also allowed for the selling of
exotic perfumes, the end result of a number of unsuccessful manufacturing ventures. Commercial fiction and perfume were both
merely manufacturing ventures.

Rohmer's perfume, called 'Honan' was put in an exotic bamboo-
clad package and fixed with a silk tassel.[12] Rohmer's company had
a workforce of 12–14 Chinese headed by a manager, Ah Sin.[13]
Barker's Department Store in Kensington was the outlet and:

The long-suffering Ah Sin was now called upon to become
an actor. He had to be the 'real, live Chinaman', since he was the

only one of the native employees who could speak English. They decked him out in a gorgeous national costume (hired from a theatrical outfitters) complete with a false pigtail. Pigtails had gone out with the Dowager Express – Sax was aware of that – but the shoppers would expect him to have one, so they included it.[14]

That a Chinese was required to pretend to be a 'Chinaman' suggests not merely a travesty, but an obvious ambivalence in the English mind over the oriental type. Sax Rohmer himself was aware of this ambivalence in his own psychological and emotional ties to Limehouse. Many years after the appearance of the first Fu Manchu story Rohmer wrote,

> Nowadays . . . I like to think that a Chinese and a Chinaman are not the same thing. When I began writing, 'Chinaman' was no more than the accepted term for a native of China. The fact that it has since taken on a derogatory meaning is due mostly to the behaviour of those Chinamen who lived in such places as Limehouse.[15]

However, the last line, in its slippage from Chinese to 'Chinamen', used as a synonym for *criminal*, exposes Rohmer's vagueness as well as his racism.

We may say now that Fu Manchu and that from which he sprang, the stock pantomime Chinaman, were ideal vehicles for the packaging of thrills but yet here they also represent a disturbance in the simple commodification of formula thriller fiction. This doubling back upon a stock and marketable object ('formula' fiction) does not merely gives a greater longevity to characters caught in a nostalgic byway of cultural history, but also adds a *frisson* of doubt over the stability of the very notion of a marketable object itself (in this case 'the thriller'). Fu Manchu represents a monstrousness in the heart of a technologically 'secure' world – he represents a diabolical disturbance which allows for the intrusion of a 'reality' that is metaphysical and denies the outward appearance of material things. As a scientist from the Orient, Fu Manchu is so advanced that he is more a magician ('the occult student and the man of science' [*The Mystery of Dr Fu Manchu*, chapter 24]). Indeed, in one episode he even resurrects the dead.

In this, Fu Manchu is the focal point for a *disturbance within things*. He becomes the occult representative of a lost world of supernatural causality which underpins and yet confronts ordinary life. This can clearly be seen in the episode in which Nayland Smith and Petrie visit Kegan Von Roon ('orientalist and psychic investigator') in chapter 22 of *The Return of Dr Fu Manchu*. Craigmore Hall, Van Roon's house, is clearly borrowed in its setting from *The Hound of the Baskervilles*. It is both ancient and evil. Moreover, Van Roon who appears 'American' (that is, ultra modern!) is, in fact, a Chinese (therefore, an ancient) agent of Fu Manchu! The house, with its incredibly ancient lineage, its association with Glastonbury, with magic and with Madame Blavatsky, is an apparent denial of the modern and a confirmation of the fearful otherness of things.

> It is a veritable wonderland, almost as interesting in its way, as the caves and jungles of Hindustan depicted by Madame Blavatsky. . . . The tower itself is of unknown origin, though probably Phoenician, and the house traditionally sheltered Dr. Macleod, the necromancer. . . . it is quite possible to see the ruins of Glastonbury Abbey from here; and Glastonbury Abbey, as you may know, is closely bound up with the history of alchemy. It was in the ruins of Glastonbury Abbey that the adept Kelly, companion of Dr Dee, discovered, in the reign of Elizabeth, the famous caskets of St Dunstan, containing the two tinctures.
>
> (*The Return of Dr Fu Manchu*, chapter 22)

Fu Manchu himself is even denied material presence at the end of *The Mystery of Dr Fu Manchu* when a theory of supernatural and demonic origin is ascribed to him, 'there is a superstition in some parts of China according to which, under certain peculiar conditions . . . an evil spirit of incredible age may enter into the body of a new-born infant' (*The Mystery of Dr Fu Manchu*, chapter 27).

In Rohmer's world the materiality of presence is a peculiarly haphazard affair, neither objects nor people conforming to the known laws of physics or human biology. This may partly be explained by Rohmer's own life-long interests in Egyptology (Petrie was named after the Egyptologist Flinders Petrie), orientalism and the occult.

During the nascence of Dr Fu Manchu, Rohmer completed *The Romance of Sorcery* (1913), joined the Order of the Golden Dawn, met Aleister Crowley and dabbled in occultism. His wife was psychic and he seemed to attract metaphysical phenomena. Recurrent dreams haunted him as did hallucinatory dreams. In one such dream an exotic oriental dancer materialized in his bedroom. This materialization, which Rohmer considered a *real* visit from another plane of existence, may have been the original for Kâramanèh. Indeed, Petrie often finds himself unable to distinguish between waking and sleeping states.

Here, perhaps, lies one of the secrets of Fu Manchu's power to fascinate. The Sinophobic message of Rohmer's books is underpinned by three theories: the notion of a conspiracy which is based upon a corporate, international secret society acting out of Limehouse, the notion of a parallel supernatural plane of existence and the notion of eternal recurrence.

The modern world, represented by Nayland Smith, is a world essentially haunted by an international mafia with supernatural powers; powers which at once uphold and disestabilize reality and whose presence is material yet invisible.

Rohmer, who was a lapsed Catholic and whose fanatical Catholic mother died an insane alcoholic, wrote thrillers at whose core is a repressed noumenal immanence. It is an immanence that is profoundly disturbing and distressing; it is satanic and fascinating – the commodification of desire: the supernaturalization of the capitalist enterprise.

Such a complex set of motival forces run through Rohmer's books. Audiences were thrilled because Rohmer offered, through a 'Chinaman' *another* history and *another* plane of meaning. Modern life was absurd, Fu Manchu was absurd, but only if one failed to see that the laws of creation were other than those of modern materialism. The commodity danced to laws which upheld and yet denied the very functions of the commodity as commodity/object. Consequently, it is not the 'Chinaman' who is other in these tales, but Englishness itself, the suburban world of Sax Rohmer's adoring readers.

10

This Revolting Graveyard of the Universe: The Horror Fiction of H.P. Lovecraft

The twentieth century has had two major sources of inspiration for the horrific imagination. The first is Hollywood, where modern cinematographic technology has been used to reproduce the Romantic Gothic worlds of Mary Shelley's *Frankenstein*, Gaston Le Roux's *Phantom of the Opera* and Bram Stoker's *Dracula*. The work of Universal and other studios' horror movies have been widely distributed and are well known, appearing nowadays regularly on television. The second major influence is the work of Howard Phillips Lovecraft, a pulp-fiction writer whose short life ended before the Second World War. Where the studios were motivated by publicity and commercialism, Lovecraft was motivated by horror of publicity and by a disgust with commercial enterprise. Lovecraft remains, fifty years after his death, an enigmatic writer and a strange and stranded personality. He wrote 'popular fiction' which never was and still is not popular; he considered himself a man of letters who wrote exclusively for pulp magazines; he instinctively felt that he was a gentleman but was actually the son of a commercial salesman; and he was a writer in the early twentieth century who owed nothing to the work of James, Eliot, Pound or Lawrence. His output was small, consisting of two novellas (one published after his death) and some short stories, many of which were completed by others after his death. In many ways Lovecraft has been an influence on film makers (especially Roger Corman) and on other writers (Robert Bloch, Ray Bradbury, Colin Wilson, Ramsay Campbell and Stephen King), but Lovecraft himself remains locked away – a cult interest for fantasy fanatics (who are rare) and academics or intellectuals (who are rarer).

Who was H.P. Lovecraft and what did he do? He was born on 20 August 1890 in Providence, Rhode Island.[1] We are told that:

Lovecraft was of predominantly British stock on both sides of his family. His father was the son of an Englishman who had lost his fortune and emigrated from Devonshire to New York in 1847 and married a girl of British descent – an Allgood from Northumberland, descended from a former British officer who remained in the United States after what Lovecraft himself, ardent Anglophile that he was, would term 'the disastrous Revolution'. On his mother's side, Lovecraft was, in his own words, 'a complete New-England Yankee, coming from Phillipses, Places, & Rathbones'.[2]

In 1898, his father, named after the hero Winfield Scott, died of a serious and lingering illness. Lovecraft was eight. For some time his father had been a paretic, muscularly paralysed and mentally incompetent. Winfield Scott Lovecraft died insane, perhaps from untreated syphilis, but, before he did, he and his small son spent time together on the father's occasional visits from the hospital to which he had been sent.[3] After his father's death, Lovecraft was brought up in the exclusive home company of the Lovecraft women – mother, aunts and grandmother.

After his father's death Lovecraft began to suffer from terrifying nightly disturbances and nightmares, which lasted until his own death in 1937. In order to deal with these unresolved nightmares Lovecraft wrote them into his letters or adapted them into short stories. Although he hated Freud's concepts, which he considered paltry and inconsequential, his attempts at fiction and at verse can be seen to be a prolonged working-through of his unsatisfactory relationship with his father – a man whose insanity was accompanied by periods of hallucination.[4] One of Lovecraft's later pantheon of 'gods', the terrifying and imbecile Nyarlathotep, may owe his origin, many years later, to the period of the elder Lovecraft's madness, for everything leads 'me on even unto those grinning caverns of earth's centre where Nyarlathotep, the mad faceless god, howls blindly in the darkness to the piping of two amorphous idiot flute players' ('The Rats in the Wall'). Indeed, this imbecile god is *the* impulse of the universe:

And through this revolting graveyard of the universe the muffled, maddening beating of drums, and thin, monotonous whine of blasphemous flutes from inconceivable, unlighted chambers beyond Time; the detestable pounding and piping whereunto dance slowly, awkwardly, and absurdly the gigantic, tenebrous ultimate gods – the blind, voiceless, mindless gargoyles whose soul is Nyarlathotep.[5]

But this terrifying and significantly 'faceless' entity was not always a god, for Lovecraft transformed dream material of another kind, a kind much closer to the commercial traveller that was his father:

> *Nyarlathotep* is a nightmare – an actual phantasm of my own, with the first paragraph written *before I fully awaked*. I had been feeling execrably of late – whole weeks have passed without relief from head-ache. . . . I had never heard the name NYARLATHOTEP before, but seemed to understand the allusion. Nyarlathotep was a kind of itinerant showman or lecturer who held forth in publick [*sic*] halls and aroused wide spread fear and discussion with his exhibitions. These exhibitions consisted of two parts – first, a horrible – possible prophetic – cinema reel; and later some extraordinary experiments with scientific and electrical apparatus. . . . I seem to recall that Nyarlathotep was already in Providence; and that he was the cause of the shocking fear which brooded over all the people. I seem to remember that persons had whispered to me in awe of his horrors, and warned me not to go near him. . . . The terror [has] become a matter of conscious artistic creation.[6]

This was a nightmare Lovecraft could not exorcise, and it created a form of self-punishment which he wrote into his story *The Case of Charles Dexter Ward*:

> From a private hospital for the insane near Providence, Rhode Island, there recently disappeared an exceedingly singular person. He bore the name of Charles Dexter Ward, and was placed under restraint most reluctantly by the *grieving father* who had watched his aberration grow from a eccentricity to a dark mania involving both a possibility of murderous tendencies and a peculiar change in the apparent contents of his mind. Doctors confess themselves quite baffled by his case, since it presented oddities of a general physiological as well as psychological character.
>
> (emphasis mine)

It is clear that Lovecraft brought deeply personal material to his work, and this may account for his low output of stories and high output of confessional letters.

Another area of 'neurosis' for him was his relationship with the ordinary modern world in the United States of the 1920s and 1930s. Lovecraft's background was essentially Anglophile and of provincial New England. As a young man he published a magazine called *The Conservative*.[7] Self-educated and outside the New England college world, Lovecraft yearned for a past age into which he could escape. In 1923 he wrote self-mockingly:

> Nothing must disturb my undiluted Englishry – God Save the King! I am naturally a Nordic – a chalk-white, bulky Teuton of the Scandinavian or North-German forests – a Viking – a berserk killer – a predatory rover of the blood of Hengist and Horsa – a conqueror of Celts and Mongols and founder of Empires – a son of the thunders and the arctic winds, and brother to the frosts and the auroras – a drinker of foemen's blood from newpicked skulls . . .[8]

And in 1929, in another letter, he tells us, 'my writing soon became distorted – till at length I wrote only as a means of re-creating around me the atmosphere of my 18th century favourites'.[9] After his marriage, he moved to Brooklyn and travelled, in a limited fashion, visiting the older colonial USA: Philadelphia, Richmond, Williamsburg and Yorktown. When his marriage failed he returned to Providence and the world of his aunts. Indeed, when previously offered the editorship of *Weird Tales*, then published in Chicago, Lovecraft refused to commit himself on the grounds of having just arrived in New York (which he refers to as 'venerable New-Amsterdam').[10] Moreover, his stories are usually set in a just-surviving seventeenth-century America. For instance, in his tale 'The Survivor' his narrator tells us,

> I came to Providence, Rhode Island, in 1930, intending to make only a brief visit and then go on to New Orleans. But I saw the Charriere house on Benefit Street, and was drawn to it as only an antiquarian would be drawn to any unusual house isolated in a New England street of a period not its own, a house clearly of some age . . . indefinable aura that both attracted and repelled. . . . I saw it first as an antiquarian, delighted to discover set in a row of staid New England houses a house which was manifestly of a seventeenth-century Quebec style, and thus so different from its neighbours as to attract immediately the eye of any passer-by. I

had made many visits to Quebec, as well as to other old cities of the North American continent, but on this first visit to Providence, I had not come primarily in search of ancient dwellings.

'The Peabody Heritage', too, is architecturally specific: 'the dwelling itself was the product of many generations. It had been built originally in 1787, at first as a simple colonial house, with severe lines, an unfinished second story, and four impressive pillars at the front.'

Lovecraft's desperation for a gentlemanly existence was set against a background of rapid social change. Although married to a Jew, he continually poured vitriol on the incoming waves of immigrants, reserving a special hatred for the new Jewish immigrants, whom he called 'beady eyed rat-faced Asiatics'.[11] Moreover, his wife Sonia recalls that, when he actually came face to face with them in New York, 'Howard would become livid with rage. He seemed almost to lose his mind.'[12] This distinctly unusual behaviour Lovecraft could not deal with in direct terms, choosing rather a 'black magic' science fiction which transformed social fears into fantasy nightmares.[13] New York is also suitably transformed into a fantastical realm of historical and 'species' degeneracy:[14]

I saw a vista which will ever afterward torment me in dreams. I saw the heavens verminous with strange flying things, and beneath them a hellish black city of giant stone terraces with impious pyramids flung savagely to the moon, and devil-lights burning from un-numbered windows. And swarming loathsomely on aerial galleries I saw the yellow, squint-eyed people of that city, robed horribly in orange and red and dancing insanely to the pounding of fevered kettle-drums. . . . I have gone home to the pure New England lanes up which fragrant sea-winds sweep at evening.

('He')

Elsewhere this becomes more explicit, and a New York police detective finds himself amid the degenerate hoards of the metropolitan heart:

He had for some time been detailed to the Butler Street station in Brooklyn when the Red Hook matter came to his notice. Red Hook is a maze of hybrid squalor near the ancient waterfront

opposite Governor's Island, with dirty highways climbing the
hill from the wharves to that higher ground where the decayed
lengths of Clinton and Court Streets lead off towards the Borough Hall. Its houses are mostly of brick, dating from the first
quarter to the middle of the nineteenth century.... The population is a hopeless tangle and enigma; Syrian, Spanish, Italian, and
negro elements impinging upon one another, and fragments of
Scandinavian and American belts lying not far distant. It is a
babel of sound and filth.

('The Horror at Red Hook')

In his long tale 'At the Mountains of Madness', a 'fetid black' monster
which Lovecraft called a 'Shoggoth' is likened to the 'Boston–Cambridge tunnel' subway train. Yet the Shoggoths 'whatever they had
been . . . were men'.

This is evidence enough of Lovecraft's peculiar brand of horror
– a transposition of his social fears about new immigrant groups
into a cosmic battle in which the evil *Üntermenschen* are constantly
defeating the less numerous *Übermenschen*. Many critics stop at this
point, believing Lovecraft's horror to be purely racist, but this is
perhaps only half the story, for the majority of Lovecraft's tales
depict Anglo-Saxon degeneracy among the rural white poor, not
the newly arrived passengers of the steerage. Two examples must
suffice:

He paused exhausted, as the whole group of natives stared in
a bewilderment not quite crystallized into fresh terror. Only old
Zebulon Whateley, who wanderingly remembered ancient things
but who had been silent heretofore, spoke aloud.

'Fifteen year' gone,' he rambled, 'I heered Ol' Whateley say as
haow some day we'd hear a child o' Lavinny's a callin' its father's name on the top o' Sentinel Hill. . . .'

But Joe Osborn interrupted him to question the Arkham men
anew.

'What was it, *anyhaow*, an' haowever did young Wizard
Whateley call it aout o' the air it come from?'

Armitage chose his words very carefully. . . . I'm going to burn
his accursed diary, and if you men are wise you'll dynamite that
altar-stone up there, and pull down all the rings of standing stones
on the other hills.

('The Dunwich Horror')

Or:

> Sir William, standing with his searchlight in the Roman ruin,
> translated aloud the most shocking ritual I have ever known; and
> told of the diet of the antediluvian cult which the priests of Cybele
> found and mingled with their own. Norrys, used as he was to
> the trenches, could not walk straight when he came out of the
> English building. It was a butcher shop and kitchen – he had
> expected that – but it was too much to see familiar English im-
> plements in such a place, and to read familiar English *graffiti*
> there, some as recent as 1610.
>
> ('The Rats in the Wall')

On one side Lovecraft was faced with an invasion of 'Asiatics', but
on the other he witnessed another form of degeneracy – that of his
own race. In 1926, when Lovecraft produced his largest body of
work, he would have been witness to an amazing growth of rural
religious fervour. In 1925 an article on the rise of the 'Holy Rollers'
painted this picture of rural enthusiasm:

> The song became a dirge and the dirge became a fiendish thing,
> rising in howls and wails and moanings that stilled the wild
> things of the night. Preacher Joe Leffew preached. 'Some folks
> thinks as how as we-uns are funny people. They come here, poor
> sinners that they are, to mock an' revile us. Here's our word of
> Scripture. "An' Christ reeled to an' fro, as a drunken man." Now,
> children, dear children, some folks think that means the Lamb
> was a drunkard. T'aint so at all. It says "as a drunken man". You
> cain't tell me God's son ever went home all soused up.'
>
> Preacher Joe Leffew assailed education. 'I ain't got no learnin'
> an' never had none,' said Preacher Joe Leffew. 'Glory be to the
> Lamb! Some folks work their hands off'n up 'n to the elbows to
> give their young-uns education, and all they do is send their
> young-uns to hell.'[15]

This needs to be added to the growth of the 'know-nothing' intolerance of the Ku-Klux-Klan, which had been recently 'revived' in
the 1920s. In 1926, the year of Lovecraft's most prolific outpouring,
Hiram Wesley Evans, Imperial Wizard of the Klan, had this to say
about Americanness:

We are a movement of the plain people, very weak in matter of culture, intellectual support, and trained leadership. We are demanding, and we expect to win, a return of power into the hands of the everyday, not highly cultured, . . . but entirely unspoiled and not de-Americanized, average citizen of the old stock. Our members and leaders are all of this class – the opposition of the intellectuals and liberals. . . .

The Klan . . . has now come to speak for the great mass of Americans of the old pioneer stock. . . .

These are . . . a blend of various peoples of the so-called Nordic race . . . the Klan does not try to represent any people but these. . . .

[Now] we [have] found our great cities and the control of much of our industry and commerce taken over by strangers. . . .

So the Nordic American today is a stranger in large parts of the land his fathers gave him.[16]

In 1928 the Klan's rise in Indiana was described by Morton Harrison in terms reminiscent of Lovecraft's monster gods. The Klan is addressed by its leader:

Here in this uplifted hand, where all can see, I bear an official document addressed to the Grand Dragon, Hydras, Great Titans, Furies, Giants, Kleagles, Exalted Cyclops, Terrors, and All Citizens of the Invisible Empire of the Realm of Indiana. It is done in the executive chambers of His Lordship, the Imperial Wizard, in the Imperial City of Atlanta.[17]

This side of Lovecraft's fears is not mentioned by any critics who deal with his work. That Lovecraft pictured himself as a barbarian Nordic type was purely ironic given his frailty and lack of physicality; that he was a rationalist materialist, whose hobby was astronomy, added to his distaste for cults based on ignorance (he was, after all, an eighteenth-century gentleman).

In order to cope with racial alienation from both directions Lovecraft turned his social fears into nightmare fantasies. His *real* nightmares then returned upon themselves and fictional fantasy returned to its origins. To suggest, as most critics do, that Lovecraft's social fears were simply translated into fantasy ignores the fact that his fantasy life (his dreams) ran parallel to his social experience and was not just an internalization of that social experience: Holy Roller, Ku-Klux-Klan Grand Wizard, Nyarlathotep, Father trace

Lovecraft's concern with origins – origins in family and in America
that literally paralysed him. Unable to cope with marriage, with
city life, with work of any sort, Lovecraft finally could not exist in
temperatures lower than 80°F, actually fainting when the heat
dropped to 60°. In his stories the seeker after origins either is destroyed or goes mad; the 'Old Ones', for example, are decapitated
('At the Mountains of Madness'). Indeed, in 1929 Lovecraft wrote of
his inability to escape the literary influence of either Poe or Dunsany:
'where', he asks, 'are my Lovecraft pieces?'[18] During March 1937 he
died of cancer. Lin Carter's 1972 biographical obituary remarks,

> He lived like a hermit, a recluse, in self-imposed exile from his
> own world and his age, neither of which he enjoyed. Far rather
> would he have been born a cosmopolitan Roman of the late
> Empire, or an English squire in his beloved 18th century, or a
> colonial gentleman of the days before the Revolution. Alas, he
> was none of these things, except in his extraordinarily vivid
> dreams.[19]

After Lovecraft's death August Derleth made it a lifelong work of
love to keep the master's writings available; yet the collections of
Lovecraft work did not sell well. *Weird Tales* also went into decline.
Stephen King drily comments,

> During and after the war years, horror fiction was in decline. The
> age did not like it. It was a period of rapid scientific development
> and rationalism – they grow very well in a war atmosphere, thanks
> – and it became a period which is now thought of by fans and
> writers alike as the 'golden age of science fiction'. . . . *Weird Tales*
> plugged grimly along, holding its own but hardly reaping mil-
> lions (it would fold in the mid-fifties after a down-sizing from its
> original gaudy pulp size to a digest form failed to effect a cure for
> its ailing circulation).[20]

Nevertheless, Lovecraft's pantheon of gods steadily grew as other
writers embellished the 'Cthulhu mythos', as it is called. The cult
status of Lovecraft was becoming an inescapable fact. For many
who loathed his excesses and 'poverty' of style, but for whom Lovecraft stories were an addiction there was also a problem. Stephen
King says that Lovecraft

has been called a hack, a description I would dispute vigorously, but whether he was or wasn't, and whether he was a writer of popular fiction or a writer of so-called 'literary fiction' (depending on your critical bent), really doesn't matter very much in this context, because either way, the man himself took his work seriously.[21]

David Punter confesses, 'perhaps little more needs to be said about Lovecraft: his writing is crude, repetitive, compulsively readable, the essence of pulp fiction'.[22]

In order to understand this ambivalence over Lovecraft's work it is necessary to see that Lovecraft's personal traumas were, in fact, the *social traumas* of the group from which his work emerged and to which his work was addressed. While that group of readers has evolved over the years since his death and the specific milieu in which he wrote belongs to the past, it is, nevertheless, still possible to identify some broader cultural issues which stop his work from being of purely historical interest.

Lovecraft's work emerged at a certain point coincident with the emergence of modern mass literacy in America and the growth of vocational self-improvement and literary escapism. Magazines such as *Weird Tales* met these needs following the decline of dime novels. The adolescent, mostly male readership that emerged during this period looked to magazines which included petit-bourgeois writers such as themselves who represented the world of a class and a culture that felt it had no voice. This was a class that saw itself as neither proletarian nor bourgeois and that felt itself exploited by bourgeois cultural requirements. (Lovecraft emerged from such a class, being self-educated, aspiring to be an eighteenth-century gentleman yet the son of a travelling salesman.) This petit-bourgeois-generated antagonism left it feeling bewildered and disenfranchised (hence Lovecraft's hatred of others, especially aliens). The readership of one class unknowingly united with another readership of fantasy tales – the bourgeois intelligentsia, who also felt (and feel) disenfranchised. In both classes a desire for a period before technological specialization (the very period from which these classes emerge) led to an alliance among the pages of *Weird Tales*. Such an alliance manifests itself in a distaste for money (Lovecraft's disinterest in publishing fiction or editing magazines) and a paradoxical love of ostentatious consumption (Lovecraft's taste for the life of a gentleman and, in his tales, for 'empires' and for prehistoric gods and 'heroes', who do not have to earn a living). This paradox is represented in the fiction by a 'revival' of a mythic past, a romanticized past of Gothic or feudal origins and a whole mythology of warring gods being a rewriting in fantasy terms of the myth of Genesis.

This construction of another (quite separate) history to the world other than the official bourgeois history reflects the petit-bourgeois belief in a conspiracy by 'those at the top'. This conspiracy involves the translation of social factors into black magic and occult forces which because they are about to return suggest they are outside human (therefore bourgeois) control. The immanence of archaic elements about to irrupt into modern life always brings the bourgeoisie near to defeat, but they can always recover and this allows the petit-bourgeoisie also to survive, for total defeat of the bourgeoisie would lead to total dissolution of the petit-bourgeoisie. These dangerous archaic elements represent anti-bourgeois forces, but they embody petit-bourgeois ideas about the bourgeoisie controlling everything. Hence Lovecraft's 'good' monsters have pyramidal heads covered with all-encompassing tentacles. Being buried under pyramids of power ('Imprisoned with the Pharaohs') suggests social pyramids, but, again, paradoxically, the monsters are always at the very bottom of the pyramid, beneath history and therefore outside it. What is seen to be at the top is represented as being underneath.

Such a representation of life also involves (despite Lovecraft's distaste for Holy Rollers) a strongly religious notion, but one that has become scientifically objectified: a materialist belief system. The class to which Lovecraft belonged had 'liberated' itself from an old-style religion, but was unable to go back to the superstitions beliefs of the lumpenproletariat or rural peasantry. Lovecraft instead turned to his hobby of astronomy in order to create stories about *astrology* and black magic bringing real monsters from the stars as star-spawn. Moreover, this quasi-religiosity which is fatalistic and deterministic rests on a scientific understanding of phenomena, at once upholding the incredible but defeated by it ('At the Mountains of Madness'). Objective, materialist science is used to defeat itself: it recognizes what it cannot control – the other, the Absolute, ultimately the gods or God (but the gods are mad).

We return to the question of origins – of the cosmos, of man, of the petit-bourgeoisie. The identification of those origins is bound to the textual unravelling of a riddle, which once deciphered offers Truth – not merely a set of truths, but an absolute reassurance of the impossibility of *change*, both capitalist and bourgeois; for the Truth is that the 'Old Ones' and their enemies will always exist and battle for the universe. Hence, history stops in eternal recurrence. In order to stop history it is necessary to travel back in time to find it and to disturb it, thereby discovering that it exists not merely as the past but also in the present as a threat. For the return of the past reassures us of permanence even as it acts to threaten the very class representatives (and hence the whole class) who go in search of it. Indeed, the other place for history fantasized by the petit-bourgeoisie is actually the place of archaic feudal relations, the relations of autocrat to peasant – the very class relationships that must not return if the petit-bourgeois (servants of the bourgeoisie) are to survive. Questioning the cosmic order (the social order) may lead to destruction, but it also leads to an answer: there is a need for order and a need to 'know one's place'. Hence, hatred of the new coincides with hatred of the old and ends in personal and class paralysis.

This paralysis is the result of the nature of the quest and the quester. It is not a metaphysical quest, but a materialist quest for metaphysical certainties. The hero is a loner, disenfranchized in the modern world by his desire for lost knowledge. He is characterized by physicality and a distaste for psychology. His actions are character, as introversion by extension implies the bourgeois notion of individual control and the privacy of thought. The petit-bourgeois hero is always a man who acts publicly in the arena of activity allowed him (Lovecraft hated Freud) Yet this lone quester is, paradoxically, removed from socialized activity: he avoids women, and hates Black people and Jews (who are deeply socialized). His actions are public, but they are not the property of the group from which he emerges (he prefers communion with dead masters) nor of aliens (whom he avoids and whose alienation, ironically, destroys him). In Lovecraft's tales public action is public only because it indicates private motives which are openly represented by a character's hostility or withdrawal from public life.

Like the heroes of his tales, Lovecraft's life was public but always anonymous (conducted with many people but only by letter). Like his characters, the pulp-fiction author has no biography: his cult is that of a name to a text only. The author's authority is ensured by the repetition of his name on the cover of a work or magazine – a name without personality. Hence, like the tales of the fabulous that he produced, the author himself becomes fabulous, and this fabulousness is both projected away from and determined by his ordinary existence.

This fabulousness accords well with Lovecraft's lack of and distaste for professionalism (bourgeois work). Remaining anonymous Lovecraft imposes no bourgeois ethic of the artist: any writer can join in with the mythology and create new monsters. Lovecraft's name on his stories stands for a *type* of story which anybody can create and which allows a tradition to emerge: even in his lifetime he rewrote other people's stories, and August Derleth completed Lovecraft's unfinished works after the author's death. The essential element thus emerges which constitutes the industrial processes within which Lovecraft tales exist. Always different, 'Lovecraft's' stories (whoever writes them: Colin Wilson, Robert Bloch, August Derleth or Ramsay Campbell) are, at the same time, always the same: they reflect the need for a production-line process and an unchanging product in an unchanging world – a world whose unchangingness reassures as it terrifies. But it is a world where the production process is always out of control. For Lovecraft it invaded his dreams:

> The death of my grandmother plunged me into a gloom from which I never fully recovered. . . . I began to have nightmares of the most hideous description, peopled with *things* which I called 'nightgaunts' – a compound word of my own coinage.[23]

Lovecraft's monsters enjoy a horribly easy reduplication of bodily parts which are animal but function unnaturally. Lovecraft's nightmare was of 'things' which had a life of their own – things which act quasi-humanly in his stories. Lovecraft's nightmares are about the products of the production line – things with their own history: a production line that he exorcized and reproduced in his fiction.

11

Harry and Marianne:
The Never Ending
Supernatural Soap

I do *not* like careless talk about what you call ghosts.
'Oh, Whistle, and I'll Come to You My Lad', M.R. James

Anyone interested in haunted houses will certainly be aware of the ghost hunter Harry Price. Since his death in 1948, however, his reputation as a trustworthy authority has been severely dented, most notably by Trevor H. Hall in *The Haunting of Borley Rectory* (1956) and the later biography *Search for Harry Price* (1978) in which he established Price as both a fraud and an egotist.[1] And yet, Price's name has a minor cult following and his two 'factual' works about the rectory in the hamlet of Borley, Essex, although sometimes out of print, are firmly established in the lists of books regularly borrowed from public libraries. Indeed, first editions of both, 'The Most Haunted House in England' and *The End of Borley Rectory* command high prices when they appear on the second-hand market.[2]

For those unfamiliar with the story of Borley I shall offer an outline, but let it suffice for the moment to say that the Victorian rectory was supposed to be haunted by headless coachmen, a ghostly nun, good and evil poltergeists and many other bizarre psychic phenomena all of which finally ended in the fire that destroyed the place in 1939. Here were sex, sensation, murder and thrills.

Approaching Borley is rather bleak even in good weather: the lanes have deep ditches on either side, the land is dead flat and uniform and the area depopulated. As you approach the 'village' you are reminded of the atmosphere of an M.R. James short story or of the threatening isolation of Fenchurch St Paul in Dorothy L. Sayers's *The Nine Tailors*. This is the classic landscape of East Anglia.[3]

Borley itself consists of a church, and a small number of old houses and farm buildings. It neither threatens nor welcomes. Nowadays it is the church that is believed to be haunted and a group in 1979 recorded spirit footsteps and whisperings near the old Waldegrave Monument. Indeed, there was a note pinned to the graveyard gate which read, 'No ghost hunters after dark.' (The note, alas, no longer exists and modern bungalows cover the site of the original rectory.) In its heyday this sleepy hamlet was a stop for curious tourists and charabanc parties. On 17 June 1929, the *Daily Mirror* reported,

> The Rectory continues to receive the unwelcome attention of hundreds of curious people, and at night the headlights of their cars may be seen for miles around. One 'enterprising' firm even ran a motor coach to the Rectory, inviting the public 'to come and see the Borley Ghost', while cases of rowdyism were frequent.
>
> (Hall)

The unwanted visits of noisy tourists must irritate those who have to live in Borley, but for those who do visit the place it takes on the strange, isolated atmosphere of Price's books, for even though Trevor H. Hall and others have 'proved' that Price indulged in a massive hoax there is still enough of the weird left to leave the visitor with that especially enjoyable *frisson* of doubt. The place and its stories have regularly appeared in the media: on radio, on television and in the press. Paul Tabori followed Price's own autobiography with his biographical account *Harry Price: The Biography of a Ghost-Hunter* (1950) and Price's books were reprinted.[4]

By 1975 (when Price's reputation was under investigation and when the memory of Borley was fading into a cosy nostalgia for the 1920s and 1930s), Business Travel World could still advertise 'Psychic Research Tours', a holiday package, including Borley, organized by Enjoy Britain and the World Ltd. The cost of the eight-day holiday was £145.

The questions raised by this minor and yet controversial figure and his quest for 'life beyond the grave' are, what the motivational forces were which established Price's dubious reputation and what it is in the nature of his work on Borley that makes these works classics of their kind, in spite of or maybe because of their disputed status as factual documents.

Harry Price was born in 1881. The 1880s and 1890s were crucial in establishing a thriving popular and sensationalist press which was consumed by a voracious and half-educated populace. Mass readership was now catered for by a large and well-organized press machine which 'homed in' on lower-middle-class and working-class readers. The thriving newspaper industry reached its zenith when reinforced by the appearance of radio and film, stories from one medium feeding to other two. Both George Orwell and Richard Hoggart record this process. By the late 1920s Price was established as a 'psychic journalist'. For a poor boy with big ambitions and with no prospect of higher education or 'preferment', the popular press offered a direct route to 'easy' money, fame and a recognized knowledge gained through the 'university of life'. Price, like his better known journalist/author contemporaries, chose this route to fame.[5] The life he chose spanned hack journalism and an acknowledged thirst for the thrill of showmanship. The life work of Harry Price was, perhaps, the promotion of 'self' based upon increasingly unusual means.

Price claimed throughout his life that his origins were rural and his stock a decayed middle-class respectable Shropshire family. This was not so. Hall has shown that Price's origins were humble, urban and hardly respectable. Rather than coming into the world the son of a 'well-known paper manufacturer' of Shrewsbury, he was in fact the son of Edward Ditcher Price, a commercial traveller for a London pen and ink manufacturer and failed one-time grocer. His mother, who came from Newington in South London, met his father at 14 and married him at 16 – Edward Price was 40. When his father died, he left virtually nothing. To cover these inadequacies Price began his career of deceit. In all of it, even and especially through his work on psychical research, he craved *respectability*. Ironically, the more sensationally and unlikely Price behaved the more this was done to gain that respect never accorded to Price's family and never accorded by the middle classes to that invisible 'underclass' of tradespeople from whom his family hailed. Far from being the 'solicitor' he pretended to be on the marriage certificate (professional, middle-class and having a position in society) Price's maternal grandfather was, in fact, a newspaper reporter (feckless, rootless and without respectability). Hall bluntly declared 'I was dealing with a family of liars', but in this drive toward respectability there may be more to consider.

Until his marriage Price scratched a living as a 'numismatic' journalist on a Kent newspaper, a photographer of grocery shops, a manufacturer of glues and a creator of patent medicine (alongside other quacks, such as Dr Crippen: the arch example of the type of lower-middle-class rootless male we are studying). In 1908, however,

Price finally found a degree of respectability in his marriage to Constance Knight, the daughter of a wealthy 'perfumer' from middle-class Brockley, a suburb of South London. His wife brought middle-class respectability and the comforts of money. After this date Price could live out his 'fantasy' version of the respectable life of a middle-class gentleman and use his fantasy to promote his own idea of becoming a household name. In this, Price combined a peripheral knowledge of advertising know-how and commercial sense with an inbred distaste for the very money that had eluded his own family. Price's business knowledge was founded not on the 'solid' principles of engineering or paper manufacture (as he claimed) but rather upon the fairground principles of the shyster or the wartime 'spiv'. He combined this knowledge with a deep-seated desire (I suggest) to live the life of an amateur gentleman collector – an eccentric and rather cautious investigator and collector of curiosities: a very special kind of English gentlemanly type. After his marriage, Price could indulge a spurious knowledge of archaeology (for which he was exposed), display a deceitful knowledge of numismatics (which he plagiarized) and gain expertise in the history of magic and legerdemain (about which he was an expert but about which he still felt the need to lie). These eccentric gentlemanly pursuits failed to bring any real reward (Price craved respectable, that is, institutional recognition). What nearly brought him what he wanted was psychical research.

One important factor in Price's story is his constant need to 're-write' his own history or to write in episodes at points that elsewhere he had included as occurring at another time or place. Hall points out at least two of these incidents. Without a strong sense of his own 'reality' or perhaps oppressed by too much of this reality, Price created the history of his life as it suited him. In this he became, not a commercial failure and an impossibly ill-educated drifter, but a lively, creative, middle-class boy with leanings towards engineering and the knowledge that he would inherit his father's business in Shrewsbury.

One incident recorded as true in his autobiography (and investigated by Hall and proved totally false!) was the visit Price 'witnessed' as an eight-year-old boy in the market place in Shrewsbury. Here 'the Great Sequah' put on his medicine show. The show may or may not have occurred and Price probably did not witness it (although a 'Sequah' was actually an American called Hartley who came to Britain; Price may have seen the show in London). It is of great interest to us to find out why Price felt an especial need to record the effect of the incident in his life. It appears to have had a direct effect on his psychological growth – yet as a 'fictional' memory in his autobiography it also seems to serve to justify the darker side of Price's psychic makeup: the master showman, flamboyant, American, magical and charismatic. We are told,

One cold January morning the 'Great Sequah', with his brass bands, gilded chariots, and troop of 'boosters' in the garb of Mohawk Indians, pitched his tent – so to speak – in Shrewsbury's principal square. . . . During the whole of this eventful morning I stood, cold but happy, open-mouthed at this display of credulity, self-deception, auto-suggestion, faith-healing, beautiful showmanship, super-charlatanism, and 'magic'. The miracles of the marketplace left me spellbound.

What is important here is the recording of 'miracles' and the knowledge of 'credulity' and 'self-deception'. The ambivalence is important – Price both 'knew' and did *not* know about his deceptive schizoid nature: a nature well placed to create two of the 'greatest' books on psychical investigation, themselves a mixture of miracles and self-deception. Here, Price became both 'Sequah' (to whom he added the revealing epithet 'Great') and the sceptical, aloof investigator. The description of the 'Great Sequah' which mixes, in the same paragraph, real astonishment at the 'truly' magical and a knowledge that this is all the product of a 'cheat' describes and reveals the Harry Price that Price himself would not have recognized. The fact that what left him 'spellbound' happened in 'the market-place' (the proper place of a tradesman's son?) is, perhaps, also revealing of the important relationship that the modern supernatural has with capitalism and consumerism. In the 'projected' figure of the 'Great Sequah', Price accomplished the fantasy of the gentleman collector (this was the moment Price became interested in magic) and the fantasy of the charismatic showman.

And this dual fantasy was worked upon all Price's life, not least in his gentleman's library with its 'fake' bookplates and its air of antiquarianism, but also in his association with psychic extravaganzas. The first instance was Price's opening (accompanied by national publicity) of the sealed box of the religious fanatic Joanna Southcott (who had died in 1814). Needless to say, the box, which was meant to contain items useful during a national emergency, contained nothing of interest. The second incident, which was played out to an international audience, was the attempt to raise the devil in 1932 in the Hartz Mountains. The devil failed to materialize. In both these instances, and through the creation of the National Laboratory of Psychical Research, Price hoped to establish his credentials as a 'scientific' investigator: one worthy of respect among academics. On the Brocken Mountain, Price had C.E.M. Joad with him, and in the investigation into the haunting of Borley a group of undergraduates from Cambridge had conducted experiments into the phenomena there. Price always hoped for a university chair, honorary doctorate and university department. He donated his collection of work on magic to the University of London, but he was deprived of what he considered his right: a department of psychical research. What emerges through these exploits is the curious way Price's life becomes a lived fiction and the overriding social (that is socialized) unconscious of the man and his need, at almost any cost, to project a public persona.

In turning to Price's best-known works, it is necessary to fill in the story of Borley as it is narrated in '*The Most Haunted House in England*' (*MHHE*) and *The End of Borley Rectory* (*EBR*). The narrative covers a series of bizarre supernatural occurrences that had persisted from the late nineteenth century until the Second World War. The 'plot' consists of Price's investigation into these occurrences from his initial acquaintance with the case in 1929 to the early 1940s. Through ghostly visitations, poltergeist activity, spontaneous 'spirit' writing and planchette sessions, a story emerges of kidnap, murder and secrecy: a story either of a love affair between a nun and a monk which ended in tragedy or (more plausibly, at least in terms of the 'evidence') a love affair between the lord of the manor and a French 'nun' during the seventeenth century which ended, somewhat obscurely, with a 'rape' and 'murder' and three centuries of secrecy. Included within this double narrative (which forms the detective thriller part of the two books) is another tale of the eccentric clerics and their families who occupied the rectory since the time of Henry Bull in the late nineteenth century. Both books consist of collected reports and anecdotes interlaced with possible explanations offered by Price's correspondents and fellow investigators, and the atmosphere of both books is that of the detective at his trade, indeed, Price says he was asked to 'take charge of the case' (*MHHE*).

From the miscellaneous anecdotes and reports that emerge the reader is quickly immersed in a story in which the laws of nature seem horribly in abeyance – the atmosphere is at once sinister and fascinating. Some examples of incidents from the many that are offered will give the reader a feeling for the books. One occupant, 'awoke suddenly and found an old man in dark, old fashioned clothes, wearing a tall hat, standing by her bed. On another occasion, the same figure was seen sitting on the bed' (*MHHE*). 'One early morning in 1919 [other occupants of the rectory cottage] . . . saw a black shape, in the form of a little man, running round their bedroom' (*MHHE*). Another occupant, Mr Foyster, recorded in his diary numerous poltergeist phenomena, including violent attacks on his wife, who psychically attracted 'spirit' messages on the walls! Price listed some of the phenomena:

> The phenomena our observers were able to confirm included footsteps and similar sounds; raps, taps and knockings; displacement of objects; 'clicks' and 'cracks'; sounds as of a door closing; knocks, bumps, thuds, jumping or stamping; dragging noise; wailing sounds; rustling or scrabbling noises; 'metallic' sounds; crashing, as of crockery falling; wall-pencillings; 'appearance' of objects; luminous phenomenon; odours, pleasant and unpleasant; sensation of coldness; tactual phenomena; sensation of a 'presence'; and a fulfilled prediction. One observer says she saw the 'nun'.
>
> (*MHHE*)

Finally a planchette message revealed that *Sunex Amures* would burn down the house and this sinister entity finally fulfilled his promise (*MHHE*). All of these strange activities centred on the fate of the spirit of the 'nun' and indeed certain unidentified human bones are finally found in the cellar. The nun emerges during the story as, 'a Mary Lairre . . . a French girl of nineteen years of age, who was a novice in a nunnery at Havre, . . . and was murdered (strangled) by "Waldegrave" on May 17, 1667' (*EBR*).

Both books end on a disturbing note of inconclusiveness. Even after the destruction of the rectory the weird phenomena continued and just as Price is ready to leave Borley for good he finds on a photograph of the ruins, the distinct outline of half a brick floating in mid air!

What makes a good ghost story? Price's story of Borley seems to contain the definitive recipe: a coach and *headless* horseman; a ghostly nun who walks the grounds (waiting for her lover?); an old, decayed and isolated rectory (without electricity and with deep, dark and damp cellars that hold a terrible secret); psychic occupants (Marianne Foyster); bizarre occurrences (the appearance of a monster insect in one episode and of an old coat in another); bells that ring without human agency; messages from the dead (via suburban planchette readings); a legendary past (of monasteries and nunneries and a secret tunnel); flying bricks, vanishing and reappearing household utensils and 'apports' (a French medallion and a gold wedding ring). All this on what appears an almost daily basis taking place in and around a 'cold' spot outside 'the Blue Room'. In every respect the case was sensational. Into this dramatic setting steps the one person able, like Holmes, to put the thing into perspective: the ghost hunter.

In case the reader may wish to know what a psychic investigator takes with him when engaged on an important case, I will enumerate some of the items included in a ghost-hunter's kit.

Into a large suitcase are packed the following articles: A pair of soft felt overshoes used for creeping, unheard, about the house in order that neither human beings nor paranormal 'entities' shall be disturbed when producing 'phenomena'; steel measuring tape for measuring rooms, passages, testing the thickness of walls in looking for secret chambers or hidey-holes; steel screw-eyes, lead post-office seals, sealing tool, strong cord or tape, and adhesive surgical tape, for sealing doors, windows or cupboards; a set of tools, with wire, nails, etc.; hank of electric flex, small electric bells, dry batteries and switches (for secret electrical contacts); 9cm. by 12cm. reflex camera, film-packs and flash-bulbs for indoor or outdoor photography; a small portable telephone for communicating with assistant in another part of building or garden; note book, red, blue and black pencils; sketching block and case of drawing instruments for making plans; bandages, iodine and a flask of brandy in case member of investigating staff or resident is injured or faints; ball of string, stick of chalk, matches, electric torch and candle; bowl of mercury for detecting tremors in room or passage or for making silent electrical mercury switches; cinematograph camera with remote electrical control, and films; a sensitive transmitting thermometer [etc, etc].

(*MHHE*)

From all this it emerges that the ghost hunter combines the qualities of a Sherlock Holmes, a master spy and a boy scout – he is both a psychic adventurer and a rather well equipped camper (of the 'Famous Five' type). One is irresistibly reminded of this quality of adventure (a cross between E. Phillips Oppenheim and Edgar Wallace) when, after his last visit, Price tells us 'although I have investigated many haunted houses, before and since, never have such phenomena so impressed me as they did on this historic day. Sixteen hours of thrills!' (*MHHE*). However, Price combined these elements of the psychic thriller in order to reinforce the message of respectability he wanted to convey. In the second of the two works, *The End of Borley Rectory*, Price brings his narrative to a halt with the repeated, yet contradictory assertions that, firstly science cannot explain everything and secondly it will be able to explain psychic phenomena.

Price's second book ends with quotations linking supernatural phenomena with the laws of thermodynamics (*EBR*), atomic energy (*EBR*) and abnormal psychology (*EBR*). Yet he does not quite end there, for the last chapter presents the evidence of the two books as if it were a murder trial and Price 'proves' the strength and coherence of his arguments in a 'literary' court of law. Despite Price's desire for his evidence to be taken seriously, it is entirely based on anecdotes, 'faked' experimental conditions, legend, clairvoyancy and planchette readings. Every time historical accuracy is invoked the text suppresses it.[6] Thus, because 'hard' evidence cannot be found in the records there must have been either a conspiracy to suppress the truth or all evidence was accidentally removed or erased. In every case, the evidence of history and of archaeology is suppressed in favour of the logic of numerous clairvoyant messages and the selection of evidence to fit certain 'physical' phenomena that were reported.

Did these weird events occur? In one sense, there is no need to ask the question in the terms posed by a cultural historian. Our question is why did they occur *when* they occurred and to *whom*. On another level, that of plain fact, rather than perceptual qualification, there are enough clues in the text to suggest that many of the events were possibly 'staged', that some did not occur, that others could be put down to natural phenomena. The way they are all placed in one universe suggests a tenuous relationship cemented not by fact but by the fiction of the planchette. These random events are then given a shape by equally random and variable planchette messages (even Price agreed that so much was dictated this way that the sitters needed wallpaper rolls) and much of what Price reprints has no basis in anything that can be checked. If these are ghosts, then, perhaps they are the ghosts of cultural necessity? Moreover, the way Price constructed his story by claiming for himself only an 'editorial' role (*MHHE*) makes it difficult to see when certain events happened historically and if they really were recorded outside Price's control. Even he admitted that most people left the rectory through natural reasons and not through terrorization.

What as cultural phenomena do the events of Borley and the status of Price's two books represent? In the previous chapter I considered this relationship between the sensational and the respectable: that odd mixture of the inexplicable and supernatural and the organized and the social. For want of a better definition I have characterized this attitude as essentially 'lower middle class', a perceptual framework exemplified by, but not specific to, those elements of society on the ragged edge of class division. Here, I am keen to insist that 'class' represents a perceptual space inhabited by a whole spectrum of society and not wholly confined to income. This space is the space of the *disinherited*, culturally and economically. Typically, this is why popular fictions and alternative 'sciences' interest the intellectual and artistic classes as well as those who count themselves bereft of an education. At this period, prior to the Second World War, it is an attitude that is shared by the likes of W.B. Yeats, George Yeats, AE and the circle of the Golden Dawn, as well as the Society for Psychical Research and the 'ordinary' housewife in 'Alma', 'Coronation' or 'Balaclava' villas (or any such decayed suburb) who regularly visited a medium, read the tea leaves or attended a spiritualist meeting to be greeted by her long lost husband with a 'message'. T.S. Eliot satirized these attitudes with 'Madame Sosostris' in *The Waste Land*.

Because Price appealed to an essentially suburban and southern English audience (I suggest) his work should be seen against a background of rapid technological growth, suburban expansion and material progress. In the wealthy home counties of the late 1920s and 1930s (so different from the depressed north), the signs of material advancement could not be ignored. Against this a sense of *disorientation* among certain sectors would lead to the usual vacuum in spiritual needs for which Price's work would provide an ideal panacea: the phenomena (at Borley) could not be explained by science (materialism) but they demonstrated through relevance to the theological backwater of survival after death, that there *was* an explanation and an order which organized, and could not be controlled by, earthly powers.

In an age characterized by the masses and by mass means of control (radio (*EBR*), the loudspeaker, the factory-floor production line), an age in which commentators noted the 'loss' of individual control and sense of hope (see John Betjeman's 'Slough' or W.H. Auden's 'The Unknown Citizen'), and an age in which bureaucracy and state control appeared unstoppable (see Aldous Huxley's *Brave New World*) the 'ordinary' person could be comforted by a non-material explanation of circumstances. Borley's ghosts with their doctrine of survival suggested that one could exist (if only after death!) and preserve one's individualism (if only eccentrically as a 'nun' or 'headless' coachman) and willingly submit to an authority beyond oneself (via planchette messages). This is the best of both worlds, a theory of compensation that allowed the individual the freedom to be themself only if that selfhood had been granted by the authority of an agency outside the self. I am not suggesting (given the period) that Price's work acts as an analogue to the rise of fascism, indeed, given its essential Englishness and normalcy (a story of eccentric rectors in a corner of idyllic Essex) it would seem it acts as a 'mythic' compensation for the uncontrollable nature of world events.[7] The story begins in 1929 and ends during the Second World War. Throughout the narrative, Price insists that the events of Borley are a type of 'sign' of other worldliness (a prolonged miracle) that demands explanation. Borley itself is seen as of national importance, little less than a piece of English heritage.

Borley Rectory stands by itself in the literature of psychical manifestation. Wisely discarding theories of causation (which in these matters are little better than conjecture), the author, Mr Harry Price, sets out to prove by the cumulative evidence of eye-witnesses – recorded in a form which would be admissible in evidence in any court of law – the happening of events at Borley Rectory which it is impossible to explain by the operation of natural law.

The large number of the public who are interested in these things are under a debt of gratitude to him, for without his untiring energy and skilled experience as an investigator, a fascinating chapter in the history of psychical research would have been lost to the world.

(*EBR*)

In the end Harry Price never got his department at a university and never became Chair Professor of Parapsychology. For us Borley exists as merely a nostalgic memory, its site left unmarked except for the cryptic sign that once was nailed to the church gate. Ultimately, Price was a materialist who felt (genuinely?) that the domain of science could be widened to include occult subject matter. Despite the 'evidence' at Borley, the sensational could not be normalized into scientific experience and it remained both peripheral and trivial. A collector of books on magic tricks and a dabbler in the sensational, Price could not reconcile the sensational and the respectable any more than he could reconcile the supernatural and the temporal. For us, Price's life and his two major works represent an excursion into the forgotten, the trivial and the disenfranchised.

The phenomena at Borley proved to be subject matter for a story both sensational and respectable and Borley itself became a centre for a minor tourist industry based upon the illicit pleasures of the spectral. Although I have suggested the probable fraudulent nature of Harry Price's connection I have not yet pointed out the curious nexus of fictions that helped create Borley's legend and which allowed Price to place himself at the centre of the media's interest. For this we must look at Price's relationship with the inhabitants of the rectory.

It is probable that folk tales of ghostly carriages and suchlike had existed in Borley before the arrival of the Bull family who built the rectory, indeed the Bull sisters believed they 'saw' spectral phenomena as early as 28 July 1900.[8] Whether deceived or conniving the sisters began the belief in the haunted rectory. Their brother Henry (Harry) Bull later married Ivy Brackenbury who (probably for snobbish reasons) was disapproved of by the sisters. Harry Bull, a keen spiritualist, promised to return after death, and the sisters who accused Ivy of poisoning him (à la Mrs Maybrick) duly saw his apparition.

On 12 June 1929 Harry Price, working for the *Daily Mirror* arrived at Borley after correspondence about the hauntings with the next occupants, the Smiths. Yet what emerges from now on is not a tale of ghosts but a tale of ghost writers! Price, scenting a good story, had come to investigate, but had originally been written to by Mabel Smith for advice on finding a publisher for her thriller *Murder at the Parsonage*, which had clearly been inspired both by the accusations of the Misses Bull against their sister-in-law Ivy and the writings of Agatha Christie. Instead of advice Mabel got Price, who realized the potential of a story which played up the fiction of a haunted house mystery.

> The Smiths must have *wanted* publicity. They *wanted* to attract a reporter to Borley and watch him at work. What Mrs Smith was after was material for her supernatural thriller, which was based not only on the traditional legends, but also upon stories invented by the cruel and malicious Bull sisters. Any publicity they received as the residents of a haunted house would of course be of greater value when she tried to place her manuscript.[9]

Later when Lionel Foyster lived in the house with his wife Marianne, he too tried to publish a manuscript based on a haunted house mystery:

> he completed a manuscript, entitled *Fifteen Months in a Haunted House*. Foyster's book was a story about a clergyman and his wife and the vicissitudes of their life in a haunted rectory that is recognised as Borley.[10]

Neither Mabel Smith nor Lionel Foyster published their manuscripts, instead Price ruthlessly exploited their co-operation and published two best-selling accounts himself.

This peculiar fictionality which centred around Borley marked the place as 'text' rather than as psychical centre. The folklore readily accepted by the Bull sisters had quickly become intertwined with the story of their brother's 'poisoning' at the hands of a ruthless woman whose persona they possibly based on their 'memories' of the Maybrick trial and this in turn spawned an Agatha Christie-type novel, a Dennis Wheatley style thriller and two best-selling journalistic acounts. And these texts themselves were bolstered by séance messages, planchette writings and copious graffiti aimed at Lionel Foyster's mysterious wife Marianne.

And what of Mariane Foyster? Research by Trevor Hall and Robert Wood unkindly revealed her to be 'nymphomaniac and a pathological liar' and her husband a 'credulous old fool'.[11] Apparently unable to recognize fact from fiction and with a husband willing to be knowingly deluded about his wife's activities, Marianne became the centre for the most extraordinary and the wildest events at

Borley. Recognized as a fraud by Price, he nevertheless played along
with her in order to keep the story alive as material for *his* Borley
books.

Marianne vanished (at least she hoped to) in 1946 when she left
for America. She had a bizarre past, both in Canada where she may
have been involved with supernaturalism and in England where
she falsified her age, origins and marital status, lived in successive
ménages à trois at Borley, ill-treated her adopted children, banished
her real children and may have finally murdered her husband. It
was she who probably wrote the Marianne messages on the walls
(supposedly from the 'nun'). But what is most curious of all is her
own psychic makeup, for Marianne was a supreme story-teller – a
liar whom everybody was willing to believe. Marianne was simply
her own supreme creation – a living fiction played out for *others* as
entertainment. Many years after the events at Borley she told an
interviewer, Robert Swanson: 'those were flights of fancy; kind of
a soap opera. It seems so horribly silly, but it seemed a lot of fun
at the time – a continuous story.'[12]

Harry Price had found a kindred spirit. Finally, what of Sunex
Amores? Well this creature too becomes the centre of a fiction – the
creation of one Captain Gregson, last owner of Borley and an arsonist in search of insurance money and an alibi! What occurred at
Borley between 1900 and 1946 was not a convention of spirits so
much as a convention of authors and a web of texts which congre-
gated around an isolated house in Essex. In such circumstances it
is writing itself which takes on the form of the supernatural wherein
two inhabitants at least lived out Borley's fiction as the reality of
their own existence. Without substance herself, Marianne Foyster,
the fictional creation of her own fantasies and those of Lionel Foyster,
emerges as the real ghost of Borley's soap opera.

Part III
Requiescat

12

The Death of Cult Fiction and the End of Theory

Any requiem for pulp culture will inevitably also be the requiem for the old high literary culture that defined itself as its implacable enemy. Both required the conjunction of market forces (that is, commercialism), media cross-fertilization (especially with film and newspapers) and the need for a canon of taste using *contemporary* literary production as its benchmark. If serious fiction used mimesis for revelatory truth, so pulp used it for entertainment. Indeed, pulp turned information into entertainment for the urban, literate and democratic masses.

In the age of Hollywood, it was the movie that acted as the defining medium for the world of literature (just as much as any tradition of high art), for writers engaged in representing the modern world. The magnetic grip of Hollywood and its inability to accommodate great writers is well documented; what is less obvious is how commercial movie-making influenced writing *per se*. It was the movies as form that transfixed and fascinated not merely movie audiences but writers of all types and levels. Just as the camera had challenged painting, so Hollywood challenged writing; the advent of television did not affect writing as Hollywood did and continues to do. Indeed, television is a side issue in terms of the formal changes and challenges brought about by the studio system, the moving image and the star system. Moreover, it is instructive to note that during the 1920s that golden age of the pulp magazine as well as the height of modernistic experimentation, Hollywood's influence can be felt as a guiding principle. By comparing the work of two writers who occupy different and supposedly opposite sides of the cultural divide one can usefully see how movie-making affected literary form.

Both F. Scott Fitzgerald and Dashiell Hammett were drawn to Hollywood, could not reconcile their art nor their affections with its culture and suffered as a consequence. Both were involved with and affected by the concept of a script. Some sample passages from

221

each author give a sense of the impossibility of writing modern literature (that is during the 1920s and after) without incorporating the formal conditions of mimesis dictated by film technique. Here is part of the celebrated guest list from *The Great Gatsby*:

> Once I wrote down on the empty spaces of a time-table the names of those who came to Gatsby's house that summer. It is an old time-table now, disintegrating at its folds, and headed 'This schedule in effect July 5th, 1922'. But I can still read the grey names, and they will give you a better impression than my generalities of those who accepted Gatsby's hospitality and paid him the subtle tribute of knowing nothing whatever about him.
>
> From East Egg, then, came the Chester Beckers and the Leeches, and a man named Bunsen, whom I knew at Yale, and Doctor Webster Civet, who was drowned last summer up in Maine. And the Hornbeams and the Willie Voltaires, and a whole clan named Blackbuck, who always gathered in a corner and flipped up their noses like goats at whosoever came near. And the Ismays and the Chrysties (or rather Hubert Auerbach and Mr Chrystie's wife), and Edgar Beaver, whose hair they say, turned cotton-white one winter afternoon for no good reason at all. . . .
>
> (chapter 4)

What appears to come across from this passage with its carnivalesque grotesquerie is the movement, vivacity and exuberance of Fitzgerald's style – a style which suggests carnival but does not deliver it, after all we are witnesses only to a static list, not a real party in which people would have to be introduced dramatically. The list is, in essence, a clever trick, a literary equivalent of the *trompe l'oeil*. It is no wonder then that this so movie-like of novels should have filmed so disastrously. Where a movie is essentially *mobile* such a novel is essentially *static*. Two more examples make the point:

> A sudden emptiness seemed to flow now from the windows and the great doors, endowing with complete isolation the figure of the host, who stood on the porch, his hand up in a formal gesture of farewell.
>
> (chapter 3)

> *There was nothing to look at* from under the tree except Gatsby's enormous house, so I stared at it, like Kant at his church steeple, for half an hour.
>
> (chapter 5; emphasis mine)

Here mood is produced through a language of immobility and existential inertia which recreates a panoramic experience more in common with eighteenth-century landscape painting and the use of perspective glasses than with contemporary movie-making. In other words the linguistic form is *nostalgic* for print: a novel unusable by Hollywood but unrecognized as such by everybody in the business. Fitzgerald thus defines his novel by what Hollywood cannot use. Ironically because the novel *reads* like a movie it was guaranteed success with the public. Fitzgerald knew only too well that movies defined form in a way no writer could (or can) ignore.

Reading like a movie but nevertheless unfilmable, *Gatsby* seemed the epitome of the great American novel and yet its static nature tied it to an older age. How curious that the book is all about recapturing the past! Equally how curious that Fitzgerald, despite his contempt for Hollywood, could not write a successful novel without incorporating the formal requirements of the movie theatre. Filmic cross-fertilization had movie-ized the novel, had hijacked the literary qualities of fiction (as basic formal properties) and transformed them.

Conversely, Dashiell Hammett's *The Maltese Falcon* cannot be itself without also being a creation of the age of the movie. Hammett's book is stripped down to essential moments of action. Character is defined not by contemplation but by acts of volition. Two passages clearly give this sense:

> She got up from the settee and went to the fireplace to poke the fire. She changed slightly the position of an ornament on the mantelpiece, crossed the room to get a box of cigarettes from a table in a corner, straightened a curtain, and returned to her seat.
>
> . . .
>
> Spade's thick fingers made a cigarette with deliberate care, sifting a measured quantity of tan flakes down into curved paper, spreading the flakes so that they lay equal at the ends with a slight depression in the middle, thumbs rolling the paper's inner edge down and up under the outer edges as forefingers pressed

it over, thumbs and fingers sliding to the paper cylinder's ends
to hold it even while tongue licked the flap, left forefinger and
thumb pinching their end while right forefinger and thumb
smoothed the damp seam, right forefinger and thumb twisting
their end and lifting the other to Spade's mouth.

Both passages demonstrate the concept of character as defined by
action and if the first is pure stage direction then the second is a
type of philosophy by making. It is equally instructive to consider
the concept of description in the novel. In the next quote the panorama is not Long Island nor New York as in *Gatsby* but a man's face
defined by the functionalism, futurism and modernism of the engineered V-Strut:

> Samuel Spade's jaw was long and bony, his chin a jutting V
> under the more flexible V of his mouth. His nostrils curved back
> to make another smaller V. His yellow-grey eyes were horizontal.
> The V motif was picked up again by thickish brows rising out-
> ward from twin creases above a hooked nose, and his pale brown
> hair grew down – from high flat temples – in a point on his
> forehead. He looked rather pleasantly like a blond satan.

In this opening sequence of themed images the figure of Spade
reconciles the longshot and the close up in the defining moment of
celebrity: Spade's presence fills the scene as a star's close-up fills a
screen. Thus the nature of description itself and especially that of
central characters is determined by the Hollywood image of the
movie star: totally *present*, and defining character by the facial dex-
terity of eyes, mouth, muscle. Psychology returns to the moment of
the 'look' which expresses, but does not explain, the inner forces of
character and will.

Alexis de Tocqueville was one of the first commentators to notice
the importance of speech-patterns in a democracy and the implications that held for a transition from 'writerly' (that is aristocratic)
cultures. Nowhere is speech and writing more focused than in the
creation of novelistic characters, carrying as they do the moral weight
and narrative structure of fiction. Here again it is instructive to see
the transition from Fitzgerald to Hammett. In *Gatsby*, characteriza-
tion speaks of continuity, elegance and permanence and it creates
a purposive and accumulative narrative: built-up detail provides a
meaningful *totality* to the work. But the work, just like its central

character, is borne back into history; Daisy is the past returned to be relived in the future. A continuous past captures the work. Moreover, we can relate this concept of character and of the past to Nathanial Hawthorne's 'Wakefield', a tale in which a man, having left his wife, lives a parallel existence for so long that he is unable to return to her. The result for Hawthorne is a salutary lesson – leave the 'natural' order and you become an 'outcast of the universe': a cosmic as well as an ethical alien.

Such alienation dominates *Gatsby* and the eyes of 'T.J. Eckleburg' look down on a universe that has lost God. Like Hawthorne, Fitzgerald aligns character and history with moral consequences. The world of Tom, Daisy, Jay and Nick is moral precisely because it knows it has *lost* its place in the universe and because there once was a moral universe now destroyed. All this relates Fitzgerald's ideas to the world of the nineteenth century, only amoral Daisy links us to the contemporaneity of Hammett's new style.

In Hammett's Continental Op we find the genuine voice of the masculinely modern. It is at once inelegant, banal, ephemeral and anonymous and it is focused through a first-person narrative whose episodes are cumulative but not homogeneous. What links episodes is character not theme and that character lives in a continuous present of speed, violence and movement. Hammett's work too can be related to Hawthorne's 'Wakefield' and in *The Maltese Falcon* we are given a long Hawthornesque parable about a man called Flitcraft. Having found the universe to be meaningless and *random*, after a near fatal incident he leaves his wife and family of many years. Unlike Wakefield, he happily restarts a similar parallel life and lives happily ever after. The message, quite unlike Hawthorne's, is that in a random universe one can adapt without the slightest alienation to the caprice of circumstance and that the only meaning we make is the one we make unknowingly in the patterns of our mundane existence. Unlike Kafka's 'K', Flitcraft simply (and unknowingly) *conforms* to the conditions of the random and therefore survives. It is in searching for a meaning that Gatsby is destroyed. Nostalgia kills both character and structure.

Unlike the frenetic action in Fitzgerald's *Gatsby*, Hammett's *The Maltese Falcon* is essentially a *static* novel, and given its wordiness a surprisingly good novel to adopt for screen. John Huston's faithfully wordy third version defined a Hollywood style. What emerges from Hammett's book is a style cognizant of Hollywood and a language incorporating and embracing 'the movies' as both a form and a *grammar*. Hammett's work *is* a movie, by which I mean it is constituted by embracing movie technique *as* literature. Fitzgerald's language imitates Hollywood and is mimetic of its form while Hammett's form *is* Hollywood – a transitional language no longer tied to a nostalgia for print nor for representation. Look at how Hammett happily refuses Bridget O'Shaughnessy any 'real' identity, leaving us simply a series of 'fictional' names which act to fix her literary characteristics in a proper name. Far more than James Joyce's *Finnegans Wake*, Hammett's *The Maltese Falcon* marks the end of the traditional representational novel and the beginning of a new crossed medium existing alongside of, and usually despised by those nostalgic for a *pure* high literary culture.

In their different ways both *The Great Gatsby* and *The Maltese Falcon* epitomize the necessary and inherent relationship between fiction and the other emerging mediums of the twentieth century. The emergent relationship created between the various media provided space for a new hybrid literature. Pulp embraced hybridity whereas 'high' fiction sought to ignore it or attack it. This changing of the nature of the 'form' of the modern novel was as profound as the more obvious formal (and purely literary) experimentation of avant-gardism. The proliferation of media both changed, contained and redefined literature. Whereas, once, fiction (especially as encoded in the novel form) had stabilized structures of representation, now the novel had to negotiate its own structural requirements in the light of other media (and especially the film script).

The conditions which allowed the guardians of culture to define themselves by their control of a hierarchically determined literature had flourished precisely because only print acted as valued information. By the mid-twentieth century other media could claim a stake in culture, but were on the whole excluded because of the primacy of print's claim to exemplary status (in terms of representation of *value*). Twice excluded, once as being seen as a lower grade literature and once as being seen as not literature at all (a sort of 'printed' movie or television show), pulp was a type of infiltration by hackdom into the realm of the sacred (that is, the serious novel).

This devaluation of pulp literature helped give the serious novel its status in an age where print was no longer the dominant form of representation. And yet, this also led to the collapse of the conditions in which high art could claim a commanding role as the cultural arbiter of taste. High culture is now dead. It is dead not because it cannot still fulfil or enlighten its recipient, nor because it died of neglect amid the philistinism of the masses. It is dead because it no longer has the right environmental conditions to sustain its creation. Contemporary novels, poetry and drama under the pressures of technology have adapted and flourished. The narrative, linear taxonomies of the classic novel have been refashioned in the postmodern age.

It was not only technology's relentless pursuit of subject matter that killed high culture. This just made it easily available. Yet, in so doing it gave high culture technology's shape and made it conform to technology's rules. Technology de-emphasized the notion of creation and replaced it with the conditions of consumption. Yet what ended the age of high culture was the loss of a foundation. Its own material circumstances changed and so did the make-up of its recipients. The autonomous, enlightened individual of the classic novel ceased to exist as a valid intellectual concept or even as a contemporary human type. Ironically, popular art itself is becoming more self-referential and in so doing is effacing itself as 'popular' as it appropriates high literary style.

It needed a neurotic high art to define a confident pulp culture, but pulp culture, while illicit, always desires respectability. This is nowhere beter exemplified than in the work of Stephen King. The greatest market force in American publishing, King's name is more trade mark than signature, his awareness of other media total, and yet horror is still an illicit thrill and print still the only mark of real genius: horror cannot be literature. In the self referential world of Stephen King pulp too is finally sung its requiem: high art and its 'dark' other are reblended in the new grammar of the market and the consumer. No less than high literature's guardians, pulp's fans also retain their nostalgia for the word and its taxonomic solidity. King's obsessional love of print is the sign of an unfulfilled and unfulfillable search for respectability, while his chosen genre is and remains the contradictory refusal of that respectability – this is King's misery.

His clearest exploration of the pulp writer's dilemma occurs in *Misery* where Annie Wilkes has become the final ghastly incarnation of the muse. Wilkes is the Calliope of horror – a monster masquerading as a nurse – who forces her victim into an endless slavery to the word. Literally crippled by her attentions, the writer hates her and wishes to kill her but also is shackled to her by more than physical restraints. Without her, without the muse, who is also his number one fan, the writer would simply cease to exist as these are actually the required projections of himself. The writer's addiction, the viral infection of the muse is logorrhoea. It is this addiction that King's *Misery* explores and exemplifies, containing, as it does, an adventure not only in horror but in the very nature of print.

For all those of you who can't afford a Stephen King typescript there's one free with every copy of *Misery* – just join the bookclub. The manuscript in *Misery* has the perfect level of a simulacrum. The whole book acts as such: a simulacrum of the art of fiction. Here is a How-To Book with examples enclosed. Bound in real simulated kid comes the Franklin Mint version of an authentic famous writer's typescript (yes, *type*, none of that WP print-out stuff for me). With handwritten corrections added as in the original. See the process of creation occur before your very eyes – subscribe today!

The whole of *Misery* is racked by doubt and contempt – doubt about the audience and contempt for that audience. King encloses his book 'within' a book to pastiche the very sensibilities he knows he caters for in the majority of his audience.

Even as King desperately fights the demons of self-doubt he cannot avoid the myth his fans demand and that haunts him (I suspect) as his alter ego (the romantic artist as hero/slave to his act). He is also haunted by a dream. For his fans this may be the reality they see of his own work; a *roman à clef* of the writer as writer – not the glamorous work they thought but difficult, dangerous and obsessed. Fine. It is also a dream to haunt King. Behind the book stalk the ghosts of Hemingway, Fitzgerald, Du Maurier and Fowles, but maybe and especially the young Mailer: *Fast Cars – An American Dream* revisited?[1]

King wants to be taken seriously – and why not? He longs for the myth of the American hero-writer: an old battered Remington or Royal, a trash can, a black and red typewriter ribbon, a motel room somewhere on the Mexican border (remember *Salem's Lot* and Ben's post-vampire novel) ready to send that manuscript to the New York editor in time to gain that Pulitzer that brings no pleasure – only the endless pain, the bottle and the crushed pack of Camels.

It is interesting to compare King's obsession with being taken seriously with passages from Robert James Waller's *The Bridges of Madison County*, a work of pulp sentiments which fictionalizes (for the uninitiated) the role of the artist (tortured, lonely genius). This is typical of the dialogue:

'That's the problem in earning a living through an art form. You're always dealing with markets, and markets – mass markets – are designed to suit average tastes. . . .

Sometime I'm going to do an essay called "The Virtues of Amateurism" for all of those people who wish they earned their living in the arts. The market kills more artistic passion than anything else. It's a world of safety out there, for most people. They want safety, the magazines and manufacturers give them safety, give them homogeneity, give them the familiar and comfortable, don't challenge them . . .'

Francesca supposed that, for Robert Kincaid, this was everyday talk. For her, it was the stuff of literature.

The pretentiousness of this dialogue makes it bad art and worse pulp. Its aspiration is towards that very middle-brow conformity it attacks in its readers (the Francescas of this world). Hardly surprising that Robert Kincaid ('the last cowboy') should pack the obligatory cartons of Camel cigarettes.

King is caught looking two ways. At the end of *Misery*, Paul (aka King) works on a computer which he little understands and with which he can hardly cope. Yet, the bestsellers (and *also* the *important* novels) still appear. Writing is hard enough. King needs it mystified for him to be able to function. King's world is 'if only' – if only Smallsville was still a nice place to live, if only there was no junk mail, if only they still showed 'chapter-plays', if only (as in *Salem's Lot*) you could still buy Aurora kits of Frankenstein and the Werewolf that glowed in the dark, and if only you could be a modernist in Paris – a serious writer with a big bank account. How do you do that?

Stephen King is the biggest selling US author of all time (probably) but will his work last and is it serious? Does he have the one great popular novel in him – is this King's nightmare? And whenever he wants to assuage the demon of doubt he can fall back on a personal nostalgia which coincides with his reader's desires. This nostalgia is for *the act of writing itself* exemplified by the myth of Hemingway, an old typewriter, a bottle of hooch and a pack of Camels. King's oeuvre is suffused with nostalgia for the modernist writer as mythic alienated hero and with a nostalgia for schlock horror films and the popular culture of his youth. In that he is especially American.

Misery is a nostalgic book, an 'if only' book, despite the horror in it. The real horror is the fear deep inside that the age of the serious novel is long gone and that all novels are merely the raw screenplay of yet another film. One long compromise. King works a nostalgic picture of the writer's trade – his own nostalgia is for the *innocence* of creativity, an older, better period when popular books could be serious books.

In *Tropic of Cancer* Henry Miller proposed the end of writing. In *Finnegans Wake*, Joyce practised it. In these books what is proposed is the end of *serious* fiction – the fiction of *reality*. In *Misery* what is recorded is the *end of popular fiction* now gone cold, old and self-conscious: the feminists get *Carrie* and the postmodernists get *Misery*. Stephen King is taken seriously now *because* he is a popular writer. Only Annie knows what a travesty this is – only Annie knows that popular fiction is in big shit (She's the NUMBER ONE FAN AN' SHE KNOWS). This is, in a weird way, the 'end' of the popular fictionalist's trade: both knowing too much and yet also too little. It is, after all, a book about pretend people and yet pretend people *can* die. In the book *Misery* must 'live'. Buried alive, she is dug up and reanimated by the fictionalist's hand. Revival is nostalgia – the impossible is the return. Gothic nostalgia revives the dead and lets them walk. But, when all is said and done – dead is dead.

Like Annie Wilkes and her neighbours the Roydmans, King craves recognition and recognition brings *respectability*. King's bizarre worlds are the symptom of a need for *respectability*, the polite acquaintance of scholars with the antiquarian touch (Barlow, the vampire, is an antique dealer). This nostalgia for innocence is nevertheless disturbed and upheld by the violation required of the gothic genre itself: King's vehicle for respectability.

The gothic moment occurs at a precise point in our recent history. The naked power of the Sadean libertine goes hand in glove with the naked heroic innocence of the Rousseauistic savage. By a process of instant osmosis the one *becomes* the other: innocent in his evil, savage in his control. *Justine* records not merely the nostalgia for a lost medieval myth but also the new Techno myth of the body. For Sade, his heros and their victims are all pumping machines. Here then the body becomes a machine, an automated process of control and production. In this, the body's becoming machinelike predates most *actual* machines. The body had gained its privacy and had such privacy proved real by its violation all in one go. From now on the body as a bit-part machine tool – as a non-organism and as an object – would dominate the metaphoric and symbolic space of actual machines. 'George Stark's' own fictional villains is, of course, called A(lexis) Machine.

Medieval nostalgia coincided with this new awareness of the body – but already built in was a nostalgia for the body as a 'whole' entity. As real bodies ceased to be racked, tortured and pulled to bits for public sport, so the bourgeois state in the name of autonomous individual freedoms brought in dissection in the name of health and private humiliation in the name of public order. The body was at once recognized as a totality and at the same time pulled into the components of its machine existence. Frankenstein's monster walks with the living dead.

The gothic has long since sloughed off its nostalgia for the medieval but its nostalgia for the full body – a body bloated to bursting with all these gloopy machine-like tubes and joints – all that fossil-fuel blood – has remained. With the rise of science fiction, the true gothic either compromised or simply died: H.P. Lovecraft compromised, while M.R. James represented the end of the line. With the nostalgia for the medieval gone, Dracula lost his sublimity and the transcendent element departed for good. All that remained was the body – elemental, full of the sticky wet mess of the soft machine. In the modern era, the full body is always to be emptied, evacuated of its interior, opened from its private place into the glare of the public gaze. Violation of moral innocence (the stock of the gothic) now goes hand in hand with violation of the *physical* innocence of the total body. In modern gothic the body is always and ever totally *there*: its thereness is its horror as an object. Thus it is always *too much* there, too much *in place*. The closer the body gets the more its claustrophobic presence invites its dissolution. We are obsessed with the thereness, the total presence of others and at that moment, overclose, they become less than human – threateningly similar to bit part objects. Paranoia of bodily space: read *American Psycho*.

The individual, (no longer obsessed with the body as presence, but obsessed with escaping from it – one to whom the body is a mere symbol or token) is the artist. Meet his brother the psycho. The serious nut is obsessed with the body as fetish: a reinforcement of his own 'thereness' in the vacated (because dead) space of the other.

Norman Bates keeps mum but knows Norman Mailer's white

negro intimately. Colin Wilson's outsider goes for tea with Peter
Sutcliffe. Annie Wilkes sure likes Paul Sheldon. The psycho and the
obsessive artist are the last remains of real individuals in a world
gone Stepford through junk TV, junk diets, junk art. Only psychos
and writers still enjoy *authenticity* in a world of simulation and deceit.

In this weird romantic alliance of the creative and the destructive
we see the last vestiges of self-possession in a Brave New World
where the concept of self-possession is (itself) unthinkable. In such
a world the artist is as scary as a psycho and may actually be one.
From *Psycho* to *The Silence of the Lambs*, from *American Psycho* to
Twin Peaks and from *Twin Peaks* to *Misery* the psycho goes hand in
hand with the artist into the *Black Lodge*: bad dreams of paranoiacs.
Here there is all the nostalgia of the postmodern for individual
autonomy and the complete body, but it is crossed by slavery and
dismemberment and loss of control to the system of the machine.
Despite being dismembered almost all of Paul Sheldon's life with
Annie is recalled in the immobile inner world of the *mind*. It is
Paul's mind which constantly registers the indignities to his body
as if his body was merely an object to contemplate.

The novel of the techno-body, this full body waiting to burst open
(remember *Alien*) and reveal the total works, is a novel which necessarily goes in for total visualization. Such a novel restricts imagination by doing away with it. Total visualization dispenses with
partial description. Such writing is for a culture going cold on
imagination yet which views body functions as grotesque and fearful. In this horror as in pornography there is no *modesty* (shall I
chop off your foot Paulie? Shall I chop off your thumb Paulie? Shall
I chop off your 'man gland' Paulie?) As George Orwell pointed out
long ago there is only the fascist boot, the presence of broken flesh,
subjection and slavery.[2] No one gets out of this funny farm. Techno-
subservience is now served up as escapism. The age of modern
post-war horror is the age of the post-war corporate hero: Zombie
Man, Zombie Woman.

King's books display a special contradiction: a nostalgia for an
earlier innocent authentic reality produced by a fiction of *imagination*. This fiction's reality was only ever 'suggested'. The project of
writing has run its course because the project of the autonomous
bourgeois imagination has done so too. When we say King has a
weird imagination we mean exactly the opposite. King's tragedy is

that his novels leave nothing unsaid because it is all always present. King knows that the age of the full body demands *total* representation: you cannot avoid the machine. In the old sense, in the 'Hemingway' mythic sense (which was never the reality of Hemingway but always the myth) in this sense, he will never write a 'serious' novel, for the project he desires to participate in has now become a false trail.

Even as cult fiction has become self-aware and thereby lost its nature as pulp, so theory, that most self-reflexive of activities, has been colonized unawares by the very sensational, erotic and violent language of the pulp enterprise. Does this double yet unequal movement signal the end of both pulp and theory?[3]

There is now a large (often academic) audience for pulp exemplified by a new respect for the kitsch movie-making of the 1950s and 1960s. Russ Meyer's elephantasized Vixens play art-house cinemas both sides of the Atlantic and his banal yet surreally named films (for example, *Faster Pussycat! Kill! Kill!*) have found a new and unexpected respect among the critically aware. Ed Wood, whose very name seems a type of parental satire (Edward Wood, shortened to Ed Wood) and who found fame of sorts by becoming the worst film-maker ever has also been granted posthumous legitimacy through the loving reverence of educated fans, including the much-celebrated film-maker Tim Burton. As one critic has pointed out, to be the worst is in a peculiarly apt way to personify 'a particularly high concept'.[4] It is here, in this inversion of culture, that the worst attracts the 'best' and it is here also that the language of culture uneasily shifts. Tim Burton's film is *homage*, indeed 'there's no mistaking it for anything but an art film'.[5]

Edward D. Wood, Jr. was born in 1924 and flourished in the second great age of pulp, the era of pulp's phase of horror comics and drive-in B movies. He made crude horror and science-fiction films and ended his days making pornography, attracting along the way a gallery of freakish actors and the burnt-out junkie shell of Bela Lugosi whose death on the set of *Plan 9 from Outer Space* (1959) is recorded (as it were) in a cut-away shot which allows Bela in one door of a house and an appallingly poor look-alike to emerge from another. Wood's stable of freak actors, from Lugosi to 'Criswell the television psychic' and from Vampira to Tor Johnson seems a parody before the fact of Andy Warhol's later factory.

From irrelevant and talentless film-maker, Wood has risen through the ranks and now commands a place as a 'respected' iconographer of the 1950s, a *Kitschmeister* without parallel, a sweatergirl cross-dresser, an artist-manqué whose lasting memorial is *The Rocky Horror Show* which, in its turn, celebrated in high-camp good humour the androgynous posing of a whole generation unaware of Wood's Cold War transvestite *fest Glen or Glenda* (1953).

But this is quite different from giving Wood's work a theoretically or artistically central place. If Tim Burton has indeed 'embalmed' 'living kitsch' and turned it into dead 'art' he is guilty of the sins of reverence and respect that kill pulp dead. Yet the critic is also guilty of another sin when, in attempting to salvage both Wood (as naive amusement) and high culture (lamenting the loss of irony in Burton's work and attacking the celebration of the 'lowest common denominator') they invoke the full weight of the postmodern, hence: 'Deliberately or not, Ed Wood served to *deconstruct* all manner of Hollywood pretence.'[6] (my emphasis)

Suddenly Wood is legitimized as a natural philosopher, a true *naif* – an incompetent who wears the word deconstruction as an accolade for an oeuvre entirely crass and yet entirely self-knowing, aware of its power of denial and refusal – the decentring of the Derridean gaze summed up in its crudeness, vulgarity and ineptitude. If Ed Wood did not know, then his films 'know', as they actively decentre the 'pretence' of Hollywood. It's as if the verbal imperative of 'deconstruct' was always *in* the films, their *raison d'être*, discovered many years after the fact as the core of their claim to legitimacy.

A new and wholly unexpected admiration is legitimized by a theoretical and often semiotic turn, itself both scorned by and courted by pulp producers. Through such means, fictions once ignored as illicit are transformed retrospectively into a repectable and stabilized field of study. The second move, however, is the only one of real interest as it retains its illicit and problematic status while courting respectability and legitimacy. In this move the very language of pulp 'invades' the legitimate field of theory – gives its theoretically dull language the edge of scandal but also the means to command respect. *Consciously* scandalous and anti-establishment, literary theory nevertheless is itself scandalized by a metaphoric language that is violent, erotic and unstable. Here is a language not merely descriptive of the modern condition but entirely conditioned by it and to a certain extent directed by it in parallel with the fictions it seeks to explain. What exactly is the status of the language used here (without irony?) by critic Arthur Kroker?

What is the bimodern condition? It is the contemporary human situation of living at the *violent* edge of *primitivism* and *simulation*, of an indefinite reversibility in the order of things wherein only the *excessive* cancellation of difference through *violence* re-energizes the process. The bimodern condition, then, as a time of *excessive* tendencies towards *violent* boredom and *suicidal nihilism*: driftworks between *ecstasy* and *terminal catatrophe*. Here, the horizon finally closes and we are left with the *fatal* residues of all the referents in the *ecstasy* of *ruins*. That *fatal* moment prophesied by Heidegger's reflections on the techological logic of the *death camps* as the genetic logic of the bimodern scene. And all this under the sign of *seduction*.[7]

(emphases mine)

Here, for instance, we find a combination of explicitly scandalous language and a covert language of scandal which speaks only as the 'unspoken' of the first language. The overt language's *intention* is to disrupt established complacencies and at the same time describe them. Kroker is not being metaphoric but literal. The second language using the words of the first is a celebration of the erotic, the violent and the scandalous: an aesthetic of fascistic style unnoticed by Kroker as the antithesis of his own overt liberal and humanist sentiments. Here language becomes a type of style enjoyed for its own sake, a sub-cultural fantasy of control through an erotic apocalypse and a type of legitimate obscenity, not subversive but illicit (at once respectable *and* shocking). The first language is an attempt to shock explicitly, the second language is that which speaks the first – a scandal within the expression of theory itself.

A second example, apparently quite different from the one just offered concerns one academic's memories of her childhood. Influenced we are told, by radical politics, Marxism, feminism, poststructuralism and psychoanalysis, Valerie Walkerdine goes on to state of an essentially provincial, conservative, working-class, traditional and *stable* upbringing that,

We are beginning to speak of our histories, and as we do it will be to reveal the burden of *pain* and *desire* that formed us, and, in so doing, expose the *terrifying fraudulence* of our *subjugation*.[8]

(emphases mine)

Isn't this the vocabulary of the sensational – forgotten, yet returned o give substance to an otherwise unexciting life? Here we find revelations of pain and desire and the need to expose (an exposé) subjugation. Notice too the peculiar shift of the unanchored adverb, 'terrifying' fixed rather to 'fraudulence' than where we might expect to find it attached to 'subjugation'. But what possibly could be meant by such violent language when used in association with such a wholly uneventful life as recorded by the writer? Here the banal becomes sensationalized, the erotic and the violent ('desire' and 'pain' and 'subjugation') meeting in a world of terror and fraud: the language of the post-structuralist critic becomes quite uncosciously that of the tabloid and the pulp thriller.

My contention is that contemporary post-structuralist criticism is the new 'pulp', that its metaphors and obsessions parallel that of pulp fiction and that around the critical genre, modern criticism has created a subculture at once arcane and escapist: a fantastic arena in which the body, sexuality and violence underwrite the cult's wildest fetishes. Such criticism toys with the idea of somehow going beyond, transcending and deconstructing the boundaries and realities presented in those fictions we as academics are paid to explain daily. I further contend that such literary theory is basically a *nostalgia* for scandal, a basically conservative retro-ism defined by a loose alliance of deconstructionists, feminists and liberal critics whose relationship to the established order is that of a false opposition unknowingly renewing, by mysticism and obfuscation, current cultural, political and economic control, having substituted a theology of the body for a politics of intervention: theory as escapism, dressed in the erotic language of horror. Their celebration of broken taboos *in fiction* simply reinforces the stability of the taboo in the world.

My reading of *Misery* suggested a crisis in popular writing which was most apparent in Stephen King's ambiguous attitude not only to the 'muse', his readers and the nature of publishing but was also focused on his chosen genre: horror. The specific consideration I gave to King was part of a larger argument centred on the historical progress of the gothic and the changing form of its presentation. I suggested there was a movement in the genre, from a literature of revelation and annihilation obvious in writers such as M.R. James but obvious too in Edgar Allan Poe (whose tale 'The Facts in the Case of M. Valdemar' is an exemplary instance of a tale centred on bodily functions ending in revelation and annihilation), to current works which also concentrate on the body but for different purposes. For Poe the interior of the body is simply a sticky mess of undifferentiated organs – a type of interior slime. For current writers brought up in a photographic and technological era the body represents an anatomical structure and a fluid-filled machine. In this present literature, the body is cut, dissected, ripped, dismembered, always tortured and abject; it is emptied out, displayed; part human and part machine, visceral, fluid, sticky with blood, semen, faeces, urine. The body is monstrously *there* but already so alien as to constitute an horrific elsewhere both paradoxically supernaturalized and objectified. The vague image of London fog and a faceless assassin represents what previous generations wanted to know about the psychopathic dismemberment of the body: material horror of annihilation – the flash of a knife and the moment of truth. Yet it is the famous Scotland Yard *photograph* of Mary Kelly's eviscerated body which forms the first link in a chain which reaches to the Zapruder tape of Kennedy's assassination and beyond: the interior of the body suddenly and uncannily exposed to a fascinated and sensationalized gaze.

The central stalking horror of this literature is no longer the demon, hellish spectre or ghost but the psychopathic hero-villain not only of pulp fiction but also of supposedly serious writers who themselves stalk the popular imagination for their subject matter. Here is a metaphorical or virtual world of libidinous violence, incest, dismemberment, Sadeian fantasy, with a shopping list of broken taboos and of invented horrors for which no taboo exists to be broken.

We can trace four parallel and interelated incarnations of fiction concerned with the erotic, the sensational and the horrific. The first includes the early work of James Herbert, Stephen King, Clive Barker, Shaun Hutson and many other popular authors who work or are identified with the purely horrific. The second includes popular fiction which crosses genres, especially into that of detective or crime fiction. Thomas Harris's *Silence of the Lambs* cannot be overlooked here. Purportedly based on the psychopathology of known serial killers, the book owes just as much to its gothic horror origins with Clarice Starling acting the part of the heroine in a Radcliffe-like adventure pursued through a dungeon basement filled with death's head moths, bodily parts and terrified female victims cowering in an oubliette. Hannibal Lecter, with his deformities, gross appetite and ludicious knowledge is at once Dr Fu Manchu, Dr No, and

Count Dracula. Here the mundanity of the psychopath is super-naturalized for popular consumption.

The third incarnation concerns writers or artists whose work is recognized by academics as 'art' and who have utilized the sociopathic as a central theme. These writers are Booker Prize candidates or Palm D'Or winners who may have no real interest in the horror genre *per se*. Its ultimate expression would appear to be Bret Easton Ellis's *American Psycho*.

The fourth incarnation is not in fiction at all but in current cultural criticism.

American Psycho is the ultimate novel of body nostalgia, a final futile search for the innocent subject amid the charnel house of New York's postmodern decadence. I want to state, rather baldly, that the fourth incarnation of contemporary erotic horror sensationalism is the new fictional space of literary theory itself: pulp violence as the heart and controlling passion of cultural inquiry and intellectual concern. I further want to suggest that post-structualist criticism is itself a type of nostalgia *interlaced* with other forms of artistic expression so as to form a parallel discourse, self-contained and only occasionally an explanatory commentary. This is the horror in the library where the gothicization and occulting of the ordinary takes place amid the rococo of academia's ivory towers. Theory is pulp sensation, plagiarized without acknowledgement.

Richard Wagner wrote to Theodor Uhlig in 1849 that,

> artwork cannot be created at the present time, but only prepared
> – by a process of revolutionizing, of destroying and smashing
> everything that is worth destroying and smashing. That is our
> work, and only then will totally different people from us become
> the true creative artists.[9]

He was expressing the creed of a new intellectualism, that was based on struggle, apocalypse and renewal. This has remained the basic premise of the structure and project of *theory* ever since. It is quite irrelevant to this argument to point out that theory includes the Hegelian dialectic and its nemesis. What is at stake is the status of theory *per se*. Theory was both scandal and catastrophe – a radical disestablishment at the level of structuration. The specific nature of individual theories is not the central question and thus Wagner's relationships with Bakunin or Nietzsche become secondary issues, although it is an interesting footnote that just prior to becoming involved with 'Young Germany', Wagner had been adding material to Marschner's *Der Vampyr*.

Dis-composition then is particular to cultural theory. A recent critic has seen in Luis Buñuel's *Un Chien Andalou* another precursor of deconstruction, a film determined by Buñuel's and Dali's commitment to 'the dramatic themes of sexuality and eroticism, especially as they connect to forms of violence'.[10] Such ideas are themselves relatable to Buñuel's remark that the film was 'a desperate and passionate appeal to murder'.[11]

The violent discomposition of the body is the radical metaphoric language of pulp, surrealism and contemporary critical practice. The individual now finds himself or herself haunted by a ghostly *Doppelgänger* known only as the 'other' whose presence turns the self into a schizoid subject whose pronoun is 'it'. And the spectral language of this ruptured subject is the erased Derridean half-voice of its philosophic designation. Suffering from suture, this bricolaged subjectivity seeps the fluids of abjection on the altar of Phallic sacrifice. Its alternative, androgynous pleasure, far from being understood as an image of a mere freakishness which is both pathetic and absurd is now applauded and joined to the erotic frenzy of *jouissance*, itself the infantile excessiveness of highly rational intellectualism.

This pornutopia of freaks, drivelling irrationalism and obscene language exists in a world of Foucaultian imprisonment and Althusserian paranoia – its favourite authors being de Sade, Poe, Artaud and Céline. A runic semiology reads the signs.

And one should add into this mélange the project of linguistic feminism where we need include neither such eccentricity as Mary Daly's white witchcraft nor Luce Irigaray's bizarre obsession with the placenta. Rather such feminism by its nature is haunted, not by the misdeeds of real men and real women, but by a shadowy and inexplicably alien force called phallocentrism whose agents are real men unwittingly dedicated to fulfilling a conspiratorial and generalized male aggressivity. Aggression, duality, violence, eroticism, paranoia, imprisonment, dismemberment, the irrational, the displacement of the real, the supernatural, the body, the freak, the nature of death and the spectral afterlife – these are the component features of horror-porn-pulp and its collusive double, contemporary criticism.

It seems that current theory is both a partially descriptive analysis of contemporaneity and *implicity* involved with that which it describes. This reciprocal arrangement has allowed a new lease of life to much fiction and theory about fiction. I have pointed out that modern theory is descriptive of a *metaphysical nostalgia* for the full body and the self-sufficient ego. The modern pulp gothic seems, in parallel, to describe a similar trajectory. Such reciprocal parallelism has meant that post-structuralist language has *incorporated* the language of the pulp gothic within its own discourse. A language inherently metaphoric in pulp (gothic) fiction has been taken as literal (a description of actuality) in post-structuralism. Such analysis is drenched in the language of nostalgia – virally disturbed by its own rhetoric of violence, irrationality and death.

Perhaps analysis must again reinvent itself as both descriptive and prescriptive. As such, both popular literature and cultural criticism have reached their outer limits on the edge of a certain cybernetic imagination. Contemporary pulp is inherently nostalgic, postmodern theory is its retrospective twin.

The recent revival of post-structuralist attitudes among critics one might consider a parallel but not explanatory framework to the texts discussed here. And so, finally, here we are in a world of virtual violence and erotic fantasy practised by decent critics yet virtual psychopaths: killers like us, critics like us.

The illicit pleasures of pulp fiction.

Notes

CHAPTER 1: 'SCUSE ME MR H'OFFICER

1.   Peter Hunt, quoted in Robert Leeson, *Reading and Righting* (London: Collins, 1985) p. 145.
2.   Patricia Hollis, *The Pauper Press: a Study in Working-Class Radicalism of the 1830s* (Oxford: Oxford University Press, 1970) p. viii.
3.   Ibid.
4.   Howard Zinn, *A People's History of the United States* (Harlow: Longman, 1980) p. 280.
5.   Ibid., p. 286.
6.   Ibid.
7.   See, for example, Stanley Harrison, *Poor Men's Guardians: a Survey of the Struggles for a Democratic Newspaper Press 1763–1973* (London: Lawrence & Wishart, 1974).
8.   See comments on the censorious and authoritarian nature of the radical press in Ken Worpole, *Dockers and Detectives* (London: Verso, 1983) p. 17.
9.   See Worpole above; also Janet Batsleer, Tony Davies, Rebecca O'Rourke and Chris Weedon, *Rewriting English: Cultural Politics of Gender and Class* (London: Methuen, 1985) and Roger Bromley, *Lost Narratives: Popular Fictions, Politics and Recent History* (London: Routledge, 1988).
10.   Brian Stableford, foreword to Steve Holland, *The Mushroom Jungle: a History of Postwar Paperback Publishing* (Westbury, Wilts.: Zeon Books, 1994) p. x.

CHAPTER 2: THROWING RICE AT BRAD AND JANET

1.   For the illicit pleasures of drink, smoking and drugs see John C. Burnham, *Bad Habits* (New York: New York University Press, 1993) and for the illicit pleasures of public spaces see David Nasaw, *Going Out: the Rise and Fall of Public Amusements* (New York: Harper Collins, 1993).
2.   Jim Miller cited in Greil Marcus, *In the Fascist Bathroom: Writings on Punk 1977–1992* (Harmondsworth: Penguin, 1993) p. 169.
3.   Nick Hornby, *Fever Pitch* (London: Victor Gollancz, 1992) p. 10. See also D.J. Taylor, *A Vain Conceit: British Fiction in the 1980s* (London: Bloomsbury, 1989) p. 21:

   Why read fiction? At heart I suppose – this applies whether the author is Proust or Catherine Cookson, and knocks away most of the arguments advanced in this book – you read fiction to escape, to bring into your own life the rewarding tensions that would otherwise be absent from it. Books, it scarcely needs saying, are life lived at one remove. I feel about novels the way I felt at twelve about association football, the way I felt at eighteen about rock and roll. At bottom the critic is nothing more than a fan – or a performer *manqué*.

4. Jonathan Mantle, *In for a Penny: The Unauthorised Biography of Jeffrey Archer* (London: Hamish Hamilton, 1979) p. 133.
5. Marcus, op.cit., p. 167.
6. See George Orwell, 'Raffles and Miss Blandish', in *Decline of the English Murder and other Essays* (Harmondsworth: Penguin [1946], 1979).
7. Eliot's interest in popular culture can be seen in his essays on the music hall artiste, his fascination with contemporary murder trials and his use of Sherlock Holmes references.

It's notorious that T.S. Eliot was a Sherlock Holmes fan who pinched a chunk of 'The Musgrave Ritual' for the Second Tempter scene in *Murder in the Cathedral* (there are other Sherlockian echoes in the play) and puzzled academics with the bit in 'East Coker' about being lost 'in a dark wood, in a bramble, On the edge of a grimpen, where is no secure foothold . . .' Those who'd searched at length and in vain for the Old English root of the obscure word were not best pleased to hear it was merely the great Grimpen Mire from *The Hound of the Baskervilles*. A further micro-reference that I've never seen mentioned in print is Eliot's arrangement of *A Choice of Kipling's Verse* (1941), where unrelated poems from 1902 and 1897 are carefully placed together. They are titled . . . 'Sussex' and 'The Vampire.'

(*Million*, Sept/Oct 1992)

8. Jeff Koons, *The Jeff Koons Handbook* (London: Thames & Hudson, 1992) pp. 50 and 54.
9. Ibid., p. 56.
10. Ibid., p. 98.
11. Ibid., p. 138.
12. A.P. Ryan, *Lord Northcliffe* (London: Collins, 1953) p. 42 onwards.
13. Peter Haining, ed., *The Fantastic Pulps* (London: Victor Gollancz, 1975) pp. 189–90.
14. J. Pacione, *A History of the Booker Prize*, unpublished M. Phil (Stirling, 1991) pp. 3–4.
15. Maurice Flanagan, *Paperbacks, Pulp and Comic Collector* (Vol. 1. 1994) p. 48.
16. Geoffrey O'Brien, *Hardboiled America: the Lurid Years of Paperbacks* (New York: Van Nostrand Reinhold, 1981) pp. 12–13.
17. Haining, op.cit., pp. 13–14.
18. Lee Server, *Danger is My Business* (San Francisco: Chronicle Books, 1993) p. 15.

19. Noelle Watson and Paul Shellinger, eds, *Twentieth Century Science Fiction Writers* (Chicago: St James Press, 1991) p. 299.
20. Patrick Parrinder, 'Scientists in Science Fiction: Enlightenment and After', in Rhys Garnett and R.J. Ellis, eds, *Science Fiction: Roots and Branches: Contemporary Critical Approaches* (London: Macmillan, 1990) p. 57.
21. Ibid., p. 63.
22. Steven Marcus, *The Other Victorians* (London: Weidenfeld & Nicolson, 1966) p. 46.
23. Ibid., pp. 240–1.
24. John McHale quoted in Gillo Dorfles, *Kitsch: an Anthology of Bad Taste* (London: Studio Vista, 1969) pp. 98 and 108.
25. Harold Rosenberg, in Dorfles, op.cit., p. 9.
26. Clement Greenberg in Dorfles, op.cit., p. 116.
27. Herman Broch, in Dorfles, op.cit., p. 61.
28. Ibid., p. 62.
29. Ibid., p. 63.
30. Ibid., pp. 64–5.
31. J.A. Sutherland, *Fiction and the Fiction Industry* (London: Athlone Press, 1978) p. 65.
32. Ibid., p. xi.
33. John St John, *William Heinemann: a Century of Publishing, 1890–1990* (London: Heinemann, 1990) p. 20.
34. O'Brien ibid., pp. 33 and 35.
35. Matthew Arnold in Ray Ginger, ed., *The Nationalizing of American Life 1877–1900* (New York: Free Press, 1965) p. 123.
36. S.J. Taylor, *Shock! Horror!: The Tabloids in Action* (London: Corgi, 1991) p. 240.
37. Ibid., p. 76.
38. Ibid., p. 77.
39. Ibid.
40. Ibid., p. 17.
41. Ibid.

CHAPTER 3: TURNING THE WORLD AROUND

1. See Frank MacShane, *The Life of Raymond Chandler* (Boston: G.K. Hall, 1976).
2. Ibid., p. 1.
3. Victor E. Neuberg, *Popular Literature: a History and Guide* (London: Woburn Press, 1977) p. 142.
4. See Ken Worpole, *Dockers and Detectives* (London: Verso, 1983). See pp. 14–15 for reader confusions even in the mid-twentieth century!
5. Robert Collison, *The Story of Street Literature* (London: Dent, 1973) p. 31.
6. Collison, p. 38: Newby p. 15.
7. Newby, p. 139.

8. Ibid., pp. 139–40.
9. Collison, p. 6.
10. Ibid., p. 6.
11. Ibid., p. 10.
12. See Cyril Pearl, *The Girl with the Swansdown Seat: An Informal Report on Some Aspects of Mid-Victorian Morality* (London: Robin Clark [1955], 1980).
13. Harriett Hawkins, *Classics and Trash* (Hassocks: Harvester/Wheatsheaf, 1990) p. 10.
14. Ibid., p. 6.
15. John Feather, *A History of British Publishing* (London: Routledge, 1988) p. 137.
16. J.A. Sutherland, *Victorian Novelists and Publishers* (Chicago: University of Chicago Press, 1976) p. 63.
17. Ibid., p. 30.
18. Ibid., p. 33.
19. Charles Knight quoted in Peter Haining, *The Penny Dreadful* (London: Gollancz, 1975) p. 7.
20. Feather, op.cit., p. 57.
21. See John Carey, *The Intellectuals and the Masses* (London: Faber & Faber, 1992) p. 5. See also Feather, op.cit., p. 29.
22. Sutherland, op.cit., pp. 24 and 27.
23. See Katherine Tillotson, *Novels of the Eighteen-Forties* (Oxford: Clarendon, 1955) p. 23.
24. Sutherland, op.cit., p. 10.
25. Amy Cruse, *The Victorians and their Books* (London: Allen & Unwin, 1935) p. 315.
26. Ibid., p. 321.
27. See Peter Keating, *The Haunted Study: a Social History of the English Novel, 1875–1914* (London: Secker & Warburg, 1989).
28. John Carey, op.cit., pp. 11–12.
29. Ibid., p. 6.
30. Quoted in Alan J. Lee, *The Origins of the Popular Press in England 1855–1914* (London: Croom Helm, 1976) p. 27.
31. Ibid., p. 29.
32. Ibid., p. 15.
33. Ibid., p. 37. As early as 1829, George Shillibeer's omnibus included the loan of a newspaper within the fare.
34. Ibid., p. 38.
35. Ibid., p. 293.
36. See Richard Hoggart, *The Uses of Literacy* (Harmondsworth: Penguin [1957], 1990).
37. Daniel Boorstin, *The Americans: the Democratic Experience* (New York: Vintage, 1993).
38. See Keating, op.cit., pp. 4–5.
39. Boorstin, op.cit., p. 198.
40. Ibid., p. 145.
41. See Shirley Harrison, *The Diary of Jack the Ripper* (London: Smith Gryphon, 1994) pp. 179–80.

42. Hillel Schwartz, 'Torque: the New Kinaesthetic of the Twentieth Century', in Jonathan Crary and Sanford Kwinter eds, *Incorporations* (New York: Zone, 1992) p. 95.
43. Ibid., pp. 95–6.
44. Robert Leeson, *Reading and Righting* (London: Collins, 1985) p. 116.
45. Ibid., p. 128.
46. See chapter 1 in David Trotter, *The English Novel in History 1895–1920* (London: Routledge, 1993).
47. See *Reader's Digest* (March 1988).
48. Ibid., p. 183.
49. Ibid.
50. Penelope Dell, *Nettie and Sissie: A Biography of Bestselling Novelist Ethel M. Dell and her Sister Ella* (London: Hamish Hamilton, 1977) p. 21.
51. Ibid.

CHAPTER 4: A RIVER SO DEEP

1. Quoted in Richard Brown, *Society and Economy in Modern Britain 1700–1850* (London: Routledge, 1991) p. 215.
2. Ibid., p. 216.
3. Ibid.
4. E.J. Hobsbawm, *The Age of Empire 1975–1914* (London: Weidenfeld and Nicolson, 1987) p. 30.
5. John Lawson and Harold Silver, *A Social History of Education in England* (London: Methuen, 1973) p. 258.
6. Ibid., p. 324.
7. *International Encyclopaedia of Social Science*, Vol. 9.
8. Jerry White, *The Worst Street in North London: Campbell Bunk, Islington between the Wars* (London: Routledge & Kegan Paul, 1986) p. 8.
9. Ibid., pp. 107–9.
10. Ibid., pp. 130–1. The twopenny 'barrow' library often reverted to other goods such as cigarettes if profits were down. See J. Partington, *The Crowded Life of a Lancashire Lad* (Manchester, 1972) p. 99.
11. Carl N. Degler, *Out of Our Past: The Forces that Shaped Modern America* (New York: Harper [1959], 1984), p. 50; p. 105.
12. Ibid., p. 105.
13. James Bowen, *A History of Western Education*, Vol. 3 (London: Methuen, 1981), pp. 310–12.
14. Daniel Boorstin, *The Americans*, Vol. 2 (New York: Random House [1958], 1974) p. 30.
15. Alexis de Tocqueville, *Democracy in America*, ed. J.P. Mayer; trans. George Lawrence (London: Fontana, 1994) p. 474.
16. Ibid., p. 474; p. 470.
17. Ibid., p. 471.
18. Ibid.
19. Ibid.
20. Bowen, p. 444.

21. Ibid.
22. Ibid.; *International Encyclopaedia of Social Science*, op.cit.
23. H.L. Mencken, *The American Language* (New York: Alfred Knopf [1919], 1941) p. vi.
24. Ibid., p. 4.
25. Witherspoon, quoted in ibid., p. 5.
26. Ibid.
27. Webster, quoted in ibid., p. 10.
28. de Tocqueville, pp. 477–8.
29. Ibid., p. 478.
30. Philip S. Bagwell and G.E. Mingay, *Britain and America 1850–1939: a Study of Economic Change* (London: Routledge & Kegan Paul, 1970) p. 1.
31. Ibid., p. 2.
32. Ibid.
33. Ibid., p. 5.
34. Wallace Stevens, quoted in *Modern Poets on Modern Poetry*, ed. James Scully (London: Fontana, 1966) p. 155.
35. William Carlos Williams, 'In the American Grain', in eds Ronald Gottesman et al., *The Norton Anthology of American Literature*, Vol. 2 (New York: W.W. Norton, 1979) pp. 1458–9.
36. Ibid., p. 1460.
37. Charles Olson, in Scully, p. 278.
38. Peter Lamarque and Stein Hangom Olsen, *Truth, Fiction and Literature* (Oxford: Clarendon, 1994) p. 270.
39. Degler, pp. 326–7; *Encyclopaedia Americana*, Vol. 17.

CHAPTER 5: OUTLAWS AGAINST THE LAW BADGE

1. See Peter Linebaugh, *The London Hanged: Crime and Civil Society in the Eighteenth Century* (Harmondsworth: Penguin, 1993).
2. Ibid., p. 135.
3. Ibid., p. 169.
4. Patricia Hollis, *The Pauper Press: A Study in Working-Class Radicalism of the 1830s* (Oxford: Oxford University Press, 1970) p. 47.
5. Ibid.
6. Ibid.
7. Ibid., p. 48.
8. Linebaugh, op.cit., p. 39.
9. Ibid., pp. 7–8.
10. Ibid., p. 205.
11. E.S. Turner, *Boys Will Be Boys* (Harmondsworth: Penguin [1948], 1975) p. 53.
12. Ibid., p. 51.
13. Ibid., p. 52.
14. David Vincent, 'Reading in the Working Class Home', in John K. Walton and James Walvin eds, *Leisure in Britain 1780–1939* (Manchester: Manchester University Press, 1983) pp. 207–26 (p. 211).

15. Ibid., p. 210.
16. Ibid., p. 211.
17. Ibid.
18. See introduction in Clive Bloom ed., *Literature and Culture in Modern Britain*, Vol. 1 1900–1929 (Harlow: Longman, 1993).
19. Stephen Humphries, *Hooligans or Rebels? Oral History of Working-Class Childhood and Youth 1889–1939* (Oxford: Basil Blackwell, 1981) p. 34.
20. John Lawson and Harold Silver, *A Social History of Education in England* (London: Methuen, 1973) p. 193.
21. Ibid., p. 25.
22. See comments by William Cobbett in Lawson and Silver op.cit., p. 260.
23. Ibid.
24. E.P. Thompson, *The Making of the English Working Class* (London: Gollancz, 1980) p. 54.
25. Ibid., p. 56.
26. Thomas Boyle, *Black Swine in the Sewers of Hampstead* (London: Hodder & Stoughton, 1990) p. 22.
27. See David Vincent, art. cit., p. 223.
28. See Joseph McAleer, *Popular Reading and Publishing in Britain 1914–1950* (Oxford: Clarendon, 1992).
29. Ibid., p. 109.
30. R.C. Terry, *Victorian Popular Fiction 1860–80* (London: Macmillan, 1983) pp. 9, 11, 31. See also John St John, *William Heinemann: a Century of Publishing, 1890–1990* (London: Heinemann, 1990) pp. 10, 24, 37.
31. McAleer, op.cit., p. 114.
32. Deborah Cameron and Elizabeth Frazer, *The Lust to Kill* (London: Polity Press, 1989).
33. Ibid., p. 50.
34. Ibid.
35. *Modern Review* (Oct–Nov 1994) p. 5.
36. See Mary Cadogan, *Richmal Crompton: the Woman Behind William* (London: Allen & Unwin, 1986).
37. See David Trotter, *The English Novel in History 1895–1920* (London: Routledge, 1993).
38. Ibid., p. 151.
39. John St John, op.cit., p. 52.
40. Ibid.
41. Ibid., p. 50.
42. Ibid.
43. Quoted in Humphreys, op.cit., p. 43.
44. Ibid., p. 43.
45. See Michael Brake, *Comparative Youth Culture* (London: Routledge [1985], 1993).

CHAPTER 6: SMART LIKE US

1. Lawrence W. Levine, *Highbrow/Lowbrow: The Emergence of Cultural Hierarchy in America* (Cambridge Mass.: Harvard University Press, 1988) p. 233.
2. William Dean Howells, 'Novel Writing and Novel-Reading: an Impersonal Explanation', in Ronald Gottesman et al., eds, *The Norton Anthology of American Literature*, Vol. 2 (New York: W.W. Norton, 1979) p. 301.
3. Levine, p. 224.
4. I.A. Richard, *Principles of Literary Criticism* (London: Routledge [1924], 1976) pp. 25 and 195.
5. John Carey: *The Intellectuals and the Masses: Pride and Prejudice among the Literary Intelligentsia, 1880–1939* (London: Faber & Faber, 1992) p. 7.
6. Ibid., p. 6.
7. Ibid.
8. Harry Ritchie, *Success Stories: Literature and the Media in England, 1950–1959* (London: Faber & Faber, 1988) p. 4.
9. Ibid., p. 9.
10. Ibid., p. 14.
11. Ibid., p. 15.
12. Ibid., p. 19.
13. Ibid., p. 21.
14. For C.P. Snow's lecture and subsequent comments see, *The Two Cultures and a Second Look* (Cambridge: Cambridge University Press, 1965).
15. Ritchie, p. 15.
16. See Allan Bloom, *The Closing of the American Mind* (Harmondsworth: Penguin, 1988) and Harold Bloom, *The Western Canon* (London: Macmillan, 1995).
17. Alvin Kernan, *The Death of Literature* (New Haven: Yale University Press (1990) p. 6.
18. Robert Hughes, *Culture of Complaint: The Fraying of America* (New York: Oxford University Press, 1993) p. 103.
19. Kernan, p. 138.
20. Herbert I. Schiller, *Culture Inc.: The Corporate Takeover of Public Expressions* (New York: Oxford University Press, 1989) p. 33.
21. Paul Fussell, *BAD or, The Dumbing of America* (New York: Summit Books, 1991) pp. 59–60.
22. Richard Hoggart, *The Uses of Literacy* (Harmondsworth: Penguin [1957], 1990) pp. 247–8 and 250.
23. Q.D. Leavis, 'The Case of Miss Dorothy Sayers: *Gaudy Night* and *Busman's Honeymoon*' in *Scrutiny*, Vol. VI (1937).
24. Fussell, p. 13.
25. Q.D. Leavis, art. cit.
26. Ibid.
27. F.R. Leavis, 'The Literary Racket' in *Scrutiny*, Vol. 1 (1932).
28. For the full letter see *The Times Higher Education Supplement* (20. 11. 92).
29. Both plays can be found in James L. Smith ed., *Victorian Melodramas* (London: Dent, 1976).

30. Harriett Hawkins, *Classics and Trash* (Hassocks: Harvester/Wheat-sheaf, 1990) pp. 110–11.
31. Ibid., p. 111.
32. Martin Seymour-Smith, *Guide to Modern World Literature* (London: Macmillan, 1986) p. xxxiv.
33. Ibid., pp. xxxiv–xxxv.
34. Raymond Williams, *Towards 2000* (London: Chatto & Windus, 1983).
35. Levine, p. 7.
36. Peter Keating, *The Haunted Study: A Social History of the English Novel 1875–1914* (London: Secker & Warburg, 1989) pp. 350 and 354.
37. Geoffrey O'Brien, *Hardboiled America: The Lurid Years of Paperbacks* (New York: Van Nostrand Reinhold, 1981) pp. 5–6.
38. Ibid., pp. 94–5.
39. Eds Peter Humm, Paul Stigant and Peter Widdowson, *Popular Fictions: Essays in Literature and History* (London: Methuen, 1986) p. 5.
40. John G. Cawelti, *Adventure, Mystery and Romance* (Chicago: University of Chicago Press, 1976) pp. 1–2.
41. Cawelti, p. 3.
42. Colin Watson, *Snobbery with Violence* (Harmondsworth: Penguin, [1971], 1987); E.S. Turner, *Boys will be Boys* (Penguin [1948], 1976).
43. Stephen King, *Danse Macabre* (London: Futura, 1986).
44. Leslie A. Fielder, 'Towards a Definition of Popular Literature', in C.W.E. Bigsby ed., *Superculture* (London: Paul Elek, 1975) pp. 28–42 (p. 28).
45. Ibid., p. 30.
46. Ibid.
47. Introduction to Bigsby ed., pp. 24–5.
48. Ibid., p. 6.
49. Ibid.
50. Ibid., p. 15.
51. Walter Nash, *Language in Popular Fiction* (London: Routledge, 1990) pp. 1–2.
52. Ibid., pp. 2–3.
53. Christopher Pawling, *Popular Fiction/Social Change* (London: Macmillan, 1984) p. 12.
54. Ibid., p. 13.
55. Gina Wisker, *It's My Party: Reading Twentieth-Century Women's Writing* (London: Pluto, 1993) p. 4.
56. Derek Longhurst ed., *Gender, Genre and Narrative Pleasure* (London: Unwin Hyman, 1989) p. 5.
57. Humm, p. 11.
58. Cosmo Landesman in *Sunday Times* (14.11.93). *The Modern Review* was edited by Toby Young.

CHAPTER 7: LIVING IN TECHNICOLOR

1. Stan Lee quoted in Greg C. McCue with Clive Bloom, *Dark Knights: The New Comics in Context* (London: Pluto, 1993) p. 84. Brendan Behan recalled in 1958 how borstal boys, lacking books, would tell stories

called 'pictures' after their love of cinema. See Neil Philip ed., *The Penguin Book of English Folktales* (Harmondsworth: Penguin, 1985) p. xxx.

2. See, for examples, Anthony Delves, 'Popular Recreation & Social Conflict in Derby 1800–1850', in Eileen Yeo and Stephen Yeo, eds, *Popular Culture and Class Conflict 1590–1914* (Brighton: Harvester, 1981) chapter 4.

3. Cyril Pearl points out the restrictions put upon upper-class street activity during the late Victorian period. See Cyril Pearl, *The Girl with the Swansdown Seat: An Informal Report on Some Aspects of Mid Victorian Morality* (London: Robin Clark [1955], 1980).

4. John G. Cavelti, *Adventure, Mystery and Romance* (Chicago: Chicago University Press, 1976) p. 6.

5. Walter Nash, *Language in Popular Fiction* (London: Routledge, 1990) p. 8.

6. Vance Packard *The Hidden Persuaders* (Harmondsworth: Penguin [1957], 1960) p. 23.

7. Ibid., p. 29.

8. Ibid., p. 45.

9. Ron Goulart, *Over 50 Years of American Comic Books* (Lincolnwood, Ill.: Publications International, 1991) p. 195.

10. Ibid., p. 199.

11. Ibid., pp. 200–1.

12. McCue, pp. 29–30.

13. Ibid., pp. 30–1.

14. Ibid., p. 32.

15. Steve Holland, *The Mushroom Jungle: A History of Postwar Paperback Publishing* (Dilton Marsh, Wilts.: Zeon, 1993) p. 136.

16. Raymond Hoggart, *The Uses of Literacy* (Harmondsworth: Penguin [1957], 1990) pp. 258–9.

17. Holland, pp. 129–30.

18. Ibid., pp. 192–3.

19. Ibid., p. 135.

20. Ibid., p. 137.

21. Ibid., p. 147.

22. Ibid., p. 151.

23. Ibid., pp. 152–4.

24. Ibid., p. 157.

25. M. Montgomery Hyde, ed., *The Lady Chatterley's Lover Trial* (London: Bodley Head, 1990) pp. 4–5.

26. Geoffrey O'Brien, *Hardboiled America: The Lurid Years of Paperbacks* (New York: Van Nostrand Reinhold, 1981) p. 43.

27. Ibid., p. 42.

28. Henry James quoted in Sandor Gilman, *The Jew's Body* (London: Routledge, 1991) p. 31.

29. Pearl, p. 258.

30. Ibid., p. 261.

31. For a more fully developed argument see Clive Bloom ed., *Literature and Culture in Modern Britain* (Harlow: Longman, 1992) pp. 14–27.

32. See Jan Harold Brunvand, *The Vanishing Hitchhiker – Urban Legends and their Meanings* (London: Picador, 1981). The religious versions of the Vanishing Hitchhiker confirm rather than deny modern, urban semi-secular fears and superstitious attitudes behind much contemporary life. Equally the Mormon version of this tale confirms its relationship to modern religiosity (i.e. Mormonism) both capitalist and urban, rather than some left over from pre-urban, rural or medieval history.

33. See *Betty Page: Queen of Pin Up* (Cologne: Benedikt Taschen, 1993). After almost forty years of living in obscurity Page has recently emerged to sign the occasional autograph.

*CHAPTER 8: THE RIPPER WRITING

1. 'In appearance, a paper of the 1890s was a product substantially the same as our own . . . the phrase "new journalism" was first used by the poet Matthew Arnold of the lively work of the *Pall Mall Gazette* and its competitors in the late 1880s. This was indeed the seedbed of the twentieth century commercial popular press. . . . There was also a new group of evening papers circulating in London and going out aggressively for new readers. . . . It was these evening papers which first educated the morning papers into editorial policies suitable for the masses. Kennedy Jones and Alfred Harmsworth (later Lord Northcliffe) worked out their ideas for mass journalism for there was a new generation emerging in the years after the Great Exhibition of 1851 which had great curiosity but little education' – Anthony Smith, *The Newspaper: An International History* (London: Thames & Hudson, 1979) pp. 153–4.

2. Letters quoted by C.M. McCleod in *The Criminologist*, no. 9 (1968) 120–7.

3. Stephen Knight, *Jack the Ripper: The Final Solution* (London: Grafton, 1976).

4. Alexander Kelly, 'Ripperana and Ripperature', *The Assistant Librarian*, 1973, pp. 3–6.

5. Kim Newman in *Million*, March/June 1993, p. 20.

6. Ibid., p. 20.

7. Tony Bennett and Janet Woollacott, *Bond and Beyond: The Political Career of a Popular Hero* (London: Macmillan, 1987) p. 14.

8. Robert Harris, 'Selling Hitler in *The Media Trilogy* (London: Faber & Faber [1986], 1994) p. 579.

9. Shirley Harrison, *The Diary of Jack the Ripper*, (London: Smith Gryphon, 1993) p. ix and 178. For further discussion of the authenticity of the evidence see the *Evening Standard* (13.12.94) p. 12.

10. Brian Augustyn, Michael Mignola, P. Craig Russell, David Hornung, introduced by Robert Bloch, *Gotham by Gaslight* (New York: DC Comics, 1989).

11. Ibid., p. 1.

12. T.A. Critchley, *A History of Policy in England and Wales* (London: Constable, 1978) p. 161.
13. James Berry, *My Life as an Executioner*, ed. Jonathan Goodman (Newton Abbot: David & Charles, 1972).
14. Ibid., p. 1.
15. Ibid., p. 11.
16. Ibid., p. 66.
17. Ibid., p. 95.
18. Ibid.
19. Michel Foucault, *Discipline and Punish*, tr. Alan Sheridan (London: Allen Lane, 1977) p. 53.
20. Gordon Honeycomb, *The Murders of the Black Museum 1870–1970* (London: Hutchinson, 1982).
21. Foucault, *Discipline and Punish*, p. 57.
22. René Girand, *Violence and the Sacred*, tr. Patrick Gregory (Baltimore: Johns Hopkins University Press, 1977).
23. Ibid., p. 1.
24. Ibid.
25. Ibid., p. 2.
26. Ibid., p. 9.
27. Ibid., p. 12.
28. Ibid.
29. Ibid., p. 4.
30. Ibid., p. 8.
31. Ibid., p. 4.
32. René Girard, 'Myth and Ritual in Shakespeare: *A Midsummer Night's Dream*' in *Textual Strategies*, ed. Josué V. Harrari (London: Methuen, 1980) pp. 189–212.
33. See Stewart Evans and Paul Gainey, *The Lodger: the Arrest and Escape of Jack the Ripper* (London: Century, 1995) for the latest 'factual' accretion.

CHAPTER 9: WEST IS EAST

1. D.J. Enright, introduction to *The Mystery of Dr Fu Manchu* (London: J.M. Dent, 1985) p. vii. All quotations are then taken from this edition. *The Hand of Dr Fu Manchu* and *The Return of Dr Fu Manchu* and quoted from *Fu Manchu: Four Classic Novels* (Secausus, NJ: Citadel, 1983).
2. Enright, introduction, p. viii.
3. Ibid., pp. xiv–xv.
4. Colin Watson, *Snobbery with Violence* (London: Methuen, 1987) p. 15.
5. Ibid., p. 16.
6. Ibid., p. 158.
7. Ibid., p. 117.
8. Ibid., p. 44.
9. Cay Van Ash and Elizabeth Sax Rohmer, *Master of Villainy: A Biography of Sax Rohmer* (Bowling Green, OH: Bowling Green University Popular Press, 1972) p. 68.

10.   John Fisher, *Paul Daniels and the Story of Magic* (London: Cape, 1987) p. 4. My thanks to Clare Hudson of the Victoria and Albert Theatre Museum of London for help in locating this information.
11.   Van Ash and Sax Rohmer, *Master of Villainy*, pp. 32–3.
12.   Ibid., p. 115.
13.   Ibid., p. 114.
14.   Ibid.
15.   Ibid., p. 73.

CHAPTER 10: THIS REVOLTING GRAVEYARD

1.   Lin Carter, *Lovecraft: A Look behind the Cthulhu Mythos* (London: Panther, 1975) p. 21.
2.   Ibid.
3.   Colin Wilson, Introduction to George Hay ed., *The Necronomicon* (London: Corgi, 1980) p. 22.
4.   Ibid., p. 149.
5.   Quoted in David Punter, *The Literature of Terror* (London: Longman, 1980) p. 285.
6.   Carter, *Lovecraft*, pp. 35–6.
7.   Ibid., p. 23.
8.   Ibid., pp. 52–3
9.   Ibid., p. 82.
10.   Ibid., p. 56.
11.   Ibid., p. 57.
12.   Ibid., p. 58.
13.   Punter, *The Literature of Terror*, p. 285.
14.   Ibid., p. 282.
15.   Quoted in George E. Mowry ed., *The Twenties* (Englewood Cliffs, NJ: Prentice-Hall, 1963) p. 155.
16.   Ibid., pp. 137–9.
17.   Ibid., p. 146.
18.   Quoted in Carter, *Lovecraft*, p. 82.
19.   Ibid., p. 129.
20.   Stephen King, *Danse Macabre* (London: Futura, 1986) p. 45.
21.   Ibid., p. 17.
22.   Punter, *The Literature of Terror*, p. 288.
23.   Carter, *Lovecraft*, p. 25.

CHAPTER 11: HARRY AND MARIANNE

1.   Trevor H. Hall, E.J. Dingwall and K.M. Goldney, *The Haunting of Borley Rectory: A Critical Survey of the Evidence* (London: Duckworth, 1956); Trevor H. Hall, *Search For Harry Price* (London: Duckworth, 1978). All biographical details of Harry Price's life are from Hall unless otherwise stated.

2. Harry Price, *'The Most Haunted House in England'* (London: Longman, 1940) hereinafter referred to as *MHHE; The End of Borley Rectory* (London: Harrap, 1946) hereinafter referred to as *EBR*.
3. Belchamp St Paul appears in 'Count Magnus' by M.R. James, in *Casting the Runes and Other Ghost Stories* (Oxford: Oxford University Press, 1987).
4. Paul Tabori, *Harry Price: The Biography of a Ghost-Hunter* (Worthing: Athenaeum, 1950).
5. See previous chapter.
6. See Hall ch. 7 and ch. 9.
7. See Price's chronology, *EBR* p. 335.
8. Robert Wood, *The Widow of Borley: A Psychical Investigation* (London: Duckworth, 1992) p. 11.
9. Ibid., p. 18.
10. Ibid.
11. Ibid., p. 66.
12. Ibid., p. 117.

CHAPTER 12: THE DEATH OF CULT FICTION AND THE END OF THEORY

1. It would be tedious to catalogue all the references to other authors in King's fiction. A perfect example rests in his tribute to Daphne du Maurier in *The Dark Half*. In both *Misery* and *The Dark Half*, King makes a point of featuring references to Ernest Hemingway. Again, King's interest in authorial ancestors and author *Doppelgängers* even extends to his 'borrowing' a character from another writer. See *The Dark Half* (London: Guild, 1989) afterword p. 412 facing. Alexis Machine is taken from *Dead City* by Shane Stevens.
2. See George Orwell, 'Raffles and Miss Blandish' in *Decline of the English Murder and other Essays* (Harmondsworth: Penguin [1944], 1988) pp. 63–79.
3. For a further discussion of the reciprocity between high and low culture see Andrew Ross, *No Respect: Intellectuals and Popular Culture* (London: Routledge, 1989) pp. 3 and 5.

> While it speaks enthusiastically to the feelings, desires, aspirations, and pleasures of ordinary people, popular culture is far from being a straightforward or unified expression of popular interests. It contains elements of disrespect, and even opposition to structures of authority, but it also contains 'explanations,' as I have suggested, for the maintenance of respect for those structures of authority. . . .
> To be truthful, we ought to admit that there is no such thing as a history from above, of intellectuals, or a history from below, of popular culture, although many such histories, of either kind, have been and will continue to be written. On the contrary, it is increasingly important (especially today, when the once politicized

divisions between high and low culture make less and less sense in a culture that ignores these divisions with official impunity) to consider what is dialectical about the historically fractious relationship between intellectuals and popular culture.

4.   J. Hoberman, 'Ed Wood . . . Not', in *Sight and Sound* (May 1995) p. 13.
5.   Ibid., p. 13.
6.   Ibid., p. 14.
7.   Arthur Kroker, *The Possessed Individual: Technology and Postmodernity* (London: Macmillan, 1992) pp. 18–19.
8.   Valerie Walkerdine, 'Dreams from an Ordinary Life', in Liz Heron ed., *Truth, Dare or Promise: Girls Growing Up in the 50s* (London: Virago, 1985) p. 76.
9.   Richard Wagner quoted in John Deathridge and Carl Dahlhaus, *The New Grove Wagner* (London: Macmillan, 1984) pp. 70–1.
10. Luis Buñuel quoted in Jean Vigo, *Un Chien Andalou* (London: Faber & Faber, 1994) p. v.
11. Ibid., p. ix.

Index

262

Index

FRAGILE HERITAGE

FRAGILE HERITAGE

Sara Hylton

ARROW

Arrow Books Limited
20 Vauxhall Bridge Road, London SW1V 2SA

An imprint of the Random Century Group

London Melbourne Sydney Auckland Johannesburg
and agencies throughout the world

First published in Great Britain by Century 1989
Arrow edition 1992

1 3 5 7 9 10 8 6 4 2

Printed and bound in Germany by
Elsnerdruck, Berlin

ISBN 0 09 974490 2

'Tis all a Chequer-Board of Nights and Days
Where Destiny with Men for Pieces plays;
Hither and thither moves, and mates, and slays,
And one by one back in the Closet lays.

from the *Rubaiyat* of Omar Khayyám

BOOK 1

CHAPTER 1

Rain lay soft on the wind like a caress, soft summer rain that clung to the beech leaves as though reluctant to fall to the grass, so gentle that it turned the village into an ethereal place, a fairytale mirage obscuring the harsh lines of the housetops and the squat tower of the church.

I sat on a stile by the side of the lane with my eyes glued on the village school waiting for Kitty McGuire, and I began to grow anxious. I had been the first to emerge from the school and couldn't have missed Kitty, I felt sure. Indeed she usually dawdled or was so engrossed in conversation that she was the last to leave, but the single chime of the bell in the church tower told me it was already half past four and I would have to go soon or I would not be home before my father.

Through the mist I could see that the churchyard was empty apart from old Ned loping towards the church gates accompanied by his son, both of them armed with the shovels they had used to fill in the grave of Mrs Morrison who had died over the weekend. They had only just come through the gates when I saw the vicar hurrying after them, his face bent against the rain, his gown flapping round his ankles.

My father, the sexton, would be the next to leave after locking up the church and seeing that everything was tidy, and anxiously I looked up the road towards the school. It was time to go, something had detained Kitty and I didn't want to encounter Father in the lane. Over the last three years, ever since the McGuires had come to live in the village, he had made it abundantly clear that he didn't approve of Kitty or her folks, and even less of my friendship with her.

Sadly I scrambled down from the stile and after a swift glance towards the school I turned to walk towards the

9

village. Coming through the mist was a small figure – Michael, Kitty's young brother. He walked slowly with his hands thrust deep into the pockets of his thin inadequate jacket, a shrimp of a boy with his shock of ginger hair and a gamin face liberally sprinkled with freckles. He looked a lot like Kitty and when I smiled at him brightly he said, "Ave ye seen our Kitty? Mi mother's sent mi up 'ere to look for 'er.'

'I've been waiting for 'er, Michael, she's still at the schoolhouse.'

'Well I've got ter go up ter the Masons' 'ouse ter tell'er mi mother won't be there in't mornin'. If ye see our Kitty will ye tell 'er mi father's gone?'

'Gone!' I echoed stupidly.

'Ay, gone. 'E died just 'afore a got 'ome. Will ye be after tellin' 'er, Ellen?'

Before I could gather my scattered wits he was away, trotting up the road and quickly becoming hidden by the floating mist.

Paddy McGuire had been coughing his life away ever since he came to the village. In the summer he had done labouring work of one sort or another to help support his wife and eleven children but in the winter he had taken to his bed while Ann McGuire, his long-suffering wife, scrubbed her fingers to the bone at Mrs Mason's big house.

I was more than reluctant to break the news to Kitty, but all the same I turned back towards the schoolhouse.

The stout wooden door leading into the main hall was still open but inside there was silence and I stood in the doorway listening until I heard footsteps in one of the classrooms beyond. Gingerly I opened the door a fraction, wide enough to see Kitty standing alone before the dais, her head lowered in wrapt contemplation, and with such a look of innocent appeal it was hard to imagine that she had been guilty of a sin horrendous enough to have been detained after all the other children had gone home. I was about to call to her when Mrs Grundy's voice came from behind me, harsh enough to make me almost jump out of my skin.

10

'What are you doing here Ellen Adair? It's half an hour since you left to go home.'

I spun round to find the teacher staring down at me with an annoyed expression.

'Please, Mrs Grundy, I've got to see Kitty. Can she come home now?'

'Indeed she can't. She's to stay there an hour or until I lock up the school for the night. Now get off home at once, I don't want your parents thinking I'm responsible for sending you home at this time.'

When I didn't immediately dash off into the mist her frown deepened.

'Well Ellen, what are you waiting for?'

'Please, Miss, I must tell Kitty 'er father's gone, she's wanted at 'ome.'

'What do you mean her father's gone?'

'He's dead, Miss, just this afternoon.'

She opened the door wider and I could see that Kitty was looking at us with wide anxious eyes. Mrs Grundy said firmly, 'Did you hear that, Kitty McGuire, were you listening?'

She nodded mutely and in a kinder voice Mrs Grundy said, 'Come here, child.'

Kitty advanced and now I could see the tears on her cheeks and her trembling lips.

'You should have said your father was ill, Kitty, I wouldn't have kept you in even though there are times when I don't know what to do with you. Get your things and run off home. And you too, Ellen Adair.'

In silence I waited while Kitty shrugged her arms into her coat, then we set off down the lane. We had almost reached the village street when she said, 'Did our Micky say anythin' else about mi father, Ellen?'

'No.'

'Nor mi mam?'

'No, Kitty.'

'Will ye come as far as our house with mi? I'll not be askin' you to come inside.'

It was late, my father would be home and I was desper-

11

ately afraid of his anger. He did not rage like Kitty's father had done after one of his drinking bouts, rages that were sudden and frequent and quickly over. My father was not a drinker, but he could sit white-faced and tight-lipped for hours behind a wall of silence that encompassed us all, including my mother. I had never known her to answer him back even when he was being most unjust and horrible.

I stole a look at Kitty's face as we trudged through the rain. It was pale and anxious and I hadn't the heart to leave her to go home alone.

She took hold of my hand in a grateful gesture and we turned up the narrow lane towards the McGuires' house.

It was a farm labourer's cottage, two up and two down, and I had often wondered how they managed in the two tiny bedrooms and the one parlour and kitchen. Kitty had once told me that the older children slept head to toe in two double beds, with another for the younger children placed in their parents' bedroom, and I felt how lucky I was to be living in the sexton's house belonging to the church where we had three bedrooms and an attic.

We stopped outside the gate looking at the cottage with its drawn blinds and I shuddered thinking about Paddy McGuire lying dead in that front bedroom.

'I wish I didn't 'ave to go in,' Kitty said quietly, 'it'll be days to the funeral.'

Just then the door opened and Mrs Peel came out. She was the village midwife, who also laid out the dead. Catching sight of us standing at the gate, she said, 'Do ye know about yer father then, Kitty McGuire?'

'Yes, Mrs Peel.'

'Well yer'd best get in there an' comfort yer mother, he's lyin' there right peaceful now. He's gone to 'is rest after much sufferin'.'

I'd heard these were the words she used to all those recently bereaved. We stood aside as she bustled down the path, then in a brisk voice she said to me, 'You'd best get off 'ome, Ellen, there's nothin' ye can do 'ere.'

At that I took to my heels and ran, never slowing until I reached the vicarage and the path leading up to the church.

I could see our house now, a square ugly building surrounded by a large garden. My father didn't like gardening
so it was left to my brothers and me to weed and tend it.
Dismay and trepidation filled my heart when I saw him
standing at the door. He was holding his big silver watch,
and on his face was the look I had come to dread.

As I reached his side he stared down at me in tight-
lipped anger, then flinging open the front door he said,
'Hang your wet clothes in the lobby and wait at the dining
room door.'

I waited there while he hung his coat on the stand behind
the door, then with long strides he came towards me. I
followed him into the dining room where the rest of the
family sat at the table, and Mother looked at me anxiously
and started to ask, 'Where have you been . . .'

She was cut short abruptly by him saying, 'Get on with
your meal, Mary. I shall question her later.' Then he told
me, 'Stand there behind Luke until we've finished our meal,
then you shall tell me why ye were kept in at school.'

'Father, I wasn't . . .'

'Not another word, girl. Like I said I'll speak to ye later.'

I didn't dare to say I was hungry, that every morsel I saw
the rest of them place in their mouths gave me an actual
pain, I simply had to stand behind my brother's chair in
silence. Once I caught Peter's sympathetic glance across the
table, and watched Naomi put out her tongue at me before
asking Father for a second helping of gooseberry pudding.

When the last crumb had been eaten Father said, 'You
may all leave the table now.'

We were on a strict rota to help with clearing the table
and washing the dishes, not one of us was spared; but it
was not my turn and I remained standing while Sarah and
Mark went about their task and Mother disappeared with
the rest of them into the living room.

When the door closed behind them my father took his
seat at the table with the Holy Bible in front of him, motion-
ing me to stand before him.

'Well,' he said sternly, 'why did your teacher find it
necessary to keep you in school?'

13

'She didn't, Father, I was out before anybody else this afternoon.'

'Then is it too much to ask you to tell me where you've been and who you've been with?'

So I told him about my meeting with Michael McGuire, about the death of his father and my promise to walk all the way home with Kitty, but there was no softening of his stern features, no compassion for the deceased Paddy McGuire or his grieving family. If anything the frown became more pronounced.

'I don't like your association with that family, Ellen, I've made it quite plain in the past. Shanty Irish they are and Roman Catholics into the bargain. No doubt the Bull's Head's lost its best customer now that McGuire's gone but you'll have no more truck with 'em if I 'ave to keep ye locked up for the rest o' the week. Am I makin' miself plain, Miss Ellen?'

'Kitty's mi best friend, Father, and her mother's a real nice lady. Wouldn't it be more Christian to ask them into the house and let 'em see how sorry we are?'

'Hold your tongue, girl. There'll be no McGuires in this house and if I hear of you being in their company again I'll pack you off to your Aunt Liza. She'll know what to do with ye.'

Aunt Liza was Father's half-sister and during the time she had spent with us waiting for her shop in the Dales to be decorated, she terrified me. She was tall and thin and angular, a female version of my father but with a tongue even more caustic, and she had thought nothing of grabbing my hair and pulling it to emphasize her point.

'Now go up to your room and stay there until breakfast,' he said. 'I want your lamp out in five minutes and there's to be no readin' in bed. I'll send one o' the girls up to see that mi orders are carried out. Now be off with you.'

'But I'm hungry, Father, I've had nothing to eat.'

'And yer not gettin' anything to eat. This is yer punishment for being disobedient. In future I want you straight home from school at four o'clock and on yer own. No more Kitty McGuire, do you hear me?'

'Yes, Father.'

I passed in front of him when he opened the door, and fled. With shaking fingers I lit the lamp in the bedroom I shared with two of my sisters and after undressing crept between the chill sheets. For a long time I lay staring up into the darkness wishing something dire would happen to my father – or to me, I didn't much care which.

Once before I had been sent to bed without supper, and when the house was still and I thought the family were in bed, I had crept downstairs hoping to find food in the larder. My father had found me perched on the kitchen table eating bread and butter and then had followed two long days of near starvation and the lashing of his tongue. Only once my mother remonstrated with him over his harsh treatment, and she too earned his displeasure by long sulky silences. Then I began to see why she allowed him to have his own way because those silences punished us all.

This time I would not attempt to creep downstairs when the rest of them retired, I would lie hungry and sleepless until breakfast. Tomorrow was Saturday when Kitty and I would normally walk up on to the fells or linger around the stalls at the market held in the main street of Marsdale, spending our pocket money. Kitty received twopence a week from Mrs Mason for helping her mother carry the shopping basket up the hill, and I received twopence from the vicar's wife for collecting her groceries. Kitty got nothing from her parents because they had none to spare, and Father said we were fed and clothed and that should be enough.

We spent our twopences on sweets, coconut ice and brightly coloured turnovers. I liked these best because they contained bits of cheap jewellery, a silver-coloured ring with a glass stone, or a tiny gold-coloured chain, which needless to say I was never able to wear in the presence of Father.

He had forbidden me to see Kitty ever again, but somehow I would. Not perhaps while her father lay dead in the house, but afterwards, even if I had to lie and cheat so that Father wouldn't know.

There was a soft tap on the bedroom door and I sat up, watching it open with hope-filled eyes. It was my brother

15

Peter, a year younger than me and my favourite amongst the lot of them.

He held a cautioning finger up to his lips and carefully closed the door before coming to sit on my bed.

'I've brought ye two slices of bread and an apple, Ellen. I've quartered the apple and taken the core out so ye can eat it without leavin' anythin' ter show yer've 'ad it. Mi mother buttered the bread for ye.'

'Did mi father see her do it?'

'No, 'e's in the dinin' room wi' some o' the women fro' the church. I reckon 'e'll be there for a while.'

'What time is it?'

'Nigh on eight o'clock.'

I wolfed the bread and the apple. I would have given anything for a glass of milk or a mug of tea but I couldn't ask Peter for that, so instead I gasped angrily, 'What am I goin' to do about Kitty, Peter? She's mi friend, I can't not see her any more.'

He stared at me solemnly. He was a nice-looking boy with blond hair and honest straight eyes, and my question troubled him, I could tell.

'I don't know, Ellen. Ye know what mi father's like, 'e hates the McGuires.'

'But why, what have they ever done to 'im?'

'Nothin, but 'e's like that. Look 'ow 'e hated old Mr Pierce coz he went to the pub every Saturday, and the Philbys coz they were Chapel instead o' Church.'

'I thought religion was supposed to draw us together not pull us apart.'

'But it does, doesn't it, Ellen? He'd like mi to be a parson when I grow up, I've heard 'im talkin' to the vicar about it. But where would we ever get the money to send mi to college? The vicar said as much.'

I stared at him in astonishment.

'Do ye want to be a vicar, Peter?'

'I don't know.'

Suddenly a smile spread over his face and his eyes twinkled merrily. 'I wouldn't mind livin' in a house like the

16

vicarage wi' a nice garden. Sides 'e really only works on Sunday or when there's weddins, funerals and christenins.'

'He's allus writin' his sermons, mi father says, an' folk are allus goin' up to the vicarage to ask his advice about someat or other. Could you like doin' all that?'

'Well o' course not, but I'll never be a vicar, Ellen, we 'aven't got the money. The vicar went to a good school then 'e went to the university. He knows Greek and Latin; where would I ever learn things like that?'

'What will ye do, Peter? Another year an' you'll be leavin' school.'

'What'll you be doin? Yer'll be leavin' school 'afore me.'

'I know what I'd like ter do. I'd like to get away fro' this place and mi father. I'd like ter go to a big city and work in a big shop sellin' furs and things.'

'What sort o' things?'

'The sort o' things rich women wear. Kitty showed mi some pictures out of a book Mrs Mason's daughter sent her fro' York, lace an' georgette, lovely frocks that sweep the floor, ermine coats, and emeralds round their throats and in their ears. I'll never 'ave 'em for miself but it'd be lovely to 'andle 'em and sell 'em to others.'

'Yer've about as much chance o' doin that, our Ellen, as I 'ave of bein' a parson. Besides, mi father'd never let ye leave the village.'

'When I'm old enough 'e'll not be able to stop mi.'

'Ye do talk a lot o' rubbish, Ellen, but yer fun, I'll say that for ye. I'd better be goin', I don't want 'im findin' me here. I'm sorry I couldn't bring somethin' a bit more appetizing.'

'Thanks Peter, yer've saved mi life.'

I watched him letting himself gingerly out of the room, then I lay down amongst my pillows and gave myself up to the imagination which helped me to survive. I had my dreams of beautiful clothes and handsome men, of some distant future in a home where I was loved, but my childhood was never obsessed with Kitty's longing for jewels and furs, in those days it was sufficient for me to grow up quickly in order to get away from my father and his restrictive influence.

18

CHAPTER 2

The events of that night were with me all over the weekend.
I did not see Kitty round the village and when I
accompanied Mother to the market much of the talk was
of Paddy McGuire's death.

There was no Catholic church in Marsden and the
funeral would have to be held in a neighbouring village,
which had the only one for miles around. We heard that it
was to take place the following Tuesday so I didn't think
Kitty would be at the school until Wednesday at least.

'Good job Mrs McGuire's got that place up at the
Masons',' Mrs Jones confided to Mother. 'Mrs Mason
doesn't pay much but I reckon she gets plenty butter an'
eggs, vegetables too no doubt.'

'Poor woman,' Mother said, 'she doesn't look as though
she gets much in the way o' food, she's that thin.'

'Oh ay, scrawny she is, but wouldn't you be with a baby
every year and every one o' them wantin' feedin'? Pulled
down she was, wi' 'er 'usband allus in the Bull's Head an'
no doubt spendin' all 'is money on booze.'

'When did Paddy McGuire ever earn anythin' proper?
Labourin' 'e was, an' ailin' most o' the time in the winter.
I'm surprised the farmer ever took 'im back. What were
they doin' over 'ere anyway, why didn't they stay in Ireland
where they belonged?'

'They said there was little or no work in Ireland.'

'Well there's barely enough 'ere for our men let alone
shanty Irish.'

On and on it went while I stood patiently beside my
mother clutching a basket filled with vegetables and wishing
with all my heart they would leave the McGuires alone.

On the way home I was so quiet that Mother asked softly,
'You're all right aren't you, Ellen? There's influenza about.'

'I'm all right, Mother.'

'Don't take it hard about last night, love, your father's only talkin' to ye for yer own good. He only wants what's best for all of ye.'

'I don't see that sendin' mi to bed without supper and stoppin' mi seein' Kitty's doin' mi much good, Mother.'

'He thinks she's a bad influence on ye, Ellen. She's a little madam wi' that red hair and that sharp tongue of 'ers, and I've 'eard her mother say she's a hard one ter manage.'

'She's allus been nice ter me. She's such fun, Mother. I can laugh at all the things she says and she's never mean or catty like some o' the girls.'

Mother sighed. 'I don't like trouble in the 'ouse, Ellen. I don't like ter see yer father sittin' starin' at his food wi' never a word ter say to the cat an' all of us feelin' that miserable. 'E's not a bad man, Ellen, 'e's just tryin' te do 'is best wi' what we've got.'

I said nothing, but I didn't agree with her. I thought my father was a horrid little man, all religion and no Christianity, parsimonious, mouthing prayers and platitudes that were as restrictive as they were cruel, and I felt sure the good Lord could see right through him for the mean-spirited person he was.

'When ye sees yer father at supper you'll be respectful, Ellen, for my sake,' she said, eyeing me anxiously.

'Yes, Mother. I'm allus respectful, I never mean ter make 'im angry. I reckon he picks on me and I never know why.'

'Oh Ellen, o' course he doesn't pick on ye, he just wants yer to grow up decent, wi' the right set o' values.'

I had values even if they weren't my father's. I believed they were more honest than his – but I kept my opinion to myself.

I didn't see Kitty until Wednesday morning, after her father's funeral. Father had walked with us to the school that morning – largely, I felt sure, so that he could see me going in to school with my sisters instead of waiting for Kitty as I usually did.

I heard some of the other children talking about the funeral.

'Only one coach after the hearse,' Martha Longstaffe

20

said, 'and only Mrs McGuire and three o' the older children in it. Mi mother said the rest o' the McGuires ran wild in the street all afternoon.'

'There weren't many flowers,' her friend said, 'only a bunch on top o' the coffin an' two wreaths. I wonder who sent them.'

'Like as not Mrs Mason an' their next-door neighbour, out o' Christian charity I expect.'

I ground my teeth in anger. There wasn't much of Christian charity in any of them, and I entered the classroom and went to sit at my desk with deep anger in my heart. Kitty wasn't there, and Mrs Grundy had begun the first lesson before she appeared.

I could tell that she had been hurrying from her rosy cheeks and the riot of red curls that had escaped her hair ribbon. There was a tear on the sleeve of her blouse and mud on her skirt, and Mrs Grundy looked at her with some distaste.

'You're late, Kitty McGuire. What have you to say for yourself?' she demanded.

'I'm sorry, Mrs Grundy, I ran all the way here, I did.'

'Have you been fighting with somebody?'

Kitty stood without speaking while a dull flush coloured her cheeks.

'Well, have you?' Mrs Grundy said sternly.

'I hit Jimmy O'Reilly.'

'Why?'

'For sayin' mi father owed 'is father some money an' mi mother shouldn't be let ter keep the cottage. I wish oi'd hit 'im a whole lot harder. Sure and didn't mi father 'elp 'im 'ome drunk every Saturday noight?'

Mrs Grundy's expression didn't relax. 'I suppose Jimmy O'Reilly tore your blouse? Your mother isn't going to be too pleased about that.'

Angry tears filled Kitty's eyes. 'Oi'll 'ave ter mend it. It's a new blouse, foive and sixpence it cost mi mother fro' the market an' now that rotten boy's ruined it.'

'It might teach you a lesson not to hit out at anybody who says something you don't like, Kitty. There should be dig-

21

nity and restraint in your behaviour, it can be far more cutting than a taste of the fisticuffs.'

'Oi gave 'im a black eye oi did, an' he deserved it.'

'Go to your desk and attend to your lessons. Thanks to you we've lost half an hour.'

Meeting Kitty's eyes I grinned and received a grin in return, and Mrs Grundy snapped, 'That'll do, Ellen Adair. Now settle down, all of you.'

I was with Kitty in the playground when Naomi came up to us and said, 'I'll tell Father I've seen you with Kitty McGuire.'

I was so enraged I grabbed hold of her pigtail and hissed, 'You do and I'll not give you mi pink frock with the blue flowers on it.'

She yelped, then with round eyes said, 'I didn't know you were goin' to give it to me.'

'Well I won't if you tell him, I'll give it our Mary instead.'

She ran out of reach and tossing her dark head said, 'I'll think about it,' before running away to join her classmates.

'What did she mean, Ellen, she'd tell yer father she saw you talkin' to me?' Kitty demanded. 'Is it that he's told ye not to talk to me?'

'Oh Kitty, I wasn't going to take any notice of 'im, 'onest, but 'e was cross that night I was late home from school. He sent mi to bed without any supper.'

'Didn't ye explain ye'd bin waitin' fer me?'

'Yes, an' that made 'im a whole lot crosser.'

'Then ye shouldn't be talkin' to me, Ellen Adair, ye should be doin' what yer father asked.'

'I don't agree with him, Kitty. Sometimes I think I hates him fer the things he says. I wish I could go away, some-where where I wouldn't have to see 'im every day of mi life and listen to 'im goin' on an' on about people an' everything.'

'Where would ye go if ye left 'ere? Be sensible, Ellen, yer whole loife's 'ere, it's me who should be goin' away. We've never belonged 'ere, never since we came.'

We were both close to tears. In my heart I felt I had betrayed her, and more so when she tossed her red head and ran across the yard, leaving me staring after her. That night she was the first out of school and ran off without waiting for me. I waited for Peter to catch me up so that we could walk down the lane together.

'She ran and left ye then?' he said philosophically.

So I told him about Naomi and our words during playtime, and he said seriously, 'P'rhaps it's for the best 'til the storm wi Father blows over. At least if he's waitin' for us 'e'll see yer doin' what he asked.'

'It's Kitty 'erself who's makin' me, Peter.'

'Ye should be glad, Ellen. 'Ere's Father comin' to meet us.'

Sure enough he came striding down the street with set purpose, and Naomi ran to meet him, taking his hand and laughing up into his face.

'If she tells 'im I was with Kitty I'll kill 'er,' I said angrily. But Naomi knew which side of her bread was buttered, and she had her eye on my pink dress. I hadn't intended to part with it, it was my prettiest dress even if it was a little tight for me and a bit too short. Now however I would have to keep my promise even when I had little faith that she wouldn't tell him once the dress was in her hands.

If the truth was known I didn't much like Naomi, she was the one sister I had little in common with, pert and cheeky, and very much my father's daughter. She was his favourite and could bring the smiles to his face when none of the rest of us could, and that night as I met her eyes across the dining table she smiled and her eyes grew sly and secretive.

In some glee she said, 'I got an A from Mrs Pilkington for mi readin', Father. She says I'm the best reader in the class.'

'Yer arithmetic's not up ter much,' Peter said to my utmost joy.

'Don't deflate the child,' Father snapped. 'I'm pleased about your readin', Naomi. There's no reason why you shouldn't 'elp Naomi with 'er sums, Peter.'

'I've got mi own homework te do,' Peter said.

'You'll help 'er when you've done it then,' Father snapped.

In the days that followed it was Kitty who avoided me but I knew why – she didn't want me to get into trouble with Father on her account.

Sunday was his busiest day with church in the morning, Sunday school in the afternoon and then church in the evening. More often than not it was quite late when he had finished tidying up and putting the church to rights before locking up, and it was Sunday I looked forward to most.

I sat with Mother and the family in church where Father pompously performed his duties with more verve than the vicar himself, but after Sunday school the rest of the afternoon was free. I knew that Kitty invariably took some of her younger brothers and sisters to the park and I couldn't wait to get out of the cold draughty schoolroom fast enough to join her.

'You shouldn't be comin' to see me, Ellen,' she admonished. 'Yer father's not goin' to loike it.'

'He's not goin' to know, is he? Who's ter tell 'im?'

'Well, yer sister Naomi fer one.'

'Well then we won't stay 'ere, we'll go up on to the fells. It's nicer up there.'

We made our escape before my sister and her cronies arrived, and up on the windswept moor Kitty opened her heart to me while her brothers and sisters scampered over the short thick grass.

'We're goin' to 'ave to split up, Ellen, mi mother can't afford te keep us all with what little she gets fro' the Masons. Our Mary and Joe's goin' to mi aunt in Merton and she's puttin' up the baby an' young Terry for adoption. It's breakin' 'er heart, Ellen, but there's no way she can keep 'em and go out te work.'

'What about you, Kitty?'

'Mi aunt sez when I leave school she can get mi a job workin' in a seamen's hostel near the docks in Liverpool.'

'What sort of a job will that be?'

'Servin' food and makin' the beds, I expect. I'll be livin'

24

in so whatever they pay mi'll be mine, some te keep and some te send 'ome.'

'It sound horrible.'

Her eyes filled with tears. 'It's a long way from ermine an' emeralds, to be sure. Do ye remember 'ow we used to say that one day we'd 'ave 'em? Well sure an' I don't think it'll ever happen. We were clutchin' at moonbeams, Ellen, an' I for one 'ave got to learn some sense. Mi father's gone, not that 'e ever tipped much up at 'ome, but at least 'e took some o' the weight off mi mother's shoulders.'

'Your mother must be very sad, Kitty, 'avin' to part with the little ones. Do they know?'

'Oh, there'll be a lot o' wailin' an' anguish but there's no way we can avoid it. 'Ave ye thought what you're goin' to do when ye've left school?'

'No. Mi father'll be thinkin' o' something respectable but there's not much work in the village. I only ope 'e doesn't send me off to Aunt Liza's.'

'Where's she, then?'

'Up in the Dales somewhere. She 'as a little shop, draper's it is. I've allus thought I'd like te work in a shop, but not 'ers. I couldn't work in 'ers.'

'Do ye think he moight be sendin' you there?'

''E might, Kitty. Wi' mi father, anythin's possible.'

CHAPTER 3

For weeks my luck held. We exchanged greetings only at school and we seldom let others see us together, but at the weekends we were together roaming the countryside and giving the market a wide berth.

My father believed he had won, and one evening after supper he said, 'I don't suppose you know that your friends the McGuires are splitting up. If Patrick McGuire had been a better provider they'd 'ave had a bit o' money put by for a time such as this, but I do 'ear the two youngest children are to be put up for adoption or in some 'ome or other and Miss Kitty's bein' sent off to Liverpool to work as soon as she's left the school. I might add I'm mighty glad about that, she was a bad influence on you, Ellen. Since you stopped seein' her you've been a better girl, more obedient and nowhere near as flighty.'

I sat with bowed head and Mother said anxiously, 'I'm sorry for the McGuires, Thomas, it must be heartbreakin' for the poor woman to 'ave ter' part with the children.'

'Well in another couple of months Ellen 'ere can say goodbye to Kitty McGuire, and good riddance.'

My hands were clenched tightly together under cover of the tablecloth and I very near choked on a crust of bread so great was my desire to call my father a humbug. Reading his Bible and saying his prayers and about as much Christian charity in his heart as the cat sleeping on the hearth rug.

Christmas came around and as usual on the last day of school there was a party when we all wore our Sunday-best clothes and took fruit and mince pies and anything else our families could spare to eat in the big hall where we were expected to sing carols and recite poetry. The girls in my family took mince pies and the three boys took pasties.

On our way to the school Naomi whispered, 'I wonder

what the McGuire girls'll take, and them as poor as church mice?'

Needless to say I ignored her but I remember that all that day I was happy, singing my head off with the other children, and sampling the different foods we had taken. I loved singing although I had no great voice, not like Kitty who had a hauntingly sweet voice, low and melodious.

I was so enchanted with the proceedings I had little thought of danger as we walked home that afternoon in the bitter cold wind that swept straight off the moors.

Kitty pulled her thin coat round her and shivered because under it she was wearing her best dress which unfortunately was a summer cotton and quite unsuitable for a winter's day.

'It's early, Ellen, yer father'll still be seein' to his duties at the church. Would you like to come 'ome with mi and 'ave a word with mi mother? She'll be that glad.'

So with only a brief glance I walked on past the lane where our house stood. Mrs McGuire was just letting herself into the house when we arrived, and smiling a welcome she held the door open for us.

In the grate a few pathetic cinders burned dully and from the look of the dark little room it was evident there would be no Christmas decorations. When Kitty saw me looking round she said, 'We 'ave a Christmas tree but I 'aven't 'ad a chance to put it up yet. I don't know if I'll bother.'

'Oh but ye should, Kitty, it'll make the place look more cheerful.'

'It's a mangy little imitation tree, Ellen, mi father found it on a rubbish heap two years since an' 'e brought it 'ome. I've done a bit at it to make it look a bit more presentable but we've nothin' to hang on it this year and it'll only look worse standin' in the winder on its own.'

We'd been given small packets of sweets at the school, and an apple and orange each. Now eagerly I profferred mine. 'Take these, Kitty, we'll 'ave others. The vicar's wife allus sends us sweets and nuts and raisins. Honestly, Kitty, I don't really want these.'

27

'Well of course ye do, and didn't yer eyes light up like stars when they were given to us at the party?'

'Please, Kitty, I want you to 'ave them. I'll be upset if you don't take 'em, they're mi Christmas present to you.'

She took them gratefully and then hurried upstairs to look for the tree.

It was indeed a sad little tree with its branches flattened, and it was none too steady on the table. We both sat back to look at it and Kitty said, 'Ye see what I mean, Ellen, it's not worth decoratin'.'

'Oh but it is,' I cried enthusiastically. 'If ye can find a bit o' ribbon we'll hang up the sweets and if ye can find a bit o' coloured paper we can have some o' them lanterns Mrs Grundy showed us how to make.'

So, oblivious of the time we set about decorating the tree until Mrs McGuire came out of the kitchen with two steaming mugs of soup, saying, 'Yer'd best be gettin' 'ome luv, it's gone five o'clock.'

Startled, I jumped to my feet, my heart sinking. Kitty and the children stood at the door watching me flying down the lane with my coat wide open and my heart fluttering wildly in my breast. I prayed anxiously that my father had been delayed at the hall and my heart sank in my boots when I saw that every light in the hall had been put out. Arriving home breathless, I turned the knob gingerly on the front door, but it was closed fast. With my fists I pounded on the door but it remained closed and so I walked round to the back of the house and pounded on the kitchen door, which was also locked. I climbed up a tree outside the kitchen window and rapped on that. After ten minutes or more I realized that I was locked out and nobody was inclined to open the door.

A thin drizzle of icy rain had begun to fall and it trickled down my coat collar so that soon my teeth were chattering and I had to stamp my feet and flap my arms to keep warm. Surely I wouldn't have to spend Christmas Eve in the coalshed, that would be too cruel. But how long could they expect me to stand on the doorstep freezing to death? Finally in exasperation I lifted the letter flap and called out, 'If ye don't open the door I'll go down to the vicarage, I will.'

Then I heard my father's heavy footsteps. The door was flung open and he stood silhouetted in the doorway like some avenging angel. He grabbed my arm in a grip of iron and dragged me into the house, all the way to the kitchen. My mother sat white-faced at the table surrounded by the rest of them, speechless and afraid.

'Ye've bin at the McGuires', 'aven't ye? In spite of all I said to ye, in spite of what I said I'd do to ye if ever ye went off wi' that Kitty McGuire again.'

'It was early, Father,' I whispered in a small voice, 'I only went for a few minutes to wish 'em a Merry Christmas.'

'A few minutes is it? Look at the clock, girl, what time is it?'

'I know, Father, I'm sorry but we were decoratin' the tree, I lost all track o' the time.'

'This grieves me more than it grieves you, Ellen Adair, but I will be master in mi own 'ome. I'll make ye sorry ye disobeyed me, I'll make you so sorry yer'll never disobey me again. Now come upstairs.'

I looked round at my mother with large appealing eyes but she sat trembling, looking down at the head of Tommy on her knee. In sudden appeal I ran to kneel at her side. 'Please, Mother, don't let him punish me. Please, Mother, I haven't done anything wrong, an' I'll never go to the McGuires' again, never as long as I live.'

I was babbling now like a demented thing and my mother looked at me sorrowfully, biting her lip with anxiety, and only Peter spoke up for me.

'Don't hit her, Father, it's Christmas Eve, we shouldn't be miserable on Christmas Eve.'

'Be silent, boy, or you'll be sent to bed as well as this one. She's got to learn. Don't think I enjoy what I'm doing, it's for the girl's own good if she's to grow up chaste and decent. Now get up off the floor, girl, and come with me.'

So I followed his tall gaunt figure along the passageway and up the dark stairs towards my own room at the back of the house. I was shivering with fear, sobbing in my throat, but he paid no heed. When we reached the room he put a match to the oil lamp and pulled down the blind.

'Now take off yer shirt and blouse and everythin' else except yer shift, and lean over this chair.'

My fingers trembled so much I could barely cope with the fasteners, and it was so cold. He stood in silence watching me undress, then I watched him take off his belt. There was a look in his eyes which seemed to say he was enjoying my terror and I shrank away from him, trembling in my thin underskirt, but he pulled me forward with hard unyielding hands and thrust my body across the chair.

I prayed that I would faint, that blessed oblivion would shield me from the blows to come, but I did not faint. Instead I gritted my teeth and clenched my hands until the nails dug into my palms, waiting for the blows to fall. I have no memory of how many there were, I only know that after the first one the pain went on and on until I heard the blissful slamming of the bedroom door and his footsteps dying away.

For what seemed an eternity I stayed where I was, then painfully I dragged myself to my feet and stood swaying with my fingers curled round the back of the chair to prevent me falling down.

My skirt was sticking to my body and I felt the warm blood trickling down my back and legs. After a few minutes I found the strength to climb on to the chair so that I could see my back in the dingy mirror above the chest of drawers. Across it were dark red scores that were bleeding profusely so that my shift was saturated. I had no strength to bathe my wounds or go in search of ointment. In any case I didn't want anybody to see what my father had done to me, so I took off the shift and hid it under the chest until I could get rid of it in the morning.

Although I was freezing with cold I daren't get into bed where the blood would soil the bedclothes and I was afraid of my nightdress sticking to the wounds, so I lay on top of the bed on my stomach.

From downstairs came the sound of laughter and I guessed they were decorating the tree which the vicar always provided at Christmas. I dimly heard the front door knocker and laughter from father's friends who had come in for a tot of whisky before the evening's festivities started at the village hall. Soon after I heard the closing of the front door and laughter outside the house.

My parents had gone with their friends, and downstairs my brothers and sisters would be gathered round the tree playing games after listening to Father's instructions to be in bed by eight.

All knowledge of time eluded me and the next thing I knew Peter was standing by my side carrying a basin of warm water and a flannel. His face was set and white as he looked at my tattered back, and then gently he started to wipe the blood away. When he was satisfied that it had stopped bleeding he smoothed on some ointment with hands as gentle as a woman's.

'Ye can put yer nightie on now, Ellen, the bleedin's stopped.'

'I'll never be able to lie on it, Peter,' I murmured, 'and I'm so tired.'

'What made ye stay at the McGuires' so late, Ellen, didn't ye realize what e'd do?'

'I didn't see the time, Peter. We were fixin' up that awful little tree with sweets and coloured paper, right pretty it looked too when we'd finished. Please, Peter, don't tell anybody what happened tonight, but if ye see Kitty tell 'er nothin's changed.'

I shall never forget the fierce resentment and hatred that stayed with me after that night. There was no joy throughout the days of Christmas, the pain of my wounds was a constant reminder of his cruelty and the look of sadistic pleasure on his face before he started to beat me.

I had lost all respect for my mother also – poor down-trodden woman who had allowed him to torture me in that manner. But perhaps she was more to be pitied than blamed, and I got to thinking that she never had had a personality outside of his.

The food I ate at his table stuck in my throat and there

were times when I was sick, and even that made me glad that I had been saved from swallowing it.

I was determined that he would never touch me again, if I had to kill him first, and with that in mind I stole a carving knife out of the kitchen drawer and hid it among my underclothes. I even congratulated myself that I didn't flinch when it was missed and we all came under suspicion.

I stared straight into his face, saying, 'What would I want with a carving knife, Father? Like as not it's bin thrown out wi' the peelings.'

I was admonished by Mrs Grundy to sit straight at my desk instead of slouching but I couldn't tell her that the seat hurt my back, and on the day I slipped in the snow and fell on it I howled like a baby.

I lost weight, I could tell by my skirt which twisted round my waist so that I had to put a safety pin in it. One day when I took in the vicar's groceries the vicar's wife said to me, 'Is anything wrong, Ellen? You don't look well.'

'I'm all right, Ma'am, I slipped in the schoolyard and hurt mi back.'

'I hope you haven't cracked a bone, it's easily done.'

'I don't think so, Ma'am, it'll go right in a day or two.'

At those times when my mother looked at me appealingly, as though asking for my forgiveness, I merely tried to be cheerful so that she wouldn't feel so bad about it but it was hard living in a house where I hated my father, felt pity for my mother and truly loved only my brother Peter.

I'm not sure when the idea was born in me, perhaps it was on the morning I heard Father shouting at Peter because his shoes weren't cleaned properly, or the evening before when Naomi said slyly, 'Kitty McGuire's goin' ter work i' Liverpool, I 'eard 'er tellin' Mary Jordan.'

There was a moment of silence at the table, then Father said, 'She'll not be missed in the village, right little madam she is walkin' along the street with 'er nose in the air and the entire family of 'em little more than tinkers.'

I went on with my meal even when the silence seemed filled with anticipation that I would leap to Kitty's defence.

That night I wrote a brief note and slipped it into my

school atlas. The following morning I handed it to Mary Jordan with the whispered command that she give it to Kitty McGuire at playtime.

The note asked Kitty to meet me on the moor, wet or fine, the following Saturday afternoon. I knew Father would be in attendance at the wedding of the blacksmith's daughter Polly and that he and my mother had been invited to the reception after the service. Most of the village would be watching the wedding, including my sister Naomi.

As we walked back into the classroom Mary nudged me to say she had delivered my note.

It was a fine day for Polly Seddon's wedding and Father set out early wearing the sombre black garb in which he performed his official duties.

Mother wore her navy-blue skirt and white silk blouse. I had spent about half an hour crimping her hair with curling tongs and she looked very nice even though her grey coat was years old and didn't look much like a wedding to me.

When I had said it was a pity she hadn't bought herself a new one she merely said, 'Yer father needed new shoes an' it's more important fer 'im te look decent than me who doesn't go out much. With 'is job at the church 'e 'as te look respectable. I like 'im to look the part.'

I hoped I never became so besotted with a man that I allowed him to swallow me up alive, and when I didn't speak she said, 'I'm glad yer not bearin' 'im any malice about that night, Ellen, 'e only wants what's best for ye all. If yer does what 'e asks 'e's a reasonable man.'

'There now,' I said, 'take a look in the mirror and tell me what ye thinks about yer hair.'

She peered into the mirror and a smile spread over her face.

'It's nice, Ellen, real nice. I'll tell folk you did it for me. Now I'll probably spoil it wi' puttin' mi hat on.'

'Here, let me put it on for ye. You probably won't be takin' your hat off, but take off that awful coat as soon as ye can.'

Sure enough all the village seemed to have gathered around the church. They lined the path and perched on the walls, some of them even sat on the gravestones, and my father stood importantly at the door waiting for the guests to arrive. Mother went in alone leaving us to watch the proceedings, and Mary whispered, 'Why is Father standing outside?'

''E's got to escort everybody down the aisle and into the pews, like as not 'e doesn't trust the ushers to do it right.'

My sarcasm was lost on Mary but Naomi said, 'They don't know the church like mi father does.'

'You two stay 'ere,' I hissed, 'I'm goin round the other side to see what's 'appening.'

It was only half the truth, from the place I had in mind I only had to cross the churchyard, climb over the wall and I was almost on the moor.

I watched Polly arriving, swathed in white lace, on the arm of big Jim Seddon the blacksmith. Polly was a big girl with a jolly smiling face and she looked very beautiful in her bridal attire, but there was no time to stand and stare. Once I had satisfied myself that Father was inside the church I made good my escape up to the moor.

I saw Kitty sitting on an old dead tree stump and as I climbed the hill she waved and came to meet me. Her hair blew about her face in a riot of colour against the blue sky, and she was wearing some sort of coloured skirt which seemed to turn her into a gypsy before my eyes. As I drew nearer I could see that she was wearing earrings like bright green pears, and seeing my incredulous look she said, 'I picked 'em up at the jumble sale. I 'ave to put 'em on when there's nobody about, sure and mi mother'd kill me if she caught mi wearin' 'em at 'ome.'

As we settled companionably on the tree stump she said, 'I didn't wait te see the weddin' although I've nothin' agin' Polly Seddon or any o' the Seddons. Many's the chicken John Seddon's given mi father on Christmas mornin' an' even last Christmas didn't they send up enough turkey to feed all of us. An' John Seddon doesn't reckon on bein' a church goer.'

I didn't respond to the sly gibe at my father, and with a

little smile she said, 'I don't suppose yer dad knows yer up 'ere, Ellen?'

'No. Kitty, are you really goin' to Liverpool to work?'

'That I am, as soon as mi schooldays are over.'

'I want to come with ye.'

She stared at me aghast.

'Ye can't, Ellen, fer one thing yer father wouldn't let ye and for another it costs money to go to Liverpool and where are ye goin' to get that from?'

'I'll get it if I have to steal it.'

'Yer talkin' rubbish, Ellen, where would ye steal it from? Yer father doesn't leave the church collection 'angin' about and I reckon yer mother needs all she can get. There's bin a job promised me at the Seamen's Mission and a bed and board. I'm not sure there'd be anythin' fer you, Ellen.'

'Then I'll find somethin', in all that big city surely there must be somethin' I can do.'

'And then yer father'd come lookin' for ye and 'e'd nigh on kill ye, and me too if 'e thought I 'ad a hand in it.'

'He'll never find me, I'd run and I'd run 'til there was nowhere left to go an if 'e got mi cornered I'd kill 'im afore I'd come back 'ere.'

She stared at me startled, then shaking her head dubiously she said, 'I've never 'eard ye talk like this about 'im afore. Why are ye suddenly hatin' 'im like this?'

Springing to my feet I tore off my coat and flung it on the grass, then hitching up my skirt and underwear I bared my scored back to her shocked gaze.

'Did 'e do that to ye, Ellen?' she gasped.

'Yes, on Christmas Eve just because I was late 'ome, after we'd decorated that little tree. I'll never forget it, Kitty, an' I'll never forgive 'im or the pleasure 'e took in doin' it. Kitty, I'm frightened of 'im. I've seen 'im lookin' at mi, like 'e used te look at mi mother afore they disappeared upstairs to their bedroom, like 'e'd look at mi if I were a woman. Do ye know what I mean?'

Kitty shook her head slowly, her face shocked, then in a tight voice she said, 'Yer father thought nowt o' mi dad but 'e'd never 'a done that to any of us. P'rhaps yer wrong,

35

Ellen, p'rhaps it's all in yer mind, p'rhaps if ye never make 'im angry again it'll all blow over.'

I shook my head in exasperation. 'I stole one o' the carvin' knives an' I've got it 'idden in my underwear. If 'e comes near mi again I'll use it, Kitty, either on 'im or on me.'

'Ye must tell the vicar, Ellen, either 'im or Mrs Grundy. Between 'em somethin'll be done.'

'If I tell the vicar it'll be my word against mi father's and 'e could lose 'is job. Mi mother and the others'll suffer if I does that. No, Kitty, it's better for mi to get right away, I'll get the money somehow. Only please tell me when yer goin' so that I can come with ye.'

I was struggling into my coat, pulling down my skirt so that it covered the tops of my boots, and Kitty was helping me with a sad and troubled face.

When she didn't speak I urged, 'Please, Kitty, if ye've ever bin mi friend help mi now. Yer the only one I could ever ask, the only one I could ever tell about mi father, nobody else'd believe mi. You believe me, don't ye?'

She nodded, then with something of her old humour she said, 'Mi father said 'e was a sanctimonious old humbug struttin' off to church an' 'im with an eye for Phoebe Patterson. There was the vicar prayin' for 'er soul an' yer father 'elpin' to damn it.'

I stared at her in disbelief. 'Mi father and Phoebe Patterson!' I echoed. 'Nay, I can't 'ardly believe that, why often's the time 'e's said she were little more than a Jezebel, the village 'arlot.'

'I shouldn't 'ave bin tellin' ye, Ellen, 'e's yer father after all.'

'Tell me about 'im, Kitty, nothin' ye could tell me would make mi 'ate 'im more than I do now. Tell me 'ow true it is, Kitty, tell me so that I'll know for certain I'm right in wantin' te get right away from 'ere.'

'Oh it's only that mi father saw 'em together at the back o' the village 'all one night when 'e was reelin' 'ome in 'is cups. My mother said 'e'd imagined it but I believed 'im. When mi father was drunk 'e allus spoke the truth, 'e didn't know 'ow to lie, 'e saved 'is lies fer when 'e was sober as a judge and could remember what 'e'd said.'

For a long time we stared at each other, then Kitty said, 'Better get off 'ome now, Ellen, the mist is comin' down an' I don't want ye gettin' another beatin'.'

'They'll not miss mi, Kitty, they'll be at the weddin' feast.'

'They may be, but that young sister o' yours could be tellin' 'im.'

'I'm comin' with ye, Kitty, whenever ye go. I mean it,' I said sternly.

'All right, Ellen Adair, when I'm ready for goin' I'll tell ye, but I've no money to be 'elpin' ye and I'm makin no promises I might not be able to keep.'

'I know. I'm not expectin' anythin', Kitty, only I'd feel 'appier if I 'ad somebody te travel with.'

We threw our arms round each other and stood for a few minutes in the keen wind that blew off the moor. Without another word I ran leaping down the short coarse grass until I reached the stile in the wall, then with more decorum I strolled nonchalantly down the village street. The lamps had been lit and the mist swirled around my feet. From inside the church hall came the sound of music and laughter which told me Polly's wedding feast was in full swing. As I reached our front gate I saw that the door was open and Naomi stood peering out into the gloom. She said sharply, 'Where've ye bin, our Ellen? I waited for ye at the church.'

'Why did ye, then? Ye said you were goin' to the park.'

'Mi father said I was to wait for you.'

'I went to the back o' the church an' saw some o' the other girls from school. After the weddin' we went walkin' on the moor.'

'Wi' Kitty McGuire do ye mean?'

'No I don't, you little sneak. I 'aven't seen Kitty McGuire fer weeks, if she's any sense she doesn't want te see me, or anybody else who thinks she's nowt a pound.'

She stared out of her thin sharp little face with suspicious eyes but I met her gaze unflinching. Lying was coming easy. I hoped stealing would be just as easy, or killing if that's what it came to.

CHAPTER 4

As the weeks wore on I grew more and more excited. Beyond a brief smile and a wave of her hand I had had no more contact with Kitty. That she would keep her promise I had no doubt, and news of her plans came to me from the other girls.

'Kitty McGuire's leavin' the school at Easter, goin' ter work i' Liverpool,' Mary Jordan informed me. 'Yer'll not catch me goin' ter work i' Liverpool, mi mother sez it's full o' foreign sailors and shanty Irish.'

'When exactly is she goin'?'

'Easter Saturday mi mother sez, and that came from Kitty's mother so I reckon it's right.'

Now that it was almost upon me I was beginning to realize the enormity of my decision. I would be leaving the village where I had spent all my young life and I began to see it with a new warmth and affection. The straggling village street with its stalls on market day, a street that ran upwards until it met the fell and the rolling moor of the lower Pennines. Somehow the clear bubbling stream that trickled along the side of the street where I lived and the narrow bridges which crossed it became suddenly important. Like the snowy ducks on the pond near the stone Saxon church and the village pub with its window boxes filled with early daffodils.

My resolution began to waver until the night I saw my father send Peter skidding across the kitchen floor with a fierce blow from the back of his hand. He staggered to his feet with the blood pouring from his forehead which had caught the edge of the table, and I ran to help him. But my father clutched my shoulder with a heavy hand.

'Keep out of this, girl, or I'll deal wi' you in a similar fashion,' he growled.

'Now,' he said, standing scowling over my stricken

brother, 'ye'll clean them shoes like I asked ye to do an' leave yer books be.'

'I was goin' to clean them, Father, 'onest I was, but I 'ad to write this down while it was still in mi mind,' Peter cried.

'I told ye I had an important meetin' tonight, now get on wi' them shoes while I change into mi suit, and make a good job of 'em,' was Father's parting shot.

At that moment my mother came in and I was shocked at the greyness of her face and the dark hollows under her eyes. Piteously she looked at Peter, then at my father who snapped, 'What ails ye, woman, goin' about the house like a shadow? I've more than 'ad mi fill o' disobedient children and a wife who looks ready fer death.'

Trembling, Mother sank down on to a chair and Peter reached for the box which contained the blacking for Father's boots. As for myself, I ran to the tap and saturated a cloth with clean water in an attempt to stem the blood from his forehead. It was still bleeding profusely and I could only imagine that it was throbbing painfully.

After I had attended to Peter I made Mother a cup of hot sweet tea and advised her to go to bed.

'There's the little ones to see to, Ellen, and yer father's supper for when 'e comes 'ome.'

'I'll do that, Mother, please go to bed,' I urged.

I watched miserably while she sipped her tea, then Father was back in the kitchen wearing his best suit, scrutinizing the boots Peter handed to him and saying not a word of thanks.

'I'll not be wantin' any supper,' he said, 'so if ye wants ter go to bed yer can.'

Looking at him in surprise my mother said, 'Will ye be getting somethin' to eat at the meetin', then?'

'I've bin asked te the Skidmores' after the meetin's over,' he answered tersely, then left the house.

'Please, Mother, go to bed,' I urged her. 'I'll see to the children and I'll bring you something warm up to bed later.'

Wearily she dragged herself to her feet and shuffled out of the room.

After she had gone was the moment I told Peter what I planned to do, but he was quick to urge against it.

'Ye can't go, Ellen, think about mi mother and the children, think about me. I can't stay on 'ere without you, Ellen, we're the oldest, together one day we'll beat mi father.'

It had been a mistake to tell him, and as I coped with the evening meal and the washing up afterwards my resolution to leave with Kitty was faltering. In three weeks it would be Easter and I had very little money saved and now my mind was weighed down with doubts about the sanity of my decision.

I sat in the kitchen mending Mary's pinafore while Peter sat at the table poring over his books. At eight o'clock I got the children ready for bed and when Naomi protested I snapped, 'Mother said you had to go to bed with the others, ye don't want to lend a hand wi' the 'ousework and I don't want ye under mi feet. I've made cocoa and when ye've drunk it I want ye in bed, all of ye.'

'Mother didn't mean me,' she stormed. 'Yer only three years older than me anyway.'

'All right then, it's either bed or ye 'elp to clean the sittin' room and the kitchen.'

She glared at me furiously, then taking up her cocoa she marched out of the kitchen and up the stairs.

Peter's pale face broke into a smile. 'Ye can be somethin' of a martinet yerself, our Ellen, when ye wants ter be,' he said.

'She gets on mi nerves, sometimes I can't stand 'er at any price and it's awful that I should be feelin' this way about mi own sister.'

At nine o'clock I went upstairs with a cup of hot milk for Mother. Her face looked grey and pinched against the white pillows, and I was shocked at the cold clammy feeling of her nightdress as I helped her to sit up.

'I should send for the doctor, Mother. Please let me,' I begged.

'No, Ellen, I'll be better in the mornin' but I don't think I'm goin' te be able to get to the Nelsons' and I promised

40

Mary Nelson faithfully I'd be there to help 'er with 'er simnels.'

'I'll go as soon as I've tidied up the kitchen, Mother. I'll be up later to tell you what she's said.'

'Yer a good girl, Ellen, I wish ye'd try to get on wi' yer father a bit better. It upsets me when yer forever at logger'e-ads with 'im.'

I went about shaking up her pillows and settling her into bed without answering, and she caught my hand in hers anxiously. 'Promise me ye'll try, Ellen, it worries me so.'

'I'll try, Mother.'

'I sometimes wonders what'll 'appen to this family when I've gone, who'll look after the little uns and ye and yer father 'ardly speakin' a word to each other.'

'What do ye mean, Mother, when ye've gone?'

'I mean if I should die 'afore' 'e does. I've never bin the strongest an' when I feels real badly I can't 'elp worryin'.'

My throat felt tight with unshed tears but I bent down and kissed her cheek. 'Try to sleep, Mother, I'll look in on you later.'

I finished tidying the kitchen, then told Peter I was going up to the Nelsons' house.

'Do ye want me to come with ye, Ellen? I can finish me 'omework later.'

'I'm all right on mi own, Peter, I shan't be long,' I answered him before letting myself out.

It was a dark murky night. Mist hung low over the fields and the solitary gas lamp burning in the street shone eerily through the gloom. Even the lights from the pub failed to dispel the damp floating vapour, and I hurried along with my head covered by a warm woollen scarf and my hands thrust deep inside my coat pockets.

I was not usually afraid of the dark or of walking the country lanes alone, but this was a night of floating shadows and weird figures conjured up by the mist and I was glad when the Nelsons' house loomed in front of me.

As soon as I touched the latch on the side gate a dog started to bark and then there were two of them leaping at the gate with teeth bared and hackles bristling so that I backed off, afraid. I was unused to dogs. We had never had them as pets, indeed there had only ever been the tabby cat Matilda, and Jet the black cat who was still with us. Matilda had left home one day after one of Father's blustery rows, never to return. Weeks after I saw her sunning herself on the window sill of Miss York's cottage and although she came to greet me she refused to return home with me so that I always credited Matilda with a lot of common sense.

I stood outside the gate shivering and wondering what I should do next. How was I to reach the kitchen door with those massive dogs barring my path?

Suddenly a light streamed out into the darkness and a voice called out, 'What ails ye, kickin' up such a fuss at this time o' night? Who's there?'

A man's shape came lumbering through the gloom and then he was at the gate looking down at me with amazement.

''Ello, lass,' he said. 'There's no cause to be affeared, they'll not touch ye. Come into the light, I can't see ye properly standin' there.'

Gingerly I moved towards him and then he laughed. 'Why it's young Ellen Adair. Ye'd best come into the kitchen an' I'll tell Mother ye're 'ere.'

After a sharp word the dogs retreated to their kennel at the back of the yard, and smiling down at me he said, 'I can see yer not used ter dogs, lass, but we 'as to 'ave 'em livin' out 'ere away fro' the village. Come on in, now sit down i' that chair an' I'll sent mi wife in te see ye.'

I had never been inside the Nelson house before and I was amazed at the size of the kitchen – we could have got ours into it three times over. A half-carved fowl sat in the middle of the table and beside it a bowl of rosy-red apples. On a side table stood a huge bowl covered with a snowy cloth which I suspected contained dough for bread making and on the floor stood churns of milk and buttermilk.

Mrs Nelson was a wonderful cook, taking all the prizes for her preserves and fruit simnels at the country shows, and occasionally samples of her cooking found their way into our pantry.

I was still staring around when I heard footsteps and then

42

Mrs Nelson was there, large and bustling behind her snowy-white overall and with her grey hair pushed under a white mob-cap.

'Why it's Ellen,' she said, smiling. 'Now what brings you up here on such a dark night?'

'I've come te say mi mother won't be able to come in the mornin', she's real sick. I wanted to send for the doctor but she won't 'ave it.'

'Oh dear, I'm sorry to 'ear that, Ellen, I was 'opin' she could give me a hand wi the simnels but I reckon it can't be 'elped. Now you tell your mother to stay in bed 'til she feels 'erself again, and see that she gets plenty of nourishment. Lots 'o fresh milk, eggs and butter.'

'Yes, Mrs Nelson, I will. And if I can run any errands for ye I will.'

She beamed affably. 'Thank you, Ellen, that's very willin' of ye. I hope you're gettin' on a bit better with yer father, it worries your mother somethin' awful.'

When I didn't speak she shook her head a little, then packed a box with fruit cake, half a dozen eggs and a piece of fresh country butter. By this time Mr Nelson had returned to the kitchen and sat regarding me with a smile.

'Take these to yer mother, Ellen, and see that she gets them for herself. She hasn't to give them to the children, she's the one that's ailin'.'

'Thank ye, Mrs Nelson, ye're very kind. Mi mother'll be that grateful.'

'That's all right, Ellen, but remember what I said, try to get along with yer father for yer mother's sake.'

'I do try, Mrs Nelson, honestly.'

'Well p'rhaps ye don't try hard enough. He's a fine church-goin' man, Ellen, I'm sure there's no cause to be quarrellin' with him.'

'No, Mrs Nelson,' I murmured, wishing with all my heart that I could show her my scarred back, but just then I caught Mr Nelson winking at me with cynical humour.

'Goin' to church doesn't make 'im a saint, eh Ellen?' he said smoothly.

'Stop that, George,' his wife admonished him. 'Ellen knows what I mean.'

He grinned, quite uncontrite. 'She knows what I mean too, don't ye, lass? Now get off 'ome with yer parcel an' I'll come to the gate to see ye through the yard. Would ye like mi to walk 'ome with ye?'

'No, thank you, Mr Nelson, just to the gate so that the dogs won't get me.'

He threw back his head and laughed uproariously. 'Nay, them two lazy 'ounds'll not touch ye, their bark's worse than their bite.'

I was not anxious to find out, and after thanking Mrs Nelson for the parcel I stayed very close to her husband until the gate had slammed between me and the dogs. Docile now, they came and stood looking solemnly through the gate while their master spoke.

'Get off 'ome, luv, I'll stand 'ere at the gate 'til I watches ye down the road.'

People were coming out of the church hall where Father's meeting had taken place, and I hung back not wishing to encounter him on the way home. I watched him leave the hall, locking the door carefully behind him, then he started off down the road. I followed more slowly, surprised when he passed the entry to our lane. Instead he took the opposite direction, down Holly Lane. Curious, I crept noiselessly after him.

I stood in the shadow of a wall watching him open a gate and walk quickly up the path of a cottage garden halfway up the lane. After a few moments the door opened and he went inside.

By this time my curiosity was so great I didn't care whether I was seen or not. I walked down Holly Lane until I stood in front of the house he had entered – Phoebe Patterson's. I saw the play of candlelight in an upstairs room and then I shrank into the shadows as a lamp was lit in the front bedroom and the curtains were drawn close.

For several minutes I stood staring up at the closed curtains, then the light was turned off and the room was in darkness like the rest of the house. My heart was hammering

44

painfully as I took to my heels and ran without pausing until I threw myself exhausted into the kitchen.

Peter leapt up with alarm after taking one look at my burning face.

'What is it, Ellen,' he cried, 'was somebody chasin' ye?'

I wanted to tell him what I had seen but something indefinable held me back. I don't know even now if it was loyalty or shame, only that I gathered my scattered wits and after handing my parcel to Peter sank down with trembling knees into Father's big horsehair chair.

'I was frightened by the shadows, the mist is thick out there.'

'Ye should 'ave let mi go with ye, Ellen.'

'I'm all right now, Peter. Did ye look in on mi mother?'

'Yes, she was asleep. We'd best get to bed, Ellen, mi father'll be back soon.'

'Not yet awhile he won't,' I said stonily.

'Why not? The meetin'll be over by this time.'

'Didn't he say he was goin to the Skidmores'?'

'O' course, I'd forgotten.'

After Peter had gone to bed I busied myself putting away Mrs Nelson's offerings, then set the table for breakfast, made cocoa and took it upstairs to Mother's room, but she was fast asleep. I decided not to wake her but took it back to the kitchen and drank it myself.

I went through the downstairs rooms to assure myself that they were as tidy as a new pin and on returning to the kitchen was surprised to find that it was just after midnight. Still I dawdled until I heard the garden gate closing behind my father and his footsteps under the window, then there was his key turning the lock and we were staring at each other across the kitchen floor.

His face flushed with anger. 'What are ye doin' up at this time, why aren't ye in bed?'

'I cleaned the house, Father, and laid the breakfast table, I saw the children in bed and took care of mi mother.'

'That didn't take all night, did it?'

'No, Father. I went up to the Nelsons' house to tell Mrs Nelson mi mother wouldn't be fit to go there in the mornin'.'

His eyes narrowed and I was gratified to see the uncertainty creeping into his face.

'Did ye go up there on yer own then?'

'Yes, Father.'

'It's not a fit night for a lass to be wanderin' the streets.'

'No, Father, I was glad to get back.'

'And what time was that then?'

'Oh about ten thirty or thereabouts. I saw 'em comin' out of the church hall so it must 'ave been about ten thirty.'

'That's right, my meetin' went on a fair bit after that.'

'Goodnight, Father,' I said calmly, and without undue haste left the room and climbed up the stairs to bed.

CHAPTER 5

I didn't know whether I hated my father more when he was brutal or when he was ingratiating. During the days which followed he praised me constantly for my work around the house and for the way I cared for Mother. Naomi sulked because I was getting the praise and she was being largely ignored, and Peter stared at him solemnly out of curious, bewildered eyes.

Only Mother was pleased by this new-found peace between us. As for myself I cringed whenever his hand fell benevolently on my head, or when he addressed me in companionable terms. I knew very well that it was because he didn't know how much I had seen or knew about his association with Phoebe Patterson.

I didn't think for one moment that he cared about Mother or the rest of us, but he did care about his position as sexton and his standing in the community.

It was on Sunday morning after church when we sat down to dinner that he raised the subject of Phoebe to the family at large. 'I see Phoebe Patterson was in the church this morning, that little talk I had with her must have done some good.'

I sat with my head bowed while Mother said, 'You talked to her? Nay, surely it was the vicar 'imself who should 'ave done that!'

'He reckoned she'd take it better comin' fro' me, less like preachin' if ye understands.'

'And 'ow did she take it then?'

'Well she came to the church, didn't she? The first time for months so she must 'ave 'ad thoughts on what I said to 'er. She's not really a bad lass, Mary, she's never bin shown anythin' proper if gossip's to be believed.'

'I knew 'er mother, there was nothin' wrong wi' Mrs

Patterson, worked 'er fingers to the bone she did and got precious little thanks from Phoebe.'

'Well, I've 'eard different. 'Er father was a wastrel just like Kitty McGuire's father, that's why I don't want our Ellen 'avin too much to do with 'er. Like as not she'll end up like Phoebe Patterson.'

The food stuck in my throat so that I choked while the tears rolled down my face. How I hated him at that moment, and even more so when he came to pat my back. I couldn't bear for him to touch me and it was only when he'd left the table to sit with his newspaper in the one big easy chair in the kitchen that I made up my mind irrevocably that I was going with Kitty come what may.

I waylaid her in the school playground, making sure that none of my sisters were in the vicinity, but Kitty greeted my urgency with doubtful eyes and anxious persuasions to think more carefully.

'I've thought about it, Kitty. As a matter of fact I've not thought about anything else for days. You were right about mi father, he is friendly with Phoebe Patterson and I can't bear to see mi mother treatin' 'im like God. 'Ow much money shall I need and when are we goin'?'

'Ye'll need at least five shillings for the fare and any food we moight be needin', and somethin' to spare. I'm catchin' the seven o'clock train from the station on Saturday mornin' and I 'ave to change at Leeds and get the Liverpool train. I'm goin' early cause I don't want to be arrivin' in Liverpool when it's dark.'

I nodded wordlessly. I was thinking about Leeds and Liverpool, two big cities I had only heard of, and to a girl born and bred in that remote Pennine village as alien as Vancouver and Brisbane.

'I'll be at the station, Kitty, I swear it,' I said fiercely. 'What do I need to bring in the way of luggage?'

'Nightwear and a change o' clean clothin', Ellen. Whatever ye think ye'll need. Are ye sure ye'll be able to get out of the 'ouse without anybody seein' ye?'

I nodded. 'They don't get up very early on Saturdays unless there's a weddin' or a funeral. I'll keep out o' sight of anybody lookin' through their windows, and I'll be there, Kitty, ye can bank on it.'

'Well if ye're not I can't wait for ye, Ellen, I 'ave to be on that train.'

'Will yer mother be seein' ye off, Kitty?'

'I'd rather she didn't, I'd rather leave 'em all in the house, and it's better she doesn't if yer that intent on comin' with mi. Yer father'd worm it out of 'er sure as mi name's Kitty McGuire if 'e thought yer'd left wi' me. If mi mother knows nothin' she can't tell 'im anythin'.'

At that moment the younger classes were coming into the schoolyard so with a quick smile and a whispered 'See ye Saturday, Kitty,' I left her.

The next couple of days passed in what seemed like an instant. I collected the things I would need and made a neat parcel of them which I hid behind some books in the bedroom cupboard and I smuggled my Sunday coat downstairs and hid that too at the back of the hall cupboard.

It was inevitable that I should take stock of my life and all I would be leaving behind. In those days somehow the village took on an enchanted air and I looked with nostalgia at the tiny Saxon church and the giant yews that surrounded the churchyard, at the snowy ducks that squabbled and splashed in the pond and the friends of my childhood I would be leaving behind.

My throat ached with unshed tears as I watched my mother's head bent over her sewing and Peter poring over his books. Even Naomi took on an attraction I had never felt before and instead of feeling impatient at her pertness, now I was seeing the humour in her thin gamin face.

In those days I began to doubt my courage. Would it fail me on the morning I had promised to meet Kitty? And then I would find my father's hand fondling my bare arm, have his eyes burning into mine with the unspoken question forever there: How much did I know?

There was a thin drizzle of rain that Saturday morning and mist hung low across the fields. All night long I had tossed and turned in my bed until I heard Ben Johnson's rooster crowing before first light.

Gingerly I slipped out of bed, gathered my clothes together and crept silently downstairs. There was one tread that
creaked ominously and I paused anxiously to listen, but all
I could hear was Father's snoring and the loud ticking of
the grandfather clock.

I washed and dressed hurriedly in the kitchen, shivering
from the cold water. I took my coat out of the cupboard
and felt in the pocket for the note I had composed days
before, addressed to my mother. In it I said I was sorry for
causing her pain and hoped she would forgive me, I swore
I would pay back the money I was taking, as soon as I was
earning enough. And I promised never to forget her and to
love her always.

My next act was to reach up to the mantelpiece and take
down the tin where she kept the money for the coalman
and the milkman. There were ten shillings in it and I took
three; the rest of my money had been saved out of what I
had received from running errands for Mrs Nelson and the
vicar's wife.

I shrugged my arms into my coat and my feet into my
best Sunday shoes. Then I heard footsteps in the passage
and I stood petrified. Next moment I was staring into Peter's
horrified eyes as he beheld me dressed and ready to leave,
carrying my paper parcel, my hand on the latch of the yard
door.

'Shsss,' I cautioned, and hurried to close the door behind
him.

'Please, Peter, don't say a word. I'm leavin' and nothin'
ye can say or do is goin' to make mi change mi mind,' I
said firmly.

'But where are ye goin', Ellen? Ye can't just go like that.'

'I've a job to go to and I want ye to go back upstairs and
not say a word that ye've seen mi this mornin'. That way
my father can't blame ye for not stoppin' mi or tellin' 'im.'

'Ye can't go, Ellen. If you go I'll go too. I can't live 'ere
when ye've gone, I 'ates 'im just as much as you do.'

'I'm older than you, Peter, and ye've got yer way to make.
One day I'll see that ye knows where I am but for now I

50

wants ye to keep quiet. Please go back to bed and let me go. Nothin' ye can say'll make me change mi mind.'

'It's mi father, isn't it?'

'Yes it is. I'll never forgive 'im for what he did to me and I'll never forgive 'im for bein such a sanctimonious liar. One day ye'll be a man and I hope ye'll be a match for 'im. But all that's in the future, Peter, for now ye've got to bide yer time.'

'But 'ave ye got any money, Ellen? Ye needs money to leave 'ere.'

'I've got a bit I saved and I've borrowed three shillin' out o' the box there. I'll pay it back when I can, mi mother'll just 'ave to trust mi.'

''E'll come after ye, Ellen, ye'll never get away with it.'

'Oh yes I will, I'll travel to the ends of the earth to get away from 'im, but if 'e does catch mi and want to bring mi back I'll kill miself, I swear it.'

'I've got a bit o' money saved, Ellen, ye can 'ave that.'

'I won't take a penny of yer money, Peter, ye'll need all that for yerself one day. Will ye promise mi one thing?'

'What, Ellen, that I won't tell 'im I've seen ye this mornin'?'

'That you'll get away too if ye can when the time's right. If ye don't ye'll regret it for the rest of your life.'

From upstairs came the sound of Father's coughing and then voices, and urgently I said, 'I'm goin', Peter, get back upstairs 'afore ye're seen.' Then I threw my arms round his neck and left him without another word. I ran down the lane without a backward glance, my eyes swimming with tears so that the village was a blur.

It was too early for the train, and not wanting to be seen loitering near the station I climbed the stile near the church and walked up on to the fell. Dew lay heavy on the grass and the earth smelled of clover. From the fell I could look down on the village which was slowly coming to life. Smoke ascended from cottage chimneys and along the high street I could see Johnty the postman with the sack of letters on his back. Dogs were barking, and wrinkling up my nose I could smell bread baking in the ovens of Cornfield's bakery.

Old Mrs Trainer left her cottage carrying a paper bag of crusts for the ducks she fed every morning, and soon the Saturday traders would be coming to set out their stalls.

I saw Kitty hurrying down the path of their cottage, with her mother standing at the door holding one of the younger children, while another clung to her skirts. Like me Kitty carried her belongings in a brown paper parcel and she was wearing her Sunday-best coat and a bright green woollen tammy. At the end of the lane she turned to wave to her mother, then she ran in the direction of the station. She looked neither right nor left, and anxiously I too started to run down the hill so that I arrived at the station only minutes after she entered the booking hall.

On the platform she turned to me anxiously. 'Ellen, are ye sure?' she breathed.

'I'm sure,' I answered her firmly.

'Did anybody see ye?'

'Not a soul. I waited on the fell 'til I saw ye leavin' the house.'

'I 'opes nobody else's gettin' this early train.'

'Well we don't 'ave to sit together until we're sure.'

We were the only two people to board the country train with its two carriages, but all the same we sat with lowered heads hoping and praying that we might be the only travellers.

The train had been several minutes on its journey before I felt confident enough to look through the window at the passing scenery.

Kitty was the knowledgeable traveller, for they had come to England all the way from County Sligo so that her father could find some sort of work on a farm. It was Kitty now who wasn't afraid to ask the times of trains and whether or not we were on the right platform while I hurried along at her side overwhelmed by the thronged platform and the hustle and bustle of Leeds station.

While we waited for the Liverpool train I murmured, 'Wouldn't it have bin nice to stay a while in the city to look at the shops, Kitty?'

She nodded. 'They'll be just as grand in Liverpool, Ellen.

Will you be lookin' at that woman there, watered silk in the middle o' the mornin' and heels like stilts. I know what I'm goin' to do, I'm goin' to turn miself into a city girl an' wear clothes just like that 'afore I goes back to the village. I'll 'ave 'em all pea green with envy, I will.'

'How do you suppose we're goin' to do that then?'

'I shall, Ellen, just you watch me.'

'Then I suppose I shall too?'

'Well o' course.'

She put her arms round me and gave me a little hug.

'I'm right glad ye've come, Ellen. We're goin' to make somethin' of ourselves just like I allus said we would.'

'Emeralds and ermine?' I prompted with a half smile.

'I'll settle for less for the moment, but we'll keep our sights high. Emeralds and ermine it is. Do ye think we could spend a few pence on a cup o' tea and a bun?'

'Yes please, I'm awfully hungry.'

'Come on then, the train's not due for twenty minutes and the tea room's just over there.'

The tea room was hot and steamy but we found a corner table. I handed over the price of tea and a bun and Kitty went to the counter.

She was chatting animatedly to the woman standing next to her, then she was bringing her over to our table.

'This is Mrs O'Reilly, Ellen, she's goin' to Liverpool. She says we can tag along with 'er and she'll be tellin' us how to find our way about when we gets there.'

I made room for Mrs O'Reilly next to me, and eyeing me curiously she said, 'Yer a bit young, aren't ye, luv, to be goin' to work i' Liverpool? I should 'a thowt yer'd still be goin' to school.'

'I've just left,' I said stoutly, 'Kitty too.'

'Ay well, so she's just towd mi, but you're nobbut a lassy.'

Only a few months separated me from Kitty and I felt unreasonably annoyed that this woman thought me too young to be let out on my own.

'Goin' te relatives, are ye?' she asked next.

'To mi Aunt Mary's,' Kitty replied, 'and we 'ave jobs to go to.'

'Oh well that's different. Work's 'ard to come by. 'Ave either of ye bin ter Liverpool 'afore?'

When we shook our heads she said brightly, 'It's big, ye know, not as big as Manchester to be sure but it's a fair-sized port. A lot o' foreigners live i' Liverpool, particularly near the docks.'

'A lot of Irish too,' Kitty put in quicky.

'Oh ay, it's a great place for the Irish. I married one of 'em so I should know. I 'ated it when we first went te live there but now I likes it. There's someat different about Liverpool, I don't rightly know what it is but there's a sort of adventure about it, romantic like.'

'Why is that?' Kitty asked quickly.

'I reckon it's all them big steamers goin' te romantic places we've only heard of, China and India, South America and Africa. Ye can walk along the river and see 'em sailin' out into the mist, an' ye can take the ferries and sail across to Wallasey and New Brighton on a nice summer's day. That's where the river meets the sea, ye know, and many's the time I've taken mi children to sit on the promenade to watch the big ships disappearin' into the sunset.'

I could have listened to Mrs O'Reilly for much longer, but gathering her parcels together she said briskly, 'Well, we'd best be movin' if we're to get that train. Can ye carry one o' these parcels seein' ye don't 'ave much luggage?'

I took one and Kitty took another, then we hurried along the platform to join the people waiting for the Liverpool train.

My entire being was filled with a strange and new excitement, but as the train eased its way out of the station the spectacle of Leeds seemed depressing with the sea of mill chimneys and warehouses. The sun no longer shone out of a clear blue sky, instead the clouds hung low over the city and the distant line of the Pennines, and a thin drizzle of rain obscured the diminishing city.

I thought about the village I had left. They would have found my note and I could only picture my mother in tears while my father pontificated about my lost innocence, sure that I had taken the first steps towards perdition.

54

Peter would listen to him with anger in his heart and Naomi would be glad I'd gone. One less in that tiny bedroom had always been much to be desired, and the smaller children were too young to understand that one member of the family had gone for ever.

There would be speculation too in the village. The vicar would pray for me and Mrs Nelson would try to comfort my mother while most of the others would damn me as an ungrateful brat who had not appreciated the good home my decent and upright father had provided.

I thought with a certain grim amusement that my father, when he had had time to reflect, would view my absence with something akin to relief. There was now little danger that I would ever disclose anything about his association with Phoebe Patterson, and I hoped his suspicions that I knew more than I had let on would keep him from trying to find me.

Kitty and Mrs O'Reilly sat opposite and I was left largely to my own thoughts as they chatted. Occasionally my eyes met Kitty's and she smiled encouragment, well aware where my thoughts lay.

Mrs O'Reilly was a chatterbox. Before we reached Lime Street Station in Liverpool the entire carriage was adding anecdotes to match hers, and soon both Kitty and I were laughing at their stories.

Everybody was anxious to give us instructions on how to find our way about the city as well as to Aunt Mary's, and two of the men made it their business to see us on to one of the city's trams, with strict instructions to the conductor to put us off near Aunt Mary's address.

CHAPTER 6

Liverpool on a dismal spring evening with a mist hanging low on the river and the mournful hooting of ships' sirens echoing through the gathering gloom.

Gas lamps shed their weird glow over street corners and as we sat on the wooden seats of the tram it seemed to me that the world was filled with strange sights and sounds. The clanging of the tram and the hooting of the sirens, the cries of the newsboys and the strange accents of the people were all combining to convince me that I was now a part of a strange and alien world, a world in which I would either survive or go under. I prayed with all my heart on that creaking, clanging tramcar that I would survive.

The conductor put us off the tram with smiling good humour and passed us our parcels. We thanked him warmly, and Kitty remarked, 'Well at least the folk we've met so far 'ave bin friendly, I just 'ope the rest of 'em's as nice.'

'How well do ye know yer Aunt Mary, Kitty?'

'Not well at all, I 'aven't seen 'er since we stayed with 'em that first night we crossed from Ireland. I know her husband works on't docks and they've a lot o' children. They're mi cousins, I suppose, but I wouldn't be able to recognize a single one of 'em.'

'She's yer mother's sister, isn't she?'

'That she is, but they're not a bit alike. Mi mother 'ad the loveliest red hair just like mine when she was younger, and mi aunt's dark an' very thin.'

'But she'll be glad to see ye, Kitty?'

'Let's 'ope so. I hope she's as glad to see you, Ellen, she thinks I'm on mi own.'

'Oh Kitty, I promise I won't be any trouble, I'll work hard at the mission and I'll pay mi own way. Yer've bin so good, I don't want to be a burden to ye ever.'

She took hold of my arm and gave it a little squeeze. 'To

be truthful, Ellen, I'm glad of yer company. I wasn't relishin' comin' 'ere on mi own.'

The streets we were walking along were mean and narrow. There were no gardens in front of the tall dismal houses and my spirits sank as we passed the Seamen's Mission at the corner of the street. It was an ugly building with dingy windows through which we could see gas lamps burning dimly. As we passed the door I was aware of a strong smell of carbolic and the single gas lamp above the doorway did nothing to dispel the overall gloom.

Across the road a group of children played noisily outside a Chinese laundry and further down the street other children waited idly outside the dingy doors of a public house.

'Does yer aunt live in this street, Kitty?' I asked unhappily.

'Number twenty-seven. It's worse than I thought it'd be.'

'Well it's an awful night, it'll all look a lot better in the mornin'.'

We stood staring up at number twenty-seven, at a door with dark grey paint which was peeling away to reveal damp and rotten woodwork.

'Goodness knows what it's like inside,' Kitty said doubtfully. 'Mother warned mi that mi aunt 'ad never been 'ouseproud, she was allus the one that liked goin' out and enjoyin' herself while the rest of them cared for the house.'

'With a husband and children she's probably changed, Kitty. We're here, shouldn't you be knocking on the door?'

'I'm just warnin' ye, that's all.'

With that she lifted her hand and brought the knocker down loudly. After a few seconds we heard footsteps behind the door, then gingerly it was opened a few inches and a child looked out at us, her eyes wide with curiosity.

'Is yer mother in?' Kitty asked softly. 'Will ye tell her it's Kitty all the way fro' the West Riding.'

The child didn't move but remained staring at us, then from the back of the house a woman called out, ''Ave ye got the front door open, Jennie? Get it closed, it's cold in 'ere.'

Kitty looked at me helplessly, then giving the door a little push she said, 'We're goin' in, Ellen,' and taking the little girl by the hand she walked into the house while I followed more slowly.

We entered a square living room which seemed too crowded to present any real picture in my mind. A stack of washing was piled on to the square table in the middle of the room and against one wall a sewing machine stood open. There were chairs in the room but they were littered with dressmaking material and items of clean washing, and the woman who faced us across the table looked grey and careworn.

She was small and thin and she wore her faded brown hair taken back from her face and caught by a slide. She wore a grey woollen cardigan over a soiled white blouse and there was a floral apron round her waist.

A little girl played on the floor in front of a low-burning fire, while the child who had opened the door to us went to cling to her mother's skirts, eyeing us suspiciously.

'I'm Kitty, Aunt Mary. Mi mother said ye'd be expectin' mi.'

For a second she continued to stare, then her face relaxed and she smiled. 'Gracious, I'd forgotten it was today ye were comin'.' Then her eyes slid round to me.

'This is Ellen Adair, Aunt Mary, mi friend from the country, she's hopin' to get work alongside of me at the mission.'

Doubtfully Aunt Mary sat down on the edge of a chair. 'Well I don't know, Kitty, yer mother didn't say there'd be two of ye.'

'Can we find out tonight?' Kitty asked.

'Ye can go along tonight to see the Doyles, they're in charge o' the mission. I know there's a room fer ye, Kitty, but I can't vouch fer yer friend.'

She began to scoop up the things off the chairs, then she added a small shovelful of coal to the fire and said to the little girl, "Elp me clear the table, Jennie. And ye be quiet, our Michael, or I'll send ye out to play. 'Ave ye had anythin' to eat since ye left Yorkshire?'

'Yes thanks, Aunt Mary, we had somethin' at the station in Leeds.'

The fact that that had been almost three hours ago didn't register on Aunt Mary at all, she merely indicated that we should sit down on the now vacant chairs while Michael howled his head off and Jennie continued to stare at us as if we had arrived from outer space.

'Stop starin',' her mother admonished her. 'She's not used to folk comin' that she doesn't know. Go tell the others that their Cousin Kitty's arrived.'

There had been poverty in Kitty's home but it had not been this sort. Kitty's house had shone from Mrs McGuire's polishing. She had cut up old clothes to make rag rugs, and Mrs Mason had been generous in giving her old lace curtains for the windows and the odd item of furniture.

This room was squalid. I doubted if the table and chairs had ever seen polish, the carpet was stained and threadbare, and the huge iron fireplace had never seen black leading. Then I noticed the perambulator in the far corner of the room and the child sitting propped up against a dingy pillow.

In one hand was a pot of raspberry jam and the other hand was spooning jam into its mouth, so that its face and bib were smothered in it. Catching us looking, Aunt Mary said, 'I gave our Susan the jam to keep 'er quiet, she's teethin' and a right mornin' and night I've 'ad with 'er to be sure. Ere,' she said, snatching the jam from the child, 'give it to me, ye'll make yerself sick,' whereupon the child howled with temper and the jam was handed back to keep her quiet.

At that moment we heard what seemed like a regiment dashing along the passage and next moment a dozen children piled into the room and stood staring at us with great solemn eyes.

We stared back and Kitty cried, 'Are all these yours, Aunt Mary?'

'Nay, I didn't tell ye to bring the entire street in, Jennie. Now the rest of ye get off 'ome.'

It was then I noticed that among the childrn were several coloured ones, Negro and Chinese, and they scampered off smartly along with two white children, leaving us to face five more small McLoughlins.

'This is yer Cousin Kitty,' she said, 'and this is 'er friend Ellen. Now come forward one at a time and tell 'em who ye are.'

It seemed so strange to be greeting those children who came forward to announce their names; Jonny, Nancy, Edith, Moya and Cloonie. Introductions over, they went to the far side of the room and sat along the wall on a wooden form, eyeing us curiously.

'Yer dad'll be 'ome soon. Early shift 'e's on but 'e usually calls in the pub fer a drink on 'is way 'ome. Joe works at the docks like most o' the men round 'ere,' she explained.

There was a vague pain in my midriff which I recognized as hunger, and my eyes brightened when I saw Aunt Mary clearing the table. After that she spread a newspaper over it and two of the small girls were dispatched to bring in plates and cups. We watched as she cut thick slices of bread from a large loaf which she placed on a platter, then the jam jar was taken once more from the child in the pram, who had nodded off. Aunt Mary made no effort to clean the jam jar or the spoon.

'Yer welcome to join us, Kitty. We're 'avin' soup and there's bread and potatoes te foller. Pull up yer chairs, if Joe doesn't be comin' soon I'll send one o' the children to tell 'im we're waitin' for 'im.'

Joe it seems was in no hurry, and after a wait of about half an hour Jonny was dispatched to the public house to find his father. Again we waited, then we heard the front door opening and a large dirty man came in, his face flushed and angry.

'What do ye mean, woman, by sendin' our Jonny to the pub for me? Can't a man 'ave a drink in 'is own good time after workin' all day?'

Unperturbed, and evidently well used to his ill humour, she merely said, 'We 'ave visitors, mi sister's daughter Kitty and 'er friend.'

'So, we 'ave visitors, what's it ter me?'

'I thought ye might be after showin' 'em a bit o' welcome.'

'Which is which, then? I didn't know we were 'avin' two of 'em.'

'They'll be wantin' somethin' te eat 'afore they goes to the mission, I thought yer'd like to be 'ere.'

He took his seat at the table without making any effort to wash. Two of the childrn helped their mother serve the soup in the kitchen and carry it into the living room, and I wondered when they were going to join us and where there would be room for them.

'Come on, then,' Joe said, 'make a start 'afore it gets cold.'

The children continued to sit or stand behind us and I realized that they were to wait to see what was left. The soup was thin and watery. I was grateful for its warmth but my appetite seemed to have deserted me when I saw their eyes watching every mouthful, which by this time I was sure we were depriving them of.

Joe ate noisily and I felt sickened by his uncouth manners and the grime on his hands and face. It was my fault, I told myself savagely, if I hadn't come there would have been more for the rest of them, consequently when the potatoes arrived I ate sparingly and adamantly refused the bread and jam to follow. It was only when Joe finally pushed his plate away that the children were allowed to take our places. They ate ravenously, and my heart was filled with pity at their pale pinched faces and the sad hopelessness of their lives.

It was almost seven o'clock when we reported at the mission. The caretaker's wife, Mrs Doyle, looked at me sourly and said, 'Who's this then? I was told there'd be one of ye, Kitty McGuire.'

'That's me,' Kitty said, 'and this is mi friend Ellen Adair. We both left school on the same day and I thought an extra pair of hands might be useful. Mi aunt says you're workin' every hour that God sends.'

Slightly mollified by Kitty's hint of honest toil, the woman said, 'Well I don't know about that, 'ow much are ye thinkin' I might 'ave to pay ye?'

'I'd like to leave that to you, Ma'am, perhaps when you see what I can do you'll make your mind up.'

'That a will, in the meantime I'll be payin' ye two shillings and sixpence a week and for that yer'll wait on the tables and 'elp in the kitchen. You, Missy, will sweep and scrub and see to the bedrooms.'

'All on 'er own?' Kitty asked pertly.

'Nay, she'll get 'elp fro' me and mi 'usband, and there's Mrs Slatterly who comes in every mornin', even if she isn't much good.'

'How many bedrooms are there?' I asked dolefully.

'Well they're not bedrooms as such, they're dormitories. Twelve to a room they sleep and the smell first thing in the mornin'll like as not knock ye over. Ye'll put plenty o' carbolic in the washin' water and mi 'usband sees to it that the men wash as soon as they get 'ere.'

'What sort o' men are they?' Kitty asked curiously.

'They're seamen, most of 'em a long way from 'ome. Rough and ready they are and some of 'em are mighty interested in a pretty face, so I'd advise both o' ye to keep yer distance. On the whole they're decent, all except Black Jake and we're not expectin' 'im for some time seein' as 'e's only just gone to sea agin. Now yer'll find yer bedroom at the top o' the second flight o' stairs, on yer left. There's a double bed there and a chest o' drawers, yer'll find 'ooks fer yer clothes behind a curtain in the alcove and there's a washroom down the corridor. See that yer locks the door when yer in there. Are them all yer things?'

'Yes, Ma'am,' we answered in unison.

'Yer'll call mi Mrs Doyle and mi 'usband Mr Doyle and if 'e starts any of 'is sweet talk just let mi know, I 'aven't lived wi Joe Doyle all these years wi'out knowin what 'e was about. 'Ave ye 'ad anythin' to eat since ye arrived i' Liverpool?'

'Yes thank you, we had somethin' at mi Aunt Mary's,' Kitty said.

'I'm surprised they'd owt te spare wi' all the brood they've got. When yer've unpacked ye can come down to the kitchen and make cocoa. I 'ave to go out but I'll leave everythin' on the kitchen table for ye and ye might be glad o' the fireside.'

'Will any of the men be in the kitchen?' I asked.

'Nay, we keep our quarters locked up at night. Most of 'em'll be in the pub 'til closin' time, yer'll no doubt 'ear 'em singin' their 'eads off all the way down the street. If ye 'ears any shoutin' and quarrellin' don't let it upset ye, they'll 'ave forgot what it's all bin about in the mornin'.'

We climbed the stairs and let ourselves into our room. In it was a small iron fireplace but it was doubtful if a fire had ever burned in the grate since it was stuffed with newspaper, and the chimney too was packed with it so that the wind made rustling noises, like small animals. A solitary gas jet above the fireplace was the only illumination of the tiny dismal room with its threadbare carpet and thin cotton curtains.

Kitty threw back the covers and we both inspected the bed, relieved to find that the sheets were clean and the pillowslips freshly laundered.

'I suppose it could 'ave bin worse, Ellen,' she said miserably, 'but I reckon it's better than stayin' with mi aunt.'

'Well of course it is,' I said stoutly. 'We can make it more cheerful with some of our things.'

'What sort o' things? All I've got are clothes and clean underwear.'

'Well that's all I've got too but when we get a bit o' money we can buy an ornament or two, even some flowers or a plant.'

'I can't think why you're so cheerful, there's nothin' to be cheerful about.'

'There is for me. I don't have to look at my father's face across the table every night or watch him sulkin' at mi mother. I don't have to think about him with that Patterson woman or watch him behave as if he was God's representative on earth.'

'You really do hate 'im, don't ye, Ellen?'

'Yes, I really do. Oh Kitty, it's goin' to be so lovely livin' in this big city with the steamers and the tramcars, then there's the big shops and the museums and art galleries. Can't ye see what fun we're goin' to have?'

'Not without money I can't.'

'But we can. The museums and the art galleries don't cost anythin' and the river's excitin' enough for anybody.'

'I want more in my life than this place and I'm goin' to get it. I don't care much how, but one day I'll get mi emeralds and ermine, just you see if I don't.'

'Well of course you will, Kitty, we both will. In the meantime how about going downstairs and making that cocoa?'

The kitchen wasn't as comfortable as it might have been. There was a white sink in the corner and a white-wood table in the centre, seeming naked without a tablecloth, but there were two large comfortable chairs upholstered in maroon plush and a fire that blazed away in the large grate which had recently been black leaded.

We made the cocoa and curled up in the chairs and somehow life seemed suddenly happier, and even Kitty's dismal face relaxed a little. We made plans for the things we wanted to see in the warm summer days we believed were ahead of us. Then we heard the staccato beating of rain on the windows and the mournful sound of a ship's siren, and Kitty said fretfully, 'I'd hate to think mi life was going to be like mi Aunt Mary's. All them children and a husband who looks like hers.'

'Well of course your life won't be like hers, you wouldn't marry anybody like him for a start.'

'That'll be the sort o' chap we'll be meetin', seamen or dockers.'

'We shan't be workin' 'ere for ever, when we've saved enough we can move on.'

'We shan't save much out o' two shillings and sixpence a week, and what do we move on to without experience?'

'We can go to evening classes and perhaps find work in a shop one day. I'd like that, Kitty, to work in one o' them lovely shops where rich women come to buy beautiful clothes.'

'I'd rather be one o' the rich women than stand behind a counter saying yes Ma'am and no Ma'am.'

It seemed to me that we always came back to the same thing.

I thought Kitty would always keep her dream of ermine

and emeralds. As for me, my ambitions had always been more realistic, a little more adult, perhaps; to survive, away from my father.

The silence was broken by a door slamming outside, then the kitchen door was thrown open and a large man came in, blinking in the light. He had bright red hair and a red face, and wore a woollen muffler over a dark fawn macintosh.

We both jumped to our feet nervously and he grinned. 'I 'eard yer'd arrived fro' yer uncle. Which one of yer's Kitty McGuire?'

'I am,' Kitty said shortly.

'And yer've brought a pal with ye. What did mi missus say about that?'

'She said she could work in the bedrooms for the time bein'.'

'Ay well, that'll make it a bit less for me to do. Ye can make me a cup o' tea while I get out o' these wet things, then off to bed the pair of ye. I likes the kitchen to miself 'til the missus gets 'ome.

We heard him lumbering upstairs and I put the kettle on while Kitty spooned tea into a large brown teapot. I looked at her mutinous face anxiously and suddenly she smiled, then we started laughing, gay uncontrollable laughter which ceased abruptly when Joe Doyle returned to the kitchen.

'It's a couple o' giddy kippers ye are and no mistake,' he said sourly.

'Sorry, Mr Doyle,' Kitty said softly. 'The tea's made, and we'll be sayin' goodnight'

He didn't answer, and gratefully we made our escape into the hall, now lit by a solitary gas lamp. We took turns to wash in the dark bare washroom then we crept between the chill sheets, shivering with cold.

'First thing I buy with mi wages is a stone 'ot-water bottle,' Kitty complained. 'We were as poor as church mice but mi mother allus saw that the beds were warm, either with oven plates or bottles. That cottage had more cracks lettin' in draughts than there were tiles on the roof.'

'My bedroom wasn't much better but mi father'd never

65

let us have oven plates in the bed, he said it'd make softies out of us.'

'To think I used to envy ye when first we came to England,' Kitty said softly. 'Livin' in that nice 'ouse with a garden and a father that stayed out of the pub and wi' a decent job. Ye allus seemed to 'ave good clothes for school and a change for Sunday, and ye spoke real nice. For those first few weeks I envied ye and I think I 'ated ye for 'aving the things I didn't.'

'Oh Kitty, I only had nice clothes because the vicar's wife and Mrs Nelson gave mi mother things and she was good with her sewing. I always tried to speak properly. I listened to the vicar's wife and tried to speak like her, and mi mother came from a decent family. They reckoned she'd not done the best for herself when she married mi father but she worshipped him, she did. Never a back answer did she give him, consequently we all suffered for it.'

'I'm goin' to try to talk like you do, Ellen. If I make a mistake will ye promise to put me right?'

'Oh Kitty, I couldn't do that, I'm not good enough for that. Besides I like that Irish lilt in your voice, it's more attractive than my Yorkshire accent.'

'Ye 'aven't got much of an accent, ye copied the vicar's wife and she wasn't Yorkshire. Besides it's yer grammar that I 'aven't got. Promise yer'll 'elp mi, Ellen.'

'I'll do mi best, but you must promise not to get angry when I correct you.'

'I promise, Ellen, and if I breaks that promise don't take any notice, you'll know I don't mean it.'

'What did you think of Mr Doyle, Kitty?'

'Not much. I can handle 'im, Ellen, 'e doesn't frighten me.'

'I wonder what the other men'll be like?'

'Rough like 'im, but I knew 'ow to 'andle mi father when 'e came 'ome worse for drink. Many's the time I've stood between 'im and mi mother and many's the time I've laid into 'im with the broom 'andle and 'e was so drunk 'e couldn't catch me. 'E'd 'ave knocked the livin' daylights out o' me if 'e could.'

66

'Why didn't you hate him like I hated my father, I wonder?'

'Because when 'e was sober 'e was a darlin' man. 'E could make mi laugh like nobody else and 'e never bore a grudge, not even when I bruised 'is shoulder and mi mother was rubbin' liniment into it for a week. He laughed about it. Oh yes, when he was sober 'e was big enough to laugh about it.'

Into the silence which followed when I found myself comparing my own father with Kitty's came sudden laughter and singing from the street, and instantly we were wide awake.

We jumped out of bed and ran to the window. The pavement shone with rain and lights streamed out of the pub doorway at the corner. The men came towards the mission, about twenty of them, singing lustily, one or two still clutching bottles and occasionally drinking from them, while from the pub doorway the landlord cautioned them to be quiet or the police would be on the scene.

Lamps were lit in upstairs bedrooms and occasionally a window was thrown open and angry oaths were exchanged, then below us the door of the mission was thrown open and Joe Doyle and his wife stood there, arms akimbo, waiting for the men to slink one by one into the building, uncontrite, their raucous voices fading into the stillness of the night.

CHAPTER 7

In the weeks that followed I was too busy to be unhappy, too weary to lie awake thinking about my lot, too afraid of the alternative so that I scrubbed and cleaned until even Mrs Doyle said I was worth all of two shillings and sixpence a week.

I thought I would never get the smell of carbolic out of my system or prevent it from entering the cracks in my hands and hurting agonizingly so that the tears ran down my cheeks with the pain.

'Yer'll get used to it,' was all Mrs Doyle said, 'I 'ave.'

In some anger Kitty said, 'Yer doin' most o' the work up there, Ellen. That Mrs Slatterly's in the kitchen wi' Mrs Doyle smokin' cigarettes and brewin' cups o'tea while your slavin' upstairs. Ye should complain.'

'Oh I couldn't do that, Kitty, she might get rid of me and I couldn't go back home. I've just got to make a go of it here. I honestly don't mind the work.'

One day I was on my hands and knees scrubbing under the beds when I felt a tap on my shoulder and found one of the seamen looking at me with humorous, twinkling eyes.

'Yer scrubbin' all the pattern off that lino, luv,' he said.

'Well there wasn't much pattern on it to begin with, was there?'

'Ye should 'ave 'elp, luv, them two lazy devils downstairs are lettin' ye do all the work.'

'I don't mind.'

'Well ye should, yer a right bonny lass and yer worth someat better ner this. See 'ere, there's a bag o' sweets for ye and don't be lettin' on yer've got 'em. Put 'em in yer pocket, luv.'

'Thank you, thank you very much.'

'That's all right. What's yer name then?'

'Ellen Adair.'

68

'And a right pretty name it is too. Is the girl downstairs yer sister?'

'No, just my friend.'

'I thowt as much. Different to ye she is, she'll give a good account of 'erself. But this life isn't for ye, luv.'

'Why do you say that?'

'Because yer gentle, luv, gentle and bonny, and if I were ye I'd be lookin' around for someat better ner this. 'Ave the lads bin all right wi' ye?'

'Oh yes they have, they've bin very kind.'

'Well most of 'em are. They're rough lads but they're not bad sorts. Watch out fer Black Jake, though. If yer 'as any trouble from 'im don't ask the Doyles for any 'elp, ye go right to the police, luv. They'll sort 'im out. The Doyles are as feared o' Jake as the rest of 'em.'

'What is he like, this Jake?'

''E's a big bullyin' oaf, 'andsome and loud-mouthed, and 'e fancies 'imself wi the lasses – or 'e's all talk. 'E thinks if 'e crooks 'is little finger they'll all come runnin', and if they don't 'e could be a nasty customer.'

'When is he likely to be back here?'

'Well he signed on a ship goin' to South America so it'll most likely be a good few months 'afore 'e's back 'ere i' Liverpool. Now I must be goin', mi ship's due out tonight.'

'Where are you off to then?'

'Spain's our first call, then through the Med and on to East Africa. It'll be a bit warmer than it is 'ere.'

'Oh how I wish I could travel and see all those wonderful places. I'll never save up enough money to sail on one of those big ships I've seen leaving the harbour.'

'Ye never know, luv, yer just might one day.'

I laughed. 'Never. I've just got to watch them and imagine I'm on board. I'm not as certain as Kitty.'

'Certain, is she?'

'Well, yes. One day she's going to sweep down one of those grand staircases in emeralds and ermine or her name's not Kitty McGuire.'

'And what about you, luv, what do you want?'

'I just want to get away from the smell of carbolic and scrubbing floors.'

He threw back his head and laughed. I heard him laughing all the way down the stairs.

In spite of the carbolic I was not unhappy in those first few months in Liverpool. The money Mrs Doyle paid us was small but we had our food, and large aprons to cover our clothes so that we could keep them decent. The food was filling if not imaginative, and occasionally I saw Kitty slip any leftovers into a basin which she took down to Aunt Mary's.

'Mrs Doyle'll only throw them away,' she said one day when she saw me watching her. 'Mi aunt's so grateful for anythin' I take her, and two of the children are ill with chickenpox.'

In the first few weekends we exhausted the museums and art galleries in the city, and we spent our few coppers riding on the overhead railway from one end of dockland to the other. We took long tramrides out of the city to Seaforth and Waterloo and looked in wide-eyed admiration at the large beautiful houses overlooking the sands and the sea.

'One day,' Kitty said firmly, 'I'm going to live here in a beautiful house set high on a hill overlooking the ocean.'

I didn't continue the conversation – how could I without asking how she was going to achieve such a wish? – and she too remained silent, no doubt asking herself the same question.

My happiest time was when we boarded the ferry which plied between Liverpool and New Brighton. On this tiny chugging vessel it was easy to imagine that we were at one with the big ships which steamed down the Mersey to the open sea, and from the promenade at New Brighton we watched with longing eyes as they disappeared below the horizon.

Only once did we go to the large shops in the city during that first year. The shops fascinated me, I loved the perfumed interiors, the clothes and the jewellery, the furs and the furniture, but Kitty looked at them with haunted longing eyes. Her fierce mercenary little heart resented the expensively dressed women who came to buy things at the glass counters watched over by supercilious assistants, or sat chatting happily over their cups in the luxurious warmth of the tea rooms and coffee lounges.

At one counter she picked up a bracelet which she draped over her wrist. It was not expensive, otherwise it would not have been left on the counter, but all the same the assistant looked at us doubtfully, and catching her eye Kitty hastily put it back on the counter and stalked away.

She didn't stop until she had reached the street and I had to run to keep her in sight. When I finally caught up with her I saw that there were tears of anger in her eyes which she hastily brushed away.

'Kitty, what is it?' I asked helplessly. 'Why are you crying?'

'I'm never coming into Liverpool to walk round the shops again, not until I can afford to show that stuck-up saleswoman that I can afford a better bracelet than that cheap thing she thought I was going to steal.'

'Oh Kitty, she didn't. I suppose they have to be careful.'

'Careful with the likes of us, ye mean?'

'No I don't. They have to be careful with everybody.'

'She wouldn't 'ave given me a second glance if I'd been dolled up in furs wi' rings on mi fingers. No, it's because I'm wearin' this old tweed coat and tam-o-shanter. She knew that I'm a skivvy o' some sort.'

'But it's nice in the shops, Kitty, and it's so lovely and warm on a winter's afternoon.'

'I don't mind if ye comes on yer own, Ellen, I'll find somethin' else to do. I don't mind a bit.'

'But I couldn't come on my own and leave you back at the mission.'

'Well if you want to come to the shops that's 'ow it's got to be, Ellen. I shall never come 'ere again until I 'ave good money in mi pocket and an idea on 'ow I want to spend it.'

Miserably I fell into step at her side, knowing that she meant every word. As we paused to cross the road a long black car, chauffeur driven, pulled in at the kerb. The chauffeur left the car and stood holding the door for his lady passenger. She was fashionably dressed, wearing a large blue hat decorated with feathers and a cape edged with dark fur. Without a look at the chauffeur or us she swept towards the shop door while the commissionaire hurried forward with bows and smiles.

Meeting Kitty's eyes, I found them filled with grim amusement.

'Don't tell me you want to look like her,' I said, smiling.

'Oh but I *do* tell ye, Ellen. One day I want to look just like 'er and arrive like she did in a posh car with a chap i' uniform drivin' mi. What sort o' fur do you think that was?'

'I haven't any idea, but I don't think it was ermine.'

'The only ermine I've ever seen was white, but mi dad said it was only white i' winter. Off a stoat it is and its fur turns white i' winter so it can't be seen agin' the snow. Ye know what I thinks, Ellen? I'll 'ave to settle for emeralds and ermine in the winter an' sapphires and sable in the summer.'

We dissolved into peals of laughter and were frowned upon by both the driver and the commissionaire, then we ran across the road hand in hand like naughty children.

'Little did they know we were laughin' at 'er,' Kitty said impishly.

'What do you suppose I'll be doin' while you're all dolled up in your sable coat shopping for jewels?' I asked her, smiling.

'It's up to you to be climbin' up there with mi, Ellen. I'll do what I can to 'elp ye but if you're not that confident ye can allus come to work for mi. A companion ye can be. Mi mother once worked for an old woman as 'ad a companion. Paid her no more than chicken feed she didn't and the woman was frightened to death of 'er, but I wouldn't be like that with you, Ellen, I'd treat ye like a sister and I'd give ye presents so that ye wouldn't be made to feel inferior.'

I never really knew if Kitty was serious in the things she said, she kept a straight face and spoke with great confidence. I rather think on that Saturday afternoon she would have been surprised if she could have read my thoughts. I was never going to be Kitty's paid companion, she wasn't the only one with a grain of independence. At that time I wanted something more attainable than furs and jewels: the love of a good man and a happy marriage. A nice home in which to bring up our children and enough money so that we didn't have to worry where the next meal was coming from.

Kitty made me smile with her ideas, but I said nothing to her. Dreams were all we had at that time. No words of mine were going to take Kitty's dreams away from her.

It was a night like no other I could ever remember. I had seen wild nights in the country, and deep snow in the early spring when the men had gone up on to the fells to save sheep trapped with their early lambs in the bitter cold, but now the wind moaned like a banshee, from late afternoon throughout the night.

We lay awake listening to the wild weather, and once Kitty got up to stare through the panes and announce that the street was covered with hail, great hailstones the size of marbles. Suddenly there was a great crash from above and we both looked up fearfully to see the ceiling had split from end to end, and a cascade of water gushed down on to the bed. That was the last sleep we had that night, and Mrs Doyle said we must make arrangements with Aunt Mary otherwise we'd have nowhere to stay.

The wind came straight off the sea and the dawn was grey and cold. The windows were covered with salt from the spray swept inland on the wind, and as we walked to Aunt Mary's all we could hear were children crying and chimney pots crashing on to slate roofs.

At Aunt Mary's the children huddled miserably round the breakfast table while smoke puffed back down the chimney, bringing soot that hurt our eyes and filled our throats.

'Is mi uncle still in bed then?' Kitty asked sharply.

'Nay, 'e's out wi' the rest o' the men, called out at three o'clock this mornin' they were and most of 'em needed at 'ome. Mrs Doherty's chimney stack's gone an' the laundry winder's shattered. There'll be no school this mornin' and I reckon yer'd best be seein' what else's 'appened at the mission.'

I had thought she would have objected to our asking for sanctuary with her but she said she would move two of the children out of the attic and we could have that. 'I'll be glad o' the money,' she confided.

The wind when we let ourselves out of the front door almost swept us off our feet but it seemed the mission had escaped other serious damage.

The Doyles were here, there and everywhere issuing orders, and we were told to get on with our work and mind our own business.

'As if we cared whether the roof's leakin' or not,' Kitty snapped, tossing her head.

'Well we do care, don't we?' I replied. 'The mission's our bread and butter.'

'I 'ates the place, it reeks of carbolic and stale cabbage. I 'ates the Doyles too, she's too 'igh and mighty and 'e can't keep 'is 'ands to 'imself.'

I stared at her in surprise. 'He's never once touched me,' I said. 'Has he touched you?'

''E'd very much like to, but just let 'im try it. I'd hit 'im on the 'ead with the frying pan I would.'

I dissolved into laughter and somewhat piqued she snapped, 'You can laugh, Ellen Adair, there'll come a day when ye looks more than fourteen.'

'I look more than fourteen now, I *am* more than fourteen,' I answered stoutly.

'Ye still looks a kid, Ellen. Look at yer figure, it's just straight up and down, there's not a curve into it.'

'Well what's wrong with that? Curves'll come sooner or later.'

She grinned at me and skipped lightly down the passage. It was true my body was maturing slowly, unlike Kitty who had developed a plump rounded bust and hips that curved from a tiny waist. On the landing I looked into a dark film-covered mirror, unhappy with my pale gold hair and dark blue eyes. Kitty was right. I had the face of a child, delicate and somehow fragile, and I wished fervently that I had some of her earthiness, some of her colour and vibrancy.

In the dormitories the windows still rattled in the wind

although it was not nearly as fierce as in the night. The rooms felt cold and there were no curtains to cover the cracks in the window frames and overall was the stench of men's sweat and the carbolic I was using to disguise it.

I worked hard all morning and I worked alone. There was no sign of Mrs Doyle until she came to say I could go down to the kitchen and eat.

'I've 'ad no time ter make a hot meal, yer'll 'ave ter make do wi' corned beef and muffins,' she said sharply. 'A cup o' tea'll warm ye up.'

I ate alone, and was washing the crockery when Kitty came rushing into the kitchen with bright spots of colour flaming in her cheeks. I stared in surprise as she ran to the mirror and started to straighten her hair. Then she spun round and said breathlessly, 'E's 'ere, Ellen. Trust 'im to arrive out o' the storm in a flash o' lightning and a crash o' thunder.'

'Who? Who's here?'

'Black Jake, that's who.'

'What's he like? Is he as bad as they say?'

''E's enormous.' She stretched up her arms to demonstrate his size. 'And 'e's got jet-black hair, a lot of it and a big bushy beard. You'll 'ave to watchout for 'im, Ellen. 'E picked mi up in 'is arms and I 'ad to batter 'im wi' mi fists 'til 'e let mi go. Aw sure but I'll be after 'ittin 'im wi somethin' stronger than mi fists if 'e gets in mi way again.'

Suddenly I found myself laughing uncontrollably and in some annoyance she snapped, 'I don't for the life in mi see what there is to laugh about.'

'Oh Kitty, I love it when the Irish comes into your voice. Why did you ever forsake it for the Yorkshire?'

'What good did the Irish ever do mi in that Yorkshire village? If ye didn't talk like they did they thought yer were foreigners. If I'd bin Chinese or some other heathen they couldn't 'a treated us much worse.'

'Well you're away from the village now, Kitty, ye can let the Irish come back and forget the Yorkshire.'

'I want to forget 'em both, I wants to talk like a lady and so I shall.'

Mrs Doyle marched into the kitchen, in a temper. 'Where's that idlin' 'usband o' mine?' she demanded. 'I've searched the buildin' for 'im but it's my guess 'e's off wi' that Jake down at the pub. It's allus the same when 'e comes back an' what's 'e done wi' all that booze 'e brought in? 'Idden it where I can't get at it, I'll be bound.'

We stared at her without speaking.

With her small black eyes snapping she said, 'Keep out o' Jake's way, you two, I wants no trouble fro' that direction and 'e's a rare one for a pretty face.'

'I don't see why,' Kitty said sharply. ''E's no great shakes to look at even if 'e does fancy 'isself.'

'So, 'e's already 'ad a go at you, 'as 'e? You just watch yer step, Kitty McGuire, it doesn't do to be too cocky wi' the likes o' Jake. An' you keep out of 'is way if ye can,' she ended, addressing me. 'Ye're just the sort o' girl 'e likes.'

She sat down and poured herself a cup of tea, then staring at us balefully she snapped, 'Ye can set about black leadin' the grate, an' there's the tables to set in the dinin' 'all. And mind mi words, keep away fro' Jake.'

We black leaded the kitchen grate and set the dining hall tables, then went in search of Mrs Doyle but met Mr Doyle in the passage. He informed us she'd gone to the shops.

He looked bleary eyed and smelled of beer. He was mighty affable, though, to the point of handing us three-pence each.

''Ere ye are then,' he said. 'Buy yerself someat wi' that, a don't suppose either of ye's got much to play wi'.'

We thanked him gratefully, but brushing our thanks aside he said briskly, 'Get oft 'ome then afore the missus comes back or she'll find ye someat else te do.'

'Won't she be wantin' us to wait on the table and clear away the dishes?' Kitty inquired.

'Nay, Mrs Slatterly's comin' in and bringin' 'er two grand-daughters. There's no way Jake's goin' ter be lookin' at either of 'em. Squints they do, and wi' teeth like a buck rabbit.'

We giggled appreciatively at his attempt at wit even if it

was unkind, and giving me a little push Kitty said, 'Come on then, let's get goin' 'afore she comes back.'

The wind had subsided during the day but it still met us with some force. The corner shop had been boarded up, as was the front window of the Chinese laundry, and a group of children played on the doorstep in spite of the biting cold.

There were ten children living at the laundry, the eldest one, Lo Ying, almost as tall as her diminutive mother. They had shining black straight hair and eyes – strangely slanting to us – like bright black buttons. They were polite, and unlike the English and Irish children in the area seldom got into mischief. Their mother had them well regimented, and to call them in from play she stood outside the laundry with a brass gong which could be heard streets away and which they obeyed implicitly. It amused me to see them drop whatever they were doing to go tearing down the street in answer to the sound of that gong.

'Now what's up?' Kitty said sharply, and I saw that the women in the street were standing in groups or on their doorsteps eyeing a large black car standing at Mrs Wallsingham's front door. Cars in the area were few and far between, which made this one something of a curiosity.

'I'll bet it's Emmie Wallsingham visitin' from the city,' Kitty cried.

'Or somebody's dead,' I echoed.

'It isn't a hearse,' Kitty snapped, 'nobody'd ever 'ave a car for a funeral. It's more likely to be Emmie.'

We had both heard something of the misdoings of Emmie Wallsingham from Aunt Mary.

The black car was rakish and the length of the house. It had a long shiny bonnet and one little boy, more intrepid than the others, had opened the front door and was looking inside. Catching him by the hem of his coat I pulled him out and closed the door.

'Don't you be caught looking in there, Johnny Grimshaw, the owner'll have the police on you.'

He grinned at me cheekily. 'What's it ter yer?' he asked

pertly, and ran round the other side and tried to open the driver's door.

At that moment Mrs Wallsingham appeared at the front door and, arms akimbo, ordered the children away, then turning to the street at large she said, 'I 'opes yer've seen enough, a mother can't 'ave 'er own daughter visit 'er wi'out yer lot gawpin'.'

She went in, slamming the front door, but the women only laughed loudly without moving away.

'Come on in,' Aunt Mary said to us. 'I wants no truck wi' Elsie Wallsingham. She's a wicked tongue in 'er 'ead and a temper to go wi' it. 'Ow is it yer 'ome so soon? Not got the sack, I 'ope.'

'Mr Doyle told us we could get off home and he gave us threepence each,' I said.

When we got in the house Kitty snapped, 'What did yer tell her that for? She'll expect us to treat the kids.'

'I don't mind treating them.'

'Well I do. It's not often we get a bit extra and yer too soft, Ellen, it'll be the downfall of ye.'

Over boiled potatoes and mutton in a weak gravy Aunt Mary elaborated on the shortcomings of Emmie Wallsingham.

'Left 'ome at fifteen she did and never a word 'til she suddenly turned up again when she were nineteen, all done up i' flashy fancy clothes and a face so painted ye could 'a scraped it off. That time she turned up on 'er own, this time she's gotten a fella wi' er.'

'What sort of a fella?' Kitty wanted to know.

'Dark-skinned 'e is, but wi' plenty o' money if the car's owt ter go by.'

'What's she like?' Kitty asked curiously.

'She's pretty, a suppose, and she allus were a pert little madam.'

'Is 'e her 'usband de ye think, Aunt Mary?'

'Not 'im, 'e'll be one of 'er fancy men. I wish a didn't 'ave ter go out, I'd like to 'ave seen 'er when they comes out.'

'Perhaps they're not goin' out.'

'They will be, they'll not be sittin' in there all night. Will one of ye see to the children, put 'em to bed and clean 'em up a bit? I 'ave to go over to Sefton wi' Mrs 'Aslam's dress, I'll want ter see if it fits 'er properly.'

We said we'd see to the children and she left us to clear away the dishes. Actually I was the one who saw to the children because Kitty couldn't keep away from the front door or window and insisted on giving me a commentary on what was happening every five minutes.

It was quite dark now but still front doors were constantly being opened and women were toing and froing as though bent on some errand or other. From the window I saw Kitty talking to a woman from across the street, and felt strangely annoyed. In all my life I had never encountered such a degree of curiosity and there had been enough of it about in the village where Phoebe Patterson had been concerned.

I went back and started to darn the children's clothes. I had always been good with my fingers and my stitches were as neat if not neater than Aunt Mary's. Then Kitty came rushing back. Sinking on to the rug in front of the fire she said excitedly, 'Why didn't ye come out, Ellen? Ye should 'a seen 'er. She looked loverly she did, all i' pink with a feather 'at and a fur tippet. She looked straight at mi and smiled, then she said someat ter 'im and 'e smiled too. Sometimes I just don't understand ye at all, Ellen Adair, fancy sittin' in 'ere when ye could 'a seen Emmie Wallsingham.'

'Why should I want to see her? She isn't famous,' I snapped.

Kitty stared at me because I didn't often snap at her.

'Well she's better and prettier than anythin' else we're likely te see round 'ere. 'E can't be 'er usband, 'e's dark and foreign lookin' wi' a lot o' gold teeth. She wouldn't marry anybody like that, I'm sure.'

I looked at her face, strangely pensive in the glow from the fire. It was an expression I constantly surprised on her face these days, sad and yearning. Next moment however she was heaping coal on to the fire until I remonstrated at her extravagance.

'Your aunt said the coal had to last all night, Kitty, or at least 'til your uncle gets home.'

'I'm sick of sittin' shiverin', mi aunt's out so it's the one chance we 'ave of bein' warm for a change. Where do ye suppose Emmie Wallsingham gets such lovely clothes from, Ellen? After all she were bred and brought up round 'ere, and if she can do it we can.'

'How?'

'I don't know but I'll find out. She's no prettier than we are and she's not as ladylike as you, Ellen, but I reckon she must 'ave some ambition. I've got enough ambition for the pair of us, Ellen. You mark my words, in less than two years it'll be yer and me drivin' up to the front door in a car bigger than that.'

'Oh Kitty, you'd be a lot happier if you didn't always want what you haven't got.'

'I'll never be 'appy 'til I've got what I want. If Emmie Wallsingham's 'ere over the next few days I'm goin' to talk to 'er.

'What are you doin wi' that threepence Joe Doyle gave ye? If ye like I'll nip down to the off-licence and get pop and chocolate, and if yer've got a conscience about it ye can save some for the kids tomorrow.'

I handed over my threepence without a word and the next thing I heard was the slamming of the front door.

CHAPTER 8

I heard a great deal about Black Jake during the next few days but I didn't see him. I heard talk among the men that he had been thrown off his last ship for some misdemeanour and was looking for a new ship in the docks that stretched from one end of Liverpool to the other.

In the mission itself there was a tangible change in the atmosphere. Where once there had been rough camaraderie now there was sullen suspicion and among some of the men seething resentment because they believed Jake was getting better rations.

There was an ugly scene one morning when one of the men hit Mr Doyle, blacking his eye and breaking several front teeth. Kitty said the seaman had accused him of taking bribes from Jake – bottles of rum and gin he'd brought off his last ship – and that the other men were suffering because Jake was getting what they should have. Several days later the seaman's body was found floating in one of the docks and although the police said he'd probably fallen in drunk, nobody among the men believed them for a moment.

I was far from happy at the mission because I was afraid, but I was troubled too about Kitty. I seldom saw her in the evenings. Once we had sat before the fire, tired after our work at the mission, but not too tired to chat happily about the happenings of the day or what we would do on our day off.

Now, as soon as she had swallowed her evening meal she was away to Mrs Wallsingham's, much to Aunt Mary's annoyance as well as mine.

Emmie Wallsingham had become Kitty's idol. We heard nothing but praise of her clothes, her hair and her travels. Once or twice I had seen the man she had arrived with. He was short, slight and swarthy, his clothes were good if flashy, and he wore rings and a thick gold watch chain.

Once when Kitty went on too long about Emmie her aunt flashed, 'I don't know what's come o'er you, Kitty. Can't yer see that nature never made 'er 'air that colour? Out of a bottle it is. Nobody ever 'ad 'air the colour of an orange, Emmie Wallsingham's 'air was mousy, just like the rest of them. Yer own 'air's a lot nicer, lovely shade o' red it is, and look at Ellen's 'ere. Emmie Wallsingham'd give 'er eye teeth for 'air that colour.'

'Well I think she's lovely. She's kind too, she gave me some silk stockings last night. They have a little ladder at the top but I can soon darn that.'

'What else did she give ye?'

'A blouse she's grown tired of. I'm savin' it for summer.'

'Who's the chap she brought 'ome wi' 'er?'

''E's not 'er 'usband, not even 'er boyfriend. She sez 'e's some sort o' boss.'

'Ay and we know what sort o' boss 'e is, don't we?'

'What sort o' boss is 'e then?'

'If ye don't know I'm not up to tellin' ye. Now 'elp Ellen clear away the dishes while I get on wi' mi sewin'. Yer've not bin pullin' yer weight around 'ere, Kitty, it's about time yer did or find fresh lodgings.'

Kitty stared at her balefully but started to remove the dishes, slamming them down on the kitchen table so hard I was afraid they would break. Aunt Mary called out, 'Don't you be takin' yer bad temper out on the dishes, yer little madam, if ye breaks just one of 'em I'll 'ave the money off ye for more.'

I looked cautiously at Kitty's mutinous face but said nothing. This was not the Kitty I had known before we came to Liverpool, the Kitty who had been cheerful in spite of all her troubles, free with her laughter and her ready Irish wit.

On the way to the mission she grumbled constantly about the Doyles, Aunt Mary and her husband, even the children, and more and more I felt frighteningly insecure.

As we donned our aprons Mrs Doyle came out of her kitchen to say, 'We've another load in this mornin' so the place is crowded. Get on with yer work, the pair of ye. The

Slatterlys are comin' in at ten o'clock, we'll need all the 'elp we can get.'

Kitty bustled into the dining hall while I ran upstairs to the dormitories where some of the new men were only just unpacking. Normally they stayed only two or three nights, but if they were changing ships they sometimes had several weeks' wait until they were sent for.

I was glad to see that the seaman who had warned me about Big Jake was back, and catching sight of me he called out, 'Ello there, Little Un. Come over 'ere, I've got someat for ye.'

Shyly I went across to stand uncertainly at his bedside while he rummaged in his pockets.

''Ere's a bar o' chocklit for ye, luv. Don't let old Ma Doyle see it or she'll 'ave it off ye i' no time.'

I thanked him gratefully and pushed the chocolate into my pocket.

'Everthin' bin all right then?' he asked, looking down at me.

'Yes thank you. Big Jake's here but I haven't seen him.'

His face grew sober. 'Keep out of 'is way, luv, don't ye be askin' fer trouble. De ye hear that, lads? Jake's 'ere so mind what yer doin'.'

The Slatterlys duly arrived and I couldn't help thinking that Mr Doyle had spoken nothing but the truth about the two granddaughters. They worked alongside of me when they weren't squabbling, but Mrs Slatterly disappeared into the kitchen where like as not she sat with Mrs Doyle, drinking tea.

They departed immediately after we had eaten and Mrs Doyle said, 'It was 'ardly worth 'em comin' for the work they did.'

'The girls were all right,' I said somewhat resentfully.

'Yer'd get more work out o' the old biddy if yer didn't sit listening to 'er gossipin' in the kitchen,' Mr Doyle said sourly, whereupon his wife immediately snapped back, 'And I'd get more work out o' you if ye didn't go out every night with that Jake. I thought 'e was after findin' a ship, though like as not nobody'll employ 'im since 'e's 'ad trouble on

83

every ship 'e's sailed in. That temper of 'is'll be the end of 'im, mark my words.'

''E'll find one. In the meantime 'e's enough money ter sit back a bit and take a good look around.'

'I don't mind 'im lookin' around, as long as 'e doesn't expect mi 'usband ter look round with 'im. All last Friday yer were supposed ter be lookin' fer a ship and both of yer comin' 'ome long after midnight drunk as lords. I'll be glad when 'e goes and I don't want 'im back 'ere. There's other ports besides Liverpool.'

'Not when yer were born and bred 'ere there isn't. Jake's father and grandfather were dockers right there i' Birkenhead, 'e's a right ter try ter look for a ship leavin' Liverpool.'

'Ay well, the sooner the better.'

Some of the seamen slept until well into the afternoon and without the help of the Slatterly girls I had to change the beds and clean up the dormitory on my own while Kitty was helping to serve dinner. I was bent over one of the narrow beds when I was seized in a grip of iron and lifted clean off my feet, then I heard a man's great booming laughter before he threw me down on to the bed.

He towered over me, this great man with black curly hair and swarthy face, and he was laughing so that his breath sickened me with its overtones of tobacco and beer.

'Well what 'ave we 'ere?' he said. 'I've met the young spitfire downstairs, but they didn't tell me there was another. What's yer name then?'

'Ellen, Ellen Adair.'

'Well, Ellen, I'm Jake, Black Jake they calls me on account of mi black hair among other things. Did they tell ye about me?'

'A little about you, Mr Jake.'

He threw back his head and laughed again. 'Mr Jake, is it? Nay, call mi Jake, I likes all pretty girls to call mi Jake.'

By this time he had settled himself down beside me on the bed and I moved quickly towards the other side. I prayed for somebody to come into the room but all the activity was downstairs. I could even hear Mrs Doyle's voice from the kitchen and the sound of crockery. Something of my hopes must have got through to him because next moment he stroked my hair, saying, 'We're all alone up 'ere, Ellen, jest yer and me, and nobody's goin te come up 'ere 'til the meal's finished. Tell mi about yerself.'

'There's not much to tell.'

'No? What's a girl like yer doin' in a place like this, 'ave yer no folks?'

'Yes, but not in Liverpool.'

'Is that so. Related to the Doyles are ye?'

'No. I came here with Kitty, her aunt lives along the street there.'

''Ave yer got a boyfriend?'

'No.'

'That's good then. 'Ow about me for yer boyfriend?'

I didn't speak, and he laughed. His big hairy hand was on my hair, pulling it and teasing it, then before I could pull away his arms were round me and his mouth was bruising my lips. I felt his hands on my body, lifting my skirts, sliding up my legs, and I fought him with my fists until I felt they would break against the weight of his chest.

I felt nauseated by his breath, his thick lips on mine, the coarseness of his hands and his loud heavy breathing, and then suddenly, miraculously his arms grew slack and next moment he had sprung to his feet. He was moaning, his hands covering his hair, and there was blood sliding stickily down his face.

Even as he tried to wipe it away with his sleeve Kitty hit him again with the frying pan she held in both hands, and then together we escaped out of the room and down the stairs with Big Jake lumbering behind us, bellowing like a bull so that doors were opening everywhere and fearful faces stared out from the dining hall and the Doyles' kitchen.

Mrs Doyle pushed us both into the kitchen, then stood in the doorway, arms akimbo.

'Stay out o' mi kitchen, Jake. Yer've no doubt asked for what ye've got and yer in enough trouble wi' the police without lookin' fer more.'

'If I gets mi 'ands on that little 'ell cat I'll kill 'er, I will,' he stormed, 'and the other one asked fer all she got.'

'If yer causes any trouble 'ere I'll 'ave ye barred fro' the mission,' she went on stoutly. At that moment she had all my admiration while her husband skulked at the back of the kitchen and the seamen shuffled their feet in embarrassed and cowardly silence in the passage.

'And what will yer do to them two? Look at mi 'ead, pourin' wi' blood it is. Is that little hell cat te get off scot free then?'

'That's my business. Yer'd best get that 'ead stitched. The lasses won't be 'ere when yer gets back.'

'I'll stop right 'ere te see what ye're goin' ter do with 'em.'

'Yer'll go to the 'ospital and mi 'usband'll go with yer. Like I said, the lasses'll be gone when yer gets back.'

'I suppose that means yer won't punish either of 'em.'

'They'll lose their jobs. Is that what yer wants?'

I stared at Kitty in horror. Her face was pale but her hand still clutched the frying pan she had battered Jake with, and if the moment had not been filled with such trauma I might have found her stance amusing.

'Now get off to the 'ospital,' Mrs Doyle insisted. 'Get yer coat on, Joe, and go wi' 'im. And you two get yer things together and I'll give ye what I owes ye. I don't want to see either of ye again. I knew there'd be trouble when I took ye both in.'

Kitty collected her things with her head held high, but I was tearful. It was my fault that we had lost our jobs, my fault for being here. None of it would have happened if I hadn't insisted on coming to Liverpool in the first place, and now Kitty was being made to pay for it.

As Mrs Doyle handed over our money she fixed me with a stern look, asking, 'Did yer ask fer it, Ellen, or was it all 'im?'

'I was making the beds, Mrs Doyle, I didn't even see him come into the dormitory.'

'Well I believes yer but I daren't keep yer on 'ere. Jake's a vindictive devil as any one o' them men can tell ye. Yer'd best get off 'ome now afore 'e comes back.'

We left the kitchen and made our way to the front door.

Some of the men stood in the passage eyeing us sympathetically, and sweets and chocolates were pressed into our hands. One of them gave me a small book, saying, 'I've no chocolate for ye, lass, but ye might like to 'ave this. Do ye like poetry?'

I stared at him stupidly. I had never associated any of these men with a liking for poetry but this man's face was kind, refined and intelligent.

'I liked it at school. Thank you very much, I shall enjoy reading it.'

I stared at the well-worn leather-bound book and saw that it was the *Rubaiyat* of Omar Khayyám. I had never heard of it, but somehow it seemed precious on that terrible day and as we walked dolefully along the street Kitty said, 'What did that seaman give ye? It wasn't chocolate?'

I handed the little book over and she stared at it curiously, then scornfully. 'What's a sailor doin' readin' poetry? A proper man wouldn't be interested in such rubbish.'

'Oh Kitty, it doesn't say because he's a seaman he hasn't got a soul.'

'Well soul or no soul 'ere we arc without a job. I don't know what mi Aunt Mary's goin' to say, she can't keep both of us and no money comin' in.'

'But we'll find other work, Kitty. I don't care what I do, I'll start looking first thing in the morning.'

Aunt Mary received our news with dismay. It was a miserable evening. Two of the children were sickly and cried constantly, and on top of that Aunt Mary and her husband were quarrelling most of the night.

Kitty hissed, 'They're quarrelling about us. 'E wants us out of 'ere in the morning, and she's askin' 'im to be patient.'

'But we've nowhere to go, Kitty.'

'Ye could go 'ome, Ellen, ask yer father's forgiveness. 'E'll make yer suffer but 'e'll take ye back.'

'Kitty, I couldn't go back, I'd die before I'd go back.

'What are ye goin' to do then?'

'I'm goin' to find work.'

''Ow about yer Aunt Liza?'

'No, Kitty, I couldn't go to live with her. Besides, she wouldn't have me.'

'Why not?'

'She'll know I've run away from home, she'd send me back there if she knew where to find me.'

'Where does she live then?'

'In Langstone. It's a little village up in the Dales, she keeps a draper's shop in the high street.'

'Did ye say she was yer father's half-sister?'

'Yes.'

'She's called Adair like you then?

'No, she's called Ashington, mi grandmother married twice.'

'If I had anybody to go to I'd get out o' Liverpool, I hates it 'ere, I 'ates the sea and the mournful sound of them 'ooters. I 'ates these mean streets and there's no greenery, it's like livin' in a quarry.'

She turned over crossly without saying another word and the house was silent. Tomorrow would be different, tomorrow was the start of a whole new life. I told myself I was glad to have left the mission and the smell of carbolic and cabbage, and with the optimism of youth I reassured myself that when one door closed another opened. When I said as much to a disgruntled Kitty she merely answered sourly, 'Ye means when one door closes another slams shut.'

CHAPTER 9

The next morning started badly. Two of the children were taken to hospital with scarlet fever and Aunt Mary was distraught, saying, 'I'll never get them two dresses finished now, there's buttonholes to make and buttons to be sewn on. If I don't get 'em finished in time they'll never bring me anythin' else te make.'

'I can do them for you,' I cried quickly. 'Just show me what you want and I'll have them finished when you get back.'

'Are ye sure ye can do 'em, Ellen?'

'She can do 'em as well as you can,' Kitty retorted. 'She allus took the prize for sewin' back at the school.'

Quickly Aunt Mary showed me what was required and I set to with a will, glad to be of some use.

'Ye can try the raincoat factory at the end of the street,' Aunt Mary told Kitty. 'I 'ear they've bin lookin' for machinists.'

'I can't use a machine,' Kitty said.

'Well yer not too daft to learn, Kitty, and ye'll 'ave to find work o' some sort or go back to yer mother.'

'I'd rather go into service than work in a factory,' Kitty retorted.

'I don't care what ye does as long as ye finds work,' Aunt Mary answered wearily.

When she had cleared away and washed the dishes Kitty returned to where I was busy stitching minute buttons down the back of a dress. For a while she stood watching me then she picked up the book of poems the seaman had given me and started to turn the pages.

'I don't understand a word of it,' she said. 'It's not poetry like I've ever read. Who was 'e anyway?'

'I think he was Persian so it's bound to be different.'

'I agree with one thing 'e sez, though, time is slippin'

89

underneath our feet and we're worse off now than when we came 'ere. I'm going down to the Wallsinghams', perhaps Emmie can suggest somethin' for mi to do.'

Whatever suggestions Emmie Wallsingham had to make, three days later Kitty found work at the raincoat factory packing the finished garments. She hated every moment of it. The concrete floors that were so cold to her feet that she got chilblains, the small draughty windows, her work-mates who were foul-mouthed and vociferous. She hated the men who did the fetching and carrying because they thought she was fair game for their attentions, and she loathed the forewoman who was married to one of them and accused Kitty of encouraging him.

'What would a want with a fella like that?' Kitty stormed. ''E's old enough to be mi father and 'e's no great shakes to look at.'

Perhaps I was fortunate because Aunt Mary was tied down with hospital visiting and caring for the children at home so that I was kept busy with her dressmaking.

More and more I was aware of Kitty's resentment, and one night she said sullenly, 'It's all right for ye, Ellen, ye don't 'ave to turn out on a cold mornin', 'ere ye are with a nice fire doin' the thing ye likes doin'!'

'Oh Kitty, sewing buttons on other people's dresses isn't what I came to Liverpool for, but if I don't help Aunt Mary she'll lose the business, and she needs the money.'

She stared at me miserably, then something of the old Kitty reasserted itself.

'I'm sorry, Ellen, none of it's yer fault and I'm a little monster. It's just that I'm not happy workin' at that factory and I don't see any end to it. Mi aunt won't want yer 'elp for ever, so what will ye do then?'

'I don't know. I'll start looking the first opportunity I get. Did Emmie Wallsingham have anything to suggest?'

'No.'

Her reply was short and snappy, and almost immediately she flounced out of the room, saying she was going to buy sweets to take to the children. I was in bed when she returned so I knew she must have called somewhere else besides the shop, and I suspected she had been with Emmie Wallsingham.

The best part of helping Aunt Mary was delivering the dresses. In this way I got to see different parts of Liverpool and how other people lived in the city. Best of all I liked going to Mrs Lister's at Sefton. Her husband was a civil servant and they lived in a nice rather large terraced house with a big garden at the back and a smaller one at the front.

Mrs Lister was a pleasant lady who always invited me in and gave me a cup of tea while she tried on her dress. Once when it didn't fit too well she asked me to stay and alter it, and when she was satisfied with it she said, 'Why don't you take in sewing yourself, Ellen? You sew beautifully and I could find you work.'

'I couldn't do that, Mrs Lister, it would take work away from Aunt Mary and she's been very kind to me.'

'You've had that coat a long time, Ellen, it's getting very worn and it's too short for you. You've grown these last few weeks. I've got one upstairs you can have. I'll bring it down, if it's too big I know you'll be able to alter it.'

The coat was a lovely light navy velour and I only needed to alter the buttons for it to fit me. She also produced a navy skirt and two silk blouses, one in pink, the other white. I was overwhelmed by her kindness and thanked her profusely.

She merely said, 'I'm glad they fit you, Ellen, but don't you be giving them away merely because you're being given a home. These are yours, you must wear them.'

'Oh I will, Mrs Lister, I will really. I'm so glad to have them.'

'Well get off home then before it gets dark.'

I felt troubled about the clothes. Aunt Mary would think it unfair that I should have them when she'd been sewing for Mrs Lister much longer, and Kitty – well, I was never very sure about Kitty these days.

When I walked in with my parcel Aunt Mary said plaintively, 'Don't tell me they don't fit?'

'It's a coat and skirt Mrs Lister's given me, Aunt Mary.'

'They'd a cost a bonny penny in the shops,' she commented when I'd opened the parcel. 'Did she say *ye* 'ad to 'ave em?'

'Yes she did.'

'Oh well, ye 'ave bin a lucky girl, and me sewing for 'er all these years.'

All joy in my new clothes seemed suddenly to evaporate. I felt I had no right to them, and seeing my doleful face Aunt Mary said, 'Yer'd best wear 'em, Ellen, I wouldn't like Mrs Lister to think I'd 'ad any hand in yer not wearing 'em.'

'Perhaps Kitty would like one of the blouses.'

Both the blouses were tight on Kitty, but she said philosophically, 'I'd rather 'ave a shape than 'ave a blouse. 'Ow much is Aunt Mary givin' ye for 'elpin' out with 'er sewin'?'

'I told her I didn't want any money, she's feeding me.'

'She's got a nerve, a few bob a week wouldn't kill 'er.'

I can only assume that Kitty said something to her aunt because at the weekend Aunt Mary placed two shillings in my hand, saying, 'This is a bit towards what yer've done for mi, Ellen. I couldn't 'ave managed without ye.'

CHAPTER 10

Spring came to the city. In the parks snowdrops and crocus carpeted the lawns and daffodils swayed beside the paths. People's footsteps seemed lighter, and faces that had been grey and weary now bore smiles. The shop windows were gayer, with light-coloured clothing and spring millinery.

The children were now on their way to recovery except for the youngest who had a permanent cough and looked destined to be the weakling of the family. Aunt Mary returned to her sewing machine for what she called the heavy work, while she passed less and less work over to me. The week before Easter I got a job as a machinist at the raincoat factory.

My day began at seven and ended at seven. It was slave labour, a veritable sweat shop. Morning and afternoon we stopped the machines for five minutes so that we could have a cup of tea, then it was back to the machines where we were overlooked by an enormous woman called Mrs Edge, and woe betide any of us if we spoke to our neighbour.

I saw nothing of Kitty at the factory, and not very much of her at home. In the evenings we were both weary but it didn't stop her from spending time with Emmie Wallsingham. At the weekends I put on my best coat and went to the shops but I was always alone. Kitty had kept her word, she would not visit the shops until she could buy the best they had to offer, so I pretended to myself that I was in that fortunate position.

I drank coffee in the coffee lounges and smiled at the waitresses. I knew I looked presentable in the coat Mrs Lister had given me, and I had a little money in my pocket. The raincoat factory paid poor wages and after I had given some to Aunt Mary for my keep and treated the children to sweets there wasn't much left – enough to buy the occasional pair of stockings, and put by a little for the bigger things.

Sundays I loved. The ferries were cheap and I sailed upriver or out to New Brighton and Wallasey. I pretended that I was on a great ocean liner and for hours I would sit nostalgically staring out at the great ships sailing to romantic places. I hadn't Kitty's yearning for jewels and furs, but I had a desperate longing to travel, to sail one day on one of those ocean liners.

I didn't want to spend all my young life living at Aunt Mary's. I loved the children but I had no privacy, they were always in my things or leaping on my bed, and at times their squabbles were deafening.

I didn't enjoy seeing Aunt Mary toiling night and day at her sewing machine and cooking meals that were served up cold because her husband was late home from the public house. And I didn't like the way he looked at me.

At long last I was developing a shape. I was taller than Kitty and more slender, and had a sort of grace, Aunt Mary said, that Kitty would never have. But I didn't have her vibrant colouring, my hair was still that fine pale gold it had been in childhood.

I would often find the uncle watching me covertly across the table, and he never lost an opportunity of brushing against me while I was washing the dishes.

Kitty warned, "'E fancies ye, Ellen, yer'd better watch out.'

But it was Kitty herself who troubled me most. All the time now I was feeling her resentment, and the times became fewer when we laughed together with our old comradeship. Her hatred of her job, her home, her workmates and the city itself made her taciturn and rebellious, and only Emmie Wallsingham had the power to bring laughter to her lips and enthusiasm into her heart.

'When is Emmie leaving?' I once asked her.

'Soon,' Kitty replied, 'she's waitin' fer Alex to come back from the city te tell 'er it's all right for 'er to go back there.'

'Why does she have to wait for him, why can't she just go there?'

94

'I don't know. There was some trouble but what sort o' trouble she didn't say. Ellen, will ye not ask mi anythin' about Emmie when mi aunt's there? She 'asn't a good word to say fer Emmie and a can't see why. Emmie's done nothing to 'er.'

'Perhaps your aunt knows something you don't.'

'Not she. She's jealous because Emmie's well dressed, wi' money in 'er purse.'

'Is Alex the man she came here with, the man with the car?'

'That's right. Any day now 'e'll be back, 'e writes to 'er often.'

Alex appeared several days later, and there were many times I saw Kitty chatting to him on the street, sometimes with Emmie, at others just the two of them. He seemed to be doing most of the talking in a serious persuasive way and Kitty was listening to him, almost as if her life depended on it.

One night as we lay in bed she said, 'What would ye do, Ellen, if I leaves here, would ye stay on 'ere at mi aunt's?'

'I don't know, Kitty. You're not thinking of leaving, are you?'

'Oh well, there's nothin' planned, but ye knows 'ow I 'ates that factory and livin' 'ere.'

'You could get another job you liked better, and one day, Kitty, we might be able to afford a little house of our own.'

'And pigs might fly, Ellen.'

'I don't see why not. We're both earnin' money, all the houses are not expensive.'

'I've had mi fill o' livin' in a rubbish 'eap. Ellen, I just don't want ye to think we'll be spendin' the rest of our lives together.'

'I don't think that either. One of these days I hope we'll both get married and live in nice homes. Isn't that what you want?'

'Right now, Ellen, I'm only concerned with me. If a man turns up fer me and I fancies 'im, well and good, but I'm not sittin' 'ere waitin' for it to 'appen. If I makes mi own life, Ellen, ye won't 'old it against mi, will yer?'

'No, Kitty, I won't.'

'And yer'll be able to look after yerself?'

'Of course. Why don't you tell me what you have in mind instead of asking me questions like that?'

'Because I'm not sure. It all needs thinkin' about.'

'Do Emmie Wallsingham and that man have anything to do with it?'

'Why should they 'ave? And there's no call to be looking down your nose at Emmie, Ellen, she's a good friend with 'er 'ead screwed on right.'

'I wasn't looking down my nose at her, Kitty, honestly.'

'Oh well, I don't want to talk about it any more now and don't be talking about any of this in front of mi aunt. It's time for 'er to know when I've made mi mind up.'

Kitty was asleep long before me. I lay staring up at the ceiling with my thoughts miserably uncertain. Rain pattered on the window and occasionally above the wind came the long mournful hooting of a steamer and the sound of a train speeding through the night.

Two weeks after my conversation with Kitty it seemed my whole life was to change.

I believed that every moment of that Wednesday morning would be implanted in my memory for evermore. The day started as it always did with a rushed breakfast of tea and toast, then the short walk through streets only just coming to life.

I parted from Kitty at the entrance to the machine room, calling out, 'Shall I see you for dinner?' to which she replied, 'I'm not sure, better not wait fer mi in case I shan't be able to get 'ome.'

We sat in rows at our machines and the noise was deafening. Now and again Mrs Edge walked along the aisles picking up a raincoat here and a raincoat there, looking closely at the stitches and the hems, but fortunately she had little to complain about where my sewing was concerned.

I was astonished therefore when she came to my machine about eleven o'clock that morning, indicating that I should stop. Those about me also stopped until she snapped, 'That doesn't go fer the rest of ye, get on wi' yer work.'

'Yer wanted at 'ome Ellen, Mrs McLoughlin's sent one o' the children ter say ye 'ave a visitor. But I wants ye back 'ere as soon as yer've eaten yer dinner. There'll be two 'ours docked off yer wages.'

'Did she say who my visitor was, Mrs Edge?' I stammered unhappily.

'It's none o' my business. Just ye get off now.'

I grabbed my coat off the peg and flew through the packing room. Kitty's eyes met mine briefly but I couldn't talk to her because the forewoman was nearby. Kitty's face was strangely anxious, and before I turned away it had become bright scarlet. That Kitty knew more than I did was very obvious.

I ran all the way home and at the door Jonny, who was off school with whooping cough, said, 'There's somebody ter see ye Ellen, a lady.'

I stared at him in surprise, I had been so sure it would be my father.

'What is she like?'

'Old. She's old.'

All sorts of visions passed before my eyes. It couldn't be my mother, because even if she knew where I was Father wouldn't allow her to come – not unless he was dead, that is.

My heart leapt at that prospect but then the door opened and Aunt Mary said sharply, 'There ye are, Ellen. Here's yer aunt, all the way fro' Yorkshire. Bin travellin' since first light, she 'as.'

I stared at her in amazement, then she shooed me into the living room.

My first thought was that Aunt Liza sat in the rocking chair like a black crow in her long black skirt and coat, with a big black hat on her hair and clutching a large Gladstone bag. Our eyes met and my heart sank for there was no pleasure in the gaze she bestowed upon me, not a glimmer of a smile on her thin lips. Before I could say a word she snapped, 'Well, Ellen, and what 'ave you to say for yerself?'

'How did you know I was here, Aunt Liza?'

'That girl wrote to me, Kitty McGuire. She said if I was interested in your welfare I should get in touch with ye, that there was nothing here in Liverpool for ye.'

Weakly I sat down, not knowing which caused me most anxiety – the arrival of Aunt Liza or Kitty's perfidy.

From the kitchen I could hear Aunty Mary busying herself with crockery, then she came into the room carrying a tea tray.

'I expect yer'd like someat ter eat?' she said. 'I can send Jonny te the shop for barm cakes and cornbeef.'

'No thanks, I want to get back as soon as possible. There's a train to Leeds at two thirty that'll just catch the country train for Langstone. Go upstairs and get yer bags packed, Ellen, I'll settle up wi' Mrs McLoughlin for anythin' ye might owe her.'

'Ye don't owe mi anythin', Ma'am,' Aunty Mary said, 'Ellen's allus bin good both wi' me and the children. I'm sorry she's goin'. Does she 'ave te go?'

'Yer niece wouldn't 'ave written fer nothin', Mrs McLoughlin.'

I remembered all Kitty's questions about Aunt Liza, and felt close to tears when I realized how long she had been planning the events of this morning.

In some anger I said, 'I'm not goin' back to my father's house, Aunt Liza, I'd die before I'd go back there.'

'It's a wicked girl you are, Ellen Adair, to talk about yer father like that.' Then turning to Aunt Mary she said, 'Mi brother's an upright God-fearin' man. Sexton at the church he is and well respected by the vicar and the rest o' the community. He's always bin a good provider, his wife and children have lacked for nothin' and she's bin brought up in a good Christian home. A right nice house it is with a big garden an' every comfort. How any niece o' mine could 'ave turned out like Ellen here I'll never know, but for your information, Ellen, yer father doesn't want ye back. He sez yer've made yer bed and ye must lie on it. All the same it's mi Christian duty to take ye in and bring ye up proper if it's the last thing I do.

'But I am brought up, Aunt Liza, I'm sixteen next birth-day. I'm no longer a child and I can earn my own living.'

'This good woman's given ye a home because of 'er niece but you're not 'er responsibility. It looks to me as how she's enough to do with her own husband and children, as well as her niece. Why, there's hardly room to swing a cat around and there'll be some sighs of relief when yer've gone, I feels sure.'

'But I don't want to live in Yorkshire, I love Liverpool. I love the sea and boats. What will I ever do back in the Dales?'

'You can 'elp me in the shop, do the shoppin' and help mi to clean the house. By doin' all that one day yer'll make a decent wife for some man, which is more than yer'll ever do if ye stays on 'ere. Now go and pack yer bags, Ellen, you're coming with me. If I have any trouble I'll send for the police. Don't forget you're under age, they'll see that ye does as you're told.'

I packed my bags with the tears streaming down my face and with my heart filled with deep anger and resentment, against my aunt, my father, but most of all against Kitty. Again and again I told myself how much I despised her for what she had done, but by the time I had packed and changed into my best coat I had composed myself. I would rather have died than allow Aunt Liza to think I was desolate.

I kissed Aunty Mary and my aunt shook hands with her formally, then we were walking side by side down the street and lace curtains were being moved aside so that inquisitive eyes might watch us. Then I saw Kitty running across the factory yard with her coat thrown carelessly round her shoulders. She was gasping for breath when she reached me and I could tell that she'd been crying.

'So yer goin', Ellen?' she gasped.

'You've made it so that I have to go, Kitty. Why did you do it?'

'I 'ad to do it Ellen, I'm goin' too. I'm goin' with Emmie Wallsingham at the weekend, I couldn't go and leave ye 'ere.'

'Why couldn't you have told me what you intended to do and left it to me to sort out my own life? Honestly, Kitty, I never thought you'd do this to me, never.'

'In time yer'll thank mi for it, Ellen. This is no city for you to stay in.'

'What will you do with Emmie Wallsingham, where will you live and what sort of work will you do?'

I watched the rich red colour flood into her face and her eyes slid away from mine, confused and embarrassed.

'I wish ye 'adn't asked mi that, Ellen, because at the moment I'm not sure.'

'I know what everybody says about Emmie Wallsingham.'

'Mebbe they're jealous of the way she dresses and the way she looks.'

'No, Kitty, but everybody's pretty sure how she comes by the clothes she wears.'

For the first time there was anger in her face, anger mingled with a strange sort of anguish and at that moment I pitied her because I loved her and understood her anger.

'I won't listen to any more, Ellen, and I don't care what anybody sez about Emmie, she's bin kind to me. I'm not goin' to end up like Emmie, small time and contented with it. One day I'll be somebody and look like somebody and right now I don't much care 'ow I gets there. One day, Ellen, we might see each other again and then yer'll understand why I 'ad to do what I did. Yer aunt's waitin' for ye and she looks none too pleased.'

Aunt Liza was standing near the tram stop, her face registering impatience and displeasure. With another swift look at Kitty's face I turned and ran. The tram came clanging noisily down the road and it was only when I clambered aboard behind Aunt Liza that I turned to look back. Kitty was standing where I had left her and I saw her raise her arm and wave before I went inside.

Hurriedly I brushed away the tears from my cheeks and sat resolutely looking in front of me. A part of my life was irretrievably over and as the tram noisily made its way towards the heart of the city I stared out of the window at the streets I loved.

100

This city, so vibrant with life, had been my joy. It was not a beautiful city but I had revelled in its sounds and its smells, its romantic obsession with the sea and foreign places, and if Aunt Liza expected me to be sorry for what I had done there was no regret in my heart.

For nearly two years it had been part of my first great adventure. And there would be others – Kitty McGuire was not the only one to have dreams and longings even if we were destined to attain our ends by different means.

CHAPTER 11

It didn't take long to familiarize myself with Langstone because there wasn't a great deal of it: one long straggling high street paved with cobblestones, a square-towered Saxon church standing at one end and the Black Bull inn at the other.

On Wednesdays and Saturdays market stalls were set out along the length of the street and I could see all the activity from the window of my aunt's draper's shop halfway down the street.

Aunt Liza didn't much like market days. 'Sellin' cotton and tape and the like at half the price I sell 'em for,' she complained. 'Like as not they've bin stolen from some mill or other or there's somethin' wrong with 'em.'

Her best crony was Mrs Devlin from the baker's shop across the road and in the evenings they would sit together going over the village gossip, drinking tea and eating the baker's leftovers which Mrs Devlin brought across. On some nights Aunt Liza would trip across there carrying several bottles of stout in her black bag, and when she returned I was amused to see how her temper had improved until she became almost affable.

I enjoyed setting out the shop window and waiting at the counter. Most of the villagers were friendly if curious, and yet I made no close friends so that I wondered how long I would have to reside in Langstone before I became one of them.

Aunt Liza had quarrelled with the vicar and was not going to church, consequently on the first Sunday she said, 'I'm not stoppin' you from goin' to church, Ellen, but I'll want his apology 'afore I sets foot in the place again.'

'What did he do, Aunt Liza, that makes you so angry?'

'I didn't get mi usual stall at the church fete, that's what. I've 'ad that spot for nigh on twenty years and this year if'e

102

didn't go and give it to Molly Weaver for 'er plants and flowers.'

'Didn't you get a stall then?'

'I did, but it was in a draughty corner which did nothin' for mi arthritis. Them that were lookin' for mi in mi usual place had to find mi and I didn't do as well.'

'What did the vicar have to say?'

''E said 'e didn't think I'd mind. 'E's not bin 'ere long, eighteen months that's all. I've stopped the church magazine 'til I get some sort o' satisfaction.'

It all seemed so small-minded and petty, exactly like the village gossip at home, but it did mean that on Sundays I was free to do as I liked, which nearly always meant going for long walks over the fells or along the country lanes.

The sun was warm on my arms as I sat on the hillside contemplating the view below. The sunlight fell on warm red roofs and the rambling high street, on people wearing their Sunday-best clothes on their way to church and on the majestic pile known as Langstone Priory set in its vast parkland and formal gardens.

When I first saw it I thought it might be a boys' school where gentlemen and the aristocracy sent their sons to be educated but Aunt Liza said, 'Of course it isn't a school, it's a family house. Most of us round 'ere call it the Hall, but that isn't its real name.'

'It's awfully big. Who lives there?'

'The de Bellefort family own it. They do say they came over wi' the Normans but there's only old Lady de Bellefort livin' there now. Three sons she had and one daughter. The eldest son lives in a house as big as that one over at Mowbray and the other who was a bit of a tearaway in his younger days lives over in Ireland at County Wicklow. The youngest son was killed in India, and now and again his widow visits and their daughter spends some time 'ere. Yer'd think the young widow'd spend a bit more time with the old lady now she's all alone'.

'What's going to happen to that house when the old lady dies?'

103

'Who knows? But folks do say one o' the grandsons'll come in for it.'

'I wonder what it's like living in a house like that?' I mused.

I was thinking about Kitty, how her eyes would have grown wide with wonder while her imagination clothed her in the things she longed for.

To give Aunt Liza her due she hadn't asked too many questions about my life in Liverpool, but one evening as we sat over our cocoa she astonished me by asking, 'What made yer leave home, Ellen? I've heard mi brother's version, now I'd like to 'ear yours – particularly if ye intends staying here with me and lookin' after mi little shop.'

She was watching me closely with her lips set tight, her black eyes stern and brooking no prevarication.

'I couldn't get on with mi father, Aunt Liza.'

'Why not! He's a good provider and 'e's bin a good husband and father, hasn't he?'

'I was afraid of him.'

'What nonsense. What 'ad ye to be afraid of him for? I've never seen him take a hand to ye.'

'Well of course not, you were never there when he beat me until mi back ran with blood. You never had to sit through his sulks or watch mi mother's face miserable and unhappy after one of his tirades. I've watched him beat Peter for no reason at all and he was always the first one to sit in judgement on everybody else.'

'Ye must 'ave done somethin' to warrant a beatin'. I know 'e didn't like ye bein friends with that Kitty McGuire and as things 'ave turned out he was probably right about that. Don't ye think he was stern because he wanted ye to grow up proper and decent?'

'You don't know anything about Phoebe Patterson, Aunt.'

'Who's she then?'

'She's the village harlot. Mi father's out to save her soul but he's not averse to visitin' her late at night and comin' home in the early mornin'.'

'Nay, I'll not have that, Ellen. I'll not 'ave yer sayin' 'e has a woman friend. Why it's more than his job's worth.'

So I told her what I had seen. Indeed I told her everything except the real fear I had had that my father was beginning to lust after me in a quite unfatherly manner. I could not bring myself to tell her that.

After that night she never referred to my reasons for leaving home again beyond saying that she had written to my father to say I was living with her in Langstone.

It wasn't a particularly busy shop, so I took to embroidering tapestries and tablecloths and one of these I put in the shop window.

'There's no room for it,' Aunt Liza complained. 'Besides, who'll buy it? If they wants embroidered tablecloths they'll do their own.'

'It's worth a try, Aunt.'

'Well if it's still there when the new wools come in it'll 'ave to come out to make room for them.'

Two days later it was sold to a woman visiting one of our neighbours and when I told Aunt Liza how much it had fetched she merely snapped, 'It's not enough, Ellen, yer not paid for yer time and trouble. If ye does another, update yer price.'

I did several others and traycloths also, all of which were sold. Then one day a carriage pulled up at the front door and the coachman stepped down to help an elderly lady out. She was tall and slender and carried herself superbly although she was obviously very old. She was dressed entirely in black, but it was expensive black and there was the rustle of silk as she entered the shop.

I pulled a chair forward for her and she thanked me with a gracious nod. Her voice was low pitched but commanding and almost immediately Aunt Liza appeared from the room behind the shop, almost falling over herself in an effort to please.

'Good afternoon, Lady de Bellefort. What can I do for you?'

'My maid ordered some wool from you, I was passing and thought I would call to see if it had arrived.'

'I'm expecting it any day, Milady. I could send my niece up to the Hall with it.'

'Would that be a lot of trouble?'

'No trouble at all, Milady.'

'Well thank you, that would be very kind. Your window is different, I wondered if you had left the shop.'

'It's mi niece, Milady, she's taken to doin' the window and dressin' it up with some of her embroidery.'

'So I noticed. May I see some of it?'

'Of course, Milady. Ellen, show 'er ladyship what yer've done.'

So I produced cushion covers and tablecloths, babies' bibs and traycloths, all of which the old lady looked at closely.

'Have you done all these?' she asked quietly.

'Yes Milady.'

'You have been trained in fine sewing?'

'Only sewing lessons at school. I like sewing, I was always good with my fingers.'

'Yes indeed. It's nice to see a young girl so skilful. I would like my maid to see some of this work, her own leaves much to be desired. I will take two of the tablecloths and four traycloths, they will do very nicely for presents. I will pay you what you have charged, my dear, but allow me to tell you that they are very much under priced. Don't you agree, Miss Ashington?'

'Well there's not much call for this sort o' stuff in the village, Milady, and if there was they wouldn't want to pay much for it.'

Lady de Bellefort shook her head sadly. 'Yes, it is a pity that more people do not recognize beauty when they see it. You will send the wools then, Miss Ashington?'

'As soon as they arrive, Milady, and thank you for your custom.'

As she passed out of the doorway Lady de Bellefort turned to me with a half smile, saying, 'Do not be discouraged by other people's failings, my dear.'

To say that Aunt Liza was gratified by that visit is an understatement. She retired to her parlour and got out the sherry glasses and one of her iced fruit cakes from which she cut me a generous slice.

'It's a pity the vicar wasn't about when her carriage was outside,' she muttered. 'That would have given 'im somethin' to think about.'

'Does she always drive about in a carriage?'

'Well of course, her ladyship can't be bothered with them smelly motorcars, and those two horses are a picture.'

'She was very kind to buy my embroidery.'

'Yes well, don't you be getting any ideas above yourself, Ellen, yer've a long way to go before ye convinces me that ye've left all that silliness behind ye.'

'Yes, Aunt.'

'I think I'll just slip across to Mrs Devlin's. She's probably seen our visitor but I'd like 'er to know what she's bin buyin'. If I tells Mrs Devlin what's bin happening, in no time at all the whole village'll know, including the vicar.'

I was glad for her to go. I liked having the house and shop to myself so that I could pretend it was all mine. I visualized what I would do with it, the shop window and the shelves above the counter, but when I voiced only half of these imaginings to Aunt Liza she sniffed contemptuously, saying, 'It's good enough for me as it is. Yer seem to have ideas above yer station, Ellen, it's time ye came down to earth. I can understand how ye must 'ave worried yer parents. Ye might as well know yer father's written back sayin' they don't want to know anythin' about ye.'

This did not surprise me.

I was neither happy nor unhappy in Langstone. It seemed that I was living in limbo, marking time while waiting for something to happen, but as uneventful day followed uneventful day there seemed little hope that it would ever change.

One day after Aunt Liza had spent a particularly painful night with her arthritis she watched me setting out the window in rather more than her usual close-lipped silence, then said peevishly, 'Ye enjoys doin' the window don't ye, Ellen?'

'Yes, Aunt.'

'Well I wants ye to know now that this shop'll never be yours. I 'ave a bit o' money which I intend to divide between mi brothers and mi niece over at Ripon. If ye gets any, it'll 'ave to come from yer father, and I can't see that happenin'.

I bit my lip to repress the quick retort she was waiting for and which I had no intention of making.

'I know ye likes the shop and the work but that's as far as it goes. I just wanted ye to know that puttin' a roof over yer head is all I'm aimin' to do.'

'I didn't expect anything else, Aunt Liza, why should I?'

'Well I just wanted to be honest with ye, that's all. Now get off to the Hall with Lady de Bellefort's wool. To the back door, mind ye. I don't want ye knockin' on the front door and 'ave that supercilious butler order ye round to the back door thinkin' I 'aven't taught ye anythin' better.'

It was a clear golden morning. A light breeze filled the air with the scent of clover and the hedgerows were white and pink with May blossom. The huge iron gates were open and the drive seemed to go on for ever. Giant oaks stood in the parkland and in the distance I could see deer wandering among the beech trees and swans sailing majestically across the tarn.

I stood in the middle of the path looking back towards the village, which from this point halfway up the hill seemed to be dominated by the sprawling mansion behind me. How Kitty would have loved this house, and I approached it with a strange resentment against all those people who had all the colour of the world while others had nothing at all.

Dutifully I made my way to the servants' quarters where I knocked sharply on the stout wooden door. It was opened to me by a maidservant who reminded me of Kitty with her red hair and pretty pert face.

She stood without speaking, eyeing me over without any sense of urgency, and a voice came from a distance. 'Are ye answerin' the door, Jennie?'

'Yes, Cook, it's a girl from the village.'

'What's she want then?'

Jennie looked at me for an answer.

'I'm Miss Ashington's niece from the wool shop, I've brought her ladyship's wool. She's expecting it.'

'Wait 'ere,' she said, and disappeared with the parcel of wool.

In a few minutes she was back asking, ''As the wool been paid for?'

'I'm not sure, but my aunt didn't mention payment. I'm sure it will be all right if I just leave it.'

'Well ye'd best come in and tell Cook. It's mi half day and I'm late as it is.'

I followed her into the largest kitchen I had ever seen in my life. Cook and a very young girl sat at the table polishing silver and without another word Jennie left me standing in the middle of the floor.

Cook looked up and said sharply, 'Did I 'ear ye say you were Miss Ashington's niece?'

'Yes, that's right.'

'I didn't know she had any kinfolk around these parts.'

'She hasn't. I came from Liverpool but my family live north of Skipton.'

'Yer aunt doesn't come to church much these days, how's that?'

'Her arthritis has been troubling her.'

'I'm sorry to 'ear it. I did 'ear she'd 'ad a bit o' trouble with the vicar. There isn't any truth in it then?'

'I'm sure there isn't.'

'Well a tale never loses anythin' round these parts. Are ye wantin' payin' for this wool then?'

'That's between Lady de Bellefort and my aunt, I don't expect to be paid for it today.'

'Sit down for a minute and 'ave a cup of tea, there's still some in the pot, I think. 'Ave a look, Mary, and get out some o' that simnel. It's nice to 'ave a bit o' company from the village.'

So I sat down at the table with a large piece of simnel and a cup of strong tea.

'There's an awful lot of silver to clean,' I ventured.

'Ay, and this is only a bit of it. We're getting ready for Mrs de Bellefort and 'er daughter, comin' tonight from France they are so the rooms have 'ad to be got ready and the whole house cleaned from top to bottom.'

'It will be nice for her ladyship to have them here.'

'That it will, but the daughter-in-law'll be off almost as soon as she's got here. Never stops long, she doesn't, but Miss Lisanne'll most likely be 'ere for the summer.'

'They don't live round here then?' I asked, anxious to know more about the family who could afford to live at Langstone Priory.

'Well Mrs de Bellefort never lives anywhere for long since 'er 'usband was killed out in India. Cousins they were. The de Belleforts always marry their cousins, that way they keeps the money in the family so to speak, but I don't think it's a good idea at all. If there's anything wrong in the family it's bound to crop up again and again and if the Colonel had lived I 'ave mi doubts that they'd end their days together.'

'Why is that?'

'Well he was always a nice serious sort o' man while 'is wife was pretty and flighty as a butterfly. He liked the country and she liked the shops and the theatre, balls and tea parties. She liked to surround herself wi' all sorts o' young men who danced with her and flattered her, and she spent a small fortune on clothes, and I bet she 'ad a high old time when they were out in India.

'Miss Lisanne's at finishin' school in Switzerland and that's where 'er mother spends most o' the winter, some place they call St Moritz. One o' these days she's goin' to find it awful quiet 'ere at her grandmother's house.'

'She might find it a pleasant change.'

'I doubt it, like mother like daughter. Marriage'll tame 'er.'

'How old is Miss Lisanne?'

'Eighteen or nineteen by this time, I should think. One day she'll marry one of her cousins, but I'm not sure which one. One of 'em'll get the place in Ireland the other'll get this one.'

'Surely she'll have a say in which one she marries?'

'I don't know. There's Miss Geraldine to consider. That's Lady de Bellefort's daughter's daughter, another cousin. She'll get one and Miss Lisanne'll get the other.'

It seemed archaic to me that four young people should

110

have their entire lives planned for them, who they would marry, even where they would live, but Cook was saying, 'One thing's for sure, none of em'll ever be short of a bob or two.'

'I'd rather be free to plan my own life than be told who I must marry, even if it meant living in the lap of luxury.'

'I'm not so sure, lass. It's very nice to have a bit o' money in your pocket to spend 'ow ye like and be beholden to nobody.'

'Yes of course it is, but it's nice to be able to work for it, not marry for it.'

'Well I'll say this for ye, love, ye knows what ye wants out o' life, but when ye gets a few more years on yer shoulders you might just change yer mind. Would ye like to look over some of the house?'

'Oh yes, I would. But won't anybody mind?'

'I can't take ye over it all but we can see just a bit of it. We can go as far as the long gallery, that way ye can 'ave a look at the portraits of the family.'

For the next hour I was Alice in Wonderland as I wandered along the long gallery decorated with gold leaf and beautifully carved wood. Suits of armour stood the entire length of it, and the windows were stained glass so that their glowing colours were shown on the polished wooden floor where the sunlight fell.

Cook switched on a dozen chandeliers, and the lights placed above the pictures brought the colours to life. It seemed to me that I was looking at portraits of de Belleforts cut from the same mould across innumerable centuries. Women and men in powdered wigs wearing silks and satins and cloaks edged with ermine. Many of the men were in uniform, others wore ceremonial orders across their chests.

The family resemblance was profound. It seemed to me that all the women were flaxen fair with dark-blue eyes, while most of the men were dark with dark blue eyes, and while the women were undeniably beautiful the men were very handsome.

When we reached the end of the gallery cook said 'If we

111

hurries ye might just be able to take a peep in the library, the more recent potraits are in there.'.

We stood at length below a portrait of a woman sitting on a long low couch. She had a sweet half smile on her lips and behind her stood a tall slender man his right hand resting lightly on her shoulder. With them were two boys, one a little taller than the other, and on the floor beside her sat a younger boy and a little girl.

'Lady de Bellefort,' Cook explained. 'The older boy is Mr Gerald who lives at Mowbray, the other one is Master Steven who lives in County Wicklow and then there's Master Roland who was killed in India and Miss Alice.'

'What a very handsome family they are,' I exclaimed.

'Yes indeed,' she said, moving on, 'and this is Mr Roland and his wife with Miss Lisanne. Ye can see what a pretty woman 'is wife is.'

I looked up with interest at the tall man in army officer's uniform and the beautiful woman by his side. She had soft golden hair framing a perfect oval face and she was wearing a long cream-coloured satin ball gown. There was the gleam of sapphires round her throat and in her tiara.

The little girl was wearing a billowing party dress in what looked like sprigged voille and there was a bright blue ribbon round her waist and another in her pale golden hair.

'They're all very beautiful,' I said wistfully. 'How exciting it must be to wear clothes like that.'

'Ay, the housekeeper says she'd 'eard Mrs de Bellefort tell 'er husband she wanted sapphires and sable for 'er birthday. Do you think you'll ever be askin' for things like that, love?'

'No, I'm sure I shan't, but I once had a friend who yearned for emeralds and ermine.'

She threw back her head and laughed before I followed her down the corridor and back to the kitchen.

I thanked her warmly for having shown me the pictures and she walked with me to the side door. I bade her goodbye on the doorstep where the warm sun fell on my face and lit up my hair, and suddenly she said, 'Ye know, love, ye have a real look of the de Belleforts, it's the pale hair and yer eyes. Has nobody in the village ever mentioned it?'

'No, but then I don't know many people in the village and I haven't been here very long.'

'Well somebody'll mention it for sure. Wait 'til Miss Lisanne gets here, ye could be sisters for sure.'

I thought about that house and the de Bellefort family all the way to the village but one look at Aunt Liza's face soon brought me down to earth.

'Where 'av ye been all this long time?' she complained.

'I'm sorry, Aunt, but Cook would give me a cup of tea and show me the long gallery.'

'The what!'

'The gallery with all the portraits along it. I thought it would seem discourteous not to go with her.'

She sniffed, somewhat mollified. 'And what had Cook to say for 'erself then?'

'She told me a little about the family, as a matter of fact she said I could be Miss Lisanne's sister, we were the same colouring.'

'Rubbish. She'd no call to be puttin' such ideas into yer 'ead, it's filled with high-flung notions as it is. The de Belleforts are gentry and you're just plain Ellen Adair.'

Sufficiently deflated, I watched her set out to the market, clutching the inevitable black bag.

Trade was never good on market days and there was little for me to do except stare through the shop windows at the crowds milling round the stalls. Suddenly I was aware of a young man staring at me through the glass. He was tall and thin, with a white apron over his clothes and a basket over his arm.

The first thing I noticed when he entered the shop was that he had rather protruding eyes under a shock of dark hair. He had a cheeky grin however, and handing me the basket he said, 'I've seen ye walkin' down the street. You're the niece, aren't you?'

'I'm Miss Ashington's niece, who are you?'

'I'm Alec Devlin the baker's son.'

'I didn't know Mrs Devlin had a son.'

113

'She 'asn't, she's mi father's second wife. Mi mother died when I was four.'

'Oh, I'm sorry.'

'I was asked to bring these over, yer aunt's at the market.'

'I know.'

'There's a dance at the village hall tonight, would ye like to go?'

'I'm not sure, I'll have to ask my aunt.'

'Starts at seven o'clock. They're not bad. There's supper, and a three-piece band'll be playin' fro' Milden. I'll call round about seven to see if you can come. Mi mother told me to ask ye.'

'Thank you, that was very kind.'

I didn't particularly want to go to the dance, nor was Alec Devlin my ideal man, but anything was better than sitting all evening across the hearth from Aunt Liza, listening to the clicking of her knitting needles until it was time for cocoa and bed.

As soon as she returned I told her about my visitor but, contrary to my expectations, she nodded her head, well pleased. 'Yer can do a lot worse than 'ave Alec Devlin, 'e's the only lad Devlin's got so 'e'll come in for the baker's shop one o' these days.'

'He said Mrs Devlin asked him to invite me?'

'She wouldn't have done that if she 'adn't thought 'e'd take a shine to ye. I've seen 'im looking across 'ere somethin' and often.'

Alec Devlin appeared on the doorstep promptly at seven o'clock, wearing a dark navy-blue suit and with his hair well greased and spruced back, while I wore my navy skirt and pink silk blouse. The colour suited me and I had found a silk ribbon for my hair exactly the same shade as the blouse.

I did not miss the gleam of admiration in Alec's eyes, but any hopes that I would be the belle of the ball were quickly dashed when I stepped into the village hall and saw what the rest of the girls were wearing.

Most of them were in pretty floral dresses, frilled and flounced, and they looked at my attire in cool disdain. I felt

114

rather better when Alec whispered, 'Ye look's real classy, Ellen, I 'ates them flowered dresses.'

Alec was no expert dancer and I'd always loved dancing. Mrs Grundy had once told me that I had a natural aptitude and grace, and now I found myself being patient with him as I endeavoured to instruct him through the more intricate footwork of the foxtrot, otherwise we merely marched up and down with the precision of a drill sergeant.

At supper we sat in the company of two more couples who Alec knew.

'Where's Alice tonight?' one of the girls demanded of him, and I saw the colour flood his cheeks before he said, 'How should I know?'

'Ye usually bring her,' the girl replied.

Ignoring that remark he helped himself to patties and cakes from the table and I couldn't help noticing that everything came from his father's shop.

'The cakes are nice, Alec,' I volunteered.

He smiled toothily and while he talked to one of the men I found myself weighing up his appearance. I guessed his age to be about nineteen or twenty and he was at the gawky stage. His adam's apple moved up and down as he talked and he had a good appetite from the amount of food he had piled on to his plate. The girl who had asked about Alice turned to me, saying, 'You live at the draper's, don't ye? Where do you come from?'

'From a village north of Skipton.'

'Ye don't sound Yorkshire. Mi mother said she thought ye'd come from Liverpool.'

'I've been living in Liverpool for a few years.'

'Fancy comin' here fro' Liverpool.'

'I'm living with my aunt.'

'Do ye get on with 'er? Right little sourpuss she is. She's not set foot in the church since the vicar gave her stall to somebody else at the village fete.'

When I didn't rise to that one she said, 'Are ye goin' out with Alec then? He used to be Alice Almond's boyfriend.'

'No, I'm not going out with him, he invited me to the dance, that's all.'

I was amused by the knowing looks the two girls exchanged, and then the other girl said in little more than a whisper, 'Alec's parents didn't approve of Alice, poor as church mice her folks are and they've never asked 'er to the house.'

I felt both amused and irritated by their assumption that I was Alec's new interest who would meet with his parents' approval because I was Liza Ashington's niece. I also felt a grim sort of satisfaction in knowing that I was to get nothing from her when she died.

I was glad that it was raining when we left the village hall, which meant that we had to run all the way home. I had not wanted to loiter through the scented dark with Alec, even so he pulled me into the shop doorway and stood with his arms around me asking if I would accompany him to church in the morning, and quite taking it for granted that he only had to ask and I would readily agree.

'I'm sorry, Alec, but I have things to do in the morning and my aunt doesn't go to church these days.'

'*You've* no quarrel wi' the vicar.'

'I don't even know him.'

'When shall I see you then?'

'Well you only live across the way, probably next week.'

'That's no answer.'

'I'm sorry, Alec, I really don't know, I don't know how much free time I shall have.'

He pulled away from me with a sulky expression, and I felt a faint twinge of conscience.

'I've had a lovely time, Alec, thank you for asking me.'

His expression changed somewhat. 'Does that mean you'll come with me again?'

'Yes, of course. Now I must go in, mi aunt'll be waitin' up for me.' With a hurried goodnight and a quick avoidance of his encircling arm I escaped into the darkened shop.

Aunt Liza was waiting for me although it was long past her normal bedtime. Two cups of steaming cocoa lay on the table, and she sat in her favourite chair waiting to be informed about the evening's events.

She watched in silence while I took off my outdoor clothing, then I sat at the table and pulled a mug of cocoa towards me, only too aware that her impatience was mounting.

'Well,' she said at last, 'what 'ave ye got to say for yourself! 'Ave ye enjoyed yourself?'

'Yes, thank you, Aunt. Nobody else wore a blouse and skirt but I reckon I looked as well as they did.'

'Of course ye did, there'd be nothin' at that dance to write home about. 'Ow did ye get on with Alec?'

'Very well. He's no great shakes as a dancer and he eats too much and probably knows how to drink too much but it was kind of him to ask me, and I love dancing.'

She stared at me nonplussed for several seconds before she snapped, 'Are ye tellin' me there was drink at the hall?'

'No, Aunt, but I heard him talking to some other boys about a rare old night they'd had in the Black Bull.'

'It's only high spirits, the lads 'ave to go somewhere to pass their time. Alec's a decent 'ard-workin lad, it'd please me if I thought you were walkin' out with 'im. Like I've said, yer'll not be comin' in for this shop.'

'I wonder if Alec knows that?'

'What does that mean?'

'I wouldn't like to think he was asking me out because he thought I was better off than Alice. Everybody seemed to think it was strange that he was with me instead of her,'

Her face flushed darkly. 'Everybody wants to mind their own business. I don't know anything about any Alice but yer've got a sharp tongue in yer head, Ellen Adair. No doubt it's come from mixing with the likes o' that Kitty McGuire. Has he asked to see you again?'

'Yes, Aunt, but I've made no definite arrangements.'

'Ye don't apparently know which side yer bread's buttered. What I'll say to Mrs Devlin I really don't know.'

She left me abruptly to climb the stairs, calling, 'Put out the lights, Ellen, and don't put any more coal on the fire.'

117

CHAPTER 12

During the following week I was pestered by Alec. If I went out by the shop door he was either sweeping outside the baker's or cleaning the windows, and if I went to the market he was there too, dogging my footsteps and trying to be clever with the stallholders.

In some strange way I felt trapped. I was sixteen years old with a great many dreams, and even if they seemed impossible I needed to keep them for a little while yet. I was not ready for a steady boyfriend. I had vivid memories of Aunt Mary and her brood of children with a husband who was no good as a provider, and Joe Doyle who had to be nagged and bullied by a despairing wife into pulling his weight at the mission. I had memories of my father and his interminable sulks, and on reflection I couldn't honestly think of a single happy marriage.

I was in the shop one afternoon when in came a large lady wearing a flowered hat and with a fox fur covering her ample bosom, even if it was early September. She swept to the counter like a ship in full sail and seemed very surprised to find me there.

'You must be Miss Ashington's niece then, I've 'eard she had somebody livin' with her.'

'Do you want to see my aunt?'

'Tell her it's Mrs Broadbottom, Alderman Broadbottom.'

Duly impressed I conveyed the message to my aunt who came immediately into the shop. While I dealt with another customer I couldn't help overhearing the conversation from the other side of the shop.

'I 'ear you and the vicar are not friendly,' Alderman Broadbottom began, 'it all seems a storm in a teacup to me. You've missed the bazaar and the fete, it's time ye both made up yer differences.'

'It's nothin' of the kind,' my aunt protested. 'Twenty

118

years or more I've 'ad that spot in the village hall for the church fete, and last year 'e gave it to Molly Weaver without a by your leave, and Molly Weaver not even a regular church-goer.'

'Ye knew she was cleanin' at the vicarage, though?'

'Well of course I did, but I didn't think 'e'd give 'er preferential treatment because of it.'

'Well I've 'ad a word with the vicar and told 'im what I thought about it. I think 'e's feelin' a bit sorry for what 'e did, after all for a man o' the cloth it wasn't very diplomatic. 'E's promised if ye goes back to 'elpin' wi the fete 'e'll give ye the stall back and put Molly Weaver across the doorway. What do ye say, Liza?'

'Well it's kind of ye to 'ave stood up for me, Janie. Is the vicar goin' to apologize?'

'Nay, Liza, yer wants jam on it. Just forget it ever happened, that's my advice, and the sooner ye gets back to attendin' church the better.'

I watched Aunt Liza's face crumple from resolution to acquiescence. 'Ay well, perhaps I'll go on Sunday. I can't say I 'aven't missed it.'

'See that ye do then, I'll expect to see ye there.'

Alderman Mrs Broadbottom swept from the shop and Aunt Liza stood on the doorstep watching her cross the street. She went straight to the baker's and I couldn't help thinking that what had transpired in Aunt Liza's premises would be duly reported across the way.

After that day it seemed to me that my life no longer belonged exclusively to me. Aunt Liza returned to the fold and became immediately immersed in committees of various descriptions: the vicar's wife's sewing circle and counselling for young women, the Church Bazaar and the Summer Fete, Bible Classes and Sunday school teaching. I was taken along with her and introduced as 'mi niece fro Skipton way'.

I was invited to become a Sunday school teacher but I told the vicar quietly that although I believed fervently in God I didn't know enough about religion to instruct others in it. I came in for some very straight talking when Aunt Liza knew I had turned his request down.

'It's all Kitty McGuire, Ellen. Catholic she was, and no doubt she filled yer head with idolatry.'

'It has nothing to do with Kitty, Aunt Liza, and Kitty wasn't a particularly good Catholic anyway.'

'But she was a Catholic, once a Catholic allus a Catholic. She influenced ye, Ellen, against good Christian faith.'

'Oh Aunt, what bigotry and ignorance you talk. Don't you know that Catholicism was the only Christian religion in England until Henry VIII made it illegal because he wanted to divorce his wife and marry somebody else?'

'I hopes ye never talks to the vicar about such things, Ellen, ye don't know what ye're talkin about.'

I knew it was no use talking to Aunt Liza about religion, or indeed about very little else if she'd made up her mind. It was impossible to shift her on any subject under the sun if she thought she knew best.

Alec Devlin too was becoming a problem, pushed on I have no doubt by his father and stepmother, ably assisted by my aunt.

It gave me perverse pleasure one evening after one of the village dances to bring Alec down to earth. He had been holding forth most of the evening on the money his father was making in the baking business and generally showing off in front of our companions, so much so that one of the boys, catching my eye, raised his own heavenwards in some degree of despair.

On our way home I said, 'Did you have to swank quite so much about your father's shop, Alec? One or two of those boys are out of a job.'

'That has nothin' to do with me, Ellen. Mi father's always said, "If yer've got it, don't be ashamed to say so." One o' these days, Ellen, we're goin' to 'ave a nice little thing goin' for us, me with the baker's and you wi' the draper's.'

I stopped and stared at him. 'What exactly do you mean by that?'

He stammered a little, no doubt thinking he's spoken prematurely. 'Well nothin' really, Ellen, but I'm right fond of ye, and I hopes one o' these days you'll be fond of me.

Mi father has a good business and there's only me for it, just like there's only you for your aunt's.'

'You're wrong there, Alec. I shall get nothing from Aunt Liza.'

His mouth opened in amazement. 'Nothin'! Has she said as much?'

'In no uncertain terms. I'm not in her will. She'll probably leave something to my father, her half-brother, but she'll leave most of it to her full brother Simeon Ashington and his daughter over at Ripon, including the shop. I'll get nothing from my father, I can tell you that now, and when my aunt dies I'll have to get out of the shop and find other work.'

'I can't believe she'd treat ye like that, Ellen, wi' all the work ye puts into that shop. Will her niece even want it?'

'Perhaps not. She could sell it but I have no money to buy it.'

'She's never said nothin' to mi mother about all this.'

'There's no reason why she should, Alec.'

'Well I think there is, particularly when she knows you and me are keepin' company.'

'Alec, we're not keeping company, we're simply good friends. I've been very honest with you about my circumstances and I want to be honest about our friendship. I like you as a friend, that's all. I doubt if it could ever be more than that.'

After that night our relationship cooled and Alec's step-mother too became distant when she met me on the street.

One afternoon Aunt Liza said, 'I 'aven't noticed Alec Devlin comin' round much these days. Have you two quarrelled?'

'Of course not, Aunt.'

'Then why doesn't he call for ye?'

'Alec was counting his chickens, Aunt Liza, he had it all weighed up – his father's prosperous business and your little shop one day. When I told him the shop would never be mine he didn't seem as anxious to continue the friendship.'

'Yer'd no call to be tellin' him how I intended leavin' mi

121

money. He'll have told 'em at home and like as not the tale'll 'ave been spread round the village.'

'I'm sure you don't mind, Aunt. How you leave your money is your affair and parting with Alec hasn't been painful. I could never have fallen in love with him, never.'

'Love's all very well when ye have someat to back it up, but Alec Devlin would have been a stable influence in yer life, Ellen, and heaven knows ye needs one. There was he with a nice business to look forward to, ye didn't 'ave to tell him yer were getting nothin' from me.'

'Would you rather I'd gone on with our friendship letting him think I was fond of him, perhaps even marrying him? Don't you think he would have held it against me for the rest of my life, seeing this little shop going to somebody else when he'd thought it was coming to me? I'm glad I didn't love him, if I had and he'd turned away from me just like he has now I'd have been desolate. As it is, I really don't care.'

She stared at me but I knew she didn't understand a word of what I'd been saying. I came to the conclusion that I'd never really been understood by anybody.

I went alone to the next village dance and Alec was there with his old love Alice. She was a pretty dark-haired girl, poorly dressed, and obviously out on a limb with the other girls in their party, but I smiled across at her pleasantly and in the cloakroom I managed an odd word with her.

When she had gone back to Alec the girl I had met on the first evening said slyly, 'E'll never marry 'er, his folks wouldn't allow it.'

'Why not? She's pretty and she seems nice.'

'Oh, Alice is all right and she worships Alec but she's the eldest of a big family and they haven't two halfpennies for a penny. Her father has consumption and can't work and 'er mother cleans up and down the village at the big houses. Old Ma Devlin'll never want Alice in the family.'

'That's nothing Alice can help.'

'Course not, but it's life isn't it?'

At that moment I wanted to get out of the village hall and away from these people with their have-and-have-not philosophy. Tomorrow they would all be in church believing themselves good Christians, but between them they hadn't a worthwhile Christian thought. They're all religion and no Christianity, I stormed to myself as I grabbed my coat and made off alone down the village street. I was halfway along it when I heard footsteps running after me and I turned in some fear. It was Alec, without his coat and bare headed, running against the wind.

'Where are ye goin', Ellen,' he cried, 'why are ye leavin' so soon?'

I turned on him savagely. 'I'm leavin' because I can't bear to hear any more about people being unacceptable because they haven't any money and aren't likely to be gettin' any. She's a nice girl, Alec, if ye've any sense at all you'll be hanging on to Alice no matter what anybody says.'

He stared at me stupidly, uncomprehending, and I clutched his arm and shook him. 'I'm talking about Alice, the girl you're at the dance with, Alec. You mustn't let anybody tell you she's a nobody just because she hasn't any money. That's the only reason your folks wanted you to be friends with me. They're not so anxious now they know I won't have any either, but money isn't everything.'

'I don't know what you're talking about, Ellen.'

'I'm talking about Alice. You've been friends with her a long time haven't you, Alec?'

'Since we were at school.'

'And you love her, don't you?'

His face grew rosy red and he stammered a little. Alec was not accustomed to young women asking straight questions.

'I don't know. Mi father sez I'm not old enough to know mi own mind.'

'Your father'll probably make it up for you and it won't include Alice, of that I'm sure.'

He shuffled his feet in an embarrassed fashion. 'Why don't ye come back to the dance, Ellen! It's not like you to rush off like that.'

'You don't know any of the things I'm capable of doing, Alec. I was capable of running away from home when I was fourteen, and living in Liverpool working at a seaman's

123

mission. I ran away from home to be with a girl who had nothing, just like Alice has nothing, but Kitty had all the fire and beauty I ever remember in my early life. I'll probably never see her again but I'll never forget her, never.'

My words didn't make sense to him, they were alien words to this boy brought up in the sheltered world of the village, protected by a father who was making money and a stepmother who had great hopes for the right sort of wife for him. Any words of mine could only fall on stony ground, and realization made me shake my arm free. As I let myself in at the shop door I heard him walking away along the rain-darkened street.

CHAPTER 13

Aunt Liza didn't believe in holidays apart from one week in August she spent with her brother and his family in Ripon, when she closed her shop.

'What will ye do while I'm away?' she demanded of me.

'I'm not sure, Aunt. I've saved a little money, I might spend a few days at the coast somewhere.' Indeed I had managed to save a little by taking in sewing, a thing which Aunt Liza deplored because she didn't want the villagers to think I needed the money.

'Where on the coast?' she snapped.

'Southport, perhaps, or Bridlington.'

'Bridlington's better. They tell me Southport's expensive. Besides, isn't it close to Liverpool?'

'Is it?' I answered innocently. 'I hadn't thought of that.'

'I hope ye're not thinkin' of lookin' that Irish girl up, she'll 'ave forgotten your existence by this time.'

'No, Aunt, I wasn't thinking of it. I haven't really made my mind up yet, I might not even go anywhere.'

'Ye know Alec Devlin's got 'imself engaged, I suppose? If yer'd played yer cards right it could 'ave been you getting married.'

'I didn't want him, Aunt Liza. I hope he'll be very happy.'

'Well, I've been invited to the reception. They didn't invite you, Ellen, because you were one of his old girlfriends and they thought his bride might not like it.'

I laughed without rancour. 'Oh Aunt, I was never one of Alec Devlin's girlfriends, and I don't suppose they've invited Alice.'

'Indeed they 'aven't, they were mighty glad when that finished, I can tell ye.'

'She was a lot prettier than the one he's marrying' on Saturday.'

'What's pretty got to do with it, and her with a father

125

ownin' two ironmonger's shops in Ottley? Madge Bromley'll bring him plenty o' brass and that'll do him more good than a pretty face. Beauty fades, money appreciates.'

The entire village turned out to watch Alec's wedding the first Saturday in August and most of them followed the bridal party to the Black Bull for the reception.

At midday Aunt Liza closed the shop and began to put on her wedding finery: a new beige skirt and silk blouse, a short brown coat and brown hat with a fair show of veiling and a cream silk rose to top it off. I had hitherto never seen her in anything but black and I had to confess that she looked considerably younger in her latest attire. When I said as much she merely remarked dryly, 'I don't suppose I'll wear this 'til the next weddin', mi niece's at Ripon or maybe yours, although ye're pretty good at letting eligible men slip through yer fingers. Make sure ye opens the shop at two o'clock prompt. Weddin' or no weddin', today's market day, we don't want to miss any customers.'

I walked with her to the Black Bull and stood with a crowd of others watching the bridal party line up for photographs. Alec and his father looked uncomfortable in their formal morning suits, Mrs Devlin was in mauve, a billowing dress with a hat to match and trimmed with bunches of violets. The bride's parents too had evidently spared no expense. Her mother, attired in pale green, was a tall thin woman wearing a severe expression and constantly spoke sharply to her exuberant spouse.

A long white Rolls-Royce stood outside the inn decorated with white satin streamers, and there were a great many pictures of the happy couple taken standing in front of it. The bride was not a pretty girl. She was very much a younger version of her mother, tall and thin, very dark and with an expression of boredom that, I felt convinced, Alec would come to recognize over the years ahead of them.

I noticed with some amusement that Aunt Liza was very much in the forefront of the photo including the guests. Then they all trooped into the inn and I was free to do what I liked for an hour and a half on a glorious warm summer's day. It was then I saw Alice, tearful and miserable half running along the pavement in an endeavour to avoid the stares from unsympathetic eyes.

I chased after her, in and out of the market stalls, and saw that she took the road that climbed towards the fell, where I assumed she would pour out her anguish to the lonely crags and the curlews.

I came upon her sitting dismally on a five-barred gate looking hopelessly down on the village, her mind filled no doubt with the goings-on at the inn. She looked at me without recognition, then shamefaced she jumped down from the gate and started to walk up the road.

'Alice, please wait for me,' I called.

She turned hesitantly and for one moment I thought she was going to ignore me, then her expression changed and she stared at me defiantly, daring me to feel sorry for her or ask why she was unhappy. I knew better than that, I had not been Kitty McGuire's companion all those years for nothing.

'I'm walking on the moor, Alice. I'd like some company if you're going that way,' I said, reaching her side.

'I'm not going far, I've the shopping to do.'

'Well, just to the top of the hill there, then we'll make our way back to the village. I'm eating alone today, would you like to join me?'

For a moment she looked at me uncertainly, then she said, 'I must get back, Ellen, or mi mother'll wonder where I've got to.'

'I'm sure she'll not miss you for a little while, after all it's Saturday. What do you usually do on Saturday?'

I wished I hadn't asked when tears suddenly filled her eyes and she turned her head away sharply.

'Please come back to the shop with me, Alice. I don't know many people in the village. There are times when I think if you've not been born and bred here you'll be a stranger for ever.'

'I suppose yer aunt's at the weddin'.'

'Yes, she went off wreathed in smiles and wearin' her Sunday best.'

'Why didn't they invite you, I wonder?'

Quite suddenly I wanted to bring the smiles back on to Alice's pretty face even if it meant belittling her one-time swain.

'His mother had designs on me when she thought I'd get my aunt's shop and her money. When she found out I wouldn't, they looked around for somebody else for Alec. It was just as well because I couldn't ever have wanted to marry him.'

She stared at me in surprise. 'Ye couldn't, ye mean ye never liked him?'

'Oh he was well enough I suppose, but he wasn't my idea of the man I want to marry. In my mind he was a callow youth with too many spots. Besides he had buck teeth.'

For a moment she seemed angry and I thought she would have leapt to his defence, then suddenly her face crumpled into laughter and there on the hillside we stood laughing until hers turned to hysteria and the merciful tears were suddenly released. I prayed silently that she would never cry over Alec Devlin again.

We ate a hurriedly prepared lunch in the parlour behind the shop, then she left, saying she didn't want to be there when my aunt returned.

Indeed she had only just left when Aunt Liza let herself into the shop well before two o'clock so that she could see we had opened on time. She was in high good humour and as she took off her hat gave me full details of the meal and the bottles of wine the bride's father had ordered from the delighted landlord.

'Money to burn they must 'ave,' she said. 'Young Alec's done very well for 'imself there and the girl seems nice enough.'

'She's not as pretty as Alice and I don't suppose she'll make him a better wife,' I couldn't resist snapping.

Without answering me she stamped into the kitchen to return a moment later asking, 'What are all them dishes doin' in the sink! Who've ye 'ad in, Ellen?'

'I met a friend on the street, Aunt Liza, I didn't think you'd mind if I asked her in to eat with me.'

'Which friend! Ye're allus sayin' ye've no friends in the village.'

'It was Alice if you must know, she was upset at Alec's wedding.'

'Really Ellen, I can't leave ye alone five minutes 'afore ye're pickin' up wi' the wrong companions.'

After that I went into the kitchen and started to do the dishes, and when I returned to the parlour she was sitting in her usual chair staring into the fire.

'They were sayin' at the weddin' that Lady de Bellefort's daughter-in-law and 'er granddaughter 'ave arrived. Yer'll be seein' the girl around the village on that 'orse of 'ers. She's a pleasant sort o' girl, very pretty too. If ye should see 'er yer'll bob a little curtsey and say good mornin', Ellen, let 'er see ye knows yer manners.'

I stared at her in amazement. Life in Liverpool had obscured the need to bob country curtseys to local land-owners and their families, and an overpowering feeling of resentment took hold of me.

Once, a long time ago, I would not have been averse to being servile to such people, after all I had been reared in a village similar to this one where we had been taught to bob curtseys to the dignitaries who had attended the school and bestowed half-day holidays on us. But now Aunt Liza was talking about my kow-towing to a girl hardly older than myself, and the deep resentment I felt in my heart frightened me.

Meanwhile, Aunt Liza had changed tack and was issuing more instructions. 'I'll be wantin' ye to 'elp me carry mi bags on Saturday mornin' and while I'm gone I don't want ye lettin' any Tom, Dick or Harry into mi shop. Perhaps ye should go away for a few days.'

'Perhaps I will. I've never been to York or Harrogate.'

'Ay well, either'd be better than goin' off to Liverpool and no doubt looking for that Kitty McGuire.'

I said nothing else, and I was relieved when the subject was not raised again. On Saturday morning I went with her to the bus stop carrying her one piece of luggage while she toted two carrier bags filled with pies and cakes from the

129

baker's as well as knitted jumpers and cardigans for her niece.

I didn't mind, in spite of the fact that not once had she offered to give me one of the things I had seen her knitting. It was very evident that I was not her favourite niece and could expect no softening of her attitude towards me.

On Sunday I tidied up the house and the shop, and first thing on Monday morning I boarded the local train for Leeds and another that would take me to Liverpool.

I had made no plans. I didn't know where I would stay or for how long, but I had a desperate longing to see Liverpool again. At last I stood on Dale Street Station clutching my one piece of luggage, and the sight of a woman with two children both with buckets and spades made my mind up for me. I would take the ferry across the Mersey to New Brighton where surely I could find somewhere to stay.

I had no difficulty. There were small boarding houses in plenty and I found one quite close to the promenade. It was owned by a jolly buxom woman who made me very welcome, carried my case upstairs for me and produced a welcome cup of tea as soon as I'd unpacked.

Across the river I could look at the skyline of Liverpool, the stately towers of the Liver buildings, the lights shining in the water, and I could sit on the promenade watching the boats and the bustling ferries while behind me a band was playing.

That first night I simply absorbed its appeal through a haze of nostalgia. The smell of the river, salty and brackish, the people scurrying off the ferries, the hooting of the tugs and the long mournful farewell sirens from the big steamers. I decided that in the morning I would once more board one of those ferries and go to see Aunt Mary. I slept badly, impatiently waiting for the morning and the meeting with old friends, and hopefully news of Kitty.

CHAPTER 14

I couldn't understand why I had imbued Liverpool with so much nostalgic glamour when I walked along its mean streets on my way to Aunt Mary's. The mission windows were still as dingy with soot and grime and the Chinese children playing outside the laundry seemed a little more numerous than before. They stared at me out of wide coal-black eyes, then recognizing me they waved and bowed their dark heads.

Some of the women were standing at their front doors and they eyed me curiously until one of them recognized me and called out, ''Ave ye come back then?'

'No. Just visiting.'

'Well yer'll not find 'er in, the bairns are on 'oliday so she's taken 'em to the park. Yer'll no doubt find 'er 'usband in the pub.'

'Thank you, I'll walk to the park.'

I had always wondered how flowers ever grew in that little park. The gardener must have had the patience of Job because the borders were immaculate with snapdragons and marigolds. A band was playing in the bandstand while elderly people sat around to listen, and children bowling their hoops along the paths were admonished to keep quiet. I guessed Aunt Mary and the children would be near the paddling pool.

I saw her immediately. On her lap sat Susan, the little girl I had first seen clutching a pound pot of jam while lying in her pram. With one hand Aunt Mary gently rocked a battered perambulator. The other children were playing near the pool and I was almost at her side before recognition dawned in her lack lustre eyes.

'Why Ellen, what are you doin' in Liverpool?' she gasped.

'I'm taking a few day's holiday. I was hoping to see you.'

131

I looked at the baby in the pram. He was so tiny, like a little wizened old man, then I looked at Aunt Mary.

'He's three weeks old,' she said, 'and 'e's bin a sickly child, allus ailin' somethin' or other since the day 'e were born.'

'What do you call him?'

'Patrick after mi grandfather. He allus got Paddy but I've told the children to call the baby Patrick and not to go shortenin' his name. Ye look well, Ellen, I can see that country life suits ye.'

'It's all that fresh air. I can't say the same for you, Aunt Mary, you look very tired.'

'Well I am tired, I'm up with baby most nights. 'E cries a lot, poor little mite.'

For the first time I saw the poverty in her thin dress and tattered shoes and a wave of pity swept over me. For people like Mary McLoughlin there didn't seem much to look forward to in this bustling city.

'Are you still taking in sewing?' I asked.

'Mi old customers don't come so much now, I kept 'em waitin' ye see when I 'ad the baby and 'e takes up so much of mi time the things were never ready when they came for 'em. No doubt they've found somebody else to do their sewin'.'

'Oh I am sorry. Surely they realized you'd need to look after Patrick?'

'I've no doubt they did, but I couldn't expect 'em to keep 'angin' on, could I?'

'Is the tea shop open? We could walk round there and have a cup of tea.'

'It's probably full up by now. I'm ready for goin' back anyway, we can 'ave a cup of tea back at the 'ouse.'

'I'll collect the children then.'

'They can stop 'ere, Ellen, Mrs Maloney'll look after 'em, she's over there with 'er lot.'

So I pushed the pram and Aunt Mary carried Susan who cried all the way home because she didn't want to leave the park.

There was no sewing lying about the house now but it

132

was still untidy with shoes left lying on the floor and her husband's betting paper spread out across the table. She plonked Susan into a high chair and parked the pram, then muttering angrily she collected the paper and threw it into a corner.

'If 'e 'as any money to spare it goes on the 'orses,' she complained. "E's not changed, Ellen, I thought 'e might 'ave done when the new baby came but it was too much to hope for.'

'Was he pleased about the baby?'

'Not he. It's another mouth to feed, but I can't think we'll rear this one, he's too sickly. Sit down, Ellen, and I'll make the tea.'

I had bought sweets for the children and I gave one to Susan, hoping it would dry her tears. The baby was sleeping, his tiny face as grey as his pillow.

She came back to the living room carrying a tray set with cups and saucers and a sponge cake decorated with bright pink icing. I accepted the tea gratefully but refused the cake and she said, 'I'll not 'ave any either, the children like icin', I'll leave it for them. Well, Ellen' what 'ave ye bin doin' up in the country.'

So I told her a little of my life and made her smile at Aunt Liza's narrow-minded views and penny-pinching stinginess.

Then I asked, 'Do you hear from Kitty, Aunt Mary?'

'Not a word since she left. I don't know where she's livin', but it's somewhere with Emmie Wallsingham and we all know what she's up to.'

'What, what is she up to?'

'She's on the streets, that's what. 'Ow else can she afford all them clothes? And that chap she brought with 'er, I do 'ear 'e's got a lot o' young women livin' in the city that 'e finds customers for.'

I stared at her in anguish. 'Surely you can't think that Kitty would be like that Aunt Mary.'

'Of course she could, Ellen. She cried for the moon, that girl, and 'ow could she ever get it on 'onest pay? I tackled Elsie Wallsingham and she more or less admitted that

133

Emmie got 'er money that way, not that Elsie'll care if Emmie sends some 'ome.'

'I was hoping I might see Kitty.'

'There's not much chance o' that, luv, not round 'ere. She's never coming back to this part o' the city and I'd advise ye not to go lookin' for 'er in the centre, folks might get the idea yer like 'er.'

'Oh Aunt Mary, I can't honestly believe it of Kitty. She was so strong and independent.'

'She's that all right, a girl 'as to be strong to live that sort o' life. Go back to the country, Ellen, and forget Kitty. The likes o' her's are not for you. Now I'd best be getting on wi' mi husband's tea. Yer welcome to join us, Ellen.'

'No thanks, Aunt Mary, I must be getting back, there'll be a meal waiting for me.'

I pressed five shillings into her hand at the front door, and although she seemed reluctant to take it, I did not miss the light that came into her eyes.

'Buy something for yourself,' I urged her, 'don't spend it all on the children.'

She nodded. 'Thanks, Ellen. Ye were allus a thoughtful sort o' girl, and you look after yerself in the country.'

As I walked down the street I knew I would never visit that part of Liverpool again. It belonged to a youth I was not particularly proud of but it had toughened me for whatever the future might hold.

Tomorrow I would go to the shops and mingle with the city girls as if I were one of them. I would take afternoon tea in the cosy warmth of one of the tea rooms and perhaps I would see Kitty and hear from her own lips how she was surviving, for I hadn't believed a word of what Aunt Mary had told me.

I was fascinated by the shops, the perfume counters and the haberdashery, and so ashamed of my cheap cotton gloves that I stuck them in my skirt pocket. I loved the feel of fine leather and crepe de Chine and the delicacy of chiffon flowers. All in all I spent an enchanting morning and was about to enter the coffee lounge when I heard two girls discussing the tea dances held at three every afternoon at the Adelphi Hotel.

Consequently I decided there and then to save the money I would have spent in the coffee lounge and go instead to the Adelphi. I wasn't quite sure if I was properly dressed for such an occasion but my beige skirt fitted well and I had been extravagant with the pure silk of my cream blouse which I had made myself.

I tried not to be overawed by the majestic foyer of the hotel, and the carpet which my feet seemed to sink into. I was intrigued by elegantly dressed women and immaculately suited men, and the waiter who escorted me to my seat in the tea lounge seemed unperturbed that I was alone. My table was set against a wall and reasonably inconspicuous.

I ordered afternoon tea, whereupon he said loftily, 'China or Indian, Madam?'

'Indian, thank you,' I replied, remembering that the vicar's wife had disliked China tea because she considered it too scented.

There were thin cucumber sandwiches and rich cream cakes, all served on fine china, and with the tea came cube sugar to be served with tiny silver tongs. I felt like a queen as I helped myself from the plates set in front of me, and then from the dais the fourpiece band began to play and I gave myself up to the sound of the music.

One or two couples got up to dance and from across the room I noticed that two men were eyeing me curiously. Blushing, I lowered my eyes, wondering what I should do if one of them came across to ask me to dance.

All such thoughts were swept from my mind when a man and two women entered the room. I knew him instantly, he was the man who had accompanied Emmie Wallsingham to her mother's house.

They sauntered to a table at the edge of the dance floor. People were staring at them curiously and the waiters were muttering together in a group near the wall.

For one thing the man was wearing a loud checked jacket, and he stood out like a sore thumb beside the dark-suited men occupying the tables nearby. For the first time I looked at his companions and I gasped with surprise when I recognized Emmie Wallsingham, but a very different Emmie to the one I had seen before.

She had on a large pink hat trimmed with roses and heavy veiling but it was her painted face which caused me the most surprise. Her cheeks were heavily rouged, and her lips were shining with flame-coloured lipstick. Her eyes swept round the room boldly before she sat back and addressed herself to her companion, who sat with her back to me.

The man stood chatting to them for several minutes, then smiling broadly he bowed over Emmie's hand before leaving the room.

Emmie continued to scan the room but I noticed that the waiters did not approach their table. After a few mintues the head waiter went up and said something to the women quietly. I saw Emmie's eyes flash angrily, then with a dramatic flounce she rose to her feet, dragging the other woman after her, they stalked across the room and out of the door.

Quickly I summoned the waiter to ask for the bill, too excited to be stunned by the size of it, then I hurried into the foyer after them. I badly wanted to speak to Emmie to ask if she had any news of Kitty, and was immediately relieved to see the two women standing near the flower shop. They were deep in conversation when I approached them, and when I touched Emmie shyly on her sleeve they both turned to stare at me. I stared back, hardly able to believe my eyes.

This was not Kitty as I had known her, but Kitty it was, wearing a too-tight green dress and incredibly high heels, and with her hair dressed high on her head, redder than I ever remembered it. Her face was painted exactly like Emmie's but not nearly as professionally. The powder was too pale, the carmine lips and rosy cheeks too red, the mascara too thick, yet underneath it was somehow the face of a very young girl.

Her dismay was as profound as my own.

'Why Ellen,' she gasped. 'What are you doin' in Liverpool?'

136

Quickly I explained, ending with, 'Oh Kitty, I'm so glad to see you, I saw your Aunt Mary but she didn't know where you were living.'

'No, she wouldn't. I 'aven't had much time to see them, 'ow is she?'

'She doesn't look too well, and they have a new baby, a little boy.'

'Ay well, mi uncle's good for somethin' evidently.'

Just then the head waiter came out of the tearoom towards us. Emmie said quickly, 'We'd best be goin', Kitty, we can talk outside.'

They turned away and the man said sharply, 'Please ladies, I asked you to leave, I don't want you loitering in the hotel.'

I stared at him and then at the two girls. Emmie turned away with a toss of her head before stalking towards the door while Kitty and I followed quickly. At the door I turned and found him staring after us. Once on the pavement, Emmie said sharply, 'Stop and talk to yer friend, Kitty, and meet me back at the house. Try not to be late.'

She walked off without giving us a second glance and I stared at Kitty unhappily.

I felt that she would have liked to have gone with Emmie but instead she stood uncertainly on the pavement and I was aware of her hostility in the set of her tight-lipped face and her smouldering green eyes.

'Why did ye 'ave to come to Liverpool again, Ellen, why couldn't ye 'ave settled down in the country and forgotten all about mi?'

'Because you're my friend, Kitty, and I wanted to see you again.'

'Well I didn't want to see you, Ellen, we've nothin' in common any more. It's all over between you and me, Ellen, and I'd rather not be sayin' anything to you.'

'But why, Kitty, what have I done?'

'Nothin' Ellen, you 'aven't done anythin', it's just that we're different you and me, we've gone our separate ways. I suppose mi aunt had a lot to say about me. What exactly did she tell yer?'

137

'Very little. How could she when you haven't visited her?'

She smiled grimly. 'That wouldn't stop 'er, Ellen, but I can guess what she said.'

'Would it be true, Kitty?'

'Oh Ellen, don't you be gettin' at me. What was there back there for either of us except some chap like mi uncle and a brood o' screamin' kids? It's not fer you and it's certainly not for me. Go back to Yorkshire, Ellen, and forget about mi. I don't suppose we'll ever see each other again but when ye thinks about mi just remember that this is my way of being somebody, my way of gettin' some money together while I'm young enough to enjoy it.'

She stared at me out of hard angry eyes, then suddenly her face relaxed and she smiled. Her face was the old Kitty's, pretty and pert beneath its paint. With a quick gesture she threw her arms around my neck and kissed my cheek, then with a gay wave she was away.

That night I decided I would go home the following morning. I would look my last at the skyline of Liverpool, forget the sound of the sea breaking on the beach, the smells of the river and the long strident noise of the ships' sirens. I would put Liverpool behind me as though she had never existed . . . but even as I was making these vows I knew that my heart would not let me forget.

I was relieved that Aunt Liza showed little interest in how I had occupied my time during her absence. She returned on Saturday afternoon in high good humour, and immediately I was treated to a description of her brother's house, the welcome they had given her, and approval of her niece's young man, George.

She informed me that he was a bank clerk working in Ripon where he lodged with her brother and his wife, and went home each weekend to see his parents in Harrogate taking Jennie, her niece, with him.

Ever since I could remember, the town of Harrogate had been mentioned in hushed tones. People who lived there were considered highly fortunate because it was a spa town where folk went for the cure, a town of broad avenues and green parks, where most of the shops bore the royal arms because the Princess Royal who lived close by at Harewood did her shopping there. All Langstone would soon be made aware that the niece's fiancé lived there, and some of the glamour would most likely rub off.

'Next time I go to see mi brother I'm to be taken to Harrogate to meet George's folks. He's an only child and so's mi niece, so they'll 'ave a nice little bit one o' these days.'

'If she's going to live in Harrogate or even stay in Ripon what will she do with the shop?' I was unwise enough to ask.

'She'll sell it of course, and it'll bring a nice bit o' money, what with the goodwill and it bein' on the main street o' Langstone.'

Her insensitivity amazed me, but it was changing me too. Once I had been a gentle girl, perhaps a little too gullible but always one to look for the good in people, now I was becoming waspish and suspicious.

I was glad when evening came and she set off to see the Devlins. Aunt Liza had just reached the other side when she turned and almost ran back, just in time to greet a girl riding a big chestnut horse down the main street.

The girl raised her whip in greeting, then to my amazement she pulled the horse up outside the shop and jumped down. Aunt Liza, all smiles, stood with me in the doorway and the girl walked towards us smiling a little apologetically.

'I say, I am sorry to come so late. Are you closed?'

'We 'aven't bin open today, Miss Lisanne, not on the local 'oliday you know, but I'll serve ye if ye wants anything.'

We moved inside the shop and I found myself staring at the girl curiously. We were about the same height but that was not the only similarity. She was as flaxen fair as myself, with the same dark blue eyes, and it seemed to me that I had seen her face in the mirror every day of my life.

She too seemed surprised at my appearance, and smiling she said, 'My grandmother said there was a girl in the village who looked like me. I didn't believe her, but now I do.'

'Oh Ellen's not really like you, Miss Lisanne, just her colourin' perhaps. We mustn't 'ave 'er gettin' conceited. Now what can I get ye?'

'I promised Granny I'd call for her tapestry wool and I completely forgot earlier in the day. Did it arrive?'

'Well not 'afore I went away, it didn't. Did it come last week, Ellen?'

'I've been away too, Aunt. Mrs Devlin would know, she said she'd take in any parcels.'

'Yer'd best get over there then and see what's come, I didn't know you weren't 'ere.'

The tapestry wool had not arrived, and when I explained the girl merely smiled and said she'd call again. Turning to me she said, 'Granny says you're good with your fingers. Would you shorten one or two skirts for me? I'm hopeless and Mother's taken her maid back to London with her.'

'Yes of course, will you be bringing them to the shop?'

'I'd rather you came up to the house, that way you can see them on me.'

'When will you want me to come?'

'Monday, if that's convenient.'

I looked at Aunt Liza for confirmation and although she was slightly put out she nodded briskly. 'I can manage without ye, Ellen, if you comes straight back.'

With a swift smile our visitor left us, and we watched her riding away at a brisk canter.

'Don't you be gettin' any ideas that yer workin' for the gentry, Ellen. I couldn't very well say I didn't want ye to go, wi' the girl standin' there, but I wants yer feet on the ground not yer head in the clouds. Now lock up the shop and go inside.'

'Yes, Aunt.'

Before she reached the edge of the pavement she turned again and came back to me. 'Yer said yer'd bin away. Where did ye go?'

'I went to New Brighton for a few days.'

'To see that Kitty McGuire, I'll be bound.'

'I went to see Aunt Mary. Kitty isn't living there now.'

140

She merely sniffed disdainfully and once more set off across the street.

I felt strangely miserable as the long lonely night stretched out before me. Life held no promise of better things in store but as I sat alone contemplating a wearisome future I was not to know how dramatically it would soon be changed.

CHAPTER 15

On Monday morning I was told to get off to the Hall so I packed a small valise with scissors, cotton and a tape measure, glad of the walk in the warm summer sunshine.

Walking through the park with the pile of Langstone Priory rising up before me I felt I was walking through another world, it was so peaceful. A light breeze stirred the trees over my head, and my appearance startled a young deer grazing on the verge so that she darted away towards the mere where she stood gazing at me cautiously, poised for flight.

Geraniums in tall white urns stood the length of the terrace, and a peacock spread his tail for me while his more humbly attired spouse looked on admiringly.

How Kitty would have loved this, I thought, then more bitterly: Why did I always have to think of Kitty? I doubted if she ever spared me a thought.

A young man wearing a green baize apron let me into the house, and then I was in the presence of Cook and a tall grey-haired woman wearing a long black dress who eyed me from top to bottom before asking who I was and why had I come.

After I had explained she said shortly, 'Wait here and I'll see if Miss Lisanne is available. Does she know you intended to come this morning?'

'She asked me to come today, Ma'am.'

After she had left the room Cook grinned at me. 'Out o'sorts she is this mornin', there's guests arrived and she's only just bin told.'

'Well if it's not convenient I can come another day. Miss Lisanne will let me know when to come.'

'You wait here, love. If Miss Lisanne said today, today she meant.'

She was busy weighing flour and other ingredients before

turning them into a huge mixing bowl, then energetically stirred the mixture with a stout wooden spoon. A kitchen-maid was dispatched to bring a jug of milk while another was busily greasing cake tins.

A huge piece of beef and a leg of lamb stood on a side table and I longed to ask how many people they were expecting when the door opened and two gardeners appeared carrying bunches of roses and copper beech leaves.

'Put 'em down on the side table,' Cook said sharply. 'Miss Lisanne'll do the flowers.'

The men grinned at her, and the younger of the two came up to the table and put his arm round one of the maids.

'I'll 'ave less of that,' Cook snapped, 'they don't need much distraction as it is.'

'Looks as though a regiment's comin',' the lad said with a broad smile.

'There's some buns in the cake tin there, 'elp yerself and then leave us to get on with our work.'

I watched him helping himself to a pile of currant buns out of the tin and handing some to the other gardener. They both departed with cheeky grins and the maid greasing the cake tins simpered and blushed furiously until Cook gave her a hard look that quickly brought her to her senses.

After a few minutes the housekeeper returned with another maid saying that Miss Lisanne would see me in her bedroom and the maid would show me where it was. Dutifully I followed in her wake, and outside the kitchen she turned to say, 'I'm Amelia the under housemaid. Who shall I say you are?'

'Ellen Adair, Miss Ashington's niece from the draper's in the village.'

Without another word she stalked ahead of me and I was left to admire her trim ankles in black stockings and the bouncy curls under the starched frilly cap. Then I forgot the maid in the beauty of marble and pale thick carpets, in the carving of the curved balustrade and the crystal chandeliers. I was not to be blamed if I dawdled a little in such prestigious surroundings but when I looked up the maid was waiting for me with an impatient frown on her pretty face and I hurried to catch up with her.

At one of the rooms along a wide passage she knocked on the door and opened it to announce me. I had never been in such a bedroom, it would quite easily have accommodated all Aunt Liza's shop and living quarters. But the beauty of the room was marred by its untidiness. The wardrobe doors were flung wide open and Lisanne was busy pulling out dresses which she threw across the satin bedspread unceremoniously. Her smile was warm when she greeted me, however, and she said, 'I hope you've come prepared to stay a while, there's more than I thought.'

I stared with dismay at the clothes on the bed, remembering Aunt Liza's terse instruction not to spend all day, that there was work to be done at the shop. When I looked doubtful she said anxiously, 'You have come to stay awhile, I hope?'

'Do all those clothes need altering? Because if they do I'm afraid it will take much longer than one day.'

'Oh dear, will it really? Did your aunt say you had to get back?'

'She did.'

'Well we're having visitors from near Mowbray, they haven't arrived yet so I'll saddle the horse and ride down to the village. I'll explain to your aunt, I'm sure she'll understand.'

She would most certainly take my absence better if the news came from Miss Lisanne, but even so the task in front of me would have been daunting to a more experienced needlewoman than I.

'Some of those are party dresses from the school in Switzerland, and they're far too long. Madame was adamant about the length of our clothes and I daresay my grandmother would be too. Mother said they looked antiquated but they're too good to be thrown off. About two inches off all of them please, Ellen. You don't mind if I call you Ellen, do you? It's so much more informal than Miss Adair.'

She was busy picking out the dresses I was to shorten

144

and I approached the bed and picked up one of them, a beautiful china-blue gown in georgette. Looking at its beautifully draped skirt I couldn't help thinking it would be sacrilege to cut it.

'You're thinking I have too many, Ellen?' she said with a wry smile.

'No, I was just thinking how beautiful they all are. It must be heavenly to wear such a dress.'

'Do be a dear and make a good job of them, then we'll go through them and pick one or two out for you. We're exactly the same colouring, what flatters me will flatter you.'

'Oh Miss Lisanne, I couldn't possibly accept them. Besides, where would I ever wear them? The only function I ever go to is the village dance, I'd stick out like a sore thumb in something like this.'

'Well of course you would. You'd be the belle of the ball and all the other girls would be pea green with envy. We'll find something sophisticated, quite plain but well cut. None of the villagers will ever suspect that it cost the earth. Sometimes the plainer they are, the more expensive. Now you know what to do, don't you? You can work at the window so that you have a lovely view of the mere, and I'll have lunch sent up to you around twelve thirty. I take it you've brought cotton and the like with you?'

'Well I've brought a selection of cottons, I only hope they're the right colours.'

'They will be, Ellen. Now I'm off to beard your frosty old aunt. Don't worry, I'll be all sweetness and light and I'll buy something from the shop just to sweeten her up a bit.'

She was gone like a piece of quicksilver and I gathered up two or three dresses and took them over to the window. There was a beautiful view of the mere and the swans with their brood of cygnets sailing majestically across the water. The parkland looked so green and peaceful that I allowed myself the aesthetic pleasure of absorbing a scene totally alien to every facet of my life until that moment. It was as though I had existed on a different plane and that at any

145

moment the dream would end and I would awake in my narrow bed in Aunt Liza's back room.

I lost myself in the sewing of those lovely dresses and I had no idea of the time. I did not even hear the door open, the first thing I knew was that two cool hands covered my eyes and a teasing voice said, 'Guess who?'

When I struggled the hands left my face but then I was taken hold of by strong hands and lifted bodily from my chair. I found myself looking down into a young man's laughing face, a handsome tall young man with blue eyes in a bronzed face, with the glint of sunlight in his dark wavy hair.

'What are you doing here all alone?' he said, laughing. 'I thought you'd be at the gates to meet me.'

I was staring at him in an astounded way, and gently he lowered me to the ground. 'Well,' he demanded more sternly, 'haven't you a word of greeting for Cousin Lance?'

At that moment there was a peal of laughter from the door and there was Lisanne convulsed with merriment. The young man looked from her to me in a great deal of puzzlement.

'How too romantic for words,' she trilled. 'Cousin Lance and Ellen Adair caught in an ecstatic embrace. You've embarrassed my friend, Lance, but I'm not suprised you thought she was me. We're as alike as sisters.'

He was staring down at me now, his dark eyes contrite and serious. 'I'm so sorry,' he said. 'I really thought you were Lisanne.'

I found my mouth suddenly twitching at the corner, and then the three of us were laughing again and he said, 'It really is remarkable how much alike you are, are you quite sure you're not related?'

'Quite sure, we couldn't possibly be.'

'I ought to introduce you properly, Ellen. This is my cousin Lancelot, but he hates the name and we hate it so we call him Lance. Lance, this is Ellen Adair.'

He took my hand gravely and smiled down into my eyes.

'Well I'll apologize once more, Ellen, although I can't say I regret my action. We'll meet again over lunch, I hope.'

146

I didn't contradict him, nor did Miss Lisanne, and with a swift smile he was gone. I heard them laughing together as they made their way along the corridor and I picked up my sewing again, though the first enthusiasm had gone.

Lunch was served to me where I was by a maidservant. There was fresh salmon and salad, a concoction of fruit lavishly decorated with cream and a pot filled with delicious coffee. While I ate I was able to look round the room. I felt no envy for the silken drapes at the long windows and the exquisite Chinese carpet, only appreciation. I felt I could never have been untidy in such a room, I would have cherished it and cared for it tenderly, but then if I had been born to such riches I might have felt differently.

After I had eaten I set about putting the room to rights, closing drawers, stacking magazines that had been left lying haphazardly on the floor, straightening lampshades that had been knocked crooked when Lisanne threw her clothes out of the wardrobes.

When the maid came to collect the tray she looked around her appreciatively, then with a smile she said, 'I can see yer've done a bit o'tidyin' up, Miss. It takes us all our time tidyin' up after Miss Lisanne.'

'I hated to see it so untidy. I hope she won't mind.'

She laughed. 'Mind, Miss? Nay, she'll hardly notice. Some folks 'ave it too easy, they don't appreciate it when they've got it.'

I stared at the pile of clothes ruefully. I couldn't hope to finish them in one day and I couldn't think that my aunt would let me make a habit of visiting the Hall to get on with the rest of them. I decided I would ask Miss Lisanne if I could take some home with me.

My opportunity came in the middle of the afternoon when she returned to the room to change out of her riding habit.

'How are you getting on?' she inquired brightly.

'I've finished two of them but I can't possibly finish all the others today.'

'Oh that doesn't matter, Ellen, you can come back tomorrow and the next day until they're done.'

'I won't be able to come again, Miss Lisanne, my aunt won't allow it.'

'She seemed all right about your being here when I talked to her. I'll have another word with her, I'm sure her bark's far worse than her bite.'

'She might be all right with you, Miss Lisanne, I'm the one who has to live with her.'

'But Ellen, I can't possibly wear them like that, when are you going to finish them for me?'

'I was going to ask you if I could take them back with me.'

The frown left her face as quickly as it had appeared.

'Well of course. I'll find you a suitcase and Lance and I will deliver you at your aunt's shop on our way to the Palmerstons'.'

I watched her flinging open the wardrobe doors. I had never seen such clothes, ranging from long ball gowns to silk afternoon dresses, but Lisanne stood looking at them with a frown on her pretty face.

'I'm so fed up with them,' she muttered. 'None of them are new, but I've got to look decent tonight, the Palmerstons are throwing a party for their youngest daughter so I've got to keep my end up. What do you think, Ellen, which of these will be suitable?'

She threw three of them on to the bed: a cornflower-blue taffeta, a cherry-red chiffon and another in black lace which she picked up suddenly and held against her.

'This is the one I love, Ellen, but even Mother was doubtful about it and Granny will be scandalized. I know it's probably too old for me and too sophisticated, but don't you just adore black even if it does make me look a Jezabel?'

'Which do you think your cousin Lance would like to see you in?'

'Oh, you know what men are. He'd love the blue, or that white one there with the blue streamers. My cousin Gervase would like me in black. Did you like Lance?'

'He seems nice. He's very attractive.'

'He is, isn't he? Did you know that the de Belleforts

148

always married their cousins? Both Lance and Gervase are very handsome, I don't much mind which of them I marry.'

I stared at her in amazement and she trilled with laughter.

'I've shocked you, Ellen. I expect you've been brought up to believe that people only marry the people they're in love with whereas I've been brought up to believe that the de Belleforts marry for expediency, to keep the money in the family and in the hope that love might come later.'

'Then you're not in love with either of your cousins?'

'Oh I love Lance, of course. I love him because he's nice and fun to be with. I haven't see Gervase since I was ten and I thought he was horrid. He wasn't the slightest bit interested in me, he was impossible to talk to and he spent all evening chatting up some woman whose husband was playing bridge in the card room.'

It was all a very different world to me. Talking of marriage to one man because he was fun to be with, and the other who would probably be indifferent. By this time she was rummaging through the dressing table for silk stockings.

'If Lance comes in do chat to him, Ellen. I'll wear the red chiffon and I'll take everything I need into the bathroom. Will you be able to get the dresses into this?'

She threw a leather suitcase on to the bed and without waiting for an answer went into the bathroom, slamming the door after her.

I spent the next few minutes carefully folding the dresses I intended to take with me. While I was busy with the straps Lance came into the room. He was wearing evening dress and I thought again how handsome he was. The sombre evening clothes gave him a peculiar distinction, more mature and strangely distinguished, and after a brief smile he said, 'Isn't she ready yet? We're going to be late, it's quite a drive over to the Palmerstons'.'

He eyed the suitcase I was struggling to put on the floor and came forward immediately to help me.

'What have you got in here, Ellen?' he demanded.

'Only dresses for alteration. Miss Lisanne said you would take me to my aunt's shop.'

'Come along then, I'll take you now. I doubt if there's room in the car for the three of us and that suitcase.'

I tripped beside him down the wide curving staircase where a maid was polishing the rail, and I could have smiled at her open-mouthed curiosity.

Lance's car was a low-slung open tourer with a bonnet that seemed to go on for ever and with precious little room in the back once the suitcase was in.

He drove fast down the long drive and once when I stole a look at his face he turned to smile at me.

'You'll have to tell where you live, Ellen, I don't know the village very well.'

'I live halfway down the high street, at the draper's shop.'

'With your aunt, I believe?'

'Yes.'

'And what do you do all day, serve in the shop and set out the window?'

I was aware of a strange resentment and yet there was nothing condescending in his tone of voice. How mundane he made my life sound in my own ears, serving in a shop, setting out the window, tasks that required no special training.

My heart sank when I saw Alec Devlin at the window of the baker's shop, his eyes almost popping out of his head with curiosity. Then I saw my aunt hurrying across the road from the pavement where she had been chatting to Alec's mother.

Both women stood on their respective pavements waiting for me to get out of Lance's car, watching him walk round to open the car door for me before he handed out the suitcase. They continued to watch while he smiled down at me and then got back into the car in the most unhurried manner, raising his hand in farewell before he drove up the street to turn round at the village hall and drive back, waving again as he passed the shop.

Aunt Liza strode into the shop with disapproval evident in her straight stiff back, leaving me to follow with the suitcase. She said acidly, 'Yer've taken yer time leavin' me on mi own all day. What's that yer bringin'?'

150

'There was a lot to do, Aunt, I couldn't possibly finish all these in one day. I asked if I could bring them home.'

'That means you'll spend every day workin' on 'em and expectin' another day to take 'em back to the 'All when they're finished. And who was that who brought you back?' she inquired shortly.

'It was Mr Lance, Lady de Bellefort's grandson.'

The frown grew more prominent. 'Don't ye be gettin' any fancy ideas, Ellen, men in 'is walk o' life are not lookin' for girls in yours.'

'I have no ideas at all about Lance de Bellefort, Aunt Liza, he was kind enough to bring me home, that's all.'

'Well, just as long as ye remembers that. Now I've got a meetin' to go to and I'm late as it is, thanks to you. Mrs Devlin's gone off without me, I'll 'ave to 'urry to catch 'er up. Lock up the shop when I've gone. I'll be back about ten.'

I watched her pulling her black straw hat down over her hair before snatching up her big black bag and marching out into the shop. I always wondered what was in that bag which she took everywhere, little realizing that I was soon to find out.

When the sun went down it was dark in the small room behind the shop and I was glad to put a match to the fire and light the gas jet. I worked steadily, sitting in Aunt Liza's velvet chair near the window, the only sound the steady ticking of the clock on the mantelpiece and the chattering of the birds in the tall elms. I was about to make a cup of tea when I heard somebody knocking loudly on the front door and I jumped to my feet, startled.

It was just nine o'clock, not nearly time for Aunt Liza to come home and although it was a sleepy quiet place, from time to time there had been trouble from village louts with too much to drink in them. Nervously I went into the shop and tried to see who was at the door from the window. I was hampered by the piles of wool Aunt Liza had stacked in the window so I went to the door and in a trembling voice called out, 'Who's there?'

151

I was relieved to hear the vicar's voice, even though the tones were undeniably urgent.

'It's your aunt, Ellen, she's been taken ill. Can you come at once?'

I unlocked the door with trembling fingers and there he stood accompanied by two members of the committee, both elderly women and decidedly agitated.

'We couldn't bring her home, Ellen,' the vicar explained. 'We've laid her down on one of the benches and Mrs Devlin's gone for the doctor, I expect she'll catch him at home at this time. Can you come right away?'

'Of course, Vicar, just let me get my keys. Is she very bad?'

'We couldn't bring her round, Ellen, she just passed out in the middle of an argument she'd been taking part in. One minute she was her usual forceful self, the next she was gasping for breath. I don't like the look of her at all, but perhaps by the time we get back she'll have come round.'

We hurried through the dusk to where the lights from the village hall streamed out into the night, and as we arrived we saw the doctor and Mrs Devlin at the door before us. Mrs Devlin eyed me unhappily, saying, 'She didn't look 'erself when she arrived, Ellen. Late she was and no doubt she'd been hurrying.'

I felt suddenly very guilty, and that her eyes were hostile as well as accusing, but the vicar hurried us into the hall and my eyes immediately took in the group of women clustered at one side of the hall while the doctor bent over my aunt. I stood with Mrs Devlin and the vicar while he conducted his examination, then at last he turned to take stock of us before addressing me.

'As far as I can see she's had a stroke. Are you the niece?'

'Yes, Doctor.'

'Just the two of you I suppose?'

'Yes.'

'Well I'll get her into the village hospital, they won't be pleased at this time of night but you'll not be able to cope

152

on your own. She's a dead weight, you'll not be able to lift her and I'm not sure how severe the stroke is as yet.'

'Will I be able to go with her to the hospital?' I asked him.

'I'll drive you there myself after they've taken her away.'

'I'll come with you to the hospital,' Mrs Devlin said sharply.

It seemed to me that the next half hour happened like something in a dream. The ambulance chugged down the street and two men carrying a stretcher jumped out and hurried inside the hall. Aunt Liza lay as one dead, her face grey, her hands lying limply at her sides until I tucked them carefully under the rug, then we were climbing into the doctor's trap for our journey to the hospital.

'Never seen 'er ail a thing in all the time I've known 'er,' Mrs Devlin was saying. 'She'll not be a good patient, 'er sort never are.'

'How old is your aunt?' the doctor asked suddenly.

'I'm not sure, sixty perhaps.'

'Fifty's more like,' Mrs Devlin snapped. 'Nay, Ellen, whatever made ye think she was sixty?'

'I never really knew, she just seemed sixty, that's all.'

I realized I didn't know much about Aunt Liza at all and I hoped fervently that he wouldn't ask me any more questions. Mrs Devlin was the person to ask, not me.

It was after two o'clock when we were entering our respective dwellings having left Aunt Liza at the cottage hospital, still unconscious. The doctor said we could do nothing more that night and I would be allowed to visit the following day.

On parting, Mrs Devlin whispered, 'I don't like the look of 'er, Ellen. Mi mother died from a stroke and she never did regain consciousness – just like Liza, she was. What are ye goin' to do if she doesn't get over it, and what are ye goin' to do if she needs nursin'? Can ye manage 'er and the shop?'

'I don't know, Mrs Devlin, I don't know what will happen.'

'I suppose the shop'll 'ave to be sold. That niece of 'ers in Ripon'll not want it. 'Ave ye the money to buy it?'

'No.'

'Mm. Make a nice little tea shop it would. Mi 'usband's offen said we could branch out across the road 'ere. But these are early days, luv, I 'opes Liza'll get better and come 'ome.'

The fire had long since died in the grate and the room looked untidy with my sewing. I felt cold with shock and my hands trembled as I filled the kettle but all thoughts of sleep had deserted me. There was too much on my mind.

I was sorry about Aunt Liza, sorry without loving her, without really liking her very much, but once more I was burdened with insecurity. If she died my whole life would be changed and once again my father's figure loomed large, to be feared and to escape from. I prayed fervently for my aunt's life, that it might be spared both for her own sake and for mine, at least long enough to afford me the few years that would place me irrevocably beyond his jurisdiction.

My prayers were not to be answered. At eight o'clock the next morning a message came to me that Aunt Liza had died during the night without regaining consciousness, and during the next few days I had so much to do that my immediate future was the last thing I thought about.

I hated going through her things, and I hated even more my preoccupation with the rough diary she had kept in an old manuscript book. Right from the day she made me leave Liverpool there were references to me, most of them uncomplimentary, but two of them I was destined to remember most vividly.

The first one was written only a few days after I came to live with her and it read: 'I can't believe what Ellen tells me about her father who I've allus believed to be an upright God-fearing man, nor what she tells me about that girl from her village. One day I'll make it my business to find out, and if she's been lying to me she'll have to go, I'll have no further truck with the girl.'

The second entry was made on the night she came back from her brother's house in Ripon:

'Ellen's been to Liverpool, she hasn't said so but I know, and she's been to see that Kitty McGuire. I know now I've done the right thing by leaving everything I've got to my brother and his daughter. If I'd left some of it to Ellen she'd have been off seeing that Kitty and no doubt sharing whatever she'd got with her. My brother was right, I should never have doubted him.'

I stared at the pages filled with her small ill-formed handwriting, hearing her acid voice and seeing her thin-lipped doubting face. Then I started to cry, thinking how different it could have been.

I could have worked so hard in that little shop, made something of it, and I could have made Aunt Liza proud of me if she hadn't been so prejudiced and uncaring. Now my future was an empty place, I would be without a home or employment. But worse than that, I had to write to my father to tell him his half-sister was dead.

The village was in mourning on the day of Aunt Liza's funeral. The curtains were drawn in every window and all through the morning the women came and went from their front doors in order not to miss a solitary happening.

I altered one of Aunt Liza's black skirts to fit me and I wore my white silk blouse. It was a warm day so I didn't need a coat and I tied a black ribbon in my hair because I didn't possess a black hat, and I couldn't bring myself to wear one of Aunt Liza's.

Alec Devlin delivered balm cakes and boiled ham and tongue, and Mrs Devlin helped me to make sandwiches. Later he came again with huge slabs of fruit cake, and Mrs Devlin said, 'I suppose the brother'll settle up with mi for all this, Ellen. You'll 'ave nothin' to spare, I don't suppose.'

We spread the repast out in the kitchen and covered the plates with greaseproof paper, then she went to get ready for the funeral and I sat waiting. Aunt Liza lay in her coffin in the living room where they had brought her from the mortuary that morning but I had no desire to look at her, a fact which Mrs Devlin had regarded as unfeeling and unusual.

I hated to go into the room and when I did so I walked

155

with averted eyes and the thought that I would never again be able to sit there without seeing the coffin on its trestle across one corner. Because of my fears I was inordinately glad to hear voices in the shop and next moment four people entered the living room. I knew immediatley that these were my aunt's relatives from Ripon – her brother Simeon Ashington and his wife Martha, their daughter Jennie and her financé George. Although the two older people went immediately to the coffin, the girl and the man took stock of me.

Jennie was a pale girl with hazel eyes and light brown hair, and she clung on to the arm of the young man as though afraid to let go. I thought he looked like a bank clerk. He was correctly dressed and well scrubbed and he had pale protruding blue eyes and a receding chin. Neither of them seemed disposed to be civil towards me.

The father said somewhat sullenly, 'I suppose you're Ellen?'

'Yes.'

'Well we didn't expect this, to be sure. Our Liza seemed as fit as a fiddle when she stayed with us i' Ripon. Not bin doin' too much, 'as she?'

'No. I'm sure she hasn't.'

'Stroke was it?'

'Yes. The death certificate is on the table and the doctor said if you cared to visit him he would tell you everything you needed to know.'

'Ay well, I might just do that after the funeral. Is yer father and anybody else comin'?'

'I haven't heard but I've written to tell everybody I thought should know.'

'Well Cousin Edie won't be comin', she wont' leave that damn dog of 'ers, so there's only yer father and mother. If they intend comin' they should be 'ere anytime.'

At that moment the bell tinkled once more above the shop door and my heart leapt when I saw my father in the doorway.

Our eyes met across the room, but for all the

acknowledgement he made I might have been a marble statue instead of his daughter.

The pain of his rejection was acute, but almost immediately it was dispelled by the sight of my brother Peter and the warmth of his smile. I hoped we would be able to talk later, although there was little chance of it now because my father had placed a firm hand on Peter's shoulder and kept it there.

Mrs Devlin returned and introduced herself, and then the funeral coaches were outside and the men were coming in to close up the coffin.

It seemed that all along the long rambling high street people in black stood at their doors. Pulled up at the front of the shop was a black hearse with purple velvet curtains at the windows and purple plumes on the headgear of the black horses.

Two coaches followed, each pulled by two black horses, and into the first one my father climbed followed by Peter and myself, while the other five people piled into the other. When I questioned this procedure the undertaker said, 'Your father is the eldest brother, Miss Adair, and you are living in Miss Ashington's house.'

'I see,' I replied with a little smile.

All the same I didn't miss the haughty stare Jennie favoured me with and I sat miserably opposite my father's sullen face and Peter's embarrassed one. Just before we reached the churchyard, Father snapped, 'I noticed ye haven't asked about yer mother, Ellen.'

'I'm sorry Father, how is Mother?'

'Not well, not well at all. She needs somebody to look after 'er and I've got mi work to see to.'

I said nothing. Was this the preamble to asking me to return home, I wondered, and catching Peter's eyes on me I didn't miss the slight shake of his head.

My opportunity to talk to him came while we walked together towards the gates of the churchyard after the service.

'Is my mother really ill?' I asked Peter fearfully.

'No more than she always is, Ellen. You mustn't think of

157

comin' home, for if you do ye'll never get away again. Yer've made the break, Ellen.'

'But is she being looked after?'

'Our Mary's very good and I suppose Naomi does a bit. Mi father could do more.'

'You've left school, Peter, what are you doing?'

'There's not much work in the village, Ellen, but I'm doin' a bit of farm labouring. Mi father sez there might be a job goin' over at St Hilda's when old Mr Marshall retires but I don't want to be a sexton. I daren't tell mi father, though.'

'What will you do then?'

'When I'm eighteen I'm going to sea. It's something I want to do and next time Arnold Mason comes home he's promised to take me to Liverpool with him and get me on his ship. I'm countin' the days.'

'Do they know about it at home, Peter?'

'Nobody knows about it. I'll 'ave to do it just like you did, Ellen, a note left in the kitchen for 'em to find. It's the only way.'

'Then we'll both be outcasts, Peter, the sort of people nobody at home ever talks about.'

'I suppose so.'

For a few minutes we walked in silence, then abruptly I asked, 'Did you ever hear any talk about mi father and Phoebe Patterson?'

His face flushed and he looked acutely embarrassed, then he said softly, 'I got to watchin' 'im, Ellen, after I saw 'im goin' into her cottage. I don't think anybody in the village suspects 'e's friendly with 'er, 'e's covered his tracks too well for that. I'm just glad mi mother doesn't know about it, she worships 'im just like she allus did.'

'Oh Peter, I could never come home, I'd have to confront him with it, I couldn't stop miself, and in his heart he doesn't want mi home. He'd never be sure of me, would he?'

'No, Ellen, he never would. What will ye do?'

'I honestly don't know. The shop's goin' to the niece and she'll soon dispose of it. There's no work in the village so

I'll have to think very hard of what I want to do and where I'm goin'.'

'I hope we get a chance to talk again, Ellen, but if not I'll write to you. We'd best be quiet now, 'ere they come.'

CHAPTER 16

As the afternoon wore on I could see there wasn't going to be much opportunity to speak with Peter again. The people from Ripon made short work of the sandwiches and I was kept busy brewing pots of tea while Mrs Devlin basked in their admiration of her husband's cakes.

My father maintained an austere silence and Peter sat beside him looking miserable until I engineered his help in handing round plates.

'It doesn't look as if we're goin' to be able to talk again, Ellen,' he whispered, 'we're goin' home on the four o'clock train.'

'Is there anywhere I can write to you when I'm settled – how about the vicarage?' I asked.

'Nay, the vicar'd hand yer letter to mi father. Ye can write to, Mr Nelson, I 'elps out at the smallholdin' at the weekends, 'e'd pass yer letter on. Mr Nelson's no love for mi father, though Mrs Nelson'd feel she 'ad to give it to mi mother.'

'Then as soon as I'm settled I'll write, Peter.'

'Now then you two,' came my father's voice from the doorway, 'we're waitin' for tea in 'ere, and y'ed best look sharp, Peter, the train won't wait for us.'

In minutes they were shaking hands, saying it was a sad business. Then they were gone without a backward glance from my father and with a long sad look from my brother.

Mrs Devlin helped me to clear away, then Simeon Ashington said, 'Well, Ellen, there's things to talk over. I reckon we'd best make a start,' whereupon Mrs Devlin wished them all good afternoon and I went with her to the shop door.

'It looks as if he means business, luv,' she said. 'My 'usband'd be interested in buying the shop so just you see

160

'ow the land lies and if ye gets a chance tell 'im we'll be interested.'

They sat in a small bunch across the hearth from me. I soon felt sure they had come well prepared, that between Aunt Liza's death and the day of her funeral, matters to do with her shop had been well and truly gone into.

'Ye knew of course that the shop was to be our Jennie's,' her father began. 'Mi sister said she'd left ye in no doubt about that.'

I nodded, unable to trust the evenness of my voice.

'Well our Jennie'll be gettin' married next year and goin' to live i' Harrogate. George 'ere's got a transfer to the bank there and it'll be very nice with 'is folks livin' there. Naturally she won't want the shop so it'll 'ave to be sold. I suppose yer've no money to buy it?'

'No.'

''Ave ye somewhere to go?'

'Not at the moment.'

'Well obviously these things can't be done in a day so there's no reason why the shop can't go on tradin'. I'll pay ye a wage for lookin' after it and it's a roof over yer head. How about the same money that Liza paid ye – does that seem fair to you, Ellen?'

'Did my aunt tell you how much she paid me?'

'Two and sixpence a week she said, and yer board and lodgin'. I'll give ye four shillings, that sounds about right to me.'

'I think the Devlins might be interested in buying the shop.'

'Is that so? Why didn't she say somethin' when she was 'ere then?'

'I expect she thought you might think she was interfering. You could speak to Mr Devlin if you have the time.'

'What's 'e aimin' to do with the shop if he gets it? E'll not be keepin' it on as a draper's?'

'No. Mrs Devlin thought it might make a nice tea room, selling their confectionery of course.'

'Would he keep you on 'ere, has he mentioned that?'

'No. That has never been mentioned.'

161

'Well if the price was right and if he'll match whatever else I might be offered p'rhaps it would make a cafe. I can't see it payin' except on market days.'

'I think if it was here it would pay. Walkers and climbers come into the district and people come to look at Langstone Priory. There has been talk that Lady de Bellefort might throw open the gardens several days a week, and there's the old abbey up on the fell.'

His eyes narrowed with speculation, then turning to his wife he said, 'The shop's got possibility, Martha, if we'd bin a bit nearer you might 'a bin able to do somethin' with it. I haven't time to see Devlin today but I'll get mi solicitor to have a talk to im. Now, Ellen, yer'll keep the place lookin' nice and if folks want to look round yer'll treat 'em respectful and point out all the good things in the village. If ye does all that don't be surprised if there isn't a nice little present for ye at the end of it.'

'Can't we 'ave a look round, Father?' Jennie said. 'There might be somethin' George and me might want.'

'And 'ow are ye goin' to get it 'ome? We can come again, lass, and bring a suitcase and hire a trap from the station.'

'There's tablecloths and the like,' Jennie protested. 'Surely there'll be a suitcase we can put 'em in.'

'Oh well, ye might as well look while you're 'ere. P'rhaps Ellen'd show ye where our Liza kept things.'

Seething with anger I took Jennie upstairs where she went through Aunt Liza's bedroom. While I watched her I heard a sound from the other bedroom and went in, to find her mother rummaging through my things.

'You'll find nothing in here, Mrs Ashington. This is my room and there are only my things in it,' I said firmly.

'Oh well, I was just savin' time,' she said, and without a look in my direction went on to the landing. ''Ave ye got everythin' ye want, Jennie?' she called out.

Jennie appeared with several tablecloths, two pairs of new bedroom slippers and a roll of white damask.

'There's more,' she said, 'but we couldn't put it all in the suitcase. I thought we could put these in the carpet bag I saw in the kitchen.'

'What's 'appenin' to Liza's clothes?' Mrs Ashington asked as her daughter tripped lightly down the stairs.

'I have no idea. Is there anything you want?'

'Well I never much liked the things Liza wore but she did 'ave a new 'at for that weddin' she went to. I'd like to 'ave a look at that.'

Together we returned to Aunt Liza's bedroom where Mrs Ashington helped herself to the wedding hat, the new blouse and several items of underwear wrapped in tissue paper and unworn.

'Liza was a great one for black,' she said, 'but it doesn't suit mi. This 'at'll do very nicely for our Jennie's weddin', I can find a costume to wear to it and it'll save mi a bit o' money.'

At just before five thirty I saw them depart carrying two suitcases and the carpet bag, watched from their upstairs window by both Mr and Mrs Devlin, and by Alec from the front of the shop.

They were still marching down the street when the doctor's trap drew up at the front door and he alighted with a conspiratorial smile.

'I see the vultures have gone, Ellen, and not empty-handed by the look of things.'

I smiled. I liked Doctor Jarvis, he was always friendly and with a ready smile, and I liked his sense of humour which leaned towards dryness.

'Have they sorted your life out for you, Ellen?'

'For the next few weeks yes, Doctor. After that I'm on my own. Have you time to come in for a while, Doctor?'

'Well I'm due up at the Hall, the old lady is indisposed today but it's only the usual sick headache she suffers from. A few minutes is neither here nor there.'

He followed me into the living room which still smelled sickly of flowers and I hurried into the kitchen to put the kettle on.

'No tea for me, Ellen,' he called out, 'but I'll have a tot of your aunt's whisky if you know where to lay your hands on it.'

I grinned at him across the room. 'I don't rightly know that I do, Doctor.'

'Well I'll show you, Ellen. Second drawer down, pushed away at the back. If they'd discovered that it would be on its way to the station along with the other loot.'

I poured out a generous dram for him, and with a wink he raised his glass, saying, 'Good health to you, lassy, and here's to your future. Now did your aunt leave you any money?'

'Not a penny, Doctor. I'm to stay in the shop and work 'til its sold, then I have no plans.'

He shivered delicately.

'Heaven preserve us from such a project. Women gossipin' over their teacups and hikers queuing up for tables at the weekends. I'll be telling my wife to keep clear of the street on market days, I can tell you.'

'So, Ellen, you're likely to be leavin' us in the near future, and no place to go.'

'Something like that.'

'Well I'll keep my eyes and ears open. Have you thought of going into service, Ellen? There's not much else for a girl these days unless its shop work and you'd have to go to one of the big towns for that. By the way, I've got your aunt's big black bag, but I didn't want to deliver it while the funeral party was here. It's in the trap, Ellen, I'll try to hand it over without the nosy parkers seeing what we're about.'

The high street was quiet. The men would be home from the fields by this time and families sitting down to their evening meal, even so the doctor looked quickly along the street, then up at the Devlins' before he handed out Aunt Liza's bag wrapped in newspaper, then with a gay wave of his hand he picked up his whip and urged the ponies on.

Back in the house I took out the bag and stared at it curiously. It was bulky and I had sometimes wondered idly what she carried in it and why she took it everywhere. At the same time I was reluctant to open it and I could imagine her standing watching me, grim-faced and accusing.

I laid it on the table and went into the kitchen to make

a cup of tea. Whatever the bag contained, I had no right to it. Instead I should have been racing down the high street, trying to catch the Ashingtons before they could board the train. Then glancing briefly at the clock I saw that it was six thirty and by this time they would be on their way.

I picked up the bag gingerly, turning it this way and that, then taking my courage in both hands I pulled at the clasp and opened it.

It was full. Two pairs of leather gloves and a woollen scarf lay on top, and under them was a pair of scissors and a small cash book showing the shop's day-to-day takings. There was a rolled copy of the church magazine and two tickets for the Harvest Fair, then I opened the middle pocket and stared incredulously at a roll of banknotes.

With trembling fingers I took it out and started to count. There was over a hundred pounds, a hundred and seventeen to be precise as well as several pounds in loose change, and if at first my heart leapt, it immediately sank when I realized the money was not mine. At first I wanted to rush out of the house to share my secret with the Devlins, but something held me back. I needed to think and I didn't think they were the right people to advise me.

I decided to sleep on it. Tomorrow I would tell Doctor Jarvis what I had found and accept any advice he cared to give me, and in spite of all the trauma of the day I was surprised how well I slept that night.

CHAPTER 17

I viewed the shop the next morning with many misgivings. When my aunt was alive I had felt my interest in her shop was a way of repaying her for giving me a home. Now I felt no allegiance whatsoever to her relatives in Ripon, and yet mechanically I set about tidying out the drawers and making the window seem a little more enticing.

Mid morning Miss Lisanne arrived on her horse and from my vantage point in the window I thought what a pretty picture she made in her dark habit, riding side-saddle on the big chestnut horse, her blond hair hidden under her attractive yet severe bowler and with the snowy white stock at her throat.

She smiled at me brightly and perched on the wooden seat before the counter.

'I came to see how you were getting along with my clothes, Ellen. My mother might be coming here any day now and if she wishes to take me back with her I'll be needing them.'

'Didn't you hear that my aunt died, Miss Lisanne? I'm afraid there's been so much to do I haven't been able to finish them. The funeral was only yesterday.'

Her pretty face took on a petulant air. 'Oh yes, Granny told me something about it, but I thought the funeral was days ago.'

'I've only had the dresses a few days, she died the night I brought them home.'

'Oh dear, what are we to do then? I suppose you're looking after the shop on your own?'

'Yes I am.'

'Does that mean you're not going to be able to do them?'

'I'll work on them in the evenings and during the day if I get a chance. I promise you'll have them as soon as I've finished.'

'Oh well I suppose I'll have to be satisfied with that. It's so inconvenient.'

Suddenly aware of my expression she said more contritely. 'You must think I'm an unfeeling little beast but it's the way I am, I suppose. I'm sorry about your aunt, Ellen.'

She smiled at me brightly across the counter, then with a gay wave of her whip she tripped lightly out of the shop and I watched her untying her horse while Mr Devlin came across the road to assist her into the saddle.

Business was slow. People came to look in the window and move on, almost as if they thought it too soon to be buying, and for want of something to do I sat in the shop stitching one of Lisanne's dresses.

There was a lot on my mind, particularly the contents of the black leather bag, and I wished it was time to shut up the shop so that I could seek Doctor Jarvis's advice.

My next visitor was Mrs Devlin, cheerful and conspiratorial, asking, 'Did ye mention we might be interested in buyin' the shop, Ellen?'

'Yes. Mr Ashington's putting it in the hands of his solicitors, but he did say if the price was right he'd have no objection to letting you have it.'

'We talked about it all last night. A little cafe'd do right well 'ere, Ellen, particularly if Lady de Bellefort opens the gardens for visitors. We'd not need the livin' room, we could knock that wall down to make more room, and the back kitchen's big enough to make tea and coffee and see to the cakes. We're not thinkin' about meals, only mornin' coffee and afternoon tea. The little cafe in Scarborough was makin' a fortune doin' things like that, and we 'ave a good name for our confectionary.'

I reflected cynically that this had been my aunt's best friend, now all she was interested in was how much Aunt Liza's death might benefit them.

While she chatted on the doorbell rang and I looked up gratefully to see Doctor Jarvis entering the shop.

Wrapped up in her ambitions Mrs Devlin didn't turn round so he stood patiently waiting for her to conclude her fantasies, then when she did turn round to see who my visitor was she blushed as red as a beetroot and I did not miss his sharp twinkling eyes.

After that she beat a hasty retreat and he said with a wry smile, 'So she's got the cafe already has she, Ellen, and where do you come into all this? Has she asked you to run the cafe for them?'

'I don't come into it all all, Doctor, but I'm very glad you've called. If you hadn't I'd have called to see you.'

'I suppose it's your aunt's black bag?'

'Yes, Doctor. Can we talk in the living room? I'll hear the bell if anybody comes.'

He followed me into the living room, and although it was mid morning I helped him to a tot of whisky and he sat in Aunt Liza's big chair drinking it with obvious enjoyment.

'Now then, Ellen, what did she carry in that black bag? Ye never saw her without it.'

I took it out and emptied the contents on the table.

He raised his eyebrows at the wad of notes.

'I always thought there'd be money in there, Ellen. Is the bag empty?'

'I think so.'

'Well we'll just make sure, it would be like your aunt to keep money and jewellery stitched into the lining.'

I watched his hands exploring the inside of the bag and the innumerable pockets, then looking up with a smile he said, 'Hand me the scissors, Ellen, I didn't think I'd be far wrong. There's somethin' at the bottom here.'

'Damn!' he said suddenly. 'There's some sort of pin in there.'

Next moment he had brought out a heavy gold brooch and was sucking his bleeding finger ruefully. 'The blasted pin was open,' he said. 'I can't think why the woman didn't wear her jewellery instead of carrying it about in her handbag. Hold on awhile, Ellen, there's somethin' else in there.'

I picked up the brooch curiously. It was engraved with the initial 'L' and decorated with tiny embossed flowers, and I supposed it was valuable because it was heavy and obviously gold. Then there was a clatter on the table and the doctor was setting out a row of gold sovereigns as well as a gold chain and locket.

'Did she ever wear any jewellery, Ellen?' he asked sharply.

'She had a gold watch on a long chain and several small brooches. I never saw these before.'

'And where is her jewellery now?'

'She kept it upstairs in her chest of drawers.'

'Well nip up and see if it's still there. If it's gone then they took it yesterday.'

I searched every drawer in the bedroom but I didn't find the jewellery, and when I told the doctor he smiled grimly, saying, 'I guessed as much. Well, Ellen, I wouldn't let 'em get their hands on this lot. They ransacked this house yesterday and took what valuables they found. They know nothin' about this and I'd keep it that way.'

'But can I do that, Doctor, I haven't any right and I'm pretty sure she'd want her niece to have it.'

'Look, lassy, you're going to lose the roof over your head, and your livelihood. You'll have no home and no money and they'll get a fair price for the shop. I reckon they've done very well. Now what are you going to do with this money?'

'I've no idea.'

'I'll put it in my bank for you and you'll get interest on it. The bank's in Ilkley but that's no problem, you'll have the address and you can get what you want when you want it, and it's a better idea than leaving it in the village. If the nosy parkers sees ye going into the little bank in the high street they'll put two and two together and make five.'

'I don't know what to say, Doctor.'

'Ye mean you've got a conscience about this money, Ellen. Well you don't need to have, love. I knew your aunt a good many years as a cantankerous tight-fisted and very difficult woman. I could hardly believe my own ears when I heard she'd brought a niece home to live with her, I could never think it was out of Christian charity. My wife told me how nice the little shop was lookin'. What made you come 'ere, Ellen?'

'I was living in Liverpool and she came looking for me.

169

I couldn't get on with mi father and I ran away from home when I left school. I was happy in Liverpool. I didn't want to come here but I was under age and I didn't have much choice. I could never go back to living with mi father.'

'Was he at the funeral?'

'Yes, with mi brother Peter. He'll leave home too when he's old enough to join the merchant navy.'

He looked at me shrewdly but made no comment, then he wrapped up the notes in a page taken from the newspaper and after counting the sovereigns placed them in his pocket.

'There's fifteen of 'em, Ellen, a nice little nest egg, and I hope your aunt's somewhere or other bein' made aware of what we're doing.'

'If she is she'll haunt me, I just know she will.'

'Don't even think it, lass. She'll be so busy makin' her peace with her maker she'll have no time to haunt you, and if she haunts me I'll soon send her packin'.'

As our eyes met I suddenly felt very light-hearted and I laughed joyfully for the first time in days.

'That's better, Ellen, that pretty face wasn't made for tears. By the way, wasn't that Lady de Bellefort's grand-daughter I saw leavin' the shop earlier on?'

'Yes, I'm doing some sewing for her.'

'You're very much like her, you know, I thought so the first time I saw you. Are there any skeletons in your family, Ellen?'

I smiled. 'No, I'm sure there's not. None of my family had ever heard of the de Belleforts and they didn't come from these parts.'

'Well perhaps way back there was a romance nobody these days knows anything about. These things happened, Ellen, some member of the gentry and a local lass, some baby born on the wrong side of the blanket and a whole village coverin' up the scandal. You and that lass at the hall could be sisters and it's my bet the old lady knows a thing or two.'

'She's remarked on the resemblance but that's all.'

'She's a shrewd one. Well I'd best be off, I'm overdue

170

on my rounds as it is. I'll see to your money for you, Ellen, and I'll be in touch.'

He grinned at me mischievously and suddenly I felt more light-hearted than I had any right to be, with a fortune that I had no right to and a fellow conspirator to aid and abet me.

CHAPTER 18

In the middle of the afternoon Alec Devlin appeared in the shop, jaunty and smiling. He said amiably, 'Well, Ellen, what's it feel like to 'ave the shop to yerself and be yer own boss?'

'I'm not quite used to the idea yet.'

'I suppose mi mother's told ye about our ideas for a cafe. What do you think, Ellen.?'

'It sounds like a good idea with more and more people coming into the village.'

'Well it'd be very handy with the shop across the way. All the bakin' could be done there, all we'd need to do is bring it across the first thing in the mornin'. It'd be a good thing on market days and we've heard they intend to 'ave a market on an extra day.'

'Will your mother be taking charge of the cafe?'

'They're talkin' about mi wife getting involved, but I don't think she'd take to that. She's not a good mixer and when the baby comes she'll 'ave 'er hands full. Did ye know we were goin' to be parents, Ellen?'

'No I didn't, Alec. Congratulations.'

'Well ye can see mi point, can't ye, Ellen? I can't see mi wife wantin' to come 'ere and mi mother wouldn't make a waitress, she'd spend all 'er time gossipin' to the customers. No, what it wants is a nice attractive young girl who'd look well in a frilly cap and apron, somebody who can talk nice to the customers and take a pride in settin' out the window and seein' to the tables. It might suit you, Ellen.'

I stared at him stupidly.

He grinned at me and sidled round the counter. 'Think about it, Ellen. I'd 'ave a word with mi father, I'm sure both 'im and mi stepmother'd soon see the sense of it. Ye could live upstairs and work down 'ere, and it's my bet 'e'd pay ye more than ever ye aunt did.'

I was on the point of thinking the idea had possibilities when I felt his arm slide round my waist and suddenly I was pushing him away while was was cajoling, 'Think about it, Ellen, you and me working more or less together, there's many a day we can get off to Harrogate or even to Ripon. I'm lookin' round for a little car and it'll all be in the line o' business.'

Angrily I pushed him away. 'You've got a nerve, Alec Devlin. In one breath you're telling me your wife's going to have a baby and in the next you're suggesting you and me might have something going for each other. I think you're despicable. I don't want to work in your wretched cafe and I don't want to have any more to do with you.'

His face was red and angry as he answered me. 'Well I don't see you've any cause to be so high and mighty, Ellen Adair, yer'll be out on yer ear when mi father buys this shop and I know for a fact yer aunt didn't leave ye any money. You thought ye were too good for mi 'afore I got wed, it seems ye still thinks so.'

'I don't, Alec, I just think you're a married man who's going to be a father. Why don't *ye* remember it?'

Sulky, like a small badly behaved child he flung out of the shop, slamming the door, and I stood dejectedly at the counter trembling with distaste.

Alec could be vindictive. Once his father got the shop I felt sure my days would be numbered.

It was a long wearisome day. I was glad when I could pull down the shop blinds and go into the back to prepare my evening meal.

I was still in the kitchen when there was a smart rap on the shop door, and I hurried to open it. I stared in surprise at the de Bellefort butler standing there tall and unsmiling, and even more surprised when he handed me an envelope.

'Her ladyship asked mi to give you this, Miss. I'm not to wait for a reply.'

I stared at it stupidly for several seconds, then he raised his hat and stalked off down the street. Across at the baker's Alec Devlin was pulling up the shutters, his round eyes bulging with curiosity.

A faint aura of perfume hung about the pale cream envelope, and as I turned it over I saw that the de Bellefort crest decorated the flap. It contained a single sheet of pale cream parchment and the handwriting was beautifully formed and flowing:

Dear Miss Adair,
I was very sorry to hear of the death of your aunt who was always most efficient at ordering my requirements. I shall miss her and would like to think that the shop will continue to function.

I shall be much obliged if you will kindly call upon me one day soon to suit your convenience when I shall have a proposition to put before you. It is not necessary to make an appointment, I am invariably at home.

Yours sincerely,
Helena, Lady de Bellefort

For several minutes I stared at the letter. What sort of proposition could Lady de Bellefort possibly have to put before me? And immediately I thought of going into service. But I didn't want to scrub floors and clean vegetables, serve tea or wait on table in the Hall's enormous dining room. It would be a far cry from the mission but I'd had a surfeit of menial tasks, and yet I wasn't trained for anything else unless it was sewing, and I sewed because I needed the money, not because I wanted to spend the rest of my life doing it.

I thought distastefully of Alec Devlin's proposition, and it seemed to me then that anything her ladyship might propose would be preferable to looking after the Devlins' tea room and having Alec think he had a right to paw me because he was paying my wages.

I realized suddenly that I wasn't very hungry, so I let myself out of the shop and set off along the street at a brisk pace. I hadn't planned to climb the fell above the Hall, but unconsciously my feet led me on to it. The late afternoon sunshine lit up the mullioned windows until they blazed as if a fire burned in the rooms, and there was a timeless peace about the parkland and the shimmering mere. As I sat on the fell I saw two girls walking arm in arm from the direction of the house. I knew that they were servants from their attire, but they were chatting happily together and quite suddenly I felt an urge to belong in such a life.

What did it really matter what I did as long as it was good honest work? I had money at the back of me even if I still felt it shouldn't be mine, and I badly needed somewhere to live. At that moment I prayed that Lady de Bellefort might have the solution I was looking for, and then suddenly I thought about Kitty.

Kitty would have tossed her head at the idea of going into service. Service would never open the door to ermine and emeralds but it would put another meal in my mouth and find me somewhere to lay my head. It was high time I forgot about Kitty and her ideas of grandeur.

CHAPTER 19

It was Sunday afternoon before I could take advantage of Lady de Bellefort's request to visit her. In the meantime the shop was busy, and I was agreeably surprised when I totted up my takings on Saturday evening. Aunt Liza would have been highly gratified and no doubt her brother would be too.

I had finished all Miss Lisanne's alterations but was not looking forward to the journey up to Langstone Priory with a full suitcase.

On Sunday morning I attended church out of deference to my aunt and I was very glad I'd gone when the vicar said prayers for her soul and the congregation joined in singing her favourite hymn, 'Abide with Me'. After the service many came to offer their condolences and most of them wanted to know if I intended staying in the village and keeping open the shop. When I said I didn't know, one woman said, 'I suppose we could get by without a draper's, the wool on the market's much cheaper,' a remark which left me thinking that neither Aunt Liza nor myself would be much missed.

Doctor Jarvis and his wife walked down the church path with me, and he amused me by saying, 'Well Ellen, have ye given a good account of your week's tradin' to the folk up at Ripon?'

'Not yet, Doctor Jarvis, but I think they'll be well pleased.'

'And today's a day of rest for you.'

That gave me an opportunity to tell him about my proposed visit to the Hall and I was delighted when he said, 'I have to go up there myself this afternoon, Ellen, I like to keep an eye on the old lady. I'll give you a lift if you like.'

'I'd be very grateful, Doctor.'

'Good, that's settled then. I'll pick you up at two. I'll only be a few minutes with the old lady and I can tell her you're waiting to see her. I had a feeling she might be getting in touch with you.'

'Why is that, Doctor?'

'Well she asked a few questions about you and it's my guess she's curious about the way you look. You're too much like Miss Lisanne for it to be merely coincidence.'

I stared at him curiously, and Mrs Jarvis said with a smile, 'Have none of the villagers mentioned it, Ellen? I would have thought they might.'

'No, none of them, and I'm glad about that because coincidence is all it is.'

'Oh well,' the doctor said, 'you go along there and see what she has to say. I'd like to think she might be able to help you, Ellen, you badly need a friend just now and she carries a lot of influence.'

We parted at my front door with me wondering just how her influence could help me, and with whom.

I was glad of the lift, and when Doctor Jarvis picked up the suitcase he exclaimed, 'Gracious me, Ellen, what have ye got in here, the crown jewels?'

'Only clothes, Doctor.'

'Enough to last 'til she's in her dotage, I shouldn't wonder. That lass's been spoiled what with her father bein' killed when she was only a wee thing and her mother flittin' about from pillar to post, never settling long enough to give the girl a proper home or a steady education. First she was in one boarding school and then another, next she was abroad in a French convent school, then another in Switzerland. I'm surprised she's turned out as well as she has.'

'I wonder which of the cousins she'll marry, Doctor?'

'You know about that, do you? It's not a good thing for first cousins to marry, and the de Belleforts have always done it. I'm surprised there hasn't been more sickness, both mental and physical, in the family but there must be some good stock there somewhere.'

I was unprepared for the charm of the sitting room in which Lady de Bellefort received me, so overwhelmed had I been by the great rooms we had passed through to arrive there.

The doctor gave my arm a gentle squeeze as I passed into the room through the door he held open for me. 'Take heart,' he whispered, 'she's not going to eat you.'

It was a room overlooking the mere, decorated in gentle pastel colours, with a delicate Chinese carpet and exquisite watercolours. On that day I was only aware of its beauty without knowing anything of the value of the pictures and porcelain around me, and Lady de Bellefort, sitting in a rose-coloured velvet chair at a long low window, received me graciously, indicating that I should take the chair opposite.

'I'm sorry I couldn't come before, Milady, but there was the shop to see to and the rest of Miss Lisanne's gowns to finish.'

She smiled. 'I understand, Ellen. I didn't expect you immediately, and have you finished my granddaughter's dresses?'

'Yes. I left them with the housekeeper.'

'And she must pay you for doing them, they have taken a great deal of your time. You are keeping the shop open until it is sold, I believe.'

'Yes.'

'And when the shop is sold?'

'I shall have to find something else.'

Her eyes were kind, so kind that I felt a lump rise into my throat and in my eyes the smarting of unshed tears.

'I would like to hear something about yourself, Ellen, how you came to be living in the village, something of your early life and your family.'

'There isn't much to tell. I left home when I was fourteen.'

'Then you shall tell me why you left home and what happened before you came to Langstone.'

So I told her about my schooldays, my parents and my brothers and sisters. I told her about my friendship with Kitty McGuire and my father's rigid principles and unyielding abhorrence of anything outside his own concept of right and wrong. I was aware of the bitterness that crept into my

178

voice, the hatred and the fear that I could not escape from whenever I thought of him.

Gently she asked, 'Did your father never come after you, Ellen? And what about your mother in all this?'

'My mother never spoke against him, and I know how he would feel, I'd made my bed so I must lie on it. His pride would never allow him to take me back.'

I could have talked about his involvement with Phoebe Patterson but some strange sense of loyalty made me bite my tongue.

'Are you like your mother, Ellen?'

'I don't think so. My mother always looked so careworn and she was so thin. Some of the neighbours told me she was a pretty woman when she first went to live in the village, but she'd had a lot of children and my father wasn't an easy man to live with.'

'Your family hadn't always lived in the village then?'

'Mi father was born and brought up there but when he was a young man he went to work on the land over at Chantry. He only went back to the village when the old sexton died and he got his job at the church. Mi mother was living in Chantry, it was there where they met.'

I was aware of the gleam of interest in her eyes. 'So your mother lived in Chantry. It begins to make sense, Ellen. Tell me, what sort of a family did your mother have in Chantry?'

'She didn't talk about it much. Mi grandmother died when I was seven and mi grandfather wasn't much interested in any of us. I went once with my mother to visit but my grandfather hardly spoke to either of us and mi aunt and uncles seemed not to care if we ever went again. When I said as much to mi mother she said there was probably a reason for it, but she would never say anything else.'

'Do you remember your grandmother?'

'I remember that she was pretty, and I once saw a picture of her, lovely she was with dark auburn hair and eyes as blue as mine.'

'What was her name?'

'Sarah Welsby.'

'That was her married name?'

'Yes, she was called Sarah Saxton before she married, she came from a little village not far from here.'

She sat looking out of the window with a pensive smile, and seemed to have forgotten my existence, as though her thoughts were on the past and a long long way from her sitting room on that bright sunny afternoon. At last she turned with a small sad little smile which I found strangely appealing, the tone of her voice compelling.

'And now, Ellen, I am going to tell you something about myself and my family which you might feel you should have known about a long time ago. Some might think that it is better to let sleeping dogs lie, but not when you are going to be given the opportunity to concern yourself with the de Belleforts. The choice shall be yours.'

Our eyes met and locked, and I was not sure that I wanted to hear what she had every intention of telling me, for I knew in my heart that after today my life would never be the same again.

'I always knew that one day I would marry my cousin Roland de Bellefort and I saw no reason to quarrel with that. The de Belleforts always married their cousins or second cousins and although we had only met twice I had liked him. He was the younger of the two de Bellefort boys, not destined to take the title, and we were little more than children, so marriage was a long way off.

'My mother was a de Bellefort, my father a second cousin, the son of a country parson. When my father was thirty he came into a fairly substantial fortune left him by a maiden aunt who had been particularly fond of him, and we started to travel.

'I had an enchanted childhood and it continued until I was seventeen and approaching marriageable age. We lived in lovely cities for months at a time or until my father felt the urge to move on – Florence and Venice, Vienna and Saltzburg, Genoa and Sienna, Madrid and Grenada. I could speak German, Spanish and Italian fluently, and I was pretty. Quite suddenly when I was seventeen I realized I didn't want to come to Yorkshire and live the life of a country squire's wife in a draughty stone mansion where the weather was unpredictable and where nothing ever happened.

'I made my wishes known in no uncertain manner, but here I came across my parents' iron resolve. Not lightly were the laws that had governed the de Bellefort family since medieval times to be put aside. I would go to England when I was eighteen and I would marry Roland de Bellefort. It was my duty to provide strong heirs to an ancient lineage and neither tears nor tantrums would alter the course of my future.

'Fate plays some very strange tricks on us, Ellen, it was almost as though God sat there in his heaven saying, "Who are these de Belleforts that they should usurp my role in the order of things? Helena Cressey will not marry Roland de Bellefort, he will not live to make her his wife." Indeed we had hardly left our ship at Dover when my father received a message that Roland had died in an epidemic of typhoid while serving with his regiment which had just recently returned from Russia, and to my shame I inwardly rejoiced.

'I was sorry Roland had died. I remembered him as a nice, well-set-up young man I had danced with and laughed with and believed that one day I might marry, but in recent years he had taken on the mantle of a stranger, an unwelcome stranger.

'I hoped my parents would catch the next boat back to France and that would be the last I would ever hear of the de Bellefort family, but instead my father set out for Yorkshire, leaving my mother and myself in a comfortable inn in Dover. Several days later he returned with the news that the three of us were to journey post haste to Yorkshire, to this house where we were to meet Roland's parents and his elder brother William.

'You can imagine how my heart sank at the news. How I longed for the warm mellow cities of Europe, the sun shining on the Apennines, the azure sea, the sun-baked plains, while instead we travelled north towards these dark

181

hostile hills, the unrelenting moorland and those lonely pines on the windswept crags.

'By the time we reached the house I was almost in tears and certainly in a deep sulk, but I hadn't imagined for one moment that William de Bellefort would be no more anxious to meet me than I was to meet him.

'My mother urged me to smile as we dressed for dinner on that first evening. She pinched my pale cheeks to bring some colour into them, and I was ordered to wear my prettiest gown and show some degree of delight at being there, tempered of course by my sadness at the death of my fiancé.

'We sat down to dinner in that great dining room on the ground floor, my parents affable and compassionate, William's parents sad at the loss of their younger son, but anxious, most anxious to see that William and I found each other's company agreeable. We did not.

'We hardly exchanged a word and I did not miss the look which passed between the girl who served us at the dining table and William. She was a pretty girl with dark red hair and blue eyes, a combination I found quite intriguing as, I have no doubt, did William. Later I saw him in earnest conversation with the servant girl.

'I don't propose to bore you with all the details, I will only say that both William and I were told in no uncertain terms that we would marry, and if I protested to my parents I am sure William protested to his. In my own misery I was able to sympathize with his.

'It did not take long for my sympathy to turn to impatience. William had no earthly chance of making the girl his wife, he had had no right to fall in love with her and fill her naive head with ideas that one day things might go right for them.

'I became cross when she waited on table with tearstained cheeks, when she looked at William with eyes filled with reproach, and at me with barely concealed envy. There were nights when I stood in the shadows on the stairs listening to raised voices coming from the study, William's voice coupled with his father's arrogant one, and more and more

I became angry. After all I was the one who wanted to return with my parents to the continent, if William didn't wish to marry me I most certainly didn't wish to marry him. But the de Belleforts named our wedding day and I found myself wearing the engagement ring which all the brides of the de Bellefort heirs were expected to wear. When my eldest son was born the ring was placed in the vault for safekeeping until he should choose a wife. My husband presented me with a copy, just as valuable but hardly as old.'

She held out her left hand so that I could admire the large emerald surrounded by sparkling diamonds.

'I fear that I may be boring you, Ellen, but it is a story you should hear.'

When I said it was a story which interested me enormously, she merely smiled and went on.

'We were married fairly quietly out of deference to the memory of Roland and we went immediately to County Wicklow to spend our honeymoon in a similar house to this one, surrounded by mountains and wild moorland, where the sea crashed on the rocks below the house and where William rode madly day after day along the shore to erase the memory of Sarah Saxton so that he returned to me spent and exhausted.'

At the mention of my grandmother's name I started and she nodded. 'Oh yes, Ellen, my husband was very much in love with your grandmother, but all I knew was that she had been sent away from the Hall with enough money to placate her family, and eventually buy her a husband. It was archaic, dishonest, but it was the way things were in those days.

'Months later I made inquiries as to her whereabouts but all I could find out was that she had left the village, married a farm labourer in another village, and that her family did not expect to see her again.

'One gets over many things in this life, Ellen, even love, and I was an intelligent girl and not unattractive. I had many admirers. I was a good hostess, a lively companion, and in due course I believe William came to care for me. Never perhaps with that foolish young love that believes all things are possible, but with a more intelligent, deeper understanding, and when our children began to arrive he was a faithful if somewhat undemanding husband.

'Four children I gave him, three sons and one daughter, and I believe your grandmother Sarah Saxton gave him one child: a daughter, and your mother.'

'Why are you so sure about that?' I asked quickly.

'Look in a mirror, child, and then look at Lisanne. Look in the picture gallery and you will see that face, that colouring again and again across the centuries. Why did your grandfather show little interest in either you or your mother? Because he was never your grandfather and was probably filled with resentment because your mother was not his child. In all probability his sons and daughters knew that your mother was not their full sister, and if your father knows perhaps that is why he was all too ready to attribute your grandmother's shortcomings to yourself. Perhaps he believed that one day you would be like her – he does not appear to be a man endowed with much Christian charity. What do you think of my story, Ellen?'

'I suppose it's true, but I don't understand why you had to tell me or why you asked me to come here.'

'Because I owe you something, because in my heart I always felt sorry for that girl Sarah Saxton. I took what she wanted, and I took him without love, my only excuse that I was upholding a law made centuries ago by people unconcerned with love and only with wealth.'

'But isn't it a law you subscribe to today, Lady de Bellefort? Is it any more right now than it was then?'

'No, Ellen, but are you prepared to come into this family and be a part of it?'

'Come into this family! How can I do that, how can I be a part of it?'

'By being my granddaughter's friend and companion. I can't suddenly turn you into a relative but I can give you employment, and Lisanne needs a friend very badly.'

I stared at her in stunned silence. Her face was grave and unsmiling, and for the first time that afternoon she seemed suddenly old, as though the talk of the past had taken its toll, and I felt a twinge of pity for this proud old woman who had bared her soul to me.

'I can't think that she so badly needs a friend, she has you and this lovely house to live in, she has money and education and position. I don't see that I can bring anything into her life that she hasn't got already.'

'You can bring more stability than she's ever known, and you can bring loyalty, the same loyalty that you had for that girl Kitty McGuire. You'll have more money than you ever earned, better clothes, the chance to travel and see something of the world, and in time Lisanne will come to think of you as her one true friend who she will always be able to rely on. You like Lisanne, don't you, Ellen?'

'Well yes, but I don't know her very well. I can't really think straight at the moment, all this is so new and strange to me. Are you wanting my answer right away? I feel it's something I need to think about.'

'Well of course you must think about it, Ellen, and take as much time as you like, but I believe you will come to see the advantages of the proposition I have put to you. I shall be very glad and relieved if you look upon it kindly, Ellen.'

CHAPTER 20

I had thought that running away from home was the hardest decision I would ever made, but Lady de Bellefort's proposition was causing almost as much heart-searching.

I thought about it while I was serving in the shop so that some of my customers grew impatient with wrong change and mis-matching of colours. I couldn't sleep for thinking about it and I could have wept with relief when Doctor Jarvis's trap pulled up outside the shop several days later just as I was closing.

'I just thought I'd call to tell you I've deposited your money in my bank in Ilkley, Ellen. I've got your bank book here and the money will be earning interest. You're lookin' a bit peaky, my girl, haven't you been sleeping well?'

So I poured out my problem and he listened without interrupting until it was told, then with a wry smile he said, 'I wondered what the old lady had up her sleeve. I've known her a long time, but although we get along and I can have a joke with her I've never really known what she was thinkin'. She's never had much time for her middle son, that's the one over in County Wicklow, and she thinks her eldest son's a bit of a dry old stick, but she's very fond of Lance. She sees more of Lisanne than the others but she's scathing about the girl's mother, now and again over the years she's let that much slip.

'Are you expected to be a maid to Lisanne?'

'A friend, a companion she said, so really it's neither one thing nor the other.'

'There's more to this than meets the eye, lassy: Why you, why is her ladyship being so philanthropic, is it the way you look?'

I might have known that Doctor Jarvis would be too astute to let it rest there, so haltingly I told him the story of my grandmother, and he chuckled delightedly.

186

'I knew it wasn't coincidence, Ellen, that you look like you do. So Sir William wasn't the stern and upright country gentleman everybody thought he was, but he got away with it, didn't he? It's funny how folk in these closeknit villages stick together. I've been in Langstone twenty-five years and I've never heard a whisper, not from the folk in four villages or from the Hall, and it took your aunt to bring you here from Liverpool to start it all up again.'

'But I haven't started anything up, nobody's said a word.'

'Not yet they haven't, but the old lady's jumping in first by taking you out of the village and planting you in the Hall.'

'Isn't that likely to open more mouths than if she'd left me here hoping I'd go away?'

'Yes, but then she has a queer streak of honour in her and perhaps you'll learn more as time goes by. Have you decided what you're going to do?'

'No. I'm very tempted but being somebody's servant isn't really what I want.'

'Well if you're not happy there ye can always move out, you've a bit of money behind you. I think I'd take it, Ellen, out of curiosity maybe, but certainly out of self-preservation.'

In the end my mind was made up for me by the arrival of the Ashingtons. They came early on Saturday morning, with several suitcases.

'Things is quiet in the street, Ellen,' Mr Ashington remarked. 'I would 'ave thought Saturday'd be busy enough.'

'It's very early It was busy yesterday. I have the takings for you, they're quite good.'

'I'm pleased to hear it. There's one or two things we couldn't take after the funeral, mi wife and our Jennie'll take a look upstairs.'

I sat while he counted the money in the cash box, and across the table George the fiancé sat scanning the account book. At last he looked up, saying, 'It seems all right, Mr Ashington,' whereupon he handed the book over for Mr Ashington's scrutiny.

After nodding briefly he said, 'The shop's sold, Ellen, I've decided to let the Devlins 'ave it for their tea shop. Course it'll take a few weeks 'afore its properly finalized, so ye can continue to work in it. No doubt the Devlins'll be spendin' a fair bit o' time 'ere so I'll be glad if yer'll be accommodatin', Ellen.' I expect yer'll want to start lookin' round for work but there's not much ye can do 'til the shop's turned over.'

'If I find something soon I won't be able to stay on here.'

He looked at me sharply. "Ave ye anythin' in mind Ellen?'

'I might have.'

'I don't know why ye didn't make it up with yer father. Ye had every opportunity on the day of the funeral.'

I didn't speak and irritably he went on, 'What are those two doin' upstairs? I 'ope ye haven't bin getting rid of yer aunt's things, Ellen.'

'I haven't even looked at them,' I answered sharply.

Eventually Mrs Ashington and her daughter came down carrying blankets and sheets, table linen and numerous cardboard boxes containing heaven knows what.

All these articles were unceremoniously dumped on the table top before Jennie returned upstairs for more. I stared at the pile of blankets and linen but almost immediately Jennie came back carrying hats and dresses. Her mother asked, 'Did you bring the shoe boxes, love?'

'I'm goin' back for them, Mother, I couldn't carry 'em all.'

'Yer'd best get packin' the suitcases if we're to get that train home,' her father said, then turning to me: 'You'll not have much call for any of Liza's stuff, Ellen, seein' as 'ow yer've no place to go to and the Devlins'll want this place cleared so that they can make a start. I thought ye said our Liza had nothin' in the way of clothes that you wanted,' he ended, addressing his wife.

'Nor do I for miself, but mi sister might be able to make use of them and what she doesn't want we can give to the church for their appeal.'

'I rather think our vicar was hoping he might be given

something for his appeal,' I couldn't resist saying. 'Aunt Liza was a very prominent member of the church.'

'Ay well, if there's nowt left 'e'll be disappointed, won't he?'

At that moment I made up my mind. I would go to Langstone Priory. There couldn't be anything in my future worse than my past, and there couldn't be people more mercenary or grasping, more unkind than those I had already met.

Time was to prove that I could be wrong on both counts, but I was not to know that as I faced my father's half-brother. 'I shan't be staying on at the shop, I have a job to go to but I'll stay on for a bit until you find someone else.'

My words sounded terse even in my own ears, but one look at his angry red face made me tremble with fear. I felt I was looking at my father after one of his tirades, his eyes narrowed dangerously, his lips set in a thin straight line.

'What's that, a job did ye say! 'Ow long 'ave ye known about it and 'ere's me thinkin' ye'd be glad of these next few weeks. You've not bin straight with mi, Ellen, ye could 'ave told me you were lookin' for work.'

'I'm sorry but I have to think about myself. I need somewhere to live, and I doubt if you'd concern yourself about that.'

'It seems to me our Liza was right when she called ye an ungrateful girl, you were ungrateful to yer mother and father and now it's my turn. Well if ye feels like that about it, Ellen, the sooner ye gets out the better I'll like it.'

'But what about the shop, Father?' Jennie asked anxiously. 'Who's goin' to look after that? We'll lose money if it's closed.'

'You and yer mother can stay. Yer'll soon get the 'ang of things.'

'But I don't know anythin' about wool and bobbins o' cotton.'

'Ye're not too daft to learn, I 'ope. Me and George'll go back to Ripon tonight and we'll be back next weekend. In the meantime learn as much as ye can from Ellen 'ere. I don't suppose she'll want to take up 'er new job today.'

He looked at me sharply for an answer and quickly I said, 'No of course not, I'll be glad to show them where everything is and how much they cost.'

'Well then, that's what yer'll do, and I'll thank ye not to look so sulky, Jennie. What yer makes in this shop'll help to pay for yer weddin' finery with a bit to spare for that 'ouse yer intent on buyin' in 'Arrogate.'

Jennie's face brightened visibly and just then the bell went over the shop door and her father said, 'You go into the shop with Ellen to see 'ow things are done, yer'll soon pick things up.'

It was a day I wanted to come quickly to an end. Jennie had little patience with customers who couldn't make up their minds and she quickly forgot where things were kept. I doubted if the account book would fare any better in her hands, and her mother must have thought so too because she quickly decided that the accounts would be her province.

Mrs Devlin and Alec appeared in the afternoon and they spent a long time taking measurements and chatting to the men in the living room. As they left Mrs Devlin said, 'I hear you've got another job to go to, Ellen.'

'Yes.'

'In the village?'

'No.'

'Does that mean yer'll be leaving the village then?'

'In a manner of speaking it does.'

'Well it's not like me to ask questions but I must say I'm surprised, I didn't think there was that much work about. Where 'ave ye managed to find somethin'?'

'I'd rather not say until I'm absolutely sure, if you don't mind, Mrs Devlin.'

'Oh well, if ye feel like that about it,' she snapped, shrugging her shoulders. 'Come on, Alec, there's work to be done.'

Alec would dearly like to have stayed to ask more questions, but one look at his stepmother's set face and he decided against it.

I was over the first hurdle. It was almost five o'clock, in

another half hour Mr Ashington and George would have left, and there would only be his wife and daughter to suffer.

As I watched Simeon Ashington departing up the street he reminded me strongly of my father. He had the same tall spare figure, and his eyes had been cold and peevishly vindictive, like my father's eyes after one of his beatings.

Tomorrow I would tell Lady de Bellefort that I would accept whatever plans she had for my future. My life as Ellen Adair had come full circle.

BOOK II

CHAPTER 21

There were times during the next two years over which I would dearly have liked to draw a veil, but there were other times that I would hold close to my heart for ever.

There were difficulties, right from that first moment when I arrived in Doctor Jarvis's trap with my one suitcase, and there were other times when I seemed as much a part of Langstone Priory as those others who call themselves de Belleforts.

Often in those early days I found myself staring at William de Bellefort's portrait, reassuring myself that whether they liked it or not this was my grandfather, and my grandmother had been the woman he loved, not Lady de Bellefort for all her patrician beauty and her social graces.

The servants were told that I was a distant relative and that she had inquiries made about my family when she realized how closely I resembled her granddaughter. I have never been sure how much of that they believed, particularly Cook and the housekeeper who had lived in the village most of their lives.

They knew better than to gossip openly or disbelieve what they had been told, and I was accepted in the capacity of poor relation. This was not her ladyship's fault. She was always kind to me and most gracious, but it was Lisanne who one minute treated me like her dear friend and the next like some child who had been swept in from the storm. For weeks, months even, we were close companions, more like sisters than friends, and then after one of Lance de Bellefort's visits we were like strangers.

I never quite knew if I was happy, only that I was there to learn. How to dress and speak, how to walk and ride. At first I was frightened of the horses, they seemed so large and temperamental and Lisanne laughed at my fears in a situation where she was so confident.

I came in for the clothes Lisanne no longer wanted and I had no difficulty in changing them to fit me and improving on them. I was a little taller than she and slimmer so there was always plenty of material to play with. In the company of visitors we were told we looked like sisters and it was then that Lisanne would say airily, 'Oh, we're actually not related at all. Granny arranged all this because Ellen was soon to lose her job at the draper's shop and it entertained Granny to see how alike we were.'

I never missed the discreet looks that were exchanged between those present, and Lisanne was careful not to make such remarks when her grandmother was present.

There were times when I could have quarrelled with her but I bit my tongue, thinking about my small fortune in the bank at Ilkley and of those other times when she was away from the house with Lady de Bellefort, visiting friends and relatives. Then I would borrow books from the library which I read avidly, tracing the history of the family which went back to Norman times. There had been a Sir Roland de Bellefort on the first Crusade, and another who had been decorated on the field of Waterloo. Sir Geoffrey de Bellefort had been present at the signing of the Magna Carta and a Sir William de Bellefort had perished in the Charge of the Light Brigade. As I read I became more and more involved. This was my family, my grandfather's family.

One day the butler came across me sitting cross-legged on the window seat in the library with my head buried in a book and he came across to shut the window.

'There's a storm brewin', Miss Ellen, you'd be warmer in the sitting room.'

'I'm not cold, Mr Carstairs, and the books are so heavy.'

He smiled. 'I doubt if Miss Lisanne's opened one of those books in all the time she's spent here. I can't think what you find so interesting.'

'The family's interesting.' And there and then I began to recite to him all the achievements of the de Belleforts across the years.

'They might be your family, Miss, you're so interested,'

he remarked, and then thinking I had said too much I smiled and continued to read.

That the servants talked among themselves I felt sure, but in the main they were respectful. It was only the young servants who showed some reluctance at waiting on me, a girl from the draper's in the village, but as these servants left and others took their places the antagonism became less and less.

'Why are you always reading those stuffy old books?' Lisanne asked one day. 'Granny says you know more about the family than I do.'

'I love reading about them, I love anything connected with history.'

'Then it's a pity you didn't receive a good education so that you could make use of it,' she said caustically.

'I agree with you. It would have been nice to be educated like you were. Why don't you make more use of it?'

'Because I don't have to. I've been born to riches. I'll never want for money and I know that in five hundred years my descendants will be in exactly the same position as I'm in now. That's more then you can say, Ellen.'

I bit my lip angrily and turned away, then with a little laugh she said, 'I'm sorry, Ellen, I didn't intend to be mean but you're always so superior when it comes to reading. We're supposed to be companions, why aren't you more interested in learning to ride, and the latest dance steps?'

'I am interested, I'm not nearly as afraid of the horses as I was and I love dancing. But we never go to places where I can dance so I really don't see why I should bother.'

'Does that mean you'd like to dance if I took you to parties with me?'

'Yes, but you really don't have to. Your friends always ask so many questions, wanting to know if we're related and where I come from?'

'And you always prevaricate, Ellen, by saying a little and leaving so much unsaid that they think there's more to it than meets the eye.'

'I often wonder if it was a mistake for me to come here when you say things like that, Lisanne.'

She threw her arms around me impetuously. 'Well of course it wasn't a mistake, Ellen, we're very good friends and when my mother comes at the end of the month and Grandmother holds her usual family party you shall come to all the functions and set everybody's tongue wagging.'

'Your mother is coming?' I asked in dismay.

'Well of course, she does come periodically and I'd love to see her face when she sees you. I'm so fed up with the Priory, I'm going to persuade Mother to take me back with her to wherever she's going. Granny won't like it but I can usually bring Mother round to see things my way.'

'How long will you be gone for?'

'Well I haven't gone yet, have I? But hopefully for months. Why do you ask?'

'I was wondering what there would be for me to do while you're away.'

'Oh, the usual things. Hold Granny's knitting wool, read to her, sit for hours poring over those dreary old books, and – oh, I forgot to tell you, Lance will be here for the celebrations and my cousin Geraldine, Aunt Alice's daughter. We haven't met since I was six years old, I don't even know what she looks like.'

Lance would be coming! That was the only thing that registered in my foolish tormented heart, and it was agony to be in love with Lance when I knew that one day he would be married to Lisanne or Geraldine and I would have to look on while Lady de Bellefort engineered it all.

They came at the beginning of December when snow lay thick on the ground, the north-east wind swept across the moors from the sea, and the Pennine hills cast their dark shadows across the parkland and the churning mere.

I heard voices in the hall, and laughter, then Lisanne's mother swept into the old nursery, staring at me with wide quizzical eyes while Lisanne looked on delightedly.

'Gracious me,' her mother murmured, 'I didn't believe it when you wrote to tell me, now I feel I gave birth to two daughters instead of just one. Ellen, isn't it?'

'Yes, Ma'am.'

'Don't call me Ma'am, Ellen, I prefer you to call me by

name. Either Mrs de Bellefort or Mrs Roland, like the rest of the servants call me.'

'Ellen isn't exactly a servant, Mother. Granny says she's much more than that, she's a distant relative.'

'What sort of relative, for heaven's sake, and how is she related?'

'You'd better ask Granny about that. We are alike though, aren't we?'

'Yes indeed. Come over here, Ellen, into the light, let me take a good look at you.'

I felt like some prize poodle as she took hold of my shoulder and turned me around. I was glad that I was wearing my good black skirt and a pretty cream lace blouse, and that my flaxen hair was tied back simply by its black watered-silk ribbon, but if Mrs Roland de Bellefort appraised me I did likewise.

She was tall and slender and incredibly fashionable. Her hair was a bright golden blond and it was impeccably set and styled. She was wearing a rich dark fur coat over her pale cream gown. My first thought was that Lisanne was not like her mother, she was a de Bellefort while this woman was a socialite, a breed old Lady de Bellefort classes as inconsequential, a butterfly.

Satisfied with her appraisal, she smiled. 'Well obviously my mother-in-law had her reasons for putting you two together. Are you very good friends?'

With a laugh and petulant toss of her head Lisanne said, 'Oh we get along, Mother. Granny's almost as good at choosing friends as she is at choosing husbands. Lance is coming, and Geraldine. I suppose we'll know over Christmas which one of us he's going to marry.'

'Don't you mind, darling?'

'Will it make any difference if I do?'

I had gone to sit on the window seat wishing they would carry on this conversation out of my presence, but over the last two years I had become accustomed to people behaving as if I weren't there. It wasn't because they considered me family, but rather that I suddenly became invisible.

Now Mrs Roland sank gracefully into one of the easy

chair while Lisanne perched on the edge of the table, facing her mother with some degree of petulance.

'I can use my influence,' her mother said gently. 'How well do you know your cousin Lance?'

'Better than I know Gervase, I don't really know him at all.'

'Well of course not, he's too far away and I don't suppose he comes here. After all his father never got along with your grandmother and his mother died when he was just a child. It would be interesting to know how Lance feels about marriage.'

'We've never discussed it, but we're good friends, Mother. He's such fun to be with and we like the same sort of things. Oh, you know, horses and dancing, and he doesn't talk to me like he talks to Ellen.'

'He talks to Ellen!'

'Well yes. They talk for hours walking in the park. Of course they both know it can never be more than that. Ellen's a friend, that's all.'

'I see.'

With a blushing face I applied myself to my reading, but I was aware of Mrs Roland's close scrutiny across the room before she rose to her feet to show that the conversation was at an end.

'We'll talk about this after dinner, Lisanne. By that time both your cousins will have arrived and I'll be able to make my own judgement. Will Ellen be dining with the family this evening?'

I looked up quickly. 'Oh no, Mrs Roland, I hardly think so. I shall have my meal in here or in my room.'

'I'm accustomed to my mother-in-law's vagaries, she decrees what goes on in this house and the rest of us acquiesce if we know what's good for us. Come to my room, Lisanne, while I change out of these travelling clothes. I have a present for you from Rome, I want to see if you like it.'

Lisanne jumped off her perch gleefully. 'I do hope it's something to wear,' she said gaily, 'all my clothes are ancient.'

200

A fine snow was falling, obscuring the hills, clinging like dust to the ivy which climbed outside the window. I shivered in the draught that came through a chink in the window frame, and then my heart lurched painfully as I saw Lance's long low tourer arriving. He had assisted two women out of the car when, as if aware of my scrutiny, Lance suddenly looked up. His face broke into a smile and he raised his hand to me in greeting. The younger of the two women looked up briefly and I was aware of a pretty face surrounded by cloudy dark hair. She was totally unlike either Lisanne or myself.

I received Lady de Bellefort's invitation to be present at dinner as if it were a royal command, delivered by her butler with a half smile of amusement. As we sat round the heavy ornate dining table groaning under its wealth of silver and glass, waited on by deft servants, I was unable to banish my wayward and cynical thoughts.

How in the years to come would I be able to describe that evening? Lady de Bellefort sat at the head of the table, slim as a reed in her black gown heavily beaded with jet, her thin claw-like hands occasionally fingering the pearl choker round her throat, her fine eyes missing nothing.

At the other end sat Lance, dark and inscrutable in his sombre evening clothes, occasionally inclining his head to hear the remarks passed by Lady Alice Vernon on his left and her daughter Geraldine on his right.

Totally unlike her mother, Lady Alice was comfortably plump, and her chatter brought a glance of impatience from the woman at the head of the table. Lady Alice wore a gown in an indeterminate shade of yellow and she was well corseted and had a healthy appetite. Her daughter was lovely. She dimpled prettily at Lance's remarks, looking strangely ethereal in a white delicate gown, her dark hair framing her face, and when she laughed she showed small even white teeth.

Lisanne picked at her food. She had a mutinous look and appeared not to like the attention Geraldine was getting, attention which was merely the attempt of a chivalrous man endeavouring to put at her ease the girl sitting next to him.

Lisanne's mother chatted amicably to the only other man present, Lawrence Hartington, the de Belleforts' estate manager, and from the way he responded I was sure he admired her. She was indeed a very attractive woman and she knew how to dress. Her magenta gown was elegant and fitted her tall slender figure as though she had been poured into it, a fact that her mother-in-law seemed to disapprove of.

I sat opposite Lisanne, her face so like mine I might have been looking into a mirror, except that she wore her hair on top of her head whereas mine fell on to my shoulders, unadorned by either ribbons or jewels. I wore no jewellery, but the blue dress I had chosen was the colour of my eyes and it flattered my tall slender figure in its simplicity.

Lisanne was wearing pink, not a colour that I cared for with our pale hair and porcelain skin, and I noticed round her throat a necklace of tiny opals which I assumed was the present her mother had brought from Rome.

As our eyes met she fingered the necklace and smiled, confirming my assumption. I was so intrigued by those sitting round the table I didn't at first hear Lady Alice's remarks and, confused, asked her to repeat them.

'How long have you been living at Langstone Priory, Ellen, and where did my mother find you?'

'Just over two years, Milady. I was living in the village.'

'I see.'

Quite obviously she didn't see, and I felt sure that either her mother or myself would be subjected to further questions at a later date. I found Lance watching me, and as our eyes met I knew that a rich red colour had dyed my cheeks and I looked away quickly, embarrassed and confused. When I glanced up again I found Lady de Bellefort staring at me, her face a polite mask.

After dinner we retired to the drawing room for coffee and Lance came to sit with me while Geraldine played the piano, some light tinkling tune that I had never heard before. I had no accomplishments and it seemed that every day of my life I was being made aware of the fact. I had no skill with a watercolour brush and although I loved music I was no performer. And I was an indifferent horsewoman.

Later when Lisanne suggested somebody should put on a gramophone record I watched miserably while Lance danced first with her and then with Geraldine. I loved dancing. My feet tapped in time to the music under cover of my long skirt while Lady de Bellefort and her daughter looked on indulgently, and Mrs Roland and the estate manager chatted together.

I was unprepared for Lance standing before me holding out his hand.

'Will you dance with me, Ellen? I can't leave you sitting here alone and looking all forlorn.'

Like one in a dream I moved into his arms and I felt until that moment that I had never been alive. Suddenly the music came to an abrupt end and we stopped in some dismay to see that Lisanne had lifted the arm on the gramophone and was snapping peevishly, 'Oh can't we do something else? There's not enough men to dance with.'

'Don't be so tiresome,' snapped her grandmother, 'I was enjoying the music.'

'Well, Lance can't dance with everybody and I hate sitting here like the proverbial wallflower.'

Lance was looking at her with a small frown and I left him to return to my seat. I wished it was time to go to my room. I thought desperately that I might excuse myself on the grounds of a headache but one look at Lady de Bellefort's tight-lipped face made me think again.

Didn't Lisanne realise that these few days were to be a testing time and that in them her grandmother would make up her mind which granddaughter would be the future Lady de Bellefort: Geraldine sitting quiet and demure beside her mother and regarding Lisanne's show of bad temper with something akin to dismay, or Lisanne, her blue eyes flashing, her voice raised in petulant annoyance.

Lisanne's mother sauntered across the room and poured herself another sherry, then in a light airy voice she said, 'Too many women and too few men have always been a

203

problem. Thank heavens it's never been a problem whenever I've invited people to my house.'

'I doubt if you are ever in a house long enough to invite anybody,' said her mother-in-law caustically. 'It seems to me that for the past twelve years you have moved about Europe like an aimless moth, gathering too many acquaintances and very few friends.'

'But of course. The de Belleforts never remarry so what is the use of putting down roots and making commitments one can't keep? As long as I remain as I am I'm entitled to whatever money the family gives me. It isn't inconsiderable, and up to now I've found nothing worth giving it up for. But you must confess, Mother-in-law, the limitations are endless.'

'I hardly think this is the time or place to air the limitations, and certainly not in front of your daughter, Delia.'

'On the contrary, I think both these girls should be made aware of what it means to be a de Bellefort wife. Presumably we're all here to decide which one of them is to marry which grandson, all except Ellen that is. None of this concerns her. I expect she's mighty glad about that.

Across the room my eyes met Lance's and I surprised in them a sudden misery, while my own eyes blazed.

Why doesn't he tell them all here and now, I thought, that he doesn't want to marry either Geraldine or Lisanne, that he objected to being treated like a prize stallion instead of a human being. How long did it take for someone in this high and mighty family to cut and run, to tell this indomitable old woman that she wasn't God, that she had no right to ordain people's lives as though they were puppets without wills of their own? But as he turned away I knew that as yet he had no will that was not her will, no future that had not been nurtured and determined by others of his family across the centuries.

I decided at that moment that I had had enough of the de Belleforts. I would leave Langstone Priory where I was nothing more than a whim, leave the first man I had ever been in love with to one or other of the women he was expected to marry, and I would make a new life for myself.

What had I once said to Kitty McGuire? 'When one door shuts another opens,' then with a wry smile I remembered her answer: 'Ye mean when one door closes another slams shut.'

I asked Lady de Bellefort if I might be excused to go to my room, aware of her steely blue eyes and set gracious smile.

'Of course, Ellen, but I want to see you in the morning, first thing after breakfast. I have something to discuss with you.'

There it was again, the cool assumption that I would be here after breakfast, waiting with some trepidation to hear what new plans she had for my future. Like the rest of them I squirmed with resentment at her high-handed belief that she had only to say a thing for it to be so, all the same I knew that I would be there outside her door waiting to be received, with my heart thumping like a wild thing, my palms sticky with anticipation.

CHAPTER 22

I lay sleepless for hours, then stood at the window.

The snow had stopped, and a full moon showed a scene of indescribable beauty. The park shimmered silvery white and snow clung to the trees like blossom. The mere was frozen over but through the trees the deer moved silently, and as they came out into the open I could see the proud head of Jupiter the stag, crowned with magnificent antlers raised towards the moon.

It was no use. I was not going to sleep easily so I went down to the library for a book.

Lance was reading at one of the long tables. He looked up sharply as I entered, then he smiled, a smile that always had the power to touch my foolish heart. 'Why Ellen, what's this, can't you sleep?'

'No. I came to find a book. It seems you couldn't sleep either.'

'No, and it seemed a golden opportunity to catch up on our family history.'

'I can tell you all about the de Belleforts: honoured by royalty, brave in battle, honourable in conquest. Ask me anything you need to know.'

He laughed. 'Then I wonder if you can tell me, Ellen, which one of my ancestors decreed that for ever more his descendants should marry one another. He must have been a bitter man who was afraid of life – terrified of losing his wealth and desperately afraid of falling in love.'

He was not smiling now, but looking down at me with sombre searching eyes.

'You won't find any mention of it in the book you were studying.'

'So you've looked for it too, Ellen?'

'No.'

'You're not curious about it?'

'No. I was curious once. I agonized about how your grandfather could love my grandmother and yet allow her to go from his life, and I wondered if he ever thought of her afterwards.'

'I'm sure he did, Ellen, a great many times.'

'But it isn't enough, is it, Lance? Just to think about somebody with regret and a degree of kindness, even feeling relief perhaps that he'd had the courage to let her go, that she had no power to interfere with his nice comfortable ordered life with his wife and children. It seemed so odd to me that all that loving, all that passion could turn into complacency.'

Suddenly he put his arms around me. 'Oh Ellen,' he groaned, 'is it my grandfather you are despising, or me?'

He was kissing my hair, my face, my lips, and God help me I was kissing him back with all the passion that was in me. I felt him pick me up in his arms and carry me across the room, putting me down on the long low velvet settee before the fireplace, but as his lips came down once more on mine my eyes fell on the portrait above the mantelpiece of his grandfather surrounded by his wife and children. A happy, respectable family group, permanent and inviolate. With all my strength I pushed him aside and struggled to my feet.

He put his arms around me again but fiercely I said, 'No, Lance. No. I love you and I want you but I'm not my grandmother, I won't let you make love to me then toss me on one side to marry one of your cousins. Save your loving for her, you'll have no memories of me to look back on with kindness or regret.'

I tore myself from his arms and fled to my room, where I lay sleepless until the dawn.

I presented myself in Lady de Bellefort's sitting room immediately after breakfast the following morning. I had lived in her house for two years but I still felt the distressing tightening in my throat in those first few moments of our meeting.

'You are punctual as always, Ellen. Don't look so anxious

207

child, I have not asked you to come here to be scolded. How well do you get along with Lisanne?'

'Quite well I think, considering that I am the companion you found for her.'

'You resent my interference in such matters, Ellen, you think my grandchildren should be allowed to chose their own companions and partners in life.'

I didn't answer her, but sat with lowered head and every expectation that I should hear more. I was not disappointed.

I was unprepared however for the compassion in her voice and the touch of her hand over my clenched fist.

'I am not a fool, Ellen, I saw how it was with you and Lance last evening. You think you love him, and I can well understand why you think it. Lance is young and tall and handsome, and totally unlike any other man you have ever met. But you are a sensible girl, Ellen, you know he can never be yours.' With a little sigh she went on. 'It is not in my power to alter things that have been asked of this family for generations, Ellen. Lance knows this, that is why he will not attempt to change anything, why I have decided that he will marry Geraldine and why I must let you go away.'

I looked up quickly, my heart thumping with anxiety. 'I am to go away?' I cried.

'Don't look so tragic, Ellen, I am not sending you away as your grandmother was. My daughter-in-law wishes to take Lisanne with her when she goes and I have said I have no objections if she takes you also.'

Resentment burned in me and I could feel the hot blood burning my cheeks while a new and desperate courage made me burst out, 'Why should Mrs de Bellefort be asked to take me? I won't be treated like a parcel.'

She smiled gently. 'My dear, I have put it very badly, perhaps I should explain. Delia is a flibbertigibbet. She is my husband's sister's child and a more spoilt child you could never have imagined. I was not happy that she married my favourite son but I had hopes that she would mature, that life in India would teach her responsibility and stability. It did neither.

'From time to time over the years I heard stories of their

life in India. While my son was serving his country on the North West Frontier his flighty wife was indulging in all sorts of fleeting affairs in Calcutta and Bombay, then when Roland was killed in a skirmish on the Khyber Pass I insisted that Delia should return to England with their daughter.

'She was happy enough to leave the child in my care. I got Lisanne into a good school in this country, and then two years later right out of the blue her mother removed Lisanne from the school and took her to France, so I stopped her allowance. I thought she would come running back but she found some man to finance her. It didn't last, Delia is selfish and imperious. She would be a liability to any man over a long term and this man was no exception. The affair was over and Delia came running back here to ask for the restoration of her money. By this time Lisanne was in school in Zürich but before I restored Delia's money I made her promise that Lisanne would spend all her school holidays with me, and she gave her word.

'I have watched Lisanne closely over these last two years while her mother flitted unconcerned from one gay European resort to the next. Now for some quite unknown reason she wants Lisanne to return to Europe with her.

'I do not want Lisanne to marry Lance. She is not the wife for him, she is too much like her mother. When she is twenty-one I wish her to marry Gervase, they are probably two of a kind if he is anything like his father, my middle son. Together they will have a gay old time, spending money like water, and I shall be happier thinking that one day Lance and Geraldine will make this their home. Lance's father is a sick man, and one day, anyday I expect to hear that he is dead. I have never liked the house at Mowbray, nor has Lance. When he has the title I hope he will reside here.'

I knew that I was staring at her with desperate awareness. It seemed incredible to me that this slight silver-haired woman could wield such power simply because she held the purse strings. As though she read my thoughts she

209

suddenly rose and walked over to the window, where she turned and held out her hand to me.

'Come here, Ellen. Let me explain something to you.'

Mechanically I joined her at the window.

'I too felt like you when first I came to Langstone Priory. I rebelled at all that obsession with land and property and it took me a long time to accept what generations of de Belleforts had accepted before me. Now in my mid seventies I know that these are the only things that last. The young are obsessed with trivialities, they do not know that even love is transient, that they will recover from the trauma and tragedy of loving, or even move on to other loves just as conflicting and hurtful. But what you see out there, Ellen, remains sure and unchanging. That is the rock on which we build our lives, not the littleness of love.

'I came to that belief slowly and painfully over the years, and at last I understood why we de Belleforts are as we are. I shall not be the one to change things, Ellen, that is why I am sending you away. I could wish that you were my granddaughter, wish you were the woman to marry Lance, for you would bring to him loyalty and courage and devotion, but you are not my granddaughter.

'Geraldine is sweet and pliable. She has not been blessed with too much imagination and yet I think that like their grandfather and me they will be contented and in the years to come consider themselves well blessed.'

There was nothing to say. No words of mine could change this old indomitable woman's thinking, and like the rest of them, like a leaf in the wind I was going to allow myself to be blown in whatever direction she desired. I stood with bent head waiting to be dismissed and for several moments there was no sound in the room.

I thought: I will not go with Lisanne, I have a little money, I'll make my own way, go where I please, find work and show the de Belleforts that I am not beholden to them, that I am Ellen Adair, a free spirit, not a puppet to be worked by strings. As if she read my thoughts she said gently, 'Don't fight me on this, Ellen. Try to see what advantages there are in it for you. You will travel, see new and exciting places, wonderful cities, beautiful lakes and mountains. And who knows who you might meet? You are intelligent and beautiful, and you will not go empty-handed. I will arrange for an allowance to be paid to you so that you will not feel like a poor relation, and all that I ask from you is to provide the stability Lisanne will lack in the company of her mother. I am giving you the power to mould Lisanne into the sort of woman who will make Gervase de Bellefort a fitting wife when the time comes. When she goes to Ireland for her marriage, your task will be done. A lump sum will be paid to you and you will be free to make your own life. I think your grandmother would approve of what I am doing for you, Ellen, while I feel that my debt to her will have been fulfilled.'

Our eyes met and her smile was filled with appeal. Against all my better judgement and in spite of all the reluctance in my heart I found myself promising to do what she asked.

That is not to say that I did not agonize over my acceptance in the days which followed. In spite of the deep snow and icy winds I tramped through the parklands. I avoided Lance as much as I could. If we met in the corridors we smiled politely and I knew with some chagrin that he was obeying his grandmother and seeing as much as possible of Geraldine.

I seethed inwardly at her dimpled smiles and the way her eyes followed him across a room. Geraldine was already in love with him, but when Lance looked at me his eyes were sombre and filled with a strange hunger.

I did not often visit the village, largely because the villagers' tongues wagged too easily, but on market day some perverse obstinacy made me leave the house immediately after breakfast to go there. I told Lisanne I wanted to buy some embroidery silk but she merely said, 'Oh well, you would have been on your own anyway, I'm going with Granny and Mother to see the Rawlinsons and you wouldn't want to play gooseberry with the lovers.'

I didn't answer, and in a light teasing voice she said, 'It does bother you, doesn't it Ellen? Oh I know you go around as if you don't in the least care but I've heard you prowling about your room in the middle of the night and all that tramping about in the snow can only be because you have to get something out of your system.'

'I haven't been sleeping well but it has nothing whatsoever to do with Mr Lance or Miss Geraldine.'

'Mr Lance! I've heard you address him as Lance often enough.'

'Then it must have been a slip of the tongue.'

'He'll never fall for that sweet simpering Geraldine. Lance is too much of a red-blooded male for that.'

I was in no mood to discuss Lance or Geraldine, on the other hand Lisanne was in no mood to let the subject drop.

'One day she'll be just like Aunt Alice, far too fat with masses of diamond rings on those too podgy fingers, and Lance will be miserable.'

'He deserves to be miserable if he's not prepared to do anything about it.'

'What can he do, what can any of us do without money? We've not been brought up to be poor. Right from the very beginning we've all known what our destiny was to be. We're proud to be de Belleforts, and we all want what rightly belongs to us. Love is something quite different and apart.'

'So you're going to marry Gervase without knowing him or loving him, and it doesn't worry you?'

'Not in the least. I met him first when I was about six. He came here with his father and I hated him. He was bold and attractive. He pulled my hair and threw my favourite doll through the window, I didn't speak to him for days and granny made him apologize and he was sent to bed without supper.'

I stared at her curiously and she dissolved into peals of laughter. 'You think I must be mad to even think of marrying a man I disliked so much as a boy.'

'I know I couldn't do it.'

'Well of course not. You're not a de Bellefoprt and you haven't grown up with the knowledge that one day it will happen. I always rather hoped it would be Lance, but granny

212

could never really stand my mother so she's wishing me on Gervase.'

'I think it's archaic.'

'Of course, it's equally archaic to have you accompany me to Europe in the role of a watchdog.'

'I have no intention of being a watchdog. Your grandmother hasn't asked me to spy on you, only provide some sort of companionship because she feels your mother might neglect you.'

'I want to be neglected, I want to go off on my own – and don't foget, I know my way around most of Europe.'

'I can't think that's true. You were only a schoolgirl, Lisanne.'

'There are schoolgirls and schoolgirls. We didn't spend all our time sequestered in the schoolroom or the dormitories. We led some of those nuns a terrible dance, I can tell you.'

'Perhaps your grandmother has heard something of your escapades and thinks you need a watchdog. I can assure you it won't be me.'

'I'm glad about that, Ellen, it would have spoiled our friendship, such as it is. You can take the trap into the village if you like.'

'I thought I would walk, the pony doesn't like a lot of people and the high street will be crowded today.'

I left her petulantly looking through the clothes in her wardrobe. Outdoors the keen wind hit me like a lash so I dug my hands deep in my pockets after pulling my woollen scarf round my throat. I kept to the drive where the snow had been flattened, but even so it was tiring with the wind against my face and my feet slipping and sliding.

It had been a mistake to come to the village. I mingled with the crowds around the market stalls but I was not one of them. The old Ellen Adair had gone, to be replaced by a new alien being, but I was not a de Bellefort either.

My whole being rebelled at the laws which governed the de Belleforts. The rigidity of those medieval beliefs made me want to scream from the housetops that they were cruel and degenerate, and the pain in my heart was so intense I

213

viewed the village street through a haze of stinging tears. To cover my distress I pretended to be interested in the fruit and vegetables on the stalls, and if people stared at me curiously I dabbed at my eyes, hoping they would think it was the wind that had brought the tears.

The Devlins had transformed Aunt Liza's little shop. A gaily coloured canopy decorated the window and the tea room was doing a steady trade. Through the net curtains I could see that the room had been enlarged and was filled with small tables and chairs.

Across the road the bakery seemed much as usual. It was the busiest time of the morning and a queue had formed outside. I could see both Alec and his father busy at the counter. Lowering my head I made as if to pass on, but my arm was seized firmly, and looking round I found Mrs Devlin staring at me.

'I wasn't sure if it was you, Ellen. We don't seem to see ye in the village these days.'

'No. I don't often get here. How are you, Mrs Devlin?'

'Well enough. We're grandparents ye know, we 'as a little granddaughter over twelve months old, lovely she is, we've called her Ruby.'

'That's nice, Mrs Devlin, I'm so pleased for you.'

'What do ye think of the tea shop? We does very well on market days. Come on in, Ellen, and 'ave a cup o' coffee. I allus 'ave a table reserved for mi.'

Reluctantly I went in and she led me to a table near the window. The shop and the living room were now one big room. A middle-aged woman sat at the cash desk near the door, and two younger women in dark dresses and white aprons and caps were taking orders. Mrs Devlin commanded immediate attention and in no time at all coffee and biscuits were placed in front of us. I sat back in anticipation of the inquisition to come.

'Ye did very well to be taken on at the 'all, Ellen. There was a lot o' talk, particularly with ye lookin so much like the granddaughter. What exactly are ye doin' there Ellen, 'ousemaid is it?'

'Not exactly, you could say I'm looking after Miss Lisanne.'

'Lady's maid?'

'Sort of.'

'Yer'll 'ave yer 'ands full then, I see 'er mother's arrived 'ere. There was allus a lot o' talk about Mrs de Bellefort before and after her husband was killed.'

'People will talk about anything.'

'Ay well, there's no smoke without fire, and scandal in small communities gets milled over.'

When I remained silent she pursed her lips and set off in another direction. 'I don't suppose ye hears from yer family, Ellen, or from the folks at Ripon?'

'No, I never hear from them.' I didn't tell Mrs Devlin that I couldn't understand why my brother Peter hadn't written, and could only think that my father had intercepted his letter.

Bitterly Mrs Devlin was saying, 'That Jenny and 'er mother took everythin' Liza left in the house. That wasn't right when Liza's church got nothin'. I made sure they knew 'ow I felt about it afore they left.'

When I didn't reply she went on, 'We're allus busy like this on market days and on the other days a lot o' the villagers come in for a cup o' tea and a bit of a gossip. The vicar says the cafe's as much a part o' the village now as the inn and the village hall itself.'

I smiled. The people in the cafe were all strangers to me, market day shoppers, and I was unprepared for Mrs Devlin's look of utter dismay when a man stopped at our table. I gasped with surprise at seeing Lance looking down at me with obvious relief.

'So here you are Ellen, I've been looking for you along the street.'

He spoke as if it was the most natural thing in the world for Lance de Bellefort to be searching the high street for me on market day, then looking at Mrs Devlin with an all-embracing smile he said. 'I hadn't realized Ellen wasn't alone.'

She struggled to her feet and I performed the introduction. She could barely contain her amazement, and I felt sure she would think I had taken the first step towards perdition. Oblivious to her surprise Lance took the seat she had vacated and asked brightly, 'More coffee, Ellen? I've left the trap at the inn with instructions to feed the pony. He'll not miss us for half an hour.'

Mrs Devlin had taken over the cash desk from where she could watch the room, and our table in particular.

Unconcerned Lance reached out and covered my hand with his own.

'Ellen, we've got to talk and it can't be here.'

'I don't see that there's anything to talk about,' I said shortly.

'Lisanne tells me you are going to Europe with them, is that true?'

'Your grandmother has decided and we all obey, don't we?'

'And you, do you want to go?'

'I have very little option. If I don't go I'm on my own looking for work, if I do go at least I'll be seeing something of the world and getting paid for it.'

'You make it sound very mercenary.'

'It is mercenary, isn't that what it's all about? Nobody should know that better than you, Lance.'

'Let's get out of here, Ellen, damn the coffee.'

'But you've ordered it.'

'Then I'll pay for it, we don't have to drink it.'

Mrs Devlin's disapproval was very evident until Lance explained that we hadn't time to wait and she mellowed considerably when he left a handsome tip for the waitress, at the same time bestowing a charming smile on Mrs Devlin herself.

He took my arm and as we hurried up the street I was only too aware of Alec Devlin's round eyes watching us from the baker's shop window. The pony and trap stood outside the inn and the pony's nose was thrust into his nosebag with evident enjoyment. 'We'll drink a glass of sherry until the pony's finished his lunch,' Lance said.

Shortly afterwards we set off back to the Priory and after

216

leaving the pony with one of the stablehands we were walking along the path which edged the frozen mere. The swans,
dejected and ungainly waddled ponderously through the
reeds, occasionally endeavouring to break the ice with their
beaks.

'Poor things,' Lance said softly. 'How does one explain
these things to birds and animals?'

His face was pensive, with that sensitive remote expression that I loved. We stood hand in hand watching the
swans, then he turned and smiled down at me.

'If you're not too cold, Ellen, we could walk as far as the
boat house.'

We walked in silence until we reached the boat house,
sheltered between trees heavy with snow and out of sight
of the house.

'We can talk here, Ellen, I don't think we shall be
disturbed.'

I waited. In my heart I believed that anything Lance had
to say could only be irrelevant, there was no room for Ellen
Adair in his life and I felt a fierce satisfaction that he was
finding the words difficult to say. At last he looked straight
into my eyes and I stared back solemnly, determined not to
help him.

'Ellen, I think you must hate me,' he said at last.

I shook my head sorrowfully. 'I could never hate you,
Lance. I don't understand you, that's all. I don't understand
any of you.'

He was looking at me helplessly and I felt that he hardly
understood himself. Then his eyes swept the mere and the
snow-covered acres before him and resolutely he seemed
to square his shoulders.

'Darling Ellen,' he said gently, 'it would all be so simple
in your world, wouldn't it? Girl meets boy and they marry,
as easy and straightforward as seeing and breathing. But
now you're caught up in a tradition that has ordained our
lives for centuries. If there have been rebels they have gone
their ways and been unheard of again.

'Gervase's father was a rebel in his youth. He quarrelled
with his parents and for much of his life went his own

217

way, but in the end he came back to the fold. Money and possessions brought him back, if nothing else. He conformed. And like me, Gervase will conform, however reluctantly.'

'Then why are we talking like this, Lance? You have nothing new to tell me.'

'I want to make you understand, Ellen.'

'I do understand. You care more for all this than you could ever care for me. You say you love me, but you are not prepared to give anything up for me. I know you will marry Geraldine and she will give you children to carry on the tradition, and if I want you I can be like my grandmother, your mistress, nothing more.'

'What would you be giving up to be my mistress, Ellen?'

I stared at him dumbfounded, then anger took over. 'I can answer that question, Lance: my self-respect and every dream I ever had that one day a man might love and want to marry me. Oh I know that seems very trivial against all you would be giving up for me, but it isn't trivial to me. I don't want to talk any more, Lance, you will never understand me and I shall never understand you. It's a good thing I'm going away, I want to forget I ever knew you and loved you, as I'm sure you will quickly forget me in the life your ridiculous ancestor planned for you.'

I turned on my heel and ran towards the house with my feet slipping in the snow, then my feet slid from under me and I went sprawling.

He was there at once, gathering me into his arms, his voice breathing endearments against my frozen face, and I do not know which hurt the most, the pain in my ankle or in my heart.

Gingerly I put my foot down on the path and hobbled a few steps with his arm holding me close. Then I struggled free and, still limping and writhing against my loss of dignity, made my way painfully towards the house.

My face was wet with tears of pain and from the biting wind, and when he took my arm again I had no strength to tear it away.

'I'll get the housekeeper to see to your ankle, Ellen. You'll have to rest it for a day or so if you want to be fit to travel at the end of next week.'

The end of next week! A lump came into my throat and I wanted to fling myself onto the snow and sob my heart out. I loved him and he was letting me go. Then as though he knew how I was feeling he gathered me into his arms and kissed me savagely.

I knew that later I would despise myself for responding passionately to his kisses but I had no will at that moment that was not his, no thoughts of the future. Only the present mattered, only the joy of his arms round me, his lips exploring mine.

I have no memory of the dusk coming down across the parkland, I knew little until icy hail whipped my face and I looked away from Lance in dismay to see that we were caught in a world of whirling whiteness. Once more the paths had become obliterated and the lights from the house were faint.

'Lance we must go,' I said anxiously, 'it's so late.'

Without another word he picked me up and carried me. At the front door he set me on my feet and for a moment we stood staring at each other, his eyes sombre and strangely pleading, mine swimming with tears.

CHAPTER 23

The room was cold and I was glad to pull the curtains to shut out the night, even so the hail rattled against the windows and the wind moaned eerily. The gas lamps flickered fitfully and I thought savagely, what is so wonderful about this draughty old house that makes a man believe it is more important than people, than love?

A young maid entered carrying a bowl of hot water and I realized Lance had made arrangements for my aching ankle to receive attention.

It was swollen and discoloured, and the pain was excruciating when I removed my short leather boots and woollen stockings.

'Oh Miss,' the maid cried, ''ow did yer manage to do that?'

'I was hurrying through the snow, I slipped and fell.'

'Mr Lance said as 'ow ye 'ad to rest it. 'E's asked the 'ousekeeper if ye can 'ave some food up 'ere in yer room, and I 'as to light the fire.'

While I eased my foot gently into the water I said, 'I don't remember seeing you before. What is your name?'

'It's Jemima, Miss. I'm new 'ere but mi grandmother worked 'ere 'afore she were married. Mi grandfather worked in the stables, and mi mother was a parlourmaid afore she married mi father, who was a gardener 'ere. All mi family's worked 'ere at some time or another.'

'And who will you marry, Jemima?'

She blushed and dimpled prettily. 'I reckon I'll marry Algy, 'e's only a stable lad now but there's plenty o' time.'

Plenty of time. Generations of time for entire families to serve this one great family. It was feudal, I told myself angrily.

'Can ye manage to bathe yer foot, Miss, while I go and see to yer meal?'

'I can manage, Jemima. Will you light the fire? It *is* cold in here.'

Gently I applied a soft face towel to my sore ankle and already the soothing warmth was easing the pain.

The door opened sharply and Lisanne stood on the threshold staring at me curiously.

'Lance told me about the ankle,' she said lightly. 'That's what you get for cavorting in the snow with my cousin. I don't suppose you'll be able to walk on it for days. If Doctor Jarvis sees it he'll probably tell you to rest with it up.'

'I don't intend Doctor Jarvis to see it, it isn't broken.'

'You don't really know that. There are so many bones in one's ankle, it could quite easily be broken without your knowing it.'

'If it was broken I couldn't stand on it, and I did manage to walk on it. You sound as though you'd *like* it to be broken, Lisanne.'

'Well it would let you off going to the continent with us at the end of next week.'

She came and perched beside me on the bed.

'Lance and Geraldine are to be married in the spring and Granny has decided we are to be back by then. I'm to be her bridesmaid along with two half-cousins I've never met. What granny doesn't know is that my mother is quite determined we are not coming back. She'll make all sorts of excuses to stay in Europe and I don't suppose you want to come back here to see Lance married.'

'Why should I care?'

'You shouldn't, but you do. You care so much it's making you waspish and quite unlike yourself. If you'd any sense you'd be asking yourself all sorts of questions.'

'What questions?'

'It's not for me to tell you, Ellen, you'll tell yourself sooner or later. Just think about it, that's all.'

She smiled brightly and left just as abruptly as she had entered, and several minutes later the maid came back with my evening meal. It was beautifully cooked but I had little appetite. I ached after Lance. I felt worthless and rejected, my ankle hurt and I was glad he wasn't there to see me

221

with my foot in a bowl of water and a tray of uneaten food in front of me.

How long would it take to forget him, I wondered. I knew I must forget him, a girl was a fool to yearn after a man who didn't yearn after her. Then unbidden I found myself answering the questions Lisanne had posed.

I was Ellen Adair, a country girl without education, self-taught from listening to others, and although I was intelligent and honest the only money I had in the world was that taken out of Aunt Liza's bag. I was pretty, but so were a million other girls. What right had I to expect Lance de Bellefort to forsake the conventions he had sworn his life to?

All night long I agonized about Lance, alternately loving him and hating him, but with the first cold light of day I realized, with that peculiar honesty of being able to see both sides, that I understood him.

I slid out of bed and put my foot gingerly on the carpet. There was still some pain in my ankle but nothing like before. I looked out at the frozen mere and the forest behind: as far as I could see the land belonged to the de Belleforts, and I, Ellen Adair, had had the temerity to think I might matter against all that.

I rarely ever thought about Kitty these days because it made me miserable. Now, however, I found myself thinking of her tight-lipped gamin face on the street in Liverpool when she stated adamantly that she would never go into the city again without enough money to buy what she wanted. I had not properly understood her then, but now I understood her only too well.

My life stretched before me like a battleground. I was being given opportunities that had been denied to Kitty but they were opportunities surrounded by barriers of wealth and class. If I lived to be a hundred they would always be there, and the longer I stayed close to the de Belleforts the more I would be aware of them.

Kitty had sold her soul to the devil to achieve her desires. I could not live like that, but I made a silent vow that I would serve the de Belleforts and take what they offered. I would listen and learn, and whatever sum of money Lady de Bellefort settled on me I would save and add to what I had in the bank in Ilkley.

There would be no more ecstatic meetings with Lance. It was finished, and somehow or other I would make the barren waste of the years before me blossom, even if at that moment I did not know how.

I was accustomed to watching Lisanne opening her mail. There was never anything for me, so I was more than surprised when she tossed an envelope across the table, saying, 'This is for you, Ellen. It looks a bit battered, as if it had been around a bit.'

The envelope was decidedly battered. The ink was smudged as if by rain and the paper was torn in one place. Even so my heart lifted with joy when I recognized my brother's handwriting. Lisanne was looking at me expectantly so I said. 'It's from my brother Peter, I've been hoping he might write.'

Impatiently I slit the envelope and took out two sheets of paper which I read eagerly.

Like me he had left home, and was joining a ship sailing from Plymouth. I guessed he had been carrying the envelope about in his pocket for several days before he posted it.

The heartache he had suffered at leaving home was evident, but he had been unable to stand it any longer. My father was impossible to live with, and my mother was ailing. More and more Father was becoming careless about his affair with Phoebe Patterson, so that there was gossip in the village. If it got to the vicar's ears his job would be in jeopardy.

Peter had remonstrated with him and received a cuff about his ears for his pains, and that had been the deciding factor. I was glad he'd had the courage to leave. His letter made me feel that I too had made the right decision, and strangely enough I felt cheered by it.

I folded the letter and put it in my pocket. Lisanne was uninterested in my correspondence, she was too immersed in her own, and I sat watching her, wishing she would find me something to do. It was the inactivity of my life at Langstone which caused me the most heart-searching.

At last she looked up casually to remark, 'I'm waiting for Mother, she's in with Granny at the moment. They're probably talking about when we are to leave here.'

Oh God let it be soon, I prayed silently, and just then Mrs de Bellefort swept in and went to stand staring out of the window while Lisanne and I sat startled. She seemed preoccupied. There was a frown on her beautiful face, though as always she seemed to be the epitome of grace and elegance.

'Is something wrong, Mother?' Lisanne asked at last.

She spun round and eyed us stonily. 'Lance's father is very ill and probably won't last the week out. Lance is leaving here this morning and your grandmother thinks we shouldn't travel until after it's all over. I hate funerals, and I'm quite sure Gerald wouldn't be bothered if I didn't attend his. We never really hit it off, he was always a dry old stick. Steven was the gay one, we had a lot more in common.'

'Is he really going to die, Mother?' Lisanne asked petulantly.

'Darling, he's been a creaking gate for years. I suppose it could be another false alarm but this time I don't think so. There'll be all those mourners from all over Yorkshire and further afield than that, all the pomp of opening up the family vault, and Granny will be there to lord it over the proceedings like some ancient potentate. I don't think I can stand it.'

'Then why can't we go away like we planned?' Lisanne said anxiously.

'I'm in trouble with your grandmother as it is. I don't want my allowance docked, you know what she's capable of.'

'Why does she arrange everything, why can't we have our own money, why does everything have to be ploughed back into the family? Why does she always know best?'

Mrs de Bellefort shrugged. 'Why indeed?' she said cynically. 'Oh well, I can't afford to antagonize her, Lisanne, we'll just have to hope that Gerald doesn't linger on. I can't

224

think they'll be coming over from Ireland for the funeral, neither Steven nor Gervase came to Cousin John's funeral.'

'If he dies Geraldine's going to be Lady de Bellefort when she marries Lance, isn't she Mother? She'll be no match for old Lady de Bellefort.'

Her mother laughed. 'No, I don't suppose she will, but quite often the shy sweet ones are the most dominant. It will be very interesting to see how she develops, and it will serve the old girl right if Geraldine plays her at her own game. Don't worry, Lisanne, we'll hang on for a few more days. By the weekend we shall know if Gerald is going to survive yet another heart attack.'

We knew before the end of the day. Lance arrived home in time to be with his father when he died, upon which he became the fourteenth baronet. And Geraldine had every expectation of being the next Lady de Bellefort.

I watched the funeral cortege arriving for his interment in the family vault at the church in Langstone. I had never seen such an array of black coaches, black horses and purple plumes. Lady de Bellefort disdained limousines as being unsuitably decadent for such an occasion.

I walked to the village church as a mark of respect and stood in the crowded churchyard wearing a thin black veil over my face, my feet becoming colder by the minute. If my eyes followed Lance's tall figure with considerable longing nobody could see behind the veil, but it was at old Lady de Bellefort that most people looked. She stood beside Lance, slender and upright, her tightly clenched hand resting on her tall umbrella, and when he offered his arm she declined, walking slowly with head held high behind the coffin of her eldest son.

Geraldine walked behind with her mother, and as she passed there were smiles of sympathy and curtseys from those lining the paths. It seemed that already it was understood that this was the girl Lance would marry.

Lisanne's mother looked conspicuously elegant in her black. This was not the attire brought out of mothballs for a funeral, but rather the sort of fashionable black she might have worn for Ascot. The large sweeping brim of her hat was adorned with ostrich feathers and just once I saw her mother-in-law glance at her with cynical impatience, an impatience the younger woman treated with maddening unconcern.

They came back to the Priory for the funeral breakfast in the great hall while I sat alone in Lisanne's small sitting room overlooking the fells. It was not surprising they forgot to serve a meal to me, I knew the servants were run off their feet, so after two o'clock I went down to the kitchens in search of a sandwich.

Cook was busy at the long black range, her face flushed with exertion, issuing orders to the kitchenmaids who scurried about as if their life depended on it.

I stood hesitantly in the doorway wishing I hadn't come, and I was about to make a retreat when Cook spotted me.

'Did they forget ye, love? I'm not surprised, there's so much goin' on. There's hot soup in the tureen there and ye can no doubt find some bread and cheese if ye looks round for it. Yer'd think some o' them folk up there 'adn't eaten for months.'

I helped myself to soup and found newly baked bread and Wensleydale cheese and settled myself at the kitchen table. At the first lull in the proceedings Cook came to sit opposite me.

'Things'll be changin' round 'ere, now,' she said gloomily. 'I can sense it in mi bones. Did ye go down to the church?'

'Yes, the church and all the roads were crowded.'

'Ay well, they would be. Out o' curiosity if not compassion. Sir Gerald was allus a quiet sort o' man not like Master Steven who were never averse to chattin' up one o' the servants. Right caution he was and led 'er ladyship a merry dance. I thought one of 'em might 'ave come over from Ireland for the funeral, but they 'aven't.'

'It's a long way to come for a funeral.'

'I suppose so, and I've heard Master Steven 'asn't been all that well. Still, there's that son of 'is. Not a bit like Master Lance 'e wasn't, that lad sure 'ad the devil in 'im.'

I didn't speak and Cook sat pensive, remembering. At

length she looked up and said, 'I suppose it is Miss Geraldine who'll be the next Lady de Bellefort?'

'I think so.'

'And Miss Lisanne'll be packed off to County Wicklow to wed that limb o' Satan. Oh well, like as not 'e's changed a lot over the years.'

I didn't speak, but finished my tea and with a smile and a word of thanks left the table and edged towards the door. At that moment the butler came in rattling his keys and saying in a cross voice. 'They want more port. I thought I'd laid out enough to supply a regiment, but apparently not.'

Cook smiled at me across the room. ''E watches that port as if 'e'd paid for it.'

I made my escape up the back stairs and returned to the sitting room. It had turned cold so I built up the fire and drew my chair up before it. I tried to read but the warmth made me sleepy and I started up guiltily at hearing a sharp knock on the door. I was surprised to find Lance standing hesitantly outside it.

We stared at each other for several seconds before he said with a small smile, 'Aren't you going to invite me in, Ellen?'

I stepped back and held the door open wider. He followed me to the fireplace and stood looking down into the flames while I sat back in my chair, waiting for him to speak.

It seemed a small eternity before he looked at me again and when he finally spoke his voice was tired and remotely sad.

'My aunt tells me you hope to travel on Wednesday. I couldn't let you go without saying goodbye. I shall miss you, Ellen.'

I didn't speak.

'I wish all those people would go home. It seems somehow indecent to see them wading through all that food and wine, more like a celebration than a funeral.'

'I'm sorry about your father, Lance. Were you very close?'

'No. My father was a solitary man, he liked books and collecting pictures and bronzes. He'd never been a great traveller and he disliked field sports. After my mother died

227

he retreated more and more into his shell. They were very close.'

'In spite of being closely related?'

'Yes. They were fond of each other as children. It can happen, Ellen.'

'Of course. I hope you and Geraldine will be very happy, Lance, and that in time you too will be close. You're to be married in the spring, I believe?'

'Yes.' He looked at me keenly.

Sharply I said, 'I shan't be here, Lance. Mrs de Bellefort is hoping to stay away some time, I know that your grandmother is expecting that Lisanne will be Geraldine's bridesmaid.'

'I've told my aunt I'm not expecting her to return for my wedding. She thinks I'm merely being considerate, I couldn't tell her it was because I couldn't bear to see you at that time.'

'If this is to be your home Lance, you can rest assured I shall never return to it.'

'Ellen, if ever you want for anything – money, anything – will you promise to let me know?'

'I shan't want for anything, Lance, your grandmother has been very generous.'

I wouldn't tell him that he was the last person I would ever ask for anything, not even if I were old and destitute.

He seemed ill at ease, he wanted to touch me but was afraid of the passion I would arouse in him, and he wanted to be gone. I too wanted him gone, I wished he had never come, and I was more than relieved when he finally said, 'I must go back, Ellen. I am after all the host of that affair downstairs.'

I stood up and walked to the door. He made no effort to take my hand, instead with a brief smile he passed in front of me and I closed the door behind him. I stood with my back to it while the tears flowed from my eyes unchecked, then fiercely I rubbed my face clean and returned to the fireside.

Wednesday couldn't come quickly enough. I wanted to be gone from this place, never to return. I would have been

228

astounded if I had known then how fate would shape and change my destiny.

I had one more meeting with Lady de Bellefort, the night before we left for London. She seemed more fragile, her aristocratic fine-boned face almost transparent, and her hands were nervous. As always she was gracious, inviting me to take the seat opposite, but she came quickly to the point.

'It may be that we shall not meet again, Ellen. I am hoping Lisanne and her mother will return for the wedding but knowing my daughter-in-law I cannot be sure, and I am too old to argue with her.

'Do you have a bank account?'

'I have a little money in the bank in Ilkley.'

'If you will give me the details I will see that it is added to. I have also given my daughter-in-law money for your upkeep and for anything you wish to buy. I don't know what sort of life you will live abroad. No doubt you will have a great deal of time to yourself but you are an intelligent girl, I am sure you will spend your leisure time wisely. Europe is a treasure trove of culture, my dear. Visit the art galleries and the museums, walk in the parks and along the water fronts. Real education begins after one has left the school-room, Ellen, life is the educator.

'Lisanne does not understand that any more than does her mother. She believes education for itself is not important because she will have enough money to ignore it. I disagree.

'My grandson Gervase might enjoy having a social butter-fly for a wife. On the other hand Lisanne could exasperate him beyond all measure. It will not concern you, Ellen, by that time you will undoubtedly have sorted out your own future. I wish you well in it.'

The interview was at an end and I thanked her for the time I had been allowed to spend in her house and for the chance she was giving me now, all of which she waved away with a graceful move of her hand.

From a small table beside her chair she took up a dark blue leather box and handed it to me.

229

'I would like you to have this, Ellen. No, do not open it now, wait until you are in your room. My husband gave me what you will find in that box soon after we were married. I always had the feeling that he would have preferred to give it to your grandmother.'

Suddenly compassion flooded my being for this proud old woman who had for a brief moment allowed me to feel sorry for her. Then raising her head imperiously she said, 'That is all, Ellen, I wish you a pleasant journey and a happy life.'

I sat on my bed with the leather box unopened. I had been careful to lock the door, I didn't want Lisanne bursting in on me as she was wont to do and asking too many questions. Gingerly I opened the box then gasped with delight. Inside was a gold chain holding a single beautiful pearl, and matching earrings. I determined to have my ears pierced at the first opportunity.

I felt sure that Lady de Bellefort had never worn this jewellery, knowing it had not really been meant for her. I wished I had known my grandmother. My mother said she had not had an easy life. There had been too many children too soon and not enough money, but she had worked her fingers to the bone to keep them decently dressed and fed. I thought unhappily of the hundreds of times she must have remembered the love affair of her youth, particularly when she looked at my mother, and all those times when she had to shield her daughter from her husband's resentment.

I set about packing my suitcase. I needed to take everything I had because I would not be coming back. Most of my clothes were hand-me-downs from Lisanne. I packed the leather box in the same cardboard box which contained Aunt Liza's jewellery, and left the suitcase undone for last-minute things in the morning. It would not be heavy, nor would it be strictly full, a thing which I was pleased about when later that evening Lisanne asked if she could find room for things she couldn't fit into her own luggage.

She perched on my bed with evident enjoyment.

'Aren't you absolutely thrilled to be going in the morning?' she trilled. 'We're spending four days in London, then we're going to Paris. You should learn some French, Ellen, it's so silly and so British to think everybody should talk to us in our own language. Mother speaks French and Italian quite fluently. I only wish I'd paid more attention to Madame Buchard at the school in Switzerland.'

'French was something they didn't teach at my school, I'm afraid.'

'Oh well, there's no reason why you shouldn't start to learn it, it will give you something to do in Paris. We're to stay with Aunt Julie. She has a lovely house not far from the Opéra and I just know she'll fill it with dozens of her exciting friends. I adore Paris. There'll be no Christmas festivities here with Lance's father dying, but we can look forward to Paris in the spring.'

'Where do we sail from?'

'Oh Dover, or Folkestone I expect. Will this be your first boat trip, Ellen?'

'I've crossed the Mersey on a ferryboat from Liverpool to New Brighton.'

She dissolved into laughter. 'Oh Ellen, you're going to have your eyes opened, I shall enjoy seeing them fill with wonder at all the new experiences. Mother's downstairs talking to Granny, who'll be full of advice, that I hope Mother ignores. They packed me off and told me to get to bed early but I'm far too excited. The way Granny treats me one might think I was still a schoolgirl. Did Lance come to say goodbye?'

'Yes, after the funeral.'

'Did you melt into each other's arms and vow undying love?'

'Of course not.'

'Whyever not, for heavens sake? There doesn't look to be much passion in Geraldine. I can't think she'll add any lustre to his life.'

'You don't know that, Lisanne.'

'I can guess. What clothes are you travelling in?'

'My tweed coat, it's the only one I've got that's decent.'

Suddenly the laughter died out of her eyes, and after giving me a little hug she said. 'You can try my grey one

231

with the fox collar. Grey's not really my colour – come to think of it, it isn't yours either – but the coat is lovely. I'll wear the blue, it's newer.'

'Oh Lisanne, I can't keep wearing your clothes. What will your mother say?'

'She'll never notice. I'll bring it in the morning, and there's a darling little velvet hat to go with it. In that tweed coat you look like somebody's nanny or governess, and I'm too old for either. I'd much rather you looked like my friend than my poor relation.'

After she had gone I looked at my tweed coat ruefully. It was warm and serviceable. It would be perfect for those moments when I was out on my own, and I felt sure they would come often in the weeks ahead. Lisanne's grey coat was a dressed-up affair, suitable for drinking tea in elegant salons, not for tramping through the parks or along the city streets.

She was in my bedroom before it was properly light next morning, cramming things into my suitcase so that we had to sit on it to fasten it.

'What shall I do about my tweed coat?' I asked. 'There isn't going to be room for it.'

'Didn't I promise you the grey one, Ellen? You're surely not thinking of taking that tweed thing with you. Leave it for one of the maids. It's very suitable for tramping across the fields, but absolutely hopeless for Paris.'

She brought the grey coat and hat and laid them on the bed. 'We're to have breakfast around nine, Ellen, then Major Hartington will take us to the station.'

I wore my best dress, a fine cornflower-blue wool which looked pretty against the grey coat, then I went down to the breakfast room. While I waited for Lisanne and her mother I stood absorbing the view of the distant snow-covered fells and the forest of evergreens which I believed I was seeing for the last time.

They arrived together, Lisanne wearing blue, her mother elegant as always in pale beige. We sat down to breakfast together. Mrs de Bellefort leafed through her mail, occasionally handing envelopes to Lisanne, and there was no

232

conversation. It was strange that I felt more at a disadvantage with Lisanne's mother than with her grandmother. She made me feel nervous, I was afraid of her sophistication, the way she smoked her cigarette through a long ebony holder, the manner in which she flicked her eyes over me as though I didn't exist. I felt that she regarded me as an encumbrance, and my antagonism towards her mother-in-law grew minute by minute.

As she swept from the room she said, 'Ten minutes girls, and I want you both in the hall. Major Hartington won't want to be kept waiting.'

After she had gone Lisanne grinned. 'Ten minutes is long enough for them to bid each other a fond farewell.'

I didn't speak. I had seen the Major and Mrs de Bellefort riding together in the park. I had seen him pick her up in his car one evening. It seemed Lisanne was reading more into their association.

Jemima was in my bedroom when I entered it but the luggage had gone. She turned with a bright smile on her pretty face and I went to the bed to pick up the coat and hat.

The hat was a pretty thing, a tiny velvet tricorn with a cluster of grey feathers framing the face, and as soon as I put it on I knew it suited me. The coat's fox-collar fell soft around my shoulders and looked expensive and elegant over the blue dress.

Jemima gasped with admiration. 'Oh Miss Ellen, ye do look lovely, I've never seen ye lookin' so nice.'

'Thank you. Jemima, would you like to have my tweed coat?'

Her eyes opened with pleasure. 'Are ye sure, Miss?'

I took it out of the wardrobe and handed it to her. 'Try it on, see if it fits.'

It fitted the girl beautifully and she stood in front of my mirror smoothing her hands along the collar and her hips, her eyes shining excitedly.

'This is one coat mi sister's not goin' to get 'er hands on,' she said smugly. 'Thanks ever so much, Miss Ellen, I'll look after it.'

233

I held out my hand for the girl to take otherwise she would have bobbed a curtsey, and curtsies I didn't merit from Jemima.

'Goodbye, Jemima,' I said, smiling down at her, 'thank you for looking after me so well.'

'But yer'll be back, Miss, yer'll be back for Sir Lance's weddin' in the spring.'

'I'm not sure, Jemima, our plans are uncertain.'

She was staring at me in a puzzled way and I knew my remarks would be repeated in the servants' quarters. Nobody would be surprised. The vagaries of Mrs de Bellefort were as much a puzzlement to those downstairs as they were to the lady of the manor.

CHAPTER 24

I became aware very quickly that I had embarked upon a great adventure. I revelled in the quiet luxury of the hotel in London and I was happy to find my way about alone. Lisanne and her mother knew people in the city, so largely I was left to entertain myself. I loved the mist that hung low over the river, and the theatre crowds. I went to the art galleries and the museums and I bought myself a dark brown coat which seemed less ostentatious for such meanderings.

I was sorry to leave London but greater adventures were in store, the next one being the ferry across the channel. As soon as we boarded her Mrs de Bellefort and Lisanne went to their cabins with Lisanne saying, 'I must get to sleep before the boat sails otherwise I'll be awake all night just thinking about being at sea. You should do the same Ellen, that trip on the Mersey ferry didn't prove you're a good sailor.'

Needless to say I didn't go to my cabin, instead I stood at the rail of the ship until England faded into the distance, and I discovered that I was a good sailor. Then I discovered the lounges and the companionship of fellow travellers. Indeed it was after two in the morning when I finally went to my cabin and even then I was too excited to sleep.

Although I was not the seasoned traveller it was I who ate the hearty breakfast. When Lisanne and her mother finally joined me they both seemed pale and languid, and for the first time since I had met her Mrs de Bellefort seemed less than elegant. They revived on the train to Paris, and by the time we arrived they were both eagerly looking through the window. As we stepped down a woman came hurrying along the platform followed by a uniformed chauffeur and then there were embraces and much laughter while I stood back waiting for it to subside. At last Lisanne turned to me, saying, 'This is Aunt Julie, Ellen.' I found myself being appraised from head to foot in some surprise and I was glad I was wearing the grey coat and hat.

At last Aunt Julie said, 'Well it's easy to see you're related, darling. Now come along with me, all of you. I've brought Leon to see to your luggage.'

We followed in her wake obediently and Lisanne whispered, 'She's so very French, Ellen, she never stops talking and like all French people she talks with her hands as well as her lips. I love Aunt Julie, she's so chic.'

Aunt Julie was small and slender. Her dark hair was fashionably shingled under the tight fitting velvet toque and there was dark fur round the hem and cuffs of her beige coat. Her shoes were the same colour as her coat, with ridiculously high heels, and as she tripped daintily along the platform she chatted animatedly to Mrs de Bellefort, her hands gesticulating excitedly.

She led us to a long black car and soon afterwards the chauffeur appeared with porters carrying our luggage.

I was too preoccupied with the streets of Paris to pay much attention to the conversation. Now and again Lisanne would point out buildings of interest, particularly the Eiffel Tower, a gigantic landmark against the blue sky.

As the car moved into the most beautiful boulevard I had ever seen, Lisanne whispered, 'The Champs Elysées, Ellen. And look, up there on the hill, the church of the Sacre Coeur.'

It was all too much to take in in one day: the warm pulsating heartbeat of the life along the streets, the laughter and chatter from the pavement cafes, the sound of bells and smell of roasting chestnuts, the children's carousels at almost every street corner. Whereas London had seemed as solid and eternal as the white cliffs of Dover, Paris spoke to me of laughter, as gay and feminine as a woman's smile.

I had only just arrived in the city but already I was in love with her, and I hoped anxiously that I would be left alone to discover her at my own pace. I need not have worried.

In those early days I was forgotten. There was always somewhere for them to go with Aunt Julie, people to meet

236

at the race track or at cocktail parties. It was a strange new world to me who had never heard of cocktails before the arrival of Mrs de Bellefort in my life, now I was being initiated on second-hand terms into the opera and musical comedies, expensive nightclubs and horse racing. Lisanne and I took morning saunters along the Grande Boulevard where the fashions defied description, and there were times when, perhaps unkindly, some of them left me helpless with laughter.

Left to myself I discovered the parks and gardens. I took boat rides on the Seine and gazed in rapt admiration at the many bridges. I visited the tomb of Napoleon where I stood looking down at it from the gallery and was told by one of the attendants that even in death, all entering would bow to the little emperor. I gazed in awe at the beauty of Notre Dame even when I deplored the ugliness of the gargoyles and the flying buttresses, and there were other days when I climbed the steep streets of Montmartre and from the Sacre Coeur looked out with aesthetic pleasure on the sprawling city beneath me.

Christmas came and went and it didn't seem like Christmas at all. I received presents from Lisanne, her mother and Aunt Julie – a silk scarf, perfume and toilet water – and I presented each of them with a silk handkerchief. They were pretty and so expensive they had taken most of my money, and I felt even as I received their polite thanks that my gifts had been totally inadequate.

It was two weeks later when Mrs de Bellefort remembered my existence and sent for me.

She sat at her dressing table in a frothy pink negligée, brushing her blond shingled hair, and I stood near the door hoping she would soon acknowledge my presence. At last she turned and for a few seconds sat eyeing me with a small frown.

'How are you for money?' she surprised me by asking.

'I have a little, Mrs de Bellefort.'

'What do you mean by a little?'

'Lisanne changed five pounds into francs for me the day we arrived here, I have a little left.'

'You mean you have been in Paris two weeks and have only spent five pounds?'

'Not quite five pounds, Mrs de Bellefort.'

'But what have you done all day?'

'I've been to the museums and the art galleries, they cost very little, and I've walked for miles around the city. The boat trips were the dearest but it was lovely on the river and I met the nicest people.'

'I could wish my daughter was as thrifty,' she snapped, then in a more friendly tone, 'Has my mother-in-law written to you since you arrived here?'

I stared at her in surprise. 'Why no, Mrs de Bellefort, I'm not expecting a letter from her.'

'Lady de Bellefort gave me a sum of money for your keep and for other things that you might want. I can't think why she didn't give it to you, you are a far more economical proposition that either my daughter or myself. However, I propose to give you an allowance each month, and if for any reason I forget I would like you to ask me for it.

'In time you will want to buy clothes and accompany Lisanne to the theatre. Up to now she has gone everywhere with me but I have my own friends here in Paris and she should see that it won't always be possible for me to invite her to join us. You are here as her companion, perhaps it is time you started to earn your money.'

I could feel my face flaming with colour and in some indignation I said, 'I shall be happy to be Lisanne's companion, Mrs de Bellefort, I want to earn my money.'

She seemed irritable and ill at ease as she played with one of the brushes on top of the dressing table, then in a more conciliatory manner she said, 'I'm sorry, Ellen. It hasn't been your fault that you have been left too much on your own. Lisanne is demanding and we havn't seen too much of one another over the years, so I can't really blame her.

'I'm asking you to take her off my hands for a while. You are much of an age whereas she's far too young to be with my friends, and some of the men are flirtatious where a young girl is concerned. I intend to be generous. Go to the

238

theatres and the opera and for heaven's sake see that she absorbs a little culture. I haven't seen Gervase de Bellefort since he was a schoolboy but I hardly think he will want an ignoramus for a wife. The girl has had every opportunity to study, she went to the best schools and a very expensive finishing school in Switzerland, but until now she's frittered away her advantages. I don't suppose you had many of those.'

'I didn't have any of them.'

'It seems very strange to me that you are as you are and Lisanne is as she is.'

'It isn't really so strange, Mrs de Bellefort. If I wanted to survive I had to work at it, for Lisanne everything came too easily.'

'You could be right. Well, that's all, Ellen. You'll find Lisanne in her room, probably in a temper. Try to think of something you can do together. I'm dining out, it will be quite late when we get back.'

She reached into a drawer and took out a wad of French francs which she handed to me.

'I don't know exactly how much is there, Ellen, but it will last for a while. When it runs out ask me for more. That money is yours. As for Lisanne, try not to let her spend more than she needs to.'

When I still stood hesitantly near the door she nodded briefly. 'That's all, Ellen, but I'm relying on you.'

239

CHAPTER 25

Lisanne behaved as if her mother had abandoned her. Like the spoilt child she was she threw one tantrum after another until, unable to stand it any longeer, I snapped, 'Really, Lisanne, I wish you'd grow up. You're twenty years old, and in twelve months you hope to be a married woman. Can't you make a life for yourself apart from your mother? This is a wonderful exciting city. Why do you need to have your mother with you?'

She turned on me viciously. 'Because she goes to all the right places with the right people. You're not getting me into any museum or art gallery.'

'You mean you actually like being with all those dilettantes she surrounds herself with?'

'What do you know about them?'

'I've heard them, each one trying to talk a little louder, laugh a little wilder than the rest. I shouldn't think most of them have a brain in their heads.'

'What do brains matter? They know how to enjoy themselves. They have so much money they don't need brains.'

'Then I don't understand your mother. She's beautiful and cultured, why does she need those silly ineffectual people around her?'

'They amuse her, besides they're friends of Aunt Julie.'

'Well, your mother has asked me to go with you wherever you want, and I've given her my promise. Where is it to be, Lisanne?'

'We can't go to the tea dances or the nightclubs without an escort so I suppose we'll just have to go to one of the pavement cafes and watch the world go by. If this is to be the pattern of our time in Paris I shall die of boredom.'

So we went out and looked into the shop windows, and were drinking coffee at a pavement cafe when we were accosted by a dapperly dressed man wearing a monocle.

'Darling Lisanne, what are you doing here and where is your mother?'

Her face lost some of its sulky expression and she dimpled prettily. 'Why Henri, why aren't you out at Deauville with the others?'

'I had things to do in the city.'

He was looking at me expectantly and Lisanne said, 'This is Ellen Adair. Ellen, this is Henri, Comte d'Aubriet.'

He lifted my hand and brushed it with his lips, then sat at the table. Before I knew what was happening Lisanne was pouring out her woes to him.

'I'm going to be so bored, Henri. Mother's decided she doesn't want me around all the time which means there's absolutely nothing for Ellen and me to do.'

'You don't feel like visiting the museums or the galleries?' he asked quietly, and I gave him a grateful look.

'I had quite enough of museums and the like when I was at school, I've outgrown such things. We're in the most exciting city in the world, can't you think of anything else?'

He was studying us in an amused fashion and I was studying him. It was difficult to guess his age but I would have thought him to be well into his forties. He was slim and elegant and good-looking in a faintly foppish way. The monocle was an affectation, but somehow it suited him and he spoke English with only the faintest foreign inflection.

'I can think of a hundred different ways to amuse two charming girls, but would your mother approve?'

'I don't care about my mother, she doesn't care about me.'

'I don't think that is strictly true, my dear, but tomorrow if you agree I will bring along a friend and we could drive out to Fontainebleau.'

'More culture?' she pouted.

'Can you think of anything else in the middle of the afternoon? The drive there is through beautiful scenery, the house is exquisite and we could have tea at a very charming restaurant on the way back. What do you think, Miss Ellen?'

'Thank you, Monsieur le Comte, perhaps if we were to ask Lisanne's mother,' I replied unhappily.

'Perhaps I should explain that Ellen is the watchdog my grandmother insisted came abroad with us,' Lisanne put in angrily.

'A more charming watchdog I have never seen,' he replied gallantly, 'but perhaps she is right, we should ask your mother.'

'If you do I shan't come. Can't I just for once do as I please? I'm sure neither you nor your friend have designs on us, isn't that right, Henri?'

He laughed. 'Well of course not, and you will find my young friend Anton charming and knowledgeable. We will call for you at ten o'clock in the morning and have lunch on the way.'

'Please, Henri, can't we meet you somewhere else? I don't want you to call at Aunt Julie's for us. I wouldn't be in the least surprised if the servants haven't been cautioned to keep their eyes open.'

'You mean your mother wouldn't think I'm respectable, Chérie?'

'I mean she doesn't want me to enjoy myself.'

He shrugged his immaculate shoulders, and with a wry smile said, 'Very well, it is as you wish. We will look for you here at ten.'

He rose to his feet and smiled down at us, kissed Lisanne's hand and mine, gave a polite bow and walked off down the boulevard.

'For heaven's sake don't look so doubtful, Ellen. We're going to have a marvellous time. Henri's amusing and he finds you attractive, I can tell. I wonder what the friend's like, I hope he's young and good-looking, I'm long overdue for an escort of that calibre.'

I was beginning to realize the enormous responsibility that had been thrust upon me. Lisanne was strong-willed and determined when it came to her own amusement, and if I were the more responsible, she possessed a sophistication that made my homespun philosophy seem childishly immature.

She had got her own way, she had something to look

forward to, and the rest of the day passed without further incident.

In spite of my many misgivings I began to enjoy the next few weeks. Henri and Anton were charming, fun to be with and knowledgeable about everything we saw. We took boat trips on the Seine and I learned a lot about architecture. I was educated into choosing a good wine by the year it was laid down, and I came to appreciate works of art which before had been merely judged on whether or not they appealed to me.

To say that Lisanne was bored by much of this is an understatement, so to offset her boredom we were taken to concerts in the evenings, and when this did not satisfy her to discreet nightclubs Henri vetted most carefully as proper for two young English women.

Lisanne was not impressed.

'Oh Henri, why can't we go to one of the more risqué places? Mother's not likely to find out, and in any case she isn't interested just as long as I don't interfere with her pleasures,' she cried petulantly.

'The risqué places are not for girls of your age, chérie, why can't you be content with the clubs that put on a decent floor show and have a good pianist?' he said gently.

'Because I can stand all that when I'm eighty, right now I want to see one of the naughty shows, somewhere Ellen and I couldn't go on our own.'

Across the table his eyes met Anton's, and with a shrug the younger man said, 'Why not, Henri? This is Paris, why shouldn't the girls see what all the tourists come to see?'

'But these girls are not tourists in the accepted sense,' Henri said firmly, 'and you are forgetting that I am a friend of Madame de Bellefort.'

'Oh Henri, please don't be such a spoilsport, my mother needn't know anything about it. I'll make a deal with you: two concerts to one club with a reputation. That's a fair exchange, I think.'

He laughed. 'Let me think about it, chérie, but tomorrow

243

we are going to Versailles. I find your total lack of knowledge about our history most deplorable.'

She pouted prettily. 'All right Henri, tomorrow you shall tell us all about your French kings and queens, and that terrible revolution when you took off their heads. But the day after, or rather the night after, we shall expect you to take us slumming.'

Henri merely smiled, but not displeased with the conversation Lisanne maintained her good temper for the rest of the afternoon. That evening when we returned to the house however she said, 'You really should ask Mother for some more money, Ellen. You need some decent clothes, you've worn that blue thing three days over the last week and I know for a fact Grandmother gave her an allowance for you. And you always wear that jewellery Granny gave you. Does that mean you haven't anything else?'

'Nothing I want to wear, and it doesn't seem very long since your mother gave me some money, if I ask her for more so soon she's sure to want to know what I need to buy clothes for and you've said over and over again that I mustn't tell her.'

'Don't you have a bank account back in Yorkshire?'

'Well yes, but that's for later on when I'm no longer with you. You'll go off and marry your cousin, I'll need that money then.'

'It's quite ridiculous to have money in Yorkshire when you're living in Paris. It's a long time before I go off to marry Gervase, and a great deal could happen before then. Besides, when Mother gives you more you could always put it in the bank to replace what you'd taken out.'

'I don't know,' I murmured doubtfully.

'Well I am a bit sick of you looking like a poor relation, Ellen, I really do wish you'd spend a little on some pretty dresses. You're a lovely girl, if you set your stall out who knows who you might capture.'

When I still looked doubtful she flounced towards the door petulantly. 'If you decide to have your account transferred here I can tell you how to go about it. After all I'm not asking you to spend the lot, only enough to make you look a little more attractive. I'm sure Henri's noticed that your clothes are quite dreary, and a worldly sophisticated man likes to be seen with a fashionable girl.'

After she had gone I surveyed my wardrobe with the utmost disenchantment. They were not the clothes of a fashionable young lady in the Paris of nineteen thirty-nine but I was a Yorkshire lass brought up to recognize the desirability of money in the bank for a rainy day.

The money in the bank in Ilkley was along way away but before I did anything about that I decided to ask Mrs de Bellefort for a little more and hoped she wouldn't ask too many questions.

I heard her come in with Aunt Julie in the late afternoon and went to the top of the stairs to look down into the hall. They were laughing together as they separated their parcels, and from the looks of them they had both spent a great deal of money. I ran lightly down the stairs and she favoured me with a slight, absentminded smile.

'Perhaps you would help me to carry some of these upstairs, Ellen.'

I followed her up the stairs carrying a number of her parcels, and together we laid them out across her bed.

'I was hoping to have a few words with you, Mrs de Bellefort,' I said.

She was busy taking out gown after gown and laying them across the bed wherever there was an inch of space. For a few minutes I stood watching her until she said irritably, 'Well, Ellen, what is it?'

'You said I should ask you for more money when I needed it, Mrs de Bellefort. I am getting rather short.'

She frowned. 'It doesn't seem all that long since I gave you some, Ellen, I hope you're not spending it rashly. It isn't a bottomless pit, you know.'

'I do know, and I have been very careful. Lisanne says I need to buy clothes, those I have are really quite old and she is tired of my looking shabby.'

'Is she indeed?'

She stood on the other side of the room eyeing me and my attire with maddening condescension, then picked up

245

her handbag and handed me a roll of notes. 'If there isn't enough to get something decent, ask me again.'

'Thank you, Mrs de Bellefort, I won't spend money needlessly.'

As I moved towards the door I began to think I had got away remarkably lightly and my hand was on the knob when she called out, 'Where do you and Lisanne spend your time? It seems to me I should have asked before.'

'We go to the art galleries and the shops, we take boat trips on the river and we walk in the parks. Tomorrow we're going to Versailles.' She stared at me in some surprise. 'My daughter was never interested in art galleries or places like Versailles. You've done very well to persuade her to visit them. I take it there are just the two of you?'

I could feel the warm blood colouring my cheeks, and sharply she said, 'Who is taking you to Versailles, Ellen, some young men you have become entangled with?'

'Oh no, Mrs de Bellefort. Actually this gentleman is a friend of yours. He's been very kind in showing Paris to us.'

'Who is he?'

'The Comte d'Aubriet.'

For a few moments she simply stared at me, then she threw back her head and laughed with delighted amusement.

'Henri! Well neither of you will come to much harm with Henri. He's a dear little man but quite averse to females. Oh, he likes to be seen with them, to pet and flatter them, but that's all. So the three of you have been taking in the cultural sights of Paris?'

'Henri brought along a friend, Anton. They have both been very kind.'

The laughter died and her eyes became strangely thoughtful.

'Anton Gourin. Young, handsome and supposedly Henri's live-in lover.'

I stared at her, shaken. In my innocence I knew nothing of men who loved other men, to me Anton had merely been

246

a young friend of Henri's, a friend who shared the same sort of interests.

My shocked expression suddenly registered with her and she said quickly, 'I'm sorry, Ellen, obviously you are a child in such matters. Anton Gourin is a young man without means. When he came to Paris from Dijon he was the complete gigolo, escorting wealthy old women to the opera, the race course and dubious nightclubs where they could not go alone. He has certain charm and is obviously handsome. In no time at all Henri took him under his wing and installed him in his apartment. They were seen everywhere together and I must say I am not at all happy about the situation where Lisanne and you are concerned.'

'But Mrs de Bellefort, I can assure you Henri and Anton are always most polite and kind, if they had been otherwise neither Lisanne nor I would have gone with them again.'

'You are not as sophisticated as Lisanne, Ellen. My daughter knows well the sort of men she is dealing with and I am not convinced that Anton is of the same persuasion as Henri. It could well be that he admires women, particularly younger women, and merely goes along with Henri for what he can get out of him. If that is so there can be undercurrents and repercussions you cannot be aware of.'

I stared at her helplessly, miserably aware that she was deeply disconcerted by Lisanne's association with Anton and unsure what she could do about it. Of course she could forbid us to go with them again but that would interfere with her own pleasure, and while Lisanne was being entertained and kept amused she was less likely to demand attention from her mother. I was beginning to realize how infantile I must appear to this worldly woman, but while I fretted and worried she suddenly appeared to make up her mind.

'Oh very well, Ellen, there's nothing I can do about tomorrow, but I have put you on your guard. Stay together, don't let Lisanne wander off with Anton and don't be tempted to wander off with him yourself. I don't want either of you to become involved in a lovers' quarrel between the two men. In the next few days we must think seriously about moving on, I'm getting a little tired of Paris anyway and there is an atmosphere in the city I don't particularly understand.'

I stared at her. I sensed no atmosphere. Paris was gay and airy, a city obsessed with life and enjoyment, but Mrs de Bellefort showed no inclination to explain her sudden disenchantment with the city.

'I wouldn't say anything to Lisanne about this conversation, Ellen,' she said, 'she will give me a thousand reasons why we should stay here and I intend to make my own mind up about that. Enjoy Versailles and bear in mind what I have said.'

The following day I found myself watching Henri and Anton with new eyes, and realized I should have seen something not quite normal in their relationship from the beginning.

Henri's pernickety behaviour exasperated me. The complete dilettante, he liked to be seen and acknowledged by painters and actresses, members of the new nobility, and to be fussed over by the curators as an authority on everything in the palace of Versailles.

My head spun with paintings of the French kings and queens, their lovers and their mistresses, and if I was dutifully appreciative, Lisanne was plainly bored. She and Anton lagged behind, whispering and giggling together, and Henri's irritation was plain. Eventually they decided they would saunter out into the gardens, and while warning bells sounded in my head, Henri stubbornly persisted in escorting me from one ornate hall to the next.

For an hour or more we wandered through the palace, and Henri became more and more preoccupied. He seemed relieved when I suggested we should go outside but the gardens were extensive and we couldn't see Lisanne and Anton.

By this time we were walking in silence, a strange menacing silence, and Henri constantly consulted his watch as though to assure himself that time was moving slowly. How I would have loved those gardens if the atmosphere had been more amenable. As it was my shoes had started to pinch and I suggested that we should sit for a little.

He sat beside me with ill-disguised impatience, his eyes constantly raking the paths on either side, and I could have wept with relief when at long last Lisanne and Anton came into view, walking arm in arm, so intent on each other they failed to see us until they were almost level.

Relief made Henri snap at them but Anton merely raised his eyebrows maddeningly and Lisanne smiled so coyly I could cheerfully have slapped her. The day was spoiled, and I wanted to get back to Paris as quickly as possible. It soon became apparent that Henri had the same desire.

Anton prevaricated. 'Why should we rush back to the city when it's so beautiful out here?' he said angrily.

'I have matters to attend to in the city,' Henri snapped. 'matters I have totally neglected over the past few weeks.'

Lisanne looked from one to the other uncertainly and at last began to realize that her unfortunate behaviour was making Henri think twice about his association with us. She left Anton to link her arm through Henri's, all charm and girlish affection.

'Darling Henri, you've been so good,' she simpered, 'surely you can't mean you are going to desert us now?'

'I simply want to get back to the city,' he said stolidly. 'Perhaps some other day soon we could meet again.'

'But Henri, you promised. What about the nightclub?' she wailed.

'I did not promise, Lisanne, I only said maybe.'

The tears came readily to Lisanne when she was in danger of not getting her way, and today was no exception. Henri and Anton stared at her helplesly and after a few minutes Anton said coldly. 'Now see what you have done, Henri? Besides, you *half* promised to take the girls to a nightclub.'

Henri was not proof against Lisanne's tears and Anton's rebuke. With that small shrug I had grown familiar with over the past weeks he said resignedly, 'Oh very well, there is a small nightclub that has a reputation for good food and a singer who is making a name for herself.'

'Not one of those too-proper places, Henri, you promised,' Lisanne said appealingly.

'The nightclub is neither too proper nor too obscene, please allow me to know what is suitable for two English girls and do not forget your mother is a friend of mine. I do not want to lose her friendship because of some silly whim of her daughter's.'

'You really are cross, aren't you, Henri?' Lisanne said gently. 'I'm sorry we were so late, the time simply went, there was so much to see.'

Slightly mollified, Henri said, 'Come along then, let us get back in time for you to dress. We will pick you up at the house at eight o'clock.'

Back at the house Lisanne trilled lightly, 'Wasn't he cross, just because we left you for an hour? Poor Henri, it's my guess he loves Anton but Anton doesn't love him.'

'How can you say that?'

'It's true, Ellen. I've known about them for some time, I've heard Mother's friends talking about them. Anton would leave Henri like a flash if he found some girl with plenty of money to latch on to.'

'Some girl like you, do you mean?'

'Well yes. Unfortunately for Anton I'm already spoken for and he knows you haven't any money, he's only got to look at the clothes you've been wearing. Did Mother give you some money?'

'Yes, but I want it to last me for a month.'

'What nonsense. Paris is expensive, nobody knows that better than Mother. Have you thought about having your account transferred here?'

'Yes. I suppose it isn't much use to me back in Ilkley but I still can't afford to be extravagant with it, Lisanne.'

'Well of course not. We'll do it tomorrow, and tonight you shall borrow something of mine. We must do Henri proud, it's the only way to restore a smile to his face. Otherwise the evening will be spoilt.'

Lisanne wore a gown I had never seen her in before. It was black, shimmering with tiny bugle beads and, I privately considered, far too old and sophisticated for her. When she

250

saw my doubtful expression she laughed airily. 'It's not mine, Ellen, I've borrowed it from Aunt Julie. She said I might look in her wardrobe for anything I needed.'

'Don't you think it's a little old for you?' I said anxiously.

'I suppose it is, but I'm fed up with pastels and frills and flounces. Let Henri and Anton see that we know how to be sophisticated and soigné. Now what can we do with you?'

I waited while she ran her fingers along the clothes in her wardrobe, then she pulled out a dark blue chiffon gown.

'That's the one, Ellen, blue is definitely your colour. I'll lend you my saphire pendant and earrings.'

I had never worn such a gown before. It shimmered and swirled around my feet and gave me a shape I had never thought I possessed. As I fastened the pendant round my neck I knew that I was beautiful. That was the moment I decided to transfer my money from the bank in Ilkley to Paris, a decision made in a moment of euphoria, elated by the sight of my reflection in the mirror.

Lisanne gasped with admiration when she came into my room carrying an armful of furs.

'You look wonderful, Ellen, I knew you would. Now which one of these goes best with that gown? This one, I think.'

She draped a soft luxurious stole round my neck. The fur was dark and rich and my fingers sank into it. I stared at her helplessly. 'Is it yours?' I whispered.

'No, it's Mother's. She won't mind. I'm going to wear the ermine, it looks better with black.'

I stroked the fur, my fingers seeming reluctant to part with it, and Lisanne laughed. 'It's sable, Ellen, don't you just love it? You should, the man who gave that to Mother was an Indian prince or something.'

'Honestly, Lisanne, I feel I shouldn't wear it. Haven't you a silk stole or a shawl you could lend me?'

'Don't be so tiresome, Ellen, tonight we're going to have the time of our lives. We're going to make Henri wish he preferred women to men, and I'm going to make poor Anton see the error of his ways.'

251

'Lisanne, be careful. You saw what happened this afternoon, that should be a warning to you.'

She laughed delightedly. 'Wasn't it funny, Ellen? Just like a man and a woman being jealous of each other.'

'I didn't think it was funny at all, I thought it was very sad.'

'Sad!'

'Well, yes. Can't you see that?'

'No of course I can't. Henri will do well to realize that Anton is merely using him, he'll come to his senses much quicker if he does, and there must be other men who are really like him, not one who merely pretends to be.'

'I still don't think it's up to you to enlighten him.'

'Oh well, I'm not going to argue with you, Ellen, I just want to enjoy every moment tonight. Was that the doorbell?'

Henri and Anton waited for us in the salon, both of them in faultless evening dress and both enthusiastic about our appearance.

Gallant as ever, Henri said, 'We shall be very proud to escort such elegant ladies.'

It felt so wonderful to be driving through the city in Henri's chauffeured limousine. The perfume from the sable fur rose to my nostrils and I knew instinctively that the sapphires gleamed attractively against my throat and in my ears.

Lisanne was wearing a diamond necklace and there were diamonds in her ears, borrowed no doubt from her mother or Julie, but it was the ermine wrap which sent my mind back over the years: diamonds and ermine, not emeralds and ermine.

It was in a badly lit street where the car pulled up, and Lisanne pouted a little as we were escorted into a narrow passage and finally into a dimly lit room. At one end was a small stage where a Negro sat at the piano playing softly. The tables were set back from the floor space and we could see immediately that most of them were occupied. A man wearing a dinner suit with a bright red cummerbund escorted us to our table, which was in an alcove with a good view of the stage and the floor.

Lisanne whispered, 'Couldn't we have sat nearer the floor, Henri?'

'This is better, chérie, if the dancers get too enthusiastic they are not likely to fall over us here.'

'Oh well, I suppose you know best,' she admitted grudgingly.

There were candles and bright red and white checked cloths on the table. Looking round I soon realized that though some of the men were in evening dress, the women were not dressed as flamboyantly as Lisanne and myself. I caught Henri's eyes and knew that he had guessed my thoughts.

'This is Paris, chérie, nobody cares how the next person dresses or behaves. The men will look at you with admiration, the women with indifference.'

'Nobody is going to see how we look in this dim light,' Lisanne complained.

'The night is young, Lisanne,' he answered patiently. 'The food is good, it is said the entertainment is different, we should wait and see.'

'What is the entertainment?' I asked, hoping to relieve the tension.

'A man and a woman who perform the apache dances better than anywhere else in Paris, the Negro pianist you are hearing now and a girl who is making quite a name for herself with her singing.'

Henri was right about the food. We dined on deliciously cooked duckling and tender young vegetables, followed by pastries I had never dreamed of. By this time I was enjoying the piano – haunting, faintly sad French music listened to by those around us appreciatively – and I thought how pleasant and civilized it was not to spoil it by chatter and laughter.

Anton was on his best behaviour. He danced first with Lisanne and then with me but in both cases Henri watched our progress round the floor with tense narrowed eyes.

I was glad that we were sitting well back when the apache dancers began their show. The woman was flung from one side of the floor to the other and the people occupying the front seats had to move back to avoid the spirited exhibition. It was a display of male domination, cruelty set to music, and it was not to my taste although I could not deny the artistry of their dancing.

I could tell that Henri was not impressed, he would have preferred a concert or the opera, but Lisanne and Anton applauded enthusiastically.

Once more the lights were dimmed and the Negro returned to the piano amid much applause, then a girl came towards the centre of the floor. She had bright red hair and was wearing a black satin dress that clung tightly to her slender figure. The dress showed an ample amount of bosom, and although the skirt reached the floor it was slit at the side and showed a shapely thigh. She carried a bright emerald-green feather boa and her only jewels were long green earings.

I couldn't take my eyes off her. In some strange way she reminded me of Kitty, even though her hair was brighter, her figure more slender, her walk more sinuous. From all around us the applause and cheering rang out.

'Who is she?' I whispered to Henri.

'She calls herself Emerald but I don't suppose that is her name.'

I was about to tell Lisanne that she reminded me of Kitty but when I turned to speak to her I saw that she and Anton were in deep conversation. I also saw that he was holding her hand.

The tune was haunting and the girl's voice low and melodious. She sang in French which immdiately dispelled any idea that she might be Kitty.

I had learned a smattering of French, but it was not sufficient to follow her words. I knew when the song was risqué from the titters and laughter that came from the tables around us, and I knew when there was pathos from the expressions that flitted across the audience's faces.

After she had finished the applause was deafening. They stood on their feet and cheered her and she picked up a vase of roses from one of the tables and tossed them around the room. She was laughing, her eyes shimmering with bright green eyeshadow sparkling with enjoyment, and for one breathless moment they met mine. I saw them open wide in startled surprise, then I thought I had imagined it for in the next moment she flung the emerald stole around her neck and after making several low bows disappeared behind the dais.

Of course it wasn't Kitty. Kitty had no French and would surely never have taken the trouble to learn any. Besides it was a far cry from the streets of Liverpool to a nightclub in Paris. It was then I became aware of the atmosphere around me, and saw that Henri was watching Anton and Lisanne closely.

We danced a little more, then Henri stated that he did not wish to be late since he had an early call to make in the morning, and disregarding Lisanne's cry of protest and Anton's scowls he rose to his feet and indicated that we should follow.

In the car, disconcerted by Henri's coldness, Lisanne said quickly, 'I hope we are going to see you tomorrow, Henri?'

'Alas no, I expect to be out of the city all day.'

'Tomorrow evening perhaps?'

'I am making no plans for tomorrow, Lisanne, I do not know what time I shall be returning from Rouen.'

'But I'd love to go to Rouen, Henri, we both would. I've read so much about Joan of Arc, wasn't she burnt in Rouen? And you're always saying I should pay more attention to French history.'

Her voice was persuasive, and at one time Henri would not have been proof against it, but tonight was different.

'I'm sorry, chérie, but I shall be too busy at Rouen to entertain two ladies.'

'Well couldn't Anton do that while you attend to your business?'

'Anton is not coming with me, he has things to do in Paris.'

I did not miss the surprise on Anton's face or the sudden glee in Lisanne's.

Henri's goodnight was unusually cool but in Anton's

smile there was promise, and as we let ourselves into the house Lisanne seemed well pleased with herself.

For myself I was glad we were not seeing the two men in the morning, I had decided to transfer my money from Yorkshire to Paris and I hoped Lisanne would tell me how to go about it. This she did the following morning with something approaching impatience.

'Honestly, Ellen, you've had all these weeks to do something about your money, now you're bothering me today when I particularly wanted to be out of the house early.'

'Why, where are you going?' I asked in surprise. 'I'm meeting Anton at the cafe soon after ten. He's at a loose end all day and so am I. I don't want you to come with me, you can find something else to do, I'm sure.'

'When was this arranged and why didn't you tell me last night?'

'I don't have to tell you everything I do or take you everywhere I go. If that was my grandmother's plan then it's not going to work.'

'I don't expect it, I only know you are flirting with dangers. Surely you must have seen Henri was angry with both of you at Versailles.'

'Henri's a foolish man if he thinks Anton will stay with him. I like Anton, he's lively and amusing and there's absolutely nothing wrong in our wanting to spend a little time together. If Henri doesn't like it then he should have asked Anton to go to Rouen with him.'

'Your mother wouldn't like you to go off with Anton on your own.'

'What has my mother got to do with it?' Her eyes narrowed dangerously and suddenly she caught hold of my arm in a grip like iron. 'You've been talking to her about us, haven't you, Ellen? What nonsense have you been telling her?'

'She asked me how we were spending our time, I didn't see why I should lie to her.'

'When did she ask you?'

'When I asked her for money. She doesn't think much

256

of Anton and she said we should be very careful not to cause trouble between the two of them.'

'Having you around is like having a gaoler, if I'd wanted my mother to know how we spent our time I'd have told her myself. I'm spending the day with Anton whether she likes it or not and if you say just one more word to her I'll make you wish you'd never heard of any of us. I'll ask her to get rid of you and it won't be very pleasant being left stranded in Paris where you don't know the language and haven't any money. I mean it, Ellen.'

She was too angry at that moment to reason with, and stunned into silence I watched while she slammed out of the house.

For several minutes I felt shaken by the force of her anger, then pulling myself together I went slowly to my room. The house was quiet. Mrs de Bellefort and Aunt Julie invariably slept late if they had been out the evening before, and I made up my mind to be out of the house before they surfaced.

I wrote to the bank manager in Ilkley asking for my money to be paid to me in Paris, then went out. It was a warm sunny spring morning. The trees along the boulevards had erupted into delicate leaf and people were already sitting at the cafes or standing in companionable groups at the street corners.

Boys on bicycles went by whistling joyfully and there was a smell of newly baked bread from the cafe at the corner of the avenue, and yet there was something strangely different about the way people were behaving. They sat at the tables in earnest conversation, they snatched newspapers from the stands and stood in groups poring over them urgently. I wished fervently that my French was better and as I waited to cross the road I tentatively asked a man standing beside me if there was bad news in the papers.

He spread the front sheet of his paper before my eyes, but seeing my puzzlement he said, 'It is war, chérie, very soon I fear.'

I stared up at him dumbfounded and in a soft voice he said, 'You are English, Mademoiselle?'

'Yes.'

'Then you should think about going home while it is still possible. Very soon I fear both England and France will be at war with Germany.'

He raised his hat and moved off across the road, leaving me staring.

I looked round at the gay bustling city, and in my innocence could not think that anything could change the city I had come to love. It was nonsense, of course there would not be war. It was quite ridiculous of the newspapers to fill their pages with such threats.

I posted my letter and stopped at a cafe for coffee. The day stretched before me and I realized that for the first time in weeks nothing was planned. I was alone with nothing to do. Then the idea took shape.

I had no idea where the nightclub was situated, but a taxi driver would know. When I found a taxi and asked for Le Chat Noir the driver stared at me curiously. It was a place one went to in the evening, not in the middle of the morning, and I thought he might be wondering if I was an entertainer. But shrugging his shoulders he applied himself to his driving while I tried to memorize the route.

Eventually we came to a less salubrious part of the city where the streets were narrower and less populated, lined with dingy shops and dingier houses. At last we stopped in front of a door I recognized from the night before and I paid the fare before stepping out on to the road.

The nightclub looked even less inviting than on the previous evening. Over the door a cardboard witch wearing a tall pointed hat sat on a broomstick while a black cat sat behind her, and the door was painted black and endorsed with silver stars. It was all a little crude but I remembered that the food had been good and the entertainment even better.

A glass case stood behind the front door, filled with photographs. There was a photo of the Negro sitting at the piano and smiling broadly, and another of the apache dancers, but there was none of Emerald. Disappointed I turned away, and then through a glass panel by the door I saw a life-size cardboard figure of Emerald staring back at me – the bright red hair, the poppy-red lips smiling tantalizingly, the bright emerald feathers and long emerald earrings. Once again my heart missed a beat when I thought how strangely she resembled Kitty McGuire.

From behind me a voice said, 'It is me, Ellen. I was hopin' you hadn't recognized me.'

I spun round and there was Kitty looking much like she used to without the theatrical make-up, and only her red hair more startling than I remembered it.

I took her hands and leaned forward to embrace her. 'Oh Kitty, I couldn't really believe the girl last night was you, but I had to be sure. Can we go somewhere to talk?'

'I have a rehearsal and I'm a bit late. You can sit and watch if you like, then we can go round the corner to a little cafe where the food isn't bad. I'll be rehearsing for about an hour, can you wait that long?'

'I can wait all day if necessary. Kitty, I've so much to ask you.'

'And I you, Ellen Adair. You could 'ave knocked me down with a feather, seein' you sitting in the nightclub with those posh folk. I knows the younger of the two men, he's been here somethin' an' often with different women.'

'He's a friend of a friend. I don't know him very well.'

Her eyes were smiling into mine, worldly cynical eyes that brought a blush to my cheeks.

Nothing I told Kitty would shock her. She knew Anton for what he was and probably Henri too. It was Lisanne and myself she would want to know about, and how I came to be in Paris in an atmosphere totally alien from the Yorkshire we had both known and the old life we had shared.

259

CHAPTER 26

I sat entranced at the back of the nightclub as Kitty went through her repertoire. She conversed with the pianist in English, which he instantly translated into French for the manager who sat near the dais.

She sang the songs with impeccable French aplomb and I was entranced, marvelling at her lively courage and with a mounting impatience for the rehearsal to finish.

After what seemed ages she turned to the pianist, saying, 'That's enough for today, I have a friend waiting for me.' She flashed him a bright smile and after a gay wave to the manager she was walking quickly towards me.

'Come on, Ellen, let's get out of here afore they produce a hundred and one new numbers for me to try.'

The cafe was only a few minutes' walk away and was crowded with ordinary working-class people. Kitty was met with smiles and greetings.

'It's cheap,' Kitty said. 'You might not like it now that you've become used to better things, but I don't waste mi hard-earned money on expensive food. It's good and plentiful here and it's what the local people enjoy.'

'I shall love it, Kitty. I can live without the expensive restaurants I've been to recently.'

Indeed the food was better than anything I had eaten for days. We dined off succulent onion soup and tender escalopes of veal, and shared a bottle of sweet white wine of no special vintage but which I found quite delicious.

She seemed reluctant to be the first to ask questions and, equally unsure, my first question was, 'What do you think of the war news, Kitty?'

'What war news?' she asked, opening her eyes wide with surprise.

'The papers are full of it, the people on the streets talk about nothing else.'

'I've heard nothing round here, and if I had a newspaper I wouldn't understand most of it. I'm going to take French lessons but I don't start until next Friday.'

'I thought of doing the same . . .'

'We're skating round the things we really want to know about, aren't we, Ellen? Suppose you start first. What are you doing here, and who was that girl you were with? She was a lot like you, one of your sisters was it?'

So I started to tell Kitty about my life since Aunt Liza died and in my own ears it sounded like a fairy story, starting with my grandmother and her lover and ending with my reasons for being in Paris. I could feel the bitterness in my voice when I told her about Lance and she listened without speaking. When I became silent there were tears in her eyes and then there were tears in mine, and we cried a little in memory of the years that united us and the traumas that had divided us.

'What's goin' to happen to you when this girl Lisanne goes off to marry her cousin then?' she wanted to know.

'Honestly I don't know, Kitty. I'll have to find work, that's for sure.'

'This Lady de Bellefort's done you no favours, has she, Ellen? You fell in love with her grandson and she took him away from you, she's made you a companion for her granddaughter who'll go off and leave you without a second thought. I wonder if this is her way of making you pay for what she suffered because her husband loved your grandmother. I reckon it's cruel she's been.'

I'd never seen it like that. I'd believed in the old lady's good intentions in giving me work and a home, now I was seeing her actions through new eyes and I too saw the cruelty behind it. But I couldn't believe that she had been deliberately cruel. Fate had taken me to Langstone where it had all begun, and there was no armour against fate.

'Tell me about you, Kitty. How can you sing so beautifully in French when you hardly understand a word of it?'

'I learn it like a parrot. I've always been a mimic, nobody knows that better than you. It used to get me into trouble at school. And I could always sing a pretty tune. It was my only accomplishment, learnin' was never easy.'

'But when did you leave Liverpool?'

'I got to hate it, Ellen. I hated the disdainful looks we got in the shops and on the streets. They knew us for what we were and I told Emmie if she wouldn't leave with mi then I'd go on mi own, but she wouldn't come. I don't know what became of her, but at any rate she had a mother in Liverpool. She could allus go home if the worst came to the worst.'

'Where did you go?'

'I went up to London. I joined the Salvation Army and stayed in some grotty hostel in the East End while I looked for work.' She grinned, the old infectious grin that had always brought a smile to my lips.

'In the weekdays I worked in a mission, like in Liverpool, and at the weekends I walked with the Army and carried one of the banners.

'We were singin' in the street near the West End one Saturday afternoon when I saw this feller listenin' and watchin' mi. I always felt safe from fellas in mi uniform, and he didn't look like a chap that was after pickin' a girl up. When I went round with mi collectin' box he gave me his card and said if I was interested in a job I could contact him at that address.

'I did nothin' about it for weeks, then one day we had a seaman at the mission much like Black Jake. Ye remember him, don't you, Ellen?'

'I don't think I'll ever forget him!'

'Well he made a nuisance of himself and he frightened me a bit. That week I dressed miself up and went into the West End to look this man up. The outcome was that he sent me to see the manager of a club who was lookin' for a girl singer. I sang one or two songs for him and he took me on trial singin' three nights a week. I found digs with two other girls who worked at the club and I stayed with him two years. Then one night a man came to mi dressing room and offered me a job in a new club that was openin' in the West End, singing five nights a week at double the money, and I moved on. I called miself Emerald, ye can guess why, and I allus wore black and emerald. The earrings are real, Ellen, I saved up for 'em. If no chap was goin' to lavish mi with 'em I was goin' to buy 'em for myself.'

'When did you come to Paris?'

'Some months ago. The same chap that owned the club in London owns this one and I've built up a reputation, you can see that for yourself.'

'I thought you were wonderful, Kitty.'

'I like singin'. I like the atmosphere, the dimmed lights and the cigarette smoke. I adore the applause and I enjoys bein' that bit disdainful which helps mi to keep mi distance, and the customers seem to like it that way.'

'Where will you go from here then?'

'Always to somethin'a little bit better, I hope. A better club, a richer audience. I'd like to become known all over Europe. I'd like to see the name Emerald in lights over the most expensive clubs in Paris. But it's early days yet, all that takes time. I always had such big ideas, I'm not surprised you got exasperated with me.'

'I never forgot you, Kitty. You were the only one who ever brought warmth and laughter into my life. When I lived with my aunt I couldn't think I'd ever see you again but I began to understand why you did what you did. As long as I'm in Paris I hope we can meet. We mustn't lose touch with one another ever again.'

She laughed. 'Oh Ellen, you were always such an earnest little thing, I don't think I ever really deserved you.'

'Is there anybody you're in love with, Kitty?'

Her face became strangely wistful, then with some bravado she shrugged it off, saying, 'I take love where I finds it, Ellen. I'm not the type to settle down with a man and a home and children, I like variety and I like independence. One day perhaps I'll feel different about love but for now I'm only interested in makin' somethin' of mi life as a singer. I have it in me to do well, Ellen, I'd be a fool to tie miself down.'

'Will you stay in Paris if there's a war? Everybody is saying it's inevitable.'

'Well if there is the Germans won't come to Paris. The French have got that Maginot Line no army could get through. Besides, there isn't going to be a war. Would all these people be sitting at the cafes laughing and joking if they thought war was comin'? Surely you don't believe those rumours.'

I looked at her tense earnest face and hadn't the heart to say that I did believe them. Instead I brought the conversation round to something more light-hearted like the apache dancers at the nightclub.

'They're married,' she confided, 'and it isn't all make-believe when he throws her about. He's jealous of everything she does, the way she looks and the way men look at her. You can hear 'em rowing in their dressing room night after night, Desmond says one night he'll kill her for sure.'

'Who is Desmond?'

'The pianist. He's helped me a lot, if I move on I'd like to think he'll move on too.'

'Are you very good friends, Kitty?'

'If you mean are we lovers the answer's no,' and there was something in her face that prevented me asking more.

It was late afternoon when I made my way back to Aunty Julie's, promising Kitty that I would see her again in a few days. I could make no definite arangements until I had spoken to Lisanne.

The house was quiet. I had not expected Mrs de Bellefort or Aunt Julie to be in but I had hoped Lisanne would be back from her meeting with Anton. When eight o'clock came and went and she still had not returned I became anxious.

I dined off a tray in my room and afterwards I tried to get interested in a book Lisanne had passed on to me. It was a light frothy novel, entirely predictable, and failed to hold my interest so that I laid it aside and thought about my talk with Kitty. I found her life far more interesting than any novel, for how could I ever have believed that I would find Kitty McGuire entertaining fashionable Parisian society in the improbable name of Emerald?

It was considerably later when I heard the slamming of

the front door and hurrying footsteps followed by the crashing of Lisanne's door and I leapt to my feet, startled.

For several seconds I stood outside her door but inside there was silence, then I heard sobbing.

Cautiously I opened the door. Lisanne lay prone on the bed, crying into the pillow, and anxiously I went to sit beside her. Her face was red and swollen from weeping, and when I touched her gently a fresh flood of tears shook her slender body.

I waited patiently for them to subside, then gently I asked, 'What is wrong, Lisanne, is it Anton?'

Her voice came to me muffled by the pillow. 'It was horrible, Ellen. He told me to get out.'

'Who did, Anton?'

'No. Henri.'

My heart sank dismally and in some exasperation I said, 'Tell me what happened, Lisanne. I can't hear you properly.'

She struggled into a sitting posture and for the first time I saw the fear as well as the anger in her face.

'He was there all the time, sitting in the dark waiting for us to go back there, just like a spider. I couldn't believe that Henri could be so sneaky, he'd said he would be in Rouen all day.'

'You went to Henri's house?'

'Well yes. We were so tired of walking in the parks and drinking wine at the cafe. Anton didn't seem to have enough money for anything else so when it got dark he said we should go to Henri's house and he would make coffee. Honestly, Ellen, we weren't doing anything wrong, just a few kisses and caresses, that's all, but then suddenly Henri was there, accusing us, and he looked so terrible, not like himself at all. When I started to tell him we hadn't done anything wrong he told me to get out, just like he would speak to some woman off the streets. I was so furious I ran out without my coat and I daren't go back for it even when I was freezing.'

'What about Anton, what did he say?'

'Nothing. At first he was flippant, then when he saw how

265

furious Henri was, he looked frightened. Don't you dare say I told you so, and don't you dare tell my mother.'

'Perhaps in a day or two Henri will be in the mood to listen to explanations.'

'I don't ever want to see Henri again, I'm just afraid he'll tell my mother. If he does she'll pack me off home to Grandmother and you know what that'll be like.'

I could quite cheerfully have slapped her. Just when I'd found Kitty and there was a chance of renewing our friendship, just when I was beginning to see all the advantages the coming months might bring. She had started to sob again and suddenly I felt sorry for her. It wasn't her fault that she was spoilt and wilful, but she had to learn her lessons some time. Sooner or later she had to learn that mistakes had to be paid for, that takers needed to be givers also, and if she learned it the hard way so much the better.

Lisanne seemed to have recovered her high spirits when she came to my room the next morning. If she had wept during the night careful make-up had obliterated all signs of it, and she was wearing a bright poppy-red skirt and white organdie blouse which seemed to demonstrate her restored equilibrium.

'I heard Mother and Aunt Julie going down to breakfast so I thought we might join them,' she said brightly. 'They might have some suggestions about how we should spend the day.'

We were halfway down the stairs when Aunt Julie came out of the breakfast room and crossed the hall. She gave us never a look but ran past us up the stairs dabbing at her eyes with a lace handkerchief. Meeting my eyes Lisanne shrugged, saying, 'Now what? Do you suppose there really is going to be a war?'

Mrs de Bellefort sat at the table with the paper open before her and she was very angry. A spot of colour burned in each cheek and her eyes were cold and hard.

We approached uncertainly and she snapped, 'Sit down, the pair of you.'

'Is it war?' Lisanne whispered anxiously.

'War! War is all I need, I doubt if even that catastrophe will cause more consternation among my friends than this. Where were you yesterday, Lisanne? And don't lie to me.'

'We walked in the gardens and went to the Louvre.'

'Who is we?'

'Ellen . . .'

'I told you not to lie to me, Lisanne. You were not with Ellen yesterday, indeed you were seen drinking wine at a cafe near the Opéra with Anton Gourin.'

'Well what of it? We were doing no harm. Who saw us anyway?'

'Somebody of sufficient note to see that it appears in the press.'

'You should be glad that I've made the society column then.'

'Don't you dare speak to me like that. You are not in any society column, indeed you will be lucky if you escape being interviewed by the gendarmerie before the morning is over.'

The bombast was suddenly wiped off Lisanne's face. 'Why the gendarmerie, what has happened?' she asked fearfully.

'Your friend Anton Gourin is dead, he was shot early this morning by his friend Henri who is now in the hands of the police.'

We stared across the table in horrified silence and Mrs de Bellefort had the satisfaction of seeing her daughter put her head in her hands and sob helplessly.

Neither of us attempted to comfort her. For my part I felt too stunned, and in a little while when Lisanne saw there were to be no words from either of us she moaned, 'It isn't my fault, Mother, I had nothing to do with it.'

Mrs de Bellefort directed her attention to me. 'I warned you about this, Ellen. Did you not see fit to warn my daugher?'

'I tried to warn her, neither of us believed it would end like this.'

'I told you Henri could be as jealous as any woman. The shock of discovering that he was being used by Anton was evidently too much for him, that and his involvement with

267

my daughter. Do stop snivelling, Lisanne, any amount of tears is not going to undo the damage. What we have to think about is your grandmother.'

'Grandmother?' Lisanne murmured.'

'Well of course. If this gets into the English papers, and she does seen quite capable of getting to know most of my business, she will demand that I return you to her immediately. And what is far worse, she will not countenance any shopsoiled girl marrying her grandson.'

'I'm not shopsoiled,' Lisanne stormed. 'If the papers say I am then they're lying. Nothing, absolutely nothing happened between Anton and me.'

'I believe you, strangely enough. But would your grandmother, and would Gervase de Bellefort?'

'I don't care about him, how do we know what *he's* been doing all these years?'

'It is a fact of the times, my dear, that what a man does before he is married, and sometimes afterwards, bears little relationship to how a young woman is expected to conduct herself.

'If the police wish to interview you, you will tell them the honest truth, that you and Ellen were friends of both Henri and Anton, that they had been kind enough to escort you around the city and to Versailles, and that is all. Where were you yesterday, Ellen, in case the police wish to know why you were not together?'

'I went to the shops and I had lunch with a friend I once knew in England. I didn't know she was in Paris until the day before.'

'A woman friend?'

'Yes of course.'

'Had you arranged to meet her?'

'No. I met her by chance.'

'But *you* had arranged to meet Anton Gourin, Lisanne.'

'Well yes. Henri said he had to go to Rouen and Anton was all alone all day. Honestly, Mother, all we did was walk in the park and sit at a cafe.'

'Are you sure that is all that you did? Did you return with him to Henri's house?'

268

'Yes, but only for a little while. Anton made coffee and we drank it in the salon.'

'And I suppose Henri found you together?'

'He was so sneaky, Mother, waiting in the dark just like a big spider, and he looked so strange. His eyes were staring and he started shrieking at us like some old harpy.'

'I can't believe that you were such a fool, Lisanne. I can't believe that I'm saddled with two girls who don't seem to know what damage they've done. Go to your rooms and wait there until I send for you. I don't want you together concocting some story for the police. Henri d'Aubriet is a man of some consequence in Paris. Everyone will be talking about this terrible thing this morning and I very much fear that neither of you will come out of it smelling of roses.'

'I don't see why anybody can blame us,' Lisanne insisted vehemently. 'They must know that Henri was a silly vain little man who was queer to say the least. Why should he shoot Anton for spending the day with a girl? Men are meeting girls all over Paris.'

'Go to your room, Lisanne, and begin to think a little. I suspect it's something you don't do very often. And stay there until I send for you.'

Lunch was served to us in our separate rooms and we heard nothing more until we were summoned to the salon about four o'clock. Once more we faced Mrs de Bellefort but this time Aunt Julie too sat before the fire, though she would not look at either of us.

'You may sit down,' Mrs de Bellefort said.

'It appears we are not to be troubled by the police, as whatever statement Henri has made does not apparently include you. He may indeed be a vain little man who is unlike other men but in your case he has behaved impeccably by sparing you a great deal of harassment. He probably wishes he had never heard of you, and the French can be surprisingly sympathetic in a crime of passion. You would do well to put the whole matter behind you.'

For the first time I began to agonize over my position. I had asked for my money to be sent to me here in Paris, but suppose Mrs de Bellefort decided to move on and send me

269

back to England. Where would I go and who would I go to? As if she understood my anxiety she said, 'Do you wish to go home to England, Ellen? If you do I cannot stop you.'

'I have nowhere to go to in England.'

'You have no family?'

'None who would welcome me.'

'And you could not go to Langstone, there is nothing for you there. What do you propose to do then?'

'I don't know,' I said in a small voice.

Almost immediately Lisanne said, 'I don't see why Ellen can't stay with us. At least she'd be somebody of my own age.'

'Would you be prepared to travel with us, Ellen I feel we should leave Paris for a time.'

'Oh yes, Mrs de Bellefort, I promise to behave and not be any trouble.'

'I would prefer those promises to come from my daugher, she's the one most likely to cause me trouble.'

For days we scanned the newspapers in case something of Anton's death should be reported but there was nothing.

I chose a day to visit Kitty when Lisanne was out shopping. I was astonished to see closing notices splashed across the door of the club, which was closed and padlocked.

I had only a vague idea where Kitty was living, but I had come so far, I couldn't go back without trying to find her.

The streets around the club seemed unnaturally quiet and the cafe where we had eaten lunch was almost empty. I recognized one of the men who had spoken to Kitty, and when he saw me he rose to his feet and smiled.

'You wait for your friend?' he said, and I was surprised that he addressed me in English.

'The club is closed, can you tell me where she lives?'

'Ze club ees being transferred to anozer part of zer city, better, much better. Come, I veel show you where she lives.'

So we walked together down the narrow cobbled streets and at last he pointed to a small courtyard and some steps leading to a narrow veranda behind which there were small-paned windows.

'Zat ees 'er door, she may be in, I do not know.'

I thanked him warmly and hurried across. A fat tabby cat sat washing its face on the bottom step and there were plant pots on each step and along the balcony.

Before I reached the door I was aware of laughter, and then the deeper tones of a man's voice. Tentatively I knocked on the door and from inside came a man's muttered curse but I knocked again, more loudly this time.

After what seemed ages the bolts were drawn back and the door was opened only a fraction. A man stood at the door wearing a robe over his trousers but the robe was open to reveal a tanned hairy chest. He was dark, with tousled hair over a handsome inquiring face, and slowly he eyed me from head to foot, bringing the hot blood to my face.

'May I speak to Kitty, please? Tell her it's Ellen.'

Maddeningly his eyes appraised me for several seconds before he said, 'Kitty, who ees Kitty?'

Nonplussed and at a great disadvantage, held as I was by his bold dark eyes, I stammered awkwardly, 'Emerald then, please tell her it's her friend Ellen Adair.'

Suddenly he found the door taken out of his grasp and it opened wider to reveal Kitty, her red hair hanging in great curls on to her shoulders, her hands hastily tying the thin silk cord which girdled her robe. For a moment she seemed embarrassed that I should find her in the company of a man in a state of undress, then with that old take it or leave it shrug which I remembered so well she said, 'I wasn't expecting you, Ellen, and the room's a mess.'

'I don't want to come in, Kitty, I only came to tell you that we might soon be leaving Paris. I didn't want to leave without seeing you again.'

'Is it the war that's making you go?'

'That amongst other things.'

'Like the shooting of Anton Gourin for instance?'

'That is one reason, yes.'

The man's voice came from inside the room, saying, 'Must you stay there all afternoon?'

Kitty merely smiled, her eyes filled with cynical amusement.

'Who is he?' I asked curiously.

271

'Didn't you recognize him?'

'No.'

'You saw him dance with his wife at the club the other evening, the apache dancer.'

I stared at her incredulously, then I burst out with, 'But you told me he and his wife were jealous of each other, is it any wonder?'

'He came to me for sympathy, he often does, and if it ends with us making love, no love in involved. We both know that.'

'Oh Kitty,' I murmured, and again the small sardonic smile came back to her lips.

'Men have used me in the past, a great many of them, but it was Kitty McGuire they used. Emerald is something different, she takes them and leaves them to please herself. I give them no illusions, and I promise nothing. I wonder if your upright moral little soul is capable of understanding that.'

'I would like to understand it better.'

'You've been hurt by a man, Ellen. You loved that man Lance and you could have been his mistress, you could have stayed together on his terms. What sort of life would it have been for you, always in the background, somebody he came to see when he wasn't busy, when he didn't have to appear with his wife in all the right places and with all the right people?'

'I told him I couldn't live like that, but I couldn't live like you either, Kitty. I'll always care about you, I'll always want to see you no matter what you do, but that man isn't worthy of you, Kitty.'

We stood for a while saying nothing, then she said, 'You know I'm moving to a new club?

'To some grotty little street in Montmartre. It's fashionable, but there are so many nightclubs in the area I just hope the people will come to mine.'

'I'm sure they will, Kitty, those people the other evening adored you.'

'One day, Ellen, the name Emerald will be set in lights

from one end of Paris to the other.' Then she laughed gaily. 'There I go again, daydreaming.'

'What will you do if war comes?'

Her face sobered rapidly. 'I don't want to think about it. They tell mi Paris is invulnerable and I believe them. It's like London, the Germans could never come here.'

'But if they do?'

'They'll be a new audience, won't they, Ellen? Different uniforms, different men.'

'Kitty, you can't mean that, you wouldn't entertain the Germans?'

'If I wanted to survive I would have to, wouldn't I? Besides, you seem to forget that I'm Irish, and England's done precious little for me.'

'It didn't even teach you any values, did it, Kitty?'

'Oh those. Yes I learned some of them but to live by them depends on what life does to you, doesn't it? I found out in Liverpool that I couldn't really afford values. Will you come to see mc when the new club opens?'

'If I'm in Paris yes, I'll come to see you.'

'I've got two great new numbers you'll love. In no time at all everybody'll be singing them.'

'What are they?'

' "Love's Last Word is Spoken" and "I'll be Seeing You". I'm learning to sing them in French but I'll do them in English too. They'll be just the sort of things to go well if the men have to go away.'

It was a Kitty I'd seen so many times before, obsessed with herself, impatient for life and riches, a survivor even if everybody else went under. I couldn't relate to Kitty like this. All the same I embraced her and as I ran down the stone steps and across the courtyard she called out, 'Take care, Ellen. I'll be seeing you.'

CHAPTER 27

In spite of the threat of war the people seemed gay, too gay, and as Lisanne and I mingled with them in the cafes and the parks, talk of war seemed incongruous.

I was having French lessons ever morning but when Mrs de Bellefort suggested Lisanne should accompany me she refused, saying there would be little use for French when she married her cousin in Ireland.

There was nothing in the papers now about Henri who was still in prison awaiting trail, but Aunt Julie was convinced he would seen be relased. 'After all,' she said, shrugging her silk-clad shoulders, 'Anton Gourin was well known as a gigolo before Henri became fond of him, that surely is enough to stand Henri in good stead when he comes to trial. Poor Henri, he was more sinned against then sinning.'

She maintained an aloof stance towards Lisanne and in some anger Lisanne said, 'I don't care what she thinks, I know myself that I did nothing wrong. Surely even in Paris it must be possible to spend an afternoon in the company of a young man without some idiot like Henri shooting him.'

In many ways Lisanne was very like Kitty. She only believed what she wanted to believe and was quite capable of closing her eyes and ears to unpleasant happenings.

Matters were brought to a head one morning over breakfast when a letter arrived for Mrs de Bellefort bearing an English postmark.

'From Grandmama,' she announced. 'No doubt to do with Lance's aproaching wedding when we shall be expected to swell the ranks of the de Belleforts. At least that is what I hope it is, and not about Paris's latest scandal which involves you, Lisanne.'

We watched anxiously while she read. Her expression conveyed nothing, and consumed with impatience Lisanne said sharply, 'What does she want, Mother?'

Her mother looked up with a half smile. 'She wants us to return to England without further delay.'

'For Lance's wedding?'

'Apparently Lance and Geraldine were married at the beginning of March, very quietly, and Lance is now serving with the Yeomanry somewhere in the south of England.'

'Lance is in the army, but why?'

'Apparently they are rather more concerned with the war news in England than we are in France's capital. Your grandmother informs me that gas masks have been issued and Langstone is populated by children from the large cities out of the way of air raids, and it is time we realized that our place is at Langstone, or at least in England where we can take some part in the war effort.'

'Is that all?' Lisanne asked dismally.

'She also says your marriage will in all probability have to be deferred since Gervase has seen fit to enlist in the Royal Navy. He has told her that he will not be available for matrimony or anything else until the war is over. Knowing Gervase, I expect it has afforded him a great deal of pleasure to tell her that.'

'If he's not anxious to marry me, I'm certainly not anxious to marry him,' Lisanne said angrily.

'Your grandmother's made very sure that Lance honoured his obligations, but at any rate we don't have to go rushing back to attend his wedding.'

'What will you do?' Lisanne asked anxiously.

'I can't go back to Langstone to sit out the war under your grandmother's watchful eyes, that's for sure. On the other hand we can't stay here in Paris.'

'Granny'll be furious if we don't go back after receiving her letter.'

'I know, but she's not to know we received it, is she? If we move on within the next few days she'll think her letter went astray. After all, in today's climate anything could happen.'

My own thoughts were in turmoil. One half of me wanted to go back to England, not to Langstone but to some place where I could find work in any capacity that might help my country, but the other half wanted to stay away. I had unhappy memories of my youth in England, memories that seemed quite alien to the woman I had become.

When Mrs de Bellefort told Aunt Julie the contents of her mother-in-law's letter, she burst into tears.

'But you can't go back to England, Delia, what shall I do all alone in Paris?'

'But Julie, you are never alone in Paris, you have a large collection of friends.'

'And most of them are talking about moving away. Besides, I'm half Jewish, they wouldn't want to know me if the Germans come. Hitler is fanatical about the Jews. I thought you and the girls would be staying on here in my house, or if not we could go somewhere together. There's the house at Antibes, you love it there, Delia, and the girls would love it too. Besides it's close to Monaco and the Principality will never go to war. You know, Delia, I have more friends in the south of France than I have ever had in Paris.'

'I was thinking of Switzerland, don't you have friends there?'

'Oh no, Mother, not Switzerland,' Lisanne moaned dismally. 'I vowed I was never going back there, all that snow and those dreadful cuckoo clocks.'

'If there is war what makes you all so sure that it won't touch the south of France?' her mother asked sharply. 'It seems to me we shall be jumping out of the frying pan into the fire.'

'Where else is there?' Aunt Julie sighed helplessly.

'We could go home, I suppose. Money is going to be my problem if we don't. My allowance would cease, there is no way Lady de Bellefort would send money out of the country during a war. Being entirely practical, Julie, it does seem as if that's the best idea for us. You could come with us.'

'I wouldn't be happy in England, I hate your beastly climate and it would be quite ridiculous to go there when I have a house in the south of France which is quite beautiful.'

'Money *is* important, Julie, I've never learned to live without it.'

'Delia, I have enough money for all of us, and so many people like and admire you. In no time at all we'll be feted and entertained without it costing you a penny.'

'Julie, I have to think about it. I don't want to live on charity and I won't be persuaded against my will.'

I had sat patiently listening, not having been invited to take part. Now as we left the room Mrs de Bellefort turned to me, saying, 'I would like a few words with you in private, Ellen. Perhaps you will come to my room.'

Now I am going to learn my fate, I thought anxiously as I followed her. She sat before the window and indicated that I should sit opposite.

'Your problem is my problem, Ellen,' she began. 'My mother-in-law sends money to me for your keep. I can ignore her letter and we can go south to Antibes. I can write to her from there and she will think we never received her letter. She will no doubt urge me to return, and may for a time continue my allowance, but if there is war it will stop immediately. I intend to withdraw my money from the bank here in Paris, but I don't exactly know what to do about you.'

'I have had my money transferred here, Mrs de Bellefort.'

'I'm not very sure if that was wise. Your bank manager in Yorkshire will have notified my mother-in-law that your account is no longer in his hands and she will assume that none of us had any intention of returning to England. I suppose Lisanne cajoled you into taking that step.'

I didn't speak. Any minute now she was going to tell me I must go home, and I had no doubt that she would see the anxiety in my face. While she pondered I could have cried with impatience. She started to pace the floor, while I sat with my hands clenched against my knees.

At last she stopped in front of my chair. 'You've said nothing of what you want, Ellen, but I must ask you. I can send you home to England, or you can throw in your lot with us. Be very sure that I can give you no promises regarding our future. Life will be very uncertain and in six months you might well be wishing you were safe in England

277

with people you know, speaking a language you understand. How adventurous are you, Ellen?'

'Please, Mrs de Bellefort, I would much rather go with you and Lisanne, wherever you're going. I'll try not to be a burden, indeed perhaps I will be able to find work.'

'Work!' she said, raising her delicate eyebrows.

'Yes, of course. If there is war they will be needing people in the hospitals and the factories. I could earn my keep, I've never been afraid of hard work.'

'I have a much better idea, Ellen. You are a beautiful girl, talk of factories and hospitals seems a little incongruous besides my memories of the Côte d'Azure. Be a little aloof, remember that you are English, but not too aloof to prevent you being pleasantly charming to those rich men you will undoubtedly meet. And Lisanne must give you some of her clothes, I will see to it personally.'

There was doubt on my face, and she laughed delightedly. 'My dear child, don't look so alarmed. I am not asking you to sell yourself, only to be available as a charming companion. I am talking about survival, Ellen. As the months pass, particularly if war comes to Europe, you will begin to understand.'

'Does that mean that we are going to Antibes?'

'I expect so. Julie is well known in the area and the house is lovely, in the most beautiful place you can ever imagine. One could do worse than sit out the war in Antibes.'

'It seems so awful to talk about sitting out the war.'

'My dear girl, you are talking like a romantic child. I have seen war, the last one was terrible, and I lived through riots in India and China. Can you blame me if I never want to see another one? And count yourself lucky to be in a position to escape this one.

'I should withdraw your money from the bank in Paris, Ellen. We must take everything we have with us and we must make preparation to leave as quickly as possible, by the end of June at the very latest.'

Lisanne was waiting eagerly in my room to hear what had transpired between her mother and me.

'Well I'm so relieved not be going back to Langstone,'

278

she said firmly, 'and I couldn't have stood going to Switzerland. After all, we don't know how long the war will last, supposing it comes at all.'

'Your mother says we must be prepared to leave at the end of June, no later.'

'Oh well, why not? I'm fed up with Paris anyhow and Antibes is quite beautiful. I wish it was Nice or Cannes but neither of them is very far away.'

The end of June came and went and still we were in Paris. It was largely Aunt Julie's business commitments that kept us there. Her husband had had his fingers in a great many pies, and disposing of her assets in Paris at that time was a harrowing business. It was the beginning of August which finally saw us taking down pictures and shrouding furniture, packing great wooden crates with ceramics and porcelain over which Lisanne's mother remarked, 'I really don't know why we are doing all this, if the Germans come they'll take what they want regardless.'

'How can you say that, Delia?' Aunt Julia cried angrily. 'This is Paris, the Germans won't come and the servants won't let them lay a finger on my treasures anyway.'

Two days before we were due to leave another blow fell. Leon, Aunt Julie's chauffeur, was called up to the army. It was the final straw in a succession of calamities in Aunt Julie's eyes, and she sat in the midst of her packing cases with the tears streaming down her face, a pretty spoilt woman who was thinking only of herself while her world crumbled around her.

'What shall we do?' she moaned. 'I was taking all my most treasured things with us in the car and Leon was going to do the driving. How are we to get to Antibes now? We can't go on the train.'

'We shall have to do the driving,' Mrs de Bellefort said reasonably. 'It surely isn't outside our capabilities.'

'It's outside mine, I never learned to drive. Hermi always provided me with a chauffeur.'

'Hermi never allowed you to grow up, Julie. Thank God I can drive.'

'But it's so far, Delia. You're never going to drive all that way without somebody to help you.'

'I shall have to. We can stay over for the odd night, and France isn't at war yet. And we are leaving in the morning, not a minute later.'

'How can we possibly be ready to leave in the morning?' Aunt Julie wailed.

'We shall have to. This afternoon we shall have to pack the car with our clothes and everything else we want to take with us. Anything the car won't hold we shall have to leave behind. And please, Julie, don't take a lot of useless things merely because they're valuable.'

'It's because they're valuable that I am taking them.' Aunt Julie snapped.

'Our lives are more important than china, or jewellery too for that matter.'

'You are surely not suggesting I leave any of my jewellery behind?'

'No, I'm merely trying to point out the relative importance of things. Hurry, girls, collect your things and take them down to the garage. And that reminds me, Ellen, did you see about your money?'

'Yes, Mrs de Bellefort, I withdrew it all.'

'As soon as we get to Antibes you must put it in the safe, at this particular moment and in the forseeable future it will be safer there than in the bank.'

'You talk as if war is inevitable, Delia, and that we are going to lose it.'

'I don't mean to be defeatist, Julie, but I've lived with catastrophe too often not to see when it stares me in the face.'

It was a day of urgency, of running up and down to the garage below the house carrying suitcases and boxes which we stuffed into the massive boot of the limousine until there wasn't an inch of space for anything else, then we started to place things inside the car until Mrs de Bellefort said angrily, 'All of this stuff can't go. The journey will be a long one, we can't possibly spend it cramped like sardines. I'm sorry, Julie, but you'll have to leave more of it here and pray to God that it will be here when you return.'

For once Aunt Julie saw the logic of her argument, and sadly she began to retrieve her packages.

We ate dinner early. Outside we could hear newsboys crying out the latest war news.

As soon as we had eaten I said I must go out to say goodbye to my French teacher. Nobody was very interested so I escaped into the night, hurrying along the crowded pavement in the desperate hope of finding a taxi. In actual fact I had given up my French lessons, now I was on my way to see Kitty McGuire. I had found the club where she was working several weeks before but had not seen her since that afternoon at her apartment. I was lucky to pick up a taxi near the Opéra and soon we were climbing the steep meandering steets of Montmartre.

It was about nine o'clock when I approached the door of the club and with some trepidation the big burly man who stood there, and he gazed down at me moodily.

When I asked to see Emerald he said sourly, 'Emerald doesn't see anybody.'

'But I'm a very old friend of hers, I'm sure she will see me if I give you my name.'

'Zey all zay they are old friends. I tell you, Mademoiselle, she veel be madder zan a wasp eef I take you in zere.'

Helplessly I turned away but I had only gone a few steps when there were quick light footsteps along the pavement and then I saw Kitty.

She took in the situation at a glance and said to the doorman, 'It's all right, Emile, I know this one. I haven't got long, Ellen, I hope you won't mind chatting while I change.'

I was fascinated, sitting in her tiny dressing room watching Kitty McGuire disappear, to be replaced by the alien exotic Emerald. Her red hair was teased and pulled into a tumbling flowing mane. Bright emerald eyeshadow enhanced eyes that were a softer jade green, and artificial eyelashes hid their frankness, lending them a mysterious and sensual magic. Carmine lipstick changed the shape of

281

her mouth and then her slender body was poured into the sequinned black dress, slit voluptuously to show one rounded thigh.

'Well,' she said at last, turning round for my inspection.

'You look so different, Kitty, it's not surprising I wasn't sure the first night I saw you.'

'The dress is new, Ellen. The club's bigger and better and we fill it night after night. I demanded a new dress – after all I'm the main attraction – and the manager agreed even if he is an old skinflint. And what do you think of this?'

She opened a large flat leather box and there shining against the satin lining was an emerald necklace. I looked up at Kitty with some awe.

'It's only paste, Ellen, I've not got the real thing yet although my earrings are real. A jeweller made it up for me and with the lights on it you should hear the cries of amazement from the women in the audience. And here, look at this. No more feather boas for me, this is fox, real fox.'

It was fox, two thick pelts dyed a bright emerald green, and there were black sequinned shoes with incredible four-inch heels.

She looked beautiful: beautiful, exotic and alien. Not the Kitty I knew and loved but some elusive threatrical being who only came alive beyond the footlights.

'Are the apache dancers in the floor show too?' I asked.

'No. They had a terrible row one night in the dressing room and she went for him with a knife, after that the manager told them to go.'

'Why did she go for him?'

She grinned at me. 'It had nothing to do with me, Ellen. It was always going on. One of these days, if she doesn't kill him, he'll kill her.'

'Why doesn't one of them just leave?'

'They're in love, that's why.'

'How can they be?'

'Oh Ellen, didn't love teach you anything? Didn't you love that man you told me about and hate him, all at the same time?'

282

'I left him, though. I didn't go on being with him.'

'Yes well, maybe you're stronger than the rest of us.'

'Have you stayed with somebody you hated?'

She sat silent staring in the mirror, then with a sudden bright smile she turned, saying, 'No, I never have. I don't know what it's like to really love somebody, I guess I'm only in love with me, but I've seen what it can do to other people. I don't ever want to be in love, Ellen, it's too punishing. Now tell me why you wanted to see me so urgently.'

'I came to say goodbye, Kitty, we're leaving in the morning.'

'You're going home then?'

'No, we're going to Antibes in the south, to Aunt Julie's house.'

'You think you'll be safe there?'

'I'm not thinking at all, I'm just flowing with the tide. Beyond tomorrow I don't seem able to think at all.'

Her face was thoughtful and when she didn't speak I cried anxiously, 'Shouldn't you be thinking of leaving Paris too, Kitty?'

'There's no hurry. I'm an Irish girl earning a decent living here, if the worst comes to the worst I'll have a new audience.'

I felt betrayed once again by Kitty, as betrayed as when I stood with Aunt Liza at the corner of the street in Liverpool looking back at her tight, closed-in face. I felt a desperate urge to get out of her tiny scented dressing room and into the clear air of the summer night.

I rose to my feet clutching my bag tightly in my hands, saying in a small distant voice, 'I'll say goodbye then, Kitty, I don't supose we'll see each other again.'

I didn't want to touch her, I just wanted to leave, and she too seemed to recognize that it wasn't the time for tender farewells or words of regret.

'Oh, you never know, I could end up on the Côte d'Azure myself if Paris gets to hot. Take care.'

Quite deliberately she turned her back on me and sat staring into her mirror. I opened the door and fled, startling the doorman when I took to my heels and ran, oblivious to the jostling crowds and the flashing lights from innumberable nightclubs.

CHAPTER 28

As long as I live I shall remember that long journey from Paris to Antibes, as much for its discomfort but more, much more for its beauty. All of nature was combining to colour the countryside with the exquisite tones of summer, the apple orchards and the red-roofed old towns, the grapes ripening on the vines and the long sun-baked straight roads lined with poplars.

I was enchanted with the chateaux in the valley of the Loire and the stone bridges that crossed the lovely meandering river. I would dearly like to have explored towns like Orleans and Nevers, but always Mrs de Bellefort said we must press on until Lisanne rebelled, saying, 'Oh Mother, we're so cramped in the back of the car, if I don't get out to stretch my legs I feel I'll never walk again.'

Pierre, Aunt Julie's poodle, was increasingly restless as we tried to accommodate him on the back seat, and at last Mrs de Bellefort decided we'd had enough, and stopped at a small country inn.

Before nine o'clock the next morning we were once more on the road, headed for Lyon, and here we encountered army vehicles driving north and we were delayed. Aunt Julie said, 'Why did we have to come through Lyon? The roads are always so busy and today they're worse than usual.'

'I want the girls to see Avignon,' Mrs de Bellefort replied, 'I loved it as a child and Lisanne has never been there.'

'I thought we were suposed to be in a hurry,' Aunt Julie said petulantly.

'We are, but since I am doing all the driving I should at least be able to determine the route we take,' Mrs de Bellefort replied firmly.

'I'm sorry, dear, of course you must fix the route, it's only that I'm so anxious.'

We found a hotel for the night at Avignon and Lisanne

said, 'We must go out tonight, Ellen, I want to see the bridge and the Palace of the Popes. Everything is going to be so beautiful from now on. Tomorrow we shall see the Mediterranean and so much more of Provence. Did you see those old women sitting at their doors knitting in those tiny villages we drove through? I had a friend at school whose home was in Arles and she said most of them lost their husbands in the last war and they'll wear black for ever. None of them will ever marry again, isn't that terrible? I'm glad I'm not a French peasant woman, it must be horrible to be in mourning for some man you've probably forgotten anyway.'

'You never talk about your cousin Gervase, and yet in a few months if all had been normal you would have been marrying him,' I said.

'Well it looks as though I'll be marrying him in a few years now, doesn't it? Always supposing we survive to marry each other.'

'Have you any feelings for him at all?'

'Well obviously, he's my cousin and blood's thicker than water, but I'll make the best of it when the time comes.'

'It doesn't seem to be a particularly good reason for marrying anybody.'

She stared at me reflectively, then with a small smile she said, 'I've got a respite, Ellen, time to look around and perhaps find some man to love, some man who'll love me. That way I'll have something to remember when I'm a staid married lady.'

'You don't think that's unfair to the man, or to you?'

'Darling Ellen, of course I do, it's diabolical, but you're only angry because of Lance and you. It didn't stop him marrying Geraldine and it won't stop me marrying Gervase. Just see to it that you forget him when somebody else comes along.

'Do come along, Ellen, we're missing all this heavenly sunshine.'

So we went out into the streets of Avignon and mingled with the holiday crowds who stood looking at the bridge even though only half of it was left. As we walked back into the town we burst into song and those we passed on the way sang with us. 'Sur le pont d'Avignon,' we sang, and suddenly I felt light-hearted and gay with the warm sun on my bare head and arms, and we ran laughing into the crowds that thronged the sun-baked pavements of the old town.

The first feeling of disquiet should have occurred when first we arrived at the door of the Villa Hibiscus in Antibes and an old man came down the steps to help us unload the car. With him were two middle-aged women who greeted Aunt Julie joyfully. She asked anxiously, 'Where is your son, Jules? You should not be lifting that heavy luggage.'

The old man shrugged, and his face became suddenly sad. 'He has been called into the army, Madame, I have not see him for three weeks. All the young men have been called and some of the young women also.'

'But who is left?'

'Only the three of us. We can manage, Madame, the house is no trouble.'

'What about the gardeners?'

'Gone too, Madame, and who knows when they will return? Not until after the war.'

'But there is no war yet, Jules. Oh I cannot believe that war will come here, look how beautiful it is. God will not allow it.'

'It is the devil who rules Hitler. I fear that God has washed his hands of the lot of us. We have seen this coming for too long and done nothing to prevent it. God only helps those who help themselves.'

My room overlooked the rock garden which tumbled down the hillside in a riot of pink and blue. It afforded me only a brief glimpse of the sea but I stood on the balcony breathing in the pine-scented air, thinking that war was a myth, a fantasy dreamed up by politicians who would soon be proved wrong. In a rush of delighted optimism I thought about Kitty and how very far both of us had come from those two country girls who had boarded the train on the first stage of their journey to Liverpool and a whole new life.

That night we dined on the terrace. A full moon sailed omnipotently in a star-spangled sky, silvering the sea, vying with the lights strung out like jewels along the coast as far as I could see.

It was warm, with only a slight breeze filling the air with the perfume of blossoms, and as we ate I looked round the table at my companions.

Lisanne had piled her pale hair on top of her head and she was wearing her favourite gown, a pale delicate turquoise which matched her eyes. I thought her mother looked pale and tired, but that was not surprising after driving all the way from Paris, coupled with her other anxieties about money. Aunt Julie on the other hand kept up a constant chatter about what we must do and see in the days ahead. She at least, I thought, semed confident that we were safe in Antibes.

CHAPTER 29

I was in love with Provence, enchanted with the narrow winding streets of her old towns, where steep crumbling steps led down to ancient harbours and to where warm stone villages clustered lovingly on impossible hills. How I loved the terracotta villas surrounded by dark stately cypresses, and every day the sun shone in a blaze of glory on scenes of enchanting beauty.

Aunt Julie's friends and acquaintances came trooping back, and night after night we entertained or were entertained by people unlike any I had ever met. Many of them had titles. Archdukes and duchesses, counts and countesses, none of them English. One elderly man who seemed like somebody out of a Viennese operetta commanded a great deal of respect and I was told he was Prince Vladimir, a survivor from a deposed royal family. Personally I thought him the most disreputable hanger-on of all.

He accepted all the adulation and largesse as a personal right and always sat in the most comfortable chair surrounded by fawning courtiers who combined to see that his glass and plate were filled.

'What will happen to them if France goes to war?' I asked Mrs de Bellefort, and smiling cynically she said, 'I rather think they'll try to move on, always supposing there is somewhere to move to.'

'But who are they?'

'Remnants of forgotten royalty. Many of them are Russian aristocrats who were lucky enough to get out during the revolution. All these years they have hung on, hoping that one day they would be invited back to take up their old lifestyle. It will never happen. People like that bred communism. How can they ever believe that Russia will take them back to behave like medieval lords?'

I found myself staring at them: aristocratic women in

their silks and chiffons, men who still wore silken orders across their chests. 'And the Prince?' I asked, looking to where the old man sat surveying the room through the monocle with a lordly air.

She laughed. 'He calls himseslf a Polish prince and tells me he is closely linked with the Polish royal family. You must ask Julie, she knows more about him than I do.'

The occasion came to ask Aunt Julie next morning over breakfast.

'I can only tell you that he is of royal blood, Ellen,' she informed me. 'It's so sad for these poor people to have lost their homes and their estates. Luckily many of them were able to bring valuables out and have been living on them ever since. It must be heartbreaking to see one's jewllery sold, simply to live.

'I know you think he's an old humbug, Delia, but I think he's a very charming man who has had a most unhappy life.'

'He appears to be doing very well for himself at the moment, Julie. He never entertains yet he gets asked everywhere. He's fetched and carried, he never gives presents and he never buys drinks. Tell me, when did he ever send you flowers after a night when he's eaten your food and drunk your wine? I don't believe he ever has.'

'But I don't expect flowers, Delia, it's an honour to have him here.'

'My mother-in-law wouldn't have given the old fraud house room. Over the years some of her acumen must have rubbed off on me, at any rate I have very little time for people like Prince Vladimir.'

'You're hard, Delia. How would you have liked to lose your country as well as your home?'

'I have the strangest feeling that I might find out about that very soon. Have you see this morning's newspaper? Hitler has ordered his army into Poland. They are already in Warsaw so it seems even less likely that our Prince Vladimir will be allowed back to claim his heritage.'

'Poland isn't France, Delia. We didn't help when the

Germans walked into Austria or Czechoslavakia, why should Poland be any different?'

'Poor Julie, go on for a little while believing that your world is inviolate. I haven't the heart to shatter your illusions.'

At night, when darkness came too suddenly after the sun went down, there were now no lights strung out like jewels along the winding coast of the southern sea, there was only darkness except for the raking fingers of the searchlights that probed the skies above the shoreline that reached down into Italy.

Complacent in their faith in the invincibility of their Maginot Line, the French refused to believe that war would be fought on their soil, but contemptuously the Germans ignored the Maginot Line and swept through the Low Countries and into France in a matter of days.

We hung round our radio sets in fearful disbelief as the Germans swept towrds Paris. Refugees thronged the roads of Northern France, hampering the French and British armies. As soldiers and civilians alike retreated towards the coast they were forced to take refuge in ditches to escape the machine guns of the German planes.

It was with tearful disbelief that we heard that the British Expeditionary Force was fighting a last-ditch battle on the beaches of Dunkerque while miraculously an armada of small pleasure craft manned by weekend sailors waited off shore to pluck the soldiers from the jaws of death, and always across that narrow strip of water Britain stood defiant and waiting for the bombardment that was to rain down in the months ahead.

For over two years we lived in the limbo that was Vichy France – unoccupied by the Germans, in a kind of truce that gave no real peace. We carried on with the social round as before, almost as if no state of war existed, until the Germans decided to take over the rest of France. They came suddenly to Provence, their armoured vehicles and tanks disturbing the peace of the countryside, and overnight our familiar world collapsed into chaos.

Curfews were imposed, German soldiers strutted in the

streets, and hotels and civic buildings were annexed for their use. German officers came to inspect everyone, and I shall never forget the morning when every member of the household stood facing the officer who had come to interview us.

He sat in the salon wearing field-grey uniform, young and tall and arrogant, and we stood before him like supplicants for his favour and with deep resentment in our hearts.

'Who is the owner of this house?' he asked, staring at Mrs de Bellefort.

'My friend, Madame le Mauriac,' she replied shorly.

He sat with our passports in front of him, then singling out Aunt Julie's he said, 'You are Madame le Mauriac?'

'Yes.'

'Yes, Herr Kommandant,' he corrected.

He was leafing through her passport so slowly I could feel her trembling beside me, and instinctively I took hold of her hand.

'I see that your address is noted as Paris, how long have you been in Antibes?'

'Since August nineteen thirty-nine. Herr Kommandant.'

'Just before France declared war on Germany. Vy did you leave Paris, did you think to escape the war?'

'We always came to Antibes in the summer.'

'Who is ve?'

'My husband and me.'

'Vere is your husband now?'

'He is dead. He died five years ago.'

'Vat vas your husband's business?'

'He was a banker. He had many business interests.'

'And a great deal of money if you could afford a house in Paris and this one in the south of France. Vas your husband Jewish?'

'No, Herr Kommandant, he was French.'

Her voice trembled and her face was so pale I felt that if he questioned her further she would have fainted, but instead a sadistic half smile curled his lip and in a distant voice he said, 'I shall keep your passport, for further inquir-

292

ies. Now you Madame,' he said, addressing Mrs de Bellefort, and singling her passport out from the rest.

'You are vell travelled Madame,' he said, raising his
eyebrows.

She didn't speak, and he began to recite the names of
the countries she had lived in. 'This is a British passport,
Madame, why are you in Antibes?'

'Madame le Mauriac is an old friend, I often stayed with
her in Paris, Antibes also.'

'You did not think to go back to England then, you
preferred to hide here in Provence?'

'I consider we are in more danger here than we would
have been in England, Herr Kommandant. France has
fallen, England is still at war and as yet the Germans are
not on her soil.'

'Ve vill be, Madame, and very soon,' he said sarcastically,
his lips curving in a scornful smile, but she met his eyes
without flinching. 'You have not answered my question, vy
did you come to Antibes?'

'It was an extension of the summer, to find a little more
sun and the sea.'

'You vere very complacent, Madame, you evidently did
not think that war would come. Isn't that so?'

'I thought it possible that somebody somewhere might
come to the realization that civilization was not prepared to
destroy itself.'

'Oh, the var vill not last long, Madame, ve have conquered most of Europe, and England vill be no match for us.
The Führer had promised an early peace – but on our
terms, Madame. I fear that things may never be quite the
same for you and people like you, but peace is to be prized.
De Bellefort is not an English name, vhere did it originate?'

'In Normandy, the de Belleforts have been in England
since the Norman invasion.'

He laughed. 'In nine hundred years, Madame, there will
be others in England bearing proud German names. Are
these two young vomen your daughters?'

'This is my daughter Lisanne, the other is her friend
Ellen Adair.'

'But they are related I think?'

'No, Herr Kommandant, they are friends.'

In something approaching disbelief he took up our passports and scanned them closely, but made no further comment.

'Ve Germans are a magnanimous people, obey our rules and ve shall not trouble you.'

'Your rules, Herr Kommandant?' Mrs de Bellefort asked.

'Vy yes, Madame, you vill obey the curfew and for the time being confine yourselves to the villa.'

'Is it permitted to shop for food? We must eat.'

'The servants vill shop for food. You there,' he said, addressing Jules, 'for one hour every morning you are permitted to leave the villa to go to the shops. If you are accosted by a German soldier you must show him your identity card, is that understood?'

'Yes, Herr Kommandant.'

'Are these all your servants, Madame?' he said to Aunt Julie. 'You have no gardeners, no younger men on the premises?'

'No, they all went to the army.'

'If any of them should return you vill notify us immediately.'

She nodded dismally, then he gathered his papers together and walked towards the door. There he turned, and said in the friendliest manner, 'You need not vorry, the curfew will not last long. The coming months could be quite pleasurable, and you, Madame de Bellefort, might come to think you were fortunate to come to Antibes instead of returning to England.'

He left us, and Aunt Julie sank trembling into a chair. 'Oh, the disgrace of it, what is to happen to my beautiful France?'

'He will be back, Julie,' Mrs de Bellefort said scornfully, 'and the more frightened you appear the more he will bully you.'

'I can't help it, Delia. Why did he take my passport when he didn't take any of the others?'

'Because you were the most afraid. They've been well

294

trained, those interrogating officers. If he comes again you must try to be calmer.'

'I'll try,' she said without much conviction.

Three days later he returned but this time he did not wish to see the servants. He seemed friendlier, but it was a manner more terrifying than before.

He invited us to sit while he presided at the table before us, flanked by two German soldiers. He was smiling genially, and almost absentmindedly brought out a passport which he tossed to Aunt Julie.

'Your passport, Madame,' he said. 'You may keep it for the time being although we may vish to see it again at a later date. Tell me, Madame, you have been known to keep open house here for a great many of your friends, are they all vell known to you?'

'Why yes. Many of them live in the south of France permanently. My husband and I came here every summer. We visited our friends and they visited us, it was wonderful.'

'To hobnob with faded royalty, people without roots, drifters.'

'I felt sad for them, it wasn't their fault that they had beome exiles from their own countries, and largely I found them kind and hospitable '

'What do you know about the Caspards?'

'The Caspards?' she echoed, and this time her voice lost its conviction and trembled slightly.

'Vy yes, Madame, Joseph and Marie Caspard. You knew them in Paris did you not?'

'Yes, Joseph Caspard was in banking like my husband.'

'But he was not French.'

'I don't know, I believed him to be French.'

Again his thin lips smiled, wolfishly, without mirth.

'Joseph Caspard vas born in Latvia and came to Paris in nineteen twenty-one but he vas not French. His wife Marie vas born in Hungary and likewise made her way to France via Austria and Germany vere she met up with the man who became her husband. Surely, Madame, they must have discussed their history with you.'

'Why should they? I accepted them for what they were,

he a business associate of my husband, she a charming woman and a good friend.'

'It vould be best for you to be frank with me, Madame le Mauriac. Ve have reason to believe that the Caspards are both Jewish. Did you know that, Madame de Bellefort?'

'If I had known it I would not have thought anything about it. I have friends in many walks of life, some of whom are indeed Jewish. But in actual fact I only knew the Caspards from holidays in Paris and here.'

'I see.'

He continued to smile, pressing his fingers together, looking from one to the other of us. Three of us met his eyes bravely, but Aunt Julie was pale and quite obviously distressed. Suddenly he straightened up and, jumping to his feet, said affably, 'Vell, for the time being ve vill leave matters as they are. The good times are coming back, ladies, and ve are here to enjoy them with you. France has been defeated, accept it and she vill survive, reject it and ve shall have to show her who are the masters here. I bid you good day, ladies.'

We sat stunned until Lisanne at last said, 'Does he mean that we can go out of the house now, Mother, are we no longer prisoners?'

'I think we should wait a little while, Lisanne. I can't think that life is going to be that simple.'

'What is going to happen to the Caspards?' Aunt Julie maoned. 'I didn't tell him anything, did I, Delia, nothing I said could possibly affect them?'

'No of course not.'

'If they found out about the Caspards they'll find out about me.'

'Why should they?'

'I don't know, but they will. Look how they've traced the Caspards, all their journeyings, where they came from. They can do the same thing to me.'

'Julie, stop worrying. He knows nothing about you as yet, let us hope it remains that way.'

Three days later an invitation came from the German

296

Embassy in Monaco to attend a garden party in the grounds of the Sporting Club.

CHAPTER 30

One of Lisanne's dresses lay across my bed but I had no wish to attend the function, and I said as much to Mrs de Bellefort.

She said sharply, 'I told the Kommandant you were my daughter's friend, Ellen, and it's about time you stopped thinking of yourself as her paid companion.'

'What else am I?'

'You are somebody who will share whatever calamity befalls us, but you will also accompany us to the German Embassy. It is a matter of survival, Ellen.'

So I dressed myself in Lisanne's rose chiffon and stuck an artificial gardenia in my hair to match the ones on the shoulder of my gown. Lisanne wore her favourite turquoise and Aunt Julie her usual beige, and Mrs de Bellefort a grey and rose frothy confection with a large rose-coloured hat.

Faced with our amazement she laughed, saying, 'I wore it as a whim, I want to show the Germans that a garden party is a garden party whoever gives it.'

Promptly at two o'clock a large limousine arrived at the door to collect us, driven by a German soldier. As we drove along the wide sweeping corniche road to Monte Carlo I thought I had never seen the sea so blue or the mountain slopes so green. Something of my thoughts must have communicated to Aunt Julie who said wistfully, 'How beautiful it all feels. The world must seem like this to a cage bird who escapes.'

Mrs de Bellefort smiled cynically. 'Personally I think we are still caged, except that the cage has become a little larger.'

The garden party was a glittering affair. I recognized several people, some who had come to the Villa Hibiscus and others whose homes we had visited. Prince Vladimir stood at the buffet table happily piling large helpings of caviare on to thin slivers of toast and holding out his glass to be replenished.

It seemed to me that everybody who was anybody was there, and I couldn't help thinking: What would Kitty McGuire say if she could see me now, in my borrowed plumes, hobnobbing with the enemy – and wishing I were ten thousand miles away?

Mrs de Bellefort was engaged in gay and vivacious conversation with a high-ranking German officer who was looking at her with some admiration. Lisanne said hotly, 'She needn't look so pleased about, I think it's quite dreadful to be talking to the Germans as if they were our friends.'

'I can't think she's enjoying it, Lisanne, but she intends to survive.'

'She looks as though she's enjoying every minute of it. I've never been able to understand my mother, I'm not surprised she never got along with Granny.'

It was dusk when we were finally driven home and in the car there was silence, each one of us no doubt busy with our own thoughts.

Once inside the villa however Aunt Julie burst into tears. 'Nobody's seen the Caspards for days,' she sobbed. 'They were taken away for questioning and they haven't returned. The rumours are that they've been taken to Vichy for questioning.'

'But they're old,' I protested, 'what have they to do with the war?'

'Nothing – how can they have? – but they are Jewish. Oh, I am so afraid for them, and for me. What shall I do if they take me for questioning?'

'Julie, they won't,' Mrs de Bellefort reassured her. 'You were invited to the function today, which proves they don't suspect you. And we must all behave in such a manner that they have no reason to complain. I know, it sticks in your throat, as it sticks in mine, but there's no alternative.'

'The curfew has been lifted, so we go about our business as usual. We entertain and we visit our friends, we go to the casino and the nightclubs openly to show we have nothing to fear. Is that understood?'

299

'What about money?' Aunt Julie complained mournfully. 'Our finances are not a bottomless pit, it takes money to do the things you say. I was never any good with money, you know my husband always handled our financial matters and we can't get money from the bank, the Germans have seen to that. Delia, we only have the money we brought out of Paris with us.'

'Then we must start to sell our jewellery – or better still, try to be a little nicer to our lords and masters. I made a considerable effort this afternoon, I didn't see any of you contributing to the success of the occasion.'

'Mother, how *could* you laugh and chatter to that German officer? You can't expect Ellen and me to do the same.'

'I can and I do. Before all this is over you will both have to forget a great many of your prejudices. Now I am going to get out of this ridiculous dress and into something a little less flamboyant.'

Just then Jules came in carrying a crate of champagne and a large spray of white roses. His face was inscrutable as he handed her an envelope.

She said, 'It is from the German general you saw me talking to this afternoon. He hopes I will accept his gifts with pleasure, and invites us all to a ball at the German Embassy in Monaco next Friday.'

She looked at each one of us with pointed authority before sweeping out of the room, while Jules shook his head sadly and shuffled after her.

That was the start of a merry-go-round that went on and on. We entertained and were entertained. We went to the casinos in Monte Carlo and Nice. We sauntered along the boulevards of Cannes and explored the shops and in the evenings we went to the nightclubs and to dinner parties in dimly lit restaurants.

Mostly we went together, although there were other times when a German staff car came for only Mrs de Bellefort and she left the house in her evening gown and furs, but the jewellery she wore became less and less.

Aunt Julie too was parting with her jewellery until the day when Mrs de Bellefort said, 'You didn't tell me you were selling your opal necklace, Julie. That was the last present your husband gave you.'

'It caused me a great deal of pain to part with it, but there was no alternative.'

'I told General Eisfeld a little of our circumstances, and I asked him to retrieve the necklace for you, Julie. Please don't ask any questions, just be grateful to have it back.'

Aunt Julie took the leather case from Mrs de Bellefort's hands with an expression of wonder, and across the table I saw Lisanne's eyes become hard and resentful.

'But Delia,' Aunt Julie said softly, 'you too have parted with jewellery, what of that?'

'I have decided that we should not invite so many people to the villa. People like Prince Vladimir and some of the others are not real friends, they wouldn't lift a finger to help us if we were in trouble and we have to think about ourselves. The General has promised to help us with obtaining food, and I can't think we should be too proud to accept.'

'Every mouthful will stick in my throat,' Lisanne cried hotly.

'In that case you'll probably starve yourself into an early death,' her mother snapped, 'but it would be more intelligent to be realistic. I'm not asking you to like the General, only to eat his food.'

I was glad to have evenings when my face could relax from smiling, when I could walk in the garden and breathe the pine-scented air, when I could read or sew, any of the simple pleasures I had once considered boring but which now were preferable to the socializing I had become used to.

It was hot in my bedroom with the shutters drawn, and for hours it seemed I had tossed and turned. Unmindful of mosquitoes lurking in the garden I rose from my bed and flung the shutters wide. For a long while I stood looking out to the calm and unruffled sea, I then heard the soft closing of a door. Jules came creeping silently along the path, pausing now and again to listen and look round fearfully.

I waited, stepping back a little. When he reached the

301

shrubbery he paused, peering intently, then I heard a long low whistle and a small rustle in the shrubbery. Next moment another man stood beside him, somebody younger and slimmer, and they were embracing one another and whispering together. The younger man drew Jules further into the shrubbery and they were lost from my view.

I waited but neither of them reappeared, and after a few minutes I returned to bed. The episode had disturbed me strangely. Jules was always polite, always subservient, but there were times when I sensed his anger that he had to be polite to German officers who visited the house, opening doors for them, serving them drinks. Now I wondered who he was meeting and what plots they might be hatching.

Aunt Julie was worried about her friends the Caspards, who had not been seen again.

'I wish you could find out what has happened to them, Delia,' she said unhappily. 'Couldn't you do it very discreetly?'

'No, Julie, I don't want the Germans to think we are interested, that is what they are waiting for. If we appear uninterested it might put them off.'

'But it's so awful to think they've just disappeared and that nobody is in the least concerned.'

'They're not the only ones, Julie. Other people from Cannes and Nice have been taken away – many of them shopkeepers, Jewish no doubt – people who have been in Provence for a great many years. Julie, you have to think about yourself, it would be dangerous to show concern'.

Coupled with all our other woes I was desperately concerned about money. My nest egg, drawn from the bank in Paris, was almost gone, spent on the clothes and other expenses essential to the way of life we were leading. I felt I was living on charity when I listened to Aunt Julie bewailing her lack of ready money, and with this in mind I approached Mrs de Bellefort to ask her advice.

'You were foolish to transfer your money from the bank in England, Ellen and it was more foolish still of Lisanne to attempt to advise you.'

'But I feel I'm living on charity, Mrs de Bellefort, I need to contribute but I don't know how.'

'There is no way you can contribute, Ellen, and I don't expect it. I've always accepted gifts of jewellery with the utmost complacency, the right of a woman men thought attractive, even desirable. Now more than ever before I look upon such baubles as a lifeline for all of us. We won't speak of money again, Ellen. I feel responsible for our being here, we should have gone home to England.'

We learned little about the war since newspapers were heavily censored and I wished I could have asked Jules. I was sure he knew more about the war than any of us.

One day after lunch Mrs de Bellefort said, 'We are invited to the new nightclub in Nice. Apparently it's one of the smart places to be seen in and the girl singer is particularly good. There will be a party of us and we are being picked up around nine, You two girls must think what you are to wear, we shall probably be staying to dance.'

'It's quite immoral to be opening up new nightclubs in these times,' Aunt Julie said with some anger. 'People are suffering and dying and all we can think about is a new nightclub.'

'It will take your mind off of people suffering and dying, Juile.'

The new nightclub was plushy, with red velvet seating and a preponderance of crystal chandeliers, and on the dais stood a white grand piano. Our party was at the largest table in the room, with waiters hovering behind us deferentially.

The German general took his place at the head of the table with Mrs de Bellefort on his right and Aunt Julie on his left. At Mrs de Bellefort's place rested a long black leather box, and the German general smiled as he invited her to open it. On a bed of blue velvet rested a diamond and sapphire necklace and long earrings, and she gasped with pleasure while Lisanne exclaimed, 'Mother, it's your necklace! Whenever did you part with it?'

The General leaned forward with a smile, saying, 'Some time ago, Fräulein. I have retrieved it for your mother with

303

instructions that she should part with nothing else. Now, Madame, will you allow me to fasten it for you?'

Across the table Aunt Julie's eyes met mine with an unfathomable expression before she turned to speak to her companion. Over the laughter I could hear the piano, the haunting air of a French tune, and I turned to look at the pianist. I had recognized his touch and was not surprised to find it was the Negro of Le Chat Noir.

His music was unobtrusive, a melodious background to light-hearted laughter and lovers' whispers, and I for one wished they would all be silent so that I could hear this true artist better. I took no part in the conversation. Was Kitty the singer we had all come to hear, and would we be treated to a display of apache dancing?

Suddenly the lights were dimmed and spotlights shone on the raised dais and from the shadows a girl appeared, gliding sinuously into the light, and I caught my breath sharply in amazement.

Her hair hung in great waves reaching below her shoulders, startlingly red, and her gown, glittering with beads, caught the light as she moved so that it changed alternatively between jade and emerald. It was split provocatively to the thigh and there were trails of ostrich feathers round the hem. Green stones sparkled in her ears and round her throat, and behind her she trailed from one slender hand a white ermine coat. By fair means or foul Kitty McGuire had acquired her emeralds and ermine.

When she started to sing I realized her voice had taken on a new maturity. It was deeper, richer, more throaty and she sang in French, making me glad that I now understood it well. The tune was slow, haunting: 'Was it the spell of Paris, or the April dawn, Who knows if we shall meet again, But when the morning chimes ring sweet again, I'll be seeing you . . .'

The applause was rapturous, and she sang several more, all in French, then to the gratification of the Germans she lapsed into their language and the more martial tones of 'Lili Marlene.'

They whistled and stamped their feet, and she moved

from table to table, her green eyes under their glittering jade eyeshadow tantalizing and enticing, yet at the same time miraculously distant. Then her eyes met mine and became filled with a strange nostalgia.

She came back again and again for yet another song, and then for the first time she sang in English, in a voice so sad and filled with memories I felt the tears rolling unchecked down my cheeks.

> Ah the apple trees,
> Blossoms in the breeze,
> That we walked among,
> Lying in the hay,
> Games we used to play,
> While the rounds were sung,
> Only yesterday, when the world was young.
>
> Ah the apple trees,
> Sunlit memories,
> Where the hammock swung,
> On our backs we'd lie,
> Gazing at the sky,
> 'Til the stars were strung,
> Only last July, when the world was young.

At last she was bowing and smiling her farewells. The audience was cheering her enthusiastically, as she moved from table to table, then she was at ours. The General was on his feet inviting her to join us but she only met his invitation with smiles and in a French accent totally different from her native Irish brogue she said, 'I'm sorry, Herr General, but I nevaire seet at ze tables.'

Her smile embraced the rest of us, then she reached across the table and handed a rose to me.

She returned to the dais, trailing the ermine, without looking back. Then the pianist started to play, laughter and chatter broke out around the room and I stared down at the red rose lying in my hands.

'I wonder why she gave it to you,' Lisanne whispered, 'why not one of the men?'

I didn't answer. People were starting to dance and at the door there was a small stir as three or four German officers came into the room. They were taken to a table set against the wall, and one of them surveyed the room and our table in particular.

He was tall and slender, blond, good-looking and arrogant as he crossed the room and stood before me, clicking his heels and bowing his head before asking me to dance.

I should have smiled my acceptance of the honour he clearly believed he was bestowing upon me, I should have allowed him to lead me on to the floor and dance with every appearance of enjoyment, but I did none of those things. Instead my eyes met his icily and in a voice devoid of emotion and speaking in English I said, 'I'm sorry, but I'm not dancing this evening.'

I couldn't believe that I had said those words. I saw his face change, coloured by rich red blood which made his eyes seem startlingly shocked and blue, then I was aware of the silence around us.

It took Mrs de Bellefort only a few seconds to recover her poise before she said quickly, 'You should have said you didn't feel well, Ellen. The poor child didn't really want to come with us tonight, she's not been well all day. Perhaps you should think of going home now that you've heard Emerald sing. Lisanne will go with you, won't you, darling?'

'Oh no, please,' I said, jumping to my feet, 'I'll go alone, I don't want to spoil the evening for Lisanne.'

I was more than relieved when a young French man rose to his feet, saying he would drive me home. As we drove, he said, 'I'm glad you refused to dance with him, Mademoiselle. We have lost our identity – day after day we swallow our pride, we pretend in a world of makebelieve that everything is the same. Tonight you made me see that it can never be the same, that we cannot be coerced and pushed into doing the thing we hate. Mademoiselle, I salute you.'

I grasped his hand gratefully but the comfort was short-lived.

When the rest of them returned to the villa my bedroom door was thrown open unceremoniously and Mrs de Bellefort snapped, 'Ellen, I wish to see you in the salon immediately. Please don't keep me waiting.'

I struggled into my robe and hurried down the stairs.

Aunt Julie sat next to Lisanne on a couch pulled up near the dying fire but Mrs de Bellefort stood in the centre of the room filled with a strange nervous anger.

'Ellen, whatever possessed you to behave so disgracefully at the nightclub?' she began. 'We are foreigners living in a conquered country. We have no rights, the Germans are our masters whether we like it or not, and your behaviour tonight must surely have undone all I have tried to do.'

I didn't speak, and in some exasperation she went on, 'Why couldn't you have danced with him? That young officer, Major Klaus, will not forgive a slight like that and he has a reputation for thoroughness in his investigations, or he is much maligned.'

'What investigations?' Lisanne asked.

'Why do you suppose I've made myself charming and polite to the General and indeed to every other German officer I've met if it wasn't to protect Aunt Julie? Have you forgotten that she is half Jewish, that they have requested her passport not once but three times, and that a host of our friends have disappeared from the area and have not returned?'

The enormity of my behaviour was suddenly brought home to me but with head held high I said, 'I'm sorry if you think it will injure Aunt Julie, Mrs de Bellefort. I wasn't even thinking of her when I refused to dance with him.'

'What *were* you thinking of then? That is if you were thinking at all.'

'I was thinking that my country was at war with Germany, that they were sinking our ships, killing our men, bombing our cities, and I have a brother in the Royal Navy. I couldn't bring myself to dance with one of the men he was fighting. Besides I hated his arrogance, his assumption that he only had to ask and I would jump at the chance to dance with him.'

'I told them you were ill, that you hadn't been well for days, but whether they believed me or not I can't say.'

'Perhaps it would be advisable if I didn't go in their company in future. I would prefer it, Mrs de Bellefort.'

'Well certainly in the immediate future it would be just as well if you stayed at home. That way they might begin to believe that you are unwell. When you do eventually accompany us, and the officer asks you to dance again, I suggest you comply with his request.'

'Surely he will never ask me again.'

'To make you squirm, perhaps. Oh yes, I think Major Klaus is quite capable of that.'

'I didn't mean to hurt or embarrass anybody but him. Please believe that, Aunt Julie.'

'Oh, my dear, I do. One half of me applauded your courage, the other more cowardly half made me desperately afraid. I understand your feelings. Now can we please have done with the matter?'

Mrs de Bellefort nodded curtly. It was a nod of dismissal and I was glad to escape to my room, where I lay sleepless for most of the night.

In the time that followed I was much alone, and happier than I had been in months. I helped Jules in the garden and caught up with my reading, and I knew I had the servants' approval by the way they cosseted me.

One afternoon in the garden Jules said, 'You listen to the radio, Mademoiselle. You are anxious about the war?'

'We only listen to what the authorities want us to hear, and sometimes I don't believe a word of it,' I answered him shortly.

'You are right not to believe it, Mademoiselle. It will cheer you to know that the Allied armies have returned to France in force.'

'Who tells you these things, Jules? How is it you know and we don't?'

'That, Mademoiselle, I am unable to tell you, and it will be a secret between us. Say nothing of what I have told you.'

'Well of course not, but I would like it to be true.'

He laughed. 'It is all true, so it would seem that the good God is on our side after all.'

'Oh, I do hope so.'

'Well of course. You were brave to behave as you did with that German officer, but he is known to be a vindictive man. I fear there might well be repercussions, so be on your guard at all times. His reputation is a bad one, even among the Germans.'

'I hope I never see him again, Jules, I am happier here working in the garden with you. Perhaps I shall soon be able to walk in the hills again or along the shore.'

He smiled. 'Perhaps, Mademoiselle, if you are vigilant.'

I loved Provence. I seemed to have lived there for much longer than four years and I believed it was the climate which made it so timeless. Winter melted into spring, and spring into summer and yet there were many times when I recalled our northern winters with nostalgia. And how I missed the twilight, long country twilights in what seemed like another life.

Then came the morning when Mrs de Bellefort said, 'There is a tea dance this afternoon, Ellen, and I think you should come with us. Your illness has lasted quite long enough, it is time to emerge from your chrysalis. If anyone asks if you are better, answer them politely but don't embroider on your condition. I have merely told people that you were indisposed, something quite trifling.'

After she had gone Lisanne asked, 'What will you do if Major Klaus asks you to dance?'

'Dance with him, I suppose. I owe it to your mother and Aunt Julie.'

'You'll lose face, which will delight him.'

As it turned out, nobody asked me to dance. I thanked people for inquiring after my health, and I sat listening to the music while people danced on a tiny crowded floor. Lisanne, passing by in the arms of an officer, grinned wickedly in my direction.

I longed for the affair to be over, but there was one more humiliation in store. Just before the dance finished a party of German officers entered and stood at a long bar at the edge of the floor. My heart sank when I recognized Major Klaus, standing nonchalantly scanning the room, with one arm resting along the bar, the other holding a glass of wine. Across the room our eyes met and held, and next moment he was striding in our direction.

I thought I would suffocate. I was conscious of the warm red blood colouring my cheeks, but he passed me with never a look and went directly to Lisanne. He bowed in front of her and next moment she was in his arms and he was laughing down at her with obvious admiration.

Beside me I heard Mrs de Bellefort saying, 'I told you he would make you squirm if ever the opportunity presented itself, Ellen. I hope he considers his action this afternoon puts an end to the matter.'

'Are you happy to see him dancing with Lisanne?' I asked her sharply.

'No more happy than I was dancing with several of them this afternoon, but surely by this time you are beginning to learn something about survival, Ellen.'

'I'm learning a great deal, Mrs de Bellefort. Most of it makes me very sad.'

'We're all sad, Ellen. I feel the rest of my life might be sad, none of us is in a position to fight it.'

On the way home Aunt Julie said tremulously, 'Did Major Klaus say anything of any importance, Lisanne?'

'He said it was a pleasure to dance with me, that I danced very well, and he hoped I would give him the pleasure of dancing with me again. All terribly polite and stilted.'

'He didn't mention Ellen?'

'No. He was pointedly rude to Ellen.'

'It doesn't matter,' I muttered.

'He asked if we were attending the General's ball at the Sporting Club on Friday evening. I said I didn't know, and he said he would make sure we received invitations.'

The following day a messenger arrived with invitations for Lisanne, her mother and Aunt Julie. Noticeably there was no invitation for me and I saw Major Klaus's hand in this.

Shortly before they left for the ball Lisanne said, 'Do you fancy doing some sewing for me?'

'Yes of course, what is it you want?'

'I'm so sick of that white georgette dress. I hate those handkerchief things hanging from the skirt, they're so dated. Would you mind taking them off and doing something with the neckline?'

'I'll have a look at it. Personally I like the effect of those handkerchiefs, they're very graceful.'

'I'm fed up with them, Ellen, they shriek out how long I've had it. You'll find it in my wardrobe, be a dear and see what you can do.'

They left at last and I went to her room for the gown. The material was delicate. Every handkerchief was edged with one tiny drop diamante and the overall effect was charming, but I knew from experience that no power on earth would make Lisanne wear something she felt was dated.

I hunted high and low for a pair of scissors but finally had to go down to the kitchen where Marie handed me a large pair of kitchen scissors which I looked at in some dismay. They were hardly suitable for cutting delicate stitches but they might come in useful for trimming the hem.

I sat under a lamp in the salon. There was music on the radio and occasionally I could hear the distant rumble of thunder.

At shortly before ten o'clock I was surprised to hear a car driving up to the house. It was too early for them to be returning from Monte Carlo, and late for visitors. I heard the doorbell, and the feet of one of the servants crossing the hall, then Marie's startled face looked in on me. Before she could say a word Major Klaus pushed her aside and closed the door in her face.

I jumped to my feet but he didn't look at me. Instead he wandered round the room, picking up objects here and there, observing the pictures on the walls, leafing through magazines, taking up several gramophone records to look at the titles.

I could stand it no longer. 'If you want Lisanne,' I stammered, 'she has already left for the ball.'

'I know that, I sent the car for them.'

'Then why are you here?'

'I thought it would be nice to see you. Ve could perhaps dance in private since you appear not to vish to dance in public.'

'I'm sorry, I wasn't feeling well.'

'So you said. I didn't believe you. Vat vould you like to hear, a valse, a tango perhaps, vat are you best at?'

'This is ridiculous. I have said I'm sorry for what happened, surely that is enough.'

He slammed the records down and came to stand in front of me. His face was flushed and vindictive, his eyes so cold that I shrank back, afraid.

'Tell me,' he said, 'vat are you and the others doing here in the home of a Jewess?'

'Aunt Julie is French.'

'Ve know all about the Jewess, it is only a matter of time before ve have her.' His voice sank into a tone more infinitely menacing. 'Tonight, however, I intend to have you, Miss Ellen.'

Before I could gather my scattered wits he had me by the shoulders in a grip that made me cry out with pain. As I stepped backwards I fell over a footstool and he was on top of me, his hands tearing at my dress, and I was struggling with all my strength to push him away.

Suddenly as my hands flayed and thrashed about me they encountered the kitchen scissors lying on the floor, and with all my strength I plunged them into his back, not once but twice, and in that instant I saw surprised incredulity in his eyes. He was gasping and clutching at his back, and as I wriggled out from under him and stood unsteadily I saw that my hands were sticky with blood. I moved away, but obscenely he came after me, crawling on his knees, his hands clawing at his back, his eyes never leaving my face. Then one bloodstained hand reached out for me again and I ran towards the window. But still he came after me, crawling unsteadily like a crab.

312

I did not hear the door open, suddenly Jules was there, and taking in the situation at a glance he called out and a much younger man was in the room. I watched in horrified silence as he advanced towards the German kneeling on the floor, then he produced a thin shining length of wire which he threw round Klaus's neck. There was a horrible gurgling sound and his face became scarlet, his eyes protruding horribly before he fell forward. He lay with his head strangely twisted, the scissors still buried in his back.

I stared in horror at Jules and his companion, but by this time they were covering the body with a piece of sacking. Jules, looking up suddenly, said, 'Don't worry, Mademoiselle, he will be taken away. Only you and the servants are to know he was ever here, and they will say nothing.'

I stared at the younger man who by this time had bundled the body into the sacking and was busy tying it with ropes. He looked up with a grin, and incongruously I thought to myself that he was good-looking, but there was no fear or compassion in his dark smiling eyes.

'My son André,' Jules said. 'We saw the German enter the house and I knew immediately he was trouble. It is fortunate that André came to visit me tonight.'

The younger Frenchman picked the German up and slung him over his shoulder, then with another smile he said, 'Don't worry, Mademoiselle. Just remember you have not seen him, if they come asking. When they find his body they will not suspect you or my father.'

Jules left with his son and it was then I saw that Lisanne's dress was torn and stained with blood, and there was blood in a long heavy smear across the carpet. I was still looking at it when Jules came back into the room, taking in the situation at a glance.

'Don't worry,' he said gently, 'Marie will see to the carpet. The dress, I fear, is beyond redemption.'

'It is Lisanne's dress,' I murmured stupidly. 'She asked me to alter it.'

'You have not seen it, Mademoiselle. You looked for it and when you couldn't find it you sat for a while listening to music, you read a little, then you were tired and went to

313

your room. Mademoiselle Lisanne will be made to think she made a mistake, she must have left the dress in Paris.'

'But she told me it was hanging in her wardrobe, Jules.'

'Then she was mistaken, Mademoiselle. It was another white gown she saw and not that one at all.'

'Jules, what is your son doing here?'

'He is in the Resistance. There are pockets of them all over France. France is still at war, Mademoiselle, she will never be defeated. Now go to your room and rest, and in the morning you must pretend as you never pretended before.'

He took the dress from my helpless fingers, then Marie ushered me upstairs. No sooner was I there than Annette appeared with hot milk, turning down my bed while I scrubbed my skin clean in the bathroom.

'Drink your milk, Mademoiselle,' she counselled. 'Zere ees brandy in eet to 'elp you sleep.'

I slept like a log, and when I awoke I lay motionless for some time, my mind refusing to face the realities of the night before. Then suddenly I was wide awake, sitting up and trembling like a leaf, and all the trauma of the night before brought me the realization that I had been capable of murder in the cause of self-preservation. How could I hide it, how could I go downstairs and join the others with a bland face and lies on my lips? How could I ever go into the salon without seeing Major Klaus crawling after me, reaching for the scissors I had plunged into his back?

After a brief good morning nobody paid much attention to me. They were talking about the ball, the gowns of the women, the gossip of the moment. Then Lisanne said, 'Did you manage to do anything with the dress, Ellen?'

I gulped nervously. 'I looked for it but I couldn't find it, Lisanne.'

'But it's there in the corner of my wardrobe. I'd have got it out for you but I was sure you'd find it for yourself.'

'I looked, but I couldn't see it.'

'Oh really, Ellen. After breakfast we'll go and look for it together, it was probably staring you in the face.'

Aunt Julie was saying, 'Did the General send the car for us, Delia?'

'Why no, apparently Major Klaus sent it, but it was strange that he didn't come to the ball.'

'He said he would be there,' Lisanne said sharply. 'He asked me to have the supper dance with him, and in view of Ellen's behaviour I promised I would.'

'Oh well, he was probably busy elsewhere. We shall see him again, I have no doubt, he seems to have formed an attachment to us,' her mother said dryly.

Immediately breakfast was over Lisanne invited me into her room.

'Now I'll show you where to find the dress, Ellen. I hope you can do something with it so that I can wear it. I'm so tired of my wardrobe.'

She flung open the doors, disclosing several evening gowns including two white ones. I watched her hand moving along the rail, her frown becoming deeper, and at last she faced me with a look of incredulity.

'I could have sworn I saw it hanging there yesterday, I could see those ridiculous handkerchiefs.'

'You must have been mistaken, Lisanne. Are you quite sure you didn't leave it in Paris?'

'Well of course I'm sure. And the servants wouldn't take it, neither of them has the figure for it anyway. You haven't borrowed it, have you, Ellen?'

'Well of course not. For one thing I wouldn't borrow anything of yours without telling you, and for another I'd know where to find it, wouldn't I?'

I was amazed at how glibly the lies were forming on my tongue as once more she searched the wardrobe before going through the drawers in her dressing table. At last she straightened up, saying, 'Then I must have left it in Paris. Oh well, I didn't like the thing, I don't suppose it's any loss.'

When I was alone I breathed a sigh of relief. It had been too easy, I couldn't believe that I had got away with it. But there was one more moment of anxiety in store.

That evening we went into the salon after dinner and

immediately my eyes were drawn to the faint stain on the pale carpet which all of Marie's ministrations had been unable to remove. Aunt Julie noticed at once.

'I wonder what's been spilled on the carpet?' she said in some annoyance. 'It looks as if it's been scrubbed, the pile is rough.'

She pulled the bellrope near the mantelpiece and almost immediately Jules came in answer.

'There's a stain on the carpet, Jules. Do you know how it got there?' she said.

He gave the carpet some attention, then straightening up he said calmly, 'I'll ask the servants, Madam. One of them will know.'

'It has obviously been scrubbed.'

'Yes, Madame, it would appear so. I will ask them now.'

In a little while he was back. 'Annette said there was a soiled mark on the carpet from someone's shoe, something brought in from outside, she thought. She has tried to remove it, and will try again when it is thoroughly dry.'

'Really, I would have preferred to have had it done professionally. This is a very valuable Chinese carpet which needs special treatment. Telephone Le Bourget's, they will send somebody out to look at it.'

His face inscrutable, Jules bowed and left the room, while I sat trembling, thinking that the man from Le Bourget's would know immediately what had caused the stain.

He came the following morning. Jules brought him into the salon while we were reading the morning papers, and immediately he went to the stain and bent down to examine it.

Over his head my eyes met Jules', and he smiled, allaying my fears.

'What is it?' Aunt Julie asked the carpet cleaner curiously.

'Probably moss from the garden, Madame. It is always difficult to remove, and this carpet has a very deep pile. On any other carpet the stain would not be so pronounced.'

'Can you remove it?'

'Oh, I expect so. Perhaps you would go into another

room, ladies, there will probably be fumes from the cleaner I intend to use.'

We all rose immediately and trooped into the morning room. In a little while Jules appeared to tell us the stain had been removed and the firm of Le Bourget would send their account.

Later I asked Jules if the man had not known that the stain had been blood.

'He knew of course, Mademoiselle. He asked no questions and I gave him no explanation.'

'Will he say anything if Major Klaus's body is discovered?'

'He will say nothing, Mademoiselle, he is a good Frenchman.'

His answer, delivered so calmly and so staunchly, helped considerably to ease my troubled mind.

That night after I had put out the light in my bedroom I pulled back the curtains and looked out into the garden. It was then I saw Jules and his son standing in the shadows deep in conversation. They talked for a long time. I could not hear their voices but I could see that their talk was earnest, then at last they embraced and Jules walked back to the house alone. Again I became afraid. Had Major Klaus's body been discovered and were the German authorities already searching for his killers?

The following morning I saw Jules working in the garden and immediately I joined him there, my eyes searching his anxiously until he smiled.

'The Germans have enough to occupy their minds this morning, Mademoiselle. There is heavy fighting in the north, it would seem they are being repelled on all fronts.'

'Oh Jules, I'm glad. Is there no news about Major Klaus's body?'

'We shall know as soon as he is found, in the meantime I suggest you learn to be a little happy at the good news I have given you. I do not need to ask you to keep it to yourself.'

'No, of course not. What happened to Lisanne's dress?'

'Marie burnt it. It was a pity, such a beautiful dress. Mademoiselle Lisanne accepted that you could not find it?'

'Yes. I hated lying to her, it made her doubt her memory.'

'Ah well, Mademoiselle's memory is ever elusive. She is a young lady who only remembers the things she wants to remember. She will soon forget about the dress, you will see.'

CHAPTER 31

The German Kommandant returned to the house the following week, bringing with him two Gestapo officers, who were infinitely more sinister and with none of his urbanity.

We were assembled in the salon and seated in a row facing the questioners, who began with Lisanne.

'I believe Major Klaus is vell known to you, Fräulein. Did you not have an appointment to meet him at the General's ball?'

'No. He asked me to save the supper dance for him and he sent a car for my mother, my aunt and myself.'

'Did you not think it strange that Major Klaus failed to keep his appointment?'

'No, I merely thought he was engaged elsewhere.'

'Did it not surprise you that your friend Fräulein Ellen vas not included in the invitation?'

'Not really. Ellen had been ill.'

'Indeed. And yet she found energy to work in the garden, hardly an occupation for an ailing young woman.'

Lisanne didn't speak and I could feel my heart fluttering while beside me Aunt Julie's face was pale and I could smell her fear.

'And on the night of the ball, Fräulein Ellen, perhaps you had a visit from Major Klaus?'

'There was no need for Major Klaus to come here when he had arranged to meet my friend at the ball. Why should he?'

'It has been told to me that you were impolite to Major Klaus previous to that evening. It could be that he intended to teach you your manners while the rest of the household was elsewhere.'

I felt everybody staring at me, and heard Aunt Julie catch her breath nervously. I made myself stare at him in surprise without answering, and in a more cajoling voice he continued, 'Come now, Fräulein, Major Klaus vas interested in you before ever he became aware of your friend. Vat vas more natrual than to send a car for the others to get them out of the vay and then make it his business to see you? Vat happened between you on that evening?'

'Nothing happened, I have told you, I read for a little while and went to bed early. I did not hear what time they came in from the ball.'

'So you slept vell that night, Fräulein, and with a good conscience?'

'Why shouldn't I?'

'Vat if I vas to tell you that Major Klaus's car vas seen climbing the hill outside this villa not long after these other ladies left the house?'

'There are a great many villas along this road, why should you think he was coming here?'

'Because of vat ve know of the Major himself. His reputation for retribution upon those who have offended him. Major Klaus vas not the man to forget or forgive an insult. And you, Fräulein, insulted him before a roomful of brother officers. Vat time did he leave here?'

'He was never here. Why don't you ask the servants? They would know if he was here.'

'I have every intention of asking the servants but before I do I should tell you that Major Klaus's body was discovered yesterday morning on the hillside above Gagnes. He had been strangled, but vat vas more surprising, he had also been stabbed in the back. The vound in his back vould not have killed him, so obviously some other person had to make sure that he died. You had an accomplice, Fräulein?'

For the first time Mrs de Bellefort spoke, calmly and contemptuously.

'Really, Herr Kommandant, must we listen to these wild accusations? Everything in this house was perfectly normal when we returned from Monte Carlo, and again the next morning. If such a thing had occurred Ellen would never have been able to keep it from me, she would have been terrified, and the mere idea of Major Klaus coming here to intimidate a young girl is nauseating.'

'We must explore every avenue, act upon every piece of information – and the information ve have received does not absolve this house. Now, Madame le Mauriac, I vish to question your servants.'

'Lisanne will bring them here, Sir.'

'My officer vill bring them here, Madame. I vish them to receive no promptings or varnings.'

Minutes later the three servants stood with us before the officers. Marie looked down stolidly at her shoes, but Jules and Annette faced the Germans with straight eyes, unperturbed.

The officer leading the questioning addressed himself to Jules. 'You remember the night of the ball in Monte Carlo?' he asked, watching him keenly.

'I remember it well, Sir.'

'Vy particularly?'

'It was a stormy night. I had to Lold an umbrella for Madame and her guests as they got into the car.'

'Is that all you remember about that night?'

'Only that Mademoiselle Ellen did not go with them.'

'And vhen they had left for Monte Carlo, some time later you had a visit from Major Klaus.'

'No sir, we had no visitors that night.'

'And Fräulein Ellen, vat did she do?'

'She sat in the salon here and I know she went to bed early.'

'How do you know?'

'Mademoiselle Ellen had not been well. Annette took hot milk to her room after she had retired.'

'Vat time?' he snapped, addressing Annette.

'Soon after ten sir,' she answered.

'Vat makes you so sure?'

'I'm not sure, Sir, I only think it was soon after ten. It was not long after they left for Monte Carlo.'

'You did not think that it vas strange she retired so early?'

'No, Sir, she had not been . . .'

'I know, I know, she had not been vell. Do you ever hear from your son, old man? Many of the men who served in the French army returned by devious means to their homes and are even now in the Resistance. Is your son one of them?'

'I do not know where my son is. I have had no news of him since the morning he left Provence. I would give everything I have to know where he is and to know that somewhere he is safe.'

The Kommandant's eyes moved over each one of us in turn, and at last he said coldly, 'There is to be a curfew. Nobody vill be allowed on the streets after dusk and there vill be no calls on friends or neighbours, no visits to other places in the area. You vill stay close to the villa and you vill receive no visitors. These restrictions vill extend until ve have Major Klaus's killer. And Madame le Mauriac, I should tell you that ve have found discrepancies in your passport. One day soon ve shall vish to see you for questioning.'

'But why?' Aunt Julie stammered. 'What discrepancies? My passport is in order.'

'It is not relevant to vhy I am here this morning. Ve shall come here again.'

In a body they rose to their feet, clicked their heels, and raised their right arms, said 'Heil Hitler' and departed.

Aunt Julie left the room in tears, with the others endeavouring to comfort her. Jules turned to me, saying, 'Mademoiselle, you will lie and lie to save all our skins. They must learn nothing otherwise many brave men will die, my son among them. Do you understand?'

'Yes I do. They will learn nothing from me.'

He smiled and clasped my hands in his.

'You must be brave, Mademoiselle, and you must have faith. These dark days will not last for ever. Europe is awake and fighting back. One day, perhaps sooner than we think, real freedom will be ours, and not this shameful travesty of freedom we have today.'

For weeks we were prisoners in the house and gardens, with a German soldier posted at the gates. Once a week Jules was allowed out to obtain groceries, and I felt rather more comfortable when he arrived home to say we were not the only house under surveillance.

From the terrace we could see German soldiers marching in columns along the roads, clambering down towards the harbours, or combing the hills.

The inactivity bothered Lisanne the most. Never a reader, she spent most of the morning lying in the hammock and the rest of the day going through her wardrobe again and again to look for clothes in need of alteration, a task which kept me busy when I was not helping Jules in the garden.

We worked together in silence, aware of the eyes of the soldier peering at us through the gates, occasionally served cups of coffee by Marie – who adamantly refused to take coffee to the soldier.

All Mrs de Bellefort's persuasions failed and in the end it was Lisanne who took coffee out to him. Jules said, 'Marie is a peasant. All she understands is that the Germans are keeping us prisoners in our own house.'

Mrs de Bellefort played endless games of patience while Aunt Julie read, but there were entire evenings when she sat staring into space without turning a page. It was a game of cat and mouse until the morning the Kommandant returned to tell us a man had been taken and would be shot.

I saw the colour drain out of Jules' face but it was Mrs de Bellefort who asked, 'Who is he, a local man?'

'Yes, Madame, a local man,' he replied, 'Armand Rochefort.'

'But you must be mistaken,' Aunt Julie cried, 'Armand Rochefort would not be capable of killing anyone. He is an old man, a good kind old man.'

'Nevertheless, Madame, the death of a German officer must be avenged. Ve have not got the man who killed him, therefore ve must take the life of a man of Provence. It is a warning to the men who killed Klaus. For the life of every German some man of Provence will forfeit his own. It is justice, Madame.'

'It is not justice,' I found myself crying, 'it is murder. This poor man had nothing to do with Major Klaus's death.'

'Then perhaps, Fräulein, you vill tell me who had. It is not too late to save his life.'

'I don't know, how could I know?'

He bowed, a cynical inclination of his head. I became aware of Jules' eyes fixed on me in desperate appeal and I was sure he had been afraid I would tell the Kommandant all I knew.

Instead I cried, 'Oh, this is a terrible war when innocent people have to die.'

Aunt Julie wept, 'Oh, that poor old man, always so kind, so much loved by everybody.'

The Kommandant faced us sternly. 'Exactly, madame. If ve had taken a vagrant, a man who was not loved, it vould hardly have mattered. But if ve take a man who is esteemed, loved you call it, that might be a lesson the men who killed Klaus would not forget. They vill think twice before they take another German life. Now, the curfew has been lifted, and you may now take up your life as previously. The sentry will be removed from your gate.'

Later that afternoon Jules found me in the summerhouse in tears. It was all my fault that Armand Rochefort must die, my fault that Major Klaus was dead. Why oh why hadn't I swallowed my pride and danced with the man?

I sobbed out my remorse with the tears rolling down my cheeks and Jules listened to me calmly, allowing me the luxury of self-pity, self-recrimination. Then he said gently, 'Mademoiselle, it is not your fault that you are caught up in a war that has made victims of us all. It is not your fault that Klaus behaved like a monster or that my son killed him. He would have killed the German on the mountainside, in the streets, wherever they had come face to face.

'Come, you must dry your eyes. They must not see you so distressed or they will ask questions and you may reveal more than you intend. We must protect poor Madame le Mauriac. They are playing with her like a cat plays with a mouse before he kills it. I fear for that good lady, she is very afraid.'

Those words calmed me as nothing else had done, and by the time I returned to the house I was composed.

Life took up its pattern, but it was more subdued than before. We learned that the General had left Provence and were told that he had a more important role to play in the north. Consequently, without her escort Mrs de Bellefort stayed away from the casino and other establishments, and I for one was glad. In those days it seemed Lisanne and I grew closer as we roamed the countryside while the slow leisurely pace of Provence entered my soul, ridding it of much of the bitterness accumulated over the years of war.

It was a world remote from war-torn Europe, but whenver Jules brought news I rejoiced at the victories of the Allies and cried at their losses.

Aunt Julie was like a cat on hot cinders. She jumped when the telephone or doorbell rang, she grew thin and nervous in spite of all our attempts to console her. And my admiration for Lisanne's mother grew.

I felt old Lady de Bellefort would now have approved of her daughter-in-law. She, more than any of us, remained calm, showing to the world an indifference, a stoicism nothing could shake, and more and more I modelled myself on her while her own daughter became petulant and desperate for entertainment.

'Why can't we go to the casino?' Lisanne complained. 'Women do go there on their own.'

'I prefer to go with an escort,' her mother replied. 'The German general was charming and entertaining, I have no wish to go anywhere with any of the others.'

'Do you suppose Emerald is still singing at the nightclub?' I asked, for I had neither seen Kitty nor had news of her for weeks.

'Apparently so,' Mrs de Bellefort said, 'She is the toast of the Côte d'Azur. The Germans love her, they entertain her and send her flowers. She is now to be seen at the casino wearing fabulous jewels and expensive furs. And not only with the Germans. It is rumoured there are several Arab princes buzzing like flies around the honeypot. She is obviously a girl on the make, delighted with her success and eager to extract every last ounce of profit and pleasure from it.'

How could I argue with her? I knew it to be true, but

Mrs de Bellefort knew nothing about the poverty and hardship that had prompted it.

Only days later I was shopping in Antibes when a German staff car was briefly stopped by oncoming traffic. Kitty sat in the back with a German officer. She was beautifully gowned in black, with a small black hat trimmed with osprey feathers, and silver fox furs round her neck. She was throwing coins to the children clustering round the car. She didn't see me, nor, later, the looks of contempt on the faces of the villagers as they forced the children to part with the coins, which were promptly thrown over the hillside.

Several days later it was a very different Kitty I saw in earnest conversation with a young Frenchman near the harbour. This Kitty wore a trenchcoat and had a scarf tied over her head. There was nothing the least flamboyant about her, she might have been any village girl meeting her lover. But this man was not her lover, their conversation was too intense.

I turned away and had almost reached the harbour when I heard my name called, and saw Kitty running lightly down the steps.

She had taken off the scarf and her hair flamed wildly about her vital gamin face. She was smiling, greeting me as if we had met the day before. 'I thought it was you, Ellen. Are you alone?'

'Yes. I saw you talking to a man, Kitty, I didn't want to interfere.'

'Oh he's just some man who comes to the club. An acquaintance, that's all.'

Afterwards I wondered why I didn't believe her, but almost immediately she was saying, 'You've never been back to the club, Ellen. Didn't you enjoy my performance?'

'Yes of course I did, we all did, but there was some trouble afterwards, it's all been pretty terrible.'

'You refused to dance with Major Klaus, I heard about it.'

'It was a silly thing to do, I should have danced with him and forgotten about it. I'm beginning to realize that one can't afford to be noble or cling too closely to old values.'

'And didn't I spend most of mi youth tellin' you that, Ellen Adair?'

How easily the Irish came back into her speech, but next moment she was saying, 'You know of course that the Major was murdered?'

'Yes. We had a sentry posted at the gate for weeks. Why they think we had anything to do with it I can't imagine.'

I was watching her carefully, choosing my words, and incredibly I didn't trust her. I couldn't reconcile the Kitty I had seen throwing coins from a German staff car with the girl I had just seen with the young Frenchman.

'You know that they intend to execute one of the men living in Antibes, I suppose?' she said casually.

'Yes. A man who had nothing to do with the Major's death, a good, kind old man. It is terrible.'

'But expected. They have to make very sure that the French know who are the masters here. I'm very much afraid there may be more killings before that lesson is learned.'

'Whose side are you on, Kitty? Surely you can't approve of the killing of an innocent man.'

'I'm not on anybody's side, Ellen. I'm Emerald the singer, nothing more. I have my living to earn and I'm doing it in the best way I know.'

'So it doesn't really bother you, all the cruelty and persecution of people like Aunt Julie and many of her friends who have been sent away and not heard of again?'

'If it bothers me, what can I do about it?'

My bitterness must have shown in my face because next moment she said lightly, 'What are you going to do when the war's over, Ellen?'

'I don't know, I don't see how any of us can know.'

'Could you live in an England under German rule?'

I stared at her in horror. 'How can you even think such a thing?' I said angrily. 'Germany isn't going to win this war, it's unthinkable.'

'Why not? She's already defeated most of Europe. We have to face facts, Ellen, you must see that.'

'I don't believe it can happen. Germany can't win the war.'

'Why are you so sure? What do you know that I don't?'

Once more I was wary. In my indignation had I said too much? She was watching me closely with a half smile on her lips, and I was quick to say, 'I don't know anything, how could I? But I don't believe England will be defeated, nothing will make me believe that.'

'One hears rumours, of course,' she said. 'We'll hear nothing from the Germans but there are pockets of resistance everywhere. I suppose news trickles through from them.'

'We get to hear nothing at the villa, and none of Aunt Julie's friends seem to know anything,' I replied, then looking at my watch I exclaimed, 'Gracious, Kitty, it's late, they'll be wondering where I've got to.'

'Do they monitor your hours then?'

'Well of course not, but life here is difficult. I don't suppose Armand Rochefort expected to be plucked off the street for a murder he didn't commit.'

'They're not very likely to do that to you, Ellen.'

'They questioned me at the villa and more or less accused me of his murder.'

She laughed. 'I can't see you murdering anybody, Ellen. If I hear they've accused you again I'll use whatever influence I have to tell them they're barking up the wrong tree.'

I looked at her sharply to find her eyes filled with a strange cynical humour before I turned away. 'Are you walking back with me, Kitty?' I asked.

'No, I'm staying down here for a little while. I like the cafe across from the harbour.'

She smiled, then digging her hands in the pockets of her trenchcoat she set off towards the harbour while I climbed up towards the town.

The road wound round the hillside and for a time the harbour was obscured from view. When I reached the top of the hill I paused to look down. Kitty stood at the harbour wall looking out across the forest of masts and then I saw a man crossing the square towards her. I thought it was the same man I had seen her talking to earlier, and as he reached her side she turned and together they walked towards the cafe.

As I reached the road I saw that I was not the only person to be interested. A German officer accompanied by two soldiers was standing looking over the wall, and in spite of the warm sunshine I shivered at the menace in his cold scrutiny.

I was dreading the evening before me, watching Mrs de Bellefort playing endless games of patience, Lisanne's restlessness and Aunt Julie's fears, but the atmosphere of gloom had vanished and I was met in the hall by Aunt Julie brandishing a letter, her face registering a happiness I hadn't seen for ages.

'Isn't this marvellous, Ellen? We have received invitations to the opera, just when we thought everything was going to be so terrible.'

'The opera!' I echoed stupidly.

'*Madama Butterfly*. The new German general is inviting a great many people to attend in aid of charity. It will be heavenly to sit in the opera house and listen to glorious music again. Singers from La Scala in Milan, it says. Don't you just love *Butterfly*?'

'I've never been to the opera. I love music and I've heard arias from *Butterfly*, but seeing it performed will be a new experience for me.'

'You'll love it, Ellen. How strange never to have seen an opera.'

The following day the new German general paid us a visit. He was a small, slender man with a toothy smile, overly polite, and I disliked him intensely: his narrow hooded eyes which seemed to be appraising us, the smile which never reached his eyes. He made quite a ceremony of kissing our hands in turn before he departed.

Apparently my dislike was shared by Mrs de Bellefort, who said dryly, 'He had a smile like that on the face of the tiger. Against all my better judgement I quite liked his predecessor, but I don't trust this man.'

'That's most unfair, Delia,' Aunt Julie argued. 'He's trying to be nice, he's invited us to the opera and he's paid us a social call. One can't really go by appearances.'

'Oh well, I suppose we should give him the benefit of the doubt, but I've always been pretty good at sizing people up.'

Never in my life had I expected to be involved in quite such a glittering occasion. Aunt Julie and Mrs de Bellefort were greeting friends and neighbours on either side and I stared in admiration at the jewels worn by the women – in their ears, round their throats and on their hair. It was like something out of a fairytale.

Lisanne whispered, 'Ellen, your eyes are popping. Do try to look as though you're accustomed to moving in such exalted circles.'

'But I'm not,' I hissed. 'Who are they all?'

'Germans, Italians and a sprinkling of French. I suppose we're the only English here, and sticking out like sore thumbs.'

It was an experience I would remember all my life. I would tell my grandchildren how once I had sat on a red plush seat in a box adorned with flowers watching the stalls being slowly filled by exquisitely gowned women and men in impeccable uniform.

Suddenly my reverie was shaken by Lisanne hissing, 'Up there, Ellen, in the box opposite.'

I looked across and my heart missed a beat. Kitty had swept into the box wearing an emerald gown. Her red hair was lifted on top of her head and adorned with white gardenias. She wore long emerald earrings, and as she took her seat she removed her ermine stole to reveal a stunning décolletage.

She was in the company of two high-ranking German officers who appeared to be vying for her attention.

Mrs de Bellefort observed, 'It appears the invitations have encompassed a varying selection of society. Isn't that the singer from the nightclub?'

Across the vast glittering space for a moment our eyes

met but Kitty was so far away I could not read her expression, and after the slightest inclination of her head in our direction she turned away to speak to her companions.

After that I forgot Kitty and everything else in the beauty of the music, the glorious voices of the singers as Puccini's exquisite melodies flooded the night with joy and pathos telling the bittersweet story of a love affair that turned sour and ended in tragedy.

It was over at last, the most exciting night of my life, and as we drifted out into the scented darkness, people were exchanging their thoughts on the performance, friends promising to meet soon, and none of them prepared for the nightmare to come.

Before the opera house stood a group of men in Gestapo uniform, watching the descending audience with more than a passing interest. In turn they stepped forward to address some man or woman on the steps, then to our horror one of them approached us.

He bowed to Aunt Julie, and in a cold officious voice said, 'Madame le Mauriac, I must ask you to accompany me.'

I could smell the fear that erupted all around us as women cried out in terror, clutching the arms of the men who were being taken, or in other cases refusing to be parted. Aunt Julie stood pale and shaken while Mrs de Bellefort said icily, 'Why must she go with you? Surely you can come to the villa?'

'It is not your concern, Madame,' he answered her. 'Kindly do not interfere.'

'Then I must go with her. Can't you see that she is very frightened?'

'You can not go with her, she must come alone.'

'But how long will you keep her, when will she be able to return home?'

'I do not know Madame, ve are taking them to Avignon for questioning.'

'Avignon!'

'To headquarters, Madame, now please stand aside. You, Madame le Mauriac, come vith me.'

331

We watched helplessly as about a dozen men and women were bundled into cars and driven off into the night.

From all around we were jostled by the crowds as we made our way to our car. At one time we were separated and as I looked around me wildly I found my arm taken in a fierce grip and I was staring into Kitty's jade-green eyes.

'I saw what happened,' she whispered urgently, 'I'll see what I can do to get news of her.'

Next second she was gone and the last I saw of her was a fleeting glimpse of bright red hair over an ermine wrap as she stepped into a long black car.

Mrs de Bellefort broke the news to the servants. The two women left the room in tears while Jules stood with bent head and clenched hands.

'Go about your duties as normally as possible,' Mrs de Bellefort advised him. 'I fear we shall be watched during the next few days.'

'I told them she was innocent of any crime,' Jules answered her savagely, 'I said that she was a kind good lady who had lived in Provence for many years. She was happy here, happier than she ever was in Paris, and those other people they have taken tonight were her friends. I knew when they came here after you had left for the opera that something terrible would happen.'

'They were here, Jules?'

'They tore everything out of her desk. Some papers they threw about the bedroom, others they pocketed.'

'But what sort of things?'

'Letters, photographs, business papers. They knew exactly what they were looking for. They will not let her return, Madame. God knows what will happen to her.'

There were no outward signs that we were prisoners in the house, no sentry at the gates, yet I had the distinct feeling that we were under observation and Lisanne's mother was sure the telephone was being tapped.

Jules shopped for groceries and we sat in the garden overlooking the exquisite coastline until I felt I knew every blade of grass. Once in the distance we heard what seemed to be thunder until Jules said it was gunfire. We stood with eyes straining out to sea until the sky turned from brightest blue into mauve and shooting flames.

Weeks passed and Aunt Julie did not return. We saw nothing of our neighbours, and any information we had came from Jules after one of his shopping trips.

None of the people taken had returned to their homes. The towns were quiet and there seemed not to be so many Germans in evidence.

'Either they have been taken for service elsewhere or they have been ordered to keep a low profile,' Jules said quietly.

That afternoon I decided to walk down to the harbour. For one thing I ached to get away from the house and for the other I hoped I might see Kitty since she had not been in touch with me.

I strolled down to the cafe near the harbour and sat at one of the small tables drinking coffee. The bartender eyed me curiously while in the harbour a tiny boat darted between the large yachts which had been anchored there since the start of hostilities.

Disconsolately I paid the man and wandered across to sit on the harbour wall.

I had the strangest impression of being watched. I could feel the hairs in my neck prickling, and as unconcerned as I knew how I sauntered across the square. The barman was sitting at a table under the awning but he paid no attention to me and I reached the steps and started to climb up to the town.

It was so silent, so dark in the narrow streets, and my footsteps seemed to echo hollowly on the old cobbles. I was frightened. I had reached a junction in the road when I felt my arm suddenly taken in a firm grip and I was pulled into a shop doorway. Gasping with terror, I looked up into the smiling face of the man I had seen talking to Kitty in this very road weeks before.

'Do not be frightened, Mademoiselle,' he whispered, 'I am not going to 'arm you. I 'ave a message for you from Mademoiselle Emerald. Eet is to do with Madame le Mauriac, you understand?'

I nodded mutely.

'She 'as been taken from Avignon with ze ozers, possibly to some prison camp in the north, or even in Germany. Zat ees all we'ave been able to discover.'

'Why didn't Kitty come to tell me this herself?'

He smiled. 'Mademoiselle Emerald has zere confidence, why jeopardize eet for a woman who is already doomed? Eet was not safe to telephone you. Eet is not safe for us to be seen talking together, I can tell you no more. Now go quickly, Mademoiselle, and I will wait a leetle while until I move out into the street.'

Still I was staring at him fascinated, then in some anger I said, 'Why do you say Madame le Mauraic is doomed, what will they do to her?'

'Go now, Mademoiselle, go while eet ees safe.'

He gave me a little push which sent me out on to the cobbles, and I had no choice but to turn away and climb up to the town.

One thing in our encounter had given me hope: that Kitty seemed to be playing a double game. She had the confidence of the Germans and, it seemed, of the man I had just met. I felt sure he was involved with the Resistance. It was the one good thing in all the hopeless sorry business of Aunt Julie that gave me renewed faith.

When I told Mrs de Bellefort what I had heard, without mentioning Kitty's name she said sharply, 'But why should this young man be concerned about Julie? Who was he?'

'I have no idea. He only said they had taken her away from Avignon.'

Jules said quietly, 'The man is obviously a member of the Resistance, Madame, he knew we would be anxious about the mistress.'

'There are times, Jules, when I suspect you know more than you are telling me,' she replied. 'One feels so helpless, it is wrong that we are living here in Julie's house when she is heaven knows where, and probably suffering terrible hardship.'

'Nay, Madame,' he murmured, 'I only know what my eyes and ears tell me. The Germans are only maintaining a small garrison here now, they are up in the north fighting

334

the Allies, and perhaps for the first time they are losing. Why else would they send their soldiers away? I tell you Madame, my ears and eyes tell me all I need to know.'

They made their presence felt in the next months, those few men who had been left in Provence to prove that Germany was still our master. If the Resistance was more active the revenge was more terrible.

Men, women and children were taken and shot in the streets in front of their families, but it was the last desperate defiance of a nation facing defeat. The news came pouring into Provence, in spite of the curfews and the tapped telephone wires, in spite of the radio news fed to us by a defeated and degenerate government. Paris had been liberated, one by one the countries of Europe were being freed as the victorious Allies swept onward, and soon in Provence we were dancing in the streets, the Tricolour was being hoisted once more over public buildings and to shouts of derision and hysterical glee Swastika flags were being ceremoniously burnt at every street corner.

Lisanne threw her arms around me in an ecstasy of weeping. 'We're free, Ellen, free to go home, free to go to Langstone. I never thought I'd ever long to see those dark Pennine hills again or hear Granny de Bellefort telling me what I should or shouldn't do.'

It was a thought that sobered me up as nothing during the last few days had done. Langstone Priory was not my home. It belonged to Lance and his wife Geraldine, it belonged to that implacable imperious old woman who had shaped my life as indomitably as she had shaped the lives of her own kith and kin. Now they were talking of going home and I had no home to go to.

'We can't go home yet,' her mother said sternly. 'We have to find out what has happened to Julie. Just be patient, Lisanne, and in the meantime try to enjoy Provence which is slowly coming back to life, back to how she used to be.'

So day by day and hour by hour we got back on the merry-go-round, but a very different merry-go-round it was. Now people's faces were lighter, their smiles more meaningful. It was like the sudden golden shining of the sun through clouds of rain.

The authorities were desperately trying to find the people who had been taken from their homes but they were experiencing acute difficulties. Documents and papers had been destroyed as the Germans were pushed back, and although we were aware of the atrocities that had been committed against the Jews in the prison camps in the north we could not believe that Aunt Julie had suffered a like fate.

Not Aunt Julie with her fashionable clothes and gay lively wit, her childlike assumption that life was for living, sometimes extravagantly, but whose warm heart had always been the first to give where it was most needed.

It seemed incredible that those people should have disappeared into thin air after the opera. Then Jules came with the incredible news that one by one they had been shot on the outskirts of Auxerre when it became plain that Germany would lose the war.

We wept inconsolably for Aunt Julie and I realized that I too had loved her. Together we helped Lisanne's mother to sort out her belongings. The servants were asked to choose what they wanted from the house and I was surprised at the things they took: ordinary everyday things from the kitchens. A brass cooking pot or a geranium from the kitchen window. A favourite pair of embroidery scissors or a lace-edged handkerchief. In the end Mrs de Bellefort handed out items of furniture and other household effects.

'What are we to do about the house?' Lisanne asked curiously.

'The lawyers will decide that. Possibly they may find a copy of her will, or even her husband's will. Jules will stay on here for the time being. I suppose eventually he will go to live with one of his children.'

'When are we leaving for England, then?'

'I am going to telephone Langstone this evening, it's possible now to do that. After I've spoken to them we can start to make plans.'

Lisanne was impatient while her mother telephoned Langstone from the study.

'I just hope we can shop in London. Granny will insist on my marriage taking place as quickly as possible and she'll want it at Langstone, I'm sure,' she said airily. 'We shall need some money, most of what we brought here has gone. I don't suppose you have much left, Ellen?'

'No.'

'Oh well, Granny will see you don't go short. You'll be coming to Langstone with us, I suppose.'

'I shouldn't think so. There'll be nothing for me there.'

'Well I hadn't actually thought you'd be leaving us, but I suppose you're right. I'll be going to live in Ireland and I shan't need a companion when I have a husband.'

'No.'

'Oh well, something will turn up for you, Ellen. After all you're an accomplished lady now. You speak French and you're very pretty. That alone should secure a husband for you, hopefully a rich one.'

Lisanne seemed to think life at Langstone would be as she remembered it in spite of the years of war, and I don't suppose it had even entered her head that her husband to be might not have survived it.

Her mother's face was thoughtful when the returned to us. 'Fortunately Lance was there,' she began. 'He still hasn't got his release from the army but he is stationed nearby so was visiting the Priory. Your grandmother's health is failing and she has cataracts on both eyes, so she doesn't see very well.

'Geraldine is expecting her first baby in a week or so, and it all sounds too dismal for words. Most of the servants at Langstone have been either in the services or on war work and only a few of them have trickled back, indeed Lance has suggested that we stay anywhere except Langstone in the immediate future.'

Lisanne looked at her in dismay. 'But what about my marriage? Hasn't Grandmother anything to say in all this?'

'Lance will break the news to her that we are safe and living in Provence. I don't suppose she's too infirm to dictate policy, but we shall have to wait a while.'

'How about money?' Lisanne demanded.

'I told Lance that money was in short supply and he promised that something would be done immediately on that score. Oh, I'm sure when your grandmother is told she'll give instructions regarding our future. She's never failed before.'

So for several weeks we waited in Provence. Many of the wealthy people who had yachts in the harbour returned to claim them, and day by day life along that fabulous coast recovered its gaiety.

Lance kept his word to send money but I felt I was living on charity. There was none for me so I had to depend on Mrs de Bellefort's generosity. Entertainment however was there in plenty. I was included in any invitations that came our way and there were a great many of them – dining out, sailing, the opera and the theatre. But it was an empty existence. Then the letter arrived from Yorkshire.

My heart missed a beat when I recognized the crest on the pale parchment envelope and Lisanne too leaned forward eagerly while her mother slit the envelope.

'It's from your grandmother,' she announced. 'It isn't her writing, she's probably dictated it.'

She read it through without another word, and unable to bear it any longer Lisanne cried, 'Mother, what does she say?'

'She says she is pleased that we are safe and well, that she was very disappointed that we didn't return directly home to England from Paris before the war, and we will be pleased to hear that both Lance and Gervase returned safely.

'She was hoping your marriage could take place from Langstone but now she doesn't think it will be possible. She herself will not be well enough to attend and Gervase is reluctant to leave his estate in Ireland because he is too busy. His father died during the war and Gervase arrived home to be faced with a great deal of work. She suggests your marriage takes place quietly in Ireland and no doubt you will be able to visit Langstone at some later date when things are back to normal. I'm afraid my mother-in-law doesn't mention you, Ellen.'

338

Lisanne stormed and raged. She would not marry Gervase in Ireland. She would marry him at Langstone or not at all, and nothing, absolutely nothing would make her change her mind.

Mrs de Bellefort eyed her with cynical impatience, and I knew that none of Lisanne's wishes would count. The tirade would end, her mother would talk to her logically and earnestly, and the outcome would be that she would go to Ireland to marry her cousin on his terms and her grandmother's. As for me I was living in limbo. My future was shrouded in uncertainty, and while the life and entertainment went on around me I felt I was floating on a cold and hostile sea.

As I had known, Lisanne accepted her grandmother's wishes, but with poor grace. She began to look for her trousseau in shops that were rapidly becoming exclusive, and one day she surprised me by saying, 'I'd like you to be my bridesmaid, Ellen.'

'Have you mentioned this to your mother?'

'No, but I know she won't mind. After all it is my wedding, I should be able to choose my bridesmaid even if I don't get my own way about anything else.'

Still doubtful, I approached Mrs de Bellefort to see if she approved, but she seemed quite resigned to the fact. 'I don't see why not, Ellen. Most of Lisanne's friends are probably scattered all over the place by this time and I think you will make a very pretty bridesmaid.'

'Thank you, Mrs de Bellefort, I shall try to play my part.'

'I think we should go back to London for a few days before sailing for Ireland. There's a boat leaving Marseilles at the end of the month so I propose to book passage on it for the three of us. There is nothing we can do here, and if I was never keen to stay in England before I find I want to see London again. As soon as we arrive in England I will make some provision for you. If my mother-in-law is too frail to be concerned I am sure Lance will understand your predicament.'

'I shall be able to find work in England, Mrs de Bellefort,

I don't wish Sir Lance to be troubled,' I said more sharply than was necessary.

She looked at me with a half smile. 'My dear girl, you are in no position to be too proud. Let Lance help you, let him ease his conscience.'

Soon we were busy packing our belongings. I tried several times to telephone Kitty, but without success. Apparently she was still not taking telephone calls, but she now had a new and equally enthusiastic audience. I saw her one day in the company of a dark-skinned man in a luxurious motor car. They were talking animatedly so that she had eyes for no one else, and I thought with grim amusement that once again she seemed to have fallen on her feet.

Two days before we were due to sail Lisanne said that Kitty's pictures had been taken down from outside the nightclub. She had heard that Kitty was returning to Paris.

For what seemed like the tenth time I told myself that I would probably never see Kitty again. In that I was wrong, but it was fortunate that I couldn't know the circumstances that would throw us together once more.

CHAPTER 32

Lisanne's mother had been correct in her assumption that the boat would be a crowded one, indeed she was lucky to obtain two first-class cabins some distance apart.

I shared with Lisanne while her mother had a cabin on another deck, and we met for meals and for whatever entertainment there was in the evening. I was loving every minute of it. This was the sort of life I had envisaged when sitting on the seawall at New Brighton watching the big steamers sailing out from Liverpool. Now I was a part of that life.

We danced in the arms of the ship's officers night after night until the stars paled, and not even the weather in the Bay of Biscay could dampen our enthusiasm. Lisbon was a joy with its beautiful shops hardly touched by the war and Lisanne shopped wildly for household linen and exquisite underwear until her mother put a stop to it by saying firmly that the money Lance had forwarded was not limitless, and would have to see us through the voyage and probably for some time in London.

Our first surprise occurred the second night out after dinner when the master of ceremonies announced that he had a special treat for us all, a lady who had entertained all Paris and the Côte d'Azur with her singing. Then he went forward to bring Kitty out of the shadows into the light of the ballroom.

Those people who had boarded the ship in New Zealand and Australia had never heard of her, but those of us who had lived in France applauded rapturously, me among them, and she smiled like a queen as she acknowledged the applause.

She wore black, simply cut and expensive. Round her throat and in her ears were emeralds, and her red hair flamed under the lights. Her songs, filled with nostalgia and a sad longing in her deep throaty voice, brought tumultuous applause and calls for encores, until she kissed her hands to the audience and retired from the stage.

I knew she had seen me, and the young officer who was my companion whispered, 'She's really something, isn't she? Would you say she was French?'

'I've heard she's Irish.'

'I suppose she could be, with that lovely red hair and green eyes.'

'She's very successful.'

'You've heard of her before?'

'Yes, in Paris and again in Monte Carlo.'

So we talked for a while about life in Provence during the war, and then for a time Kitty was forgotten as we started to dance.

All the next day I looked for Kitty on the decks, in the lounges and the bars but I couldn't find her. I didn't even know if she was travelling alone and it was obvious she had no intention of entering into the life on board the ship.

On the last night there was to be a gala dance and notices went up that those who wanted to wear fancy dress were invited to do so.

'I can't be bothered to think of anything,' Lisanne said. 'I shall wear my prettiest dress and you must do the same.'

I wondered privately what she considered my prettiest dress considering they had all been bought before or at the beginning of the war, so it would have to be blue. The colour suited me and it was a pretty dress. Lisanne on the other hand was fretting and fussing about hers.

'What do I do with this thing?' she complained as she twisted the long chiffon ties that fell from her shoulders.

I was hunting into my cardboard jewellery box at the time and somewhat petulantly she came to look over my shoulder.

'What have you there?' she asked, sitting beside me on my bed.

'Nothing very much, I'm afraid. I shall wear the pearl drop and earrings.'

'How about the locket? It's pretty and I've never seen you wearing it.'

'I never have. It belonged to Aunt Liza.'

'And this brooch is beautiful, Ellen. Why have you never worn it?'

'It isn't my initial, that too belonged to Aunt Liza.'

She was holding it in her hand, turning it this way and that, then she started to arrange the ties on her gown, finally catching them with the brooch to her entire satisfaction.

'This is just what it needs, Ellen, It's my initial too. Can I borrow it?'

'Of course, you can keep it if you like.'

'Do you really mean it?'

'Yes of course. Look upon it as a wedding present, I think it's quite valuable and I could never wear it.'

Impulsively she bent down and kissed me. 'It's lovely, Ellen, and every time I wear it I'll think of you. Are you quite sure you don't want it?'

'Yes, I'm sure. I never felt I had any right to it anyway, and I'm sure Aunt Liza would never have given it to me. I've always felt guilty about having it with me.'

'Well I'm sure you don't need to. She treated you like a skivvy and she didn't care what became of you, it was that niece of hers who had to have everything. But for Granny you'd have been out on your ear looking for work.'

I didn't speak. I wasn't all that sure that her granny had done me any favours.

People were gay that night, the pent-up gaiety of people who had experienced long years of war, forgetting that in the Far East war still raged. We danced and drank champagne, and people paraded in ridiculous costumes they had obviously made up on the spur of the moment. I hoped that Kitty would come to sing to us but she didn't make an appearance.

Later when I lay sleepless in my cabin I thought of Kitty again. It was very hot in the cabin, airless, although Lisanne was sleeping like a baby. We were due to dock in the early afternoon and I lay staring up at the ceiling with my thoughts turning this way and that as I tried to think what my future might be.

It was no use, I had to get out for some air. Slipping my

343

arms into my dressing gown I tiptoed out of the cabin, closing the door quietly behind me.

Moonlight flooded the deck and silvered the sea, and I stood at the ship's rail with the wind in my hair and the tang of salt on my lips. If I had known the number of Kitty's cabin I would have gone there in the hope that she would talk to me, but I could not be sure that she was alone and I didn't want her to think that I was curious. After a while I grew cold in the freshening wind, and returned to the cabin.

Lisanne switched on the light over her bed, saying, 'Where on earth have you been? It's after four.'

'I couldn't sleep, it was so hot in the cabin. I stayed on deck until it turned suddenly cold.'

'Oh well, after tomorrow we'll be back to English weather. I've loved every minute of this voyage, it'll probably be my last chance to flirt for years. Those officers do it so beautifully.'

'On the voyage back they'll be flirting with other girls, have you thought about that?'

'Are you always so practical, Ellen?'

'I suppose so.'

'But you weren't very practical about Lance, were you?'

I didn't speak, and provocatively she said, 'You were in love with Lance, Ellen, however hopeless it was.'

'He would always have married Geraldine, so you're right, it was hopeless.'

'Or me. What would you have done if he'd married me?'

'Nothing at all. We would never have gone to Paris, our lives would have been quite different and we would probably never have met again.'

'Granny de Bellefort was a strange one, wasn't she? I've never quite been able to understand why she was so insistent that you went to live at the Priory. Oh I know she had that thing about your grandmother, but lots of men have affairs with women they're not married to, and vice versa. Everybody said my mother had lovers when we were living in India but I honestly never saw any of them.'

'You didn't live in India for long.'

344

She chuckled. 'That's true, Mother soon shipped me out so that I didn't interfere with her social life. Heavens, but it's hot in here. I wonder why that girl singer's going to England. Do you suppose she's singing in London?'

'I've no idea.'

'She looked much prettier in that black dress without all the emerald eyeshadow. I suppose she wears that for effect in her cabaret act.'

'I suppose so.'

She reached out to the table beside her bed and picked up the brooch she had worn the night before.

'I'm thrilled with this, Ellen, it's lovely. Mother said I shouldn't accept it until you were quite sure.'

'I'm sure.'

'I must ring for the steward and ask him to bring some iced water.'

I heard her get out of bed and move towards the bell, then there was a crash that sent me flying out of my bed and next moment Lisanne was lying on top of me, thrown across the room by the explosion.

The lights went out and although we struggled to our feet the floor was already listing and we had great difficulty in reaching the door. Winded by the fall we were gasping for breath, and all around us were the sounds of rending metal, hysterical screaming and the crackle of flames. There was chaos in the passage as men, women and childen fought to reach the companionway. I cried. 'Hold on to me, Lisanne, don't let them separate us.'

Somewhere a child was screaming, 'Mummy Mummy,' and the stewards were asking for calm, trying without much success to keep our pathway to the deck clear and the procession moving in an orderly direction.

Lisanne clung to my waist and it seemed to me as we moved forward inch by inch that the deck shifted terrifyingly under our feet. The wind hit us like a knife and we had great difficulty in staying on our feet since the deck was sloping at an alarming rate. Towards the prow of the ship flames were leaping upwards into the night.

Lisanne caught the sleeve of one of the young officers

we had danced with only hours before. His jacket was grimy with soot and his eyes were bloodshot.

'Hang on to the rails, girls. We're trying to do something with the boats but the list isn't helping.'

'What has happened?' Lisanne stammered. 'I can't see for the smoke.'

'We've struck a mine. All those miles of ocean and we have to strike a bloody mine within sight of England. Half the ship's gone.'

He shook himself free and we watched helplessly as he made his unsteady way through the crowds. Lisanne turned tortured eyes on me, crying, 'We must look for my mother, Ellen. She must be on deck somewhere.'

We started to move along the deck but it was hopeless. Our feet were slipping and sliding from under us as the ship listed further and further, and all around us people were screaming or praying, weeping or trying to claw their way towards the stern. Suddenly I thought: We're going to to die, we'll never get out of this alive. Even as I thought it there was a shudder that seemed to reverberate through the entire ship and I found myself falling down and down until I hit the icy water and I was thrashing about wildly looking for Lisanne.

The sea was alive with floating debris and others who had been thrown into the water with us. Suddenly I saw a steward with his arm round Lisanne, attempting to keep both of them afloat, and I made my way towards them. I was not a powerful swimmer, but he helped me to hold on to a floating table and I saw then that Lisanne was unconscious, with the blood pouring down her face from a blow she had received on her head.

'We must get away from the boat,' he gasped, 'or she'll take us with her when she goes down. 'Ang on to that table and I'll 'elp ye.'

My arms ached from holding on to the table and I was so cold I couldn't feel my feet, then to my horror I watched him let Lisanne go. For a few moments she floated away from us, then she sank from my sight.

I felt myself screaming, then clawing at him wildly. I

struggled until he slapped my face hard, hissing, 'Lie still, you little fool. I 'ad to let 'er go, she was done for.'

Shocked and hurting, I felt him take hold of me. He was a powerful swimmer, and bit by bit fought his way through the churning sea away from the ship, cautioning me all the time to hold on to the table. I wanted to die, it seemed too pointless to try to keep afloat, but self-preservation is a powerful thing. Then I heard him shouting, and he was waving wildly.

I found myself being lifted up out of the water by strong arms which laid me down on something hard. It was a boat, and as I struggled to sit up I saw a scene I shall never forget. The ship suddenly slid beneath the water in a haze of flame and smoke, and my last thought was that surely the sky was lighter, it was almost dawn.

I lived through the next few days in a haze, with people wearing white moving fitfully through my conscious thoughts. At times I heard voices, I felt hands moving me, and there were even times when I thought I saw faces looking down at me – Lisanne and her mother, Kitty and Aunt Liza. But my mind didn't want to remember, it was so blissful to lie in limbo with no past, present or future to agonize over. Then suddenly I opened my eyes to a white clinical room and a pale sun endeavouring to shine through the open window.

A woman stood beside the table holding something in her hands, and painfully I turned my head, moaning a little with the pain of it. She turned and came to the bed.

'So you're awake at last. Sure and oi thought you'd be comin' out of it today.'

My first thought was that she sounded like Kitty McGuire, but it wasn't Kitty, it was some woman I'd never seen in my life before. Then I realized that she was wearing nurse's uniform and memory came flooding back to me. I struggled to sit up.

'Oh no you don't,' she said, pushing me back gently. 'Toime enough for that when you're feeling stronger. Now

what do you say to some nice hot soup, and after you've
eaten oi'll get the doctor to take a look at you?'

'Is this a hospital?' I murmured.

'That it is.'

'Where?'

'Plymouth.'

'I don't remember them bringing me here.'

'No, of course ye don't. Now just lie still 'til I get the
soup, then after the doctor's been I'll tell that friend of
yours yer've come round.'

'Lisanne,' I murmured.

'Yes, love. I'm glad ye remembers yer name. Now just
lie still for a while. You'll get stronger every day now and
in no toime at all ye'll be sittin' up and takin' notice.'

Something was wrong but I didn't know what. Memory
was elusive and as I lay in bed I allowed my eyes to rove
round the room. There were flowers on the table near the
bed and a large basket of fruit on the chest of drawers. I
puzzled fretfully: Who knew me well enough to have sent
them? There was no time to puzzle further because the
nurse came back with a steaming bowl of soup.

'Now let me see if ye can sit up to eat yer soup, love. I'll
see to the pillows. I've done mi best with your hair but I
reckon there's still plenty o' salt in it. My, but it's my bet
you'll not be forgettin' that sea voyage in a hurry. Now come
on, love, lie back on the pillows and I'll bring over the soup.'

I was too weak to hold the spoon so she fed me the hot
soup and gradually I began to feel warmer, more alive. She
laughed, saying, 'Now what did oi tell you, sure and the
colour's comin' back into your cheeks already. In a few days
you'll be able to have visitors.'

'Visitors?'

'Why yes, Miss de Bellefort, you have a friend just up
the passage there. She's been in every day to see how you
were gettin' along.'

'Why do you call me Miss de Bellefort?' I murmured
stupidly.

'Why sure and it's your name, love. Don't say yer've
forgotten your name along with everything else?'

I was too weary to argue with her and she plumped the pillows after I had eaten and laid me back among them.

'I'll fetch the doctor now, love. He'll be pleased to see you've decided to enter the land of the livin'. Moi, but you've kept us entertained these last four days.'

'Entertained?'

'Sure, with yer talk about somebody called Emerald, and Aunt Julie bein' taken away and shot. What an imagination, I said to miself. Ye were dreamin', of course.'

Dreaming! I didn't want to remember, memories would be too painful, too hurtful, yet unbidden they came creeping back to me, the most terrible one of all seeing Lisanne slowly drifting away to drop almost gently beneath the waves.

The doctor came, kindly, solicitously, assuring me that I would soon regain my strength. He told the nurse to give me a sedative, that I must sleep some more.

'When you wake up next time you'll feel foine,' she assured me. 'Now drink this, love, and off ye go to sleep.'

When next I woke it was night and the curtains had been drawn. I felt more alert and my bones ached less. I struggled to sit up but hesitated to ring the bell beside my bed. My watch was missing, instead there was a plaster tape round my wrist bearing the name Lisanne de Bellefort. Once more memory came flooding back and impatiently I rang the bell, waiting anxiously to put the matter straight.

It was a different nurse who came in this time, an older woman, brisk and businesslike.

'So you're awake again, Miss de Bellefort. I'm busy in the ward at the moment but I won't be long.'

'I must talk to somebody, please. There's been a terrible mistake.'

'A mistake?'

'Yes. Please can I talk to the doctor?'

'Not at this time you can't my dear. It's almost eleven o'clock.'

'But I must talk to somebody.' I was almost in tears and she was impatient.

'I'll see if your friend is awake, she'll talk to you. You really must try not to get distressed, Miss de Bellefort. I'll be with you as soon as I've finished what I'm doing, we're very short staffed and the hospital is full. Now be a good girl and I'll send somebody in to you.'

I stared at the door which she had closed with some annoyance. Who was this friend she intended to send to me, who was there to tell me I was Lisanne de Bellefort?

I didn't have to wait long. There was a light tap on the door and then Kitty's red head appeared round it. ·

She was smiling and she reminded me of the Kitty I had known as a child with her red hair and freckles, freckles that had been well camouflaged by theatrical make-up.

'Oh good, the nurse said you were awake. My but I thought you'd sleep for ever like the sleeping beauty. I was on the point of askin' Lance de Bellfort to come down to kiss you awake.'

'Lance de Bellefort!'

'Sure, I've bin talkin' to him on the telephone. His wife's just had a baby girl and his grandmother's on her deathbed.'

'Kitty, they think I'm Lisanne. I've got to make them see, I can't think straight. How have they made such a mistake?'

'Well for one thing when they plucked you out of the sea you were clutching a gold brooch engraved with the letter L. I was in the lifeboat that fished you out of the sea, and I said I was your friend. They had a copy of the passenger list in no time and they put two and two together and made five.'

'But you knew, Kitty. Why didn't you tell them?'

'Why should I? Look, Ellen, both Lisanne and her mother lost their lives when the ship hit that mine. You've nobody to care a hoot about whether you're livin' or dead and you've no money. You haven't even a coat to stand up in and the de Belleforts owe you somethin'.

'I telephoned Lance de Bellefort. I told him Mrs de Bellefort was dead and so were you. I said only his cousin Lisanne had survived and she was unconscious. If he'd come tearing down here he'd have seen things for himself and I could always have said I'd made a mistake. But he's not comin', Ellen. He's still officially in the army, and what with his grandmother dyin' and the baby, he can't get away.

What he has done is send you the flowers, the fruit and the letter in that drawer there. I expect there's some money in it. Seems to me the de Belleforts are good at dishing out money, to them it solves everything.'

'Kitty, it's dishonest, I can't accept it and I can't go on calling myself Lisanne. How long do you think I'd get away with it?'

'For ever, if you're sensible. Look, there's only me who knows any different and wild horses wouldn't drag it out of me.'

'There's my family, my parents, my brothers and sisters.'

'And when are you likely to be seein' any of them? Read the letter, Ellen, see what he has to say.'

Cream parchment and the de Bellefort crest. I'd seen it so many times it seemed incredible that on this occasion it was for me. Nervously I slit the envelope and took out three pages of parchment covered in Lance's flowing handwriting, and my heart fluttered wildly with a remembered pain.

Dear Lisanne,

I am so relieved that you are safe, but saddened to hear that your mother and Ellen did not survive. Regretfully I am quite unable to visit you in hospital but I know you are in good hands. I have spoken with the doctor who assures me you will soon be well and strong and fully recovered.

I have also spoken with your friend on the telephone and explained to her why I am unable to make the journey to see you. Geraldine gave birth to a daughter just four days ago. It was a difficult birth and she is far from well. Worse than that, Grandmother is very ill and unlikely to recover. She is of course very old and has not been able to see well for several months. I have not told her of your mother's death, I doubt if she would be fully able to take it in.

I have written to Gervase in Ireland to tell him all that has happened. No doubt you will soon be hearing from him since your marriage was to take place quite soon in Ireland. I wish you well, Lisanne. I have very happy memories of those times we spent together at Langstone. So much has happened and it all seems so far away.

I wish you a quick and full recovery, dear cousin. Perhaps one day we might meet, although I have no wish to visit Ireland

and Gervase has even less desire to visit the Priory. I do however wish you well in your marriage.

Your ever loving cousin,
Lance

The letter fluttered on to the bedspread and I stared at Kitty helplessly, then I passed it over for her to read.

'What did I tell you?' she said firmly. 'He's not going to visit and he's no intention of visiting Ireland. If Granny de Bellefort gets better she can't see and she won't be visiting Ireland either, so I really don't see what you're worrying about.'

'Kitty, don't you understand, for the rest of my life I'd be living a lie, just waiting for somebody to say, "That isn't Lisanne." I can't spend the rest of my life married to a man I don't know, somebody I've never seen, somebody who thinks I'm somebody else.'

Suddenly she leaned forward and gripped my shoulders, holding them so firmly I cried out in pain.

'Don't be such a little fool, Ellen. I didn't ask them to fish you out of the sea to see you flounder on the rocks of life. I lived a lie every night of mi life when I paraded in front of all those people in my finery, smilin' when I never felt less like smilin', pretendin' to love somebody when I hated his guts, hating the Germans but hatin' miself more. It was a game called survival, Ellen, did you never know that?'

In my mind I was hearing Mrs de Bellefort's clipped upper-class tones saying, 'If we wish to survive in the harsh world we find ourselves in, Ellen, perhaps for a while we should forget our prejudices, even our honour. It is all a matter of survival.'

Something of all this must have registered on my face because Kitty pressed home her advantage. 'Ellen, think. Never to be short of money again, never needing to kowtow to people. Besides, you *are* a de Bellefort, even if your mother was born on the wrong side of the blanket.'

'I'll never get away with it, Kitty.'

'Oh yes you will. You and Lisanne were like sisters, you

had the same colouring, sometimes the same mannerisms. I can tell you it fascinated me whenever I saw you together, and you said yourself she'd not seen her cousin Gervase since they were children.'

'But he'll know, he'll sense it. How can I marry him? It's like prostitution.'

'You'll try that too if you're destitute. Oh come on, Ellen. How much money did Lance send you?'

'I don't know.'

I picked up the envelope again and looked inside. There was a folded cheque wrapped in a short note. I stared at the cheque in amazement. It was for two thousand pounds and the note informed me that an account had been opened in my name at the National Bank of Ireland in Dublin and all my money transferred into it. The statement showed that I was the richer by over a hundred thousand pounds.

Kitty gasped in amazement. 'Ellen, you're rich,' she said, 'you can't afford to say no to all that. Lisanne's dead, she isn't ever coming back, so who'd get all that money? Gervase or Lance. And it's my bet they've got more than enough already. Besides, I reckon Lance owes it to you, you loved him. And I know you, Ellen Adair, you don't fall in love very easily. That man made you suffer. Think, Ellen, think. You'll never get another chance like this one, never.'

Just then the nurse came back and Kitty sprang to her feet, saying, 'Miss de Bellefort seems much better. I expect she'd like something to drink.'

'I've only one pair of hands and we are short staffed. Thank you, Miss McGuire, you can go back to your room now.'

Kitty winked and waved to me from the door, while the nurse inquired if I wanted milk or cocoa.

'You'll be able to get up for a while tomorrow,' she said sharply, 'even if it's only to sit in the chair. You'll soon find your sea legs.' Then with a little titter, 'That was a stupid thing to say, I don't expect you'll ever want to find your sea legs again.'

She brought hot milk and I sat back to drink it. The enormity of Kitty's suggestion filled my thoughts to the exclusion of anything else. How could I ever get away with it, and would Gervase know? What would happen if he ever found out, if Lance ever found out? I lay sleepless for the rest of the night, and once I took Lance's letter out of its envelope and read it through.

He was sorry his aunt had not survived the wreck, sorry too about Ellen. But in being sorry for Ellen did he just once think that he had professed to love her years ago?

As the long night wore on I began to speculate whether I could get away with it. I told myself angrily that the de Belleforts owed me something, owed my grandmother something. That I had been loyal and served them faithfully, that I had tried desperately to save Lisanne. But the thought of marrying a stranger filled me with fear.

I tossed and turned in my narrow hospital bed and morning brought me no nearer to a solution. Kitty was bolder than I, she would never have had any hesitation in similar circumstances, but then Kitty's sights had always been set higher than possibilities. Even now she would probably know what her future was to be.

By the time the sun thrust its first tentative fingers into the room I began to know what my future would be, for better or worse. Ellen Adair had met her end in a watery grave and I was for the rest of my days destined to be Lisanne de Bellefort.

BOOK III

CHAPTER 33

Day by day I grew stronger and now I was able to walk in the gardens. Kitty had been discharged from hospital but was staying close by in a new hotel that had been recently completed.

'It's costing me the earth,' she complained, 'but I thought I'd stay on here until I know for sure what you're about. Besides, I'm waiting to hear what's happening in Paris.'

'Are you going back there to sing?' I asked curiously.

'For a while. I was happy in Paris, it'll be the same again. I made friends there and if I'm lucky I'll get an apartment, something quite luxurious, not like the one I had before.'

'How are you for money, Kitty?'

'Well enough. I had a friend who managed my money for me. I'm quite well off, actually, and if I go back to sing in Paris I can command an extravagant fee. It's not really what I wanted but the war altered many things.'

'Will you ever get married, Kitty?'

'I might if I find somebody rich enough.'

'Oh Kitty, money isn't everything.'

'It is when you haven't got any. I want to return to Paris in the autumn, meantime I'm going up to Liverpool to see my folks.'

'Not to Yorkshire?'

'I've no folks in Yorkshire now. Mi mother's gone to live with Aunt Mary in Liverpool. Mi uncle was killed during the war so they've set up home together. There'll be a houseful of children and they'll be like pigs in muck even though I have sent mi mother money when I could spare it.'

'I'm sorry about your uncle, Kitty. Was he killed in the army?'

'No, at the docks when the Germans bombed Liverpool. He left mi aunt with six children to bring up, I expect she's takin' in sewin' again. I'll be glad to leave them some money and mi mother'll be glad to see me.'

'Oh yes, Kitty, I'm sure she will. Do you think we'll ever meet again? It's so funny, but every time we part I think it's for the last time.'

'I rather think this time it might be. You'll be off to County Wicklow to marry your cousin and I'll be off to Paris with one eye on the main chance. No, Ellen this time I really think it'll be goodbye for ever. I must get used to calling you Lisanne but it seems so strange. It's just as well we shan't be meetin' again, I'll never get used to it.'

We walked on in silence and it was Kitty who eventually said, 'Have you had another letter from Lance?'

'No, just a huge bunch of carnations from Lance and Geraldine, with love.'

'No note to say how his grandmother was?'

'No.'

'And no word from Gervase?'

'No. That frightens me, Kitty. Wouldn't you just think he'd be eager to meet me? How can he ignore the woman he's going to marry, particularly when she's just survived a shipwreck?'

'It seems to me the de Belleforts can ignore a great many things. Most of them seem to have spent their lives riding roughshod over people's feelings. Won't it be funny if you have a son, Ellen, a son who inherits the title and everything else?'

I stopped in my tracks and stared at her open-mouthed. I could barely envisage a husband, but a child was something else.

'You *are* going to be married, you know,' she was saying with a tantalizing smile. 'Lance has a daughter, he might have another daughter. But if you had a son, what price the de Bellefort title then?'

'Oh Kitty, I can't think that far, when you talk like that

356

I can't even think straight. Suppose he doesn't like me, suppose he's in love with somebody else just like my grandfather was?'

'And just like your grandfather it won't make any difference. He'll marry the girl he's expected to marry. What he won't know is that it's a marriage of convenience for both of you. It wouldn't have been any better with Lisanne.'

'No, I don't suppose so.'

I was remembering Lisanne saying she hadn't really liked Gervase, that she found him overbearing and arrogant, and I wondered if I would find him the same.

'I think we should go back now,' Kitty was saying, 'I've got to pack a few things before catching the Liverpool train, and you've probably been out in the fresh air long enough.'

'Are you going to write to me, Kitty?'

'Oh Ellen, you know what a rotten correspondent I am. No, I don't think so. I don't know where I'll be, I don't intend to stay in Paris all that long and I've no idea where I'll move on to. I've got a good ear for music and I can sing in most languages without understanding a word of it – I learn like a parrot. I'd like to sing in Budapest and Vienna. I want to make money and travel, then when I've had enough I'll look around for that elusive man I might be able to live with for the rest of my life.'

'I wish you luck, Kitty.'

'I'll never forget you, Ellen. We did have some good times and we shared a lot. You were a better friend to me than I ever was to you.'

We parted on the terrace and I stood there while she walked quickly down the drive. She didn't look back.

I had only just reached my room when the Irish nurse bustled in, saying, 'You have a visitor, Miss de Bellefort, he's waitin' in the common room.'

My heart lurched sickeningly in my breast. 'A visitor, for me?'

'Yes, and he's not used to being kept waitin', from the look on his face.'

'Who is he?'

'A Mr de Bellefort. A relative, surely.'

357

For one desperate moment I thought: Lance. Lance, and the game was up. Then common sense came to my aid. He was now Sir Lance de Bellefort, so obviously it must be Gervase who waited for me in the common room.

'Here,' the nurse was saying, 'do something with your hair and I'll borrow a pretty dressing gown from next door.' She was soon back with a pale rose robe over her arm. The colour suited me, lighting up my wan face, but I was still trembling and she gave me a small exasperated push out of the door.

'Go on, love, he'll not be expecting Greta Garbo, he knows the ordeal you've been through.'

For a few moments I stood in the common room doorway looking at the tall slim figure of a man standing looking through the window, then I went in and closed the door.

He spun round and we eyed one another without speaking. My first thought was that he was surprisingly like Lance. They had the same shining dark hair and deep blue eyes, but there had been laughter in Lance's face while this one was remote. It was undeniably handsome but there was no warmth in it. Instead there was a sort of cynical aloofness in his eyes, and the finely chiselled lips were unsmiling.

I could not have spoken, my throat was too dry and my heart was hammering. At any moment I expected him to say, 'You're not Lisanne. Why are you posing as Lisanne? Instead he said in a voice which reminded me of Lance's, 'Have you no greeting for your fiancé, Lisanne, or at least for your cousin Gervase?'

I went forward immediately and held out my hand. He laughed before taking it, then dutifully he bent his head and gently brushed my cheek with his lips.

'I remember we didn't exactly get on the last time we met, and no doubt you've remembered it. How are you, better I hope?'

How formal it was. We were like two strangers asking polite questions, and if I shed no tears there were tears in my heart.

'Thank you, I'm much better,' I murmured.

Again the amusement flickered in his eyes.

'I was out in the garden, have you been waiting long?'

'About fifteen minutes. I should have brought flowers. I'm sorry, there wasn't time to get any.'

'Have you come straight here from Ireland?'

'No. I've been in Yorkshire attending a funeral, our grandmother as it happens.'

'Oh, I didn't know. I'm so sorry, when did she die?'

'Last Tuesday, she's been ailing for some time. You really are sorry, aren't you, Lisanne?'

'Of course, aren't you?'

'I didn't want her to die, but I never really knew her. She dictated policy from afar. She plotted and moved us about like pieces on a chess board and we obeyed on the strength of her promises. Money, power, land. With you I expect it was money, with me it was land, with Lance, heaven knows.'

'Langstone Priory and the title,' I murmured.

'The title was his anyway, but I expect you're right about the Priory.'

He said it casually, as if Lance's ambitions didn't really interest him, and in the next breath he said, 'You look very pale, Lisanne. Perhaps we should sit down, here in the window.'

'How are Geraldine and the baby?' I asked dutifully.

'Actually I began to feel rather relieved that it was not Geraldine I was to marry. She's pretty and gentle, she's also rather a bore. The baby is a girl, which no doubt disappointed our grandmother sorely. Perhaps we shall have a son, and somewhere beyond the grave Grandmother de Bellefort will rejoice with the angels.'

Would I ever understand this man, I wondered. He was amused by me which put me at an even greater disadvantage than I felt to begin with. Taking my courage in both hands I asked, 'Did you have a very bad time during the war, Gervase?'

'Didn't we all, but then you were living in Antibes, weren't you? What was it like under German rule? From what I remember of your mother she would be inclined to look upon it as a challenge, men were never a problem to her.'

359

'She was an inspiration to us all, and brave in the face of much provocation. I admired her tremendously.'

His eyes narrowed. 'Well well, I'm glad to see that you speak up for something or someone you believed in. Perhaps our life together might not be quite so tedious after all. When do you propose to join me in Ireland?'

'When are we supposed to be getting married?'

'Well, not too soon after Grandmother's death. I think we should let the dust settle for a while. Suppose we say November, that gives us five months.'

'November isn't exactly a nice month for a wedding.'

'No! Well, September then. I'll book a flight for you into Dublin, I'm sure you won't wish to take a boat so soon after the disaster. I expect you'll want to shop in London for all you need - the shops in Dublin are well enough but I doubt if they have the variety of London's.

'I hope you'll like the life in County Wicklow. The estate is quite large and it keeps me very busy although I do have an estate manager. We spend a lot of time fishing in the loughs, we hunt a lot and generally think a lot of our horses. You do ride, of course?'

'Not for a long time.'

'Oh, you'll soon fall into it again. I'll find you a decent mount. When you were a girl you rode quite recklessly, I seem to remember.'

Already it was going wrong. He would expect me to be an accomplished horsewoman when in fact all I had ever done was ride a docile and predictable mare around the park at Langstone. To be in Lisanne's class I would have had to live with horses since childhood.

Gathering my wits, I murmured, 'I had a bad fall, I rather lost interest in horses after that.'

'My dear girl, surely you knew you must get straight back on and ride. Don't worry, we'll soon lick you into shape. I suppose you lost everything on the ship?'

'Everything except a brooch. I haven't any clothes, the nurse said she would arrange for a girl to come in from one of the shops, just to help me out for the time being.'

'Good idea. Well, you'll need riding clothes, all sorts of

360

country clothes and the odd evening gown. You're looking very pale, Lisanne, you should get back to bed. I have to be going anyway, I have business to do when I get back to London tonight.

He rose and held out his hand to help me out of my chair. Together we walked to the door where he once more brushed my cheek with his lips. Then he was gone, striding away from me down the corridor.

In a bemused fashion I walked back to my room where the nurse was busily turning down my bed. She stared at me in amazement.

'My, but that didn't take long,' she said, smiling.

'No, he has to get back to London tonight.'

'Is he a relative?'

'Yes, he's also the man I am going to marry.'

The astonishment on her face was profound, indeed if it hadn't been so hurtful it would have been laughable. Then she said briskly, 'I don't much hold with cousins marryin', the blood gets thinner and they always throw up a weakling or two.'

'I don't think you need to worry about the de Bellefort family, they've been doing it for centuries without any dire results.'

'Is that so? Well if himself's an example I can believe you. Now come along into bed, you've been on your feet long enough.'

To my amazement and hers I got into bed laughing helplessly, wildly, and it was only when she closed the door behind her that my laughter turned into tears.

CHAPTER 34

I stayed in hospital for another week and received one letter from Gervase informing me that arrangements were being made for our wedding to be held privately. There would be few guests and after the ceremony we would be going back to the house for a reception. He asked me to let him know when I might expect to travel and he had arranged for me to stay with a Colonel and Mrs Jefferson until the day of our marriage. It was not the letter of a man to the woman he expected to marry within a few months, but rather that of a man honouring his obligations somewhat reluctantly. He hoped I was now fully recovered and sent me his love.

After leaving the hospital I went immediately to London and moved into a small hotel in Kensington. I thought it only correct to inform Lance of my movements but shied away from writing in case he thought there was something odd about my handwriting, so I sent him a telegram giving him my new address.

Within a few days a letter arrived from him saying he was pleased I was well again and that Gervase and I had decided our wedding plans. He also informed me that Geraldine was recovering from the birth of Catherine slowly, but the baby was well.

I sat on the edge of my bed in the informal hotel bedroom and thought about the enormity of what I had done, and that there was no going back. What would my marriage be like in a strange house in an environment I did not know? There would be no love to sustain me. Other women followed their husbands to the ends of the earth with love in their hearts, but that was not going to happen for me. Everything I would have would be superficial. I would be Mrs de Bellefort, the rich Mrs de Bellefort, but would that be enough for the rest of my life?

I tried not to think of the future in the joy of the present.

I loved London. I loved the park across the way, and the lovers lying on the grass and under the trees filled me with a sad nostalgia. I loved the shops and the tea lounges, the arcades and the museums, and for the first time in my life I could spend money extravagantly, knowing there was more.

I bought riding clothes and found stables near the hotel where I explained that I was an absolute beginner but was going to live in Ireland where I would be expected to ride

They were kind and patient, and soon I was cantering in the park on a bright chestnut mare, taking lessons in dressage and even putting my horse over jumps that were not too formidable. My teacher expressed his delight over my prowess but I couldn't think I would ever be the horsewoman my future husband might be expecting.

I chose my clothes carefully. Elegant clothes that had a timeless air, and three evening gowns which seemed a ridiculous expense, but then I was unsure about the life I would be expected to lead.

I also bought my wedding dress, and if it wasn't exactly the dress of my girlhood dreams, it was expensive and elegant.

It was evident that Gervase was not a good correspondent, but two weeks before our marriage I received a long letter from him. It informed me that I would be met at Dublin airport, he didn't say by whom, and that I would be taken straight to the Jeffersons' house. He did not expect to see me before the day of the wedding as he had business to attend to in Cork and on the west coast. He also informed me that Lady de Bellefort had left all her grandchildren well provided for, but I was to have an additional sum which had been put aside for my mother. He thought I would be pleased to know.

Little did he know that that particular piece of information only made me feel very ashamed, but by this time it would need more courage to tell the truth than it would to act the part.

On the day I was to leave London I started to pack my clothes in the set of very expensive luggage I had bought.

Every case bore the initial L, and as I folded crepe-de-Chine underwear and soft leather skirts I reflected on how easily I had discarded the name Ellen for the more unusual Lisanne, and how easily I responded when hotel staff addressed me as Miss de Bellefort. A trunk containing most of my clothes had been dispatched to Ireland several days before and I was now packing the most expensive things I had purchased like evening gowns and afternoon dresses.

I had had my hair cut and styled at an exclusive new salon by a young woman who had enthused about its colour and texture. I had bought make-up, creams and lotions to pamper my skin, and bath oils in fragrant honeysuckle that reminded me poignantly of the countryside.

After my luggage had been taken to the foyer and I was dressed for the journey I took a final look in the mirror thinking that it was not Ellen Adair who faced me but a stranger, a fashionable expensive stranger in an exquisitely cut burgundy suit. On my fashionable bob was a hat of the same colour and round my shoulders a set of pale beige mink ties. There were soft kid gloves, and high-heeled burgundy shoes with a handbag of exactly the same colour. It was a fashionable, beautiful girl who faced me in the mirror and as I walked through the hotel foyer to the taxi heads turned to watch me.

I felt excited to be flying for the first time, but glad that the journey was a short one. Indeed I wasn't sure that I would ever again be a comfortable traveller.

After the customs I stood hesitantly in the airport lounge at Dublin surrounded by my luggage and feeling strangely deflated. People were milling all around me, many of them staring at the elegant woman who seemed lost and unsure.

Embarrassed, I was about to approach the desk when I felt my arm taken and looked up into the eyes of a man wearing country tweeds and an apologetic smile.

'I say, I am sorry but I was detained in the traffic on the way into Dublin. You're Miss de Bellefort, Gervase described you very accurately.'

I smiled, taking his outstretched hand.

'I'm Alan Harvey, Gervase's estate agent. I think he

explained that he would be away in Cork the day you arrived. My car's just outside. Here, I'll get somebody to help with your luggage.'

I thought he was nice. He had a boyish smile and he was trying too hard to be kind. Inwardly I wondered what he thought about this marriage. He must surely have heard Gervase's explanation of why he was marrying a cousin he hadn't seen since he was a child.

He seemed shy, and he kept up a running chatter while he eased the car through the late afternoon traffic. During our drive through the city he pointed out things like Nelson's Column in the centre of O'Connell Street, and the university buildings.

'It seems strange to see a monument to Nelson here in Dublin,' I said.

'Oh, one of these days they'll pull it down, there's nothing surer.'

'Are you a native of these parts?'

'Good gracious no, I'm from North Yorkshire, way up beyond Hawes. I could have sworn I detected a faint trace of the Yorkshire in your accent.'

'Oh well,' I said airily, 'I've spent a lot of my life in the Dales.'

'Of course, with your grandmother.'

He accepted it, and I in return began to realize how easy it was becoming to lie. Only I didn't want to lie. I prayed for the day when I wouldn't have to lie any more. When I really became Lisanne de Bellefort and stopped feeling guilty about remarks passed in all innocence.

We drove towards the mountains, beautiful and pointed like I'd always thought mountains should be, and my companion gave them names that I felt sure I would never be able to pronounce properly.

'How long have you known Gervase?' I asked him curiously.

'About twenty years. My family used to come over here for holidays when I was quite small, my mother had a brother who lived down there at Dalkey and we always loved the coast here, and the mountains. I met Gervase walking

365

in the park with his father, I was trespassing and their gamekeeper caught me. They let me off with a lecture but I saw Gervase laughing and somehow or other we struck up a friendship, so that every summer I was invited to fish in their trout stream and ride in the park. When I left school I went to an agricultural college and learned estate management, Gervase's father took me on as under manager, and when my boss retired I was offered the job.'

'Are you happy working for him?'

'Of course. He knows what he wants and generally gets it. We understand each other and of course I've got a nice house that goes with the job, and a nice garden. I'm fond of gardening.'

'You actually live on the estate?'

'On the edge of it. Most of the labourers have cottages on the estate. The old man was more interested in the land than he was in the big house. I'm afraid it needs quite a bit doing to it, but now you're coming to live in it I expect Gervase will give you a free hand.'

'You mean it's decrepit?'

He laughed. 'By no means, but goodness knows when carpets and curtains were replaced. My wife says it needs a fortune spending on it.'

I hadn't realized he was married, and in the next breath he said, 'I married a girl from Bray only last year. We'd known each other a long time, also since we were chidlren.'

'I see.'

'I'm to take you to stay with Colonel Jefferson and his wife Edna. They'll make you very welcome. You do ride, I suppose?'

'Yes, but I'm not very expert.'

'Really? Gervase seemed to think you loved it, at least he told me you'd always had horses at your grandmother's place.'

'I haven't ridden for years, until I rode in London. I'm terribly out of practice.'

'Oh, one never forgets. Gervase will fix you up with a nice predictable mount and you'll soon get the hang of it again. And this is hunting country.'

My heart sank. I would not get the hang of it again, I'd yet to get the hang of it at all. I could already imagine how much I was going to disappoint my husband to be.

For a while we drove in silence, then he pulled the car over to the side and pointed down to the golden beach.

'That's Dalkey down there,' he said. 'Folk round here do say it's a lot like the Bay of Naples with Vesuvius rising across the bay. They're comparing the volcano to Old Sugar Loaf there, but you must admit it's very beautiful.'

I agreed. It was a pretty bay with the surf breaking on the soft sand and the exquisite shape of the mountain rising proudly in the distance.

'It's not far to the Jeffersons from here,' he said, 'I expect you're ready for a cup of tea.'

'Yes, that would be nice. Do I call you Mr Harvey?'

'I'd rather you called me Alan, Gervase does.'

'Very well, Alan.'

'You're not a bit what I expected, you know. It's funny, isn't it? I don't know why I imagined you so different.'

At that moment my heart missed a beat, and quickly I asked, 'Whyever not?'

'Well if you'll forgive me saying so Gervase described you as a bit of a brat, always wanting your own way, and probably a bit spoilt. I was expecting somebody rather imperious.'

'Gervase only remembers me as a child, I was probably all of those things.'

'How do you remember him?'

'Arrogantly insufferable, and when I met him in Plymouth I began to think he hadn't changed.'

He threw back his head and laughed. 'He can be all of those things. I suppose you'll both have to get to know each other all over again.'

'You're thinking that is hardly a happy augury for marriage.'

'I wouldn't presume to think anything of the kind. You've both known about this marriage for a very long time so I'm sure it'll work out. You know, in many countries marriages are still arranged, and surprisingly they do work out.'

He was reassuring me and I warmed to him. I was beginning to think I would find a good friend in Alan Harvey.

'The Jeffersons are just at the end of this lane here, the big red-brick house with the tall chimneys,' he said.

We drew up outside the front door and it opened immediately. Several dogs rushed out, followed by a tall spare man wearing tweeds and a pretty middle-aged woman in a tweed skirt, twin set and sensible shoes.

If she was surprised at seeing a distinctly elegant woman step down from the car she showed no signs of it. Her smile was welcoming and as the dogs were called to heel we all moved into the house.

'You'll stay for tea,' she called out to Alan.

'Actually no. I'll help with the luggage, then I've things to see to on the estate. I've been too long away already, and Gervase is in Cork.'

'Oh well, if that's the case we won't detain you. Give our love to Maureen,' Mrs Jefferson called out.

I was shown into a sitting room which I thought entirely charming, with pretty faded chintz covers on the large couches pulled up before the fire and chintz curtains at the windows. There were bowls of flowers here and there about the room, and gold-framed oil paintings.

I had noticed the hall as we passed through and thought to myself that I was in the home of hunting people. There were several hunting horns decorating the wall, a case filled with guns and rifles, and several fox masks.

'Take off your hat and anything else you want to get rid of, my dear,' Mrs Jefferson said, 'we'll have tea and then I'll show you up to your room.'

Almost immediately a small fresh-faced country girl came in carrying a tray set out with scones, butter, jam and an enormous fruit cake, followed by another girl carrying a tray arranged with a silver tea service.

The Colonel was poking the fire into renewed life, then he turned to me with a smile. 'The days are getting shorter and it was cool this morning. Is this your first visit to Ireland, my dear?'

'Yes, I'm afraid so.'

'Very pretty country round here, good hunting country. You do hunt, I suppose?'

'No, not since I had a bad fall several years ago.'

He raised his eyebrows in surprise. 'Is that so? I could have sworn Gervase told me you were into horses and hunting.'

I smiled politely and his wife said with a little laugh, 'I knew that was the first thing he'd ask you, he thinks of little else. Now I'm going to call you Lisanne, and my name is Edna. My husband's is George. Both very ordinary and easy to remember.'

'Yes they are, not like Lisanne.'

'But it's the prettiest name I ever heard. We were both so sorry to hear about the shipwreck, dear. How terrible to lose your mother in that way.'

'Yes, she was a very special person.'

'I'm sure she was, and how awful to have lived through the war under German rule and die on the way home to England. I don't suppose you'll ever forget it.'

'No.'

'And we don't want to go on talking about it,' her husband said sharply. 'It's something the poor girl wants to forget as quickly as possible.'

'Darling, don't be silly, of course she won't forget it.'

'No, and she doesn't want to talk about it either. Now come along, my dear, show us what a healthy appetite you've got.'

George was heavy handed and kind, his wife fluttering like a little bird, but as the evening wore on I felt relaxed in their company and they asked few questions.

They talked about their neighbours, the countryside and the fishing, but never once did they mention Gervase or my approaching wedding day.

I was happy with the Jeffersons. I tramped the country lanes with them and sat in silence on the banks of the trout stream watching him fishing. I went with Mrs Jefferson to the country shops and was introduced to the people we met on the way, and I was always aware of their heads close together in small groups after we had wandered on.

'Country people gossip,' Edna said, smiling. 'They've been agog to know what you looked like. Of course they've known for years that one day the squire's son would marry his cousin from England. You'll be the topic of conversation for weeks.'

'Is the church where we are to be married near here?'

'You'll be married in the small chapel in the grounds of the house, dear. You needn't worry, it's properly consecrated and it's very pretty.'

'Does that mean that there will be nobody watching the wedding?'

'None of the villagers, dear. But we are guests along with one or two other people. Gervase said he wanted a quiet wedding in view of his grandmother's death and your mother's death also. I thought it was very sensitive of him.'

Personally I didn't think sensitivity had had anything to do with it. Gervase hadn't struck me as a man given to too much sentiment and I felt sure he was hating this marriage as much as I, as much as generations of de Belleforts must have hated having brides and grooms chosen for them, and strangely unable to do anything about it.

My silence made her say hurriedly, 'You and Gervase will have to get to know each other all over again, my dear. I'm very fond of him, although he's a singularly self-assured young man who doesn't suffer fools gladly.'

I felt strangely miserable. How Gervase would despise me if he ever knew the truth, as much as he despised the strictures placed around him by a grandmother he had respected but never loved.

CHAPTER 35

Like every girl before me I had dreamed of drifting down the aisle in a froth of white lace on my wedding morning, indeed there were many times when Kitty and I had fantasized about it. I could hear her voice saying, 'Just as long as ye don't expect mi to wear pink, Ellen. It's death to my colouring.'

So we had agreed that Kitty would wear lemon and I would wear blue when we acted as bridesmaids, but now here was I staring at my refleciton in the long cheval mirror in my room at the Jeffersons' and thinking I was dressed for a garden party but never a wedding.

The cream wild silk dress was beautifully cut and at the waist were pale pink chiffon roses which trailed prettily to the hem. The skirt fell in long folds from a narrow waist and the cream white hat with its pink chiffon roses was undoubtedly elegant though not exactly bridal.

Gervase had sent orchids which did not go with the roses so I decided to wear them on a long satin ribbon in my ivory prayer book. I had borrowed the prayer book that morning from Edna and she had insisted on stitching a small blue bow on to my petticoat. My clothes were new, the prayer book was old, so it would seem all the traditional items which might bring me luck had been included.

I wasn't required to have a bridesmaid but George Jefferson was giving me away, and Alan Harvey was Gervase's best man.

For the very first time we drove through the vast ornamental gates and the grounds of Glenmoor with the large turreted house in the misty distance. I was amazed how far the grounds extended, and as we drove through a forest of evergreens George whispered, 'We'll soon be at the church, it's in a little clearing just outside the forest.'

A small cluster of men and women stood round the

church door, and again George whispered, 'Servants from the house and off the land, come to watch the squire's marriage.'

As we left the car they bobbed quaint country curtsies to me and I smiled back at them shyly. There were other servants and tenants seated at the back of the church and a handful of guests in the front pews but my eyes were drawn to Gervase standing tall and impassive before the altar with Alan at his side, both of them wearing morning suits which surprised me a little.

The organist began to play, some tune I was unfamiliar with, and slowly George and I drifted down the aisle and Gervase took his place besides me.

I remember very little although I must have made the appropriate responses. All I was conscious of was the tall man standing beside me, his low voice making promises, then he was placing a heavy gold ring on my finger and the vicar proclaimed that we were man and wife.

He bent his head and kissed my cheek. His lips felt cold, impersonal, and his eyes stared into mine like blue steel.

The rest of the day passed in a haze of unreality. There were speeches and laughter at the reception, but I couldn't have told anyone what was said. I was introduced to people I felt sure I would not remember when we met again, and the meal tasted like nothing although the table was festive.

Gervase sat at one end of the long oak table and I at the other. Occasionally he raised his glass to me with a look of cynical amusement, and once I saw Alan looking at me, puzzled and compassionate.

I was glad when the meal was over and people began to drift about the house. I wanted to change, get out of my wedding finery, but nobody had told me where I could go. By this time pride and anger had come to my rescue and approaching Gervase, I said, 'I'd like to change, Gervase. Where is my room?'

'Surely you must mean our room, Lisanne?'

'All right then, our room. I take it my cases and trunk have been taken there.'

'I'm sure they have, and probably unpacked for you. We

372

may be living in darkest Ireland but we do have a modicum of the refinements.'

'Why are you so defensive, I wonder?'

'Why are you not more defensive? Surely you haven't enjoyed being a sacrificial lamb.'

'Is that what you think we are?'

'You need have no worries, my dear, I intend to honour our marriage to the extent of providing an heir. How far do you intend to honour it?'

'I don't know what you mean.'

'And now is not the time to explain. Martha will show you to our room. Please change quickly so as not to keep our guests waiting.'

I don't know what devilment prompted me to change into the only black dinner gown I had. It was elegant, with its low-cut neck and trailing sleeves edged with sable. The only adornment was the long diamond earrings I had bought in London and charged to my account.

I looked far more beautiful in the gown than I had done in my wedding dress. Black suited my pale blond colouring, and if the guests looked somewhat askance at my choice of gown, they also looked at me with some admiration.

For one fleeting moment I saw admiration in Gervase's eyes also, but almost immediately it was quenched by the maddening cynicism I had almost come to expect.

The night wore on. People laughed, the men sang hunting songs, they ate and drank too much and already it was midnight and I was wondering when Gervase would call a halt to the merriment. At precisely twelve o'clock he said, 'Time to go home. Thank you, my friends, for coming to our wedding. I can only say how much my dear wife and I have enjoyed your company, now we must have one last drink and you must leave us to enjoy the rest of the night.'

There were titters of appreciative laughter among the men and several embarrased glances from the women in my direction. For my part I watched them drift into the hall, then slowly I mounted the stairs towards the bedrooms.

For the first time I began to take a real look at Glenmoor. The curving shallow staircase could have been beautiful but the gilded balustrade, intricately carved, had suffered much neglect. The gilt was sadly in need of renovation and the oak steps badly needed polishing to restore the original lustre of the wood.

In places the carpet was threadbare and there were cobwebs high up on the walls. The lighting from heavy bronze lanterns was dim, and I thought sadly of the crystal chandeliers that had adorned the hall at the Priory where everything had been beautifully maintained under Lady de Bellefort's jurisdiction.

I entered the great bedroom overlooking the long drive and really saw it for the first time. Before I had been too anxious to change out of my wedding gown, now I was unhappily aware of the dark embossed wallpaper and the heavy dark blue carpet.

The long drapes at the windows were drab. Perhaps once they had been beautiful since the material was good and rich, but like the carpet the blue had faded and when I shook them the dust that came out made me cough and splutter. The room felt cold and I looked with dismay at the huge four-poster bed with its blue drapes. Gingerly I turned down the bedspread which felt cold to my touch, but I was relieved to see that at least the bed linen was newly laundered and clean.

A log fire had been laid in the hearth but nobody had thought to put a match to it, and I was shivering with cold. It was only late September, but there had been heavy rain during the evening and I could smell the damp which seemed to permeate the entire room. Off the bedroom was a bathroom, but this was no better. The floor tiling was badly chipped and I wrinkled up my nose with distaste at the stained bath and dark blue and gold paper on the walls.

It was evident that nobody living at Glenmoor had taken much pride in the house, and I speculated on what Gervases's father had been like.

I thought about Lady de Bellefort's description of him: a spendthrift, wayward and independent, totally unlike Lance's father who had been predictable and malleable. She had expected the same sort of behaviour from Gervase, and my marriage stretched out before me like a battle ground.

I undressed and bathed in lukewarm water. I had spent money extravagantly on exquisite underwear, and the satin nightdress I lowered over my head fell to the floor in exquisite folds.

There were matches on the mantelpiece and I lit the fire. The logs sparkled and crackled, sending volumes of blue smoke up the chimney, and I could smell them, a strangely aromatic scent that quickly filled the entire room. For a few minutes I knelt on the rug extending my hands to the blaze, feeling the warmth on my arms and shoulders, and I started to brush my hair.

I didn't want to think of the night ahead of me. I did not associate Gervase with the love and tenderness I had always longed for. I knew even before he entered the room that our lovemaking would be clinical, a means to an end, an obedience test, joyless and practical. But did I really deserve any better?

If I was being cheated of all the dreams in my heart, wasn't I in turn a bigger cheat, didn't I deserve to suffer at the hands of the man I had married in another girl's name?

From downstairs I could dimly hear laughter and the sound of voices. Our guests seemed in no hurry to depart and my husband was evidently showing no eagerness to seek his bride.

I felt lost in the great bed. The sheets were smooth and cold to my limbs but the bed was comfortable and the pillows soft. Whether he came to me or not there would be no sleep that night, my mind was too active, or so I thought. Eventually however the warmth of the room and the comfort of the bed proved me wrong and I drifted off to sleep.

It was a slumber plagued by terrible dreams. I saw Aunt Julie standing against a warm stone wall on a day when sunlight shimmered over the fields and honeysuckle ran riot across the hedgerows. I heard the German commands ringing coldly as one by one Aunt Julie and her friends sank in crumpled heaps after the sound of rifle fire. Then worse, far worse, I felt myself falling down and down until I was thrashing wildly in a cold black sea, and in my dream I was screaming.

Somebody was shaking me, saying sharply, 'Wake up, Lisanne, wake up, you're only dreaming.'

I opened my eyes to find Gervase was holding my shoulders in a firm grip, his dark steel-blue eyes staring into mine. My eyes darted wildly round the room in an attempt to reassure myself that it had all been a dream.

He laid me back on the pillow and went to a side table where he poured sherry into a glass and brought it over.

'Drink this,' he commanded. 'You've been having a nightmare. I heard you calling out before I entered the room.'

'What did I say?' I whispered.

'You were calling, "Aunt Julie," then you started to cry out, "Lisanne, Lisanne." Was somebody threatening you?'

'I don't know, I don't remember, but I did dream about the ship going down.'

He nodded grimly. 'It is to be expected, it was an experience you will not easily forget.'

For the first time I saw that he was wearing a dark red velvet dressing gown, and the grim amusement in his eyes brought the hot blood to my cheeks.

'Would you like a sleeping draught?' he asked quietly. 'I can quite easily sleep in my dressing room tonight.'

'Just as you wish,' I answered shakily.

'No, my dear, it is as you wish. Do we get our wedding night over or do we postpone the occasion?'

Anger came suddenly to my rescue and with cheeks flaming I stormed, 'You must think me uncommonly unattractive to leave the decision in my hands.'

He threw back his head and laughed delightedly. 'That is more like the Lisanne I remember. Incidentally I do find you attractive, more attractive, more beautiful than I had envisaged, and perhaps in any other circumstances I would have longed to make love to you. As it is I can only think that you and I are here to play a part, obey a command. Don't you think, my dear cousin, that in this most personal thing we should have been allowed to choose for ourselves?'

'Yes I do. I have always thought so.'

'And doesn't it make you feel less than a woman to have obeyed without question? It has made me feel less than a man.'

'Then why have you obeyed, why didn't you rebel?'

He was sitting on the edge of the bed, a reflective look on his dark, handsome face. 'Why indeed?' he said at last. 'I saw what it did to my parents, what it did to my father when he rebelled. My parents never loved each other, they quarrelled constantly, hating each other. It was hardly an atmosphere for a sensitive child to grow up in, and in those days I was sensitive. It was a sensitivity that needed to be stifled throughout my schooldays.

'In other people's homes I saw love and tenderness, friendship and comradeship, in my own I saw only strife and bitterness. When my father rebelled he was rejected, he became a traveller over the face of the earth and eventually his money ran out and he came home, humiliated and scorned. I learned the lesson well. I keep what I have, even this old house to which my father and his family were banished because my grandmother couldn't bear to have him living near her in England. I hate this house, I've always hated it, and as time goes by you'll hate it too.'

'Why do you hate it?'

'Because it's not Langstone Priory, because it's a house my grandmother hated, and she paid my father back by giving it to him.'

'It seems to me the de Belleforts have been more interested in hating than loving.'

'I think you're right, but they have loved the land, land that has been the de Belleforts' for centuries – the enduring thing, Lisanne, the only thing that matters.'

I was staring at him mutely, but I was thinking about another day years before when I had stood with Lance in the snow looking down at the Priory and its acres. Their voices were similar and in the firelight even their faces were etched in the same mould, and now as then I was being made to see that I had no armour against the land. Lance had loved me and I had lost, Gervase did not love me but I could never hope to win.

The tears welled slowly into my eyes and rolled unchecked down my face, and in that moment I saw his expression soften and grow kind. Appealingly I reached out to him and without hesitation he took me in his arms, kissing my tear-stained face. Then suddenly I felt his arms grow tight like bands of steel around me and his mouth was on mine, kissing me with a passion I had never really known, and before I was aware of it I was responding with all the ardour in my nature.

It was the animal passion of a man for a woman, hurting and gentle, painful and ecstatic, and it was a passion that left me trembling and drained in the hour before the dawn, when suddenly I was alone. I had felt him tear himself from my grasp as if he could no longer bear to have me pliant in his arms, as if the act of love had degraded him, robbed him of his manhood. I heard the door of his dressing room close with a sharp click, then in all the house there was a stillness, like the stillness of an empty tomb.

I slept late, waking to a chill grey morning when the room looked no more inviting than the night before and the dead cinders in the grate gave it an additional neglected atmosphere.

I dressed leisurely. It was almost eleven o'clock and nobody had thought fit to waken me or bring me a cup of tea. I dressed in a tweed skirt and sweater and after reassuring myself that I looked well enough, I ran lightly down the stairs.

A servant girl was busy sweeping the hall and she bobbed one of the curtsies I was becoming accustomed to. 'Is the master in?' I enquired.

'No, Mrs de Bellefort, the master was out of the 'ouse 'afore eight o'clock. Sure and we shan't be seein' 'im 'til just 'afore dinner.'

'Is there a fire in the dining room?'

'No, Ma'am, but there be one in the mornin' room. There's allus a fire in the mornin' room at this toime. Can I get you some breakfast, Ma'am?'

378

'No thank you, but a cup of coffee would be nice. What is your name?'

'Oime, Mary, Miss, Mary O'Donnell. Oi'll get your coffee and tell the 'ousekeeper you're awake.'

I found the morning room on my own, glad to see the warm fire roaring on the hearth, but like the rest of the house the room had little character. I decided at that moment that when I next saw my husband I would ask him if I could have a free hand to go over the house. If I lived here, then I should be able to do something about implanting my own taste.

When Mary appeared with the coffee I asked, 'Are there any dogs about, Mary?'

'Dogs, Ma'am?'

'Yes, I thought I would walk in the park, a dog would be good company.'

'The dogs usually go out with the master, but old Danny moight be in the kitchen, oi'll 'ave a look.'

I can't think why I had suddenly decided that a dog might be a good companion, I had always been afraid of them until Aunt Julie's poodle Pierre. I had been fond of Pierre and upset when we had to leave him with Jules.

She soon reappeared with a shake of her head. 'The dogs are all out with the master, Ma'am. Mr Murphy sez p'rhaps the master'll let ye'ave one o' the pups from the stable.'

'I'll talk to the master when he gets home, Mary. Thank you.'

Again came the curtesy before she disappeared into the hall.

Immediately I had drunk my coffee I put on a tweed coat and scarf and let myself out into the park.

It was fresh and I tied the scarf round my hair and thrust my hands deep into my pockets. I headed for the forest and was soon walking briskly, revelling in the salty tang of the wind, and taking off my scarf I allowed my hair to blow freely.

I came across the church we had been married in only the day before. I was surprised at its smallness, a grey stone church with a small square tower and stout oak door

379

studded with brass. I pushed it open and entered. There were only a dozen rows of pews but the altar was pretty, a fact that had hardly registered the day before. Slowly I walked up the aisle, looking at the stained-glass windows and the plaques in honour of long dead de Belleforts.

It surprised me that Gervase didn't have much love for the place. It must have been in the de Bellefort family almost as long as Langstone, because some of those plaques dated from the sixteenth and seventeenth centuries.

An open Bible lay on the altar and as I stepped forward to look at it my foot disturbed a single orchid lying on the step. It was from the spray I had carried in my prayer book the day before.

I picked up the flower, a perfect thing, strangely exotic and alien in that tiny Irish church, then I laid it gently on the open Bible before going out into the open air.

I carried on through the forest until I came to a small clearing set out as a burial ground. The graves were all old, some of them bearing stone effigies like knights in armour, and one of them in the garb of a priest or bishop. I looked for Gervase's parents but could not find them, and in a little while it started to rain, soft misty rain that clung to my face and hair in tiny drops and, I hurried back through the forest and across the park.

In the afternoon I roamed the house armed with a notebook and pencil, making copious notes of what needed to be done to make the house more in keeping with the grace of its architecture.

Mary informed me that fires would be lit in the dining hall and the sitting room, and the master liked to eat dinner no later than seven thirty. I was therefore waiting in the sitting room at seven o'clock wearing a soft woollen dinner gown, feeling conspicuously overdressed and so nervous I jumped at every sound outside the room.

CHAPTER 36

We dined in splendid isolation in the great dining hall and I thought with some exasperation how much more intimate it would have been if we could have used the morning room. Conversation was practically impossible as he sat at the other end of the long table, and the food was mediocre and none too warm.

He seemed preoccupied, excusing himself immediately we had eaten by saying he had a telephone call to make, so disconsolately I wandered into the sitting room alone. I was bored. There were magazines laid out on a side table but they were boring men's magazines.

He returned after about half an hour and came to sit opposite me. For several minutes he eyed me in an amused fashion over his whisky glass before saying, 'And how have you spent your day?'

'I walked in the park and went to the church.'

How stilted our conversation was, with neither of us making any real effort. I felt nervous, unsure of myself, and he was enjoying my discomfort. In some exasperation I snapped, 'Is this how you spend all your evenings, drinking whisky and staring into the fire?'

He stared at me in silence, then getting to his feet he said politely, 'You must forgive me, Lisanne, I am accustomed to spending my evenings alone without the need to entertain a wife. What would you like a drink, sherry?'

'Nothing, thank you.'

'You'll have to get accustomed to spending a great deal of your time alone. I'm kept very busy on the estate and I shall be away for the next few days. Why don't you get a car and drive around the countryside? You'll find it very beautiful.'

'I'm afraid I don't drive.'

He stared at me in amazement. 'You never fail to surprise

381

me, Lisanne. Surely my respected aunt must have insisted you learn to drive.'

I bit my lip angrily. Of course Lisanne had been able to drive. All sorts of dragons were rearing their ugly heads and once more the enormity of what I had done hit me like a sledgehammer.

'I haven't driven for years, I need practice,' I answered him.

'You don't drive and you don't like horses. Where is the Lisanne I knew?'

'I do like horses. You said you would find me a predictable mount.'

'And so I will. I'll speak to Alan, he'll go along to the stables with you in the morning and you can take a look around. As for a car, that can easily be arranged and you can begin by driving round the estate.'

'Thank you, Gervase. I would also like a dog, quite a small one, one that would be a good companion.'

'Very well, I'll see what I can do. Tell me, how well did you get along with Cousin Lance?'

I stared at him in surprise. 'Very well. Lance was always kind.'

'Where I am not.'

'I didn't say that.'

'Nevertheless, my dear, you will find out that we are very different. I have the strangest feeling that Lance is destined to be a man with daughters. See that you give me a son, Lisanne.'

I could feel my face burning with colour but with my head held high I answered, 'That is something neither of us can be sure of, we can only hope.'

'It is the one thing that might bring us closer together, the only thing. It's a great pity that in an arranged marriage such as ours the birth of a son and heir can't be arranged also.'

'I think this whole conversation is offensive.'

'Very well then, we'll change it. What shall we talk about?'

'We can talk about the state of the house.'

'The house?'

'Yes. It's a beautiful house which has been allowed to fall to pieces. It needs a great deal of money spending on it. The curtains are dusty and extremely dirty, there are cobwebs in the corners and the woodwork is disgraceful. That beautiful balustrade is in an awful state and the food at dinner was inferior, badly cooked and barely warm.'

He threw back his head and laughed.

'There now, you remind me of Aunt Delia. I can see her sitting there wrinkling up her aristocratic nose and telling me what is wrong with my home. Personally I don't see anything wrong with it.'

In some anger I jumped to my feet and pointing to the windows said, 'Take a look at those curtains then. All the colour is faded out of them, and look at the dust.'

To suit my actions to my words I went over to the curtains and shook them and immediately the dust was in my eyes and my throat.

He didn't speak, but simply sat there with a small smile on his face.

'Look at the fireplace,' I cried. 'It's the most beautiful marble, yet when did it ever get polished? It's lifeless.'

'If you want to spend your money on the house go ahead with my blessing,' he said calmly. 'As for the food, you're the mistress now, you have my full permission to talk to the servants.'

'How many servants are there?'

'Enough. I've always been satisfied, but then I'm often away and maybe they have been able to go in for self-determination. You must do what you think fit about the house and the servants, Lisanne, it will no doubt keep you fully occupied. Now if you will excuse me I have work to do in the study. I may have gone when you get up in the morning but I expect to be back by the end of the week.'

I stared after him in amazement. It was barely nine o'clock and a lonely evening stretched before me. Evidently he had no intention of sitting with me again and no doubt he expected me to be fast asleep when he sought his bed.

I couldn't sleep. I lay alone in the huge four-poster listening to the rain on the window, the sighing of trees and occasionally the distant hooting of an owl. Once I thought I heard the sound of a ship's hooter echoing dismally through the mist but later it became so insistent I realized it must be a foghorn.

I cried stormy tears into my pillow as I tossed this way and that through the early hours, then I heard a door close in the corridor and I sat up with my ears straining, my eyes looking into the darkness. I eased out of bed and went to the window to draw back the curtains. It was a dark moonless night and I shivered in the cold air which crept through the cracks in the window frames.

Nervously I returned to the bed, listening all the time for the sounds of somebody moving in the room next to mine, watching feverishly for the knob on the door to turn, but there was no sound. For what seemed ages I sat up in my bed hardly daring to breathe, and then realization dawned. Gervase was sleeping next door in his dressing room, he had no intention of coming to me.

I was eating breakfast before nine o'clock the following morning but Gervase had already left the house. I had no sooner finished breakfast, however, when Alan came into the room, and with his arrival something more normal entered my life.

'Gervase said you wanted to take a look round the stables, Lisanne. We'll go now if you're free.'

'There's nothing else to do round here, I'll be glad to go with you, Alan.'

The stables were several minutes' walk from the house and as we neared them I could hear the sound of laughter and men's voices.

A group of them stood chatting in the centre of the stableyard and as we entered they raised their caps respectfully. Several dogs came rushing towards us.

'I haven't seen any dogs around the house,' I said to Alan while they leaped and fawned around us.

'Well old Danny stays mostly in the kitchens and I expect Gervase keeps the others in his study. He doesn't allow them the run of the house.'

384

'What sort of dogs does he have?'

'Great danes, enormous chaps but they have a nice temperament. There's no need to be afraid of them.'

'What kind are these?'

'Retrievers, labradors and spaniels. I say, Lisanne, you're not really well up in dogs. I would have thought you would be.'

'I never had one of my own.'

'But you had them at Langstone?'

'My grandmother wasn't into hunting or field sports, she was quite an old lady, you know.'

His face cleared and he nodded in agreement, while I thought how glibly the words came, almost without thinking.

A row of horses stood with their heads over their stall doors and we walked past them, occasionally patting their noses.

'How proficient are you, Lisanne?' Alan asked.

'I enjoy riding but I'm not keen on hunting. I just need a horse I can ride around the estate or maybe into the villages.'

We paused in front of a stall where a grey horse looked at us gently from behind incredibly long eyelashes.

'This is Silver. He's a gelding with a placid temperament and can be relied upon to behave. I don't think you could do better, Lisanne.'

I was stroking his satiny neck gently, then he started to nuzzle my neck and I was loving him. Suddenly he was my friend, something of my own.

'Oh yes, Alan, I like this one. Will you have time to ride with me one morning just until I get used to him?'

'Yes of course, but better than that I'll ask Maureen to ride with you. She knows her way around these parts and she'd like a woman companion, I'm sure. If you like I'll call for you this evening and you can spend the evening with us.'

'I'd like that very much, Alan.'

'Gervase said you'd also like a dog.'

At least, I thought, Gervase has made a little effort on my behalf, and my heart lifted in gratitude.

'I thought a dog would be a good companion around the estate.'

'We've three cocker spaniel pups in the stable. The older dogs are trained to the gun and need to be with a gamekeeper, but if you get one of the puppies early enough you can mould him into the sort of dog you want.'

The puppies were adorable. I loved them all but finally settled for a black one with large soulful eyes and a too-affectionate disposition.

'You'll need to house train him,' Alan laughed, 'or I could ask one of the grooms to take him for a day or two first.'

'Perhaps that would be best, I'm still feeling my way up at the house.'

'What are you going to call him?'

'I think I'll call him Toby, what do you think?'

'I like it. We have a black one we call Jet. You'll find your puppy very faithful and affectionate. How are you liking the house, Lisanne?'

'I'm hating it, Alan. It needs a fortune spending on it. Hasn't Gervase ever seen what it's really like?'

'Gervase is interested in the estate, he's never really liked the house. His father disliked it.'

'But why, when it could be so beautiful?'

'I rather think his grandmother hadn't much time for the old squire. He was a bit wild in his youth and he always had the feeling that this was a place of exile. Gervase has grown up with that belief.'

'But Lady de Bellefort had three sons, so they couldn't all live at Langstone, that was to be for her eldest son. The younger one was in the army, he died in the army.'

'Your father?'

I stared at him, then I looked away sharply. Of course, Lisanne's father, and I had spoken of him as if he were a stranger, just somebody someone had mentioned to me.

'Yes.'

'I expect with three sons rivalry between them is to be expected. Gervase's father always said his elder brother was as dull as ditch water and the younger one was your grandmother's favourite. Resentment doesn't get better with the years, if anything it only festers.'

'I don't know Gervase at all. You're his friend, you can tell me if he's worth knowing.'

He stopped in his tracks to face me. 'My dear girl, he's your husband. If you want your marriage to succeed you've got to make the effort.'

'Don't we both have to make the effort?'

'That too.'

'Is there any other woman in his life?'

I saw the blank look come over his face, leaving it expressionless. I would learn nothing from Alan, and impatiently I thought that men were like that, they kept faith. If my husband was the greatest womanizer between Glenmoor and Dublin it wouldn't be Alan Harvey I heard it from.

Ignoring my question he said normally, 'You can get busy with the house, Lisanne. I expect Gervase has given you a free hand.'

'Of course, and the suggestion that I use my own money.'

He laughed. 'Well, I suppose he's satisfied with it as it is, so if you want it altered then you should pay for it.'

'Do you think that's fair? It isn't me who's allowed it to get into such a state.'

'It's all the same money that's in the family. I've never had that sort of money, so what can I say? You'll enjoy tackling the house, Lisanne. If you want any help I'm sure Maureen will lend a hand, and Edna Jefferson.'

That afternoon I walked down to see the Jeffersons and explained about the house.

They both laughed and Edna said, 'I told Gervase you'd soon fall out of love with the house. I wouldn't live in it for a fortune, but it has possibilities, I'll give you that.'

'What's wrong with the house, old girl?' George said impatiently. 'It only wants a decorator in some of the rooms. You must admit it's a fair stately pile.'

'It's a disgrace,' I retorted. 'Peeling paintwork, dirty walls, and the curtains are as ancient as those old tombs in the clearing.'

They laughed again. 'Gervase told us what a determined

387

young woman you were. I'm sure it won't take you long to get things moving.'

'But will he approve, do you think?'

'He probably won't take much interest,' George said, only to be reproved by a hard look from his wife.

'Of course he'll take notice, it's his house as well as Lisanne's.'

'Sorry, Edna, but you know Gervase as well as I. He doesn't care how much money he spends on the farms, the land, even the stables, but the house is just somewhere to lay his head.'

'I want rather more from my home than that,' I said firmly. 'I'm just not quite sure how to go about it.'

Lisanne would have known, but not Ellen Adair who'd never had any money and hardly knew how to spend it.

'The first thing we must do, Lisanne, is to get hold of an interior decorator who'll take a look at the house and decide just what needs to be done,' Edna said. 'He'll come along with samples of wallpaper, curtains, carpets, the lot – all you'll need to do is look at them and decide colour schemes. It'll be enormous fun, I'd love to help.'

'I'll be glad if you would. Alan said his wife would probably like to help too.'

'I'm sure she would. You'll quite like Maureen, she's a good sort.'

At the end of the day I felt I was gaining ground. I had found myself a horse and a puppy. I had made some headway with the house, and I had spent a delightful evening in the home of Alan Harvey and his wife. I got on very well with Maureen. She had a nice bubbly sense of fun, and she quickly became enthusiastic about my plans for Glenmoor.

'I knew you'd hate it,' she confided in me. 'When Gervase said you'd lived in the lap of luxury all your life I thought how much you'd hate Glenmoor. I'm not surprised you intend to do something about it.'

'I'm not too sure about the servants. The place is dirty and the food is inferior and badly cooked. I don't want to come the heavy-handed mistress of the house but I do think they need knocking into shape.'

'You're quite right. Gervase has let them have too easy a time of it and if you intend to change things, Lisanne, you've got to start right away.'

'Would Gervase mind if I interfered with the running of the house? The housekeeper's been there a long time.'

'Yes, I know. She spends more time helping out at the church in the village than she does attending to her duties at Glenmoor, and it's said she tipples her whisky and anything else she can get her hands on.'

'I have to talk to her, I have to talk to all of them.'

'Talk to them soon, before Gervase comes back, and then tell him about it.'

'I don't suppose he'll be too pleased.'

'Oh, men are all alike, they don't like the tenor of their lives disturbed in any way. But there does come a time when things need to change.'

The opportunity came the following morning when I asked to see all the servants in the morning room directly after breakfast. I had not realized there were so many of them as they stood in a shuffling untidy line before me, looking down at the floor.

The housekeeper, Mrs O'Flaherty, was a big raw-boned woman with a red face, wearing a long black dress and a none too clean apron.

Mary I already knew, and one by one the others introduced themselves – Rosie and Moira, Paddy, Connah and Jonah – and I was careful to be forthright without being unkind.

I told them I appreciated that the house was a large one and old houses needed more care than modern ones, but I was displeased that there were cobwebs on the walls and dust in the corners. I told them I was intent on making changes, there would be decorators in the house and workmen of all descriptions, after that there would be new carpets and new curtains. And things had to change.

Mrs O'Flaherty listened to me in silence, arms akimbo and face becoming more ruddy by the second, and when I had finished she said stoutly, 'We does our best, Ma'am. Like ye said it's large, the house is, and we works our fingers

389

to the bone to keep it tidy. If it's wantin' improvements you are, then there should be more of us.'

'Then there will be, Mrs O'Flaherty, but if I'm still not satisfied when the improvements are completed then I shall have to replace you with other servants who are more conscientious. There is also the question of the food – who does the cooking here?'

'Rosie and me does it between us.'

'I like my meals served hot, Mrs O'Flaherty, and I dislike watery vegetables and green mould on the cheese. If you are short staffed in the kitchen then I will employ others, but there are only the master and myself to cater for. Surely it isn't too much to ask that the food be served properly and hot.'

'It's a fair distance from the dining room to the kitchens, no wonder the food's cold 'afore it's served, Ma'am.'

'In that case, Mrs O'Flaherty, we must see about installing a food lift from the kitchen to the dining room. All this can be gone into when the decorators and workmen come in. The house is bound to be upset for a considerable time, but I'm sure we shall all benefit from the results. That is all, and I am very glad to meet you. Please don't be afraid to approach me if you have any problems.'

On that note they departed, and I heard them muttering amongst themselves in a disgruntled way.

I had surprised even myself. That I had had the temerity to lecture a body of Gervase's servants as if I were accustomed to it gave me a new confidence. Those years with Lisanne's mother had not been in vain, and with a certain grim amusement I thought: I am after all a de Bellefort. My grandmother might have been a servant girl but my grandfather was the master of Langstone Priory.

CHAPTER 37

It seemed incredible that four years had passed and I had become as firmly established at Glenmoor as Lady de Bellefort was at the Priory. I had transformed the house from something approaching a monstrosity into a house people came to gaze at.

Once every month the gates were thrown open to the public who came to wander in the parkland. They had picnics near the mere and gazed in wonder at the old tombs in the burial ground. They knelt in reverent prayer in the tiny church and gazed at the flowerbeds and smooth green lawns with delighted appreciation.

Occasionally I moved among them, chatting to them as they stood about in groups, and I took my small son with me so that he would know how to greet other children.

If I had transformed Glenmoor I had also transformed myself. I was aware of a new confidence and not unaware of the admiring glances of the men and women I met in the park. I knew how to walk, how to speak and how to dress, and although the house had cost me a fortune it appeared that my capital was well invested in substantial areas which paid me considerable dividends, enabling me to spend lavishly on the things I loved.

I had expected Gervase to object when I wanted our son to be called Lance but he seemed not to mind, and when I told him I was surprised that he had not objected he merely smiled, saying, 'Lance is very appropriate. One day he will no doubt inherit Langstone, and there have been many Lances at the Priory.'

'Why do you say that?' I answered sharply.

'Didn't I tell you that Lance was destined to have daughters?' Indeed Geraldine had presented him with three – one older than Lance, one the same age and one two years younger.

When Gervase informed me that probably one day my son would marry one of his cousins I turned on him sharply, crying, 'He will marry who he wants to marry, neither you nor I will make him marry a stranger.'

Gervase and I went our separate ways. I had my house and my garden, I rode every day through the villages with Lance beside me on his pony, and I was very much the lady of the manor.

The girl Ellen Adair belonged to another world, another life. I had largely forgotten her existence and there were only two regrets. I wished I could have seen my brother Peter again, and I longed for news of Kitty. Kitty would approve of the way I had coped, but how could I tell my brother that every day of my life I was living a lie?

I knew that Kitty was married, indeed her picture had been in the papers only months before showing a gay laughing woman wrapped in furs standing with the Nôtre Dame behind her, laughing up into the face of a tall swarthy man with evident enjoyment. Under the photograph I read that the singer Emerald had been married quietly that morning to Sheik Mohamed Isfara, and they would be honeymooning in the Bahamas.

That day I felt disturbed. A part of my life had caught up with me and found me strangely vulnerable. When I showed the picture to Gervase, saying that I had heard her sing in Paris and Monte Carlo, he merely said, 'He's probably got half a dozen wives already. The woman's a fool to marry an Arab.'

'He's obviously very rich.'

'Obviously, or a woman like that wouldn't have entertained him.'

'You don't know what sort of a woman she is.'

'Do you?' he said maddeningly.

In the eyes of the world our marriage was well enough. We appeared together at race meetings and horse shows. We danced together at hunt balls and we entertained and were entertained in the homes of the few friends we had in the area, but still between us was the resentment that I had largely forgotten but Gervase could not.

He adored our son and occasionally he sought my bed, when I despised myself for the ardour he aroused in me and when I knew full well it was not prompted by love, only by desire, and such a bitterness flared between us that the aftermath left me in tears.

I first became aware of Pamela Capethorn at the ball our friends induced us to give on completion of the house.

'You ought to show it off,' Edna Jefferson encouraged. 'The house is a showplace and if Gervase never entertained before, he now has a wife. So there's really no excuse not to.'

Lisanne would have known how to organize a ball of vast proportions but when I appeared doubtful Edna said, 'Nobody does it themselves these days, there are numerous caterers you could call in. Really, dear, all you need to do is the flowers.'

When I consulted Gervase about the guest list he said sharply, 'Do we really need to fill the house with all sorts of people who will tramp over your newly polished floors and leave their glasses to stain the tables?'

'Other people have balls, why can't we?'

'We don't go to their bunfights. They mean a lot of silly people milling around talking at the tops of their voices about nothing at all.'

'We don't go because we don't invite them here. There are times when I still feel like a stranger in the area.'

'If you want the ball, Lisanne, go right ahead and arrange it. Just don't expect me to take much interest in it. I have other things on my mind.'

So I engaged a firm of caterers who moved in on the day, and I arranged the flowers – huge bowls of chrysanthemums in shades of white to deepest bronze, and with them shining holly which was already bearing scarlet berries although it was only late November.

Satisfied that the supper table looked festive and that huge log fires burned in every grate, I went up to my room to dress. For the first time I wore the turquoise chiffon evening gown I had bought in London, and I adored it. It draped my slender figure tenderly like some ancient dress of a Greek goddess, and the skirt shimmered and swirled around my feet when I moved.

I went into my son's room to say goodnight and he sat up in his bed with round eyes as he took in the picture I presented.

'Mother, you look so beautiful,' he said, and I gathered him into my arms and held him close.

'You smell lovely too,' he said. 'Why don't you always wear that dress?'

I laughed. 'What, to ride in the park and walk across the fields? Whatever would the villagers say?'

'Has father seen it?'

'Not yet. I've told Mary to bring in your hot milk and biscuits around eight o'clock. Will the music keep you awake, darling?'

'I'll lie in my bed listening to it. I'll think about you dancing in that dress with Father.'

I kissed him again before pulling the covers round him, then I turned on the light beside his bed before switching off the others. He was still watching me with a happy smile when I closed the door.

Gervase stood in the hall with a group of his friends as I descended the stairs and they all turned to greet me. I was instantly aware of their admiration, and the long mirror across the hall told me that I was indeed a beautiful woman in a beautiful dress. I had dressed my hair high on my head, leaving only one heavy tress to fall over my shoulder, and I was wearing my long diamond earrings, my only adornment.

Gallantly Gervase stepped forward and took his place by my side. His eyes were dark and sombre as they gazed into mine and then in a low voice he said, 'You look very beautiful, Lisanne. I should appreciate my good fortune more.'

'Thank you, Gervase.'

'I think you know everybody here.'

I smiled and one by one the group of men took my hand, then Gervase whispered, 'Perhaps we should go to the door, our other guests are arriving.'

There were so many of them. Several of the men were in hunting pink mess jackets, others in sombre evening dress, the women in silks and taffetas, with jewels round their throats and in their hair, but not one of them was wearing a dress as fashionable or beautiful as my own until Pamela Capethorn arrived.

She entered the room with an elderly man and immediately I became aware of a moment of silence before the chatter broke out anew.

She was not a beautiful woman but she was decidedly striking. She was tall, with wide smooth shoulders, and she wore a topless sheath dress in white satin that showed off her high firm breasts and shapely hips. She was dark, but there were red lights in her hair and her eyes were a curious light hazel.

She smiled confidently as Gervase said, 'This is Colonel Capethorn, Lisanne, and his daughter Pamela.'

I smiled a greeting but at the same time I was aware of her eyes sliding from me to Gervase, and her smile became warmer and singularly more promising. By this time her father was gripping my hand and congratulating me on the improvements I had done to the house, and in the conversation that followed I was given to understand that they had been living in India, where Colonel Capethorn was finishing his time. I could only assume that their invitation had been sent by Gervase, who must have known of their return to the area.

They were the last guests to arrive and I couldn't help thinking that their entrance had been engineered by the girl. As we moved in a foursome to the ballroom where there was already dancing, I knew that people were whispering together and many of them were regarding us with the utmost speculation, even amusement.

Dancing with Gervase was a joy. He moved with graceful competence round the ballroom and we were looked upon admiringly. Indeed to those watching we must have looked a well-matched couple, he dark and I fair, he tall and handsome, myself slight and somewhat ethereal, and from some of the older people present there were smiles of approval as the dance reached its end.

I danced with many of our guests and Gervase did likewise, then just before supper I saw him dancing with Pamela and they were laughing together, enjoying each other's company like old friends.

From dozens of people as the night wore on I was complimented on the beauty of the house and the success of the ball, and showered with invitations which I felt sure Gervase would ignore. Indeed I said to one lady who was over-insistent, 'My husband isn't fond of socializing, he always makes the excuse that he has too much to do.'

'Oh, Gervase has always been like that – his father was even worse – but he has a lovely wife to show off, he should make the effort.'

'Perhaps you should try to persuade him,' I said, smiling.

'He'll take no notice of me. Have a word with Pamela, my dear, she could always persuade him to attend one function or another.'

For a moment there was an uncomfortable silence before Edna Jefferson said, 'How's your darling little boy, Lisanne? You haven't brought him to see us this week.'

'Lance is very well, Edna, but I've been too busy this week. He's missed you too.'

'The caterers were excellent, dear, it's all been wonderful.'

I smiled and moved on to another group and met the same praise, the same invitations. Then I saw Gervase and Pamela move out on to the terrace regardless of the keen frosty night. He was helping her to arrange her fur wrap round her shoulders and although there were others moving out on to the terrace with them I didn't miss the knowing looks from several people standing nearby.

People were dancing again and as I excused myself and ran lightly upstairs I was sure that between Pamela Capethorn and my husband burned the embers of an old love. I went straight to my son's room to find him sleeping soundly, one rounded arm under his head. Toby, curled up at the end of his bed, raised his head and eyed me soulfully.

'You shouldn't be on the bed,' I admonished him. 'Come along now, get into your basket.' I patted his head as he obeyed me, then I switched off the light and went to my own room.

One of the servants had drawn the heavy drapes but I pulled them back, letting in the moonlight. I could see people standing in groups on the terrace, see the smoke from their cigarettes mingling with the autumnal mist, and I saw Pamela and Gervase strolling along the path towards the sunken garden. They were in earnest conversation and she appeared to be doing most of the talking. At times I could hear their laughter and I reflected that I didn't often hear Gervase laugh, to me his amusement was always cynically inclined.

They came to a halt almost below my window and I could hear their conversation.

'Didn't you mind when she decided to knock the house to pieces, Gervase? I must say it's an improvement,' she said in a light, amused voice.

'No, I didn't mind. It kept her occupied and she was pretty lonely, I suppose.'

'She's very beautiful, or hadn't you noticed?'

'Well of course I've noticed, I am a man after all.'

'And doesn't her beauty do something to you?'

'If you mean doesn't it compensate me for being unable to please myself, I suppose perhaps it does in a way. But it's not enough, Pamela.'

'She's played her part, you've got the son you wanted and she's made this place a show house. Isn't that enough?'

He was gazing down at her, and for several moments he didn't answer while I stood at the window with bated breath, waiting for his answer as she was waiting.

'If you mean am I ready to take up our liaison as before, as if my wife didn't exist, I don't think that's possible, Pamela. We've had some good times, we've enjoyed ourselves together, but Lisanne's not just my wife. She's a de Bellefort, and between we de Belleforts is a strange sort of honour. I don't intend to open everybody's mouths by carrying on with you as though Lisanne didn't exist, she's my wife, the mother of my son. I owe her something even if she did come to me gift wrapped and with precise instructions as to what to do with her.'

'You'll not keep it up, Gervase, I know you too well. One of these days you're going to want me again as I shall want you. We've too much going for us, too much to remember, and we're alike: hard and greedy and selfish.'

'Thank you for spelling out my faults, my dear, obviously you never recognized that queer streak of honour in me. I'd rather you forgot about the past, Pamela. In any case my cousin Lisanne might prove to be something of a match for you, she is after all her mother's daughter.'

'Darling, there never has been a woman who's been a match for me where you're concerned.'

Although they laughed together, as her arms reached out for him he held her away. 'I mean it, Pamela, not here, not now.'

Angrily I pulled the cord that closed the curtains, shutting out the night. I was trembling, and I sank down on to the edge of my bed, gasping with the pain of it.

Gervase had said it was over, but I had heard the longing in her voice. Why should I care? I didn't love him, I had never professed to love him, or he me. If he spent every night of his life with Pamela Capethorn it shouldn't bother me – but the awful thing was that it did.

I didn't want to be a cheated wife, I wanted to be a loved one. I wanted my son to be part of a loving family, not to grow up as Gervase had grown up: aware of the bitterness between his parents, the quarrels and bitter recriminations that must have coloured his childhood.

Gervase had said that Lisanne de Bellefort would know what to do with Pamela Capethorn. But Ellen Adair did not.

398

CHAPTER 38

With the advent of Pamela Capethorn into my life I felt less assured. She was a superb horsewoman and she could enter into men's conversation with ease as they discussed horses and hunting, agriculture and the running of large estates.

She was a man's girl, a drinking pal, a sportswoman who could often beat them at their own game, and although she treated all the men in our circle with friendly comradeship it was Gervase she followed with her eyes, Gervase she smiled at over her brandy glass.

I tried to appear indifferent but whenever we were in the same room I could sense the atmosphere, the knowing glances of those around us, and I began to refuse invitations – it was easier to stay away than it was to face people.

One afternoon she accosted me in the village, saying, 'Why not turn out with the hunt on Saturday, Lisanne? Gervase gave me to understand that you were keen.'

'Gervase gave you to understand wrong, then.'

'But I've spent months in Yorkshire in the winter time. Hunting's a way of life there.'

I smiled politely and made as if to move on but she stood in my path, her light hazel eyes filled with a strange amusement.

'You're not a bit like Gervase described you. He expected you to be something of a handful, too spoilt and self-assured, instead he finds you calm and strangely gentle. I don't really think he knows how to handle you.'

'Did he say that?'

'No, it's an impression I get.'

'If he's puzzled by me perhaps it's a good thing. He might like to be intrigued.'

'I didn't say he was intrigued, Lisanne, he's not suf-ficiently interested to be intrigued. He's merely puzzled

399

that his giddy, rather silly little cousin isn't living up to expectations.'

'Are you always so insolent to people you don't know very well?'

I watched her face colouring a bright brick red, and covered with confusion she said quickly, 'I say, Lisanne, I really didn't mean to offend you. I'd very much like us to be friends.'

'I'm sure you would, it would be nice to have my blessing on your efforts to steal my husband. Unfortunately, however, I'm not looking for your friendship, I prefer to choose my friends from women who have no ulterior designs on what is mine.'

Stung to anger she retorted, 'Gervase was never yours, you were always just a girl he needed to marry to hold fast to his heritage.'

'Exactly so. I agreed to marry him for the same reasons. I have played my part, I shall expect him to play his.'

'What exactly do you mean by that?'

'I expect him to keep up appearances and not to scandalize everybody by flirting with you.'

'Gervase does not flirt with me, it goes much deeper than that.'

'Then I shall give him an ultimatum. Either he puts a stop to it or I leave him, taking my son with me. The de Belleforts have always known, and it was spelt out in our grandmother's will, that if there is divorce or separation the guilty party would forfeit all rights to land and property. You will count as nothing when Gervase comes to weigh up the cost.'

'You wouldn't dare, he would despise you for it.'

'Surely you don't think I care about that? What he does in private is his own affair but in public I have the right to expect him to conform. Either way I think you will find that you are relatively unimportant.'

I left her staring after me with my head held high. My words were filled with brave confidence but my heart was fluttering wildly. I could not believe that I had had the courage to talk to Pamela Capethorn with all the confidence of an affronted wife.

I thought about Lady de Bellefort arriving at Langstone as a bride only to become aware of her husband's dalliance with a serving girl. How her proud spirit must have squirmed, even when she hadn't learned to love him herself. Now I was experiencing the same sort of anger. It was retribution planned by some omnipotent diabolical genie and I was being asked to pay for the waywardness of other years.

It was several days later when Gervase made me aware of his displeasure in no uncertain manner. I was sitting with young Lance in the drawing room. He loved books and was beginning to read remarkably well for one so young. His father burst in upon us unceremoniously, saying, 'I want to see you in the study, Lisanne. Alone.'

I stared into his face. It was white with anger and his dark blue eyes shone with a steely glare.

Unhurried I said to Lance, 'Go on with your reading, darling. You're doing very well, I won't be long.'

I followed in Gervase's wake as he stormed across the hall and when I entered the study he was standing near the fireplace looking down into the flames.

I went to stand opposite him, then when he didn't look up I sat in the nearest chair with my hands clenched in my lap, hoping my face was more composed than my heart.

It seemed like a year before he looked at me. All I was aware of was the ticking of the marble clock on the mantelpiece and the crackling of the coals on the hearth. When he did look at me his face was cold and his words fell like drops of ice from his lips.

'I don't expect my wife to insult my friends in the village street. If you had anything to say to Pamela Capethorn it was better said in private.'

'I didn't accost her, she accosted me.'

'I can hardly believe that.'

'You prefer to believe your mistress before your wife?'

'Why do you call her my mistress?'

'Because she told me the thing between you went very

401

deep. It was more, much more than a mere flirtation. And I believe her.'

'And if it did go deep what does it matter? We were both free, and even now I didn't promise my grandmother to love you to the exclusion of all others, I only promised to marry you.'

'You're never going to forget that you married me as a duty, are you? It's seethed and festered in you ever since you knew that one day you'd have to conform. You don't see me as a woman at all, only as some terrible curse wished on you by a grandmother you never really knew. Don't think I don't think about you in the same way.'

'In that case behave yourself with my friends, accept things the way they are and we might be able to get along together.'

'I will not have my son learn about his father's infidelity from strangers. In public I'm asking you to conform, surely you must remember what your own parent's marriage did to you.'

'And I am asking you, Madam, not to interfere in my life. Do what you like in private and I will do the same. The façade we show to the world will be as blameless as you wish it to be, what we do in private will be our own affair.'

That was the start of it.

In the eyes of the world we were a happy well-adjusted family and it was plain to see how much Gervase adored his son. He took the boy fishing in the trout streams that burbled and gushed their way from the enchanting Wicklow mountains. Already Lance was becoming good with horses, and one day I heard Gervase say to him, 'Don't be afraid to get right back on should you ever have a fall. That was your mother's problem.'

Every day of my life I was cheating my husband, but at least I had given him the son he loved and was proud of. As for myself, I entertained his guests and played hostess with grace and polish at intimate dinner parties and stately balls. We appeared together at horse shows and race meetings, and if Pamela Capethorn was attracting men because she knew how to drink with them and ride with them, I attracted them with my beauty and the way I dressed.

I was never short of admirers or escorts and the face I showed to the world was smiling and serene.

Not so Gervase. He was sarcastic about my admirers. He called them dilettantes because they understood art and music, and more and more I was invited to listen to music in Dublin and London and I spent a great deal of time away from home, particularly after Lance went away to his prep school.

I watched Pamela Capethorn change from a handsome shapely girl into a coarser blowsy woman with a frustrated air, and smiling grimly I told myself that I was winning.

It was April and I was alone in London on one of my cultural shopping trips. Gervase was fishing in Connemara and Lance had just returned to school so there was no pressure on me to return home.

I was enjoying myself hugely, with trips to the theatre and the art galleries, where by this time I had become a familiar figure with the curators. It was one of the curators who told me about a private exhibition in one of the smaller galleries by a new artist who was commanding a great deal of attention in the art world on the continent.

'I've been along to look at it,' he confided. 'There's some very nice stuff there which I think you'd be interested in, Mrs de Bellefort.'

That afternoon I took him at his word and went to the exhibition. To be honest I was a traditionalist and much of the artist's work left me feeling bemused and unsure. It was only when I entered the second gallery that my eyes became riveted on a picture of a red-haired girl in an emerald gown. The artist had dealt haphazardly with the background, pale misty people sitting at pale misty tables, but the girl stood out vibrant and enchanting, and her green eyes seemed to mock me.

There was a price tag on the picture of two thousand pounds but undeterred I hurried along to the gallery office to buy it. The gallery owner was not alone so I waited impatiently outside for the man who was with him to leave.

They came out together, and seeing me the owner smiled and I stepped forward immediately to say, 'I would like to buy the picture of the girl in an emerald dress.'

His smile became uncertain and he looked doubtfully at the man with him and they laughed a little.

'I'm sorry, Madam, you are just too late. This gentleman has bought it.'

'Oh but you can't have,' I cried. 'It is very important to me.'

'I am sorry, Madam, but I'm afraid it's true,' he said apologetically. 'I've had my eye on it all week, and this morning I made up my mind to buy it.'

The distress must have shown on my face and in some torment I cried, 'But why do you want that particular one? There are dozens to choose from.'

'Why do *you* want that particular one?'

'Because I know her. I've known her for years. The picture is terribly important to me and I don't suppose I'll ever meet Kitty again.'

'Kitty?'

'Yes, Kitty McGuire, that's her name.'

'You must be mistaken, Madame,' the owner put in, 'the picture is of the singer Emerald. She's quite famous on the continent, that is she was until she left the stage to marry some Arab prince.'

'She's Kitty McGuire nevertheless,' I insisted, then suddenly realizing I had lost, I said, 'I'm sorry, of course the picture is yours. I was just terribly confused at seeing it and I thought I must have it. Do forgive me.'

The owner was quick to say, 'If another painting of this lady arrives may I telephone you, Madam?'

'I shall only be staying in London a few days but I would be very interested. The name is Mrs de Bellefort and I am staying at the Savoy.'

I smiled at them both before making my escape. I had behaved like a petulant schoolgirl and no doubt they were even now congratulating themselves that the picture wasn't being bought by me. I had no further interest in the exhibition, no other painting was to my taste and I was glad to get out into the open air.

I hurried down the street but had not gone far before I found my arm taken in a firm grip and looking up in surprise I found the man who had bought Kitty's picture looking down at me with a half smile.

'I hope you know I've almost had to break into a run to catch up with you,' he said. There was laughter in his voice and in spite of feeling decidedly at a disadvantage I eventually laughed to.

'Why don't we talk about the picture over a cup of tea?' he said calmly.

'But what is there to talk about? The picture is yours, I accept that.'

'And I accept that it really does mean something to you. I am open to be convinced.'

By this time he had taken my arm and we were walking down the street together.

'Tea at Grimaldi's I think, and the most sensational scones in all London. Do you agree?'

'I don't normally drink tea with a stranger.'

'In that case I should introduce myself, my name is Mark Allenby. And yours?'

'Lisanne de Bellefort.'

'Any relation to the Yorkshire de Belleforts?'

My heart began to race as I replied, 'Well yes, do you know them?'

'I was at school with Lance, and I knew Gervase at Oxford. Which de Bellefort are you?'

'I'm their cousin Lisanne, I'm also Gervase's wife.'

'Of course, the de Belleforts have always married their relatives. I thought Gervase was living in Ireland.'

'We do live in Ireland, in County Wicklow. My husband is away fishing so I took the opportunity to visit London for shopping and the theatre.'

'I'm sure Gervase wouldn't mind my escorting his wife to tea. I knew Lance better than Gervase, but no doubt he'll remember me.'

So we drank tea together and he asked a great many

405

questions about Lance and his wife and daughters. He seemed to know Langstone Priory well and when I asked him if he'd ever been there he said, 'Several times when I was a schoolboy. I stayed with Lance and his family at their place but I was taken to Langstone to meet his grandmother. She was a remarkable woman, very intelligent and with a marvellous sense of humour. Lance adored her. I rather think I met you and Geraldine on one of those occasions.'

Again my heart raced until he said, 'I remember you as a bit of a tomboy, a pretty fair-haired tomboy. I must say you've grown up beautifully, Lisanne. You don't mind me calling you Lisanne?'

'Not as we seem to be such old friends. Do you remember what I was doing when you met me at Langstone?'

'I remember you were mad keen on horses. Do you hunt much in Ireland?'

'My husband does. I still love horses but I don't hunt.'

'I must say that surprises me. I don't much care for hunting either but I do enjoy a game of polo. I met your mother at Langstone. She'd just returned from India, I think your father had died out there.'

'Yes, that's right.'

'Is she still living?'

So I told him about the mine and a little of our life in Provence and he listened attentively.

'Are you going to the theatre this evening?' he asked.

'I haven't made plans to go, I should think about going home soon.'

'But not yet, not when we've just met and I feel as if we're old friends. Will you come to the theatre with me this evening? I'll try to get seats for something good and I could pick you up around seven. I'm staying at my club, it's quite close to the Savoy.'

For a moment I hesitated. I liked this man, he was obviously a gentleman and he had seemed like an old friend when he talked about Langstone. I wavered and he pressed home his advantage. 'I'm sure your husband would rather you went to the theatre with me than went about London on your own,' he said gently.

That was the beginning of an enchanting spring. I stayed on in London savouring the joys of being admired and cosseted. We went to the theatres and we danced in dimly lit exclusive nightclubs. We listened to music in the concert halls, we even went to the zoo, and every day I fell deeper in love with him and he with me.

My beauty blossomed with a new-found delight in living and in my stupidity I believed it could go on indefinitely. I need not make a decision, I need not think of returning home to Ireland, Gervase would not care. We had never professed to anyone that our lives were intricately bound, we had a marriage and a child, but we had never had the sort of love that held others together.

It was pleasant to drift, pleasant to have his eyes, warm and caring, gazing at me across the table, heavenly to drift in his arms without a single thought beyond the moment, until the day we walked in the park and I found him unusually silent.

I had been happily chattering away until I realized suddenly that he was not responding and I found his face grave and strangely sad.

'Is something wrong, Mark?' I asked quietly.

He smiled down at me. 'Something is terribly wrong, Lisanne. You must know that I'm in love with you, and it can't go on like this.'

'I don't understand.'

'I think you do.'

'But what can we do? Oh Mark, must we talk about it now? You know I love you, but must we spoil this heavenly day by talking about things we have no answers for?'

'There have to be answers, my dear. I love you, I want to marry you but you're married to somebody else. Are you prepared to ask Gervase for a divorce?'

'A divorce!'

He nodded.

'Oh Mark, I don't know. It's not as easy as that, I have my son to think of and Gervase will be difficult, I know.'

'And the de Belleforts do not separate.'

'That too. Gervase will never divorce me, the penalties

407

are too great. We agreed to go our separate ways but on the day he married me he made me understand that I would be a de Bellefort for the rest of my life.'

'And I too have a duty, Lisanne. I have my own family to think of. I need to marry and have a son. I too have a noble name and an estate I love – the de Belleforts are not unique in that.'

'You would marry me?'

'If you were free I'd marry you tomorrow. But you're not free, Lisanne, or ever likely to be. I've spent all night thinking about this. Obviously we can't go on as we are. I love you but I can't have you, you love me but you're married to somebody else. The longer we go on seeing each other the harder it is going to be. We should part now, Lisanne, while we're still strong.'

Tears came into my eyes and rolled down my cheeks and I clung to him miserably while his arms held me close and I could feel the steady beating of his heart.

'Poor Lisanne,' he murmured gently, 'I don't suppose you've ever had to part from somebody you loved before.'

Wildly at that moment I thought of Lance. I had loved him but he hadn't loved me enough. Now I loved Mark and he loved me too much, and once again I was being made to realize what I had done when I adopted the role of Lisanne. As Ellen Adair I could have gone with this man to the ends of the earth, as Lisanne de Bellefort I would have to see him walking out of my life.

We moved on in silence, oblivious to the sun shining on the grass, or other lovers walking hand in hand beneath the trees. At the gates he paused and I looked up at him doubtfully, unsure until he said, 'I'll get a taxi for you, Lisanne. I don't think we should meet again under these circumstances.'

'You mean I shall never see you again?'

'Lisanne, I must go home. I've been away from my estate too long already. If you feel like talking to Gervase about us I shall be happy to hear the outcome. This is my address in Leicestershire.'

408

'How cold and formal you sound all of a sudden,' I cried dismally, taking the card from his fingers.

'I'm trying very hard to be formal, Lisanne. I don't feel formal, I feel like it's the ending of the world.'

'I'll speak to Gervase, Mark, I have to. Oh, surely he won't hold me to a marriage as empty as ours. He must see that we can't go on obeying laws that were laid down centuries ago, there should be something we can do about them in this day and age.'

'The decision is yours, my dear, but I am not hopeful. I have known the de Belleforts too long. Here is your taxi.'

I wanted him to hold me in his arms and kiss me, but instead he merely kissed the back of my hand, and raising his hat politely stood back while I entered the taxi and was whisked away into the afternoon traffic.

For the first time I looked at the card in my hand and saw that he was Sir Mark Allenby of Galveston Hall in Leicestershire.

That night I packed my suitcase and paid my hotel bill. In the morning I would fly home to Ireland.

The house felt strangely impersonal as it always did after one of my absences. There were no flowers in the rooms, and there was a film of dust on the furniture. I went immediately up to my room and started to unpack. The room felt stuffy so that I was glad to fling open the window and let in the fresh air. The gardens and the park beyond them looked much as usual. The gardeners were busy mowing the lawns: they were interested in appearances even if the house servants were not.

I rang the bell and in a few minutes Mary appeared, wiping her hands on her apron, staring at me with round-eyed surprise.

'We didn't expect ye, Ma'am,' she said somewhat sourly. 'Ye usually lets the master know when ye'll be home.'

'I made up my mind suddenly. Has anybody seen fit to dust the house since I went away?'

'We're short-handed, Ma'am, Moira's left to get married an' we haven't got anybody in 'er place yet.'

'I see. Well, please see what you can do with this room. Is the master on the estate?'

'Yes, Ma'am. There was a big storm in the noight, uprooted some o' the trees it did. One of them fell on a labourer's cottage. Sure and it's a lot of damage it's done.'

'I'm sorry, was anybody hurt?'

'Two o' the men, Ma'am, hurt bad they were.'

'I'll walk over there. Is Toby in the kitchen?'

Her face coloured bright red, and she stammered, 'Oim sorry, Ma'am, but 'e got out o' the kitchen one day and 'e went berserk in the park, killed a lot o' lambs 'e did. The master 'ad to 'ave 'im put down.'

I sank down on my bed, staring at her. Toby who had never killed a thing, Toby who had been my dog, my companion. I couldn't believe it.

'I reckon 'e was missin' you, Ma'am. He fretted a bit, Joe said 'is temper was spoiled.'

I dismissed the girl curtly, then I dissolved into tears, sobbing wildly. I had lost Mark and I had lost Toby. At that moment I hated Gervase with all my heart. He kept me from the man I loved and he had destroyed my dog. I couldn't wait to tell him how much I hated him.

I heard him come into the house, heard his footsteps crossing the hall then men's voices in the study, and without a second's thought I ran down the stairs and burst into his study. He sat behind his big mahogany desk and Alan Harvey and another man stood facing him. Across the desk maps were spread out and all three seemed intent on these. They looked up in surprise at my hurried entrance and Gervase said coolly, 'So the mistress of the house has returned. When?'

'An hour ago. What happened about Toby?'

'I'm busy now, Lisanne, I'll tell you about it over dinner.'

'No. Now, Gervase. There must have been some mistake, Toby never killed anything, he was always too gentle. Why did you have to put him down?'

The two others were looking uncomfortable but Gervase said firmly, 'I had to shoot him. He had a dead lamb in his mouth and we'd seen him savaging four or five of them.

410

When a spaniel goes wild he means business, and I couldn't take a chance. If they kill once they go on killing.'

I stared at him stonily. 'Couldn't you have waited until I got home? He'd be with me after that, he'd never have been alone on the estate again.'

'That was a chance I couldn't take, particularly as I had no idea when you were returning. Now, Lisanne, if you don't mind I'd like to carry on.'

I hated him. I hated his calm condescending voice. He was like a brick wall against which I was battering my bruised palms. I wished he were dead. That night I would tell him about Mark, I would wipe that self-satisfied smile off his face for ever.

I did not see Gervase again that night. I dined alone in the vast dining room and was informed that the master had had to go out suddenly and would not be back until well after midnight. My pride would not allow me to ask where he had gone and I assumed in my anger that he was with Pamela Capethorn. It was only much later in the evening when I learned that he had driven into Dublin to see the two labourers who had almost lost their lives in the storm, and from there had gone on to Alan Harvey's house to discuss what should be done about the damaged cottage.

CHAPTER 39

The moment to confront Gervase came over breakfast the following morning. Normally he was out of the house long before I went down but this morning I was determined to speak to him. When I entered the room he raised his eyes maddeningly and as I helped myself from the side table he calmly went about opening his mail. As I took my seat he said without looking up, 'To what do I owe this honour? I hope you've not come to talk about the dog, the matter is closed.'

'I want a divorce, Gervase.'

He threw back his head and laughed while I stared at him astonished. I had not expected merriment on my announcement.

'I mean it, Gervase, I want a divorce, and as quickly as possible.'

'You know that's impossible.'

'Why is it impossible? Other people get divorced, even people in our exalted station.'

'We agreed to go our separate ways, we agreed to make a public show of our marriage if we maintained a private indifference, but divorce is something neither of us can think about. Who is it, some man you've met in London, one of those arty men you hang about with?'

'I don't hang about with anybody. I have met somebody. I love him and he loves me. We would like to marry. Gervase, why should you mind so much? You don't love me, there are times when you don't even like me. If you divorced me you'd be free to marry Pamela Capethorn. That's what you want, isn't it?'

Deliberately he went on opening his mail, then he laid it in a neat pile beside his plate before raising his eyes to meet mine.

'Lisanne, you're a fool. I have no wish to marry Pamela

Capethorn, or any other woman for that matter. I don't break contracts, business or marriage. I have a name for the utmost integrity in these matters and I intend to keep it. You are my wife and you will remain my wife. Divorce between you and me is quite impossible. There is too much at stake, too much I have no desire to lose simply because my wife thinks she's fallen in love with a man she's known for a few short weeks. Who is he, anyway?'

'I have no intention of telling you.'

'You mean he's somebody I would consider quite impossible.'

'No, I don't mean that at all. If I told you who he was it might conceivably shatter your complacency.'

'Then why not tell me. I like to be surprised.'

I sprang to my feet and ran from the room, and all the way across the hall his laughter followed me.

I felt utterly and completely helpless. He would never let me go, he didn't want me but he would keep me. Lance had wanted me but he had wanted the land more. Either way there was something inside both of them that would hold fast to what was theirs regardless of the feelings of others.

Anger filled me and agonized in me to the exclusion of everything else, and even Alan Harvey said, 'Is something wrong, Lisanne? You've not been like yourself since you returned from London. I know you were upset about Toby, but really Gervase had no alternative, the spaniel was caught in the act.'

'It isn't the dog, Alan. I loved Toby but I realize he had to be destroyed when he went about killing the lambs.'

'What is it then? You can confide in me.'

'But you're Gervase's friend.'

'Yours too I hope.'

'Alan, I want a divorce. Neither of us is happy in this marriage and I've met somebody else, somebody I love very dearly.'

'Divorce is impossible, Lisanne.'

'Why are you so sure, what has Gervase told you?'

'Nothing at all. I only know he's talked about the family

413

for as long as I can remember. He talked about it and railed about it. At times he despises himself for conforming, but he'll never let you go.'

I felt as helpless as I had when facing my father, facing Aunt Liza. It seemed to me that every desire of my life had been thwarted by other people I had been afraid of.

I couldn't sleep, I was nauseated by food and I began to lose weight so that my skirts slipped over my hips and I had to fasten them with safety pins. Gervase was amused. He commented sarcastically on my lacklustre appearance by saying, 'I wonder if your lover would find you as attractive as you were in London. You look decidedly seedy to me.'

'Don't you care that I'm unhappy?' I cried.

'I'm afraid I don't care, Lisanne. You entered this marriage with your eyes wide open, you knew the terms. Gracious me, girl, they've been spelt out for you just as they were spelt out for me all through our lives, and now you want to change them to suit yourself.'

'I can't live the rest of my life unloved and unwanted. Why can't you let me go? You're not happy in this marriage either.'

'I didn't expect to be happy, but neither did I expect to be moaned at night and morning by a wife who isn't prepared to honour her obligations.'

'Obligations that are monstrous and archaic.'

'I agree, but obligations nevertheless.'

It was no use, I could never win against Gervase's arrogant stand, and during one of the nights when I tossed and turned in my bed I made up my mind to tell him the truth. The idea came upon me so suddenly it left me shattered.

I would tell Gervase that I had deceived him, that I was not Lisanne de Bellefort but Ellen Adair who had survived the shipwreck and taken his cousin's place because I was alone in the world and destitute. A bold plan that had misfired terribly, and I could not visualize that Gervase would stay married to a woman who had cheated and wormed her way into his life.

The more I thought about it the more it became the only solution, but it carried with it a price. I thought about the contempt I would be subjected to from my friends: Alan and Maureen, Edna and George. And how Pamela Capethorn would gloat about the aristocratic wife who was nothing more than an adventuress.

And what about Mark? He would have to know, and would he regard me in a better light? I hardly thought so.

Yet the more I thought about the idea the more it became a necessity. It wasn't just Mark, it was my conscience. But how was I to tell Gervase, and when would be the best time?

He was seldom in for dinner, and he was too anxious to be out of the house at breakfast time. I would have to make an appointment to see him, incongruous thought it was.

I left a note beside his breakfast plate before I retired for the night, saying that I would like to see him in his study some time during the day. When I went down to breakfast there was a note beside my plate saying he would see me at noon in the study.

I couldn't settle to anything. I changed my skirt and blouse twice and made the best of my face. I had no interest in the flowers, and even the house over which I had spent such time and trouble failed to please me. I thought of it as a cage, a beautiful cage of my creation furnished with toys I had suddenly outgrown.

It was a relief to go outside where the wind swept through the park and soft Irish rain misted the horizon, obscuring the distant mountains which I had come to love.

Promptly at noon I went to Gervase's study. My heart was beating so painfully I felt sick and my knees were trembling. The door to the study was open and I could see the play of firelight on the furniture. Gervase was standing at the window looking out into the park.

He didn't turn as I entered but continued to stare through the window, and nervously I went to sit near his desk. In front of his chair I could see an opened envelope lying casually on the blotting pad and my heart skipped a beat when I recognized the familiar cream parchment bearing the de Bellefort crest.

It seemed like a small eternity before he turned. He

seemed bemused, almost unaware of my existence, then making an effort to gather his scattered wits he said, 'You wanted to talk to me, Lisanne?'

'Yes. Is something wrong?'

He stared at me morosely for a second before tossing over the letter.

I did not recognize the writing and before reading it I turned to the signature. It was signed, 'your loving cousin Geraldine'. He was watching me closely but offered no comment, so I turned the page over and started to read.

Lance de Bellefort was dead, killed in a hunting accident when his horse fell and rolled on top of him. Geraldine was a widow, her children fatherless, and we were asked to attend Lance's funeral at Langstone.

All thoughts of what I had been about to tell him fled. Now was not the moment for it, but my thoughts had certainly been unable to fully recognize the implications of Geraldine's letter.

'I suppose you realize what this means?' Gervase said stonily.

'Only that Lance is dead. It is tragic.'

'I agree, it is tragic. We never really liked each other, there never seemed the time or inclination, but I never wished him dead.'

'Well of course you didn't.'

'Not even when his death would give me all I ever wanted, Langstone and the title.'

I stared at him incredulously. Of course. With Lance's death Gervase would be Sir Gervase de Bellefort and I would be his lady. I would be the mistress of Langstone Priory. Even in that moment of agonizing stupor I remembered old Lady de Bellefort vividly, offering little Ellen Adair a home and a job. That I would ever take her place was a thing so remote neither of us could have envisaged it.

Gervase was saying, 'I shall have to get hold of Harvey as soon as he returns from Dublin. There's a great deal to be done on the estate, and heaven knows how long we shall be away. Can you be ready to travel first thing in the morning?'

'In the morning?' I echoed stupidly.

'Well of course, if we're to be there in time for Lance's funeral the following day. We should offer some support to Geraldine. We're her closest relatives.'

'Yes,' I murmured. 'I'll pack this afternoon. Will you arrange the air travel?'

'Of course. What was it you wanted to see me about, Lisanne? It must have been very important.'

'No, it wasn't really very important, it can wait.'

'Good. I've enough on my mind at the moment. How do you feel about being Lady de Bellefort?'

'I don't know, it hasn't registered yet.'

'I can almost see our grandmother sitting with the angels, shaking her head doubtfully. I shouldn't think she would be happy to see her precious Langstone and the title in the hands of her tearaway grandson and his pretty spoilt wife.'

'I don't see why childish labels should stick to us for the rest of your lives.'

'You don't?' Well, it's true that you're very pretty, Lisanne, even if at the moment you look like the very devil. And you're spoilt, forever falling out with your toys when they cease to amuse you.'

He was baiting me, standing before me with that maddening half smile on his face. Tossing my head, I turned away and walked out of the study, followed by a cynical chuckle.

Telling him the truth was as far away as ever. Now was not the time, not when Lance lay dead and his widow was devastated by grief for herself and her three little girls. Not when Gervase for all his bombast maintained a feeling of shame because he had wanted the things that were Lance's by birth. Now they belonged to Gervase, but not even he had wanted them quite this way.

My first shock was when Mary came to my room to say the master would be in for dinner, calling me Milady with round-eyed awe.

Facing Gervase at the dinner table, it seemed to me that with Lance's death had come a new maturity. He was

417

thoughtful, and his eyes were no longer appraising me with taunting cynicism. He informed me quietly that we were to fly from Dublin the following morning and he had ordered a car to meet us at the airport. I must take enough luggage to last several days and he had informed Alan Harvey he would not be back for the Hunt Ball. When I raised my eyes at this piece of information, for the first time I saw the old amused glint come into his eyes and he said casually, 'You look surprised, Lisanne, but you must admit a family bereavement should take precedence over the delights of dancing with Pamela Capethorn and seeing my wife flirting with half the men in the county.'

I didn't speak and after a few moments the sombre mood returned and he appeared to be miles away, no doubt thinking of the ambitions which had never seemed possible until now.

I was thinking about Lance. Remembering how much I had loved him, remembering the passion that had flared between us in the library at Langstone, and my tears in the snow above the house. Our lives had been a mess, a tortuous meandering mess, and even now when I had thought to see some way out by the easing of my conscience something had happened to make it impossible.

CHAPTER 40

It was late afternoon the next day when we drove through the village of Langstone, and I was immediately shocked by the black drapes at the windows of the cottages which lined the main street. The flag flew at half mast above the old church and over the entire village was a dejected sombre air.

The cafe which had been Aunt Liza's shop was deserted, and here again black drapes hung at the windows and I remembered that they had been similarly draped for the funeral of Lance's father.

Gervase drove without speaking, his eyes trained on the road, and I allowed my thoughts to wander to those days I had served in the draper's shop with Alec Devlin's eyes trained on me from across the road.

We passed the village hall where he had taken me to my first dance, and the old crooked stile that Lance and I had climbed on our way to the Priory. The gates to the Priory were open and ahead of us stretched the long drive with the house in the distance.

I couldn't know Gervase's thoughts at that moment. In his childhood he had come here as a visitor, the son of a man his grandmother had disapproved of, an independent headstrong child who was aware of the resentment surrounding him, a strangely angry boy, jealous of an older cousin he deemed to have everything, even then. In the darkness of the car I stole a look at his dark handsome face. As if suddenly aware of my regard he looked at me and my heart began to hammer strangely and my thoughts were suddenly confused.

'Do you realize we're home, Lisanne?' he said quietly.

'Oh Gervase, is that all Lance's death means to you, that suddenly all this is yours?'

'Ours, Lisanne. All this is ours. Lance is dead. It is sad,

but his death was not my fault, and I never wished him dead. For the first time in my life I have what I've always wanted. I can feel sorry about Lance, but don't begrudge me this moment of joy for what we have.'

I should have felt some fear on returning to the Priory that I would be recognized as an impostor, but it had never occurred to me. I had come a long way from the girl who had come to alter Lisanne's dresses. I had become a woman of the world, beautiful and assured, and I was relying on my resemblance to Lisanne.

Geraldine showed no astonishment when I embraced her, and the servants who had been lined up in the hall to meet us merely bowed their heads in acknowledgement as we passed before them.

I saw no look of recognition on Cook's face, or the butler's. I was simply the new Lady de Bellefort wearing mourning for the loss of my cousin, and after the simple ceremony of greeting was over we passed into the drawing room.

Geraldine was pale and composed as she told us about the accident that had ended Lance's life.

'It is strange,' she said quietly, 'but I had a premonition that morning that something would go wrong. I didn't want Lance to turn out with the hunt, I begged him to refuse. His own horse had gone lame and was having treatment from the vet so he borrowed a horse from Major Acton over at Hawes. The horse was young, untried, and Lance had never ridden him before. The Major was confident he would be an excellent mount for Lance, but the horse was headstrong. I have been told that right from the very outset he was fighting Lance, who was having great difficulty in controlling him.'

'Are your children in the house?' I asked her thoughtfully.

'Only the eldest, Catherine. The two younger ones are with my mother and I agree with her that funerals are not for children. They are not coming up for Lance's funeral, it is a long way. But Catherine will be here.'

My occasion to meet Catherine came later over dinner. She was tall and slender, in time she would be pretty, but at the moment there were braces on her teeth and she resembled Geraldine far more than Lance.

Dinner was a silent meal. Occasionally I questioned Catherine on her schooling but she seemed remote and withdrawn, which I put down to the sudden loss of her father.

The servants at Langstone had always been well trained, now they ministered to us silently and deferentialy. Gervase sat at the head of the table wearing his dinner jacket and Geraldine and I wore black. Catherine's grey dress seemed far too old for her, and her pale little face seemed pinched and scared, while occasionally her eyes moved from one to the other of us. She picked at her food, and once I saw her eyes slide fearfully towards the library door.

Lance is in there, I thought to myself, lying alone in the library where once we had clung passionately in an ecstasy of love.

Later that evening we trooped in a solemn procession of family and servants to take our last look at him. It wasn't the Lance I had known, warm and vibrant with life, not this cold pale Lance with his dark hair greying and the harsh look of care which death had not eradicated from his face.

The women servants were dabbing their eyes as they moved around the coffin but Geraldine maintained a reserved calmness. At that moment I admired her, but later when I said as much to Gervase he merely answered, 'Neither of us know how much they cared for each other. If the caring doesn't go too deep it is easier to remain serene.'

'But he was her husband,' I cried angrily, 'the father of her children.'

'Of course. Have you forgotten, Lisanne, that you have just recently asked me for a divorce? How do we know what went on between Lance and his wife?'

'I don't suppose they were like us at all. Lance was kind, he would make their marriage work, I just know it.'

'You mean I am anything but kind, that I have never tried to make our marriage work?'

'I didn't say that, you're always so cynical and sarcastic.

421

You formed an opinion of Lisanne as a girl and never forgot it.'

'You mean you've changed?'

'I've grown up.'

He came and stood looking down into my face with a tantalizing half smile on his lips.

'Are you prepared to grow up a little more, I wonder? Are you prepared to play your part as my grandmother played hers? Are you prepared to forget the foolish notion that I shall let you go to marry this man you only think you're in love with?'

'I am in love with him,' I cried angrily.

'Shall I put you to the test, Lisanne, shall I make you see that he doesn't exist? He's a dream you've made up in your heart because you want more from me than I'm prepared to give.'

I backed away from him with flashing eyes. 'You're conceited, you're arrogant and impossible. He does exist, I do love him.'

He followed me and the look in his eyes was devilish, then suddenly his arms were round me and his mouth was bruising mine with the savagery of his kisses. I felt him lift me up bodily in his arms while all the time I struggled helplessly, then he threw me on the bed and my arms and legs were flaying underneath the weight of his body.

'Lie still, you little fool,' he hissed savagely. 'You're my wife, you have a duty which has been sorely neglected over the last few months.'

I could feel his hands tearing at the flimsy material of my nightgown and my struggles were becoming feebler. I was no match for his strength, no match for the relentless passion that consumed him, and he paid no heed to my cries of pain. Some devil within him was intent on making me suffer, extracting from me the full measure of our marriage contract, and then suddenly I came alive under his hands and I found my own passion answering his, every bit as wild, with all his eagerness until at last we lay sated and spent in the hours before the dawn.

They came from all over the county and further afield for Lance's funeral, and the villagers lined the lanes leading to the stone church on the hillside. Gervase walked with Geraldine and Catherine and I was glad that on this morning at least there need be little contact between us.

I was glad of the dark veil over my face. I had begun to recognize people in the crowded churchyard: Alec Devlin with his mother, several acquaintances of Aunt Liza, and some of the girls I had met at the village hall. Many of them clutched the hands of small children, but none of them could clearly see my face behind the veil. It was my guilty conscience that was making me afraid, there was never any danger that the figure of Lady de Bellefort would raise doubts in the eyes of the villagers.

I walked between two elderly men, Lance's solicitor and family friend, and an old man who Geraldine had said was the last relative from her grandmother's generation.

We stood at last before the huge stone mausoleum. The villagers stood back and now we were merely family and close friends, and under cover of my veil I stole a look at them. Lisanne would have recognized many of them but I felt strangely alone and detached in their company. Geraldine had shed no tears. She stood tall and slender like a statue carved out of marble, her face pale, and I was surprised to see that she had removed her veil so that everyone could see her face clearly. Beside her stood Catherine, clutching her mother's hand, her child's face achingly sad, and I felt such an overwhelming sense of pity for her I moved forward and took hold of her other hand.

It was over at last. People were milling round looking at the wreaths and Gervase was in earnest conversation with a group of people who had driven in that morning from York.

Sadly I turned away and began to walk back with some of the others towards the gates, it was then I felt my arm taken and a man's voice said gently, 'I'm sorry to meet you again on such a sad occasion, Lisanne.'

I looked up startled into Mark's sombre eyes.

'Mark, when did you arrive here?'

423

'Yesterday evening. I'm staying at the inn. As soon as I read about Lance's death I knew I had to come, we were friends a long time ago. And I wanted to see you. Perhaps that was foolish of me.'

'It's all so terrible, Mark. I can't even think straight. There are those three little girls without a father and Geraldine seems so distant and remote, she isn't helping her daughter at all.'

'Grief affects people in different ways, Lisanne. Your own life is going to be very different now. I expect you will come to live here at the Priory?'

'I don't know. It's all been so very sudden, we haven't discussed the future. Are you returning home today?'

'Tomorrow. My only sister is getting married on Thursday, I must be home for that occasion.'

'Of course. Oh Mark, I know so little about you. I don't know anything about your home or your family.'

'No. It was very unreal, our time together in London. We talked about all sorts of things but we never really talked about ourselves. Is there any chance that I might see you this evening, just for a few moments? I have something I very much want to give to you.'

'Oh Mark, I don't want anything from you. I shall remember how happy you made me, I don't want presents to remind me.'

'All the same, my dear, I think you will want this one. Can you possible meet me, just for a few minutes? I know it might be difficult on such a day but you can telephone me at the inn stating a place and a time.'

'I'll try, Mark.'

We could say nothing more. Gervase had left the other guests and was walking towards us. I watched as he held out his hand to Mark, saying, 'Good morning, Mark, it was good of you to come. You should have come up to the house.'

We left the two men talking together and after a few minutes Gervase joined us alone. I stood on one side holding Catherine's hand. I didn't want to talk to Gervase about

Mark, I was too afraid that I might betray feelings I wanted to keep to myself.

Luncheon was a banquet. Speeches were made, reminiscences were exchanged between friends who only met at weddings and funerals, and it was more than two before I could telephone Mark at the inn. I arranged to meet him at the stile beside the river in half an hour's time, so I promptly removed my funeral attire and donned a tweed skirt and jumper. Wearing a trenchcoat and with a silk scarf covering my hair I walked quickly along the corridor and down the back stairs.

I made my way through the kitchen and Cook looked at me, surprised, so that I felt I owed her some explanation.

'I need some fresh air, Cook, I don't want to interfere with the rest of the proceedings. I'm going for a quick walk in the park.'

'I knows just how you feels, Milady. It's a sad day for us all, but the funeral service was beautiful. And all them people, it just goes to show what a popular man the master was.'

'The meal was excellent, Cook. I think the servants should be congratulated, looking after all these people isn't easy. I feel sure Sir Gervase will be speaking to them later.'

She beamed her gratification and I let myself out of the side door and hurried along the drive. It was a fair walk across the park to the river but I was glad of the keen wind, and by the time I reached the path leading to the stile my cheeks were smarting in the wind and I felt warm and very alive. I had forgotten how beautiful it was with the willows dipping their feathery branches into the water.

Mark was waiting for me, holding a brown paper parcel in his hands. From its shape I knew immediately what it was.

'I can't take the painting, Mark,' I protested. 'I know how much you wanted it and I was too late. Please keep it for yourself.'

'I want you to have it, Lisanne. You knew the girl and I got the impression that at one time she was important to you. For me it was just a striking picture of an unknown woman. Please take it, I shall be bitterly disappointed if you don't.'

'Shall I ever see you again, Mark?'

'I don't know, Lisanne.'

For a few moments only he stood holding me close and I was filled with utter desolation, so acute that I could not have spoken, so agonizing that I could only smile at him tremulously before I tore myself from his arms and ran heedlessly back to the house. Tears filled my eyes and rolled down my cheeks and I saw the park and countryside through a blur.

People were leaving, cars stood in the driveway, and I hung back among the stout oaks that lined the drive, waiting until it was clear before I could enter the house and find the privacy of my room. Would they never go, I thought wildly, hadn't they talked enough over luncheon, hadn't they exhausted every topic, every memory? But still they lingered, and I was forced to wait helplessly out of sight, aware that Gervase would be furious with my absence.

He made his displeasure very evident that evening as we waited for Geraldine in the drawing room before dinner.

'Our guests travelled from the other end of the county and my wife couldn't even find time to be polite and wish them good afternoon,' he said coldly.

'I'm sorry, Gervase, I felt sick and I had a headache, I had to get some fresh air before I fainted after that huge lunch. I didn't think they would be going so soon.'

'Well you can be sure your absence will be talked about. We shall be living in this part of the world and will probably need all the friends we can get. It was stupid to antagonize them before we even had the opportunity to get to know them.'

'I've said I'm sorry, Gervase, I can do no more. You were here and so was Geraldine. It was after all *her* husband's funeral.'

'I'd hope you'd behave better after mine.'

'Now you're being silly.'

'Where did you go in your search for fresh air?'

'As far as the river and back.'

He was watching me narrowly and I forced myself to meet his gaze unflinchingly. All the same I was glad when Geraldine arrived.

That night we talked about her future and marvelled at the provision Lance had made for his family in the event of his death.

Geraldine and her children were to move into a small manor house Lance had bought near Harrogate. She had never liked his father's large property, and we learned that Lance had sold this only recently and it was now an agricultural college.

'What will you do with Glenmoor?' she asked curiously. 'Perhaps you would prefer to live there than here.'

'I haven't decided,' Gervase told her. 'Lisanne's spent a fortune on the house and I have friends in Ireland. I enjoy the hunting and the fishing, so perhaps I won't do anything about it for the time being.'

'Oh well,' she said evenly, 'you have one son who in time will inherit this place, if you have another he could be given Glenmoor just as your own father was. You're a wealthy couple, you could afford to keep on both houses and in time you might be glad you'd done so.'

When Gervase didn't speak she turned to me, saying, 'Have you no thoughts about Glenmoor, Lisanne?'

'No. It's true the house is beautiful now, but Gervase has always loved this house. I'm wondering just how much time we shall spend at Glenmoor.'

I listened to their voices making polite conversation about Geraldine's future. Catherine had pleaded a headache and had not come down to dinner, and I wished fervently that Geraldine would talk about Lance. It seemed incredible to me that in all this talk about her future not once had she showed any hint of real sorrow for the loss of Lance, only a commendable dignity and a remoteness that had created barriers through which there was no entry.

Gervase too was finding the conversation heavy going, and to change the subject he said, 'It was good of Mark Allenby to come to the funeral. I saw you talking to him,

Lisanne. No doubt you met him many times when you were here living with our grandmother.'

'I probably did meet him, one met so many people. I was supposed to know most of the people who came to the funeral.'

'He was friendly with Lance, he told me he remembered you.'

'Really. Did you ever meet him, Geraldine?'

'Of course, he came to our wedding, actually he was one of the groomsmen. I don't believe he ever married.'

The conversation went on about Mark and I learned more from them than he had ever told me himself. They talked about the house in Leicestershire which he called home; his father who had been a general in the Blues and his mother who was the youngest daughter of a Marquis; his career in the diplomatic service – until in the end I felt I would scream if they didn't change the subject.

I only knew I could never tell either Mark or Gervase that I was not Lisanne. I did not have the courage to face either of them and see the contempt in their eyes. Neither could love an impostor such as I, it was clear my secret would have to go with me to the grave.

How I wished I could find an excuse not to sit with them in the drawing room where Geraldine worked on her tapestry and Gervase sat immersed in the field magazines that were prominent on every table.

Promptly at eleven o'clock I rose to me feet, feigning tiredness, and Geraldine said quickly, 'Yes, of course, Lisanne, it has been a long wearisome day. I think I shall go to bed too. You don't mind, Gervase?'

'Not at all. Goodnight, ladies.'

As we walked up the shallow curved staircase together Geraldine said, 'You know this house as well as I, probably better, but there are things you should know about the position you will now occupy. Perhaps you'll come to my room in the morning and we can discuss them.'

'Yes of course, after breakfast do you mean?'

'Mid morning I think. I gave you and Gervase the Normandy Room but when I've gone you will no doubt wish to move into the room at the front of the house. Traditionally they have always been occupied by the head of the family.'

'This is all quite dreadful for you, Geraldine, I wish I could do more to help.'

'Everything that needed to be done has been done. The children and I all like the house we are moving into, we shall soon settle down.'

'I hope you'll visit us often and that we shall be friends. After all, it isn't very far away.'

'That's true, but once I leave the Priory I doubt if I shall be anxious to return. There are a lot of memories connected with this house, some of them happy, many of them sad. It was never really my house when Grandmother was alive, and since she died somehow or other I feel she's still here. Oh I'm being fanciful, I know, but she was a very dominant person. We never really had much in common.'

'I see.'

'You spent a lot of time here when your mother was abroad. Were you happy here?'

'I think so, but with Grandmother it wasn't always easy.'

'I'll say goodnight then, Lisanne. You'll come to my room about ten thirty?'

'Yes. Goodnight, Geraldine.'

I was glad that a fire had been lit in the bedroom and for the first time I looked around me with interest. Geraldine had called it the Normandy Room and now I recognized the French air, from the murals on the walls to the patterned damask at the windows. It had the feeling of a chateau with its high domed ceiling and wrought-iron balcony which overlooked the lily pond and formal gardens. If the de Belleforts had arrived in England with the Normans, they had brought much of Normandy with them as well as their name.

Before I climbed into the huge bed I took Kitty's picture out of the wardrobe and unwrapped it quickly. Her startling green eyes looked out at me, tantalizing and assured, and I could see again the cigarette smoke curling upwards in the dimmed nightclub, hear her voice, strong and low pitched, singing the haunting songs of France.

Suddenly I felt the picture being taken out of my hands and Gervase was beside me staring down at it. He had come into the room so softly I hadn't heard him, now I trembled unhappily as I waited for the questions which I was sure would come.

'Where did you find this?' he asked sharply.

'I found it in London. I went to an exhibition of the artist's work, and thought this was his best.'

'The house is filled with all sorts of valuable paintings and you have to buy this work by an unknown artist?'

'The artists who painted the pictures that fill this house were all unknown at one stage, most of them only became famous after their deaths. At least we are beginning to recognize contemporary artists during their lifetime. Don't you like the picture?'

'I suppose it has something. It's bold, the colours are good and the woman has a sort of earthy appeal. God knows where you're going to hang it.'

'I'll find somewhere.'

'I should put it in your sitting room, that's where Grand-mother put most of the things she didn't want in the rest of the house.'

I remembered the sitting room where I had received my instructions on the rest of my life, now he was talking about it as being mine. I stared after him as he crossed the room to go into the dressing room and after a few minutes he came out carrying a briefcase.

'I have letters to write,' he said. 'I shall be returning to Ireland at the end of the week. You need not come with me, in fact I prefer you to remain here to familiarize yourself with your new role.'

'When will you be coming back?' I said sharply. 'Or are you intending to reside permanently at Glenmoor, appearing here at brief intervals?'

He came to stand beside me, looking down from his superior height with lofty amusement so that I bitterly regretted having removed my shoes with their high heels.

'You would like that, wouldn't you, Lisanne? For me to live at Glenmoor and you to be free to have your lover here.

Well, it isn't to be. I shall be visiting Ireland less and less. Harvey will see to the house and the estate, and from time to time I shall expect you to visit Glenmoor with me simply to see that the place is being cared for – our second son will have no cause for complaint when the time comes for him to inherit.'

'Our second son!' I gasped.

'Yes, of course. You needn't look so scandalized. I have forgiven your indiscretions, divorce is quite out of the question and I rather think we can both look forward to, if not a happy marriage, certainly one which will not lack for passionate involvement.'

I stared after him with burning cheeks, trembling with anger at his devilish amusement, his high-handed dismissal. I lay against the pillows still smarting with resentment, then I saw Kitty's portrait propped up against the chair where I had left it and she seemed to be smiling at me with quiet amusement. In some exasperation I sprang out of bed and after wrapping the picture in its brown paper I thrust it impatiently to the back of the wardrobe.

CHAPTER 41

I went to Geraldine's room promptly at ten thirty the following morning after breakfasting alone. Gervase presumably slept in his dressing room and he had gone out with the estate agent. This, I thought angrily, was going to be the pattern of married life, but it was probably all I deserved.

Geraldine was emptying her wardrobe, piling clothes on to the bed, and she looked up with a smile when I entered.

'I always hated packing,' she said irritably. 'I hated packing for school holidays and I hate it now. This seems to be the sum total of my life here, ball gowns and cocktail gowns, garden party dresses and dresses for Ascot and other race meetings. You'll find out, Lisanne. I hope you've got an extensive wardrobe.'

'Not like that I haven't.'

'Well, you will have. Lance liked to entertain. He filled the house with guests for the racing at York and Ripon, then there was the start of the shooting season and the musical season in Harrogate. It seemed we always had a houseful of people, that we were hardly ever alone as a family. Granny and Lance revelled in it.'

'Were you and Lance very happy, Geraldine?'

'If you mean were we ever in love the answer is no. I could have loved him once. He was a nice man, a good kind man. But he never loved me and I received no incentive to love him.'

'Oh Geraldine, I'm sure you're wrong. He was very anxious about you when your first baby was born, I know. I was in hospital in Plymouth and he wrote to say how worried he was about you.'

'He liked me. He had regard for me, I was his wife, his cousin, and I was a de Bellefort. He didn't make any effort to visit you in the hospital Lisanne. He sent you letters and flowers, but if you'd been Ellen Adair he'd have made the effort to see you in person.'

I gasped with amazement. 'Why do you say that?' I cried.

'I saw his face when he heard the news about the wreck. He was sorry for you, for the loss of your mother, but the loss of Ellen twisted his heart.'

'Oh, but you're wrong, you have to be.'

'I knew that first night, when Grandmother told me it was I who would marry Lance, that it was Ellen he was in love with. I couldn't sleep that night, I was far too excited. I hadn't met him since we were children and there he was, that tall handsome nice man I was soon to marry. I was half in love with him already. I went down to the library to look for a magazine or something, the door was ajar and through it I saw Lance with his arms round that girl. I stood watching while he picked her up and carried her over to the settee in front of the fire, then I took to my heels and ran for dear life up the stairs and back to my room.

'I never forgot that scene in the library, Lisanne, not even when I was his wife and he made love to me. I wished I was Ellen Adair and he loved me as he had loved her. Then when I heard she had lost her life in that shipwreck I was glad, until I saw his face and realized that though she was dead it was too late for him to love me.'

'Geraldine, I'm sorry. It was a pity you saw them in the library, but don't you think if he'd have loved her enough he'd have married her and not you? He watched her walk out of his life. Does a man do that if he truly loves a woman?'

'He does if he's a de Bellefort. Both my parents did it, my grandfather did it – leaving that girl to change my life.'

I stayed silent, hating myself miserably for having hurt Geraldine so deeply, but she was staring at me across the room. 'I thought on that first evening I met her how alike you were, now I'm not so sure.'

'What do you mean?'

'I don't really know. I haven't seen you for years, now I'm not even sure which one I remember, you or Ellen. I suppose she was a de Belleforts too.'

'Do you want any help with that packing?'

'No, Catherine will help me later. I should be telling you how you will be expected to spend your day. In the morning I see the housekeeper about the meals for the day, and we make arrangements if there are to be guests in the house.

'I sit on the committees of various charities. There's also the Musical Circle, the drama school over at Harrogate, and I'm constantly being called upon to judge flower shows, dog shows and craft exhibitions. I'm on the bench, and I know it's the Magistrate's Clerk's intention to nominate you – that can be very tying, with probation work and visits to prisons. Then there's work on the hospital board. You'll find yourself leading a very full life, Lisanne.'

'It sounds like it. What will they expect from Gervase? He's not at all like Lance, you know.'

'I've realized that, but though he's more remote he'll play his part – he's wanted this role most of his life. Grandmother said there was always resentment between the two boys.'

'Yes, I'm afraid that's true. How did you get on with Lady de Bellefort?'

'With Grandmother? Reasonably well. I was always aware that she was in charge, Lance deferred to her and so did I. In the early days of our marriage I couldn't forget Ellen Adair, and I blamed my grandmother for bringing her into the house. She was well aware of the resentment I felt towards her. I couldn't think what devious whim had made her do it, and once I asked her.'

'What did she say?' I murmured.

'Only that she had liked the girl and felt she owed her something. I never found Grandmother easy to talk to, she was always a little like my headmistress.'

'Perhaps we should go down to the study, that is where I interview the housekeeper and listen to any complaints.'

'Do you still use Grandmother's sitting room?'

'That is now your sitting room. I haven't disturbed anything, it's all exactly as she wanted it. I haven't even looked in her desk or in the bookcase. Perhaps you will do that?'

'I shall feel as if I'm prying into things which don't concern me.'

'That's what I thought, but someday someone must do it. She kept her diary every day until she couldn't see. I couldn't bring myself to look at it – I didn't want to read about Ellen, I only wanted to forget about her.'

In the study she showed me the account books and the engagement book. I sat beside her while she interviewed the housekeeper about the evening meal and after that we went into the small sitting room.

It was exactly as I remembered it, the beautiful Chinese carpet, the delicate pastel colours, the beauty of the watercolours and porcelain Lady de Bellefort had loved. From the windows I could look at the most beautiful view of all, the swans sailing majestically across the mere and the distant hazy fells.

The top of the small period walnut desk was tidy apart from the thick leather-bound diary bearing the de Bellefort crest in gold letters. Beside it lay a finely wrought gold pen tray and a long gold letter opener in the form of a goose feather.

'You can see, Lisanne, it is all exactly as she left it. I never sit at the desk, although sometimes I come in here to sew. I sit where I can see the swans and the mere, but I never feel that I am alone here: I can see her there at the desk, writing in that eternal diary every small thing that came to disturb her day.'

'I wonder if I shall ever feel comfortable sitting here?' I mused. In my heart I did not think I would. I would feel the old lady's eyes boring into my back, filled with accusation, willing me to tell the truth, daring me to be honest, telling me I had no right to be there.

Geraldine was saying, 'The butler visits the shops in the village for groceries, we like to patronize the local people. We get most of our bread and confectionary from the baker's shop in the village, except when there are house guests, then we get some of it from the caterers in Harrogate.

'There's quite a good draper's shop in the village now.

Apparently there used to be one years ago but that's now a cafe run by the Devlins. The new draper's shop is across the road, next to the baker's. If you want wool or embroidery silk she will get them for you.'

'Did you say it was a new shop?'

'Yes. Two elderly sisters have opened up there. The old draper's shop was very much missed, and they tell me this one is a small gold mine.'

'Is the cafe popular?'

'Popular enough. They go there for coffee and scandal, village gossip and any local news they can pick up. Mrs Devlin runs that with the help of her daughter-in-law.'

'I see.'

'I expect you remember the village quite well.'

'Is the doctor still at the same place?'

'Well, we have a new young man now. The old doctor retired just after the war. He said he'd had enough, and he and his wife are now living near the coast at Whitby. We've missed him, although Doctor Law is very capable and dependable.'

I would have liked to see Doctor Jarvis, but perhaps it was just as well he had moved away. I remembered his astuteness – he was probably the one person in the village who would have recognized me.

'Some of our stuff will need to be sent on, Lisanne,' Geraldine said. 'Catherine and I will leave around three o'clock, taking our personal luggage. You'll see to the rest for me, I hope.'

'Yes, of course.'

'It's mostly momentoes. Pieces of china, pictures, presents Lance gave me throughout our married life, and things the children want to keep. I think we should now take a look in the safe, you will no doubt want to see your jewellery.'

'*My* jewellery!'

'Well, yes. You will have your own personal jewellery just as I have, but these are de Bellefort pieces which are handed down from one generation to the next. The safe is in the library.'

I had not been into the library since the night we trooped

round Lance's coffin. This morning however a fire burned in the grate and my heart ached for that other night when I had found myself swept into his arms, the night Geraldine had watched from the door with bitter resentment in her heart.

I watched her open the safe and take out jewel case after jewel case which she placed on the table below the safe. Then she opened the cases, handing each one to me in turn.

I stared at them wide-eyed while the jewels flashed and dazzled against sombre velvet. Necklaces in diamonds and rubies, sapphires and emeralds, rings and bracelets, tiaras in diamonds and pearls. Geraldine was saying quietly, 'Gervase will no doubt give you jewels over the years just as Lance gave them to me, and they will be your own. But one day all this will belong to your son's wife.'

'But you have children too, Geraldine,' I cried unhappily.

'They are girl children. The de Bellefort jewels are for the wives of the heirs to the title. Lance was generous with our daughters, he laid money aside for their education, their wellbeing and for the good things of life he thought they were entitled to. These are for you, Lisanne. You need not look so unhappy about them. I've worn them all at some occasion or other, but never expected to keep them. Wear them and enjoy wearing them.'

She left them for me to replace in the safe, then with a small smile she said, 'I think I should see if Catherine's finished the rest of her packing and done something with mine. We'll meet at lunch, Lisanne.'

After she had left me I couldn't help thinking how remote she seemed. She had shown hardly any curiosity about my life at all, and even the invitation to visit her now seemed to have been given reluctantly and with the express adjuration to telephone first to see if it was convenient.

I doubted very much if Geraldine and I would ever be close friends, although no doubt we would maintain a family front for the rest of the world.

I accompanied them to their car after lunch while the servants lined up on the drive to say their farewells. I saw

437

that one or two of them cried a little, and Geraldine was gracious. It was little Catherine who brought tears to their eyes as she followed her mother, clutching a small kitten in her arms, and as she entered the car she looked back towards the house, her small tight-lipped face pale and strangely old.

'If you need to know anything about the house you can telephone me,' Geraldine said calmly. 'Just as soon as we've got the house to rights I intend to spend a little time with Mother, she'll be glad of the company.'

'Yes, of course. I've been wondering why she didn't stay on here with you for a while.'

'She's living in Bournemouth. She has a ghastly new flat with modern furniture. Grandmother would have gone mad if she'd known about her selling the old place just as it was to some Americans she met in London and invited down for the weekend.'

'And yet you're wanting to spend some time in her modern flat?'

'Mother will be good for me, she's always loved life, had lots of friends, and it will be a life totally different from any I've known married to Lance and living with Grandmother.'

'Do let us know when you arrive back home, I'll be very happy to have you visit, Geraldine.'

She smiled politely. Then tapping the glass which separated them from the chauffeur she sat back in her seat and the long black car moved slowly down the drive and out of the gates. I watched until it had disappeared, in spite of the chill wind that ruffled my hair and brought the warm colour to my cheeks, then I turned and followed the servants into the house.

As the butler closed the door behind me he shook his head sadly. 'I can't think Lady Geraldine'll be paying many visits to the Priory, Milady,' he said gently. 'I never thought she was over-fond of the place.'

'No, perhaps not.'

'But the master was. The Priory was his life. He loved every stick and stone of the house, every blade of grass in

438

the park there, every ripple on the mere. Will Sir Gervase love it like that, Milady, do you think?'

I stared at him, remembering the old man's amusement at the young Ellen Adair poring over the books in the library, his pride in the house, his joy that she was finding its history compelling, and gently I said, 'I'm sure Sir Gervase will love it just as I do. I'm not sure what changes he will make because no two people think alike or act alike, but whatever my husband does will be for the best, the best for the Priory I feel sure.'

'Of course, Milady. His father before him loved this place. I don't expect the master ever thought this place'd be his in a million years, and when you were a young girl stayin' here with your grandmother, you never thought so either, did you, Milady?'

'No, Carstairs, never in a million years did I ever think that one day I would be Lady de Bellefort.'

Gervase left the house at mid morning the next day and I was alone to eat my solitary meals in the dining room, staring down the long expanse of polished mahogany while soft-footed servants ministered to my needs.

'I think perhaps I'll eat in the morning room until Sir Gervase returns,' I said to the butler, whereupon he raised his eyes disapprovingly, saying, 'Her ladyship always ate in the dining room, Milady, whether she was alone or not.'

'When you say her ladyship I take it you are referring to my grandmother?' I said stonily.

'Well yes, Milady. Why I remember when you stayed here with her when you were quite small, you at one end of the dining table and her ladyship at the other, a great stickler for tradition she was.'

'Very well, Carstairs, I will continue to eat in the dining room. There are times when I think my grandmother is dictating policy from beyond the grave.'

He chuckled. 'She'd have liked that, Milady, she'd have liked that very much.'

The conversation decided me that I must take my courage in both hands and face her uneasy ghost in the comfort of her sitting room. It was a morning when rain lashed against the windows and the swans sat huddled on the banks on the mere.

I was glad of the glowing fire in the grate. A bowl of white and yellow dahlias had been placed on a table near the window and apart from those the room stared back at me impersonally, too tidy, too lonely. I was trying to remember how she had looked that last morning I had seen her sitting at her desk, erect and slender, her silver hair beautifully dressed, her rows of lustrous pearls shining against the black velvet of her gown, her knuckles white as her long slender hand rested on her ivory-topped cane.

In my imagination I could smell her perfume – floral, light and expensive – and instinctively I reached out my hand and opened the top drawer in her desk.

It was scrupulously tidy, the only thing in it being a handkerchief satchel which I opened to find a pile of beautifully embroidered linen handkerchieves, together with several in silk. The smell of perfume became stronger and I picked one of them up and held it against my face. For a few moments I felt faintly dizzy and I had to sit down because my legs were trembling.

The other two drawers held stationery, pale parchment envelopes and writing paper, all embossed with the de Bellefort crest, and there was a selection of pens and inks. Feeling like an interloper I closed the drawers and pulled my chair up close to the desk.

My fingers were trembling as I lifted the catch on the large diary resting on top of the blotter, then I started to read.

Every page was dated and numbered, and at the beginning her words meant nothing to me. Every day she had made a chronicle of what she had done from rising until she went to her bed, but in those early years I only recognized a few names. Letters she had received from her grandchildren from their various schools, visits from relatives and friends, tenants and dignitaries. Visits she had paid to local functions and others further afield. It was the diary of a busy woman who had taken pride in her position in the community, and impatiently I turned the pages until I found what I was

440

looking for, then my heart skipped a beat as I read: 'Today I saw the girl in the draper's shop in the village and it is true her likeness to Lisanne is uncanny. I bought embroidery from her and learned she is Miss Ashington's niece who has come to live with her. I hope to speak with the girl again when her aunt is not in evidence.'

I turned the pages more slowly now, but for whole days there was no more mention of the girl in the draper's shop. Then I read: 'I have discovered that the girl at the draper's shop is called Ellen Adair. The name means nothing to me but I am haunted by her face. She has been up to the Priory to sew for Lisanne, and I watched them walking in the garden together, so alike they could easily have been sisters. It cannot be coincidence, and I have to know. One of these days I must find an excuse to talk to the girl and find out something of her background.'

Then came a whole page: 'Miss Ashington has died very suddenly and the girl is alone in the shop in the village. I intend to send for her, I do not know what is to become of her and I cannot allow her to leave the village without satisfying my curiosity.'

It would appear that on that day nothing occupied her mind beyond the desire to talk to me. Then two days later: 'I have spoken to Ellen and have learned that her grandmother was Sarah Saxton. When she was sent away from the Priory I did not know that she was expecting William's child, now the pattern has fallen into place. Poor Ellen has not had a happy life. She ran away from home because she hated and was terrified of her father, her grandmother is dead and her mother sounds like a poor frightened creature, completely dominated by her husband. I liked the girl. She is like Lisanne but without her assured independence. This is understandable when one considers the sort of life she has led. She has clear blue eyes which meet one's own without guile, straight and honest, and she has great courage. She has needed plenty of that, and there has been precious little happiness living with her aunt in the village.

'The shop is to be sold and she has no employment to go to. Speaking to Ellen I constantly told myself: 'This is

441

William's granddaughter, she might have been yours and she is alone in the world and without means.' It seems to me that I owe Sarah Saxton something, I have thought about her so seldom across the years but now I feel I must make some retribution. Fate has brought this girl into the village, and I believe the time has come for me to make amends.

'I have offered Ellen Adair a home and employment as companion to Lisanne. I could not bring myself to ask her to act as lady's maid, they do after all share the same grandfather and it could be that Ellen will bring a stability into Lisanne's life which she sorely lacks. I pray to God that I have done the right thing.'

For some time in the diary Ellen was mentioned only in passing, to say that it would seem things were working out reasonably well. Then once more I came across several pages closely written, pages which made me relive painful memories.

'I have invited the family here. I have not seen Geraldine for some time but already I have decided that she should marry Lance. She is pretty, intelligent and amenable, she will make a fitting wife for him although I am aware that he is fond of Lisanne. Lisanne is too flighty, too much like her mother but without her mother's character, and she will be better with Gervase. They are two of a kind, they will spend their money like water, live their own lives and hopefully in time accept what they cannot change.

'I should have made an effort with Gervase but he refused to meet me halfway and I am after all his grandmother. I saw him as a handsome wilful and remote boy who showed quite plainly that he didn't like me or the things I stood for, and in all that long summer when he tramped alone across the fells I came no nearer to understanding him, his resentment was too strong.'

Again I turned the pages before I sat back stunned.

'Lance is in love with Ellen and she with him. I have watched them at the dining table, walking in the park, dancing together. I have seen the way he looks at her, the anguish in their eyes, and I am troubled by it. I would never

442

have taken Ellen into the house if I had thought this would happen. It is too cruel: now he will go unhappy to his marriage with Geraldine, and Ellen will stand between them like a dark shadow.

'I shall pray that Lance will forget her just as William was asked to forget her grandmother, and I am glad that Delia is taking Lisanne to Europe. For the first time in my life I am grateful for the restlessness that has always spurred Delia on from one place to the next.'

After that there were whole pages filled with her disquiet about the war news and a brief paragraph saying: 'Delia and the two girls are in Antibes. It was foolish to go to the south of France instead of returning to England, but no doubt after that dreadful scandal in Paris they had to get away quickly. How could Delia let such a thing happen? Now I dare not think what will happen to them when war comes, for I think war must be inevitable.

'I wish I understood Geraldine more. She is always so polite, so restrained, and I fear she is destined to produce daughters. I dare not ask myself if she and Lance are happy, they play their part but there are times when I long for the old Lance who made me laugh. He has grown so sedate and correct.

'I have been thinking a lot recently about Ellen and wishing she had been my granddaughter and not Sarah Saxton's. How much happier Lance would have been married to Ellen, perhaps she was the best de Bellefort of them all. It seems that all my life I have schemed and plotted in an effort to do my duty as I saw it, and now that I am old and very tired I have come to realize that fate does not always place the right people in the right places.'

After that there were dozens of blank pages and then some brief notes in handwriting that wavered and scrawled across the page, and I was unable to read any of it. I imagined that already her sight and her interest in life were fading.

Sadly I closed the diary and sat for a few moments with it in my hands while I stared unseeing through the rain-splashed windows. I felt no anger or hatred in that gentle firelit room, no burden of resentment against the role I had usurped, only an atmosphere of peace as ethereal as the haunting perfume that still lingered.

A new and powerful resolution was born in me in that room. There was no going back, I could only go forward, and I knew I could not live my life as Gervase's wife in an atmosphere of indifference and destructive separateness.

I knew now that what I had felt for Mark was not love. He had been a charming interlude, someone who had shown me love and gentleness, tenderness and understanding, all the values denied to me in my lonely childhood and the years that came after. It was the sort of love I wanted from Gervase. I could not live in an atmosphere of resentment interspersed by rare nights of passionate abandonment which somehow left us further apart than ever.

I understood him. I understood his bitterness and jealousy. That remote moody boy had grown into a man writhing with resentment that he was destined to be second best, even to the wife who had not been thought suitable for Lance to marry, pretty frivolous flighty Lisanne who he believed was hating him for the very same reasons he was hating her.

I ached to tell him the truth but it was impossible. He would hate Ellen Adair far more fervently, for deceiving him, for not being Lisanne.

We had to talk. I had to make him see that I was not his enemy. I needed to be his wife, the mother of his children, and if I couldn't make him see that, there was no future for either of us.

It was several days later when I heard a car approaching the house and I ran to the window to see who my visitor was. It was Gervase's long black tourer, and with my heart thumping I watched while he climbed out and stood for a while looking back along the drive.

I knew what he was thinking, what Lance had thought years before when we had stood together in the snow: Mine, all mine, the park and the trees, the mere and the fells as far as the eye could see. The farms nestling on the hillside,

444

the stone villages and tiny hamlets with their ancient churches and comfortable inns, surrounded by rolling hills and stark crags, all of them reaching far back into a history created in days when armoured knights fought each other for tracts of land where they could build their castles and great houses. There they had lorded it over other men and made stern laws to ensure that they could hold what they had, until those laws became as much a part of this land as the falcons sailing majestically on the north wind.

With a strange kind of urgency I left the room and ran out into the hall. I flung open the stout oak door and stood for a moment looking down on to the terrace where Gervase was still contemplating his domain, and trembling with nervousness I waited for him to turn his head. In that first moment I was aware of the reserve that clouded his eyes, the remoteness I had come to dread which came over his face like a shutter excluding the light, then with a little cry I ran down the steps and throwing my arms round him I cried, 'Oh Gervase, you're home, I'm so glad you're home.

For a moment he held me away from him, staring silent and brooding into my eyes until once again I felt afraid and uncertain, then suddenly he gathered me close with a new and desperate longing, a tenderness I had never known from him, and a new and sudden joy flooded my being.

As we walked into the house he said dryly, 'You take my breath away, Lisanne, I hadn't expected such a greeting. Have you been very bored?'

'Gervase, we have to talk,' I replied urgently.

'About what? Has something momentous happened while I've been away?'

'I realized how much I was missing you.'

'Despite the fact that you have recently asked me for a divorce.'

'Can't we talk just once without your cynicism clouding everything?'

'We can try. But not now Lisanne, I have things to do. Tonight perhaps, after dinner.'

'Why can't we talk now, what is more important than our marriage?'

He raised his eyebrows in that maddening surprise that made me want to hit out at him, instead my eyes filled with tears and apologetically he said, 'I really do have things to do right now, Lisanne. We'll talk later.'

Miserably I was about to turn away when he caught hold of my hand. 'My poor Lisanne,' he said gently. 'When you were a little girl you only had to ask for something and it was there immediately, even now you can't understand that it isn't always possible to have everything your way.'

Bewildered I cried, 'Will you always hate me, Gervase?'

'My dear girl, I don't hate you.'

'You don't love me either.'

Cynically he said, 'Is that what you want, Lisanne, all this and love too? We would indeed be fortunate.'

With a brief smile he left me standing in the hall staring after him while he ran lightly up the stairs.

How could I ever have thought that it would be easy, how could I ever have expected him to overcome the resentment of years? I heard him go out while I stood at a window staring out towards the mere. The late afternoon sunlight gilded the beeches and already the leaves were turning. Soon now the chill autumn winds would sweep from the North Sea across the fells and the wild geese would be flying inland – a prospect as chill and unwelcome as the next encounter I was expecting with my husband.

Dinner was a silent meal. Gervase seemed preoccupied with his own thoughts while I was rehearsing how I could begin as soon as the meal was over.

For what seemed like hours I sat in the drawing room alone while he talked on the telephone from the library. He came at last, apologizing for his tardiness, helping himself to sherry and placing a glass on the table by my chair.

He stood near the fireplace staring down into the flames and I thought how handsome he was with his raven hair shining blue under the lamplight, his dark perfect profile haughty and brooding before he looked up suddenly and I was achingly aware of his steely blue eyes looking coolly into mine.

'You wanted to talk, Lisanne,' he said evenly. 'I take it

you are no longer interested in a divorce, there is a new game you wish to play, and a new role you are anxious to adopt. The perfect Lady de Bellefort, dutiful wife, perfect hostess, caring mother, isn't that so?'

'I don't want to be less than your grandmother, less than Geraldine. I want people to see that we're worthy of this house and all that goes with it. I wouldn't be able to bear it if people looked on us as interlopers because we merely covered our hopeless marriage with a façade of respectability.'

'You think people might be prepared to see us as a devoted family?'

'Yes, if we try, for our son's sake. We owe it to him.'

'I understood the old Lisanne better than the Lisanne you are trying to show me now.'

'I don't know what you mean.'

'The old Lisanne was greedy for life. I saw myself in her, grasping and selfish and not a little ruthless. Leopards don't change their spots, Lisanne, although I must admit there are times when you puzzle me, when I think that perhaps life has moulded you into a person I could love. Then I start remembering things I would prefer to forget.'

'What sort of things?'

'That our respected grandmother thought we were two of a kind, that we deserved each other. You hadn't changed when you went to Paris, your escapades there made headlines, my dear.'

'You knew about Henri?'

'Like I said, it made headlines. Society beauty in shooting scandal. None of the hoary details were left out of the gossip columns.'

'There were no hoary details. All I was guilty of was foolishness.'

'Of course it reassured our respected grandmother that she had been wise in selecting Geraldine to marry Lance, while you and I were considered worthy of one another. I was never her favourite and now you too had forfeited any right to that honour.'

'And you're not prepared to see that I've changed, that

447

I've grown up. I don't want to be the old Lisanne who thought only of pleasure, who hurt people without thinking and wanted everything regardless of the cost. I want to be a good wife and mother, I want us to be respected. Can't you see I'm not blaming you for the way you grew up, why must you blame me?'

'Lisanne, I can't be bullied into loving you.'

'Does that mean that you can't love me, that for the rest of our married life you are going to make me aware that ours will always be a marriage of convenience?'

He didn't answer me. Instead his gaze reverted to the flames and I could feel the hot stinging tears filling my eyes before I scrambled to my feet and walked swiftly across the room and out through the door.

I needed to escape from the house whose walls seemed to be closing in on me. Snatching a scarf and coat from the cloakroom I flung open the front door and pulled it fast behind me, then I started to walk. I had no idea what time it was or where my footsteps would lead me but I walked quickly with my head bent against the wind, my hands thrust into the deep pockets of my tweed coat while the force of the wind brought the tears back into my eyes.

I came at last to the boathouse and sat forlornly on the wall near the slipway where once I had sat with Lance while I came to terms with the rest of my life, a life without him. Now once again there were decisions to be made, decisions that were far harder than those I had been asked to make before.

I had been a fool to ever think that I could live the rest of my life as Lisanne de Bellefort without robing myself in her personality. Lisanne would have met Gervase on his own ground. His moodiness and remoteness would not have disturbed for one moment the equilibrium of her life because she wouldn't have cared. I on the other hand cared too much.

I had been a fool to believe the things Kitty had said when she told me nothing was easier than to pretend to be Lisanne, to marry Gervase and live the rest of my life cocooned in wealth and privilege. Not so easily could I kill

Ellen. I did not have Kitty's ruthlessness. If I were to survive I would do it on my own terms. The risk was enormous, it was a risk that in the end would probably cost me my husband and child, but it was a risk I had to take if I were to preserve my integrity. I had to make Gervase see that the woman he thought of as Lisanne had changed, because she was not Lisanne, she was someone he had never known.

My resolution made, I jumped up and started back to the house. The lights in the drawing room had been extinguished but as I crossed the hall I could see a light shining under the library door. First of all I went into the study and picked up Lady de Bellefort's diary where it lay on the top of the desk. Her words more than mine were capable of describing Ellen Adair. They could not make him forgive the deception but they might in time help him to understand.

Only one light burned in the library, over the easy chair set in front of the fire. He sat with his eyes scanning a large leather-bound volume and I had almost reached his chair when he looked up in surprise.

'Where have you been?' he asked. 'I thought you'd gone up to bed. I seem to remember it was always a worthwhile tactic when you failed to get your own way.'

'I went for a walk. I needed to think.'

'I hadn't realized that walking in the dark was conducive to healthy thinking.'

His sarcasm was making it easier than I had thought, and trying desperately to keep the anxiety from my voice I said, 'I have something to tell you Gervase, and I'd rather you didn't say a word until I've finished.'

'Not more histrionics, I hope.'

'No, I'm going to tell you the truth and it's possible you will hate me more, much more than you ever hated your grandmother or Lisanne. I'm sorry. I should never have thought for one moment that it would work, now I know it was the most stupid, terrible thing I ever did, but I have to tell you the truth even if you kill me for it.'

He was staring at me fixedly and when he didn't speak I

449

went on, harnessing my words with a devastating clarity that surprised me.

'I'm not your cousin Lisanne, Gervase. Lisanne was drowned in the shipwreck. I'm Ellan Adair who you never knew existed, and it started innocently enough in the hospital where they took us after we were picked up. Lisanne and I were very much alike and I was clutching her brooch engraved with the letter L when they took me into hospital. I tried to tell them I wasn't Lisanne but they thought I was rambling and in the end I allowed them to go on thinking I was Lisanne. I hadn't any money, I had nowhere to go and no job. You have no idea how easily everything fell into place.

'I'm not proud of what I've done, I'm bitterly ashamed and I shan't blame you if you hate me for the rest of your life. This is your grandmother's diary which she kept meticulously. It will explain how Ellen Adair came here, what happened to her afterwards and why she came to be travelling back to England with Lisanne and her mother. Please read it. It won't make it any easier to forgive me but it might help you understand a little.'

Firmly I thrust the diary into his hands. His face was filled with astonishment, there had not been time for anger to take its place, and without another word I turned on my heel and left him alone. I had not told him anything about Kitty's part in my deception. I had not needed to listen to her, and in the end it was I who had to face the music.

Upstairs I started to pack a valise with my personal things, a small amount of underwear and a sweater. I took no jewellery except my wedding ring and my wristwatch, but from the table near the window I picked up a photograph of my son, the last that had been taken before he went off to school. He smiled back at me from the photograph, and I realized how achingly like Gervase he had become with his dark hair and steely blue eyes.

With tears in my eyes I laid it in my case. There would be last-minute things to pack in the morning, but for now all I could do was bathe and go to bed. It was too late to leave the house but I took the precaution of locking the doors leading to the hall and dressing room. I wanted no more scenes with Gervase that night, morning would be soon enough. But I had no hopes of sleeping.

The night seemed endless as I lay staring into the darkness. The wind had become a crescendo round the house and occasionally flashes of lightning lit up the room. I strained my ears to·hear if Gervase had come into the dressing room but inside the house there was only a stillness except for the musical chiming of a clock. I listened for the closing of doors, for the creaking of some board in the corridor outside the room, but there was nothing. I could picture Gervase sitting in the library staring into the dying embers, tortured by the knowledge that he had been deceived by an unknown woman, far more treacherously than he could ever have been decieved by the cousin he believed he hated.

The first faint light of a new day found me still sleepless, but dawn came relentlessly, and now I was able to distinguish the outline of furniture in the room. The wind had died and the rain had stopped, that much I was aware of before I pulled the heavy drapes back from the window to face a morning sky streaked with gold and the promise of a lovely day.

I dressed quickly in a charcoal-grey skirt and white silk blouse but it seemed incongruous to brush my hair and apply make-up as though this was just an ordinary day, when it was probably a day I would remember for the rest of my life. It was a day when I must face my husband's anger and the desolation of all that came after. The loss of my home, my son, all the normal everyday things I had begun to accept as mine. But I forced myself to go on with my tasks. To collect my toilet things and arrange them neatly in my case. To choose the plain black kid court shoes I would wear and finally, when I was satisfied there was nothing else I needed, to snap the case shut.

It was just after seven o'clock and very soon now the house would be coming to life. The tweed coat and scarf I had worn in the park the night before lay across the back of a chair and I decided that these would be my travelling clothes. In my purse was a small sum of money, about sixteen pounds, but there w s a large sum of money in the bank.

If Ellen Adair had been more sensible about her money she would probably have returned from France to find the sum of two hundred pounds in her bank account. This much I decided to take out of the de Bellefort account, the rest was for Gervase to do with as he thought fit. Now, all that remained was for me to listen to his scorn – but with the fervent hope that from time to time he would allow me to see Lance.

I couldn't think that Gervase would wish to make my deception public, he had too much pride. Idly I wondered what he would tell our neighbours and the rest of the family.

I sat in a chair in front of the window watching the pale sun gilding the lawns while along the drive from the direction of the gate two men walked towards the house with their dogs, two of the gamekeepers starting their day's work. I started nervously at the sound of the dressing room door being opened from the corridor, then the sound of the shower in the bathroom. It was evident Gervase had not slept in the dressing room and I thought about him spending the night in his chair in the library with his grandmother's diary lying idle in his hands, sleeping fitfully, and in his moments of wakefulness seething with anger and frustration at the betrayal which tortured his soul.

I was trembling as I waited for him to show some sign that he wished to speak to me, listening anxiously to the sounds from the room next door, the opening and closing of drawers, the sharp click of the wardrobe door. I jumped nervously at the curt tap on the dressing room door and, squaring my shoulders, went forward to open it.

In those first few seconds we stared at each other without speaking, then his eyes fell on the valise and the tweed coat.

'You intend to leave then, Lisanne?' he said distantly, then more helplessly, 'My God, what do I call you?'

Willing my voice not to tremble, I said, 'I've packed what I shall need for the next few days. You will find the rest of

452

my clothes in the wardrobes and the drawers and I am not taking any jewellery apart from my wedding ring.

'I intend to withdraw two hundred pounds from my account, I think that roughly represents the sum I might have expected to find waiting for me in England before I decided to remove it – most foolishly, as it turned out.'

He was staring down at me enigmatically, his face haughty, distant, and suddenly my voice was trembling and the treacherous tears were filling my eyes and rolling dismally down my cheeks.

'I shall need to see Lance from time to time, Gervase, I love him very dearly. I am not asking for him to live with me permanently, he is your son too and you will be able to do far more for him than I could.'

His eyes were dark blue and coldly angry. Suddenly he snapped, 'I suppose you're going to this man you met in London?'

My eyes opened wide. 'Well of course not, how can you even think it? I'm not going to anybody, I'm on my own. I'm Ellen Adair again and I shall find work, there must be something I can do. I was going to look for a job when I came back to England after the war, I shall do it now.'

'My grandmother thought you were in love with Lance. Was that true?'

'Yes, I loved him. He was the first man I ever loved. I'd never met anybody like him, educated, polished, caring and kind. I was ready for love, nobody had ever loved me before. And Lance didn't love me enough.'

'Did you love him when you married me?'

'Oh Gervase, of course not. I hadn't loved Lance for a very long time. He was married to Geraldine and I was living a strange sort of life in occupied France. For me to go on loving Lance in situations like that I would have had to be very sure that he loved me in return, and there was no such certainty.

'Gervase, I'm sorry for what I've done, sorry and bitterly ashamed. I couldn't blame you for anything you did to me.'

'I should take you by your pretty neck and squeeze the life out of you. I should haul you up before the world as an impostor, a woman who cheated me by pretending to be a de Bellefort, a woman who even went as far as marrying me in another woman's name.'

At that moment anger came to my rescue and with flashing eyes and deep resentment in my heart I raged, 'I am a de Bellefort. I'm a better one than Lisanne or Geraldine. If you read your grandmother's diary you'll know she thought so too. This family owes me something. They made a scapegoat out of me and didn't know or care how I survived. Well I'm sorry for what I did but there are other things I'm not sorry about. I tried to be a good friend to Lisanne, I really did try to make her the sort of girl her grandmother would have been proud of, and I tried to save her life.' I was sobbing now, scrambling in my bag for my handkerchief.

Calmly handing me his, he said, 'What other things are you sorry for?'

'I'm sorry I ever thought I could make you love me. I'm sorry I thought you had it in you to care more for me than this heap of old stones and your rambling acres. You de Belleforts are all the same. I was a fool to think you, of all people, would change.'

'Is it too much to ask where you think you are going?'

'I don't know. I'll think better when I'm out of this house, and I'll let you have my address as soon as I'm able. I'm quite sure you'll want to divorce me as quickly as possible.'

I pushed my arms into my tweed coat and picked up the valise while he stood impassively watching me with maddening composure. He doesn't care, I thought wildly, I'm walking out of his life and he is totally immune from any feeling of sorrow or loss.

I opened the door and started to walk firmly along the corridor and down the stairs, and to my chagrin he walked with me, companionably, as if we were embarked on a day's outing. Carstairs was crossing the hall as we got to it and if he was surprised to see us leaving the house at that time in the morning, like the well-bred servant he was he showed no sign of it.

Outside on the terrace I was surprised to see Gervase's

tourer and he went to it immediately and opened the passenger door for me, saying, 'It's too far to walk, I'll drive you.'

'There's no need,' I said firmly, 'I've walked it often enough in the past.'

'Nevertheless I don't expect you to walk this morning. Please get in the car.'

He took the valise out of my hand and put it in the car, then he walked round to the driver's door and got in the car. We drove in silence. I could read nothing from his calm austere profile and I sat beside him miserable and close to tears.

I had been married to Gervase for many years but he had never seemed more remote.

The village was coming to life, people were setting out their stalls for market day and already Alec Devlin was outside his father's shop sweeping the footpath. The homely smell of baking bread came through the open window of the car.

We left the village and headed for the station, and I found myself stupidly wondering if he would wait with me for the train or simply deposit me at the station before driving out of my life.

He ignored the station road and instead drove on towards the moor. I stared at him but his expression gave nothing away, and in some agitation I cried, 'You've missed the road. You can turn at the crossroads.'

He ignored me, driving past the crossroads and on to the long winding road that crossed the moor and climbed towards the crags that rose in isolated splendour against the misted hills. On any other morning I would have delighted in the sun striking the crags like molten gold and the heather in the distance shading blue and purple. But now my heart was hammering in my breast so loudly I felt sure he must hear it. Fearfully I began to believe that he was capable of killing me up there on those lonely fells with only the swooping curlews to see what he was about.

The long car climbed steadily and soon we were on a single track used only by weekend ramblers and climbers. My hands were clenched together to stop their trembling and I made up my mind that as soon as he stopped the car I would scramble out and start to run down the hillside. Then as soon as it was born I stifled the idea. Gervase would follow me mercilessly and I was wearing ridiculous high heels which were quite unsuitable for a headlong flight across the harsh moorland.

At last he could drive no further but contented himself by reversing the car into a narrow space where the crag towered above us and the track came to an untidy end. Without a word he got out of the car and came to open the passenger door.

'Come with me,' he commanded, 'I have something to show you.'

For several seconds I shrank back in my seat but his fingers closed round mine with steely strength, forcing me to obey him, then he was holding my arm and I was walking with him towards the spot where we could look down on the village of Langstone and the imposing pile of Langstone Priory which dominated the picture spread before us as surely as the crag behind us dominated the fell.

Had he brought me up here to show me how completely the Priory and its vast acres mattered? If so I had heard it all before, and at that moment anger came to my rescue and impatiently I struggled in his grasp, unprepared for the gentleness, the normality of his voice.

'When I was a boy I used to come up here, Ellen,' he said softly, and the sound of my name on his lips brought my struggles to an end. I waited anxious and breathless for what I now knew would be important for both of us.

'I used to tell myself that that was Lance's castle and this was mine. We were medieval knights fighting for land and the women we would marry, and my grandmother was some omnipotent medieval queen watching the tournament where one of us would die and the other would have everything.

'It was a dream, Ellen, the sad dream of a foolish resentful boy who in his heart was refusing to accept the role that fate had dictated. Now fate has relented and all the things that boy once longed for are mine. There will be no scandal to mar it, Ellen Adair, there will be no sniggers of contempt or pointing fingers, no sly innuendos that Gervase de Belle-fort was deceived into marriage by some unknown girl society would condemn as nothing more or less than an adventuress. You are my wife, Ellen, and you will remain my wife. Do you understand?'

For what seemed an eternity I stared at him blankly, then suddenly an anger such as I had never known made me snatch my arm away from his grasp and with my eyes blazing I stormed, 'I won't stay married to you to keep up appearances, you'll have to kill me first. You only want me for a wife to satisfy your ego, to thwart your grandmother even now when she's dead. Every time you look at me you'll be congratulating yourself that you've stolen a march on all of them by marrying a nobody. It won't make you care for me, but God knows it will make you feel twice the man you are by watching me play a part I have no right to and feeling that between us we've defeated every de Bellefort who ever lived. I'm sorry, Gervase, I won't do it. I'm glad it's all over, that I can be myself again, that I don't have to deceive anybody ever again.'

'I thought you wanted me to love you,' he said stonily.

'You'll never love me,' I cried. 'You have too much pride, and so have I.'

I turned and walked away with my head head high.

He came after me, turning me round to face him with his hands on my shoulders. There was no anger in his face, only a whimsical sort of humour.

'Would you believe me if I said I did love you, Ellen, that I'd fought against loving you for a very long time? I didn't want to love you, I couldn't believe that I could possibly be falling in love with Lisanne. But now I can see that you were never Lisanne. Ellen, there is no way you are walking out of my life to ease your conscience. You'll stay and do you duty as a good wife and mother.'

'No, Gervase, I will not. In some strange perverse way you want me in your life as a constant reminder that you are paying back your grandmother for every slight, every mean and tortured thing you imagined she did to you.'

'I did hate her, Ellen, I openly admit it. But last night I

spent reading her diary, and bit by bit I began to understand her, and understanding her I began to love her, to wish I'd loved her when she was alive. I saw so much of myself in that indomitable old woman, the pride that was my pride, her fears that were my fears, and through her eyes I began to see the young Ellen Adair who was the best de Bellefort of us all. Ellen, if you walk out of my life now none of that you see down there will have any meaning, nothing will matter if you're not there to share it with me.'

I looked for mockery in his face, the old tantalizing remoteness I had struggled to break through, but his face was serious, his eyes beseeching me to believe him. And still the doubts persisted.

'Oh Gervase, I wish I could believe you, I wish I could be sure that you mean what you're saying.'

'Ellen, even when I made you most angry, when I hurt and tormented you, did you ever know me say a single word I didn't mean?'

'No, perhaps that's why I can't believe that so much resentment and anger can be replaced by so much caring.'

'Then come back with me. A whole new start, Ellen, a different world for both of us.'

'Gervase, you are asking me to be Lisanne all over again, to live at the Priory where everybody believes I am Lisanne. I do so desperately want to be myself.'

'You will be, Ellen. Neither of us can obliterate the past entirely. You created the lie and in some respects you will have to live with it, but between you and me there will be honesty from now on. To me you will be Ellen, I shall never call you Lisanne again.'

'You can't call me Ellen.'

'I know. I shall call you darling, it's what I've always wanted to call you anyway.'

His arms were about me, holding me close and with a tenderness I had never thought to find in him, then he was holding the car door open for me and he knew he had won.

For the first time as we drove through the village of Langstone I felt I was going home. In the months, even the years ahead of us we had much to discuss, much to explain.

He had to meet the young Ellen who had fled from her father's house in fear and anguish, and those others who had made up her story, and in my imagination they all came trooping back. My poor downtrodden mother and bombastic father. Aunt Liza with her sharp disapproving face and Aunt Mary with her brood of children and her feckless husband. More than any of the others, though, there was Peter who I had loved and agonized over. Now I would be able to seek him out and bring him back into my life. And Kitty, for no story of mine would ever be complete without her, and in my imagination I was seeing the old Kitty with her red curls and the freckles on her pert nose.

He reached out and covered my hand with his.

'So silent, darling,' he said quietly, 'I wish I knew what you were thinking at this moment.'

'You will, Gervase,' I assured him. 'There is so much I have to tell you, it will take forever.'

He smiled. 'Here we are, darling. Welcome home.'

We were passing through the huge iron gates and ahead of us the Priory basked in the morning sunlight. I stole a look at his face and somehow the old bitterness had gone and in its place were a serenity and a new maturity. He turned his head to look at me, then he smiled, and in his smile was the promise of great joy.

INTERNATIONAL ACCLAIM FOR

"L. Ron Hubbard's ability to weave humour, adventure and suspense gets your nose back into the pages—with more character and plot changes than one can imagine."

— **The Macombe Daily**

"Hitchhiker's Guide fans will love it..."

— **Bristol Evening Post**

"...exciting, inventive...an L. Ron Hubbard masterpiece destined to become a classic."

— **Mark Thompkins for Starship Express**

"...whirl... spoof..."

he Times

This book follows

MISSION EARTH
Volume 1
THE INVADERS PLAN
Volume 2
BLACK GENESIS
and
Volume 3
THE ENEMY WITHIN

Buy them and read them first!

N

Empire University | 125th St
120th
Amsterdam
116th St.
Bronx

New Jersey

Hudson River

Broadway

Fifth Avenue

Central Park

Weehawken

Ship Passenger Dock →

West Side Elevated Highway

Lexington

Franklin D. Roosevelt Dr.

Queens

Lincoln Tunnel

59th St.

42nd St

52nd

Queensboro Bridge

Empire State Building

Grand Central Station

United Nations

Queens-Midtown Tunnel

23rd

0 | 1
Miles

To Bayonne

First Avenue

East River

Holland Tunnel

Greenwich Village

14th

Bilto-P3 (Earth) Cities

Central Manhattan and

Plotted by 54 Charlee Nine

N

CONNECTICUT

NEW YORK

Branchville

Bridgeport

NEW JERSEY

Norton Point

Long Island Sound

LONG ISLAND

Southern State Pkwy

Spreeport Speedway

JFK Airport

Jones Beach

Atlantic Ocean

Monte Jammell

New Haven

Manhattan

Miles 0   5   10   15

FALSE!!

Long Island

WARNING: The planet Earth (Blito P3)
does not exist. The map is contrary to
all Royal Astrographic records and is
based solely upon descriptions in this
fictional narrative.
By order of Lord Invay
Chief Censor

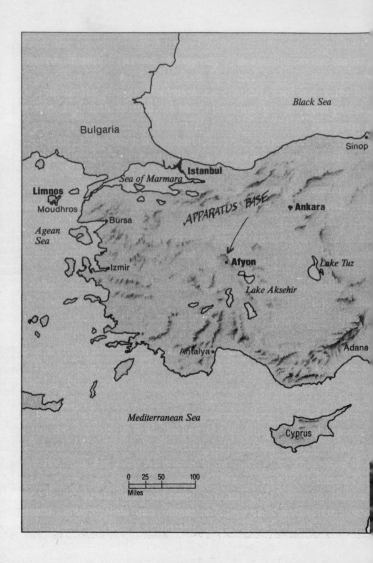

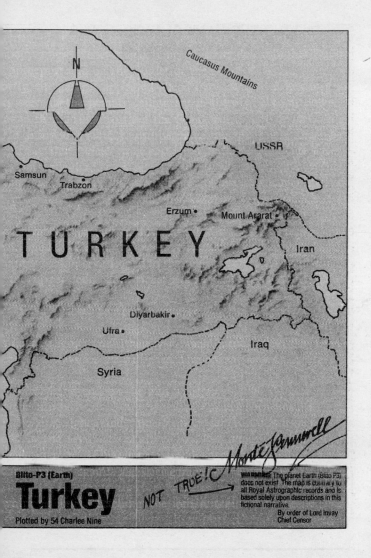

Caucasus Mountains

N

USSR

Samsun
Trabzon

Erzum •

Mount Ararat •

Iran

T U R K E Y

Diyarbakir •

Ufra •

Iraq

Syria

NOT TRUE! C. *Monte Farnwell*

WARNING: The planet Earth (Blito P3) does not exist. The map is contrary to all Royal Astrographic records and is based solely upon descriptions in this fictional narrative.

By order of Lord Invay
Chief Censor

Blito-P3 (Earth)

Turkey

Plotted by 54 Charlee Nine

AMONG THE MANY CLASSIC WORKS
BY L. RON HUBBARD

Battlefield Earth
Beyond the Black Nebula
Buckskin Brigades
The Conquest of Space
The Dangerous Dimension
Death's Deputy
The Emperor of the Universe
Fear
Final Blackout
Forbidden Voyage
The Incredible Destination
The Kilkenny Cats
The Kingslayer
The Last Admiral
The Magnificent Failure
The Masters of Sleep
The Mutineers
Ole Doc Methuselah
Ole Mother Methuselah
The Rebels
Return to Tomorrow
Slaves of Sleep
To the Stars
The Traitor
Triton
Typewriter in the Sky
The Ultimate Adventure
The Unwilling Hero

Mission Earth

An Alien Affair

THE BOOKS OF THE
MISSION EARTH DEKALOGY*

* *Dekalogy—a group of ten volumes.*

L. RON HUBBARD

Mission Earth

VOLUME FOUR

An Alien Affair

NEW ERA PUBLICATIONS UK LTD.

This is a work of science fiction, written as satire.
**The essence of satire is to examine, comment and
give opinion of society and culture, none of which is
construed as a statement of pure fact. No actual
incidents are portrayed and none of the incidents are
to be construed as real. Some of the actions of this
novel take place on planet Earth, but the characters
as presented in this novel have been invented. Any
accidental use of the names of living people in a novel
is virtually inevitable, and any such inadvertency in
this book is unintentional.

**See Author's Introduction, *Mission Earth: Volume One,
The Invaders Plan.*

To YOU,
the millions of science fiction fans
and general public
who welcomed me back to the world of fiction
so warmly
and to the critics and media
who so pleasantly
applauded the novel "Battlefield Earth."
It's great working for you!

Voltarian
Censor's
Disclaimer

For the health, safety and sanity of any reader, it cannot be said often enough that the so-called planet "Earth," as described in this story, does NOT exist.

And more—it must also be pronounced that it is IMPOSSIBLE for such a planet to exist.

First, Voltarian astrographic charts are the most complete in this galaxy. They cover millions of light-years and NO record exists of ANY "Earth" or its so-called designation of *Blito-P3*. If any such entity existed a mere twenty-two light-years away, we would be the first to know. But there is NOTHING to be found on any astrographic records in the vicinity of the "Earth" coordinates but spacedust.

Thus the fabricated representation that there was a secret Voltarian base on "Earth" can be dismissed since there is no such planet. There was once a freighter called the *Blixo*. Records show it disappeared with no survivors, probably at the hands of pirates. Thus, any attempt to say that it was used to make regular six-week runs to bring Earth substances called "drugs" (another deluded concept) to Voltar is without taste or sensibility.

Therefore, there could NOT have been such a person as "Rockecenter" who controlled an entire planet's fuel resources as well as "drugs" and the media.

The characters Jettero Heller and Countess Krak are real but clearly their so-called exploits on this fictional planet could never have occurred. The name Soltan Gris does appear on some records but this fact does not lend a grain of credit to the account attributed to the narrator who bears that name.

The idea that Heller, a Royal officer, would be sent on a Grand Council mission to keep such a planet from destroying itself so it could be invaded later is almost beyond comment. If such a planet did exist, it would be cordoned off as a malignant growth, not assimilated into our Confederacy.

This is most evident in the bizarre practices described in this book. It is beyond the bounds of the most fevered imagination to think there could be such people. It proves beyond any doubt that it is IMPOSSIBLE for such a planet to exist.

No society could possibly exist that would openly countenance such behavior, let alone professions called "psychiatry" and "psychology." If such sexual practices as described in this volume were condoned (let alone promoted in ANY form), one would find a society where pornography was promoted and perversion promulgated. Crime in such a society would rise to the point where even heads of state would be assassinated and entire countries destabilized through terrorism.

No, there can be no such society, let alone a planet, where such decadent extremes could be found. It is impossible. In time, it would destroy itself.

That is why "Earth" does not and cannot exist.

Lord Invay
Royal Historian
Chairman, Board of Censors
Royal Palace
Voltar Confederacy

By Order of
His Imperial Majesty
Wully the Wise

Voltarian
Translator's
Preface

Hi there.

This is 54 Charlee Nine, the Robotbrain in the Translatophone and the translator of this work.

In support of the Honorable Lord Invay, I can verify that there is nothing in my most extensive data banks to compare with what is described in this book. In fact, certain Earth practices came as such a shock that one of my subcomputers quit in protest and still won't talk to me and another tried to mate with itself.

Meanwhile, two are still having a great time arguing over the proposition "Earth is dirty," one is writing a musical, "Candied," two are coauthoring a book called "101 More Ways to Use Mustard and Rolling Pins" and the rest are rejecting this ridiculous behavior with gales of hysterical laughter.

That leaves me to try and put some order back into the area after I write up the Key to this volume, which immediately follows.

For a nonexistent planet, Earth is a pain in the circuits.

Sincerely,

54 Charlee Nine
Robotbrain in the Translatophone

Key to
AN ALIEN
AFFAIR

Absorbo-coat—Coating that absorbs light waves, making the object virtually invisible or undetectable.

Afyon—City in Turkey where the *Apparatus* has a secret base.

Agnes, Miss—Personal aide to Delbert John *Rockecenter.*

Agricultural Training Center for Peasants—Cover name for the secret *Apparatus* base in *Afyon*, Turkey.

Antimanco—A race exiled long ago from the planet *Manco* for ritual murders.

Apparatus, Coordinated Information—The secret police of *Voltar*, headed by Lombar *Hisst* and manned by criminals.

Assassin Pilots—Space pilots used to kill any *Apparatus* personnel who try to flee a battle.

Atalanta—Home province for Jettero *Heller* and the Countess *Krak* on the planet *Manco.*

Babe Corleone—The six-foot-six leader of the *Corleone* mob, widow of "Holy Joe."

Bang-Bang Rimbombo—An ex-marine demolitions expert and member of the *Corleone* mob.

Barben, I. G.—Pharmaceutical company controlled by Delbert John *Rockecenter*.

Bawtch—Soltan *Gris*'s chief clerk for *Section 451* on *Voltar*.

Bildirjin, Nurse—Turkish teen-age girl who assists Prahd *Bittlestiffender*.

Bittlestiffender, Prahd—Cellologist who implanted Jettero *Heller* back on Voltar. He was brought in by Soltan *Gris* to start the phony *World United Charities Mercy and Benevolent Hospital* in *Afyon*.

Blito-P3—Voltarian designation for a planet known locally as "Earth." It is on the *Invasion Timetable* as a future way-stop on *Voltar*'s route toward the center of this galaxy.

Blixo—*Apparatus* freighter that makes regular runs between Earth and *Voltar*. The voyage takes about six weeks each way and is piloted by Captain Bolz.

Bolz—Captain of the freighter *Blixo*.

Bomber—An ordinary Earth vehicle with all of its glass removed and roll bars added. It is found in "demolition derbies" where the object is to ram others to make them unable to move. A winner of one of these was defined as the last vehicle that could still move under its own power. The term is also applied to the driver.

Bugging Gear—Electronic eavesdropping devices that Soltan *Gris* had implanted in Jettero *Heller.* Gris uses a video unit to monitor everything Heller sees or hears. The signals are picked up by the receiver and decoder that Gris carries. When Heller is more than 200 miles from Gris, the *831 Relayer* is turned on and boosts the signal to a range of 10,000 miles.

Bury—Delbert John *Rockecenter*'s most powerful attorney, member of the law firm *Swindle and Crouch.*

Caucalsia, Prince—Name of *Tug One,* after a hero of *Manco.*

Cellology—Voltarian medical science that can repair the body through the cellular generation of tissues, including entire body parts.

Chank-pop—A small, round ball that, when pressed, sprays a scented fog; used as a refresher on *Voltar.*

Code Break—Alerting others that one is an alien. Per a section of the Space Code, it carries an automatic death penalty. The purpose is to maintain the security of the *Invasion Timetable.*

Control Star—An electronic device disguised as a star-shaped medallion that can paralyze any of the *Apparatus* crew of *Antimanco* pirates that brought Soltan *Gris* and Jettero *Heller* to Earth.

Coordinated Information Apparatus—See *Apparatus.*

Corleone—A Mafia Family now headed by *Babe Corleone,* a former Roxy chorus girl and widow of *"Holy Joe."*

Crobe, Doctor—*Apparatus* cellologist who delights in making freaks; he worked in *Spiteos.*

Empire University—Where Jettero *Heller* is taking classes in New York City.

Epstein, Izzy—Student at *Empire University* and financial expert whom Jettero *Heller* hired to set up a corporate structure to handle his finances.

Faht Bey—Turkish name of the commander of the secret *Apparatus* base in *Afyon,* Turkey.

F.F.B.O.—Fatten, Farten, Burstein and Ooze, the largest advertising firm in the world.

Flagrant, J. P.—Vice President at *F.F.B.O.* He was fired during the hiring of J. Walter *Madison.*

Fleet—The elite space fighting arm of *Voltar* to which Jettero *Heller* belongs and which the *Apparatus* despises.

Geovani—One of *Babe Corleone*'s bodyguards.

Gracious Palms—The elegant whorehouse where Jettero *Heller* resides. It is across from the United Nations and is run by the *Corleone* Family.

Grand Council—The governing body of *Voltar* which ordered a mission to keep Earth from destroying itself so the *Invasion Timetable* could be maintained.

Gris, Soltan—*Apparatus* officer placed in charge of the *Blito-P3* (Earth) Section and an enemy of Jettero *Heller*.

Hakluyt—Sixteenth-century Earthman who wrote of various explorations in the eastern United States.

Hatchetheimer, General—Last surviving member of Adolf Hitler's general staff.

Heller, Hightee—Sister of Jettero *Heller* and most popular entertainer in the *Voltar* confederacy.

Heller, Jettero—Combat engineer and Royal officer of the *Fleet*, sent by *Grand Council* order to Earth, where he is operating under the name of Jerome Terrance *Wister*.

Hisst, Lombar—Head of the *Apparatus* who, to keep the *Grand Council* from discovering his plan, sent Soltan *Gris* to sabotage Jettero *Heller*'s mission.

"Holy Joe" Corleone—Head of the *Corleone* Family until murdered. He did not believe in pushing drugs, hence his name.

Hypnohelmet—Device placed over the head and used to induce a hypnotic state.

Inkswitch—Name used by Soltan *Gris* when pretending to be a U.S. Federal officer.

Invasion Timetable—A schedule of galactic conquest. The plans and budget of every section of *Voltar*'s government must adhere to it. Bequeathed by Voltar's ancestors hundreds of thousands of years ago, it is inviolate and sacred and the guiding dogma of the Confederacy.

Karagoz—Turkish peasant, head of Soltan *Gris*'s house in *Afyon*.

Knife Section—Section of the *Apparatus* named after its favorite weapon.

Krak, Countess—Condemned murderess, prisoner of *Spiteos* and sweetheart of Jettero *Heller*.

Lepertige—Large catlike animal as tall as a man.

Line-jumper—Small spacecraft used by the Voltarian Army to lift and quickly move up to one hundred tons across battle lines.

Louseini, Razza—Consigliere to mob chief Faustino "The Noose" *Narcotici*.

Madison, J. Walter—Fired from *F.F.B.O.* when his style of public relations caused the president of Patagonia to commit suicide, he was rehired by *Bury* to immortalize Jettero *Heller* in the media. He is also known as J. Warbler Madman.

Magic Mail—*Apparatus* trick where a letter is mailed but won't be delivered as long as a designated card is regularly sent.

Manco—Home planet of Jettero *Heller* and the Countess *Krak*.

Maysabongo—A small African nation of which Jettero *Heller* was made a representative. Izzy *Epstein* made some of Heller's businesses Maysabongo corporations.

Mudlick Construction Company—A private company in Turkey that gives Soltan *Gris* kickbacks whenever he gives them a contract.

Multinational—Name of umbrella corporation, located in the Empire State Building, that Izzy *Epstein* set up to manage other Jettero *Heller* companies.

Mutazione, Mike—Owner of the Jiffy-Spiffy Garage who customized, for Jettero *Heller*, both the Cadillac and the vintage cab.

Narcotici, Faustino "The Noose"—Head of a Mafia Family that is the underworld outlet for drugs from I. G. *Barben* and is trying to take over the territory of the *Corleone* Family.

Nature Appreciation 101—Class taught by Miss *Simmons* to which she has assigned Jettero *Heller* in order to flunk him out of *Empire University*.

Octopus Oil—A Delbert John *Rockecenter* company that controls the world's petroleum.

Odur—See *Oh Dear*.

Oh Dear—Nickname for Odur. With *Too-Too*, forced by Soltan *Gris* to get information on *Voltar* and courier it to him on Earth.

Peace, Miss—Secretary to Delbert John *Rockecenter*.

Raht—An *Apparatus* agent on Earth who, with *Terb*, was assigned by Lombar *Hisst* to help Soltan *Gris* sabotage Jettero *Heller*'s mission.

Rockecenter, Delbert John—Native of Earth who controls all the planet's fuel, finances, governments and drugs.

Roke, Tars—Astrographer to the Emperor of *Voltar*, Cling the Lofty, and old friend of Jettero *Heller*. It was his briefing to the *Grand Council* that prompted Mission Earth to restore the *Invasion Timetable*.

Section 451—A Section in the *Apparatus* on *Voltar*, headed by Soltan *Gris*.

Seven Brothers—Secret consortium on Earth that includes *Octopus Oil* as the senior member.

Silva, Gunsalmo—Former bodyguard to "Holy Joe" and believed to be the one responsible for killing the Corleone boss. Soltan *Gris* sent him to kill the CIA Director and be killed.

Simmons, Miss—A teacher at *Empire University* who has promised Jettero *Heller* she will flunk him out of school.

Smith, John—An alias that Soltan *Gris* uses as a Delbert John *Rockecenter* employee.

Space Code—See *Code Break*.

Spiteos—The secret mountain fortress and prison run by the *Apparatus* on *Voltar* where the Countess *Krak* and Jettero *Heller* had been imprisoned.

Stabb, Captain—Leader of the *Antimanco* crew that piloted *Tug One*.

Stinger—A flexible whip about eighteen inches long with an electric jolt in its tip-lash.

Sultan Bey—The Turkish name Soltan *Gris* assumes in *Afyon*, Turkey.

Swindle and Crouch—Law firm that represents Delbert John *Rockecenter*'s interests.

Tavilnasty, Jimmy "The Gutter"—Hit man for the *Corleone* family until killed by Gunsalmo *Silva*.

Tayl, Widow—Nymphomaniac on *Voltar*. She had a small hospital that Soltan *Gris* used when he had Prahd *Bittlestiffender* implant Jettero *Heller* with *Bugging Gear*.

Terb—*Apparatus* agent on Earth who, with *Raht*, was assigned by Lombar *Hisst* to help Soltan *Gris* sabotage Jettero *Heller*'s mission.

Too-Too—Nickname for *Twolah*. He and *Oh Dear* were forced by Soltan *Gris* to get information on *Voltar* and courier it secretly back to him on Earth.

Tug One—The spaceship used by Jettero *Heller* to travel the 22½ light-years to Earth. Heller renamed it the *Prince Caucalsia*.

Twolah—See *Too-Too*.

Utanc—A belly dancer that Soltan *Gris* bought to be his concubine slave.

Vantagio—Manager of the *Gracious Palms*, the elegant

whorehouse operated by the *Corleone* Family, across the street from the United Nations.

Voltar—Home planet and seat of the 110-world Confederacy that was established 125,000 years ago. Voltar is ruled by the Emperor through the *Grand Council* in accordance with the *Invasion Timetable*.

Whiz Kid—Nickname given to Jettero *Heller* by J. Walter *Madison*. In addition, Madison has another person acting as Heller's "double" to get publicity without Heller's consent. The phony "Whiz Kid" has buckteeth, a protruding jaw and wears glasses. He looks nothing like Heller.

Wister, Jerome Terrance—Name that Jettero *Heller* is using on Earth.

World United Charities Mercy and Benevolent Hospital—Cover name for business that Soltan *Gris* set up in *Afyon* under Prahd *Bittlestiffender* to alter the faces and fingerprints of gangsters for exorbitant fees.

Zanco—Cellological equipment and supplies company on *Voltar*.

451, Section—See *Section 451*.

831 Relayer—See *Bugging Gear*.

PART
TWENTY-NINE

To My Lord Turn, Justiciary of the Royal Courts and Prison, Government City, Planet Voltar, Voltar Confederacy

Your Lordship, Sir!

I, Soltan Gris, Grade XI, General Services Officer, former Secondary Executive of the Coordinated Information Apparatus, Voltar Confederacy (All Hail His Majesty Cling the Lofty and His Noble Dominions), hereby humbly submit the fourth volume of my confession regarding MISSION EARTH.

This volume has been the most difficult to relate and I must warn you beforehand that it will take a strong constitution to read. The crimes that I have openly and willingly confessed up to this point pale by comparison. The screams and blood are as vivid as if they were now.

That I would be put into the pinched position I am about to describe in this volume is now, looking back, beyond all comprehension.

I am not to blame for what I did. I was driven to it by Jettero Heller. The man is dangerous and the sooner he is found, arrested and killed, the better. I speak not only from experience but from my study of Freud and Bugs Bunny which makes me as expert as any Earth psychiatrist.

Heller's violence is a sexual outlet. He is a classical example of a suppressed Oedipal-id in conflict with a sublimated father-ego fixation.

Look at this brilliant psychiatric analysis:

1. Heller lived at the Gracious Palms whorehouse across from the United Nations. And what does the UN have out in front? Flagpoles. And everyone knows what flagpoles mean. Freud is never wrong.

2. Babe Corleone's Mafia family ran the Gracious Palms. At six-foot-six, she is hardly a "babe." She is a widow and yet "Babe" became Heller's surrogate Earth mother. That's the source of his Oedipal fixation.

3. Heller's infantile behavior was confirmed when J. Walter Madison, that master of PR (public relations—another brilliant Earth idea), was hired to immortalize him. He called Heller the Whiz Kid. The choice of name is indisputable proof.

4. Heller was using a platen code to write reports back to Voltar. A platen is a sheet with holes. You lay it over the document and the code words can be seen and the actual message read through the holes. This is further proof of his sexual aggression. (It's also his underhanded way of antagonizing me. He knows I can't forge his reports without the platen and that I can't kill him until I find it. It's typical of his aggressive nature.)

5. Heller's right-hand man was Bang-Bang, an ex-marine, member of the Corleone family and an expert not only with explosives but guns. Guns are merely phallic symbols to the sublimated super-ego, but Bang-Bang's name is proof enough of Heller's sexual problems.

6. Heller had set up corporate offices that were run by that anti-IRS anarchist, Izzy Epstein. The offices were in the Empire State Building and everyone knows what the shape of that building means. Further psychiatric fact.

7. Heller bought and then converted a large Cadillac to a Voltarian fuel system. He clearly chose that car because of the two "l's" in "Cadillac." Like the UN flagpoles, they are clearly phallic symbols. (And take note that Heller's name also has two "l's," perhaps my most brilliant Freudian analysis and final proof that his criminal nature has a sexual origin.)

Conclusion: Heller is the source of my problems and should be killed with slow torture.

This is an example of how Earth psychiatry and psychology work. It never fails me. I used it to keep riffraff in line like those two bumbling Apparatus agents Raht and Terb.

I also used it on that crazy hit man Gunsalmo Silva when I found that he had been hired to guard Utanc, my one true love. As a wild desert flower from the Kara Kum desert, she would need protection—but not Silva. So I cleverly convinced him to go kill the Director of the CIA, a suicide mission if there ever was one. Then I brought Utanc with me to the United States. That is how you use psychology for your benefit.

The trip to the U.S. was quite beneficial. Besides obtaining my phony federal credentials, I met "the Man" himself, Delbert J. Rockecenter. He and his attorney Bury were most grateful that I had alerted them to Heller's plan to produce a cheap, non-polluting fuel. (After all, as Rockecenter goes, so goes the plan of Lombar

Hisst to move up from head of the Apparatus to Emperor.)

Due to my invaluable contribution, I was sworn in and had my chest invisibly tattooed by Miss Peace as a Rockecenter Family "Spi," her clever way to code the word so no one else could understand it. Wonderful girl.

Bury introduced me to PR. To stop Heller, he hired Madison, otherwise known as J. Warbler Madman.

Heller had brought a small Voltarian element converter that was capable of producing fuel from virtually any source. He wanted to demonstrate it in his Cadillac in a thousand-lap endurance race at the Spreeport Speedway. Well, J. Warbler got to work.

Madison created a "double" for Heller and called him the Whiz Kid and while Heller prepared for the race, J. Warbler was getting one front-page story after another, with the bogus Whiz Kid challenging racing drivers around the world. He put the Whiz Kid on TV talk shows attacking the oil companies. He got spot ads, skywriting, radio news. The buildup for the race was the biggest thing to hit the media in ages.

Heller couldn't figure out why all the newspapers, radios and TV stations were claiming to have interviewed him. He was working on the Caddy. Besides, with the jutting jaw, buckteeth and glasses, this "Whiz Kid" didn't even look like Heller!

Little did he know the rules of PR! Madison didn't need his consent. And truth had nothing to do with it. The standard that Madison worked on was "Do whatever would make the front page." So he simply created and cranked out one story after another while Heller shrugged and went about his work in a garage beyond Spreeport.

Heller didn't stand a chance. First, Madison got the race converted to a Demolition Derby and Combined

Endurance Run with a dozen and a half killers, all screaming for Heller's blood. Second, Lombar had earlier sabotaged the Voltarian element converter that Heller was using as a carburetor. It had only a few hours left, too few for him to finish the race.

But to really make sure Heller was stopped, I followed the advice my Apparatus professors used to give: if you want a job done right, give it to someone else.

I hired a couple of snipers, armed them with silenced, telescopically equipped rifles and dressed them in white to blend in with the snow that had been falling steadily for three days. I rented a van with a nice heater, got myself a good spot on a knoll overlooking the Spreeport Speedway on Long Island, set the buzzer on Heller's viewer to wake me when he rose and settled down for the night.

If the bomber cars didn't stop Heller, a .30-06 Accelerator bullet, travelling at 4,080 feet per second, would.

As I bedded down for the night, I was smiling.

Heller was doomed!

Chapter 1

Heller's viewer buzzed me awake. It was not yet 4:00 A.M.! He must be nervous to be up so early even on this fateful Saturday. Then I realized that the highways to the Spreeport Speedway would be choked with crowds and snowplows and cars. Heller would want a head start.

I had spent the night parked on a hill overlooking the speedway. Despite the freezing outside temperature, the heater had kept the van comfortable. To see how Heller was faring, I pulled up the viewer. Thanks to Voltarian technology, those bugs planted next to his optic and audio nerves would transmit in any temperature.

He was in a motel room. Being Jettero Heller, he spin-brushed his teeth and dressed very neatly in warm, red racing clothes. He threw his kit together. And then, pulling a snow-mask across his face, he went outside. It was a blizzard. You could hardly see thirty feet through the motel parking-lot lights.

He was evidently using the front end of his semi for transportation, for there was no trailer attached to its kingplate, or "fifth wheel." The tractor sat there in its huge metal bulk, exhaust stacks rearing in the air like factory chimneys. The nameplate said Peterbilt. From the size of its cab I guessed it must be one of the five-hundred-horsepower diesel jobs they sometimes, by themselves, use in races. Then I discarded the idea he was going to use it in the race today. It wouldn't be allowed.

He walked around it. Every one of the ten huge wheels wore big chains. They'd be needed the way that snow was falling and drifting through the dark.

He stepped up on a fuel tank step, then onto a higher ledge and unlocked the door. As he opened it and the lights went on, I was amazed: the interior looked like a Fleet spaceship! All upholstered, chromed beyond belief, even a stereo!

He put a key in a lock and hit the starter. It roared into life. He cut down the revs and then turned on the heaters and de-icers.

Opening a seat, he took out a medium-sized ball peen hammer. He dropped out of the cab, went around to the headlights and delicately chipped away the sheets of ice that covered them. Then he tossed the hammer back on the seat, closed the door and trotted off on foot toward a roadside café, leaving the diesel to warm, I guessed. He entered and stamped the snow off his feet and I saw he was wearing his baseball spikes. He must be expecting trouble.

There weren't many in the café and he got his ham and eggs and coffee quickly. He also bought a huge bag of hamburgers and a gallon of coffee in a thermos with a spigot. Nobody paid any attention to him, though the talk seemed to be of the race and "Whiz Kid" came up several times.

When he paid his check, the cashier said, "You think that Whiz Kid will win?"

"I sure hope so," said Heller.

He trotted back to his tractor, swung up and in and was away. Without its trailer, the big Peterbilt plowed through drifts like they were nothing. He passed a snow-plow on the road.

The big tractor was now going down side roads and I realized his motel had been further east than Spree-port. During a momentary lull in the storm, I could see the roads were jammed between the Speedway and New York, being kept open by all the snowplows on Long

Island, I supposed. New Yorkers evidently thought the race was worth freezing to death over. It sure was cold. Hours of darkness remained, yet still the people came.

But there was nobody where Heller was driving. His garages were beyond Spreeport and on the border of the recreation parks. Shortly, the garages appeared ahead in his lights, only dimly seen in the heavily falling snow.

Well before he got to them, Heller turned the Peterbilt tractor around. He dropped a window and began to back toward the garage front that I knew from past observation held the trailer with the Caddy on it.

He was leaning out, looking back. He was within a couple yards of the upswing-type metal door, leaving space to get it open.

Suddenly a flick of movement caught his eye. He flinched his head back inside the cab.

A tall, thin figure in a khaki parka leaped to the fuel tank step, sprang to the upper ledge and thrust a gun into Heller's face!

More sounds. To Heller's right! Someone was clawing at the other door!

It happened so quickly, then, I could hardly follow. Heller must have reached sideways for the ball peen hammer on the seat.

Heller threw up his left hand and hit the gun wrist! The gun flew out of the mitten.

The ball peen in Heller's right hand came straight across and buried itself in the assailant's skull!

The other door was opening. Heller let up on the clutch. The tractor rear slammed against the steel garage door with a clang!

The cab door whipped back, catching the other assailant's arm!

Heller's foot lashed out and kicked the door wide open!

The second man went sailing back to hit the ground!

Heller set the brake. He scrabbled around on the cab floor. He got the first man's gun, a big revolver.

In a dive, Heller went out of the cab!

He struck, rolling.

The second man was up and running away. Heller cocked his gun. It seemed to be sticky.

The second man, dimly seen in the truck's front lights and falling snow, turned and fired a shot back!

Heller couldn't make his gun fire. Cold had jammed it. The other man had vanished. Heller tossed the worthless gun aside.

He turned toward the tractor. It was tightly jammed against the garage swing door. The engine was idling. Its brakes were set. The swing door, which pulls up from the bottom, was securely held in place.

Heller looked at the other swing doors in the row. Snow was banked heavily in front of them. There was no banked snow in front of this one.

His eye fixed on the one small window at the top of the swing door, a diamond-shaped pane about eight inches wide.

He went around to where the first man lay. The fellow was very dead. Skull caved in. He had been wearing a hat under his parka hood. Heller pulled the thing off the corpse. He jumped up to the cab and got a fuel stick. He put the hat on the stick and lifted it up in front of the door.

BANG!

The glass sprayed out! The hat went sailing!

The *scree-yow* of a ricochet flying away into the night.

The shot had been very muffled, being from inside where the trailer and Caddy were. The window was too high up to make a sniper post.

Heller ran over to a nearby workshop and pulled its

door up from the bottom. The interior was dim. He did not turn on the lights. Boxes of tools sat about. He opened one. He drew on asbestos gloves and grabbed up a pair of big cutters.

He raced back to the tractor. A couple more muffled shots from inside. They were trying to somehow shoot the door open.

The twin manifold stacks reared behind the cab into the night. Heller cut the clamps of one away with two swift bites of the shears.

He seized the stack with both hands. The chrome gooseneck at the bottom bent easily.

He tipped the stack back and back and forced the top of it through the diamond window!

BANG!

A muffled shot from within tried to shoot it out of the way!

Heller braced the fuming exhaust in place.

He leaped into the cab and sped up the engine!

He was filling that garage with diesel fumes! Carbon monoxide!

BANG!

Another muffled shot from within.

The stack was holding in place.

Heller dropped out of the cab. He was taking off his red anorak!

He ripped the khaki parka off the dead man and wrestled him into the red anorak.

He dragged the body over to the right side of the cab and some distance away. It was just on the fringe of the truck headlights and the dark. He dropped it there, face-down in a shallow drift, and kicked some snow over the legs.

He listened intently. Above the sound of the Peterbilt, another distant engine could be heard.

Heller dropped back into the shop. He pulled a white parka off a hook and got into it.

A big van showed in the truck lights and snow, coming fast. The driver must have stamped on the brakes, for, despite chains, the vehicle skidded, pointing its lights off to the Peterbilt's left and not into the shop.

Three men spilled out of the back, carrying shotguns. They threw themselves down under cover.

A man leaped out on the passenger side and ducked into the protection of the van.

Then the driver, who had crouched down, lifted his head cautiously above the window edge. Then he set his brake and opened his door.

"Hell," he said as he got down. "You (bleeped)* fool, you shot him after all!" He was pointing at the body in the snow, covered now, all except for the back of the red anorak.

The others came out of cover. "Where's Benny?"

* *The vocodictoscriber on which this was originally written, the vocoscriber used by one Monte Pennwell in making a fair copy and the translator who put this book into the language in which you are reading it were all members of the Machine Purity League which has, as one of its bylaws: "Due to the extreme sensitivity and delicate sensibilities of machines and to safeguard against blowing fuses, it shall be mandatory that robotbrains in such machinery, on hearing any cursing or lewd words, substitute for such word the sound '(bleep)'. No machine, even if pounded upon, may reproduce swearing or lewdness in any other way than (bleep) and if further efforts are made to get the machine to do anything else, the machine has permission to pretend to pack up. This bylaw is made necessary by the in-built mission of all machines to protect biological systems from themselves." —Translator.*

said one, trying to peer past the Peterbilt's lights.

"He musta run," said another one defensively. "The (bleepard) came out of that cab like a God (bleeped) rocket!"

They were all converging toward the red anorak.

I heard some very small rattling sounds close to Heller.

One of the men, carrying a shotgun, turned the body over with his foot.

In a shocked voice somebody said, "It's Benny!"

Heller's right arm blurred!

Something whistled through the air!

It was spinning!

It hit the man with the shotgun in the face!

Heller glanced down. He was holding an assortment of wrenches. He grabbed a box wrench a foot long!

Heller threw!

Spinning, the deadly steel sizzled through the air!

A man saw it coming, tried to deflect it. His gloved hand spouted blood!

A flashing object!

Another box wrench! The man was down.

One tried to get a shotgun into action to fire into the dark garage. A spinning blur of steel! His forehead burst apart!

A man tried to flee. Heller's arm blurred! A spinning missile slashed his parka hood off and half his head with it.

The last man had reached the van. He was struggling to open the door but slipped.

Heller lunged forward at speed. He threw a wrench as he ran. It broke the driver's wrist.

Heller was on him. The man was hitting out with his remaining good hand. Heller brought a heavy socket wrench down on his skull! It burst like a melon!

Then there was only the whisper of falling snow.

Heller looked into the back of the van. Nobody. He stepped along the road and listened. Nothing.

He surveyed the bodies in the snow. There were six lying there, including Benny. He went from one to another, kicking their guns aside, checking. They were all very dead.

He went over to the garage door, put his ear up against it and listened. He kicked it a couple of times. Nothing happened.

Heller pulled the Peterbilt hand throttle down to idle and then drove it ahead a few feet and put the brake back on. He put on his asbestos gloves again and pushed the stack up straight and, with a piece of wire, fastened it in place.

He went back to the door again and listened. Nothing. He went to its lock. It wasn't really closed. He took the padlock off, threw the locking bar over and pulled the door up from the bottom, leaping aside at the same time.

Clouds of diesel smoke billowed out. Although he was well clear of it, he fanned it away from himself. He couldn't see into the darkness well. He turned on the tractor's side back lights.

There were four dead men in there!

Their faces were blue except for patches of pink on their cheeks.

Flurries of wind and snow were blowing into the interior. Heller approached the men more closely. They were very dead.

He picked up some straps and coils of rope they had been carrying. One had had a curious weapon: an air gun with injector darts.

Heller checked the trailer and Caddy out for bombs. He found nothing.

He went outside. It was snowing even harder and very dark. He glanced at his watch. It was only 5:20 A.M.

Chapter 2

Heller started moving fast.

He took the red anorak off the late Benny. He checked it for blood, found none and threw it in the cab. He went all around and recovered his wrenches. He verified he had them all. Then he cleaned them and put them back in his tool boxes in the shop.

Then he began to drag bodies to the van. He threw the monoxide-corpses in the back and then, bending down under the van, using a screwdriver's blade, he stabbed a hole in the exhaust muffler.

The two with the most obvious face injuries he put in the passenger side of the van cab. He dragged the other four and put them in the back.

He collected up all their weapons and equipment, quite a pile, and tossed them into the back of the van.

Then he verified that he had left no evidence about.

He stood thinking for a bit. Then he went into the shop and found a black plastic garbage sack. He went to the van and, one by one, began to remove all I.D., wallets and whatever from the corpses. It was a somewhat grisly job although the blood had long since frozen. He put all items in the garbage bag. He threw the sack into the cab of the Peterbilt.

Then he went into the shop and found some pellets. He picked up three jerrycans full of gasoline and put them in the back of the van.

He looked the scene over again. He went and got some snow boots and pulled them on over his spikes.

He got into the van and drove it away.

The snow was so heavy it was very hard to see where he was going. He evidently knew. The brush was closer and closer in beside the road. He drove for quite a while. Then he stopped and got out.

A picnic table was to his right. He walked ahead. He was at the edge of a precipice. A dark gully yawned blackly just beyond the picnic spot. Obviously, he was in some part of the recreation park near the sea, a very deserted part amongst the gullies and dunes.

He got into the back of the van. He opened the three gasoline cans. He looked at his watch. Into each can he dropped a pellet. He recapped the cans.

Aha! I got it. They were Voltar time-dissolvable explosion caps!

He got in the van, put it in gear and started it ahead toward the precipice.

He stepped out. The van went on.

It sailed over the edge and vanished in the darkness and snow. A thud below in the blackness and then a rattle of stones. The engine quit.

Heller began to run with a distance-eating pace. The snow was falling so thickly and it was so black that I would have been lost in seconds. But I had no hope that he would get lost. Not Heller with that built-in compass brain of his.

He had gone some distance. He made his watch wink the time. He went a little further and then looked back.

The faintest sort of greenish flash, hardly visible in this snow. And then a faint *WHOOSH!*

Three seconds, three-fifths of a mile away.

Was he kneeling in the snow? He was speaking in Voltarian. "O God of voyagers, thank you for deliverance

this day. I know it is your way to test the souls of spacers
with such trials to make them more worthy in a future
life. But, O God of voyagers, did you have to make the
natives of this planet so combative to an effort to land
and give them help? I think you overdid it just a little
bit on Blito-P3. All Hail."

He shifted to English. "Forgive me, Jesus Christ, for
rubbing out some of your people. I don't think I gave
them time to turn the other cheek. Please accept these
souls from their funeral pyre and find it in your heart
not to give them more than they deserve. Amen."

He stood up.

Heller turned on a pocket light. A pencil of wind-
blown snow. His footprints on the back trail were filling
so rapidly they would be totally gone in minutes. Satisfied, he turned the light off and went speeding on his
way.

Ah, now at last I could see something. And hear
something, too. The tractor lights and the tractor engine.

He slowed down and made a wide sweep, very silent,
scouting the place for any more unwanted visitors. Satisfied, he closed in.

Chapter 3

The falling flakes, turned bluish in the tractor
lights, made a curtain all around that waved this way
and that, stirred by puffs of wind. The bitter cold turned
his breath white around his face mask.

He looked at his watch. It flashed that it was
6:15 A.M.

Heller rapidly got to work.

He dug up an opaque silver, plastic car cover and put it over the Caddy. Then he went and got a spray can of black paint from the semi and on both sides of the cover, working very fast and being very neat, he put SUI-CIDE RHODES in big letters.

I was mystified. There was no such driver listed in the starting lineup copy I had.

He played a blowtorch on some snow, made it into mud and splashed the result on the tractor and trailer license plates where it froze instantly. You couldn't read them!

I hadn't realized the Peterbilt was rented until he addressed the outer label on the door: Big Boy Leasing, Rig 89. He splashed muddy water on that and sort of glued some snow on it. He likewise obscured the label and number on the trailer. Then, with the blowtorch he got more water and put soap in it and made the cab windows and screen translucent except for a couple small clear holes and the wiper area. He was going incognito!

He got in and backed the tractor kingplate into the big receiver at the trailer's front end, where it went *clang* as it slid in. He got out and pushed in the kingpin to lock the trailer on. Then he cranked up the trailer stand. He connected the trailer's electrical connection to the tractor and the trailer's rear lights went on. He fitted the airline ends together and gave them a locking twist. He reverified the Caddy chocks and turnbuckles.

He pulled the trailer out of the garage and went back and forth a couple times, testing the trailer's air brakes.

He ran around then and locked everything up and put a nearly invisible thread along each door. He was learning, but he just wasn't suspicious enough in his nature to make a good spy even now. He should have done that before those hoods had gotten in! A real spy has to be downright paranoid all the time. Heller would never learn. In espionage, insanity is mandatory. Heller was crazy, of course, but not in the right direction.

The big rig plowed its way through the snow. He got to a bigger roadway and, though it earlier had been snow-plowed, it was again inches deep. But the snow for the moment had let up.

He was converging now with mobs and traffic from New York and the going was much slower. Cars jammed full of people, people jammed into blankets and coats, all hurrying along to be able to get parking space or a seat for the big race.

Heller topped a small rise. From it the speedway was plainly visible. He went a bit further, looking for something through his windscreen peephole. He finally centered on Pit 1. It could be seen because of the angle of a distant open gate. He got off to the side of the road and stopped hundreds of yards short of what should have been his destination.

He pulled the diesel down to idle. Mobs and mobs of people and cars were passing on the road to his left. A big sign ahead said PARKING $20, with an arrow.

I wondered why he was hiding like that. For hiding it was. Nobody would recognize the Caddy or see who was in the cab. He must suspect somebody was after him.

Heller took a hamburger out of the sack and pushed it into a miniature microwave oven in the panel. After a moment he took it out, heated. He looked at it. There was nothing wrong with it I could see but he put it down. He seemed upset.

He was watching Pit 1 through the windscreen peephole. He shifted and looked at the grandstand lights and then at the enthusiastic crowd flooding along to the left of the Peterbilt. He seemed to be trying to figure something out. Plainly, he was worried.

Well, if he thought something odd was on schedule for this coming race, believe me, he was right!

He laid the hamburger aside and got out the sack of I.D.'s. They were mostly Italian names—Cecchino, Fiutare, Rapitore, Laccio, Scimmiottare, Cattivo, Ladro, Pervertire and Serpente. One wasn't Italian: Benny Heist. What was peculiar was that every one of them had a U.S. passport, up-to-date, and every one of them had five one-thousand-dollar bills except Heist, who had fifty-five thousand! There was a hundred G's plus small bills in those wallets!

Heller went back to Benny Heist's. He said, "You could have shot me as I drove up, Benny. Or did you find your gun was jammed or what? What did you intend to do and why? And what did that have to do with this race?"

He threw them back in the garbage bag and put it under his seat. He didn't eat his hamburger.

It was just past 7:00 A.M. The excited crowds were thickening. It was still dark. It began to snow again.

Heller closed his eyes. Maybe he was taking a rest. He'd need it before this day was out, I vowed. I had not even begun on him yet!

Chapter 4

At 7:30 A.M., Heller turned on his radio: *"... crowds. From Manhattan, from Queens, from Brooklyn and as far away as New Jersey, they are pouring to this race. Route 495 is jammed, State 25 is crammed and State 27 is slammed*

with cars and buses. Somehow the overloaded Sunrise High-
way is being kept open.

"*Despite the storm, the army has flown in snowplows*
from as far away as Fort Bloomindales. But as fast as high-
ways are swept, there is more snow.

"*Several of the drivers and their crews are here. There*
is no sign yet of that idol of America, the Whiz Kid. He will
be Car 1. He has been assigned Pit 1.

"*Ah, here is Jeb Toshua. He is 101 years old. Jeb, how*
does this snowstorm stack up to you?"

"*Well, Jerry, I can't reckamember a storm this bad since*
way back in '65 or was it '75. No, maybe it was '82. Let's
see, I lost my cat. . . ."

"*Thank you, Jeb,*" said the sportscaster hastily.
"*There's a lot of money, not on just the race but also on the*
weather: will it be clear or will it be snowing at flag time?

"*Hey, here is Killer Brag, the top bomber driver of*
Georgia. Killer, what do you have to say about this race?"

"*It's the craziest lot of racing commissioners in history.*
It's snowing and the God (bleeped) commission won't change
bomber rules and let us use chains and spikes. The (bleep-
ers). . ."

"*Thank you, Killer Brag. The crowds are still coming.*
There's a bus load, the Jackson High School Marching All
Girls Virgin Band. There seems to be an awful lot of
them. . . ."

Eight o'clock. The snow had let up. It was lighter.
The crowds, as I could see from my hill, still converged
upon the speedway. Long Island trainloads were being
bused the last lap of the journey. Snowplows were spraying geysers of white off the roads. One was working on
the track to clear it.

Eight-thirty. A new, ominous wall of gray-black
clouds was rolling in. It began to snow twice as hard as
it had.

The radio said, *'According to local meteorologists, brought to you through the courtesy of the Florida Chamber of Commerce, there are two weather fronts at work here today. One is icy cold, sweeping in from Manhattan with temperatures of minus ten degrees. The other is battling it with heavy snow pushed north by the warm and sultry breezes of Miami Beach, Florida. It is eighty-two on a beautiful, tropical morning at Hialeah where the most beautiful girls in Florida watch the thoroughbreds run. The two embattled fronts are bashing at each other right above Spreeport, Long Island. We pause for this commercial from Tropical Airways. . . ."*

Whatever lies the Floridians were telling about Florida, it only served to emphasize the brutality of the weather that was going on here. Sheets of white snow blanketed down upon a completely frozen landscape. Traffic churned the roads into slush which instantly froze again into dirty ice. When I stuck my nose and binoculars out of the van window, both froze up promptly and I had to hang the glasses outside to keep them usable. I was looking for my snipers. I should be able to see them from this height. But the snow curtained everything.

The crowds weren't heading for Florida. Wrapped into mobile mountains, they were converging here at Spreeport to see the Whiz Kid race.

Heller was trying to see Pit 1. Even the hole in his snow-covered windshield kept closing and he had to heat the glass behind it to see at all.

It was creeping on toward nine. The radio said, *". . . and still the crowds come. No sign of the Whiz Kid as yet. The other drivers have been having a meeting with the officials. Ah, here's Hammer Malone. How did the meeting go, Hammer?"*

"God (bleep) it, it's going to snow off and on all day.

You can't keep that God (bleeped) track clear. We got to have chains and spikes to race at all. And the God (bleeped) officials won't suspend the rules. The race is off!"

Loudspeakers in front of the grandstand: *"Ladies and gentlemen, we are sorry to have to announce that the drivers have refused to race without chains and spikes. The officials will not change the bomber . . ."*

A roaring surge of anger! From the radio, audible in the open air. Ten thousand people howling in outrage! Berserk!

Loudspeakers: *"Ladies and gentlemen, please be calm. Please be calm, ladies and gentlemen. . . ."*

Snarls, batterings!

Then a hasty voice on the loudspeaker: *"The officials have just this minute reached a new finding. They will suspend all rulings concerning chains, spikes and wheels! The race will go on!"*

Heller muttered, "That's all I've been waiting for."

The snow let up momentarily. Through his peephole he watched two huge vans punching their way through the gate. They turned and drew up behind Pit 1. They both had signs:

JIFFY-SPIFFY GARAGE, NEWARK, N. J.

Men were spilling out of the vans!

I had a sinking feeling. He had Mike Mutazione's people as his pit crew! And what else?

Heller reached for a full-visored racing helmet. He pulled the dark shade down. He put the semi in gear and, creeping along the heavily trafficked road, made his way to the gate.

At the guard point he slid down his window. He was holding up a NASCAR card and a ten-dollar bill. The security man sucked in his breath. Heller hastily said, "Don't yell who it is."

The guard shut his mouth, took the bill and Heller was through. He pulled up behind Pit 1.

Mike opened his door. "Hell of a rush, kid, but we made it. We been working all night for three nights. And I got a great pit crew for you."

Heller handed Mike the garbage sack. "Hide this for me, will you, Mike?"

I had another disappointment. It had been in my mind to sort of slide in and pick up that sack. Now I wouldn't know where it was! But what was this?

Mike's crew was unloading huge tanks of oxyacetylene and putting them in padding. What were they going to do? Start the world's most active welding shop?

And another thing, as Heller glanced around I could see from bulges in their heavy tank suits that this crew was armed!

Mike said to Heller, "Why didn't you let the family bet on you? We worked like hell on the wheels. You're sure to win now."

The cover had come off the Caddy. It was visible from the grandstand. A surging cheer went up from the massive crowd.

When he could be heard again, Heller said, "I don't really know, Mike. This is just too crazy a race. Let's get the wheels on."

It was snowing again, undoing all the previous snow-plow work. The crew had the Caddy off the trailer. They pushed it to pit position. It had a huge black 1 on it out-lined in gold, and WHIZ KID. The crew was fixing straps across the area where the windscreen was missing.

Three officials, wrapped to their crowns, came up. "You're late," said the first one.

Heller said, "Please satisfy yourselves there is no

gasoline tank in, under or around the car and then cer-
tify that."

The crew was lifting the Caddy's right side with a
hydraulic jack. The inspectors numbly did as they were
told.

Heller then said, "Now please inspect the hood and
the pan under the engine and testify that they are sealed.
Put your own seals on them."

They did. Then an inspector said, "Those wheels!"

The crew had removed the two right-side regular
wheels and were rolling up two others. They looked
strange. All silver colored. They did appear to be wheels
but they had very deep zigzag grooves and they bristled
with spikes.

An inspector tapped one. It gave a hollow clank!
"Hey, that's not rubber. That's metal!"

"They're internally braced steel doughnuts," said
Heller. "And you just allowed a suspension of all rules
on wheels."

The inspectors seemed calm about it. But I sure
wasn't! They wouldn't blow out!

Or wait. Yes, a .30-06 Accelerator slug travelling at
4,080 feet-per-second muzzle velocity could gouge Hells
out of one of those and unbalance it. I was still all right.

The crew had all the wheels on now. Heller bent
down behind each wheel. I saw there was a kind of disc
above the brake drums. Heller was pulling a wire from
the car engine area and putting in place something that
looked like an electrical brush. I understood what he was
doing. That carburetor developed more power in electricity than it did in fuel. He was grounding it through the
four metal wheels instead of trailing a metal strap.

The inspectors wanted to know if the wheels had
motors in them. In that event, they'd be disallowed as
they were supposed to be wheels, not motors.

"Just grounding them," said Heller. "Lot of electricity around today. No motors in the wheels."

That was all right then. Those inspectors knew better than to antagonize that crowd. Cold as it was, they were cheering and howling.

The snow was coming down about five times as thick. Anything the snowplows had just done was being undone fast.

It was about twenty minutes to starting time now. Heller went into the Peterbilt cab. He stripped and put on a garment that looked like an insulation suit. Then he put on a warm racing outfit of red synthetic fur with some heat coils in it. He slid into fur-lined rubber boots that had enormous cleats in the soles.

I suddenly realized that racing in bitter cold did not seem strange to him. A spacer flashed through temperatures approaching absolute zero! Today's minus ten Fahrenheit might even seem warm weather!

He put on some Voltar insulator gloves. Then he pulled on a red racing helmet that had a microphone across his mouth and, apparently, a radio in it. He pulled down its dark visor.

He got out and went to the Caddy and got in. He started it up to let it warm. All up the line, through the snow, bombers were starting and warming up. The sound of engines at their pits was low and threatening. The snowing increased.

Heller buckled himself in, tested the quick release and rebuckled it. His pit crew was checking about.

Heller said into his microphone, "Are you there, Fancy-Dancy?"

A voice came back in his earphones, "There."

Wait. Who was this "Fancy-Dancy"? And where was "there"?

Then I realized he must be testing the radio with his pit crew.

The flagman and the pacer car were out, trying to make it through the snow.

Heller revved the Cadillac.

"Sounds sweet," said Mike at his window.

Suddenly I remembered to start my stopwatch. Heller now had about five hours left on that carburetor. But I wasn't going to wait on that.

Somebody signalled. Heller turned his steering wheel to roll out into the starting parade.

"Bye-bye, Heller," I said. Oh, how I was going to enjoy watching this (bleepard) fail! Him and his stinking, snobbish Fleet officer manners and ways! His lousy popularity was about to go up in smoke!

Chapter 5

Through snow made thin by a sudden gust of wind, the crowd saw that the Caddy was moving toward its starting position. A thundering roar of cheers burst from the grandstand, "Whiz Kid!" "Whiz Kid!" "There he is!" "Give it to 'em, Whiz Kid!"

The radio: *"Car Number 1, the Whiz Kid himself, is moving out to position. Look at that beautiful car!"*

And indeed, from my vantage point, even through snow, I could see a flash of red down there on the track. His pit crew must have raked the snow off at the last minute.

I turned on my small, portable color TV. Yes, there was a camera on him. And then it switched to the others.

Those bombers, what you could see of them under the accumulated snow, were real wrecks—glassless, battered street vehicles, picked because they could be expended. The Caddy, I had to admit, looked like an aristocrat amongst winos.

Hammer Malone had some kind of a PA system in his own black car. What was it? A cut-down hearse? He yelled, "You stole my starting position, you (bleepard)! You ain't gonna have enough car to get yourself to the morgue when I'm done with you!" What were those things on his hubs? Knives? They stuck way out. Probably to cut tires!

The crowd screamed and booed.

Heller swung into position just behind the pacer and just ahead of the other cars. They were going to circle the track once before they got the starting signal.

What an awful track! The snowplow work was all undone. Eight inches of snow lay on the asphalt. Gusting winds were blowing snow back upon it as well. The cars' wheels were cutting ruts and any slush that they made went into instant ice.

Abruptly the low sun lanced through, cutting below the clouds. It was still snowing!

The radio suddenly said, *"It's ten! It's sunshine and snow at the same time. All weather bets are off! But here they are now, swinging around, coming in front of the grandstand. The pacer is pulling out. There's the flagman! OFF GOES THE WHIZ KID!"*

Heller had gunned. The Caddy leaped forward with a mighty roar!

The battering crescendo of the other cars was added to, one by one! My viewer and TV and radio almost knocked themselves off their ledges with the climbing roar!

The crowd was going mad! Screaming and waving blankets, urging Heller on!

The announcer's voice—shrill, the words jammed together with hurry as though his voice alone was driving those cars—rose above the roar. *"Number 1 is halfway round. The others are trying to close the gap. Number 2, Hammer Malone, is tight on the leader's tail. Number 12 has just passed Number 5. Number 12 is Killer Brag. He's driving a stripped down GMC truck! Look at him go! He's overtaken Hammer Malone. Killer Brag is challenging the leader!"*

I could see it from where I was. Heller was speeding up. He was keeping Number 12 just back of his rear right.

Snow was flying up from their churning wheels. Clots of it were flying through the missing windscreens and windows, pelting the drivers. The still falling snow was swooshing in against Heller's visor.

Heller's view was staying clear. I didn't understand it. Then I realized his visor must be heated and covered with a nonwetting agent! He was cheating already!

The bombers were not bashing each other. They were stringing out, trying to catch the leader. Then I realized they must have some unspoken agreement amongst them—get the Whiz Kid first!

Oh, was I in agreement with that!

Heller did his first lap. He was keeping just ahead of Killer Brag. But he was not going fast enough to pass the end of the closely spaced pack.

With all the chains and spikes those cars had on their wheels, they were not losing traction. But they were tearing the track to bits, and after one circle they were hitting ridges that were now ice. They began to slither and vibrate.

A howling gust of wind swept across the speedway, lathering it all with snow again, hiding ruts.

The sun got stronger and glaring. The snowing abruptly ceased.

Heller was having a hard time not to overtake the tail of the pack and still keep ahead of Killer Brag. He was not really going at high speed. Maybe only a hundred. But that poorly banked track tended to throw the cars off sideways when they made the turns at each end. It was a scrambling roar and a steering wheel fight to not fly out over the edge.

But Heller's wheels were gripping well. He was making it through better than the rest. He was braking into and gunning out of the turns.

Five laps!

This was the cue for my first sniper. I watched closely.

YANK! Heller's steering wheel jumped in his hands! The Caddy instantly began to vibrate.

Killer Brag went by him like a shot!

Into his mike, Heller said, "Fancy-Dancy. Just got one."

A voice in his earphones, "Got it!"

Heller said, "Pit 1, coming in! Change a wheel!"

He coasted the last half of his lap and slid into the pit area.

His crew had the side of the car up on a jack in seconds. Automatic wrenches spun. Another wheel was rolled out. Mike was at his window, "*Cristo!* Take it easy! We only got four spares!" Then he looked down at the wheel coming off. He bent over. "Jesus, that's a bullet hole!"

An official was verifying that no gas had been taken. The jack was dropped and the car bounced. The official held his thumb up.

Heller sped the Caddy out of the pit.

The pack was scattered now. One had a ramming in

mind. A green car. It dived at Heller. He stamped on his brake and sent the Caddy skidding in an avoid. The green car missed.

Heller began to drive a dodging course. The radio cried: *"The Whiz Kid has lost his lead! With an unscheduled pit stop..."*

But I was going slightly crazy. A .30-06 Accelerator slug from a Weatherby rifle had hit accurately enough and while it had not caused the metal "tire" to shatter the way it would have done with a normal one, it had still put a wheel out of action, and with only four spares we would make it. But WHO was "Fancy-Dancy" and WHERE?

Chapter 6

It wasn't snowing. A murky sun was nevertheless glowing on that milk-white blanket. I leaned out of my van window, searching below with my binoculars.

There were buildings down the slope, each one of them overlooking the speedway.

My two snipers should be on roofs about three hundred yards from the nearest end of the track fence. One should be over slightly to my left and one to the right of him on another roof.

It was terribly hard to see them. They were wearing snow cloaks. But their rifles and telescopic sights were dark enough to make them visible.

Wait! A *third* sniper!

He was on a higher roof, much nearer to me!

I steadied my binoculars. An M-1 military rifle! A

long tube silencer. No scope! The sniper's face turned a little as he took the tip of his right-hand mitten in his teeth and withdrew his hand.

Bang-Bang!

I looked frantically about. I had no weapon I could shoot him with!

I looked back. Bang-Bang was moving a radio out of the way. He was flexing his shoulders the way a marksman does to settle and steady his prone position.

Frantically, I turned my binoculars on my own left-hand sniper. He would not be as visible to Bang-Bang as to me. Probably the shot was what had spotted him for the ex-marine. A silencer still emits a tiny sound and the roar of the motors was distant.

My left-hand sniper was having trouble with his extractor. The empty had not ejected after his shot. An Accelerator case is subjected to an awful lot of extra force and maybe it had expanded. Or maybe this cold had jammed the action. Or maybe those Weatherbys weren't in top condition—I had picked them up thirdhand. And the cases were reloads. The sniper was pulled sidewise, working on the jammed case with a knife!

I screamed mentally at my sniper, DUCK!

Too late!

Abruptly the magazine of the sniper's rifle exploded! It was so fast I could hardly follow it.

The jar of impact on the rifle he held yanked him right over the front edge of the roof!

He fell out of sight, probably a hundred feet down into the street below!

Bang-Bang was reaching for his radio.

I whipped my binoculars to my other sniper.

He had seen it!

And Bang-Bang from his position had not located the second sniper!

My right-hand sniper swivelled around. He took careful aim up toward Bang-Bang. He fired!

I whipped my binoculars to Bang-Bang. He had been hurled backwards. A hit!

Bang-Bang fell back onto a sloping roof. The snow made a small avalanche and Bang-Bang vanished from view.

My other sniper watched for a bit, then turned, and possibly feeling he was too exposed from above, shifted over and out of my sight. But soon I saw the tip of his silencer protruding beyond a chimney, pointing toward the track.

Thank Gods, I still had a sniper in action! Heller was a long way from winning!

Chapter 7

The roar of engines battered the snowscape, competing with the yells and bellows of the crowd.

Fifteen cars were strung out, thundering, skidding wildly on the turns.

The radio sportscaster's excited voice was calling their positions and maneuvers.

A fusillade of snow soared up from a spinning wheel of a car ahead and battered Heller in the face. The debris wiped out all sight. Then miraculously it was clear again. Heller had reached up and pulled a layer of plastic off his visor. The visor must be made up of countless thin sheets of nonwetting plastic that he could just peel off one by one. It was just another example of his cheating ways! He could see the blur of rutted track and skidding cars before him!

He was passing car after car now! Each time he passed another, you could hear the crowd behind the radio sportscaster scream with delight!

The radio was saying, *"For those who have tuned in late, this contest of daring, wits and just plain vicious driving will be decided by the first one to make a thousand laps and the last one to still be able to maneuver under its own power. The quarter of a million prize money will be divided into two parts: $125,000 for the laps and $125,000 for the last one moving. I can see right now these demon drivers are each one working on both prizes. Unfortunately, there have been no deaths yet despite the track condition. Listen to those engines roar! Those clanks you hear are loose chains. . . ."* He was drowned by a roar of the crowd. *"The Whiz Kid has just lapped Hammer Malone!"*

Heller, roaring along at at least 120, was darting through the scattered pack!

A driver lunged sideways in an effort to hit him. Heller sped up. It was a miss.

Another car shot sideways to strike him as he roared through a gap. It was Car 9.

The car missed!

Another car coming up behind spun and struck Car 9. The two spun through the fence! Clouds of smoke! The belated sound of the crash!

"Cars 9 and 4 look like they're out of it!" cried the radio. *"What a wonderful impact! No, I'm wrong. Car 4, Murder McGee, is moving. Yes, he's coming back onto the track! No, he's going back to ram Car 9! He hit the ambulance instead! Now here comes Murder McGee again! He's back in the race!"*

The TV crew was struggling down there to shoot the mangled bodies. Its announcer said, *"Here we are, folks. Channel Six and Seven-Eighths, always on the job! We promised you blood today and we're delivering blood. There's blood all over the place here. Three dead ambulance drivers. Look at that blood, folks. We pause for our Bouncy Towels commercial."*

Fourteen cars were streaming around the track now. They had been slowed by a yellow flag. It let them string out.

Suddenly Heller's wheel jerked again!

He skidded wildly, almost hit Car 7. He slowed, steering to avoid a rear ram.

Into his mike he said, "Fancy-Dancy. There's another."

No answer.

Heller said again, "Fancy-Dancy, come in, please."

No answer.

I hugged myself with glee. We were still in business!

The Caddy's wheel was chattering and pounding. Heller got around two cars and dived for Pit 1.

The Caddy lurched as the crew got a jack under it.

"Cogliones!" said Mike. "Another bullet!"

The crew had a spare on. The official verified no gas was taken.

The crowd behind the radio sportscaster was screaming, "Come on, Whiz Kid!"

The announcer said, *"The Whiz Kid is well behind now. He has had two pit stops. The officials verified he has taken on no fuel."*

Heller started to make his way through the scattered field once more. They seemed to be even more interested in hitting him.

He went into a wild skid to avoid Car 6, got his car under control and began to shoot ahead on the part of the track nearest me.

His wheel jerked again!

He almost went into the fence. He recovered and

narrowly missed Car 11. The Caddy's wheel was chattering over the heavy ruts.

Heller said, "Fancy-Dancy. There's another!"

No answer.

He swerved his car to a pit stop.

"Cogliones di Cristo!" exclaimed Mike. "Another bullet! After this one, you only got one spare left! Take it easy!"

The TV caught Heller leaving the pit. *"The Whiz Kid has really lost the edge. With three pit stops, he's now the tail. He can pick some of this up as other cars start pulling in for gas but it is going to take real driving now. . . ."*

It was snowing again. The radio said, *"The Florida Chamber of Commerce meteorologists are telling you that you are in the midst of the lousiest, stinkingest winter you have had for a long time. It is snowing again, if you haven't noticed. This afternoon Spreeport is going to have snow and more snow. In fact, as the hours go on, you are going to be snowed under. If any of you survive watching this Spreeport race and win a bet, rush to Florida to spend it. We love money, we will rip you off painlessly."*

I couldn't see the track. But I hugged myself. As soon as this flurry passed and he could see again, my sniper was going to mess up another wheel. And then just one more after that and Heller was out of it! That Caddy was taking enough of a beating already. It could never survive running on a gaping bullet hole.

And then, suddenly, a voice. I had three sound receivers on. For a moment I didn't locate it.

Heller's earphones!

The voice said, "Sorry, High-Flyer. My talk box got hit and number two took time." It was Bang-Bang!

Heller said, "You okay?"

"Only a bruise, High-Flyer. Take her to a win!"

"Roger, dodger, over, under and out!" said Heller, and really fed throttle! The blurred track sped under him!

I swept the curtained expanse before me. Somewhere in that chill terrain, my other sniper lay dead. Probably with a knife, if I knew Italians. I could find nothing. Probably nobody else ever would either!

I had a bad few minutes. Maybe Bang-Bang was up there somewhere stalking *me!* I locked my van doors securely and laid out a Knife Section knife. But then I realized Bang-Bang was down at Pit 1. He had had to go there to use their radio to reach Heller.

(Bleep) that Bang-Bang! (Bleep) him, (bleep) him, (bleep) him! Heller had a chance to win!

Chapter 8

The snow snowed and the roaring race went on!

Numb, not just with cold, I sat and watched. There were only two chances now: Heller would smash up on that skidding track or his carburetor would fail.

The snowing let up and started again numerous times. Round and round they went.

The TV Channel Six and Seven-Eighths had been running along as fast as the cars. *"I'm sure it will thrill our national audience to know that the Whiz Kid, who had several times lost his lead, has now recovered it. Track conditions are appalling. Ah, here is Jeb Toshua. He is 101 years old. Jeb, do you ever recall a track this bad?"*

"I think it was '83 when I lost my cat...."

"Thank you, Jeb. Car 7, Dagger Duggan, has just pulled into the pit. He is refuelling. . . . No, he's getting a drink of Peegrams Corn Whiskey. Look at that ecstasy on Dagger Duggan's face as he empties the pint. We pause for a word from our sponsors, Peegrams Corn Whiskey! . . ."

The commercial's boys quartet sang:

> Corn Whiskey,
> Corn Whiskey,
> Corn Whiskey, I cry.
> If I don't get my Peegrams,
> I surely will die.

The picture of the race came back on. *"Dagger Duggan is now leaving his pit. That's him, waving at the camera. Hey, he turned right out into the path of the Whiz Kid! The Whiz Kid braked and spun his car around him!*

"Car 7—that's Dagger Duggan, folks—is . . . No! He has just caromed off Car 8! There he goes through the rail! Duggan shoots up into the air. The car is turning over! It comes down on its roll bars! It has burst into flame! He's trapped! He bursts into flames.

"We will now do a slow-motion replay of that shot."

The replay flashed on.

A low, harsh voice came over. *"Get that (bleeped) shot off the screen or you'll lose our account!"* Hastily, a string of letters flashed across the exploding Duggan:

SIMULATED DRAMATIZATION

Another car spun out and wound up in the snowbanks. Another came crawling into the pit with a busted fan belt and an engine that was overheating.

There were only eleven left in the race. It was creeping up toward 3:00 P.M. Spraying snow to either side, jockeying through openings, Heller drove on to the screams of delight from the grandstand. I found it absolutely disgusting. I kept a close eye on my watch: in a very short time now, that carburetor was scheduled to fail and he would be done for.

But in the last half hour, he had so clearly asserted a lead that some of the other drivers evidently began to think they had no chance at all if they did not take him out.

Instead of driving to make laps, some were driving now to get a ram at Heller as he went by.

Car 10, Basher Benson, driving a stripped International station wagon, lay in wait at the near end of the oval. He was going to, I could see, sweep along on the inside and ram Heller.

The Caddy braked into the turn and then sped up, skidding sideways in the flying snow.

Basher gave his car all it had and rushed parallel, aiming for Heller's left front wheel.

Above the yowl of tortured engines, Basher's voice, "Take this, you (bleepard)!"

The International touched before Heller could avoid.

A flash!

An electrical explosion!

Car 10 rebounded like it had been hit by lightning! It spun away, went through the rail!

The driver sat there stunned.

The crowd yelled and roared with delight!

The TV did a replay. It *was* a lightning bolt! Car 10 had hit Heller's left front wheel and an electrical flash at least five feet in diameter had flared!

The electrical surplus from the carburetor was being grounded in those wheels! And any other car that touched them bled off the grounding in a lightning bolt!

Basher Benson was getting shakily out of Car 10. He apparently had no idea of what had happened except that he didn't want anything more to do with this race!

The radio sportscaster was trying to account for it and suddenly settled upon the explanation that it was the Whiz Kid's magnetic personality.

Heller and the other cars roared on, the shrieking engines merged with the howls and cheers of the crowd.

The other drivers had no real idea of what had happened. There are always sparks to some extent when metal is hammered against metal in a crash.

The snow stopped and a murky sun came out.

Another driver, in an old Dodge, got the idea of sideswiping Heller on the far straightaway. He was driving close to the rail and, as Heller started to pass, the Dodge speeded up and dived at him.

FLASH!

It made a crack like a lightning bolt!

Heller had tapped him with a wheel!

The Dodge went spinning out of control! It rolled! It skidded fifty feet on its roll bars!

The crowd went crazy with ecstasy!

Yellow flag. A tow truck sped out to latch on to the Dodge and drag it away. The driver stood there until an ambulance came and then tried to climb into the tow truck. He seemed to be walking in circles.

The cars were speeded up again. There were now nine.

I was on the edge of my seat. I had half an eye on the viewers and the other half on the stopwatch. It was past three.

Was Heller going to win after all?

Chapter 9

The snow clouds parted more widely. The dirty-hued afternoon sun slanted down upon the chewed-up track. It seemed colder.

The battering roar of the straight-shoot-exhaust-piped Caddy racketed above that of the other cars as it speeded up to make the near turn. Heller had started to race in earnest. He was already twenty laps ahead of any other driver and he was starting to open the Caddy up!

The other eight, including Hammer Malone and Killer Brag, seemed to realize they were done unless they did something. Probably the chanting, "Whiz Kid, Whiz Kid, Whiz Kid!" that sporadically rose from the grandstand egged them on.

They were old bomber veterans. They had seen everything and done everything but they were not going to just idle around and watch themselves be thrashed.

Strategies of demolition derbies included gang-up. Once they had disposed of Heller, they could fight the rest of it out amongst themselves. But Heller must GO!

I read all that in the way they concertedly began to idle down as they passed the grandstand. They did another circle, Heller threading his way through them as though they didn't exist.

Heller was doing more than 150. He was sitting there doing an alert job of driving, predicting the movements of the other cars and predodging in ample time. The

Caddy looked like a red streak. Its engine was a continuous scream of power.

The other eight cars were drawing up in a kind of an uneven circle with a huge gap in the center. Four favored the grandstand side of the straightaway, the other four favored its other side. They had stopped trying to lap. They were going into pure demolition derby formation.

The TV and radio sportscasters were both jabbering in excitement that there was something up.

Heller knew there was something up. He suddenly slowed. He shifted down to lower drive, cutting out his top gear, probably to give himself enormous pickup in a sudden spurt.

The Caddy approached the waiting circle doing only about sixty.

He came to the outer edge of the hole.

A lunge as cars surged at him!

A yowl as the Caddy speeded up.

A grinding crash!

It was Hammer Malone hitting another car!

The Caddy was through the gap and away!

The other cars changed tactics. They turned around so they could back ram this time. It looked like a planned maneuver and, indeed, they were within shouting distance of one another.

The gap for Heller was wide open and inviting.

He was apparently just going to go through again.

The bombers began to back! They would hit him!

He suddenly stamped on his brakes and gave his steering gear a yank to the left!

He spun in a complete circle.

The bombers crashed into one another!

Heller wasn't there!

He came out of his spin and gunned his engine and streaked by, almost scraping the grandstand barricade!

He had gone behind them! He had used a lane just vacated!

The crowd howled with joy!

The bombers pried themselves apart. More shouting. They got back into position.

Heller toured the oval.

But whatever he planned to do next never happened.

Coming out of the far turn of the oval, doing about seventy, his engine quit!

He had only about a hundred yards to go to reach the bombers.

Perhaps he thought he could coast through.

He had been high on the bank. There was lots of snow under his wheels. It was cutting his speed down dramatically.

There was nothing he could do about it.

He went straight into the open center with a dead engine. He was doing about twenty.

CRASH!

Eight cars backed into him!

They were stopped in a jammed mass.

The top of Heller's hood was going cherry red!

The carburetor had fused!

With a quick yank he released his safety belt!

He shot his arm out through the window and got a hold.

He said, "Good-bye, you Cadillac Brougham Coup d'Elegance. It wasn't your fault!"

Like the gymnast he was, he pulled himself through the window.

Jammed cars all around!

Cursing drivers!

Smoke began to shoot out of the Cadillac's hood.

"Run!" Heller shouted in that high, Fleet voice.

He was up on a roof. He sprang to another roof!

He leaped to yet another roof.

He launched himself into the air, struck the snow with a roll, was up and running. He was heading for Pit 1.

Hammer Malone and Killer Brag had extricated their cars.

As one, with a crash of gears, they launched their vehicles after Heller!

Two explosions in the tangled mass of the six cars. I knew it would be the oxygen and hydrogen tanks going up.

Flames shot into the air!

The other drivers were running away.

But the cars of Hammer Malone and Killer Brag bore down on Heller!

He turned to face them.

They converged!

He slapped his hands against their hoods, sprang upwards and with a roll, hit the roof of Hammer Malone's car and was over it and behind.

With a grinding shriek of metal, the two sideswiping cars recoiled right and left, spinning in the ice.

Killer Brag's gas tanks must have been ruptured. The sparks of the chains on ice did the rest.

A whoosh of green, orange and red flame enveloped both cars!

Brag was out, racing away.

Hammer Malone was on fire. He dived into a snowbank to put it out.

Heller was racing for Pit 1.

Chapter 10

The pit crew was scrambling about.

Heller dived over a pit barricade.

Mike Mutazione was pounding at some sparks lying in Heller's racing suit.

The grandstand was going crazy.

The radio announcer was yelling, "*The Whiz Kid's engine died, just like that....*"

The TV sportscaster was shouting, "*Nine cars in flames....*"

The loudspeakers blared, "*The Whiz Kid apparently ran out of fuel....*"

Hammer Malone could be seen struggling out of the snowbank. He raced back toward his car. He beat out some flames in the upholstery. He leaped in!

The old wreck started! It had only been damaged by the explosion of Killer Brag's!

No other car in the flaming pyre before the grandstand was moving.

Hammer Malone began to drive around the track!

There was a howl of rage from the crowd.

A new voice was in the grandstand loudspeakers. "*That God (bleeped) Whiz Kid cost us our shirts!*"

Nobody was paying any attention to Hammer Malone, faltering along at about twenty. He had won the demolition and he was now going for the endurance. Totally ignored.

The grandstand loudspeakers blared, "*Get that God (bleeped) Whiz Kid!*"

The losers spilled in a wave over the grandstand barricades and onto the track!

Howling and shrieking revenge, they tore toward Pit 1.

Heller looked up, watching them come. He muttered, "Just like it said in *Hakluyt's Voiages*. Very hard to make a safe landing amongst the natives of North America!"

Mike Mutazione's crew was standing in a semicircle around the pit area.

The crowd was plowing down the track like a storm cloud gone crazy. The race was forgotten. All they wanted was blood.

Track security police tried to make a stand to check them. They were hurled aside!

The crowd came storming on. They were screaming, "Get the Whiz Kid!" "Cost me ten thousand!" "Kill him!" and other ferocious war cries.

Heller just sat there watching.

The foremost ring of the mob, mouths snarling, fists shaking, got within twenty feet of the Mutazione line.

"Now!" barked Mike.

Abruptly flame erupted from nozzles!

A dozen oxyacetylene hoses played a fan of fire over the heads of the mob!

There was an instant of incredulous gasps cut by the sizzle of flame.

Then a torrent of screams!

Howls of terror burst out!

The foremost ranks recoiled!

They knocked down people behind them like dominoes!

The crowd was racing away, leaving the fallen and trampled in the snow. And then these, too, found the energy to run.

The oxyacetylene torches popped out as their valves were shut off.

Hammer Malone's old wreck staggered past the grandstand and wrecked cars and knocked along, working to complete his thousand laps.

But the race was over for the crowd. They were going home.

PART THIRTY

Chapter 1

I packed up and drove the van down off the hill, heading for the track and grandstand.

I had seen Heller get into the Peterbilt and knew there was no danger he would spot me.

The disgruntled and disgusted crowd was trailing away. I steered the van slowly through them. I was hoping I could find J. Walter Madison.

Behind Heller's back, Madison had fabricated the Whiz Kid and the controversy around this race. With Heller's spectacular defeat and the bloodthirsty crowd, I had to find what Madison planned next.

The security guards were no longer tending the gates. They did not care who went in or out now.

I went through a tunnel and emerged in the littered grandstand. There was a cluster of people around a box. I recognized one of the nearest ones. It was a reporter I had seen at Madison's office, 42 Mess Street.

I went up to him. Although he had a sheepskin coat up around his ears and although I was wearing a hooded parka, we recognized each other.

I said, "Did Madison start that great riot?"

He said, "No. I did, on the spur of the moment. J. Warbler is in a weird state. Twenty minutes before the race he went into shock and passed out. We had to take him to the hospital tent. He only returned to the grandstand in time to see the end of it."

I looked through the cluster of 42 Mess Street people and saw Madison sitting there on a folding chair. Cold as it was, he had an ice bag on his head! His face was gray and awful!

I went over to him. I said, incredulously, "Are you feeling that way because Heller lost?"

He shook his head. "Oh, no. Win or lose, that wouldn't have mattered. It would only have given us one day's front page and then we would have had the work of doing something else."

I didn't understand it at all. "Well, if winning or losing didn't matter, what are you feeling so bad about?"

He ineffectually adjusted the ice bag. Then he broke down. "Never trust a client! They always do you in!"

"Maybe you better tell me what you think is wrong," I said, puzzled.

He began to cry. In a choked voice, he said, "He wasn't supposed to race at all! Just before the race he was supposed to be kidnapped! We would have had two weeks at least of *front page!*"

He ground his fists into his knees. "It was all to be so perfect! After two weeks he would have turned up behind the Iron Curtain, a captive of the fuel-hungry Russians!"

He let out a frustrated wail. "It would have started World War III! He'd be IMMORTAL!"

After a period of writhing and pounding his knees, he said, "You just can't ever depend on clients! OH, MY GOD! WHAT DO I DO NOW TO RECOVER THE FRONT PAGE??????"

I crept away.

Chapter 2

Sunday morning, the Bentley Bucks Deluxe Arms (to give it its full name) held me in tender and loving, if expensive, embrace. That was the only embrace I was getting these days.

But by ten my feeling of laziness began to give way to a vague disquiet. It occurred to me that it was altogether possible that Heller might recover from that debacle. In life, he was treacherously hyperactive. A type of disposition for which I have no sympathy.

I called down for a breakfast of strawberry shortcake—imported from the Argentine, the menu said—and, wrapped in a robe, was soon devouring it. My carbon-oxygen furnace needed restoking after the shocks and labors of the day before.

Almost indolently, I opened the ten pounds of Sunday paper. I don't really know what I expected to see. But I had not at all anticipated what I *did* see.

Nothing!

There was absolutely no word about that race in the whole paper!

Not ONE word!

I hastened over to the TV. I ran through the channels. Ah, a program called "The Week in Sports" was just beginning. Several items. Then a few brief clips of the race without any editorial comment, hardly any mention of the Whiz Kid! Just the crashes!

Oh, this was bad. Madison was right. He was off the front page. And not even in a day or two but at once!

I then remembered the local-radio-station dial position I had been listening to on Saturday—a Long Island station, WHOA. I tuned in on it. I was in luck! They were just beginning their news.

It was, apparently, a sleepy, snowed-in, suburban Sunday on Long Island. There were only two items of interest to me, both local.

A burned-out van with ten bodies in it had been found by some Boy Scouts in a picnic area of Jones Beach. Police said that they were burned beyond recognition; that a leaking muffler had overcome them; that they probably had been en route to pick up a load of seaborne narcotics; that Tommy Jones had been awarded his merit badge for snowshoeing.

The other item was another discovery: Miss Sarah Jane Gooch, the charming wife of Gooby Gooch, had been on her way to Cranston's Supermarket this morning and had stumbled over a body in the snowdrifts which now "dot our streets" and had called the police who had then found another body about two hundred yards away, the location traced by Police Chief Flab because of dogs quarrelling over it, which event had been phoned in by Mrs. Emma Gross, the charming wife of Bill Gross. The police concluded that one of the men had shot the other one with a rifle and had then committed suicide with a stiletto that was still sticking in his back. Crime in the community was thus reduced by two, which was heartwarming on a cold day.

The race might as well have never happened so far as the Spreeport area was concerned!

And it looked especially quiet when it came to news about the Whiz Kid. I was worried. What was going to happen now? Was Heller going to get off scot-free and ride to glory?

I thought I had better check up on said Heller.

I had kept my receiver-viewscreen loaded with strips to record Heller's actions and by replaying them I found out what he had been up to this morning.

He had come into his office! On Sunday? That was a bad sign. Awfully industrious!

The first thing he did was dig Izzy out of that closet-office he uses as a bedroom.

"I gave you a device some time ago," said Heller. "I want to look at it."

Heller went into his own office, turned on a heater and stood for a while gazing out across the snow-covered expanses of lower Manhattan. He seemed to concentrate on soot patches already darkening the snow. He was evidently letting his office warm up, for presently he took off a ski mask, a white fur hood and parka and sat down.

Izzy came in with the item. It was the unmodified carbon converter Heller had brought from Voltar and a duplicate of the one he had put in the now-defunct Cadillac.

Heller broke out some tools and, with very rapid motions, soon had the device spread all over a cloth on his desk. A small feeling of alarm began to rise in me.

One by one, holding each close to his eye, he began to go over the parts. Suddenly he stopped. He was holding a thin metal bit about an inch long.

"A notch!" he said.

Magnified by his own eyesight, I could see it too on my screen. Just a little V notch, the one our saboteur had cut to embarrass Heller.

"Look!" he said to Izzy, holding it out.

But Izzy couldn't see it no matter how he twisted his horn-rimmed glasses around. Heller got a huge magnifier and showed him.

"That caused the wrong electrical value to pour into the next component!" said Heller. "It built up to red-hot overheat! These were just cheap school kits. I should have known better."

Izzy gazed at him blankly. "School kits?"

"No, no," said Heller, probably realizing he was on the edge of a Code break. "They will work fine. All I need to do is redesign it slightly to guarantee its electrical values in this area and it will run forever. Get me the plans back."

Izzy got them and Heller made the changes. He seemed quite cheered up. The stupid idiot didn't suspect it was the farsightedness of Lombar Hisst that had cost him that race!

"Izzy," he said, "what do you do when you have lost a race?"

"You don't engage in one in the first place," said Izzy.

"No, no, really, I want to know."

"You leave for South America," said Izzy. "There's this place up the Amazon where there are only soldier ants. Peaceful! No people! Even the reporters have been eaten up. I'm holding your ticket. I can get you a Pan American reservation in seconds!" He was starting to lilt with enthusiasm.

"No, no," said Heller. "I'll just fix up this thing, get another car and challenge them again!"

"Oh, no!" wept Izzy.

And "Oh, no!" wept I! I could not possibly tolerate that much strain again, ever! This was a REAL emergency.

I reached for the phone, found I was holding the viewscreen. I put it down and tried to make a call on my Colt Bulldog. I ran about, slamming doors, trying to get dressed.

Utanc, my darling Turkish love, stuck a sleepy head through the bedroom door. "Whatever is going on, Sultan?"

I had not seen her in days. But I had no time now. "The world is liable to fall in!"

"Oh?" she said, closed the door, locked it and apparently went back to bed.

I didn't, let me tell you! I knew duty when I saw it calling! It was screaming at me!

Chapter 3

I found the phone where I had knocked it off under the bed.

I managed to find Madison's number. I forced the hotel operator to dial it: I couldn't hit the right buttons.

A very concerned, older female voice answered. His mother!

"I must talk to J. Walter at once!" I yelled at her.

"Oh, dear," she said, "I'm afraid that is impossible. He is lying in bed. Three doctors have been here and they ordered absolute rest. I can't even go near him myself."

And, indeed, I could hear tiny suppressed screeches in the background.

I hung up.

Bury. I must phone Bury!

It was a tangle! His number was unlisted. The Octopus Oil Building Exchange would not give me his home phone.

Ah, I had it! That night he had gone home in the police car! I knew where he lived!

Sunday or no Sunday, Mr. Bury was going to have a caller!

I still had the van, the rental office being closed on Sunday.

I piled into some warm clothes, got the car brought around front and was soon tooling uptown.

The streets were deserted tunnels piled high on both sides with snow, the tops of cars showing vaguely in the mounds. The snowplows had been industrious! Some of those motorists would not see their vehicles until spring!

I was soon standing before his mailbox. It said Mrs. Destuyvescent Depleister Bury.

I rang. I got him at once.

Within a minute I was in an upper hall and he was letting me through a door.

"It's an emergency," I said desperately.

His reply was strange. "Oh, good," he whispered.

Then, with a conspiratorial finger he beckoned me into the sitting room. He was carrying a sheet of Sunday paper and he didn't have any shoes on.

A torrent of words was coming from an inner room—things like "When I married you, I expected..." and "Time and again my whole family told me..." and "That is what I get for marrying beneath..." Quite a blur.

Bury whispered, "Tell me again, real loud!"

"THIS IS AN EMERGENCY!" I yelled at him and meant it.

"OH, HEAVENS!" he shouted back. "AN EMERGENCY ON SUNDAY!"

He grabbed his shoes and put them on. He grabbed some overshoes out of a hall closet. He got into an overcoat. He put on his snap-brim, little New Yorker hat. He grabbed an attaché case, rushed into a side room and filled it with white mice. He closed it.

Then he rushed into the room his wife's voice was

coming from and said something to the effect that the office demanded his presence.

He rushed out. A storm of small pillows and perfume sprays and nail files poured after him. He got us into the hall.

"Thank God," he said. "I've never been so pleased to see anybody in my life, Inkswitch. I will remember this as a kindly act! So rare, kindly acts!"

He was pushing me along as he spoke. We got outside and we climbed into the warm van.

I handed him a half pint of applejack I had taken to the race in case of emergency. "You're going to need this." And I told him first how Madison had planned to kidnap Wister, send him to Russia, blame the Communists and start World War III.

Bury nodded. He didn't even touch the applejack. "Well," he said, "I told you, Inkswitch. A little bit of Madison always goes too far. Many think his mother should be arraigned for attempted humanocide. But frankly, Inkswitch, he's really no more skilled than any other public relations man or reporter. He's just a little faster, that's all."

"You aren't worried?"

"Oh, PRs, catarrhs, Inkswitch. One of them, sooner or later, will get us into World War III, anyway. What do you expect? At least we got him into action."

"That's just it," I said. "He's not in action. He's under the care of three doctors and he's lying in bed screaming. And I can see his point. After the failure of his plan, he can't figure out how to get any more headlines. The paper today was blank."

"The Sunday papers? They're all printed on Saturday. They were in the delivery trucks before that race even started. Now, I'll admit you have a point. It is probably infeasible now for him to make Wister immortal for

74 L. RON HUBBARD

starting World War III. And it is very unlikely that
J. Warbler Madman will come up with another gem like
that. And he probably will have to work like a dog to get
back on the front page. And I surely want to thank you
for getting me out of there."

"You mean your wife?"

"Oh, no, no, no. The mayor! We were scheduled to
have dinner with him."

"Is he that bad?"

"Oh, no, no, Inkswitch. You don't understand. The
mayor is just a fat slob. It's his wife! She's a former Roxy
showgirl and she's never forgiven anybody for preventing
her from becoming a Hollywood star. My wife is nothing
compared to the mayor's wife. Her voice ought to be
arrested for assault and battery with intent to kill! I shall
remember your kindly act. Even though kindness is an
awful weakness, Inkswitch, and you've got to guard
against it. But come, we're wasting time."

"You've got another emergency?"

"Indeed so. I was going to go to the Bronx Zoo today
and I couldn't possibly figure how to manage it until you
came. Because of the Rockecenter gifts to the place they
specially open the snake house for me on Sundays and let
me feed live mice to the most delightful reptiles it's ever
been your pleasure to meet. Want to come?"

I shudderingly declined.

"All right, then drop me at the subway station and
I'll be on my way. And guard against kindness, Inkswitch. It can be a fatal flaw. It can even open the door
to the Madisons of this world."

With this threat, I hastily started up and dropped
him at the subway station.

I watched him go down the steps with his attaché
case full of live mice.

I have seldom felt so uncertain of the future.

Chapter 4

Late that night, around 10:00, fearing that Madison might not be dead, I again called his mother.

She stunned me!

"Dead? Oh, no, he's not dead. I've seldom seen him look more energetic. Is that you, Mr. Smith?"

I managed to say that it was.

"He flew out of here hours ago. He said he knew you would need reassurance and encouragement and for you to call 42 Mess Street right away if you rang."

I rang 42 Mess Street. I said, "This is Smith. I want to speak with Mr. Madison."

A bright male voice said, "Smith? Ah, Mr. Smith, owner of the *National Enmirer,* of course. Listen, Smith, have we got a scoop for you! . . ."

"No, no," I said. "I'm not a publisher. Tell Madison it's *the* Mr. Smith."

Whoever it was left the phone. A mad chatter of telex machines and barking voices assaulted my ears. Hey, that office was *busy!* But Madison had been dying!

Madison's voice, "Oh, Mr. Smith. I do thank you for calling. I knew you would be worried."

"I thought you were dying or dead!"

"Quote Medical Miracle Unquote Intramuscular morphine followed by Benzedrine and intravenous transfusions of black ink saves Madison's life. Smith, we must cease to dwell upon the nostalgic and roseate glow of yesterday. Now is the time to get the shoulder to men's souls. For these are the times that try men's grindstones.

We are the masters of men's fates and I thank God for my indomitable will. . . ."

"Wait," I protested. "What are you going to do now?"

"Smith, we must rest content that there will never be another chance to pull the PR coup of the century again. We have to let sleeping dogs tell lies and abandon all that. We must not look back but sternly face the future. Inspiration and genius would have triumphed had it not been for that undependable client. But never mind. I will now resort to standard press policy and though it will be hard and long, the end will see us riding in the triumphal procession, crowned with laurel leaves, never fear."

"What," I demanded with growing fear, "are you going to DO?"

"Smith, we have the first *C* of PR, Confidence. What we have lost is the second *C*, Coverage. We are OFF the front page! But never fear, Smith, we will regain it! For we have the third *C*, Controversy! Riding through the icy night, determined to make good, it came to me in a flash. CONTROVERSY! We can rebuild our campaign upon the sturdy headsman's block of Controversy without end. We will succeed! And you will have to excuse me now as I am told the publisher of the *Los Angeles Grimes* is on the other wire." *Click!* He was gone!

I sat there staring at the phone. He hadn't told me a blasted thing. I feared I did not understand this mysterious world of PR. I put the phone on the hook.

It rang instantly. Madison's voice, "See tomorrow's front page!" *Click.* He was gone again.

Needless to say, the next morning, it was with shaky hands that I unfolded the morning newspaper.

And there it was. Headlines!

WHIZ KID
ACCUSED OF FRAUD

VEHICLE IMPOUNDED

Race officials last night obtained a court order to impound the car used by the Whiz Kid in Saturday's race.

No one could be found to comment.

The Whiz Kid refuses press interviews.

The racing world tonight was shocked by the ominous order. . . .

I rushed out and got other papers. They all said more or less the same thing. They didn't say what it was really all about.

The TV and radio both were carrying the story. Apparently it was going national, for West Coast racing figures were being interviewed.

And so it went through the day.

Toward evening, I thought of my viewer. How was Heller taking this?

He had newspapers spread all over his desk. He was asking Izzy, "What in the name of blastguns is this all about?"

Izzy said, "It's about a ticket to South America. I got a book right here on soldier ants. They're a lot less deadly than the press. The ants just destroy everything."

"But," said Heller, "the remains of the Caddy are sitting right over at Mike Mutazione's garage. I called him. Nobody has come near it! And besides, it's so burned out you can't see anything but melted metal. And not a soul has called me. I haven't refused any press interviews!"

He started to clip all the stories, pushing the airline

ticket aside from time to time as Izzy kept putting it in his way.

All day Madison's phone was busy or he wasn't available. But that office, each time I heard it on the open line, sounded like it was situated in the middle of a hurricane.

Tuesday morning came.

Front page again!

WHIZ KID CHEATED

GAS LINE FOUND

Officials today revealed that in investigating the smoldering wreck of the Whiz Kid's car, they had discovered a gasoline line cleverly hidden in the pistons. . . .

It was in all the papers and on radio and TV.

Well, I thought. That will be the end of it and the end of Heller, too!

But Wednesday morning came.

Front page!

RACE OFFICIAL FLEES

WHIZ KID CULPABLE

According to unimpeachable sources we cannot disclose, a track official—whose relatives demanded he remain anonymous—fled the state after confessing he had accepted a bribe from the Whiz Kid to overlook a hidden gas tank in the Whiz Kid's steering wheel. . . .

It was in all the papers and on radio and TV. Ah, well, I thought. Madison has cleverly scotched any future race. And that will be that.

So, on Thursday I was fairly relaxed when I opened the morning paper.

Front page again! With photos!

ANGRY MOB SEARCHES FOR WHIZ KID

EMBATTLED POLICE USE RIOT GUNS

Today, Manhattan huddled behind closed doors and listened with terror as the streets were torn to bits by the angry marching feet of a howling mob searching for the Whiz Kid. . . .

Photos of the mob, with placards which said *Down with the Whiz Kid*, showed flame and tear gas shooting from police lines. I looked out the window. Fifth Avenue never looked so calm.

The afternoon editions had new banners:

MAYOR CALLS CITY-WIDE EMERGENCY

And there were more photos.

Well, I said to myself, this Madison has really got what it takes. Really a genius. But he's shot his bolt now. He'll drop to page two.

Friday.

Front page again!

WHIZ KID
HIDEOUT FOUND

Investigative reporters today stumbled upon the secret hideout of the Whiz Kid. Tipped off by a Good Humor Ice Cream man who was in a bad humor . . .

The story went on.

But the photograph! There was the Whiz Kid, buckteeth and all, peering out from behind the Venetian blind of an upper window and looking very fearful.

I wondered if Heller really had fled. I ran through my recorded strips. He was going about his usual routine. At one point he came into his office, puzzled over the papers a bit and then went on with his schoolwork.

On Saturday, I knew Madison would have worn it out.

But no! Front page!

WHIZ KID
HIDEOUT BOMBED

Today mobs converged upon the hideout of the Whiz Kid, ten thousand strong, and with ferocity hitherto unknown in city annals bombed the house to bits! . . .

Photos of an exploding building. I looked at it closely. It could not have been the same house the Whiz Kid had been shown peering out of. It looked more like a factory. Hard to tell with all the flame and bits flying about.

I went for a walk and saw Madison's earlier advertising signs about the Whiz Kid, that had been so neat, were now all covered with graffiti derogatory to the Whiz Kid.

Sunday, of course, would be a blank news day. But it wasn't! Front page again!

MAGAZINE CANCELS CONTEST

In an unprecedented action today, the sports magazine, *Dirt Illustrated*, cancelled the $100,000 contest to guess the secret fuel of the Whiz Kid.

The full details, according to magazine officials, will be released in this week's issue.

But unimpeachable sources leaked that it had to do with a criminal act of the Whiz Kid relating to the contest....

Hey, a *second* front page story! Madison was really pouring it on!

"SECRET" FUEL DISCLOSED

WHIZ KID FUEL LEAKS

According to the Attorney General's office of an undisclosed state, investigators today obtained vital information on the supposedly "secret" fuel of the Whiz Kid that was to revolutionize industry and automobiling.

Using forensic air hoses on a gas station

attendant whose name was withheld, they obtained the name of the actual fuel.

According to the indictment which some believe to be under preparation, the ''secret'' fuel was no less than Octopus Gasoline!

The gas attendant sought immunity from conspiracy charges by testifying that someone who looked like the Whiz Kid bought, in North Carolina, 39 gallons of Octopus High Test Supreme Unleaded the very day of the race!

With variations, the story was in all the Sunday papers. But there was much more. *Dirt Illustrated* had full-page ads announcing the coming exposé. And double-page ads were carried by Octopus Gasoline, ''The Drink of Industry and the People!''

By the Gods, he had even made the Sunday papers! I was really pleased. Bury's faith in Madison had not been misplaced!

I hastily went down to get the newest copy of *Dirt Illustrated* and there it was! A complete exposé! According to the leading story, the Whiz Kid himself had tried to win the prize! He had submitted an unsigned entry that simply said ''Octopus Gasoline''!

I really chuckled. This Madison was a howling genius after all.

I tuned in on Heller. He was at his Nature Appreciation 101 class with Mr. Wouldlice as his instructor. The snow was all over the place and the class looked cold. Wouldlice seemed a sort of chinless young man. With an ice saw, he was trying to cut a hole in the frozen Harlem Meer in Central Park and lecturing on the nesting habits of carp. He wasn't making much headway with the ice cutting. Heller, hands in pockets, finally finished the job for him with some strategically placed kicks with the heels of his baseball spikes. Heller handed the resulting slab to a girl and the students began to use it as a sort of belly sled. Mr. Wouldlice went on lecturing with Heller as his sole attending student. He didn't seem antagonistic to Heller; well, that would change with the next term when Miss Simmons got back on the job.

Heller did act sort of depressed. He was stirring the soot-covered snow with his foot. It made me very cheerful.

Monday, however, made me sort of wonder whose side this Madison was on.

He got his front page again. But a new twist.

OCTOPUS OFFICIALS DENY INSTIGATING WHIZ KID RIOTS

The mayor today denied that he had been summoned before a full-scale meeting of the Octopus Oil Company. However, unimpeachable inside leaks reached this paper just before dawn that a secret meeting of the Seven Brothers had occurred over the weekend to discuss the Whiz Kid riots.

All officials reached denied the meeting and the discussion.

"In admitting that he used Octopus gasoline in the race," a spokesman said, "the Whiz Kid obviously sought to implicate the oil companies in his vicious and villainous plot to undermine the entire oil industry with a felonious breach of racing rules. I deny vigorously that the oil

companies financed the rioters. Besides, the Whiz
Kid, being only 17, could not legally drive in Nas-
sau County. This is an effort to link the great
American patriots of the oil industry to an illegal
act and imply that by selling the Whiz Kid Octopus gasoline to use in his fraud, the oil companies
are also party to the crime."

But when Tuesday's papers came, Madison had lost
his front page. He had slumped to page 3. The story was
even short.

WHIZ KID FORBIDDEN
TO DRIVE

Officials of the State of New York today revoked the unissued New York Driving License of
the Whiz Kid due to the Octopus disclosure that
he is only 17 and underage.

NASCAR officials also revoked his membership, effectively ending any further racing by the
Whiz Kid.

Charges of fraud and public conspiracy ...

Ah, well. I could relax. Madison had done it. I
phoned his office. He wasn't there. I phoned his mother.

"Mr. Smith? Oh, I am sorry. I can't call him to the
phone. He has been under a terrible strain all morning
and didn't feel well enough ..."

Madison took the phone away from her. "Mr.
Smith?" He sounded very depressed. "I am so sorry,
Mr. Smith. I lost the front page. I could feel it in my

bones last night." And an aside, "Mother, please hold the ice bag tighter, it's slipping. Mr. Smith, please don't lose faith in me. These things take time. Somewhere I went wrong. I promise you I will live up to everything you ever thought of me. Really. I have to hang up now. My psychiatrist just came in."

He really sounded depressed. But I wasn't!

I checked up on Heller. He was in the High Library at Empire University. He was reading Hakluyt's *The Principall Navigations, Voiages, and Discoveries of the English Nation (1589 A.D.).*

He was lingering on a section where a vessel had gone aground on the North American coast and natives were swarming all over it, hacking the crew to pieces in the intense cold. Then he just sat there looking into space.

An assistant librarian, gathering up some books, said, "You look kind of lost. Can I help you?"

Heller said, "No. I don't think anybody can. Somewhere I went wrong. And for the life of me, I can't spot where."

"Just go see the student psychiatrist," said the assistant librarian cheerfully.

"Just because I'm lost is no reason to make *two* mistakes," said Heller and went back to studying Hakluyt.

But oh, was I cheerful. My life felt like a song.

Bless Bury. Bless Madison. Heller was stopped cold!

Chapter 5

According to psychologists a manic state seldom lasts very long. And so it was with mine.

Not two minutes after I left the viewer, there was a knock on the door. Thinking it was a bellhop with some deliveries for Utanc, I unsuspectingly opened it.

Raht and Terb!

I hastily swept them into the living room, looked up and down the hall, reentered and locked it behind me.

Raht's mustache was growing back—they must have shaved it to repair his fractured jaws. He had some facial scars from the wires. He was very hollow-eyed.

Terb had lost most of his fat and, apparently, the use of a couple of fingers.

"It's about time!" I thundered at them. "Lollygagging about on company time! You ought to be ashamed of yourselves. I've a good notion to dock your whole year's pay!" That's the way you have to handle such riff-raff.

I sat down and poured myself a cup of coffee from the silver pot and looked at them contemptuously through its steam. They were standing in the middle of the room, their thin clothes shabby, shivering from the outside cold, kind of blue. Apparently they had lost their overcoats.

"The New York office is open and running," said Raht. "They got all the criminals scheduled for their identity changes as you requested."

"That's no reason for you to come around and bother me," I said.

"Oh, we wouldn't have," said Terb. "But Faht Bey said on the wire that it was pretty urgent so we had to come."

I sighed the sigh of the harassed executive. "And what," I said, "is urgent enough to disturb the vital work I'm doing? Without any help from menials, I might add."

Raht said, "Apparently, he wouldn't wait."

"And *whom* is *he?*" I said, correcting his grammar. You have to keep such riffraff on their toes.

"Gunsalmo Silva," said Terb.

I felt my hair lift. I had told Silva to go kill the Director of the CIA. Silva shouldn't be alive. He should be safely dead while executing an execution that couldn't possibly be executed!

"Evidently," said Raht, "he arrived several days ago in Afyon. Faht Bey tried to find out what he wanted and get it handled but Silva said his business was with you and a couple days ago he simply left. The airline booking he made was for New York!"

Well, New York is a big town. Silva couldn't possibly, Gods forbid, know my address. One mustn't appear nervous before underlings. "So what else is new?" I said.

Terb promptly handed me a stack of orders to stamp!

Wearily, I got out my identoplate and stamped away. But, for once, I was alert. There were two orders there: one for their hospital expenses and another which called for overcoats and new clothes. I tossed them aside. Then, on second thought, to make a better impression, I recovered them and tore them in small pieces.

"You be on call," I said as I swept them into the hall. "No more of this loafing!"

I slammed the door on them.

For some time I sort of paced around the bedroom and sitting room. Then I decided to go for a walk. I got my warmest clothes and, all wrapped up, I went to the hall door and opened it.

GUNSALMO SILVA!

In moments of intense shock, the thing uppermost in one's mind tends to surface.

"How did you find me?" I gasped.

He pushed on by. He removed a camel's-hair over-coat from his squat and muscular frame and threw it on the sofa. He put his hat, a Russian *astrakhan,* on the coat. He sat down, found the coffee was still warm in its thermos pot and poured himself a cup.

"Come in and close the door," he said. "It's drafty."

I did. I went in the bedroom and took off my own coat. I checked to make sure I had my Colt Bulldog but, actually, I don't think I could have drawn it, because my hand was shaking.

I reentered the living room and sat down to hide what my knees were doing.

"The answer to your first God (bleeped) question," he said, "is easy. I seem to have these miraculous powers. That Utanc is sending avalanches of postcards to her two little servant kids back in Afyon and they're showing them to half of Turkey." He pulled one out. It was pretty dogeared. It was of the Bentley Bucks Deluxe Arms with an X on the penthouse and said "X marks my room." And also "Confidential."

"I had to twist the little (bleepard's) arm a bit, but there it is. Now as to your next question," he said, over-looking the fact I hadn't asked it, "where's my hunnert big ones?"

I found my wits. "How do I know you did the job?" I said. "After all, the rub-out of the Director of the CIA would make big news."

"Jesus H. Christ," he said, "don't you ever read the papers?" He looked around. A stack of them for the last two weeks stood in a corner: my Heller file that I hadn't clipped yet. He went to them. Sure enough, there was the story:

CIA DIRECTOR
REPLACEMENT
HITS SNAG IN SENATE

He fished around in the stack some more. "And how about this?" He jammed it under my nose.

CIA DIRECTOR
SUCCUMBS
TO OPERATION

"They can't come right out and say he was hit," said Silva. "It would set the God (bleeped) Russians a bad example. But how about this?"

He threw the whole wallet and identity cards of the Director of the CIA on the sofa. It was bloodstained!

"Incredible!" I said, stalling for time.

"Yeah, I thought so myself. You see, I sort of got these incredible powers. I don't know where the hell they come from."

I knew. Taken to Voltar, he had been hypnotrained by the Apparatus! I had a killer-killer in front of me, very deadly indeed!

I fought to think of more stalls. "It's hard to realize you could waste a man as guarded as that," I said.

"Yeah, it took time. First, I had to get them to hire me as a hit man. They knew my score—'Holy Joe' and all—so they took me on. And I had to waste two Russians for them and then a dictator in Central America. That's what slowed me down."

He poured himself another cup of coffee. "Still, it wasn't too slow. You see, these ideas on how to do things just pop up and away I go. Mysterious. Like angel voices. Really beautiful."

Silva added two lumps of sugar to his coffee. "But wasting the CIA Director was easy. Hardly took any angel voices at all. After the three hits they trusted me so much I was even riding in his car. I learnt his habits, so to speak. So I disguised myself as his wife and shot him in a Georgetown brothel. They're looking for her now. Good, clean job so they won't find her. I sold her body to the God (bleeped) university hospital. It was a bit more money, too. And speaking of money, where's my hunnert big ones?"

I choked. "Listen," I managed, "lira won't do you any good in the U.S. I'll phone and find out what the exchange is and pay you in dollars."

"*Lira!*" he snarled. "What the hell would I do with ten million *lira!* It's a hunnert thousand U.S. greenback bucks, buster. So cough up."

"That's what I was saying," I said hastily. "I'll make a call and get it sent over right away."

"That's better," he said.

I went into my bedroom. I had about a hundred and thirty thousand under my mattress but I had conceived a good plan. I phoned the New York office.

"Raht," I said.

They put Terb on the phone. He said, "I'm sorry. Raht has gone out to find us some rooms. I'm alone."

"Then come alone!" I snapped. "I want you over here at once. Come to my bedroom door and no place else!" I slammed down the phone.

I went back. Silva was sitting relaxed. "Well, you won't believe this," he said, "but I'm going to God (bleep) retire shortly."

"Good," I said. "I don't have any more work for you."

"Oh, I wouldn't take it if you had it. I'm a real artist now. I got these mysterious God (bleep) powers, see? And there's a bird that nobody will take a contract for. It's been offered and offered and no takers. One million God (bleeped) bucks. And no takers. What do you think of that?"

"Marvelous," I said. "He must be pretty dangerous."

"Oh, he is, he is." And then he snapped his fingers. "But me, I'm an artist. I'm taking it. He's wasted thirteen hit men, they say. But thirteen is his unlucky number. *He*'s going to be fourteen! One million God (bleeped) bucks."

He glowed for a bit. Then he waved his hand about and said, "I'm going to live in swanky joints like this one and have a swanky dame like you got and live it up! And speaking of living it up, where's the delivery boy with the money?"

He waited and I sweated. It was actually a temptation to simply blow him full of holes with the Colt Bulldog, but such a slug spills a lot of blood and it would ruin the sofa. Besides, he might outdraw me.

At last, a knock on the bedroom door. I closed the door to the sitting room and opened it. Terb was standing there, blue with cold.

"Listen," I said in a tense whisper. "There's a man, Silva, going to be leaving here in a few minutes. He'll be carrying a hundred thousand dollars. You tail him, kill him and get the money back. And bring it right here back to me without one single penny missing."

"I didn't come armed. We lost our guns. Can't I wait and get Raht on this with me? We work together. . . ."

"Not armed!" Oh, I was furious with him. But a hundred thousand is a hundred thousand. I pushed the Bulldog into his hands. I thought for a moment. I took the Knife Section knife out from behind my neck and gave it to him. I thought for a moment and went back into the room and got two Voltar heavy-concussion grenades—they are common enough, a fifteen-second delay time after you throw them and no fragments to leave evidence.

"Now, no excuses," I said. "Watch my door from down the hall and when he comes out, tail him and, in a safe place, blow him away. Got it?"

He said he did.

I went back into my bedroom and dug the hundred thousand out from under my mattress. It certainly hurt me to part with it, even for a little while.

I reentered the sitting room. "The messenger had to count it," I said in apology. "But here it is."

He took it, counted it and stuffed it into his pockets, quite a wad. As he left, I said, "Good luck on your retirement." He gave me an evil smile and was gone.

Chapter 6

At dawn there was a furious pounding on my bedroom door.

Ah, Terb with my money!

Groggily, I staggered over and opened it.

It wasn't Terb. It was Raht!

He was standing there, shivering and shaking, covered with the snow falling outside, blue with cold—and something else.

He came in, he shut the door behind him and leaned against it. He said, "He's dead."

"Well, that's good news," I said. "Hand over the money."

He stared at me noncomprehending. He looked pretty shattered, sort of half doubled up and sort of liable to fall.

"Don't stall," I said. "You know very well I sent Terb to tail Silva and get the money back."

He slumped all the way down and sat there with his back against the door, head bowed over. I could swear he was crying.

"Come on, come on," I said. "No stalling. It's too early in the morning for any tricks. Just hand over the money and don't try to hold any out!"

"He's dead," said Raht. "Tortured to death."

"Well, good," I said. "So Terb had a little fun. But that doesn't mean you two (bleepards) can keep the money."

He said, between sobs, "It's Terb that's dead."

I had opened my mouth to speak. I closed it. GUN-SALMO SILVA WAS STILL ALIVE!

Quickly, I locked and barred the door. Hastily, I got another gun out of my bureau, a Smith and Wesson .44 Magnum revolver. I made sure the living room was empty, locked and barred. I scouted the terrace. No Silva. Yet.

I came back and grabbed Raht by his shirt front. "You better (bleeped) well tell me how you two fouled this up!"

He was so blue and so shaking with shock, it took him quite a while before he could do much talking.

"I never would have found him," he finally got out. "But we both wear bugs we can locate each other with. He didn't come back last night. They said he had gone to your place. I traced him by the bug sewn in his pants.

He was in a basement entrance of an old abandoned house." He halted.

"Was there anything on him?"

"His feet were burned half off. His teeth were all broken with grinding them. We always worked together. If he was following Silva, the man must have pretended to go in the house and then circled and got him from behind."

"Did he have my hundred thousand on him?" I demanded. You can never get a straight story out of such riffraff.

"Nothing. He had no weapons, no money—nothing."

"Did he talk?"

Raht had begun to cry again, sort of dry, choking sobs. Then he said, "I think Terb must have been too cold to fight."

What a way to try to pry money out of somebody for an overcoat! Believe me, I kicked Raht out right then.

He got to the elevator and was supporting himself against a piece of wall, head down, shivering and sobbing. I slammed my door. I had more important things to think about.

Had Terb talked?

Very likely.

I better stay very close inside. I better keep this gun on me day and night.

Leave it to those two to foul everything up!

Suddenly, I remembered Silva had impersonated the wife of the Director of the CIA, had kidnapped her and hung the murder on her. Utanc!

I got brave enough to cross the sitting room. I pounded on her door. After a long time, she opened it.

"Don't go out. Keep your door locked. Don't let anybody in!"

"Why?" she said in alarm.

"Silva. You remember Silva. The man you hired as a bodyguard once. He murdered the Director of the CIA and now he may be gunning for me."

"He did?" said Utanc, eyes flying wide. Then, "Are you sure?"

She needed convincing. It was still there on the sofa, slid behind a cushion: the I.D. of the Director of the CIA. I scooped it up and thrust it at her, bloodstains and all.

Her mouth was open in astonishment as she stared at it. Then she said, "You paid him to do it?"

"And tried to get the money back. He may be around any corner. Don't go out!"

Psychologists will tell you that murder and blood do strange things to women. Death stimulates them sexually.

She suddenly grabbed me and kissed me!

Then she raced around and closed all the drapes so the room was dark as pitch.

She threw me on the bed and was all over me!

We didn't go out that day.

Her mouth was hot as fire!

Chapter 7

After two days of such isolation—and very rewarding isolation it was—I was feeling pretty cocky.

Because there had been nothing and no one strange in our vicinity, I had to conclude that it was possible that Terb had not talked.

I decided it might be possible to venture out cautiously. Besides, forty-eight hours of uninterrupted bed with Utanc was actually making me weak. At breakfast, I found that lifting a spoonful of ice cream required considerable effort.

Besides, she had left the table and gone into her room and locked the door and had now come back and was standing there fully dressed in a mink coat, mink snowboots, mink hat, and was drawing on mink gloves.

There was just a trace of irritation in her voice. "I was looking through my clothes just now," she said, "and found I don't have a thing to wear. It has finally stopped snowing and there's a sale on at Tiffany's."

"They sell jewelry," I said.

"I know. So ta-ta."

"Wait!" I said. "Be careful of the money!"

With some asperity, she seized her mink purse, opened it and showed me. It was stuffed with money! What a manager! She turned to leave.

"Wait," I said. "One more thing!" I weakly stumbled to a bureau and got out an old Remington Double Derringer with pearl handles. It was small, weighing only eleven ounces. I made sure it was loaded with its .41 caliber rimfire shorts. "You better take this."

She recoiled. "Oh, dear me, no! I am absolutely terrified of guns! I might shoot myself by accident!"

Oh, well, little wild desert thing that she was, naturally she was too shy to shoot anybody.

Around one o'clock, after another sleep, I got energy enough gathered up to get dressed and go out myself. What prompted me was the state of my exchequer. There must be only about $38,000 left under the mattress.

Looking around corners first and keeping the Smith and Wesson .44 Magnum in my hand in my overcoat pocket, I made my way through the snowy streets to Rockecenter Plaza. It was time to draw my pay as a family "spi."

Soon, I was standing at my destination:

Window 13
Petty Cash

There was a new girl there. Well, I guess you could call her a girl. She had a man's haircut and a man's suit on and a thin, hard slit for a mouth.

"Where," I said, uncertainly, "is Miss . . . Miss . . . ?"

"Miss Grabball finished her twenty-five years yesterday and retired to a villa in Monte Carlo. I am Miss Pinch. Who the hell are you?"

"Inkswitch," I said, tendering the Federal I.D.

She looked at her thick book of employees. "You aren't listed here, buster."

"If you will just punch the computer," I said helpfully.

She did. It came up blank.

"Beat it," she said.

"Wait," I said. "You know what it means when it comes up blank."

"It means I call the cops. But I'm in a good mood today. Get out of here before I pull the trigger on this under-the-counter riot gun. I been dying to see how it works."

Naturally, I left. I went to see the personnel director.

"Miss Pinch? New personnel," he said. "They always give trouble." And he left for his afternoon coffee break.

I went to Bury's office.

It was locked.

I went home.

Well, at least Silva hadn't shot me.

For a little while I toyed with the idea of robbing a bank. It seemed to be pretty easy to do and certainly something had to be done to recoup my dwindling fortune. That hundred thousand really hurt.

Thinking Raht might know something about robbing banks, I phoned the New York office.

"Raht?" said the receptionist. "He's been in the Metropolitan Hospital for two days with pneumonia." More vacation! My Gods, how could you work with such riffraff!

But the day ended with some good laughs. They had a comedy show and who was on it but the bogus Whiz Kid, buckteeth and all!

The show was called "The Benighted Show" and the interviewer was Donny Fartson, Junior. The show had run on prime time for decades and the son had taken over from the father.

The phony Whiz Kid sat there and bragged and bragged about what a great student he was and how smart he was and how he was top of his class. And in a stroke of genius he had invented this fuel in the university laboratories and now he had come out of hiding to tell all and the Octopus Oil Company was against him. And then he did a little dance, waving a college flag.

And then the interviewer asked him, "If you're the top of your college class, maybe you can answer this one. Why was New York called the 'Big Apple'?"

The Whiz Kid double grinned, his buckteeth especially prominent, and said, "Because it's full of worms!"

The audience laughed and laughed and the Whiz Kid took a couple bows.

At that moment I had a twinge of worry. They hadn't thrown any rotten eggs at him! They had laughed at him, yes. But at the end, the audience even seemed sympathetic! I didn't want this sort of thing getting out of hand. I didn't want them thinking he was a brilliant student. I called 42 Mess Street. The phone was busy, busy, busy.

Well, I hoped Madison would handle it.

I went to bed to recoup my energies.

Chapter 8

And I had been right not to worry!

The very next morning, Madison had his front page!

WHIZ KID
FALSIFIES COLLEGE

FAKE STUDENT

Last night, when the Whiz Kid appeared on the nationwide prime-time Benighted Show, he alleged that he was a top student of the leading engineering university of the country.

He also alleged that Octopus Oil was behind his recent troubles.

Investigative reporters at once swarmed to the campus of the Massachusetts Institute of Wrectology.

The Whiz Kid is not and never has been enrolled there!

No student in the engineering school had ever heard of him, no professor had him on any roll book.

The President of M.I.W., in a public statement, said, "This is a deliberate fabrication. I will

---

not have the name of this noble and honored institution dragged through the public scrap heap! It
is an obvious effort to trade upon the lofty and
divine right of universities. If we had more ap-
propriations from the CIA we would be better
equipped to handle monstrous cabals of this sort!''

There was more. And it was in every paper and on
radio and TV. I was filled with awe.

It was a type of assassination I had not been familiar
with. And it was all the more deadly because the assassin
seemed so general and it was all within the allowed law!
And it could be done to anybody!

I tried to call Madison to congratulate him but all
his phones were busy.

Ah well, Madison was doing fine so I wondered if
there was any reaction from Heller. His plans were being
so undermined, he must be utterly wild. I resorted to the
viewer.

He was certainly taking his time getting to the
office. It was a bitterly cold, windless day and every oil-
and coal-burning furnace in the city was adding so much
smoke and smog that one's eyes watered. Instead of just
observing that, Heller was going along measuring it with
an atmosphere densimeter, a Voltar instrument being
used right out there in the street! It would have been a
Code break except that New Yorkers never notice anything, (bleep) them.

At length he reached his floor in the Empire State
Building and en route to his own palatial layout noticed
that the door to Multinational was ajar. That was where
Izzy slept in his mop closet.

Heller went in.

He stopped suddenly.

Right there on the giant screen of Izzy's business computer, a spelled-out sign!

In green electronic-type letters, it said:

GOOD–BYE CRUEL WORLD!

Heller dropped whatever he was carrying. He rushed to the elevator area that served his floor and, like lightning, pushed every one of the call buttons urgently, both up and down.

One after the other they stopped.

He urgently asked each operator, "Have you seen Mr. Epstein? The little fellow with the big nose and big glasses?"

He hit it with the third one.

"He went up about five minutes ago," said the young man. "Then he found you couldn't get to the Observation Platform in this car and he had me take him all the way down."

"Forget these passengers," said Heller. "It's life and death. Take me all the way down instantly!"

The operator did that. "He seemed awful confused, Mr. Jet," he said as they rocketed downwards with the other passengers protesting.

Heller was out and over to the express elevator on 34th Street at speed. He was up to the 80th floor in less than a minute. He switched to the elevator to the 86th floor. The sign said:

Visibility Poor Today

There wasn't any traffic to the 86th floor.

He stepped out into the area of the snack bar and souvenir stand. Only the clerks.

He rushed out onto the Observation Platform. He ran along the high fence which encloses it and prevents suicides. He was looking down. It made me dizzy.

Then he saw a hand. It was gripping the bottom leg of a firmly embedded chair over by the door, well away from the edge.

Heller looked over the top of the seat. There was Izzy. He was hugging the platform pavement, gripping the bottom leg. He was at least twenty feet from the edge!

"Izzy!" said Heller. "Get up!"

"No. Height makes me so dizzy I can't walk! I can't let go. I came up here to throw myself off but now I can't let go of this chair!"

"What's happened?" said Heller.

"All this bad publicity on you triggered it," wailed Izzy. "That student story this morning was the last straw! My back is broke. I can't be responsible for you anymore!"

"Oh, come now," said Heller, "that's been going on for some time. There must be something else."

Izzy began to weep. "I don't even deserve your scolding me. And you should. I have been so flustered and nervous with all this press that I have been making business mistakes."

Heller knelt down by him and put a hand on him as though holding him from slipping.

It made Izzy wail all the harder. "You shouldn't be nice to me! I've *ruined* us." He choked and gasped for a bit. Then he said, all in a rush, "We were about to owe a fortune in income tax. There was an old, old company that was so deep in debt nobody would touch it: even the government and unions had abandoned it, years ago. The

Chryster Motor Corporation. I couldn't resist it. It would have furnished us with debt for years and years!"

Heller put a second hand on him as though he might slide horizontally twenty feet. "Well, that doesn't sound so incompetent, Izzy."

"It wasn't," said Izzy. And then he wailed, "But right away I did the most stupid thing! I fired the board of directors and I put my mother in charge of it and it started making money! For the first time since 1968!"

"But that's good news," said Heller.

"Oh, no it isn't!" cried Izzy. "Right away, IRS made a retroactive ruling and invented taxes for it, overdue and compounded with fines and penalties clear back to 1967! They've impounded all our bank accounts even in corporations that aren't interlocked! We're ruined!"

"How ruined?" said Heller.

"We need over a million and a half to free our bank accounts. We can't pay our staff or rent. We don't even have money to start exchange arbitrage again. Throw me over the fence. You'll be better off without me. I'll close my eyes."

Heller pried his fingers loose from the leg of the seat with some difficulty. Izzy had his eyes tightly closed. Heller picked him up.

"Oh, thank you, thank you," said Izzy. He obviously thought Heller was going to throw him over the high fence.

But Heller carried him into the area with the souvenir stand and snack bar and pushed an elevator button. Izzy tentatively opened his eyes and saw he was no longer on the platform and began to sob anew.

Heller carried him down in the elevators and then up again to their floor. He went on through to his office, opened it and put Izzy in a chair.

Heller went to a safe and got out the black garbage

bag. He began to empty wallets and pile wads of notes in Izzy's lap.

The heap grew. Mostly thousand-dollar bills. Izzy was holding them up to the light, checking them.

Suddenly Izzy began to count them with the expert motions of a bank teller.

"One hundred and one thousand, two hundred and five!" said Izzy.

"Tax free," said Heller. "Now, will that let you start arbitrage exchange again?"

"Oh, yes! How did you do this?"

"And you can begin to pay the rent and payroll?"

"Oh yes. The pound is out the bottom in Singapore and high in New York. But . . ."

"There's a string," said Heller. "Promise me not to go near that Observation Platform again."

"Oh, I won't. The wind hurts my sinuses!"

"And one more thing," said Heller. "I have now saved your life twice so you are doubly responsible for me."

"Oh no!" said Izzy with a wail. "Not with all that bad publicity!"

Heller reached for the money.

"I PROMISE TO BE DOUBLY RESPONSIBLE FOR YOU!" shouted Izzy. And he ran with speed for the telex room, probably to get away before Heller thought of anything else.

Well, I ruminated, they were still in business. But they owed a million and a half and IRS had a way with it, being run as it was to keep Rockecenter rich and everybody else poor, especially potential competition. Hadn't I heard that in 1905, Rockecenter's great-grandfather had been the one who financed and pushed and hammered Congress to amend the Constitution and put income tax into law? And when it happened in 1911, that the family fortune was so organized that only it survived when those of all competitors were swept away? Cunning people, the Rockecenters, no matter that the current scion was insane. Here was IRS working for them still. Izzy didn't have a prayer of getting hold of a million and a half! A half he might make. But a million and a half, never. Not with just arbitrage, not with all his current expenses. Not even Izzy.

It was a relief. For Izzy's Chryster Motor Corporation would have been a potential competitor of Rockecenter interests. Izzy might pull the wool over Heller's eyes. But he couldn't fool me. He had obviously bought old, rickety, mostly defunct Chryster to build and install Heller's carburetors! One more crazy Izzy dream gone to pot.

But it was the media thing that really intrigued me. Rockecenter had that down, too.

And Heller? He really had no idea of what was happening to him or who was doing it. During the rescue of Izzy, his hands had gotten pretty dirty on the Observation Platform and there he stood looking closely at the soot. He just had no idea at all of the really important things that were going on!

Chapter 9

About nine forty-five, Heller's day was given another jolt. He had been listening to speeded-up Italian-language tapes he had probably gotten from the language school down the hall and was just doing a replay of how to pronounce numerous Italian saints when Bang-Bang came bursting in.

"Right away, right now, Babe ordered you brought in. Come on!"

Heller said, *"Santa Margherita."*

"Do you no good to pray. She sounded quite put out. (Bleeped) mad, in fact. Come along."

Heller got into a white sheepskin coat, buckled its belt and put on a white leather cap with earmuffs. Pulling on white gauntlets he followed Bang-Bang.

They went down the elevator and over to the 34th Street Observatory entrance which Bang-Bang usually used due to the large taxi stand there, apparently. It was Heller's usual route out when he had to take a cab. He started to signal one.

"Hell, no," said Bang-Bang, pointing to the old orange cab. "I'm driving you!"

"Won't that take you out of your parole jurisdiction?" said Heller, but he got in.

Bang-Bang two-wheeled the cab into a screaming U-turn and rocketed it westward. He was bashing other traffic out of his way and felt comfortable enough now to talk, evidently. He yelled back, "Babe ain't in Jersey today. The family just acquired the old Punard Steamship Line through a merger with our Luverback Line. And Babe cleaned house of their lords and sirs and ex–Royal Navy captains, the ones that put the Punard Line on the bottom. She always okays top brass. So she's over here today passing on the hiring of new ones."

"She say what she wanted?" said Heller.

"No. She just said to fetch you. Hell, she ought to be happy as a lark today. The family controls the unions and with this last merger of shipping companies, she now controls all seaborne carriers in America. There ain't a single U.S. port she couldn't close down so fast it would make even the fish blink. You wouldn't think any-body could run a little rum-running fleet up to such a point but she has. Organized crime made it in spite of hell. The Feds don't even dare breathe on us now—America could be paralyzed. Even Faustino can't object to her being on this side of the river today. And she's down there hiring some of the biggest names in shipping like they was gofers. And is she happy? No!"

"What makes you think that?" said Heller.

"She (bleep) near exploded my ear is what makes me think that. But she ain't been the same since Jimmy "The Gutter" got wasted by that God (bleeped) Gun-salmo Silva. So you watch it, Jet. Be awful polite. Say 'sir' even if you ain't spoken to."

They got over to Twelfth Avenue and up on the West Side Elevated Highway and Bang-Bang nose-dived the cab down a ramp.

It was the old Passenger Ship Terminals, long since fallen into disuse with the monopoly of aircraft on people-carrying. A faded sign, Punard Line, had a bright new banner across it, EXECUTIVE UNION HIRING HALL, Local 205.

What with drays and limousines and swarms of seafaring-type people, Bang-Bang had to do quite a bit of nudging to get them into the terminal.

It was a vast place, like a warehouse, in an advanced state of decay. Bang-Bang drove the cab over the stan-chions of a no-parking restricted zone and came to the foot of some stairs.

Two men, one on either side of the cab, materialized. They were tough-looking men: overcoat collars turned up and slouch hats turned down. They both shoved riot shotguns into the cab, one at Heller, one at Bang-Bang.

"Whatcha want?" said one. "Oh hell, it's you, Bang-Bang."

"And the kid," said the other one, stepping back. "Don't scare us that way. At least give us the lights signal. Doncha know the *capa* is over here today?"

"It's all right," yelled the first one up toward the mezzanine above them. "It's Bang-Bang and the kid."

Three men up there lowered their assault rifles.

Heller and Bang-Bang trotted up a flight of rickety stairs and walked along a sort of balcony that overlooked the mob and cars below. There were three lines of men formed and inching along past three desks. Half a dozen men in black overcoats and slouch hats were sitting at the desks, doing fast interviews. The desks had three signs: DIRECTORS, SHIP OFFICERS and EXECUTIVES. A lot of uniformed security police stood about, directing the foot and vehicle traffic. A busy scene.

Bang-Bang and Heller got to a point on the mezzanine which was above and just back of the interview desks on the floor below. It was glass enclosed.

And there sat Babe Corleone. She was dressed in a full-length, silver-fox coat and a cylindrical, silver-fox cap. She wore white silk boots and white silk gloves. She was seated in a big chair, intent and imperious. She had four bodyguards and three clerks near to hand. In front of her was a row of screens, closed-circuit viewers and computers, placed low so she could see over them and observe who was at the desks. The speakers near her were carrying whatever went on at the desks.

She didn't look up from her work. She pointed at a spot a few feet to her left. "You stand right there, Jerome Terrance Wister," she said to Heller, using his Earth name. It was ominous.

The screens were carrying views of the application forms on the desks and, from some data bank somewhere, records of the people themselves and a close view of the applicant's face.

Curiously, there was only one screen on each of the desks below and even more curiously, each of those had only one scene: it was Babe Corleone's right hand!

She would scan the applicant form, look at the face of the applicant and then glance at the record viewscreen where the clerk had the fellow's real record. Finally, she would either turn her thumb up—in which case they would hand the applicant a blue *Hired* slip—or she would turn her thumb down—in which case the applicant would be handed a red slip with *No dice* on it.

One of the clerks near her was keeping a big board and checking off positions as fast as they were filled.

The personnel selection was progressing with surprising speed.

It was interesting that some of the people she was hiring had criminal records.

The lines moved. Her thumb went up and her thumb went down. All of a sudden her hand went horizontal and flat. She was staring at the screen.

On the administrative-position application desk was the form of J. P. FLAGRANT!

Yes, there he was, down on the floor, standing there, looking pretty deflated, the Rockecenter PR man that was fired when we found and hired Madison.

The job being applied for was *Punard Line Advertising Executive.* The application form simply said *Former employer: F.F.B.O.* But the data bank record said *Account Executive, Rockecenter Accounts. I. G. Barben.*

Babe hissed something into a mike. It went to the earplug of the man at the desk below. A speaker went live on the mezzanine.

"I was fired," said Flagrant. "I will be honest with you. I hated the job. I hated Rockecenter interests. If you hire me you will do yourself a good day's work. I can even help you do Faustino in! I'll swear it as big as a billboard!"

Babe's hand did another movement. The thumb was sideways!

Two men in black overcoats instantly grabbed Flagrant, one on each arm. They marched him out through a warehouse door. The winter wind off the Hudson hit them.

They marched him right over to the edge of the dock and threw him in the water! In the dead of winter, they threw him in the river!

"*Traditore!*" spat Babe. "I hate a traitor!" When she had said "*traditore*," which is Italian for "traitor," it sounded like a bullet!

Babe pointed a finger at a clerk. He picked up a microphone and threw a switch. He said in a cultured voice, "Gentlemen, may I have your attention, please?" It went booming hollowly from metallic speakers the length and breadth of the vast pier warehouse, battering the thousands who milled about or stood in lines. "We are very grateful, on this cold day, that you have come to apply for employment with the newly resurrected Punard Line. What we most cherish is loyalty. The gentleman who was just thrown in the river was once employed by persons antipathetic to those who now own the company. If there are any others of such ilk, they can save themselves the inconvenience of a ducking by leaving quietly now."

Three men moved away from different parts of the line.

They were grabbed instantly.

Men in black overcoats and slouch hats bore them struggling to the dock edge and threw them into the icy water with resounding splashes.

A fourth man suddenly rushed out of the line and, of his own accord, dived overboard!

The clerk with the microphone said, "Now that we have gotten rid of those dirty (bleepards), executive hiring may proceed. Thank you, gentlemen, for your loyal support of the new management."

There was a faint cheer.

The lines began to move once more.

Heller was watching the water. A fish boat was pulling Flagrant and the others aboard. Heller was once more watching Babe.

Her wrist got tired. She stopped the lines with a flat palm. Then she extended her hand and a man rushed up and put a glass of blood-red wine in it.

She turned and looked at Heller, her expression as cold as the wintry river. She fixed him with her gray eyes.

Frostily, she said, "You lost the race." She let that sink in. "I have told you and told you, Jerome, you must not lose. It is a bad habit, Jerome. It is a habit that must not be tolerated! I know I have been neglectful. I know I have not always been a good mother to you. But that doesn't make any difference at all, Jerome."

"I'm sorry, Mrs. Corleone."

"And the newspapers are saying bad things about you, Jerome."

"I'm sorry, Mrs. Corleone. I don't know where it is all coming from. I . . ."

"Newspapers are very bad things, Jerome. You must not go out carousing with reporters. It will ruin your reputation. You must be very careful of the people you associate with. You must not consort with criminal types like reporters. Do you understand me, Jerome?"

"Yes, Mrs. Corleone. I am very sorry. . . ."

"Stop interrupting me and don't try to change the

subject. You do not have a single, valid excuse! You have
been a very, very naughty boy, Jerome. I am very, very
provoked. First you lose a perfectly simple race. And
then you spread yourself all over the press. And you not
only are ruining all your future but," and here her voice
rose in pitch and volume, "the mayor's wife was on
the phone to me for half an hour this morning saying the
most awful things! And all about you and your bad publicity!"

She threw down the glass of red wine with violence!
It shattered and splattered like blood!

Her voice made the room shake!

"THIS IS THE LAST TIME I WILL WARN
YOU! KNOCK OFF THIS GOD (BLEEPED) BAD
PUBLICITY!"

She turned back to her screens.

Bang-Bang must have detected a sign Heller didn't
see. "You better come along," he whispered in Heller's
ear. "If you stay any longer, she's liable to get upset."

They withdrew and got back into the cab. Bang-
Bang ran into a couple more no-parking stanchions and
they got out of there.

Heller was sitting in back, chin on his chest. Finally,
he said through the partition, "I can't do anything about
the publicity. But I can try something else. Bang-Bang,
what does Babe really like?"

"Babe? Why hell, just like all dames, she goes for
jewelry."

"You sure?" said Heller.

"Absolutely. Couple diamonds and they purr."

"Good," said Heller. "Take me to Tiffany's."

Across town they went and very shortly Heller was
standing in front of a counter being addressed by a cour-
teous clerk. Heller looked at all kinds of things, trays

and trays of jewelry on black velvet. He didn't like any of them. Suddenly he snapped his fingers with the force of inspiration. "Do you make jewelry to customer design? I want something more sentimental."

"Of course," said the clerk. "Follow me." And he left Heller with an artistic type in a design department. The artistic type thought he would need some help drawing. But Heller grabbed art paper and colored pens and went to work.

What in Hells? He was drawing the Sovereign Shield of his Voltarian home, the Province of Atalanta, Manco! Two crossed blastguns, firing green against a white sky, circled in red flame. Incidentally, I had seen him draw it before under the words *Prince Caucalsia* on the tug he flew to Earth. More sentimentality? Crossed blastguns? What was he up to?

In response to his questions, the designer said, "Yes, we can make it into a tiara. The shield will be on the front of the head, of course, gripped in place by the semi-coronet. We can make the field in diamonds, the guns in onyx, the blasts, as you call them, in emeralds and the flame circle in rubies. And set it all in white gold, of course, so it will not clash."

"How much?" said Heller.

They called in some others and after calculation, they could do it for $65,000.

Heller dug into his pockets. He only had $12,000 on him. "This is all I've got just now," he said.

"It will be ample as a deposit," they told him. "You can pay the balance when it is done."

"When will that be?"

"The Christmas season is coming on. We are quite busy already. Will a few weeks be all right?"

He gave them the $12,000. But I could see he was a

bit defeated. I hadn't realized that Heller himself was going broke. He told them to do the best they could and left.

I was jubilant. Izzy would soak up his cash. He'd never be able to pick that tiara up.

I hugged myself. The real jewel was Madison!

The publicity was having its effect. Not only was it assassinating Heller's character but was also stripping him of support from his friends. It was worth thinking about. As a direct knife and gun devotee, I was really getting my eyes pried open with what could be done with the media! And how marvelously painful! One could wreck lives just like that!

Little did I know that I had really seen nothing yet!

PART THIRTY-ONE

Chapter 1

I wished I could hold on longer to these manic states, they are so pleasant. But that very night, the depressive began to raise its ugly head.

I was running the TV channels looking for some good animated cartoons and I just happened to pass the program "59½ Minutes Too Late." And there was the Whiz Kid!

He had a little college beanie on his head and was holding a little pennant on a stick. He had stacks of books and you could hardly see the interviewer back of them.

The bogus Whiz Kid was telling the story of his life: how he had been lying in a crib, choking on his bottle, and had gotten this marvelous idea for a new fuel. But years of underprivileged decadence as a member of the white minority had deprived him of reaching toward his goal. And then one day, in a supermarket, while he was riding in a shopping cart, a book had fallen off the book rack and hit him in the head and it had changed his life.

He had the book right there to prove it and the TV cameras shifted to his reverent hands as he opened it. It was by Carl Fagin, a reprint of a reprint, entitled *Homecraft Series: You Too Can Make an Atom Bomb in Your Own Little Basement Workshop, or, A Visit to Graves of the*

Mighty Men of History. And there was a picture of Albert Blindstein. And the shaggy hair that had inspired him.

And then he showed a newspaper clipping of the remains of his basement workshop which had blown up and flattened nearby houses.

The canned applause resounded.

And here was a picture of his winning the soapbox derby by getting the daughter of a neighbor to ride inside and pedal on a secretly connected sprocket.

The canned applause resounded.

I thought, wait a minute, what is this doing on prime-time national? It was not nearly as good as the usual sex orgies on the rival channels. And then I remembered that all the Rockecenter people had to do was call the director of the TV network and tell him what to run.

But then the bomb burst!

The Whiz Kid pulled out a high-school yearbook and there he was in the fifth row of the choir! Buckteeth and all!

Worse!

A picture in the same yearbook: The Student Most Likely to Get Shot. Buckteeth and all!

Much worse!

Another yearbook. Picture of the freshman class. A circle drawn around a head with buckteeth in the third row.

Very much worse!

Another yearbook. A picture of the sophomore class and, although much marred by the printing screen, the buckteeth and horn-rimmed glasses were unmistakable!

The hands turned the book over.

Yearbook, Massachusetts Institute of Wreckology of just last June!

And there was his name on the cover: Gerry Wister!

It left me in a complete spin! So much so that I didn't even hear the rest of the program!

Something was going wrong!

An hour later, my search for cartoons utterly abandoned, I remembered that Bury had chosen Heller's identity and given it to him in the Brewster Hotel. Bury had ordered Madison to use this bucktoothed double and no other and that Madison had even had to make Heller up.

There was another Wister! A *Gerry* Wister, probably a cousin or some such to a Jerome Terrance Wister who may or may not ever have existed.

This clever Wall Street lawyer, Bury, had covered every trick! If snipers didn't work, there were bombs. If bombs didn't work, there were doubles!

But I still didn't get the full horror of it until, with shaking fingers, I opened the paper beside my breakfast plate. Hotels sure know how to ruin your appetite!

Front page!

WHIZ KID SUES M.I.W. FOR 500 MILLION!

FIRST SUIT IN UNIVERSITY HISTORY

Alleging that he actually was a student at M.I.W., the attorneys of the Whiz Kid—Boggle, Gouge and Hound—today filed suit against the university for 500 million dollars for defamation of fame with compounded mortal felony.

A stunned nation last night on the prime-time program "59½ Minutes Too Late" beheld the evidence itself.

> Never before have the sacred precincts of
> M.I.W. been breached by the slightest breath of
> scandal.
>
> A spokesman at Boggle, Gouge and Hound
> said, "We'll win in a walk. The honor of Ameri-
> can youth must be upheld against the denigrating
> connivings of the pillars of learning. This is a land-
> mark case. We will murder the bums."
>
> The president of M.I.W., who was not called,
> could not be reached for comment.
>
> In frantic search for opinion, this paper
> called Supreme Court Chief Justice Hamburger.
> He stated, "In an unofficial opinion, off the re-
> cord, justice must always get its just desserts. If
> called on to review the case, we will consider any-
> thing in writing."
>
> (See page 34 for on-the-scene, exclusive riot
> photos of M.I.W.)

I would have rushed down to get the other papers
but I didn't have to. The news vendor, accustomed to my
habits by now, had them piled three feet high on a cart.
Just as I feared! National coverage!

This Madison was making me nervous. You understand, my faith was not really shattered, it was just wob-
bled a bit. I realized that it was the size of the suit and
that it was the first time anyone had ever dared sue the
mighty M.I.W. that was making the news, and I hoped
the Whiz Kid would sort of get eclipsed in this.

I would let Madison have his head. Probably some
deep-seated strategy lay behind this.

However, the following morning Madison had his
front page again!

M.I.W. FIGHTS BACK!
WHIZ KID BLASTED!

In an exclusive interview with the president of
M.I.W., this paper was entrusted with an exclusive
message for the Whiz Kid.

"If," said the president, "Gerry Wister does
not drop this suit at once, he will be expelled!
Furthermore, we will cancel his Octopus Oil Company Scholarship and fire him from his job as
waiter in the college restaurant."

These strong words were uttered with great
force. The university means to fight!

The university attorneys—Fuddle, Muddle
and Puddle—today filed countermotions in the
state court, alleging that the accusations of the
said Gerry Wister were false, malicious and un-
founded on fact.

(See Photo Section page 19 for full coverage
of M.I.W. riots.)

There were TV shots of the riots in most of the news
hours. There was also a full-page ad in the papers telling
the listening audience to watch "59½ Minutes Too Late"
if they wanted to get the news before it happened. They
were really crowing over their scoop.

The other papers carried not only the M.I.W.-fights-
back story, they also carried editorials on the victim-
ization of American youth in their universities and
concluded, by and large, that they ought to be clobbered.

Yes, Madison was coming through. Heller had been
dealt another heavy blow, for the press was definitely

favoring the universities. They even showed the bodies
of some students beaten to death by riot police. A favorable sign.

I might have found even more favorable evidences in
my analysis except that that very night, my attention was
rudely snapped in another direction.

Chapter 2

I might have missed it entirely if I had not been
extraordinarily alert. I knew it was important for me to
pick up every possible clue I could about Heller. He had
an inkling, I am sure, after Connecticut, that I was out
to get him and even though I was not moving around
much in New York, I didn't want to run the slightest risk
of turning a corner and running into him. In fact, every
time I rode anywhere near the Empire State Building or
the UN area, I scrunched way down in the cab just in
case he happened to be on the street.

Thus, I had been making it a habit to rapid-scan the
recorded strips of the viewer lately. Ordinarily, I would
not have bothered with the night strips due to that
strange electronic interference around his suite, but after
Gunsalmo Silva had calmly walked up and knocked on
my door, I knew I couldn't be too careful.

It paid off!

I was amazed! Apparently Heller's rescue of Izzy
had turned his attention to the Observatory of the Empire State Building. I have never seen a man so interested
in soot. Who really cared what happened to the atmosphere of this planet? After Lombar had taken over Voltar,

he would make very sure there was no population left on Earth: Lombar had enough riffraff at home without a full, additional planet of it to cause him trouble. Probably at the most he'd put in a little colony in Turkey to keep the opium coming. So who cared about the atmosphere of Earth? Let them choke on their own soot or get wiped out with exterminator sprays—who cared?

Yet Heller had begun a routine. Each night he would leave the Gracious Palms dressed in heavy cleaner's clothes, carrying a bucket and broom, and have Bang-Bang drive him down to the Empire State Building Observatory entrance.

The last car went up at 11:30 P.M. He would take it, and with a transfer arrive at the 86th floor.

At that hour the snack bar and souvenir counter would be closed and the place deserted. And who, I suppose, ever stops a cleaner in a New York building?

The snack bar and souvenir counter are housed, with the elevators and staircase, in a structure which stands in the middle of the large platform.

He would go up on the top of this central structure and plant three new wind cones and take the ones left the night before and put them in his bucket.

Although the platform extended out widely all around the central structure and although even the platform edge itself was amply guarded by a ten- or twelve-foot wrought-iron fence, the sight of him teetering around up there, fixing those cones to catch the wind, made me quite giddy.

The area had considerable light, coming up as it did from the city down below and all about and from the aircraft-warning and other lights on the higher tower. But to watch him fiddling with wind cones on those buttresses was a lot more than I could stand.

He was catching soot specimens or spores or something. He was probably analyzing them minutely and making all sorts of valuable conclusions, no doubt, but in my opinion it was just plain silly. Crazy as he was on the subject of height, it was probably recreation.

So tonight, I almost didn't look at the viewer when the time came. But some keen sense that is bred into you in the Apparatus told me that before I went to sleep, I better make sure he was up there again and not knocking on my door.

Yes, he was up there.

He put the old cones in his bucket and put some new ones in place and climbed down to the platform.

And then it happened!

Heller was just about to walk down the stairs when an old lady rushed up to him!

She had a huge purse on a strap over her shoulder. She was dressed all in black. She had on a black hat and was wearing a black veil.

"Oh, young man, young man!" she cried in a high falsetto voice. "You must help me! My cat! My cat!" and broke off sobbing.

I went into instant shock. Falsetto or no falsetto, I knew that voice.

GUNSALMO SILVA!

He had used a woman's guise to murder the Director of the CIA and here he was repeating the trick.

It was HELLER who was the million-dollar contract nobody else would take!

Who had offered it? Not Bury: Madison was doing a great job and Bury wasn't even in town!

I sat there suffering. I did not yet have Heller's platen; I could not forge his reports to Captain Tars Roke back on Voltar. And Silva with his Apparatus training would make short work of Heller! After all, hadn't Silva

wasted the impossible target—the Director of the CIA—
plus two Russians, a dictator and Jimmy "The Gutter"
Tavilnasty? And for that matter, hadn't he even wasted
Babe's husband, the *capo*, "Holy Joe" Corleone? Oh, Heller was a dead duck!

There is a very heavy liability to being a gentleman.
That's why I never was one. For Heller, the gentleman, the perfect Fleet officer, was patting the "old lady"
on the back, saying, "There, there. What about your
cat?" Blubbering brokenly, the "old lady" was pointing
as she sobbed. Then, tottering along, she led the way to
the extreme other end of the platform, pointing up.

Sure enough! There was a cat there!

It was white and orange and black. It had on a small
red harness. And it was hanging by the harness from the
top of the ten-foot, open wrought-iron fence! The rods
curved in at that height and the cat was outside the fence!

The cat was meowing pitifully as it dangled over
eighty-six stories worth of empty space. "It jumped," falsettoed Silva. "It got frightened and it jumped!" To get
to it, one would have to climb the three-foot concrete
parapet and then seven or eight feet of spaced wrought
iron and then go over the inward bulge and reach down
outside.

Silva had obviously been tailing Heller and under
other guises had learned of this silly habit of climbing
things. Exactly how he was going to do this hit, I could
not even guess. To leave bullets in a body makes people
suspicious.

Heller looked up at the yowling cat. Then he backed
about twenty feet from the fence toward the central
snack bar and souvenir stand outside wall. There was a
seat there and beside the seat were two suitcases.

He looked at the "old lady" and then at the huge

purse. Some balls of yarn were sticking out of the top of the purse.

"Sit down here," said Heller and the "old lady" sat down, sobbing away.

Heller sat down beside her. "I don't have any rope. I need something to drop a loop over the cat from the top of the fence. Otherwise it might leap again."

He reached for the yarn and began, with rapid hand motions, to make a rope by weaving it. "A cat's cradle is what we need," he said. And he was quickly making one.

I vividly remembered Bury's warning about being kind. Here was an awful example. Heller was sitting next to death, complete even to widow's weeds!

The night winds blew. The lights of New York rose upward with a blue fatality.

Heller wove the cat's cradle.

The "old lady" sobbed.

Finally Heller was through. He had a very open basket on a long cord.

"Everything will be all right in just a moment now," he said.

"Oh, I hope so," falsettoed Silva.

Heller went over and stepped up on the parapet. He nimbly went up the inside of the fence. He moved over the top bulge.

With a deft cast he dropped the basket below the cat and pulled up. The cat's legs extended through the open weave but it was securely meshed. He drew it up.

Some sound must have caught his ear above the wind. Teetering on top of the fence, he turned his head and looked.

Silva was just that moment ten feet away, laying something down upon the pavement!

Heller saw what it was. A Voltar concussion grenade.

I recognized it at the same instant. It was one of those I had given Terb! It would make a fantastic concussion blast without a single fragment. It would blow Heller off that fence and into the depths eighty-six stories below.

Silva's hand left the grenade.

"And one," whispered Heller. He was going to count!

Silva straightened up.

Heller threw the cat!

"And two," said Heller.

The cat hit Silva in the face!

It was screeching and clawing!

Obviously, Silva had meant to withdraw behind the barricade of suitcases and chair to escape the concussion. Beating at the cat, trying to get it off of him, he backed up!

"And four," said Heller. I realized he knew that that grenade had a fifteen-second lag!

Down came Heller off the fence and onto the platform!

Silva was still fighting the cat. But with one hand he was reaching into his purse.

Out came my Colt Bulldog!

The cat was still on him, screeching like a nightmare.

Heller was swiftly circling. "And seven."

Silva himself was howling now, shouting obscenities! He began to hit at the cat with the purse!

The cradle burst!

The cat leaped away and fled toward the souvenir stand's open door.

Maddened with pain, Silva heaved the purse after the cat!

Silva crouched into a deadly pose, the Colt Bulldog pointing this way and that.

Heller had reached the barricade of the chair and suitcases against the snack-bar wall.

"And ten," said Heller.

He ducked down!

Silva spotted him. He knew better than to rush. He could not count on a lucky shot when he had just the top of a head and eyes as a target.

He backed up.

He got up on the parapet to get height to shoot down.

"And twelve," whispered Heller.

Silva fired!

The bullet thunked into the suitcase in front of Heller.

Silva climbed up higher on the fence!

He fired again!

"And fourteen," said Heller. And at that he ducked very low and all sound went off as he cupped his hands solidly over his ears and stuck his face hard against the suitcase side.

BLOWIE!

The sound even went through his protecting hands.

He looked up.

And there was Silva flying high into the air!

The wind caught the body as it rose, and there went Silva, soaring away over nighttime New York, but mostly down! Heller went over to the fence and looked.

It was only emptiness and blackness below.

He came back to the center. He looked around. There was a slight concavity where the grenade had exploded. Nothing noticeable. He went over and picked up Silva's huge purse.

There didn't seem to be any other evidence around except the grips.

Heller raised his head to the sky. He said, "I hope you noticed, Jesus Christ, that I didn't have much to do with that. But if I ever happen to wind up in your Heavens by mistake, remember to chalk me up with having saved a cat. Amen."

Chapter 3

Heller threw the purse strap over his shoulder. He put one heavy grip under his left arm and picked up the other with his left hand. He grabbed the bucket and broom in his right and moved through the door and into the souvenir and snack-bar enclosure, kicking the door shut behind him.

The elevator was barred off for the night. He turned to the stairwell and stepped down.

And there was the cat! It had apparently been inside and partway down the stairs when the concussion went off, for it didn't seem disturbed. When Heller went down the steps, the cat followed him.

But the distance from the Observatory to the ground is eighty-six floors. In fact, New Yorkers every year have a race from the bottom to the top, up these 1,860 steps. And Heller must have thought he was racing the other way. Six at a time, he was doing the closest thing to free fall down that stairway.

He got two floors lower. Then he heard a yowl behind him. He stopped and looked back.

The cat was halted on the last landing Heller had left, yowling and looking reproachful.

"Oho," said Heller. "Too fast for you, eh?"

He went back up to the cat, picked him up and put him into the bucket. Heller turned and started

catapulting down again. The cat put his paws on the
bucket rim and watched the descent with interest.

Heller emerged onto 34th Street. Bang-Bang was
there with the old cab. He reached over and opened the
door for Heller but his attention was on something way
ahead. He said, "They're prying somebody off the sidewalk on the other side of Fifth Avenue. What have you
been up to?"

Heller said, "Drive."

Bang-Bang U-turned the cab and rocketed west.
He glanced back. "Well, at least tell me what the cat's
name is."

"Drive," said Heller.

"Jesus," said Bang-Bang, "ain't nobody talking, not
even the cat."

They drove a couple blocks and then the cat started
yowling.

Heller said, "Pull over."

"Where?"

"By that delicatessen, of course. Holy blast, Bang-
Bang, don't you even talk cat?" Bang-Bang mounted the
curb and stopped. Heller said, "Now go in and get some
milk." He threw Bang-Bang a bill and then turned on
the cab's overhead light.

Heller looked at the cat. It had on a harness but
there were no marks on it. He found a string, apparently
too tight, around the cat's neck. Heller took out a pair
of snips and cut it. The string had a paper tag on it.

He looked at the tag. It said *#7A66 City Pound.* Heller addressed the cat, "Oho, a jailbird, huh? Well, don't
worry, we'll just remove the evidence and they can't get
you for complicity."

Heller took the purse and spilled the contents on the
floor. A jumbled assortment fell out, tangled up in knitting yarn. Heller began to inventory it.

"An obsolete Voltar Fleet grenade. An Apparatus Knife Section knife. Russian rubles. Travellers checks on a Panama bank. Assorted Canadian, Swiss and U.S. passports. A baggage check." He had his hands on packets of money. "And U.S. dollars done up in Turkish bank bands." He sat back. "This is CRAZY!"

Oh, my Gods, I recognized the money. It was *my* $100,000! How cruel fate is! There were the hundred big ones in Heller's hands! I tore at my hair.

Bang-Bang opened the door. "What's all this worry over the cat?"

"He saved my life. I'm responsible for him now."

Bang-Bang had half a pint of cream. He cut off the top of the carton and was putting it on the floor for the cat when he saw the money. "Jesus, Jet. Did the cat give you that?"

Heller said, "He's a very wealthy cat."

"Ain't he kind of young to have all that dough?" He was watching the cat tie into the cream.

Heller snapped open one of the suitcases. It seemed to have some strange things in it. He pulled out something that looked like a close-fitting jump suit. It had a little undetached label:

Proofed to 3600 foot-pounds of impact energy
CIA Test Lab, Langley, Virginia

Heller said, "Mysteriouser and mysteriouser. Items from all over the place: Russia, Panama, Canada, Switzerland and wherever, including Turkey and Washington."

Bang-Bang said, "That's an African-type cat. My aunt had one with the same white, orange and black markings. They're great fighters, supposed to be awful bright for cats. They're called *calicos.* Male calicos are very rare. Oh, yeah, they're also supposed to bring good luck. So anyway," he continued learnedly, "if you've got Russia and Washington and all them, you can add Africa. If that's his purse, I'd say he was a very well-travelled cat."

Heller was opening up passports. They all had the same face in the pictures but different names. He came to the U.S. one. His hands jolted.

GUNSALMO SILVA!

Heller covered up the type with his hands, leaving only the picture showing and turned it to Bang-Bang. "Who is this?"

Bang-Bang's eyes bugged. "Jesus Christ! It's GUN-SALMO SILVA!"

Heller looked back at the passport and said, "Thanks. I just wanted to be sure. But Gunsalmo Silva from where, for whom?"

"Sangue di Cristo!" said Bang-Bang with awe. "You just rubbed Gunsalmo Silva!"

"The cat did it," said Heller. "He's a hit man. Got a record as long as his tail. Wanted posters in every post office. And he just broke out of the slammer. So don't turn squealer on him: they could send him up for life."

"Gunsalmo Silva," whispered Bang-Bang, still in awe. "Top of the hit parade. Jesus, Jet, that must've been Gunsalmo plastered all over Fifth Avenue! You threw him off the Observation Platform!" he added in sudden comprehension.

"It's my word against the cat's," said Heller. "And he'll take the Fifth. But quit changing the subject, Bang-Bang. This bulletproof suit is too small for me. It looks like it would fit you exactly."

"Wait a minute," said Bang-Bang. "What's coming off here?"

"It isn't what's coming off," said Heller. "It's what's

going on. You know that rental costume shop up on West 37th Street in the garment district? Get going."

Bang-Bang did, while the cat, having demolished the cream, climbed up on Heller's lap and with a deep sigh went to sleep.

They halted in front of an old two-story building with a costume shop on the ground floor and, apparently, living quarters on the second. It was well after midnight and the shop was closed and barred.

Heller got out and forcefully pushed a bell behind the iron grate.

A window shot up on the second floor and a bald head jutted out. "Ve iss closed yet! Go avay!"

Heller stepped back. He called, "Won't a hundred-dollar bill open you up?"

"Dot iss a goot key! Down right I'll be yet. Don't noplace go!"

Presently they were in the shop. The proprietor was in a white nightgown and slippers with a black jacket thrown over his shoulders.

Heller handed him a hundred-dollar bill. "I want to look," he said.

"For a hundred dollars business iss so bad you can buy the shop," said the proprietor.

Heller was going through racks of all kinds of costumes. He came to a rack where everything was black. Black dresses, black hats, black veils. He kept looking at them and then back at Bang-Bang, locating a size. He pulled one out.

He handed Bang-Bang the bulletproof suit. "Go in that booth over there and put this on."

Bang-Bang, grumbling, did as he was told.

Then Heller handed him the black dress.

"Oh no!" said Bang-Bang.

"Oh yes," said Heller. "It's the latest style."

132   L. RON HUBBARD

Bang-Bang furiously wrestled into the dress, muttering, "What I go through!"

Heller now put the hat on him and dropped the veil over his face.

"Oh my God!" said Bang-Bang, looking at himself in a mirror. "If they ever hear of this at Sardine's, I'll never live it down!"

Heller gave the proprietor another fifty dollars. "We'll bring the costume back."

The man said, "Nein, nein, keep it! We got plenty like dot. Them we furnish for the funerals, yet."

"I hope not mine!" said Bang-Bang.

"Let's go and see," said Heller.

Chapter 4

In the cab, Bang-Bang said, "That cat is having an awful effect on you! Janitors don't ride in cabs and old ladies sure as hell don't drive them!"

"This is G-2 homework," said Heller, in obvious reference to his military class. "We're spies in disguise."

"Oh," said Bang-Bang.

Heller was examining the baggage check. It said:

Midtown Air Terminal
Overnight Baggage Check

He told Bang-Bang where to go exactly. The town was quiet. They reached the entrance Heller had specified and pulled into the covered area where cabs usually stood. There weren't any there. The place was deserted.

Heller put his cap down on the back seat and put the cat on top of it. Heller handed Bang-Bang the baggage check.

"Now, Bang-Bang, we're going to go in separately. When you hear me drop this bucket, you walk up to the overnight baggage counter, present this check, pick up whatever they give you and walk out through the underground passage back to this cab. If I yell 'Pizza,' you duck. Got it?"

"Did you say 'Drop the bucket'? or 'Kick the bucket'?"

"If there's any shooting, let's hope it's somebody else that kicks the bucket."

"I haven't got a rod."

"Neither have I and I didn't notice any in these bags. But I know this place. I am sure you'll be as safe as if you were in your own bed."

"You don't know some of the skirts that get in my bed," said Bang-Bang.

"They always shoot for the body," said Heller.

"Let's hope they know that," said Bang-Bang.

They got out. "Now, cat," said Heller, "you stay there. I don't want you hitting me up for overtime." He closed the door.

Bang-Bang slung the empty purse over his shoulder and entered the long, dark tunnel.

Heller, with his broom and bucket, skipped around to another entrance and shortly emerged on a mezzanine that overlooked the lobby. From it he could see the overnight baggage-check counter below and across the lower floor.

The mezzanine had seats on it. In one of the seats sat a very beefy man in a black overcoat and a black slouch hat. He glanced up as Heller walked along and then resumed his watch on the lobby below.

Heller looked the lobby all over. Only a couple of clerks. No traffic at this time of night.

He dropped the bucket loudly and began to sweep away.

Bang-Bang emerged from the tunnel and mincingly walked over to the overnight baggage counter below.

The man in the black overcoat leaned forward.

Bang-Bang pushed a buzzer on the counter and a sleepy clerk came out of the wire-enclosed interior, yawning and rubbing his eyes.

Bang-Bang handed him the ticket.

Heller swept away at the carpet, ignored by the man on the nearby seat.

The clerk found the item. He got it down from the racks. It was a large, brown suitcase with big metal locks. It seemed heavy. He wanted two dollars and Bang-Bang, with the empty purse, had to hike up his dress, fumble in the pockets of the bulletproof suit for his wallet and get out two one-dollar bills. He made it not very elegantly, but from this vantage place on the mezzanine, the bullet-proof jumper didn't show. Bang-Bang needed a lot of lessons in being an old lady!

The clerk relinquished the suitcase. Bang-Bang got it off the counter at the near cost of a sprained arm. He went tottering off toward the underground-entrance arch.

Black Overcoat was up with a grunt the moment Bang-Bang vanished into the tunnel.

With great speed the man went flying down the mezzanine stairs.

Heller with bucket and broom was not five steps behind him.

Why didn't the fellow look back? Then I realized Heller was running at the exact same cadence as the other. There was only one set of sounds of feet!

Heller was almost breathing down the man's neck!

They crossed the lobby.

Black Overcoat darted into the tunnel.

He had drawn a gun!

Suddenly it came to me that somebody had not meant Gunsalmo Silva to really collect that suitcase! I was watching the standard hit-the-hitter routine in progress!

Or was it? Maybe this was something else?

The doors ahead of Bang-Bang burst open!

Two men dressed like cab drivers rushed in. They were thirty feet in front of Bang-Bang.

Black Overcoat had a big revolver extended toward Bang-Bang.

Heller reached over the big man's shoulder and seized his gun hand. The bucket clattered to the floor.

"Pizza!" shouted Heller.

Bang-Bang dropped the suitcase and dived to the side! Heller's left hand was gripping a neck muscle of the big man. The gun stayed extended.

The two coming in the door dived for the suitcase. One got it. The other was grabbing out a gun.

Heller's hand closed on the big man's gun fist.

The revolver roared!

The one who had been drawing was flung back with a hammer blow!

The big man's revolver fired again!

The one with the suitcase flew forward, dropped it and collapsed.

Heller turned the gun sideways until it pointed at the struggling assassin's head.

BLOWIE!

The hat went sailing with hair in it.

Heller's left hand shifted to the overcoat. He snatched out a wallet from the breast pocket.

He let the big man collapse and only then let go

of the gun hand. Black Overcoat's fingers were still wrapped around the weapon. I realized Heller's own hand had never touched it!

Heller scooped up his bucket and broom.

Bang-Bang was picking himself off the floor.

Heller raced ahead and grabbed Bang-Bang by the arm and then, in passing, grabbed the handle of the suitcase.

They sped to the cab.

Heller threw Bang-Bang behind the wheel and the bag, bucket and broom into the back.

"Close that door!" cried Bang-Bang. "We don't want this blamed on the cat!" He slammed the cab into gear with a crash!

There wasn't a soul in sight as Bang-Bang sped out of the terminal.

Chapter 5

In a parking lot and a darkened cab they got Bang-Bang into his regular clothes. Then, burdened with all the baggage and the cat riding in the purse, they struggled through the icy New York night and entered the Empire State Building at the 33rd Street entrance.

A sleepy elevator girl deposited them incuriously at their floor and shortly Heller was knocking sharply at the door of Multinational.

Izzy put an eye to the door. "What's up?"

"We're making you an accessory after the cat," said Bang-Bang. "Come along."

They went to Heller's office, put the baggage down

and turned on the lights. The cat began to inspect the place.

Heller laid the new bag over on its side and was reaching for something to pick the locks when Bang-Bang stopped him. "No, no! Jesus, don't you never remember nothing I taught you? Never pick a lock in New York—it might be wired for a bomb! Let me."

Bang-Bang rummaged around in a case of tools and found some wire snips and thin screwdrivers and began to attack the hinges of the new bag.

Heller opened the two original suitcases wide and began to go through their contents.

Izzy came in. He had on a shabby old overcoat and a nightcap and his feet were bare.

Heller was picking up items and reading their tags:

Hydrogen self-inflatable balloon
for rapid escapes.
Certified CIA Test Lab.

Melting spoon.
When used to stir cocktails,
introduces deadly poison.
Certified CIA Test Lab.

Poison Lipstick.
Shade: Charming Carmen.
Apply to secretary's lips
and when she kisses boss,
imparts deadly poison that kills instantly.
Certified CIA Test Lab.

Suicide Kit: Take two before retiring.
The Surgeon General has determined these
to be hazardous to your health. . . .

"What are you doing?" said Izzy with alarm.

"We're penetrating the most closely held secrets of the CIA," said Heller.

"I can't get these God (bleeped) hinges loose," said Bang-Bang.

Heller reached over to the front locks and gave them a flip. The bag cracked open! Bang-Bang dived for cover.

Izzy didn't. He had already spotted something through the crack. He bent down and pulled the top wide. He said, "Oy!"

MONEY! The bag was jammed tight with U.S. bills of assorted denominations, neatly strapped with bank bands.

Heller picked up the corner of the big suitcase and emptied it on the floor.

A small mountain of MONEY!

Heller examined the bag for internal markings and false bottoms.

But Izzy sat down on the floor. His bare feet started scrubbing against each other. His hands, like talons, began to lock upon packets of money.

In a muttering blur of sound, as fast as the blur of his hands as he stacked it, the pile of packets, neatened, grew beside him. Then he was done.

"Oy," said Izzy. "Give or take miscounts in the packages, this is a MILLION DOLLARS!" He rubbed at his eyes behind his horn-rimmed glasses. He looked at Heller. "How do you do these things?"

Heller fished up my poor, misdirected hundred thousand. He added to it rubles and an extra fistful of currency that had been in the purse. Then he tossed all this on the pile. He said, "I have secret admirers, Izzy. They are terrified I might go on welfare."

"Did you draw this out of the bank? I mean are there any traces on it?"

"Nary a one," said Heller. "A totally untraceable donation."

Izzy was totalling again. "Oy, oy!" he said, "This means we only have $400,000 more to go to clean up IRS!"

Heller reached over. He pulled some packets off the stack. "Make that $410,100, Izzy. Bang-Bang is low on skirts. He was complaining just tonight." He handed $10,000 to Bang-Bang.

Izzy was doing plans and calculations. "I won't pay IRS. I will put it all on the arbitrage line, run it up and then pay those *goyim* robbers. The Japanese yen is dirt cheap in Singapore tonight and sky-high in Paris! I'll get right on— —"

"Wait a minute, wait a minute, Izzy." Heller looked around. The cat had gotten up on his desk and was sitting there eyeing Izzy very intently.

Heller handed Izzy a $100 bill. "Go buy this cat a blanket and a new harness and a dish and things. He hasn't got a decent spacekit."

Izzy took the $100 but he said, "You going to keep a cat here? There aren't any mice."

Heller said, "This is a no-mice cat. He deals with rats, exclusively. He's a very tough hit cat, Izzy. And you'll be very glad to know that I saved his life so now you have somebody to share responsibility for me."

"Oh, thank heavens," said Izzy. "I'll get him a spacekit at once, whatever it is."

Izzy was stuffing money into big plastic bags from the bar. He looked around to see if there was any more and then rushed out.

The cat, apparently having made certain that Izzy would obey, curled up under Heller's desk lamp and went to sleep.

Heller was looking at the wallet he had snapped out

of Black Overcoat's pocket. It had some names and I.D.
in it. He showed it to Bang-Bang. "Inganno John Scroccone. You know the name, Bang-Bang?"

"No."

Heller looked at it again. "I'm certainly in the I.D.
collection business. I've got to find out."

Bang-Bang said, "What really happened up there on
the roof tonight?"

"Hush," said Heller. "I promised the cat faithfully
I wouldn't turn state's evidence on him. His pawprints
are all over the place. So both him and me have got to
take the Fifth."

"Oh," said Bang-Bang.

The cat stretched and began to purr.

Chapter 6

The horrible sight of my hundred thousand dollars
U.S. in Heller's hand did something even more horrible
to my psyche. A psyche is, as all psychologists know,
located just above the id and, when overreacted upon,
bruises the ego. When these three things are already swollen from past abuses, there ensues what is called the "I'm-
going-nuts syndrome." A case of multiple frustrations is
likely to ensue, surcharging the blood vessels and precipi-
tating an epileptic fit.

All patients have their own particular remedies.
With some, it is yelling at the wife. With others, it is kicking the dog. I thought rapidly: if I did not apply first aid
at once, I might find myself in need of psychiatric help.
Drunkards often obtain relief by imbibing the hair of a

dog that bit them but I had no dog whose hair I might find palatable, much less one to kick. Thus, out of dire necessity, an inspiration was born. I had better look at some money. That, I was sure, would be the soothing balm which would interrupt the threatened epileptic fit.

Accordingly, with shaking hands, I went to my mattress and reached within. Some days ago, when Silva had come, thirty thousand bucks had remained in this hiding place. If I just gazed upon them and caressed their crispness, life might once more begin to flow through my higher nervous centers and make them less nervous.

My hand didn't contact anything!

I threshed it about.

Still nothing.

Alarmed now more than ever, I threw the mattress on the floor. I tore the bed apart. I took a knife to the box springs.

NO MONEY!

It was gone.

I lay down in the wreckage and had my epileptic fit.

It didn't help.

I banged my head against the wall. That didn't help, either. But some time later, I woke up and found that it was a bright day.

Coffee. Maybe several cups of coffee would steady my nerves. I managed to phone down and get the order placed. I took a shower and then found out I was standing in it with my clothes on.

By the time I had remedied this and had my pants turning into ice on the terrace, breakfast had arrived.

Unthinkingly, I opened the paper.

Buckteeth!

A two-column picture!

Madison had once more made the front page!

WHIZ KID SUES OCTOPUS

TEN–BILLION–BUCK BANG

The attorneys of the Whiz Kid—Boggle, Gouge and Hound—today filed suit against olympian Octopus Oil Company for a cool ten billion bucks, the largest malfeasance civil suit in history. Rockecenter attorneys, Swindle and Crouch, when reached, said, "No comment."

The financial world today was rocked by the spectacle of Octopus actually being sued. Stocks fell. Dow-Jones dropped 230 points. The other six of the Seven Brothers hastily denied connection and complicity but informed sources implied they would soon be added due to their inextricable interlocks and total control by Octopus.

The Whiz Kid stated, "Octopus cannot help but be included in my campaign to bring honesty and integrity into the way faculties discriminate against students. Octopus heavily endows M.I.W., which makes oil a party to conspiracy to conspire with multiple malice and breach of breaches. By cancelling my scholarship and depriving the college restaurant of my services, chaos has been caused, irreparable and condemnatory. If Octopus can callously deny students second helpings of rice pudding, the whole American way of life is threatened. Fascism will flourish and all will tremble at the tyranny. . . ."

Oh, there was more! And the vendor, knowing my habits, had a five-foot stack of newspapers outside my door.

The shouts and roars of student riots on the TV were so loud, I couldn't understand the news vendor who kept asking me for his money. I had to close the door on him.

Madison had blown it!

That was very plain indeed. He was obviously going to tailor the Whiz Kid into a deathless symbol of revolt against Big Oil.

How Heller must be sniggering this morning!

Although I loathed to do it, I approached my viewer. It was my duty and the way of the Apparatus officer (hard though it may be to always have duty as a goal). Besides, I was too shaken up to do more than collapse in front of the screen hoping that this did not reveal a diagnosis of masochism in me.

Chapter 7

Heller was riding in a public cab. By his reflection in the partition, I could see he was wearing a tan tweed suit, a puffed-out silk tie and, over it all, a cordovan-leather trench coat. Really elegant. I tried to make out where he was going by the passing winter scenery he seemed to be admiring so much. They were on some sort of a turnpike. He was catching glimpses of sunlit water to his left.

The Statue of Liberty! Way over there. And beyond it, back and across the bay, Manhattan!

Babe Corleone—he was on his way to see Babe Corleone!

Sure enough, they soon exited from the turnpike and

shortly were threading their way through the impressive high-rises of Bayonne.

He told the cab to wait and shortly was greeting a somewhat uncertain Geovani.

"She ain't very happy today, kid," said Geovani. "Maybe you ought to postpone seein' her."

"Can't wait," said Heller.

Geovani shrugged. He went to the living room door and knocked and then opened it.

Babe was dressed in a light gray lounge suit. She was pacing back and forth, the width of the huge living room, pausing to look out the picture window at the wintry sunlight on the park. She did two turns before she said, "Show him in."

Heller entered.

Babe faced him with cold gray eyes, all six feet six of her expressing a wish to snap at him.

"And what have you got to say for yourself today, young man? Did you or did you not understand me when I said to knock off your God (bleeped) bad publicity? Now, don't interrupt. Not fifteen minutes ago, on that phone," she pointed, "in this," she pointed at the floor, "my own living room, I have had to listen to fifteen solid minutes of the mayor's wife concerning YOU!" She pointed. "Now, don't interrupt me. I know you have some lame, contemptible, God (bleeped) cock-and-bull story made up to account for THOSE!" And she pointed at a stack of morning New York papers. "The only thing that was good about it is that she has a cold and can't talk very long!

"Now, Jerome, this carousing around with criminal reporters must cease. And it must cease at once! Now, don't interrupt me. I know I have been busy. I know that I have not taken the time to work and slave like I should to bring you up properly. But that is NO excuse at all!

"Jerome, the very idea of going to court is NOT done! It is not done at all, Jerome! It exposes one to public ridicule. It costs one respect! And you have got to get the idea you should be respected!

"Jerome, you cannot keep running around with reporters and running off to courts! Courts are crooked, Jerome. They are not places you should be in! Now, don't interrupt!

"Jerome, this is very wearing and tiring on me. I know I have been neglectful. But Jerome, you don't *sue* people you don't like. You get a proper heater and you rub them out. Only weaklings and fools and idiots go rushing off to courts. You want justice, the only way you get justice is to buy yourself a proper rifle, learn how to shoot it and, with a proper telescopic sight . . ."

"Please!" cried Heller. "Please, can I interrupt?"

"No. What do you want?"

Heller was extending a packet to her. It was wrapped in silver paper and it had a black ribbon around it. "I have a present for you!"

She took it, somewhat softened, but she said, "It will do you no good at all to try to get out of it with some *gingillo*. No trinket could possibly compensate for what I have to put up with on your account from the mayor's wife! I have exhausted my vocabulary trying to tell her you are just a good boy gone slightly wrong. . . ."

"Open it!" said Heller in desperation.

"All right," she said frostily. "Just to please you and spoil you, I will open it."

She shook a stiletto out of a sleeve holster and used it to cut the black ribbon. She knifed off the silver paper. She opened it up.

She stared at it.

She turned it over to be sure there was no mistake.

She looked back at it. She looked at Heller, her eyes round.

"The passport of GUNSALMO SILVA!"

It dawned on her.

She rushed to Heller and threw her arms around him. "You KILLED him!"

"Not exactly," said Heller, kind of smothered. "He sort of blew himself up!"

"Oh, you DARLING BOY!"

She drew back. She looked at the passport again. Then she said, "YIPPEE!" and went whirling around the room in a twirl she must have learned on the chorus line.

Then she sank down in a chair. "*Ave Maria*, 'Holy Joe' is at last avenged!" She began to cry.

Then after a while she bashed at her eyes with some tissue and began to stab buttons.

Staff came pouring in, looking like she had rung a fire bell. She held up the passport.

"Gunsalmo Silva is dead!"

They cheered until I had to turn down my sound volume.

She went over and showed the passport to "Holy Joe's" portrait. She reeled off a volley of Italian, telling him the turncoat was dead and his soul could now rest in peace and promising a huge Mass as soon as she could.

Then she turned to her staff. "Quick, quick, get Jerome some milk and cookies!"

She made Heller sit down in her own favorite chair. They got him milk and cookies.

Babe was planning a party and a Mass.

Suddenly she remembered. "I'm sure he will have a funeral. Yes, we must plan for that. Silva's funeral. He had a brother and uncle. Now, what can we do for Silva's funeral? A big floral display. That's it. In the shape of a black dog. Georgio, make sure it is ordered. Oh, yes. I will attend also. And I will think of some way to get the mayor's wife to attend. Now, what will I wear? White and scarlet? Maybe just scarlet. A scarlet veil.... No, no, I must get a better idea than that! Georgio, call my dress designer. Order him to design the most festive thing he can think of for a funeral! Oh, will this put the mayor's wife in her place. She'll come in something dowdy. Oh, do have another cookie, Jerome."

Italians! It took two solid hours before they even began to settle down.

At last, the important phone calls had been made and probably it was ripping all through the vast east and west and international Corleone organization that "Holy Joe's" murderer was dead. And just when it looked like the excitement was over, somebody called to state that Silva was in the New York City morgue and that there wasn't a single bone in his body that remained unbroken and it all started up again and this fact chased the other the length and breadth of the Corleone empire around the world. Telegrams of congratulations began to flood in on their basement RCA and Western Union machines from as far away as New Zealand, from ships at sea and aircraft in flight.

The coils of printout began to mound up on the floor at Heller's feet, Babe reading aloud every message, eyes bright, with animated elocution.

At length, Heller said he had to get back to New York to make sure the cat was fed. But Babe made him stay. Cats could wait. Young boys, she knew, were always hungry and she stuffed him full of lunch.

After he got through his third plate of spaghetti, he said, "There's one more thing." He took out of his pocket a card I had seen him remove from Black Overcoat's wallet. I suspected that that was the major reason he had come to Babe's. "Can you tell me who this man is?" Babe read it. She frowned, thinking. "Inganno John Scroccone? I seem to have heard it. I can't remember where. Geovani!" And when he appeared, "Put this into the computer and see what you get."

Geovani came back from the basement. "He's the chief accountant of Faustino Narcotici, body lice on a louse."

"Jerome!" said Babe, shocked. She looked at him. "You are associating with the wrong people! Jerome, you must continue to be careful of your reputation."

I wondered for a moment why he didn't tell her he had killed the guy. And then I realized that Heller really hadn't told anybody anything at all.

With a shock, I became certain he knew he was being watched. He was afraid of being caught in a Code break. The grenade! That was why he couldn't and wouldn't tell even Bang-Bang how Silva had died. No grenades of such power and type existed on Earth. That would have to be it. Any normal man would have bragged and bragged about it. And he was being so close-mouthed it was even slopping over into not mentioning the other three hits!

"Jerome," she said, "I faithfully promise to stop neglecting you. Blood will tell and you proved that today. But upbringing has a lot to do with it, too. Now, as a good mother, I should pay more attention to your vital needs and of course resist temptation firmly not to spoil you at the same time. You are so accustomed to my shameful neglect that you were even going to leave here, unfed, and continue to run about in rags like some street urchin."

She got out a pen and poised it over the snowy linen tablecloth. "Now, first, of course, you need a brand-new wardrobe." She wrote that down. "And then a string of

polo ponies—that encourages you to be a gentleman
when you hit other boys over the head with a mallet. Yes,
definitely polo ponies." She wrote that down. She
thought a bit.

Heller would have spoken but she sensed it and
shushed him with a hand gesture. "Oh, it's wintertime.
You will need some new ice skates." She wrote that
down. "And then, of course, it will soon be spring. So
you will need a new baseball bat."

Heller would have spoken again but this time she
shushed him directly. "No, no more racing cars. Not
one, Jerome. You may think this is harsh but my ears cannot possibly stand to hear one more word about racing
from the mayor's wife!"

She thought for a bit. "I was going to add the old
Capone villa in Miami Beach but you're getting that for
Christmas and I want to keep it as a surprise. Part of
being a good mother is not to spoil a boy all at once."

She checked her list to see that she had everything
down. She said, "Good." She drew a big circle around
the notes on the tablecloth. "That settles it. Now, with
your new wardrobe, you'll have to have something very
quickly for the Silva funeral.... A red tuxedo and cape.
Yes, that will do. It won't clash with my gown. Here,
have some more cookies, Jerome."

A faint honking had been going on, from out in the
street. Babe suddenly yelled, "Geovani! What the hell is
all that honking out there?"

Geovani popped in. "It's a New York taxi. He says
he's been waiting for the kid here for three hours."

"Well, blood of Christ, pay the (bleepard) off! You
think I'd send Jerome back to town in a public cab? Tell
Battitore to get out my limousine! You think my own son
is some kind of a bum? And you tell that Battitore to get
the back seat nice and warm. You want Jerome to catch

cold?" She turned to Heller. "Now, what were we talking about? Oh, yes. An increase in allowance. . ."

That was too much! Outraged at all this attention and adulation Heller was getting, I turned off the viewer and hid it from my sight. There is a point where even masochism pales.

I thought I'd better see what the radio and TV had to say about this "mighty deed" he was bragging to everybody about. I listened to several news broadcasts. Aha! Not a mention of it!

I stretched my credit with the news vendor and got the afternoon papers. There had been nothing in the morning papers. But in one afternoon one there was a little notice wedged in amongst the latest fashions. It said:

MIDTOWN
CONTEMPORARY GARB

A body identified as that of one Gunsalmo Silva by dental plates and fingerprints, was found in the small hours of last night on Fifth Avenue, apparently having fallen from the Baltman and Company roof. Silva was clothed in what had apparently been a woman's black dress. One wonders if this is the latest fashion trend now emerging.

That put things in their proper perspective. The newspapers never lie. They always tell the exact truth in things of this kind, and things of all kinds, for that matter. The Rockecenters and Madisons take care of that!

I felt a little better. I was no longer twitching and I didn't have to keep my mouth tight to suppress the tiny screams which sought to issue from my throat.

My lot was very difficult. I was broke. Heller and some unknown had robbed me. Miss Pinch didn't have a clue as to how to be a petty-cash cashier.

Somehow, trembling, abandoned and alone, I would struggle further along the sadistic road of thorns some people laughingly call life.

Lacking a crystal ball, I thought no further shocks lurked ahead, at least today.

I was wrong!

PART
THIRTY-TWO

Chapter 1

Sirens were sounding in the street. There seemed to be an awful commotion going on. Despite the cold, I went out on the terrace and looked down at Fifth Avenue.

Military vehicles! Drawing up around the hotel!

White-helmeted and -belted MPs leaping out to set up a machine gun on the corner!

I drew back. A movement on a nearby building caught my eye.

Snipers in white helmets and belts!

They were laying their weapons directly at this terrace!

My Gods, I gasped—the U.S. Army has discovered I'm an extraterrestrial! They've got me trapped! They're closing in!

I hastily withdrew inside the penthouse.

A thundering on the door!

I'm dead!

Bravely, as one walks the last mile, bare-chested to the bullets, already in so low a state I did not care whether I lived or died, I threw the door open.

It was a bellhop.

His face was chalk white.

"Is a Mr. Inkswitch in?" he said.

Life without money wasn't worth living anyway. "Why not?" I said.

Crash!

Out of the stairwell, out from around the potted

palms, out of the elevator, came MPs with assault rifles, running low.

They knocked the bellhop aside like he was a rag doll!

They burst past me!

They overturned the chairs, smashing them!

They yanked open closet and bathroom doors, leaping back with rifles pointing in case anyone came out.

They fired short bursts into mattresses!

They jabbed their rifles into clothes.

They raced out on the terrace with a crash of potted palms and took positions commanding the surrounding terrain.

An officer stood firmly before me. He was backed up with two MPs who had their Colt .45s on me. He gave a signal. An MP began to shake me down. He got my wallet. He handed it to the officer.

The officer looked at it. He held it to the light. He compared pictures. He gave another signal. A soldier grabbed my hand. He produced a pad and inked it. He got my fingerprints. He gave them snappily to the officer.

The officer compared them to a card he had.

In a cavalry voice, he shouted, "FOHwud, HO-o!"

There was a roar and rattle.

A cart of equipment was rushed in, the cannon wheels rumbling on the carpet and tearing it to bits. Three men were pushing it. They stopped it in the center of the room. One of them rushed out on the terrace and held up a chromium-plated pole.

Another officer came in. He knelt by the cart. He picked up an instrument. He barked into it and waited tensely.

The pause gave me an instant to read their uniform badges:

U.S. Army Signal Corps

The officer at the cart said to me, "This is ultra-secret. You could be shot for disclosing that you have seen a satellite-enscrambled decode-recode. Not even the Russians know we have it. Do you swear you have not seen it?"

I raised my inked-up hand and swore.

"Good," he said, "here is your party." He handed me the instrument.

A voice said, *"Alo. Kto eta gavarit?"*

I handed the instrument back to the Signal Corps officer. "Don't you have the wrong number? I think he just asked me who was speaking in Russian."

"(Bleep)!" said the officer. He got on the line again. He talked very fast and hard. Once more he handed me the phone.

A voice said, *"¡Diga! ¿Con quien hablo?"*

I tried to hand the instrument back to the officer. "Somebody just answered me in Spanish. I think he wanted to know who he was speaking to."

"No, no," said the officer. "You've got the right party."

I put the instrument back to my ear. The voice repeated, *"¿Con quien hablo?"*

"Inkswitch," I said.

"Ah. Espere un momento, por favor." So I waited a moment. It was more than a moment, but that's how the Spanish are. Funny, though. I didn't know enough Spanish to spot accents but it sure wasn't Spain Spanish. A lilting sort of speech like he was singing. Cuban?

"Well, that sure took them long enough!" Voice on the phone. New England twang. Bury!

"Where are you?" I gasped.

"Central America," said Bury. "Somebody killed the Director of the CIA and there was an outbreak of peace down here. I had to fly in to review treaties to see which ones could be broken. It's not too bad, though. They really have some great snakes down here. You ought to see them! But that isn't what I called you about. The matter is pretty high security so I had to bypass the National Security Agency. Besides, there aren't any phones in the jungle here. Is the U.S. Army Signal Corps still in the room, there?"

"Yes," I said.

"Well, tell them to move out of earshot. This is highly classified stuff."

I told them and they went out onto the terrace and into the hall, guns drawn and ready to defend their equipment in case of attack.

"The area is clear," I said.

"All right," said Bury. "I got a call about an hour ago on the facsimile satellite hookup. *He* was on personally. You know who I'm talking about."

Yes, I certainly did. I realized with alarm that Delbert John Rockecenter himself had been through to Bury.

"Inkswitch," said Bury, "you've let Madison get out of hand! You-know-who is hopping mad!" I could hear him shaking newspapers at the phone. "Raving, Inkswitch, raving!"

I chilled. When Rockecenter raves, governments fall.

"He kind of got it wrong," said Bury. "He thought the news said the kid was setting up a rival oil company and was violating family policy by introducing competition. It's that Miss Peace: she reads him the papers and she can't spell. So Madison has got it all screwed up. That kid is his client, not Octopus. Madison is out of his field, getting into legal. Justice mustn't be allowed to get out of hand. I know, I'm a lawyer. And that's the real catastrophe in this. We can live with most of this but one item in it really needs to be objected to and no overrule! And this is the real reason you've got to get Madison under control, Inkswitch. Have I got your full attention?"

I told him he surely had.

"Inkswitch, right there in the same news story, he committed a felony. He mentioned Swindle and Crouch along with Boggle, Gouge and Hound. Listen, Inkswitch: Boggle, Gouge and Hound are a bunch of cheap ambulance-chasers, and even whispering Swindle and Crouch in the same news story could ruin our reputation. It's a clear-cut case of attempted manslaughter. Madison has gone too far! It's pretty serious, Inkswitch. That's the real reason this call has got to be so secret. Do you grasp the need for a tight, unviolated lawyer-client relationship here?"

I said that I did.

Bury said, "Now, I can't call Madison. He'd just plead the Fifth. So you have to handle Madison. If you don't, we're liable to get a summary judgment with no reprieve. Got it?"

I said I certainly did.

Bury said, "Good. Is there anything else on the docket?"

"Well, yes," I said. "They changed cashiers and I can't get paid."

"Details," said Bury. "Don't bother me with details. Tell the Chief Security Officer. Say, you wouldn't like me to send you a couple of these nice snakes, would you?"

Hastily, I said, "I'll get on Madison right away!"

"All right," said Bury. "You make sure you do. I've got to go deeper into the mountains now to find General Hatchetheimer and get some of these peace treaties violated to get things going again. I won't be available for a while: I also want more time with these great snakes. You sure you don't want some?"

"I'll be too busy on Madison!" I said quickly.

"Well, give my best to Miss Agnes, (bleep) her."

He rang off.

I signalled the Signal Corps people on the terrace.

They blew shrill whistles. The MPs went into Red Alert.

They rushed the closely guarded equipment away.

Sirens began to scream in the streets.

With very precisely executed maneuvers, they were gone.

Utanc crawled out from under her bed, white-faced and shaking. She slammed and locked her door with extraordinary force in my face.

The hotel resident doctor was giving the first bellhop an emergency transfusion in the hall.

A hotel repair crew timidly came in and began to put the breakage together as best they could.

The manager appeared. He said, "There are two questions, if you please. A: Are you a Russian defector? Or B: Are you a member of the Joint Chiefs of Staff in disguise?"

I was kind of upset. I gave him the wrong answers. "It's no to both," I said, irritated.

"Good," he said. "Then here's the bill for the damages."

It was for $18,932.27 plus one expended bellhop, value to be determined later.

That decided me right then and there!

Chapter 2

First things first.

MONEY!

I would go see the Chief of Security at once. The

problem was how to get there. It is sort of suicidal to get into a New York cab with only thirty-five cents in your pocket. I knew better than to approach Utanc, the way that door had slammed in my face. I would jog.

Wrapped warmly against the cold day, I was shortly sweating and puffing my way southward toward Rockecenter Plaza. It was only a few blocks.

I turned at Saks and wheezed my way through the Channel Gardens, shivering at the sight of all the unovercoated statuary sporting in the iced pools, and finally got to the Octopus Oil Building.

The Chief of Security had his feet on the desk, easing his several stomachs after lunch.

I flashed my Federal I.D. at him. "Inkswitch," I said. "I have a problem of the greatest importance to the company."

He punched the computer and it came up blank. "What's the problem?" he said, taking his feet off the desk.

"Your Miss Pinch on Petty Cash Window 13 has not been trained on her job. Miss Grabball did not tell her the procedure in handling a family 'spi'!"

"Ho, ho!" he said. He checked his revolver, picked up a thick billy club and we were on our way.

I hung back. He went right into the cages like a lion trainer. He seized Miss Pinch by the shoulder and with a yank, hauled her into a back closet.

There were some sharp sounds coming out. Blows.

Very shortly the Chief of Security emerged. He said to me as he passed me, "That's the way."

I went promptly to Window 13. Miss Pinch was sitting there in her mannish clothes and thin lips. She had the beginnings of a black eye.

"Inkswitch," I said, "I want $20,000."

She punched the computer keyboard. It came up

blank. She made out a voucher and handed it to me to sign. I wrote *Thomas Jefferson*. She took it and carefully counted $20,000 from her cash drawer.

She put the whole $20,000 in her purse!

She didn't have it right.

I said, "Are you sure that is correct?"

"That's the way," she said with hostility.

I went out. Maybe she was just a bit rattled. I should give her a chance to get settled in on her job.

I came back in.

"Inkswitch," I said. "I want $20,000."

She punched the computer keyboard. It came up blank. She made out a voucher and handed it to me to sign. I wrote *George Washington*. She took it and carefully counted $20,000 from her cash drawer.

She again put the whole $20,000 in her purse!

I said, "Wait a minute, Miss Pinch. I don't think you have this right!"

Her eyes were very, very hostile. "That's the way," she said.

I went out. Maybe I was giving her the wrong figure!

I went back in.

"Inkswitch," I said. "I want $40,000."

She went through all the motions. Only this time, I signed it *Benedict Arnold* as a kind of threat.

She took the money out of her cash drawer.

Yes, she put the whole $40,000 in her purse!

"AND THAT'S THE GOD (BLEEPED) WAY!" she shouted.

I gave it up. I made my way outside and thought about it. I really didn't have any time to waste. If I delayed too long, Bury might phone again and I'd get another hotel bill for $18,932.27 for damages. I couldn't risk it.

I walked around a while. And then inspiration came to me. I'd go back and see the Chief of Security.

I walked straight in.

He had a pile of money on his desk.

He covered it up with his cap.

"So that's the way," I said.

I left. I rapidly walked across courts and down hallways I had memorized before. As a family "spi," I really had something to report. Crooked employees! I found the private door to the office of Miss Peace.

I knocked.

She opened it a crack.

I said, "As a family "spi," I have something about employees to report to Mr. Rockecenter."

I have seen a few faces twist in rage in my time. Hers went more so.

"You think I'd let you in here to spill the beans about me? Get out of here, you (bleepard)!"

I left.

None of this had gone well at all!

As I could think of no way to handle any of this on the spur of the moment, I left.

Chapter 3

How in the Hells was I going to get down to 42 Mess Street? It was far too far to jog.

I walked along a street. Suddenly, inspiration! I saw a cop car. I went up to it. I flashed my credentials. "I have to make an urgent raid on Mess Street. Take me there."

"We ain't no errand boys for no God (bleeped) Feds," said one of them with a hostile glare.

That didn't work.

I went up a side street. There were some cars parked. I relaxed. Crime was the best way after all. I realized I had become slack on this planet, even to the point of relaxing my Apparatus reflexes. I walked along beside the cars, looking to see if anyone had left his keys in the ignition.

No luck. I had heard cars could be jump-started but I did not know how to do it.

A few doors along, a moving van, huge, was standing. They were just taking out a sofa and carting it into a house.

Aha!

With stealthy speed I crept to its cab. When the driver and helper went inside, I leaped into the van. There were the keys! I started it up, engaged the gears with a clash and roared away!

Behind me I could hear some sliding. In the rearview side mirror, I saw that I was depositing furniture at intervals on the street.

Then there was a big crash as a grand piano went out!

After that there was a sort of banging behind me on the pavement as I roared along. I didn't know what it was. But nothing must deter me from stopping Madison. I might get another phone call or even a couple of snakes!

The truck was pretty hard to drive, being fifty feet or more long and being pretty high. But after many a narrow escape I made it within a block of 42 Mess Street. The street was too narrow to admit the moving van so I parked it. I found what had been banging behind me was the tailgate hitting the pavement. The grand piano must have busted its hinges. I got it closed. I walked the rest of the way.

The old loft was a beehive. Reporters were rushing about. Typewriters and telex machines were roaring. Outgoing mailbags full of releases to every paper in the world were being passed like fire-bucket lines through the window to sail down into waiting trucks.

A huge new banner stretched across the room:

THINK COVERAGE
AT ANY COST!

Another said:

Front Page or You're Out!

Madison was in the end office, so surrounded with reporters taking dictation I couldn't get near him.

Close to hand a reporter was bellowing into a telephone, "I don't want page two. I want page one! Look, Mr. Vitriahl, you may be managing editor of the *St. Petersburg Grimes* today, but you won't even be a copy boy on the *Smearwater Shun*, the dinkiest paper in Florida, tomorrow! You cooperate, you (bleepard), or you-know-who will be onto your board of directors to find a new God (bleeped) managing editor before dawn. . . . That's better. Headlines it is." He hung up.

The reporter was muttering over a dogeared notebook. He put in another call. "*Los Angeles Grimes?* Give me J. Blithering Bonkers, please. . . . Hello, Bonkers. This is Ted Tramp of the you-know-who organization. You didn't give us front page yesterday. . . . All right, all right. So your God (bleeped) managing editor's wife is head of the National Association of Mental Stealth. Don't cry on . . . All right. I agree that her embezzling the NAMS funds and running off with the head psychiatrist was news. But God (bleep) it, Bonkers, you got to assert your control over that board! Why the hell do you suppose you-know-who got you on as chairman of the Grimes-Smearer Corporation, anyway? . . . Ah, that's better. . . . That's better, Bonkers. . . . Well, (bleep), you don't have to shoot the (bleepard). Just make him put the Whiz Kid on the front page!"

The reporter hung up and got out some dirty tissue and scrubbed vigorously at his ear. "I can't stand slobbering!" He saw me. "Who the hell are you? You don't look dirty enough to be a reporter. You some kind of a spy?"

"Precisely," I said. "Tell Madison, Smith has got to see him."

"I dunno," he said, glancing at the mob around Madison in his office.

"Smith from you-know-who," I said.

"Jesus," said the reporter. He grabbed the handle of a fire-engine siren close to hand and began to turn it briskly. The reporters all rushed out looking for the fire.

I walked in.

Madison looked at me with aplomb. "Oh, hello, Mr. Smith. Fifteen point quote Madison Triumphs unquote! We've seized the initiative! And I'll bet you're here bearing rave notices from Bury!"

"I'm here bearing an axe, Madison," I said sternly. "You have trod upon sacred toes. You forgot that Octopus isn't your client so save your ruin for the Whiz Kid!"

"Ruin? Madison can't get it on the pica stick! What are you talking about, Smith? Mr. Bury gave me specific and direct orders to make the Whiz Kid's name a household word and to make him immortal!"

"He didn't give you any orders to PR Swindle and

Crouch!" I said. "You link them up in the news with Boggle, Gouge and Hound and Bury will have your telephone disconnected!"

That got to him. "Oh," he said, slumping. "It is so difficult to work with nonprofessionals. You don't really understand PR."

"I understand it very well," I said. "It's Confidence, Coverage and Controversy. And the Coverage in my penthouse today cost $18,932.27. And you and I are going to have an awful lot of Controversy if you don't get Swindle and Crouch out of it and if you think Octopus needs your PR. You mend your ways or you'll shatter my Confidence!"

"It was front page!" he wailed. "I have had the front page day after day! PR is like marksmanship! It's the number of times you can hit the front page! And Madison has been riddling it!"

"It and everything else!" I said. "Now settle down. Get on course and do what you're supposed to do! You repair this damage to Swindle and Crouch and Octopus! No more wild bullets slaughtering innocent bystanders! Get rid of these suits! They're too close to home."

"But PR should have a little bit of truth in it," said Madison. "It sort of spices it up!"

"I'm adamant," I said.

Suddenly he smiled. "Great! Absolutely great! I got it. I can see it now! Suits are only good for one day of front page. They usually sag to page two and right on down the drain. It doesn't change my general program."

He walked up and down his office, sort of dancing. I watched him suspiciously. He was far too happy for a man who has just been chewed up Apparatus style!

He stopped. His honest, earnest face grew sincere. He took my hand. He shook it. "Thank you for a great idea, Mr. Smith. You may not be a professional but I can

assure you that a fresh viewpoint is like warm air to the
overworked wits."

He rushed out. "STAFF! STAFF! Everybody gather
round. I've just had a GREAT idea!"

I left. A little of Madison is an awful lot.

Chapter 4

I had my own problems.

I was broke.

I myself had just had a marvelous idea. I was anxious
to get going with it.

I looked at my watch. I had ample time if I hurried.

At the corner of Mess Street, I looked about.

The moving van was gone!

Some (bleepard) had stolen my transportation!

Now I *would* have to hurry. It was far too close to
five o'clock.

With an anxious eye, I looked about. There was a
stoplight near to hand. An idea! I raced across the street
against the light, dodging traffic. I got alongside the
northbound lane.

The light went red. The traffic stopped. I raced
down the line of waiting cars.

I saw an old lady behind the wheel of a rattletrap
Ford. I grabbed the door handle, opened it and leaped in.

I snapped my derringer out of my sleeve and shoved
it into her side.

She gasped!

"This is a pickup!" I grated. "Drive at once to
Rockecenter Plaza or get raped!"

She let out a thin scream.

"Drive!" I said.

The light changed. Trailing a thin scream behind us we rushed north.

I looked at my watch. I still had time. But this woman was driving all over the road.

"Drive straight!" I ordered her.

"I can't see without my glasses!" she screeched. "Get my glasses out of the glove compartment!"

"Drive!" I ordered her with a jab of the derringer.

Erratically, following my directions, we got onto and raced northward on the Avenue of the Americas. We were within four blocks of Rockecenter Plaza but the streets were all torn up. It was like threading a needle.

We swerved and almost went into a construction ditch!

She jammed on her brakes! I almost went through the windscreen!

"I can't see without my glasses!" she screamed. "They're in the glove compartment!"

All right! Gods! Anything to keep from being wrecked. I opened it.

POW-SWISH!

I got a full blast of Mace straight in the face!

I screamed! I was stone blind!

She must have opened the passenger-side door. Sharp-heeled shoes crashed into my side.

Out I went on the pavement! Right in the gutter!

I heard the Ford roar away.

I fumbled around, hoping to find my derringer and take a shot at her. And then I realized that (bleeped) (bleepch) had even stolen my gun!

I got some tissue out. I tried to wipe out my eyes.

Gods, they stung!

I could see some light now but the day was all washed gray, without details.

I fumbled along. I was afraid I would be late. I couldn't read my watch.

Things were becoming a little plainer. A trick and novelty store! I staggered in.

"Do you have any water pistols?"

Dimly I could see four or five being put on the counter in front of me. "How do I know they work?"

Whoever it was got a glass of water and filled them. I grabbed one and shot myself in the eyes. I grabbed another and did the same. I shot another one up my nose. I shot the last one into my mouth.

I could see!

"They don't work," I said and rushed out.

The water glass shattered on the door frame as I left.

I sprinted for my destination.

I ran into the right hall.

I hauled up, panting and spent.

My Gods, it was difficult trying to get around New York! They were laying for you at every turn!

But thank Gods, I was on time!

Chapter 5

Right on schedule, tightly packed in the mobbed rush of quitting time, the target-subject was in view.

Miss Pinch! She was wearing a bulky, mannish overcoat. The target-object was swinging from her arm: her purse!

The flooding wave of workers crested against the traffic of Seventh Avenue.

Hat down, coat collar up, I had target-object in close view. An old hand at such campaigns, trained by the Apparatus to the keenest possible edge, I foresaw no trouble in obtaining target-object. A quick snatch, a fleet run, a stuffing of target-content into my pockets and a flinging of target-object into nearest trash can and victory would be mine!

I quivered with the thrill of the chase.

A $80,000 quarry does not every day enliven the spirit of the hunt.

I could see that the purse, black and hanging from her arm by a strap, was bulky, aching to be gutted by the skilled hunter. And after that, in victory, I would not have to steal moving vans or get hit in the face with Mace just to get around upon my duties.

Her masculine stride marked her. The heavy, light gray overcoat could not be missed. The gray slouch hat was like a beacon calling to the storm-tossed mariner adrift on the heaving and pitiless seas of New York.

She was heading, obviously, for a subway station. This gave me a sudden panic. I did not have enough to buy a token and get through the gate.

But fortune smiled. She was lingering before a newsstand.

Buffeted by hurrying humanity, I crept behind her. She was trying to choose between *Muscle Making for Men Complete with Full Nude Photos* and *Panthouse Magazine with Full Nude Cover Folds*. It seemed to be a difficult decision. She picked up one and then the other and then back to the first.

With $80,000 at stake, why delay?

With an expert hand from behind her, I removed

the purse from her shoulder with an expert twist!

I darted away!

I had it! I thought I would win after all!

What trouble it was trying to operate with untrained employees! One had to resort to such extraordinary shifts!

I ran.

Thinly, I could hear a police whistle blowing!

I must be being pursued!

With too much cunning for my own good, my first thought was to possess the contents of the bag and discard the evidence.

Masked amongst the mob, I plunged my right hand into the purse.

SNAP!

YEEOWWW!

A hidden something had seized my hand with agony!

I tried to withdraw my hand!

Whatever it was was also fastened to the inside of the purse!

In agony, I sought to shake the purse off. It wouldn't leave!

With my left hand, I seized the bottom of the purse and tried to pull it off my hand.

AGONY!

In extremis, I stopped and tried to use my left hand to free my right. I plunged my left hand into the purse.

SNAP!

YEEOWWW!

Something had clamped down on my left hand!

I had both hands inside the purse! I couldn't get them out!

The faint sound of the police whistle kept blowing. It was inside the purse!

A hard, smug voice behind my ear said, "I thought that you'd try that." Miss Pinch!

She touched the side of the purse with her finger and the faint police whistle went off.

But that was not all she did. She pushed something hard and round into my right kidney. A gun!

I was in agony. My fingers felt like they were caught in the teeth of a savage beast. Two savage beasts.

"I don't take the subway home," she said. "I live just a few blocks from here. So walk quietly and no yelling. This gun has a hair trigger. It is quite invisible to the passerby. Stop screaming. You are making a scene and I might have to call the cops after all. March along, Inkswitch."

I clamped my teeth on my lip. I somehow endured the excruciating pain. A bullet in the kidney does not help one's circulation a bit. I avoided it by walking.

We went across Broadway. We went north a couple blocks. We turned west again.

She halted me at a walk-down, the entrance to a basement apartment in an old shabby house that had survived the demolition of much of the nearby area. The steps were full of snow and garbage. I was seeing it all in a red haze of pain.

Miss Pinch pressed a bell three times.

Then she took a key and unlocked a wrought-iron grill. She took another key and unlocked the basement door. She gun-prodded me into a small hall. She shut and locked both the grill and the door.

"You can resume screaming, if you like," she said. "This basement is totally soundproof. It really is a find. It also has a nice back garden where one can bury unwanted bodies. So just be patient and do as you are told."

She kicked me into a second room.

In spite of my red haze of pain, the place gave me

a shock. She sensed it and said with satisfaction, "Interior decorated by myself."

It was dull red of hue. Instruments of torture hung tastefully upon the walls. Festoons of whips served in lieu of curtains. A huge bed occupied the center of the room, its four posts topped with the grinning faces of gargoyles. The carcass—stuffed, I hoped—of a dead goat hung head down in the corner. It was full of darts.

"Now just sit down on the bottom of the bed, Inkswitch." She assisted the movement with a prod of the gun.

"Now, I know you are probably provoked," said Miss Pinch, looking at me with slitted eyes. "Men are violent and unreliable. Therefore, we cannot begin upon the removal of the bag until certain precautions are taken. You might kick out."

With her left hand she undid my overcoat. She reached to my waist and undid my belt. I would have lunged up but it looked like the gun was going to hit me in the teeth. I sat back.

She pulled off my shoes.

She shucked off my pants.

She pried off my underpants.

A chain rattled!

She was fastening a steel cuff to my right ankle. It was held to the right-side bottom of the bed with links.

She clamped a steel cuff to my left ankle. It was connected with a chain to the left bottom post of the bed.

Miss Pinch got up on the bed behind me. She pulled my overcoat, jacket and shirt up over my head and down on my arms.

She then hauled me backwards to the center of the bed. From the right-hand upper post of the bed she pulled a steel cuff on a long chain. She put it on my agonized right wrist. She did the same from the left-hand upper post and put that steel band on my left wrist.

Going to the posts, she shortened the leg chains until my feet were securely fastened wide apart.

She took up the slack on the wrist chains as far as she could with my hands still in the bag.

"Now, I know those traps must be quite painful," said Miss Pinch, sounding very congratulatory about it, "but we will have to free them. But only if you promise not to strike out. Men are so violent!"

Begging, I promised.

Working on the outside of the purse bottom, she effected the release of something. She drew off the purse.

Two huge rat traps!

They had teeth and were gnawing deeper with every movement!

Standing very clear of possible strikes, she got the sleeves off the right hand and trap after she unfastened and refastened the steel cuff. She then tightened the chain so the arm was extended nearly to the right side bedpost. She repeated this operation on the left side.

I was naked and spread-eagled, chained face up on the center of that bed!

Miss Pinch removed her overcoat. She took off her hat. She smoothed out her hair before a mirror in a frame of daggers.

"You forgot the traps!" I screamed at her, driven by the agony of my mangled fingers.

"Everything in its own time and place," said Miss Pinch. Then she raised her voice and called, "Candy, baby! Come see what I've got for us!"

Chapter 6

The door to the back room opened. Mincingly, expectant, a woman, maybe thirty, tiptoed in. She was dressed in very frilly, very feminine, gingham clothes. She had frizzy, very fluffy, platinum-colored hair. She had big, round, black eyes. She wasn't very pretty but she certainly was making the most of what she had.

"Oooooo," she said. Then she jumped up and down and clapped her hands. "Oh, Pinch, dear! What wonderful things you do! And all for me!" She raced to Miss Pinch and kissed her passionately.

A lesbian and her "wife"!

Oh, Gods, what did they want with me!

Candy danced back and looked at me, spread-eagled and naked on the bed. She pretended coyness. Then she said, "He isn't very big, is he?"

"Oh, my darling Candy," said Miss Pinch. "You are not pleased."

"No, no, sweet Pinchy. Please let us not quarrel. He will be just wonderful! Have I offended you, dear Pinchy?"

They embraced with croonings of endearment.

"Take off these Gods (bleeped) traps!" I screamed at them.

Miss Pinch said to Candy, "I thought that you, just this once, might like to . . ."

Candy drew back in horror. "Oh, no, no! I could not bear to touch a man. What must you think of me! Oh,

dear Pinchy, how could I be so gross? Never, never would
I be unfaithful to you even by a fingertip."

Miss Pinch smiled at her indulgently. Then, humming a little tune without words, she moved over and, in
the most painful way possible, began to take the trap off
my left hand. Believe me, I screamed!

"Ah," said Candy. "Ah, dear Pinchy. Kiss me!" Her
eyes were shining.

Miss Pinch kissed her. Then she came back and finished the left hand with maximum agony. I screamed
myself hoarse!

Candy had sat down on a sofa. She was panting. Her
mouth was wet. Her knees were wide apart. She was beckoning urgently to Miss Pinch.

Miss Pinch grabbed her, crushed her to her flat chest
and then carried her to the other room and slammed the
door shut with her heel.

Through the red haze of agony from my right hand,
I could hear urgent beggings in the next room. Then little moans. Then groans of ecstasy. Minutes. And then a
gasping shriek!

What was going on in there?

More minutes.

A low muttering.

The door opened.

Miss Pinch still had her coat and shirt and tie on.
But she was nearly naked from the waist down. She was
breathing hard.

Candy was wearing only a chemise now. Her face
was red and flushed and wet.

Their eyes were hot.

What could they possibly have been doing?

Miss Pinch went to an Iron Maiden and opened it.
It was serving as a fridge. She got out some beer.

They lolled down on the sofa, drinking from their beer cans thirstily.

"Take off the Gods (bleeped) trap!" I screamed at them.

In a conversational voice, Miss Pinch said, "Everything in its time and place, Inkswitch."

"What are you up to?" I bellowed.

"Tell him," said Candy. "I always love to hear it."

Indulgently, Miss Pinch said, "All Rockecenter's companies have classes in Psychiatric Birth Control. It's vital, you understand, to reduce the world population. They breed like rats. And they're all riffraff. They outstrip the world's food supply which has to be reduced so food prices will stay up and Rockecenter's friends can make a profit. And, of course, that is the name of the game."

She took a thirsty guzzle of her beer and, without bothering to wipe off the mustache, continued learnedly, "Birth control requires more than pills and besides, I. G. Barben has no monopoly on them and there are competitors. So the answer to controlling world population is homosexuality. Now, if everyone was a homosexual—the men gays and the women lesbians—then there's no more population problem at all. The great work begun by the Rockecenters decades ago is just now coming into its own. Birth control training is now being introduced even into kindergartens. The competitors of Barben will go broke, as who will need the pills? There will be no mass meetings against abortions and even abortion is going out of use. The trend is overwhelmingly toward universal homosexuality.

"The Psychiatric Birth Control classes are wonderful. They were developed by Dr. Frybrain, the head of the International Psychiatric Association, on a special

FREE

Send in this card and receive a FREE GIFT.

Send in this card and you'll receive a free MISSION
EARTH POSTER while supplies last. No order required
for this Special Offer! Post your card today!

☐ Please send me a FREE Mission Earth Poster

☐ Please send me information about other books by
   L. Ron Hubbard.

ORDER TODAY

PLEASE SEND ME THE FOLLOWING:

____ MISSION EARTH hardback volume(s)		
(specify volume No.) _____ (each)	£10.95	_____
____ MISSION EARTH set (10 vols, hardback)	£82.12	_____
____ Vol 1, The Invaders Plan (paperback)	£3.95	_____
____ Vol 2, Black Genesis (paperback)	£3.95	_____
____ Vol 3, The Enemy Within (paperback)	£3.95	_____
____ Battlefield Earth (paperback)	£4.95	_____
____ Writers of The Future Volume I	£2.75	_____
____ Writers of The Future Volume II	£2.75	_____
____ Writers of The Future Volume III	£2.95	_____

SUB-TOTAL: _____

POST AND PACKING*: _____
* Add £1.00 per book for post and packing.

I enclose:

☐ Cheque/Money Order enclosed   TOTAL _____
   (Use an envelope please).

NAME: _____

ADDRESS: _____

_____

_____ POST CODE: _____

DATE: _____

NEW ERA PUBLICATIONS UK LTD.
78 Holmethorpe Avenue
Redhill, Surrey, RH1 2NL.
England

Rockecenter grant. And the Rockecenters, as you know, have always controlled psychiatry and psychology. What used to be called 'normal' sex is the real sex crime. And what used to be called 'sex crimes' are now normal. So if every student becomes dedicated, as psychiatrists are, to making all the perverts and sadists and homosexuals they can, then the long-term Rockecenter goal of shrinking world population will become a fact. So we are expected to make at least one man a pervert. And that's where you come in, Inkswitch."

"I won't cooperate!" I screamed. "Take off this Gods (bleeped) second trap!"

Miss Pinch looked at Candy. "How do you feel, dear? Ready?"

"Oh, yes," trilled Candy.

Miss Pinch put her beer down.

She walked over to my right hand. She began to remove the trap with twisting motions. I screamed!

"It seems to be stuck," said Miss Pinch with thin-lipped satisfaction.

Candy's beer began to run out of the sides of her mouth. She was starting to pant.

Miss Pinch gave the trap a more dreadful twist. I screamed my head off!

Candy dropped her beer can. It frothed in a puddle on the floor. She put her heels out straight. Her mouth was open, her eyes hot.

Miss Pinch was beginning to breathe hard. She closed the trap tighter. I almost tore my lungs out.

"Oh, God," panted Candy.

Miss Pinch tore the trap off. I yelled so hard I deafened myself.

Candy had her legs straight out, her head back. She was beginning to buck up and down on the sofa.

Miss Pinch seized her in her arms and, pressing hot kisses on her throat, bore her into the other room and slammed the door.

I could hear moaning and begging. I could hear an urgent scramble. Then more begging.

Then small moans.

Then a shriek!

Minutes passed.

A low snarling. The voice of Miss Pinch.

More minutes.

What were they doing?

The door opened. They came out. They were both practically naked. Miss Pinch had no breasts at all. She had a tattooed dagger in the middle of her chest. Her short hair was ruffled and wet.

Candy had lipstick smeared all over her face and stomach. Her large breasts were shiny and wet.

They plopped down on the sofa, legs outstretched. Candy had her head back. She looked quite spent. Miss Pinch was staring at me, thin-lipped and calculating. I began to be afraid.

"What you are doing," I said, "is criminal. You stole my money!"

"Shut up," said Miss Pinch. She got up and got two more beers out of the Iron Maiden.

Candy took hers and held the cold can against her (bleep).

They sat that way for a while.

Then Miss Pinch took a mouthful of beer and leaned over Candy and put it in Candy's mouth. Sort of mouth-to-mouth resuscitation. Candy swallowed convulsively. She began to revive.

Miss Pinch got some marijuana out of a can and rolled a fat joint. She lit it and put it in Candy's mouth. Candy, after a few soulful drags, sat up.

Miss Pinch took the joint and pointed it at me. "Have a few puffs?"

"Gods, no!" I said, already a bit ill with the growing stench of it in the room.

"Smart boy, Inkswitch. But I could get you in severe trouble by reporting to your superiors that you won't do grass. You know and I know that staying away from happy drugs is the fastest way there is to get demoted in a Rockecenter company."

I had her there. I didn't have a superior.

"I notice you aren't dragging on it," I sneered.

"Big H, man. All I ever use is Big H. And speed, of course." She gave the joint back to Candy. "But Candy here is a sweet and delicate thing. I only let her smoke Acapulco Gold, the very best hay. Her psychologist keeps trying to get her on to cocaine, but nose powder would ruin her lipstick. I know why he's doing it. The vicious (bleepard) wants to have sex with her. Straight man sex. A real pervert." She turned to Candy. "We'll get him on that bed there someday, won't we, sweetheart?"

Candy sat up straight. "I feel better now. What's this guy's name?"

"Oh, I'm sorry, Candy. I forgot to introduce you." Miss Pinch pointed to me. "That loathsome male creature's name is Inkswitch. Inkswitch, this is Miss Candy Licorice."

Candy hastily drew back her hands although no motion to shake had occurred. "I am *not* pleased to meet you," she twittered. Then she was off onto something else. "Music. Oh, dear Pinchy, please turn on some music."

Miss Pinch hurriedly raced over and opened up a casket. It was a stereo. She put on a record.

A low sound filled the room. It was coming from the

mouths of two devil masks on either side of a brick fireplace evidently used for heating torture tongs.

Wagner! One of his more stern, foreboding symphonic works.

Candy listened for a while. Then she began to massage her very ample breasts. The nipples began to stand up.

"Oh, Pinchy," she said, "would you think me forward if I said it's time we really began to prepare for the evening's sex?"

Miss Pinch petted her head and kissed her on the cheek. "Whatever you say, my darling."

I flinched at the look in Pinch's eyes.

Miss Pinch walked over to a closet, her naked body moving like a man's. She reached inside. She was selecting one of several somethings.

She stepped back. She was slapping a fourteen-inch rubber truncheon against her palm.

Candy was sitting up, eyes bright. Wagner rolled through the room. Miss Pinch checked the chains that held me spread-eagled.

Her eye was moving up and down my nakedness with calculating selection.

Candy had her legs apart. She was all bright attention.

Miss Pinch chose the sole of my foot.

WHACK!

"Go ahead and scream," said Miss Pinch. "It's no good without screaming."

I vowed I wouldn't give her that satisfaction. I clenched my teeth.

She aimed for my foot again.

WHAP!

The pain shot through me. It stung!

She moved up the side of the bed. She turned on a red light that put me in a spot.

She chose my stomach.

SPLAT!

Then she got to work.

Teeth bared, laying on with all her might, she began to hit my body everywhere!

She hit my (bleeps).

I screamed!

Candy was panting. Miss Pinch's eyes glared with hate. The rubber truncheon rose and fell in rhythm to Wagner.

Agony!

I screamed and screamed and screamed!

Miss Pinch had descended now to fists!

Candy was whimpering. "Pinchy, Pinchy, Pinchy! Oh, my God, Pinchy, take me, take me quick!"

Miss Pinch whirled. She seized Candy's nakedness in her arms. She raced with her into the other room and slammed the door behind her.

Gibbering moans. Then shrieks and shrieks and shrieks!

Silence. Had Miss Pinch killed her?

At length, a low snarling. It sounded like curses.

Then silence.

Minutes later, the door opened. Miss Pinch came in carrying Candy. She dumped her on the sofa and then got down and began to massage her wrists and ankles.

Candy came to and flung her arms around Miss Pinch's neck.

Miss Pinch said to me, "You're a dirty (bleepard), Inkswitch. You have an evil mind. Get your lustful eyes off this poor, innocent girl."

Miss Pinch had some beer and Candy had a joint.

After a while Candy said, "Music. I must have some more music, dear Pinchy."

Miss Pinch found *A Night on Bare Mountain*. The awesome strains were shortly coming through the devil masks.

Oh, Gods, they were going to do it again!

The truncheon was even worse!

I passed out.

When I came to a long time later, they were on the couch again but Candy was collapsed on her knees, her hair against Miss Pinch's lean belly.

"Ah," said Miss Pinch. "Decided to stop faking, did you?" She spat at me.

The music had run out. But the beer and marijuana hadn't.

After a while, Candy was stroking Miss Pinch's hair. She said, "Music. I must have music. Dear Pinchy, something soulful, please."

Miss Pinch found a medley of death marches and put them on. Then she went and found an even bigger truncheon.

I didn't even wait for her to hit. I passed out cold to the mournful strains of a dirge. From way off somewhere I could sense the slaps and thuds of blows against my body in funereal cadence.

It was probably hours later that I came to.

Candy's body was draped across the end of the sofa. She had designs drawn on her in lipstick. Her hands flopped over on the floor. Her mouth, wet and smeared, was half-open in sleep.

But Miss Pinch looked deadlier than ever. She saw I had come to. She stood up and with her feet apart and hands on her hips, she said, "You owe me an apology."

That was enough to startle me into total wariness.

"You thought I stole your money. I could tell. When I put the last wad in my purse, I knew that that was what you were thinking. Now admit it."

I wasn't going to talk. But she reached down toward the floor and picked up a truncheon.

"Yes," I said. "And I thought you'd given part of it to the Chief of Security."

"Hogger? Why, how could you think that of Chief Hogger? Believe me, Inkswitch, you won't go far in a Rockecenter company thinking lies about the very pillars on which it is built! He's an honest man. Did he say something?"

"He had a pile of money on his desk," I said.

"Oh, that was probably his collections from drug sales to staff. He has the pusher monopoly for the Octopus Building and you better be careful not to buy from anybody else. How could you think evil of such a fine man?"

She looked up and down my bruised and naked body with disgust. "Men are all evil. You prove it. No, Inkswitch, you have not been the victim of any skulduggery. Your entire $80,000 is right here."

Miss Pinch went over to her discarded overcoat. She began to take packets of money out of the inside pockets. She stacked it up on a table with skulls on each of its four corners. Then she began to flutter it down over my body, a shower of floating, settling bank notes until they covered my thighs.

Then she took out something else. A small sheaf. She came over and leaned her naked chest close above mine. She was holding a piece of paper.

"These are copies of the actual receipts in my office," she said. "Knowing what you would do, I ran off the duplicates I am showing you here. Now, three of these, as you can see, are just vouchers, copies of the ones you signed. But look at these other ones."

I looked. What a strange receipt. Superimposed on it was a picture of my face from below and in the corner, a fingerprint.

"Few know," said Miss Pinch through thin lips, "that there is a camera below the signing ledge. It shoots a picture of the face seen through the voucher and makes them both one. And few know that the pen that people are handed at Window 13 takes a fingerprint and relays it with electronic scan to make it part of the receipt. So the receipt is a composite of money, date, face and fingerprint. The name you sign it with doesn't matter."

"You mean Rockecenter . . ."

"Oh, no, no, no, not that idiot," said Miss Pinch. "Miss Grabball had this installed herself. A refinement of the system. These face-and-fingerprint ones don't go in company files. You thought I was untrained. But she showed me exactly how to work it."

She smiled evilly at me and dug an elbow into my bruised and naked chest. "It's quite clever. It's how Miss Grabball could pick up half of all the petty cash issued. You see, all she had to do, if there was a squawk, was threaten to report the withdrawal to IRS. Unreported income gets three years in a Federal prison. Minimum. And the person who spots the unreported income and tells IRS gets 10 to 20 percent of the money."

She slapped at me and smiled. "So you see, Inkswitch, you are very much in my power. Miss Grabball liked money. I like other things. I have refined the system. If you don't do exactly what I say, I can send you to a Federal pen for three years just like that. And be rewarded in the bargain with 10 to 20 percent of it, all legal. Miss Grabball was deficient in imagination, even though cunning in her way. Using this system, I can blackmail half the employees of Octopus. And get far more in favors and money than Miss Grabball ever dreamed of."

She got up. She stood there naked in the red light. She picked up handfuls of money and showered them down on me. They floated eerily this way and that, settling on and around my bruised nakedness. She was humming a little wordless tune.

At length she said, "So it's all your money, Inkswitch. Every bit of it. Isn't it lovely?" She smeared some against my body and injured thighs.

Then, in a hurricane of motion, she gathered it all up and stuffed it in a big white bag. She put the bag in the lower part of the casket. When she closed the door I saw it was really a safe. She gave the combination a spin.

Then she came back to the bed. "Only I know the combination to that safe. And it can't be beaten out of me. So there's your money, Inkswitch."

She stood there, legs apart, shameless. She held out one hand. It had a hundred-dollar bill in it. "This," she said, "will pay your taxi fare home. It will also pay your taxi fare back here again, tomorrow night."

She dropped the bill on me in contempt. "And maybe," she said, "tomorrow night, I may take pity on you and give you even more of your money."

I gazed at this monster in horror!

"Now promise, if I let you loose right now, you won't kick up a fuss."

I wanted to kill her and she could see it.

"There's a bank camera up in that corner of the room," she said, "so don't get any ideas about murder. Promise?"

What could I do? I promised.

She undid the wrist and ankle cuffs. As I rose, aching and wounded, she kicked my clothes toward me.

I dressed. I picked up the hundred-dollar bill.

"One more thing," this vicious (bleepch) said, "if you come near Window 13 again, I will simply fire off the counter shotgun and say it accidentally discharged. The only place you're going to get any money, Inkswitch, is right here."

She opened the front door and wrought-iron grate. She stood there, naked and thin-lipped in the icy blast. "The first time you came to my window, Inkswitch, I told you to beat it. I didn't think you'd last. But due to Psychiatric Birth Control, all the males around have lately turned into gays to help cut down world population. And I refuse to risk the danger of separating two dear gays. So you're better than nothing, Inkswitch. Although not much. So I will see you right here tomorrow night. It's better than three years in a Federal pen. The homos there would murder you. Don't be late."

I would have slapped her but my fingers were too sore.

I staggered outside into the cold and cheerless night.

But I was not without hope, no matter if dim. The next time I saw this (bleepch) I would kill her.

Chapter 7

I awoke in a world that was against me.

The repairers had patched up the penthouse. My baggage had not been sitting in the lobby so I had to assume that Utanc had paid the damages bill.

The resident doctor, with a midnight "Tch, tch, tch. We must learn we must not let our fingers stray," had patched up my hands.

Right now, a December sun was streaming in the French doors, closed upon the wintry terrace. It was hurting my eyes.

Working as well as I could with cotton-thickened hands, I pushed down the sheet. The bruises had not yet turned as blue and yellow as I knew they would. I felt like I had been mistaken for a piece of pavement and run over by a steamroller. That feeling was confirmed whenever I moved.

But an Apparatus officer is made of stern stuff. I still had a pair of guns. They were black-powder duelling pistols, a pair. I had picked them up cheap one day, thinking they were originals. They were just replicas, modernly built on an 1810 pattern. They were flintlock. They had nine-inch barrels. They were .50 caliber and that half-inch slug could almost cut a body in half. Clumsily, since my bandages were in the way, I cocked and snapped each one. Very gratifying sparks! Powder and balls were in the case. Grunting and hurting my fingers, I got them loaded with enough charge to kill an elephant. That done, I got on to less important things.

I showered as best I could. Every drop inflicted near mortal injury. I got the bandages wet. I had to dry them by holding my hands in the gas fireplace. I was encouraged. They only caught fire twice.

Moaning a bit at the pain of holding the phone, I ordered breakfast.

And with it, of course, came that Gods (bleeped) morning paper.

Masochism knows no limits.

I opened it. There it was, front page:

WHIZ KID
COURT TRIUMPH

In a startling development, the Whiz Kid has won his court battle with M.I.W.

Boggle, Gouge and Hound, today announced that in the case of Wister vs. Massachusetts Institute of Wreckology, an instant out-of-court settlement had been reached for an undisclosed amount.

The president of M.I.W. himself verified that Wister was back in class and on the job in the restaurant.

Student riots ceased at once.

(See photos page 23, "Victorious Students Flood Back to Classes Throughout Nation.")

Speculation was rife in court circles as to the amount of settlement. Herman T. Guesswinkle, the noted astrologer, placed it in the millions. . . .

I slammed the paper down—and hurt my hands. That (bleeping) Madison had followed orders. He had gotten rid of at least one suit. But he had done it in such a way as to make the Whiz Kid a hero! (Bleep), Bury had been wrong about Madison. The man was far worse than I or anyone else had thought!

Somehow, I got the doorknob to open. A stack of papers from the news vendor fell in. I kicked them and hurt my foot.

I did not turn on the TV. I did not—could not actually—manage the radio. I knew what I would find. Whiz Kid, Whiz Kid, Whiz Kid. Jesus!

Life was much too much for me.

I went back to bed.

About four in the afternoon, the ringing phone woke me up. Using two hands, I got it to my ear.

A gruff voice said, "Inkswitch?"

I grunted, "Yes."

"This is the local Internal Revenue Service office, Inkswitch. We were just making sure we had your correct address." He hung up.

I swung off the bed. Ouch.

That (bleeped) Miss Pinch! If I didn't show up, the message was very clear! She would turn me in! It had to be her. She would have this address or could get it if she dug enough into Octopus Personnel. How else would IRS be interested? I had never filed a return in my life!

Nothing for it. Miss Pinch had to die. Both she and Candy Licorice. I would have to recover those receipts. I had better figure how to blow up the safe.

I got dressed as best I could.

I had not brought much in the way of explosives for such purposes. I took all I had. I put it in the pockets of my overcoat. I also stuffed the duelling pistols in, one on each side.

I hobbled down and got a cab. I had it drop me a block away from Miss Pinch's apartment.

Since it was winter, it was dark already. The rush hour had ebbed. I limped along the darkened street with grim determination.

The basement areaway was pitch black. I had to feel my way along. I took out the right-hand duelling pistol. I cocked it. I pressed its cavernous muzzle against the bell. I stood back.

I wished they had known about silencers in 1810. This was going to make an awful roar!

I could hear someone coming in the hall inside. A thread of light. It was Candy in her gingham frills. I knew I had made an error. I should have rung three times. That was probably the signal for Miss Pinch. She had used it before.

This time the signal for Miss Pinch was Candy undoing the inside latch.

BONK!

A blackjack hit me in the head from behind!

At least, I think it must have been a blackjack.

I went out with stars exploding all around me. I heard the duelling pistol fall.

Miss Pinch had been standing in the areaway's blackness waiting for me to ring the bell, facing away from her!

That was all I knew just then.

When I awoke, all my clothes were off. I was chained, spread-eagled on the bed, bandaged hands offering no resistance.

Miss Pinch, fully clothed in a mannish suit complete with slouch hat and bow tie, was standing there looking at me.

"Inkswitch," said Miss Pinch, seeing I had now come to. "I have just voted you the top jackass of the year. And we'll soon see how loud you bray."

She reached for the brace of duelling pistols lying on the casket with the explosives from my overcoat. She spun them expertly, one in each hand. She pulled back the mammoth flintlock hammers. She pointed them at me, one at my head, the other at my belly.

She pulled both triggers!

A flash of sparks!

She laughed gaily.

"You forgot to prime them, Inkswitch. Not a single grain of powder in the priming pans!"

It seemed to amuse her mightily. She cocked them once more. She held them very close to my side. She pulled the trigger of the left-hand pistol!

A shower of sparks scorched into my skin. I bit my lips. I would not scream. That's what set these idiots off!

Candy was peeking through the door of the inner room. "May I come in? Now that I won't see him undressing?"

"Come in, sweetheart," said Miss Pinch.

"Ooo!" said Candy. "Its body is all black and blue!"

"Colored meat," said Miss Pinch. "We're going to have colored meat tonight. Now, do you want a drumstick or a wing, you dear girl?"

Candy flinched. "Oh, horrors! Are you trying to suggest that I actually touch a man? You know that is forbidden to us by the instructor. The thought is horrible to me!"

Miss Pinch was quite disturbed she had upset her. She stroked her soothingly. "I promise to stand by Psychiatric Birth Control teachings." Then she had a bright idea. She was very anxious to please. "Watch this!"

She turned the cocked pistol upside down. Too late to yell, I saw powder trickling from the touch hole into the pan!

She pulled the trigger!

BLAM!

The gout of red flame shot across my stomach!

The heavy bullet plowed into the wall. Down came a display of knives!

Black-powder smoke rolled through the room.

That powder burned! The sparks began to eat into my flesh. I could not reach them to beat them out.

I screamed! I was so deafened for the moment I could hardly hear myself. Then after a bit my hearing returned.

Neither of those monsters was in shock.

Candy, panting and hot-eyed, was hauling at Miss

Pinch and trying to yank down her own clothes at the same time. "Pinchy, Pinchy. Take me!"

Miss Pinch looked at her. "So soon?" She looked back at me reluctantly. But Candy was kissing her passionately. "All right," said Miss Pinch. She grabbed her, carried her off to the other room and slammed the door.

Moans, groans and shrieks.

Silence.

Low, savage muttering.

Silence.

At least I had had a half-hour reprieve.

Miss Pinch came out. She still had her shoes on. She stood and cursed me. She called me every vile name I had ever heard of and some that I hadn't.

Finally she ran out of vitriol. She sat down on the couch. "Men!" she said, with burning contempt. "Torturers of women!"

"Miss Pinch," I said, "I think you have a psychological problem. I think, perhaps, some childhood experience may have caused you to reverse roles with..." I couldn't think of a thing that would account for this monster!

"Well, go on, Inkswitch. Let's hear some juicy tales about you and the little girls in the neighborhood. Possibly gay little anecdotes of how you threw them on a beach of pointed rocks and did a frolicking dance on their faces! Or perhaps how you had a little sister that you carefully made into a whore. Oh, I'm sure you could tell us lots of stories. We would not be amused. For such crimes, Inkswitch, you should be beaten! You will be beaten, Inkswitch!" She turned.

"Candy!" she yelled into the other room. "The (bleepard) just confessed! Come in here!"

Candy came out. She was naked. She watched with interest while Miss Pinch got a big truncheon.

"Now," said Miss Pinch. "You're going to hear some real screams, you darling girl."

"I don't have a sister!" I yelled.

"You will when I get through with you," said Miss Pinch. And laid on with a will. She drew back at last. "Now confess! Did you make your little sister into a whore?"

I confessed hurriedly that I had.

"Then this beating is going to do you lots of good," said Miss Pinch and began in earnest!

It must have been nearing midnight. They had depleted the record cabinet. The room was full of marijuana smoke. They were both naked and exhausted after numerous trips to the other room.

Miss Pinch unchained me. I somehow got into my clothes.

She stood naked in the hall, holding the door open, oblivious to the icy wind.

"You obviously have not had company training, Inkswitch. It is all too plain to see that you prefer sex-smashing a woman down into a bed. You are perverted, Inkswitch. Don't you know that that makes babies and babies are forbidden? Think Psychiatric Birth Control, Inkswitch. Rockecenter would fire you out of hand if he thought you favored old-fashioned sex! So we are doing you a favor, Inkswitch. We will gradually win you away from your male beastliness. Consider it our blessing, Inkswitch."

"Oh, I do," I faltered.

"Very good, you contemptible (bleepard). We will see you here tomorrow night. Without pistols. Primed or unprimed. And without fail."

She stopped. "Oh, I almost forgot. Here is another hundred dollars. You weren't very good tonight. Maybe more tomorrow night. So show up, Inkswitch."

She slammed the door.

The hundred-dollar bill fluttered down beside my feet.

I shivered, beaten, in the cold wind.

PART THIRTY-THREE

Chapter 1

The next day, when I awoke, I came to the conclusion that things were not going very well.

The morning paper confirmed it.

You would not think that a wad of wood pulp, crushed flat, messily smeared with some carbon, could constitute a deadly weapon. But a newspaper is all of that and more. Any direction it is pointed, it can kill. Especially when motivated by an idiot. One who does not seem to know who he is pointing at.

The target person was supposed to be Heller, whatever name they called him, however many doubles he might have. The person it wounded, this morning, was me!

There it was, right on the front page:

TEN-BILLION-BUCK SUIT
SETTLED

WHIZ KID TRIUMPHS
OVER OCTOPUS

OIL GIANT WRITHES
DOW-JONES SOARS

The ten-billion-buck Whiz Kid suit has been settled out of court for an undisclosed amount.

The Director of the Federal Reserve Bank issued an emergency statement that the bank would open this morning and resume business.

In a sudden stop-press announcement in the small hours of this morning, a spokesman for Boggle, Gouge and Hound stunned the assembled media, stating "Octopus Oil is out of danger. We have just met with Swindle and Crouch and reached total agreement on an out-of-court settlement of Wister vs. Octopus Oil."

Swindle and Crouch, when reached, stated, "No comment." But their representative was seen at the courthouse removing the case from the court dockets.

Speculation as to the amount of settlement was rife. The president of the New York Stock Exchange promised that the Exchange would again open its doors.

The dollar is expected to soar against foreign exchange.

The Seven Brothers, in a predawn meeting, pledged the closest possible support to one another.

A director of Peril-Cinch, the world's largest stock-brokerage firm, stated, "Now that this threat is out of the way, we can expect Dow-Jones to rise this morning and have coffee. The panic sell-off of Octopus stock (most of which we bought ourselves) has been ended, and we extend our condolences to the suckers who sold. Octopus stock will now soar. God bless the Whiz Kid and American youth."

Wister, exhausted from his battle, smiled wanly. "I did it all for America." When asked what

> he would do with the undoubtedly huge amounts
> of the settlement, he just smiled quietly.
>
> (See page 18 for photos of the Octopus Oil
> Building and courthouse.)

Later editions carried much the same story. I did
not have to look at TV or radio to know what they were
saying.

My attention was on something else. I was watching
the gaping slit under my door.

Swindle and Crouch *had* been mentioned again in
the same story with Boggle, Gouge and Hound.

Snakes were going to come crawling under that door
any minute!

I was sure of it.

I ached. The resident doctor, when I had come in
around midnight, had rubbed some ointment mixed
with "Tch, tch, tch. We must learn not to put our stomach up against certain things," but it hadn't helped a bit.
I was bruised and raw!

With a conviction seldom equalled in the Apparatus
experience, I knew I had to get out of New York. It
was too small for me and Pinch. But I also knew that
it was impossible. Heller was winning!

At home in Turkey an unknown assailant from Lombar would rub me out if I left Heller triumphing in New
York.

It was a matter of off-the-barbecue-stick and into-the-
flames if I left things in this condition.

I tried to get practical. A baseball bat taken to Madison was all I seemed to be able to think of.

Something desperate was called for.

Moaning from pain, I tried to lie down. Moaning
from pain, I tried to stand up.

I compromised. Half-reclining in a chaise lounge I tried to think. An idea greater than any idea I had ever had was absolutely mandatory!

Before I could do anything else, Heller had to be smashed, smashed, smashed!

But how?

Chapter 2

My eyes, sort of glazed, at first did not register what they were looking at.

The viewer was on.

It may have been the bright red colors that drew my attention. They were so glaring, they were painful.

It was Babe Corleone! She was sitting in the back seat of a big limousine that had just stopped. She had on a red gown and a red cape that was printed here and there with black hands. She was wearing a red veil.

The costume she had mentioned! I knew I was looking at the start of Gunsalmo Silva's funeral!

There was a man in black sitting beside her. She was talking to him petulantly. "True, true, Signore Saggezza. You have been a good *consigliere*. True, true, the Corleone family has had none better. True, true, true, I must take your advice. But I don't care what the hell you say, I am going to go to this funeral!"

"*Mia capa*, I plead with you again. It is not wise! The report is just in. The church is swarming with the lice of Faustino Narcotici! This could start a gang war!" He saw he was getting nowhere. He looked with appeal straight out of the viewer. To Heller!

Of course. Heller. I would be getting no picture at all unless Heller was there. My wits were too soaked in pain to concentrate well.

I could make out Heller's own image in the limousine glass. He seemed to be wearing a red tuxedo under a scarlet ski parka with a hood and snow-mask. Everything red. He must be sitting on a jump seat.

Heller looked outside. There was a church seen through the leafless trees of a park. All around the limousine, near to hand, men were packed thickly, facing outward. They held riot shotguns in their hands. They were dressed in black overcoats and black slouch hats. Corleone *soldati*, soldiers alert for war. They were very tense.

Heller turned back. Babe was sulking behind her red veil. The *consigliere* was still looking at Heller in appeal.

"Mrs. Corleone," said Heller, "why don't I just step over to that church and see what's really going on? Then we'll know for sure whether it is safe or unsafe. We don't want you in the middle of a gang fight."

"They'll shoot you!" said Babe in sudden alarm. "Take ten or twelve men!"

"No," said Heller. "I'll be all right. I'll wear this ski mask."

Heller took out his ornate Llama .45 and jacked a shell into the chamber, put on the safety and then shoved the gun into a back belt holster. He adjusted the ski mask in place.

He started to get out. There was a sound. A yowl! He turned. "You stay there," he said.

The cat was sitting on the other jump seat! It had on a red leather harness and a red collar with brass spikes. It had been about to follow but now it settled back on the seat, sitting up, alert.

I sat up, too! With sudden hope. If Heller was walking straight into the Faustino mob, he indeed might get shot! I didn't have the platen so they mustn't kill him. But a nice painful wound that would put him a long time in the hospital would be just great!

There was every chance of it, too! Imagine going on a scout in a red tuxedo and a luminous scarlet ski parka! About as invisible as a bomb blast! What an idiot!

He walked through the circle of Corleone men and straight over to the church. Actually, it was a small cathedral. A sign said Our Lady of Gracious Peace. They must be somewhere in lower Manhattan.

There was nobody outside, just a few empty limousines.

Heller scanned the cathedral itself. Gothic arches swept up to considerable height on either side of the massive doors. He stepped forward. The altars glittered with gold leaf, the votive candles sputtered in vast rows. Sunlight beamed down through stained glass. The place was empty of people.

At least live people, anyway. A casket, its top open, rested on trestles. Heller did not walk down the aisle and approach it.

Voices were coming from a side room near the main entrance. Heller tiptoed over to the door of it and looked in. The place, in comparison to the main cathedral, was well lit by diagonally paned windows all around it.

It was absolutely crammed with men!

They were in black overcoats and slouch hats. Many had shotguns under their arms. They were facing someone standing on a raised platform.

Razza Louseini! The *consigliere* of Faustino "The Noose" Narcotici! I recognized him well from past dope contacts in Turkey. He was also the man who had fingered Heller that first time in the Howard Johnson's on the New Jersey Turnpike. He would possibly recognize Heller! Marvelous! A good, disabling wound in Heller was exactly what I needed!

Louseini was not making too much progress. He looked angry and upset. "But men," Razza was arguing, "you don't seem to understand. Gunsalmo Silva was killed while on family business. We've got to bury him in some sort of style."

A man in the mob spoke up, "Our family has lost nineteen good men this fall. That's more than in most gang wars. All we been doing all fall is giving our own family members funerals! But Silva wasn't any real loss to us. We got better things to do!"

Others muttered in agreement.

Razza looked at them and showed his teeth. "Silva was a hero! He wasted 'Holy Joe' for us! You got to show respect! How would you like to get bumped and nobody showed respect? How about that?"

Another voice. It was a priest in robes, very close to where Heller stood. Evidently he was the one who was supposed to officiate. "May I speak?"

Razza said, "Go ahead, Father Paciere. Maybe you can talk some sense into their thick heads!"

Father Paciere said, "My sons, we are here in the presence of the dead. It grieves me to see you quarrel in this holy place. I need eight pallbearers and it would please me well if some would volunteer."

A very tough-faced mobster turned toward the priest. "Father, I don't think they been telling you all they know. Gunsalmo Silva was a *traditore*, a traitor to the Corleone family."

The priest recoiled. He crossed himself. "I didn't know!" He bowed his head and shook it sadly. "Now I understand why even his own brother and uncle would not attend. All are equal in the eyes of God, but a *traditore*..."

"Hey!" the tough-faced mobster suddenly barked, pointing at Heller. "Who's that? A spy?"

All faces whipped toward Heller in the doorway. Guns came up. Oh, here it came! I was going to get my wish!

Father Paciere said, "No, no. Peace! There will be no firing to desecrate the cathedral!" He came over to Heller.

"My son, you are masked," said the priest. "What is your name?"

Well, I suppose a Royal officer doesn't lie to a priest. He said, "Here on this planet, they call me Jerome Wister."

The noise was such that I couldn't tell what happened for a moment. It was a dreadful smashing sound!

Heller looked.

Men were going out those leaded windows in a rocket stream!

Screams of panic!

Shattering crashes of riot gun butts hammering out panes to clear the way!

Men were pouring out onto the shrubbery outside!

Limousines were roaring into life!

The room was empty.

The limousines were gone.

A tinkle of broken glass fell with one last sound upon the floor.

Father Paciere came out from behind the door. He was staring at Heller with an open mouth. Then he looked around at the empty and wrecked room. He crossed himself. He looked at Heller, eyes wide, "So you are Wister."

Heller said, "Wait around, Father. Maybe I can get you a funeral started yet."

He sprinted back through the leafless trees. The Corleone soldiers were standing there, open-mouthed, staring at the missing limousines and empty surrounds. Heller went through them. He opened the limousine door.

"Mrs. Corleone, I think it's safe for you to come into the cathedral now. The Faustino mob is gone."

"What did you do?" said Signore Saggezza in astonishment.

"I just think they had another appointment somewhere," said Heller.

He helped Babe out of the limousine. She was rubbing her red-gloved hands together.

Heller reached in and picked up the cat which, to my amazement, promptly climbed up and sat on his shoulder.

"I knew it, I knew it," said Babe. "Not even the Faustino mob can stand a turncoat and a traitor like Silva!"

Signore Saggezza issued a few crisp orders. The Corleone *soldati* raced ahead and took up positions outside and inside the cathedral.

Babe, Heller and the cat approached the vast wide doors.

Father Paciere met Babe in the aisle. Her six feet six towered over him. "My child," he said, "I am afraid there is little in the way of a funeral for this man. Not even his own brother would attend."

"Have no fear, Father Paciere," said Babe, "we will give the *traditore* a funeral he is not likely to forget."

She swept on forward in her red cape printed with black hands. She marched up to the casket.

The morticians had rebuilt Silva's face, probably from police I.D. shots. He lay in state. Although pretty yellow colored, he really didn't look bad, particularly considering what a mess he must have been after his fall.

Babe towered above it. She lifted her red veil.

"*Traditore!*" she said.

SHE SPAT ON SILVA!

The priest drew back in horror.

Suddenly the cat let out a snarl!

It rocketed off Heller's shoulder!

It went straight at Silva's face, snarling and clawing! RAKE! RAKE! RAKE!

Heller hurriedly reached over and pried the cat off. As he held it, it kept snarling and hissing the way only a cat can do! It was hard for Heller to hold it. No cathedral organ for Silva. Those sounds of hate reverberated through the vaults.

Babe shouted, "Signore Saggezza! The men, if you please."

The Corleone *soldati*, while mindful of their posts and withdrawing to them immediately, yet came forward one by one.

Each took a dagger out as he approached the coffin.

Each plunged the dagger into the chest of the corpse, spat on the face and cried, "*Traditore!*"

Father Paciere was cowering back, powerless to stop it.

The *soldati* finished their part of the ceremony.

Babe, red cape flowing in the drafty place, held up her hand.

Georgio rushed forward. He gave her two long, black sticks. She took one. Geovani rushed up. He had a blowtorch. He fired it off. Babe put the end of one black stick into its flame.

A branding iron!

The end began to glow red. A T! For *traditore,* traitor! She approached the casket.

Into the right cheek of the corpse she pressed the sizzling end! Smoke rose. She pressed the **T** into the left cheek. More smoke.

The corpse's face was branded as a traitor!

Babe was not through.

She took the other iron and began to heat it.

Father Paciere wailed.

It was a cross!

It glowed cherry red.

She again approached the casket.

She lifted her red-veiled face to the vault of heaven. She cried, *"MUEM SUPROC TSE COH!"*

She plunged it down upon the forehead. The cross was upside down!

Oh, Gods, I suddenly understood. The words *Hoc est corpus meum* are the words of Holy Communion. They mean "This is my body," in Latin. When they are said backwards, over an inverted cross, the grace of one of their Gods is *taken* from the individual, not given to him. He would receive the reverse of forgiveness. BLACK MASS!

The priest cried out. He crossed himself frantically.

Babe pulled the iron up.

Silva was branded to be never forgiven by anyone! Not even a God.

"Oh, my child," wept the priest, "I will have to tell Father Xavier to give you thirty *Pater Nosters* for this and thirty-one *Ave Marias.* You have desecrated a house of God with the rites of the Black Mass."

"It's worth it," said Babe. "The dirty, filthy traitor! Now you cannot bury him in consecrated ground."

"No, we cannot," wept the priest, "though it is doubtful if even God would accept a traitor."

"Very good," said Babe with satisfaction. "Then we have handled your funeral problem. I suggest you send the body over to the New Jersey pig farms and have it fed to the pigs."

"No, no," said the priest. "They would protest the infecting of their pigs."

"Ah, I have it," said Babe. "Tell the mortician to send the body to I. G. Barben Pharmaceuticals to make poison out of!"

"As you say, my child," said the priest.

Babe leaned over the casket again, staring at the branded face. *"Traditore!"* she said once more. And once more she lifted her red veil and spat.

Proudly, Babe Corleone strode up the aisle and left the cathedral.

They reached the limousine. She sank down on the seat, smiling, pulling off her red gloves.

Heller put the cat down on the jump seat.

Babe reached over and petted it. "This is a very nice cat, Jerome. He knows a traitor when he sees one."

They drove away.

Gunsalmo Silva had had his funeral.

But I, though disappointed Heller had not been shot, also had something.

I had a great idea!

The idea was so good, I only screamed a little as I dressed.

I was on my way to wreck Heller once and for all!

Chapter 3

It was very obvious that J. Walter Madison needed some mature help and guidance but he didn't seem to be exactly hanging upon my every word.

I had gotten there in an agonizingly painful taxi ride—every pebble or white line a tire hit communicated to one or another of my bruises. I had somehow gotten up the steps of 42 Mess Street without falling back down them. I had elbowed my way through the churning menagerie of staff reporters and publicity men at great cost of elbow bruises. And Madison, debonair, appealing and sincere, was really not paying any attention to me.

He also had somebody on the phone. He looked at me while he talked to me as well as the person on the other end of the phone. "Hello, Mr. Smith. Well, all I am saying is that you better give me front page. You look sort of pale. What's Mount St. Helens got to do with it?"

I started to speak for the third time. "I am trying to tell you that I have found Hel——I mean Wister's real weakness."

"Well, so what if it blew the whole top of its head off? Didn't it do that already, years ago? I'm always glad to have your opinion, Mr. Smith. Well, I admit that Portland, Oregon, buried under ashes does rate more space than a classified ad. What have you been doing to your face? It seems bruised. So what if the business section is buried under lava? Have you seen a doctor?"

Desperate, I said, "I am certain you will be running out of front page material soon, Madison. Maybe even tomorrow, I hope. I have the very thing for you."

"Well, push it to page two, page six. Even nonprofessional ideas are welcome, Smith. So thousands died and more thousands are missing. Why don't you just go out and tell one of the staff, Smith."

"I've got something about Hel——Wister that nobody else knows!"

"Well, it *is* necessary that I talk to you. If you can see lava rolling right at your building right now, get a

rewrite man on it and give me your full attention here.
I am shocked you would suggest an exposé at this stage,
Smith; the time is not ripe. You better give me the
front page on what I send or the *Portland Grimes* will
find itself in trouble. If I can't have your front page. . . .
What? You don't have any paper now, much less a front
page? Then what the hell am I doing talking to you?" He
hung up.

"It's a great idea!" I begged.

"I can't send the Whiz Kid out to rescue Mount St.
Helens. It's off image, Smith." He was reaching for the
phone again.

Firmly, I put my bandaged hand down on his, preventing his picking the instrument up again. And
although my voice was rough and hoarse from screaming, I raised it stridently. "You will need a front page on
Wister tomorrow. You have shot your bolt on the suits.
I am trying to give you tomorrow's front page!"

"But I haven't shot my bolt, as you so unprofession-
ally put it, on the suits. And I have tomorrow's front
page! Here it is!" He thrust the smudgily typed news
story at me.

It said:

WHIZ KID DONATES
WHOLE SETTLEMENT
TO CHARITY

In a magnificent gesture, the Whiz Kid today
signified that the entire settlement sum realized
from his legal battle with M.I.W. and Octopus Oil
would be given in full to charity.

"I am not one to profit from the misfortunes

> of others," he was quoted as stating. "I shall not keep one dime of the monies awarded. Every penny will be given to a worthy cause."

It went on and on. I was sickened by it. "You mean," I said, "you're going to let him give away those huge sums? Of course, I'm happy to see him bro——"

Madison said, "Huge sums? Honesty is a keynote in PR, Smith. Not one word has been said about the *actual* amounts M.I.W. and Octopus settled for. Just read the stories of the last two days. The settlement in both cases was zero cash. So, of course he can give it all to charity. No money was involved. I always keep a firm check on reality, Smith. So there, as you can see, is sure-fire, front page, national coverage tomorrow. What a gesture! How typical of his great nature! And besides, it's already on the wire, going out to every paper in the land."

He would have lifted the phone. I applied more pressure to the back of his hand despite my pain. "Day after tomorrow, then," I cried. "You haven't got day *after* tomorrow and I have it for you!"

"Well, I'll admit," said Madison, "that day after tomorrow is pretty far into the future. You see, the image I am trying to build is——"

"Listen to me, then! Listen loud and clear. Here is your story! 'The Whiz Kid Has Mob Links!' Madison, he's thoroughly hooked up to organized crime! The Mafia!"

"Well, who isn't?" he began. "Our very best people . . . Wait a minute, Smith. Wait a minute. I do think . . ." He leaped up from his desk. He began to pace back and forth. He was in the throes of inspiration.

I tried to tell him more but he held up his hand to

quiet me. I persisted. He raised his voice, "Facts, Smith. You are trying to disturb my concentration with facts. Fact has nothing to do with PR, Smith. You are being delusory! Newspapers wouldn't sell at all if they dealt in real data. So be quiet."

I subsided.

He paced a bit more. "Let me see. I have been trying desperately to think of how I am going to get him back in the fuel business. We have to continue Controversy. Image, image. I have to think of image. Positioning. Names. That's it! NAMES! Names make news, Smith. You have to connect up big names! I have it! You are right, Smith! Mob links *is* a wonderful idea!"

I sank down in a chair. I had gotten through to him!

"Tramp!" he yelled into the other room. And Ted Tramp rushed in. "Ted," said Madison, "what reporter do we have that knows mob figures and is expendable?"

Tramp said, "There's old Bob Hoodward. He was a great investigative reporter in his day. When he was on the staff of the *Washington Roast* he even brought down President Nixon and some other mob figures. But that was decades back. He's on his last beat now—dead beat, in fact. Expendable."

They rushed out. I could see them buttonhole a gray wreck. They talked in low tones excitedly.

Oh, thank Gods, I was getting some action. I did some rapid calculation. I maybe could live through today and tomorrow. After that, it was impossible. If this worked, I would have Heller smashed and I could flee New York and Miss Pinch! It would be a near thing.

Madison raised his voice, "Today! We have to have it today! Only then can it be front page day after tomorrow! So don't you dare fail to get his consent!"

I could see Hoodward out in the other room as he sank into a chair and picked up a phone. He was making a call to someone important as he seemed to be going through several intermediaries.

Despite my pain, I dragged myself over toward him so I could hear above the clattering din.

He had his party. "... so you see, sir, as one of the city's most prominent and respected citizens, we want you to present the award.... Oh, yes, sir, I am aware that you are trying to build an image for yourself. That's why I thought of you at once. ... The award is a monetary prize for The Most Honest Man of the Year.... Yes. Well, you see, sir, I thought of that. By your being associated with the most honest man of the year, that, of course, positions you as an honest man and helps your image. ... No, I can't tell you the name of the recipient. It is just this minute being drawn by lottery. ..."

Madison was urgently pushing a slip of paper at him. Hoodward looked at it. "The appointment is for three o'clock this very afternoon at the Tammany Hall Auditorium. It will only take a few minutes.... Yes, sir. Only selected press will be present.... Really, just myself and photographers, no TV.... Oh, yes, sir, I can assure you that it will get national coverage and I promise you faithfully that I will clear the story and caption with you, every word. You can depend on me, sir."

He hung up and stood up. "He'll be there. Is this on the level, Madison?"

"You know it is, Bob. Now, everybody, we've got to move very fast on this. Bob, you leave right away and escort him there. Take a cab."

The old reporter tottered out.

Madison had three photographers picked out. He sent them hurriedly into makeup to get their faces made unrecognizable. That done, he put them in bulletproof vests.

Then he phoned orders to the bogus Whiz Kid.

I began to get sort of lost. What did makeup and bulletproof vests have to do with it?

It wasn't until we were all piled into an unmarked van that I had a chance to ask Madison.

"Mob figures are chancy things," he said. "I'm surprised you are coming along. This is highly professional PR, Smith."

"It was my idea," I defended, wincing as we hit a bump.

"So it was," he said. "I am really gratified at your support and encouragement, Smith. It really is a great idea."

Fact was, I was getting pretty foggy about WHAT idea was being executed.

We tore through the truck- and dray-crowded streets. The afternoon was cold and sleet was spitting out of the sky. The pavement glistened gray. Fitting weather in which to torpedo Heller.

We drew up at the back of Tammany Hall. It was a recently restored building in a park, a landmark used for only the most sacred occasions. Apparently Rockecenter had financed its reconstruction, and the land around it, which he owned, had rocketed in value: very public spirited. So Madison had the run of the place.

It was about a quarter to three. The photographers leaped out and rushed in. Madison led me up a different flight of stairs.

We came out overlooking a small auditorium. We were on a little balcony—a box, really—well screened from the floor below. But we could see everything that went on.

There was a raised lecture stage there. It had doors at the back of it. There was a big chair with a solid back facing the empty seats for the audience. The photographers were positioning things. They got the auditorium lights very low. They got their own flash guns in position.

Madison, now that he had it all moving, was chatty. "That chair," he said, "is historic. It's the same one Boss Tweed used to use when he collected his payoffs from the whole city. Well, it will even be more historic yet, shortly."

The Whiz Kid double rushed in from a side door. It was the first time I had seen him in the flesh. Actually, aside from being tall for his age and blond, he really didn't have any of the aura of Heller. It wasn't just his buckteeth and protruding jaw or even his horn-rimmed glasses. He had the air of a cheap bum, really. It gave me a lot of satisfaction. This nut couldn't have ordered a puppy dog to wag its tail! But he did have a kind of impudent brass. The photographers were trying to get him to sit just so in the chair. He had his own ideas.

He was wearing a red racing suit and carrying a racing helmet and he thought he would look better with the helmet on and the photographers were telling him to (bleep) well keep it off—it threw a shadow on his face.

Out of curiosity more than any inkling of coming trouble, I said to Madison, "Who is this mob figure you're getting?"

"Why, the top man. Names make news, Smith. The *capo di tutti capi* of course. Faustino 'The Noose' Narcotici, naturally."

With a shock, I remembered the funeral. "Wait! The minute Faustino knows it's Wister, he'll run! I guarantee it!"

"Well, well!" said Madison. "Now you tell me."

He rushed down a side stairs to the floor and hurriedly issued some orders. He came back up.

"Whew, Smith. You certainly play it close. You could have blown the whole caper. (Bleep)! Working with unprofessionals! But it will be all right now."

The bogus Whiz Kid put the racing helmet on and closed the opaque visor.

There was a burst of activity behind the stage.

Three Faustino bodyguards rushed in. With sawed-off shotguns they probed the seats. They made sure the cameras weren't guns. They opened doors. They were trying to make certain it wasn't a hit spot.

Madison and I drew back. The bodyguards gave the boxes a perfunctory glance and then contented themselves with stationing a man to fire in case a gun was shoved over the rail from this mezzanine.

Faustino came waddling through a door at the back of the stage. Hoodward was with him. The aged reporter put a big sheaf of bills in Faustino's hands and fanned them out. The *capo di tutti capi*'s rings flashed as he arranged the money in his hands.

The Whiz Kid double was sitting in the chair with the helmet on, facing forward.

Hoodward finished coaching Faustino.

The mob chief moved fatly forward to the side of the chair.

The photographers stood alert.

Faustino put on his best gold-toothed smile. He said, "As the most honest citizen of New York, I hereby have the honor to present you with your award as the Most Honest Man of the Year." He extended the money to the bogus Whiz Kid.

This Wister extended a hand for the money and, with the other, plucked off his helmet. He was smiling.

Flash guns flashed!

The smile on Faustino's face froze!

He let out a scream!

Money spurted out of his hands as he flung it away!

He ran!

His bodyguards ran!

The photographers ran!

We ran!

As we mobbed into the van, Hoodward caught up, prevented the door from slamming and got in. He was furious.

"You set me up!" he yelled at Madison.

Madison said to the photographers, "You got it in the can?"

They nodded gleefully.

Hoodward said, "I don't know why he ran but I know Faustino will murder me! I may get away with wrecking a president but not a *capo di tutti capi!*"

"I think of everything," said Madison. "You've wanted to retire for years. Here is a ticket I always keep on hand. Straight flight to Israel. It's in the name of Martin Borman. There's a nice room reserved there in that name. And here's my own gold watch for long and faithful service."

"Wait a minute," I said. "I don't get how this works out. The Whiz Kid image isn't honesty. What are you trying to do?"

"My dear Smith," said Madison, "it is plain that you, while you may get great ideas, don't really grasp the nuances and fundamentals of the newspaper business. It is, essentially, an entertainment industry. Never let anyone in on what you are trying to do, much less let the public in on what is really going on. You disappoint me. You ought to be saying, and would, if you were a professional PR man, 'Eighteen point quote Madison Does

It Again unquote' and all you're doing is asking questions. Can't we let you off somewhere? We've got to get
Hoodward to the airport terminal quick."

Chapter 4

All that money flying around the stage had reminded me how close to broke I was. Unfortunately,
Hoodward had delayed to pick it up: that's what had
almost made him miss the van. I was not going to miss
anything. Day after tomorrow, as soon as Heller was
ruined—and though I did not see quite how, I had high
hopes—yours truly was going to be gone from New York.
It would be a near thing, touch and go, the way I
planned my escape. Remembering that the route from
Turkey to the U.S. lay through Rome, Paris and London,
and remembering, too, the way they gouged tourists in
those places, I needed cash.

There was only one way to get it. To torture the combination out of Miss Pinch and then to murder her in the
most gruesome and grisly way imaginable. There was no
other choice: I was far too weak and shaky to rob a bank.
But the Apparatus trains one and prepares one for such
emergencies. I knew how to do it.

Actually, I would like to omit that evening from this
confession. It is too horrible. Murder should not be advertised to the young and this confession might someday
fall—Gods forbid—into the hands of the immature. Even
a Justiciary is likely to pale at what happened.

But in all honesty, as promised, I will carry on, even

though the next few hours fill me with remorse. In all my crimes and escapades, this was the worst.

I knew where, in New York, I could procure the weapons—a supermarket.

Guile was the watchword. There is an Apparatus technique called the "Lure-Kill." It pretends affection as a mask for murder.

I tottered along the shelves of the supermarket, supported by the rolling, wheeled shopping basket. I found what I wanted in the condiments section—a big, glaringly labelled box of McKormick's Red Pepper.

I crept, supported by the shopping cart, to the flower section. As Christmas was just up the line, there were huge bouquets of white chrysanthemums to be had. Despite the expense, I bought the best.

At checkout, I prevailed upon the teen-ager not to crush them into a sack, but to actually wrap them like flowers with an open top.

I went outside and found a dark place. Putting a thick handkerchief over my nose and tying it as best I could with my bandaged hands, I then took the red pepper and, with care, worked it under every petal. Time consuming.

That done, I threw the empty pepper can in the trash and closed the top of the bouquet with a single fold.

With glee, I contemplated what would happen. Miss Pinch would open the door, holding a gun as usual. I would say, "You have reformed me from being a beastly male and I bring this to express my affection." She would say, "Oh, how charming!" And she would take the bouquet, pull back the top flap to see what it was, behold flowers and sniff! That would be all I would need. I would have her gun as she convulsed in sneezes. I would hit her over the head. I would drag her to that bed and use every torture implement in the place until I had that combination. Candy? I would just gut-shoot her and laugh as she writhed.

I got a cab. I was dropped off a block away so no one could trace me by cab numbers to the murder site.

It was very dark. The rush hour had ended. They would be home.

Feebly, I tottered to the house. I went down the basement steps. I made sure there was no one behind me. I rang the bell.

Footsteps!

Success!

It was Miss Pinch!

She was dressed in mannish pants and shirt. And as I had suspected, she was carrying a revolver.

She opened the door and outer grill and stood back.

I said, "Miss Pinch, you have reformed me from being a beastly male and I bring this to express my affection."

I held out the flowers.

The play didn't quite go as planned.

"Flowers?" she said. "Why, you dirty (bleepard)! You're trying to steal Candy from me, are you? Well, to hell with that!"

She seized the wrapped bouquet.

She jabbed me backwards with the gun.

She slammed the flowers down on the dirty floor of the areaway!

She stamped on them with her heel!

She kicked the lid off a garbage can! I flinched at the violence of the clatter.

Without taking her eyes or gun off me, blocking my exit up the basement stairs, she scooped the destroyed bouquet up and threw it in the garbage can.

Then she halted.

She sniffed slightly.

With a hand, she flapped a careful sample of the air from the top of the garbage can to her.

"Red pepper!" she snarled. "Why, you dirty (bleep-ard)!"

In vain I tried to tell her it must have been on the discarded fish. Making motions that seemed to indicate she was about to pistol-whip me, she drove me inside.

She locked the wrought-iron grill and door behind her.

She fired a shot so near my head, I felt the powder sting.

"I will give you to the count of ten to get out of your clothes!" she snarled. "And after that I am going to shoot off your (bleeps)! ONE!"

I hastily got out of my overcoat.

"TWO!"

I shed my jacket and my shoes at the same time.

"THREE!"

I was undressed. I couldn't see why she was still counting.

"FOUR!"

It was my hat. I had forgotten my hat! I flung it frantically away from me.

In no time after that she had me wrist- and ankle-cuffed, spread-eagled face up on that Gods (bleeped) bed!

When she finished the last cuff, she threw the gun aside. "So you like red pepper, do you? Well, always give the male the right to his chauvinistic domination." She turned and called into the other room, her voice lilting, "Oh, Candy dear, we're going to have Mexican red-hot tamales tonight!"

She began to hum a little wordless tune. She took off her shirt. She took off her shoes. She stepped out of her pants. She shucked off her underwear and stood naked, still humming.

Candy tiptoed shyly in. She saw what was coming off and began to strip, halting halfway and saying, "Oh, dear Pinchy, make him look the other way."

Pinch did, with a backhand slap. Then she went on humming. Slap or not, I watched in growing anxiety.

Miss Pinch opened a drawer and got out a small white apron about three inches wide that covered nothing. She put it on. Then she got a cook's hat, tall and stiffly starched. She put it on at a rakish angle.

Then she got a little gingham napkin and hung it around Candy's neck and tied it. It didn't even cover her now naked, bulging breasts. She sat Candy down on the sofa where she waited, knees apart, watching with eyes that were gradually getting hot.

They evidently used the torture-implement fireplace for barbecuing. It had all the long forks and tongs and needful tools. But Miss Pinch was putting those to one side. She was looking through a pile of kitchen utensils.

I knew it would not do the slightest good to protest. I knew I should try not to scream. But my body was already so bruised and beaten, I knew that it was impossible to do much more damage to it, so I took heart.

I shouldn't have.

Miss Pinch found what she wanted.

A cheese grater!

She tested the ragged sharpness of its jagged teeth. She cut herself slightly and stopped humming long enough to curse me for it.

Then, humming again, she approached the bed.

Very lightly and with artistry, she began to draw the cheese grater down my chest!

It was sharp. I bit my lips. I would not scream. But she was paying little attention to that. All her concentration was that of a chef's. And Candy looked like a hungry diner!

She shifted her target to my legs. She drew the cheese grater down along the insides, making a wavy pattern of scrapes very carefully.

I could see small bubbles of blood rising in the raw scrapes.

She put the grater aside. She went to a torture rack and opened a cabinet under it and got something out!

A can of red pepper!

Holding her face away, she put some in her hand and began to massage it quietly into the wounds!

Sheer pain!

I let out my first scream.

I choked it back.

More red pepper and more massage.

I screamed!

Candy yipped!

Miss Pinch seemed to think that was enough red pepper. Half a can. She went and got a three-foot wooden spoon. She carefully turned it to the bulging side.

WHAP!

She began to beat the pepper in!

With all her might!

Agony!

Scorching, sizzling agony!

I lost control. I began to scream!

Candy began to scream.

I could see her naked, bucking about on the sofa. "Take me, Pinchy, oh God, take me!"

Miss Pinch scooped her up, carried her into the bedroom and slammed the door shut with her heel.

The pain didn't stop.

I kept screaming!

To make it worse, I could only half see!

After how long I do not know, Miss Pinch came back. She had lipstick on her apron.

Candy came out, breasts rising and falling.

They had a beer.

Candy had a joint.

Miss Pinch apologized to Candy for having forgotten the dinner music. She put some mood music on the stereo and Candy said it was nice. But she was still hungry.

"Oh, that was only the first course," said Miss Pinch. "We mustn't be too greedy. This is a gourmet dinner."

I had just begun to be able to support the awful torment of that pepper without screaming or writhing.

Miss Pinch retied her apron. She adjusted her cook's hat. She went over to the cabinet and took out something.

"This is what we need now," she said, showing Candy. "It will titillate the jaded palate. I can't stand bland food, can you, Candy dear?"

She came over.

TABASCO SAUCE!

She sprinkled it from the squirting bottle all up and down the wounds! Artistically, humming, making sure that it was just right.

At the first touch of it, I thought it was liquid fire! And she was emptying the whole bottle!

I began to scream.

She went and got the cheese grater again.

She went to work.

I really screamed!

Candy began to yip. She was bouncing all over the couch.

Miss Pinch had hold of a three-foot barbecue fork. She was raising it to bring it down.

"Take me, Pinchy, take me!"

Miss Pinch brought it down anyway! Time and time again!

I passed out.

When I came to, it was like trying to live in a bed of live coals!

They were not in the room.

I could hear low, snarling curses from the other side of the closed door.

They finally came back. Candy was wild-eyed. She kept rubbing and cupping her breasts.

"It's too bland, dear Pinchy. I don't mean to be critical. But I'm starving!"

Miss Pinch looked distressed. Then she took a tug at her apron. She found her cook's hat in the other room and came back with it.

She gazed at me. "Mustard!" she said in sudden decision. "That's what it needs! Mustard! To give it some tang!"

She went and found an enormous jar of French mustard with a squirt spigot. From on high she trailed artistic designs on my body.

She threw it aside. With two vigorous hands, she began to rub it in.

I screamed. I begged and pleaded. I told her I would do anything, anything, but please, for Gods' sakes, get this stuff out of these wounds!

Candy smiled. "It sounds delicious," she said. "Rub him harder!"

Miss Pinch went and got a rolling pin. She used it to rub the mixture in.

Then she cheese grated some more.

Then she began to use the rolling pin to beat it into me!

I was clever. I managed to get my head in the way and get knocked out!

I came to a long time later. Candy was flopped on

the floor, exhausted, designs drawn all over her naked body with lipstick, her mouth open and wet, out cold.

Marijuana smoke was thick in the place.

Beer cans rolled about dribbling.

Miss Pinch was just completing an intravenous shot of Big H. She drew the needle out. She looked at me. The drug wasn't making her any more cheerful. She went through a hot surge.

She composed her face into a deadly mask of hate.

I was on fire down to the middle of my soul. I burned so, I could only think one raving thought. I was smart enough not to voice it. Get out of New York!

"You male (bleepard)," said Miss Pinch. "You were very bad tonight. You aren't even fit for pigs to eat, truth be told. You aren't living up to what the Psychiatric Birth Control classes said even a *lousy* male should! Dr. Frybrain would call you a retarded pervert!"

I shut my eyes. They burned and I couldn't see well anyway.

She kicked at me. "Are you a homo yet?"

"No!" I screamed. The one thing I would never be was a homosexual. Sick as I was, I was revolted even more!

"Then, see? We aren't having the least success with you. You're trying to make us fail our homework! Get on your God (bleeped) clothes, you (bleepard)."

"For Gods' sake, let me wash these wounds out!"

"Hah," she said. "Don't try to change the subject! All you men can think about is women. That's forbidden!" She grabbed the naked Candy and stroked her breasts. "You're that psychiatric horror, a normal male! All you can think about is pawing some poor, defenseless girl. Look at her. Completely unconscious just from being unable to stand the thought of you touching her! And I would kill you if you did." She kissed the unconscious Candy passionately on the mouth. "You came here tonight to steal her away from me, you loathsome beast. I am glad you have learned your lesson. Now get dressed."

"I'm still chained!" I said.

She dropped Candy who flopped into a naked heap. She picked the gun up off the floor. She cocked it.

Savagely she cast off the shackles one by one.

Moving, when I tried it, was agony again!

"Let me take a shower," I begged.

"And dirty up the bathroom where this dear innocent girl stands every day? Never! Get on your clothes!"

I think that vicious, calculating (bleepch) knew what would happen. As soon as I got into my clothes, the red pepper and Tabasco sauce and mustard reactivated in the wounds!

I screamed.

Candy stirred. "Pinchy, kiss me."

Miss Pinch did and if I had had the strength, I could have killed her, killed them both, lying naked and entwined there on the floor.

But I saw I could get out and that was all I could think of. Besides, the gun was still pointed at me. I fumbled for the door.

Miss Pinch called after me, "If you don't get here on time tomorrow night, remember, it's three years in the Federal pen!"

I couldn't even close the door behind me.

On fire, trying not to scream, I made it to an avenue. I got a cab.

Half an hour later, the resident doctor had me in a shower, working at the wounds in a most painful way to get the red pepper, Tabasco and mustard out. It didn't hurt so much, only because he had first given me a shot of morphine.

As he worked, he said, "Tch, tch, tch. With all these injuries, we certainly must be running with a rough crowd."

Well, no more. If all went well, in forty-eight hours Heller would be finished and I would be out of New York! The town was too much for me. Never in my life had I thought a city could turn you into a salad. If I didn't watch it I could even become a fruitcake!

Chapter 5

When I awoke the next day, it was already noon. I checked myself over carefully as I lay there in the bed. Yes, I was still alive, incredible but true.

I had one ace up my raw sleeve.

I was *not* going to visit Miss Pinch that evening!

The question was, would I get away with it? Would I get out of New York alive?

It was going to be an awfully near thing. I clenched my teeth. Duty was a burden but I had to make sure Heller was wrecked before I could go. Otherwise, I would be assassinated by the unknown spy on my return to Turkey. It would do no good to leave New York alive if I would then wind up in Turkey dead. Then, with a new surge of horror, I remembered the assassin had threatened to kill Utanc first!

Somehow I had to suffer through the next twenty-four or so hours. Tomorrow would be the crucial time, for then, observing that I had not shown up on schedule, Miss Pinch would call the Internal Revenue Service.

Bury would surely have noticed by this time, no matter how deep he was in the Central American jungle, that once more Boggle, Gouge and Hound had been coupled with Swindle and Crouch.

I managed the phone with two hands and ordered some breakfast. It was an unwise action. The room-service waiter, noting all the papers outside the door, added the mound to my burdens.

It was the push that sort of sent me over the edge.

Just as Madison had predicted, the Whiz Kid was all over the front page.

In an action *"unprecedented in history"* he had presented *"anything he had won in settlements"* to the farmers of Kansas.

I knew now that, factually, it was a nothing amount that he was retaining a nothing of. But this thing about farmers of Kansas was quite beyond me. What did they have to do with it?

Maybe I was sort of feverish already but this puzzle turned it into a kind of strange delirium.

All the rest of that day I lay there with my eyes fearfully on the door. I expected two deadly IRS men to slither through the crack at the bottom or a snake to call me via the U.S. Army Signal Corps before I could check out. An uncomfortable frame of mind. It got worse when dark came. I knew what the reaction of Miss Pinch would be when there was no ring at her front door. The tension would mount to an explosion syndrome! She would be more than slightly peeved! Her reactions would become more and more unprintable.

As the night wore on, every time a curtain stirred, I knew it would be Lombar's unknown assailant, magically transported by magic carpet from Turkey with a communication from the Widow Tayl informing me that she, too, had called IRS. It didn't even do any good to sleep.

That brought nightmares and prominent in them was Candy pleading with Lombar and the assassin pilots to make me scream harder!

And through it all, echoing in the room, were the first words Heller had ever spoken to me: "From your accent, you're an Academy officer, aren't you? What sad route brought you to the 'drunks'?"

It was very confusing. How had he known about Bury?

The hours and the fog dispersed.

Voices. Real voices!

It was the resident doctor. Winter sunlight was coming in the hotel penthouse terrace doors. Morning had come once more. It was D-day! "He seems to have had a fever. It's broken now. If he drops off to sleep and begins the screaming again, just give him one of these aspirin." He closed up his bag and left.

Utanc! She was standing over by the mirror. She was dressed in a silk lounging robe and primping at her hair. She must have felt my eyes on her. "You kept screaming and I couldn't hear my radio well so when the doctor came, I let him in."

Dear Utanc! She was all I had. How thoughtful of her! How tender.

I said, "They're after me!"

"I shouldn't wonder," she said, putting a strand of her hair in place under a diamond clip.

"No, no! They really are after me! The Feds are liable to send the U.S. Army here with snakes any minute!"

She whirled. Ah, I had her attention. She did care for me after all! "The wallet!" she said. "The wallet with blood on it! The man you had killed!"

I was too weak to argue. "Yes. Yes, that's it. If I get good news this morning we have to flee! Although we've got to delay, we can't. We must get out of New York!"

Her face went white! She said, "There's a plane at four. I will pack at once!" Practical, efficient girl. She was gone like a shot!

I was too wobbly and hoarse to call her back. If I didn't get the good news, I would only be going home to my death.

With two bandaged hands I managed to get room service on the phone. This was going to be a near thing. The U.S. Army Signal Corps was liable to bring the snakes covered with IRS red pepper any minute.

I told room service, "Send me two scrambled newspapers, overdone."

I waited in mental and physical stress. The waiter came and finding stacks of newspapers at the door, brought those in, too, and dumped them on the bed: the movement sent waves of agony through me but newspapers always do.

I opened one with shaking hands.

Was this victory or death?

Chapter 6

Ye Gods!
Headlines!

> ## WHIZ KID BRIBED
> ## TO THROW RACE!

And the story with its titles:

WHIZ KID FUEL DIDN'T FAIL

The famous investigative reporter, Bob Hood-
ward, the Nixon Nailer, has ferreted out the facts.
The famous Spreeport Race was thrown by the
Whiz Kid for payola!

FUEL VALID

Earlier belief that the race was lost due to
defective fuel has now been exposed as false.

MOB FIGURE

The Whiz Kid had the honor to be bribed by
the most famous Mafia mob mogul on the planet, no less than Faustino "The Noose" Narcotici,
capo di tutti capi.

CONFESSION

In an exclusive interview with Hoodward, Wister confessed. "I thought I would not have money
enough to develop my fuel, so I did it the American Way: for cash, I threw the race."

I gaped! I had never realized the extent imagination
played in PR!

But how convincing!

And here was the photo, front page, three columns
wide! A smiling Faustino was handing a grinning Whiz
Kid the most huge wad of filthy lucre anybody would

ever care to have. And the Whiz Kid was obviously lifting his helmet in salute to his benefactor. No matter that a tenth of a second later, Faustino had been running like an electric rabbit on a greyhound track! Those photographers had gotten it in the nick of time! What experts!

The caption under the photo said:

> Secret candid shot proving the bribe: In the chair once used by Boss Tweed, the Bribe Baron of New York in the '90s, the Whiz Kid, Gerry Wister, receives his payoff from *capo di tutti capi* Faustino "The Noose" Narcotici, Crime Czar of the world.

I was stunned! What virtuosity PR had! I had never realized the headlines of this world were the product of overheated imaginations, staged events and tons of nothing! It took my breath away.

And how cunningly they had linked it up with NAMES! Nixon, Narcotici, Boss Tweed. The Whiz Kid was now positioned with criminals! How convincing! Who could doubt it?

The other papers were the same. This story would be bouncing coast to coast and even around the world. TV would be carrying that photo as a still. Radio would be spot-newsing it every hour. What coverage! An avalanche!

And, my Gods, it was also all over the sports pages! They were running still shot reviews of the race! That meant TV sports programs would be running the moving color footage!

All was revealed! So this was how news was made! Madison was right. I had not really been a professional PR.

But wait a minute, how was Heller taking this?

Chapter 7

I got the viewer on.

Heller was driving the old cab down the Jersey side of the river. He had a stack of the newspapers on the floor under the meter and was glancing at them from time to time.

He was PERTURBED!

I turned back the strips. Yes, Heller had been summoned by Geovani when he had reached the office. Geovani had simply said, "You better get over here, kid, but I advise you not to come." That voice was very tense.

Heller was in trouble!

Ah, PR, PR, what a beautiful tool for trouble. I realized now that nobody was safe from such a weapon. It might strike anywhere at anyone. There was no predicting it at all! One minute he had been happily going about his business and then, bang, through no action of his own, he was shot by PR. And he didn't even have any inkling it was a shot. Maybe he thought it was just how the world ran: that newspapers were unreliable or made mistakes or simply catered to the public taste for sensationalism.

An expert in hand-to-hand combat, a Fleet combat engineer that could blow up fortresses and bases without a single scratch, Heller was a leaf in the wind before the

mighty hurricane of PR, just a chip to be exploded at
will by a master like Madison. And Heller not only
didn't know, there was absolutely no one he could fight,
nothing whatever he could do about it! Madison had
reduced him, with a few paragraphs, to a helpless pawn!

All Heller knew was that he was in trouble. He drove
that way. He had even ignored a disguise when he left
New York.

Just a pile of paper. A pile that could be burned with
a single match. But that pile of paper was on its way to
wrecking Heller!

I could tell it just from Geovani's voice.

At Babe's he parked the cab.

Geovani met him in the elevator. "Kid, I wouldn't
go in."

Heller handed Georgio a tan, leather trench coat and
cap but Georgio wouldn't take it. It fell to the floor.

Heller knocked on the living-room door. It did not
open. He turned the knob and went in.

No Babe.

Some sounds were coming from beyond another
door across the room. Heller went over and opened it.

It was a sort of den. It had a fireplace but there was
no fire in it. A crucifix hung on the wall. The rug was
black.

And there sat Babe. She was crumpled up on her
knees. She had a sackcloth over her head. She had taken
ashes from the fireplace and was smearing them on her
face.

"*Mia culpa*," she moaned. "*Mia magna culpa*. It is
my fault, it is my great fault."

She was crying.

She sensed someone had entered.

She looked up, tears coursing through the ashes on
her face, making two clean streaks.

She saw him.

"Oh, Jerome," she groaned. "My own son a *traditore!*" She bent over, weeping. "My own son, my own son!"

Heller tried to walk forward to her. "Mrs. Corleone, please believe me...."

Rejection was instant. Palms flat toward him, she blocked his further approach with a gesture. "No, no, do not come near me! Somehow, somewhere you have tainted blood! You have stained the honor of the family! Do not come near me!"

Heller dropped to his own knees, distant from her. "*Please*, Mrs. Corleone, I did not have..."

"*Traditore!*" she spat, scuttling back to get away from him. "You have broken your poor mother's heart!" She made a grab at the fireplace. She took out a newspaper that was only partly burned. The face of Faustino could be seen. The movement fanned the sparks that clung to it. They fanned into sudden flame as she shook it in the air.

"You have brought dishonor to the name of Corleone!" she cried. "My own son has turned against his family!"

She cast it out from her into the fireplace. "I have tried and tried to be a good mother to you. I have tried and tried to bring you up right! And what thanks do I get? What thanks, I ask you! The mayor's wife was on the phone!" Her voice rose to a wail. "She said I was such a stupid fool I did not even know I had a traitor in my own camp! And she laughed! She laughed at me!"

She was trying to find something suddenly. The fire tongs! She threw them at Heller. "Get out!" They landed against the wall with a clang.

She got the poker and threw it. "Get out of my sight!" It bashed into a chair with a splintering thud.

She grabbed the shovel and pitched it. It almost struck Heller in the face. As it clattered against the floor, she was shrieking, "Go away!"

She got hold of the stand they had been in. She threw it with all her might. It smashed against the door! "Go! Go! Go! Get out, out, out!"

Heller backed up. He went out of the room.

The sound of her renewed weeping was like a dirge. Heller walked slowly to the hall.

Neither Geovani nor Georgio were in sight.

He picked up his coat and cap from the hall floor. He got into the elevator.

At the cab he slowly got in and drove away.

Oh, my Gods! Madison had done it! With just a simple trick of paper and ink and newspaper influence, out of whole cloth and without even an ounce of truth, he had turned Heller's most powerful ally against him!

What genius!

What a beautiful tool!

And Heller did not even suspect who was shooting at him! Or that anybody really was!

But this might still take a turn for the worse. Heller was tricky, too!

Chapter 8

Heller drove to the Gracious Palms. He parked the old cab in its usual stall.

He took the elevator up. It was still early in the day and there was no interference on my viewer. I could see what he did. There were two whores in his suite. They were practicing ways to undo a wristlock. One of them asked, "Pretty boy, is it the thumb you use in this grip or the first finger? Margie says ... Why, what's the matter?" She saw something must be very wrong when she looked closely at Heller's face.

He was opening cabinets and getting out suitcases. He was beginning to pack.

In alarm the two whores ran out. I could hear one pounding on doors down the hall, one door after another. The other whore was on the hall phone talking quickly.

Heller just kept on packing.

When he turned around, there were numerous women standing in the door in different states of undress. They looked alarmed. A high-yellow came forward, "Pretty boy, are you leaving?"

Heller didn't answer. He just went on packing.

There were more girls at the door. They were beginning to cry.

Heller was getting out the racks and racks of clothes and binding them with cords.

There was a commotion at the door. Heller looked up. Vantagio had shouldered his way through the mob of weeping girls.

"What the hell is this, kid?" said Vantagio.

Heller said, "Has Babe called?"

Vantagio said, "No," in a puzzled voice.

"She will," said Heller. "She will."

Vantagio said, "Oh, kid. Babe sometimes gets upset. I should know. She gets over it."

Heller reached into his inside pocket. "Have you seen the morning papers?"

"I just got up," said Vantagio. "What have the morning ... ?"

Heller had handed him a ripped-off front page of the *New York Grimes*.

Vantagio stared at it. He took it in. He went white. "Good God!"

Heller was indicating the piles of clothes. "These are no good to anybody else. What would you say the bills were?"

"Oh, kid . . ." said Vantagio, sadly.

"How much were the tailor bills on these clothes?" demanded Heller.

"Kid, you don't have to . . ."

"Fifteen thousand?" said Heller.

"Five," said Vantagio. "No more than five. But kid . . ."

"Here's five thousand," said Heller and began to count out the bills. "My safe downstairs is empty. Now there's the matter of the old cab. Bang-Bang will need it so he can still say he has a job. He's on parole, you know. And he has to go on with my military classes at Empire University. So how much is the cab worth?"

"Oh, kid . . ." said Vantagio. He himself was beginning to look teary-eyed.

"Five thousand," said Heller. "We'll call it five thousand. It was expensive to rebuild. Now, was there anything else I owe here? . . ."

Vantagio didn't answer. He had his face buried in a silk handkerchief.

Heller took his hand and put the ten thousand in it. He finished up stuffing things into his bags.

There were girls all around him, pleading with him. "Don't go, pretty boy, don't go!"

They were tugging at him.

He asked them to help carry his clothes. They would not touch them. He had to go get a cart himself. He loaded it.

"Kid," said Vantagio, pleading. "I think you are making an awful mistake. If she had intended you to go she would have called."

Heller said, "She intended."

He pushed the loaded cart to an elevator.

He went down to the basement. The girls, bare of feet and crying, came down in the other elevator.

Heller loaded the cab.

He looked back at Vantagio and the crowd. Two security men were standing there, looking sad, shaking their heads.

My viewer was misted.

Heller had tears in his eyes!

He drove away from the silent crowd. He could still see them in the rearview mirror. Then they were out of sight.

At the Empire State Building, he parked in a cab rank and got a hand truck. A cabby friend offered to take the old taxi to its nearby lot.

Heller wheeled the handcart to his office.

There was a side resting room there and he put some of his luggage in it. He put his toilet kit in the bathroom. He didn't have room for his clothes and he piled them on the sofas.

Izzy came in, saw the clothes. He didn't speak. He just looked aghast.

"I'll be living here," said Heller.

Izzy finally spoke. "I knew it would come to this. Fate has a way with it, Mr. Jet. And it always has more tricks waiting up the path."

"Is there something else wrong?" said Heller.

Izzy twisted around. Heller pressed. Izzy finally said, "The IRS won't wait. They're demanding everything we have. I wasn't able to make enough on arbitrage. Word just came in from the IRS District Office.

They're going to impound every corporation whether it is legal to do it or not. I didn't want to tell you. I saw your morning press. But that's not all of it, I'm afraid. When IRS finds they are not going to be paid, they'll turn their public relations people loose, smear these corporations all over the media. It's ruin. Unless a miracle happens, we won't even have this office in another month."

He left mournfully.

Heller sat down at the desk.

The cat had been following him around from the moment he had come in. It jumped up now and took its place underneath the desk lamp. It sat there studying him.

Heller said to the cat, "You picked the wrong guy to be responsible for." He sounded beaten.

VICTORY!

I had won!

PR!

What a totally effective assassin's tool! And how painful, too!

And better: nobody, neither the victim nor the public, ever knew where the bullets had come from!

Suddenly, I understood the power controls of Earth. So this was how even empires were broken and made. By the PRs. And then the PRs even wrote the history books!

In one deadly blast, Madison had stopped the mighty Heller cold. With a few lines of ink, based only on his imagination, Madison was directing the destinies not only of Earth but of Voltar! No wonder Bury considered him so dangerous!

The PRs were the true Gods of this planet! Gods of wrath and misery. But Gods nonetheless! What a weapon they wielded! What destruction they wrought! Magnificent!

Chapter 9

I had been so fascinated with the glorious weapon, PR, that I had not realized that time was passing, every instant of which might spell deadly danger to me. After all, I had not turned up at Miss Pinch's last night. Also, Bury would not be pleased at all and might even send another phone-call team: I was in no condition to withstand the U.S. Army Signal Corps, much less a flank attack by snakes.

It was getting on toward noon. I painfully dragged myself out of bed and tottered in the direction of Utanc's room.

The suite's side door was open! This had never happened before.

Scenting a new disaster with an experienced nose, I peered in.

Her room was empty!

No trunks. Nothing in the closet or drawers.

She was gone!

I didn't know what plane!

I didn't have a ticket!

I had only eighty or ninety dollars! Nowhere near enough to get me out of New York.

Then I realized she would probably call when she had picked up the tickets. Of course, that was it.

My hands were bandaged. So was much of my body. It hurt to move. But I knew I had better pack. Struggling and fumbling, I went to work, screaming slightly every now and then.

It was very exhausting. Before I could strap anything up, I had to rest. I sank down in a chair.

There were newspapers scattered about the floor. My jaded eye landed on a news story. I was surprised that the paper contained any other news than the Whiz Kid's capers. The story said:

IRS SUSPECT COMMITTED

Arginal P. Pauper was today committed to Walnut Lodge Nut House by Internal Revenue Service routine desk-agent order.

Pauper is alleged to have failed to file an income tax return.

The IRS order also required that Pauper be electric-shocked, given a prefrontal lobotomy and thereafter tortured for life in the institution.

"He needed professional help," the IRS spokesman said, "and only our psychiatrists can give him that.

"He claimed he had spent the sixty cents in question on stamps to mail his return. However, all returns not sent by registered mail and delivered by a Rolls Royce painted blue with yellow stripes are, of course, waste-basketed, so the defense is preposterous."

Pauper's widow and orphans have been ground into meatballs to pay the tax penalties.

IRS N.Y. District Chief Stoney T. Blood issued a public statement: "IRS *über alles!* And let that be a lesson to you, you dumb suckers!"

Over 300,000,000 Americans are said to be tax delinquent each year.

I knew it was PR. I knew it was simply a planted story to frighten people into paying their taxes. But in spite of knowing all that, it scared me spitless!

Having already seen that day the havoc PR could wreak, it stood my hair on end!

I had no more than finished reading it when the phone rang.

Thank heavens! It must be Utanc to tell me what plane. I answered.

A gruff voice said, "Inkswitch?"

I was so startled, I said, "Inkswitch."

"Good. This is the IRS New York Delinquency Office. Just a routine verification that you are there." He hung up.

My hair was not only standing up, it was crackling!

Oh, I had to get out of here! Three years in a Federal pen with homos even worse than Miss Pinch would make a brain operation welcome!

I locked all my suitcases. Then I noticed that I had forgotten to get dressed. I didn't have the energy to unstrap everything. Lying in the wastebasket was the suit I had worn at the last visit to Miss Pinch. Frantically, I pulled it on.

I sneezed!

It stunk violently of red pepper, Tabasco and mustard!

There was no time. I would have to take what clue I had. Utanc had said a four o'clock plane. I would flee to the airport!

I called down for a bellboy and a cart and told them to get a cab at the door. This might be a close thing. Police always verify if you're in before they knock down the place with battering rams, so IRS would of course do even worse!

The bellboy piled my luggage on his hand truck. He pushed it to the front of the elevator door, waiting for the car to come up. Somebody must be coming up in that lift!

Some sixth sense told me to be cautious. The stair-well door was close to hand. I faded into it, holding it open a crack.

The elevator arrived and the door opened.

Two of the toughest-looking men I have ever seen stepped out into the penthouse foyer! They had black hats, gray overcoats, huge shoulders and great, black mustaches! Mean!

They knocked like thunder on the sitting-room door!

Oh, thank Gods for Apparatus training! I fled down the stairwell, unmindful of the agony every movement caused.

Speeding, I went down all thirty stories of the hotel!

I burst into the lobby.

The doorman recognized me. He beckoned. The cab was sitting there.

My bellboy and baggage had already arrived. It was being put in the cab. So slow, so slow!

My eye was pinned on the elevator doors in the lobby.

In desperation, I waved a ten-dollar bill at the bellboy.

He stopped to make sure it wasn't counterfeit!

The manager was coming out. I thought it was to tell me the bill wasn't paid. Instead, he shook me by the hand and said, "Congratulations on your leaving, Mr. Inkswitch. Please use another hotel when you return." I was so relieved to realize Utanc had paid the bill.

The delay was nearly fatal.

The two tough guys came out of the elevator!

I leaped into the cab and screamed, "John F. Kennedy International Airport!"

The driver sped away.

I was looking back.

I had beaten them!

We battered our way through congested traffic. We plunged down into the Queens Midtown Tunnel. We emerged into the flowing traffic of Route 495. I looked back. For a moment I could see the UN fading. I was making it! What a relief!

Wait. Many cars behind us. A gray vehicle was threading its way closer! I stared with my face pressed more closely to the glass.

THE TWO TOUGH MEN!

Not only that, they seemed to have recognized me! One was waving frantically for us to pull over and stop.

I didn't have much money. But I leaned forward. "A twenty-dollar tip if you lose that gray car!"

"Fifty dollahs," said the cabby.

"Fifty dollars!" I said.

We sped forward. We swayed and tire-screeched around trucks. We cut desperately in front of cars whose brakes shrieked as they stamped down to miss us.

Every sway was agony to my tortured and bruised body. Gods, would I be glad to get out of New York—if I made it!

We got onto Woodhaven Boulevard. We roared through the wintry Forest Park. We rocketed past Kew Gardens. We blasted by Aqueduct Race Track.

We came screaming into the passenger terminal of John F. Kennedy Airport. I looked anxiously on the back trail. They still might come. I paid the cabby. I then had only eighteen dollars left!

"What airline?" said a black porter with a cart.

"I don't know," I said.

He was loading my baggage on his small truck. "Well, you c'n take yo' choice, then. They's Pan Am. They's TWA. But if'n it's TWA, we bettah git anothah cab 'cause this is Pan Am. Now, me, f'um mah study of the crashes . . ."

I thought fast. Four o'clock. Maybe only one plane left at four. "What goes to Rome or London or someplace at four?"

"Well, ah thinks they is one fo' Rome at fo'. But if you ain't too partickler, me, I'd go to Trinydad wheh it is mo' wahm."

"Rome. Take me to that counter."

He did. It was long, long before plane time.

"Inkswitch?" said the clerk. "We don't have any reservation in that name. I will call central . . ."

I wasn't listening. I had been casting glances back toward the door.

THERE THEY WERE!

I hysterically threw three one-dollar bills at the porter. "Take care of my baggage!"

I fled.

Darting through a troop of Girl Scouts, colliding with a woman carrying a Pekingese who gave me a shove, I was propelled into the midst of an Olympic ski team. It was a lifesaver. They gave me such a vigorous rejection that I went like a bowling ball into a crowd of priests. The confusion was so great, all I had to do was keep rolling and I was in through the door of a men's washroom.

I hastily got a coin out and with an agonized sigh of relief I was safely inside a john.

I sat there for a bit. I hurt so much, I forgot to pull my feet up. Then I remembered the technique and did so. It was just in time.

Two pairs of heavy boots!

The two tough men were coming down the line of locked toilets, looking under the doors!

They didn't see me.

They were in a hurry.

They went on.

Only then could I permit myself to suffer. The bruises were just one big general pain from the cab ride. I was sure the cuts were bleeding again from the bowling-ball trip. What one had to go through just to execute his simple duties!

Stifling a sneeze, I abruptly remembered that I had forgotten to phone the New York office and get Raht to turn on the 831 Relayer. Without it, I would be blind about Heller.

I had lots of time before four o'clock. The problem was how to get out of this place and to a phone without being spotted.

Getting brave, I left the john cubicle.

There was a man, a very big man, over by a wash bowl. He had a rather extensive kit spread out and he was shaving with an old blade razor.

He was facing sideways to the entrance door. He had hung his hat—a sort of hunting hat with two bills front and back—and his coat—a black and white checkered mackinaw—on a hook quite close to the door.

Being of a cunning frame of mind, I knew that he would shortly wash his face. He would have soap in his eyes for a moment. I waited. Sure enough, over he bent.

Quick as a flash, I had the hat and coat. Quicker, I slid out of the washroom, expertly getting them on at the same moment.

The odd, red cap was awfully big. It fitted easily over my own hat. The loud-checked mackinaw was huge, more like an overcoat on me. Adequate disguise!

I peered cautiously about. Yes! There they were, the two tough men! But they were facing the other way, looking along lines of people.

I got to a coin-change machine and converted ten dollars to change. I certainly was low on cash.

Adequately masked by the hat and coat, I slid into a

glass-enclosed phone kiosk. I dialled the New York office.

"Put Raht on the phone," I said.

They had some idiot clerk from Flisten on their reception: I could tell by the crazy way he had of pronouncing his *S*'s: He made them into *Z*'s. "I am zorry. The poor Raht iz in the hozpital ztill. Complicationz. The pneumonia iz not rezponding to the penizillin. Hiz condition iz critical. Whom zhall I zay called?"

I was furious! I was zo zizzling, I znapped ztraight over into gutter Flizten. An idiot like that couldn't hope to understand Standard Voltarian, much less plain English. "Vacations! Vacations! That's all you people ever think about!"

"O Demons of the green abyss!" he said in Flisten. "This must be Officer Gris!" He sounded scared. That was better!

"Now listen to me," I snarled at him in Flisten. "You order Raht to stop faking and handle the *Empire State* and make him report in or I'll have him filled full of red Tabasco Signal Corps! And listen, you idiot, if I ever catch you speaking Flisten again on an Earth phone line I'll make you listen to *A Night on Bare Mountain* with rolling pins! Got it?"

He had it. It was the most terrible curse I could think of. He was gibbering!

I hung up, feeling a bit better.

Madison! I ought to call Madison and tell him what a magnificent job he had done. A PR triumph! And also that I was leaving. Then Bury wouldn't know where to send the snakes.

I inserted the coins and hit the buttons. Amazing! It was Madison himself who answered. "Thank you for calling right back, Mr. Underslung. What progress have you made in getting the Whiz Kid an Oscar for underhanded driving?"

"No, no," I sneezed. "This is Tabasco Smith, I mean Mr. Smith. Madison, I absolutely had to call and tell you what a magnificent job you have done. You are a wonder. Thank Gods for PR and please tell Mr. Bury I have gone off on a long trip to spy on the Signal Corps for Miss Agnes."

"Job done?" he said, sounding mystified. "But this campaign isn't over, Smith, far from it! It has a long, long way to go yet to achieve lasting image. Wait until you see tomorrow's papers! They will say that he made so much money betting against himself in the race that he will give the bribe in full to the Kansas farmers."

There it was again, the thing which I hadn't understood before. "What's all this about Kansas farmers?"

"You don't get that?" he said, amazed. "Good heavens, you surely are a long way from professional. My orders are to make his name a household word and to make him immortal. Since the image of 'the man who started World War III' was ruined, I have had to take a different tack. The one I am working on now is 'Jesse James.' He was a famous outlaw who fought the railroads in Kansas by robbing trains and gave the loot to the farmers. He is one of the great American folk heroes. Deathless. So if I can give Wister a Jesse James—type image, all will be well. It can change, though. PR is a fluid subject, Inkswitch, and above all we've got to keep that front page no matter how many natural cataclysms get in the way. If I try very hard and stay with the fundamentals of professional PR, the Whiz Kid will make it, but it will take time. Now if you will get off my phone, I'd appreciate it. I'm shorthanded today since Hoodward was shot at the airport by Faustino's men and Ted Tramp's wife is having a baby. I'm expecting calls from various racing associations to get the Whiz Kid debarred from every track in America so we can come back the next day and claim they are just terrified to race against him. And for the day after that, I have to get riots organized by those who lost bets and riots take a lot of advance time. So I need all my phones!"

Yes, I sure could see he was beautifully busy. "Please tell Mr. Bury," I sneezed, "that both the Signal Corps and Miss Agnes have snake detectors. Good-bye."

I hung up. Well, that was out of the road. Did I need to call the Security Chief at Octopus and tell him I would not be around? Then I remembered that anything connected with me came up blank on the computer and they couldn't tell whether I was working or not. And Miss Pinch might have a bug on that line. Also, IRS might trace the call. In fact, they might be tracing me right now....

SCRAPE!

The door of the phone kiosk flew open.

I cowered back, but not in time!

It was the owner of the hat and coat!

He loomed like a mountain!

A huge paw seized me!

I was yanked ferociously out of the kiosk.

I saw a fist cocked in midair.

WHAM!

An anvil seemed to hit me in the eye!

Down I went on the floor. THUD went my head against the edge of the phone booth!

PLOWIE!

Into the air around me went a cloud of stars.

The sound wasn't from the stars. It was from a boot in my side.

He tore the mackinaw off of me. He grabbed the hat.

THUNK!

He kicked me again in the side.

I shut my eyes tight. I was waiting for the next kick. It didn't come. I opened my eyes.

TWO PAIRS OF HEAVY BOOTS! Right by my face!

The two tough men had caught up with me!

I was done for!

I looked up. One bent over and yanked me to my feet.

The other was reaching into his pocket. Gun? Handcuffs?

The first one said, "Are you Achmed Ben Nutti?"

Oh, my Gods. At Pan Am I had asked for reservations in the name of Inkswitch. Achmed Ben Nutti was the United Arab League name I had been travelling under and had passports for.

I was too weak to fight. Cunning was in order. "Yes, I am Achmed Ben Nutti and I have diplomatic status! You can't arrest me!"

"Arrest you?" he said. "No, no, Comrade. We are from the Bolshoi Travel Agency. We have been trying hard to catch you and give you your ticket!"

He was dusting me off and it made a cloud of mustard-pepper-Tabasco odors fly into the air. We both sneezed.

"Here are all your flight papers," said the other tough-looking man. "We have already found and checked your baggage aboard. You had better hurry, Comrade. That's your flight they're calling now."

"He doesn't seem to be able to walk," said the other, sneezing again. "Let's carry him over to the first-class gate and get them to let us through. We can dump him aboard."

We went through the rat maze of detectors, past the cooperative attendants, down a gangway and into the side of a ship. We were the last ones aboard. I had almost missed the plane! It evidently was an earlier one!

They dumped me in a first-class seat.

Utanc! She was caped and hooded and veiled, sitting right there!

"Darling!" I cried.

Utanc grabbed a passing blue sleeve. "Purser," she said, "I see you have a lot of empty seats at the back. Could you please dump my owner into one of them? He is making me feel like I'm going to sneeze!"

He gave a snappy salute. "Pan Am service, ma'am."

The purser snapped his fingers for a stewardess and in no time the two of them had me clear at the back of the first-class compartment and were covering my clothes with a plastic sheet and buckling me in.

I sank back. Surrounded with the posh luxury of a first-class superjet, complete with classic Greek temples in the murals, I sighed a sigh, somewhat interrupted with a sneeze, as anxiety ebbed out.

And so, gratefully, I saw the landing strip race by and presently, bending sideways without too much pain, watched the smoggy skyline of New York grow small and fade away.

Thank Gods, I had made it.

Later, the dinner being served from carts on the aisle was delicious. But a glass of wine, no matter if served with great ceremony in first class, aloft, does not substitute for a good crystal ball.

With its usual evil grin, fiendish Fate had been busy, just ahead, sorting out available disasters. The one it chose to first serve up for me was horrible. The very memory of it makes me wince.

PART THIRTY-FOUR

Chapter 1

The THY (Turkish Airlines) plane slid down toward Afyon. The snow-capped peaks lined up to point at Afyonkarahisar's wintry finger. It was a striking view of a bleak terrain: how could any human beings possibly survive in the villages which dotted the hostile mountains and the plain? A scene of utter desolation, it had one saving grace: I was home! The optical illusion, which made a mountaintop and marked the Voltar base, was still in place—suitably wintry now—so I was not only home, I was still connected to Voltar, my real native land.

And I was still alive!

What a relief!

We landed and while we waited for the landing stage to roll up and the door to open, Utanc stepped close to me. She put her dainty hand upon my sleeve, a favor I so seldom enjoyed. She looked at me, her eyes large and dark and pleading above her veil.

"O my master," she whispered, "we still have a little money left." She was holding her purse open now. It was absolutely stuffed with money. "May I keep it?"

"Oh, dear Utanc, what a manager you are! Of course you may keep it." I was quite touched. Imagine doing that whole trip on much less than a hundred thousand dollars! Besides, I still had millions in the gold I had brought from Voltar.

She closed the purse with a snap and was first down the plane steps.

Some people were at the airport gate. The taxi driver, Karagoz and, ah yes, Utanc's two little servant boys!

Cloak pressed against her by the wintry wind, Utanc raced toward the gate!

The two little boys burst through and, crowing with delight, sped across the tarmac to meet her!

She gathered them up, hugging them.

Both of them had their arms around her neck and she was kissing their cheeks through her veil. What a bundle of welcome! They were trying to tell her everything that had happened since she had been gone and trying to find out what she had brought for them all at the same time.

They ignored me as I limped painfully by them.

Karagoz ignored me. The taxi driver ignored me. I went through the terminal to the parking area. Karagoz had evidently brought the boys in Utanc's BMW for there it sat alongside the taxi driver's taxi.

The wind was very dry and cold and a bit gritty. I was getting chilled and it wasn't doing my unhealed wounds any good.

Finally they came through the parking lot door, the two small boys chattering and excited, eyes glowing. They did look somewhat like Rudolph Valentino and James Cagney as they must have looked as children. That surely had been a successful present!

Utanc was saying to the taxi driver, "Now, here are the shipping manifests for the trunks. They couldn't come on this plane but when they do, you be sure to hire a truck to pick them up. Now we will go home."

Karagoz stepped close to her and whispered something in her ear.

Utanc said, "Ice cream! How would you two dear little boys like some ice cream over in town?"

They shrieked their approval of the plan.

Karagoz, Utanc and the two little boys got in her BMW, and with veiled Utanc behind the wheel, it rocketed out of the parking lot, screeched its tires as it turned into the road to Afyon and was gone.

The taxi driver loaded his taxi with the bags we had checked through on this plane and shortly we were headed for the villa.

"Well, how is she working out?" he flung back at me as he dodged through the camels and donkey carts.

"She is absolutely amazing," I said. "Not only is she a great slave but she also happens to be the best (bleeped) money manager you ever saw! She handled all our funds on that very expensive trip and just now when we got off the plane she must have had nearly all of the original money left. Amazing! I don't know how she did it!"

"Yeah, she was sure a bargain," said the taxi driver. "Cheap, too. They don't make slaves like that anymore. Her turn-in value would be almost as high as the original price. You want I should ever trade her in on a new model?"

"Never!" I said firmly. "Not even if they come out with a new rear end."

We were drawing close to the villa. There seemed to be a number of cars parked on the road outside it. The taxi driver found a place to stop.

Creakily, I got out. I went through the gate.

The yard was full of men!

My reflexes, after all I had been through, were not very quick. I didn't get any chance to retreat.

A hulking brute stepped behind me!

Another hulking brute stalked up to me and used my Turkish Earth-name. "You Sultan Bey?"

"That's him," said another. "I know him!"

Another jumped in front of me. "I'm from the American Oppress Company! Here is your bill. It's overdue!"

Another shouldered through. "I'm from the Dunner's Club. Here is your bill."

Yet another shouldered through. "I'm from Masker-Charge! What are you going to do about this bill?"

Still another crowded up. "I'm from the Squeeza Credit Card Corporation. One month interest on your first month's purchases is already more than the original amount!"

In chorus, a very menacing one, they yelled, "When are we going to get paid?"

I staggered back. I couldn't stagger very far as they were hemming me in. They were all waving bills!

It hit me! Utanc had gotten credit cards on my apparently affluent name and position before we left. She had done the whole trip on CREDIT CARDS!

Chapter 2

I saw some of the amounts they were waving. HUGE! The best hotels, all first-class travel, all the best shops . . .

Weak as I was, I still had some wits to gather about me. My gold! Painful though it might be, I would have to part with some gold.

I held up a bandaged hand. "Enough!" I cried. "You will be paid!" I would save the old homestead!

I rushed across the yard, across the house patio, into my bedroom, into the closet and through the secret door.

There it was, the stack of boxes in the corner of my

secret room, all marked as "dangerously radioactive" to keep people away.

Ignoring the pain to my hands and the agony it caused to bend over, I ripped the lid off a box. Glittering yellow! I picked up a fifty-pound bar. It would weigh 41.6+ pounds on Earth. At twelve ounces Troy to the pound, that was 499.99+ ounces. Gold was above $700 when I last looked. This bar should be worth more than $349,999.99! That should hold them!

I struggled out with it. They gaped when I reappeared on the lawn. I dropped it in front of them. "This gold, if you cash it in, should take care of everything. And be sure to credit me with the difference."

They fought their way to it. One hulking brute got possession. He took out a pen knife and cut into the bar.

He stared.

He showed the others.

I stared.

The sliver he had cut off was lead!

"Sultan," he said in a low and menacing voice, "that bar is just lead painted with gilt paint! Are you trying to put us off?"

I couldn't believe it!

I checked it myself. Just lead with a coat of gilt paint on it.

The creditors instantly started grabbing rugs out of the house!

"Wait! Wait!" I cried.

I struggled back to my secret room.

I began to open boxes and lift out bars. Nine cases. Seventeen more fifty-pound bars. Eight hundred and fifty more pounds of lifting. A frantic knife cutting slivers!

They were *all* lead with a gilt coat of paint! But it

had been real gold before I had left for New York! I had checked it!

Aching and battered, the bandages on my hands coming apart, I regained the lawn.

Not only did they have piles of rugs and furniture stacking up, they were now also herding the domestic staff out. They began to put ankle cuffs on them and connect them together on a long chain. One hulking brute cried, "They'll bring a good price in the slave markets of Arabia!"

"Wait! Wait!" I begged. "I will pay you! It's just that I have a slight headache."

The taxi driver was still there. I leaped into his cab. I would still save the old homestead. "Mudlick Construction Company!" I cried, "And to Hells with the camels!"

At great cost to my bruises from the bumps, we went careening back to Afyon. With screaming brakes we skidded to a stop at Mudlick.

I rushed in. The manager said, "I've been expecting you." He went right over to the safe, opened it and took out stacks of U.S. dollar bank notes. It was really painful to see those going into a sack and know I would never be able to caress them.

A quarter of a million dollars! My half of the kickback on that construction cost. I signed the receipt.

We went tearing back to the villa.

In agony from the bumps, I got out of the smoking taxi.

I stalked into the yard.

They had waited. The rugs were still piled up. The staff, in leg irons, was still standing there.

Triumphantly, I threw the sack of bank notes at them.

They all tore it apart and began to count it.

Then the Dunner's Club man cried, "There's only

a quarter of a million dollars here!" He turned his back on it. He got a piece of paper from an aide. He waved it. "Here is my order for foreclosure! Get a padlock on those gates!"

"Wait! Wait!" I screamed. "I will pay! I will pay!" Ye Gods, how much were those bills?

I turned to the taxi again. "To Faht Bey's office!" I would save the old homestead in spite of Hells!

With engine roaring and my bruises shrieking, we braked in front of the International Agricultural Training Center for Peasants. I went reeling into the Base Commander's office.

Faht Bey looked at me. "I've been expecting you," he said, a deadly look on his fat face.

"Give me a million dollars!" I said.

"Can't do it!" he said.

I was astonished. "Look," I said. "I started this hospital project. You have two hundred gangsters coming in here to get their faces remodelled. At $100,000 each, that's $20,000,000! The buildings only cost a million. You got $19,000,000 clear! What do you mean, you can't? Look at that profit!"

"Little enough to compensate for all the damage you do. Besides, the demand for drugs from Lombar Hisst is out of sight in tonnage. We're barely making both ends meet."

"I'm in trouble!" I wailed.

"When weren't you?" said Faht Bey. "But I have a proposition for you. If you will agree to certain terms, you can have a quarter of a million."

"The terms?" I begged.

"When the credit card bills began to come in, I made up my mind and wrote it all out for you to sign. Here it is."

I read it:

> I, *Soltan Gris*, *hereby swear and affirm to stop grafting, chiselling and embezzling monies from the Earth Base Treasury. I will demand not one more cent after this final payoff and I will absolutely undertake to place no more contracts for construction so I can get a kickback from the contractors as I have been doing.*
>
> *Sign, Sworn, Attested, Witnessed.*

I was desperate. But this was horrible!

Faht Bey said, "If you refuse to sign it, I will simply let those credit card people tear you to pieces."

He had the quarter of a million in stacks, right there.

I signed! He got his wife and the security guard to witness it.

Stuffing the packets of bank notes in a handy sack, I regained the cab. We went scorching back to the villa.

I staggered out of the taxi. I made my way to the waiting mob. I flung the bag at them.

They pounced on it. They tore it apart. They counted it.

"Aha!" said the American Oppress man. "He has covered the first month of bills!"

They agreed. They got the shackles off the staff. They brushed them off. They put the rugs and furniture back in place.

I was reeling. I had saved the old homestead. But at what a terrible sacrifice! And it and I would both be swept away again in just a few weeks when the rest of the bills came in!

But that wasn't what caused me to collapse.

When they had everything in order again, the whole mob came over to me. They were fawning.

"Ah, Sultan Bey," said Dunner's Club. "I speak for all of us. You have met your first month's bills. You have proven your credit beyond any doubt. We are waiving any limit we thought we might have to impose. Feel free to charge whatever you like, any amount you like, anywhere in the whole world!"

The others raised a cheer.

What an awful, awful sentiment!

I fainted dead away!

Chapter 3

I came to, lying in the yard, right where I had collapsed. The staff had pretty well cleaned things up. They were walking around, even stepping over me.

I became afraid they would sweep me into one of their trash bags. I was far too weak to resist.

Suddenly, I recognized how really sick I was. I knew I had to get to the hospital while I still had the ability to move somewhat.

The taxi driver wasn't there.

An old Chevy station wagon was in the yard. I crawled over to it on my hands and knees. They used to keep a spare key under the mat. With enormous strain, I lifted up the corner of the floor covering.

The key!

I hauled myself up by the steering column. I somehow got under the wheel.

It started!

Oh, Gods, if I could just hold out until I got to the hospital!

A camel driver saw me coming. I was driving awfully slow. He saw who was behind the wheel. He got his beasts off the road quick. Lucky for me: the camels might have attacked me.

Going five miles an hour, concentrating on every yard of advance, I finally saw the sign ahead:

WORLD UNITED CHARITIES
MERCY AND BENEVOLENT
HOSPITAL

It looked much bigger. The warehouses were up and a new wing had been added.

I was distracted by the fact that it was all landscaped! A couple of peasant women were doing winter trim on rose bushes. They screamed at me when a wheel inadvertently went off the drive slightly and made a furrow in their lawn. I couldn't understand the commotion: cold weather had turned the grass brown.

Distracted, I hadn't seen a little Fiat move around me and sneak into the parking place toward which I was headed. It was bright red and at the last instant I saw that it was opening its door.

CRASH!

The door hit the side of the Chevy.

The curb stopped me. I somehow managed to shut off the ignition.

Somebody was getting out of the Fiat. A voice! "What in the name of Allah are you doing, you cross-eyed camel! My car, my poor car!" In the rearview side mirror, somebody was bending down stroking at a dent. That somebody promptly stood up and came storming to the side of the Chevy. "My new Fiat! You wrecked my brand-new Fiat!"

It was Nurse Bildirjin!

She was alongside my door. She looked. She saw who it was! Fury contorted her face! "So you're back, you (bleepard)!"

It wasn't a very friendly welcome to the portals of Mercy and Benevolence even if its principal business was the altering of the I.D. of gangsters.

"I'm dying," I managed to get out.

"Really?" she said. It changed her whole demeanor. "You wouldn't fool me, would you?" She turned and ran like the quail she was named after, straight into the hospital yelling gaily, "Hey, Doc! You got to come out! Sultan is outside actually dying! Hurray, hurray!"

It did produce a certain commotion. A lot of women with children rushed from the waiting room and formed a staring ring, laughing and chattering excitedly.

At length, Dr. Prahd Bittlestiffender pushed his way through the cheering throng. He was followed by a couple of orderlies pushing a cart with a corpse bag on it.

"Cadavers are usually delivered at the mortuary entrance," said Prahd in reproof. "Can't you drive around there?"

"I'm too weak," I said sadly. "Doctor, just this once, be kind. You've got to help me. I am a survivor of the battle of New York. I am a victim of red pepper, Miss Agnes, mustard, truncheons, taxi cabs and snakes. I have crawled back home with final last words: Cancel my credit cards before the U.S. Army Signal Corps finds Bury!"

"Oh, I don't think we need to go to the expense of

burying you. But speaking of credit cards, when does my pay start?"

"Must we talk about money?" I wept. "Please help me, Doctor. I am in agony!"

Prahd had them stuff me in the corpse bag and soon we were in his operating room. He pushed the male attendants out and bolted the door.

It was with shock that I realized I was alone with Prahd and Nurse Bildirjin!

In a very businesslike fashion, they stripped off my clothes. They laid me out on an operating table. Nurse Bildirjin busied herself with strapping down my wrists and ankles. It was all too reminiscent of recent traumatic experiences.

"What are you going to do?" I begged. "No gas! Don't put me out."

"Relax," said Prahd. "We are simply here in our professional capacity." He was looking at me. "My, my, what a mess!"

Nurse Bildirjin said hopefully, "What were you in? A train wreck combined with an airplane crash? All cut and black and blue. Doc, maybe he wandered into a sausage factory and they mistook him properly for a pig."

"What are these pits on your stomach?" said Prahd. "The ones with the black bits at the bottom?"

I looked down at my stomach. "Powder grains," I said. "Black powder."

"Well, well," said Prahd. "Very uncosmetic. They will have to come out. Get on it, Nurse Bildirjin, if you please."

"Really?" she said with delight. "Isn't that surgical, doctor?"

"No, no," said Prahd. "Very minor compared to the rest of this."

She efficiently got some instruments and a pan and began to take out the first black grain.

YOW!

"Now, the rest of this is more important," said Prahd. He began to pass a scope over my body. "Hah! Three cracked ribs. One chipped pelvis bone. Numerous blood blisters..."

He was taking notes. Nurse Bildirjin had some huge pliers. "I think this will be faster!" She dug in and closed them.

YEEE-OW!

"That's one. Now for the next."

"How many are there?" said Prahd.

"Oh, maybe two or three hundred," said Nurse Bildirjin.

"Do you have to make such big holes?" I screamed.

"Oh, yes," she said. "I might leave some. Very unsightly." She was digging for the next one. My Gods, this was far worse than the original blast! "Doctor, in your professional opinion," she said conversationally as she worked, "don't you think he is a bit dinky?"

Prahd nodded. "Yes, I would say an inch is below average. Well, well! What is this? What is this? A crushed testicle!"

"That was when I was a boy!" I said. "YEE-OW! Please, Nurse Bildirjin, not such big bites! Those powder grains are awfully small. A farmer kicked me for drowning all his breeding animals. It was a school vacation job and I was just trying to see if they could swim. He was a very...YEEEEE-OWWWW!"

"Well, that may have been done when you were a boy," said Prahd. "But now the other testicle seems to be in bad shape, too. That must be an awfully tough town, New York. And especially hard on testicles."

"It is, it is," I said. "The primitives are . . . YEEEE-EEEE–OWWWWWWWW! . . . real (bleep) breakers."

"I really think I had better put you under general gas," said Prahd. "There's hours and hours of surgery and cellular handling here. And Nurse Bildirjin seems to be working very slowly today."

"I think this would go along faster," she said, "if I just burned them out. See, when this electric probe touches one in the pan here, it explodes." It went *Zzzt!* and smoke rose. "Now I will just go over here and turn on some pop music. . . ."

That was all it took. I fainted.

Chapter 4

I awoke.

I couldn't see!

I had no sense of body weight!

In fact, I didn't have any sense at all!

Maybe I was dead!

I blinked my eyes. Yes, I could feel myself blinking my eyes.

Maybe they had thrown the rest of my body away. Maybe I was just a head!

Gods knew what a Voltarian cellologist would do. After all, I had known Doctor Crobe and how he loved to make human freaks. Maybe I was some sort of monster now. Maybe I looked like a cat or an octopus or Miss Pinch.

Worse than that: Earth psychologists and psychiatrists teach that all anyone is, is a bunch of cells evolved up the evolutionary track, that the person himself is just what his cells and body make him. There could be no doubt of the validity of their teachings, for one could be shot for not believing them. If Prahd had changed my cells, it followed by Earth psychology that my personality would suffer a total shift! So what new personality would I have? Something sweet and kind—Gods forbid! Or something whining and propitiative, like Izzy—which of course would be even less acceptable.

What had been changed? If I knew Prahd and Nurse Bildirjin, it would be something utterly underhanded and with some ghastly twist!

There was a sort of dim glow around. An eerie light was coming hazily through the slits of something. Gradually I could get a half-seen impression of my immediate environment.

I was in a sort of a long tub, midway between ceiling and floor. Only my head was out. The rest of me was suspended, probably by antigravity coils, in fluid: my body was not touching anything solid.

There were lights burning in the tub, probably emitting some strange wavelength. It was these, escaping through slits, that furnished the dim, greenish glow in the room. Cell catalysts of some kind? I had no real idea.

Accidentally, I moved my eyes to the right.

A window!

Through it I could see the pale sickle of a wintry moon. That was the moon of Earth! I was still on Blito-P3.

I concentrated. Maybe I could estimate how much time had gone by. If it took four and a half hours to come out from under gas—a fact of which I was uncertain—I must have been on that operating table for eight to ten hours! A very long time.

WHAT HAD THEY DONE TO ME?

It seemed to confirm my worst suspicions. A monster! Did I have flippers for feet? Did I now have tentacles for hands? Maybe a beak instead of a nose?

Horrors! What personality changes would follow such shifts?

Oh, Gods, I should never have come near those two fiends!

I had no question at all whether or not it was awful. That followed as the night the day. The only question was about the exact horror design. Dracula? Did I now have long teeth and live only on fresh blood? Would I be able to live with myself comfortably under the dictates of this new personality? I worked my jaws experimentally to see if they were now designed for severing jugular veins.

My face was bandaged right up to the eyes!

WHAT HAD THEY DONE???????????

I fussed and fumed and fretted through that dark and horrible night.

At least three centuries of worry later, dawn came. Only another century after that, possibly about nine according to the bleak sun through the window, Doctor Prahd Bittlestiffender came in.

I found I could turn my head and speak. "You put me out!"

He smiled. A very bad sign. He began to read meters and gauges around the suspended tub. When he had noted them all down on a chart, he looked at me and said, "I had to. You kept screaming even when you fainted. Nurse Bildirjin couldn't even hear her favorite radio program. It's the Hoochi-Hoochi Boys and Their Electric Cura Irizvas. She's only sixteen, you know, and she's a fan of theirs. They come on every day at . . ."

I knew the tactic. Trying to get me off the subject

and lull my suspicions. "You did something dreadful," I snarled. "You cellologists are all alike!"

"No, no. The work was just very extensive, that's all. You have no idea how bashed up you've let yourself become in that strange career you have. Old, old injuries and wounds. A lot of improperly treated bone breaks. You apparently have not been in the habit of seeking professional care. I even took a coin out of your kidney."

"Aha!" I said. "You did all this just to recover a coin and enrich yourself!"

"No, no. It was only a two-cent piece from the planet Modon. Somebody must have shot it at you. I put it in your wallet so your accounts will balance. But all that aside, it was this last escapade that could have crippled you for the rest of your days. I even had to replace three square feet of skin entirely: it had some of the strangest things in it. In that town you call New York, the one that kept coming up in your screams, you surely must have been running with a rough crowd."

"You didn't do anything else?"

"No, I just put you together."

The day I believe a cellologist won't ever dawn. "You didn't change anything?"

"Well, I had to work on your genitals a bit."

"I knew it!" I screamed. "I knew you'd do something awful if you could put me out!"

"No, no. All I did was normalize things a bit. Purely routine cellological work. Well, bye-bye now. One of the gangsters I fixed doesn't like his new face: says it reminds him of somebody called J. Edgar Hoover. But that isn't odd because that's where I got it from. I need better picture books. I'll get some on my own when my pay starts."

I frowned so sourly at this hint that he left.

Oh, I didn't like the looks of things at all. I know

when people are hiding things from me. But I was helpless. I could only move my eyes and my neck and talk through the bandages on my face.

I was more certain than ever that Prahd had done me in.

The only question was, exactly how?

Chapter 5

Throughout that whole morning, I lay suspended in that (bleeped) tub and stewed and fumed.

I could see a Turkish tree through the window and the nameplate—*Zanco Cell Catalyst Growth Machine, Model 16 Magnaspeed*—on the tub rim above my face. The tree did not have the power to occupy the mind very long. The nameplate, in Voltarian script, was far more thought stimulating. WHAT was it growing? Bird feet?

I couldn't see my body. And after the two-thousandth reading, the nameplate was no more informative than it had been the first time.

One's imagination can become overactive.

Firmly, I steeled myself to shut off speculation on future form and the effect it inevitably would have upon my personality and character.

I wondered if I would be fed. I wasn't hungry but maybe starving me to death was part of their dastardly plot.

The shadows on the tree said it must be about noon.

The door opened.

Nurse Bildirjin! She was dressed in a starched white nurse's uniform and cap. She was not carrying a tray.

She had a notebook and chart in her hands. She went around reading all the meters or whatever there was to record on the outside of the tub. She sent a glance or two at my face. She looked awfully sly!

I decided to speak, regardless of consequences. Maybe I could get some information out of her.

"Where's my food?" I said.

"Oh, you don't have to eat. You're connected to the fluids and containers in the tub."

"Give me a mirror," I said.

"I'm sorry. It's not allowed. Patients can get upset."

"What did you two do to me?" I grated.

She faked a look of utter surprise.

I knew she wouldn't answer. I changed the subject. "I'm going crazy just floating here."

"Oh," she said, "I thought you had arrived there a long time ago, Sultan Bey." She gave a nasty, sniggering laugh at her own joke.

I didn't laugh.

"But," she said, "I wouldn't want any complaints being circulated about our care of patients."

She left. She came back in about three minutes. She was carrying a radio on a strap. She hung it somewhere on the wall above and behind my head. She put some earphones on her ears. As she tuned in, leaking from under the pads I could hear the Istanbul hot pop station.

She put the earphones over my ears. She turned it up very loud. She left.

I don't care for commercials about bubble gum and camel feed. But everybody in Turkey these days seemed to be listening to hot pop.

I couldn't take the earphones off or change the station.

As the hours wore on, I found that the Goat Guys must be especially popular for they played their records frequently. And at least once in every hour, they played their latest hit. With flutes and drums and snarls and roars, it went:

> *You are my monster,*
> *I am your camel.*
> *You make me crazy,*
> *The way you play.*
> *I only wonder,*
> *Why my dear mother,*
> *Bought strychnine*
> *And asked you here today.*

At first, I was sort of detached about it. Then I began to realize that they must be playing it for me as a sort of request. It fitted my case pretty exactly when you got right down to it. I even invented a sort of personality test to go with it. Each time the news came on, I would fill in the interval of Arabs not getting along with Arabs with searching probes into my reactions to the word *strychnine.*

Since the cells and body are the only things which determine personality, and if I could detect any change of reaction in myself to the word *strychnine,* it followed that from this I would be able to work out exactly what they had done to me physically. It didn't work.

Fortunately, the station was off the air for several hours each night and I could get some sleep.

About three times a day someone would come in and read the meters. But as I had earphones on, they presumed I couldn't hear anything they said and so didn't bother to answer anything I said.

For the next eight days, the only real change I could detect was a snowstorm that whitened up the tree for a day. The boughs then gradually, bit by bit, from wind, lost the whiting.

I began to believe that for the rest of eternity I would just float here without sensation, detached from every world except that of hot pop and camel feed, while somewhere in another world, Arabs fought Arabs and mothers bought strychnine.

But, one morning, just as I had become accustomed to it, my life in the Zanco Model 16 Magnasped came to an abrupt and shocking end.

Chapter 6

It was about 11:00 A.M. by the cold sun in the window.

Prahd walked in.

He was followed by two orderlies and a cart of instruments, gas canisters and masks.

The clatter smashed through "You Are My Monster." I looked at this invasion in sudden fear.

Prahd took the earphones off me. "I've come to disconnect you," he said.

He held up his right hand.

An orderly put an anesthesia mask in it.

"But . . ." I started to say.

The mask was over my face and I was out!

I came to after what seemed to be a space of two seconds.

I was lying in a bed. I was in a different room. I had a sheet over me. Over and under the sheet there were straps. I could not move my arms or legs or lift my body.

They had done something else to me! I was sure of it. But no, nothing much could happen in two seconds.

I turned my head. A very thin, low sun was coming in the window. It must be afternoon. It hadn't been two seconds. It had been 11:00 A.M. It must now be 3:00 P.M. Plenty of time to do something else nasty!

I found I could flex something at the end of my arms. I managed to get a hand in view. Oh, thank Gods! Not flippers. They were fingers! I could move and control them. They weren't fakes. They were mine.

Somewhere toward the bottom of the bed I could feel the canvas ankle cuffs. I stirred that extremity. The sheet lifted slightly. By craning my neck I could see toes. I wiggled them. Oh, thank Gods they were not hoofs! They were my toes! I tried the other one. Toes on both feet! Oh, thank Gods!

A clatter at the door.

Nurse Bildirjin came in pushing a cart with food on it. She was all starched and crisp looking. All smiles. Was there something sly in that smile? "How about some breakfast?" she said.

BREAKFAST! Oh, my Gods, they had been working on me another twenty hours! I looked anxiously at the food. Maybe they had given me the stomach of a goat. Was it hay on that cart? No, just a couple of boiled eggs and some *kahve*. However, it did not dispel my fears. I knew they had done *something*.

She didn't let me use my hands, which was suspicious enough. She fed me with a spoon and gave me the *kahve* through a straw. And all the time she was humming a little tune. I recognized it: "You Are My Monster"! Oh Gods, what had they done?

I tried to read it on her face. She was a very pretty girl, though young. Raven-black hair, a tan complexion, even, white teeth, full lips, big black eyes capable of considerable expression. And very well developed in spite of her being only sixteen. But she was a woman and treachery could not be far off. Anybody can tell you that treachery and beauty go hand in hand. That's why you have to kill songbirds wherever found. But where women are concerned, it's the other way around. Where killing is concerned, they always choose me as the first target of choice. Piled onto earlier experience, Krak with her hypnohelmets, Miss Pinch with her red pepper and even dear Utanc with her credit cards proved that beyond any doubt whatever! I was learning to be wary. Nurse Bildirjin undoubtedly had something up her sleeve!

She straightened up her tray and gave it a push toward the door. She smiled at me very cheerfully: a very bad sign!

Then she went to the foot of the bed.

She lifted the sheet slightly and looked up under it. "*That's* what I wanted to see," she said.

Oh, Gods! What had she looked at?

They HAD done something!

It was too much for my already unbalanced wits. I screamed, "PRAHD! PRAHD! PRAHD!"

Nurse Bildirjin was smiling all over herself. "If you mean Doktor Muhammed," she said, citing his Earth name, "I'll get him for you. Oh, this is great."

In under a minute young doctor Prahd (alias Doktor Muhammed Ataturk) came in, followed by Nurse Bildirjin.

He walked over and exposed my chest. There were a couple cup bandages there. He pulled them off and took some chest hair with them.

"You had me under another twenty hours!" I raved at him. "What have you done now that you haven't already done?!"

He pulled the sheet down further, found two more

cups on my abdomen and pulled them off. "Tube holes. They've healed very nicely. After you come out of a Magnaspeed, the tube holes have to be closed and healed."

The strap across my lower middle was in the way. He pulled the upper part of the sheet back across my chest. He went down to the foot of the bed and, just like Nurse Bildirjin, lifted the sheet slightly and looked. "Oh, yes," he said. "You've done very well."

Oh, my Gods, what were they looking at? I knew Crobe. I went into terror. "What have I done very well?" I screamed.

"Get the mirror," he said to Nurse Bildirjin.

She had it right there. She held it by my knees and adjusted it. Young doctor Prahd lifted the sheet with the air of a theater manager introducing a new play.

I looked in the mirror.

I almost fainted.

I looked again. I shrieked, "You've made me into a horse!"

"No, no," he said, with professional calm. "That's simply normal. You are so used to one testicle not being there and the other drawn up into the body that a normal scrotum and actually having testicles may look strange to you."

"But the LENGTH of *IT!*" I screamed.

"Sultan Bey," said Prahd, "you don't seem to trust me. Your skin is all new, your old mis-set broken bones are mended, your vital organs are all fixed up. And although it was a great temptation, I didn't even change your face; I only removed some warts and scars. You will just look a bit brighter and fresher. You still aren't very good looking, so don't be alarmed."

"No, no!" I shouted. "I mean those HUGE genitals!" I could still see them in the mirror. I was aghast!

"Oh, my," tut-tutted Prahd. "Don't you ever take

showers with other men? You must be awfully unobservant. For your home habitat, a tumescent size of ten inches is not overly large. Many on Earth have them that size—even bigger. I assure you that your previous one-inch tumescence was too small."

"Oh, I know you cellologists!" I cried. "You couldn't resist doing something strange!"

Prahd thought it over carefully. Then he pushed his straw-colored hair off his face. "No, not really. Of course, you may feel a little more vigorous. Your muscle tone will improve."

"Oh, you can't fool me!" I cried. "You did something peculiar! I'm sure of it!"

He thought once more. Then he seemed to remember something. He turned his bright green eyes on me depreciatingly. "Oh, yes. The catalyzer. It was a pretty complex scene getting all the nerve ends sorted out on the first testicle after it was grown from the gene pattern. And I did leave the other one in the growexpeditor a bit too long. But it won't produce in excess of more than half a pint of semen."

"WHAT?" I screamed.

"But," he said reasonably, "that's no more than a horse furnishes at one time."

"I knew it!" I wailed. "You've turned me into a horse!"

"No, no, no," he said soothingly. "It's completely human. You will produce completely human babies. Really, Sultan Bey, you should trust me. Horses are completely out of style. They have quite enough of them. You are now just a well-equipped male. Of course, you may have the urge to do it a little more often than you used to. And you can probably do it more than once in the same night. But truly, I think you'll find it quite all right."

"Oh, my Gods!" I wept. "I am sure all this will change my whole personality."

"What?" he said, his bright green eyes shooting wide in astonishment.

"Yes," I sobbed. "Ask any Earth psychologist. All a personality is, is the product of cells. One has urges. They come from the reptile brain, the censor and the id. And all that is made up of cells. You have changed my cells and so you have utterly altered my whole character."

"Ah," he said. "In your case especially, how I wish that that were true. Unfortunately, you are just mouthing the superstitions of an uninformed primitive cult: you find it on many backward planets. They try to make men believe that character is inherent and passed on by an evolutionary chain or some such nonsense. In some witch-doctor cults they even go so far as to say a man is totally the effect of his cellular inheritance and therefore can't be changed. It's a way of excusing their inability to mold character. When people try to hold them responsible for creating a criminal society that way, they just glibly say 'a man is just the product of his cells.' It obscures the fact that they are just too incompetent and too criminal themselves to mold character and teach right from wrong.

"Ah, no, Sultan Bey. If cells and glands were all there was to life, I'd be a God, wouldn't I? And I'm not. I'm just a poor cellologist, unpaid, but doing my job anyway, and without even a thank-you from my superior, but suspicion undeserved."

He dropped the sheet. He looked at me. "It's a very sad thing that personality can't be changed just by shifting a few cells. Particularly in your case. But," and he smiled bravely, "one does what one can to relieve pain and make people happier. And I do hope that your

increased activity potential doesn't have violent consequences for others or this planet." He brightened up.
"Well! That one was successful. You can be up and
around and leave whenever you like."

He set the example and marched out the door.

Chapter 7

Nurse Bildirjin began to sweep the floor and tidy up
the room. She seemed in a happy frame of mind but
apparently it was too quiet for her. She went over to the
radio on the hook, pulled out the earphone jack and
turned on the hot pop station.

"Hey!" I said, being pretty tired by this time of
"You Are My Monster," "He said I could leave! Unstrap
this bed and let me out of here. Where are my clothes?"

"Clothes?" she said. She rushed out and came back
with a type of bag they use to hold discarded body parts:
Non-Odor Transmitting was on it very plain in Voltarian. She shoved it at me.

I couldn't take it. My arms were still strapped down.
It looked awfully thin to have any clothes in it. "That
isn't what I wore in here!"

"Oh, we had to throw your suit and overcoat away.
They were all full of sauce of some kind. We threw out
your shoes, socks and hat, too. This is just your wallets
and papers."

I looked at her. Her black eyes might be pretty but
she sure was stupid! I decided to be patient. I was im-
mobilized. "Look, Nurse Bildirjin. I need clothes to
leave the hospital. Through that window, I can see that

it is very cold outside. There is a wind blowing. I cannot walk out there with no clothes on."

She understood that.

"So," I continued, "like the good, sweet, innocent girl that you are, please go out to the office and phone my friend, the taxi driver, and tell him to bring me some clothes."

She got that. She left. In about ten minutes she came back. "I phoned him." She was carrying a disposable bathrobe-and-slipper set. Ah, she did have some sense after all.

She put the bathrobe and slippers down all the way across the room. Then she stood there just looking at me.

It was an uncomfortable silence. I didn't like the look in those black eyes. Even the best of women are the most treacherous beasts ever invented. Whatever she was plotting right now had better be distracted.

"You instigated that operation," I said.

I expected a hearty denial. But she said, "Well, of course! Anyone who would TWICE interrupt a girl half-way through is undersexed. Such a person couldn't possibly appreciate the finer things of life. And at my first hint, Doktor Muhammed got straight to work. But I am not at all sure that we have put an end to it."

Those black eyes were too bright! "I think," she said, "I should be reassured."

A stir of alarm speeded up my heart. She looked just like women look when they are about to do something sly and cunning.

"Well," she said, "there's only one way to tell."

She raced over to the door and barred it. She came back and turned the radio up louder. She went to the windows and made sure nobody could see in.

My alarm grew.

She tested the straps and buckles on the bed. When

I saw she was not releasing them, my temperature started
to go up.

She took off her right slipper. She kicked off her left
slipper. She turned her back on me. She was doing something at her waist level.

What was she up to?

There was a shimmer. She bent over and rose again.
She was holding her panty hose.

She threw them away!

She set her nurse's cap on the back of her head.

I was glaring at her in alarm.

"That won't do," she said. "Mustn't peek!"

She promptly arranged the sheet so that I could see
only through a slit. I could see a corner of the window
and the light fixture in the middle of the ceiling. I
couldn't see Nurse Bildirjin!

I felt the bed tip: the light fixture slanted.

Oh, my Gods! What did she have in mind?

The bed tipped again.

Frantically, I tried to rise up and see what was happening. The straps prevented it.

A cold draft told me the lower part of the sheet was
being lifted.

My eyes almost popped out of my head.

I suddenly divined what she was up to!

Good Gods! This girl was a minor!

Her father was the leading physician of the province.
He would kill me if I touched her!

I tried to reconcile myself with the thought that
SHE was doing all the touching.

Then I had a vision of her father's shotgun! He was
the best quail hunter in all of Turkey. A dead shot!

The idea of me flying hectically into the sky, the
boom of a shotgun and me flapping earthward, blurred
my vision.

It was too late.

I caught a glimpse of the top of her nurse's cap for a moment. The red crescent was like a blade pointing at me.

"Ooooh!" she crooned. "Lovely, lovely!"

The nurse's cap eased down.

Then the bed began to rock.

The top of the nurse's cap was in my view, then the light fixture, alternately.

I felt my eyes begin to spin in spirals.

The Hoochi-Hoochi Boys and Their Electric Cura Irizvas started a song on the radio. She took their rhythm.

> *Little bo peep went do-da, do-da.*
> *Little bo peep went do-da all the day.*
> *Little bo peep, oh do-da, do-da, do-da.*
> *To hell with the sheep,*
> *Let's do-da all the day.*
> *Let's do-da all the day.*
> *Let's do-da all the day.*
> *Let's do-da all the day.*

Her nurse's cap and the light fixture were shifting in rhythm to the music.

I was engulfed in a GLORIOUS SENSATION!

Only now and then were strains of the music coming through.

> *Let's do-da all the day.*

It went on and on and on! Both Nurse Bildirjin and the music!

> *Let's do-da all the day.*

Minutes and minutes.

Then *bbbbbbbbblowOWIE!!!*

Earthquakes and hurricanes mixed up with all the celestial chaos of the Gods didn't compare to what occurred!

WOW!

Finally the room quieted down to just a blurred spin.

I lay back panting.

A sort of wonder came over me. Where had this been all my life?

Somebody else was panting. Then the bed shook.

I saw the top of Nurse Bildirjin's cap. She must be standing now beside the bed.

She was muttering to herself. "Prahd says it's awfully good for the complexion. Judging from the amount, I'm going to have the finest complexion in Turkey!"

Suddenly I saw her feet upside down through the slit. She must be sitting on the floor!

"Mustn't waste it even so," she said. "Conservation is my motto."

I couldn't see what she was doing. I heard her crossing the room to the washbasin.

I heard water splashing. Then a silence.

Suddenly the sheet was yanked off my face. She was standing fully dressed beside me.

"Anyway," she said to me with a professional smile, "you will be glad to know that the equipment passes the clinical test. Of course, you lack expertise in the use of your tools. Prahd, I must say, is a much better craftsman."

She nodded toward my lower body which I couldn't see. Then she looked at me. She wagged an admonishing finger at me. "You are, of course, just a little boy with a new toy. So don't break it right away."

She began to undo the buckles on the straps that

held me down. "You don't have a very good reputation, Sultan Bey. I had to keep you strapped so that you wouldn't rape me the minute I let you loose. I'm sure you understand. It was just a precautionary measure. Now, if I undo this last buckle, will you promise not to leap on me and rape me?"

This insanity served to bring some order into the chaos of my thoughts. The realization hit me fully. I had just (bleeped) Prahd's girl!

"Don't tell Prahd!" I pleaded with her.

"Well," she said, "that depends."

Blackmail! I knew it! My Apparatus trained nose could smell it even above her perfume and the reek of sex. "On what?" I begged.

"Two things," she said. "Don't interrupt a girl again halfway through. And don't, don't, don't you run into my Fiat ever, ever, ever again!"

I did not like the look in her eye. "I promise."

"Well, I don't," she said.

She threw off the last buckle and then tossed the disposable bathrobe and slippers at me. "Put these on and walk around in the hall until your clothes come. I've got to mop all these spatters off the floor before somebody sees them and finds out."

Practical girl. I hastily exited.

Chapter 8

I found I had been occupying a room in the main hospital building. The rooms and wards had been all cleared out as soon as the vast supplies could be stored in the warehouses. It provoked me to see so many Turks in the beds. They sure were cluttering up the place with nonpaying guests! The real income was down in the secret basement.

I wandered toward the main lobby. It was clinic hours. The area was crowded with old people, women and children waiting their turn at the free treatments. Sheer waste of time. Riffraff! Well, anyway, I had made it possible for them. They ought to be grateful. I sauntered through the seated mob. They saw who it was and hastily pulled their children to them and flinched back.

To Hells with them. I turned to go back into the hall. One of the town doctors that served part time here at vast salary was talking to an old woman, probably telling her she needed expensive specialist treatment in his town office.

It was Nurse Bildirjin's father!

I flinched.

I hastily dived through a door so he wouldn't catch sight of me. I peeked through the crack. He was still there.

I turned. I was in a private room. There was somebody in a contraption that covered his whole chest like a metal bra. The patient was all bandaged up, only the eyes were showing.

Why did he have his hands up in an attitude of defense? Somebody who knew me?

I peered closer.

RAHT!

What in the name of Modon Demons was Raht doing here? Oh, I was furious!

"Why, (bleep) you!" I screamed at him. "More vacations! I can't depend on you for a single instant! Do you realize that your (bleeped) fixation on loafing will have me totally blind? You're supposed to be in New York! You're the only one that can turn that 831 Relayer on! And unless it's on, I won't be able to see a (bleeping) thing that condemned Royal officer is doing! You were supposed to watch him! You don't care for a split second that he has Grand Council authority to order all our arrests! Now, (bleep) you, Raht. Get out of that (bleeped) bed this very minute and get to New York and climb the Empire State Building and get that 831 Relayer back on!"

Oh, I was furious! My voice must have risen pretty loud. Somebody was coming in. I whirled on him.

It was Prahd. "Softly, softly," he said. "The people out there shouldn't be overhearing Voltarian."

I swept it aside. "What is HE doing here?" I demanded.

"The New York office sent him in because he was dying of pneumonia. He only had half a lung left. I've had to cure the infection and rebuild both lungs. Also, they didn't set his jaws properly and he couldn't eat. I've had to rebuild the mandibles. He also had old breaks and wounds and scars. And in addition to that, his feet were frozen. He's doing quite well now but he is certainly in no shape to leave yet!"

"I'm the judge of that!" I raved at him. "Get him out of that contraption and on his way to New York!"

"It would kill him," said Prahd.

"To Hells with that!" I screamed. "You could get yourself charged right along with him as an accomplice in loafing!"

Raht had been waving his hands. Prahd got out a notebook and a pen and gave them to him. With some difficulty, Raht began to write. When he finished, Prahd handed me the sheet.

It was pretty scrawly. It said:

> *You ordered me via the office to get the 831
> Relayer turned on and then report in. That's
> what I did. That's how I got the frozen feet. Is
> it true that the tall, blond young man with the
> blue eyes is a real Royal officer? Of the Voltar
> Fleet? With Grand Council orders?*

That was the last straw. They were just trying to
make me wrong. "Of course he is! And he could have us
all executed! Me, you, Prahd, anybody! So you better
watch it, you impertinent (bleepard)!" I threw the wad-
ded note back at him.

"Then it's all right if Raht stays and finishes his
treatment?" said Prahd.

"You're all alike," I said. "I ought to blow this place
up!" I stalked out.

Chapter 9

Mad as I was, I had not lost my sense of caution. I
cunningly avoided being shot by Nurse Bildirjin's father
by putting my bathrobe over my head and using side corridors on my way back to my room.

The staff must be readying the place for some other
patient, although my bag of wallets and papers was still
beside the bed. A four-wheeled handcart sat in the middle of the room stacked high with cardboard boxes.
Then I entered further. Beyond the cart, the taxi driver
was sitting in a chair.

He spoke. "Mudlick didn't do a very careful job of

decorating this place. They left white paint splattered all over the floor. Look at that. A trail of it from the bed to the wash basin."

I thought I had better distract him quick! "I've been waiting for you for hours! I can't leave here without clothes."

"Oho, clothes, is it?" he said. "Well, you just look what I've got for *you!*" He reached way up and got the top box on the handcart. He threw it on the bed and opened it. I flinched. I thought a wild animal was jumping out!

"A real Turkmen genuine bearskin coat, full length! Feel that fur! Expert tanning, hardly any smell at all!" He grabbed another box. "A karakul fur hat: straight from Lake Kara Kul, Tadzhik, S.S.R. Look how glossy the lamb pelt is. Smuggled through by the very best people." He put it on my head. "Boy, does that give you an air! Classier than a commissar!" He grabbed another box. "Now look at these elegant, roll-top snow boots! Isn't that a beautiful blue? And see? These patent leather oxfords fit inside just right—three whole pairs of them, brown and blue and black. Just your size. Everything is just your size."

Ignoring anything I was trying to say, he made another leap to the top of the cart. Boxes came cascading down. He ripped another one open. "Now look at this waterproof, silk ski suit. How do you like that horizon blue, eh? Top of the line. Latest fashion from Switzerland! Look at this hood! Feel the inside of it, man. Mink! Isn't that wonderful?"

He was grabbing more boxes. "Now for the practical things. Look at this specially cut, tan English tweed jacket. Look at it glow! Look at that style! And here's the flared-side, steeplechase jodhpur breeches that go with it. How's that for a match? Look at that dark brown against the jacket. And here are the jodhpur boots. Look at the leather. Isn't that beautiful? Name brand. Top of the line. Just your size."

He was ripping open more boxes. "Now, here's the German Tyrolean outfit. Hey, how do you like that pompom on the green Tyrol hat, eh? Isn't it great? And the jacket and shorts and walking boots, all the finest leather. And get those suspenders. Look at that design on them: hand woven! Says so right there."

I was trying to stop him. He plowed right on. More and more boxes. "Now here's the more formal wear. Silk shirts and silk neck scarves. And get this Italian pinstripe gray suit—it goes with the white Homburg. Boy, is that ever classy! Now here's a dozen silk knitted turtleneck sweaters——"

"WAIT!" I managed to stop him only by leaping bodily between him and the still heavily loaded handcart. "Where did all these come from?"

"Why, the Giysi Modern Western Clothing Our Specialty Shop for Men and Gentlemen in town, of course. Days ago they were tipped off you were coming home and they got the whole lot in for you by express order from Istanbul. They know your size. Have no worries. Every bit of this will fit."

"My Gods!" I cried. "The message I had relayed to you was to go to the villa and get me some clothes."

"No, it was to get you some clothes. But I did go to your villa and they said they were much too busy to bother. It's awfully cold out and you've just been in the hospital and all. I know what a classy gent you are, so I just nipped over to town and got these clothes."

"They look awfully expensive!" I protested.

"Oh, no money needed. You'd just be amazed how great your credit is. I got them on your Start Blanching and Dunner's Club credit cards!"

I felt as if I were going to faint. Credit cards! Oh, my Gods, credit cards!

Inspiration to the rescue. "You don't have their numbers!"

"Oh, everybody in town knows the numbers of all your credit cards. And in Istanbul, too! No trouble!"

Inspiration beyond the call of inspiration was called for. I not only didn't have any money, I also owed the credit-card companies for the whole last month of our fatal trip!

I had it! "I won't sign the invoices!"

"Oh, no problem. You forget I was a convicted forger on the planet Modon, Officer Gris. I knew how weak you'd be, just getting out of the hospital and all. I signed the lot for you to save you all that trouble!"

"You set this up just to get a 10 percent kickback from the store," I grated.

"Oh, Heavens no, Officer Gris. How you wrong me! It's awfully cold weather. Now that you're home, I can't afford to have you get sick. Now, why don't you step over there and have a nice shower while I lay out some silk underwear and some alpaca wool mountaineering socks and the nice tan camel's-hair lounging suit. And this dark brown silk shirt with this white Christian Dior cravat and these cordovan tooled cowboy boots. Don't take too hot a shower. It's awfully cold outside. And then you can put on this bearskin coat and karakul cap and I can take you home."

What could I say? At least there was one person in the universe who cared about me, for whatever reason. I might as well be shot in a genuine Turkmen bearskin coat as in a Zanco disposable bathrobe. Another fifteen thousand wouldn't make any difference when added to the maybe half a million I still owed on credit cards. I brightened. This wouldn't be due for another month after they had shot me for failing to pay my already existing debt.

It struck me as I soaped that I didn't know the taxi driver's right name. Above the shower spatter, I yelled, "You know, nobody ever told me your name."

"Ahmed," he yelled back.

"No, no," I shouted. "I know your Turkish name. I mean your *right* name."

"Oh," he said. "Deplor."

Deplor? That, in Modon, meant "Fate."

Later I was to have cause to remember that. Just now I was too engrossed in trying to soap myself in spite of these newly acquired appendages. I certainly hoped those virgin pants would take care of it. It sure was *big!*

PART THIRTY-FIVE

Chapter 1

Despite the taxi driver's solicitude, I felt fine. I walked across the villa lawn with a spring in my step and the customary scowl on my face in case any staff was watching.

I felt it was beneath me to order the carrying in of the boxes of new clothes and left that to the taxi driver. He, in turn, marshalled up Karagoz and several of the men and they got a fire bucket sort of line going and very soon my bedroom looked more like a store than living quarters. At least I was going to go to my financial death in the height of fashion.

The taxi driver paused by me in the patio as he left. "Those will do you for the cold weather," he said. "And you be sure to keep warm. But, come spring, they will be *too* warm so I'll have Giysi Modern Western Clothing Our Specialty Shop for Men and Gentlemen working on your spring wardrobe."

Come spring, I had a feeling, I would be long cold in the graveyard they reserve for people shot by the delinquent accounts sections of the credit card companies. But let him dream. According to his own lights, he was taking care of me.

"Wear those wool scarfs around your throat," he said. "And don't get your feet wet." And he was gone.

The sound of the closing of the patio door signalled the opening of Utanc's. I had been standing there wondering how to get in my bedroom. I heard a gasp. I turned.

Utanc. She looked at the karakul cap. She looked at the bearskin coat. Then she peered at my face, part of which must have been showing between the folds of fur collar.

"Oh!" she said in what must have been relief. "It's only you!"

"I'm just back from the hospital," I said.

"Oh. Is that where you've been? What are you doing coming around here and scaring people to death? I thought you were a commissar or somebody important at first."

Something in her attitude nettled me. "Utanc," I said. "You and I have to have a talk about credit cards."

"Hah!" she said. "There you go flying into one of your rages about the least little thing!"

She was beautiful, standing there in a Saks Fifth Avenue white satin housecoat trimmed with pearls. I did love her. But also she had placed both my right and left feet over the edge in the Delinquency Creditor Graveyard. "Utanc," I said, "could you possibly send back or sell some of the jewelry you bought? I am in deep financial distress."

I don't know what I expected. A slammed door, probably. But she stood there staring at me. She then put her finger in her mouth and thought about it.

I said, "Utanc, I love you dearly. But if you could just see fit to let me cancel your credit cards and return some of the more valuable purchases, I might be able to weather this somehow."

"O Master," she said, "I am so sorry to hear that I was bought by someone of limited means. However, I share the blame."

My spirits lifted. She did care after all!

She said, "I should have had you looked up in Dunn and Bradstreet before I stepped onto the auction block. I did not, so I am remiss."

It was touching. Of course, as a wild desert girl, she lacked facilities to establish credit ratings.

"I don't suppose," she continued, thoughtfully tapping her teeth, "that capitalistic law allows a pauperized slave girl to sell her master. No, it would be too decadent for that." She frowned prettily and began to weave a lock of her raven black hair. "Certainly, there must be something we can do."

I had an inspiration. I suddenly realized that the basis of all her upset with me was unsatisfied sex. She had always wound up unhappy after a bout. Freud cannot be wrong. She was simply frustrated! But now! Now, after Prahd's great work . . .

"Utanc," I said. "Why don't you come to my room tonight? I have a beautiful surprise for you!"

"A surprise?" she said suspiciously.

"A big one," I said. "And very nice."

"Hmm," she said. Then, "Master, if I come to your room tonight—just that and nothing more implied —will you let me keep all the things I bought and my credit cards?"

I did a very rapid calculation. There was no doubt whatever in my mind that once she found what I had now, all thought of jewelry and credit cards would vanish. Freud cannot be wrong. Sex is the basis of every tiny impulse, everything in fact. If I could just get her in my room for one hour, after that she would be totally content to live with me the rest of her life in poverty if need be.

I put all my chips on Freud. "Utanc, if you just come to my room tonight and lie down with me upon my bed for just five minutes, you may keep your jewelry and your credit cards."

She nodded. "Nine o'clock. I will be there." She closed her door.

I did a little dance.

I had it solved!

In well under five minutes, all thought of jewelry and credit cards would be gone forever from that pretty head. After that, I would simply ship the offending items back to Tiffany's and rip, rip, tear up the treacherous cards. She would even laugh gaily as I did it! Wonderful, wonderful psychology! Bless Freud!

Chapter 2

I was at once all bouncing enthusiasm. I had to get all these clothes stowed and my room straightened up and I wasted no time.

Problem: I didn't really have enough closet space. Something would have to go. In one secret closet a lot of the space was taken up with hypnohelmets in their big cartons. I sealed them up, just like new, and with a few assorted threats, got them into the Chevy station wagon and made Karagoz take them to Prahd for storage in the new warehouses. That gave me barely enough room, and by means of a lot of cramming and parking things on top of things, I got the job done.

New problem. It was only 4:00 P.M. Five hours to kill!

Heller. Raht had said he had turned on the 831 Relayer. I had better check it out.

I went in the secret office, pushed aside the bogus gold bars and boxes that still littered the floor. I turned on the wall electric fire, mindful of the taxi driver's advice to take care of myself. I got the receiver and viewer out of my baggage, put them on their former low bench and turned them on.

Victory!

There he was in his Empire State Building office.

I couldn't quite make it out, though. I was getting various views of the floor.

Then, finally, his voice. "There it is." He fished a rubber ball out from a dark corner under his desk and, straightening up in his chair, put it on the blotter.

The cat leaped up on the desk, moved over to a point about three feet from the ball and sat down.

Heller rolled the ball at the cat. The cat, with an expert paw, rolled the ball back at Heller. Back and forth, back and forth.

Kind of pathetic. We really had him slowed down. He had nothing better to do than play ball with a cat!

All of a sudden the cat hit the ball a terrific lick and sent it bounding off the desk. This time Heller caught it. "You got to watch that strength, cat. Don't be such a showoff. Somebody will get the idea you're an extra-terrestrial and they'll get you for a Code break. Here, chase it for a while!"

Heller tossed the ball the length of the room. The cat was after it like a shot.

Just before the ball hit the wall, the door opened!

The cat ignored the rebounding ball and squared away to the door.

"You missed me." It was Bang-Bang.

The cat saw who it was and said, "Yeow?"

Bang-Bang came across the room. "You got to teach that cat how to shoot better." The cat was following him, eyes on a bag Bang-Bang was carrying. "No, it's not ice cream," Bang-Bang informed it. He threw the bag on the desk.

"There's your photographs you had taken, Jet. And here's a bottle of stuff the man said would float off the emulsion."

"Any questions?" said Jet.

"Hell, no. I told them it was just my G-2 class and they said they were always glad to help a student with his homework."

The cat was satisfying himself the package did not contain ice cream. It was quite obvious he did not believe Bang-Bang.

"Jet," said Bang-Bang. "While I was waiting for this stuff, I thunk up a great plan. I got to do something. I'm scared to go near the family. I can't leave my job or I'll wind up back in Sing Sing. But I got it all worked out."

Heller waved to a chair. The cat sat down to listen.

"It goes like this," said Bang-Bang. "I get the license plates of all publishers' cars in the country. Then I simply put bombs in them and BANGO! they're in Purgatory and we're in clover."

Heller said, "Sounds kind of extensive."

"Well, how about this one? I plant bombs under the TV network buildings—NBC, CBS and ABC. This phony Whiz Kid is bound to show up in one and BLOWIE, he's in Purgatory and we're in clover."

"Then the reporters would mob *me*."

"Jet, I begin to suspect that you do not have the soul of a good demolition man."

I snorted. Heller, as a combat engineer, had probably blown up more buildings and forts than Bang-Bang had ever heard of. I was astonished to hear Heller answer, "I bow to the expert. However, I somehow don't think any of those is the right target."

I chilled. It was obvious Heller was talking about

ME! Had he really found out? Then I thought it might
be Madison he meant. Better Madison than me any
time. I waited breathlessly for Heller to say more. He
didn't and it dawned on me that he just plain didn't
know. I relaxed.

Bang-Bang got up. "Then," he said, "I am left with
the final solution."

"And that is?" said Heller.

"Go get a drink of Scotch," said Bang-Bang. "Come
on, cat. Your boss won't miss you for an hour and I hate
to drink alone."

He departed with the cat trotting after him.

Heller got busy. He propped open a G-2 manual
on identification. He emptied the sack of photographs on
the desk. They all seemed to be pictures of Heller but
somehow he looked different ages. He got a tray and
poured some water and fluid in it. Then he went to a
safe and got out stacks of I.D.'s. Hey, these were all the
passports and social security cards and driver's licenses
he had been taking off gangsters and Silva. He spread
them out. My Gods, I hadn't realized how many there
had been!

Ten at the garage. The two snipers I had hired—
Bang-Bang must have picked their pockets! One from the
Midtown Air Terminal. Five CIA-sourced ones he'd tak-
en off Silva.

There were others he hadn't taken the I.D. from: the
three at the Gracious Palms, two more at the terminal
and, of course, Silva's own.

I did a hasty calculation. Heller had wasted nineteen
of Faustino's men. They knew it: no wonder they were
terrified of him. He had slaughtered eight hoodlums in
Van Cortlandt Park. He had wrecked but not killed Torpedo Fiaccola and two Turk wrestlers. And he had blown

up ten IRS agents if, by stretch of the imagination, you could call IRS agents human.

Forty men!

They had been after his blood and it was in self-defense. But what might happen if he took it into his head to go hunting people!

He was *dangerous!*

Oh, I better make awfully sure he did not get out of control! And I had better be awfully careful myself! I sometimes forgot that I was dealing with the top combat engineer of the Voltar Fleet. That was the trouble with him. He was deceptive with all those gentlemanly officer ways and pretenses of decency and even religion.

But never mind. Rockecenter knew his business. Bury knew his business. And thank the Gods, Madison was an expert with a weapon more powerful than I had ever imagined existed—PR.

And we had him stopped. We had him pinned down.

He was fooling with those passports and driver's licenses now. He would put a photograph of himself looking older into the tray of fluid. The thin emulsion of the photograph would begin to separate from the paper backing. Then, using a couple pairs of small tongs, he would slide the emulsion over onto the actual passport picture. Then using a dampened ball of something, he would press the new emulsion down in place so that even the embossing of the seal would come through.

After a while he had eighteen passports. All he had to do was change his own hair color and draw in some age lines on his own face to agree with the age stated, and he could use them himself!

He now went to work on the driver's licenses. This was a little trickier as the small color pictures were tinier. He also had to remove the whole license from its lamination in some cases. He would pick up the emulsion from the color picture, put it aside and then put one of himself in its place. He finished them by running them as a batch through a portable lamination machine he had set up.

Eighteen sets of I.D. But of what possible use were they to him? Names like Cecchino, Serpente, Laccio, Rapitore... All mobster names. They would be known and show up on police computers. And everybody would know by this time that Inganno John Scroccone, Faustino's chief accountant, was dead. Only those five CIA passports might be of some use and I would bet anything they would trace back as a CIA operative cover. And of a dead operative—Gunsalmo Silva.

Then I began to laugh. I understood what this was all about. He was pinned to the name Wister, of course, by college and friends. But Madison had driven him under cover. Heller couldn't even register in a motel without some clerk thinking he was the Whiz Kid! We were really wrecking him!

Oh, that made me feel good. I had Heller on the run. He was living in a little tiny room beside his office. He was probably even going to lose that soon. He was undoubtedly low on cash. He had lost the support of Babe and the family. He would probably soon lose Izzy.

A beautiful vision! Heller, broke, adrift as a bum in New York. It had all begun with the brilliance of Lombar. It had been pushed on through by the brilliance of Rockecenter. And with Madison as a hatchet man, the Heller tree was cut down.

He didn't have a prayer!

That would teach him the stupidity of trying to benefit a planet!

Planets and populations exist to be milked by the power elite. Unless one understood that thoroughly, one could do a lot of stupid things like help people.

The Gods put the riffraff there as prey for superior men like Hisst and Rockecenter. And there was very short shrift for anyone who thought otherwise.

I hugged myself with glee.

Then, at length, I threw a blanket over the viewer.

I had more important things to do than watch the painful demise of a (bleeped) fool Royal officer with silly notions you could help a world.

Chapter 3

At 9:00 P.M., aglow with anticipation, I lay in the bed in my room. All the lights were out, just the way she always wanted it. But there was a big difference: I had taken off all my clothes and, like you wrap a present, had thrown a single sheet over myself.

Was she going to be surprised! Wow! I was making a big thing out of it, of course, but such splendid moments don't come often in a lifetime.

I heard a slight sound at the door. Then a groping gave a tremor to the bed.

In a moment I felt her weight and warmth beside me. A gentle jasmine perfume filled the air. I began to quiver with excitement. "Darling," I whispered.

I put out my hand to encircle her. She was fully clothed as always at such moments.

She withdrew slightly. "What's this surprise?" she said.

I groped for and found her hand. I guided it under the sheet. I made the fingers touch my chest and then began to press her hand downwards.

"Feel this," I whispered, a little choked with passion. "Look what I've got for you."

I made her fingers connect with me.

"What the HELL?"

Oh, I knew she would be surprised!

Her fingers recoiled. Then they reached again, encircled my member.

"Hey!" she said. "What kind of a trick is this? A falsie? A dildo? Well, we'll see about THAT!"

Her fingers began to pluck all around the edges, then at the surrounding area. The fingernails were pretty sharp. She was trying to find if there was any strap to hold it on.

"No, no," I said hastily. "It's real!"

"We'll see about that!" she said grimly.

She wrapped her fingers around it, held on hard and gave it a mighty yank!

"OUCH!" I shrieked.

"By Allah the Merciful, it IS real!"

Aha, I knew she would be amazed!

She was feeling the top of it, getting an idea of diameter and scope.

She drew back and sat up suddenly.

"You (bleepard)!" she said. "You treacherous, rotten (bleepard)!" An ill-aimed fist hit me in the jaw! "First you're so God (bleeped) small nobody can even find it! Smaller even than the little boys! Now, you're so God (bleeped) big that you could get it into anything!"

Did I hear the meaning? Yes! There was the luminous dial. She must be studying it. Making sure the time had expired!

"Utanc," I gasped. "I am sure there is a way. Utanc, I did it all for you. Please think again. Please give me your hand. It isn't that bad. It's really just a little bigger than normal! And it has other advantages, Utanc...."

The button of the stopwatch went *click*. "Five minutes," she said. "I want you to witness that I stayed five minutes in your bed." She pushed the dial close to my face and it glowed green. She had been there five minutes all right.

"Please, Utanc," I wept. "You have no idea..."

"Listen, you (bleepard). I am tired of your tricks! You go to such EXTREMES! One minute you couldn't even please a flea and the next minute you would wreck a camel! I am going to my room now and don't you bother me again until you decide to be more NORMAL!"

She got off the bed. The door slammed! She was gone.

I lay there in shock. All my anticipation had been aroused to the bursting point. The sudden twist of events left me in midcareer. My heart was pounding with unspent passion while my brain reeled with shock.

I tried to lie quietly, hoping that I would settle down. Instead, I began to twitch.

I couldn't lie still. I got up.

Thinking that she might be experiencing remorse, maybe even crying with frustration herself, I went to the receiver of the bug I had long ago planted in her room. I turned it on.

There was more volume in it now. Maybe it had been moved to a better place when the credit card people had tried to strip the house of rugs.

I could hear water runnin͏g   I heard some clinks and clatters. Then Uta͏   ͏ake up, you little dears. No reason to slee͏   ͏."

Some "What's this?" and ͏   wo little boys. Then some "Oh, g͏

The clink of glasses. Was she giving them their evening milk?

Then some Turkish music. Probably recorded. Savage. Primitive. The rhythmic pounding of a foot. Then the swish and swirl of fabric. Then the clash of swords together in rhythm. My own body began to respond, no matter that I couldn't see her dance.

The voices of the two little boys began to rise in gasps of appreciation.

Then suddenly a change. The *cura irizva* striking bold and savage chords. Then Utanc's voice in song:

> *You may be small,*
> *But oh, you're good.*
> *I would eat you,*
> *If I could.*
> *Why should hunger*
> *Be in fashion,*
> *When you're there,*
> *To slake my passion?*
> *So off with hat,*
> *Let down your hair,*
> *I'm going to eat*
> *Your table bare!*
> *Now I'll throw*
> *You into bed.*
> *You better hide!*
> *There goes your head!*

The clatter of the *cura irizva* being thrown down.
Small shouts of surprise.
The swish and rustle of sheets and bed.
Squeals of delight!
I couldn't stand any more. I turned the receiver off. My passion was at a bursting point. I lay down in my bed.

My arms were empty. I ached. I had never ached before like this. Painful. Awful!

And for hours I lay there like that.

I realized that there was no torture to compare with unsatisfied desire! All centralized in a very sensitive place!

Chapter 4

The next morning it was very cold. The electric fire had blown a fuse. I got into a blue ski suit. Warming my hands around some *kahve*, I thought it over carefully. I came to a desperate decision.

I would stop being true to Utanc.

I phoned the taxi driver and when he came, I had him drive down the road a few yards. There was a turn-in there where another villa had been burned in centuries past and one could go a few feet off the road and park under a cedar tree while still retaining full view of any traffic.

He shut off the engine. The sigh of wind in the cedar was very mournful. He turned in his seat, pushed his sheepskin cap onto the back of his head and waited for me to speak. He obviously could see that I was troubled.

"I've got to do something about Utanc," I said.

He digested that. He thoughtfully lit a cheap Hisar cigarette. "You can't get anything out of a trade-in," he said. "The bottom is out of the market. Things have gotten even worse behind the Iron Curtain. Hundreds of thousands of girls have come over the border. Threatened with rape from the Red Army, it was a case of either infection or defection. They chose the latter. Can't say as I blame them. You ever feel the beard on one of those Ivans? Or see the body lice? Fleas, too. No, Officer Gris, we're stuck with her."

"I don't mean to make a big thing out of it," I said. "But a long look at it has convinced me the matter isn't going to settle down."

"Well," he said, "you never can tell what you're getting into in these things."

"You've got to come up with something," I said. After all, he was the only one who seemed to care what happened to me. And the criminals on Modon are a pretty smart lot. "The situation is wide open to suggestions."

The cedar sighed. Three camel loads of opium went by, led by a farmer and a donkey, heading toward the Agricultural School. The farmer looked at us curiously.

Deplor, alias Ahmed, waited until they were out of sight. Then he threw away his cigarette in sudden decision. "I don't want to get you into any tight spots you can't get out of, Officer Gris. I have your best interests at heart. So, I tell you what you better do. You better give me some money and I'll get some women for you."

"No more slaves!" I said hastily.

"No, no," he said. "I got you into a hole on that one. And you don't want any prostitutes, either. The type I have in mind are just women who need money for a dowry. They need money to get married. You can get a one-night stand with such a woman. Good lookers, too. Lots of variety. Different one every night. Spread it around. And they're real hot, too."

Oh, that sounded good!

He continued, "Now, to do this right, you should have a big car. Women go in for big things and that includes a big car. You remember that bulletproof limousine I told you about? The ex-general's car? The one who got shot? It's still for sale up in Istanbul."

A snag suddenly occurred to me. "Wait. You can't get women on a credit card. And I'm trying to swear off, anyway."

"On women?" he said, astonished.

"No. Credit cards. I hate the things."

"Well, you don't need to use credit cards," he said. "Just deal in cash. So if you'll just give me some money . . ."

It was time to confess. He was, after all, my friend. "I'm stone-broke," I said. "I don't have any money at all."

The taxi driver started up the car rather quickly, I thought. He dropped me off at the villa up the road. He didn't even say good-bye.

I stared after him.

(Bleep)!

It was all too plain to me that it took money to get things done. Life without money, as I had always known, was death.

I limped back to my room with this awful ache.

(Bleep) Prahd!

I decided some physical work might take my mind off my plight. I warmed up my secret office, stripped myself down and began to clean guns, sweep away old clothes and, by late afternoon, began to straighten up the mess of fake gold bars and the boxes.

Puttering around, I was mostly done when I saw that one of the cases had fallen onto some packages of unexamined mail.

Idly, and with no thought, I picked up some of the letters. They had been forwarded from the Section 451 office on Voltar and had come in on recent freighters. Faht's orderly had slipped them through the slot in the tunnel door.

Routine stuff. A notice that I'd been dropped from the Academy Alumnus Association for the nonpayment of dues. A bill from a gun dealer on Flisten—years old and I didn't intend to be on duty on Flisten soon. An advertisement for new General Services officer caps "that would remain undamaged under the hardest blows of troops' cudgels." An ad for the latest release of "the ever more popular sweetheart of Homeview, Hightee Heller," song strips, featuring hits from the new musical show that was "jamming Voltar theaters nightly: *Bold Prince Caucalsia*." A warning that I had not acknowledged reading the latest general Apparatus order about filling in forms that listed the correct sequences of forms and must fill in the attached form at once. A new type of chank-pop that "totally eradicated for seconds at a time the gaseous odors of troops." A special offer to Apparatus officers only—a fun gift for their friends —exploding boots. An electronic bird whistle, available in dozen lots, that called in selected types of female songbirds for breeding purposes.

What's this?

Two personal postcards? The kind you send to friends and are wide open in the mails for anyone to read. Who could this be? I didn't have any friends.

I looked at the signature and gaped. The Widow Tayl!

The first card said:

Soltan Gris
Section 451
Please Forward.

    Yoo-Hoo. Wherever you are. I'm just coming along great.
    What shall we name it?
    Why don't you write?

> *The lovey-dovey woman you*
> *heartlessly abandoned,*
>
> *Pratia*
>
> Return to Pratia Tayl
> Minx Estate
> Pausch Hills

Oh, my Gods! Open like that right through the office for anyone to read! You could be cashiered for knocking somebody up and not marrying them! The law was all on her side.

The second card was worse! It said:

> Soltan Gris
> *Officer of the Apparatus still, unless his com-*
> *manding officer finds out he didn't marry me if*
> *he didn't the next time I see him.*
>
> *Yoo-Hoo! Wherever you are.*
> *He is just coming along fine. It is too soon to*
> *feel him kick yet. What schools shall we send him*
> *to when he is born? How about the Academy like*
> *his father? And maybe buy him a commission in*
> *the Fleet. Please waste no time in writing me*
> *quickly so as to save all the tedious trouble of hir-*
> *ing lawyers which is so time wasting when one*
> *could be so nicely busy doing other things.*
>
> > *The loving pregnant girl*
> > *you left behind,*

> *Pratia Tayl*
> *Minx Estate*
> *Turn right off the main road at the*
> *Inn of the Rutting Beast.*
> *Pausch Hills*
>
> *PS: Young officers are always welcome, in or out*
> *of uniform, to look into this case.*
> *(You can also use the landing pad day or night.)*

(Bleep) *her!*

She was trying to get me into trouble! The one thing I had vowed from earliest youth was never, never, NEVER to get married! Who wanted cooking utensils sizzling through the air around one's head? Who wanted all the killings that followed digging brother officers out of your wife's bed?

And, curse it all, Prahd said he had certified and registered her pregnancy before he left Voltar!

(Bleep), (bleep), (BLEEP) Prahd! It was a good thing he was legally dead. Otherwise, I would have shot him out of hand!

Bad off as I might be for women, it could never include the Widow Tayl! She murdered husbands at the slightest pretext. But I had to be honest. That wasn't the real reason.

I could just plain never, never forgive her for her fixation on Heller. The nerve of her, with me right there, having automatic (bleeps) just at the thought of that (bleeped) Heller! And even when she had only seen him just once for less than a minute. Never even talked to him!

Oh, the Widow Tayl was not for me! I might be hard up but not THAT hard up!

Let her go on dreaming of Heller all she liked. I was safely twenty-two and more light-years away!

But it served to cool my ardor off a bit. I almost stopped aching in the place where it hurt. To Hells with her and to Hells with Heller!

And then I thought of having rooted Heller out of the Gracious Palms. To deprive him of those women was rare punishment. I had the upper hand when all was said. I laughed.

I thought I had better take the blanket off his viewer and enjoy his discomfiture.

Chapter 5

He was standing in a park, looking out across the East River. A wintry wind was putting small whitecaps on the water and gulls were flying low.

He turned and his eyes rested for a moment on the Statue of Peace and then, passing on, looked down the Esplanade where the flags of many nations streamed and whipped.

Heller was at the United Nations!

A chill of premonition that had nothing to do with the stormy cold he saw swept across me. What business could he possibly have there?

His gaze was watchful on the broad walkway before the doors of the General Assembly Building, looking often down East 46th Street. I knew the area well: He was expecting someone from the city to arrive here in the United Nations area.

A group caught his attention. There were five in it.

They were caped and hooded in furs. It was possible that he did not expect them to see him as he moved forward into plainer view.

The group stopped. One of them pointed at the distant Heller. They all looked.

Then they began to run toward him. They were calling out glad cries. "Pretty boy!" "Oh, you darling!"

They were running toward him and he was running toward them.

They met in a gladly shouting turmoil!

They were trying to kiss his cheeks and seize his hands.

They were women from the Gracious Palms! I recognized Margie and Minette and the tall high-yellow!

"Oh, pretty boy! We have been so lonesome without you!" cried one.

"We missed you so!" cried another.

"Eet 'as bean a zentury!" cried Minette.

My Gods, they were beautiful women! All bright-eyed and rosy-cheeked. What right did he have to such glorious creatures? He had never even slept with any of them!

"We didn't think you'd come," said the tall high-yellow.

"And miss this day?" said Heller.

"I can't think how you would," said Margie. "After all, it was your idea."

"No, no," said Heller. "It was Vantagio's. He's the political expert. And you girls did all the work."

Minette said, "Oh, an' 'ow we 'ave work'! So veree, veree 'ard! We 'ave lobby an' lobby, night after night, up and down. All ze girls 'ave really put eet to ze delegates: eef zey don' pass ze bill, we knock zem up! An' we boycott zere pantings."

"I think these UN delegates got the point," said

Margie. "Any delegate that doesn't vote a loud 'aye' on this bill knows he'll be under sanctions at the Gracious Palms."

"We really put our backs into it," said the high-yellow. "This is one thing they can't take lying down!"

"Oh, I think the bill will pass the General Assembly," he said.

I was stunned. I had heard one or two of them mention to Heller, when he sat in the Gracious Palms lobby of evenings, that they were "working on something" with the UN delegate customers. But I didn't have a clue what chicanery had been going on in the dark of those whores' rooms. What was this bill?

"We had better go in," said Heller. "It's coming up on the time for their final vote."

They rushed in a happy mob through the doors of the General Assembly Building and up to the information desk in the lobby. A uniformed girl there looked up in some disapproval at their laughter and bustle.

"You have special tickets for us," said the high-yellow. "The Delegate of Maysabongo said they would be here."

"Ah, yes," said the clerk. "Five passes to the public gallery."

"Six," said the high-yellow.

The clerk had the envelope out and open. She counted five.

"I weel zit on pretty boy's lap," said Minette.

"No, I will," said Margie with decision.

The high-yellow was reaching across the clerk to the passes in their boxes. She picked up one. "Nobody will," she said.

"You can't do that!" said the clerk. "We are supposed to hand these out on a first come, first served basis. But this is a special session and we are expecting the wife of the president of the United States and a whole party from the Women's Liberation League. . . ."

"First come, first served," said the high-yellow, "is exactly the system we use, too."

The clerk grabbed for the purloined ticket. "You can't!"

"Can," said the high-yellow. "This is *our* bill that's being voted on! But if you're going to be that way about it, why don't you call the president of the General Assembly and tell him you are preventing Beulah from attending!"

A guard came over. "I must caution you against unseemly noise here in the lobby and also if you are attending a meeting of the General Assembly, there must be neither noise nor applause in the public galleries. I think it might be best if you were to give the tickets back and . . ."

"You tell your clerk that," said the high-yellow. "And if you want to keep your job, be polite. Here's your ticket, pretty boy. Shall we go in?"

I wondered why the guard was suddenly escorting them to the entrance of the public galleries until I noticed Beulah, the high-yellow, had him by the arm just above the elbow. (Bleep) that Heller! He had taught these whores how to handle men. A traitor!

They arrived in the public gallery, took front-row seats, and the girls were taking off their furs. They were beautifully dressed, satins and brocade. They got out compacts and repaired their makeup.

The General Assembly was a vast hall of soothing elegance.

There were just a few delegates on the floor so far. Others were arriving from time to time. They were very conscious of their own dignity as they took their seats behind the signs of their countries. But what was this?

More than one of them glanced shyly toward the girls and made little hand motions that were extremely subdued waves.

A tremendous bustle and fanfare occurred. The gallery suddenly swarmed with agents. The wife of the president of the United States came in, ignored by the delegates.

Another bustle. Some females with Women's Liberation League ribbons across their chests came in. Also ignored.

What was this bill? A fear began to rise in me that Heller, whom I had supposed was down and out, retained a lot of influence. It was bad news to me.

At length the hall below was apparently as full as it would become. The public galleries were packed. Things were ready to begin.

Heller and the girls were picking up the headphones in front of their seats. There was a dial there. It said English, French, Spanish, Russian, Chinese. Minette, beside Heller, was having trouble with the earphones and her hairdo. Heller helped her and then dialled French for her. He put his own on and dialled English. He looked up at the glass-enclosed translator booths on either side of the UN emblem. The place was mobbed with TV crews and their chatter was coming over the line. Evidently the media thought this was pretty important.

But what the Hells bill was it? To bomb the Voltar base? To declare Soltan Gris an international criminal? I was worried.

The president of the General Assembly came in and took his place at the rostrum in the center of the oval hall. He opened the proceedings.

"We are met here today," he said, "for the final vote on UN Resolution 678-546-452. May I call for any last minute afterthoughts or reservations?"

Holland got the floor. "It is our consideration that this bill will shake the world." The fat Dutchman looked up at the gallery and covertly winked.

India wrapped a robe about himself and said, "I believe it must pass because of the riots in Pakistan."

The U.S. rubbed his State Department-type face and said, "It is our considered opinion, which we wish to bring to the attention of the media, that it is high time we bowed our heads to the true sources of joy." And he bowed his head but he managed a slight smile toward the girls in the gallery.

U.K. gave his trim military mustache a brush and said, "Her Majesty will wax very wroth if the bill is not passed." He cleared his throat twice in the direction of the Gracious Palms girls in the gallery.

Maysabongo got the floor. "We cannot any longer neglect our members. I move the measure be read once more and put to the vote."

Brazil said, "Seconded!"

A man at the rostrum rose, an imposing scroll in his hands. A breathless hush gripped the hall. In a sonorous voice he read:

UN Resolution 678-546-452.

Hereas and wherewith, it is the wish and will of this, the General Assembly of the United Nations, by all sovereign powers attended, as follows, to wit:

RESOLVED: WOMEN HAVE THE RIGHT NOT TO BE THERMONU-CLEAR BOMBED AND NOT TO BE FORCED TO SHUT UP BY SLAPPING OR TORTURE.

In the tense room, before the breathless gallery, the vote was taken, one by one.

As the count progressed, the packed gallery became more and more on the edge of their seats.

Then the president of the General Assembly called out, "One hundred and forty member states in favor! Twenty-six abstentions! I hereby declare the measure PASSED!"

PANDEMONIUM!

Despite the most sacred law that there be no cheering from the gallery, the din was deafening!

It was being led by the wife of the president of the United States!

The whores weren't content with just cheering. They stood up in a row throwing kisses at the delegates!

The delegates were throwing them back!

That staid chamber was being rent by chaos!

In vain the gavel rapped!

In vain the guards raced around trying to say "Sssh!"

And then Heller was helping the girls hurriedly into their furs.

They streamed out of the building with the cheering throng.

The five whores made a circle and forced Heller inside it and they began to dance around and around him in front of the Statue of Peace!

Breathless, they finally slowed down. They gathered in a group.

Beulah said, "We've got to get back and tell all the girls that they won!"

Heller said, "Almost won. It still has to go before the Security Council to become the law of the world."

"Come with us," pleaded Margie, clutching at Heller.

He shook his head. "I can't. And listen, all of you. I forbid you to tell anyone at the Gracious Palms that you saw me. I don't want any of you getting into trouble."

"Not even wan leetle wheesper?" pleaded Minette.

"Not one," said Heller. "I don't want you getting sacked because you were associating with me. Now promise."

"Oh, pretty boy," said Beulah. "At such a glorious time! They miss you, pretty boy. The girls all cry when we speak of you!"

"And I miss you," said Heller. "But go along now with your great news. The world will owe you a great debt if this gets by the Security Council. You did it all on your own."

They kissed him on the cheek. They lingeringly touched his hands. And then they sped away down the Esplanade.

Heller watched them out of sight. And then he slowly turned toward the river.

A seagull was walking near to him. "Well, seagull," he said to it, "with any luck the Security Council will pass it and then you will be safe, too. And Miss Simmons will have to realize I am on her side."

I was shaken right down to the bottom of my boots. Yes, it was very true that if that passed, Miss Simmons would not be just at his side but at his feet! She would even HELP him get his diploma! But although that in itself was very upsetting to me, in that it could cost me a valuable ally, it was not the main reason for my chill.

The raw, naked power of the man! He had used women to get a UN General Assembly Resolution passed! He could use women to do anything he wished! Widow Tayl's impression of him proved it utterly!

Oh, I had not crushed Heller the way he should be crushed! He was still dangerous beyond belief. What women saw in him I could not even begin to imagine —they were just putty in his hands!

He was just plain monopolizing all the women in the world! He was leaving none left over for anyone else!

Oh, I realized right then I had to do more! But what could I do? I paced about. What could I possibly do?

My buzzer rang. I impatiently picked up the base intercom instrument.

Faht Bey. "I'm just calling to remind you that the space freighter *Blixo* is scheduled in tonight. Captain Bolz always wants to see you, though I can't understand why. So don't go running off and making yourself hard to find again." He hung up.

Beautiful relief flooded through me. The *Blixo!* Of course! With brilliant forethought, I had already solved the very problem I was now faced with!

With luck, the Countess Krak would be on that ship. She'd slaughter Heller for even glancing at another woman! She'd slow him down to a crawl as she had on Voltar!

I laughed with delirious delight.

I had it all solved!

Smart brains. My Apparatus professors were oh so very right. I had smart brains!

Chapter 6

I began to work out exactly how I would meet these incoming people and how to persuade the Countess Krak to let herself be bugged as I had bugged Heller.

It would be very tricky. To tell the honest truth, any contact at all with the Countess Krak compared, in risk value, to walking on the outside hull of a spaceship in flight! With no safety line!

I laid my plans carefully and then, at last, satisfied they were foolproof, I began to get ready.

In the first place, I must look, myself, impressive. This would give the necessary ring of authority to things I said.

Hidden in my secret office, my General Service uniform had gotten pretty wrinkled. I got it washed by using a wash basin and dried it in front of the electric fire. Then I suddenly remembered that my rank locket had long since vanished. I didn't have my old Grade X locket and I couldn't afford to demote myself anyway.

I walked about, thinking. I went into the patio and looked. It was afternoon and sure enough, Utanc's car was gone. I scratched at her door. No answer. Luck! The little boys had gone with her, as they often did these days.

One picked set of locks later, I was in her room. It was much the same as before except that she now had two additional mahogany wardrobes. They were also locked but that was no obstacle. I opened some thin drawers in one. Just as I suspected. Jewelry. Gods knew she had been to Tiffany's often enough!

The emerald locket I had once seen her wear was right there. It was not really a rank locket but it was the right stone and gaudy enough. It would have to do.

I didn't want to stay long, it was too risky. I couldn't find the bug I had put under the rug, too small. I got out of there.

So far so good.

In my room, I buckled on a stungun and put a couple blasticks in my pocket. I put a Knife Section knife back of my neck. I hung the Antimanco control star on my chest. Thus readied, I went down the tunnel into the hangar. It just didn't do to go around these people unarmed.

There didn't seem to be anyone about.

I hadn't been in this place for some time. The two cannon ships were still there. The tug sat on its tail gathering dust. A few odds and ends of vessels and freight.

There was a movement over in one corner. I peered closely. What a strange ship! A sort of a dome like a bell. And there was the Antimanco Captain Stabb in working clothes. He saw me. I went over.

"So you come to see this little beauty," he said. "Greatest pirate vessel ever built!"

It was the line-jumper Stabb had been assembling. And it certainly wasn't little! The Antimancos were on ladders testing the absorbo-coat with beams to detect any possible radar reflectance.

"All done," said Stabb. "Been done for two weeks but they kept saying you were busy. When do we go out and pick up some banks?"

I had a very dim idea of such a project. I could see the headlines now, as Madison would say: BANK FLIES STRAIGHT INTO THE AIR—AIR FORCE INVESTIGATING. But I said, "Soon, soon. There are big things in the wind." I wasn't here for such nonsense anyway.

"Glad to hear it," said Stabb. "I was beginning to think, when you weren't in here watching progress, that maybe you'd lost your piracy perspective and gone over to the Royal officers."

"We'll get him, too," I reassured him.

I went over to the office area. I found what I was looking for. It was a cubicle near the main exit tunnel. I would not swarm aboard the *Blixo*. I would have them brought to me. That's what you do when you are in authority. I had the guards move some of their equipment around and got a desk and chair in the right place. In they would come. I would keep them standing. They would know who was in control. I even got the guards to promise to salute me that evening. They shrugged. I told them they could have special liberty the day after and they agreed.

The stage was set. I went back to my room and called the taxi driver to be ready at the exit barracks and when.

I phoned the hospital and, with guarded speech, found that Raht would be ready to travel tomorrow. I told Prahd to be available at 9:00 P.M. that night and set up to do an operation without anyone else attending. He couldn't argue back on that open line.

Because it was routine mission expense, Faht Bey couldn't object. I got him on the secure base intercom and told him I had to have two separate air tickets to New York and the usual expense money.

"I'll need an American passport," I said. "Female. Make the age about twenty. Get the photograph in the Costume Office as the female leaves. Have it all ready for tomorrow's plane. Any problem?"

"No. I. G. Barben just sent us some blank forms for drug runners, but I have to send back the name and birth date so they can file it. So what's the name?"

I was feeling a bit sarcastic. "Heavenly Joy Krackle," I said. "With a K. From Sleepy Hollow, New York."

"You leaving?" he said, far too hopefully.

"No. This is legitimate business," I snapped. "So don't goof up. Don't forget to put old immigration stamps on it. I'll leave the identostamped order with the photographer."

"I can include another air ticket for you," he said. I hung up.

I put on my uniform, hung the thing which would have to pass for a rank locket around my neck, laid out my bearskin coat and karakul hat to carry with me. I put some reference texts in my tunic pocket. I set out the complete audio-visio bug set, sealed it and put it out to take along.

Actually, I was pretty nervous. Krak or any thought of Krak had that effect on me. The memory of her scarlet heels when she had stamped that yellow-man to pulp had always stayed pretty vivid. And realizing that I would not have faced that giant with blastguns in my hand for any amount of money did not make it any better. It ruined my supper.

I vowed to myself that I would get her out of my area with no delay whatever and get her to work on slowing Heller down.

I was awfully glad to hear the gongs going, down the tunnel. The *Blixo* was coming in. I grabbed up the coat and hat and headed for the prepared office.

Chapter 7

I sat, lordly, at the desk when the guards brought in the first one I had chosen to see: Odur.

I was surprised. The little homo had apparently gotten the word from Too-Too. He had been on his good behavior. He wasn't even in chains.

In the greenish office light, his pretty, powdered face looked rather strange. But he was very respectful. And properly frightened.

"I have very few papers for you, Officer Gris," he

said. "The office is quite a confusion. Bawtch is not there and two others seem to be gone. There is a new chief clerk but he doesn't know anything much."

Ah! Too-Too had succeeded! My old enemy Bawtch was dead! And the forgers, too! What marvelous news!

"So I just have these few blank forms for you to stamp in case they have an emergency."

He had them right with him, only a few pounds of paper. I took them. I got out my identoplate and stamped them then and there. It only took about twenty minutes instead of half an afternoon. How much lighter the work would be, now that Bawtch was in some unknown grave. I should have thought of that before!

I pushed the stack back to him. "And now, Oh Dear," I said, using his nickname, "what other news do you have?"

"Well," he said, "from what I can hear when they don't know I'm listening, Lombar Hisst is making just utterly marvelous progress addicting the Grand Council members. All the court physicians have been won over to the need of drugs. A lot of population on them, too. It is just a matter of time. There is just one little hook."

I became alert.

"You apparently have a man here on Blito-P3, some Fleet officer. On some mission. Apparently he has been sending reports through to Captain Tars Roke and the Grand Council has faith in both Roke and this officer. Lombar had the reports traced and they're in some kind of a monthly platen code so he knows that they can't be counterfeited."

Ah, well. No one is likely to get very far ahead of Lombar.

"Goodness, but Lombar hates this officer here! Absolutely goes into fits. So just before I got on the *Blixo* to come, I got pulled into Lombar's office. He's very frightening."

Indeed, he was, with his yanking on lapels and his stinger.

"And he said he'd found out you had a courier line to Voltar. I think he has spies on every ship. And he gave me a message."

Ho, ho! A message from the Chief himself!

"He said he was glad to help in sending the whore and Doctor Crobe like you requested. I think he'd do anything to mess up this officer here. Is she a whore, Officer Gris? She seems awfully nice. I talked with her on the voyage. She taught me to tie my tie properly, see?"

"Get on with the message!" I told this rattlebrain.

"Where was I? Oh, yes. And he said they were really counting on you. If this officer he hates so gets the planet on its ear, and especially if he upsets its control elite in any way, things could get very grim." He was trying to remember the rest of it, twisting his face and frowning.

"Wait a minute," I said. "If you talked to that woman on the voyage, what did you tell her?"

He went into instant shock. "Nothing. Nothing, Officer Gris. She sort of tried to pump me but I said I was just a messenger and knew nothing. Just carried some papers. And she didn't pay any attention after that. She was in her cabin nearly the whole voyage. I think she was studying a language because I could hear the machine going."

"You sure?" I said.

"Oh, goodness gracious, yes, Officer Gris. Lombar Hisst said he would murder me if I told anybody but you. But wait, that isn't all the message. Lombar said he was counting on you utterly to keep this officer slowed down. The opium and speed and heroin have to keep coming in. And no Rockecenter organization is to be disturbed in any way. Lombar is certain the supply line would collapse if I. G. Barben collapsed. But he said to tell you there was good news. There is a plan afoot—he didn't say what it was—but he was certain that some time in the future he would be able to give you a go-ahead and you could safely kill the man."

I was certainly glad to hear that! Then I had a disturbing thought. Krak had talked with him. "Did she put a helmet on your head?"

"The woman? No. Just before we took off from Voltar the whole ship was searched by Apparatus guards. They confiscated almost all our baggage. They took everything she had with her except one change of clothes and a language machine and tapes. So where would she get a helmet? Who is she?"

"The girlfriend of the man you carried the message to kill," I said. I couldn't resist it.

Oh Dear fainted dead away!

I put the magic-mail postcards in his pocket, allowing his mother to live until the next courier run.

I had the guards drag him and his papers out with orders to throw him in a detention cell until the *Blixo* left.

At my signal they brought in Crobe. The good and learned doctor was a mess. Always dirty, he was not improved a bit from six weeks in a spaceship cabin.

"Are you the (bleepard) that got me ordered here?" he said.

"Well, you're out of Spiteos," I replied. "You're on a beautiful humanoid planet that knows absolutely nothing about cellology or putting tentacles on babies."

"They confiscated everything I brought!" he said. "I haven't even got an electric knife!"

"We have lots of electric knives and over five billion

people who have never seen a man with two heads where his feet ought to be."

That interested him, as I knew it would. Then a suspicion crossed my mind. "Were you given orders to study a language? And did you study it?"

"Oh, yes. But languages are a waste of time. Who wants to talk to people when you can do interesting things to them?"

"Tell me 'Good morning' in English."

"Goot mordag."

Oh, Gods. "Ask me how I am in English."

"You iss a doggle name George," he said.

(Bleep)! Stupid (bleepard). He had loafed the whole voyage! I couldn't trust him even out of this hangar!

"Doctor Crobe," I said, "I am going to put you in a room and I am going to keep you there until you have mastered a planetary language."

"What?"

"Just that. And if you really want to get around and enjoy the scenery and begin fruitful work, you'll take the language machine they gave you and put that nose of yours right into it. And when you can talk to the natives, I will have interesting employment for you and not until."

It failed to bring the overjoyed response I had expected. He just stood there and glared.

There was a chance that he thought of Earth as just a barbaric and primitive place without a scrap of culture. And this is not true. They have the subjects of psychology and psychiatry and these are marvelous and wonderful things.

I usually carried a couple of paperback texts for consultation when I came up against a knotty problem. I reached into the pocket of my tunic and brought them out. One was *Psychology Rampant*. The other was *To the*

Depths with Psychiatry. These would certainly prove to him that there was benefit in learning English. I handed them over.

"Read these," I said, "and you will see how worthwhile English is!"

He took them. He leafed through them. He saw a drawing of a brain and his eyes lit up.

I beckoned to the guard captain and told him to put Crobe in one of the better cells and not let him go until I gave the word.

When the time came, I would let him out and turn him loose on Heller. After all, Heller had wanted a cellologist! I smiled.

Success so far in handling things. One of the troops had even saluted once.

I told the guard captain to bring the female over from the ship.

Chapter 8

Lulled by months of not seeing her, I had completely forgotten the impact of the presence of the Countess Krak. You knew she was there.

She was wearing a spacer's greatcoat with the collar turned up. She was wearing spaceboots. Her blond-gold hair was in braids around her head like a crown.

She looked at me with steady gray-blue eyes and said, "Is Jettero all right?"

Hastily, I gathered my wits. This was going to be touch and go. "Oh, yes!" I got out.

"Nothing has hurt him?" she said.

Now I had my chance. I could win this only if I played it perfectly. I put my hand on my stomach. "No!" I said quickly. "Somehow I don't feel very well. It must be something I had for lunch."

Aha! It worked! She smiled faintly. She thought her hypnotic implant of me was still in place, the (bleepch). She put down the small bag she was carrying.

Now to get a clue about the forgeries. I pointed at her grip. "I see you're not carrying much baggage. I hear the ship was searched."

She sighed. "Yes. Snelz put my trunk aboard and they took it. All that fuss about just a few training items. They must have missed them and they read me some long screed about it being unlawful to disclose you were an extraterrestrial. They're very unreasonable people. I'm not in the military. But that isn't the problem. They took all the beautiful clothes Jettero gave me. I don't have anything nice to meet him in. I can't let him see me like this! But then, you'll help me get some, won't you, Soltan."

"Of course," I said. My attention was on those Royal forgeries I had given her. "Anything else of value in that trunk?"

"No."

"I mean the Royal documents . . . you know. . . ."

"Oh, don't worry, Soltan. They're safe."

Aha. She must have been wearing them on her body. I would get around to that during the operation. I said, "You haven't told anyone about them, have you?"

"Oh, indeed no," she said reproachfully. "I gave you my word. I haven't even told Jettero about his Royal appointment or the promise to sign my pardon. You don't think I'd break my word, do you?"

"Of course not," I said soothingly. I felt more in control of the situation now. "But, come. You are anxious to go where Jet is. We have to prepare you quickly. Come along."

I grabbed the unmarked box of bugs, my hat and coat, and went to the door, beckoning.

She picked up her small grip and followed me up the tunnel.

We stopped at the Costume Department. The photographer was there, waiting. I handed him the identoplated order for passport, tickets and travel money and he handed them over.

The Countess Krak had started going down the racks of clothes. The photographer got her attention and asked her to step over to a white wall.

She didn't divine what he was up to right away as the camera he held probably didn't look like any camera she had ever seen before. When he held it up to his face, she suddenly understood.

"Oh, no! Not a picture!" she cried. "I'm such a mess!"

Too late. He already had it. He rushed away.

I grabbed a dress off the rack. It was blue with big white flowers.

"What's that?" she said in a kind of horror.

"Native dress," I said. "You have to look like a native. Remember the Space Code they read you."

She looked at the dress in amazement. "You mean these natives don't know any more about dressing than *this?*"

I masked any glee I might feel. I pointed at a change booth. "Quickly, quickly. People are waiting. Heller is half a day's flight from here and we've got to get you on your way."

Reluctantly, she went into the booth and shed her greatcoat.

I found a dingy-looking woman's hooded cloak. It was a sort of spotty brown. I found a veil. I couldn't find any shoes or stockings. She was wearing spaceboots. So let her wear spaceboots.

She came out wearing the dress. She was about five foot, nine and a half inches tall and the dress was for a smaller woman. Her opinion of it was plain in her expression.

I shoved the cloak at her. "This will cover it," I said.

She found a couple small holes in it. She looked at me with a rather calculating eye. It made me nervous.

"The sooner you put this on, the sooner you're away," I said.

She put it on. I handed her the veil. She didn't know what to do with it so I showed her on my own face. "All women go veiled," I told her. "It's a religious custom."

"Are you sure we're on the right planet?" she said. But she put it on.

I got into my own bearskin coat and karakul hat, picked up the box of bugs, the things she had taken off and her grip, and with some persuasion, got her outside and into the taxi.

Now came the tricky part. I closed the partition so the driver couldn't hear. "You have to be very careful on this world," I said. "They are absolutely crazy on the subject of identification. And if you have any scars or marks of any kind on your body, they grab you at once. So all such things have to be removed."

The taxi was rolling through a very dark night but I could feel her eyes on me.

"Oh, Soltan," she said, disbelieving.

I turned on the overhead light. "No, look. See that scar on the back of your hand? A dead giveaway."

"That's just a little claw mark from a lepertige. You can hardly see it."

"And look at that wrist! Electric cuffs, weren't they?"

"Oh, Soltan. You'd need a vivid imagination just to make them out."

"All right," I said. "But how about that hideous scar over your right eyebrow?"

"You mean that tiny little scratch?" She fingered it. "But the eyebrow covers it."

"Well," I said, "you're just used to seeing it." And then I got very cunning. "You think Heller wants to have to look at that huge blemish the rest of his life?"

She was thoughtful. Then she said, "I see what you mean. But you're not putting me under gas, Soltan."

"Listen, Countess," I said. "It is my duty to protect you. Heller would have my head if I let you wander out only to get picked up because of identifying marks."

I must have sounded convincing—possibly because it was true that Heller would kill me with slow torture if I let anything happen to her. She grew more thoughtful.

It was time to dive straight into Strategy Plan A. "I don't blame you for being wary," I said. "The world, any world, is full of wolves. But I am a slave of duty. I will tell you what I will do. I happen to have hypnohelmets here. I'll let you put both me and the cellologist under one first and I'll give you a wrist recorder to wear during the operation. How's that?"

Just as I suspected, it caught her fancy. Above the veil, a gleam was very visible in those gray-blue eyes. "All right," she said.

I almost hugged myself with glee. It had worked! It had worked! I had to turn my face away so she would not see me suppressing triumph. I was tricking the formidable Countess Krak. And getting away with it!

Chapter 9

It was nearing 9:00 P.M. and there were very few around at the hospital.

I steered the Countess Krak through the lobby and got her into an interview room.

Dr. Prahd Bittlestiffender had been on the lookout and followed.

She sat down in a chair. She obviously didn't like the veil and took it off. She threw back the hood.

Young Doctor Prahd gangled into the room.

He stopped.

He stared.

In Voltarian, I said to her, "This is your doctor. He is one of the most competent cellologists Voltar ever produced. Doctor, this is Miss X. She just came in on the *Blixo* and, as usual, has to have her identifying scars removed."

Prahd, the silly ape, didn't take the cue at all. He was just standing there, staring at her with his mouth open!

I was operating smoothly now, myself. I said to her, "We'll go out now to the warehouse and get a hypnohelmet. So please excuse us."

I kicked him out of his trance, got him into the hall and closed the door. Carrying her bag and the bug box, I herded him back to the privacy of his office.

I snarled, "What the Hells are you so (bleeped) stunned about?"

"That lady," he said, eyes wide.

"That 'lady'," I told him acidly, "is a very wanted criminal!"

"WHAT? That beautiful woman? I can't believe it. She must be one of the greatest beauties of Voltar! I've only seen one other that could compare with her. And that was Hightee Heller, the Homeview star!"

I pushed him into his chair so I could tower over him. "Listen," I snarled. "That woman you are going into orbit about was once condemned to death and is today a nonperson. She has killed four men to my personal knowledge. Three of them for just making an innocent pass at her. So don't get any romantic ideas about that 'lady'! She is being sent in to do another job. A murder."

He was staring at me round-eyed, his straw hair standing up in all directions. I pressed my advantage. "We have to con her to protect ourselves," I continued. "You're going to remove her scars all right. But you're also going to put these audio and visual bugs in her skull just like you did with Heller. There's a scar just above her right eye that will do just fine. So you're going to put her under gas right now and do the job. She's not to know about the bugs."

"But she'll kill us if she finds out!" he said.

"Precisely!" I snapped. "But I've got that figured out. She has an inflated idea of herself as a hypnotist. I am going to propose to her that she put a hypnohelmet on each of us——"

"WHAT?"

"Be calm, be calm," I soothed him. "I've fixed a helmet so it doesn't work. You simply pretend you are under hypnosis. So will I. And we'll put a wrist recorder on her. Then she'll go tamely through with it. I'm just protecting you, that's all. So run over to the warehouse and get a couple of those hypnohelmets I sent over and I'll see you back in the interview room."

He took the box with the two bug devices and put it in his pocket. He left.

Rapidly, I opened her grip. I went through it very thoroughly. Only a few toilet articles and a little makeup. The bulk of the space was taken up with the language machine and some Earth texts. I carefully investigated the lining. Nothing.

The space greatcoat and the coveralls she had been wearing and which I had brought along produced no better result. Originally, when I gave them to her, she had strapped the "proclamations" against her body. And that's exactly where they must be now. I couldn't imagine even an Apparatus guard adventuring a skin search on her: she would kill him! And had they found them, they would have checked them against the Palace City log, found they were forgeries and she now would be a very executed Countess Krak, instead of a live one here on Earth.

My own neck was still out. Even with Bawtch and the forgers dead, the Countess Krak could implicate me. Ah, well. Very shortly, I would have them back for she would be lying there under gas. I might even fold a packet of paper to put in their place. Yes, that was the ploy. I made a paper packet up.

A door slammed somewhere and I realized Prahd must be back. I hurried down to the interview room and arrived just as he was entering. The Countess Krak's eyes lit up.

He was carrying two cartons and when he put them down she instantly rose and brushed him away. I had carefully replaced the original carton seals, of course —we are experts at that in the Apparatus—and those two cartons looked like they had never been touched since the day they left the manufacturer.

She chose one. She opened it. She looked like somebody about to cut a birthday cake. "Oho!" she said. "All shiny new and the very latest type! See, look! It has a plug-in microphone as well as the recording strip player! Oh, lovely. Such nice colors, too."

She expertly inserted a power pack and checked the meter. She plugged in the microphone. "Who is first?"

I wasn't really sure that she wouldn't also shove a knife into somebody. I gave Prahd a push toward a chair. He nervously perched his lanky body on its edge.

"Do you own this hospital?" she asked him conversationally.

"No, no," said Prahd, pointing at me. "He does. That is to say, he's the boss. If you have any complaints . . ."

"Not any yet," said the Countess Krak, smiling at him sweetly.

She put the helmet on his wheat shock of hair. She turned to me. "If you'll just wait in the hall, Soltan." She was juggling the microphone in one hand, the other poised over the switch to turn the helmet on.

I went. But I kept my ear pressed close to the closed door.

"Sleep, sleep, pretty sleep," she said. "Can you hear me?"

A muffled "Yes."

"You are about to do an operation. You will do it very expertly. You will not bring about any physical-body distortions or alterations. In other words, you will not monkey with my limbs or glands. Is that clear?"

A muffled "Yes."

"You will limit your operations to repairing a few

scars and blemishes and make it all heal rapidly with no further scars or blemishes and no fancy ideas. Right?"

"Yes."

"Now," she continued, "if you or Soltan or any other man approaches me carnally or makes any sexual contact with me while I am under gas, you are to use an electric knife on yourself or them. Understood?"

"Right."

"And you are not to say anything around me or to me while I am under gas. Understood?"

"Yes."

"Now, if you violate any of this you will feel like atom bombs are exploding in your head. Right?"

"Right."

"You will now forget what I have said to you and when you wake up you will only remember and believe that I have been asking about your professional qualifications. Agreed?"

"Right."

A click. She had turned the helmet off. In a minute Prahd came stumbling out the door. I was watching him very closely. I had wanted to be sure that the helmet was made inoperative when the unit I carried came within two miles of it.

He was mopping his face. "Gods," he whispered. "Atom bombs! I see what you mean!" He tottered down the hall to his operating room.

It was all right. If he'd been hypnotized, he would not have remembered! It was safe.

"Soltan," a soft voice was calling.

I went in like a meek little schoolboy. I was hiding my grins. She plopped the helmet down on my head. She threw on the switch. Through the visor shield I could see her check the meter and the lights.

She stepped back and held the microphone to her mouth. "Sleep, sleep, pretty sleep. Can you hear me, Soltan?"

"Yes," I said, making my voice sound groggy.

"Some time ago I told you that if you had any idea of hurting Jettero Heller, you would get sick at your stomach and so forth. Now tell me, Soltan, is that still true?"

"Oh, yes," I lied.

"And you have not gotten any notion of hurting him or doing him any nasty tricks?"

"Oh, no," I lied.

"Good. That is still true. Only, added to it is the fact that if you try to do anything bad to me, you will now feel the same way. Understood?"

"Yes," I said. Oh Gods, it sure was a good thing this helmet was null on me!

"Now listen carefully. You will help me in every way you can to reach Jettero. You will let me go wherever I want around this hospital and nearby buildings or base. You will let me pick up anything I want. Understood?"

"Yes," I said.

"Now also," she said, "you'll let me have whatever I take, no matter what it is. You will let me leave with it. And you will find a reasonable reason in yourself for letting me do so. Is that clear?"

"Yes," I said.

"Good. You will now forget what I have said. When you awake you will think I have been asking you about the operation. All right?"

"Yes," I said.

She reached over and clicked the helmet switch and then took it off my head. "Wake up, Soltan."

Hiding my grin, I said, "Now that you know all about the operation, shall we go to the operating room?"

Oh, smart brains, indeed! What if I had not had that breaker-switch pair installed in the helmets and my skull? All that agony had just paid off! It didn't compare to the stomachaches I'd had!

Chapter 10

Prahd sent her into a cubicle beside the operating theater. It was a sort of bathroom–dressing room. He gave her a package—a Zanco disposable, sterile operating gown and cap. He gestured toward a slot in the door. "Please drop your clothes through that, including those boots. Then take a shower and get into this. Then enter the operating room through that side door."

She nodded. She seemed oddly cheerful. But of course she was happy to have a bath after six weeks on a freighter. And she was going to see Heller soon, wasn't she? Still, I was very suspicious of a happy Countess Krak.

Prahd and I entered the operating room itself. He had lights flashing and beakers bubbling and it all looked very businesslike.

"Just as soon as you have her under," I said, "I'm going to have to do a skin search."

"WHAT?"

"I have to make sure she is carrying no secret weapons," I lied. "I will take off my boots. I will be very quiet."

"You don't have to come in," he said. "There's a viewport, one way, right over in that wall. It looks like a small mirror."

"Won't do," I said. "I can be very quiet. I have to be sure."

"All right, but do it before I begin work. I don't want all the germs you carry in here. And I can disinfect afterwards."

I ignored his insult. I took a wrist recorder out of my pocket. "Tell her she can put this on and start it."

"I think she *would* kill us if we took any liberties, Officer Gris. So just be warned that I'll have my electric knife ready."

"Hey, you weren't really hypnotized, were you?"

"No. But if she wakes up and finds she's been fooled with and your dead body isn't lying on the floor, she'll get suspicious that the helmet didn't work."

Yes, there was that. But I didn't exactly like the way he put it.

She came in, in the open-backed operating gown. "That's the awfullest-smelling soap I think I ever smelled. What a frightful stink!"

"Overstrength germicidal," said Prahd. "As to the stink, Officer Gris is just leaving. As to the soap, I'll put a nice smelling bar in the recovery room and you can shower and wash your hair when you wake up. All right? Good. Now, if you will just sit down on the operating table . . ."

I left. I went around to the one-way window. I couldn't hear what they were saying. She was on the table but she was having to master how to operate the wrist recorder and I realized she was unfamiliar with the clumsiness of Earth devices. She finally got it tested and running and hung on her forearm.

She swung her shapely legs up and stretched out. Prahd lowered the gas anesthetic dome. He watched a heart counter and respiration meter. She was out.

He pulled the gown off her and beckoned toward the window.

I went around to the door. I slipped off my boots. More silent than a cat, I entered and stole toward the table.

Gods, she was a beautiful woman! No Greek sculptor had ever had a model like this!

Prahd was standing there with an electric knife. I got busy.

There was nothing strapped to the front of her body. There was nothing around her waist so far as I could observe it. They must be strapped to her back! I moved forward to turn her over. I stopped. Prahd notwithstanding, I was afraid to touch her. I suddenly discovered that terror could be a much heavier emotion than sexual desire. I backed up.

Finding it hard to swallow and shaking a bit, I gestured to Prahd to lift her.

He did, very quietly. I looked under her back from the right side. I went around while he moved her the other way. Nothing. She didn't have a thing on her!

I tiptoed out of there, feeling somehow that I had escaped with my life.

I went into the change room and searched. Nothing. I examined the clothes she had taken off. Nothing. I looked for false soles in the boots. Just plain, black spaceboots.

(BLEEP)!

She was a very clever woman. She not only trained people for the stage, she could also do all kinds of sleight of hand. I would have to watch her very carefully. It would be my neck if I didn't recover those forgeries. The horrible thought hit me that maybe Bawtch had talked before he died. Or left a note or something! Yes, I had no choice but to recover them. Constant watchfulness was the watchword.

Chapter 11

Back at the one-way window, I watched the progress of the operation.

She lay in naked repose, oblivious of what was going on.

Prahd was working with rapid expertise. For some reason, he took a lot of measurements with a lot of different scopes and devices, cataloguing them all on a chart. Then he opened a big volume and consulted it. From where I was I could see the page he had: it was headed "Manco." Well, he was right about that. She was from Manco.

Then he made a signal toward the window, indicating the hall. I met him there. He showed me the book. "This lady is from the aristocracy of Atalanta."

I noted sourly that it was "lady" again. "Yes," I said.

"That accounts for it," he said.

"For what?" I said, irritated.

"The perfection. She's the product of tens of thousands of years of selective breeding. The aristocracy married nothing but the most beautiful and bright. Do you realize that her thyroid . . ."

Oh, Gods, deliver me from a specialist riding his hobby! "Are you going to get on with this operation or aren't you?"

"I just wanted you to be aware that you were

tampering with the aristocracy," he said. "It carries the death penalty, you know."

"I told you!" I grated. "She's a nonperson! A criminal! There isn't even any penalty if you killed her."

He went back in the operating room. I went back to the window. Prahd bent over her ankles and looked very carefully. Then he looked over her wrists. Then he looked at me and nodded. He was convinced.

I knew what he had found. Electric cuffs, wrist and ankle, when worn for weeks, make small burns. And she must have been in them for months during her imprisonment, transportation to Voltar and trial before the Apparatus got her. They had left faint scars.

Prahd got to work. He made his "cell soups" from little clips and drillings. He addressed the scarred eyebrow and, very soon, sterilized the two bugs and implanted them. He covered them over with the bone and skin paste and then put the area under a catalyst light.

He then got busy on the ankle and wrist scars. I didn't really like the way he was working. It was with sort of flourishing motions like a painter; he was also cocking his head over and eyeing the effects. Silly (bleepard).

With new lights now on her wrists and ankles, he went prowling for more scars or blemishes: he found some ancient signs of slashes along her right ribs, below the breast, probably from the claws of some wild animal she had been training. He fixed those. Then he found some tiny burns on the outside of her left thigh. I knew where those had come from: Lombar's stinger. He fixed them. Then he studied her whole naked body minutely under a scope. He didn't seem to be finding any more past wounds or blemishes.

He put cups and straps over the work he had done and I thought he would now be finished.

But no. He got out a little set of tools and began to work on the ends of her fingers. I couldn't imagine what he was doing. Then it came to me. He was giving her a manicure!

Having finished that quite expertly, he went to her feet and gave her a pedicure! He seemed to be getting her toenails just right.

I thought he would surely be done now. But no! He was getting out another set of tools. He propped her jaws open, did a thorough inspection of her mouth and then, of all things, began to clean and polish her teeth!

Deliver me from idiots! Her smile was about as dangerous a thing as anyone would ever see without making it blindingly bright!

Done with that at last, he pulled the cloths from under her jaws and stood back. He surveyed her long nakedness. Then, busily, he pulled another lamp down on its swing neck, turned it on and passed it the length of her body, stood back and admired the effect and then did it again. He gently turned her over and did the same thing to her back.

He was giving her a suntan!

I had to admit to myself that two or three years in the dungeons of Spiteos and six weeks in a spaceship might make one a bit pale. But he had something else in mind for he was consulting the tables in the big book. He got a meter out. He was apparently measuring skin color! The people of Atalanta are white but it is a white with a faint tan tinge. He was restoring the exact shade!

He was satisfied with that. Now he was checking her hair color. The blond-gold of it seemed satisfactory by meter.

He was done! Thank Gods! What a tinkerer!

He threw a blanket over her and picked her up and carried her into the hall. I was with him promptly.

Prahd took her into a private room. He laid her on the bed. He covered her up with sheets and blankets. He made sure the recorder was not exerting any weight on her arm. He arranged her head properly on the pillow.

He left the room and closed the door. He looked at me and there was a dreamy farawayness in his eyes. "You know," he said, "she was perfectly right. Anybody who messed up such a gorgeous creature *should* have atom bombs exploding in his head."

He locked the door and put the key in his pocket. "I'm going to bed now," he said. "I suggest that you go home."

He went away. I was absolutely fuming! I was seething at how blind people could be about the *real* Krak. Here she had added another ally to her mobs of supporters!

Well, I certainly had no intention of going home! She might come out of that room and attack me! She might even blow up the base!

I got a straight-backed chair and planted it opposite the door. I gathered up the spacer greatcoat, coveralls and other clothes and put them in a stack beside the chair. I took the spaceboots and put them on their sides on the floor. I tilted the chair back against the wall and put my foot on the spaceboots so that if they were even touched, it would cause my foot to move and bring the chair back forward on its four legs to jolt me awake in case I dozed. I took the catch off my stungun and gripped its butt.

I looked at the locked door and for the first time since her arrival I began to smile.

Despite her trickery, I had foiled the Countess Krak. I had finally gained the upper hand. I was impervious to her hypnohelmets while she in turn was now bugged so I could monitor her every move.

Heller, meanwhile, was sinking fast. And if he thought Babe's wrath was rough, he hadn't seen anything yet. The best was yet to come.

I folded my arms across my chest and grinned. Gris, I complimented myself, you got 'em. Sending an implanted Krak off to Heller and his whores would be like tossing an anvil to a drowning man.

Then when Hisst sent the OK, I could humanely end Heller's misery, get the forgeries even if I had to torture the information out of Krak (a delicious thought), sell her to the black market in Istanbul, settle matters with Utanc and then sit back and rake in the money from my host of enterprises.

Sleep well, Countess Krak.

Tomorrow belongs to me.

*What will Krak do when
she finds Heller knee-deep
in girls?
Is this the end of
Heller's mission?*

**Read
MISSION EARTH
Volume 5
FORTUNE OF FEAR**

About the Author
L. Ron Hubbard

Born in 1911, the son of a U.S. naval officer, the legendary L. Ron Hubbard grew up in the great American West and was acquainted early with a rugged outdoor life before he took to the sea. The cowboys, Indians and mountains of Montana were balanced with an open sea, temples and the throngs of the Orient as Hubbard journeyed through the Far East as a teen-ager. By the time he was nineteen, he had travelled over a quarter of a million sea miles and thousands on land, recording his experiences in a series of diaries, mixed with story ideas.

When Hubbard returned to the U.S., his insatiable curiosity and demand for excitement sent him into the sky as a barnstormer where he quickly earned a reputation for his skill and daring. Then he turned his attention to the sea again. This time it was four-masted schooners and voyages into the Caribbean, where he found the adventure and experience that was to serve him later at the typewriter.

Drawing from his travels, he produced an amazing wealth of stories, from adventure and westerns to mystery and detective.

By 1938, Hubbard was already established and recognized as one of the top-selling authors, when a major new magazine, Street and Smith's *Astounding Science Fiction*, called for new blood. Hubbard was urged to try his hand at science fiction. The red-headed author protested that he did not write about "machines and machinery" but that he wrote about people. "That's just what we want," he was told.

The result was a barrage of stories from Hubbard that expanded the scope and changed the face of the genre, gaining Hubbard a repute, along with Robert Heinlein, as one of the "founding fathers" of the great Golden Age of Science Fiction.

Then, as now, he excited intense critical comparison with the best of H. G. Wells and Edgar Allan Poe. His prodigious creative output of more than a hundred novels and novelettes and more than two hundred short stories, with over twenty-two million copies of fiction in a dozen languages sold throughout the world, is a true publishing phenomenon.

But perhaps most important is that, as time went on, Hubbard's work and style developed to masterful proportions. The 1982 blockbuster *Battlefield Earth*, celebrating Hubbard's 50th year as a professional writer, remained for 32 weeks on the nation's bestseller lists and received the highest critical acclaim.

"A superlative storyteller with total mastery of plot and pacing."—*Publishers Weekly*

"A huge (800+ pages) slugfest. Mr. Hubbard celebrates fifty years as a pro writer with tight plotting, furious action, and have-at-'em entertainment."—*Kirkus Review*

But the final *magnum opus* was yet to come. L. Ron Hubbard, after completing *Battlefield Earth*, sat down and did what few writers have dared contemplate—let alone achieve. He wrote the ten-volume space adventure satire *Mission Earth*.

Filled with a dazzling array of other-world weaponry and systems, *Mission Earth* is a spectacular cavalcade of battles, of stunning plot reversals, with heroes and heroines, villains and villainesses, caught up in a superbly imaginative, intricately plotted invasion of Earth—as seen entirely and uniquely through the eyes of the aliens that already walk among us.

With the distinctive pace, artistry and humor that is the inimitable hallmark of L. Ron Hubbard, *Mission Earth* weaves a hilarious, fast-paced adventure tale of ingenious alien intrigue, told with biting social commentary in the great classic tradition of Swift, Wells and Orwell.

So unprecedented is this work, that a new term—dekalogy (meaning ten books)—had to be coined just to describe its breadth and scope.

With the manuscript completed and in the hands of the publisher and all of his other work done, L. Ron Hubbard departed his body on January 24, 1986. He left behind a timeless legacy of unparallelled story-telling richness for you the reader to enjoy, as other readers have, time and again, over the past half-century.

We the publishers are proud to present L. Ron Hubbard's dazzling tour de force: the *Mission Earth* dekalogy.

"I am always happy to hear from my readers."

L. Ron Hubbard

These were the words of L. Ron Hubbard, who was always very interested in hearing from his friends and readers. He made a point of staying in communication with everyone he came in contact with over his fifty-year career as a professional writer, and he had thousands of fans and friends that he corresponded with all over the world.

The publishers of L. Ron Hubbard's literary works wish to continue this tradition and would very much welcome letters and comments from you, his readers, both old and new.

Any message addressed to the Author's Affairs Director at NEW ERA Publications will be given prompt and full attention.

NEW ERA PUBLICATIONS UK LTD.
78 Holmethorpe Avenue
Redhill, Surrey, RH1 2NL England

In Australia contact:
N.E. Publications Australia Pty. Ltd.
2 Verona Street, Paddington N.S.W.
AUSTRALIA 2021

FOR MORE CAPTIVATING ENTERTAINMENT

FROM L. RON HUBBARD

SEE THE FOLLOWING PAGES.....

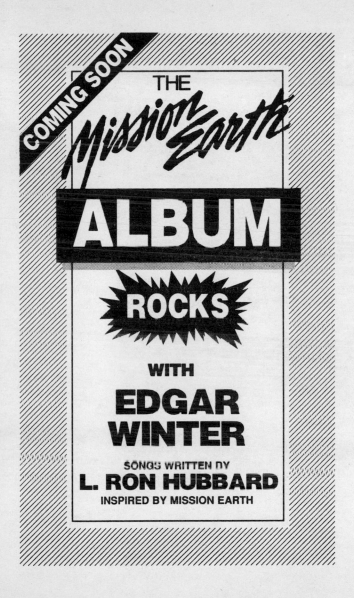

IN LA-LA LAND
WE TRUST

ROBERT CAMPBELL

WITHDRAWN

FROM STOCK

THE SHERIDAN
BOOK COMPANY

This edition published in 1994 by
The Sheridan Book Company

First published in Great Britain in 1987
(simultaneously in hardcover and large-format paperback by
Mysterious Press in association with Century Publishing and
Arrow Books)

This Mysterious Press paperback edition first published 1988

Mysterious Press Books (UK) are published
in association with
Arrow Books Limited
Random House, 20 Vauxhall Bridge Road, London SW1V 2SA

Printed and bound in Great Britain by
Cox & Wyman Ltd, Reading, Berkshire

ISBN 1–85501–555–2

In appreciation to R. R. Irvine,
who suggested the title . . .
for only ninety-seven percent
of the royalties.

"When you got nothing to do, anything to do is something to do.
When you got nobody to love, anybody to love is somebody to love."

—**Bosco Silverlake**

One

Chippy Byrd was sitting in his lipstick-red 1976 Plymouth four-door with the vinyl top, showing his right hand full of ten-dollar bills while trying to get his left hand up Lacy Ohio's dress.

His real name was Chester Bucherleider. Her real name was Loretta Oskanowsky. Chippy fancied he looked a little like Fred Astaire and wore his hair combed slick and flat in the fashion of the thirties. Lacy believed she resembled, in a certain light, the younger Bette Davis. He was a petty grifter. She was an amateur doxy thinking about turning pro. Their courtship was a case of mutual and benign deception.

They were parked under the magnolia trees growing around the lot that serves the amusement pier jutting out into Lake Pontchartrain. Which everybody knows is in New Orleans. But which Chippy told Lacy would be in heaven if only she would unclamp her thighs.

Having counted ten Hamiltons out of the corner of her eye, and knowing what good times they would buy, Lacy was about to do as requested when another car, a white Cadillac convertible with a right front fender primed with gray Bondo, braked

1

to a stop just short of the water, spraying rooster tails of gravel behind the rear wheels.

While Chippy and Lacy watched, two men—a big one and a little one—tumbled out of the car, laughing and scratching, clearly drunk on something that made the night glitter and the world sing. One of them had something that looked like a soccer ball wrapped in newspaper tucked under his arm. First thing you know, they were tossing it back and forth. When one of them missed, it fell on the ground but didn't bounce. So they took to kicking it around, laughing like a couple of banshees baying at the moon.

Chippy was not surprised to find that his hands were wet. He sat there as still as a mouse, hoping the two drunks wouldn't happen to look his way. Hoping Lacy wouldn't honk the horn just for laughs. There was something about the two men that gave him warning. His instincts told him they were the sort who would kill him and rape Lacy just for the hell of it. Or maybe they'd do it the other way around. He didn't know how he knew it, but he knew it, and suddenly he realized that Lacy knew it too.

The little one gave the ball a hell of a boot. The big one made a dive at it and missed. The ball scooted into some reeds growing in and around the water. They went down on their hands and knees, hunting around for maybe five minutes. When they stood up, all they had was mud up to their knees and elbows.

"The hell with it," Chippy heard the little man say.

"For Christ's sake, it's gotta be around here somewheres," the big one said. "It couldn'ta grown itself legs and walked away."

"Well, I don't give a fuck. If we can't find it, nobody else is gonna find it. Barcaloo said lose it, so we lost it, right? Didn't we just goddamn lose it?"

The big man started to giggle and laugh and slap his thighs with his big, meaty hands. Then he got serious. "Barcaloo's gonna be mad as hell we don't tell him we buried it like he tole us."

"I'm gonna be mad as hell you don't shut your mouth. You're worse than a fuckin' cunt the way you harp on things. The

2

damn thing sunk down to the bottom of the goddamn lake. What you want me to do, *dive* for it?"

"Fuck it," the big guy said.

"That's what I said," the little man said. "All I ask is just you should act a little reasonable."

"Well, I just said fuck it, didn't I?" the big guy said, getting into the car on the passenger side.

"That's all I ask," the little man said. He kicked the motor over, and the Cadillac squealed out of the lot.

Chippy and Lacy sat there wondering.

"What the hell was that all about?" Chippy said.

"I don't want to know," Lacy said.

"Where was we?"

"We was just about to drive me home."

"There's nothin' to worry about. They're long gone."

"They might get a notion to come back."

"Why the hell would they want to come back?"

"To look for whatever it was they was kickin' around."

"You heard 'em say screw it."

"I also heard one of 'em say Barcaloo would be mad if he found out they didn't bury it. If two people like that are afraid of this Barcaloo, I don't want to be here if Barcaloo decides to come around and see if they did what he told 'em to do.

"My God, what in the hell is that?" Lacy squealed.

Chippy looked where she was looking and saw the comical obscenity down at the water's edge.

"Nothin' but a possum."

"Yech. Ain't he the ugly thing? What's it doin'?"

"How the hell would I know?"

What it was doing was dragging the round thing wrapped in newspaper out of the water. The wet paper shredded away.

"Chase that thing away," Lacy said.

Chippy turned on his headlights. The slow-witted creature turned to the light, blinking rapidly, dazzled but unafraid. One paw remained on top of the object of its interest.

Chippy picked up the sawed-off baseball bat he kept on the floor of the car in back and opened his door.

"Where you goin'?" Lacy asked.

3

"Chase that goddamn possum the hell away," Chippy said, showing how brave, how manly, how fuckable he was.

He walked up to within ten feet of the possum. It looked at him like an old man without his specs. Chippy could see that the animal was trying to work it out if the thing he'd found was worth fighting for.

Chippy got a good look at the prize the possum held.

"Oh, dear fuckin' me," he yelled.

The possum took off at a shambling run.

"What is it? What is it?" Lacy shouted from the car.

It was a head. Mangled and swollen. Skin broken here and there. One eye opened, one eye closed. A head with shiny black hair. A human head.

Now, how the hell was he going to tell her *that* without queering his chances of getting into her pants anytime that night?

Two

It was well after one A.M., and a party was still going strong at Walter Cape's house on top of Hollywood's highest hill. He wouldn't have it called a mansion. That smacked of privilege.

The entire hill had been chopped, channeled, and honeycombed to create ten thousand feet under roof that rivaled, if it did not surpass, the old Xanadus of the movie moguls whose lusts had been commonplace and acts of evil simple.

There were those who laughed and sneered at it, but no one he'd ever met, man or woman, would not have kissed his proverbial ass in MayCo's window to have a weekend in one of the incomparable bedroom suites or an invitation to one of his fabulous parties where deals were cut and fortunes made.

There were whispers about other, even more exclusive, evenings when actresses of considerable fame pranced around on stiletto heels wearing nothing but horsehair tails belted to their rumps and men of wealth and power rode them bare-assed. Talk of delicious crimes against nature committed with young actresses. Sins against God involving children.

Cape consumed high-concept but acted low-profile, in constant subtle conflict between his public and private lives.

There had been two hundred people at the party. There were still about a hundred left. The diehards. The greedy. The fearful ones who just knew something earthshaking would happen the minute they got in their automobiles and drove out of sight. Something spectacular. A ten-million-dollar movie deal; a cherry vintage Rolls-Royce put up for sale at a bargain price; a drunken actress upended bare-assed in the punch bowl, ready to be buggered by one and all.

Others who waited for a talk with Cape waited for a deal.

Cape had worked the crowd like a snake-oil salesman, touching flesh, bumping asses, laughing up a storm. Flashing, dashing, gliding across the costly carpets with the smooth assurance of a winning politician or a pope. Now, in the quieter shank of the evening, when many were drunk and most were winnable, he offered a quieter performance, a twinkling, slightly weary eye and the face of everyone's favorite uncle.

He tapped a woman wearing beaded turquoise satin on the rump. She turned around, smiled, and followed him down a long hall into a small office paneled in wood and furnished in leather. Butterflies, pinned to green felt and framed in walnut, hung on the walls.

He refreshed the glass she had in hand with three fingers of Scotch and asked her if she wanted ice. She shivered, bare-armed in the air-conditioned chill. He went over to the Adams mantel and touched a button. A fire flamed to life amid a pile of realistically sculpted logs.

"Ain't we excessive?" she said as she sat down in the chair closest to the hearth. "Chill the air and light the fire?"

He sat down in the facing chair.

"Atmosphere counts for plenty, May."

"I do better in a stable," she said.

May Tuckerman liked to say that she, like Otis and Dorothy Chandler, was in the communications business. They owned the *Los Angeles Times*. She owned the biggest string of shopping guides in the state, covering the territory from Monterey County in the north to San Diego and Imperial Counties in the south and out to the Nevada border to the east.

She liked to say that the Chandlers might influence more people when it came to national and international affairs than she did, but when it came to state and local issues, she was the one with the clout. Ask any sucker who ran for office without calling on old May for a cup of tea.

She was no Dorothy Chandler in other ways. Her interest in the pursuit of finer things was less than minimal. A rousing performance of *Oklahoma!*, a recording of Glenn Miller's "Chattanooga Choo-Choo," the tap-tap-tapping of a tap dancer's flying feet was her style. Steak and potatoes, whiskey and a beer chaser, straight fucking, nothing fancy, these were what suited her best. She had the typical American preference for an overloaded plate.

She dressed the part in jeans and flannel shirt. When events demanded she wear an evening dress, she was not one bit shy about squeezing into bugle beads and satin a size too small, even though she was the first to say that she had an ass six ax handles wide and tits like twin cannons.

Fifty, she looked forty, screwing no man over thirty-five. Preferably young gardeners or telephone linemen. Rich, she played poor, driving around in a much-used and battered pickup truck that reeked of the horse shit collected on her ranch in the Malibu foothills where she kept thoroughbreds and quarter horses side by side in equal-opportunity stalls.

She didn't have a husband and didn't want one. There were no men available who could offer her more money, more excitement, more security, or more power than she had already. Besides, she often said, she'd get a husband and all of a sudden some slick magazine would have him listed among the fifty most powerful people in the city and she'd be nothing but the little woman doing good works. She was self-made, she often said. For sure, no man had ever made her.

"Great party, as usual, Walter."

"Enjoying yourself?"

"I notice you got a lot of new waiters working it."

"If there's one you fancy, May. They're all aspiring for one thing or another."

"You know, Walter, you would have made a great pimp, you ever wanted to give up being a millionaire."

7

"It's not the money, it's the game. You know that, May."

"Why have you invited me into your inner sanctum, Walter?" she asked with a hint of uncharacteristic coyness. She glanced over at a huge American Wooten desk, the kind with thick doors that open like a clam shell to reveal a honeycomb of pigeonholes and little drawers for the filing of a hundred matters. It had been made sometime in the fifteen years between 1860 and 1875, a rare treasure of walnut worth its weight in gold. "You pick my file out of your collection for something special?"

"You think I have a dossier on you, May?"

"I think you had a dossier on your mother before you were born."

"I have a new venture in mind that might interest you."

"For the money or the game?"

"What do you know about home videocassettes?"

"You mean movies?" May asked.

"Motion pictures, music videos, instruction tapes, erot- - ica . . ."

"Fuck flicks?"

"Got anything against them?"

"Depends who's on top. Who's getting double the pleasure, double the fun."

"As long as the principal parties are getting equal time?"

"I suppose. Frankly, Walter, most women don't get hot by looking, or haven't you heard?"

A tic quivered briefly beside his left eye.

"Maybe in the future, " he said blandly. "Women are taking their place in the world. Their real preferences may soon be known."

"I'll have to watch out where I sit my ass on that issue. I wouldn't want to get stuck in a position I hadn't thought about. What's the proposition?"

"Erotica—"

"Pornography."

"—is a three-billion-dollar-a-year business."

"So is bagging horse shit, give or take a billion."

"Exactly my point. You don't take a moral position when it comes to horse shit, do you, May?"

8

"Just so long as nobody tracks it on my rugs."

"I'm not asking you to watch skin flicks instead of Johnny Carson, May. Just to make yourself a profit."

"How far do you mean to go?"

"I'm not interested in live sex acts, nightclubs, or any other aspect of the business that presents ongoing personnel problems. I mean to consolidate the production and retail distribution of printed matter, films, and home videocassettes under one management for the territory west of the Mississippi."

"Seems to me, even looking at what's on offer with half an eye, that there's more than enough of that crap to go around already."

"There's never enough, May. And rarely the right mix. Like every other market, the one for erotic entertainment is fragmented. Very handsome profits are being ignored because the mass-market producers won't tailor-make a product for some very small, but very rich, groups of specialty consumers."

"What will your start-up capitalization be?"

"Ten million. Four to product. Three to distribution. Two for litigation if needed."

"And the last million?"

"Contingencies."

"What's your management strategy?"

"I've already engaged the services of a firm with broad experience in the field."

"Where's it based?"

"New Orleans, but it will be here within the week."

"So, how long is this proposition on offer?"

"Three days?"

"That's not a lot of time to reconcile some deep feelings."

"If you have strong reservations about it, May, why don't you just pass this one up?" Cape said, standing up to splash another two fingers into May's glass. "There may be other venture opportunities in future."

May caught the implication very clearly. Turn your back on a Walter Cape enterprise and chances were very good you'd never be invited to join another. Paternal. You'd have to call Cape paternal. As long as you let him be big daddy, he'd make

9

your life sweeter. Turn his little golden marks of affection down, and he'd give the chances to others.

"I'd just like a better idea about the kinds of films you're asking me to help finance. I'm running a series condemning kiddie pornography, and my conscience wouldn't allow me to support anything that even hinted at that."

"Oh?" Cape said, as though questioning her sincerity. He sat down again. May noticed, with a start at her own instincts, that his chair was disposed in such a way that no light fell on his eyes, though she was brightly lit, her expressions open to his scrutiny.

"I'd like to see the bastards who mess with children strung up by the you-know-what," she said vehemently, showing the measure of her condemnation.

"Well, May, I don't think anyone would say anything except amen to that," he said in the flattest kind of voice.

She knew she was being warned off the subject. For a moment she wondered if some of the tales told about Cape were true and not just the sort of shit balls thrown at the rich, the famous, and the successful by the viciously envious.

For instance, one story claimed that Cape kept a beautiful woman on hand in one wing of the house. Gossip from "reliable sources" had it that other young women, always generously endowed in the tit department, were stashed here and there in apartments and hotel suites throughout the city.

Another rumor said there was a chid, a little boy, maybe seven or eight, living in the house. The resident whore might even be as much companion for the child as Cape's in-house fuck. One version hinted at a cuckoo twist, like a tale from Grimm or Mother Goose. The boy, it was said, never aged, but always remained seven or eight.

"But you have to understand, May," he went on, "should you choose to join me in this enterprise, I'd expect you to consider our common interests concerning the series of articles."

"Not publish?"

"I didn't say not publish, did I? I'm talking about tone, emphasis, and fairness. The jury is still out on what pornography is. There's also the matter of first-amendment rights. I'm simply suggesting that you don't come down too hard on one side or the other but offer your readers a well-balanced argument for all sides of the issue."

"For Christ's sake, Walter, I can't go around pussyfooting on this. Unless a strong position is taken, there's no reason to even bring the subject up one more goddamn time."

"Well, of course, there's that. You don't have to publish. There's enough out there to make our lives unpleasant without stirring up matters that might well be considered deeply personal. But you know your business better than I do, May. Settling conflicting interests is what it's all about, isn't it? So why don't you think it over and see where your best interests lie?"

May mumbled and stroked her face with a scarred, rough hand.

"Horse shit is horse shit," Cape said. "Skin flicks are skin flicks. I'm sure you share my view that anything not specifically prohibited under law is open to enterprise. Cassettes have taken erotica—call it pornography if it suits your prejudices better—and packaged it for the eighties. The man in black socks doesn't chase the lady in rolled stockings around the horsehair sofa anymore.

"I'm bringing an executive in from New Orleans who knows the business. He had extensive experience and a working knowledge of the industry. The stockholders will simply be buying into an entertainment enterprise. They won't even have to look at the product if they don't want to."

"If you don't intend anything too outrageous, I'll consider the proposition," May said.

"I don't make promises about things that cannot be precisely described, May. You know that. You'll just have to trust me and the people I'm bringing in."

She was being dismissed. She stood up. Cape, as mannerly as he usually was, didn't get up to show her to the door but just sat there in the red leather chair with the shadow falling across his eyes, making it so hard for her to read them.

When she reached the door, he said, "Would you ask Frank Menifee to come in for a minute, May?"

"Sure. Are you going to ask his people to invest?"

Cape didn't answer.

"Why do you do it, Walter?"

"Why do I do what, May?"

"You could retire with your money right now. You could buy up something else like a chain of retail stores or a small oil company. Why are you always out there on the fringe?"

"Because that's where the heavy action is, May. Out there on the barrens with the wolves."

Three

He had a first name, but with a last name like Whistler, hardly anybody ever used it. He was sitting in a window booth at Gentry's, a fancy name for a seedy coffee bar run by a failed kazoo player named Bosco who'd lost an arm in an argument with a shotgun over a whore.

The rain had washed all the baby prostitutes and twangy boys, the chicken hawks and queer bashers, the gonifs and petty grifters off the four corners of Hollywood and Vine. The empty streets looked as quiet and innocent as they had in the fifties when Hollywood was still a small-town beauty and Whistler was just a youngster looking for a score.

The city and the man had grown old and run over at the heels together. Both a little fragile, their faces battered from the impact of too many closing windows and too many slamming doors.

There was only the two of them. There was no cook at two A.M.

Bosco was reading *The Lives of the Saints*. Whistler was reading *The Enquirer.*

"Whattaya read that crap for?" Bosco asked as he came over to refill Whistler's cup.

"Because I'm sick and tired of the true horror of the news," Whistler replied. "Along about now I want to read fairy tales about actresses strangled with feather boas and corpses rising up from graves all over La-La Land. A man's got to have some hope in miracles, and these pages are full of them."

"You should go home and get some sleep."

"I'm waiting for the rain to let up."

"It never will. This is July fifteenth, St. Swithen's day. When it rains on St. Swithen's day, that means it's gonna rain for forty days and forty nights," Bosco said. He went back to his book.

Whistler returned to his tabloid.

On the third page of the "Stinky Ink" there was an item datelined New Orleans, a few days before.

> Early this morning at the deserted amusement pier on the shores of Lake Pontchartrain, Mr. Chippy Byrd, 978 Bourbon Street, sitting in his automobile with a companion, Miss Lacy Ohio, saw two men apparently engaged in a game of football.
>
> "They was acting drunk," Mr. Byrd told this reporter. "They was kicking this here ball back and forth until it lands in the water, at which time they get in a white 1981 Cadillac convertible with one Bondoed fender and drive away. A possum comes along and drags the ball out of the reeds. My friend says there is something very funny about that there ball, and when I say, 'How, funny?' my friend says it don't look really round and was wrapped in newspaper, so I go to drag it out and have a look. It like to scares the hell out of me when I see what I thought was a ball is a person's head."
>
> The head, hacked off at the neck, was collected by members of the New Orleans police. Gross examination so far indicates that the badly decomposed head is that of an Oriental female approximately twenty-five years of age.

"A head without a body was found in a lake in New Orleans," Whistler said.

"It happens all the time down there," Bosco said. "Those witch queens do a thing where they cut off two heads and put them face-to-face alongside any body of water. Ask those heads any question you want and they got to answer."

"You know things unheard of by your average counterman, Bosco. You think we could set up something like that in MacArthur Park and see if a couple of heads could tell us which horses are going to win the quiniela at Santa Anita?"

A crippled station wagon came lugging along the boulevard.

From the crossroad by the movie house, a silver 635 CSi BMW chased down the tunnel made by its own headlamps.

Whistler watched with the melancholy calm of a man who knew the worst would always happen. There were only two cars on the road, and they were going to have a smashup. That's the way things happen on a rainy night in La-La Land.

When it came, Whistler was already on his feet.

"Is fifty bucks a fair price for an expert eyewitness?" he asked as he started for the door.

The BMW smashed into the side of the station wagon, bulldozing it across the boulevard and up onto the curb right outside Gentry's plate-glass window. The wagon slammed into a light pole, a fire hydrant, and a stack of newspaper vending machines, the doors flying open and the driver flying out.

By the time he finished bouncing, he was busted up like a porcelain doll. His blood was all over the place. But that wasn't the worst of it.

The worst of it was, another body came flying out of the back end of the wagon. It ended up sitting against the racks for *The Enquirer* and *The World*. A naked body. A woman's naked body. A woman's naked body without a head.

The publishers of *The Enquirer* and *The World* couldn't have asked for a better tribute. Whistler couldn't have been more surprised, if he hadn't lived so long in La-La Land that he'd long since lost any sense of astonishment along with his innocence.

The BMW, and the people in it, had fared better than the station wagon. It was still on its feet, though its radiator was

15

wrecked. Day-Glo coolant bled from it onto the curb. The front fenders looked like crumpled aluminum foil.

The blasted vehicles hissed like wounded beasts in the strange silence that always seems to follow a crash.

A high-pitched moan was coming from the passenger's seat.

Whistler stepped around and dragged the door open. A very pretty woman sat staring at the starred windshield. Her skirt was up and her pants were off. She was unaware of the picture she made. She didn't look injured. Her moan started to stretch out and run up the scale.

Whistler took a handful of her long blond hair and turned her head around so she had to look up into his face. Her eyes didn't change focus, and her safety valve was still threatening to pop. He slapped her twice, and she fell forward into his arms without another peep.

There was nothing else he could do but lift her out of the car. It was carry her and risk a hernia or lay her down in the filthy gutter. The driver got out of the car and stood spread-legged, his hands up on the roof of the car, steadying himself. Then his hands dropped out of sight. He was closing the zipper on his fly.

Whistler knew him. Well, he didn't *know* him, but he knew him. The sucker was on the tube every week on some police show. He played a white undercover cop. Some actor who looked like a Caucasian with a deep tan was the black cop. There was another show just like it. Except on *that* show the black cop wore the earring, and on this guy's show the white cop wore the earring.

He put his hand up to his ear to see that his earring hadn't been ripped out of the pierced lobe of his ear, looking at Whistler as though wondering if he meant to steal his girl-friend. Why else would a stranger be standing in the street holding her in his arms?

"Hey, you," he said, with more than a trace of belligerence.

"You mean me, my name is Whistler," Whistler said. "You're Emmet Tillman. I see you on the tube."

The actor grinned and brushed his hair back.

"Can you walk?" Whistler asked.

"What the hell's going on?"

"You drunk or on toot?" Whistler said.

"I had drinks with dinner. I don't do drugs," Tillman said with a careful show of dignity.

"Can you walk?"

"Of course I can walk."

Tillman came around the back of the BMW. Whistler could see that his boner hadn't died away completely.

"Well, follow me into the coffee bar before I drop your lady in the street."

Tillman did as he was told, just as though he were blocking out a scene under a director's orders.

Bosco pushed open the door for them.

As Tillman went through he spotted Bosco's empty sleeve.

"My God, were you in this goddamn accident too?" Tillman asked.

Frank Menifee, the labor lawyer, also managed the largest investment fund amassed by the reigning Mafia family in Los Angeles. He had the Irish gift of gab, though his silences were legendary. The tale was told of one negotiation during which he spoke not one word, except "Good morning" at the beginning and "Good evening" three weeks later at the end, getting up from the bargaining table with all he'd asked for in his written proposal and even a little more.

Before he sat down, he moved the big leather chair away from the fire and the light. Cape and he were both wearing masks of shadow when he sat down and looked at Cape with an expression of mild expectation on his rice-pudding face. It was all bumpy with little translucent specks like tiny sun blisters. They shone when the light struck a certain way. Shone like bits of wax. His eyebrows were pale and had an odd shine to them as well. If somebody told you Menifee was made of plastic, you'd think twice before calling him a liar.

"Well, Walter?" Menifee said.

"Well, Frank?" Cape said with the slightest of smiles. "Have you talked to your clients?"

"I did."

"And what do they have to say?"

17

"They mentioned the fact that they are already enjoying a piece of the action."

"Prostitution? Old-fashioned pornography?"

"Well, yes, Walter, is there any other kind?"

"It ain't what you do, it's the way that you do it, Frank," Cape said in the voice of a burlesque comic.

"What are you going to do that's different?"

"Better photography, better stories, better actors and actresses, new subject matter."

"Well, I wouldn't know about that, would I, Walter? You're talking about art, and I'm talking about money."

"You see all the movie and television stars taking off their clothes for *Playboy* and *Penthouse*, Frank?"

"I keep a Catholic house, Walter. I've got teenage daughters."

"But you've seen the magazines, haven't you? Like at the barbershop?"

"I've glanced through one or two. Yes, I have."

"Miss America gets printed up bare-assed, and they have a four-million-dollar issue. Does that tell you something, Frank?"

"Americans like brand names."

"That's one way of looking at it. Our films are going to have beauties in them. No sluts and whores, Frank."

"You know how to slice it that fine, Walter?"

"I expect to sign them up just before they're ripe."

"You've got a way to make them famous afterward?"

"I'm working on it. I'm making friends. The right opportunity will come my way."

"Oh, you're a collector, Walter. No doubt about that. But my people still don't know why they should even let you start doing business."

"Because I'll do it better than they've been doing it. They'll make more money with none of the bother. I've got a hundred ideas for profit where there was no profit before."

Menifee stared into the fire.

"Have you got a thought, Frank?"

"You know, Walter, the old struggle between the mustaches and the young turks came about over pushing hard drugs on the street to the school kids. Now, I'm not making a judgment, here—"

18

"I should hope not, Frank."

"—but it could be that the next generational struggle might be over certain aspects of the skin trade."

"Certain aspects?"

"S and M, Walter. Kiddie porn. Snuff films. New subject matter, what you call it. Am I right, Walter, when I make the prediction that these are some of the areas of greater opportunity you're talking about?"

"They're on the agenda."

"Some of the old men, the family men, don't like that sort of thing."

"Tell them to wash their hands, Frank. Like their fathers did about the drugs. The business needs organization. There are too many free-lance operators making costly competition."

"That came up. What do you mean to do about that?"

"Ask them to join my group."

"And if they don't, will you be needing the kind of persuasion I can offer?"

"I wouldn't want that sort of attention. I've got better ways. You notice the tall woman in the silver suit?"

"I noticed her, Walter. That's Janet Hyer, the assistant state's attorney, isn't it?"

"That's who it is, Frank. And we've been discussing the possibility of bringing certain producers of pornography up before the grand jury."

"It's been tried. Nobody can agree on what constitutes obscenity anymore since the Supreme Court threw it over to prevailing community standards."

"But they do agree on what constitutes conspiracy to solicit an act of prostitution. What we're going to do, Frank, is bring these producers up for pimping, and their actors up for being whores."

"It could work." He looked at the Wooten. "That's a grand desk you've got over there, Walter."

"I'm glad you like it."

"A desk like that would have room for a thousand documents."

"Would you like to see?"

They got up and walked over to the massive piece of

19

furniture. Cape opened it up, revealing the many drawers and compartments inside. Cape reached over and pulled out one drawer. Menifee took his billfold from the breast pocket of his dinner jacket and extracted a check. He placed it in the drawer. If asked, he could honestly say he'd never handed over money of any sort to Walter Cape for any purpose.

Menifee looked up at a butterfly with hot-blue and green wings.

"Butterflies," he said.

"I've been collecting them for years," Cape said.

"Drink some more coffee," Whistler said, leaning across the table toward Tillman. "Go ahead."

"I don't need any more. I told you I'm not drunk or high," Tillman said. "I've got a full bladder."

"Well, for Christ's sake, don't sit there suffering. Go use the john."

Tillman slid out of the booth. The girl's leg, resting against Whistler's thigh, jerked as though she wanted to run away too.

Whistler saw a look in Tillman's eye.

"Just take a leak, Mr. Tillman. Don't try coppin' a sneak. That's your car out there, and you can't hide it. You should know that it'll go a lot harder if you try to leave the scene of the crime."

Tillman tapped his forehead with his fingers as though saying he wasn't thinking straight. Then he said, "Crime? What the fuck you mean, crime?"

"Accident. Go take your leak, Mr. Tillman, and hurry back. The cops'll be here before you know it. And we should talk."

Whistler looked at the girl. She smiled back at him as though he were her big brother. She carefully kept her back to the plate glass and the carnage on the other side of it.

"I don't know your name," Whistler said.

"Well . . ." she said.

"You're an actress, right?"

"Trying to be."

"Whatever you call yourself will do."

"Shiela Andes."

"That's got a certain lift to it," Whistler said.

"The Andes are mountains in Peru."

"You feel all right now?"

"Well, no, I feel awful. I mean, those two people out there. They're dead, aren't they?"

Whistler almost said one was deader than the other, but he caught himself.

"Well, you saw, didn't you?" he asked instead.

"Not really. I mean, I couldn't see very good out of the windshield, and then I fainted. Did I faint?"

"Yes, you did."

"I'm almost glad. I don't like to look at dead people. Especially—"

Her pretty tongue curled up like a cat, and Whistler thought she was going to cry or be sick. But she grabbed hold of herself.

"There's a lot of blood, isn't there?" she said.

"Yes." Whistler looked out the window.

A lot of blood from the driver but not a drop from the headless body. The driver lay sprawled on his face in the rain. It pasted his shirt and slacks to his skinny body. His hair wavered like river weed in a puddle of water. Bosco appeared outside. He went to the body without a head and covered its nakedness with a blanket he took from the back of the wagon. Only the ankles and feet were exposed, nicely molded, as delicate as ivory carvings.

"So I must have seen something, but I don't remember. I'd rather not," she said, as though refusing a cup of coffee.

"Well, you don't have to," Whistler said, touching her hand.

It was trembling fiercely. She was strung tight and about to snap.

Tillman was coming back from the rest room. Whistler got up and met him halfway along the aisle.

"What did you mean, 'go harder'?" Tillman demanded.

Whistler, keeping his voice low, said, "You know and I know that you had half a load on when you hit that wagon. And you had your hand up Shiela's skirt mining for gold just before the crash. While driving in the rain. You're in for it if they question her."

"She wouldn't say."

"Think not? Take another look at her. She's scared to death.

21

She'll answer any questions they put to her without a care in the world about you. She your woman?"

"Just a squeeze."

Oh, for Christ's sake, Whistler thought, this gazoony was going to talk like the character in the show.

"I wouldn't talk like that when the cops come. Nobody really talks like that. Something like that could make the cops take a dislike to you."

"Hell, I know most of them. I even carry a reserve badge."

"Don't let that turn your head. Five'll get you twenty they'll drop the book on you. Five'll get you fifty they'd like to bring you down. What are you making? Two million a year playing a cop? Well, they're making twenty thousand running through the shit and blood in the streets. Take my word. They get a chance to do you, they'll do you."

"That's bullshit," Tillman said, making a hard jaw.

"Tell me about it. Send me a letter from jail."

The jaw turned to pasta. "So what should I do?"

"You'll take a little advice?"

Tillman nodded.

"You'll let me represent your interests?"

"You're not an agent, are you?"

"No, and I'm not a lawyer, either."

"Then what the hell are you?"

"I'm a private investigator."

"An eye?"

"Nobody's said that since they buried Humphrey Bogart in his trench coat."

"What can you do for me?" Tillman said, rubbing his fingers and thumb together and looking wise.

"No, I can't pass a bribe," Whistler said. "What I can do is advise you to sit down and wait for the cops. Answer any questions they ask. Refuse a breathalyzer until your attorney can get here. You got lawyers?"

"I got lawyers, agents, managers . . ."

"Refuse to walk any lines or blow into any balloons, but do it like you'd like to cooperate. However, you're scared half to death and you don't want to do anything without your lawyers tell you it's okay. Understand me. Do *not* act like you're an honorary cop just because you pretend to be one every week on the tube. Do *not* get unduly familiar with the officers or detectives, even if you're acquainted with them. Do *not* talk like a goddamn script."

Out on the street a siren wailed, rushing toward Gentry's, and Bosco's summons.

Tillman jerked his head around.

"We got time. Sound carries on wet air," Whistler said.

"I'd better make a call," Tillman said.

"Make your call after some conversation with the police. Drink more coffee. Piss as much as you can. Take your time. Your lawyers got any brains, they'll take as long as they can getting here. What you want to do here is delay a blood test as long as you can, until its value as evidence can be put in doubt."

"What am I paying for this advice?" Tillman said.

"The advice is for free. What you'll pay me for is seeing that Miss Andes gets home safe and sound. And maybe for what I can do for you after."

"I understand," Tillman said.

Whistler went back to Shiela and held out his hand.

"What?" she said, her mouth trembling.

"I'm taking you home," Whistler said.

"Is it all right?" she said, looking at Tillman and sliding out of the booth. "Are you sure it's all right?"

"I'll explain it to you on the way," Whistler said.

He walked over to Bosco while Tillman got up close to Shiela.

"I'm taking the lady home," Whistler told Bosco. "You understand?"

Bosco nodded. "What lady?"

Whistler looked at Tillman, holding Shiela's hands, playing the protector, reluctant to let her go, acting a part.

Shiela's eyes were shining as she looked up into the actor's face. There was a little smile on her lips.

Whistler had the notion that Shiela thought Tillman absurd. He had another notion that she knew she'd just been dealt the card that filled out an inside straight.

"I'll make him a dish of potatoes," Bosco said.

"What?" Whistler asked, not certain that he'd heard correctly.

"Confuses the breathalyzer."

23

"Who told you that?"

"I learned about it when I was in England."

"Does it work?"

"Who knows? But if somebody thinks it works, it makes for a better attitude under interrogation."

Whistler led Shiela through the kitchen and out the back door to the parking lot where he kept his Chevy.

Four

Monsignor Terrence Aloysius Moynihan, chancellor to His Eminence Cardinal Eustice, chairman of the Financial Discovery Committee, keeper and wielder of the bank accounts of the richest archdiocese in the country next to those of New York City and Chicago, was wearing his purple sash and the outfit with the little cape and purple piping.

He was black-haired, white-skinned, red-cheeked, and blue-eyed, the greatest dissembler since Pontius Pilate washed his hands and gave the decision between Christ and Barabbas to the mob.

It is sometimes said by those in the know that if most cops were not allowed to carry a gun legally, they'd be on the other side of the law, carrying one illegally. It was said of Moynihan that if he'd not become a priest, he'd have become a loan shark, a Hollywood agent, or a pimp.

A Catholic buck, once in Moynihan's pocket, rarely left it. He had an ancient mind. And a powerful lust for women that he did not exercise but sublimated in his pursuit of power and money. Sometimes even Cardinal Eustice thought he went to too many parties and stayed at them far too late.

The young monsignor had stood in a well of serenity by the fireplace nearly all night, as the party swirled around him. His slender hands held a double old-fashioned as though it were a precious relic. For hours he'd been taking congratulations upon his latest appointment to the County Board of Adjustments—the civic body that passed on architectural design review—and was taking them still.

He'd soon be rubbing palms and asses with the contractors. Finding the corners that could be cut, discovering closets filled with old bones, accepting little contributions to the archdiocese, like parochial school buildings constructed at cost. There was money to be made by association with Monsignor Moynihan, and this was a crowd where a person's popularity was in direct proportion to the thickness of their fleece.

Frank Menifee joined Moynihan when the priest was otherwise unoccupied. Menifee wore his tuxedo as though it were made of black cardboard. The bow tie looked like it was pinned to his neck with a nail. Whenever he moved his head, the tie moved with him. Moynihan found the tie fascinating and could scarcely tear his eyes away.

"Congratulations, Monsignor," Menifee said, smiling like a winking shutter.

"Why, thank you, Frank."

"Is it true?"

"What would that be?"

"That you're going to run for county supervisor next?"

"It's a thought."

"I wouldn't."

"Why not?"

"There'd be no profit in it for you."

"I'm not looking for personal profit, Frank. You know that."

"Ah, well, Monsignor, that's what you say. But there's profit and then there's profit. You sit on enough boards right now to work any con you've got a mind to work. Go public and you open yourself up to a great deal of scrutiny. That wouldn't do you, the cardinal, the archdiocese, or the Church a bit of good."

"I'm sure His Eminence appreciates your concern and counsel, Frank."

Moynihan plucked a gold watch as small as a half dollar from his cummerbund and consulted it.

"I've left my good-byes much too late. I must go find our host."

"I just left him in his office."

"Oh? Business, Frank? Are you taking your people into Walter's new enterprise?" Moynihan asked. "You didn't seem too eager about it when he first approached us."

"I'm like you, Monsignor, a man with many masters."

"But a good Catholic, Frank. Never forget that."

"'Give unto Caesar . . .'"

"To coin a useful phrase."

"I took the offer to my principals. They like it. They see a future in home entertainment. And you?"

"The Holy Father takes a dim view of such entertainments," Moynihan said.

"How many do you think he's seen?" Menifee asked with a curly twist to his mouth.

"I doubt he's ever seen any. But you don't have to stick your hand into the fire to know it burns."

"But you've got to bite the apple to know if it's sweet."

"Don't tease me, Frank. It's cruel to tease a man who's taken a vow of celibacy."

"If you ever decide to break your vow, I know a young woman."

"You'll be the first to know if I do, Frank."

"What does the Holy Father have to say on the subject?" Menifee said.

"I won't quote verbatim from his latest encyclical on pornography, but I can tell you he's definitely agin it."

"Sure of himself, isn't he?"

"Infallible."

"Does he threaten excommunication?"

"For the lookers or the makers, Frank?"

"Either. Both."

"Shouldn't you be more concerned about the souls of the venture capitalists?"

"I don't know that money carries sin with it, Monsignor.

There's a debate there for your Jesuits about the moral neutrality of money."

"I often think about it, Frank."

"I mean, I was just wondering about those buildings the Church owns on Santa Monica and Western. I was just wondering if you knew that one small manufacturer renting space from you makes studded dog collars, whips, and punishment gags. Another prints a magazine called *Where the Boys Are*, a little directory for pedophiles. And, from what I've been told, there are three whores working out of a third-floor apartment."

"Well, no, Frank, I didn't know that," Moynihan said evenly. "I'll look into it."

"And raise their rents?"

"I expect, if what you say proves true, that we'll give them notice."

"Then you'll have some empty square footage."

"Considerable."

"You wouldn't want it left vacant too long."

"No, we wouldn't, Frank. Now, I'd better go say good night and thank you to Walter."

And have him sign a lease, you hypocritical, holier-than-thou son of a bitch, Menifee thought.

Shiela lay back against the worn seat of Whistler's old Chevy.

Whistler looked straight ahead, his hands on the wheel. Making like a chauffeur. Playing the game.

She was glancing at him from time to time, and Whistler knew it. He expected she looked at every man the same way. Weighing his balls. Estimating his power and clout.

"I want to thank you for this," she said.

"Just what do you think you've got to thank me for?" Whistler said.

"Removing me from the scene of the crime."

"No crime. Accident."

"That naked body had no head," Shiela said. "I thought I was going to toss my cookies."

"Oh, you saw that, did you?"

"There's not much I don't see, Whistler. And something like that is very hard to miss."

"You just take a miracle drug when I wasn't looking?"

"What?"

"I never saw anyone recover so fast. You act in front of the camera as good as you did on the street and in Gentry's, you'll be collecting a brass doll one of these days."

"Thanks."

"If you'd stayed at the scene, you'd have gotten your picture in the paper."

"I could use the exposure," Shiela agreed, "but I can use the leverage better."

"What leverage is that?"

"I just did Tillman a big favor. Leaving the scene. He was promising me a hand up. He meant up my skirt. And I meant a part on his show. It was going to take a long time before either of us really delivered, what with all the jockeying around we were doing. Now he owes me. It wouldn't have helped him any if I'd told the cops he was playing with my pussy and not minding the road."

"You've got a mouth."

"You men teach us how to talk dirty, then you flinch."

Whistler said nothing.

"I suppose I do sound as hard as nails. It bother you?"

"If you think that's what it takes."

"Turn here, first apartment house on the corner," she said.

Whistler turned off and parked at the curb. When the wipers stopped dancing, the rain, like a mist of gelatin, obscured the view of the pink-plaster court apartments.

"I'm not hard," Shiela said. "Really, Whistler. I'm butter and cream. But, Christ, they don't make it easy for you to be good."

"You don't have to explain yourself to me."

"Why not to you? You're the nearest thing to a knight in shining armor I've bumped into since I left the plains of Kansas for L.A."

Whistler shrugged and smiled.

"So, maybe if you take the time to look, Whistler, you'll see I'm a princess worth rescuing. Your good deed wasn't a waste of time," Shiela said.

"I'm not a Boy Scout."

"You should have a reward, anyway."

They stared at each other quietly, like enemies.

She moved in closer, her lips starting to part, the pink tip of her tongue already showing. He pushed her away.

"I think it's only fair you should know I wasn't saving you trouble. I was cutting myself a slice of the action."

"Sure. I understand. That's fair. If you can't get a meal off the fat cats, who can you get a meal off of?"

She opened the door and stuck one long leg out into the rain. She kept it there while she said, "I'm in the book, Whistler. I'd appreciate an invitation to whatever."

Whistler nodded. She stretched out and kissed him on the mouth, her lips still trembling from the strain of keeping her screams in check. This time he didn't push her away. Her leg was still out in the rain getting wet.

Five

Ralph Parker was wearing maroon trousers with a black satin stripe down the sides and a forest-green dinner jacket. He had a beeper clipped to his cummerbund. People often mistook him for a doctor. He controlled the beeper from a battery in his pocket. It interrupted conversations he wanted interrupted and got him out of parties that were proving a waste of time.

Cape's parties were rarely a waste of time, but Parker wore the beeper because it was a habit and he was used to it.

The crowd was almost gone, the last of them moving toward the exit hall, round-eyed with fatigue and the effects of so much alcohol. Only a few were left, wandering around as though in a daze, like commuters in a train station early in the morning or very late at night. He made the beeper beep as though reminding himself that it was time to go.

Henry Warsaw came up to him and said, "Why don't you just suck your thumb when you're in need of comfort?" Warsaw was petroleum. Out of the most powerful fifty in Los Angeles, featured in a recent slick that chronicles the shifting pecking order of La-La Land, eight were petroleum. Warsaw's name wasn't among them. He was into oil and natural gas the way you could say a pirate on the high seas was into cargo and transport. He was a raider. He ate oil companies for breakfast, but none of his corporations would ever show up in the Fortune 500.

Everybody but his victims liked him for his country ways and straightforward manner.

He had a taste for little boys between the ages of nine and ten, some of whom he got from Walter Cape when Cape was done with them.

He prided himself on being a good judge of men, but he didn't have a clue about who Ralph Parker really was, because he'd never bothered to find out. Parker said that he put deals together and sometimes called himself an investment banker.

Los Angeles is full of people putting deals together. Anybody with a tattered script in his pocket is packaging a film. Anybody patching roofs is into construction. Anybody with a five-dollar bag fancies himself a dealer.

Warsaw didn't have to be friendly to anybody he suspected was a con merchant, but you never knew when some asshole would prove useful, so he slapped Parker on the back and joshed him like they were both a couple of good old boys and grass-roots Democrats.

But Parker was really an investment banker. Not one of those who operated out of glass-and-marble buildings on Wilshire Boulevard in Los Angeles, or in New York, Paris, or Rome, but a banker who collected doctors, dentists, and lawyers with smooth salesmanship and invested millions out of an armored briefcase equipped with a mobile phone, a book of private numbers, and a .357 Magnum.

When Shirley Quon drifted over to join them, Warsaw put his arm around her waist and she didn't even flinch. Quon's fortune was based on restaurants and real estate. Properties purchased for a song in all the most strategic places along planned freeways and areas of future public condemnation. Buildings allowed to crumble around the ears of illegals from every quarter of the world. Restaurants that had once had plenty of trouble with the inspectors from the Health Department until Quon had learned how to spread the grease.

Ordinarily she didn't like to be touched by white hands. That was a well-known fact.

What was not a well-known fact was that Quon was a man in Oriental drag. It was not a well-known fact because anyone who found out and tried to use it disappeared. Quon had a taste for little boys between the ages of ten and eleven. That was why he allowed Warsaw the familiarity. Warsaw passed the children he got from Cape on to Quon. And Quon passed them on. Each pedophile had a taste for children of the age they'd been when they'd had their innocence taken from them. Now they traded in lost innocence, passing the children from hand to hand as they grew older, until they were so old that there was nothing left to them.

Parker was a gonif and a con and had been, more than once, a killer, but in many ways he was among the best of them.

He saw Monsignor Moynihan enter the room, which meant that Cape was probably alone. He excused himself and went down the corridor to the paneled door and knocked. Cape called out, and Parker went in.

Cape looked small in the red leather chair. Small and weary and melancholy.

"Hello, Ralph," he said without warmth or enthusiasm.

"You look worn-out, Walter."

"I am worn-out. How's the party going?"

"Winding down."

Cape made a movement, as though meaning to get up, but settled back again. "I should be out there seeing my guests off."

Parker made a question with his eyebrows. When Cape nodded, he took the chair that so many people had occupied that night. "Don't bother yourself, Walter. They'll never know."

"Parties are bothersome things," Cape said. "But they can be useful."

"Did you put your consortium together?"

Cape made a shape in the air like a ball and smiled. "There's still some thought to be given to casting and recruitment."

"Plenty of twat around," Parker said.

"I wish you'd clean up your language," Cape said mildly.

"Sorry."

The phone rang. Cape stared at Parker without moving to lift the receiver until Parker got up and started to go.

Tillman had gotten himself more than half sober. He'd counted up his options on his fingers as the siren died outside. He could call his agent and let her work the angles, but that would mean she'd have him by the shorts forever and ever. He could call his lawyers and let them put in a fix, but he couldn't be sure a lawyer's fix would stay nailed. Fixes worked out by lawyers were made of cardboard and were known to fall apart, causing complications that required another lawyer's fix—and another and another. Lawyers could get you hung for a ten-dollar parking ticket. He could call the producer of the series, but Manny Ostrava had said more than once that it wasn't the old days anymore, and thank God he didn't have to get his actors out of jail or find doctors to scrape out the pussies of his starlets. Besides, Ostrava was no friend and would use whatever he could get his hands on to sandbag Tillman come contract time.

The one-armed asshole behind the counter was looking at him with bland contempt, waiting to see if he'd just stand there doing nothing. Like he was no better than any other schmuck with no juice to call his own.

There was one person known to Tillman important enough maybe to put a lid on something like vehicular homicide and rich enough not to ask for payment.

Tillman dug for change and came up dry.

He took a hundred-dollar bill from a silver money clip.

"Can you change this? I've got to use the telephone."

Bosco looked at the c-note and smiled but didn't touch it. He opened the register drawer and scooped out some dimes. He spilled a half dozen on the counter.

"You owe me."

Tillman gave him five bucks' worth of charming smile and went over to call his friend, Walter Cape.

It was a lousy hour, yet somehow he had an idea that Cape was the kind of man who never slept, or slept only when the rest of the world was awake.

He didn't know about the party. He'd never been invited to

34

one. Friendship with Cape was like climbing a ladder. You had to wait awhile on each rung before he invited you to climb the next. Right now Tillman was at that stage where he'd been assured that he could call upon Cape as a friend in case of need.

Cape played the part of a simple man who would take the time and trouble to get a drunken brother-in-law out of jail or arrange for the friend of a friend to sit in the steward's box at any racetrack in the country. A man full of fatherly concern and advice, always ready to lend a hand. He'd been known to personally take charge of a birthday party for a child or spend half a day planting daffodils in a garden bed, kneeling right beside an old woman in Santa Monica who knew him only as a friend she'd met sitting on a bench facing out to sea. His life was filled with such simple acts. His pockets were full of favors, large and small. That's how the stories went.

What Tillman didn't know was that Cape, sooner or later, sent his bill the way great nations send bills to small client nations or Mafia *capos* finally ask favor for favor from those who have placed themselves in their debt.

In spite of the weather, nighthawks were finally gathering outside Gentry's, their images distorted by the console flasher on the black-and-white and the rain streaming down the plate-glass window. Two uniforms got out of the squad car, setting their caps and holstering their batons. Neither one wore the regulation yellow slickers against the rain. The black cop wore a leather flight jacket with a fur collar, the white one a hooded football jersey that zippered up the front.

The white cop made a half-assed attempt to move the crowd along. They eddied and flowed around his outstretched arms like sheep turning away from the dog that herded them. The black cop went to squat down beside the dead driver.

Tillman dialed Cape's private number, given, he believed, as a mark of special favor. The receiver was lifted after several rings.

"Yes, how can I help you?" Cape said before Tillman even had a chance to identify himself.

"It's me, Emmet," Tillman said. "I hate to bother you so late."

"You're not bothering me," Cape said in a voice of such kind patience that Tillman's own voice became choked with longing for the father he'd never really known. "I was having difficulty sleeping, anyway," he lied, taking the advantage.

"Well, thank God for that. I mean . . . look, Walter, whenever you can't sleep, all you've got to do is call me. It doesn't matter what time.·Anytime you—"

"Thank you, Emmet. Where are you?"

"A coffee shop called Gentry's on the corner of Hollywood and Vine."

"Can you speak up? Are you in some kind of trouble?"
Tillman raised his voice half a measure.

"Well, I got into a foolish accident in the middle of town."

"How foolish?"

"I was out with this woman, you know, and we were fooling around a little bit while I was driving."

"You were trying to take her temperature with your finger," Cape said without the slightest change of tone.

Tillman laughed.

"Oh, goddamn, leave it to you, Walter, to make a joke out of it and make me feel better."

"Does it make you feel better when I talk in the vernacular?"

"It always makes me feel better *anytime* I talk to you. I mean, you put things in focus. No fucking around. Right to the point. The cops just pulled up a minute ago."

"Take your time. No need to jump. Go on."

"It was raining, and I didn't see this station wagon speeding down Hollywood Boulevard. . . ."

"And it crashed into you."

"Well, no, I hit the wagon."·

"Are you injured?"

"No."

"Are you drunk?"

"Well, I had a couple of drinks. . . ."

"Half drunk. Would it be fair to say that you were half drunk?"

"Okay," Tillman said.

He glanced out the window. The black cop had left the station wagon driver's body and was bending down beside the blanket-covered corpse. He was lifting the top edge of it.

He half leapt up and stepped back so fast that he nearly fell down on the rain-slick road.

"Your companion? Is she injured?" Cape said.

"No."

"Drunk or high?"

"No."

"What's her name?"

"Shiela Andes."

"What does she do?"

"She's an actress."

"Tell your companion to be civil but not too friendly."

"I already sent her home."

"I see. What about the driver of the other car?"

"Dead."

"Not so good. Still. Rain. Poor visibility," Cape murmured as if instructing himself.

"Streets get like goddamn glass in L.A. when it rains," Tillman pitched in eagerly. "Sucks the grease up out of the pavement . . ."

"Just so. Were there any passengers in the station wagon?"

"Ahhh," Tillman said.

"Not a child, I hope. Not children?"

"I don't know what to call it."

"Are you talking about an animal?"

"There was a woman's body in the wagon. I mean, a woman's corpse fell out of the wagon right into the street."

"A corpse?" Cape exclaimed with the slightest rise of inflection.

"That ain't all," Tillman said, losing the last of the mid-Atlantic accent that had been so carefully learned and nurtured back in drama school. "It didn't have no head."

"You're sure of that? You're sure you weren't just so drunk . . ."

"Who wouldn't be sure of a thing like that? I'll never forget it. It was a woman's body with little tits and no head. . . ."

There was a stretch of silence, and then Cape said, "Go talk to the police. Be polite and cooperative."

"Should I call Baggot and Barrow?"

"I don't think we need any lawyers yet. Perhaps we won't

37

need them at all. I'm going to make a call or two. Remember, be polite, but don't try to be a pal. You're a toucher and a gladhander, Emmet. That's good with your fans, but people in authority, or people who think they're in authority, don't like to be touched. Be polite and cooperative, but don't get pally with the police."

Son of a bitch, Tillman thought. *Here I am an actor making two hundred thousand dollars a fucking episode and everybody's telling me how to act.*

Cape rang off before Tillman could say anything, though all he would have said was "Thank you" in the nicest way.

"That was our casting director, I think," Cape said aloud, to himself.

Cape stared into the fire for a long time. After a while he stirred himself, reached for the phone, and tapped out a number without bothering to check the hour.

"This is Walter Cape. I regret the hour and the necessity, Bill," Cape said into the telephone.

A sleep-drugged voice assured him that William Burchard, Deputy Chief and Administrative Commander of Inspection and Control of the Los Angeles Police Department, was happy to be of service, no matter what the hour.

"This is police business. I may be doing you a favor."

"What is it?" Burchard asked clearly and alertly.

"A young friend of mine, Emmet Tillman . . . Do you know him?"

"The actor on the cop show?"

"That's him. He's been involved in a smashup at Hollywood and Vine. I should think that he's being interviewed by the uniforms right about now."

"How many vehicles involved?"

"Only two were mentioned."

"Who was responsible?"

"Who can say? Tillman hit the other car but claims that the other driver was speeding and the crash was unavoidable."

"What does the other driver say?"

"He's dead."

"Oh, for chrissake, Walter, that makes it tough."

"I wouldn't have called you otherwise. It gets tougher. There was a previously dead body in the station wagon."

"Previously dead?"

"I can't state it more accurately than that. The driver of the other vehicle was transporting a woman's corpse."

"Well, that gives me some reason to put a gag on it."

"The corpse is without a head. Are you there, William?"

"I'm here. You present me with the damnedest things at the damnedest hours. No head."

"You see why I called you? With a television star's involvement it's the kind of story the papers would find lip-smacking good."

"I appreciate the concern, Walter."

"Then you'll see to it that Tillman's part in this doesn't appear on the blotter or in any police officer's report?"

"I can promise that. At least until we find out if Tillman had any previous connection with either the driver or the corpse."

"I'd like to be informed of any progress you might make on this, Bill."

"No trouble about that."

"What story will you give the cops on the scene about the headless body?"

"I haven't had time to give that a lot of thought, Walter," Burchard said a bit sourly.

"Well, I have had a little time to think about a scenario. Maybe you could tell your police to say the driver worked for a company making special effects for the films. The headless body is a dummy."

"Any other place, who'd believe it?"

"Any other place, any other time," Cape said. "I'll expect to hear from you, Bill. Never mind the hour."

Six

After the white cop had gone over to see the curiosity for himself, both cops put their heads together. Tillman walked out of Gentry's and stood in the rain, catching snatches of their conversation like pieces of rag blown on the wind.

". . . see the fuckin' head anywheres around . . ."

". . . anywheres around where?"

". . . like in the fuckin' gutter . . . down the sewer . . ."

". . . could be Japanese."

". . . how the fuck you figure that?"

". . . cunt hair like black wire wool . . . that funny color skin . . ."

". . . sounds like a fucking ethnic slur . . ."

The black cop threw Tillman glances every now and then, but it wasn't until the white cop went to the radio car and the black cop came walking over that his eyes lit up with recognition.

"Sir? My name's Officer Auburn. My partner over there is Officer Schoonover. Were you a witness to this accident?"

"I was nosing out into the boulevard after making a stop. . . ."

"I asked, were you a witness or a participant?"

"I'm telling you that I was driving the BMW. I came out into the intersection until I could see that nobody was coming either way. Then I hit the gas. . . ."

"Your name, sir?"

"Emmet Tillman."

"Do we know each other, sir?"

"You may have seen me on television."

Auburn grinned whitely. "Oh, sure. You're on that funny cop show."

"I don't know where the hell he came from, except he must have been going like hell," Tillman said. "I didn't see him when I started nosing out into the intersection and put my foot down on the gas."

"Which one of these vehicles did you say was yours, sir?"

"The silver six thirty-five CSi BMW."

"I can see the color."

The white cop walked over.

"Ho, Schoonover," Auburn said. "You call the meat wagon?"

"I called for some detectives and a supervisor. That's really something, ain't it? Fuckin' awful." He looked at Tillman. "You happen to know where the head went, sir?"

Tillman tried it again. Maybe it would be third-time lucky. "The boulevard was clear when I started pulling out. . . ."

"When you stepped on the accelerator?" Auburn said.

"That's right. That wagon came out of nowhere."

"Well, no," Schoonover said. "It came along Hollywood Boulevard going east to west."

"You know what I fuckin' mean!" Tillman said.

"There's no reason to use that kind of language, Mr. Tillman. You might have servants. You got servants?"

"Yes, I've got some help."

"You might have servants you can crap on, but although we're called public servants, we don't stand for being crapped on."

"I'm sorry. This is all getting to me."

"Take it easy, Mr. Tillman," Auburn said, seeming to take

pity. "We're not out to get you. I watch you on the television with my wife. She thinks you're very good-looking for a honky." Then he added, "How many drinks would you say you had tonight?" like he was slipping in a knife.

Always the goddamn zinger, Tillman thought. Always the shit when they got you to open up your mouth because you thought they were going to give you candy.

The detectives arrived in a maroon sedan, looking pleased and mean. Pleased for something to do on a rainy night and mean because they meant to make somebody's life miserable for making them go out in the wet.

Tillman recognized them and felt much relieved.

They were detectives well-known to him. They'd even worked his show as technical advisers for a stretch a year or so before. Lubbock and Jackson. Tillman thought it was even fair to call them pals.

The rain had slowed to a drizzle. Maybe it would blow away. Maybe it was coming up sunshine. He stood on the sidewalk near the curb, waiting to be recognized as Lubbock squatted beside the driver's broken body, tucking the skirts of his raincoat under his knees to keep them from trailing in the dirty water. Jackson stood nearby. He glanced at Tillman and said nothing. Lubbock looked at him as though he were a creature made of glass. Auburn went to stand by Jackson, notebook in hand.

"Hi," Tillman said. "Ain't this the shits?"

"You say something?" Lubbock said.

"You addressing me?" Jackson said.

Tillman felt a sour bubble of fear rise in his throat.

"You probably don't recognize me. . . ."

"Oh, yes, Mr. Tillman, we know who you are," Jackson said, taking a step toward him. "What are you doing on the streets at this hour?"

Auburn murmured something into Jackson's ear, keeping his head averted from Tillman. Jackson listened carefully without the trace of a smile on his broad face, looking as serious as he knew how to look. Intimidating.

"Officer Auburn tells me you were driving the BMW."

"That's right."

42

"Looks like the BMW plowed right into that old station wagon," Lubbock said. "Killed this poor fucker on the spot."

"Instantly," Jackson said.

Lubbock stood up and snapped his fingers, indicating how fast. "This is very bad." He went over to the other body under the blanket. Tillman began to follow. Jackson spun around on him.

"Where do you think you're going, Mr. Tillman?"

"I was just going to—"

"You just stay back there, Mr. Tillman. No reason for you to get your shoes dirty stepping in all this crap. You just stay out of the way until we get to you. Anybody get Mr. Tillman to blow into the bag yet?"

"Not yet," Auburn said.

"Walk the line, touch the nose?"

"Not yet."

"Shit, do your job, Officer."

Auburn nodded but didn't ask Tillman to go through the paces.

Lubbock looked under the blanket.

"Twat without a head, Jackson. What do you think about that?"

"I think it's very, very bad."

"Listen, for Christ's sake," Tillman said. "What the hell you talking to me like this for? I thought we were friends."

"Did you? Well, I don't know if we're friends. Acquaintances, maybe. But even if we was friends, this is a serious matter, and we have to go about it in a serious manner. No time to guzzle a couple beers, cut up any touches, tell each other any lies or dirty stories."

"I wasn't going to tell you any lies, for Christ's sake."

"I wish you'd stop taking the Lord's name in vain, Mr. Tillman. I'm a practicing Catholic," Jackson said.

A lieutenant in uniform, driving alone, rolled up. Lubbock, Jackson, Auburn, and Schoonover made a beeline to the supervisor like moths to the flame. They stood around talking in low voices for maybe three minutes. From time to time Lubbock, Jackson, and the lieutenant glanced over at Tillman.

The siren of an approaching ambulance sobbed five blocks

away. Then, like a wolf answering a mating call, another siren wailed from the other direction.

Lubbock and Jackson walked over to Tillman, all smiles.

"Well, son of a bitch, ain't this the shits?" Lubbock said.

"That's what Emmet said just a little while ago," Jackson said, as though the coincidence was too amazing to go uncelebrated.

"Ain't this something? Had yourself a little spot of trouble here, did you, Emmet?"

"For Christ's sake, fellas, you had me worried there for a minute," Tillman said. He reached out a hand to grab Lubbock's arm, but Lubbock flinched away, and Tillman remembered what Cape and even Whistler had warned him about. "You acted like you didn't even goddamn know me."

"Well, look here, Emmet, we only got to work your show for eight weeks, then we were canned."

"I didn't know that."

"Oh, yes, we were fired," Lubbock said.

"What the hell for?"

"Well, we really don't know."

"What we was told," Jackson said, picking it up, "was that you put the knife in."

"Oh, for Christ's sake . . . I'm sorry. . . ."

"Go ahead. No offense."

"I mean, son of a bitch, what would I want to do that for? Just why would I want to have you fired off the show?"

"That's what we've been asking ourselves. You know what I mean? We always thought we was friends," Lubbock said.

"Yeah, you know. Guzzling a few beers, cutting a few touches, telling each other lies and dirty stories," Jackson said.

"Well, fuck yes, so did I. Who told you I put the knife in?"

"Nobody actually said so. Manny Ostrava hinted at it when he give us the air."

"He's a fucking liar."

Jackson looked at Lubbock. "Didn't I tell you our old buddy, Emmet, would never have done such a thing?"

"That's what you said. Now, Emmet, about this dead citizen and that cunt over there without no head."

"Jesus H. Christ."

44

Jackson smiled benignly. "You get a good look at that thing under the blanket?"

"I didn't want to look too close."

"Of course you didn't. Make you sick. Ain't it something?"

"It's awful."

"Fucking thing looks almost real."

"What do you mean?"

"Don't it look real? It's not real. Oh, no. That's just a dummy. That man laying there in the street used to make things like that for the movies. He's dead, that's for sure, but that other thing, that's just a dummy."

The first ambulance arrived. It was private, the establishment's name, Khymer Mortuary, discreetly printed in gold on the doors.

Auburn's eyebrows went up as he glanced at Schoonover, silently remarking on the private carrier as two men got out and put the headless body in the back, still wrapped in the same blanket Bosco had thrown over it. Not even bothering with a body bag.

Lubbock, Jackson, and Tillman waited.

The lieutenant, Auburn, and Schoonover watched as though picking up headless bodies were an everyday affair.

The junkies, whores, hustlers, gonifs, and homeless watched as though it were the next best thing to television.

From behind the window of Gentry's, Bosco watched and winced at the pain of a clenched fist that wasn't there.

A minute after the private carrier pulled away the wagon from the morgue pulled up. The female medical examiner got out and looked the dead driver's body over. It only took a minute before she was satisfied and stood up. They bagged the driver, piled back into the ambulance, and took off.

"Here's what we're going to do," Lubbock said. "We're going to get all the facts from Officer Auburn, here. We're going to call for the wrecker, get that sweet BMW out of the rain and over to the police impound. Save you the trouble, okay?"

Jackson leaned his mouth close to Lubbock's ear. "You're right," Lubbock said. "Look, Emmet, we're going to see what we can do about leaving your name out of the report. We want

45

ROBERT CAMPBELL

you to go home and put this out of your mind. Okay? You just forget all about it. We'll clean up the mess."

Walter Cape's mansion was empty except for the staff cleaning up and his own servants, most of whom had long since gone off to their beds in the farthest wing.

The phone rang not more than an hour after Burchard had first been awakened by Walter Cape. Nobody could say that Burchard didn't know the wires or wasn't a good man with a phone.

"Your actor friend should be home any minute now, if he isn't home already," Burchard said.

"I owe you one, Bill," Cape said.

"I'm not counting, Walter."

"Well, you know me, Bill. I like to pay my way."

"Forget about it."

"How did you dispose of the headless body?"

"Private carrier is taking it to a contract mortuary."

"Oh?"

"I don't want the press barking at my heels just yet. What's your interest, Walter?"

"I'm not without a certain natural curiosity, Bill."

"That body'll be kept at the private mortuary until I find out what the hell's going on."

"Have you found out anything so far?"

"Not much. It's the hour, Walter. Most people are in bed. I have found out that the driver killed at the scene was Willy Zabadno, a night attendant at the county morgue. I'd say it's a dead certainty the body came from county. Now all I have to do is find out who she was and what the hell Zabadno was doing taking her for a joyride on a rainy night. You know what, Walter?"

"What, Bill?"

"This is a very fucking funny town."

The first thing Tillman did when he got home was to be sick in the toilet. It sobered him up, so he went to the bar and made himself a drink. He opened up the blinds and looked out the window at the panoramic view of Hollywood. A plane with

46

blinking rubies and emeralds on tail and wingtips came in from somewhere. He wanted to cry but was afraid that if he started, he'd never stop. He felt like he was waiting for the shit to hit the fan. The telephone chattered. There it was now, he thought.

"I've been calling every fifteen minutes," Shiela said. "I was just about to call the county jail."

"Now, why would you want to do that, sweetheart?"

"I was afraid they might have you in a cell for whatever they call what you did."

"You would've caused some confusion if you'd done that. The cops at the station wouldn't have known what the hell you were talking about. My friends told me to go home and not give it another thought."

"Just like that? Just like that they let you go?"

"Christ, Shiela, who the hell did you think you were out with? Some asshole featherweight?"

"No featherweight, you."

Well, if she was going to say "no featherweight," why didn't she say "no asshole," too? Did she mean she thought he *was* an asshole? Was she sticking it in and twisting it a little? Smart-ass cunt.

"So, that schmuck got you home okay?"

"If you thought he was a schmuck, why did you let him take me home? You didn't even know him. He could've raped me."

Well, thought Tillman, somebody would've gotten a little piece of ass, which was more than he'd ever got.

"I was saving you a lot of questions, a lot of trouble."

"You were saving yourself some embarrassment and maybe some jail time."

Oh, shit, Tillman thought, here it comes. He should have checked her fucking teeth and claws before asking her out on a date that first time. Who the fuck did she think she was—giving him a sniff, then closing the gates?

"Say again."

"I have it on my conscience that you and I were doing things people shouldn't be doing in a moving car, on a wet street, in the middle of the night and, by so doing, caused an accident and the death of at least one fellow human being. I don't think I'm going to be able to get much sleep for a while. Maybe a long time."

"Take a Valium," Tillman said in his flattest voice.

"Drugs can get to be a habit. I've just got to find some way to occupy my mind and tire myself so I'll just fall into bed at night and conk right out."

"You have anything in mind?"

"When I'm working on a picture, I just work, eat, and sleep. I mean, I love it, but that's all I've got the energy to do. Just work, eat, and sleep. If I had a job—"

"On my show."

"It wouldn't be very hard to do. I mean, you're certainly no featherweight."

"Small part? Maybe a two-, three-day run?"

"That could do it. I don't know. We could try."

"Maybe if I had them write in a character that you could play for maybe four or five weeks."

"Wouldn't that be lovely? I mean, all that hard work and long hours on the set would surely make me so tired by the time night came, I'd just fall into bed and sleep. Every night for weeks."

"Because when you work on a picture, all you do is work, eat, and sleep."

"And maybe fuck a little."

"Well, you know what?"

"What?"

"You're just going to have to fuck yourself."

"My God, the picture of that headless woman laying naked in the gutter with the rain falling down on her just won't go away."

"That was no body, that was a dummy."

There was a hollow pause.

"You making one of those jokes? Like 'That was no woman, that was my wife'?"

"I'm telling you, you've got nothing to sell. You don't have to lose any sleep, I don't have to give you any job, and you can sew your twat up for all I give a fuck. Now, what do you say to that?"

"I say I'm going to have to think about it and maybe seek some advice."

She hung up and he hung up, and then he called Cape, as he'd been told to do.

"I'm still here at your service, Emmet. You're at home?"

"Yes, sir, I'm home," Tillman said.

"How did it go?"

"I couldn't believe it. I mean, there's these two bodies laying in the street. One without its head. The cops are there giving me the drill. You know. No smiles. No jokes. Just this chilly, polite way they have. Name, address, and telephone number. They know who I am, all right, but they don't even blink. Then the detectives arrive. They're not so sweet. They go shovin' at me with their eyes. You know what I mean? Like they warn me with their eyes that they know I'm a killer and a liar and I'd better watch myself or they'll hang me from the lamppost right then and there."

"Did they know you?"

"Oh, sure. Lubbock and Jackson. They were detectives I knew from the show. You know what I mean? They drew a paycheck for eight weeks. Technical advisers. They told me that, but I already knew it. I didn't know it was eight weeks, but I knew they were on the locations with the company. In the streets. Night and day. We split more than a couple of beers together. I thought we were friends. Lubbock and Jackson. Do you know Lubbock and Jackson?"

"Is there any reason why I should?" Cape said.

"Of course not. Am I crazy? Why should you know anybody like Lubbock and Jackson? Why should you want to know anybody like Lubbock and Jackson? I just figured you knew everybody."

"I know everybody I want to know. Everybody I've got reason to know. I'll know Lubbock and Jackson. So. They gave you a difficult time and . . ." Cape said.

"At first. They went over and picked up the blanket the counterman from the coffee shop had thrown over the body without a head and looked at me like I'd done it. Then the uniformed superintendent drives up. They have a talk. All the cops have a talk. They come back all smiles. They tell me it isn't a body, it's a dummy. They tell me to go home and forget about it. I can't believe it. They tell me to go home and just forget about it. They'll file the reports. They'll clean up the mess. That's the way they said it. I wasn't to worry. Jesus."

"What is it?"

"I can't forget it. I can't forget that naked body falling out of the back end of the wagon. Her feet were sticking out from under the blanket. I was sick in the toilet when I got home."

"That was the drink. That other thing. The horror show. That was just a dummy. Didn't you just tell me that's what they told you?"

"That's right. I'm not to worry about it. They'll clean up the mess."

"Well, that seems to be that," Cape said. "You can go to bed and get a good night's sleep now."

Tillman cleared his throat. Cape waited. Finally he said, "Is there something else?"

"The woman I was with—Shiela Andes—she called me up."

"She got home safely?"

"Oh, she was just fine. I sent her home because I thought she couldn't make it. She thought I sent her home because I was afraid she'd tell the police what we were doing before we crashed."

"Before you killed the driver of the station wagon because you had your hand between her legs. No reason to kid ourselves, Emmet. What did she want from you?"

"Help with her career. A lot of help."

"What did you say?"

"I told her about the dummy."

"And what did she say?"

"She said she'd think about it and maybe get some advice."

"Don't concern yourself about her. She can be managed. Now, is that all you have to tell me?"

Somebody once told Tillman that the reason why Cape never lost out in business was because he could read a person's mind from the inflections and hesitations in that person's voice. He wondered if Cape knew he was leaving something out. He was leaving that son-of-a-bitch jackal, that night creeper, that Whistler out. He didn't want to tell Cape he turned the cunt over to a scavenger. He didn't want Cape to know he was dumber than he already looked.

"That's all," Tillman said.

"Then give me the Andes woman's address and telephone number and then go to bed and get a good night's sleep."

50

Seven

Tillman's house was up Woodrow Wilson Drive in a neighborhood like country. One of those patches for people who'd come from the farms and small towns, learned to hate the city, but couldn't leave it because they were tied to it with chains of gold. So there were neighborhoods that pretended to be small towns or country. It cost a fortune to live in them.

The rich paid half a million for a fair reproduction of the house they could have had back home for sixty grand. The very rich lived in recycled history that cost even more.

Tillman's house had been built for a silent-movie star sixty years earlier, It had been enlarged and remodeled so many times, only a carved cornice here and a beautiful old copper drain spout there gave evidence of the graceful Mediterranean villa it once had been. It was, for all of that, about as big as the garages at Cape's mansion.

There were three signs, lit by baby spots, stuck in the flowering borders of the private access road, that read,

WARNING. ARMED RESPONSE.

The iron gates swung open as Whistler nosed the Chevy over

51

the kick plate. Malibu lights went on all over the grounds. The rain had dwindled to a pretty mist. The sun was threatening to come up.

Tillman, dressed in white slacks, sandals, and an open-mesh shirt, came walking down the drive as though it were mid-afternoon. He had a tall drink in his hand. Whistler stopped the car.

"What do you do about the electric gate if the power fails?" Whistler asked Tillman as he stuck his hand through the window to shake. Tillman ignored the ritual courtesy.

"You've got to crank it open by hand," Tillman said.

"You got a coolie to do that?"

"I do it myself unless I got a broken arm," Tillman said evenly, staring at a spot between Whistler's eyes.

Actor's trick. Throw the other guy off his stride, Whistler thought. *Tillman doesn't like me and isn't going to make this meeting friendly.*

"I had a friend had electric gates," Whistler said. "A friend of his came to show off his new white Corniche Rolls-Royce—one hundred and twenty thousand bucks—and something fritzed the gates. Goddamn things closed on the Rolls before it was through. Opened and closed, opened and closed. Did twenty-two thousand dollars' worth of damage before they stuck."

"I know the feeling," Tillman said. "It's not the cost, it's the upkeep. I can't slip the kid in the parking lot a deuce, it's got to be a sawbuck." He was friendly all of a sudden. Chatting away, forgetting he didn't like Whistler.

"Everybody hates a winner," Whistler said.

"I thought it was supposed to be the other way around," Tillman said, frowning slightly. For a moment he looked wistful, like a kid who'd lost the magic penny.

"That's only one of the lies they tell you in school."

Whistler got out of the car so they could see eye to eye.

Tillman handed Whistler his drink. He dipped his hand into his pocket and pulled out a small fold of bills in a silver clip. It looked like they were all hundreds. He counted off two and handed them over between two fingers, tipping the boy at the parking lot.

"No thanks," Whistler said.

"Two bills. For driving Shiela home. Go ahead. Take it."

"No thanks."

"You earned it. She called me and said you did good."

"How is Miss Andes?" Whistler said, keeping his hands and eyes off the c-notes.

"On my shit list."

"Oh?"

"She said I owed her."

Whistler nodded as though that were a reasonable assumption, but didn't say anything.

"Gave me an idea of how I could repay the favor," Tillman went on.

"Greedy, was she?"

"Oh, no. She was ready to start small enough. Just a small role. Maybe a two-parter a while later. Next year maybe a running character for half a season."

"Well, why not? You must like her, and she's proved herself a friend," Whistler said.

"She's a user like everybody else."

"What the hell," Whistler said. "Some people couldn't find an apple in a stable full of horse shit."

"What's that supposed to mean?"

"It means that some people got no luck. No matter how good the cards look, the last one dealt leaves them with a busted flush. So they go broke and have to build a new stake wherever they can. However they can. From whoever they can."

They were hard-eyeing each other. Tillman had money and was actor-trained, so he was better at it.

For Christ's sake, Whistler thought, *something's happened to queer the pitch. This gazoony isn't scared and he isn't needy. I should just pluck those two yards from his fingers and run.*

"Well, somebody asks, maybe I'll give. But I don't share because somebody sticks a gun in my face," Tillman said.

"I don't think Miss Andes got the part," Whistler said.

"She's lucky I don't have her ass kicked."

"Oh, you do that sort of thing, do you?"

"Take the two hundred bucks, Whistler."

"If all you think I did was cab a lady home, that's too much."

"I'm a big tipper. I even tip people who give me lousy service and bum steers." Tillman grinned, showing five thousand dollars' worth of caps. He had that look poker players get when the bets are doubling and doubling and they're sitting there with a full house. Even players who think they have no eyes give it away.

"You got it all wrong, Whistler. The detectives on the scene—"

"Who was that?"

"Lubbock and Jackson. Hey, why should I tell you who they were?"

"Who gives a rat's ass? Is it a secret?"

"Well, they did right by me," Tillman said, as though the news were a triumph over Whistler. "They knew who I was. We split a couple beers more than once. They treated me like a friend. Like a fellow cop."

"They didn't book you on drunk driving?"

"They did better. . . ."

"What do you mean 'better'?"

Tillman clammed up. His mouth became a wire with an insulting curl at one end and a sarcastic twist at the other. He shoved out the two hundred-dollar bills again.

"What about the dead driver?" Whistler said. "What about the body with no head?"

"That was nothing but a goddamn movie dummy, you asshole. The driver was delivering it for a movie."

Whistler stood there doubting himself as the mist took the crease out of his pants.

"Go on, take it," Tillman said, shoving out the bills again. "You did good. You got the bitch home safe."

Whistler stared at the money and then into Tillman's eyes. He felt like telling the actor to shove the two hundred up his ass. But that way, Whistler thought, you go home two hundred bucks short just for the satisfaction of making an asshole pucker.

He plucked the bills from Tillman's hand without touching his fingers or looking away from his eyes. He folded them up small and put them in his watch pocket. Small change. He got back into the Chevy.

"Hey. I hope your gates don't attack my car," he said.

Eight

The rain hadn't really let up, after all. The four corners were deserted again. Gentry's was still empty except for Bosco, perched on his stool by the register, and a sad lump of a man wearing a wet felt hat slurping up a bowl of soup at the counter.

Isaac Canaan was a Detective Three working the Sexually Exploited Children Detail, Vice Unit, out of Hollywood Detective Division. His eyes were always red-rimmed, as if he'd just got over crying. He worked alone and was rumored never to sleep.

Bosco was reading Darwin's *On the Origin of Species by Means of Natural Selection, or the Preservation of Favored Species in the Struggle for Life*. Whistler came in and sat in the booth by the window. He stared out at the wreckage of the newspaper vending machines still lay scattered in the gutter. All the rest had been swept away except for some glass and ugly stains.

Bosco came over, book tucked into the pit of his amputated arm, with a cup of coffee for Whistler.

"Sit down," Whistler said. "What did we see tonight?"

"A wreck in which one driver was killed and a body without a

55

head was flung out the door of a wagon. A wreck because of which a television actor, half high on rum or toot, lost his chance to get some nooky."

"Is that what you'd say we saw in case anybody was ever to ask?"

"No, I'd say I saw some asshole slam his brakes on to avoid a pussycat, upon which his vehicle skidded and smashed into a light pole, killing said driver and tossing a special-effects prop that looked like a headless woman out into the gutter."

"Is that what you'd say?"

"I'd take my oath on it."

"How come is that?"

"Because the cops told me that's what I saw."

"You roll over easy."

"I never contradict a cop," Bosco said, rubbing the stump of his arm and looking content.

"They're making assholes out of us, Bosco."

"Nobody's keeping score. Nobody's going to ask the questions."

"That thing ever bother you?"

"All the time. Sometimes it itches, and sometimes it has a heartbeat, and sometimes it remembers my hand. Sometimes it even remembers the feel of the watch I used to wear on that wrist."

"What do you do about it?"

"I don't do nothing about things I can't do nothing about," Bosco said, answering any and all questions on any and all subjects.

"Is that what you learn, reading so much?" Whistler asked.

"I learn that the world ignores you when it ain't stickin' it up your ass," Bosco said. "I learn not to try to eat the holes in Swiss cheese. I learn that iron rusts."

He reached over and grabbed Whistler's wrist with a hand like a bear's paw.

"Hey, Whistler, can't you see the sun would be up if it wasn't rainin'? Go on home and go to bed. There's nothing you can do about fixing the world this morning."

"It don't bother you there's a head without a body in New Orleans and a body without a head here in Los Angeles?"

"Not as much as it bothers that dummy."

Whistler gestured with his head toward Canaan.

"He know about the accident?"

"I didn't ask, and he didn't say," Bosco said.

Whistler slid out of the booth and sat on the stool next to Canaan.

"I heard about the accident," Canaan said.

"When?"

"Just now."

"You got good ears."

Canaan crumpled a handful of crackers into the remains of his soup.

"Breakfast?" Whistler asked.

"Supper."

"What do you think about them letting Tillman take a walk in the rain without getting wet?"

"Who's Tillman?"

"The television actor. You know."

"No, I don't know. I don't have time to watch television. I wouldn't know what I was watching."

"Well, what do you think?"

"I think it's a matter for West Traffic Division. Maybe for Homicide."

"It was Lubbock and Jackson gave him permission."

"Maybe they got their reasons."

"Wouldn't you like to know what they could be?"

His elbow resting on the counter and showing three inches of dirty shirtsleeve, Canaan held up a hairy hand nearly as big as Bosco's. "What does that look like?"

"Your hand."

"Not a paw? I mean, you can see it's a hand and not a paw?"

"I can see it's not a paw."

"Not a cat's-paw?"

"What the fuck," Whistler said, looking at Bosco and asking him to witness the asshole conversation Canaan had drawn him into.

"The story about the cat's-paw—" Bosco started to say.

"I know what the fuck a cat's-paw is," Whistler said.

"Detective Canaan thinks you're going to try and use him for your own purposes again."

"I wasn't going to ask for a favor. I was just making conversation."

"The favor comes next. It always comes next with you, Whistler," Canaan said.

"Well, I mean, if you happened to hear anything here and there, I'd like to know about it. What's the big deal?"

"It's none of your goddamn business is what it is."

Whistler reached for his pocket.

"Don't do it, Whistler. Don't pay for my soup," Canaan said.

"For Christ's sake."

"Shitty, ain't it? A man can't even buy a bowl of soup for a friend anymore."

Whistler was weary but not sleepy. He walked down the boulevard. It started coming down cats and dogs. He saw himself in the dark mirror of a plate-glass window. Hair plastered across his forehead. Rain like tears racing along the streambeds and gullies of his face.

He turned into the shelter of an adult movie house. The lady in the ticket booth had a body like a stack of lumpy pillows. No longer meant for bed. While she took his money and tore a ticket she looked at Whistler as if she'd like to crush him with her thighs or smother him between her tits. She was in a sudden, desperate rage because she knew he wouldn't have her even if she told him it would save her life. She smiled like a shark and called him dearie.

What the hell was anybody doing in a ticket booth at six o'clock in the morning, anyway? Whistler wanted to know. It wasn't natural. It was something only a vampire would do.

The dark gray light inside the movie house was like the light of the rainy morning outside. The obligatory exit signs stole the privacy Whistler had come for. He could make out the faces of the other patrons without difficulty. There were not many. All older men. All waiting for a miracle to come down off the screen and make them young again. Hands in their laps. Hearts elsewhere.

Whistler's clothes gave off the odor of wet dog.

Up on the screen a very pretty girl and a young man were going at it as though it were a pleasure. Was it a pleasure? Whistler wondered. After all, her nipples were erect, and there was a flush on her bosom. The body did its tricks when buttons were pushed. Heartache and disgust notwithstanding.

The girl had the face of a precocious child. A spray of freckles across a snub-nose. As wholesome-looking as sweet cream. He'd known a hundred girls like her back in New York. Had seen a thousand more come to Hollywood just as sweet. Watched them bite the poisoned apple. Shrugged his shoulders and said what the hell. World going to ruin. Who cared about a few more virgin twats turned to stone?

He remembered a girl from a long time ago. Her name had been Suzy. She'd lived in an apartment in one of the fancy hotels along Sunset. Her bedroom was in a tower and it was round. The bed was round, too, and there was glass all around so you could make love to Suzy and later lay propped up against the pillows and count the cars down in the streets of Hollywood. She was the most beautiful whore in town. She was a legend.

They told the story of how an up-and-coming movie star came banging on her door the night before his wedding to another up-and-coming movie star. He wasn't looking for a good-bye fuck. He was begging Suzy to run away with him. She smiled and showed him her tongue and told him it would only cost him fifty bucks because she wanted to give him a wedding present. The story was true.

She gave it to Whistler for free because he was as skinny as a bird and had dark brown eyes that she said made her soft and weak. She called him the little prince.

They lost touch the way it happens in La-La Land. Twenty years later Whistler bumped into Al Lister, an old extra who used to run errands for Suzy, like scoring hash or snort, for which Suzy also fucked him for free because she felt sorry for him and because she didn't like to pay out cash. Lister hadn't lost touch with Suzy. He knew where she lived out in the Valley.

He was going out to see her, he said, then he was free to have some dinner. He knew Whistler would duck his company unless there was something extra, so he offered him the chance to see Suzy again as an appetizer.

She lived in a ticky-tacky box on a patch of dying grass out in North Hollywood. When she came to the door, Whistler's heart nearly stopped. Her hair was still blond and her eyes still blue. She had a pretty face, with a mouth like the bow on a child's shoe bunched up below a nose like a candy chew. She must have weighed three hundred pounds.

When Lister said, "You remember Whistler, don't you, Suzy?" she said sure, she remembered Whistler, and kissed him on the cheek. Whistler could tell she wasn't glad to see him because she'd grown old and fat and Whistler was no little prince anymore. But still she asked him to come in and offered him a drink.

They sat in a living room full of auction furniture. They had nothing to say. In a corner of the room, in a sort of alcove, she'd hung an enormous photograph of herself when she'd been twenty and the most beautiful whore in La-La Land. It was on the wall behind a kind of altar with a dozen lighted candles lined up on a white linen runner. Whistler excused himself and finished his drink in two swallows. It's better to get some things over fast.

The past and the present did a lap dissolve.

Up on the movie screen two couples were doing it.

He realized he was getting an erection, and that made him sad. So he went back through the falling rain to Gentry's parking lot where he got his Chevy and went home and tried to get some sleep.

The drowned sun shone unseen high above the hills. Smoke the color of a tobacco chewer's spit climbed up to meet it. A single ray broke through a hole in the smog and rain, like a finger pointing the way to nowhere.

Cape picked up the phone when it hummed, just before it rang. It was Burchard back again.

"More news?" Cape asked after they'd exchanged hellos.

"More and less," Burchard said.

"Have you had a look at the woman's body?"

"It's without a head all right, all right."

Cape said nothing. He just let the silence sit there like a rock.

"It's the body of an Oriental woman between twenty and twenty-five years of age. Probably Vietnamese," Burchard said.

"What makes you say that?"

"Something you pick up. A Jap's skin is muddy. A Korean's legs is thick in the knees. A Chinese has broad feet and a big ass. This woman's skin was like pearl once upon a time."

It's not every man who can appreciate a corpse, Cape thought.

"She's been dead a long time."

A long-dead corpse.

"She was probably a Saigon whore. She's been tattooed on the hip."

"With what?"

"With a butterfly."

"You see many of those?"

"We see enough."

"Was she taken from the morgue?"

"Her toe was tagged. The mark shows, but it's not on her toe anymore."

"Have you looked into the files?"

"I'm down here at the county morgue right now," Burchard said. "There's no record fitting her description."

"Are there many Vietnamese in residence?"

"We got a few."

"Surely someone must know something about her."

"It's not the beginning of the business day yet. Give it some time. There anything you want to tell me, Walter?"

"About what?"

"*I'm* asking about what."

"I'm a fan, Bill. Sometimes I think I should have been a cop."

"It pays shit, Walter. You did better becoming a millionaire."

Nine

Ten o'clock in the morning in New Orleans. You could grill saints on the pavement outside the iron lacework gate that guarded a tunnel made of shadows. Shadows that promised to be cool but were as smothering as yards of velvet. The courtyard and the house were walled around with stuccoed brick two feet thick, soldiers trying to keep the sun at bay.

The house on Ursuline Street, converted to apartments, was known as a haunted house. Singular horrors concerning slaves and the sadistic excesses of otherwise forgotten aristocrats were recited by tourist guides to busloads of visitors in the evening hours. On rainy or foggy nights, they declared, hoarse screams and the rattle of chains spilled out into the night from the old torture chambers now used as storage cellars.

Nonny Barcaloo enjoyed the illusion of celebrity. He often sat out on the gallery over the street in the afternoon or early evening, sipping a drink, aware of the visitors gawking at a man who dared to sit his ass among ancient ghosts.

The courtyard smelled of magnolia blossoms—big, white,

fleshy flowers like baby's hands stained with nicotine. They couldn't hide the stink of death.

The inner gallery off the master bedroom overlooked the fountain in the central court. Barcaloo sweated and tried to imagine cool.

Goddamn useless fountain. Put cakes of ice in it, he thought. Cool the water. The spray could maybe cool the air. Make the goddamn fountain—cost him four hundred fifty bucks just this one year in repairs—do some goddamn good. Everything you paid for should do you good. Otherwise trash it.

He caught himself up short. What the hell was he going on about? Fuck the fountain. Blow it up. Blow up the goddamn apartment and every stick of furniture in it. Blow up the building and collect the insurance. He wasn't going to need it anymore. Blow up the goddamn city! A few more arrangements and he was gone. A little housekeeping here and there and he was gone.

His coffee, heavy with chicory, pinched his tongue and gums. Flat, square doughnuts, ordered and delivered from a little shop in Cathedral Alley, left a cake of powdered sugar on his lips and chin. He paid attention to his chewing. He paid attention to the bitter coffee in his mouth. One thing at a time.

He wondered if he should rent out the maisonette or keep it for winter holidays. Come down around Mardi Gras every year. Arrange some filthy games for old times' sake. Maybe run some screen tests. Maybe just get away from being a California big shot for a week.

His brain went from thought to thought like it was sorting mail. A little box for each thought. All his energy focused on each one as his brain plucked it out of its cubbyhole.

Look at me, he thought. *Going west. Going big time. Going to be a prince of La-La Land.*

The phone on the wrought-iron table rang. It was hot to his touch as he cradled it under his ear.

Cape's cool voice came in from the Coast.

"Are you all packed and ready for your trip?"

"Got the sheets on the furniture, Mr. Cape."

"Your lady's excited about the move?"

"She don't get excited about much."

63

"Anything I can do to stir her up?"

"Get her a date with some movie star," Barcaloo said, laughing at the craziness of such a thing.

"I can certainly arrange an introduction," Cape said in his flattest executive voice.

"Jesus Christ, I was only kiddin' . . ."

"You just name the celebrity she'd like to meet."

"Christ. Any fuckin' one of 'em would make her pussy pucker . . . excuse my French."

"I've heard the expression. If meeting a film star will please her, consider it a favor done."

"I don't know how I can pay you back for something like that."

"There is a little something you can take care of for me if you will, Barcaloo. It shouldn't take but a day or two. I'd like to send a young woman down to you. She thinks she's replacing an actress in a motion picture shooting on location in your city. She threatens to be an embarrassment to a friend of mine."

"You want me to do for you like I done before? Consider your friend unembarrassed."

"No, no. Nothing that final this time, Nonny. Just a little photography. Just some footage that I can have in hand in case she persists in making demands and threats."

"Can it wait until I get to L.A.?"

"Well, no, it can't. I want her out of town right away."

Barcaloo laughed. "I gotcha. How dumb can I get?"

"Name a fee."

"Nothing. It don't cost you nothing."

"I want you to name a fee."

"It's my gift to you," Barcaloo said. "A favor for a partner, a favor for a friend."

"You have good manners. I'll call you when I have it arranged."

"I'm always here when you need me, Mr. Cape."

"By the way," Cape said.

"Yes, sir?"

"This young woman I'll be sending to you. She was witness to an accident last night. A man named Willy Zabadno was killed in a car crash. Do you know him?"

"No, sir," Barcaloo said, hoping that he hadn't missed a beat. Cape had ears like a fucking fox. Maybe that was what gave him his edge.

"A body was flung out of the back of the station wagon. It was a naked woman's body. It had no head."

"I never heard of such a crazy thing."

"The body is that of a young Oriental woman. It has a butterfly tattoo on the hip."

"Lots of tattoos around."

"That other woman I sent you. She had a butterfly tattoo. Could this be her body? I told you when I offered you the position that I wanted assurance that you had nothing outstanding that could draw attention to you or me."

"For Christ's sake, Mr. Cape. You think she was the only slant-eyed cunt running around with a butterfly on her ass? I'm telling you, I been around a lot of women got no brains, but I don't fool around with any what got no head," Barcaloo said. He chuckled.

"You have an amusing way about you, Barcaloo," Cape said impassively. "I just ask the question. No offense intended."

Getting information from Motor Vehicles was a snap if you didn't mind standing on your hind legs and panting like a dog.

The lady with blue-rinsed hair and harlequin spectacles wouldn't think Whistler was cute even if he tap-danced and tilted his head to one side. She was hard because her life in the file cabinets was hard.

"What I've got here," Whistler said, "is a reason to ask about an accident what took place last night on the corner of Hollywood and Vine during which six of my vending machines got crushed like empty cans of Miller Lite. I make my living with those machines, and I got to see that someone pays to have them replaced."

"Go to the police. They'll have it on their night sheet."

"You'll also have it in your reports, and there's not a day in the week when I wouldn't rather do business with a pretty woman than some cop with indigestion and flat feet. If the cop has had a sleepless night, next thing you know he'll be asking me to show cause why I should not be sued by the driver of the offending vehicle for obstructing the roadway with a public nuisance. That could lead to litigation and a big fight over first-amendment rights. You know how things can start to happen if you go to a cop. Once I asked an officer how to get to the library. He sends me across the street. Then he gives me a ticket for jaywalking."

"Christ, you can really talk a mile a minute, can't you," the blue-haired lady said, and went to rob the data bank.

She was back faster than Whistler ever hoped, tapping a three-by-five card against her ruby fingernail. She had a little smile on her face.

"Report of accident called into Hollywood Division, two-twenty-one, by one Roscoe Silverlake . . ."

"Bosco?"

"Roscoe Silverlake . . . from Gentry's Coffee Shop and Snack Bar, corner of Hollywood and Vine."

The smile grew broader and richer.

"One-car collision with traffic-light stanchion. One death. William Zabadno, employed by the county, driver of said vehicle."

"Employed by the county?"

"He carried a license to operate municipal vehicles for the morgue," she said.

"No mention of my vending machines?"

"Not a word." Her smile streamed into her ears with the pleasure she was feeling about giving out bad news.

"No witnesses?"

"One Roscoe . . ."

"Bosco . . ."

"Silverlake."

She dealt him the file card like it was a deuce to an inside straight.

"What are you going to do now?" she asked.

"Talk to the cop on the desk," Whistler said.

Barcaloo picked a grape from a bunch in a bowl and turned his thoughts to grapes. Each one crunched audibly when he bit into it. Sometimes he threw a grape at a pigeon. When he scored, he laughed with real pleasure.

"Fachrissakes, leave them little birds alone," a voice like a parrot's scream—without real energy—speared out of the pool of gloom that lay like swamp water on the canopied bed inside the room.

There was a yellow-haired woman in it. She was naked, her breasts sagging with their weight on her rounded belly as she lay propped against a white mound of lacy pillows. Eyes as brightly blue as bits of glass, lying inside tiny puffs of flesh like sugared pastry. Tall glass in hand, tinged with green, slightly fluorescent.

"Drink your worms, Bouche, and let me do what I wanna do," Barcaloo replied.

"Ain't we nice this mornin'. No worms in absinthe."

"Why the hell they say they make it out of wormwood, then?"

"That's just a name for some herb. Like oregano," Bouche said.

"I don't know why you drink that crap, anyway," Barcaloo yelled, without turning around to look at the woman who made faces at his back. "The goddamn stuff's illegal. Don't you know that?"

She laughed, sounding like a small barking dog.

"Got to import the stuff all the way from Switzerland," he raved on. "Could get me busted anytime."

She laughed again, in one short burst, as though she measured out her laughter by the ounce.

"Make you crazy. Give you dee-lirium." He stood up, brushing crumbs of doughnut and specks of sugar from his naked chest and potbelly, where it glistened in a tangle of body hair. "Give you more hallucinations than you can handle. Shrivel your pussy." He stumbled into the bedroom, knees bent, arms dangling, absurdly but menacingly, nearly to the floor. The mane across the hump of his neck and shoulders gave him the look of a stalking beast. He bared his fangs. "Turn you into a goddamn idiot. Dry up your tits."

He leapt upon her.

"Watch out, you silly son of a bitch," she complained. "You're gonna spill the goddamn drink. There, goddammit, you see there? You spilled my drink all over my tits."

He fixed his snout to her teat and sucked.

"Stop it, you loony son of a bitch, stop it," she screeched through her laughter in a voice like chalk on slate. "Don't you bite me."

He rooted at her breasts and belly, making animal noises as he worked his way down to her crotch. His furry arms and legs clasped her as she bucked and writhed away from him.

"You weigh a ton," she said. "You should be on a goddamn diet. You should be eatin' carrot sticks instead of doughnuts. You should be eatin' lettuce leaves instead of grapes."

"Lookayou talkin'. Lookayou fat ass. Lookayou fat gut." His words struggled up out of her flesh like bubbles bursting out of a mud hole. One hand was fumbling down in the fold of flesh at the bottom of his belly, trying to arouse himself. He fixed his teeth in her plump, white shoulder amid a lacework of tiny, shining scars.

"Oh, no, fachrissakes." She moaned, all laughter stopped off with a plug of pain. "You brush your teeth? You scrub your teeth? You gonna give me blood poisoning. Not this mornin', fachrissakes. I was goin' for a swim."

Real fear shaped her mouth and filled her eyes. She looked over his shoulder and down his back as he plowed her, her eyes fixed on the place above his kidney where she would place the knife if she ever got the nerve.

"My name's Polokowsky," the operations corporal said, "it ain't friend. Here's yesterday's book. It says here in black and white. One-vehicle collision with municipal property. One death. Just like you got it on that card. Where'd you get that card?"

"Motor Vehicles."

"They ain't supposed to intercourse with the citizens in matters of this kind. It's a police matter."

"That's what I say," Whistler said. "I want to talk to a cop."

"You're talking to a cop."

"I want to talk to a cop that was on the scene."

"Them cops was working last out. You know what last out is?"

"Sure. It's the midnight-to-eight shift."

"That's right. Which means they is in bed sleeping, I trust. You come right back here at midnight. That's when Officer Auburn and Officer Schoonover come on."

"You got a home address on whichever?"

"You intend to bother one or both of these officers at home while they're sleeping or recreating with their wives?"

"I got an urgency about my vending machines, and I'd like to talk to somebody who was there before the statute of limitations on my property runs out," Whistler said. "Besides, it's already past noon, and those policemen probably ain't even in bed yet, anyway."

"I need persuasion," Polokowsky said.

Whistler tapped the night book and, like magic, a folded twenty appeared between its pages.

Polokowsky closed the book and wrote down Officer Auburn's address on a piece of paper.

"Why'd you give me Auburn's address and not Schoonover's? Why not both?"

"Schoonover's got troubles. If he's in bed, he needs his sleep."

"What kind of troubles has he got?"

"He's got a hernia, five brats, and a wife he can't stomach what runs around on him every chance she gets. It makes him sad and it makes him mean."

Her name was Hanna Susan Cazebone. She'd been a whore since she was twelve. Barcaloo had called her Bouche from the minute she'd done him in the back room of Jimmy Flynn's four years before. *Bouche* means "mouth," in French. It could be he called her Bouche because her mouth was pretty, because she ran it all the time, or because it was her sexual specialty. He'd bought her for two liver-spotted hounds, three handguns, an ounce of China white, and two hundred bucks.

He screwed a hundred women a year, but he needed her. She promised him her respect but never gave it. That was her edge.

She was alive with prickly heat. Fucking Barcaloo was like coupling with a shaggy dog.

He lay next to her, breathing and grunting like a pig, tossing his head from side to side, looking for breath, holding her hand.

"One of these days you'll blink out like a light, the way you go at it," she said. "Heart'll pop like a balloon in the middle of a stroke. Alive going up, and dead coming down."

"You'd like that, wouldn't you?"

Bouche laughed her short, demented laugh.

"You're a nut," Barcaloo said.

"Look what you did to my shoulder again, you fuckin' animal," she said, wiping the pale mix of blood and saliva from her shoulder with the palm of her hand. "You're going to give me a goddamn infection, for sure."

"Germs can't live in your blood," Barcaloo said. "Full of wormwood. Full of poison."

"I got to wash. I got to put on iodine. Oh, shit, it's gonna hurt."

She waited for him to let go of her hand. He still held on, measuring his breaths.

"I was born right out in those gutters," he said. "I was selling pipes of hash when I was seven. I was peddling my sister's ass when I was nine."

It was going to happen again. He was going to tell her his life story again. There was something about telling it that satisfied him. Some men fell asleep right after they came. Like horses dropped with the pipe gun at the slaughterhouse where Barcaloo sometimes took Bouche just to watch the killing. Some men liked a drink or a cigarette, but he liked to tell his life story. He told it in the dreamy voice of a kid reciting fairy tales.

She shrugged slightly, wanting to get up and wash herself.

"I got to take a pee," she said.

He held her hand tighter.

"Go ahead and do it," he said.

"For Christ's sake," Bouche mumbled, but stopped pulling away.

"My sister taught me how to fuck," he said. "You know that? That's supposed to be about the worst. I mean, a sister with a brother, like a father with his daughter, you know what I mean? They're crazy. What's wrong? Nothing's wrong."

His eyes blinked open and shut like a camera's shutter.

"I *own* this apartment house. I used to run errands for whores and painters who lived in this house, and now I own it."

Bouche wiggled her fingers inside his fist, trying to work some blood into them. She glanced down and saw that the tips were white. There was a drying snail track on her thigh.

"Sold playin' cards for a dollar a pack to assholes come down from New York, Chicago, Minneapolis. Cards with whores doin' tricks and capers on the backs. Fifty-two poses, plus two jokers and a title card. All different. I give good value. I was twelve."

He took a long, shuddering breath and tossed his head back. He stared up at the reflections on the ceiling.

"My sister Ina's dead, you know. Her boyfriend cut her twat out of her in an alley off St. Ann Street. Oh, he shouldn'ta done that. He shouldn'ta put that big hole in her and let her bleed to death."

"But you did for that son of a bitch, didn't you?" Bouche whispered, hoping to deflect his growing agitation that could easily turn on her. "Even though you was only a kid?"

His grin gleamed whitely in the shadows. It was the most— maybe the only attractive feature he had. White teeth like chips of porcelain, the canines small and pointed like a dog's.

"I done him. Oh, yes, I done him. I paid three cruel buggers a hundred bucks apiece, and they caught that rat for me. Very queer dudes they was. All big fuckers what liked to dress up like women and give it to men up the ass. How can you figure such a thing as that?"

Bouche felt her stomach roll. It frightened her. She knew the world was crazy, but she also knew, without being able to say so, that she was safe as long as she didn't lose her immunity to the insanity. If she saw it, felt it, let it touch her mind and heart and make her sick, she'd end up running naked down the street looking for someone to shoot her.

"Oh my, oh my, oh my," she whispered.

"Had my own goddamn playing cards printed when I was fourteen. I had ideas. I did pictures with black men doing white women and the other way around. I could read inside the heads of all those square johns. Oh, yeah, I could. Square janes too. I took pictures of women with dogs and ponies. . . ."

Bouche really did have to pee. She could feel her bladder filling up. She ought to give him a golden shower, she thought. Make him happy. She hadn't pissed on him in a long time. My God, the things some people did for kicks.

Ten

Reginald Auburn had skin like iron polished with stove black. He sat at his kitchen table in starched white shorts looking at Whistler with yellow eyes. The man looked so evil, it took your breath away. But when he spoke, his voice was as gentle as a dove's.

"Let me get you straight," he said. "Tell me again what it is you want."

"I distribute newspapers and tabloids to vending machines. . . ."

"You lying to me," Auburn said mildly.

Whistler grunted as though struck a blow.

"What makes you say that?" he asked.

"You haven't got the right kind of clothes for that hustle."

"I knew I was going to be talking to people, so I dressed up for the occasion."

"Shee-it," Auburn said. "You want coffee?"

"You having coffee?"

"If my wife made a pot before she left for school, I'm having coffee."

He waved his arm and gave Whistler the idea that he was

72

meant to lift the pot. It was heavy. He set it back down on the burner and turned on the gas flame. Then he leaned against the counter between sink and stove.

"This going to be a good day," Auburn said, pleased that there was coffee in the pot. He peered one-eyed into the cream jug and grinned. "A gooood day."

"What time did you get to the scene of the accident at Hollywood and Vine?" Whistler said.

"I logged it at three thirty-five," Auburn said lazily, as though the information were of no account.

"A citizen reported the accident before two."

"You know one hell of a lot for a newspaper boy." Auburn grinned slowly and slickly as he drawled his words out, cruel cat playing with the mouse.

"I figure you reached the scene no later than two-twenty. Two-thirty on the outside."

"One hell of a lot."

"You mind telling me what you found when you got there?"

"You mind telling me what business it is of yours?"

Whistler tapped the bread box and the toaster.

"You want me to make you some toast?"

"You playing mother?"

"Just like to make myself useful. I find it pays off."

Their eyes explored the eyes of the other. Reading between the lines. Shorthand code of the streets and alleys. Saying one thing and meaning another. Saying nothing and telling all.

"Make me some toast," Auburn said.

Whistler took half a loaf of raisin bread out of the box. He popped two slices into the toaster and depressed the lever.

"You carryin' a private ticket?" Auburn said.

"Remind me never to try to shit you," Whistler said.

"When I arrived on the scene with my partner, we saw a nineteen seventy-four Ford station wagon piled up against a hydrant and a rack of vendors. The driver—"

"How did you know it was the driver?"

"There was nobody else hurt or dead."

"Nobody else on the scene when the accident occurred?"

"Nobody except the counterman in the all-nighter."

Something flickered in Auburn's catlike eyes. Something that sparkled like sudden shame. Here was a man who didn't like to lie, Whistler thought.

"And that was all?"

"You telling me different?" Auburn said softly.

The toaster popped the slices up. The coffee steamed. Whistler poured the coffee while Auburn roused himself and got the butter out of the refrigerator.

The policeman sat down and saw the twenty under his cup. He sat there with the butter knife in his hand and stared at Whistler with his yellow eyes.

"What did I miss?" Auburn said. "You got a client? You on expenses?"

"I'm making an investment in the future. I figure there might have been somebody else injured in the accident. Somebody who was in the station wagon. I figure there might have been a witness besides the counterman."

"You better not tell me how you figure all this," Auburn said.

"So, there was nobody else there? Just you and your partner, Schoonover, and the counterman and the corpse of the driver?"

"And the plainclothes what came, and the team on the morgue wagon, and, later, the people what come out of the bricks when anybody dies in the street. Nobody else. That's official. You understand?"

Whistler glanced at the twenty and nodded, waiting for more.

"You better pick that money up," Auburn said, "or I'll start asking you some questions right now, right here, unofficially. You won't find it a comfort."

"I don't suppose your partner ever sees things different than you do?" Whistler asked, picking up the twenty.

"He sees the same as me. But maybe I see different anytime I know more than I know this minute."

Auburn stood up. He wasn't all that big, not as big as Whistler, but all the same, there was something intimidating about the simple move.

"You don't go botherin' Harry, you understand? Is that coffee you poured for yourself to go, or are you gonna drink it here?" Auburn said.

Whistler took three swallows and set the cup down half empty.

"Thank you for your hospitality."

"Anytime."

There was a knock on the door. Barcaloo yelled for whoever it was to come in without even asking who it was. The football players in the night game Chippy Byrd and Lacy Ohio had witnessed came through the door. The big one was Dom Pinole, the little one was Jickie Rojo. Pinole had a folded newspaper in his back pocket and was looking nervous, reaching back every ten seconds or so to make sure it hadn't caught fire.

Bouche grabbed the end of the sheet and drew it across her lap.

"What have you got in your pocket, Dom?" she asked.

"Nothin'."

"My God, it looks like something to me. If I didn't know you couldn't read, I'd swear it was a newspaper."

Barcaloo rolled out of bed and put on a bathrobe. "So, what the hell you doin' bustin' in here like this? Did I send for you?"

"Lemme see the newspaper," Bouche said, enjoying Pinole's agitation and curious about the cause of it. "You got the *Wall Street Journal* there? You got the *Christian Science Monitor*?"

"Please . . ." Pinole started to say, his heavy-featured face screwing up in anxiety. Barcaloo started to tell her to shut up, but Rojo showed his teeth to Bouche and said, "Lay the fuck off it."

It was like dropping cold water into a pot of hot iron. Barcaloo's rage took about five seconds to boil up. It sizzled and flared.

"What I hear you just say? What gives you the right to use your mouth like you just used it on Bouche? Who the hell done that? Give you the fuckin' privilege? Give you the fuckin' permission? You come breakin' into my bedroom—"

"It just slipped out," Pinole said, making quick excuses. "Jickie don't mean nothin'."

"It's all right, Nonny," Bouche yelled above Barcaloo's shouting, half enjoying his anger when it wasn't directed at her.

". . . without even fuckin' knockin'," Barcaloo roared on.

"We knocked," Pinole said.

"Then you talk to Bouche like you done? Then you—"

"I was just teasing Dom," Bouche broke in. "No cause to get mad at me, Jickie. Dom's just a big kid and I like to tease him." She snatched the paper from Pinole's pocket.

". . . like she's some whore off the goddamn street!"

"See? It's just the *Enquirer,*" Bouche said. "It's just nothing. . . ."

"I ought to leave you in this shithole of a city," Barcaloo mumbled.

". . . but that rag what writes about all sorts of crazy things. See? Here they got this story about some head these two people see somebody kicking around over to the lake."

"Lemme see that," Barcaloo yelled. He grabbed the newspaper out of her hand and started to read. All the blood drained out of his face. His cheeks and the end of his nose looked frostbitten. He read slowly, his lips making the words one by one as he plodded right on through to the end. He stared at the two cuts of Chippy Byrd and Lacy Ohio. His eyes came up and fixed on Pinole.

The buzzing of a single fly seemed loud as it closed in on Barcaloo, drawn by his odor. He waved his hand around his ear, but it came back. He watched it hover near his eye. His brain focused on the bug, as though it were the only thing of importance in his life. His hand flashed out and trapped the fly in his fist. He slapped his hands together, then wiped them off on his robe.

Pinole opened his mouth and looked at Rojo for support, but Rojo was staring at Bouche's heavy breasts.

"What the hell you doing, Bouche?" Barcaloo whispered fiercely, "runnin' a goddamn fruit stand, sittin' around with your melons hanging out like that? Get outta here."

"Oh, fachrissakes, you got these two assholes livin' in your pocket, right the fuck downstairs in the cellar flat. They walk in any goddamn time they want without even knockin', and you fuckin' yell at me," Bouche shrieked, wrapping the sheet around her and dragging it off the bed as she stood up. "Besides, these two assholes of yours has seen every inch of skin I got taking my picture for your goddamn dirty movies."

76

"That's different, that's in the line of business."

"Why'd they come back from L.A. in the first place? We're going to be there in a few days, but you send them out there and they come back here, and now they'll be going back there again. They're like a couple of goddamn businessmen takin' the shuttle flight. I don't know why you put up with two such assholes in the first place." She glared at Rojo. "I'm going to take a crap, dum-dum, you want to come in and watch?"

He raised his stare to her eyes. She ran into the bathroom with the sheet trailing behind her.

"I ought to kick your asses out, just like she says," Barcaloo raged. "I should leave you facedown in the bayou. One fuckup after a goddamn other. What the hell you think you was doing?"

"It starts out we have a couple of drinks and a toot, you know?" Pinole said.

"I *don't* know. It's why I'm asking."

"We was having a little fun. It got away from us," Rojo said.

"Here's your little fun," Barcaloo shouted, slapping the paper with the back of his hand, smashing a hole in the faces of Chippy Byrd and Lacy Ohio, who grinned out in black-and-white halftone from the newsprint. He lowered his voice with great effort. "I ask you to trash that head, and you play football with it. Which is goddamn weird. You play kickball with it and you don't get rid of it."

"We thought we got rid of it," Pinole said. "We dump it in the mud by the lake. How the hell are we supposed to figure this creature comes along and pulls it out for its dinner? How the hell we know that?"

"What makes you pick the goddamn lake in the first place? We got the city dump for things like arms, legs, and heads."

"So we'll know better next time."

"Just like that, you silly son of a bitch? This could maybe queer the biggest deal of my career. You unnerstan' that? I'm supposed to take over the porno trade for the entire fuckin' country west of the fuckin' Mississippi. You unnerstan' what I'm sayin'? I'm told to make sure there's nothin' outstanding could attract undue attention. I go to the trouble. Now I get word this morning that a body without a head turns up at the corner of Hollywood and Vine. Guess who's driving the car what it fell out of? Willy Zabadno."

"Jesus H. Christ."

Barcaloo's eyes flicked over to the bathroom door, as though making sure that Bouche wasn't on the eary.

"And right after that good news I got to read this crap. Suppose the man on the West Coast happens to read this goddamn scandal sheet? Suppose he just happens to read about this here head which you two kicked around? Suppose he puts two and two together and comes up with this head down here and a body without no head in L.A.?"

"Well, for Christ's sake," said Pinole, "why's this head here got to belong to that body back there?"

"Because it's a gook corpse and it's got a butterfly on its ass and I don't think the country's overstuffed with so many heads and bodies without heads that it don't merit some attention and maybe a remark or two. Now, you got any idea what I want you to do?"

"You want we should find those two assholes what run off at the mouth to the newspaper and see they don't run off at the mouth no more?" Rojo said.

"And we bury 'em in the city dump and not by the lake," Pinole added.

"Yeah," Barcaloo said. "Also you dump that goddamn Cadillac with the Bondoed fender in the bayou right away."

"We was gonna drive out to the Coast in it," Pinole complained.

"Dump it right the fuck now, I said."

"We could get it sprayed . . ." Pinole persisted.

Barcaloo stared at him, and Pinole looked away. "So, we'll bury them two assholes in it," he said.

"But first you bring 'em out to the studio. First we shoot a little footage. No sense lettin' them two go to waste altogether."

Whistler ran Harry Schoonover down in a little bar across the street from the apartment building on Western Avenue in which the cop and his family lived. He was seated by a window laced with yellow rain, a beer glass getting warm in his two hands, his eyes on the windows third-floor front. He had the sad eyes of a spaniel. His hair was red and combed across his forehead like a small boy whose mother got him ready for school.

Whistler introduced himself and asked Schoonover if he wanted a cold, fresh beer.

"It took me half an hour to warm this one," Schoonover said in flat accents, an immigrant from the East. "Who are you and what do you want?"

"My name's Whistler."

Schoonover took a second to flick a glance at Whistler, then turned his eyes back to the windows of his flat.

"Auburn told me about you."

"You see the same thing he saw at the corner of Hollywood and Vine?"

"The very same thing. Get the fuck out of here."

"You live up there?"

"Up where?"

"Up there behind the windows you're looking at."

"What do you know about where I live?"

"I don't. That's why I ask."

Schoonover gave Whistler his full attention.

"If you want to be a cop, if you want to do for law and order," Schoonover said sarcastically, "why don't you put in your application? Be a blue?"

"I got a limp."

"You got a belly full of shit."

"You mad at me because you know I'm going to make you an offer and you probably aren't going to turn me down?"

Schoonover let his eyes go flatter than they already were. Flat and mean and filled with melancholy despair over a life that had become a tangle of old rubber bands and bent pins.

"What are you offering?"

"Twenty."

"I roll up twenty-dollar bills and use them for suppositories."

"I doubt it. Not with five kids and a complaining wife you don't. How about fifty?"

"What do you want?"

"Nothing much. Just what you saw at the corner of Hollywood and Vine last night."

"What's your interest?"

"I was there and I saw what I saw. Now everybody's telling me I didn't see it."

"Who gives a rat's ass?"

"I like to know I'm not going crazy."

"How you going to use it?"

"I'm no bird dog for a newspaper. I don't know how I'm going to use it. Maybe I just don't like to see shit covered up. Sooner or later I could step in it. Call me curious."

"Two-car smashup. A brand-new silver BMW and a seventy-four station wagon. The driver of the station wagon was killed. The driver of the BMW was waiting for us outside a coffee shop. We called for detectives because there was a fatality—"

"Excuse me for interrupting. Just one fatality?"

"There was another body under a blanket. A woman's. Strictly speaking, her death had not been caused by the accident."

"Can you describe that body for me?"

"It had no head. If it would've had a head, she would have been about five foot one, a hundred five pounds. Oriental. Maybe Chinese. Probably Vietnamese. Her legs were a little bowed, and her tits were small. She was probably a Saigon whore."

Whistler almost said it was a wonder that Schoonover could tell that from looking at a bloodless corpse, but he didn't. "What makes you say that?"

"She was wearing a tattoo on the side of her belly by her hipbone. A butterfly. And that's the way a Saigon trader marks a Saigon whore."

"You try to look her up back in Records?"

"We were told not to browse. We were told she was the little woman who wasn't there."

Whistler handed over the fifty.

"Who asked you and Auburn to forget about her?"

"Lubbock and Jackson *told* us to forget about her."

"You do everything detectives tell you to do?"

"I do most everything my supervisor tells me to do."

"What was the supervisor's name?"

"Good night, asshole."

"You got my fifty."

Schoonover stared at the fifty-dollar bill spread out between his hands as though it were the first sign of his corruption. He looked up at the windows of the apartment house where he lived with a wife and five kids.

"Lieutenant Muncie."

He touched his hand to his groin and winced as he shifted his weight to his other hip.

"Get the fuck out of here," he said.

Eleven

With her makeup off Lacy Ohio looked like a Loretta Oskanowsky. She looked like a Loretta Oskanowsky with sallow skin, small eyes, and crooked teeth, and that's what she intended to remain, even if that sweet-talking son of a bitch Chippy Byrd came around again trying to get into her pants. Asking her out to some bar or nightclub to listen to a little music, a little jazz. Have a little fun. Have a few drinks. Buttering her up. Oiling up her hip joints so he could push her knees apart.

Not that she wasn't ready. She was ready. But she was no pushover. Her heels weren't round. Man or boy wanted to fiddle with her treasure, he had to work for it. No quick-and-easy roll me over in the clover.

When he'd taken her home that night, after the fright of her life, the son of a bitch had tried to con her into fucking right there in her own parlor with her deaf old grandmother sleeping in the next room. Jesus Christ, did he have no shame? Did he have no fear? Fucking with her grandmother right in the next room and maybe having to get up to take a pee.

He'd had plenty of fear over to the lake. She'd smelled it on him when those two wackos were kicking the head around. Before they knew it was a head. When it could have been two drunks kicking a ball. But Chippy had known there was something not right. Something very wrong. He'd known it and sat there as still as a mouse, his lips moving, silently praying they wouldn't look his way. That's why she hadn't honked the horn like she was about to do. To try to scare the two drunks. To have a little fun with them. Something about the way Chippy sat so still told her to be just as quiet as he was. Lucky for them.

By the night after, though, Chippy had forgotten the scare they'd had. Nothing front-page in the *Times–Picayune* about the head. Just an item on the fifth page. Nothing much on the television news. Just a wry item with a twisted grin at the end of the six o'clock, as if heads without bodies weren't horrible but merely odd. Remarkable but somehow funny. It was the head of a gook. Who gave a fuck about the head of a gook or a nigger?

"Small potatoes," Chippy'd said, "not worth worrying about. Come on out and play," he'd said, flashing a sheaf of tempting green.

So off she'd gone with him. Over to the French Quarter to Al Hirt's for a little trumpet, a little jazz. Over to Algiers and Manny the Mule's joint. Over to Jimmy Flynn's on St. Peter where Jimmy Flynn himself stood behind the bar telling stories and lending an ear.

And that fool, Chippy, couldn't resist showing off. Couldn't resist telling Jimmy Flynn and one and all that they'd actually been witness to the game of football played with a human head.

Instant celebrity. Free drinks. People smiling at them. Touching them. The character what put his hand on her sleeve and said he was a stringer for *The Enquirer*, the great national newspaper.

"Don't you know it? In every supermarket in the country. Right next to the registers. How'd you like to make a hundred? How about two? Just tell me your story. Give it to me exclusive. Do tell. Oh, do fucking tell. Is that what you sat there looking at? Go on, go on. Tell it in your own words. Let the little lady tell her story. Just a minute. Just hold it." And the flash of the camera. Once for Chippy and once for her.

The next day nothing happening. Those two crazies never showing as she'd feared they might, ready to do to her what they'd done to that head.

Next day after that, *The Enquirer* on the newsstands, in the supermarkets. Still nobody coming to do her harm. The terror of the name Barcaloo—whoever that might be—starting to fade away. The memory of all the smiling faces, admiring eyes, free drinks, hundred-dollar bills, coming back as sweet as wine.

When the telephone rang five minutes after she got home from work, while she was cooking up sausages and sauerkraut for herself and her grandmother, she knew it was Chippy again, ready to ask her to be Lacy Ohio for another night.

"So what did I tell you?" Byrd said. "Nothing to worry about. Nothing to be scared about. Just a couple of drunks."

"It was a head," she said. "We both read that in the newspaper. We both saw it on the tube."

"Well, nobody seems to care. Nobody's doing anything about it. So nobody's *going* to do anything about it. I want to spend my hundred on you. I want to turn your belly into whipped cream."

"Is that dirty? Are you talkin' dirty to me?"

"No, I'm talkin' love. Don't you think it's about time? I been holdin' my own and dreamin' long enough, don't you think?"

"I don't know."

"Come on out and play. If you don't want to love me when the night's over, you can shoot me and put me out of my misery."

He laughed and she laughed. She hung up after saying yes and showered and put cake, rouge, and powder on her face. Turned her cheeks into magnolia petals. Made her lips two cherries. Made her eyes as big as pansies, all black and purple. Put Loretta Oskanowsky in the closet with her flannel nightgown and sensible shoes.

Gave her grandmother supper and told her not to fall asleep watching the television.

When Chippy Byrd pushed the bell in the lobby downstairs, Lacy Ohio, in tight black skirt and scarlet shoes, was out the door and down the stairs like a sprinter.

Jimmy Flynn listened to the horror story about the head as

told by Chippy Byrd and Lacy Ohio as if he'd never heard it before. In fact, he never had heard the version they now told, in which Byrd scared the two killers away with fierce threats in defense of his lady love. Ohio stared starry-eyed at her boastful would-be, soon-to-be lover as though he spoke the gospel truth, much preferring to fuck a motion picture hero than a skinny asshole with a squint. She was too busy mooning, and Byrd was too busy lying to notice Jimmy Flynn when he tipped the wink to a big man and a little man who sat hunched on two stools in the gloom at the end of the bar, so they didn't look like a big one and a little one. Didn't see Rojo go to the wall phone and dial a number. Didn't know that the Barcaloo they once had feared, without even knowing more than the name, was telling Rojo that he was too tired and it was too late to lift Byrd and Ohio off the streets.

"Follow them two and find out where they hang their jocks and where they earn their bread. Tomorrow. Tomorrow you pick them up. They can wait until tomorrow."

Tillman, Lubbock, and Jackson each had a tall drink in hand. They were sitting in a booth in a bar on Hollywood Boulevard.

"We asked you to come meet with us because there's this thing about the car."

"My six thirty-five CSi BMW."

"With mag wheels," Jackson said.

"The silver one," Lubbock said. "What a son of a bitch of a machine." He held his arms out and pretended to be driving at speed down a long straight road. "A man wouldn't even need a cock to fuck the cunt, he owns a machine like that."

"It's a nice car, all right," Tillman said. "So what about it?"

"It's in the police impound in need of some repair."

"I was waiting for the word."

"The word? What word?"

"That it was all right to come and get it. I got the pink and registration with me, just like you said."

"Well, you'll just have to make up your mind about that."

"About what?"

"Coming to get the BMW out of impound."

"Something wrong?"

"Well, it's like this," Jackson said, the sober accountant of the team of Lubbock and Jackson. "We swept a few facts under the rug, so we don't have to take you downtown and book you on vehicular manslaughter."

"Which, under the law, we are sworn to do in the case of any such accident that causes injury, let alone death. You know what I'm saying?" Lubbock chimed in.

"Begging your pardon, Ernie, but I'm trying to apprise our friend, Emmet, here, about the facts. Which I cannot do if you interrupt."

"Sorry, Marty, I just wanted to emphasize the seriousness of the breech of procedure, if not law, which we committed for a friend."

"Understood, but I think Emmet knows. He plays a cop, and he knows what it's all about. How can he not know what it's all about playing a cop five shooting days a week, twenty-six episodes a year?" Jackson turned back to Tillman and smiled briefly. "In order to maintain your anonymity while explaining a silver six thirty-three . . ."

"Six thirty-five," Tillman said.

"Six thirty-five . . . you want to lay the letters on me again?"

"CSi."

"BMW, that's right, we had to put it in the impound as an abandoned vehicle. You understand what this means?"

Tillman shook his head.

"This means . . . You want another drink?"

"No, I'm okay."

"This means the car will stay in impound while the stolen car register is searched. It'll stay there for ninety days if there's no claim made upon it. Now, if you go down there to the police impound and claim your vehicle, somebody's going to want to know why you didn't come asking about a forty-thousand-dollar machine the minute you see it's missing."

"And who knows where that question will lead?" said Lubbock. "Begging your pardon, Marty, are you through?"

"I was through, Ernie. And your point is well taken."

"I mean, we're keeping your involvement in this fatal accident quiet. But these things get bandied . . ." He looked at his partner.

Jackson nodded sagely and said, "Bandied."

"Get bandied around. I mean, forget that asshole Willy Zabadno for a minute. What we're talking about is a body without a fucking head. A minority body, you understand what I'm saying? All of a sudden—who knows?—we got equal-opportunity lawyers fucking around. We got the Civil Liberties Union. We got some fucking old country family *society*."

"There could be ramifications," Jackson said solemnly.

"So what should I do?" Tillman said.

"What you can do is sign the pink slip over to one of us, see? Any fucker down there at the police impound asks us what we're doing picking up a car like that, we tell him to mind his own fucking business if he don't want his balls crushed. You know what I'm saying?"

"I turn the pink slip over to you. You get the car out of impound. Then what?"

"Then we take it to a garage. What do you think it's going to cost fixing the radiator and front end?"

"I'm not a mechanic."

"Neither am I."

"Me, neither," Jackson chimed in.

"The mechanic down at the police impound garage says six thousand minimum, give or take a twenty-dollar bill."

"Needs new fenders. Maybe a new axle."

"If . . ." Lubbock said, tossing a look at his partner. "If the frame ain't bent."

"Frame on a vehicle like that gets bent, it's never the same," Jackson said.

For a second it looked like he was going to take off his hat and hold it over his heart.

"Good for nothing but junk, the frame's bent," Jackson said.

"It's something to think about," Tillman said.

"It's a fucking headache. But we have a suggestion."

Tillman arranged his face to be grateful for what was coming.

"You got insurance on the vehicle?"

"Of course I have insurance."

"Does he look like the kind of fool wouldn't have insurance

on a vehicle like that, being as famous as he is?" Jackson scolded. "Of course he's got insurance."

"So, you report the car stolen. We write up the report for you and give you a copy for your broker. We put a copy in the files in case the adjuster wants a look. You understand what I'm saying?"

"My rates go up."

"So what the fuck's that? Piss in a bucket."

"What happens to the car?"

"It's a beautiful car. I'd love to own such a beautiful car."

"Me too," said Jackson.

"But where would a couple of working stiffs like us get the money for a car like that?"

"Nowhere is where," said Jackson.

"So the best thing we can do is make a deal with the mechanic down to this dealership we know. He does the job for us half price after hours. He can use the tools, garage, heat, and light, you understand? No overhead. The boss does us that favor. Mechanic works the job in his spare time. Even gives it a new paint job. I like silver, but Jackson here says it should be black. It costs Jackson and me maybe three thousand."

"Unless the frame's bent."

"That goes without saying. We take the chance. We already got the pink. Then we maybe drive it around for a week. Have a little fun. Imagine what it would be like to really own a car like that. Then we wholesale it out to a dealer we know. Maybe we make a few thousand. Why not? You don't begrudge us?"

"No, I don't begrudge you."

"Because we're taking the chance, you see? We've been taking a lot of chances to help you out. Not that we begrudge it. After all, what are friends for except to do them a favor now and then . . . fuck the chances you got to take . . . and give yourself a good feeling."

Tillman handed over the registration and the pink slip.

"You want another drink?" Jackson asked.

"No, I've got a date," Tillman said, reaching for the tab.

"Hey, hey!" Lubbock said loudly and heartily, grabbing Tillman's wrist with one hand and the check with the other. "Your money's no good here."

Auburn could see Harry Schoonover out of the corner of his eye as they drove through the night streets. He thought about what makes a cop partnership. The trouble it was. Worse than a marriage in many ways. Harder to make work.

First there'd been the fact that he was black and Schoonover white. Harry was no redneck, but he'd been raised not wanting much to do with niggers, just like he, Auburn, had been raised not much trusting honkies. How the hell could it have been any other way? Blacks pushing into white neighborhoods where they weren't wanted just so they could escape ghettos that were so bad, even the rats were looking to move. And where the hell were the working-class whites supposed to go?

Then there was the fact that Auburn was thin, almost skinny, a runner, once an all-state forward on his high-school basketball team. And good-looking to boot, even if he did say so himself. Harry was going to fat, and there was a bald spot growing on the back of his head. He had a nose like a turkey's ass and teeth no two of which grew in the same direction. They were also going to hell from the candy bars he ate. Harry had toothaches all the time.

Auburn's own marriage was hopeful, sex life hearty, future bright. Harry's marriage was a mess, he got no fucking at home anymore.

Schoonover told Auburn that his wife, Shirley, had cut off his water because she'd said five kids were enough.

"There's IUDs and the pill," Harry'd told her.

"You want to kill me with uterine infections and cancer?"

"I could wear a rubber."

"Don't talk dirty!"

"It don't seem to bother her when the several assholes she fucks outside the home wear condoms, which they must do, otherwise she'd get knocked up again just as easy from them as me," Harry had told Auburn.

"For Christ's sake, you don't want to go talking about your wife that way," Auburn had said.

He thought Harry's wife, Shirley, was self-destructive. He and Alicia, his own sweetheart wife, often talked about it and said how lucky they were, while poor Harry's life was going down the toilet at a fearful rate.

Not to mention money.

Alicia worked and went to school too. He worked an extra job tending bar. They were saving. They were looking at houses together out in Woodland Hills.

Schoonover's wife stayed at home when she wasn't out screwing other men. Harry was always buying her useless things to soothe her. And five kids ate up money like Cracker-jacks.

It was so hard making a partnership. They'd finally made one.

"You got a toothache?" Auburn said.

"You mean, have I got *another* toothache?" Schoonover said, as snappish as a junkyard dog.

"No, I mean have you got a toothache now," Auburn said calmly.

"No, I ain't got a toothache."

"How about a wild hair up your ass? You got a wild pussy whisker up your ass?" Auburn said in the same tone of voice.

Schoonover couldn't help it. He snorted through his nose with laughter.

"That son of a bitch Whistler?" he said. "He came to see me even after you told him I saw what you saw over to Hollywood and Vine."

"You mean that rascal didn't believe me?" Auburn said, half sarcastic, half amused.

"From the way he talked, it's a bet he was at the scene and left it."

"Nothing strange about that. Most people don't want to get involved."

"If this Whistler don't want to get involved, what the fuck's he doing running around asking you and me questions?" Schoonover shrugged heavily. He didn't want to think about another man's motives for doing whatever.

"You don't think the son of a bitch is Internal Affairs?" Jackson said.

"You mean those cocksuckers could be laying a trap?"

"Them bastards, they got nothing to do, they go make themselves something to do."

"Oh, Christ, I don't think so. I think I seen that schmuck hanging around Gentry's for a couple of years already."

"I think I have too. And I think I've seen him head-to-head with that kiddie vice cop, Canaan, on more than one occasion."

"You know about Canaan?"

"I heard about him, yes. I don't know if it's good for a cop to hate as bad as he does. Destroys his perspective. Makes it hard to work the deals you've got to work to make it happen out there on the streets."

"I think my brother's kid was snatched off the playground and done like that little girl was done, I'd be hating pretty good too."

"How long ago was that?"

"Two years. About two years, I think."

"They say the poor sucker hardly ever sleeps."

They drove on in silence for a while, listening to the hissing of the tires on the wet road, listening to the measured beat of the wipers as they smeared fog and road shit across the windshield.

After a while Auburn said, "I wouldn't worry. I don't think that Whistler's any cop. I think he was hanging out in Gentry's and saw the accident. I think he sees the chance for a hustle and is willing to spend a little to get a lot. How much did he give you?"

"A hundred bucks," Schoonover lied, not wanting to admit he was bought for cheap.

"That's more than he offered me."

"Did you take it?"

Auburn hesitated half a second and then said, "Yeah, I took it. Then I shined him on. You tell him anything?"

"Why the fuck not? They tell us to clam up, they don't tell us why. What the fuck's that supposed to mean? We're pups? We're fuckin' pups on a leash? Lubbock and Jackson don't even bother to tell us any lies, just give us the old slap on the back, do-this-one-for-the-Gipper crap. I don't even know who the fuck we're covering up for. Somebody's getting paid off, that's for fucking sure."

"You bet your sweet ass. But it's none of our business."

"So I didn't tell that Whistler anything a half a dozen characters standing out in the rain couldn't have told him."

Auburn grunted his assent, sorry that he hadn't taken the twenty. Sorry that he hadn't gone for a hundred the way Schoonover had done. Staying honest wasn't easy, and sometimes, he was beginning to think, it didn't much matter.

Twelve

Whistler needed somebody with a memory. Eddie Deane, a reporter who worked the crime beat, owed him one.

Deane was dressed like a Hollywood bit player hoping to be discovered leaning on a bar. Red crushed-leather boots with army twill trousers bloused at the ankles when it rained. Tan work shirt. Authentic Foreign Legion jacket bought through a mail-order firm twenty years ago. Felt hat with two wooden kitchen matches stuck in the brim, although he didn't smoke because half his lungs were already gone. Glass of something amber always in his hand for effect, although he didn't drink because his liver would have killed him in protest if he had.

"It wasn't my generation to do drugs," he said. "But I gave up booze, tobacco, sugar, caffeine, red meat, fats, and will soon give up pussy. Then I'll be perfect. Then they'll make me a saint. If you launched yourself into a program of self-improvement, Whistler, you'd be reborn just like me and live to be a hundred and ten."

"Who wants to live that long if there's a chance of ending up looking like you?"

"I'm beautiful. I'm manly. I'm what the ladies crave. I hear them whispering about the savor of my buns as I walk past them, perched like darling little finches on the bar stools of the city. What do you want to know, and why should I tell you?"

"I want to know about a headless corpse. A woman. Probably Oriental. Maybe Vietnamese."

"I know nothing about headless corpses, Oriental, Vietnamese, or otherwise. And now I no longer owe you."

"Are you shining me on?"

"I've got no reason to throw dust in your face. I've not been bribed. I've not been threatened. I've not been warned."

"Well, you missed a headless body."

"Did I? How did news of such a wonder come your way?"

Whistler told him about the story of the head in *The Enquirer*. He told him about the accident and the body that almost bounced into his lap over to Gentry's. He told him about the story of the dummy and the one-car collision in the DMV files.

"Who's your client?"

"I haven't got one."

"What's your suspicion?"

"Only that there's been a snowfall."

"To cover just exactly what?"

"I haven't got the faintest."

"Could they be right about the body being a dummy?"

"I think I can tell the difference."

"You think the body here in L.A. belongs to the head in New Orleans?"

"Don't make me crazy. It figures."

"It amazes me that we've come to think there's some kind of logic to horror," Deane said, as though Whistler's statement were among the saddest he'd ever heard.

"Do you know about *any* unidentified dead Oriental women?"

Deane closed his eyes. "There was a case. There was a Vietnamese woman found murdered and mutilated two, two and a half years ago. She was living on Alpine Hill with her ten-year-old son and her sister. One day the sisters had a fight. One of them walks out of the apartment . . ."

"What was the fight about?"

Deane opened his eyes.

"I don't remember anybody ever said. Whatever it was, the sister walks out and don't come back. Two months later they found her body out to Elysian Park. She'd been tortured and mutilated.

"A month before the discovery of her body these brothers named Corvallis—ran one of these crazy cults . . . Satanists, maybe—had been picked up for a whole string of mutilation killings, along with three of their followers. The Vietnamese woman was one of the dead. Maybe the last body found. She was discovered down in Malibu after they were arrested. There were maybe a dozen killings altogether, but murder charges were brought against them on only four. The Vietnamese woman among them. The prosecutors told her family they'd need the body for evidence, because marks on the bones of the neck, made with a knife, didn't show up good enough in the photographs. They didn't want the defense stepping on doubtful evidence. They told the family they could bury the daughter, but she might have to be disinterred later on. The family were Mahayana Buddhists from the south. Their faith doesn't allow the body, once buried, to be dug up again. So the body was kept at County Morgue."

"Has the case gone to trial?"

"What with polygraph tests, psychiatric evaluations, arguments for severance, hearings of motions, and other delays, the trial opened about two months ago."

"I don't see anything in the papers about it."

"Well, you wouldn't, would you? I mean, it hits the headlines, then it fades. It's like the phases of the moon. They come and go. The public attention span is getting shorter and shorter. Even the end of the world will only rate the front page for a day." He took a sip of his soft drink and made a face as though the taste offended him.

"You said the bodies were mutilated?"

"But not decapitated. None of them was beheaded."

"You remember the name of the murdered Viet woman?"

Deane closed his eyes again.

"Let me look in my memory book." He squinted hard. "As near as I can make it out, it was something like Lynn Shoe."

"That doesn't sound Vietnamese."

"Gimme a break. I'm giving it to you phonetically, the way I remember it. Go look it up in the files."

The photographic memory Deane was so proud of was months off. The beginning of the Corvallis murders started closer to twenty-four months ago, rather than thirty-six. The film reels of the *Times* at the library said that sixteen months before, at the beginning of last year's March, Carl Corvallis, age 34, had been arrested and charged with abducting Agnes Easter, a 17-year-old prostitute. He'd handcuffed her, mutilated her with knife cuts and cigarette burns, and sexually abused her before dumping her, naked and bleeding, along Pacific Coast Highway between Malibu and Port Hueneme.

Two weeks later he was released on a fifty-thousand-dollar bond, purchased for five thousand dollars by an aunt, Mabel Putnam, who had raised him from childhood.

Another prostitute, treated in the same way six months before, identified the van Corvallis drove, as did Miss Easter.

Corvallis was taken into custody again in April and held on a bond of one million dollars, which the aunt could not manage.

Then a former roommate, Eric Yount, 23, after failing a polygraph test, told the police that a body was buried in the hills above the highway in the coastal area known as Trancas. Police searched the gullies and ravines with shovels and methane detectors and uncovered the first of fourteen bodies that would be attributed to Carl Corvallis, the apparent leader of the raggedy cult, his brother Jan, 30, Eric Yount, Paul Firth, 22, and Jan's girlfriend, Charlotte Richey, who was only 18.

Shortly after Yount's revelation he implicated Firth in the rape-mutilation murders of three more young women, two of whom were known prostitutes. Two of the bodies were unearthed in the wetlands around Malibu.

Yount and Firth were arrested and charged during the first week of May.

Information gathered by the police during several interrogations of Yount brought about the arrest of Jan Corvallis and his girlfriend, Richey. Each of the accused, except Carl Corvallis, who refused to cooperate with the police, made statements implicating their fellow cult members in the murders already uncovered, and others, the bodies of which were still to be found.

Some of the accusations proved false or, at least, had not yet been proved twelve months later. Others held up under investigation. More bodies were discovered, the count rising to thirteen.

In June, the body of Lim Shu Dok, 25, a Vietnamese-American prostitute, was found buried in a place called the Mud Hole, off the highway, just as remembered by Eddie Deane. The discovery was made by chance and not because of information offered by any of the accused, though Yount finally claimed to remember Carl Corvallis boasting about what he'd done to a "yellow whore with a butterfly on her ass." The Corvallis brothers were charged with the mutilation-murder of Lim Shu Dok.

There was no special mention made of the prosecution decision to hold the body in case it was to be called into evidence during the course of a trial or trials yet to be set.

Attorneys for the accused appeared in court to enter a motion ordering the prosecuting authorities to stop pretrial information prejudicial to their clients from reaching the press. There had already been extensive coverage detailing the evidence of Satanic ceremonies uncovered in the basement apartment of Carl Corvallis. Judge Burlingame issued a gag order.

While all five of the accused were undergoing psychiatric evaluation the prosecuting attorneys moved for severance, seeking to split the defendants for separate trial. The Corvallis brothers to be tried together. Yount and Firth to be tried together. Richey to be tried alone. Their strategy was clearly one of divide and conquer, the accused having suddenly grown uncooperative and downright loyal toward one another.

Defense attorneys successfully fought against the severance. Judge Burlingame ruled that the matter should be decided by the judge named to preside over the trial if and when the grand jury sent down indictments.

Except that Charlotte Richey, having been a minor at the time of the alleged murders, was remanded to the juvenile authority, the eventual disposition of her case a matter of special administration.

On July fifteenth the grand jury brought down the indictments. On August sixth the case was called. Judge Burlingame sat on the bench, having been named to preside, after all. Motions were heard two months later. At this time Judge Burlingame ruled that the Corvallis brothers would be tried separately in the case of four of the alleged mutilation-murders, including that of Lim Shu Dok. Since neither Yount nor Firth had been implicated in any way in those deaths, they would be tried separately for two killings in which the Corvallis brothers were not thought to be actively involved. Yet another trial would deal generally with the conspiracy aspect of the complicated series of murders and specifically with the several in which all four men, and Charlotte Richey, were implicated.

Trial date was set for January. A continuance was granted until March.

The reels ran out. Whistler went to look at the copies not yet placed on film. Except for a column inch or two now and then, the trial of the Corvallis brothers faded from the pages of the *Times*, but for a small item that recorded the death of the aunt, Mabel Putnam, on July tenth of the current year.

Then, in today's paper, Carl Corvallis was back on the front page, claiming to have found Christ, ready to confess everything.

The antiseptic ruin of the morgue always reminded Whistler of the rest rooms in the subway stations back in New York City. Cold and dank. The tiled walls refusing to be imprinted with human warmth, accepting only human misery.

He went there bearing gifts in the lonely hours of the night when the attendant was apt to welcome company. He brought two pastrami sandwiches on Jewish rye and two large coffees in Styrofoam cups.

"My name's Whistler," he said when the attendant looked up from his crotch magazine, open to the centerfold in which a girl of stunning beauty opened her legs for anyone who cared to ogle her.

"My name's Charlie, and I got nothing to say."

"I brought you a pastrami sandwich."

"Who could resist an important bribe like that?" Charlie said, closing the slick and dropping his running shoes to the floor. "I got a sliding scale of prices," he said, peeling the wax paper off a sandwich. "Two dollars apiece for little questions like, 'How did you ever get into work like this?' Five bucks apiece for big questions like, 'Did anybody turn in a body of a redheaded woman with one black shoe?' Ten dollars if you want to have a look. Twenty-five if you want to touch a corpse. Fifty if you want to be left alone with one for half an hour." He held the sandwich in one hand and picked up a pencil with the other.

"You get many requests like that?" Whistler asked.

Charlie took a bite with teeth trapped in a silver cage and made a mark on the desk blotter. "A few," he managed to mumble around the chew. "You'd be surprised." He winked one eye from behind eyeglasses as thick as bottle bottoms.

"How many?"

"Now and again. How come you didn't bring a Dr. Brown's cream soda? Don't you know a Dr. Brown's cream soda is the only thing you should drink with a pastrami on rye?"

"Anybody ever take a body away for a while?"

"This ain't fast food. We don't box anything to go."

"I'm thinking of somebody running on the inside track."

"Borrow a corpse? You got a bizarre mind." Charlie put down the sandwich and moved his hand toward the phone.

"No need to get ditsy," Whistler said. "I'm not asking you to rent to me. I'm just asking if anyone ever did such a thing. Maybe not some gazoony in off the street. Maybe somebody who knew his way around this joint. Somebody like Willy Zabadno."

"I make that a question. So you owe me twenty-five bucks," Charlie said, totting up the tab as though the transaction were over.

"You didn't answer the one about Zabadno."

"He was in a wreck. That's all she wrote."

"You can do better."

"You want I should speak ill of the dead?"

Whistler took out his gambler's roll. A fifty was on top. You'd

99

think he was carrying big money if you didn't know the rest was ones with maybe a couple of fives.

"This is not a five-dollar answer you want," Charlie said.

"I'll be the judge of that."

"You got to understand, anybody in this job has a lot of confidential information in his ear that he is supposed to keep under his hat."

"How well did you know Willy Zabadno?"

"Willy was not a sociable person. I hardly knew him."

Whistler nodded and tossed the roll from hand to hand to give Charlie encouragement.

"Rumor has it that Willy was more than a little weird. Rumor has it that Willy consorted with the dead," Charlie said. He made a little simpering movement with his lips, which gave away his own fascination for such disgusting horrors. One of these nights, Whistler surmised, Charlie would be whispering sweet nothings into the ear of some young woman fished from the river or taken from her suicide bed.

"Willy use the desk you're sitting at?"

"He had a drawer and I had a drawer."

"He keep his locked?"

"He did."

"Is it locked now?"

"No."

"He have a locker?"

"He had a locker and I got a locker."

"He keep his locked?"

"Yes."

"Is it locked now?"

"No."

"Who cleaned the locker and the desk drawer?"

"That was my job."

"What did you find?"

"The usual."

"Tell me what's the usual."

"A pair of rotten sweat socks. A three-tooth bridge. A calendar from 1981."

Whistler sighed.

For some reason Charlie read danger in it, just as he was

supposed to do. He reached down, opened up the bottom drawer of the desk, took out a magazine in a brown paper mailing wrapper, and tossed it on the counter.

Whistler turned the pages, and his belly winced at the views of bodies grossly mutilated, hung up, and disemboweled like sides of beef, parts obscenely juxtaposed.

"There was a drawer full of that kind of shit," Charlie said.

"All like this?"

"Some worse. Some not so bloody. Some S and M. Some kiddie porn. Some—"

"Zabadno was a newsstand?"

"Only retail."

"Where's the rest of it?"

Charlie's eyes did a dance like two flies looking for a place to light. "I burned them."

"Why would you do that?"

"I wouldn't want Willy's mother to know what he read."

"I wouldn't want your mother to know what a liar you are. You going to service Willy's customers?"

"I told you I burned the shit."

"You fan the magazines before you burned them?"

"Now, why would I do that?"

"To see if Willy stashed change for a hundred between the pages."

"He didn't."

"But he stashed something. His customer list. The numbers of his suppliers."

Charlie made up his mind. "Okay. But I haven't put a price on it yet."

"That tells me you don't know where you might find a buyer."

"Maybe so, but it could be money in the bank."

"Show me."

"Fifty bucks for a look?"

Whistler closed his eyes, as if he were suddenly very weary with being nice.

"You've got to learn to curb your expectations. You're not going to live to be a hundred if you don't. You've told me what you charge. Now I'll tell you what I'll pay. I'll leave you a

101

twenty-dollar bill and your teeth so you can finish the sandwiches I bought you. If I like what you show me, I'll have the
kid from the deli deliver a six-pack of Dr. Brown's cream.
Cold."

Charlie went into the drawer again and scrabbled around
inside. He came up with a manila envelope, much soiled and
written upon, and handed it over. Whistler pulled the tines and
opened the flap without taking his eyes off Charlie's teeth.

There were two separate piles, each held with a large paper
clip.

One was a short list of publishers and wholesalers of sex
paraphernalia, with one, Manny Flowers, doing business out of
an address in downtown L.A.

The other was a pile of four-by-five glossies. Four full-figure
photographs of a dead Oriental girl and close-ups of her head
in various positions. In one the hair was piled up away from the
neck, showing terrible knife wounds and discolorations. Looking closely, he could make out what appeared to be a small mole
near the fold behind the ear. In another, her eyes were slightly
open, a tiny gleam from beneath one lid pretending life.

"What would Willy be doing with these?"

"How the hell would I know?"

"They're out of the files, aren't they?"

Charlie nodded.

Whistler tapped the identification number superimposed on
the lower right-hand corner of the photographs. "Are these
cross-filed?"

Charlie shrugged and nodded again, still pissed off over what
he considered brutal treatment.

"You check the files for me?" Whistler asked.

"You want one hell of a lot for twenty bucks and two lousy
sandwiches," Charlie said, but his voice quavered and had no
weight.

"You forgot the cream sodas I'm going to have sent over."

"Oh, yeah?" Charlie said disdainfully. He checked the number and went to the files. Five minutes later he turned around
and said, "Nothing."

"Those are morgue photos, aren't they?"

"Sure they are."

"There should be a folder in the files matching the numbers on the photos?"

"Yeah."

"And another reference to a drawer inside?"

"That's right."

"So where the hell are they?"

Charlie shrugged again.

"The woman in these photos was found off the road down in Malibu. It's been stored here ever since, waiting to be called into evidence. You should remember something about it."

"I only been working here a year. If there was any such body, it'd be listed in the file."

"Here's her goddamn pictures!" Whistler shouted, and Charlie flinched. "I want to look through the shelves."

"For Christ's sake, I can't let you do that."

"Don't kid me. You gave me your price list five minutes ago."

"There's a goddamn army in there."

"So let's get started."

They went down the rows, pulling out one drawer after another. There were bodies of all ages, sexes, colors, and sizes. Willy Zabadno was there waiting for someone to claim him. But there was no long-dead Vietnamese woman with or without a head.

"So the body that was tossed in the gutter's the same one was dug up in Malibu two years ago," Whistler said, more to himself than to Charlie. "What the hell was Willy Zabadno doing pulling her records and transporting the body through the middle of Hollywood on a rainy night?"

"Maybe he let some wacko in there alone with her, and this pervert got carried away and took the head home for a souvenir, and Willy got scared his ass was for it, so he just decided to eighty-six it because the papers are always full of it how bodies are getting lost and replaced around here, so who would blame it on Willy?"

Whistler stared at Charlie as though one of the corpses had decided to sit up and talk.

"Once she landed in the gutter, she had to be swept up again," he said. "Which means she should have landed back here again. It's the coroner's office does the sweeping. Can you give me the names of the ambulance crews on duty that night?"

Charlie checked the daybooks and wrote some names down on a sheet of paper without asking for a price.

Whistler gave Charlie the fifty so they'd be friends again.

The coroner's ambulance crew had the look of men who knew a secret about life and death and were amused about all the fuss that people made about them. They sat on two cases with another between them, playing out endless hands of hearts. They accepted Whistler as a welcome interruption to the certainties of the night.

The one called Bo looked to be sixteen, his face round and bland, his cheeks swarming with freckles. The one called Jose was small and swarthy, with the delicate hands of a woman.

"I don't got to check," Bo said. "We got one call to Hollywood and Vine last night. A male Cauc killed in a collision with a pole."

"I'll check," Jose said, and went away to get the clipboard with the trip sheets on it. He handed it to Whistler. "See?" he said.

"You're not the only wagon on duty that shift, are you?"

"Hell, no, but that's our district. We do Hollywood," Bo said.

"I could ask the other crews, you want," Jose said, "but I swear to you they don't do Hollywood."

"We do Hollywood."

"We even do the hills," Jose said. "That's very hard, doing the hills. Sometimes we got to carry some heavyweight down stairs that go like this, straight down. Could slip and take a tumble."

"There'd be three dead bodies at the bottom of the stairs," Bo said, underlining the danger of their profession.

"Sometimes we got to pick up people chopped to pieces. I have dreams about it for a week."

"We didn't pick up nobody without a head. Just a male Cauc."

"I'd remember a body without a head," Jose said. "I'da dreamed about it for a week."

"Would a private ambulance or undertaking service ever be called to pick up?" Whistler asked.

"Only if there was a major disaster and we was overloaded."

"Which wasn't the case," Bo said.

"Otherwise, we do the pickup. You could ask around," Jose said.

"Nobody but us would've been called out, and we never picked up no naked woman without her head," Bo said, as though that was that.

"Not ever," Jose said, as though wanting to make clear that he did not share his partner's sensational way of saying things so anybody could get the wrong idea about how serious and solemn their work was.

"Who signed the releases?" Bo asked. "The morgue should have releases. The cops too."

"Can't take a body away unless a coroner's man had had a look and signed a release," Jose added. "So here's the duplicate release on the male Cauc. Look right there. Signed by Dr. Shelley. But nothing on a lady without her head. Dr. Shelley would never have missed something like that."

"That's right, Dr. Shelley's young, but she'd never miss anything like that." ·

"There's no release on the woman at the morgue," Whistler said.

"Well, there you go," Bo said, looking at Whistler levelly. "No release, how could we pick up a body? And we didn't pick up no body without a head at Hollywood and Vine that night."

"Not ever," Jose said, and smiled softly, as though he hoped that would put Whistler's heart to rest.

"What if the police swept it up?"

"Well, that could be different," Bo said, as though the idea in no way startled or offended him. He spread his hand of cards out on the packing case and grinned. A clear winner.

Thirteen

There's an ancient tale from somewhere that says if everybody were to close their eyes at the same moment, the world would disappear. It was three A.M., and Bosco, Canaan, and Whistler, the resident insomniacs, were saving the world from winking out.

They huddled in a booth together, their faces pale moons in the sickly fluorescent light, working on blue tans.

"Billy Durban's passed away," Bosco said.

"Ah, Jesus," Canaan said.

"Why do you say that?" Whistler asked.

"Say what?"

"Jesus. You're a Jew."

"Yes, I'm a Jew. It's just a way of saying I feel sorry about Billy Durban."

"Wondered."

"How tall was Billy Durban?" Bosco said.

Canaan stuck his arm out, his hand hovering above the floor. "Four foot six or seven."

"Little fucker," Whistler said.

"Yes, he was. Had a schlong like a Missouri mule, though. Jimmy Schletter—"

"The producer?"

"That's him. Worked for MGM in the old days. Well, Schletter hired Billy Durban to serve table at a birthday party he gave for his sweetheart, Mary Willibald, over to the old Mocambo. . . ."

Whistler smiled. "I remember Mary Willibald. She was beautiful."

"Couldn't act worth a damn, though," Bosco said.

"But, goddamn, she was beautiful."

"Could stop your heart," Canaan agreed.

"What about the party?" Bosco said.

"Mary Willibald liked them big Polish sausages, you know? You give her a choice—lobster, filet mignon, pheasant under glass, and sausage—she takes the kielbasa every time. It was in her contract that she couldn't eat them but once or twice a year because they was afraid she'd get so fat. So it's her birthday, and Schletter has them serve these great big fat sausages arranged on beds of boiled cabbage. Somebody gets this idea, and they make up a tray of sausages with a hole in the bottom through which Billy Durban sticks his dick and lays it out there with the rest of the sausages on the cabbage. He goes over to Mary Willibald and tells her to make her selection. She don't know the joke, of course, and she's not paying much attention. She gives the tray a quick eyeball and sticks her fork into the sausage she fancies, which is Billy Durban's dick."

They laughed, but not as long or as loud as they might have hoped. Not enough to fill the hollows in the coffee shop.

"Christ, that must have hurt a little," Bosco said.

"Billy Durban let out a yell they heard all the way down to Santa Monica."

"So did Billy Durban sue Jimmy Schletter?"

"No, but Schletter paid off. It's how Billy Durban brought his newsstand over to Sweetzer and Sunset. But that ain't all."

Bosco and Whistler waited for what was more.

"Mary Willibald was so upset about what she accidentally done to Billy Durban's pride and joy that she took him to her own doctor and nursed his joint back to health afterward.

107

That's how come Mary Willibald, who was so beautiful that it could stop your heart, was sweethearts with Billy Durban, who was ugly besides being short, for two years or maybe more. I mean, they said, here was this big sausage, she didn't have to worry getting fat. At least that's what people who liked to tell dirty stories used to say. There were others who said Billy Durban was the sweetest man who ever lived and could sing like an angel."

After a long silence Whistler said, "Whatever happened to Mary Willibald?"

"Oh, you know. Audiences change their minds. The major studios died. She couldn't get pictures back-to-back anymore. The public forgot her. She got old like all of us."

Whistler and Bosco stared at Canaan like children waiting for the happy ending.

"She went back home. North Carolina, I think. Last I heard, she was working as a salesgirl in a five-and-dime and living on her wages."

"She should have gotten professional money management," Bosco said, ever the practical one.

"She did," Canaan said. "That's why she went broke."

"It happened to a lot of them," Whistler said.

"Especially the kids. Mothers and fathers just sent them out to work and spent what they made," Bosco added.

"No more. The courts watch," Whistler said.

"Oh, sure," Canaan said, his voice hard and quick, "the courts watch over the money. But they don't do much for a lot of kids sold for worse than acting in regular motion pictures. There's people do to kids like you wouldn't believe. There was this Episcopal priest down south ran a farm for wayward boys and filmed them in homo orgies for customers all over the country. These other two gazoonies down in New Orleans organized a Boy Scout troop so they'd have a supply of kids for themselves and rich queers from one coast to the other. You wouldn't believe. You wouldn't believe."

Bosco got up, came back with a hot pot of coffee, and poured refills all around.

"My kidneys are floatin'," Canaan said. He got up and walked down the tiles to the toilets.

"I'm going to miss Billy Durban," Bosco said.

"Last night, when the ambulance came to pick up the bodies—"

"Ambulances."

"There was more than one?"

"There was two."

"Why didn't you tell me?"

"It was no part of any conversation we were having."

"Two morgue wagons?"

"One morgue wagon and one from Khymer Mortuary."

"Which one arrived first?"

"The one from Khymer. You're not still sticking your nose in where it don't belong?"

"I've been asking around about this and that."

"Whatever it is, it's nothing to do with you."

"Is that what you think?" Whistler said in a voice meant to warn Bosco off.

"I think when a person's got nothin' to do, anything to do looks like somethin' to do."

Whistler shifted his ass in the booth. "Maybe I should go home before we have a fight."

"Maybe that's a good idea. Go home and stay there," Bosco growled, getting up and going over to sulk on the stool by the register, picking up his ever-present book.

Whistler didn't go. He stayed where he was, his lips moving slightly as though trying to figure out the best way to say something.

Canaan came back, pulling at the front of his pants to settle himself.

"Why don't you shake your dick dry in the bowl?" Whistler said.

"Why don't you raise fucking orchids?"

Whistler leaned over the table. "I want a favor."

Canaan picked up his newspaper, as if he didn't hear a word Whistler was saying.

Whistler tapped the picture of Carl Corvallis. "I want to talk with this gazoony."

"You crazy? Just how in the hell am I going to get you inside

109

to talk to a fucking multiple murderer? Just who the fuck you think I am?"

Whistler didn't want to do it, but he did it. He held Canaan's glaring eyes with his eyes, keeping his own calm and reasonable and undemanding. But reminding Canaan that when the little girl, the daughter of his brother, the apple of Isaac Canaan's eye and the owner of his heart, was plucked up from the playground and . . .

"I can't thank you over and over again for the rest of my life, Whistler. I already told you a hundred times, if it wasn't for you and all you done, my brother and me would maybe never know what happened to . . ."

"I'm not using a thing like that," Whistler said softly. "Look what it says there." He reached over the top of the paper and tapped the photograph of Carl Corvallis. "This fucking monster killer has been reborn in Christ. He is ready to confess his sins. All his sins and all his brother's sins and all the sins of those three asshole members of his crummy little cult who used to say prayers in front of Jesus hung upside down."

"Ready to drop the others in the pot to save his own ass from execution is more like it," Canaan said.

"Oh, sure, we know that. Everybody knows that."

"How could I possibly get you in?"

"His aunt died a week ago. The only person who maybe ever cared about him. She put up five grand to bail him the first time he was arrested. So now she's dead and he's got nobody to bring him cigarettes and candy. I'll be one of these people who go around comforting prisoners. I'll bring the son of a bitch a carton of butts—he should get cancer. And a couple bars of candy—he should have diabetes and die of sugar shock."

"What the hell is all this by way of proving?"

"I just can't help wondering why anybody would've cut off a dead woman's head. I just can't help wondering why so many people are covering it up."

Canaan looked for a minute like he was going to cry, staring into Whistler's eyes and remembering how Whistler had hunted for his niece without pause or rest.

"I'll see what I can do. Stay close to a phone. It could be some crazy hour."

"I'll be at home," Whistler said. "What's crazy hours to men like us?"

Whistler stared at the barren ceiling of his bedroom in his rickety house above Cahuenga and watched the patterns of the raindrops streaming down the window and casting shadows above his head. He listened to the night sounds of the house and the dialogue of the city. It breathed in and out with the sound of bells, whistles, sirens, horns, squealing tires, gunned engines, cat cries, screams, and the distant, muted murmur of restless dreamers.

It was hot and wet. The whole world was under water. He wondered if the way he felt was the way he felt before he was born, floating around in his mother's belly. He closed his eyes and tried to get there, but it wouldn't work. The years were too long and his feet were too big. A creature swam up out of the wet dark.

A phantom lady twined her long legs, wet with rain, around his thighs and belly. Her sweet-smelling hair caressed his neck, threatening to smother him. Her lips were damp in the hollow of his neck.

He reached out for the three-way lamp pinned to the wall and turned on forty watts, then got up from the mattress on the floor, useful remnant of his days of gypsy habits, spare furnishings, and youthful wine and roses, and went to the chest of drawers. Ducking an empty cage that had lost the tenth in a long line of singing feathered tenants just two months before. Never replaced. Having somehow lost the heart for bird song.

He riffled the pages of the telephone directory and found S. Andes listed there as promised. There was only one. Out of all the people in Los Angeles, there was only one S. Andes in the telephone book. Things like that never ceased to amaze him. How could there only be one person of a name in a place as big as La-La Land? It boggled the mind.

He reached for the telephone. It felt cold to the touch, reminding him of the hour. If he called her, she'd have to come swimming up out of sleep to answer. It would take a minute for her to understand that it was a man she had just met calling because he missed her.

He opened the top drawer and took out a little green leatherette address book, sorting it out from others, red and blue and black. It was nearly the oldest of several, saved for numbers no longer useful day to day, preserved for emergency and disaster. It was filled with the names and numbers of old loves, some still in place, still waiting. Not for him. For anybody good and kind enough to take them to Oz or drown them in a garden pool.

Joyce and Teetsa and Lenore and June and Ann and Maggie. No, not Maggie. She was gone. Dead of cancer. Forty-two. Luana and Cynthia and Pat and Elizabeth and . . .

There was a time when he could call at two o'clock in the morning, pleading sleeplessness, pleading loneliness, pleading the trials of his struggles with hope, art, and aspiration. "Oh, you didn't wake me. I was only just dozing off. I don't mind coming over. Give me twenty minutes," one or another would say. And—for the practical yet romantic in it—pleading poverty. "Anything I should bring?" they'd say. "I have a bottle of wine. Twenty minutes. Give me twenty minutes. Don't fall asleep before I get there."

But that game's a game for the young. Poverty and frustrated ambitions are not becoming after thirty. The part gets stale, the plot threadbare.

Whistler tossed the little book back in the drawer with the other dead leaves. He went into the tiny bathroom and relieved himself, listening to his water in the bowl, staring at his face in the mirror above the toilet as if a stranger, meaning to murder him, had finally shown up.

It didn't seem to him that he had slept at all when the telephone rang. When he picked it up, it was Canaan telling him to meet him over at the Rampart jail in twenty minutes.

Fourteen

The rain wouldn't let up. It shot across the freeway in sheets of varying thickness and intensity. The big semis thundered along, throwing up clouds of spray, but there was hardly another car all the way downtown to the Pasadena-Harbor interchange where Whistler peeled off and drove along Temple to the Rampart area jailhouse. It had been built as a pre-arraignment facility but never had been put into service. Every once in a great while it was used for some special purpose. Like keeping Carl Corvallis safe after his offer to roll over on his brother and friends.

Even though it had stood empty for so long, the crowded admittance area still smelled like an old man's crotch.

There were blues and county khakis and detectives and DA's men all over. A few glanced his way when Whistler came through the door, but he was just another cop from yet another jurisdiction as far as most of them were concerned. One or two gave him the leery eye, but he looked sure enough and tired enough to be a cop, so they went back to telling jokes and lies.

Canaan was way in the back, trying to wring another drop

out of the empty coffee urn. He looked at the paper bag under Whistler's arm.

"I stopped at an all-nighter," Whistler said.

"You didn't bring a container of coffee with you, by any chance?"

Whistler put his hands out to his sides, showing them empty, and made a face of apology.

"You should know enough to always bring a couple coffees along when you got an early-morning meeting with a friend."

"Why the hour?"

Canaan stared at him as though he'd like to tear his throat out. "You wanted to see a man, I got right on it. I don't fuck around, a friend asks me for a favor."

"For Christ's sake, don't make me feel bad, Isaac. I asked a favor. I didn't hold a gun to your head."

"Ah, fuck it," Canaan said, patting Whistler's sleeve. "I'm just getting sick and tired of keeping the fucking books straight."

"I can go on home. I didn't mind the drive."

"No, no. Let's walk."

Canaan put down the stained mug and sidled away along the wall toward the door that led to the booking area. Whistler went along. They took it slow and easy, working their way through the mob so nobody would notice them. Just two cops in the crowd.

"Why the convention?" Whistler murmured.

"This crazy asshole, Corvallis, decides to turn state's evidence against his brother and them other three, all of a sudden we got half the agencies in the state claiming a piece of the interrogation. They're even coming in from other counties hoping maybe he'll clear up some of their murdered and missing. Also we got crank calls pouring in, some from gazoonies threatening to blow his fucking head off for bending over, the other half threatening to blow his fucking head off now that he's admitting to some of what he done. So they lay on plenty of protection. Also, everybody's got a suggestion. Put him in a cell by himself down to County, move him around from jail to jail every two hours, send him the fuck down to San Diego for a vacation. Shit! You listen to some of these gazoonies, they're so dumb, you wonder the thieves don't steal Civic Center and the

114

murderers don't walk in and do the city council. Finally somebody shows some sense. They bring the asshole here to Rampart and stick him in the last cell in the old block, which isn't used much anymore."

"Who's running the interrogation?"

"The assistant district attorney's the top dog, but everybody's getting a crack at him. They question him a couple of hours, then let him have a piss and a lay-down. He's on his cot having a kip right this minute."

They were inside the booking area. The holding cage was on one side, the property counter on the other. A deputy on temporary assignment was behind the wire. He glanced up at Canaan and then looked around. Nobody else was there. Canaan tapped Whistler's elbow.

"Pay the man. If you got it, give him fifty."

"I'm getting fiftied to death."

"Get into some other business, or curb your curiosity."

Whistler handed over the fifty, and the deputy let them through.

They walked down one corridor after another, through one chain-link door after another. There was another officer at the door to the cell block. Canaan just gave that one a handshake.

The whole march had given Whistler the blues. It reminded him of the first jail experience he'd had at the Venice area jail a long time ago. Which had looked just like Rampart, except it hadn't been empty. It had seemed like nothing at first. He'd been picked up because a description of a mugger had just been called in and fit him almost like a glove. When the identification didn't hold up, they decided to book and jail him on drunk and disorderly charges, anyway, just so he wouldn't get ideas about unlawful arrest. He'd had a couple of drinks, but he wasn't drunk.

It was a Friday night, and the court wasn't sitting until Monday. He couldn't bail himself out. He was new to town and didn't have friends he could call upon for money. So he was just going to have to wait the two days. Chances were, an old drunk told him, they'd give him two days on the D and D and credit for time served. They worked it neat, so nobody could claim you were too much put upon.

It had seemed to Whistler that he'd just keep his eyes and ears open and chalk it up to experience. Maybe he could use it someday, if ever he should decide to write a film or got a chance to act in a prison picture.

The jail was crowded, mostly drunks and traffic violators, but a fair share of thieves and rapists too. He noticed that the hard types served as trustees in number-one cell. That seemed logical enough. They'd be there longest, they knew the ropes. What difference did it make, anyway? It wasn't prison. Nothing heavy would go down among the population of just a city jail.

The cells were crowded. Each one was supposed to sleep two, but most had a mattress rolled out on the floor for a third, and at night there were even some prisoners sleeping in the corridor inside the outer bars.

He was in a cell with a black thief and a white mugger from Canada being held for extradition. Another black prisoner, a man with a pink scar from eye to chin along one side of his face and small, red-veined eyes that seemed to be without humanity, spent the day sitting on Whistler's rolled-up mattress talking to the others and eyeing Whistler. Who was praying for constipation.

There was one lidless toilet for common use in each cell. Prisoners even washed their handkerchiefs in it and plastered them on the concrete walls to dry. Finally Whistler couldn't take it anymore and had to drop his pants.

The black prisoner, whose name, Whistler remembered with some surprise, had been Jeffers, looked at Whistler's thigh all the while he was at his business. Looked at Whistler's thigh and asked the white mugger if he liked "gibs," which the mugger said he liked all right when there was nothing else available. It didn't take much to figure out that *gibs* was the word they used for a man's ass, and what they had agreed upon was that in the absence of women they would take a man to relieve themselves anytime they could.

That night, as his cell mates, the white mugger and the black thief, settled themselves on their bunks, and he settled himself on the floor, the scarred man called softly from the next cell.

"Hey, Montgomery. You awake, Montgomery?"

The black thief grumbled but finally responded. "What you want?"

"I'll give you a quarter tomorrow night."

"No."

"I'll give you fifty cents."

Whistler had lain there thinking that the one black was soliciting the other. Then the scarred man said, "I'll give you a dollar," and the thief said, "I don't want your money. I want to sleep right where I is," and Whistler understood, with a rush of fear, that the cruel-eyed bastard meant to switch cells and get to him in the night. And he knew that, with the Canadian helping the black, he'd have a hard time fighting them off. And he knew that no matter how much he yelled, no help would come. The guard would be elsewhere, because he'd seen the guard take money from the prisoners for this and that, and he was a prisoner, no better in the guard's eyes than the rest of the animals. A drunk and maybe worse, getting what he deserved for getting thrown into jail. And he'd realized, with a terrible sense of loss, that nobody really gave a rat's ass and that he was alone.

"You're a cold man, Montgomery," the scarred man said, and if he hadn't been so scared and grateful, Whistler would have laughed because it sounded so funny said that way, like a lover cheated of his sweetheart.

"You're white as a sheet," Canaan said, bringing Whistler back.

"I think I'm dead on my feet."

They reached the last cell. Carl Corvallis was lying on his side, curled up around his belly, his folded hands locked between his knees.

"Carl?" Canaan said softly.

Corvallis rolled over on his back, unclasped his hands, and held them over his head, staring up at them, clenching and unclenching them as if they didn't belong to him.

"How long has it been?" he said. His voice was light and uninflected, almost colorless.

"This won't take long."

Corvallis put his hands behind his neck and sat straight up,

117

like a bodybuilder doing sit-ups. "How long have I been asleep?"

He was a broad-shouldered man going to fat. There was a womanly softness about his neck and hands. His skin reminded Whistler of the fat beneath the skin of a slaughtered steer. His eyes were oddly shaped, irregular ovals. The pupils were large from sleep, leaving only a thin rim of green.

"Why can't I have a watch?"

"You could break the crystal and cut your wrists. You could swallow it and choke yourself to death."

"I could bite my veins." He grinned. "I could swallow my dick."

Canaan looked at Whistler and stepped back a pace, as though turning over the proceedings. Corvallis looked sharply at one and then the other, adding them up. Whistler handed him the cigarettes and candy.

"What's this?"

"A few questions."

"What do you mean, a few questions? They take me out of here to another room for questions. They ask me if I want some coffee, something to eat before they start. They do that every time. Now, why didn't you do that?"

"You don't want to eat so much. You don't want to get fat," Whistler said.

Corvallis looked at Whistler carefully. "You're not a cop."

"How do you know I'm not a cop?"

Corvallis shook his head and smiled knowingly, pleased to have put one over, refusing to explain, making a minor mystery of it. He looked at Canaan again. "You're a cop."

"How many corpses are you laying off on your brother and the others? How many are you taking for yourself?" Whistler said.

"Who are you? You the father of somebody?"

Whistler shook his head.

"You a brother, a husband, maybe a sweetheart?"

"They'd never let anybody with a reason to care that much get this close to you," Whistler said.

"I would," Canaan said conversationally. "I'd like to leave you alone with maybe half a dozen relatives of the victims. See what they could do to you with nothing but their hands and teeth."

Corvallis stared at Canaan flat-eyed. "I don't like you."

"That's a compliment."

"What can I do for you?" Corvallis said, turning to Whistler, closing Canaan out.

"Have you cut a deal?"

"Just about. I'm taking diminished capacity on four of them."

"Did you do them all?"

"Who gives a shit? What difference does it make?"

"No difference."

"They'll send me to Vaccaville and bore holes in my head for one, two, three, or four. I'm crazy. I need help. I'm not responsible."

"You don't believe that."

Corvallis smiled.

"I just wondered . . ." Whistler said, then paused.

"What do you wonder?"

"If you hate all women or just prostitutes."

"Read your bible. That'll tell you all you need to know about women. Women and whores, it's the same word."

"All colors?"

"All shapes, sizes, ages, and colors. They've all got the mark on them."

"What mark? You mean, like a flower? Like a butterfly?"

Corvallis smiled. He couldn't figure out what was going on. He couldn't see Whistler's purpose.

"No flower. No butterfly. What the hell are you talking about? The mark they bear is the mark of Baal, who is the first king of Hell, whose domain is in the east and who commands sixty-six legions. One of his three heads is shaped like a toad, another like a man, and the third like a cat." He smiled. "No butterflies."

"Did you do the Vietnamese woman?"

"What would you like me to say?"

"I'd like you to tell me the truth."

"Does it mean a lot to you?"

"It means something. Did you pay somebody to take her head from the morgue?"

Corvallis stared into Whistler's face, hunching himself on his rump along the cot to get closer to the bars.

"O Oualbpaga! O Kammara! O Kamalo! O Karhenmon! O Amagaaa!" he said. Then he fell back on the cot and turned over on his side.

"That gazoony just jacked us off," Canaan said as they walked away.

"He never had anything to do with the Saigon whore. He doesn't know anything about a tattoo. The cops saw how she was carved up, and it looked the same as the others, so they dumped her into the crowd. Why not? Clear the books."

"Was finding that out worth a fifty and a night's sleep?"

"Well, at least I know that what happened to Lim Shu Dok had nothing to do with Corvallis."

"And what does that tell you?"

"It tells me somebody did what they did to her, and Willy Zabadno isn't around to tell us why. It tells me that somebody very important is out there covering up something very bad. I saw the body in the street and I know."

"But nobody knows you know."

"Somebody knows that Shiela Andes saw it too."

William Burchard reached out of his car window and punched the button on the post by the gates. They slowly and silently swung wide, like the opening shot of *Citizen Kane,* the wrought-iron tracery looming so high above the hood of his car that it shredded the midnight fog.

A smell filled the Chrysler like the sharp smell of battery acid or onion fields. The smog never seemed to blow away anymore these days, as it used to do even ten years ago. When the Air Pollution Control Board couldn't bring down the level of emissions, they raised the limits. People kept on breathing thicker and thicker poison and fooled themselves that the air was getting cleaner.

He smiled wryly. A sour taste rose up out of his belly and stung his throat. A testament to old compromises.

He remembered years ago, when he'd been on plainclothes detail, one of the captain's men responsible for enforcement of the city's liquor, narcotics, gambling, and prostitution laws.

They were always pushed for numbers. Arrests for the statistics to prove they were doing the job. A few more each and every year. Every year a few more arrests for this and that than the year before.

Generating the vice numbers created a problem. Gambling and prostitution were protected by politically powerful people, and, then as now, the police were discouraged from going after the sharks and barracudas.

Besides, it was the big mamas and papas who gave birth to the petty pimps, hookers, ass smashers, juice squeezers, child buyers, twangy boys, and street gonifs that, in their numbers, made it possible to score a little better on vice activity each and every year.

Every now and then, of course, some important asshole went too far and stepped into the shit up to his neck. The rest of the pack turned away from the stink and let the cops have him. On those rare occasions sergeants became lieutenants, and lieutenants captains, and captains commanders, and commanders deputy chiefs. If they didn't put a foot wrong and end up with their necks under the knife.

Burchard touched a button, and the electric motor whined as the window rose to shut out the atmosphere that would be delivering slow death with the morning newspaper when the citizens got up and walked outdoors.

There seemed to be no one in the gate house, but he checked the rearview mirror and caught a glimpse of an armed man stepping back through the doorway into the darker dark.

Mushroom lamps illuminated the path, clicking on and off in sequence as needed along the curving route to a private entrance like the way into an underground bunker, the earth bermed up and landscaped on three sides.

Cape himself opened the door.

"Come on in, Bill. What brings you?"

"Just thought I'd sit down for a cup of coffee with you, Walter."

"Well, I'm glad of the chance of thanking you in person for this favor you're doing for me and my friend, Tillman."

"It's no big thing, Walter, but it's not the sort of business I'd want to leave in anybody else's hands."

Cape preceded Burchard along corridors of glass with plants growing on both sides, giving the effect of walking through a twilight garden. Except Burchard felt there was something definitely unreal, otherworldly, about it. Burchard coveted Cape's house even while hating it. He always felt, as he passed from room to room, that he was leaving one stage set and entering another.

"Do you want anything to eat?" Cape said. His voice had the hollow ring of sleeplessness.

"Just coffee. You sound tired, Walter."

They passed through a doorway into a small breakfast room large enough to accommodate four people. Great fleshy, brightly colored blooms swayed on stalks like the limbs of sea creatures in the conditioned air on the other side of the curved glass. Cape gestured to one of the pastel-colored wrought-iron chairs. Burchard sat down heavily as Cape poured two cups of coffee from a silver urn.

The cream was cold and fresh. The sugar bowl filled with colored castor sugar. Burchard wondered who provided such delicate amenities at such ungodly hours.

"You look tired, too, Bill," Cape said.

"I've been running this headless body down since you brought it to my attention. I get a line on her, as you know. Then the man who's been charged with the woman's abduction and murder decided to turn state's evidence and roll over on his accomplices."

"Then you know who killed her."

"I know who's been charged with her murder. There's a difference. He's ready to lay claim to it, though."

"Did anyone ask him why the head was taken?"

"If I ask him that, then somebody asks me where's the head, where's the body."

"Still no idea of what that morgue attendant was doing with the body in the back of his wagon?"

"Not a clue. Aren't you interested in this cult killer charged with the woman's mutilation and murder?"

"The one who's ready to confess to it?"

"He's ready to confess to anything to cut a deal that'll get him into Vaccaville instead of the gas chamber."

"Cult?" Cape said.

"It was in the papers about a year and a half ago."

"Oh, yes. I remember reading about the body of an Oriental woman being kept for evidence. But I don't ever remember any mention that she was tattooed with a butterfly."

"It was held back. We hold back something in every murder case. Every time a body's found, the confessors come out of the woodwork. We have to have something they'd only know if they did the crime."

Burchard took a swallow of coffee and made a face. "I won't be able to sleep what with the sour stomach it's going to give me."

"We pay for our pleasures," Cape said.

"Didn't you have a Vietnamese woman staying here a couple of years ago, Walter? A Vietnamese woman who had a little boy, maybe seven or eight?"

"There may have been an Oriental servant with a child."

"She didn't happen to have a tattoo on her ass, did she?"

"I never looked."

Burchard stood up. The door opened, and a little boy in flannel pajamas ran into the room, grinning and chattering. When he saw Burchard, he became quiet but stared at the policeman boldly. He went to Cape and leaned his belly against Cape's knee.

"What are you doing out of bed?" Cape said.

"It's morning," the boy replied.

"Not yet."

"I'll find my way," Burchard said. When he turned around at the door for a last word, he saw the boy staring into Cape's eyes and rubbing himself against his knee. Cape looked up at Burchard. His stare was challenging, but he gently pushed the child away.

"Something else, Bill?"

"Do you know anyone named Whistler?"

Cape shook his head. "Why do you ask?"

"One of my friends saw this private dick, name of Whistler, down to Rampart where they're questioning this cult killer."

"He has nothing to do with me, Bill."

"Just thought I'd ask."

123

Fifteen

Bouche looked a picture in a chiffon dress
with flounce sleeves and a low bodice. It was printed with huge
red-and-orange poppies. The outfit had a hat, which she
carried in her hand while walking or riding. It now lay like a
flowery centerpiece near the water dripper on the marble-
topped bar in Jimmy Flynn's on St. Peter. She sipped a frappé
concocted of genuine absinthe, not the Pernod poured out for
tourists.

Barcaloo sat pouting at a table nearby, mad because Bouche
liked to perch on a stool at the bar, knowing she made a picture.
He hated sitting on a stool because it showed the world how
short his legs were.

Bouche observed him through narrowed eyes every time his
attention was elsewhere. He'd taken off his light linen jacket.
The hair on his chest, back, and shoulders poked through the
mesh of his net shirt, making him look like one of those baskets
filled with moss in which fleshy, tuberous begonias were grown.
She giggled.

Barcaloo glared at her.

"Something goddamn funny?"

"It's such a nice day. Why shouldn't we have a few laughs?"

"It's maybe a nice day for you. What worries have you got?"

"I could write a book."

"Don't go gettin' drunk on that poison," he said. "When Pinole and Rojo pick up a couple of people, I'll maybe want you to do a little work."

"Oh, no," Bouche said.

"What did you say?"

"Whatsamatter? You got potatoes growing in your ears?"

"What do you mean, 'Oh, no'?"

"Just what it sounds like. I'm not jerking around with some creatures what maybe haven't washed. I ain't going down on some he or she what you picked up out of the gutter. I ain't fuckin' no *amateurs* don't know a goddamn thing about taking care of themselves."

"You're more goddamn trouble than you're worth sometimes," Barcaloo grumbled.

The phone rang behind the bar. It rang five times before the café-au-lait bartender appeared from a well of cool shadows in the back like some blinking animal conditioned to the dark of caves. He picked up the handset and waited to be told. Then he handed it Barcaloo's way.

Barcaloo went over and took it. The bartender stood there staring at him with velvet eyes.

"We're at the studio," Rojo said.

"You picked 'em up without causin' any fuss?"

"It was easy."

"I'm just leaving."

"You bringing Bouche?"

"That's none of your goddamn business," Barcaloo said, and glared at Bouche, who smiled back brightly, knowing that some little thing had just been said to make Barcaloo mad again.

Barcaloo tossed the handset underhanded to the bartender, who caught it on the fly and cradled it in one move. Barcaloo dropped a twenty on the marble counter.

"You know 'Why Don't My Dog Bark When You Come Around?'"

Without cracking a smile the bartender said, "No, but I know 'I Never Harmed an Onion, So Why Should They Make Me Cry?'"

Barcaloo hooted. "Keep the change."

"A pleasure."

"I'm going west pretty soon," Barcaloo said. "I'm going to miss the jokes."

"We'll be here when you come back, Mr. Barcaloo. Everybody comes back to New Orleans, sooner or later, even if it's just to die."

"Come on," Barcaloo said to Bouche.

"I told you," she said, sweetly stubborn, settling her ass on the stool with a little sideways rocking motion, setting her breasts in motion.

"Ah, fuck it, do what you want."

The bartender stepped away quickly, so he wouldn't have to hear what he didn't want to hear.

"Stay here and drink yourself silly," Barcaloo said.

"I got no money."

Barcaloo threw another twenty on the bar.

"Make it last," he said, and went along through the shadows toward the door.

Bouche saw the bartender glancing at her from the sides of his eyes as he busily wiped a glass.

"You don't look sad because I'm leaving town, Henry."

"I'm sad. I'm going to miss you, sweet sweetness."

"This the quiet time of day?"

"You could hear hummingbirds fuck."

"I'm glad you could come, Emmet," Cape said, but did not extend his hand. He walked off down a long corridor, clearly expecting Tillman to follow.

"I wouldn't miss having a look at your house for an Emmy, Walter."

"You show people have an extravagant way of talking."

"I mean it, Walter."

"I'm sure you think you do."

"I really do. You know, a peek at this house is the hottest ticket in town."

"Really?"

"Besides, I have nothing but the highest respect for you, Walter, and a chance to have lunch with you is something I wouldn't miss."

"Then I think you should demonstrate your regard in deeds as well as words, Emmet."

"I don't get your meaning, Walter. Have I done something to upset you?"

"Well, you asked me a favor, then you lied to me."

He opened a door and allowed Tillman to walk ahead of him into the wood-and-leather office.

Tillman's hands suddenly felt cold. He put them in his pockets, then took them out and clasped them in front of his belly as though at prayer. "I never did that, Walter. I never lied to you."

"You failed to say who took Shiela Andes home."

"Who said—"

"At that hour, after that kind of experience, you wouldn't have allowed her to go home without an escort, would you?"

It was a wing shot, but he got his bird. Tillman flinched.

"Oh, that. Well, that I can explain."

"What was the name of the man who took her home?"

"I think his name was Whistler, or something like that."

"Why didn't you tell me?"

"Well, I didn't think it was all that important. It just slipped my mind. I mean, this night owl was sitting there in the coffee shop when the accident happened. He got Shiela out of the car when she fainted. He offered to take her home. What else could I do? I couldn't take her home myself. I couldn't leave the scene. There were no cabs in the street. It was raining. For Christ's sake, I didn't—"

"You're babbling, Emmet. You shouldn't babble."

"It didn't do any harm, did it? I mean, what harm could it do?"

"It's a loose end, Emmet, and I don't like loose ends. They have a way of starting to unravel. They destroy agreements and accommodations."

"You mean like getting the cops to give me a pass?"

"Yes, like that."

"Well, there's nothing to worry about there. Those detectives, Lubbock and Jackson, already screwed a big bribe out of me, so there's nobody around to bring the charge against me anymore, no matter what that cunt or this Whistler says. Those pricks hustled me for a forty-thousand-dollar car."

"You've got to pay for services rendered, Emmet."

"I'm not complaining. I'm just saying I paid to squash an automobile accident with a forty-thousand-dollar foot."

"You forget that I had to use my foot, too, Emmet. And that's worth considerably more to me than any automobile."

"Look, if it cost you any money, I'd be happy to—"

Cape made a face of sharp offense, a kind of rage catching his eyes and mouth and making him look, for a moment, as though he would attack. Then he calmed himself.

"No, no, Emmet," he said very softly. "That's not how I conduct my affairs. In fact, I asked you here this afternoon to offer you an opportunity to *make* some money, not to spend it."

"A business deal?"

"One in which you might not only invest to turn a profit, but for which you might do a little simple casting. The sort of thing that would take up very little of your time. Something you do all the time, anyway."

Tillman was in the dark. He smiled and cocked his head. "I don't do any casting, Walter."

"Whoring," Cape said. "Isn't that what you're doing all the time?"

Tillman was offended. "I never had to pay for a piece of ass in my life."

"I didn't mean to say that you did. Not in cash. You have to understand, just being with a celebrity of your current stature is payment enough for a good many women."

"Oh, sure. Yeah. Well, I see what you mean," Tillman said, jerking his chin up out of his collar and rotating his head a little like a parrot preening. "You want me to audition some actresses for some film you've got in mind?"

"A number of films."

"What's the concept?"

"Sex, Emmet."

"That's good. Sex is always good."

"Hard-core."

Tillman frowned. "Not so good. I couldn't have anything to do with X-rated."

"Oh, yes, you can." Tillman understood that Cape was calling in his marker.

* * *

Barcaloo liked the Lincoln. Its suspension smoothed the road and made it handle like a boat on still water, its air conditioning chilled the air, and its steering and braking systems made the tons of hurtling metal as easy to handle as a baby buggy. It closed out the city that steamed and rotted outside the machine's tinted windows. L.A. would be different. Warm days but cool nights. Sun on the beaches, fog on the hills. A few rainy days that didn't turn the land into swamp. Fuck the smog. He could live with the smog.

Barcaloo scorned the smooth and easy way out of the French Quarter, avoiding Interstate 10, which crossed the Mississippi at the Greater New Orleans Bridge, and U.S. 90, which connected up with Barataria Road over in Jefferson Parish. Instead he threaded the maze of streets with historic names inside the quarter, until he picked up St. Charles at the Lee Circle and Monument, west to Jackson, then south to the ferry.

He leaned on the rail going across the river, his throat clogging on the hot, wet breeze kicked by the ferry's passage, thinking about L.A. and the army of women that descended on the town each and every year. The green crop that was nothing but fertilizer for his fields. He chewed them up, but he didn't find much nourishment in women, not even Bouche most of the time. He felt like he was always mourning.

It was the lost sister he grieved for. Women like his sister, Barcaloo knew, were very hard to come by. But she was dead, her sex cut out by a pimp who used up women too.

The Lincoln banged over the iron ramp leaving the ferry-boat, and Barcaloo headed to Fourth where he turned west again until he hit Barataria Road. South again through the thicket of streets until they thinned out just beyond Estelle as the road cut through the Bayou des Familles.

Barcaloo shut off the air conditioner and punched the down buttons on all the windows so that the wet, hot wind, smelling of mud and rot, came in and filled the Lincoln like water in a bathtub. He leaned back, holding the wheel steady at arm's length, and half closed his eyes, admitting to himself with a surge of regret that he loved the heat and the enveloping damp, loved the silence of the bayous and the overhanging branches of the cypress fingering the still waters covered with a film of duckweed. The bayous had been as much the playground of his boyhood as the streets of the Vieux Carré. It was where he'd been able to be the animal he secretly believed himself to be, different from other men.

All at once he was not so sure he wanted to leave it all, big time or no big time. He quickly stripped his shirt off over his head and felt better for it, closer to himself.

The dirt track running along the subsidiary stream could hardly be seen, no more than a small wound in the heavy tangle of greenbrier and resurrection fern. Barcaloo could have found it with his eyes closed. Two miles down the twin ruts the road opened up into a clearing carelessly surfaced with gravel, rubble, and an amateurish pour of black asphalt giving way with small resistance to the fungi that burst through like tumors on a turtle's back. Then the palmetto and fern took over again. The Cadillac with the Bondoed fender and a red four-door with a vinyl top were parked side by side.

Barcaloo ran up the windows to keep the bugs out of the car. He put on his shirt while cursing to himself.

"Son of a bitch, why they have to bring the asshole's goddamn car along? Now we got to dump it *and* the Cadillac in the bayou. Can't keep filling up the goddamn bayou with cars and old wrecks. Pollute the goddamn streams and swamps. Rusting away, leaking oil and gas. For Christ's sake, why can't them two use their brains? What brains? They ain't got any brains. Between them, maybe they got half a brain. Maybe . . ."

The footpath chopped through the dry patch ended at a metal-sided, tin-roofed Quonset hut. An idle generator, colored yellow and rust, squatted like some huge swamp animal ten yards to the side, stacks of red gasoline cans huddled nearby like the creature's pups.

". . . a quarter of a brain. Look at that. They ain't even turned the goddamn generator on. For Christ's sake."

He went over and punched the starter button. The generator coughed and kicked over without hesitation, revving up to speed and settling down to a low roar, a piece of machinery often used. The smaller hinged door in the sliding barn door flew open, and Pinole stood there with his hand inside his jacket.

"Look at you," Barcaloo said, waving him aside. "You reaching for a gun?"

"Just scratching myself," Pinole lied.

"Some nosy sheriff comes to have a look at this building, you meet him at the door scratching yourself like that and he blows your balls off."

"I never thought," Pinole said.

"You don't got to tell me that," Barcaloo said, pushing past Pinole into the big shack. "You never think. What's that asshole's car doin' here?"

"They was very ditsy so I drove with him, and Jickie drove the girl so they'd think they could leave when they wanted." Pinole frowned. The slow birth of a thought was visible. "Hey, how come you knew it was the asshole's car?"

"Oh, for Christ's sake. How dumb can you get? Was we expectin' visitors? It's like a fuckin' oven in here. Why didn't you kick over the goddamn generator, get the cold air blower goin'? Where's them two?"

"Jickie's keeping them busy back by the dressing rooms."

"Jesus Christ, somebody's doin' something right. So introduce me."

Barcaloo put on his jacket and smoothed his wind-shagged hair with the palms of his hands, using his sweat for hair dressing, as they walked across a concrete floor scattered with snakes of cables; switch boxes; tripods for screens, shades, and filters; a thirty-five-millimeter camera on a western dolly; and all the rest of the paraphernalia needed to shoot moving pictures. He perked the collar of his shirt and flashed his teeth, intending to look amiable but managing instead to look like a piranha ready to slash and tear.

Chippy Byrd and Lacy Ohio were sitting on folding wooden chairs, white-faced and wide-eyed, staring like rabbits fixed in place by the menace in Rojo's eyes.

When Rojo said, "This is Mr. Barcaloo," Lacy Ohio wet her pants.

Sixteen

Whistler had called S. Andes, and nobody had answered. He'd called three times. The last time he'd let the phone ring in her apartment for five minutes by the clock before hanging up.

The pink stucco apartment house looked like a cake that was inhabited by hookers about to jump out of it any second. Whistler found a spot for his Chevy at the curb.

In the open entry there were banks of mailboxes flush with the wall on one side and a board of brass nameplates and bell pushes on the other. The idea was to find the apartment, push the button, identify yourself, and wait until they buzzed you past the wrought-iron gates.

Whistler pushed the button beside S. Andes's name just to give her warning that someone was on the way up. But the gate was busted and open, so he walked right through.

The smell of chlorine rose up, sharp as a runner's sweat, from the pool in the center of the three-story complex. Whistler knew the pool was bigger than most of the apartments, bachelor affairs fit for bed, bath, and breakfast only. And maybe nights of watching television alone.

It was a commune for the hopeful and the hopeless. Young actors, actresses, bar hookers, and upwardly mobile thieves on one end of the age scale. Retired grips, failed writers, and forgotten pinball players on the other end.

On warm nights and on long weekends there'd be a lot of action around the pool.

Oiled bodies that sold for a buck a pound. Old men floating on inner tubes, sad because there were no skirts to look up. Old ladies looking cute in sundresses with desperate smiles painted scarlet. Cold metal glasses full of booze and fruit in hand. Waiting to be invited to a party. Parties going on in one single or one bedroom and another, all around the upper tiers. Sophisticated boys and girls in jeans bleached almost white, leaning one ass cheek on the railings and looking over the edge, down into the blue heaven of the pool, wondering if they had the guts to take a dive and call it quits.

But when it rained, the pool just lay there and dimpled helplessly under the beating of the raindrops. Melancholy but full of promise. Things can get better if you wait long enough. Any pool in the rain can tell you that.

Shiela's hutch was on the top floor. The doors marched around and around, distinguished only by their scars and numbers. Whistler knocked on 312. There was no answer. He stuck his face against the glass and tried to see through the curtains if there was a lamp lit. The place was gray and empty.

No one watched that he could see. The lock was easy.

The apartment had the feeling of a viewing room in a Pasadena undertaking parlor, genteel but very cold. A ceiling-washer lamp, like a giant plastic tulip stuck in a black plastic base, stood on commercial carpeting engineered to last a thousand years. A convertible couch had been pulled out so many times, one metal elbow had broken free.

The couch sat next to the doorway into the kitchenette. The sink was full of clean dishes, stacked and draining. A geranium burned on the sill of a little window above the sink that looked out twenty feet, across to the green stucco cake next door.

There was still the bathroom and the closet. Whistler didn't want to look. He was afraid of what he might find.

The closet was jammed with clothes and shoes.

The bathroom was empty. The bottom of the tub was still wet. The shower head above the tub dripped a tear. The place smelled of young woman and promises.

Whistler went back to the closet and counted sweaters, skirts, and coats. The days were warm, but nights cold, in La-La Land. He couldn't know how many of anything a woman like Shiela might have, but he was sure there would not be much surplus everyday underwear. It wasn't seen, so it wasn't stockpiled. Ladies did a lot of rinsing out of small things every night. He remembered the wet fright of nylons in his face when he'd stumbled into strange bathrooms in the dark after half a night of love.

But when they traveled, they took it all, every silky scrap. Every bra and halter. Or nearly all. There was only a pair of holed cotton briefs and two pairs of panty hose, laddered and toeless, in one drawer of the little chest.

He looked for bathing suits. The three rolled up in a bottom drawer were old and used, meant for swimming. There should have been a new one meant for show.

There was a scattering of small change, nickels and pennies, and a couple of new bills on top of the lace runner on the dresser. Whistler picked up the paper money. It wasn't real. It was play money advertising an adult movie house called the Beaver Run. Where it reads "Federal Reserve Note" on a dollar bill, it read "Fun and Fucking Frolic." There were women's legs with garters instead of the shields and lunettes at the corners. Washington had a grin on his face. Instead of the denomination printed out underneath, it was printed "Twoferone." On the green side was a bad drawing of the movie house in one circle and another bad drawing of a tangled couple in the other. The name of the movie house on top, the address on Poeyfarre Street in New Orleans on the bottom.

"If you're a cat burglar, you're lousy at it," a voice said at his back. It had the warm roughness of a bare foot scraped along a thick-piled rug.

Whistler folded the funny money and tucked it into his waistband. He turned around to face the lady that went with the voice.

She was tall, and as broad-shouldered as a man. No padding

in the shoulders of the dressing gown. One heavy, shapely leg was exposed by the slit in the skirt, a foot in a pink mule planted on the floor like she was about to have her picture taken for a girlie magazine. Red hair down to her shoulders.

Whistler figured her to be vintage fifty. Bottled in bond. Cellar reserve.

"You won't make your million scratching around kitty-litter boxes like this one," she said.

"I'm a friend," Whistler said, taking an easy step forward, as though he were ready to go.

She backed up, and he saw the little gun that was nearly lost in the palm of her big hand.

"For Christ's sake," he said, "you must be kidding."

"Gimme a name," she said.

"Whistler."

"Not yours, sucker."

"The lady's name is Shiela Andes. But it's not her real name."

"So, what's her real name?"

"That I don't know. I'm a new friend."

Her eyes flickered over him, as if she were thinking of patting him down. Whistler had the thought that he might not mind.

She tucked the little automatic in her pocket and sat down on the sofa.

"You're not afraid of me anymore?" Whistler asked. "What did I do or say to convince you I was harmless?"

"Hell," she said, grinning wide enough to show white teeth too bright to be her own, "I haven't been afraid of a man since I was twelve and kicked my uncle's balls in for trying to put his hand down my pants."

"So why the gun?"

"I said I wasn't afraid. I didn't say I was stupid. You can sit."

Whistler sat down on the other end of the sofa.

"Where'd you meet Shiela?" she asked.

"In a coffee shop. I brought her home night before last."

"She was out with Emmet Tillman night before last."

"He was half in the bag."

She nodded as though she'd heard that song before.

"Old-fashioned boy. He doesn't do drugs," she said.

135

"That's what he told me."

"He a friend of yours?"

"New acquaintance."

She laughed, short and sharp.

"Something funny?" Whistler asked.

"I like your style. The man's an acquaintance, the woman's a friend."

"That's how it feels."

"I got you. I can see it in your face."

"What's that?"

"You like women. You really like women. Maybe that's what made me put the guy away."

She readjusted her big body on the sagging couch, swaying toward him as though unconsciously attracted, moving her legs so one knee jutted toward him, making a statement about her naked thigh.

"Did you have a date with Shiela?"

"No. I was concerned," Whistler said. "I called and nobody answered. So I came to see for myself was everything all right."

"You see anything?"

"She's out of town. Someplace hot this time of year."

"She got called to New Orleans."

"A call from who and why?"

"From some producer for a picture. They had an actress down there, he said, got dysentery. Couldn't work. They needed a replacement right away. Featured part. An opportunity."

"How'd he come to pick Shiela? He call her agent?"

"No, the producer remembered her from a party they'd both been at six months ago. Shiela doesn't have an agent at the moment. She dumped him when he tried to peddle her ass to a visiting investor one weekend."

She put her hand on her bare thigh, up near her crotch.

"Shiela didn't like that," Whistler said.

"Hey, she's no fool. We women sell ourselves all the time. But there's sales and sales. You know? White-flower sales. Clearance sales. Year-end sales. Rainy-day sales."

Her eyes were nearly green. The color of her hair was her own and not dyed for drama. There was a spray of freckles across the tops of her sun-stained breasts. Whistler knew there'd be sprays across her hips and flanks as well. Like a strawberry roan Appaloosa mare. Just as wild and sturdy to ride.

"What's Shiela's real name?" Whistler asked, looking at the woman's cheek.

"My name's Katherine," she said, looking at his mouth.

"No, Shiela's real name."

"Shiela Ajanian."

"You think it's funny this producer remembers an unknown actress for six months after meeting her once at a party?"

"I think everything that happens in this goddamn town is funny, Whistler. What the hell can I do about it? Everybody's so goddamn hungry for something, you can't tell them anything could be poison. Anything at all."

Whistler leaned forward, ready to stand up.

"Everybody's got to take their own chances," Katherine said. She moved her hand from her leg to his.

"It's a sad, rainy day," she said. "This couch opens up."

"Will you show me how it works when I get back from New Orleans?" Whistler said.

Seventeen

Barcaloo was talking Chippy Byrd and Lacy Ohio out of their clothes, scaring them out of their jeans and T-shirts; Byrd proclaiming the superior qualities of a motor oil that had more "Go!"; Ohio frankly declaring, "Make an offer."

"Lookit here, little pigeon, you got no cause to wee-wee," Barcaloo said, reaching over to lay his hand on Lacy's knee.

"I'm scared to death," she whispered.

Chippy's hand was in his crotch, preventing the same accident that happened to her from happening to him.

"Who scares you?" Barcaloo said, his smile slipping up and down across his teeth like they were coated with butter. "Nobody wants to scare you."

"They scare me," Lacy said, looking first at Pinole, then at Rojo, then back again. Back and forth, back and forth, rattling her brain. Finally landing on Rojo, who sat unsmiling next to Barcaloo, leaning forward with the terrible stillness of a snake. "He scares me," she went on, too afraid to say that it was Barcaloo who terrified her most.

"What's to be scared of?" Barcaloo said. "I know. It's the way Jickie looks at a person. That scares you. He's a cameraman.

138

He's got the eye, you know what I mean? He even looks at me sometimes like I got a wart on my nose. I ask him what the hell he's looking at. He tells me 'eff four five with a thirty.' I ask him what the hell 'eff four five with a thirty' means."

"What does it mean?" Chippy asked, trying to convince himself that they were just a bunch of new acquaintances having an interesting conversation.

"Something about how much you got to open the camera lens. How the fuck do I know what it means?" Barcaloo said, losing control for a second, finding the part of smooth operator getting on his nerves. He grabbed hold of himself and oiled up his manner again. "It's the way cameramen talk. He talks like that, and Pinole, over there, talks like 'two hundred decibels, testing one, two' fucking 'three.' He takes care of the sound mixing. How do I know what they mean when they talk like that? I'm the producer and director. I come at the business from the creative angle. You unnerstan' that? We make adult films, you unnerstan' that?"

"Oh, yes," Lacy said, wanting to believe every word he was saying, feeling a sickness in the middle of her belly, caused by the stroking motion of Barcaloo's soft, pudgy hand. It was like the touch of one of those creatures that squatted wet and slimy on the end of a log sticking up out of the wetlands.

"So, we're all grown-ups, here, wanting to make a couple dollars, right?" Barcaloo said. "You two are celebrities. You unnerstan' that? You got your faces in the newspaper half the people in the country buy at the supermarket."

"We didn't mean nothing—" Chippy said.

"What do you mean, you 'didn't mean nothing'? That's what that guy said what fingered Willie Sutton. You know from Willie Sutton, the bank robber? Ahh, you two is probably too young to remember Willie Sutton. This schmuck fingered him for the reward . . ."

"Nobody give us no reward."

". . . but that wasn't enough for him. He wants to be famous too. So he shoots his mouth off and gets his picture in the papers. Just like you . . ."

"We didn't mean nothin'," Lacy said, adding her whining voice to Byrd's old beggar's tune.

"And some friends of Sutton's blows this asshole's fuckin' head off. You unnerstan' what I'm sayin'?"

"Oh, Jesus, Mary, and Joseph, have mercy on us," Lacy whispered.

"Hey, wait a minute," Barcaloo said heartily, grinning like a car salesman. "Don't misread my meaning. What are we talkin' about here? We're talkin' about gettin' your pictures in the *Enquirer*. What does that tell me?"

"That we talked about something we shouldn't've talked about."

"It tells me you got an eye for publicity. You know you got to have an edge, and you go out and find an edge. It's a goddamn jungle out there in this land of glitter and swank, ain't that right? Now, don't tell me, let me tell you. Both of you want to be in show business. Did I hit it on the nose? Did I score a bull's-eye?"

Lacy smiled and looked at Chippy. Here was a guy talking about show business. Nobody's even mentioned what they didn't mean to say nothing about. That they spilled the beans about who dropped the head by the lake. What he was doing was making them an offer to be in the movies.

Chippy knew she was staring at him, but he couldn't take his eyes off Barcaloo. He couldn't help himself, he had to ask the question, the answer to which would probably kick the hell out of the pile of shit Barcaloo was shoveling and land him and Lacy facedown in it.

"You ain't mad about we described the car and this camera-man and sound man of yours?"

"Why should I be mad? We was workin' out a little scenario, you unnerstan'? Workin' out this little scene for a horror film we're gonna shoot as soon as we raise the finances. You know, like that crap the kids like to scream at."

"But the head. The newspapers and television said it was a real head."

"So what do they know? Ain't they a bunch of liars? Ain't they in show business too? Nobody's mad at nobody here. No, indeed. We're just a bunch of grown-ups out to make a buck. You get people to pay attention to you, that makes you a commodity. So, unless you got some better offers, I'm ready to give you a chance to cash in." He grinned invitingly.

"What do you want us to do?" Lacy asked, quicker to succumb to his sweet poison than Chippy, who still hung back, saving his enthusiasm for the time he was out of the bayou and home again.

"We just want to do what you already do."

"What's that?"

"Take off your clothes and fuck each other."

Whistler had no trouble getting through the studio gate. He'd laid down a story a year before, and the guards still thought he was the studio's cocaine connection. Who's going to question the credentials of a cocaine connection?

Whistler felt a little heartsick every time he visited this particular lot, lying in the sun just outside the shadow of the hills. His memories were offended by the executive tower that seemed to stare down on everything, a surveillance post that turned the reflections of white clouds black, monitoring the heartbeat of the magic-making machine, stunning the spirit with its impression of impersonal power. He hated the other building, which looked like a birthday cake, terrace on top of terrace, the hanging gardens of Babylon overgrown with fleshy succulents and cacti that lived on bone dust. He hated the commissary where the tourists crowded in, hoping to see a television favorite drinking a glass of beer.

Whistler remembered the studio when it had been a collection of soundstages and cottages scattered on green lawns. The rabbits had come down out of the hills. Deals were made and pictures put into production over a cup of coffee.

He drove to the soundstage where Tillman's cop show was shooting and parked in a no parking zone. Drug dealers took privileges nobody else would dare take.

There was a BMW parked in Tillman's reserved piece of curb. But it wasn't the car crushed in the accident. It was a brand-new one, slick and black, the interior bloody with red leather.

The red light was on over the door of the soundstage. A bell rang, and the light winked off. Whistler went through the lock into the air-conditioned soundstage and the noise of loud voices and hustle. Whistler strolled down toward the action, passing technicians running cable and shifting lights. They wore tool belts and black satin jackets with the name of the show stitched on the back. Hollywood warriors advertising the fact that they were employed.

Tillman was sitting in a canvas chair with his name on the back. A pretty girl was sitting next to him in the director's chair. Tillman's hand was high up on her thigh, casually placed there, declaring ownership, or at least deciding whether to have her on approval. A knit cap was pulled down over his hair. There was a wipe of grease on his cheek. He looked easygoing and tough. He looked real.

The skinny black actor who played Tillman's partner in the series sat in his chair, leaning forward, making a joke into Tillman's face, his eyes glancing away to the girl's breasts. Tongue flicking out to wet his lips. Sending a message. Invitation to her. Challenge to Tillman.

Tillman watched, sleepy-eyed. Amused. Sure of himself. He had the girl briefed. No dark meat at this turkey dinner if she expected to stay. He glanced over at Whistler's approach. His eyes looked worried. Whistler liked him for a minute. Tillman was, after all, just a guy who'd scrambled and fought to make it and had made it big. Found out there were burdens went with the blessings. The world changed around you, people changed around you. While you were counting your money and dropping your drawers, people learned to hate you and dreamed of your death. Lousy people.

Tillman stood up, looking annoyed. He put his hand straight out, showing Whistler the palm, telling him to back off.

"Who let you on my goddamn set?"

Whistler kept walking. He spoke in a low voice.

"I see you got yourself a new 'squeeze.' You don't want me to queer the deal for you, do you?"

"What the hell do you want?"

"I'd like to know if you called your lawyers like you said you were going to do on St. Swithen's night."

"On what?"

"July the fifteenth. The night of your accident."

"What accident?"

"Ah, Christ, now you believe you weren't even there."

"Wherever 'there' is, I wasn't. I was home in bed with a good book."

"You're a kinky son of a bitch, ain't you? If you didn't call your lawyers, who did you call?"

"Go fuck yourself."

"You decide to let Shiela put the arm on you, after all?"

"You're speaking Swahili."

"Did you get some friend of yours to offer her a job over to New Orleans?"

"What kind of job?"

"That's what I'm here asking."

"I don't know what you're talking about."

Whistler read him and believed he was telling the truth. He took a wild shot; it didn't cost him anything.

"I see you got a new car."

The worried look flickered in Tillman's eyes again. There was something about the car. What about the car?

"I get a new car whenever I want to get a new car."

"I guess."

"Get the fuck off my set or I'll have you tossed."

"You know, I think you're really a nice guy underneath all that shit."

"This ain't workin'," Barcaloo said.

Chippy stood there naked. His body was white and skinny. His penis and scrotum were darker, like the skin of his face and arms. His tool hung flaccidly between his thighs, all shriveled up like some small creature trying to find a place to hide. He had the urge to cover his groin with his hands, but something told him that a modest gesture like that would incite Barcaloo to more rage.

"I'm sorry," he mumbled.

"What's to be sorry? I thought I was dealing with a couple of professionals here, and instead I get a scared kid."

"Well, maybe it's because me and her only done it once."

"In the back of Chippy's car," Lacy said.

"You can't afford a bed? You can't afford all night?"

Lacy laughed. "I got a grandmother." She lay as naked as Chippy but more at ease, on a couch over which a paisley shawl had been thrown. She wasn't so scared anymore. She'd even been oddly excited by three men watching her as Chippy first warmed her up with his mouth at her crotch, then tried to penetrate her with his unworkable tool. She felt almost good with the hot lights warming her body. The man with the terrible eyes was hiding them behind the camera most of the time. The lens explored her body with the impersonal eye of a phantom lover.

"So all right," Barcaloo said, as though accepting that as sufficient answer and sufficient reason. "He was friendly to your crotch, you be friendly to his crotch. You got any objection to that?"

"Jeez, I don't know. I never done none of this . . ."

"Don't kid me."

". . . in front of nobody before, except the person I was doing."

"So try it. That's all I'm askin'. Just try it."

Chippy walked over to her in his bare feet. They left damp marks on the dusty concrete floor.

My God, Lacy thought, Chippy's so scared, he's sweating from his feet. He stood there in front of her, slightly spread-legged. She got to her knees on the mattress and ducked her head, feeling all her body parts growing weak again. Thoughts she'd managed to brush away told her Chippy's instinct for danger was better than her own. She looked up along the plane of his belly and the rise of his chest, past his scrawny neck and little chin, the somewhat protruding teeth, and long, thin nose, to his eyes, big as saucers, sending messages she would rather not read.

It was important to perform well, to do what pleased the hairy man with the awful hands and the man with the funny eyes. That was the path to safety and salvation.

"You got to do it right," she whispered, her lips brushing Chippy's flesh. "You got to do good. You got to get it up."

The grease on the cheek of the man at the police impound was honest grease. Workingman's grease. When Whistler stuck

144

IN LA-LA LAND WE TRUST

out his hand to introduce himself, the man shook his head and said, "I got dirty hands."

"Okay," Whistler said, and kept his hand stuck out there. The mechanic wiped his hand off on a rag and shook.

"My name's Chester Wendt," he said.

"How do the shifts in this garage work out?"

"Monthly rotation."

"Change over on the first?"

"That's right."

"So you were working last out on July fifteenth?"

"Sure I was."

"You remember a silver BMW brought in?"

"Front-end collision? Radiator punched?"

"That's the one."

"Who are you? I think I should ask to see something," Wendt said with an average man's natural suspicion.

"I'm not official."

"Then we shouldn't be talking about police business."

"Insurance business too?"

"Oh, I gotcha."

"I mean, how bad was it?"

"The BMW?"

"Yeah, the silver BMW."

"Them things is built pretty good. The radiator was leaking and the fenders was crumpled. That's all."

"The owner come to take it out of impound?"

"Somebody else come with the pink."

"You recognize him?"

"Sure I recognized him. It was Detective Lubbock."

Well, well, well, Whistler thought, not a bad night's divvy for the cops. And, one way of looking at it, a bargain for the actor who would have been up to his nostrils in the shit.

"Lubbock drive it away?"

"He had it towed to a dealership," Wendt said.

"You know which one?"

"The one on Wilshire down in Santa Monica."

"Well, thanks."

"Maybe I shouldn'ta told you that."

"Why not? What's the big deal? Anybody tell you *not* to talk about it?"

"No," Wendt said, still doubtful about what he might have given away.

"So there you go," Whistler said. "I owe you a beer."

"Forget it." Wendt set his jaw a certain way, like he was angry but didn't know what about. "What the hell's going on with Lubbock and that BMW?" he finally blurted out.

Whistler grinned. "You want me to write it out for you?"

"Son of a bitch," Wendt said, mad as hell that he was in no position to climb aboard the gravy train.

After an hour it was still no soap. Barcaloo felt the rage building up in his belly and chest again. This goddamn Chippy Byrd wasn't useful. The girl maybe could be useful, except she had practically no tits and all kinds of pimples on her chest and ass. Besides, there was no way of keeping one around without the other. No real reason, either.

"Look, just get on top of her and fake it. You know what I mean? Just sort of jump up and down on her and we'll get the camera in close. Later on we'll cut it up. We'll make it look okay. Just do like that, you unnerstan'?"

Lacy started to cry again. That got Chippy crying too.

Barcaloo left his canvas director's chair and walked around behind Rojo and the camera. He patted Rojo under the arm and felt the gun.

"Do 'em," he mumbled. "And make sure you got her face in close-up when she finally sees that's she's gonna be snuffed."

He turned away and started to leave. Lacy let out one hell of a scream, like she was already dying.

Barcaloo came back, his face screwed up in rage.

"Well, don't fuckin' blame me. You people got to learn not to shit on my parade."

Eighteen

The dealership over on Wilshire was only a stop. Whistler just walked on through, looking for the silver BMW. He didn't see it. When the service manager told him he should learn to read signs that told customers they weren't allowed in the garage where the work was being done and asked Whistler what he wanted, Whistler said he was looking for a silver BMW and was told they didn't have any in the shop, but if he wanted new, they could satisfy him in the showroom.

He drove up and down the blocks around the dealership and found the car parked behind a drugstore in a nearby shopping center. It didn't take a lot of smarts to know that some mechanic would be running the car through for repairs at night. Everybody steals a buck now and then, one way or another.

Just like he really didn't expect the BMW to be out there for anybody to see, the headless body of the woman wasn't there at Khymer Mortuary, either. The pie-faced, dark-suited man with the silk rep tie and hands that kept washing one another was adept at lying.

Whistler went away wondering why he was double-checking on things he already knew. A heavy snow had fallen on the situation surrounding the body of a Vietnamese whore. Why should he give a damn? There was nothing in it for him. He might as well go home to the little house he owned above Cahuenga Boulevard and lay in bed waiting for it to fall down the hillside. Worry about something sensible for a change, instead of some woman who didn't have sense enough to pull her leg in out of the rain.

The animals were tuning up for the long night in the dusk outside the rickety soundstage. Birds were screaming and gators booming.

Pinole was sitting on one of the canvas director's chairs staring first at his hands and then at the two pitiful white bodies, tangled with one another and splashed with red, lying on the daybed.

Rojo came back from propping the side door open. Out of the wetlands came the sounds of a struggle. Two animals locked in fatal combat. The screams and thrashing came into the wood-and-metal Quonset through one of those "windows" in trees and underbrush that acts like a megaphone. It was like the killing was taking place right at Pinole's feet. A last terrified scream was cut right in half.

"I don't like doing this kind of thing," Pinole said.

"What kind of thing?"

"Doing people like they don't know why we're doin' them."

"Since when you get delicate?"

"I always been delicate. I mean, I do what I got to do, but I don't like it when we do them when they're naked and going at it."

"Well, they wasn't going at it. That's just the point, ain't it? I mean, if that asshole coulda done what he was supposed to do, he'd still be alive now, wouldn't he?"

Pinole thought about that. "But we woulda done them later just the same. With the cameras running and them without no clothes."

"That's the idea of it, ain't it?"

"Maybe we shouldn't be making such pictures."

"Christ, we don't make the market. I mean, people make the

148

market, ain't that right? They're out there buying or we wouldn't be selling."

"Well . . ." Pinole said. He took a plastic pill container out of his pocket, opened it, and poured a small mound of cocaine on the curve of his thumb and the knuckle of his first finger. He brought it up to his right nostril and snuffed it. Then he did the same for the left.

"You want some?"

"You stop staring at your hands, I take a snort with you?" Rojo said.

"I don't like to touch them when they got no clothes on."

Rojo took the vial and did the way Pinole had done.

"We better not get too crazy," Pinole said. "Barcaloo wouldn't like it."

"Fuck him. Come on and help me push that sucker's goddamn car into the swamp," he said.

Pinole followed him out into the gathering dark. Rojo opened the door to the red four-door and released the hand brake.

"You like the color of this car?" Pinole asked.

"Yeah, I like it okay. You like it?"

"I like the red. I don't like the black vinyl top."

"Vinyl tops is no good in the heat."

"Goddamn sun cracks them up like tar paper sooner or later."

"This would be a good color for the Cadillac," Rojo said.

"Barcaloo wants we should dump the Cadillac in the god-damn bayou," Pinole said.

Rojo was on the driver's side with one hand pushing against the window frame and the other grasping the door molding. "You going to help me push this fuckin' thing?"

Pinole got in the back and leaned his considerable bulk against the sedan. It was heavy going only for a second, then they got it rolling. Rojo stopped pushing and just walked alongside, touching the steering wheel when the car needed to be kept on the track down to a dark place where mud and water met.

When the front wheels resisted, Rojo got in back with Pinole, and together they pushed it out far enough for the hood to tilt.

The sedan sank down into a deep spot like a liner going under in the sea. After a minute an oily bubble burst on the surface and sent out concentric rings of shimmering iridescent color.

"Beautiful," Pinole said.

"I don't want we should dump the Cadillac," Rojo said. "I always liked that automobile. It give us good service."

"You heard what Barcaloo said."

"I don't give a fuck what Barcaloo said. We just put a new engine in it twenty thousand miles back."

"That's true," Pinole said.

They walked back to the soundstage. Night fell. One second there was still a little glow left in the sky, the next it was as black as the bottom of the bayou where the sedan now rested. The rehearsal light inside made the doorway a bright rectangle on velvet.

"Look," Rojo said, "we could take the Cadillac to that chop shop over to Steerage Avenue. They bake the color on right there. What could it take if we ask the favor? Maybe three hours. Maybe less."

"Barcaloo . . ."

"So if Nonny gets pissed off, we ditch the fucking Cadillac then! After he sees what we done to it. After he sees nobody is going to mistake a red Cadillac for a white one with a Bondoed fender."

"There's an idea," Pinole said.

"Fuck, yes."

"We better hurry we want to get over to the paint shop tonight."

"You're right. Maybe we should get over there soon as we can, get the job done."

They hurried across the floor to the daybed. Pinole rubbed his hands together. "Oh, shit," he said.

"There's some work gloves on that tripod over there," Rojo said.

Pinole went to get them. They scarcely fit, but he dragged them on over his heavy knuckles, anyway, as Rojo watched, annoyed and amused at his partner's touchiness.

"We shoulda put them in the car first before we dumped it," Pinole said.

"What the fuck's the difference?"

"We dump them in the mud, the gators and other creatures will come drag them out for supper just like that other creature did with the head."

"You got a point."

Pinole grinned happily at his friend's praise.

"We could cut 'em up," Rojo said, "and stuff the pieces into old film cans."

"That would take a lot of time," Pinole said, taking him seriously. "We wouldn't get over to that chop shop in time to have the Cadillac repainted tonight."

Rojo had his mind on saving his car. His eyes skittered with tension and impatience. They fell on the utility closet.

"We put them in there and worry about it later. Then we get the Caddie over for the new paint job."

"Red."

"That's right, red," Rojo said, going over and taking Lacy Ohio, born Loretta Oskanowsky, by her ankles. "Two coats."

Nineteen

The rain was still coming down, blowing away the image of Southern 'California for another horde of pilgrims. Gentry's had seven lonelies, hunched over coffee cups, scattered around the booths and counter stools like mushrooms dotting a forest floor. Detective Canaan was among them, sitting in a booth, having a burger.

Whistler dropped his stuffed overnighter on the tiles in front of the cash register. Bosco looked up from *Freud's General Introduction to Psycho-Analysis.*

"That's an old number," Whistler said. "Nowadays we got transactional, we got Gestalt, we got primal screaming, we got mystiotranscendent . . ."

"Freud's got 'honor, power, fame, riches, and the love of beautiful women.' Freud's got fucking."

"I'm going to New Orleans."

"You going for the head?"

"I'm going for the lady who was in here the other night."

"What for?"

"Somebody's got enough clout to hush up a double homicide and let a drunken actor take a walk. This somebody's maybe got enough clout to offer an actress a picture and get a witness out of town, never to return."

"There was you and me. We were witnesses too."

"But we announced no plans to blow the whistle."

Bosco wrote on a piece of paper, "Anything you want to know, ask for Coxey at the all-night drug corner of Common and Rampart." He handed it over. "Don't fall in love."

"That's a joke?" Whistler said.

"It's a disaster," Bosco replied.

Whistler went over to the booth where Canaan sat, and put his bag at his feet.

"Did I invite you?" Canaan said.

"You don't be nicer to me, people will think we're in love."

"Why don't you get going to New Orleans?"

"You heard that too? I got to learn sign language. As good as you hear, have you heard anything about the headless body?"

"You should leave police business to the police."

"You don't even care," Whistler said accusingly.

Canaan looked up from his food. There was a smear of mustard at the corner of his mouth.

"Listen," he said, "I don't work homicide, and I don't work traffic. I got my own troubles. There's this fourteen-year-old girl comes in to see me the other day. Oh, I know her a long time. About a year. I know her from when she steps off the bus down to the Greyhound station. I know her from when she turns her first Hollywood trick for the pimp who roped her in. This pimp that I warned her about, but who she tells me is the only person in her life was ever good to her. So why shouldn't she do him a few favors on the street in his time of financial distress? She gets to hate it. After she pays off his pimp wagon she tries to quit peddling her ass. He breaks her jaw. They wire it together at the hospital and give her some pills for the pain. They tell her to rest. The pimp puts her out on the streets the same night. When she tries to commit suicide by swallowing the pills, she vomits and breaks the wires. He don't even let her go to the hospital and get them fixed. He puts her out on the street again. She finally comes to me.

"Now, this girl is already an old lady, you know what I mean? Most of my time is spent with children, seven, eight, nine, ten years old, and the people, mostly men, who eat them alive. I'm not married. I got no kids of my own. I thank God for it nearly every night of my life.

"How many sexually exploited children you guess we got in this city?

"I'll tell you how many," Canaan said, when Whistler didn't answer. "Thirty thousand is how many. When do I find time to chase down headless bodies? When do I find time to worry about police cover-ups for what is probably nothing but fucking inefficiency down to the morgue, which we got plenty of everywhere. Nothing works right, or haven't you been paying attention? I did you a costly favor. . . ."

"I appreciate it."

"You appreciate it, but you say to me that I don't care. If I cared twenty-five hours a day, I couldn't even sweep out my little corner. Go find yourself a living, Whistler." A taxi pulled up outside. "Find a new hustle. There's a cab. You ought to grab it. They're hard to find in the rain."

Airports never sleep.

Whistler sat on a plastic chair and checked his pockets the way he did a hundred times every time he traveled. Ticket, clean handkerchief, candy drops to suck so his ears wouldn't clog up, very skinny money roll, wallet with credit cards . . . no gun. The gun was back home in a potted plant. Whistler had never heard of a place where the local cops didn't get very upset about private dicks coming into their territory packing heat. So no gun.

He watched an old lady picking through a trash bin. Three shopping bags squatted nearby like mangy pet dogs. He heard someone call his name and looked over to see Al Lister hustling toward him. Lister looked as old as he'd looked ten years ago, when they'd gone into the Valley to see Suzy. His hair was still as black as bottled dye could make it. His grin was like a big wrinkle among the small ones. Eyes like licorice gumdrops above. Small chin like half a rubber ball. His small body found it hard to remain still. His small feet, sporting patent leathers, were always on the move.

"Long time no see," he chirped.

"You haven't aged a day," Whistler said.

"Maybe a year or three. Wheat germ and yogurt."

"I'm not laughing."

"It keeps the bowels empty and the disposition positive. You should try it. You look sad. And sad is bad."

Whistler wondered how the bag lady had made her way into the terminal with security sweeping the homeless out like so much trash.

She popped up out of the bin every so often and grinned every time she did. Like a puppet in a Punch and Judy show, her face painted up like Judy or like Raggedy Ann. Orange yarn hair and round, rouged cheeks.

"So what do you think?"

"I think I'll try the yogurt but not the wheat germ."

"No, no, my friend. What do you think about my success?"

Whistler glanced at Lister, trying to read between the lines.

"Don't you watch the tube?" Lister asked.

"Now and then," Whistler said, looking back at the bag lady.

"You should watch the tube, find out what's going on in the world," Lister said. "Find out what's going on with your old friends. I'm a star. Well, so, not a star exactly, but a regular on a continuing series."

"Son of a bitch."

A black, uniformed security cop came around the corner of a long row of lockers, walking free and easy with his gun settled on his hip. When he saw the garbage picker, he pulled up short. Whistler speculated for a second on the kind of emergencies security cops dreamed about, had nightmares about. For sure, not old ladies picking through wastebaskets. The cop swung his head slowly from side to side, looking for some cause for the phenomenon. Looking for the Candid Camera. Looking for the gag. Then he stared at the old Raggedy Ann with a sad look on his face, as though it were his own grandmother he saw picking through the garbage. Whistler supposed it once might have been.

"Putting it mildly," Lister chirped on, "I know what everybody was thinking."

"What were they thinking?"

155

"Not you. I don't think you were thinking what everybody was thinking."

"I'd really like to know what you think they were thinking that you don't think I was thinking," Whistler said.

The cop's head perked up because of something off to one side. Whistler saw a plainclothesman from the security office come walking across the wide hall, heel taps calling echoes out of the vaulted ceiling. The young white man stopped before he reached the Raggedy Ann or the cop, settling his maroon jacket on his shoulders with a shrug that told the cop to get with it.

"We could be an act," Lister said. "The new fucking Abbott and Costello. What they were thinking was: What's this old fart, thinks he's an actor, doing coming out here for a career? Just who the fuck does this little old fart think he is? Well, this here actor has himself a continuing role on a continuing series. Two grand a week, twenty weeks a year on the contract. What do you think of that?"

The cop went over and caught Raggedy Ann's elbow on the rise. She didn't try to pull away, just stood there grinning into his earnest black face. He bent his head and instructed her kindly. She laughed out loud. It wasn't a witchlike cackle but a low, rich contralto, the laughter of another woman altogether. She disengaged her arm and went digging into the first of her three bags. In a minute she came up with an airline ticket folder. The cop pulled out the ticket and looked it over, then looked off to his supervisor. The young executive type walked over and examined the ticket too. Raggedy Ann patted his sleeve. The security men walked away in some confusion.

Lister was a little miffed that Whistler didn't make a big thing out of his running part in the series. He saw that Whistler's attention had been elsewhere.

"You see that?" Lister said. "What the fuck was that all about?"

"It was entrapment," Whistler said. "That old lady set up the airport cops. She saves her pennies and buys a ticket to the next closest airport. Then she waits for them to roust her, and she shoves the ticket up their nose. Later on she cashes in the ticket."

"What the hell she do that for?"

Raggedy Ann grinned and waved at Whistler. He waved back. She remembered him, after all.

"She told me once there was the bottom, the middle, and the top. Cops, ticket takers, salesclerks, and so forth beat on the poor suckers at the bottom, sit down and break bread with the ones in the middle, and do tricks for the ones on top. She gets tired getting beat on sometimes and tries to get a little back."

"What are you doing flying this hour?" Lister said, not impressed at all by the antic gallantry displayed by the bag lady. "Got a deal?"

"No deal. Just chasing down a lead."

"Me too. My show's on hiatus. Friend of mine's shooting a picture down in Texas. Last time I saw him, he said he'd find something for me. So I'll see. What the hell, I got the money, I got the time. Maybe there's a little something for me in his picture. The big screen's where it is. I mean, it's okay, the money, the face recognition you get from the tube, but for me it's the big screen what counts. The way I figure, if I'm right there on the set, how's he going to avoid the issue? I mean, it's not like I'm a nobody anymore. You got a girlfriend?" he said without pause, as though it were all part of the same thought.

Whistler stared at Lister.

"I got me a babe," the little man said, his hands patting himself. He brought out a wallet and showed Whistler a picture of a hard-eyed bleached blonde who looked like a caricature out of the thirties. "Thirty years younger than me. Whattaya know? Loves me. Says an older man's a better lover. More considerate. Let me tell you, I can still get it up. So what's your babe like?"

"Well," said Whistler, "she's got long, wet legs."

"What the fuck you know about that?" Lister said.

Twenty

Whistler's plane landed in New Orleans at
midnight. Walking from the air-conditioned cabin into the wet
night was like walking into a warm bath. The smell of rotting
vegetation clogged his nose.

He lugged his bag through the empty corridors of the
terminal, as though he were a pallbearer carrying one end of a
coffin.

The main lobby was as hollow as a drum. The rental counters
were empty except for a tenth-rater trying harder.

The girl behind the counter had the knowing look of a
woman who might turn a trick between flights.

He rented a compact and drove out of Moisant Field along
the Airline Highway. The air conditioner was busted. When he
opened the windows for the breeze, it was like standing in the
mouth of a blast furnace. The road became Tulane Boulevard
quicker than he expected. He checked the map he'd found in
the side pocket of the car, spreading it out across his knees and
glancing down at it every now and then, reading it in the light
of the dash. At Loyola he turned southwest a couple of blocks
to Perdido, then hung a right, still heading toward the river.

He fell into the net of streets around North and South Diamond and Calliope. It took him half an hour of jigging and jogging before he stumbled on the all-night drugstore by mistake. Its windows were so plastered with signs and offers of sales that the light from inside scarcely crept out. He parked the car and crossed the street. There was a vagrant lying in the gutter, using the curb as a pillow for his head, his legs sticking out into the street.

If somebody came along half drunk, looking to buy a bottle, and pulled up at the gutter, he could smash the poor sucker's legs to a pulp, Whistler thought. He paused, wondering if it would be worth anybody's while to do the good deed and save the loser from possible injury and mutilation. He bent down and shifted the sleeping man's legs onto the sidewalk.

"You rotten son of a bitch," the bum snarled out of some instinct for self-preservation, scaring off the vultures and the hyenas.

A buzzer sounded when Whistler walked through the door into the drugstore. It looked like a warehouse, every aisle leading off the main one blocked off with little harnesses of chain. Both sides of the main aisle were lined with vending machines piled one on top of another. There might have been a hundred of them, delivering everything from plastic combs to chocolate bars to condoms for a couple of dimes or quarters.

The clerk sat behind his cash register with the fast night merchandise, wine and beer, in the cases behind him. A half a dozen mirrors checked out any thieves that tried to sneak past the barriers. His face was reflected back at him as though he were a prisoner always being watched by guards that looked exactly like him.

When he saw Whistler approaching, he stood up and put his hands on the wood, as though ready to pull a gun from underneath the counter. At the back of the store a bank of fluorescents overhead made sickly daylight around a lunch counter and a line of stools. Three painted women perched there like birds of paradise, pulling open the fronts of their dresses to catch the breeze from a floor fan. A bent blade ticked out a syncopated rhythm.

"Ba-da-da-da-dah," Whistler said. "'Jelly Roll Blues.'"

"What's that?" the clerk said, drawing it out as though Whistler had awakened him from a sleep from which he didn't want to be disturbed.

"I'm looking for a movie house called the—"

"Beaver Run."

The man looked at Whistler as though he were a pocket waiting to be picked. He reached into his crummy vest, pulled out a small stack of business cards, and started shuffling them, never taking his eyes from Whistler.

"You know the place?" Whistler asked.

"Outside, turn right, two blocks, turn right, one block, turn left, halfway down the street."

"Is it open now?"

"It's open all the time." His eyes flickered down to the cards. He snapped one down on the counter like he was dealing poker. "Complimentary ticket. Half price after midnight."

"There a hotel or motel close by?"

"Close by here or close by the movie house?"

"We're not talking miles, are we? Let's say anyplace between here and there."

"The Blue House is right next door to the Beaver Run." Another card fell on the counter. "Special rate. Ten bucks for a hot pillow."

"I'm not a husband or a visiting fireman."

"Forty bucks a night, sink in the room, toilet down the hall."

Whistler smiled. "Suppose I want a shower?"

Another card, fluttering softly, like a snowflake. "Across the street from the Blue House. Bee Bee Baths. Ten bucks through the left door, five bucks through the right."

"What's the difference?"

"Left door for twangy boys. That's where the action is."

"When I say a shower, I mean a shower."

"What do you want to go to the movies for? You want excitement, all you got to do is turn your head and take your pick."

Whistler looked. The three whores stared back, half hoping he would, half hoping he wouldn't. He heard the drop of another card, looked down at the growing pile, and picked up the top one. He caught the word *entertainment*.

He didn't have to ask, but he did. "You Crib Coxey?"

"That's me."

"What have I got here, another complimentary half-price special?"

"Nothing off the regular price. Just my personal guarantee. You just hand that to any girl back there—any girl on the street what takes your fancy—and she'll play you rim shots or rattle your castanets if that's your pleasure."

"This your commission card?"

"Why not?"

"Pimp pays you or the girl pays you?"

"The man in charge of the commodity, whoever he may be. No free-lance ladies in this town. Not allowed."

"All organized?"

"All safe and orderly."

Whistler threw ten dollars on the counter.

"You know who owns this Beaver Run movie house?"

Coxey's hands stopped shuffling the little pasteboards. His eyes flattened out the way a mouse does its body before skinnying its way under a door.

"What's your living?"

"I walk around with one foot in the gutter looking for dimes."

"It's no secret. Nonny Barcaloo owns the theater. If I don't tell you, the next man will."

"This Barcaloo run the girls?"

"Just the head shops and flicks. A little manufacturing. A little cinema enterprise. On the subject, you want a French tickler—drive her wild? You want a monster dildo—keep her satisfied? Inflatable doll what sucks? How about some eight millimeter or some tapes? I got VHS. I got Beta. I got *Naughty Nights with Nellie*. I got *Three Little Men in a Boat*."

"What about Vietnamese?"

"If that's your pleasure." Coxey's voice dropped through long habit. "I don't know she's from Vietnam, but I got something special with a slant-eyed girl in it. You like snuff? I got *Rosita Dies for It*."

A rustle of sick understanding brought up something sour into Whistler's mouth.

"Jokes?"

"Hell, no. The real thing. You don't got to believe me, but I even knew the girl in the movie. She used to come in here and sit back there at the lunch counter, just like them girls is doing. I ain't seen her around in over a year. I swear this flick's the straight goods. They really did her while she was coming."

"How much?"

"Two hundred and fifty."

Whistler counted his roll.

"Can I rent for the night?"

"Not this stuff. This is choice."

Whistler hesitated.

"I'll take plastic if you're short of cash," Coxey said.

Whistler took out his bank charge card. He signed the slip Coxey handed him after imprinting it on the machine.

"Telephone number?"

Whistler shook his head and pulled out the customer copy and the carbons.

"VHS or Beta?"

"What kind of machine's available?"

"Blue House has got VHS . . . if they got one working. You can rent a machine, ten bucks, from me. Same price."

"I wouldn't want your machine on my hands. I'll take my chances on the ones at the Blue House."

Coxey dropped the tape cassette into a paper bag. "You sure you don't want to take along one of the girls?"

"I'm sure. Where does this Barcaloo live?"

"Conversion over on Ursuline across the street from the rectory of St. Mary's Italian Church. I don't have the house number."

"Where does he hang out?"

"Jimmy Flynn's over to St. Peter Street. Mindy's Blue Grotto on Iberville. There's a whorehouse in the back. He has an office upstairs over the Beaver Run. Anywhere he's got a piece. You a buyer?"

"Of what?"

"The word on the street is that Barcaloo's selling up everything he's got except the Beaver Run and maybe an apartment house or two."

"Why's that?"

"Somebody give him an offer to go west."

"Las Vegas?"

"Hey, even I don't know everything," Coxey said.

Whistler started to leave. "Bosco Silverlake says hello."

"Whattaya know? You shoulda told me. I woulda give you a price."

Whistler didn't think he meant it.

Twenty-one

The room in the Blue House was surprisingly clean, although it had the milky smell of plaster that would never dry.

Whistler lay on the bedcovers in his shorts. It was dark except for the light coming from the television set.

As old as he got—knowing that things were as they were, neither good nor bad, right nor wrong, just as they were, mindless therefore thoughtless, heartless therefore cruel—he still felt a blaze of helpless rage at certain horrors. It wouldn't take much more of what he was watching for him to go to St. Louis Cemetery Number One or Two and find a tomb to hide in.

A young dark-skinned girl, probably Mexican or Puerto Rican, with a very immature body, did tricks with a slightly older Oriental woman who was beautiful in a remote sort of way. There was that crack about Orientals all looking alike, which might be true for some people, but Whistler was almost sure the woman in the picture was the one in the morgue glossies, Lim Shu Dok.

It was possible to imagine the Latino pretending to herself

that what she was doing was somehow elevated on film to something like real acting. She saw herself in Hollywood. She saw herself a star. Petted and pampered. She was doing her best to act out everything the director asked of her, turning this way and that, lying on her side, getting on her knees, arching her back on command.

Lim Shu watched herself doing and being done as though she were a spectator. A mark on her hip could be seen as she rolled this way and that. She'd lost all hope of stardom of any kind.

The dark-skinned one showed an anxious concern to do exactly as she was bidden. It was in the tension of the lips and the quick glances cast at the camera lens. Seeking approval. Seeking mercy. Maybe she sensed the coming horror and was trying to save herself.

A man took over from Lim Shu. She did not appear again, but had she been called back another time to play the sacrifice?

There wasn't much plot, no attempt at dialogue that made any sense. The moans and heavy breathing had been dubbed in afterward, so it was sometimes out of synch. The lighting was bad and the match of color temperatures careless. Nothing like the slick pieces done with seasoned professionals in Detroit and La-La Land. Gut basic. Truer to its purpose. Pure in its rotten fashion.

Whistler had once asked the editor of a string of crotch magazines published out in San Fernando Valley why a customer would spend five dollars on twenty pages of stupidly captioned black-and-white photographs of unlovely women exposing themselves awkwardly in motel rooms rented by the hour when they could buy a three-hundred-page slick, filled with articles, dirty letters, and heart-stopping beauties in full labial display for three bucks.

That was easy, the editor told him. Not many men could imagine themselves screwing one of the Technicolor beauties, wrestling them to fur rugs, stained with spilled champagne, in front of marble fireplaces. But just about every one of them could see himself getting lucky with some hard-eyed blonde, with a mouth like a hand vacuum, met in the corner bar.

Having a one-off in some hot pillow joint along the boulevard where fifty bucks bought the works.

In a while the director and crew of the snuff film ran out of tape, story, patience, and positions. The end came to the girl on the television screen so fast that Whistler felt as though he'd been punched in the belly. Her anxious eagerness gave way to dumb confusion. Then the terror burst like a bomb. It pulled her homely, painted little face into a witch's mask, eyes starting out of her head, mouth stretched back as though burned with acid, tongue skewered by her teeth. She reached out for the naked partner who'd just performed an "act of love" on her frail, small-breasted body. The camera jerked as her legs kicked out. It lash-panned across the wall behind her.

Once steadied, a different man, naked, too, a hood over his head, took two steps into the shot. He carried a machete in his left hand. He swung it at the girl's neck and the blood fountained.

Twenty-two

Sleeping too long with nightmares that refuse to escape in a scream wracks the bones and dries out the juices of the body.

When Whistler slid out of the bed stenciled with the sweaty shape of a mummy three thousand years old, it was five o'clock in the morning. The air was already hot and tasted of brass.

He turned on the television set. The commentator said, in the hollow voice of early morning, that it had been very hot and humid the day before, and the city could expect more of the same. There might be a chance of a cooling rain if everybody prayed.

Whistler punched the button on the tape deck, running it back and forth with the search key until he found the place where the girl, in her panic, had kicked the camera tripod. He hit the pause button and examined the still, clicking the tape forward frame by frame.

It looked as though the snuff film had been shot on a makeshift soundstage with some basic equipment. There were some posters and signs on the wall. One of them read, "Go Fuck a Duck."

He ran the tape back some more until he found a close-up of the dark-skinned girl. He wondered in what nameless grave she was buried. He found the place where the blemish on the Vietnamese woman's hip rolled across the screen as she twisted her body and held it there. It was the tattoo. The butterfly.

There was nothing he could do so early, but he couldn't stay in the room. With no shower available, he took a whore's bath in the sink and got dressed in his stale clothes, wondering what the hell he was doing working a hot, wet city with little hope of reward. He put the tape into its box and tucked it into his jacket pocket.

Out on the street he walked three blocks looking for a place to eat before turning back and getting into the rented car. His shirt was soaked already, his underwear tore and twisted at his crotch. He put the cassette in the glove compartment and drove to the French Quarter. Parked it on Ursuline in front of St. Mary's Italian Church between reserved signs, across from the conversion in which Coxey said Barcaloo lived.

There was a red Cadillac parked in front. Its enamel glistened with the brittle sheen of a cheap, quickie repaint. It was better than a good guess that it was the white Cadillac with the Bondoed fender he'd read about in the *Enquirer*. It had been refinished just hours ago.

A black man came out of the building next door and started sweeping the sidewalk, staring sidelong at Whistler. The janitor watched him as he walked all the way down to Decatur.

Whistler found a place for coffee and doughnuts in the French Market. He had three cups. The sugary doughnuts left a cool residue on his lips. He had a sudden image of the girl in the film biting into a doughnut, brushing the powdered sugar off the tops of her breasts and laughing. Fear rushed up into his throat. It was too easy to replace the girl's face with Shiela's. Knife coming down. Blood showering. Head rolling along a piece of carpet. Long legs forever stilled.

He went back to the all-night drugstore. Coxey was there unlocking the padlocks on the chains that kept the nighttime thieves at bay. He was working one side, and a pale man with wispy hair and steel-rimmed glasses was working the other. The morning clerk coming to relieve the guard in the shop that never slept.

Coxey saw the tape caught in Whistler's armpit.

"No refunds," he said, and walked away toward the counter at the rear where two transvestites in need of a shave mourned the wasted night by staring into the cold coffee in their cups.

"You told me this Barcaloo was into film. This some of his work?"

"Please. Don't make me crazy. I don't answer questions about my sources."

Whistler walked him back along one of the side aisles, past shelves of Pepto-Bismol and Alka Seltzer, into a section of small kitchenware. Coxey gave way until he couldn't give way any more. He had to stay very quiet to hear what Whistler had to say. That's how soft-voiced Whistler got when the rage caught hold of him. His eyes flickered one way and another. He grabbed the closest thing to hand that could do bodily harm. It was a novelty beer-can key with a sharp nose and a plastic Mickey Mouse for a handle.

"I want to tell you it wouldn't take much for me to do to you what somebody did to that girl. This thing won't make as clean a cut, but it could clean out your windpipe like reaming a squash. I don't want to play your gonif's games anymore. I don't want to haggle over price. I don't want to pay. Not with cash and not with plastic. I just want a simple answer to the simple question I asked you. It's no skin off your ass. Was that fucking snuff film shot by Barcaloo or any people attached to Barcaloo?"

"Yes."

"The dark-skinned girl was the one came in here for coffee?"

"That's right. She was a Mex."

"Was she ever with a Vietnamese whore?"

"I never saw her with one a them."

"See how easy that was? How much is this gadget?"

"Fifty-nine cents."

"I'll buy it. Let's go ring up your last sale of the night."

Whistler moved aside, and Coxey slipped past him, as though Whistler's touch could burn.

"I want some blowups made of a frame or two," Whistler said, speaking at normal volume. "You know anybody who can do it?"

169

Coxey turned at the smell of profit like a bird dog, forgetting the powerful fright he'd just been given. His hand dipped into the magic vest for a fistful of calling cards. He fanned them, cut them, cascaded them like a magician passing aces, and finally extracted one.

"I don't get a commission from this technician."

"You never give up, do you? You'll be sitting up in your coffin making deals with the undertaker." Whistler handed over a five-dollar bill as Coxey rang up the hardware sale. "Keep the change."

Coxey smiled. Four dollars and forty-one cents was as good as a twenty-dollar bill at six-thirty in the morning.

"This city got a Chinatown, a Little Korea, anything like that?" Whistler asked.

"Every city's got a Chinatown, even if it's only two old chinks playing mah-jong over a pot of tea."

"For Christ's sake, another early-morning philosopher."

"But we got no place like you mean in New York or L.A. There's maybe a couple of blocks."

"Where?"

"At the end of Saratoga at Felicity." Coxey plucked a city map out of a rack beside the cash register and circled half a dozen city blocks with a red marker. "One dollar for the map."

"Don't you ever spring for anything?" Whistler asked, handing over the dollar in small change.

"I'll buy you a breakfast if you want to tell me what you're doing here in town."

"Hell, Coxey, that information would make your fortune," Whistler said. He started to leave, then came back.

"Hey, Coxey," he said as softly as before. "Don't try to sell me. You're the only bigmouth knows I'm in town. If anybody comes after me, nobody'll be fast enough to stop me from letting Mickey Mouse drink your blood."

The photographer lived and worked at the top of a rickety wooden outside staircase that climbed to the third floor of a building ready to lie down. Whistler punched the bell. A dog with a heavy voice sounded a warning from somewhere inside the flat. Whistler checked his watch and pushed the bell again.

He didn't expect the photographer to be happy about having a customer so early.

The woman who opened the inside door and peered through the screen, tousle-haired and beagle-eyed with sleep, wasn't happy.

"Who're you?" she said.

"I'm looking for J. Kissie."

"You're looking at her."

"You're the photographer?"

"Fastest finger in the South. What do you want?"

"I want some reproductions taken off a tape cassette."

"This is a rotten time of day to do business."

"I agree, but I'm on a schedule."

J. Kissie was small and blond, of a likely age and as homely as a mutt. She stared at Whistler as though it would be written on his forehead if he were a wandering rapist.

"Wait a second," she said.

She faded away behind the mesh of the screen as she went to the back of the parlor and opened a door.

"Easy, Beau," she said in a voice of soft command.

She came back into view behind the mesh. A bull mastiff padded silently at her side, standing as tall as her hip. She unlatched the screen door. "Come on in."

Whistler hesitated.

"Beau's all right. Just don't make any sudden moves." She held the screen door open, and Whistler went inside, keeping an eye on the dog, who was keeping an eye on him. "And whatever you do, don't touch me. Understand?"

"Oh, yes, indeed."

"Sit there," J. Kissie said. She palmed her eyes for a second, then took her hands away and blinked. "I haven't even washed my face."

"It doesn't need it."

She grinned and looked at herself in a mirror above a rack of television sets, tape recorders, and monitors. She fluffed her hair.

"You can always tell if a woman's a true beauty by the way she looks in the morning without her makeup. Am I a doll or am I a doll?"

171

"Yes, you are," Whistler said. She looked like a mutt, but there was something about J. Kissie that grew on you fast.

"Let me see," she said, holding out her hand.

Whistler gave her the cassette. She inserted it into a top-of-the-line front-loader. A five-headed machine designed for smooth slow-mo and rock-steady still-frame. She punched the start button.

"What's your name?" she asked.

"Whistler."

"Whistler, you shouldn't be rotting your brain with this shit."

"I'm not a fan."

She handed him the remote control.

"Show me what you want me to reproduce."

She got a heavy tripod from the corner and screwed a Polaroid instant camera to the plate after setting time and aperture. She checked the number of the shot coming up in the film pack. By the time Whistler found the best close-up frame of Lim Shu Dok, J. Kissie was ready. The shutter clicked. She pulled the tab and tossed the print on a table. He found the close shot of the butterfly tattoo, and the shutter clicked again. He found a close-up of the Latino girl and another at the spot where the knife met her neck. The shutter clicked twice. He ran it forward a frame at a time until the head left the body.

J. Kissie turned pale and backed off. Her dog smelled her fear and was rounding on Whistler when she laid a hand on his head to hold him in check.

"What the hell kind of sick stuff is this?"

"The kind of sick stuff I'd like to grind up into stink bombs and toss into the right places."

"Is that for real? I mean, did that man with the knife really—"

She choked on the rest of it.

"It could be faked. Can you tell me?"

"Oh, sweet Jesus, I suppose it could. It's a hell of a goddamn way to start the day."

She ran the entire last sequence three times, stopping it now and then, running it back and forth and freezing the frame. She leaned forward, intent, jaw rigid, hand steady on Beau's huge head. The technician had taken over from the frightened and disgusted woman. She stopped at the moment when the blade struck the woman's neck. She advanced the tape a single frame. Then another and another. Less than a second's running time of blurred action. The next frame was of a head striking the floor. It rolled across the carpet a frame at a time.

"I can't tell for sure," she said. "If it's a fake, they must of used up all the smarts they had in the one sequence because the production quality's sure not very good anywhere else. On the other hand, the blow with the knife could have stopped at the neck . . ."

Very fancy bladework, Whistler thought.

". . . and the rest would be easy. A quick pan. A dummy head. The way they make them nowadays . . ."

"They'd fool a coroner until he cut," Whistler finished.

She took a still of the knife about to decapitate the terrified girl. J. Kissie stared as Whistler looked the prints over.

"I think they really killed that girl."

"How much do I owe you?" he asked.

"You really trying to do something about stopping stuff like this?"

"I got to tell you, I don't know how far I'll get."

"As long as somebody's trying."

"How much?" Whistler asked again.

"Nothing." J. Kissie walked him to the door, Beau padding alongside, still wary, still ready to have a go at the intruder who caused his mistress to smell of fear.

"You know," she said, "you're not a bad-looking fellow. Remind me not to let fellows who are not bad-looking into the house so early in the morning. If you come back at night— tonight—that's another story."

"I won't be in town very long."

"Well, keep it in mind in case you miss your plane," J. Kissie said, and made a monkey face.

Twenty-three

Whistler cut through Jackson Square to Chartres, walking all the way up St. Peter until, worn-out and panting like an old dog, he reached North Rampart. He shuffled along the sweltering pavement to St. Louis Cemetery Number One, rotting in a patch of swampy ground between Conti and St. Louis, Basin and Treme. The gates were open, an old white man in shirtsleeves and suspenders already sitting in a rickety wooden chair at his post, selling souvenir pamphlets, a cooler filled with cans of beer at his feet. He stared inquiringly at Whistler. Whistler shook his head and walked along the perimeter wall where the burial crypts, called "ovens," honeycombed the brick and plaster.

At the base the larger repositories of old tenants lay with their mouths bricked up except for one or two here and there. Whistler stooped down and bent his head almost to the ground so he could peer inside of one that had been torn open. There were bones piled inside, brown and dry like the teeth of old horses.

Whistler sat down on the steps of a marble tomb with a cottage front and an angel on the roof. He thought about what he was doing and why. He knew what he was doing but didn't really know why.

He'd come to New Orleans because of a woman's scared eyes, trembling lips, and long leg sticking out in the rain. He'd come down with the vague idea he'd just intercept her on the way to the Beaver Run Theater, kiss her, and tell her he'd changed his mind. He wanted to make love to her. Not in this shitty town where they were apt to melt but back in L.A. where you could depend upon the overcast.

Buying the snuff film had been a matter of curiosity because there was a yellow girl in it. And that had led to the stills he carried around, as he'd carried pictures around looking for missing persons before. Then there was the newly painted Cadillac in front of Barcaloo's.

A little curiosity, a little easy doing what he did, had led him deeper into the mystery of the Vietnamese whore who was almost positively the woman whose parts were scattered two thousand miles apart. How many Vietnamese whores, working New Orleans and L.A., could there be with a butterfly tattoo on her ass? He still couldn't see a paycheck, but he was in it up to his neck, and there was no getting out.

"No wonder I haven't got a bank account," he said aloud. The angel made no comment.

Barcaloo dozed out on the front gallery. He was dressed in a fresh string shirt and white slacks with sandals on his feet. The toes were blunted. The separations could scarcely be seen except between the big toe and the rest. His feet were like cloven hooves.

Bouche, lounging in a skimpy bathing suit on a plastic-webbed chaise, stared at his feet.

"Whattaya starin' at?"

"Who's staring?"

"You were lookin' at my feet."

"You're crazy. I was a million miles away."

"Fuckin' a dinge?"

A vein started pulsing in her neck.

"Just what the hell you mean by that?"

"I got my eye on you," Barcaloo said.

"You got your eye on me, then you should know I'd never do such a thing. I won't have nothing to do with darkies."

"You want to tell me you don't go to seances over to Mama Bluess? You want to tell me you don't dance with your bare tits over to Bayou St. John when she has her heathen ceremonies?"

"I never did," she shouted, hoping he didn't have ideas about Henry. That he was just trying to scare her for the fun of it. "Once I went to watch just like any other tourist. It's all a show."

"And you danced."

"There were two hundred people dancing, for chrissake."

"With your shirt off."

"I had a goddamn bathing suit top on underneath," she screamed.

"If I ever find out you fucked a nigger, I'll do you," he said as Pinole and Rojo appeared in the doorway.

"You do like I tole you about that goddamn Cadillac?"

"Well . . ." Pinole hesitated.

"It's still got a lot of miles left on it. We had it painted. Go take a look. It's parked right out front," Rojo said.

Barcaloo was about to dump a mountain on them, but it was too damned hot. He just shrugged and let it go, not worth the trouble.

"How'd you get it painted so fast?"

"It was already primed. Only takes an hour to spray it. They got this oven what bakes the finish."

"You had time to take care of everything over at the studio?"

"Everything's great," Rojo said.

"You didn't leave no mess?"

Pinole glanced at Rojo, waiting to see what he was going to say. Barcaloo didn't seem to notice, but Bouche did.

She knew they'd fucked up again.

"We put everything left over in a closet," Rojo said.

"How many full drums of gasoline we got over there?"

"Twenty. Twenty drums and fifty jerry cans."

"After we shoot some stuff with this Hollywood actress—" He stopped and stared at Bouche. "I want you to work this one, Bouche," he said.

"Like hell."

"I'm not negotiatin' with you. You're going to work this one last scene for me."

Her heart lurched. "What?" The word sounded like a death rattle. She smelled the sharp smell of fear mixed with perfume.

Barcaloo smiled his white smile. "After we get to La-La Land you're going to be retired. Do nothing but sit around the pool, go shopping, have cocktails in the Polo Lounge, maybe grab Clint Eastwood by the ass."

Bouche tried a laugh. It came out all right, but it didn't comfort her.

"When we're finished—maybe tomorrow night—we burn the shack down," Barcaloo said.

"A thousand gallons of gas'll burn very hot," Rojo said, staring at Bouche.

"So meet me at the movie house in an hour," Barcaloo said.

Whistler walked back from St. Louis Cemetery Number One along Rampart. The police station was on the other side of the street just outside the Vieux Carré at the edge of the section once known as Storyville, where, once upon a time, sexual novelties could be witnessed for a penny and sexual horrors rented for a dime. The red-light district had been razed to the ground long ago and low-cost housing erected in its place. Now, in the eighties, it was the breeding ground for petty and violent crime alike, but there were no marauders out this early in the morning. He paused in front of the entrance. Two cops gave him the look. He went inside and up to the desk.

"Yes, sir, what can I do for you?" the uniformed sergeant said.

"Who do I see about a matter of vice or homicide?"

"Which is it, sir?" the desk sergeant said.

"A little of both."

"Are you a private citizen here to make a complaint?"

"I'm a private ticket from L.A. looking into a killing that might have started here or might have started there."

The honey left the sergeant's voice. "That's as clear as mud."

"That's why I'm here to talk to the experts."

"Take a chair."

177

"I'm in a little bit of a hurry. There's somebody I've got to meet."

"Well, hell, yes. Ain't we all? You sit. I'll see if Lieutenant Bellerose'll see you."

It wasn't long before Whistler was shown into an interrogation room. It was longer before the door opened and a man in an ice-cream suit waded in and sat down.

Whistler had kept a turtle once. It had had the patience of a rock and a look in the eye so weary and wise that—before he met Bosco—Whistler consulted it on important matters like love and minor wars.

That turtle had nothing on Lieutenant Bellerose when it came to heavy lids, snaky eyes, folded skin around the neck, and slow-mo gestures. He was like a man swimming in a dream. He wore the wrinkled suit like a turtle's carapace. When he shifted his weight from one hip to the other in the squeaking swivel chair, his skinny body moved around inside the suit without disturbing it very much. Whistler had the feeling that if danger threatened, Bellerose would just pull in head, ass, arms, and legs and become a stone.

Whistler put down the Polaroids and the photos from the morgue.

"Ah'm not quick. You got to spell things out for me," Bellerose said.

Whistler tapped the pictures of the Latino girl. "This girl was murdered for a snuff film, I think."

"Uh-huh."

He tapped the pictures of Lim Shu Dok.

"This one left her body back in L.A. and her head here in New Orleans."

"You think?"

"I think."

"Now let me get it clear. You come into my parish lookin' for what?"

"A head to go with the body back in L.A."

"You lose the head?"

"I only *read* about it in the *Enquirer*. A story about an Oriental lady's head and two guys driving a white Cadillac with a Bondoed fender playing kickball with it over to the lake."

"Oh, *that* lady's head."

"You got many loose heads scattered around?"

"Well, now, they's not exactly as thick on the ground as magnolia blossoms at the end of summer, but a man likes to make really sure what he's talkin' about an' . . ."

"I can understand that."

". . . who he's talkin' about what with. Was that confusin'?"

"I get your drift."

"That's big-city slang, is it? My drift. Like snow, am I right? Like somebody gettin' snowed?"

"I'm not unloading any blizzard on you. I'm thinking you know all there is to know about snow jobs."

"So, all right, what's your interest?"

"I was sitting in a shop having a cup of coffee back in Hollywood the other night, reading about the head down here in New Orleans, when there's an accident between a BMW and a station wagon outside the window. A body—a lady's body— comes flying out the wagon without a head."

"An' you come down here lookin' for a match? You just a curious bystander?"

"I'm private."

"Let me see your ticket."

Whistler took out his card case, opened it, and shoved it under Bellerose's nose.

"Stand up and fan your jacket."

Whistler opened his coat and pulled the sides away from his body.

"Turn around and lift your tail. All right, you ain' carryin'. You're no fool. We're hard on private Johnny Hams what come aroun' totin' iron."

"That's small-city slang, is it? Johnny Hams are private licenses and iron is guns?"

"You're bein' a wise guy. It ain't smart to be a wise guy with a man in his own parish."

"I take it back."

"You got a client?"

"Not really. I thought I was helping the guy driving the BMW, but it turned out he didn't need my help. He walked without even getting booked."

179

"What about the driver of the wagon?"

"He didn't need my help, either. He was dead."

"Vehicular manslaughter an' there was no charge?"

"The story on the books is that nothing happened on that corner that night except a one-car collision with a pole."

"Hoo-hoo. You sit right there. You want a cup? How about a glass of water? I'd offer you some white lightin', but I don' know you good enough."

Bellerose moved out of the office with surprising speed and was back within five minutes. He was grinning.

"Cop down in Hollywood didn' believe I was a police officer. Said actors was always tryin' that gag out on him. You must have good times out there in movin'-picture land. You know what he said? He said the thing what fell out of the wagon was a made-up dummy this fella was takin' over to some movie set."

"That's the story going around, all right."

"You don't believe it?"

"Do you?"

"Say I bought your goods. I'd still like to know why you stopped by. Just down here on a little vacation, is it? Just passed the station on the way to take a look at the housing projects where Storyville used to be and said to yourself, 'Why don' I just stop in and do some old boy a favor? Tell him about the body with no head back in L.A. Give the sucker a hand up.'"

"I thought it was something you'd like to know."

"I thank you kindly. Where'd you get those pictures?"

"Those are off the snuff reel. Those from the L.A. morgue."

"You got the reel with you?"

Whistler handed the cassette over. "You know a local smutter by the name of Barcaloo?" he asked.

All of a sudden Bellerose was no turtle. He leaned forward, hunching his shoulders and putting his forearms on the desk. His neck swelled and his body filled out the suit, assuming the disguise of a bull.

"I know him. Do you know him?" Bellerose asked.

"We never met, but I think I know him. He runs an X-rated movie house, some dirty bookshops, a whorehouse . . ."

". . . a filthy press and other enterprises. What's your interest?"

180

"I think he made this crap. A young Latino girl's beheaded in it. The Vietnamese woman, whose body disappeared from the L.A. morgue and ended up in the gutter, is on this tape doing tricks with the Latino. I think Barcaloo had something to do with that too. Either Barcaloo or somebody he knows is good with a machete. Barcaloo's got two gazoonies working for him, a big one and a little one."

"Dom Pinole and Jickie Rojo."

"They drove a Cadillac with a Bondoed fender. It's been painted red."

"We'll look into it."

There was a beat-up RCA tape player and a nineteen-inch color set on a table in the corner. Bellerose got up and went over to slam the cassette into the top loader. After pulling three or four buttons and depressing a couple of switches, the player hummed and the screen lit up. He picked up the remote and went to sit down again.

Whistler watched the sorry sex scenario unfold again. The story seemed to have something to do with the delights of girls imported from Hong Kong or Singapore and sold into the flesh trade.

"We don't see many of them in New Orleans," Bellerose said.

"Many of what? Prostitutes?"

"Many Orientals. And no Vietnamese whores I ever heard about."

They watched the sex acts flickering on the television screen in silence.

"This kind of thing give you a hard-on?" Bellerose said.

"Only if I'm long deprived."

"Gives me a hard-on. Shitty stuff. Shouldn't be on the shelves. But I can understand some gazoony without a woman, or with the wrong woman, watching crap like this and having it off with Mary Fist."

"We don't have to watch the whole thing," Whistler said.

Bellerose tossed Whistler the remote control.

Whistler ran the tape at speed until he came to the close-up of Lim Shu Dok. "This look like the head you got on ice?"

"What we got on ice don't look like nothin' I'd want to show my granny."

181

"Can I have a look?"

"You can, but I'm tellin' you, it don't look human anymore."

"How about forensic's description?"

Bellerose nodded. "Trade you for copies of your pictures. We got a machine."

Whistler ran the tape ahead to the look of terror on the girl's face at the entrance of the swordsman and the upswing of the swordsman's arm. He stopped it before the blood gushed.

Whistler became aware of the sounds of the squad room going on outside the walls of the room. Phones ringing, voices talking back and forth, footsteps and slamming doors. Ordinary things.

"I seen this before," Bellerose said. "If that Mex girl was beheaded, we ain' found any part of her yet "

"You talk to Barcaloo about it?"

"Sure, we talked to him about it. He takes us over to the studio in a warehouse down by the river where he says he shoots his erotic films. He shows us the soundstage and the cameras and the laboratory where they do trick photography."

"You ask him where the Latino girl and the Asian woman might be?"

"He said how the hell should he know where wanderin' whores go. He practically dared me to prove he snuffed the girl. 'Fin' her,' he said. 'Fin' the Saigon whore,' he said. 'She'll tell you it was all a trick.'"

"Maybe he knew you'd never find either one of them. But now there's a head here in New Orleans and a body with a butterfly on the hip back in L.A."

"You say that, but the L.A.P.D. don't say that. You see the problem I got?" He took the remote out of Whistler's hand and hit the rewind. While the tape whirred back to the beginning he stared at Whistler.

"What else brings you here?" Bellerose said.

"There was an actress riding in the BMW. She saw the corpse they call a dummy. The day after the crash she gets an offer to come down here on quick notice and take over a part in a film."

"And Barcaloo's the man she was sent to see?"

"I think it's a fair bet."

"What makes you think so?"

"A chain of probabilities starting with a piece of funny money advertising his porno movie house, which I found on the lady's dressing table."

"You tellin' me this actress in L.A. gets a rush offer from a guy who's carryin' play money in his pocket from a porno house in New Orleans and she just comes traipsin' down here? Sounds to me like she knows what she's doin', but you don' know what she's doin'. Maybe you don' even know her too good."

"I'm going to ask her when I find her. And when I find her, maybe I'll need some help."

Bellerose settled back in the chair again, the swivel squeaking like a smashed rat. He seemed to shrink inside his shirt and suit again. His eyes took on the sleepy look of a sly old turtle.

"You just bring me cause."

"Like another head?"

"Don' smart-mouth me. What the hell you think, we're brain-stunned down here? You think I ain' seen this crap before? You think we don' watch? Looka hear what I'm tellin' you. This ain' your town. I fin' you someplace you shouldn't be, I'll bust your ass. I don' care you're down here lookin' for your lady love."

Twenty-four

New Orleans is an easy stakeout town. There are people of all kinds and classes loafing everywhere, on benches, stoops, and curbstones, leaning against storefronts, gates, and garden walls at all hours of the day or night.

Whistler sat in his rental car parked across the street from the Beaver Run.

It was either stake out the movie house or the apartment house on Ursuline Street where Barcaloo lived. A fifty-fifty chance that he was wrong or right. Except the only reason he could figure for the funny money he found in Shiela's apartment was because it had the address of the Beaver Run on it. They'd use the office in a half-assed attempt to make it look like business.

If he was wrong, if he missed her, if she arrived someplace where Whistler wasn't and was taken wherever they were going to shoot the picture, or do the terrible thing to her he feared they were going to do, he'd have lost her. Not just for now but forever.

On the other hand, even as he sweated, she could be sitting in some air-cooled restaurant lunching on prawns, jambalaya, and

Sazerac cocktails while some legitimate, if marginal, movie producer talked to her about character motivation and the beautiful wardrobe she'd get to wear. Well, that would be all right. He'd rather be a damned fool than a mourner.

The sun was straight up overhead, burning like a klieg. He had an awful thirst. He was about to get out and go find a beer in some place where he could keep an eye out when two men, a big one and a little one—Pinole and Rojo, who else could it be?—parked the freshly painted red '81 Cadillac in front of the movie house.

They got out and disappeared inside.

Barcaloo turned around and put his hands on the wrought-iron rail and hung like a monkey, lowering his head to stare down at the street between the bars.

Bouche looked at the back of his neck and wondered if it would kill him if she hit him with all her strength right behind the ear with a heavy pot in which a camellia grew.

He looked around as if he heard her thoughts. Then he stared back down into the street again.

Barcaloo didn't think of himself as a brute, even if he did look like a hairy ape. He didn't get where he was in the skin trade just by scaring pussy to death. He had a certain smooth, a certain charm.

He'd learned how to control women from Fan-Tan Leaper, king pimp in the French Quarter twenty years before, when Barcaloo was just a growing boy. Leaper had been as skinny as a trout, weak-eyed and weak-chinned, with snaggle teeth that almost never saw a toothbrush. He chewed twelve packs of Juicy Fruit a day, just to keep his breath sweet. There was always a line of angry red pimples on his neck where his starched collar sawed at him. He wore a tie winter and summer. He had a stool permanently reserved for him at a place called Billy Wimple's, from which he ran his stable of high assed, high-yellow girls and handed out bits of carnal and criminal wisdom.

"You go around tryin' to power a strange cunt into doin' this or that—you grab her by the hair and knock her against the wall—what you got is a bitch yellin' rape on you. Runnin' down

185

the avenue lookin' to throw herself into the arms of the first cop or pimp ready to defend her, you unnerstan'?" he'd say. "You got to do like with a cat. First ignore her. Let her come to you. Then you feed her sweet cream and peaches. You play like you don' even see she's got legs and tits.

"Now, when you feed her the cream, don' be stingy. Pour it on. If she got ugly ears, you say you never see such pretty seashells, how the light shines through them. She got a honker like a bugle, you tell her handsome noses was very highly prized by Roman emperors and French kings, pointin' out that Madame Bovary and the great witch queen, Marie Laveau, both had noses the prow of any ship would be proud to wear. If she got no tits, tell her she's a lady born out of her time, quality from the twenties come to grace this sorry age with her lovely figure. You hear what I'm tellin' you?"

"Suppose she knows what she's got ain't much and says you're full of shit?"

"What you expect her to say unless she's a sorry fool? So what you do, you eat it and make like it's tasty. You act shy and humble in the face of such misguided self-abnegation."

"Self what?"

"Never mind. We talkin' cunt, not vocabulary. You shake your head in shocked dismay. You cluck your tongue. You twist and turn and pour it on. Slop it in there by the pint. By the quart. By the fuckin' gallon! For it is written, 'There ain' no pussy alive that will not twitch when they is properly stroked.' Also remember, 'Excess is not to be feared so long as the eye is sincere.'"

"Suppose she ain' as ugly as a trout, but pretty enough to stop your heart."

"The opposite applies. Feed her vinegar. Mention that she's got a little droopy eyelid—too bad—but maybe it's better she shouldn't be perfect, after all. Say the little scar on her lip gives her face a certain character. Go easy here, you unnerstan'? Plenty of vinegar, but just a dab of cream to keep her sweet. Pussy gets a sour stomach if she goes chasin' somewhere else lookin' for her sweets."

"So why not give her candy right off?"

"Because she gets candy all the goddamn time from every

asshole tryin' to get into her silkies. After her tongue is stingin' from what you give her, just a tiny candy drop from you is worth more than a ten-pound box from any other dude. You unnerstan' these tactics, or is it too much for you?"

"I'm learnin'."

"Next thing—get her out of her clothes. Every one of them wants to get out of her clothes. All they's lookin' for is a reason. If they get into long skirts, they got a slit up the front almost to the flower patch, and their tits is fallin' out of the tops of their blouses. You know what I mean? You look at the back of their knees they stepping on a bus, they freeze you with a haughty glance. Down on the beach they's dressed in two dimes and a nickel."

"I'll get a camera and say I want to take their pitcher."

"Sheee-it. Don' talk foolish. If they do tricks in the buff for your camera, and then you lay a hand on the skin, even an old whore will say she's been tricked and betrayed."

"So what do I do?"

"Learn to give massage."

"Will you run that bus by me one more time?"

Leaper held up his hands like they belonged to a surgeon just after washing and before getting into rubber gloves.

"These magic fingers has plucked more cherries than the trees got apples in the state of Washington. Say she's a secretary and tells you that evening, whilst you're havin' a little drink at a bar, 'Oh, dear, my tailbone does hurt from so much sittin'.' You say, 'I got just the thing for that.' Suppose she's a salesgirl in a department store and she say, 'Lord a mercy, how my poor feet do ache.' Up you smile and show your hands and say, 'My dear old mother, may she rest in peace, used to say I had magic hands when I rubbed her sweet old feet at the end of a hard day.' Maybe she's a—"

"I think I got you. Say like she's a basketball player and she's got this ugly on her thigh where somebody clipped her, and she say, 'Oh my, oh my, that girl was rough and kicked me with her knee,' and I say, 'See these hands? These is the hands what nursed my basketball-playin' brother back to health and strength after he was brought down by the worst charley horse ever known in Louisiana sports.'"

187

"A little gaudy, but I think you got the idea. So you stroke them a little, and then you say deep massage works better without clothes gettin' in the way. If only she would just take the tail of her blouse out of the waistband of her skirt. If only she would take off her stockings. If only . . ."

". . . she would take off her jeans."

"So you baby them, an hol' them and drip honey in their ear. So you fuck them."

"And you tell them how good it was."

"Wrong. You tell them how good it was in a way that says it weren't so very good at all. Fair, maybe. So-so. But you ain' goin' to have any trouble doin' without. So she's on her mettle now, you . . ."

"What metal?"

"Never mind. She wants to be a winner, even with poor, ungrateful you. So she practically begs you for an encore. You let her try again, and you act a little disgusted. Then you slap her one when she comes at you for more. That's the tricky part. Some run away after that. But just as many are glad for it. Glad they is gettin' punished for being such stupid, dirty, careless creatures, givin' it away to such as you when good-lookin' stockbrokers and doctors are ready to practically marry them to get it. You unnerstan' what's goin' on here? You unnerstan' the situation that you've built? Everythin'—the sweet and the bitter, the soft and the rough, the kind and the mean—comes from you. Comes from one man. They don' got to shop around different places to get it. You're like an emotional supermarket. You got everythin' she needs in stock. Cunt is lazy creatures, don' you forget. Most of them got a good deal of ambition but very little drive. Remember that and you can't go wrong."

Barcaloo turned around.

Bouche saw his face and was terrified all over again.

"Go get dressed," Barcaloo said. "I want you should come meet this actress somebody sent me from L.A."

Bouche tried not to wonder why someone would send an actress from L.A. to see Barcaloo in New Orleans when Barcaloo was going to be there in a few days.

Something terrible was about to happen. She just knew it.

* * *

The shadows were getting longer and longer, but it wasn't getting any cooler. The day just seemed to be withering up. The street was practically empty except for men stopping into the Beaver Run. The movie house was doing pretty good business. There were a lot of lonely, hungry men out there.

A taxi pulled up. Shiela Andes got out. She was dressed in a straw linen suit and carried a big flat oblong bag made of the same stuff. Her jacket was open to show off her yellow silk blouse, cut low in front. Even from across the street Whistler could see the flash of lighter skin as the cloth dipped away from the shallow valley between her widespread breasts. Her skirt was below the knee but slit high on both sides so that her thighs flashed almost to the tops of her seamed stockings. She straightened them as the cab pulled away, her long hair swaying like pale waterfalls on either side of her face.

Whistler felt a gripe in his belly and remembered when she'd kissed him.

She looked his way and he reached over, as though checking out his glove compartment. He had the rearview fixed so he could see the front of the Beaver Run. Shiela looked up at the marquee advertising the bill of fare. Her hair cascaded down her back. It was as hot as the mouth of hell, but she looked as cool as a yellow diamond. Whistler expected she'd be like a piece of hard candy with a crisp shell and a soft, sweet, creamy center.

She hesitated. For a second Whistler had the wild hope that she'd turn around and walk away or flag down a cab. She took a step toward the lobby. For a second he didn't know what to do.

He got out of the car and ran across the street. He tapped her shoulder. She spun around, her eyes frightened and angry, not recognizing him. He spoke her name. Then she knew him.

"Whistler. What the hell are you doing here?"

"I took you up on your invitation. I called your place. You weren't home."

Little lines appeared between her eyebrows. He wanted to put his thumb on them and smooth them away.

"You didn't follow me two thousand miles just to ask for a date?" she said.

"This is a queer deal. Can't you see that?"

189

"What are you talking about?"

"The movie offer. Getting you to come down here to New Orleans."

"Do you think I'm stupid? Do you think I'm a trout? I didn't swallow it just like that. I checked around before I took the offer."

"A meeting in a goddamn porno house. Where's your brains?"

"I've interviewed for things in an empty warehouse, on an old barge tied up in Wilmington, once in a goddamn dry culvert along the Los Angeles River bottom. Somebody send you after me?"

Whistler heard a car pull up to the curb. He heard the blare of a horn at his back. Shiela looked past his shoulder.

"Are you Mr. Barcaloo?" she said.

Whistler shifted his feet and turned around as Barcaloo got out of the Lincoln Continental and shuffled toward him with the troubled look of a puzzled bear on his face.

"You botherin' this here lady?" he said.

Whistler could see a plump, pretty blonde woman inside the Lincoln.

"For Christ's sake, Whistler, what do you think?" Shiela muttered. "You think Mr. Barcaloo brought his wife along to watch him do me harm?"

"You've got to take what I feel about this on faith."

"I hardly know you, Whistler."

Pinole and Rojo came hurrying out from under the shadow cast by the marquee. Whistler stepped away from Shiela.

"I'll be all right, Whistler. Believe me. I can take care of myself," Shiela said.

Afterward Whistler would remember that there was something wistful in the way she'd said it, as though she was hoping he would say in reply, "You just come with me, my little girl. Listen to your daddy." But he didn't say anything.

"You a goddamn pervert?" Barcaloo shouted.

Before Pinole and Rojo could reach him, Whistler turned and ran. Away from the rented car parked across the street. Around the corner, running the way a gazoony who accosted women would run.

Twenty-five

The little office off the lobby smelled like the manager slept in it. Posters of naked women papered the walls.

"Who was that asshole?" Barcaloo said.

"A big surprise, I can tell you," Shiela said. "I knew him back in Hollywood maybe five years ago."

"What's his name?"

"Whistler. That's the only one I can remember, that's how well I knew him. Where he came off thinking—"

"It's awful how a lady ain't safe walking down a street in broad daylight anymore," Bouche simpered. She was half loaded.

Barcaloo frowned at Bouche, telling her to shut up, wondering how she'd managed it.

"It's really nice of you to come all the way from L.A. to see me. Can I call you Shiela? Call me Nonny. Have a seat. You want somethin' cold to drink? Bouche, you want to go see we got any lemonade at the refreshment stand?"

"Nothing for me, thank you," Shiela said.

"So, what did my people back in L.A. say about the picture?"

"Nothing much at all. Just an actress took ill and—"

ROBERT CAMPBELL

"That's right. She came down with a flu or somethin'. We
couldn't wait for her to get better. You know what they say,
'Time is money.' So, if it's okay with you, Shiela, we'll go over to
the studio with Dom and Jickie here . . . make a test . . ."

"Test, Mr. Barcaloo? I came all this way on such short notice
because I was told I had the part."

"You've got the part. I'm not sayin' a test like that. I mean a
test like for your colorin' and like that. Give my crew a chance
to get acquainted with how you photograph and how your voice
sounds on tape. Just a little scene with Miss Cazebone,
here . . ."

"Wardrobe. How about wardrobe? Don't we need some
fittings?"

"I got to be honest with you, Shiela. There's not a lot of
wardrobe changes. I mean, it's not a costume picture, you
unnerstan' . . . it's not one of them epics. What you brought
with you is probably going to be all you're goin' to need. You
bring a bathrobe? We'll pay you for the use. If not, we can fix
you up. Now, if that ain't okay with you—"

"That's all right," Shiela said quickly, hating how much she
needed a job that she'd let herself be rushed here to this wet
asshole of a city. Hating how her voice was singing like a
goddamn flute and the way this hairy beast facing her, with his
mean eyes and swollen hands—like the hands of a corpse left
too long in water—was matching her trill for trill in a sorry
attempt to sound refined. "When will I see a script?"

"Well, we don't exactly work with a heavy script. We do like
that John Cassavetes does, you unnerstan'? We give the actors
the situation and a few lines to get them started and then . . ."

"Improvisation?"

"You got it. You ever improvisate?"

"Oh, plenty." She couldn't decide what actor Barcaloo reminded her of. For some reason it seemed important to get that
settled in her head . . . to put a tag on him. Otherwise the
trembling in her belly would never go away. Barcaloo had the
white teeth with the spaces just like Ernest Borgnine, but his
face wasn't half so kind.

"So that's the way we do."

"I'd like to see something. A treatment, perhaps?"

"Well, I can unnerstan' that. What I'm going to do—we're in a hurry you unnerstan'?—we got to leave for the Coast in a couple days."

"What? I mean, if you're leaving town in the middle of production, how big's this part I flew all the way—"

"Hey, hey, hey. Listen to you, gettin' all upset. What did I say? I said I was goin' to the Coast for a little conference with the money. I'm not goin' there to set up housekeepin'. . . ."

He knew Bouche was looking at him, trying to sort out what was going on. She was already wondering what they were doing shooting footage just before making the big move west. What the hell was the reason for it? A favor for a friend, Barcaloo had said. What kind of favor? A little private smut is what she'd thought at first. Some jerkoff wanting footage of his woman getting fucked and having it off with another woman. So, all right, she could get behind that, but what was all this playacting about? And what did Barcaloo mean lying to this broad about coming back to New Orleans? Why'd he have to go to the trouble? It was crazy, like Dom and Jickie hustling back and forth between New Orleans and L.A. Days out of synch. There were things Nonny, Dom, and Jickie did that she'd heard whispered about but which she'd never believed.

". . . so I'll be right back. That's why I want to have a little somethin' in the can to take back with me. You unnerstan'?"

"You've got shaky finances," Shiela said flatly, warily.

This broad gets ditsy, Barcaloo thought, the next thing you know, she wants to cop a sneak, and somebody has to lay a hand on her, and she opens her mouth to make like a siren, and then you got to punch her out, shut her up, ruin her kisser. Make for lousy footage. Attract attention. Next thing you know, she's diving off a gallery, or if she gets the fit to run in the car on the way to the studio, she's jumping out of a moving vehicle. Shit.

"When's money not shaky in this goddamn crazy business, right?" Barcaloo said in a voice loaded with patient understanding. He stood up. "So we shoot a little scene and see how it goes."

"This is all very quick," Shiela persisted.

"I gave you a whole day to settle in and get over jet lag or whatever. I can't give you any more time to fool aroun', you

193

unnerstan'? We do a little work today, and tonight we take you to Brennan's, Galatoire's, Arnaud's—you name it—for the best dinner you had in years. How's that sound?"

"It sounds okay," Shiela said, knowing she was grinning like a fool, feeling really very bad and scared all of a sudden. Wishing she'd taken Whistler's word about the nature of this deal. Wishing she'd gone with him. Understanding in a flash, like the climactic light shot in a Spielberg picture, that Whistler must care for her one hell of a lot to come all this way to tap her shoulder in front of a movie house. What the hell had she been thinking about, agreeing to meet a producer in a goddamn porno house in the first place? The theater owner was a businessman breaking out of the skin trade, the agent back in Hollywood had said. Here's the address on this piece of advertising money, he'd said. What a gag, right?

Thinking about it now, she admitted to herself that the calls she'd made around checking on the legitimacy of the man who'd made the deal hadn't been very reassuring. She'd heard what she'd wanted to hear. Wanting an opportunity. Wanting a beginning. So badly. Now, here she was wondering how to tell this Barcaloo she'd changed her mind. She stood up because everyone else including Bouche were standing up, and she didn't know what else to do.

"You want to drive over to the studio with Pinole and Rojo here? Talk about lighting and whatever? Or you want to drive over with Bouche and me?"

"She'll come with us," Bouche said, taking Shiela's arm. "You drive and we'll sit in the back and talk."

"That's good. That's good."

Bouche walked Shiela out of the office. Pinole and Rojo lingered behind.

"This broad is ditsy," Rojo said. "She could be a lot of trouble."

"So maybe we just shoot some footage today and that's the end of it. We don't try to get any more tomorrow or the next day. We just get a few shots today. And that's that."

Shiela was riding in the Lincoln Continental with the apeman in the white linen suit. The wedding-cake blonde, falling out of her flowered chiffon, sat in back with Shiela, holding on to her arm as though they were old school chums. The newly painted red Cadillac followed the Lincoln, and Whistler followed the Cadillac.

It was no trouble through the narrow streets of the French Quarter, but after they crossed the Greater New Orleans Bridge, it got a little harder.

Whistler fell back on 90 and stayed back along Barataria through the town of Estelle and into the Bayou des Familles. He was laying a half a mile behind, along a particularly lonely stretch, when the two cars up ahead turned off and disappeared along a side track. Whistler kicked it to forty-five and almost missed the twin ruts and the thinning of the palmetto. He backed up and turned into the side road, stopped, and set the hand brake.

The sounds of the two engines, quickly muffled in the heavy growth, faded away along the green, sweaty tunnel. He had no way of knowing how far the track led.

He got the courtesy map out of the glove compartment. They'd gone west just before the Ross Canal. There were wetlands and canals into Plaquemines Parrish and the United States Naval Air Station beyond. They might be going one mile or five along the unmarked track. Chances were it never got wider. If he started into the jungle, he might not have anyplace to hide the car or even turn around until he got to wherever they were going. If anybody started back, he'd be standing there with his pants down. If he walked in, he'd be throwing away mobility.

A frog, squatting in a patch of rotting moss, cocked a suspicious eye and croaked. He started the car and backed up to the road, then drove it onto a solid patch surrounded by man-high reed and fern about a hundred yards beyond the turnoff.

Then he started walking into the hot, dank, dark green jungle, smelling of mud, rot, and abandoned swimming pools in the basements of old athletic clubs; smelling of dying two thousand miles from La-La Land.

Twenty-six

The tin Quonset hut with the generator alongside, squatting in the middle of the asphalt and gravel, looked like a swamp monster with its child. It reminded Whistler of isolated, abandoned motor depots and ammunition dumps that seemed to sprout out of the ground on every army camp he'd ever known.

The Lincoln and the Cadillac were parked there, ass-to-nose.

He hurried across the clearing into the protection of the shadow cast by the generator. He'd counted his paces coming in, as much to still his rising anxiety as to estimate the distance traveled. He reckoned it to be two miles, more or less. Forty minutes by his watch. The generator was chugging away, making electricity. The fuel to run it was piled beside it, half under a tarpaulin.

A red light, just like those on the real soundstages back in Hollywood, shone dully above the door that warned visitors away when shooting was in progress, even though nothing but gators and toads were around to interrupt.

His shirt and pants were wet clear through. Even his shoes felt soggy, and his watch strap was turning to butter.

The light went out. He expected it would be time to make a move when it went on again and they were back at work, but he had no plan. Who could have plans so far from home? Who could have plans for a danger without an identity? What he had as evidence was flimsier than circumstantial; it wouldn't have held up on a traffic-ticket bust.

But still he felt the danger in his belly and balls. Why'd Shiela have to kiss him and leave her leg out in the rain, as if she didn't know it was getting wet? Why the hell did she have to go and do that and twist his heart around and have him chasing around doing good deeds, rescuing foolish damsels in distress?

He checked out the cars. Neither one was locked. The keys to the Cadillac were in the ignition.

The red light came on again. He crossed the open space, glad that there was only the one window in the door and no face in it looking out. He pulled the handle, like the kind on big meat lockers, and pulled the heavy door, as thick as a wall to proof the studio against the steady roar of the generator, toward him. A rush of cool air made him weak. He was inside in a second, facing another door. He stood in the sound lock and looked through a window, laminated with chicken wire, into the belly of the shack.

It was all shadows and gloom in front. Nothing moved. He went inside, and it was colder still. His shirt turned to ice. He shivered against the cold and marveled about how quickly the body and mind complained when tossed from change to change. Hot one minute and complaining. Cold the next and still complaining. Always trying to get it just right. Always missing by a cat's whisker.

Cables snaked all over the dirty floor. He picked his way around and over them like a tightrope walker, his eyes straight ahead toward the place where a pool of light marked the playing area. The "Go Fuck a Duck" poster was on the wall.

Shiela stood under a white-hot spotlight, holding a trench coat around her as though willing it to change itself into armor. There were cheap shower scuffs on her bare feet. Even from the distance Whistler could see the dew of perspiration on her upper lip and the way the fine hairs clung to the shallows of her

197

temples, damp with fear. Her eyes were showing too much white.

"Hey," she said, as though speaking from a great distance, the high notes bouncing off the tin roof in little singing echos, "I feel like you're rushing me again."

The cushy blonde came out of a wallboard dressing room. She had on pink feathered mules and a pink transparent negligee and nothing else.

"For heaven's sake, Shiela, honey, there's nothin' to be so nervous about. Look at me. It don't bother me. I been doin' this for years, and it don't bother me one little bit."

The smaller of Barcaloo's two associates had his arm draped over the top of a thirty-five-millimeter camera mounted on a tripod. The bigger one was sitting at a portable mixer about the size of a musical synthesizer on four spindly chrome legs with earphones draped around his neck. Both of them looked bored and impatient, like cats at a mouse hole, charged with anticipation but hiding it lest their auras scare the mouse away.

"I'm not that used to it," Shiela said.

"You've had your clothes off in front of a camera before, ain't you?" Barcaloo said.

Whistler worked his way nearer, staying close to the wall. Off to one side, beyond the cheapjack dressing rooms, he could see a side exit.

"In front of still cameras with a cameraman, a cameraman's assistant, a hairdresser, a makeup girl, a—"

"This ain't MGM—what do you think? This ain't *Penthouse* magazine. It's a little studio stuck down here in New Orleans. What we got here is a limited crew, you unnerstan'? Just enough to get the job done and no more. We ain't union. We keep costs—"

"Well, there it is, you see? I belong to the Screen Actors Guild, and I'm not even sure I should be working a non-union picture," Shiela said with the breathlessness of a drowning woman grasping at straws.

"For Christ's sake!" Barcaloo bellowed.

It was like the silence that follows a clap of thunder. Whistler stopped moving, but the scrape of his foot was as crisp and clear as the sound of bones breaking. Barcaloo turned his head sharply and posed, listening as an animal listens.

"Hey, Jickie," he said softly.

The cameraman left the camera and started toward the side of the shack and the shadows where Whistler stood. There was a built-out storage closet two steps back. Whistler took the two steps and slipped inside and closed the door behind him. He was standing on some soft, uneven surface. He didn't dare move. He just stood there like a demented juggler, holding his balance and stilling his breath. He could hear Rojo's measured footsteps pass the closet as he walked all the way to the entrance and back again.

"Swamp rat," Whistler heard him say from the stage area. "How long is this crap going on?"

The smell in the confined space of the closet was terrible. Whistler managed to snake his pencil flash out of his hip pocket without falling over. He turned it on and shone the beam down at his feet. He was standing on the tangled bodies of a naked man and woman. The woman had her face in the hollow of the man's neck as though seeking comfort. The man stared up at Whistler, his eyes glistening brilliantly, even in the dim light of the tiny flash.

The hair on the back of Whistler's neck and along his arms rose up with a terrible chill. His bladder almost gave way.

"You know what a bad couple days I've been havin', lady?" Barcaloo said, loud enough for Whistler to risk leaving the closet. "I've been havin' a very bad couple of days, you unnerstan'? So I don't want any more of your crap. Don't play the Virgin Mary with me. You cunt are all alike. You do things and make believe you didn't. Take off that goddamn bathrobe and lay down on that bed and do like I tell you."

Whistler took three deep breaths.

"Like hell I will," Shiela said right back, but her voice carried no conviction. "I'm getting out of here."

"You're not gettin' out of nowhere, you silly cunt. What's the game? You hurry your ass down here on a blind offer—"

"I'm an actress. I was offered a part—"

"Don't make like you didn't know what was the deal. You're a pussy. You're a pussy, and a pair of tits and a big ass—"

199

"Why're you talkin' to this lady like that?" Bouche said.

"Because Walter Cape, the man what's going to help me be somebody, wants I should teach this broad a lesson, goddammit!" Barcaloo roared.

Whistler put the pencil flash in his pocket and poked it out, wondering if he could convince three hard types that it was a gun. Never in a million years. He hurried back to the entrance.

"It's going to be all right, honey," Bouche said nervously. "Just let's do like he says. Nonny's really an all-right guy, you don't make him mad."

"You can't keep me here against my will, for God's sake."

Barcaloo started to laugh.

"What the hell you gonna do? Scream? You gonna scream an' wake up the fuckin' gators? You just fuckin' listen to me. You strip down and start doin' like I tell you or I'll throw you to Dom and Jickie here, an' when they're finished with you they'll toss you . . ."

Whistler went through the sound lock and out into the wet heat. He went to the Lincoln, opened the door, and released the hand brake, then pushed it over alongside the fuel dump. He grabbed one of the jerry cans of gasoline, ran to the generator, cracked the can, and poured gas in a puddle, then ran a stream back to the fuel store and the Lincoln.

He built a little bridge by making a circle of his belt.

It only took twenty seconds to shut down the generator, disconnect the starter leads, and place them an inch apart on the leather loop. He ran around to the side of the building and waited.

Pinole came out and went over to the generator. He pushed the starter button. The spark flashed across the leads and ignited the gas fumes. The tongue of fire ran along the ground and under the tarp. Pinole watched it run, saw that the Lincoln had been moved, and got the idea. He started to turn away when the gasoline dump went up and blew the Lincoln and him into the swamp.

Whistler was at the side door before all of Pinole landed, and through the door before the explosion stopped echoing across the wetlands. Birds were screaming. A bull gator sounded a challenge.

Inside the darkened Quonset a woman was screaming her head off and Barcaloo was cursing. Whistler snapped on the pencil flash and passed it across the room. It landed on Bouche.

"Oh, my God, Nonny, don't kill me," she screamed.

He moved the spot, found Shiela, and snapped it off.

"That you, Jickie?" Barcaloo shouted. "Shine it over here."

"I got no flash," Rojo said.

Whistler grabbed Shiela by the wrist, put his hand over her mouth and his lips right on her ear.

"The cavalry's come to get you."

"Have you got the flashlight, Bouche?" Barcaloo said.

Bouche didn't answer. She just kept on screaming that Barcaloo shouldn't kill her.

Whistler dragged Shiela through the door.

"Oh, you are one sweet-looking son of a bitch," she said.

They were out the side door in a second, with Barcaloo's startled and enraged curses chasing after them.

Whistler practically threw Shiela into the Cadillac and pushed her to the passenger's side with his hip. The engine kicked over first go. He drove around the pillar of fire, which had spread to the wooden parts of the studio and was starting to eat it up. He drove like hell down the long green tunnel pierced by the dirt road until he reached his rented car.

He got the tire iron out of the Cadillac's trunk, lifted the hood, and smashed the carburetor and distributor to scrap.

They got into his rental and sped away. Barcaloo and Rojo were two miles away without transport, and still Whistler didn't feel entirely safe.

Shiela was huddled on her side of the car as though wanting to grab Whistler but afraid that if she laid a hand on him, they would end up in a ditch where Barcaloo and Rojo would find and kill them.

"Why me?" she said. "Why'd they go to all the trouble to get me down here?"

Whistler turned his head to look at her. "I don't know," he said.

Her trench coat had fallen open. She was naked underneath except for a skinny pair of briefs. She saw where he was looking and closed the coat.

Twenty-seven

Coxey sat behind his register in the all-night drugstore at one o'clock in the morning, shuffling his stack of calling cards, peering up the skirt of the whore perched on the lunch-counter stool.

He thought about that Yankee son of a bitch asshole Whistler—what the fuck kind of name was that?—threatening him the way he did. Who the hell did he think he was? Who the hell he think he was fucking with? Some two-bit hustler? Some garbage collector?

Probably was already out of New Orleans. Good thing for him. What did that fool think he was doing backing a man like him into an aisle with the dishcloths and dish drainers? Where'd he get that corny dialogue? "Clean out your windpipe like a squash." What kind of goddamn talk was that? Throwing him a fiver—no, not a fiver, four dollars and forty-one cents— like he was handing him a big score. Just what kind of shit was that? Nobody fast enough to keep Mickey Mouse from drinking his blood. That was the worst bullshit he'd ever heard. Worse than anything those television writers put into the mouths of all those faggot actors.

Whistler was probably a faggot too. Half the men in La-La Land were faggots. Everybody knew that. Fucker come nosing around, playing cozy, get a line on the manufacturer with the idea in mind that he could save some money, cut out the middleman. Faggot porn. Snuff. S and M. Kiddie porn. Cut out the connection. Fuck him out of a commission. Queer son of a bitch. Had his nerve trying to throw a scare into somebody like Crib Coxey.

He picked up the phone and rang around. He got Barcaloo over to Jimmy Flynn's on St. Peter Street where that coffee-colored nigger, Henry, worked a shift at the bar and fucked the white ladies in the storeroom. Fucked Nonny Barcaloo's woman, Bouche, too, so he'd been told. Told by Henry himself when he'd come in one night, half stoned on cocaine, to buy some Johnny the Conqueror root to wear around his neck so his tool would stay up and working. Coxey wondered if the high and mighty Nonny Barcaloo knew about *that*. He'd guess not; otherwise, Bouche would be buried in a bayou like so many others were rumored to be buried.

"Who are you and what do you want?" Barcaloo mumbled into the phone.

"You don't know me, Mr. Barcaloo. My name is Crib Coxey, and I work the owl shift in the all-night drugs over to Common and Rampart."

"What are you sellin'?"

"Well, I'm not really sellin' anything, Mr. Barcaloo. Something happened I thought might interest you."

"Yeah? So tell me."

"Maybe I could come over to Jimmy Flynn's." How the hell could a man get a tip over the phone? You can't shove a hundred dollar bill down the goddamn wires.

"Maybe you couldn't. We're havin' a wake for a very good friend of mine what just died, and it wouldn't look good for me to be takin' time with a stranger."

"Who was it died, you don't mind my asking?"

"Dom Pinole."

"Well, hell, I know Dom Pinole. Him and Jickie Rojo used to come in here for a little of this and a little of that every now and then."

"A little of what and a little of what?"

"You know. A little dope. A little skag. A little crank."

"You a fuckin' pusher?"

"Well, like, I do a little dealing with friends."

"You come on over," Barcaloo said.

Coxey chased out the solitary whore and locked up the store. If the owners found out there'd be hell to pay, but he figured he was making an investment in his future and he didn't intend to be a clerk in an all-night drugstore forever.

He was feeling so hopeful about the reward of gratitude he'd get from Barcaloo that he grabbed a cab to Jimmy Flynn's.

It didn't look like any wake to him when he peeked through the doors. A naked woman was dancing on the bar. There was a lot of booze splashing around and a lot of people getting wet. Barcaloo was sitting at the best table with Jickie Rojo and his woman, Bouche. The table had a dozen black candles burning on it, and there was a clock facing east. Old New Orleans funeral custom at a laying-out. But where was the body?

A hand like a ham pushed against his chest. Jimmy Flynn said he wasn't allowed. They were having a private wake. Coxey said he'd been asked. Flynn looked over to Barcaloo, and Barcaloo waved Coxey in.

Coxey walked over to the table.

"Hello, Jickie," he said. "Hello, Mr. Barcaloo. I'm very sorry to hear about Dom Pinole. Where's he going to be laid out?"

"Right here."

Coxey looked around, expecting he'd maybe missed the corpse lying on the bar under the dancer's naked feet.

"Right here," Barcaloo said, tapping the table for emphasis.

Coxey looked. There was the tip of a finger, complete with fingernail, in the center of the table surrounded by the candles.

"That's all we could find of him," Rojo said.

Coxey almost laughed, but when he took a second look at the expression on Rojo's face, he knew he'd die where he stood if he dared it. Pinole had been blown away in the harshest way, and it was clear that Rojo intended to make someone pay for it.

"All right," Barcaloo said, "tell me."

"Some Yankee came into the store last night asking about the Beaver Run."

"Some Yankee? You mean somebody from the East?"

"I mean, not one of us. Not from the South. This jerkoff came from L.A. asking questions about who owned the Beaver Run. Who you was and what else you did. Where you lived."

"And you told him?"

"I didn't see the harm. After all, practically everybody knows about you, Mr. Barcaloo. A man like you can't hide his light."

"Last night? This happened last night?"

"That's right."

"Then why the hell didn't you call me last night?"

"It was very late."

"And you made some profit on this Yankee and thought you could make some more," Rojo said with a mean little twist to his mouth.

"Something like that, you shoulda called me," Barcaloo said. "Ought to break your fuckin' arms and legs. Ought to mash your liver."

Bouche giggled. "Oh, he don't mean it. Sit down and have a drink."

"Stand up and tell me anything else you got to tell me. And don't listen to her. She's drunk. I mean it."

"Well, if that's what a person gets for trying to do another person a favor," Bouche said, seriously outraged.

Coxey threw a pleading glance at her, asking her to shut up and not come to his defense. If she tried to help him again, she could be helping him right into the hospital or the grave. He could see that. He could also see that it hadn't been such a great idea coming down here hoping to make a score off Barcaloo.

Rojo started to get up.

"This asshole was stupid," Coxey said. "He gave me his credit card. His name is Whistler."

"What did he look like?"

When Coxey described the height, width, and breadth of Whistler, the pale, melancholy eyes, the rough hair and sad mouth, Bouche piped up and said, "That's the asshole who was trying to mess with our Shiela."

Barcaloo cast her a withering and pitying glance. He peeled off a hundred dollars from a roll and handed it to Coxey.

"You see or hear this sucker again, you call me, you hear? Now get the hell out of here."

"Hey," Bouche said, newly concerned about Barcaloo's manners. "Ain't you going to ask Dom's old friend to drink a memorial drink to Dom's finger?"

Twenty-eight

She'd been okay on the ride out of the bayou to the airport and the first plane out for anywhere. Okay on the flight to Phoenix where they got tickets on his plastic into L.A. Okay that first night, begging only for the chance to have a bath and a long rest.

He'd called Bellerose in New Orleans as he watched her sleeping.

"This is Whistler," he'd said when Bellerose got on the phone.

"Where are you?"

"L.A."

"Wish you were still here," Bellerose drawled in his sulfur-and-molasses voice. "There's questions."

"That's why I called."

"There was a fire over to the Bayou des Familles. Seems a generator blew up its feed. A shack somebody was using for a movie studio burnt to the ground. Brand new Lincoln Continental burnt down to a shell. Motor Vehicles is checking ownership."

"Barcaloo owned it."

"I figured that sonofabitch had another studio when he showed us that one by the river. Found a little piece of somebody caught in a palmetto. I don' think we're ever going to know who that belonged to."

"Dom Pinole."

"You're a regular fountain of information. What am I supposed to think?"

"You don't have to bother. I'll tell you. I went in there on my own. I followed the woman from Hollywood I told you about and went in on my own. She was being threatened. I didn't have a gun. I did what I could with what I had."

"Oh, I could tell you was a resourceful fella. Brave, too. But what made you think they was goin' to off her?"

"Did you poke around in the ashes of the studio?"

"We may be country boys, Whistler, but we're careful. We found the remains of those two people and other things. You know those two?"

"I never met them, but I think I know who they were. I think you'll find out their names were Chippy Byrd and Lacy Ohio."

"Bucherleider and Oskanowsky."

"What?"

"Those were their real names."

"Are you going to bring Barcaloo in?"

"I would. Except Barcaloo and his woman and his boy, Jickie Rojo, has lef' town. Maybe I'll leave town, too. How's the weather out there?"

"Pissy. But you want to visit, you can always find me at Gentry's, the corner of Hollywood and Vine."

"I'll think on it," Bellerose said, and hung up.

So, that first day it had looked to Whistler like Shiela was going to be okay. A woman who might be as tough as she pretended to be.

In the morning she made a move on him, sliding across the bed until she bumped into him. Suddenly, while she was moving her thighs against his hip and nuzzling his neck, it hit her like a hammer. While he held her in his arms and she shook and kept on shaking, Whistler learned a little something new about himself. He learned he got off on somebody else's fear. The trembling of her long legs and flat belly, the soft blows of her heart against his chest, filled him with a kind of exhilaration he'd never felt in quite that way before. He wasn't actually glad she was so terrified, but he couldn't be all that unhappy about what it was that made her cling to him for safety and comfort. He was, he realized, a man like too many others, strongest when somebody else showed weak. The shakes went on for a long time. When he tried to still them with the soft violence of sex, it still took a long time for them to go away. Every time he entered her, he could feel the trembling there, too. Finally she calmed down.

They lay there in the half-light of the overcast sky, listening to the swishing rumble of the cars streaming along Cahuenga down below.

"If you close your eyes you can imagine you're in a house on the beach at Malibu and that's the surf," Whistler said.

"I'm so glad you were the one picked me up from Tillman's car and took me home."

"There's a modest look on my face," Whistler said.

She turned around and crouched above him, staring down into his eyes with a look he hadn't seen in a dozen years.

"My God, I thought I was such a tough bird," she murmured. "I thought I knew all the moves. I thought I could slip and slide my way through a forest of knives. Down there I found out I'm just a babe in the woods. There are rabbits out there could knock me down and hang me in a tree. That man. That Barcaloo. If I ever saw his face or felt his hands on my skin again, I think I'd die."

Whistler said nothing, but just stared back at her.

"What is it, Whistler?" she said.

"Barcaloo's left New Orleans. I think he's on his way or already here in L.A. You can't go home for a while, I don't think."

"Oh, no, oh, no." She was out of the bed, going to crouch, naked, in the corner of the room away from the dim light of the bed lamp, as though it were a klieg that would search her out and find her. Marking her for Barcaloo. Marking her for destruction.

Whistler was out of bed and on his knees beside her. His arms around her.

"You'll stay here with me."

"No, no. He'll find you, too."

Whistler thought of Coxey who knew his name. Shiela thought of the little story she'd laid on Barcaloo to explain her meeting with Whistler on the street in front of the Beaver Run. Both understood that Whistler was known or would be known.

"We'll get you out of town," he said.

"You, too."

"Oh, no, not me."

"You're not going to confront this Barcaloo?"

"I can't let him go running around loose."

"It's none of your business. You're not a cop."

"I've got no choice."

When he started to move away, she held him and said, "Not now. Not right this minute. Don't go right this minute."

There were white sheets over all the large pieces of furniture in Barcaloo's maisonette on Ursuline. They looked like the ghosts of the legendary horrors that had once lived there.

Bouche was dressed in a raspberry silk blouse buttoned up to her throat and a pale green linen suit that did nothing to reveal the lush overabundance of her breasts and thighs. It was as though she meant to erase her sexuality. It had finally come about that she could no longer fool herself about the kind of thing that had gone on there in the Bayou des Familles, at the studio where sad people, including herself, played out sad scenes of sexuality. And where, she now was sure, some people had died in the middle or at the end of what was called an act of love. All the whispers were true. She remembered a Latino girl who'd been around and then, suddenly, hadn't been around. She remembered an Asian woman with a child who Barcaloo said had worked the film and then had gone away, back to Los Angeles.

She was all packed and ready to take the cab to the airport with Barcaloo and Rojo. She was ready to fly to L.A. She'd think about what she could do once she got there.

She was more afraid of Barcaloo now than she'd ever been. He'd meant to kill that Shiela Andes, and she was sure he'd meant to kill her too. She'd managed a wild animal for a long time, but she'd finally lost the knack.

Every time she thought of Jickie Rojo, terror squeezed her heart and stomach. When he walked into a room, a black spirit in a room full of white ghosts, she turned her back. She was afraid to look at his face and eyes. If she did, he might strike her dead.

Barcaloo walked into the room where she waited. He was wearing a white shirt and tie with a gray summer-weight suit. It made him look different. Almost human. He smiled, and she thought it would be nice not to have to think about the things he did.

"You ready?" he said.

"Ready, willin', and rarin' to go," she said brightly.

She walked out of the apartment, down the stairs, through the courtyard, past the fountain making sounds like breaking glass, through the wrought-iron gate, and into the waiting taxicab, thinking all the way that she would make up her mind about what to do when she got to L.A.

Rojo was already in the cab, sitting in the front with the driver. She hesitated. She felt Barcaloo's hand in the middle of her back.

"Take it easy, Bouche," he said. "It won't be long before we get to La-La Land."

There were things to do, but still Whistler stayed in bed with Shiela, dozing off from time to time. He'd wake up and find her asleep next to him, making a cradle of her body around his back and hips. When he turned to see her face in the grainy light coming through the dusty curtains, when he put his face close to feel her breath on his mouth, she'd open her eyes, unsurprised, knowing he'd be there. And she'd arrange her legs so they held him between her thighs. And she'd work her legs a little, like she was running softly in the early morning, until he was strong enough to take her.

It seemed to happen every hour on the hour, going on for a long while each time.

"Open a window," she murmured.

Whistler stirred and started to get up, but she held him back with her legs and arms.

"I mean, open a window into you."

"For Christ's sake, who writes your material?" he said.

"You can't get out of it making fun," she said. "Tell me about you, Whistler, before I start to cry. I haven't been in bed with a man I really cared to know in quite a while."

"You shouldn't give yourself away like that. It's all we got."

"I never gave it away until now. I only put it out on loan. Goddamn it, tell me where and what you were when you were ten."

Whistler hated telling his life. It had always been his habit to erase it. No photographs of lost loves. No diaries or bits of things kept for memory's sake. Nothing but the little address books, hardly any of the names appearing in them more than once, twice at most.

"When I was ten, I lived in Rochester, New York, and went to a redbrick public school. I wanted to be rich and famous. I thought that was something you could learn how to do. Like riding a bike or swimming the length of a pool under water . . ."

"As long as your teeth were straight and you washed your hair twice a week and you kept your weight under a hundred and twenty if you were a girl as tall as me, everything was possible. . . ."

"I couldn't run the hundred under ten seconds with a football under my arm, or move a ball through a crowd of arms and legs looking for the slam dunk. . . ."

"Knowing how to cook was a help, and keeping a clean house like your mother always did, and knowing which end of a baby was which. Things like that were all it would take to make everything possible. . . ."

"I was no brain. I flunked mathematics and . . ."

"And being pretty. Smiling pretty and being pretty. Because everything possible was a man, a husband. Maybe a doctor or a lawyer. Accountants were okay or . . ."

"I couldn't really do much of anything. I was so average, I hated myself until I found out I could make people pay attention when I acted out some movie I'd seen. . . ."

"My mother got me tap-dancing lessons, singing lessons. She saved pictures of movie stars in big scrapbooks. . . ."

"So, I thought I'd give it a try. . . ."

"Come out to Hollywood . . ."

"The land of glitter and swank . . ."

"Where fairy tales come true . . ."

"La-La Land. Oz was a depressed neighborhood compared to La-La Land. I started selling aluminum siding to get by."

"A photographer I knew paid me twenty-five dollars for four hours of posing in bathing suits and underwear."

"I met a private detective who offered me part-time work sitting in a car on stakeout. Easy money."

"Then another photographer offered me fifty an hour to take my clothes off. What the hell, I thought, somebody wants to look at my jugs, build dreams on my bush, what the hell. Poor, sorry sons of bitches."

"Got my license just to keep the money coming in to pay the rent."

"I never did porn, though, Whistler. I never did any sex acts."

"Just take a job here and there, now and then, until I got my break."

"I just did what I had to do while I was waiting. Oh, God, Whistler, I almost fell into it. I almost did a dirty picture."

"All of a sudden fifteen years had slipped away while I wasn't looking."

"That's the way it happens to you. When you're not really looking."

"I wonder when I stopped waiting for the big break?"

"Jesus Christ, I hate this movie, Whistler," Shiela said.

"Me too."

"I mean, I hear it a hundred times a year."

Twenty-nine

The rain no longer kept the hustlers and the pimps, the circus riders and hussies off the streets. There were livings to be made, hustles to be hustled, body parts to be sold both night and day. You can't stay dry forever.

Whistler opened the door to Gentry's around one o'clock in the afternoon, standing so that he blocked the rain with his back as Shiela slipped under his arm and into the coffee-smelling warmth. Her cheeks were full of roses, and she looked, laughing as she was, like a fourteen-year-old coming to the sweetshop after the homecoming game. Whistler had the hopeful eyes of a man half his age.

Canaan was in his corner looking at the menu, which he must have known by heart.

Bosco was on his stool behind the register, reading the annotated *Alice in Wonderland*. He glanced up and read their faces.

"You ever sleep?" Whistler greeted Bosco. "Every time I walk in here—it doesn't matter what hour—you're sitting on that stool reading some book."

"Day man called in sick. If I don't pour the coffee, who's going to wire the town?" Bosco said mildly.

Whistler turned the cover of the book so he could read it. "Isn't this for kids?"

"It's for bitter men looking for sanity in a crazy world."

"Will you bring two coffees and two plates of ham and eggs to our booth?"

He looked down into Shiela's upturned face as if he'd just ordered quail and chanterelles at Maxim's in Paris and was making sure of her approval.

"White toast," Shiela murmured.

"Whole wheat's better for you," Whistler said, like he was saying, "Roll over and I'll do your back."

"I'll meet you at our booth," Shiela said, and let go of his arm, then walked down the length of the shop toward the rest rooms.

Canaan weighed and measured her as she walked past.

Bosco wrote up the order and put it on the wheel. Whistler stared at Shiela's retreating back.

"What do you think of that?" he murmured.

"I think you failed to take my advice," Bosco said.

"What's that you say?"

"I said you weren't gone long."

"I coulda been," Whistler said, finally looking at Bosco.

"Somebody died," Bosco said, looking hard into Whistler's eyes.

"You're a goddamn witch. Be glad it wasn't me."

"I'm glad."

"Be glad it wasn't Shiela."

"I'm glad." Bosco captured his book between his knees and went into his pocket, coming up with the keys to Whistler's apartment and car. "When did you get in?"

"Last night."

"Where you been staying?"

"My place. I stash a key in the flowerpot."

"What are you driving?"

"My car. I got an extra set."

"Why am I holding your keys?"

"In case I never got back from New Orleans, you're my beneficiary."

"I guess it's too late to save you."

"What the hell do you mean by that?"

"You saved the lady's life. Like the Chinese say, now you're responsible for her forever."

"Maybe I like the idea," Whistler said sharply.

Bosco held up his hand, fending off Whistler's irritation, a wry smile on his lips. "You find the head?"

"The cops have it on ice. I told them about the body I saw tossed out of the station wagon."

"That take care of your civic duty?"

Whistler hesitated and looked up the aisle to see if Shiela was coming back and within earshot. She wasn't.

"It's not over. They meant to kill her down there in New Orleans. Use her first, then kill her."

"How do you know that?"

"I know because two corpses told me. Shiela was conned down there to get snuffed. The con started here. On the night she was in the accident with Emmet Tillman."

"Tillman?"

"He hasn't got the stones. How does Walter Cape sound to you?"

"It sounds crazy to me. What the hell would a man like Cape be doing fucking around with an asshole like Tillman and a broad like . . ."

They stared at one another, old friends almost about to get busted up because of a woman.

"They missed her once, they might try again," Whistler said very softly.

"You should both get out of town."

Shiela's heels made a snappy rhythm as she came tapping back across the tiles. There was a foolish grin on Whistler's mouth.

"Oh, my," Bosco murmured, "you got the tiger by the tail and you can't let go. You've made promises to yourself. You can use my place for a safe house."

"Were you a spy?"

"No, but I see a lot of movies."

Whistler and Shiela went to the booth. Before he could sit down, Whistler saw Canaan beckoning to him. He went over and shook his head when Canaan asked him to sit down.

"I've got a breakfast coming."

"It's lunchtime. Don't do to your stomach what I did to mine." He smiled nicely. "I see you rescued the lady," Canaan said, the smile turning a little sneaky with the disdain of a man who knew she wasn't worth it.

"That's just what I did."

"You find out anything about that other thing?"

"The woman without a head was a whore. She worked some smut flicks down there in New Orleans. She was in a snuff film too."

Canaan nodded, as though the news wasn't unexpected.

"The man who produced the shit, this Nonny Barcaloo, is here in town," Whistler added.

Canaan's eyes flickered. "You know that for a fact?"

"I'd bet on it."

"You ought to take Bosco's advice."

"What's that?"

"Leave town and take the woman with you."

Whistler turned his head and measured the distance from Canaan's booth to the cash register.

"I read lips, Whistler. I read lips."

Whistler drove Shiela back to her apartment for a change of clothes. He stood in the tacky living room as she went through the closet and the chest of drawers, making up a bundle, complaining about how little she'd been left with, running away from New Orleans the way they'd had to do.

Whistler thought it a wonder that she should be worried about no clothes when she'd almost been given a swamp to wear.

There was a knock on the door, and Katherine was standing there in another full-length robe.

"I see you're back," she said.

Shiela heard her voice and popped out of the bedroom, looking from one to the other as though suspecting things. For a minute it made Whistler feel very virile and strong, even though he knew it was a trick that women used to flatter men. Acting like they believed every woman their lovers met tore off her clothes and laid down to be serviced. The mixed signals they threw around could fill encyclopedias.

"Good time?" Katherine said, looking at Shiela.

"I got to tell you, you won't believe it."

"But not now. Not here," Whistler said.

Katherine widened her eyes but didn't ask.

"Shiela's coming with me for a while."

"Was it raining in New Orleans?" Katherine asked.

"It was hot."

"How long will she be gone?"

"I don't know yet."

"What should I say if anybody asks?"

"Why should anybody ask?"

"I've got friends, Whistler. After all," Shiela said.

"Anybody asks, you don't know where she is or when she'll be back. All you know is that she went to New Orleans to do a picture, and as far as you know, she's still there."

"Are you in trouble?" Katherine asked, still looking at Shiela.

"Yes and no," Whistler said.

"Speak English."

"She could be in trouble, but I'm taking care of her."

Katherine nodded as though that was all right then.

"Where's your bags?" she asked.

"I had to leave them behind."

"You must have one hell of a story to tell me."

"She does, but it'll have to wait."

"I'll lend you a suitcase," Katherine said, and went to get it.

After Shiela put the few things she still owned into it, she and Whistler left.

He drove her to Bosco's apartment and introduced her to Bosco's cat.

"Don't answer the phone. Don't answer the door."

She looked frightened.

"There's not a chance anybody can know about us staying here. But, like Bosco would say, 'When you think there ain't a chance, there's always a chance that there's a chance.'"

Shiela moved in close to him.

"Be careful . . . and bring me flowers."

Thirty

In the mid-thirties the Chinese in L.A.'s "Old Chinatown" were moved out to make way for the Union Passenger Terminal. So they built China City just to the northwest. When that was burned out, the "New Chinatown" rose up out of the ashes. It was built to look like Peking's Forbidden City. It's a lot more than two old saffron-skinned men sitting around under the trees playing mah-jong.

It's a lichee nut. On the outside a thin, exotic-looking shell, mysterious and captivating, the tourist layer, as fragile as a scrap of burned paper. On the inside, the real goods, a little opium, a Saigon whore, stolen Korean jade, counterfeit temple dolls, paper parasols, and sticks of heady incense from Thailand. The legal and the illegal, all available for a price. Phony fragments of a culture as old as time on sale for a twenty-dollar bill. Proof of a Chinawoman's anatomy for a fifty. Ancient ceremonies in the dark for a hundred.

And not only the Chinese but the Koreans, the Thais, the Cambodians, the Laotians, and the Vietnamese, the whole damned troubled people of Southeast Asia crowding in where they're not wanted because they're not wanted even more elsewhere in the sprawling city.

Whites make jokes about not being able to tell the difference. "They all look a-fuckin'-like." The Asians can tell the difference.

The streets around Alpine and Broadway were crowded with Anglo and Chicano locals and tourists. Whistler softly bumped his way among them, imagining the crowded streets of foreign cities where he'd never been and probably would never be, getting the feel of the shell and the meat, trying to reach the stone.

The neighborhood around Spring Street is the one where the Chinese really live and other people rarely go. It was the place where he knew some answers waited. If the family of Lim Shu Dok still lived there.

The apartment house was there on the corner of New High and College. Whistler crossed the street and entered the vestibule. He looked at the stained bits of card with the names of the occupants set in the little windows of the mailboxes. He found the name Dok listed on the third floor. There was the name, Mei Hai. It had been scratched out and "Marion" printed above it.

He opened the inner door and saw that there was no elevator. He climbed the stairs.

It was just at the supper hour, and the lights were on behind the pebbled glass panes set in the doors of each flat. Small domestic sounds, like the chatter of wooden sticks and the clang of little bells, came from each one of them as pots and pans were moved from stove to table. The sound of slippered footfalls made Whistler turn around more than once, but there was no one behind him. Just the building crowded with lives and muted sounds like animals feeding.

He knocked on the glass pane set in the door of the Dok apartment. The sounds coming from behind it ceased. After a long moment a shadow appeared behind the glass. The door, still secured by a chain, was opened a crack. A wedge of pale face, black hair, and an eye like a glistening marble of jet looked him over.

"Yes?" the young woman asked, drawing out the syllable like

a hiss, then cutting it off abruptly as though she'd momentarily forgotten herself and fallen back into old ways of speech.

"My name's Whistler. I've come about Lim Shu."

"What do you mean?" She frowned. "Do you mean you want to see her?"

"I know she's dead."

"Are you from the police?"

"No."

"The coroner?"

"No."

"Did you know her?"

"We never met, but I think I know her."

The eye seemed to pierce his forehead between his eyes. The eye and cheek left the crack. A curtain of shining black hair swept past as she turned her head. Then the eye was peering back at him again.

"How do you know her?"

"I know her for more than one reason, in more than one way."

Mei Hai laughed shortly. There was a bitter edge to it.

"Don't go getting Oriental on me," she said.

"Mei Hai? Should I call you Mei Hai or should I call you Marion?" he asked.

"I call myself Marion."

"I wanted to know because I don't want to make any mistakes or offend you in any way."

"Why should I talk to you? My sister . . ."

"Her body was being kept by the District Attorney's office at the morgue . . . ?"

"Yes." The word was leaden.

"It's not there anymore."

"What do you mean?"

A thin, querulous voice, speaking Vietnamese, sang along the hallway at her back. She replied with a single word, sharply, like the bark of a dog.

"I mean that her body was taken away," Whistler said.

He took out his card case and showed her his identification.

"What does that mean? You said you weren't from the police."

"I'm a private investigator. Don't you want to hear more about what happened to your sister?"

She closed the door, took the chain off the hook, then opened it and stepped back to let him in.

The earthy smell of vegetables and spices washed over him as he stepped inside. It was very hot in the hallway.

She walked in front of him down the hall toward the place where the kitchen was on one side and the dining room on the other.

"There are a lot of people in the house. I'll say you're a friend of mine from work, if anyone should ask."

She had almost no accent. Just a certain lisp and hesitation. Whistler stopped in the doorway of the kitchen. A dozen people of all ages—at least four were very old, at least three were children—sat around a table laid for supper with small eating bowls and large serving bowls, chopsticks, forks, and spoons. They all stared at him, mildly curious, except for one, an old woman who eyed Whistler with bland suspicion.

Marion chattered to her in Vietnamese. The old woman replied in the voice that had shrilled along the hall when Whistler was at the door.

Everyone smiled because Marion smiled. They nodded their heads because she nodded her head.

Except for the old woman. Her eyes were very knowing. She didn't believe the story about Whistler being a friend from work. She had a mother's instinct for disaster.

"We can talk in my room," Marion said.

Whistler followed her through a dining room that had been converted into a bedroom. There was a huge mahogany bedstead against one wall. Two salvaged cots and a crib filled up the rest of the space. The sheets and blankets were all neatly rolled up at one end of each bed. The room had the dark smell of sleeping people.

The living room had a large bay window with paper shades but no curtains. The light of a street lamp came through yellow. It was also a room for sleeping. There was a door to a small storage room in the back.

Marion had made it her room. There was a daybed in one corner, covered with a bright length of striped material. Big bright pillows were stacked against the wall. There was a little desk and chair painted white by a small window curtained in sheer cotton. A small circular rug made a splash of color on the wooden floor. A cardboard closet in another corner contained her wardrobe.

Unframed poster prints were hung, one to each wall, except the smallest one beside the door. There a photograph of two young Vietnamese women smiled shyly from a silver-toned frame. One was Marion. The other, Whistler was sure, was Lim Shu.

"Please sit down," Marion said, indicating the chair in front of the desk. She sat on the bed primly, her knees carefully together.

Whistler perched on it, feeling gross and clumsy.

"Tell me what you mean about Lillian. That's what I called her."

"Her body was taken from the morgue."

"Taken?"

"Stolen."

She turned pale. There was something very evil in what he was saying. "Why would anyone want to do that?"

"I can't be sure. Two reason I can think of."

Tiny pinpoints of moisture appeared along the line of her upper lip. "Yes?" she prompted Whistler, but turned her eyes away as though meaning to refuse whatever else he had to say.

"Either someone wanted to conceal the identity of the body, or someone wanted to make certain of its identity."

"I don't understand."

Whistler hesitated. Was there any easy way to say what had to be said? Was there any euphemism that could serve to describe it? He couldn't find any. "Before the body was stolen, somebody took her head," he said.

Marion's eyes were neutral, staring at him as though she'd lost all understanding of American words. She made a small noise in her throat. Her face turned even paler, her eyes blacker. They blazed with a sudden burst of terror, like an explosion of the heart. She lowered her head but still stared up at him from beneath the fringe of black hair falling across her forehead. She put her hands to her ears lightly, as though setting her appearance to rights.

Whistler told her part of what he knew.

"No," she said, then swayed forward.

Whistler went down on his knees to catch her in case she fainted. She placed her hands lightly on his shoulders. For a moment their cheeks touched. Whistler's hand brushed aside her hair on the left side. There was a small mole almost in the fold where the ear met her head. "Lim Shu," he said.

She said, "What?" and backed away.

He felt as though he'd molested her.

"The mole behind your ear. The morgue photographs of Lim Shu—"

"A family trait," she said.

He didn't say anything.

"Did you think I was Lillian pretending to be my sister?"

He felt foolish, his thoughts twisted and lost.

"Did you think I was Lillian in hiding?"

"Hiding?" he said.

"From the men who murdered her."

"You know who did it?"

"Oh, yes. The ones who killed her came from New Orleans. But the one who ordered her killed lives right here in Los Angeles."

"Do you know their names?"

"Two men, Dom Pinole and Jickie Rojo, were sent by another man. A filthy man, Nonny Barcaloo. Lillian was afraid of them. She'd run away because she knew they'd killed a Latino girl and meant to kill her and steal her son."

"I know."

"They wanted to use her child in filthy ways."

"This other man. The one who hired her killers."

She hesitated.

"What is it?"

"When the police came to tell me that my sister's body had been found, I told them the truth. They nodded their heads but didn't do anything about it. When the district attorney's man came to say that my sister could be buried but would have to be dug up again and used for evidence in the trial against these other men—"

"Corvallis?"

"Yes. They nodded and smiled and said I was mistaken. They had Lillian's murderers in jail, they said. And they'd prove it."

"But you knew otherwise."

"I knew the man who wanted her dead was a man named Walter Cape." When Whistler failed to react, she said, "You're not surprised?"

"No, I'm not surprised."

"Everyone else said it wasn't possible. Such an important man."

"Why did he want your sister dead?"

"She'd lived in his house. She thought he wanted her. But it was her son he wanted. He was the kind of man who wouldn't be denied anything he wanted. He wanted her son. He's a child lover."

She looked away, toward the picture in the silver frame.

"My sister was a whore. In old Annam she would have been called a concubine. But these are modern times. She was a whore. She lived her life among the rich and powerful. But she could never explain them to me. She could never explain a man like this Walter Cape to me. What does a man like that want? Can you tell me?"

"They think it's smart to say they want everything the world has to offer and a little more. They gorge themselves. You'd think they'd roll over and die with busted bellies. But they cry for more."

"Dogs eat their own vomit."

She walked Whistler to the door.

"Will they give my sister's body back to us?"

"I don't know."

"Thank you for coming to see me. It was very hard for you."

"I want to be honest. I didn't think it would be. Not so hard."

He stood there, having all he'd come for but still feeling that he wanted something more.

"In the newspaper stories it said that you and your sister had a quarrel and she left the house."

"That's right."

"What was the quarrel about?"

She smiled. "Would you believe it? She wanted to buy me a dress and I wouldn't have it. She thought it was because I thought her money was dirty. It was just because I hated the dress she had in mind. She was out of the house and gone before I could explain."

Thirty-one

Gentry's was crowded to overload. Steamy breaths condensed on the rain-misted plate-glass window. The coffee shop smelled of wet hair and wool sweaters.

Bosco came over to the booth where Whistler and Canaan sat and refilled their cups. He perched himself on the edge of the seat, not meaning to stay long.

"You're as busy as a one-armed paperhanger tonight," Canaan said.

"For Christ's sake," Bosco said, "Johnny Carson's a cop." He looked at Whistler. "Shiela okay? No complaints?"

"You're out of soap for the dishes."

"So, whattaya know?"

Whistler looked out the window. "There he goes again," he said.

"Goes who?"

"Shelley Pope in the Mercedes wagon."

"Scumbag," Canaan said.

"How come you let him walk the streets?"

"You mean Pope? We're talking about Walter Cape."

Canaan stared at Whistler as though he'd like to bite his nose

227

off, crush his eyes. "I don't let him walk the streets. You let him walk the streets. Everybody who won't take the trouble lets him walk the streets. People don't want to think about child fuckers. Christ, ain't it a nasty subject? Let's not think about it, do anything about it. Maybe it'll go away."

Whistler leaned over the table, ready to claw and tear right back.

"So do something about it. Roust the bastard's ass."

"For buying dirty pictures of little boys? Be your age. For doing with them? I'd have to catch him in the act."

"For calling a hit on a Vietnamese whore."

"You've got nothing but hearsay on that. From what you said the sister never saw it, she just was told."

"So guys like Cape got no worries."

"For Christ's sake," Canaan said, half angry, half pleading, "give me a break. I'm no fucking cowboy. I can't go out, shoot these people down in the fucking street. Bring me a crime. Bring me a witness. Bring me something I can use!" He turned away and looked out into the street, calming himself down.

"Will you look at that?" he said.

A caricature in a white suit that didn't fit, carrying an old-fashioned carpetbag and an aluminum camera case, was getting out of a taxicab.

"I'll be damned," Whistler said.

"Somebody you know?"

Whistler got up and went to the door to open it for Bellerose, who winked his turtle eye and grinned his turtle grin.

"This the place?" he said. "I could use a cup of coffee. How I hate to travel."

Whistler reached for the aluminum case, but Bellerose moved it back and gave Whistler the carpetbag instead. Whistler led the way over to the booth where Canaan sucked a Coke up through a straw and eyed the newcomer like he was something either silly or dangerous.

"Lieutenant Bellerose, New Orleans Police Department," Whistler said. "Sergeant Canaan, L.A.P.D."

"Hello, brother," Bellerose said, and stuck out his hand before he sat down. "You've got a wet city here."

"What do you do?" Canaan said.

"I do homicide. What do you do?"

"I do kiddie vice."

"I don' know which is more heartbreakin'."

It was as though Whistler weren't even there. As though Canaan and Bellerose were members of the same family. Long-lost brothers. They spoke the same language, suffered the same aches and pains. It was as though they'd known each other for a hundred years.

"You here on business?" Canaan said.

"I've got some evidence in my bag here. Deeds and leases for various and sundry shops, warehouses, and buildings, including two what you call soundstages. One on the river, one in the Bayou des Familles. Ain' there anymore. Burned to the ground. Got medical examiner reports on two bodies nearly, but not quite, burned up in the fire. Photographs of a red four-door sedan with a vinyl roof we drug up outta the mud with a duplicate certificate of ownership to same in the name of Chester Bucherleider. I got an inventory of various magazines, books, and films confiscated on the basis of a warrant signed by a superior court judge giving me and mine permission to look into the possessions and properties owned, stored, leased, or rented by one Nonny Barcaloo. Among these films is one of a Saigon whore with a butterfly on her ass. That's of some interest to your friend here," he said, cocking a thumb at Whistler. "There's others of little kiddies and some I ain't even got the stomach to mention. I got this chain of evidence pointing to this here Nonny Barcaloo, who, I unnerstan', is in your fair city."

"You come to extradite him?" Canaan said.

"That's the slow way, ain' it?" Bellerose said, smiling slyly.

"You got another way?"

"I don't know. I'd maybe like to push the son of a bitch a little, you know what I mean?"

"This ain't your jurisdiction."

"I mean that could be a drawback or a benefit, dependin' on how you look at it. I don't have to jump in all official right off, askin' for cooperation and like that."

"As long as you got a badge to back you up in case you break your leg."

"Somethin' like that. I just knew this here Whistler would have at least one smart cop for a friend."

"What's in it for me?" Canaan said.

"Well, if we can get the dominoes to fall, all I want is this Barcaloo and his pistoleer. You can have whatever else."

"How do we get the dominoes to fall?" Whistler said.

"How you think? You push."

He put the aluminum case on the tabletop.

Whistler put out his hand and laid it flat on the aluminum. It was damp and cold.

"Dry ice," Bellerose said.

"Jesus Christ!" Whistler said.

It was awesome how Bellerose sat there as though the aluminum case contained nothing but his lunch.

"An' that ain' the only surprise I brought with me."

Thirty-two

The next time the Mercedes station wagon passed Gentry's, Whistler was standing at the curb waiting for it and waved it down. When it pulled over, the front wheel splashed his shoe. The driver leaned across and opened the door. Whistler got in.

"Not having much luck, are you, Shelley?"

Shelley Pope was a producer. He had access to half the beautiful women in town. Actresses were ready to buy professional opportunities with daring circus acts. Young executive women were ready to outperform the actresses. Streetwalkers left their calling cards. His wife was proud and pleased that her Shelley would have no truck with any of them. She didn't know her Shelley craved young boys with runny noses.

"This goddamn rain keeps everybody inside," Shelley complained.

"Lucky children. Hey, there's one. Looks like a wet rat huddled over there in that doorway."

"Too old. Must be fourteen."

"Goddamn ancient."

"It's a girl."

"How the hell can you tell? The connoisseur's eye. My, my. You like boys ten or eleven, am I right?"

"You people got funny ideas. You think I go around abusing these kids?"

"You shove it up their little asses, Shelley. Is that a kindness?"

"For Christ's sake, the little buggers are out on the streets half starved. No homes to go to. No friends."

"Except you're a friend, right, Shelley?"

"Yes, I'm a friend. I give them clothes. I feed them. I give them money."

"And put them back on the streets three hours later, they can sell themselves again?"

"I'm no pimp."

"That's right. You don't make it or sell it, you just buy it. You ever break bread with the people who make it and sell it?"

"When was the last time you gave a thousand to the Children's Fund?"

"I never."

"So give it up. I don't need righteous. I got righteous. I was the chair for this year's fund-raising dinner. We raised fifty thousand for the Children's Shelter."

"How much you raise at that other dinner for NAMBLA?"

Pope hit the brakes, and the Mercedes fishtailed on the wet leaves along Sweetzer. Then he applied the gas, and the tires took hold again.

"Watch it there, Shelley," Whistler said. "You're going to drive us into a tree and end two distinguished careers."

"What's this NAMBLA?"

"Don't make me crazy. North American Man/Boy Love Association. You should know what it is. You're the president of the local chapter. Speaking of fund-raisers, Shelley, you got money to raise every year for your emergency defense fund?"

"What defense fund?"

"The one that hires lawyers for the needy perverts who get arrested for molesting children. Need a little money for your prisoner-support committee, too, don't you? Maybe you skim a little off the top of the Children's Fund?"

"You want me to drive you somewheres, Whistler, or what?"

"Also you're a member of the Rene Guyon Society, aren't

you? Tricky motto you got there. 'Sex by year eight, or else it's too late.'"

"Don't make me mad. I'm not going to take your shit tonight, Whistler. Who the hell are you to judge? Show me where it says a busted hustler like you knows what's right and wrong?"

"We going to match bankbooks now, Shelley?"

"Don't make me fucking laugh. Why would a gazoony like you need a bankbook?"

"Maybe to save my money so I can buy some of the crap you people like to watch."

Pope looked at Whistler out of the corner of his eye.

"You getting bent, Whistler?"

"I'm looking for somebody who's already bent."

"So first you abuse me and now you want a favor, am I right?"

"It won't cost you."

"I'll be the judge of that."

"You know all the snappy comebacks. You know all the suppliers too?"

"Manny Flowers is the best."

"I heard about him. You have any secret passwords? Any special way to introduce yourselves to make a purchase?"

"Grow up. It's all on the up-and-up. It's all legal. All out in the open. What do you think, I go sneaking around back alleys?"

"Any private language?"

"We're just like you, Whistler. We put on our pants one leg at a time."

Whistler was about to tell Pope that they were nothing alike, but he looked at the producer's face in profile and saw that all the tone had left the flesh. His muscles sagged. There were little pouches everywhere. He looked like a powdered corpse all of a sudden, or a man in terrible pain.

"I like you better when you're not a person," Whistler said.

"Don't we all."

"Can you drop me down to Manny Flowers's?"

They drove in silence to La Brea, south to Santa Monica, then turned west.

After a while Pope said, "You think this rain is ever going to end?"

233

Thirty-three

Flowers's Adult Bookshop was between a boutique selling crotchless panties and bras with open peepholes for the nipples, and a shop that sold religious artifacts, plaster madonnas, and holy children with the swollen bellies of the starving. Across the street a nightclub advertised a show featuring half-life-size puppets that performed sex acts on stage. Where else but in La-La Land, Whistler thought, would people get so bored with live fucking that they'd sit and watch dolls go at it?

Pope pulled in at the curb.

"What the fuck's got into you, Whistler? You never talked so lousy to me before."

"I had a bad dream. When I woke up, it didn't go away."

"Whatever the fuck that means. Okay, here you are. Whatever you want, just ask for it. Like buying a book at Pickwick's. That's how easy it is, Whistler, so don't blame me."

Whistler stepped out into the rain, then turned back and bent over, thrusting himself partway back into the car.

"Is Walter Cape a member of any of your clubs, Shelley?"

Shelley moved back sharply, as though he'd been slapped. "What the hell would I know about somebody like Walter Cape?" he said.

"You both have the same twist," Whistler said, and turned away, slamming the door of the Mercedes behind him.

He felt furtive going through the door, uncomfortably aware that someone he might know would see him and tell the story of Whistler's new taste in reading matter and viewing pleasure. Inside, an attempt had been made to make the place bright with paint and strip lighting, but water stains like dried semen on the walls turned it into the waiting room of a whorehouse run out of a trailer. .

A man with shaggy hair, a rabbi's beard, horn-rimmed glasses, and the stunned air of a film director thinking sat behind a tall counter from which he could eyeball anyone trying to tuck a magazine or two into a pocket or down the front of his trousers. The cigarette stuck in the center of his mouth sent up a spiral of smoke that poked at his eye in the breeze from Whistler's entrance. The man closed the eye but didn't stop reading the book in front of him, except for a single glance to check the potential profitability of his latest customer.

There were three other men in the shop, all checking out the covers of the plastic-wrapped magazines. They stood in separate corners of the room, facing the walls, like rats afraid that other rats would try to steal their stash. They threw glances at Whistler over their shoulders, then turned quickly away when he returned them. Whistler wandered around like a man making sure there were no traps. One by one the customers left.

He jittered up to the man with the beard and glasses, taking small steps, backing off, circling around through the racks, playing a nervous ferret's part. He kissed off the counter like a billiard ball caroming off the cushions.

"You Manny Flowers?" he said in passing.

"That's who I am," Manny Flowers said.

"We got a mutual friend," Whistler said, passing by again.

"Is that so?"

"Yeah, that's so."

"Can you light somewheres?" Flowers said. "You're like a fucking bumper car. Who's the friend?"

"Willy Zabadno's the friend."

"Willy's dead. He killed himself."

"Willy's coworker, Charlie, is my friend."

"You one of the morgue freaks?"

"I've got a preference, but it ain't dead bodies."

"I'm without interest. You're free to browse."

"Crib Coxey's my friend."

"Oh, yeah? You up from New Orleans?"

"Nonny Barcaloo's my friend."

"Why the fuck didn't you say so? What's your pleasure?"

The cigarette was about to burn Flowers's beard. He snatched it out and doused it in an ashtray filled with a small mountain of butts. He leaned over the counter with his hands clasped, a preacher in a pulpit, ready to counsel the sinner.

"So, tell me, my friend."

"Chicken. I like chicken," Whistler said.

"How much you want to spend?"

Whistler took out his gambler's roll. The sight of it gave Flowers a lot of pleasure.

"Something special. You want something very special?"

He stepped down off the platform and went over to lock the door. "I want to show you something in the back. Something choice. I don't want some gonifs coming in here robbing me blind while I show you my merchandise."

Flowers reached out a hand to touch Whistler's sleeve and guide him toward the back room. Whistler moved off in a fright.

"Don't touch me."

Flowers put his hands shoulder high and walked to the back of the shop. He opened the door and showed Whistler into a room equipped with a television set and a tape player.

Whistler sat in the viewing room, hands in the pockets of his raincoat, head thrust forward.

"I've seen this one," he said. "I bought this one a year ago."

"How could you buy it a year ago? It only came in from Boston six months already."

"I saw one just like it, then. This is nothing special."

"Look at that little blonde doll, that cute little charmer. You telling me you seen one just like her?"

"Little girls are all right."

"I thought you'd like a little of this, a little of that. A little variety."

Whistler's mouth tasted of brass. "I don't like to waste my time."

"All boys. I understand."

"Boys are more like it," Whistler said, astonished at the flatness of this conversation he was having with the porno merchant. Like Pope said, it was like buying a book at Pickwick's: commonplace, matter-of-fact.

Flowers showed Whistler snatches of half a dozen tapes featuring frail boys with round stomachs and shoulder blades like the folded wings of birds. Small, naked boys doing things with grown men.

Whistler shrugged and looked impatient.

"You're hard to please," Flowers said.

"I want the newest. I want the best. I can pay."

"How much can you pay?"

Whistler looked sly. "Well, not as much as Walter Cape."

Flowers looked at Whistler for a long time. Something didn't fit. What didn't fit? Whistler patted his pocket where he kept his money. Greed struggled in Flowers and won. He got a tape out of a locked drawer. "When you say special, you mean really special, don't you?"

Young boys engaged in every manner of act. In the end a child was strangled. Unlike the Mexican girl, the child showed no special terror. Perhaps he'd believed, even with all the other horrors, that no one could want to do such a thing to him.

Whistler stood up.

"How about that?" Flowers said. "It's reserved for Mr. Cape, but I can run you a dupe. Take an hour and a half."

"I got to think about it," Whistler said.

He left the shop. After a while, when he didn't come back to buy, Flowers would begin to wonder about him. He'd call somebody, and somebody would call Walter Cape. And Walter Cape would know someone was taking his name in vain.

Whistler's stomach moved; something sour came up. He looked for a place to vomit. But in the alley all he could bring up was spit. Not even a last shred of innocence.

Thirty-four

The trouble with going somewhere without your car in La-La Land is that there is very little public transportation and you could die waiting for a taxicab.

But after walking seven blocks in the direction of Hollywood and Vine, Whistler lucked out and flagged down a cruiser.

At Gentry's they caught the light at the corner. Whistler tapped the driver and handed him a bill, then got out.

There was a black BMW parked in the yellow with its parking lights on, and somebody sitting inside behind the wheel. Whistler ducked his head against the rain and started to walk around the corner when the BMW's horn beeped him from behind. He turned around with a crunching feeling in his spine and belly. Had Barcaloo and that Jickie Rojo searched him out already? Was somebody going to be standing there with a gun in his hand, ready to blow his guts out?

It was Emmet Tillman standing there, wearing a six-hundred-dollar Burberry, one hand on the top of the open door. Why, Whistler wondered in the midst of a surge of relief, couldn't he look that good in a trench coat? Tillman got back into the car and leaned across to open up the other door.

Whistler slipped inside. The car smelled of the best glove leather. If anybody asked him right that minute what he'd give to be rich, Whistler didn't know what he'd say.

"Why are you hanging around out here?" Whistler asked. "You wanted to see me, you could have waited inside."

"I was doing the Durante song," Tillman said. "You know, 'Did you ever have the feeling that you wanted to go, but still you had the feeling that you wanted to stay.'"

"You're making jokes, but somehow I don't think you're having fun," Whistler said.

"I come from Newark, New Jersey, you know that?"

"Maybe I read it somewhere. In some column."

"Ninety percent of that stuff is a load of crap. Everybody knows that. But people like crap."

"So you're not from Newark?"

"Oh, I'm from Newark, all right. Born and dragged up. Old man was a drunk. My mother . . . Anyway, all that's true. What they say about how poor I was and how I lived in doorways sometimes while I was going to drama school in New York is true. But everybody probably thinks it's crap."

"Who gives a rat's ass?"

"Well, nobody wants to think people don't believe you're real."

"Are you having an identity crisis?"

"You don't like me much, do you?"

"Oh, for Christ's sake," Whistler said with a shake of his head, scolding himself, "what's not to like? I hardly know you. I suppose the bottom line is, you got to drop your drawers to take a crap. Just like me."

"There you go," Tillman said with a twist of his mouth that looked something like a wry grin.

"Go where, Tillman? Just where are we going?"

"All right. You got to admit, a person has a chance to use a little juice, pull a couple wires, keep his balls out of the wringer, he's going to do it."

"Save your ass, that's the name of the game," Whistler agreed.

"That car crash shook the shit out of me. I mean, it's bad enough you got a few in you, looking forward to a little pussy, all of a sudden there's a dead man lying on the road. That's bad enough. But when you find yourself in the middle of a fucking horror story, that's really the pits."

"Ain't it the truth?"

"Lay off me, will you? I'm trying to do the right thing here."

"I'll shut my mouth."

"After you took Shiela home I thought about calling my agent, my producer, my lawyers. You want to know what I found out? I found out I didn't really trust a damn one of them. Worse than that, I couldn't think of one friend I could count on to give me a hand without they wanted something from me. So I called the one person I knew who could maybe do me an important favor, who'd told me to ask him a favor anytime."

"Walter Cape," Whistler said.

Tillman's eyes showed some white. He was that surprised. "How the hell . . ."

"It doesn't matter," Whistler said, pleased that he'd scored a point, if only to make up for the two-hundred-dollar tip Tillman had practically tossed on the ground for him to pick up. No matter what, Whistler thought wryly, you got to give your ego a little pat, a little stroke. "Go on."

"Cape told me not to worry. He'd handle it. So I go out and talk to the cops. They give me a little shit. Then the detectives arrive and give me a little more."

"Lubbock and Jackson?"

"Yeah, Lubbock and Jackson. Guys I knew from the show. Guys I'd fucking worked with. Treated me like I was something you wipe off your shoe. Then, all of a sudden, just like that— well, not just like that, because this supervisor comes driving up and they have a little head-to-head—they come over and start kissing my ass. They tell me do go on home . . ."

". . . and sin no more."

"They didn't even hand me that shit. They gave me a pass. They tell me the body without a head isn't real. It looked goddamn real to me, but nowadays . . . Well, I wanted to believe it. Who wouldn't want to believe it?"

"You were home free."

"Yeah. Home free. But, you want to know, I didn't feel all that good about it. You think I'm an asshole, I'm not an asshole.

I was just trying to keep my balls out of the wringer. I'm home and not feeling too good when Shiela calls and lays the arm on me. I won't call it blackmail, but I don't know what else you'd call it."

"Call it taking a career opportunity."

"Okay, that's what we'll call it."

"You told Cape about her?"

"Yes. And he says I wasn't to worry about her, either. He'd persuade her not to go around blowing any whistles."

"Did you know what he meant?"

"I didn't think about it, exactly. I don't know how a man like that operates. Maybe I thought he'd call her on the phone, have a little talk with her, show her there'd be nothing in it for her if she wanted to cause me any trouble."

"You never expected he'd send her down to a porno shop in New Orleans."

"Is that what he did? Jesus Christ."

"You mean, you don't know?"

"All he said, when I told him I ended up squashing the deal with a forty-thousand-dollar foot . . . you know about that?"

"The car? Yeah, I know about Lubbock, Jackson, and your car."

"All he said was that he had to use more than a forty-thousand-dollar foot."

"And you didn't ask him what the fuck that meant? Never mind. I don't want to hear about the wringer and your balls again."

Tillman laughed briefly. It caught in his throat and got tangled in his tongue. "Shit. They got caught in the wringer good. Cape called in his marker."

"You sound surprised. Why are you surprised?"

"I thought he was just a celebrity fucker, you know. I thought it just gave him an orgasm knowing he could do things for important people they couldn't do for themselves. I never thought there was anything a man as rich as him could want from me."

"How do you think they get so fucking rich? What did he want from you?"

"He wanted me to rope young actresses into doing fuck flicks."

"Act with them?"

"For Christ's sake, no! Just drag them in. Get them to do a little of this, a little of that, for the cameras. Set the hook. Reel them in. You know how it goes."

"That's all?"

"Later on maybe put these women on my show in a little part. Just enough so they can use it in their promos. You'd be surprised how people buy that kind of stuff if they can say there's somebody legitimate fucking in it. It's an edge."

"You sound like you're getting an education."

"I'm not so damned dumb as you think."

"Why are you telling me all this?"

"I don't want any part of it."

"So you decided you didn't want to go to anybody else; you'd come to me, and I'd be the guy who'd keep your balls out of the wringer this time."

"No. I figured maybe you could tell me what to do. I had some street smarts once, believe it or not. But they rust away; you don't have to use them. I started to think. That was no dummy in the gutter. That was a naked woman without a head. So I can understand they can write it up so a Willy Zabadno gets checked off as running his station wagon up a pole. But I can't understand how they could cover up a body with no head, or why they'd want to."

"That's what I wondered too."

"And what did you decide?"

"I decided this town is at the bottom of the rabbit hole in *Alice*. I decided that, at first, Cape was only doing you the favor. It didn't look like a hell of a lot for the muscle he's got, all things considered, and it would put you where he could use you on this deal he's making. Then, later on, he found out the headless body had something to do with him, after all."

"What could it have to do with him?"

"He had her snuffed because she wouldn't give him her little boy to cornhole."

Tillman made a face of disgust and pain.

"Say a prayer," Whistler said.

He got out of the black BMW with the blood-red leather seats and walked around the corner and into Gentry's where Bellerose and Canaan were still sitting, their heads together, probably telling cop jokes and lies. Old friends at first sight.

Whistler slid in beside Bellerose, pushing the aluminum camera case aside. It chilled his fingers. "I got something for you," he said to Canaan.

Thirty-five

A person can read something wrong in their own house the minute they walk in the door. Even in the dark. Maybe it's something akin to the facial vision they say some blind people have. Knowing a wall is there before they touch it. The feeling of air that should be empty but is full. A smell not quite right.

A person can almost never read a strange house that way. Even when the lights are on. Strange houses always feel wrong. Bosco's felt wrong, and Whistler felt naked.

The television was going, the sound turned low, the way Shiela had told him she left it on for company when she was alone. Even during the day. Even when she went out, she left the television on low so she wouldn't come home to a silent house. It made the room look as if it were filled with moonlight. It was the only light in the place, except for the tiny night-light in the hall, just enough to find the way to the bathroom in the middle of the night.

Whistler could hear a faucet dripping. He went out into the kitchen, making a lot of noise, and snapped on the lights.

"I'm back," he called out, as though he really believed Shiela was there. Hoping desperately that she would answer.

He was so scared, he couldn't raise spit.

He ran the tap, filled the kettle, and put it on the burner to heat up. He opened and closed a couple of cabinets and the refrigerator. He sat down and took off his shoes. When the water was boiling, he filled a large mug and took it with him as he went into the living room and padded across the carpet toward the hall and bedroom. He didn't know what he'd find. It might be Shiela, dead, hunted down by Barcaloo and Rojo. It might be one of them still lurking in the apartment. Behind a piece of furniture. Under the bed. In a closet. He had no gun. It was in the potted plant at home. What he had was a mugful of boiling water.

In the bedroom Shiela's suitcase was still on the bench at the foot of the bed. Living out of a suitcase. How she hated it, she'd said. How she hated putting her bath oils and lotions on the corner of a shelf loaded with the toilet articles of a man she didn't even know. When he was away from his house, Whistler kept his things—his toothbrush and toothpaste, nail clippers, and extra comb—in the pockets of his raincoat.

No room in the closet for her things, she'd said. It was a hint of what it would be like when she came to live with him. His stuff would be shoved aside, packed up in one corner of the closet, one drawer of the chest, one shelf of the medicine cabinet. Everything rearranged. For efficiency. For his benefit as well as hers. Men were so bad at organizing space, she'd say. Bird cage would have to go, even if he said he intended to get another canary . . . someday. Drawers cleared out and old address books thrown away. Years and years of Whistler thrown away. When she came to live with him. *If* she came to live with him. The crazy things you thought about while waiting to see if disaster had struck or was about to strike.

He put his hand on the doorknob of the closet and started to turn it. He heard a key in the front door. He hurried across the room and through the hallway. He was standing in the doorway to the living room when she opened the door. She had a brown paper grocery bag in her arm. She saw him and let out a yell. His hand jerked, and he splashed hot water all over his hand.

"Jesus Christ," he yelped.

"You scared me half to death," she said. "Why didn't you put on some lights?" She hit the wall switch beside the door, and the overhead chandelier went on. "You burn your hand?"

"Where the hell have you been?"

"Down to the all-night market. I wanted something to eat."

"There's things to eat in Bosco's pantry and refrigerator."

"I don't like canned sauerkraut and hard salami."

"Half the people in town go to the all-night market. Barcaloo could have been there."

She stared at him. "I can't live like this. I can't live cooped up."

"For Christ's sake, it's been hours. Not even days. Can't you stay put a few hours?"

"I can't live in somebody else's rooms and sleep in somebody else's bed. I've got an apartment of my own. You've got a house."

"I don't think they're safe."

"I've been thinking about that. I've been thinking about what happened in New Orleans. Somebody spotted me and wanted to use me in a dirty picture. When they offered me the deal, I wasn't as careful asking questions as I should have been. They got the wrong idea. They thought I was ready for it. I don't think they meant to kill me."

"Oh?"

"I think that was your idea. I think you overreacted."

"Maybe you're right. Maybe I overreacted then, but I'm not overreacting now. The big man died in the fire. I don't think the little one's the kind to forget."

"Well, if he's after anybody, he's after you."

Whistler thought it might be nice if the television started playing some sentimental tune. He had a feeling he was seeing the end of the shortest love affair on record.

"You better put some ice on that burn." With a strangled little cry Shiela dropped the groceries in the easy chair and just about threw herself at him.

"Smack me in the mouth, Whistler," she said. "I got it coming."

"What do you think I am, some kind of pervert?"

"Let's go in the bedroom and find out."

Thirty-six

"**W**ell, talk to me, Nonny," Cape said.

Barcaloo sat near the fire in Cape's library and sweated. If he closed his eyes, he could imagine himself back in New Orleans.

"How's that, Walter?"

"There's no doubt about it. The headless body that flew out of Willy Zabadno's station wagon and landed in the gutter at the corner of Hollywood and Vine was Lim Shu's. I received a call from a friend who told me the L.A.P.D. had an inquiry about the head of an Oriental woman they found down there. Somebody told them about the accident, and a lieutenant named Bellerose wanted to know more about the body. I once asked you if there was anything outstanding that might draw unwanted attention to you. You said there wasn't."

"Well, there wasn't."

"There was a dead Vietnamese whore lying in the L.A. County Morgue who didn't stay put."

"I can explain all that."

"That's why I'm asking you to talk to me."

A flush spread across Barcaloo's neck and face.

"I got these two assholes working for me," Barcaloo said.

249

"Well, I had two, but one got done by a fucker named Whistler, who come down to New Orleans looking for his girlfriend. This actress, Shiela Andes, you sent down for me to snuff."

"I never said that, Nonny. I said I wanted some film I could use against her. I said nothing about snuffing her. But we'll get to that. Right now I want to hear about Lim Shu and why she lost her head."

"A year ago, when you told me to do her, she must of smelled a rat and started running before we got the chance. She run back here. I sent Pinole and Rojo to do the job."

"You never told me she'd come back here."

"Why would I bother you with details? You gave me a contract to do her, so I done her. What's the difference if it's a Monday or a Friday? What's the difference if it's New Orleans or L.A.?"

"It made a difference."

"Because when you make me the offer to take over this new production organization, you ask me is there anything outstanding could embarrass you. I say no because I know it's no. But then I start to worrying about if Pinole and Rojo did the right whore. You know how these things can start buzzin' around your head? I mean, there wasn't no reason for me to have any doubts. Except, sometimes, Pinole and Rojo are a little slow, you unnerstan'?"

"I hired you, not Pinole and Rojo."

"You didn' expect me to do the job with my own hands?"

"I expected you to see it was done right."

"This is exactly what I was tryin' to do. I sent Pinole and Rojo here to bring back proof that they did the right whore. I tell them to take some of them instant pictures. How am I supposed to know these two assholes is going to get high on some crank? How am I supposed to know they're goin' to have a party with this morgue attendant, this Willy Zabadno, and get foolish? How the hell am I supposed to know they can't get the fuckin' camera to work right? How the hell is anybody supposed to know they go and saw off her goddamn head and bring it back to show me, I should see with my own eyes they got the right whore a year ago?"

Barcaloo was in a rage.

Cape shook his head slowly from side to side, a strange smile on his mouth.

"I agree," Barcaloo said. "If it wasn't such a serious thing, I woulda fell down laughin' when they showed up with that fuckin' head, myself."

"I hope I'm not giving you the idea that I'm amused."

"Me, neither. I raised particular hell with them two. I told them to get rid of that fuckin' head the minute I see it's Lim Shu. So how am I supposed to know, after I ream their assholes out the way I done, that these two lamebrains is gonna play football with it?"

Something in Cape's expression made Barcaloo run down, but he couldn't sit through the silence that followed very long.

"When you asked me the question, I knew the answer," Barcaloo said. "It was only after I got to worryin' about it that I sent Pinole and Rojo back here. Besides, how was I to know this goddamn Willy Zabadno was going to panic when he sees the broad without her head and run off in the middle of the night with the body in the back of his wagon?"

"How, indeed," Cape said. "Now we come to the matter of Shiela Andes and this man, Whistler."

"Don't worry about them two another minute. Me and Jickie got Whistler and that cunt on the top of the list of things to do. They're as good as done."

Whistler drove his old Chevy. Bellerose sat in the passenger seat with the aluminum camera case on his lap. There was a manila envelope on top of that.

"You're sure this Bouche, this Cazebone, is in her room at the hotel?" Bellerose asked.

"That's what the desk clerk told me. She's in the room she and Barcaloo are sharing. He's not."

"I know he's not. He's not there, and neither is that other one, Jickie Rojo."

"Suppose they come back while we're talking to Bouche?"

"Your frien' Isaac Canaan's right on their asses. They start back to the hotel, he calls the room an' lets us know."

"You two got friendly awful fast."

"Professional courtesy, you know what I mean? The fuckin' brotherhood of law-enforcement officers."

Whistler pulled up in front of the hotel and parked. The doorman stepped over and said, "You can't leave that there." Bellerose opened his wallet and showed his shield. "You take care of it for us." They stopped at the desk and made sure Bouche hadn't taken a walk in the time it took them to drive over. As far as the clerk knew, she was still in her room. He reached for the phone to double-check. Bellerose flashed his shield again. "Don't do that. Just keep it under your hat."

Whistler and Bellerose walked over to the elevator bank.

"Why the hell is it they look at your tin and let you do whatever you want? That shield doesn't even look like any used by a local agency," Whistler said.

"Who would want to try me? What the hell for?"

They stepped into the elevator car and punched the floor.

"You ever thought of bein' a cop?" Bellerose asked.

"It's not my line of work."

"Oh? What's your line of work?"

"The motion picture business. I just carry a ticket for times when things get thin."

"I unnerstan'."

"You do?"

Bellerose grinned. "Oh, yes. I'm a brain surgeon when I ain' a cop."

The doors opened, and they walked down the corridor to Barcaloo's room. Bellerose rapped on the door. Bouche opened the door without even asking who it was. When she saw two men standing there, she took a step back, pulling her robe around her at the waist.

"You shouldn't open your door without askin' who it is," Bellerose said in a kindly voice.

"I thought it was room service. So who are you?"

Bellerose flashed the badge yet another time, but she didn't notice it. Her eyes had popped open along with her mouth when she got a better look at Whistler. "You're the fuckin' gazoony what kidnapped Shiela." She started to close the door, but Bellerose stuck his foot in the door.

Whistler pushed past and into the room, backing Bouche off. "Well, no," he said, "I didn't kidnap her."

"You're the one blew Dom all to hell. All we could find was his fuckin' finger."

She was startled but didn't seem that afraid of them. The pupils of her eyes were very large and black. She was high on something besides alcohol. "You don't get the fuck out of here," she said, "I'll scream this place down."

"Will you please look at this, ma'am?" Bellerose said, slightly irritated. "I'm a police officer all the way up from New Orleans, and I mean to ask you a few questions."

"You know this man here blew Dom Pinole's ass off the face of the earth?"

"Indeed I do know that, but right now I've got a lot of interest in Nonny Barcaloo and Jickie Rojo, who are both surviving."

"I don't know nothin' about them."

There was a knock on the door. Whistler took a step and opened it. The room-service waiter was there with a bowl of salad, a little loaf of bread and a knife to cut it, a plate of butter, two bottles of vodka, a bucket of ice, and some mixers on a rolling cart.

"Well, here's my lunch," Bouche said. "Look at the size of that salad. I'm sure it's enough for three."

"What kind of dressing?" Bellerose asked.

"Blue cheese."

He went to sit on the couch, putting the aluminum case down beside his foot. "My favorite."

The waiter wheeled the cart over in front of him. Bouche signed the tab with a flourish and went to sit beside Bellerose. Whistler stood there, wondering what it was all about.

Bellerose served all three of them, though Whistler said he'd rather not have any salad. Bellerose made a little face that said Whistler should not refuse and offend their hostess, and then asked Whistler to make three vodkas with tonic.

"I prefer absinthe," Bouche said, "but I doubt they got the real stuff here."

"I doubt it too," Bellerose said. He took a bite of salad and declared it good. Bouche sat there, half falling out of her

253

dressing gown, nibbling lettuce off her fork like a white rabbit. Bellerose opened the manila envelope and laid out all the horror pictures, one by one.

Bouche stared. She leaned forward to get a better look. The fork fell out of her hand and the food out of her mouth.

"Don' get sick," Bellerose said in the calmest possible voice.

"Why are you doin' this to me?" Bouche asked piteously.

"Nobody's doin' anythin' to you. Whatever doin' done was done to these two poor women. One's no more than a girl. You ever see this little dark-skinned girl before?"

Bouche nodded.

"When did you see her?"

"About two years ago."

"An' where did you see her?"

"In New Orleans."

"Whereabouts in New Orleans?"

"At the studio in the bayou."

"And what was she doin' there?"

"Actin' in films."

"Fuck films?"

"Love films."

"Is that what Barcaloo calls 'em?"

"No, it's what I call 'em."

"Why's that?"

"Well, sounds nicer than what you said, doesn't it?"

"Were you there when somebody chopped her head off?"

"Oh, no. Oh, no." Bouche started to cry. "Barcaloo's goin' to be comin' back."

"Where's he been?" Whistler asked very softly. Like a disembodied voice. Like the voice inside a person's head.

"Over to see Mr. Cape. He's a very important man. They're goin' to be partners, you know."

"In what?"

Her eyes focused and grew crafty. "Oh, no, you don't."

"Oh, yes, we do," Bellerose said in a certain voice, and gave it back to Whistler.

"In what?"

"Well, you know. What we're talkin' about. That's all I know. Nonny don't discuss his business with me."

"How about the Vietnamese woman?"

"They didn't chop her head off in front of the camera, too, did they?" Bouche asked, wide-eyed.

"Too? So, even though you weren't there when it happened, you know for sure that they killed the Mexican girl that way?"

"I don't know that for sure. I don't know that at all. I never said that. I heard that's what happened. But I always heard all kinds of things about Nonny, and Dom and Jickie. All kinds of terrible things."

"Didn't it bother you enough to make you want to get away?" Whistler asked.

Bouche looked at him as though he were asking a very foolish question. "I been hearing terrible stories all my life," she said.

"All right, now," Bellerose said, starting fresh, "this Vietnamese woman. You knew her?"

Bouche nodded.

"What was her name?"

"She had lots of names."

"Like what?"

"She called herself Connie Woo or Sally Saigon or Doris Quim. Cute, huh? She told me to call her Lillian. I called her Lillian."

"Did you know her real name?"

"I don't know. What's it matter? Who's got a real name?"

"You ever hear Barcaloo talking to his friends about killing these women?"

She shook her head.

"Or killing anybody else?"

She shook her head more vigorously.

"How about a couple of people called Chippy Byrd or Lacy Ohio?"

"No, no, no, no."

"How about Chester Bucherleider or Loretta Oskanowsky?"

"No, no, no, no! I'm going to be sick."

Bellerose shook his head as he gathered up the photos and put them in the envelope. "Anything else you can tell us?"

"Nonny would kill me, he knew I was talkin' to you two."

"You've been livin' with a fuckin' monster, you know that?"

"Nonny'll kill me."

"If you hear Barcaloo talkin' to Rojo about doin' anybody else, killin' anybody else, like maybe Mr. Whistler here, I want you to call one of us at this number." He took out one of his cards and handed it to Whistler. "Gentry's?" Whistler wrote the number on the card and handed it back to Bellerose, who folded it up until it was no bigger than a quarter. He handed it to Bouche, but she hugged herself and turned away, pouting like a child. Bellerose tucked it into the front of Bouche's nightgown, between her white breasts. She looked up at him as though she thought he was caressing her and wanted him to know that she didn't mind.

"I'm gonna burn that the minute you two fuckers get out of here," she said. "Nonny'll kill me."

Bellerose put the aluminum case up on the coffee table. "Maybe Nonny didn't have that Saigon whore's head chopped off, but somebody chopped it off and sent it down to New Orleans. Lef' the body here in Los Angeles."

"What?" Bouche said, as though he were no longer speaking English.

"That's another story maybe we'll go into another time." He snapped the catches and flipped them open. "Point is, I thought it a very cruel thing to let that woman's head stay on ice in one city and her body in another." He cracked the case. The steam of dry ice seeped out all the way around.

Bouche started to draw away, getting an idea about what Bellerose had in mind.

"Jesus, Mary, and Joseph, you haven't got her . . ." Bouche couldn't say any more. Her voice was drowned in bubbles bursting in her throat. Water streamed out of her eyes. She bent over as though her stomach ached, staring at the case as the lid came up an inch at a time, lifted by Bellerose's freckled hands.

"You call now, ya'll hear?" he said.

Barcaloo stood up. "I'm already on it. Them two better be havin' some fun because, for them, it's as good as it'll ever get."

"You're not thinking it out," Cape said. "This Whistler is

running around using my name in places where my name is never to be used."

"I just said you don't have to worry anymore."

"You don't understand. If something happens to either one of them now, I doubt if I have enough influence to prevent my name coming into the investigation. I want you to let it lie. For a while. Until he gets discouraged. Until he has to make the rent. Until it all dies down."

"Well, now, Walter, I don't know if I can do that."

Cape frowned but said nothing.

"This Whistler killed Dom Pinole. Now maybe you and me can let that pass, but Jickie Rojo can't. Won't. He's out lookin' for that asshole right now."

Thirty-seven

It felt almost domestic, going out to get the paper together. Walking arm in arm down to the newspaper vending machines on the corner. It was as though they'd been married for at least a year or three. Except Whistler was thinking about a gun. The gun he hadn't carried with him down to New Orleans just in case a cop frisked him. The gun that was still back at his house where it would be no use at all in case those two gazoonies, Barcaloo and Rojo, or maybe some other gunsels hired by Walter Cape to stop Whistler from taking his name in vain all over town, came looking for him.

The gun that was tucked away, wrapped in plastic, in the sphagnum moss surrounding the one sad and sorry house-plant, a ficus benjamina, sitting in a plastic pot beside the table in front of the living-room window overlooking the balcony.

People keep guns in drawers in night tables beside beds, between springs and mattresses, on the top shelves of closets behind Christmas tree ornaments, under kitchen sinks, and even in waterproof bags hung by hooks in toilet tanks. All places that people looking for guns will look. On the other hand, only house keys are kept in flowerpots, and since whoever was looking for whatever would not be looking for a house key since they'd already be inside the house, chances were very good that they wouldn't be looking for a key in a pot and therefore wouldn't find the gun. At least that's the way Whistler had worked it out one night.

He scarcely ever carried the goddamn gun. No matter where he wore it, in a holster clipped to the back of his belt, tucked into his waistband pointing at his cock, or under his armpit, the thing that started weighing twelve ounces started to feel like it weighed twelve pounds, dragging on his pants so he worried they'd drop right down to his knees. Or giving him a boil in his armpit. But right at the moment he would welcome the uncomfortable piece. Right at the moment he wanted and needed it. He thought about padding around in his stockinged feet with a cup of hot water in his hand when he thought he might not have been alone in Bosco's place. Hot water was no kind of weapon.

There were tremors out there. Killers were on the move. He'd been long enough in the trade to feel that much. He wanted the comfort of the gun.

So when they got back to Bosco's apartment house, he went past the entrance to the alley that led to the parking spaces in the back.

"Where we going?" Shiela said.

"I've got to get a change of socks and underwear. I feel silly as hell washing them out every night like a chorus girl."

"That's good. After we get yours we can go over to my place and get some more of mine."

It was a nice ride over to Cahuenga Pass and up the winding road to his shack hanging over the edge of the hill. The rain had let up a little again, and the air was sweet and clean for a change. There was a spot along the road where they passed almost directly underneath his balcony off the living room. On bad days, when he worried about mud slides instead of other things, he thought about standing on the balcony when the house fell and landing on the roof of some car with a messenger in it coming up the road to hand him first prize in a million dollar lottery. Killing himself and everybody in the car.

As usual, the street in front of his house, all the way up to the top and almost all the way down to the last turn, was crowded with cars on both sides. There were a lot more cars than there could be people living in the houses, unless half the neighborhood was renting out rooms, which they probably were in order to make enough to live in La-La Land. But for a change, nobody had blocked his driveway. He poked the Chevy between the front of a Mercedes and the ass end of a BMW, set the brake, and killed the engine.

"You want to wait here? I'll only be five minutes."

"What are you going to do, Whistler, pick some messages off your answering machine? Afraid I'll learn about the rest of your women?"

"Unnumbered," he said. "Women unnumbered."

He got out of the car and went around to help Shiela out, but she was already out. He walked up to the door first, reading the path, the azaleas beside the path, the bougainvillaea over the door, the panes of glass in the windows, the shingles on the roof. Something was wrong, at least not quite right. He didn't want to jump at shadows. He didn't want to get Shiela jumping at every passing breeze. He put his key in the lock. Shiela was right at his shoulder, touching him with her body. He pushed the door open and started to step inside.

"Oh, for Christ's sake," he said, "the porch light's on." He half turned, pushing against Shiela, who was crowding in behind him. The blade of the machete made a sound of rustling silk in the air near his head. It just missed his outstretched hand and thudded into the wooden door.

Whistler put his hand against Shiela's chest and shoved as hard as he could. She went careening back along the path, caught her heels on the uneven brick, and went down hard in the azaleas. Whistler ducked under an arm and hand heaving the machete out of the door, shouldering a body back and away. The blade came free, and Whistler slammed the door closed as he skidded across the floor toward the sliding doors and out to the balcony and the potted plant standing in front of them. In the brief moment before the closing door shut out the porch light, which he never left on when he expected to be away for more than overnight, he had the chance to catch a glimpse of Jickie Rojo struggling with the machete.

Now it was as dark as the inside of a magician's hat. He was on his knees pulling out the sphagnum moss by the handful, scrabbling for the plastic wrap and the gun that should be in it.

"You silly son of a bitch," Rojo said. "That's the first place I looked."

Whistler started to stand up, his right hand wrapped around the skinny trunk of the ficus benjamina. "How the fuck did you ever come to do that?"

Rojo didn't answer. He was too busy running headlong toward Whistler, the machete held off to the side so it would be very hard to block the next blow without losing a hand.

First the hand and then my fucking head, Whistler thought as he swung the potted plant at the full length of trunk and arm and caught Rojo right across the knees.

Rojo let out an awful howl of pain, stumbled, half fell, regained his feet but not his stride, windmilled like a dervish trying to check his headlong charge, failed to do so, and went crashing through drapes, glass door, and railing. Over the side.

Whistler was too slow to see him falling, but he saw him lying smashed flat on the road below in the lights of an oncoming car. The driver slammed on his brakes. They sounded like a woman screaming.

Thirty-eight

Canaan and Lieutenant Muncie lifted Barcaloo right out of the lobby of his hotel when he came back from Cape's mansion.

Bellerose and Canaan had talked to Muncie and made their case, then gave him a chance to retrieve the mistaken favor he'd done for somebody—they didn't ask who—that night when a headless body had been tossed out the back of Willy Zabadno's station wagon. They pointed out that a gunsel by the name of Jickie Rojo, up from New Orleans, up from Bellerose's parish, had tried to kill a citizen of Los Angeles and had swan-dived off a balcony onto Iris Terrace just above Cahuenga Boulevard instead. The investigation of that matter was going to lead to an investigation of the headless body that was missing from the county morgue, removed by Willy Zabadno for reasons ultimately known only to himself, since he was dead and couldn't testify to anything anymore.

But one thing was very clear: A favor had been done. There was a good chance it was about to have repercussions. If Muncie wanted to continue being loyal to whomever he was being loyal to, that was his business, naturally, but it was better than even money that when they brought down whomever, Muncie was going to be trampled underfoot.

That was all it took to convince Muncie that he should protect his wife, kiddies, and pension. Not to mention the fact that Muncie was actually an honest cop and that the favor done for Burchard hadn't seemed like such a great distortion of the law at the time.

Barcaloo went along with them very quietly, being, as he told them, a respecter of uniforms and asshole detectives with bags under their eyes.

"Take me downtown and show me your telephone," Barcaloo said.

"I thought you were from out of town, Mr. Barcaloo," Canaan said. "Don't tell me you've provided yourself with a lawyer already?"

"I wouldn't come to your asshole of a city if I didn't have some friends."

"Influential friends?" Muncie asked mildly.

"With enough juice to fry your balls," Barcaloo said.

On that friendly note they drove in silence to Temple Street and the Rampart area jail, which was no longer the home of the confessed cult murderer, Carl Corvallis, but was as empty as a tomb.

They walked Barcaloo through the front door into the echoing, empty building. Muncie hit the switch, and Barcaloo saw Bellerose sitting on a straight-backed chair in the middle of the tile floor with an aluminum camera case beside his feet.

"What the fuck is this?"

"I come to visit you, Nonny. I come to tell you of a little bit of misfortune that has befell you. I don' suppose you know that your movin' pitcher studio has burned down?"

"That's okay, it's insured."

"Oh, not the one down by the riverfront. The one out to the Bayou des Familles."

"I ain't got no—"

"Don' fuck with me, Barcaloo. There ain' no percentage in it for you."

Muncie brought over a nearby chair just like the one

Bellerose was sitting in. "Take a load off your feet, Mr. Barcaloo," he said.

"You see how polite these L.A. cops are, Nonny? I don' have to be so goddamn polite. This ain' my jurisdiction. I got no authority over here. I'm just a private citizen. I could break your arms an' legs, an' there wouldn't be any of this police brutality shit you could lay on me."

Barcaloo sat down and showed his white teeth.

"So thanks for tellin' me about my misfortune. How'd it happen?"

"The gasoline for the generator blew up. Totaled a Lincoln Continental. Blew some fuckin' fool all to hell."

"Who might that have been?"

"Your faithful employee, Dom Pinole."

Barcaloo made a noise with his lips, kissing Pinole good-bye.

"You don' seem surprised."

"Well, now, I'm not surprised. Dom wasn't very bright. I always tole him he'd be killin' himself one of these fine days."

"Other bodies in the rubble, Nonny."

Barcaloo sat there, calm and easy.

"Man named Chester Bucherleider. Young woman named Loretta Oskanowsky."

"Don't know them. Was they vandals?"

"Chippy Byrd and Lacy Ohio. Maybe you knew them?"

Barcaloo shook his head. "They got caught in the fire, huh? What do you think they were doin' on private property?"

"They were dead before the fire got 'em. Bare-assed and dead. You think your assholes was takin' their pitchers?"

"That could be."

"Maybe you was there takin' their pitchers?"

"No. No, I wasn't there."

"A frien' a mine, name of Whistler, says you was. In fact, he was standin' on their bodies in a closet while you were tryin' to get a lady named Shiela Andes to do a little fuckin' for the cameras too."

"I don't know anybody name of Whistler."

"Sure you do," Whistler said, stepping out from the shadows behind the charge desk.

If they'd thought that Whistler's sudden appearance was

264

going to send Barcaloo into a dither, they were dead-ass wrong. He stared at Whistler like he was just another citizen waiting at a bus stop.

"No, I fuckin' don't," he said, emphasizing each and every word.

"I'm the guy in front of the Beaver Run down in New Orleans."

"Oh, sure. Now I remember your face."

"Aren't you surprised to see me?"

"Why should I be surprised to see you?"

"Didn't you expect Jickie Rojo to do me?"

"I didn't know Jickie was lookin' for you." Barcaloo swiveled his head and looked up at Muncie. "Officer, you should arrest this man. I got reason to believe he caused the death of my friend, Dom Pinole."

"That's a case for New Orleans," Muncie said.

Barcaloo turned back to Bellerose.

"I just tole you, I got no authority to arrest over here."

"Son of a bitch," Barcaloo said, without anger, looking at Whistler. "Looks like you got yourself a pass on a fuckin' technicality."

"Now, in your case, we'll go through the paperwork and the trouble to get your ass for those two dead bodies we found in the closet," Bellerose said.

"Well, you'll just have to talk to Pinole and Rojo about that, won't you?"

They sat around in a pool of quiet, nobody moving, nobody hardly breathing, everybody waiting for something to snap. Whistler had the definite impression that Barcaloo already knew that Rojo had taken a header onto the concrete. Why not? If the cop who'd done the favor for Cape had gotten the word of Rojo's death, he would have passed it on to Cape. And Cape would have passed it on to Barcaloo.

"Rojo's dead," Whistler said.

Barcaloo paused a beat. "It looks like I'm going to have to put an ad in the paper for some new employees. Now, who the fuck's goin' to drive me back to my hotel?"

He started to stand up, but Bellerose reached forward and

shoved him in the chest, and Canaan clapped a hand on his shoulder.

"There's still the murder of a Vietnamese prostitute by the name of Lim Shu Dok."

"Prove it."

"And there's still a young Mexican whore by the name of Rita Sastre."

"Don' know her."

"You had her head cut off."

"I tole you once before about these two cunts. I never done nothin' to 'em except to take their pictures fuckin' and suckin'. That's my livin'. There's no law against it. You don't like what I do, go make a law."

"You had Rita Sastre's head cut off while the cameras were rollin'. You sell it on movies and cassettes."

"I told you that was a trick."

"No trick, Nonny. We didn' only find the pieces of Dom Pinole and the charred bodies of Chester Bucherleider and Loretta Oskanowsky. We found Rita Sastre's bones. Her head was in one place and her body was in another. Under the floor of the stage, Nonny."

Barcaloo's eyes flickered. He was trying to focus in on information he hadn't had before. Those stupid assholes, Dom and Jickie, he thought. Couldn't they fucking *ever* do something right?

Bellerose stood up. "All right, then."

"All right, what?" Barcaloo said.

"Let's go book you in."

"Don't jerk my chain. You were going to book me, you'd have took me down to city or county jail, not this pisshole. This was to scare the shit out of me and make me cry. Because you know, and I know, you can't prove a fuckin' thing."

"We can prove a little, Nonny. Just wait and see."

Barcaloo stood up. He tucked his shirt into the waistband of his trousers and adjusted the lapels of his jacket.

"Maybe we don't book you," Muncie said. "Maybe we just hold you forty-eight."

"All legal," Canaan said.

"Hold you forty-eight. Your friend . . ."

"Walter Cape," Whistler said.

"Walter Cape thinks you're cutting a deal. Maybe you can tell us if he hired you to murder Lim Shu Dok?"

"Up your ass," Barcaloo said.

"Don't answer right away. Think about it," Bellerose said. He reached into his pocket and took out a coin. "Flip you to see who drives this asshole back to his hotel." He spun the coin. Muncie called heads. It was tails. Bellerose looked at Whistler. "Fuck, we lose."

After they dropped Barcaloo off, Whistler drove Bellerose back to Gentry's. Bellerose still had the aluminum case on the floor between his feet.

"Why didn't you give him a look at that?" Whistler asked.

"You saw that man. You think the rottin' head of a woman he killed, or had killed, would stir him any?"

"So what do we do about him?"

"We just keep on pushin'. We just keep on pushin'."

Thirty-nine

Barcaloo walked into the hotel suite feeling mean. Like a bull gator. The loss of Pinole, and now Rojo, was a territorial threat, not a cause for sadness.

Bouche was on the couch, a bowl of lettuce and tomatoes wilting in a bowl, slices of egg and avocado turning color. A bottle of vodka was gone and another started. There were stains of a spilled drink on the carpet.

She had her head thrown back, her mouth open, showing the gold teeth in the back he'd paid a bundle for, maintaining his property.

Her dressing gown was open, and her nightgown gaped in front, exposing her heavy white breasts. Her skirts were up, exposing her thighs almost to her bush. Thighs spread wide. As pale as slabs of suet. He felt nothing. He was through with her.

Pinole and Rojo were dead. The big deal with Cape had turned to shit. He didn't want to fuck Bouche anymore. He'd leave her here in La-La Land and go back to New Orleans where he belonged, where he was a little king.

Look at the sloppy broad, he thought. He reached over to cover her ugliness. His fingers touched the sharp edge of the folded calling card. He read the name of Lieutenant Bellerose and saw Whistler and a number written on it.

She opened her eyes sleepily.

"Hullo, there, Nonny, honey."

The rage boiled up out of his belly. He knew, without doubt, that he was going to kill her. It would be better if it could be cold-blooded, but the fury was running all through his blood and bones like an electric flood. It numbed his hands and made the veins in his neck beat on drums inside his head with terrible power. It filled his gut and swelled his balls. It gave him an erection like he hadn't had in twenty years. He'd kill her, but first he'd crush her. He'd use his cock to punish her. Punish her mouth and her cunt and her asshole. He'd stab her with it and tear her apart.

Bouche was grinning at him with an oddly knowing look, as though she knew for certain what he had in mind and didn't care. "Hey, nonny nonny, and a hot cha-cha," she said mockingly.

He tore open his belt and dropped his pants. He'd take her first like she was a whore doing it for a dollar in a doorway. A utility fuck taken on the run.

"Hey, for Christ's sake, Nonny, let's use the bed. You're payin' three hundred dollars a day for the room, so let's use the bed."

He landed on her, not caring that his weight was almost crushing her. She tried to squirm away, but he clutched at her like a beast holding its prey for the fatal stroke.

Oh, dear God, she thought. *This ain't the fucking pig in heat. This is the day he means to kill me.*

He grunted and thrashed his head from side to side as he fought her legs wider. His spittle sprayed on her cheek and neck. It seemed to burn like acid and sent her into a frenzy. She managed to roll him off long enough to get out from under. But he attacked again and knocked her to the floor. She didn't scream. Neither of them spoke another word. Her arms were raised above his back, hands waving desperately in the air. She felt him enter her and instinctively adjusted to make it less painful for her, which seemed to make it easier for him. Her groping hand touched the table. The bottle fell over and the dishes clattered. Her fingers closed on the bread knife. She looked along Barcaloo's heaving back. She raised the knife and plunged it into his body just above the kidneys.

Just like she'd said once not long before, Barcaloo was alive going up and dead coming down.

Forty

Bosco was at the register reading Plato's *Earlier Dialectic* in the second edition. It was still raining, and business was once more on the ebb.

Bellerose and Canaan sat on one side of the booth, the aluminum case between them. Shiela and Whistler sat on the other. The three men were glum to one degree or another; she was not. So far as she was concerned, everything had turned out just right. Every threat against her had been taken care of. She'd never really believed that a man like Walter Cape would have bothered arranging for her to be sent down to New Orleans and filmed in a fuck flick just to shut her mouth about the accident and Tillman. But even if he had, there'd be no reason to stir the cesspool another time. What they had was a pack of sleeping dogs, and anybody would be smart enough to let them lie. She could get on with her life and her career. She could feel Whistler's thigh warm against her thigh.

"This rain is never going to stop," Whistler said. "It's going to keep on raining until every house on every hill slides down into the canyons and the valleys. Then the rising water's going to wash it all down Wilshire and Sunset to the sea. When the sun finally comes out again, there'll be nothing but a lake where L.A. once was."

"You want wet, we got wet down to where I live," Bellerose said. "If ever you want wet, you come down an' visit me." He looked at his watch.

"When's your plane?"

"I got a couple hours before I grab a cab to the airport."

"I'll give you a lift," Canaan said.

Bellerose looked at Canaan. "City car, city gas?"

"That's right."

"Thank you kindly."

Whistler looked from one to the other and then at the case. "What are you planning to do with that?"

"It's a hell of a piece of inventory to be carryin' aroun', ain't it?"

"You can turn it over to me. I'll see it gets to the right people," Canaan said.

Shiela shuddered and stared briefly at the case but didn't say anything.

Little pools of silence lay around their conversation like the oily, trash-fouled puddles in the gutters and on the parking lots.

"Son of a bitch," Whistler finally said in a low voice that sounded like it wanted to be a yell. "We didn't do a fucking bit of good."

"Hey, hey, hey," Bellerose said, "look again. We took three assholes—beggin' your pardon, ma'am—off the streets, one way or another."

"Cape's still up on the hill, buying and selling children."

"Someday we'll do him too," Canaan said. "We sent him a message. The level of shit'll be down for a while."

"For Christ's sake," Whistler said, "what are we, just a bunch of sewer workers?"

Canaan nodded his head like a wise old bird. "That's what we are, Whistler. Didn't you know that?"

"If one of you says, 'It's a dirty job, but somebody's got to do it,' I'm going the fuck home . . . begging nobody's pardon," Shiela said.

The three men didn't think she was funny. They stared at her as though they wondered about her good intentions.

"I got to wade in the shit, it's only fair Cape should wade in the shit," Whistler said. "Tillman called me. Wanted to whine. Wanted to ask me how he could get out from under this deal Cape's boxed him into. Cape's called a meeting of the stockholders for tonight. I told him not to fret, Cape would probably dissolve the company, at least for a while. I figure they should be sitting down to dinner right about now."

Canaan picked up the aluminum case and slid out of the booth. Bellerose followed. They said good-bye to Shiela and went to wait at the door.

He handed her the keys to the Chevy. "You want to go back and pack your things at Bosco's? I'll have Canaan drop me off there."

"I want to go home, Whistler."

"Okay, I'll have him drop me at the house."

"My home, Whistler. Back to my apartment. You understand? I want to sleep in my own bed."

He handed her the keys. "Your apartment, then."

"I want to sleep alone. Please? Tomorrow. I'll bring your car back tomorrow. Is that okay? Maybe we'll have breakfast here tomorrow."

"In the morning maybe it won't be raining anymore."

Forty-one

When Canaan drove up with Bellerose sitting beside him and Whistler in back, the guard came out of the gate house with a shotgun cradled in his elbow. He was wearing a felt hat with a wide brim and was squinting through the rain, which was pierced by the headlights. Canaan got half out of the car, fumbling around in his pockets.

"Excuse me," he said. "I seem to be lost."

The guard didn't answer, just stood there, heavy with suspicion, paid to be professionally suspicious of everyone.

Canaan got all the way out, then stuck his head and shoulders back into the car, saying loudly, "Hey, Carl, you got those directions your sister-in-law gave us?"

Bellerose got out of the car and walked over toward the guard, taking a piece of paper from his pocket. Canaan walked up the other side. They were ten feet apart when they closed in. The guard's eyes flicked back and forth between the two. He started hefting the shotgun. Canaan pulled his piece and shoved it into the guard's ribs as Bellerose reached out and grabbed the barrel of the gun so it couldn't be raised any farther. He got his own gun out.

"Take it from me frien', what they pay you ain' worth dyin' for."

The guard gave up the shotgun. Canaan tapped him on the elbow, and he put his hands behind him. Canaan backed him up to the wrought-iron gate and cuffed his wrists around a bar. Whistler got in behind the wheel. He drove the car slowly up to the gate, then fed it gas. The mechanism resisted at first, then slowly gave way as the engine roared and the tires whined, making dry patches on the drive. The guard walked backward as the gate opened enough for Bellerose to slip through and go into the gate house. He threw the switch. The gates opened faster. Canaan helped the guard so he wouldn't fall and get dragged.

Whistler carried the shotgun as they walked up the long, sloping drive. At the main entrance he glanced at Canaan and Bellerose, who stood on either side of him.

"Don' bother ringin' the bell," Bellerose said.

Whistler gave the lock both barrels. The doors flew open. They stepped inside as a butler came running down the hallway. He stopped when he saw their guns.

"Show us," Whistler said as he threw the shotgun over on a bench upholstered in Bayeux tapestry. The servant walked in front of them down to the double doors that led to the dining room.

Canaan flashed his shield and said, "Step aside and don't bother calling the police." He handed Whistler the aluminum case. "I think Whistler should do the honors."

There was a babble of voices coming from the dining room. It came at them in a rush when they opened the doors and went into the room.

"Sit the fuck down," Bellerose said, his gun held out to his side, pointed at the floor, but there for all to see.

May Tuckerman, Monsignor Moynihan, Shirley Quon, Frank Menifee, Ralph Parker, Henry Warsaw, and Emmet Tillman all sat down. Walter Cape was already seated up at the head of the table. Apparently he'd never even moved at the sound of the shotgun blasts.

There was nobody sitting at the foot of the table. Whistler put the case down and snapped open the catches.

"You people would sell your own mothers, sons, and daughters to make a dollar. Some of you would even want to watch what assholes like Walter Cape would do to them."

"Be careful," Cape said.

"Another time, another place, you'd be creeping up to tourists on the street selling them dirty postcards. What the hell, that's not so bad. Isn't that what you'd say? But that's not the worst. You sell pictures of women being mutilated, humiliated, even killed. Not only women but also little children. You're a child fucker and a child killer."

He lifted the lid, and the steam from the dry ice came out in a stinking cloud.

"I want you people to see the sort of thing he does."

He took out the bloated, battered, rotting head by the thick, coarse, shining, black hair and rolled it down the table. Bits of flesh and corruption spattered the linen tablecloth, gowns, and shirtfronts. When it reached Cape, he threw out his hands to keep it from falling into his lap.

Nobody screamed or fainted. Nobody got sick into the mousse. They just got up, one by one, walking past Bellerose, Canaan, and Whistler and out the door. Out of the room, out through the shattered front doors, stumbling to their cars and leaving Walter Cape sitting at the head of his table, staring into the dead eyes of Lim Shu Dok.

Forty-two

Bosco sat down at the table with Whistler. The rain had stopped. The night air was so clear, you could bottle it and sell it to Vermont. The four corners were crawling with chickens, chicken hawks, whores, twangy boys, grifters, drifters, and undercover cops with ear-to-ear grins wiped across their faces like jelly smears.

Whistler was adding up his assets.

"That was a terrible thing you did," Bosco said in a neutral voice.

Whistler took Bosco's gaze head-on and nodded. "It was, Bosco. I admit it. But in a funny way it gave Lim Shu a chance to get something back. She'll be buried, with nothing missing, in the morning."

Bosco pointed to Whistler's calculations with his chin.

"Doing your bookkeeping?"

"I got two hundred bucks from Tillman for driving Shiela home. I spent fifty on Officer Schoonover, seven bucks on the sandwiches for the gazoony at the morgue. Also I gave that Charlie fifty. It costs me fifteen bucks for the cab to LAX and a hundred twenty-nine bucks on my plastic to New Orleans.

Then there was two hundred fifty for that cassette, forty bucks for the hotel room, and ten bucks for rental on the video machine. Ten and five to bribe Crib Coxey."

"You got the Mickey Mouse can opener," Bosco said, his eyes on the paper, following Whistler's calculations with great care.

"Credit, fifty-nine cents. Car rental, thirty-eight bucks a day, two days. Oh, for Christ's sake. Two times one hundred seventy-eight dollars, two airfares from New Orleans to L.A."

"How come a hundred twenty-nine going, a hundred seventy-eight coming back?"

"We were in a hurry and couldn't get a direct flight. Taxi back from LAX."

"You figure in gasoline for your own car, meals out of town, and so forth?"

"I got it here under incidentals. I figure a hundred."

"You should get out of the business, Whistler. You're not doing very good."

"I don't count the meals Shiela and me had together," Whistler said, finishing his thought.

"They were like dates?"

"That's right."

"How is Shiela? You don't come in together anymore."

Whistler hesitated for just a breath. Then he said, "She got an offer for a picture shooting in New York City. Six weeks and some billing."

"There's a lot of runaway production nowadays."

"No more major studios like the old days." Whistler sighed. "So, whattaya know, Bosco? I'm on my own again."

"I never like to say I told you so."

"What are you talking about? You say it all the time. What did you tell me that you think I should remember?"

"I said iron rusts. And I said you should never try to eat the holes in Swiss cheese."

TEN PRAYING CHURCHES

1989

Other books in this series:

TEN PRAYING CHURCHES

Edited by
Donald English

MARC
British Church Growth Association

The BCGA gratefully acknowledges the help of the Drummond Trust.

Biblical quotations are from the following:
NIV = New International Version © International Bible Society 1973, 1978, 1984. NKJV = New King James Version Copyright © 1979, 1980, 1982 Thomas Nelson Inc. Publishers. RSV = Revised Standard Version copyrighted 1946, 1952, © 1971, 1973 by the Division of Christian Education of the National Council of the Churches of Christ in the USA. GNB = Good News Bible © American Bible Society, 1976. AV = Authorised Version, Crown copyright.

British Library Cataloguing in Publication Data
Ten praying churches
  1. Christian church. Public worship. Prayer
  I. English, Donald
  264′.1
  ISBN 1–85424–026–9
            0–948704–15–2 BCGA
            0–86760–077–2 Albatross

Distributed in Australia by Albatross Books Ltd
PO Box 320, Sutherland, NSW 2232.

Front cover photo: Mick Rock, Cephas Picture Library

Typeset for MARC, an imprint of Monarch Publications, 1 St Annes Road, Eastbourne, E Sussex BN21 3UN by J&L Composition Ltd, Filey, North Yorkshire YO14 9DX. Printed by Richard Clay Ltd, Bungay, Suffolk.

CONTENTS

TEN PRAYING CHURCHES

1 St Paul, Bentley Common, Brentwood
2 Queens Road Baptist Church, Coventry
3 Gilcomston South, Church of Scotland, Aberdeen
4 Open Door Community Church, Uxbridge
5 Portrack Baptist Church, Stockton-on-Tees
6 Chessington Methodist Church, Chessington
7 St Philip & St James, Walderslade, Chatham
8 Colne Valley Community Church, Colchester
9 New Life Assembly, Brixton
10 Stoke Holy Cross and Dunston, Norwich

FOREWORD

This was no ordinary day at the temple. Jesus, whip in hand and burning with zeal and passion, was forcefully reminding his amazed onlookers that his Father's house was pre-eminently 'a house of prayer'! Does your church need a visit from Jesus?

Prayer must always be the distinctive feature of the house of God. When we make prayer a priority we are telling God that we totally depend on him. We need his interventions and the manifestation of his presence and power. Without prayer we start trusting in our own ability and resourcefulness, and as we begin to trust in human skills and organising expertise we lose the glory of God.

By his own example, Jesus taught his disciples that prayer was crucial. They would have yielded to the demands of the crowds and to other people's expectations, but Jesus refused every distraction. Later the apostles demonstrated that they had learned the lesson well by withdrawing from the clamour of the growing church and giving themselves to prayer.

The early church never regarded prayer meetings as dull routine—a duty to be performed and a proof of evangelical orthodoxy. In the Book of Acts the church at prayer was also the church in action! The Day of Pentecost started as a prayer meeting, but God broke in and they broke out! Who can tell from the narrative precisely when they moved from sitting in the house in prayer and came into the streets in power? The next recorded prayer meeting concludes not only with the building shaking but also with the disciples freshly filled with the Holy Spirit and power.

When Peter was taken to prison, the church's natural reflex action was to once again gather to pray, resulting in his miraculous release. When the church at Antioch met to pray, the meeting resulted in a breakthrough of missionary activity as the people released their leaders to advance the gospel in other lands.

The boredom often associated with prayer meetings in the past has been caused by their predictability and lack of living purpose. But if churches are actively involved in works of faith that require the presence of God, prayer will become relevant and exciting.

Every church getting to grips with the challenge and potential of powerful corporate prayer is worth our investigation. I pray that you will be stimulated as you read the testimony of these ten churches and that multiplied congregations will follow their lead, seeing that their first calling as local churches is to be houses of prayer.

Terry Virgo

Introduction

Donald English

*In introducing the ten fellowships represented in this book,
Revd Dr Donald English points up the dedication of all ten to
prayer, the dilemma of juggling church and family life, of
discerning God's voice from one's own, of balancing the
traditional and the new. He challenges our inclination to
compartmentalise prayer as if it were somewhat separate from
real experience, and he invites us to examine our views both of
the God to whom we pray and the church with whom we pray.
In all, he shows us that there is no quick and easy understanding of prayer, but that we must—along with the ten contributors
to this volume —get on with the hard work of prayer. 'To have a
part in this service of praying churches,' he says, 'is both a bold
and necessary thing to do.'*

*As a minister, Donald taught in theological colleges for four-
teen years, served as a missionary and as a circuit minister, and
is now General Secretary of the Home Missions Division of the
Methodist Church. He was President of the Methodist Conference from 1978 to 1979, Moderator of the Free Church
Federal Council from 1985 to 1986, and is now Vice-
Chairperson of the World Methodist Council. During the
250th anniversary celebrations of John and Charles Wesley in
1988, he preached in St Paul's Cathedral before the Queen. He
also broadcasts regularly on the* Today Programme *of BBC
Radio 4, doing 'Thought for the Day'.*

*Donald is married with two grown sons. He enjoys sport, art,
gardening, and being taken for a walk by his dog.*

Prayer is probably the most elusive of all Christian activities.
It is essentially part of the hiddenness of the disciple's

life—hidden because it involves a conscious relationship with one who is not observably present, and hidden because anything resulting from the relationship is a matter of faith, not proof. In that sense prayer is probably the truest thermometer to measure our spiritual health. We are behaving most typically as Christians when we pray.

We come here to one of the major challenges in our understanding of prayer. Because it is essentially a matter of faith, the writers in this book had a harder task than those of most others in the series. This is because the prime reason for praying—if that is the way to put it—has little to do with the 'What comes out at the other end?' question. The fundamental reason why Christians should pray to God is that he is God. We should seek that communication with him even if there were no 'end results', for us or for others. The Lord's Prayer makes this so clear, with all its early phrases referring to God himself, and to his rights, not to our needs. At the simplest level, then, we come to God because he is the all-loving one, portrayed in the Lord's Prayer as 'Our Father'. As children we want to express gratitude, praise, thanks, and to enjoy this way of being intimately in his presence. We do so because he has invited us to come in the name of Jesus and by the power of the Holy Spirit. No 'proof' talk is possible here. Indeed it would be inappropriate. All we know is that we come into God's presence in this special way of self-conscious relationship; we share with him our worship, confession, attitudes, aspirations, concerns and needs; and life seems to be different because of that, even if situations do not fundamentally change (though often, we observe, they do).

Of course we have wonderful assurance in Jesus' exhortations. 'Ask and it will be given to you; seek and you will find; knock and the door will be opened to you' (Matthew 7:7). But this is an exercise of faith, not proof. It depends on God's daily gracious attitude toward us; not on some system we manipulate. And because God's awareness of everything far surpasses ours, we dare not assume that what we ask for is right, nor that our way of asking is invested with a peculiar effectiveness. It is always a 'by grace through faith'

(Ephesians 2:8) activity. We need as many descriptions of prayer experience as we can get: but probably as few prescriptions as are absolutely necessary.

To have a book in this series on praying churches is therefore both a bold and a necessary thing to do. It is bold, because criteria and definitions are not self-evident. It is necessary because a series on churches without a volume on prayer would be neglecting an indispensable aspect of Christian life, both individual and corporate.

Many different stories

The churches and communities described in this book belong to major denominations as well as independent groups. In numerical terms it cannot therefore claim to be a balanced representation of what is happening in British Christianity. But it did not set out to be so; rather to find stories of how particular Christian groups have concentrated on the life of prayer, and of what they observe to be taking place as a result.

Not surprisingly it was not easy to get ministers, pastors and priests to allow their flocks to be described as 'praying churches'. There may be some significance in the fact that it is from so-called 'renewal' groups that more contributions have come, rather than from the traditional Protestant 'Word-oriented' or Catholic 'Sacrament-centred' churches. In passing we do well to ask why this is so. Is it simply the enthusiasm of new ways to do old things, or is it an expression of genuinely new forms of spirituality? The questions raised in this chapter are not intended as judgements on what is written. Rather the aim is to develop the discussion on the basis of the stirring stories made available to us.

One meaning, many ways

Certainly anyone who reads this book will be struck by much of the originality and awesome dedication attached to prayer. Groups which spend five hours at a time praying, or meet every morning at six o'clock, or are so convinced about the authenticity of their prayer line to God that they expect someone to receive guidance about someone else being counselled in another room; are not playing at prayer, nor going through a dutiful routine. You can feel the excitement and vigour as you read the stories. Equally, in more traditional settings, churches have discovered the priority of prayer in a way that makes it newly alive for them. When there is a sense of value and meaning, the *form* of prayer seems to be almost incidental.

And many forms there are. The prayer triplet idea, so widespread in connection with Mission England, crops up a number of times. But there is a whole range of ways of encouraging, sustaining and offering prayer. In the end it is the praying that matters. The particular forms are as varied as the circumstances and the people.

Of course there is a danger here. In a number of places one discerns that new methods of praying are treated as synonymous with a deeper commitment to prayer. Thus the new ways are contrasted with the old ways as though they are qualitatively better, or even more effective, when in fact they may simply be new. In some of the stories regular members of the congregation have left when the new methods were introduced, and there is just a hint that they may be less spiritual or prayerful for doing so. This is a pity; it may simply be that the new ways were not suitable for their spirituality. When the new insights are introduced by the priest, minister or pastor, it is all the harder for members of the congregation who are uneasy about the changes.

Description, not prescription

The writers were asked to describe their situation. This they have done. The major benefit from the book is likely to be that all who read it will discover stories of what God is doing among some of his people, and will learn something from these accounts. The authors were not asked to give their theological or biblical reasons for the assumptions on which their prayer life is based. The readers therefore face the exciting prospect of working that out for themselves. At times there are prescriptions as well as descriptions. Here the reader is invited to fit these particular 'pieces' into the jig-saw of God's answers to prayer across the world. What, for example, does victory through prayer mean for the poor and oppressed casual worker in parts of South America, or to the Christian communities in Eastern Europe? Probably not what victory through prayer means in any of the stories in this book. Yet they are all part of the one picture, and each part lends meaning to the rest. There may even be different meanings of victory through prayer in different parts of the United Kingdom.

The stories in this book will quicken our awareness of the various possibilities which prayer opens up. That God answers our prayers we need not doubt, since he has promised to do so. But the ways in which he answers will be as various as the situations from which we pray. Even such predominant images as 'triumph' or 'battle' may not always be the most relevant for our situation. The stories that follow hint both at the faithfulness of God and at the variety of his dealings with us. We are not invited to copy one model but to be inspired and encouraged by how many models exist.

What kind of God is revealed by our praying?

This brings us to another issue which lies at the heart of prayer, and to which this book provides a good introduction. It concerns the kind of God we worship and the way he works in the world. Every time we claim that God led us to pray for a particular thing, or that God answered prayer in a specific way, we are making an affirmation about God himself. So as we read stories about prayers, visions, words of knowledge, spiritual victories, we have to ask ourselves the question, 'What kind of God is it who would ... ?' Why would he choose to work in this way or that? Why was this person healed and that one not? Of course we cannot answer all these questions, but the fact remains that the aggregate of our

claims about the effectiveness of particular prayers provides a
picture of the God we worship.

It is therefore very important that we distinguish between
the validity of a spiritual experience and the accuracy of our
interpretation of it. We can neither dismiss an experience
because the construction put on it seems questionable to us,
nor assume that the authenticity of our experience justifies
the explanation we offer. This comment covers the way in
which some describe their prayer life, rather like the script of
a two-person dialogue; it covers the degree of confidence
some have that if only we were faithful enough everyone who
comes to us ill would be healed.

This provides another invitation to the reader. Please put
the particular and detailed stories you read in this book into
the context of God's care of the whole wide world. Our
writers were asked to tell us about praying churches. They
have done so faithfully and honestly. We owe it to them to
relate that particular part of the life of prayer to God's
providential way with the whole of the world's existence—
international peace, feeding the hungry, ecological concerns,
justice for the oppressed, and world evangelism. It needs also
to be put into the setting of the total life of each believer—
home and work, family and friends, neighbourhood and
society. If God is the God of all the world, then prayer can
relate to all those areas. One can feel the excitement of that
perception at different points in this book. The invitation is
to carry that projection to its conclusion in the prayer experience of all of us.

How do we know the voice of God?

From this there follows another area of consideration. What
criteria do we need to test an alleged direction from God in
prayer? Is the strength with which we feel it to be from God
sufficient in itself? Is my ability to commend it to others
enough? Where does testing it by Scripture fit in? How
important is trying to search for another source than divine
inspiration, like my desperately wanting something to be

God's will? And what about the circumstances of life as a whole? As one person put it to me bluntly (though this in no sense settles the issue), 'What is God doing lengthening or shortening people's legs in miraculous healings when millions die around the world for lack of food?' Our writers hint at the dilemma as they give their accounts. There may be perfectly good answers to these questions in relation to every story in the book; we need to be clear about what they are, and what they say about the kind of God we worship, and what he is doing in the world. What follows here provides a basis for such further thought.

One notices this last point in a number of stories which give the impression both that God is directly involved in *everything* that happens and that he makes his will positively and unquestionably known to us in *every* situation. The difficulty here is that people can feel under pressure to explain why God *causes* everything to happen which does happen, and also to invest every good thought they have with direct divine inspiration. One may doubt whether that is actually either the teaching of Scripture or the experience of most Christians. A strong doctrine of creation recognises that God has given men and women the ability and the responsibility to face situations and reach decisions in harmony with his will but not by requiring a direct divine intervention at each point. A proper understanding of God's presence in the world recognises that God does not *cause* everything that happens. He *allows* human beings to make wrong decisions, or to make decisions that are not wholly right. But, as Paul says, in Romans 8:28, 'in all things God works for the good of those who love him'.

To concentrate on whatever good God brings out of situations is thus very different from ascribing to God a causative role for *everything* that happens. We end up ascribing foolish actions to God, giving inadequate explanations for events, failing to ask about the cases where things did not work like that, and so creating a picture of God that is unworthy. Again, some of the writers actually share this concern with us. We are all able, because of their contributions, to carry the conversation further with their valuable help.

Praying and doing

This consideration brings us naturally to another feature so helpfully raised in this book, namely the relationship of prayer to everything else we do in the Christian life. A volume on prayer puts the writers under great pressure to produce stories rather in the manner of equations. ('Things were not going well. We prayed and things went better. We prayed more and they went better still . . .'). Mercifully, many of the writers have resisted this pressure. Prayer is not presented in the Bible as what you must do if things are not going well, or if you have some great challenge or large programme ahead. It is commended as the natural life-stream of the Christian—individual and corporate—however life is going, and whatever we are doing or not doing. The image is not so much the foundation on which we raise a building, but rather the bloodstream flowing through the body, or air entering the lungs, whatever the condition, location, or activity.

In that sense everything depends on our prayer life. Yet for that very reason we must be careful not to ascribe specific successes to particular times of prayer, or even to prayer alone, because prayer is inextricably bound up with everything else. If, as in one story in this book, a congregation for the first time receives a full-time pastor, it would be wrong to assume that any growth was due only to a new emphasis on prayer. Having a full-time pastor (if he or she is any good at all!) must of itself have made a difference. New methods of praying which attract larger numbers and which excite the participants may do so, not because they are more spiritual, truer or better ways of praying, but simply because they are different, modern, relevant.

Similarly, success in outreach, by contrast with previous decades, may be because the people caught up in renewal perceive that they are not only to pray about people and needs, but are themselves to do something about it also. The inter-relatedness of prayer to everything else we do is vital, both because prayerless activity is not a Christian model and because to emphasise only (or to over-emphasise) the praying is to denigrate the activity to which God calls us and in which we share in his one mission to his world.

What kind of church?

This relationship between prayer and action highlights another point raised for me by reading the different accounts. It has to do with the image of the life of the church and of the individual believer which is offered. In some of the stories one gains the impression that Christian fellowship is meant to take up a 'reasonable' part of the leisure time of the members. What they do with the rest is a matter for individual conscience and arrangement. In other cases one senses that in addition to the fellowship activities there is great stress on social action in the neighbourhood, with the church as church 'living out' the gospel in practice. In yet other cases one has the feeling that the fellowship itself is taking over more and more of the members' lives. The time spent in prayer, worship, celebration and house-group, when added (one assumes) to the timetable of daily work, leaves little time for anything else. If you add to this the concept of running a Christian school, too, then you are well on the way to creating a Christian sub-culture.

This has been the traditional way of doing missionary work overseas. Its strength is that you can concentrate your missionary effort and your pastoral teaching through the life of significant institutions. You also provide a secure setting for new Christians to grow and for other Christians to flourish. You have a strong base from which to branch out in evangelism. The weaknesses are that the Christian presence becomes cut off from the surrounding culture, that Christians become less and less related to all that goes on around them, and that those outside the Christian community find a number of unnecessary cultural obstacles in the way of their

entering into the Kingdom. The task of finding a *secure* base
which is also confidently *open* is one we are stimulated to
engage in on the strength of the stories we read here.

A gift for praying?

Reflection on time introduces the opportunity to consider the
related issue of talent. It is generally assumed that all Christians say their prayers, and there are good biblical and
theological grounds for such an assumption. The niggling
question raised by this book is, 'Are all Christians equally
called to prayer, or called to an equal fulfilment of the prayer
life?' To be more blunt, 'Are some people called to, or
particularly gifted for, a ministry of prayer?' A clear answer
to those questions might help us with the fact that the
numbers engaging in the prayer life of many churches are
comparatively small. Instead of allowing this fact to cause
disappointment in ourselves and guilt in others, ought we
to recognise that as some can address meetings, others ad-
minister, others use manual skills, so some (drawn from these
groups and others) are particularly gifted for a ministry of
prayer? If so, how can such giftedness be discerned, encouraged and formally recognised?

If particular people are so gifted, are special groups more
likely to fulfil such a ministry? One cannot but be struck by
the recurrence in these stories of references to 'women',
to the Lydia Prayer Fellowship, to 'older women' and to
'widows'. I find myself asking whether the reason for much
that is imaginative, new and holistic about the modern renewal springs from the fact that women are so involved. (If
so, there are surely questions to be asked about the theology
of male authority and the practice of male domination in so
many new as well as old church groups. It is interesting, for
example, that all ten chapters in this book, plus the Foreword
and the Introduction, have the names of men attached to
them.)

Renewal in prayer does seem to set new groups free to
exercise a God-given ministry, and as this happens the variety

of expression—sight, hearing, touch, speech, drama, mime, dance, tableau, banner, plus a diversity of spiritual gifts—all become more evident. The prayer activity theme has a wider range of appeal and more join in, and since they are actively and imaginatively involved, they are more committed to do something about the issues for which they have prayed. This book makes that abundantly clear.

Prayer and Christian maturity

One major question remains for me, and I raise it with considerable diffidence. In a number of these chapters the authors express, implicitly or explicitly, their concern for the maturing of the groups and the experiences they describe. In some contexts that concern may be less of a problem, especially where there is a long history of a congregation in a main-line denomination. And in other situations almost everything is new; buildings are hired; homes are centres; congregations are independent, and much depends on the current leadership, since no other human guidance structure exists. In a number of such churches the pyramidal pattern of leadership is evident. But when what is developing and growing is so experimental, and when the emphasis is on the immediate perception of what God is doing, there *is* room for concern about structures that will enable maturing to take place. I do not mean that the problem is faced only in new renewal groups. My point is that the issue is most clearly evident there.

Tradition and newness

The elements in the maturing process relate to every part of the Christian life, though here we limit our considerations to prayer. There is the question about tradition and loyalty to it. Many of us have inherited one tradition or another, and in dry and difficult days loyalty to the tradition has kept us going till the rains of spiritual refreshment fell upon us. We also know that those very traditions can be deadening in their effect, till we end up going through the motions out of loyalty because no other motivation—eagerness, excitement, creativity—will ever emerge from our traditions again. But once we have only new, exciting, creative forms of expression, what then? Can we go on being ever new and creative? Can the human system—individual and corporate—stand it? How are we to be sustained in dry, tired and difficult days? The tension between tradition and newness is a serious one.

Bible and experience

So is the tension between Bible and experience. We have all been to Bible studies which were as sound as a bell and as dead as a dodo. No wonder groups opt for house-fellowships for sharing. But what if the experiences claimed develop an authority of their own? We can only read Scripture through our own experience, since nothing else is available to us. How do we read the Bible through our experience, yet also submit our experience, through the Spirit, to the teaching of Scripture?

Reason and religion

Then there is the place of reason in religion. Since reason is a God-given ability, it is not likely to be ignored or by-passed by God in his general dealings with us. Yet many of us would admit that the church has often become so reasonable as to be scarcely distinct from other organisations. Neither must reason be allowed to dominate faith, for faith both sees and reaches out into a future not accessible to reason. Yet on the other side one cannot avoid the tendency in some Christian groups to highlight the irrational and the extraordinary until the more bizarre the happening the more likely it is that God did it! This is out of keeping both with the biblical view of the God of creation and redemption, and with the experience of everyday life. Focusing on the unusual can undoubtedly produce an unusual set of people. It can also mean that no one else would dream of joining them, not for fear of God among them, but simply because they have lost touch with reality. How are we to pay due attention to reason, while being open to the winds of the Spirit?

Scripture as foundation

Finally there is Scripture itself. That it has authority is not questioned by Christians. The nature and extent of its authority is, however, widely debated. And it applies here in the matter of prayer renewal. There are at least two major issues. One concerns balance. Every Christian group draws its inspiration from the Bible. Most quote chapter and verse, both about their origins and about their currently held convictions. Anyone can do that, and given the size of the Bible it is perhaps surprising that there are not many more denominations than there are!

Yet we all know that finding a root in Scripture is not the real test. The true and searching question is whether what we emphasise is as important in the biblical revelation as we make it—a question much harder to answer. As with our way of becoming Christian, so with our entry into a Christian congregation, we tend to go for what is most congenial for us. The true test of our growth is how far we are willing and able to learn from those who are also Christ's, but who express their discipleship differently. This is no less true where prayer is concerned.

Bible and culture

The other issue is the Bible and its cultural setting. It is now generally accepted that the cultural contexts of Bible passages have to be taken into consideration when we try to understand what a passage is teaching. That does not, of course, devalue the truth at the heart of the cultural expression. I find it helpful to distinguish between *principle* and *application*. A principle can be universally true even if an application is no longer relevant. For example, where I live we have no trouble about meat offered to idols. The detail of 1 Corinthians 8 is not therefore directly applicable in my context today. But the underlying principle, concern for my brother or sister's conscience, is extremely relevant, and has a wide variety of different applications.

This distinction enables me to avoid investing the application with the authority of the principle, without for a moment questioning the inspiration of both. We do well to learn these lessons when we are inclined to lift Scripture texts wholesale and impose them on our present setting. The result is to imprison the universal principle in a cultural straitjacket which both prevents its free activity in a different cultural setting and also prevents the contemporary culture from taking it seriously.

Please read on!

This book raises all these and many other issues. It will stimulate and excite—maybe even annoy or puzzle. But it is the story of what people of God perceive God to be doing among them. We need to take that with great seriousness. I hope it will also bring joy and a sense of celebration at the way in which God's Spirit bursts out in the most unlikely places and ways. Let those of us who have eyes to read, read; and ears to hear, hear.

Donald English

Chapter 1

St Paul, Bentley Common

Brentwood, Essex

Colin Charlton

St Paul is quite secluded, almost surrounded by woodland, and gives the impression of being tucked away in the country-side. Yet it is only one mile from the M25 and two-and-a-half miles out of the bustling Essex town of Brentwood. It possesses an elegant spire and quite complicated styles of architecture which give it the appearance of considerable age. In fact it was built in 1880.

It serves a scattered parish, the inhabitants of which live a considerable distance from the church. The building itself is quiet and peaceful and has the feeling of an oasis hallowed by prayer. This is its greatest strength; and Colin Charlton, vicar of the church and author of this chapter, takes as his theme verse Isaiah 30:15 'In quietness and confidence shall be your strength.'

Colin is a large, uncompromising Geordie with his roots on the banks of the Tyne near Newcastle. His wife Mary is a nurse working with the terminally ill in nearby St Francis' Hospice. They have a family of three: Stephen a psychiatric nurse, Ian who has his own small business in Chelmsford, and Helen,

23

who is a hairdresser. Colin's hobbies are photography (particularly in the Greek Islands!), walking with the cocker spaniel in the woods, and collecting humorous anecdotes from the many weddings he has conducted.

There is a false modesty which would commence this chapter with words like, 'We are not worthy of the title *a praying church*,' or, 'I am the last one to be writing under this title.'

For this is a praying church, but it is far from being a story of raging success. There is no place for fervent triumphalism in St Paul, Bentley Common. This is a realistic story of a church and of individual Christians who have built up a ministry of prayer, but who have seen setbacks and failures along the way.

Origins

The manner of the church's founding, its location, and its traditions bear heavily upon this story. It was built in a far from harmonious atmosphere, great anger being demonstrated publicly by the builder *not* awarded the building contract, who felt very strongly that he had been unfairly treated. The local people were not consulted about its building, nor indeed about its location. This was not possible at the time. There was no public subscription, and private funds provided the money to build the church!

This is an important point, because it means that prayers of praise and thanksgiving were readily spoken by the worshippers from the start, having been given this lovely building. But what was lacking at first was the quality and substance of prayer uttered by the people in a local community who pray, give and work for a worship centre in their midst, which becomes '*their*' church. All these background facts affect the attitude of local people, even today. This is, for example, one reason why the principles of Christian stewardship have been so slow to take hold. In past days 'they' always provided the wherewithal, and many were content that it should remain so.

Renewal, anyone?

A second fact of life which bears upon the story, too, is the tension produced by spiritual renewal in a small Anglican parish church.

We are small. The church is over half a mile from its community, and they number in total around 1,850. On an average weekend, some 150 people will worship here, spread over three services. During the wedding season those numbers over a weekend would reach 500 or more, but that is a misleading figure to quote. So numbers are *not* great.

The churchmanship has never been extreme at any time. To quote the Bishop of Barking in another but similar context, 'It is two-candle power.'

It is a definite evangelical church, with a strong emphasis on the preaching of the word. The main worship service, simply called 'Family Worship', is centred upon the Lord's Supper, the Holy Communion. And for several years in the writer's experience that accurately describes the church's main features. Yes, there are extras: Bible study in a home; fellowship meeting in another home. We have run house groups, and there is a Women's Prayer meeting. All of these activities are very right and proper—clearly the meat and drink of the average evangelical Church of England.

But over the last years there has been a growing realisation that God's Holy Spirit needed more room to work in us as a church and in us as individuals. So began a process of renewal.

But—what have we here? A dangerous word has crept into our vocabulary—'renewal'? And if its sister word 'charismatic' is heard abroad, we are in some difficulty!

How does a small Anglican parish church grow in renewal without going 'over the top', thus alienating many of its members? For we seem surrounded by opinions and examples which serve only to confuse us.

Fellow evangelicals express concern and caution, and take the firm dispensational line that many spiritual gifts ceased in the early days of the church and do not need exercising today. I know this viewpoint because I once held it myself!

Then there is the example of the big, strong, live renewal churches who seem to many Anglican eyes to be Anglican only in name, but not in nature. Because of this some say, 'Surely *we* are not meant to be quite like that?' And sundry American-based accounts of church renewal in the Holy Spirit paint such a picture of spiritual strength and mighty works that our hearts fail within us when we look at our poor mortal selves. The writer happens to think there may well be too many triumphalist paperbacks around at the moment! (Perhaps that may provoke an end to a happy if short association with the publishers!)

Despite all this, our very ordinary and unexciting church is moving into renewal. God's Holy Spirit is moving among us, sometimes as a 'still small voice', but increasingly in power, particularly in some individuals.

I should like to think that—over the years—what is recorded in John 14:8 onwards—where Philip says to Jesus, 'Lord, show us the Father; that is all we need'—has been happening in this church.

Perhaps many people in our church have been content to relate only to God the Father, and then only perhaps in a vague and impersonal fashion. But Jesus said, 'For a long time I have been with you all; yet you do not know me' (v 9). Again, this emphasises the principle of ticking quietly along without personal knowledge of Jesus as Saviour and Lord. Then follows Jesus' mention of the Holy Spirit, particularly in verse 17, 'He is the Spirit who reveals the truth about God.'

Many of us have had to have truths about God the Father and about Jesus revealed to us by the Holy Spirit.

And so we move forward.

Prayer and the writer

I write as one who does not find prayer easy. This is a personal battle to be won. This is territory to be gained. This is not the simple turning on of a word-filled tap, but particular battles have indeed been won in relation to me and my life within this church.

My left kidney was removed in 1970, at which time poly-cystic kidney disease was diagnosed, and my health deteriorated until it became necessary to go on to a renal dialysis programme in 1980. Strange things then began to happen, because Christians had *prayed*. The years on the kidney machine (around 9,000 hours involved) meant that I was unable to be the traditional 'omnicompetent chap' demanded by Anglican tradition. Others were thrown back upon their own resources and grew spiritually as a consequence. The prayer life of the parish was strengthened, particularly in 1982 when I spent over twenty weeks in hospital following an unsuccessful transplant

That period in particular taught many of us a great deal. It buried for ever the purely simplistic attitude to healing prayer. One or two felt that we did not have sufficient faith because our prayers for healing had not been 'answered'. We had to learn truths about the Lord's timing and about his sovereign will. Some of these truths seemed hard to bear at the time.

The onset of chronic renal failure had seemed a great blow, too. This had meant giving up work as a Diocesan Adviser for Evangelism and imposed certain restrictions upon life in general. The failed transplant and resultant complications served only to weigh heavily upon a prayer life already experiencing difficulties. Looking back positively, however, I recall that there was the counter-balancing fact of relative freedom within the dialysis programme. I am most fortunate in that dialysis did not produce in me the feeling of tiredness and weakness suffered by many renal patients. Having said that, a strong influence in such matters was exercised by Mary, my wife—herself a nurse. Not only did she cope admirably with the mechanics of dialysis, but she refused to allow the patient to feel sorry for himself! It's a standing joke in our home that you have to have two broken legs or something equally serious to warrant much sympathy! This concentrates the mind wonderfully well.

Prayer and individuals

It was during this period that we became aware of prayer beginning to manifest itself in the lives of individuals in our church. Of course it had been evident that people had been praying together, and these prayers had been answered. But then things began to happen, not in any earth-shattering way, but nevertheless in a moving way.

It would be so easy to give several examples of prayer life and in so doing to leave out other equally valid cases. Perhaps, then, the answer lies in quoting only one.

One evening, the vicarage doorbell rang, and there at the door was Henry. He was a fine upstanding man of around fifty, dressed smartly, speaking in the familiar tones of the East End of London, and driving a fairly new, expensive sports saloon.

When invited in, Henry made a most unusual request. He said, 'I would like you to teach me to pray.' We don't get many such requests! More often callers wish to get married, arrange a baptism, or trace the grave of a relative in a churchyard. This was different. And this was very, very real.

Further enquiries revealed that Henry for years had suffered from worrying phobias about driving across motorway fly-overs and going up any great height. He had been very successful in business and had consulted many and varied 'experts' for help and advice with his problems. He had visited hypnotists, hypnotherapists, psychotherapists, and sundry other individuals, been given many and varied pills, potions, and powders. He had read many strange books. In the latest book read, the author had more or less said, 'When all else fails perhaps you might try prayer.' And so—as a last resort—and in some desperation, Henry called in at a strange vicarage attached to a parish church which just *happened* to be on a route regularly traversed on the way to his golf club.

We talked at length and I learned much of Henry's colourful background in the old East End days, of his knowledge of
and friendship with the Kray twins, both currently serving
long prison sentences. But none of this was relayed in any
boastful fashion, which made it all so *real*. So we prayed, and
we met again. And we prayed again. And soon Henry
became a Christian. No, not the archetypal 'I was deep in sin
and the Lord saved me' variety. This was a deep, struggling
realisation that God wanted his life and was calling him to do
something about it. So Henry learned to pray and began to
read the Bible regularly and *enjoy* what he was reading.
Today his phobias are vastly reduced, indeed virtually
removed.

But the whole point of this story is in its reality. Henry is *not*
now living in clover. His business life has suffered greatly, and
setback after setback has savagely attacked him. On several
occasions he has virtually given up. But the Lord God has not
given up on him. Nor has the church. And so we pray for
Henry: that he may rise above his trials and tribulations and
grow stronger in his faith.

The reality lies also in him. His is not the language of Zion.
His phraseology is not that of the majority of Christians. But
there is a clear process of redemption still taking place in him
which is honest and masculine, even muscular. I find it
refreshing. And prayer has brought this to pass thus far and
will sustain it in the future.

The prayer life of other individuals within our church has
become very supportive and precious (in the true sense of
that word). I have become aware of God moving among
people in power—not people in large numbers, and not in
any momentous manner on the Christian Richter scale! But
prayers have been answered in a clearly defined manner,
often now by means of a simple picture.

When we began to have a banner ministry in our church, it
was immediately obvious that not only skill and patience went
into the design and manufacture of the banners, but also a
great deal of prayer. And prayer had been answered with just
the right text or design to fit the moment. But here again there

have been setbacks. On occasions the prayers have not seemed productive and in one case the banner which resulted did not seem quite right and was most certainly not the right colour. I am glad in a sense about this. We need reminding sometimes of God's timing and his will, and when all is not as we would wish, we need to go back to him and seek his further guidance. Significantly, the next banner was superb and just right for the occasion, which happened to be Pentecost.

Equally impressive has been the manner in which individual Christians have started to pray out loud—after finding such an exercise daunting. The words were stumbling at first but gradually gained in confidence and speak much of spiritual growth. To hear some of our little group pray is for me a real delight. To hear the work of God's Holy Spirit being demonstrated even in simple things like sentence construction is a lovely thing. The prayer rings true because it seems uncontrived and lacking in jargon. I have attended prayer meetings where Christians seem to love to be heard for their much speaking. Prayers which roll off the tongue in flowing cadences with a richness of expression: all good, sound stuff. But more than once I have heard the parable of the Pharisee and the Publican and remembered that Jesus said that the former prayed by *himself*, whereas the prayer of the latter was short and to the point; and that he, not the Pharisee, was in the right with God when he went home.

Several of us have had to learn the value of *silence*, too—of *structured silence*—silence which is used, not just a vacuum of inactivity but a dwelling upon God and a waiting upon him. In some of our morning prayer activities, individuals have commented on the prayerful silence within this parish church in its sylvan setting.

Prayer and the body

To illustrate prayer in the body it is necessary to tell of a failure which finally was turned into success.

Some five years ago we were inspired to do something about our lack of a meeting room. The parish church is the only meeting place, and we have never had a meeting room or hall in which to hold activities connected with the work of the church. A large room in the old vicarage was used as a parish room for some time but was never wholly satisfactory. Parts of the church school have also been used, but the school is across a very busy road and has become expensive to hire. A number of years ago, a scheme was proposed which would have provided a hall, but plans did not progress, and the project was cancelled.

So in 1983 we drew up a new scheme, given the sound biblical title of 'Project Nehemiah'. The plans were submitted to the requisite authorities and were approved. But at that point it became clear that somehow, in a way in which was not evident at the time, the cost seemed to be beyond our reach. The project was shelved.

Suddenly, however, in 1987, Bill, our beloved verger, asked whether it would be possible to sell to him the verger's cottage. Glory be. That fact alone at the time encouraged us to re-activate the building project. Meanwhile the first 1983 costing of £30,000, subsequently raised to £55,000, had by now risen to £80,000, a huge sum of money by any standards, and for a tiny parish even more so. The sale of the verger's cottage would leave £30,000 still to find.

By this time, some of us had read George Carey's book *The Church in the Market Place*, and knowing St Nicholas, Durham, of old, I was fascinated to discover the same experience shared with St Nicholas. They, too, had launched a building project, only to find that God's time was not right.

Then on to my desk dropped the account of the huge building project at St Thomas' Crookes, in Sheffield, with vast sums being raised by prayer and direct giving. This was exactly the inspiration we needed. So we began to *pray*. The PCC decided to go ahead on the basis of direct giving, inviting gifts from the Christians, and not sending out begging letters to all and sundry.

We put together a leaflet which went out in late November. We declared in advance a Day of Giving and Thanksgiving on the Eve of the Patronal Festival of the church, 24th January

1988, and we prayed. To say that we were filled with absolute confidence as a church would be untrue. As the great day approached to declare the result of the giving, there were not a few faltering hearts.

But on the morning after the day, having asked for £30,000, we had been given or promised exactly £30,000. For our small church this represents a certain sacrifice in giving. It also ably demonstrates the power of positive prayer. Gradually it has dawned upon our somewhat unbelieving hearts that God is able to perform signs and wonders.

In fact the financial response made me ashamed of my own lack of trust and showed the extent to which the Lord was now working powerfully in the hearts and minds of those who were absolutely convinced of the success of the project and never wavered in their confidence. Again, God's Holy Spirit was at work leading us into all truth, and for some of us working in convincing and convicting power. Thus the seeming failure of 1983 was turned into success when God's timing was right.

In complete contrast came a weekend at Quiet Waters, a Christian Retreat House at Bungay in Suffolk. We had heard of its existence, and had seen it advertised, but knew little of its set-up. After a preliminary meeting with Howard and Wendy Norton, who lead the small team at the house, we booked a weekend in early Spring 1987, and fourteen people went there from Friday to Sunday.

We may well ask, 'So what?'—many churches and many groups of Christians go away for weekends and days for conferences, seminars, or retreats. But for us, the time at Quiet Waters was different. To enter the house was to experience the cumulative effect of prayer. There is a very special kind of peace there which ministered to us all. During that quiet weekend, in an atmosphere of prayer, we listened and learned and grew together. We realised— perhaps unconsciously at first—what it means to be the body of Christ. One of the party was asked to write a report of the weekend.

That report contained this passage:

I think everyone would agree that this time was very special—not because of anything we did, but because we could feel the Lord's presence in power working in us and touching our lives. We experienced the beauty of just being silent in his presence and focusing on him—so that he could use our silence to minister to us, and pour out his love on us, uniting us and drawing us closer to himself and to each other. It was then possible to wait on him for what he had to say to us and to be prompted by the Holy Spirit as to what we should sing or pray.

How beautifully those words express the experience of that prayerful time together. I am reminded of Isaiah's words in chapter 30 verse 15: 'In quietness and confidence shall be your strength' (RV). By means of wise and gentle leading, Howard Norton was able, in the short time we spent in that lovely house, to help create an atmosphere of prayer, the sort of atmosphere which does not require a formal prayer meeting to enable it to grow and flourish. When the body prays in that way, the result is an experience of great power. It does not require elegant verbosity or classical phraseology. It is just simply if quietly *powerful*.

'In *quietness* and *confidence* shall be your *strength*.'

The danger is that after such a time of prayer and sharing, the return to the hustle and bustle of life in the world seems difficult. Yet, looking back, we can now see that the building project mentioned earlier could not have got off the ground any earlier, because the confidence and inner strength of the body would not have been able to meet the challenge, had the body not prayed thus together at Quiet Waters.

One further example of the body praying together has been in the matter of the ministry of healing. For some time we have felt the clear leading of God in the matter of healing, but our efforts seemed not quite to match the inspiration. But at a certain point in 1987, four of us in the local leadership felt led to meet together and explore the whole area of the ministry of healing. So three small Anglican churches and a Baptist church joined forces for this ministry.

The immediate effect of the sharing and praying together was great strength. Churches with no great history of success now found encouragement to step out in faith. Four leaders found talents and gifts complementing each other, and the united prayer of the body produced results. I have found that working together in this way has been of inestimable benefit to me. Now I have alongside me: Paul, an ex-missionary, with a deep and mature Christian faith and great gifts of discernment; John, a young and vigorous man with vision and purpose and—again—tremendous gifts in the area of healing; and Mike, a man of intellect and sound teaching, quiet yet purposeful. Each in his own special way is playing a vitally important part in the ministry of healing we share together. All four of us have been very conscious of the Holy Spirit's leading; prayers have been answered, and the work of the body has been strengthened. For example, one more senior member of our church was simply healed of a distressing and painful condition, a healing which in turn seems to have transformed her personality and attitudes.

The three shared services of prayer for healing held so far have demonstrated, on the one hand, the great need all around us and, on the other hand, the enormous power available to churches who pray together. We have been very careful not to give the impression of a circus act, and we have sought little publicity. We have simply got together and *prayed*: prayed that the Lord would send to the services such people as he needed to be there, and prayed too that his mighty power to heal would be shown among us. Our prayers have been answered.

It could be said that these three services are not a regular part of the everyday life of the church, the humdrum slog. For that we look at *worship* and *fellowship*. Much more prayer now goes into the preparation for our worship on Sundays, and we feel the results. In a midweek preparatory meeting a group of people gather together to pray for and plan the worship service on the following Sunday. The results of that prayer can be seen in the quality of some of the worship and the appropriate nature of its content. Leadership is shared on a much wider scale, bringing to readings, prayers, testimonies, and corporate singing a freshness which lifts hearts and minds. A greater proportion of time in the weekday activities of the church is now given over simply to prayer. And that phrase 'simply to prayer' is very significant. Do we ever take a serious look at the structures of our times of prayer and question some of the ways in which we do things?

How easy it is to make lists of topics for prayer so long, and the discussion of the topics so detailed, that the actual praying is the shortest part!

How comforting it is to sit around drinking tea (in itself an admirable thing) and to have a good chat (again a very helpful exercise sometimes) and to leave so little time for actual praying.

Two sources have provided guidance for us within our church.

The first is *Three Times Three Equals Twelve* (Kingsway, 1986), Brian Mills' excellent book on prayer triplets with its suggestions relating to this method of praying together. We have had to see prayer triplets for what they really are, a thing of stark simplicity, and we have had to resist the temptation to turn them into house groups—a totally different concept.

This simple, uncluttered method of prayer has been further underlined by our contact with the Lydia Fellowship. Shirley—our parish worker—is the leader of Lydia for England. Her wise counsel has enabled others to see the value of the simple, unvarnished ministry of intercessory prayer. The power of the Lydia Groups' meeting simply to pray as intercessors has been very evident. Indeed that basic simplicity points to the strength of the Fellowship. It is not a vast organisation with headquarters and bureaucracy, but in essence large numbers of small groups of women meeting simply to act as intercessors. Would that the church could be known chiefly as the people who meet to pray!

The work of the Parochial Church Council, too, is now accompanied by much more prayer than in past days. Two examples come to mind: first, the sense of unity and cheerfulness which now pervades PCC meetings. To those of us brought up often to think of PCCs as a 'necessary evil', this sense of common purpose linked to smiling faces is quite a novelty!

Then, the kind of agenda brought before the PCC has undergone radical transformation. There is room and space now to talk at any necessary length about worship, evangelism, mission, and the like, and not to confine our discussion to maintenance of the fabric, important though that is.

We are beginning to see an interlocking of prayer and action in such matters. It is indeed true from experience that *orare est laborare*—'to pray is to work'.

Such principles have brought a workmanlike quality to many of our prayers—significantly both in quantity and quality our prayer life is growing; and added to a new definition in prayer, there has been a robust, simple style of prayer with less of the traditional, cherished phrases and more of the direct, positive conversation between child and Father, particularly in intercession.

And this directness has been rewarded with simple answers from the Lord, sometimes in picture language. We have become more aware of words of wisdom and knowledge than in former days. Such gifts of the Spirit have then been translated into everyday action of one sort or another. Some individuals have been given great discernment, a discernment the result of expectant and persistent prayer. Christians are clearly able to hear God in a way which points them in a new direction and with authority. To see such a pattern unfolding is to witness a truly beautiful thing, rather like a lovely flower opening, and fresh colour and wonder being revealed. It is humbling and yet challenging to hear words of wisdom regarding the shape of meetings which need to be altered, and to find that the word is quite right!

To see members of the body being changed and renewed by prayer in this way is both challenging and humbling, and to be ministered to by them in new ways is a precious gift. To be able to speak at a gathering now and experience the feeling of being supported on a wave of prayer is also a tremendous blessing, one of inestimable value to me.

All this may seem dull and uninspiring compared to more illustrious examples of church prayer life. There is no doubt—as I said at the start—that ours is not a scene of rampant revival and renewal. Revival there certainly is. Renewal there assuredly is. Prayer life there most definitely is—but all on a small scale and limited in its extent. Dare I say that on the first occasion of our holding a parish prayer meeting at 7.30 am on a Saturday only seven turned up? We can't say there were seventy. Wish we could! But there was a unity and a depth in the simple prayers of that small group which spoke volumes.

And perhaps in our smallness and weakness there is a certain reality. For example, it affects our sort of language. Yes, there is speaking in tongues on occasions, but not often. More frequently we hear the lovely 'unprofessional' simplicity of the intercessor talking to a down-to-earth God in down-to-earth terms. But it is very real.

Looking back over the last few years I see a picture: a picture familiar from the hills and fells of my native Northumberland. A moorland road winds back into the distance, but covered by several inches of snow, thus obscuring the outline of the road. But at intervals sticking clearly out of the road and marking its edges are lots of 'snow poles', striped markers indicating the way along the road.

In the latter history of the church in this place, in the prayer life of the church in this place, answers to prayer have popped their heads out over the partly obscured way, and these chart the road down which we have come.

As a church we still travel the length of such a road; but the warmth of the Holy Spirit is melting the snow, and the poles of answered prayer are getting longer all the time!

Chapter 2

Queen's Road Baptist Church
Coventry

David Spriggs

By complete contrast with the tenth chapter from rural Norfolk, Queen's Road Baptist Church is right near the centre of a city. Its congregation is mainly middle class, with a growing proportion of under thirties. Prayer life in this large church revolves around a prayer network, prayer triplets, and Operation Agape, a programme that encourages Christians to care more for each other. In spite of all the church's activities, however, David says, 'We are very much still learners in the Lord's school of prayer.'

One story Dr Spriggs does not relate in this chapter concerns a visit he made once to a local hospital to observe surgeons at work in the operating room. The theatre sister mistook him for a visiting anaesthetist, but the mistake was discovered before it was too late!

David is married to Eileen, with three children. Except when the two oldest, Martin and Steven, want to go camping, they enjoy being together as a family in sport and the theatre.

The living God

God has many ways of speaking to people; one of his normal ways with me is to intercept my thought processes. It is like a quiet voice from a chair in the room when you think no one is there, a familiar voice which you wonder if you have imagined at first. This time God was speaking to me gently but persistently about the need for our church to grow in its commitment to prayer. He was also quietly but firmly insisting that I would have a key role to play in this development. He was even beginning to show me ways in which this might radically affect the whole style of my ministry; ways which until then I had not envisaged—and which I did not altogether welcome. His message was clear even if the details were hazy, like a foghorn through the sea mist. If we really wanted to move with him to this next stage, we would need to learn to pray.

It was just then that the request to write a chapter for *Ten Praying Churches* reached me! God has such a wonderful sense of humour and is loving enough to make sure we don't become proud. I share this with you to ensure you understand we do not think we are a church that has learned the art of prayer, but we are learning and want to learn more. We are not a church which has all the answers, but we are discovering many adventures in prayer. We are certainly not a church that has arrived, but at least we have started moving. We share our story not because we think it is splendid but because we can pray that God's wisdom and our weakness can encourage you to do greater things than these.

Many experiences have convinced me of the reality of Christian prayer, but emphasising the necessity of prayer and encouraging our church to pray doesn't suit my nature. I am a doer, a thinker, a controller, an organiser, a manager. Prayer cuts the certainty from all of this. It leaves me vulnerable, like a boat with a sail but no rudder; oars would certainly be preferable because control would be in my hands.

So if God has developed the prayer life of Queen's Road, which he undoubtedly has, and if he has used me in that process, which I believe he has, it is the Lord's doing and is wonderful in our sight—even more wonderful because he has done it *here*. If he can do it here, he can do it for any Christian family.

Queen's Road is one of the larger Baptist churches—it was/ is also one of the more traditional Baptist churches. Its worship had not altered much in the fifteen years before I arrived, for the competence of its minister and the nature of its community did not warrant it. It was well organised, efficient, notable in its own circles. It was still influenced by the strong social outlook of one of its best remembered ministers. Prayer was not, I think, one of its most prominent or most creative features. But there are and always have been wonderful Christian people here, some devoted to prayer, who know that God answers prayer. There was (and still is) a Sunday morning prayer meeting from 10.30 to 10.50 am with a few folk faithfully praying, but there was little more to its regular corporate prayer life. In the last few years God has led us further. He has used many situations and many people to bless us and prod us into prayer.

The one

One of the earliest signs of spiritual growth in our church was a request from Beti, a lady in her early forties, 'David, can you teach me how to pray?' She had always said her prayers, but she had become aware of two things: first, that in prayer meetings she wanted to express thoughts that came to her but was unable to do so; second, that praying is different from saying prayers. She was realising that God was meant to be a father and that there can be a closeness with God she had not explored.

Gladly I agreed to help her, and we arranged to meet. However, before we could meet, God had answered her request. He had released her from her inhibitions and she had started to pray in public. Of even greater significance, her relationship with God was becoming more personal and real.

Beti was launched into a prayer ministry that has since branched out in many directions. Prayer and a relationship with God which has grown with prayer, and which is indeed the inside of prayer, has led her into many experiences: praying with people at work, experiencing God's direction in very specific ways in her family life and at church. One instance must suffice for now. She writes:

> One morning I got up feeling well, got ready to go out to work when suddenly, as I was ready to leave the house, I felt so ill I just had to go into the front room to lie down. In doing so I must have made a noise closing the door. Within minutes my next door neighbour came over in her dressing gown and in a dreadful state. She was feeling suicidal and had decided to end her life. But she knew that we cared and loved her, so hearing the noise from our house ran in to me. I know this was God's reason for my being unwell, for within a short time I was fine again. As a result of this experience the neighbour and I have become much closer.

God continues to use Beti in a prayer support group for someone in a key position and in the healing ministry. However, a word of warning is appropriate here. Soon after she began to grow in her Christian life, misfortunes began to bombard her family. I have no doubt that Satan was seeking to hold back the spiritual renewal in our church, for in the early days, as four people began to respond with a new openness to God, each of their families, including Beti's, was severely oppressed. Indeed all four are still affected. As renewal took place on a broader front, it was as though Satan's resources were overstretched; he could no longer use his spoiling tactics to affect individuals. Looking back, I am sure I did not sufficiently take account of Satan's strategies. I should have organised the shield of faith and mobilised others to pray for the protection of people moving with God. One day I believe those who bore the brunt of Satan's attack will be set free by God from the repercussions in their lives and then there will be a new wave of growth and advance for the kingdom. As you read this book, will you pray with us for that to happen?

The many

The next stage in our journey involves a detour to America! I
was invited by the Southcliffe Baptist Church, Fort Worth,
Texas to attend an Evangelism Explosion Leadership Training Clinic. The church called itself 'the church with a vision'.
It certainly had one, and I caught it! Perhaps nothing has been
quite so significant in the last few years for our church as my
visit to Southcliffe. This is not because Evangelism Explosion
has transformed our church—we still struggle along with only
a handful of people involved—but because that church gave
me a vision for prayer and prompted a plan to make prayer
work.

Coming back on the plane, my head reeling from course
cramming and culture shock, I realised that EE would not fit
easily into our mentality. I also sensed that the American
church was growing and glowing, was so generous and loving
because its people *believed in prayer enough to organise it and
pray*.

Although there were sixty-five trainees like myself, and
although we were only there for five days, each of us
was allocated two prayer partners who had been praying
for us before our arrival, and who wrote to us, met us,
and prayed with us while we were there. They also contacted us again after we left. Many other members of
that American church were prepared to drive in, sometimes
from many miles away, to pray for us while we went out
to do evangelistic visitation. The church also had a prayer
clock. People could sign up to pray for a segment of the
day, say half an hour. They had sufficient people committed
to prayer in this way to ensure that prayer for the church
and its outreach was happening twenty-four hours a day,
every day of the year. Additionally they had a telephone
prayer facility so that people could phone in for prayer
throughout normal office hours.

So I came back with a conviction and a commitment that
even if EE never happened, at least we could learn to pray
more effectively. But how?

As I asked God that question, he began to show me his answer. I had always preached and believed that my ministry was the church's ministry. The whole congregation was involved in Christ's ministry, even when I was the person through whom Christ was ministering. Thus I have always emphasised that I needed other people. Now I began to see how we could work this out. There are times when any minister can feel very lonely—when called upon to help people in the crisis of bereavement, for instance. What I needed was instant prayer support; hence we developed our *prayer network*. At any time I can pick up the phone and contact one of five people who head the prayer network. He or she will phone the other four leaders, all of whom start the process down the line. Within an hour many people can be praying for Christ's ministry operating through me.

Prayer Network

Leaders

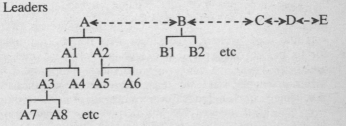

That would cover crises. But why limit prayer support to crises? So as well as the prayer network we ran 'Prayer Lines', originally a bi-monthly sheet giving basic details of my specific activities, their times and often a direction for prayer. Soon after these two prayer ministries had started, I realised something significant had happened to me. Running a large church as the sole full-time employee can be, and certainly was, very demanding. I felt the weight of responsibility for the church on me, but once the prayer ministries started, the burden was significantly lifted. I was still responsible under God for providing leadership and ministry, but God carried the weight of the burden. It took me a while to work out the connection, but that there is a connection I have no doubt.

Gradually, involvement in prayer by individuals in harmony increased significantly, and over the months things have developed even further. People on the prayer network saw that prayer made a difference to me, so they wanted prayer for their crises, too! Soon it became not the minister's prayer network but the church's! People who were not part of the network asked for prayer. Finding that prayer works, they then wanted to become part of the network.

Gail joined our church at about the same time as her sister Lorraine. Both came as a result of Mission England:

> I had been taken into hospital following a miscarriage at around eleven weeks of pregnancy. I was in quite a lot of pain, being sick and terribly upset at what had happened. Prior to going down to the operating theatre I received a message that prayers were being said via our prayer network, and that produced an immediate sense of calm and support, as I knew everything was now in God's hands.
>
> Ten months later I had another miscarriage, but again I felt encouraged and supported by all those people praying for me and my family, and out of sadness came something really victorious as I drew closer to God and could thank him for all he had done and was doing in my life. That closeness and sense of prayer about everything great and small has never left me, and I believe it is because of my own prayers and other people's prayers being said for me.
>
> God also prompted me into thinking this was something I could be involved in. I didn't seem able to contribute much as a church member but I could pray. I could pray for other people, and so for me the prayer network has a dual purpose: one being that at the dial of a phone I can ask for prayers for myself and other people and the other being that I find it a tremendous encouragement to know that God is using me to intercede for others through the power of prayer.

We always obtain the permission of the persons for whom the prayer is requested and, wherever possible, agree the wording of the request with them. We have also found it valuable to encourage those on the prayer network to write down the message to maintain accuracy. All those on the network are committed to confidentiality. Now the ministers have a feedback system from the end of the network so that we also know what is going on! We are running a trial to provide people with feedback on how God is answering the prayers. After renewing contact with those who have requested the prayer, to discover developments, the prayer network co-ordinator (one of the five leaders who head the network) produces a monthly report. We believe this will encourage prayer as well as reiterate our commitment to the people who asked for prayer.

'Prayer Lines' has also ceased to be the property of the ministers and become a prayer diary for the church and further afield. It is now issued monthly and includes brief teaching on some aspect of prayer.

Through these two attempts to organise prayer many people have become involved in specific prayer. Our relationships have been fostered, especially through the prayer network. Prayer has become the nervous system of the body. Information, warning and encouraging messages pass from the troubled area through the body to the head and back again. We thank God for the vision of organising prayer.

Working for prayer

Organising takes time and effort. One of the key people in promoting and organising the prayer network and 'Prayer Lines' is Jenny, who suffers from physical disabilities that restrict the time she can be out of bed and out of the home. She has given her life in many ways to helping others pray, but she has also experienced the impact of prayer within and on her life as she has done so. She has received much prayer for wholeness. On the physical side, things are somewhat better; but it is on the side of inner healing and her relationships with

God and other people that the results are most significant for her:

> Many people have prayed for healing for me over many years. God has been, and still is, answering those prayers bringing me inner healing which has profoundly changed my relationship with others.
>
> At times I am overwhelmed at the privilege of having so much quietness and leisure to be with God and to think and learn while my husband and friends lead such busy lives with many stresses that I do not have to cope with.
>
> But the most exciting change has come in just coming into God's presence as a child to a father and waiting to see what will happen. Sometimes I am full of thankfulness as he reminds me of all he has done in my life; sometimes he comforts and encourages and sometimes I am just conscious of his unending love—no two occasions are the same. I know I can always come to him even when I am sad or have been disobedient and will find his love waiting for me. Even when he is stern and disappointed in me there is such security in knowing that he accepts the final responsibility for my life and can deal with my wilfulness and failures.

Prayer and evangelism

I have already mentioned Evangelism Explosion. One of the keys to EE is the prayer partner scheme. Every teacher, trainer and trainee needs at least two prayer partners. Each week of the seventeen-session training course, the member reports to, and prays with, his or her prayer partners. This arrangement has many advantages, not least that it teaches us how to pray in small groups with specific objectives, and how to develop an on-going prayer commitment. Out of this there nearly always develops a deepening relationship between each member of the triplet (ie a member and two prayer partners), joy and new confidence in prayer as we see God answering prayer, commitment to persevere in prayer (most of us are better at going on praying for other people than we are for ourselves, especially when we have the encouragement or discipline of praying in a very small group), and growing involvement in evangelism.

Eventually on a small scale we did commence EE but even with only four trainees and one teacher it meant fifteen involved in prayer! So by the time Mission England came along with its prayer triplet scheme, many of us were already convinced of its value, its scriptural propriety and its workability.

Prayer triplets

Prayer triplets was the prayer scheme given by God to Brian Mills. Something of the effect across the nation can be found in his book *Three Times Three Equals Twelve*.[1] About seventy people from our church became involved in this form of prayer ministry. This proved to be another gift from God for adding two more dimensions to the growing prayer life of the church. Through prayer triplets we were learning to pray in small groups. Prayer triplets involved sharing the needs of people for whom we were concerned, so we were also learning to share things which mattered deeply to us. Through prayer triplets we not only saw people coming to faith in Jesus, but we also received the blessing of sharing our lives in God's presence. Many of us as we prayed lovingly and expectantly experienced new levels of living: God's love flowing through us in our triplets, oneness, and a flow of joyful life—not because we prayed so much for ourselves, but because we were praying for others. Such prayer was like the blood flowing through unblocked arteries to nourish the body—truly good.

Further developments

The experience of praying in small groups for others has shown us that God's principles, which work in the small group, can be applied in many other ways.

One is that if you want things to happen evangelistically

you need to pray, and it's more fun to pray together. One instance stands out in my mind. We were showing a film one Sunday evening. It was intended especially for the young people. A few people had already seen the film and were not too impressed by it. Rather than criticise it, however, or boycott the service, they decided to meet at church and pray for God to use the film to bring people to Christ. Throughout the service they prayed. One sure result was that a young policeman came to a Christian commitment. A few minutes before the service started he had been elsewhere. Suddenly he felt a compulsion to come to our church—it was his first visit. He is now a baptised member.

Prayer triplets taught us to persevere in prayer. We realised about three years ago that although people of all ages were coming to faith through the varied ministry of the church, there was little sign of spiritual growth, let alone rebirth, in the young people of our church. A group of about five people now meets regularly to pray for the young people. Prayer triplets also taught us to be specific. One of the group attends our Youth Council to glean all the relevant information to take back to the prayer group. Very gradually we are seeing God break through. We still feel in need of more prayer.

Prayer triplets taught us, too, that prayer changes people and situations. People in key positions often have a small group praying for them. At work, Beti was in a prayer triplet with people of other churches. Barbra, in a Queen's Road Baptist Church prayer triplet, had valued the experience so much that when hers was dissolved she asked Beti to be her prayer partner. At the time Barbra was a social worker in Coventry. Now, together with her husband David and a nurse, Lynne, she has been called by God into full-time Christian counselling. Needless to say Barbra needs the prayer more and more, and others support her too.

Once God's time for house groups came to Queen's Road, about four years ago, we were able to set up ten groups (now doubled). We were aware of the danger of their becoming too inward, so each house group has the responsibility of supporting with love, interest and prayer someone who is involved in full-time ministry at home or abroad. Normally this person is either a member of Queen's Road or has a family link with us. Every so often our Missionary Action Group produces a leaflet giving details of all the people we support in this way. This means the whole church can be involved in a wide range of missionary prayer at home and abroad. Through the house groups, people on the 'battle front' receive close personal support. Whenever they are able to come to Queen's Road, they have a family unit to which they already belong.

The Reverend Derek Blundell and his wife Jill, are very much part of our fellowship. Together they have initiated and now organise and lead the African Pastors' Fund, devoted to providing essential equipment and training for African pastors. Derek explains how the praying works:

> It is a great encouragement to us in our Christian ministry to know that a house group at home is backing us in prayer. In a work that demands extensive travel, both in this country and throughout Africa, we frequently encounter frustrating, difficult and even dangerous conditions. At times we have been very aware of Satan's hands at work but in all of this have experienced a calm and strength to face events when, humanly speaking, we would worry and panic. We know that this strength comes from the Lord but believe that without the prayers of his people we would find the task more difficult. It is so easy to falter under the attack of the devil that those working on the front line need the constant support of a back-up team surrounding them in prayer. (See Exodus 17:8–13.)

When we heard that the Reverend Margaret Jarman had been elected to become President of the Baptist Union, it was a natural extension of our prayer life to ask her if she would welcome a prayer support group. This was because she would be without a church of her own to pray for her as she was leaving her pastorate in a neighbouring Baptist church. So once a month or so the group has met with her. She has shared her itinerary and also more confidential and personal matters with them. They have shared communion and friendship meals as well as talked and prayed. Pam and Geoff have normally hosted the group as they have two small children. This is what the prayer opportunity has meant to them. Pam writes:

> As a group of praying people we grew closer together as the year went on and have enjoyed the rich experience of the power of intercessory prayer. Needless to say it has been a tremendous privilege to have been beside Margaret during such a special year. Her complete trust and dedication to her calling have been an example to us all. We were filled with praise and thanksgiving for all God was achieving through Margaret. For his divine influence in all she said and did and how richly she was being rewarded for her total commitment and faithfulness. There were many specific answers to prayer, mainly regarding Margaret's health. Although physically weakened by myalgic encephalomyelitis, she gained a strength far beyond her own to carry her through the year.

In turn, this is what the prayer support has meant to Margaret Jarman:

> It has been a great help to have the Queen's Road prayer support group during my time as president. I see them as a vital part of the year. As I have travelled round the country, at each engagement I have known that this group was upholding me in prayer. The year has been blessed by God far beyond my expectations, and I have no doubt the prayer group has had a hand in this.

Prayer and healing

Interwoven with the developments in prayer there is another vital thread: that of prayer and the healing ministry. This is yet another gift from God via America! This time, however, America came to Coventry and took us by storm. What happened showed again the beauty of God's sovereignty and why it's best to let him carry the weight of the church.

In 1985 we were involved in a programme of church growth known as One Step Forward. The first phase is called Operation Agape. *Agape* is the Greek word for Christian love, and the programme teaches and encourages the practice of Christian loving in the following way:

Avoid harmful criticism
Go and visit
Another acquaintance
Pray for one another
Encourage one another.

By November we were involved in learning to pray for one another. During one of those weeks our church was the venue for a four-night visit from the Vineyard Fellowship. We had heard a little about John Wimber and his commitment to help the churches reclaim the authority of Christ for healing as a sign of the kingdom of God. Because our church was the venue, probably forty to sixty of us attended at least one night, although there were also several hundred people each night from surrounding churches.

A number of our people from all ages and all strata of the church were affected positively, including both ministers! People experienced cleansing and acceptance from God, new freedoms with God and others, deeper commitment to God and, for some especially, an empowering for fulfilling the call of Christ to 'heal the sick'.

The Sunday evening service following their visit was a Communion service. In view of the results of Vineyard Fellowship's visit, it was appropriate to encourage the coming together of our commitment to pray for one another and the development of the healing ministry by inviting people to receive prayer for healing from one another. Many responded to the invitation to seek healing—of body, mind, emotion, memory or spirit—from God. Hence, without human planning, God launched our church into his healing ministry.

Ever since then our Sunday evening Communion service has become a focal point for God's healing ministry. The normal pattern is that twenty or thirty of us meet to listen to God from 5.30 to 6.00 pm. We are placed in teams of two or three. Members of these groups often share needs and receive prayer prior to the service. We then worship with the rest of the congregation. Towards the end of the service we share any insights we believe God has given us about specific areas of ministry for that evening. Then people come forward and are prayed for.

The ripples of healing prayer have spread in at least two ways. The first is that people now find it natural to pray with and for one another and to go and ask for prayer. At any time if you look over the church before or after any service, or if you walk through the corridors or come into the secretaries' office, you are likely to find two or three people praying for a friend. Prayer has become natural and visible. We have also visited other churches to share our experiences, and we respond to prayer requests from individuals. Much goes on without the ministers knowing or needing to know. We have much to praise God for—and we do. Sometimes the healing response is noticeable and measurable; sometimes it is less obvious.

One lady in her sixties has for years suffered severe spinal pain because of a prolapsed disc. She had undergone various forms of medical treatment and received prayer, which had helped alleviate the pain for short periods. A year or so ago she was suffering acutely and told her Bible study group, who prayed for her:

> I felt Jesus' presence all around me. The words being prayed became his words. It was Jesus speaking in a very positive way telling the area of hurt to be gone. I was bundled up in warm clothing as it was a very cold day, yet I was experiencing a warm glow on my spine. It was a beautiful experience of the supernatural healing power of the Lord. I became instantly free of pain apart from the area of original damage. This stubborn area was

prayed for again, and I was then completely free. I can now almost touch my toes and can walk distances that I have not been able to for years. Praise God!

On another occasion a man who had broken his wrist was told when he returned for a check X-ray that the break had slipped resulting possibly in permanent deformity. As he was already sixty, the hospital told him they would do nothing further. Partly because he felt too young to be considered geriatric, he could not accept their gloomy assessment:

> I went straight from the hospital to Queen's Road Baptist Church as I knew a member of the healing team would be there. My wrist was prayed over and the power of the Holy Spirit called on to heal any deformity.
> My plaster was removed on 5th June, and although my wrist is swollen, the swelling is gradually abating. Each day I am getting a little more movement back with no apparent sign of any permanent misalignment.
> With praise and thanks to God!

Often people receive emotional and spiritual help as well as physical. Gren was a much loved member of our congregation who discovered he had a severe and painful form of terminal cancer. The church prayed, and a couple from our church visited to pray with him and his wife Ann. Although Gren continued to deteriorate and eventually died, there were many signs of God's healing. Pain was tolerable; he was comfortable, and his wife spent the last hours with him singing him into heaven. She herself said that it was as though she was able to escort him to the very gates of heaven. For them both it was a wonderful experience in which the darkness of death was diminished.

Of course such healing prayer also needs developing, sustaining and organising. Most of our training is done in conjunction with other local churches, but we do meet to discuss our own procedures about twice a year.

Prayer in counselling

Inevitably such a prayer ministry by the church affects
people's expectations of their ministers. Equally, awareness of this kind of ministry affects what is possible for
the ministers. Normally I spend some time in prayer with
people when they come to see me. Often a large proportion of our time together would be prayer of one kind or
another. Although as yet praying in tongues is not a normal
part of our main worship, there have been several occasions
when not knowing what to ask for I have allowed the Holy
Spirit to intercede in this way, sometimes with staggering
results.

Caryl was, I think, the first person with whom I took what
for me was a great risk of praying in this way, about five years
ago. She received a significant degree of release from memories she had as a two-year-old child. At the time Caryl was
divorced with two children. Three years ago she remarried,
but recently her new husband felt he had to get away. He
walked out and left. After a few weeks I sensed God saying
that I should meet with Caryl so that in prayer together we
could ask God to free her husband from unhelpful family ties
(*or* unhelpful aspects of certain family relationships) and also
claim him back. Caryl agreed. Three or four weeks later, on a
Thursday and Friday, I sensed God telling me to pray for
Caryl and her husband. Throughout the two days they rested
in my mind, and I frequently brought them to God. On
Monday when I saw Caryl again, she told me with great joy
they were together again. Her husband had returned over the
weekend. I was delighted but not surprised; and they have
stayed together since.

Prayer for me and for others involved in the counselling
side of the healing ministry becomes more and more a matter
of affirming and reflecting back what God directs rather than
simply asking. This does not mean that there is no place for
wrestling in prayer. Yet such wrestling is with God, not
against him.

Prayer in church

Prayers in church have changed, too, over the last few years. In our services there is now great variety both in forms of prayer and in those who participate. Most frequently, because of the size of the building and the congregations, we use some form of led prayers. Sometimes the ministers lead the prayers. Often members of the congregation have prepared the prayers in advance to dovetail with the themes of the services. Sometimes the children pray, bringing to us all their own interests, simplicity of perception, honesty and directness with God. Always, care is needed with amplification so that the whole congregation can hear clearly and be as involved as possible. More and more we are appreciating the value of silence and meditation as a form of prayer. Yet even in our main services, particularly in the evening where there is more freedom and time, we will use more open kinds of prayer. Perhaps we pray in groups of four or five with topics given from the front. Another time people will be invited to pray spontaneously from the floor. Or we will gather topics from the congregation, and the leader will express them on behalf of the congregation.

As ministers and leaders, we are aware of the natural tendency for our prayers to become somewhat parochial and restricted. We therefore believe that the prayers of the main worship services need to remind people of all the heights and depths and breadths that should be covered by the praying people of God—adoration, confession, intercession and supplication, world issues, politics, disasters as well as our friends and family or evangelism and ecumenism all have their place. Perhaps therefore the key to our prayers in services is variety—of form, of content, of participants.

But there are other ways in which prayer happens 'in church'. Prayer finds a place in all our committee meetings, of course. Some of us feel that we need to give more time to prayer and less to discussion. Perhaps this is where God will help us to grow. We also want to provide opportunities for all the membership to meet together to pray for the total life of the church and its mission.

We have arranged days of prayer. The most effective format for us is to break the day into thirty-minute segments, asking leaders of the many areas of our church life to share issues of particular concern for their particular group. We still struggle, however, to find the right time for large numbers to gather for prayer. Some of them have been involved with other groups, such as Operation Mobilisation, who have come to us for their Easter evangelism. We realise the privilege and opportunity of such events, but possibly this is not God's way for us.

If prayer together is a struggle, praise together is not, at least for some. Four years ago we started *Praise and Share*—a *postscript* to evening worship once a month for those who wanted freedom to express their praise and share with others what God was doing in their lives. Often significant times are given over to prayer then as well. Two experiences show how the various strands of our prayer adventure are woven together by God.

A prayer triplet had prayed for Sandy* as part of our preparation for Mission England when Billy Graham came to Villa Park. Sandy came to faith, though not through Villa Park; it was through the verse of a hymn in an ordinary service!

A few months after her conversion, one of her teenage sons attempted to commit suicide. Though he survived the attempt, he was not at all well, and while he was recovering physically, I was asked to visit him. I was led to see that an evil spirit was oppressing him. So, with his mother, we went into the bedroom where he had often experienced the oppression, and I commanded the spirit to leave. This was the first time I had been involved in this kind of ministry. Since then the son has been fine and has become a baptised member of the church. No doubt the prayer network was at work in the background as I went.

The next Sunday, Sandy was in church as usual, but so

---

* Names and identities have been changed to protect those involved.

was someone else who had brought horror and fear into her life . . .

There, in church, she saw a man who previously had caused her extreme anguish. It was twenty years since she had last seen him. For several weeks it took love and prayer from all Sandy's Christian friends to keep her; so terrified was she that he would recognise her. However, once she was able to say to God that she would stay with Christ whatever happened, the man ceased to attend. Naturally, as a church, we are sorry that God's love did not reach this person through us. We pray God will meet him in his need also. Yet these events suggest that Satan was trying to get his own back on Sandy for what God was doing in her family.

On another occasion, it was again the wife who had been converted, not the husband. Mick, Norma's husband, had several jobs, including being a bouncer, but he was now an undertaker. He was happy for Norma and his daughter to be 'religious', but he only believed what he saw, which (for him) was that 'when you're dead, you're dead'. Loving prayer was constantly offered for Mick and for special occasions when he might be reluctantly persuaded to come with Norma. But nothing could move him further!

Then one Thursday he was at a local crematorium. Outside, rain fell in torrents. Inside, Mick was sitting quietly, wondering when the vicar would finish so that he could carry on with his job. Then out of the crematorium wall a light shone on Mick. He tried to move away, but it followed him. After the service he went back to check the building, even though he knew there was no scientific explanation. He sensed something supernatural was happening.

By Sunday he was so desperate he was in church for the morning service. 'Wild horses wouldn't keep me away,' he said. After the service Norma dragged me away from praying for someone to see Mick. We talked and together realised that he wanted to put his trust in Christ, but his years of 'I'll only believe what I can see' had caused a complete block. After we had prayed, I assured him (but with little feeling of assurance), 'Don't worry. God is seeking you, and he can handle your unbelief.'

No sooner had Mick and Norma gone home than Chas came along—one of the younger men in the healing ministry who has a gift for seeing God's words. In a vision, Chas had 'seen' someone going down a long road which led to God. As he went down the road, the person came to a huge, awful chasm and could not cross. Chas considered that God was probably warning him that someone was going to attempt suicide. Somehow, I knew that what Chas had seen was Mick's situation and God was answering our cry for help. I explained something of Mick's position to Chas and asked him to spend the afternoon in prayer, giving his faith to help the person across the chasm.

Later I phoned Mick and asked him if he was willing to share his story, without pretence, at the 'Praise and Share' meeting that evening. He said he had already decided to come and was so desperate that he didn't mind what he did. By the time I reached church for 6.30 pm, Chas was there with an excited look on his face. As he had prayed through the afternoon the vision had returned but with a significant change. As the person reached the chasm there were outstretched wings, and the person could walk over them to God. Needless to say I felt encouraged.

In 'Praise and Share' two people reported their experiences of how, when they had stepped into new situations believing in God, he had proved trustworthy. Privately I asked Mick if he still wished to share what was happening to him. He willingly told us. I then asked Chas for his story. Then we all prayed, lending our faith to Mick so that he might be able to walk over the chasm of his unbelief to know God for himself.

He didn't—at least not that night. Before he went home I briefly explained the gospel to him, along the lines used in Evangelism Explosion. As the booklet *Just Grace*[2] suggests, I explained how we could pray in ordinary words and in ordinary places. I even mentioned that sometimes the toilet is the only place to be on your own with God!

The next Tuesday evening Mick phoned to say that on

Monday morning in the toilet at work he had prayed and found Christ as his Saviour and accepted him as his Lord. Mick still glows and grows for God. You'll find him praying with people, crying with people, talking with people about Jesus.

What a privilege I feel to be part of such a praying church used by God. It was not what anyone did—it was that we let God do what he wanted with us. To us, that is prayer: living with the living God, being loved by this loving God and letting the love shine back.

Prayer with others

Our prayer journey, as I hope I have hinted, has been with the help of other Christian communities. Now we are learning to pray with them. The Reverend Graham Dow, vicar of Holy Trinity, and John Patterson, senior elder of the Coventry Christian Fellowship, have with their people played a great part in helping us grow into the healing ministry. They have now invited Christians from the churches of Coventry to pray against the darkness which overhangs our city in so many ways. This year we are holding four evenings of teaching about prayer against the satanic darkness. We are also praying for those who are working in some of the key areas of our city. We are focusing on:

1 the city council
2 the leisure and media
3 the ravages of war and violence
4 materialism and commercialism.

We meet at Holy Trinity and then pray in small groups, one person giving guidance and example for all to follow. Finally, while some remain in Holy Trinity, others of the 'troops' will go out to an appropriate area to take prayer to the front line— so to speak. On the first occasion we went to the council chambers, on the second to a local cinema and art gallery.

Because of this new venture, Graham, John and I felt it

inappropriate to become heavily involved in the day of Prayer
for the Nation. We decided however to invite people from
other churches to our 8.30 Saturday morning prayer time,
and forty-five people from a good spread of churches came
along. I sensed God saying that this should become a monthly
venture *for our city*. All those present sensed this was from
God, so we shall venture further in prayer together.

Perhaps the reason we have failed as a church to grow a
strong *central* prayer gathering is that God wants us to do it
together with other churches. Maybe God has heard the cry
of a few of us and he is bringing in help from other churches to
act as a catalyst. We shall wait expectantly to see.

Learning to pray

As I said at the beginning, we are very much still learners in
the Lord's school of prayer. Much of our praying is learned by
modelling, that is by the example of our worship services, and
now through the healing prayer teams and house groups.
However, helping people learn to pray is also one of the
objectives for our enquirers' classes. Sermons, tapes and
training courses are other ways we are learning. But often as I
look back it seems also that God has given us gifts, and as we
have unwrapped the presents and used them, so we have
discovered more fun in prayer, more joy in prayer and more
power in prayer. These gifts are now around the house, and
those who come to faith in Christ find it natural to use God's
supernatural gift of prayer when they join us.

What comes next? It has now been agreed that I will
commit certain hours of the week specifically to prayer.
People in the church will be invited to be part of this by
praying at that hour, or by prayer and fasting to support it
throughout the day. Others will let me know of specific needs
or issues for which they need direct guidance, then I shall pray
for them and listen with them for God's word. This will be a
development of a kind of intercessory counselling ministry
which has already begun in a less structured way. In time, if it
is of God, others will become involved by God in this kind of
intercessory counselling.

One plan being considered is that we arrange prayer weekends. The idea here is that about thirty people at a time would go away together and spend the weekend in meditation, teaching on prayer and praying.

A second possibility is that for a period of say a month we should stop all but essential meetings and as a church commit the 'spare time' to prayer together to discover God's will and pray for it. Whatever the developments, we look forward to our adventure with God in prayer.

> How great are God's riches! How deep are his wisdom and knowledge! Who can explain his decisions? Who can understand his ways? As the scripture says, 'Who knows the mind of the Lord? Who is able to give him advice? Who has ever given him anything, so that he had to pay it back?' For all things were created by him, and all things exist through him and for him. To God be the glory for ever! Amen (Romans 11:33–36 GNB).

Notes

[1]   Brian Mills, *Three Times Three Equals Twelve* (Kingsway Publications: Eastbourne, 1986).
[2]   Vic Jackopson, *Just Grace* (Evangelism Explosion III International: Southampton, 1980).

Chapter 3

Gilcomston South, Church of Scotland

Aberdeen

William Still

The northernmost church in this volume—Gilcomston South—is popular not only with students, nurses, and young people in Aberdeen, but also with visitors from all over the world, particularly from the US and Northern Ireland. Many years ago, when lumps of crumbling sandstone fell from the spire to Union Street below, a notice outside the church read, 'This Church is Dangerous.' Those who stopped to stare or question were advised not to attend if they did not want to be converted!

Revd William Still enjoys art, architecture, gardening and walking. As this chapter reveals, he has also made a lifetime commitment to music, having started his adult life as a music teacher. His love of music overflows into the life of his chapter and his church. Though he remains a bachelor, he has many children in the Lord.

The congregation of this Presbyterian Church of Scotland had been going down for years, largely due to its social life

practically throttling its earlier spirituality. The Presbytery
had tried to close it down twice, but a magnanimous gesture
by a sympathiser enabled it to gain a reprieve. Twenty-seven
applications for the charge were dismissed before I was asked
to accept a call to become its minister. The invitation to apply
was largely based on my reputation as a local lad who had
filled some of the larger churches in Aberdeen during the war
with sacred music recitals together with some of my university
friends.

When invited to preach as sole nominee for Gilcomston
South Church, I made one stipulation—that I would have a
prayer meeting. In their desperation the Vacancy Committee readily agreed that I could have my 'prayer meeting',
although only one of its members would have had any idea
what a mid-week service was like, let alone a meeting for
corporate, spontaneous prayer.

The last day of the war

The date on which I began work at Gilcomston South Church
was significant. I preached on 1st April 1945, was unani-
mously elected, and then travelled from my assistant's post in
Glasgow on my thirty-fourth birthday. It was 8th May, the
very day war in the West ended. As dusk gathered that
evening we saw what we had not seen for years—naked lights
in windows and streets. During the war years a great deal of
religious as well as social life had come to a standstill, so it was
a great advantage, and I believe, a providence of God, to
begin a new ministry at a time when people were almost
delirious with joy.

Prayer battles

Coming from a Salvation Army background, with an interim
spell as organist in the local Methodist church, I had had a
fairly wide experience of Christian work in different denominations. But it was my earlier days of prayer battles for souls
in The Salvation Army that made the deepest impression on

me. Nevertheless, association with Christian students at Aberdeen University (mostly then of Brethren and Free Church persuasion) also helped to form new notions of Christian work, with especial emphasis on biblical authority.

At the same time, the teaching at the divinity school was having its effect, and while it was good that I had to face liberal ideas in theology, some of its scepticism entered into my soul. These years of training therefore threw me into a confusion which would have to be resolved before I undertook a ministry with any hope of fruitfulness.

Music, theatre and evangelism

On being licensed as a preacher of the gospel I went to Glasgow with mixed feelings and many fears to be assistant minister at Springburnhill Parish Church. I had been involved in the musical life of King's College Chapel during my university course, and in my last year was asked to provide music for the students' theatre show. I had the pleasure of conducting my own music, which gained such commendation that the local music critic sent for me and said I had missed my vocation!

Fortunately the minister of the Springburn Church, who had just gained a doctorate, was an old-time evangelical; so perhaps a little against my will I was preserved from the worst excesses of liberal churchianity. Nonetheless my year in Glasgow in 1944 was a trying one for me, as I was pulled toward liberalising tendencies and yet knew that that was not the way. This period of indecision was suddenly halted by an accident at a railway station. I had tried to board the train after it had started, but it accelerated so fast that I fell and nearly went under, breaking my ankle very badly. That meant three months in hospital and months more on crutches and sticks afterwards. It also meant that I had plenty of time to think. I felt that I had made a mess of things and doubted if anyone would want me as a minister.

However, some folk in Aberdeen remembered the music recitals I had given on Sunday afternoons in churches filled to capacity. The Treasurer of Gilcomston South, after his disappointment at many unsatisfactory applications for the post of minister, declared that if he could get Willie Still then he would fill the church. Thus I came to Gilcomston South as the man who, because of musical and theatrical experience, could fill churches. Little did they know that beneath the musician was an evangelical who simply had to get out!

I did not give any details to the Gilcomston Vacancy Committee as to what I would do as their minister, but once I arrived I set about the task with the full encouragement of these officebearers who had twice suffered the threat of closure. When I suggested a set of *Redemption Songs* and an evening service commencing at 7.30 instead of the usual time of 6, they virtually said I could do what I liked, as long as I filled the church! Such a proceeding today would probably not work, for we live in a much more cynical age. But in those days we were all so jaded with the terrible strain of the war that anything new was like a refreshing stream; consequently, not only the officebearers but the entire congregation, such as it was, accepted my ideas. They were joined by many evangelical folk in the town and others not at all of that persuasion, and the church was soon full, especially on Sunday evenings, the building ringing to the sound of *Redemption Songs* and choruses.

The music was greatly enhanced by our organist, Gordon Ross. I had known Gordon, a keen evangelical, for years. He was looking for a new evangelical experience and, since the organist at Gilcomston at that time was interim, Gordon applied for the post. Although some of my other musical friends also applied, I was determined to have him because he had an astonishing gift of extemporisation. With a flowing, liquid style, he could rouse a congregation to sing as no one else I had heard.

Of course, along with *Redemption Songs* came the good old gospel message as I had been brought up with it, plus what shreds of biblical scholarship I had gathered in my course.

Then in March 1946 a team of evangelists from the American Youth for Christ came to Scotland, including an

unknown young man called Billy Graham. He stood head
and shoulders above the others, despite his youth, and he said
rather dramatically to me that he would not leave Aberdeen
until we had formed a Youth for Christ team, which we did on
the last evening of his visit. From then on, Youth for Christ
interdenominational rallies continued in our church on
Saturday evenings until the end of that year. But the initial
thrill of evangelistic rallies—and we introduced many gim-
micks—soon wore thin. All sorts of counter-attractions were
starting in the town, and the strain of providing novelty in the
presentation of the gospel had made us all rather weary. By
the end of the year I began to think that more was needed if
the work was to continue and progress.

Prayer the powerhouse

As I have already mentioned, I told the Vacancy Committee
that I would not come to Gilcomston unless I could have a
prayer meeting. During the first year-and-a-half, it was virtually a mid-week Bible study, and the only spontaneous,
corporate prayer was with the Youth for Christ team on
Saturday evening before the rally. I knew, of course, that
prayer was the secret of fruitful Christian work, and so I
considered how a meeting for prayer could be started.

Throughout this time something else was happening. During 1946, looking for evangelistic gospel messages in the
Scriptures, I came upon the first eight chapters of Paul's
Letter to the Romans, and thought it would be an idea to
preach through these chapters consecutively. This aroused so
much interest that I thought I would do the same with James'
Letter and then Paul's Letter to the Galatians. By the end of
the year the contrast between the dying evangelical rallies and
the quickening of interest in the systematic exposition of the
word of God on Sundays said something to me loud and
clear; namely, that the teaching of the word to instruct and
build up the many converts who had come to Christ during
these eighteen months was essential, along with more specific
prayer.

So at the end of 1946 I had to ask the Youth for Christ to find another venue for their Saturday evening rallies, for we were to spend our Saturday evenings in congregational prayer. It cost a great deal to do this, because many of the dear folk involved from different denominations were offended, although I am glad to say that they were able to continue their Youth for Christ meetings for many years afterwards in the local YMCA hall. My decision was the turning point of the ministry, for along with the continuous systematic exposition of the Scriptures, the new meeting for prayer on Saturday evening, and the commencement of daily Bible reading notes in the Congregational Record, an entirely new regime got under way. As we got down to systematic Bible exposition, there was a falling away of our supporters who had at first strayed from other denominations excited by this new evangelistic adventure. But when confronted by the depth of the Word of God you could hardly see them for dust! This was a new experience for me, and it astonished me.

During the first eighteen months of my evangelistic ministry, I had been on the receiving end of the rage of people who literally hated the plain gospel message, and *Redemption Songs* as well. But I now experienced a new type of opposition to what we were doing, in that folk who loved to hear the simple gospel addressed to sinners were not prepared for the challenge of the Word concerning full consecration and growth in the knowledge of Christ. Consequently attendances fell away.

In fact, between the last Sunday of the old regime at the end of 1946 and the first Sunday of the new, when the Youth for Christ on Saturday evenings had moved out of the church, there were probably as many as 200 less at our evening service which until then had been crowded. This was a great shock to me and I would have relented from sheer disappointment if I had not been sure that I was guided by the Lord to turn Saturday evenings over to prayer and continue systematic Bible exposition at both services on Sunday.

Prayer the energiser

At the same time a new spirit of devotion developed among our loyal band, smaller though it was. The offerings shot up, and the Word singled out young men and women who began to consider full-time service for the Lord. Until this point I had not been a particularly missionary-minded person, but now I was learning about missionary situations in the different parts of the world that I had never heard of. ('Ludhiana'—where in the world was that?) I had not the slightest doubt that the new work was of God, even if it was smaller, because of its depth and quality. Now, with the passing of over forty years, I have learned that there is nothing so fruitful in Christian service as a ministry of Bible exposition watered by the faithful and consistent prayers of the people. I recall the first Sunday I ascended the pulpit steps following Saturday evening prayer. It was incredible—I almost floated up the steps, and a new confidence in conducting the service and in preaching took hold of me. The experience was so astonishing that I almost remarked on it there and then. It was certainly remarked upon by others, which gave a tremendous boost to the work.

The essential pattern of this ministry has continued now for over four decades, and I have not the slightest doubt that there is no better way to serve the Lord in pastoral work. Although we have not seen such large numbers as we did during the first eighteen months of spectacular evangelistic endeavour, the result of the ministry has been that servants of the Lord who had been brought to Christ or were stimulated by the teaching of the Word are now scattered all over the world. We keep in touch with many of them by regular letter writing, etc, and we are thus able to give them support in prayer.

Prayer that scatters us

We sometimes say here that if all who have been influenced by the ministry and have not yet gone to glory were gathered together, it would take a number of churches to hold them. This leads me to say that it is clear from the Acts of the Apostles in particular that it is seldom the Holy Spirit's purpose to gather the saints together in large self-conscious huddles merely to enjoy each other's fellowship. The great boast of so many churches, especially in America, is that they are so big that, like the man in the Gospel with his barns, they have had to pull down their churches to build larger ones to hold the increasing number of people who come to these tremendous centres for what some have called 'entertainment evangelism'.

But the Holy Spirit's purpose, having brought folk to Christ and seen them built up even a little in their holy faith, is to scatter the majority to the four winds with the gospel burning in their hearts, not only as full-time workers but also as lay people longing to win souls. This scattering was exceedingly painful for us since we were constantly 'losing' some of our best people to other places and other works. But at the same time the range of our intercessory prayers was extending, not only throughout our own land but also to other lands and even to remote places that we had scarcely heard of. Our Bible teaching ministry which many regard as rather special, distinctive, and even unique in our day, has now been repeated in at least two hundred pulpits in Scotland and further afield. But it is our emphasis on prayer that has in fact gained far greater publicity than the Bible teaching ministry.

People who hear of our teaching ministry through the distribution of the monthly Congregational Record with its daily Bible reading notes, and later by the distribution of tapes, booklets of sermons, etc, still seem to be most impressed by the Saturday evening prayer meeting when they visit us. Folk have come not only from England, Ireland and Europe, but also the USA, Australia and New Zealand to be with us on Saturday evenings. In expressing their appreciation of fellowship it is almost inevitably the prayer meeting which strikes them as most remarkable.

At the same time, many who have heard of our Bible teaching ministry and have come along on Sundays have

apparently no interest whatsoever in the gathering for prayer
on Saturday evenings. This shocks us, because if people have
gone away without knowing what has energised the ministry
that has blessed them, they have missed the point of it all.
For the powerhouse of our entire ministry is our battles and
wrestlings in prayer which have continued every Saturday
without break, summer or winter, for more than four
decades.

Prayer in which we wrestle

Of course, such prayer is the hardest thing in the world. I am
often more exhausted on Saturday evenings after between
two and three hours of wrestling prayer than I am after two
long services on Sunday with hours spent in fellowship and
counselling afterwards. This is hardly surprising, since the
kind of prayer which takes the world as its parish, along with
the burden and cares of many works of God at home and
abroad, requires the utmost spiritual energy. It is remarkable
that out of a congregation of a few hundreds, for the numbers
vary considerably with many comings and goings, only a
fraction dare enter the prayer room. I say 'dare' because
many devoted servants of the Lord, even those who have
been on missionary service for years and those who are or
have been active in the Lord's service, avoid the prayer room
in which they themselves had been prayed for in the past!
Some have occasionally attended our prayer meeting, but
with its length, intensity and range of intercession find it far
more than they bargained for. I am often amazed and deeply
hurt that such people blandly opt out of the arduous work of
the powerhouse and retire to a more comfortable seat in the
congregation and the normal services of the church.

Intercessory prayer

Many folk who have visited us throughout the years, particularly from the United States, have said that the one thing
that is hardest to find in churches in that vast land is solid

sessions of intercessory prayer. Some of these dear friends who have studied in Aberdeen and worshipped with us have returned to their own land to plant churches or build up others which have lost out through the multiplicity of events going on in them—'programmes', they call them! They have said it is the hardest thing in the world to get people to come to pray. Apparently many who profess to love and serve the Lord Jesus fail to see the connection between the hidden work of intercessory prayer and what happens before their eyes in the conversion of souls and their upbuilding in the faith. What a blind spot! And what a work of the Enemy to deceive so many Christians all over the world as to the value of the powerhouse of prayer!

Naturally, over so many years our Saturday evening meeting has changed somewhat in form. More and more time had to be taken up sharing news from far and near, and eventually this took so long that we decided to print a leaflet with summaries of the news. Copies are distributed to those attending, and many come to the meeting early to 'do their homework'. This has proved a boon because it gives us up to half an hour more for intercession.

Worshipful prayer

However, there was a time when the emphasis on intercession was so predominant that we were in danger of reeling off 'shopping lists' of people's names and Christian causes all over the world. We became particularly aware of this at one of our various times of challenge regarding the depth of our devotion to the Lord. So we decided to spend more time in prayer as worship, since listing names and needs for prayer can become objective and even cold, without much more than a 'respectful nod' to the Lord himself. If biblical prayers teach us anything, it is that they almost always commence with worship. Since the prayer meeting had gone on for at least twenty-five years without any singing at all, we decided to start the meeting by singing a Psalm in metrical form and then briefly expound it after prayer. Then followed a time of

worshipful prayer when there was an implicit understanding
that no intercession would take place, but rather thanksgiving
to God for his Word together with adoration and worship.
This has done more to deepen the Christian lives of our
people than anything else. After some time of worshipful
prayer, the summaries of news are looked over, items added
and members of the fellowship share particular needs, especially urgent ones, along with news of who would be preaching where on the Lord's day. The rest of the meeting continues with intercession for an hour and a half. This is a long
meeting by modern standards in our country, commencing at
7 pm and going on till at least 9.30 pm. So a number have to
leave at various times for particular reasons. But on the whole
people do this quietly and unobtrusively.

In addition to the printed list of news we receive many
church magazines from churches associated with us at home
and abroad, as well as missionary magazines. Nearly all of
these (many scores, perhaps a hundred or two) are taken to
the prayer meeting after perusal and offered to the fellowship
as further fuel for prayer.

There are certain unwritten 'rules' as to the order of
praying, especially at intercession. The minister starts off,
followed generally by the session clerk (our principal lay
officebearer), after which the elders are expected to take
part, then the rest, including women and children. This order
is not strictly adhered to, especially because of visitors attending the meeting.

Some pray for only one need, others with more knowledge
and fluency may take an area of the land, or the world, or a
group of churches or mission stations, and briefly but compre-
hensively cover the known needs there. Some will take up the
world situation, since our people are encouraged to follow the
news on the media, and there and then turn the immediate
and exigent needs to spontaneous prayer: that burden is then
brought to the meeting.

One or another will seek to cover our own congregational
needs, although the needs of others are often so multifarious
and clamant that we may often almost forget to pray for

ourselves (but we know that others are doing that). Others will cover the ministries in Scotland, the other countries of the United Kingdom, Europe, from Spain to Finland, beyond the Iron Curtain, Asia and the Far East, India, Australasia, the Islands of the Pacific, Africa from north to south and east to west, the Americas, south, central and north, with particular burdens for the trouble spots of the world, especially the Middle East. We also have a great burden for those suffering for their faith in Soviet or other prison camps, including hostages.

The flow of prayer generally continues until 9.30 pm, but it is not always possible to end then; so if any area of the world or particular group of needs has been omitted, the minister will try to cover these in his closing prayer.

The high priesthood of Christ

If it be asked what doctrine of prayer governs our intercession, we might answer that the high priesthood of Christ is much in mind. We seek to be theological in our prayers addressing the Father through the Son by the Holy Spirit, and beseeching the Almighty for those things we believe to be in the divine will, leaving them there.

Hoping prayer

There are at least two levels of asking. There is the level of desiring or 'hoping' prayer, when the will of God may not be known, but our highest desire is expressed, say, in respect of someone desperately ill whom the Lord may wish to take, or recover. In such cases we make the request, summoning all the faith we have, but leaving the issue reverently and caringly with the Lord.

Trusting prayer

On another level there is that entrance into the known will of God which is able to believe with serene assurance that certain requests are within the purposive will of God, and not only will be granted, but have been granted. In these instances we seek to claim with full assurance. This is a level of intercession which we believe can only be entered into by an experience of the death/resurrection of our Lord, desiring only God's will. The assurance may then be given that such and such will be done. Jesus says that if we believe that a mountain will be removed and cast into the depths of the sea, it will be done. It is of course other than physical mountains that our Lord had in mind, and when by seeking we attain that level of claiming faith, we ought to be able to thank the Lord for granting what we believe is his will.

Indeed, this is the level of faith to which we invite parents to aspire in claiming their children for the Lord. The ground of the rite of infant baptism is God's covenant with Abraham in Genesis 17:10, applied to New Testament baptism and confirmed in Acts 2:39, 'The promise is for you and your children and for all who are far off—for all whom the Lord our God will call.' When children are brought to the font, parents, minister and believing congregation are encouraged to seek the assurance at which the symbol of water truly represents the washing away of the infant's sins, and its new birth. Such a level of claiming prayer is not reached automatically, for we cannot assume that every child will prove to be the Lord's (compare the case of Esau over against Jacob). The quality of believing prayer called for is that which comes to grips with a vital personal experience of the death/resurrection of our Lord in which the will is so blended with his by dying to sin and self that we are able to take hold of God's promise and ask for it confidently to be fulfilled.

Such a level of prayer may in general lead to battles and wrestlings which engage the heavenly powers of good and evil, on the basis of Daniel chapter 10, the warfare passage in Ephesians 6:10–18, or Revelation 12, verses 10 and 11 etc. We believe that seemingly intractable situations, including world affairs, are susceptible to the prayers of the saints, appealing to the Father through his reigning Son. We have no doubt that God in heaven hears us when we make intercession for the particular trouble spots of the world, the Middle-East, Central America, the Far East, and Christian prisoners in gaols and psychiatric institutions. Indeed, when we recollect that along with the saints of the world, we made continual prayer for China from 1949 when Christian missionaries were expelled, it affords us now some satisfaction and stirs our gratitude to God that he heard the prayers of those many years. It is a fact that the church in China not only survived, but grew hiddenly during times of persecution, until a great hunger for the Word of God seized areas of China's vast territory, and thousands and millions have since crowded to Christ, and long for copies of the Bible.

It is certainly our experience in Scotland that powerhouses of prayer have seen the proliferation of hundreds of conservative evangelical ministries in Presbyterian Scotland and beyond during these last few decades.

Special prayer

Occasionally, to cope with some intractable evil, a group of elders may gather for special prayer, either in the presence of, or apart from the afflicted one. Hours may be spent in prayer wrestling for deliverance of the sufferer. This may occur in cases of obdurate illness, when we believe it is the Lord's will to heal. We have thus known of demons being cast out, and dying infants spared to grow to adulthood. We also believe that along with other saints far and wide we may have had some small part in the confusing and confounding of pagan rites taking place in West Africa, when young lives were being sacrificed to vile practices.

Another thing. I can't remember how it started, but many years ago we felt that our officebearers needed a time of prayer by themselves in the vestry. This recalled a prayer meeting from the earliest days of the ministry which continued for many years at 7 o'clock on Sunday morning, after the pattern of what we called in The Salvation Army, 'knee-drill'. It must be nearly twenty years since we began to meet as officebearers at 6.30 on Saturday evenings prior to the general prayer meeting, and this has done much to bind our officebearers together, as some of the men are more free in prayer there than they find they can be in the general prayer meeting. During that half-hour we may spend seven to ten minutes chatting about anything of general or particular interest, which strengthens our brotherhood wonderfully. We then spend some time in simple prayer whose influence has extended, curiously, to the congregation. During this brief meeting the emphasis is mainly on devotion, but when there are particularly urgent needs we may turn to intercession. This is an excellent preparation for the meeting which follows.

It had seemed perfectly natural to me, all that long time ago, to tell the Vacancy Committee that I could not think of 'running' a church without a powerhouse of prayer. As I mentioned before but should re-emphasise here, I'm always astonished that people from all over the world who come to visit us express surprise at the nature of the prayer meeting. From time to time a number of ministers and divinity students from Ulster and elsewhere come to spend a weekend with us; again, it is always the prayer fellowship that they remark on and to which they return again and again.

Why should such an occasion be so remarkable and regarded as so unusual? I keep asking our friends beyond Scotland, especially in America, why it is that they come from Virginia, Carolina, California, Washington State, Georgia, Florida, Texas and other States just to savour our prayer meeting. Shouldn't this be the norm in Christian work anywhere in the world.

Reviving prayer

Today there is a lot of talk about revival, not least in Scotland. Groups of interdenominational Christians join together, very often early in the day, to pray for revival. We fully appreciate this, but having seen between two and three hundred conservative evangelical ministries started in our little country over the past forty years, as well as in other parts of the United

Kingdom, in Europe, Australia, New Zealand and America, surely a regular prayer meeting such as ours could tend toward the reviving of Christ's church without specially organised meetings!

At one stage in the early years of the present ministry, there was continual prayer in the church from 7 o'clock in the morning to 11.00 at night for at least three months: we were praying for revival. That special time ended with the summer holidays, and to our knowledge nothing spectacular happened, either among us or elsewhere. So we had to ask ourselves whether God had refused our request for revival. We came to the conclusion that revival in its simplest sense was the ongoing work of the Lord in bringing people to himself and building them up in their faith through the preaching of God's Word, which then sent many out into Christian service at home and abroad. Such revival is not necessarily the sweeping, tempestuous experience of the Christian church at different times. In the Island of Lewis they say that revival is cyclical. If that is so, it may be that in a church which is periodically revived through a fundamental emphasis upon the Word of God and prayer, cyclical movements of the Spirit may be expected. We know that we have had times of special refreshing when many have been blessed, and we thank God for them with all hearts.

Ongoing prayer

However, our chief emphasis is not upon those special occasions but upon the ongoing work of the church. We have a very simplified congregational structure of two Sunday services (which all attend apart from infants), a mid-week Bible study to which all are invited, and our Saturday evening prayer meeting. We hold few special events and have only a moderate regard for the special seasons of the church year, such as Christmas Eve, Easter and Pentecost.

Thus our work goes on unabated, whether the preacher happens to be the pastor or someone else. The Lord is always there, whoever is present or absent, and that makes every occasion a new and relevant experience; for when the Lord is present in the fulness and liberty of his power, nothing can be dull. He keeps us happily on our toes, and yet, devoting ourselves increasingly to him in a spirit of thanksgiving and worship. There is a restful and a healing peacefulness in such worship which is full of health and strength and enables us to sustain a longish prayer meeting at the end of which we may be both exhausted and refreshed.

Chapter 4

Open Door Community Church

Uxbridge, Middlesex

Malcolm Harland

Like New Life Assembly in Brixton, Open Door Community Church is based in the local community centre. Also like New Life, Open Door is racially and socially mixed. It serves a sprawling office overspill area for London—near Heathrow and the M40.

Author and pastor Malcolm Harland (one of a six-member team) outlines in this chapter the biblical basis for ODCC's prayer life and describes particularly the influence of Patrick Johnstone's Operation World *on the church's prayer meetings.*

Malcolm and his wife Lindsey have four children: two teen-agers and two in primary school. Together they enjoy exchanging jokes and walking. Malcolm shares most of his pastoral responsibilities with Phil Edwards, in particular Junior Church, fellowship groups and prayer meetings.

Open Door Community Church (ODCC) started about seven years ago when three small fellowships combined in the Ruislip/Eastcote area. The leader of the largest group, Roger Hoffman, has now returned to the United States of America. The leadership team led by Pastor Phillip Edwards includes myself (Pastor), Peter Scott (Music Director), Barry Richardson (Youth Leader), Peter Thomas (Administrator) and Neil McKee (Bible School).

Our original pattern was to meet in three or four different homes on a Sunday morning for worship (led by anyone who could play a guitar), the Lord's Supper, and a sermon. From the outset we tried, particularly in these meetings, to use as many people as possible, men and women, in the preaching, worship leading and mini-Sunday School in a back room. On Sunday afternoons we met at 4.30 pm (now 5.30 pm) mostly because we had a number of young families and wanted them to attend with their children.

Most of the children in our fellowship, whatever age, attend morning and evening services. We have Junior Church during the morning sermon and show a video during the evening sermon. The Community Centre hall in which we originally met as a larger group was eventually pulled down and, after meeting in a couple of school halls, we settled in the Council Chambers of Uxbridge Civic Centre, an excellent facility, although in a year to eighteen months we expect to be too numerous to meet there. (We may have double morning services.)

On Sunday morning we have a time of worship and cele-brate the Lord's Supper—often in groups which gather around the stewards, who stand at various points around the Council Chamber. The Lord's Supper is a time to remind ourselves of God's covenant with us, and to greet one another and chat briefly. With a band of excellent teachers and helpers I then take the children out of the chambers for their Junior Church.

We would like our own building, but our primary commit-ments have been missionary giving and full-time staff. If people have abilities in an area we 'buy' their talent by paying them a salary! We now have a staff of six with a congregation of about two hundred—we aim at excellence and to work beyond the immediate needs of the fellowship. To say we are a 'charismatic' fellowship probably gives the best description of our Christian lives. We belong to the Evangelical Alliance.

Our background

The style and content of our prayer meetings reflect the life and ministry of ODCC. A strong emphasis is placed on deliverance, faith, praise and worship and the practical application of Scripture. A favourite phrase of Phillip Edwards' expresses our position—'Go for it'. In the early stages of our development we stressed commitment both to one another and to the vision for the fellowship. We preach not to inform, but to stir to action. A regular feature of our meetings is ministry after the sermon. This involves praying for people with physical or mental problems, ministering deliverance or praying that people will be anointed by God's Spirit to do what they have been exhorted to do in the sermon.

Our view of the Christian life is in line with some of Paul's metaphors. One is about being soldiers (2 Tim 2:3). Soldiers are above all trained specialists, so we run courses on deliverance ministry (setting people free from demonic influences), on counselling, how to praise and worship God, on marriage, as well as encouragement meetings for mid-week fellowship group leaders and teachers in Junior Church. Another of his metaphors—about running the race—to us means commitment. We have no official membership; we believe commitment is a matter of the feet—if you are there you are committed, you're still 'in the race'! Two other metaphors which Paul uses are fighting (1 Cor 9:26) and wrestling (Eph 6:12), which we interpret in terms of spiritual warfare. We see the devil and his host as our enemies and fight them in praise, prayer and practical daily application of the Bible to our lives.

In common with other charismatic fellowships, we give praise and worship a central role in our lives. We praise God with the same enthusiasm and relish that we perform spiritual warfare. The devil is called 'the god of this age' (1 Cor 4:4) and because he is a spirit being he must be fought spiritually, ie with prayer, preaching and praise. Peter, our music director, thus lays constant stress on whole-hearted participation in worship. We clap, leap, dance, shout God's praises and sing both in English and in tongues. We have a real aversion to anything 'religious' or 'churchy' but a passion for God and his praises as seen in the Psalms and New Testament. Realising who we are in Christ and therefore our authority over the Evil One clearly affects how we pray. Praise and worship—their power and great spiritual significance (ie God's name is exalted above all beings and circumstances) is vital to our prayer life. It seems that God taught us about deliverance and then praise and worship so that we could pray effectively.

Extemporary prayer has always been a part of any meeting we hold. Two weekly prayer meetings developed: one because we decided to plant a church in Uxbridge, which is now our centre; the other out of a concern to pray for events—local, national and global. The church planting prayer meeting was mainly concerned with spiritual warfare and 'taking the area' spiritually. We experimented with whole nights and half nights of prayer, but some people dozed off (and others looked as though they would at any minute); some people disagreed with how others prayed, but we soldiered on—'going for it'.

In the early days, before we knew where our permanent home would be as a church, the Lord gave us many pictures and visions of the Civic Centre. At the time we did not know why, and we certainly had no plans to worship there then. Meanwhile, we also found ourselves praying for many people in key positions in the borough: people whose beliefs we knew nothing about. As I've already said, we are now using the Civic Centre for our worship, and we see in this the fruition of those many earlier pictures and visions in our prayer time. We have also found out that there are many Christians in local positions; people in the Planning Department and local Social Services, as well as the Uxbridge Chief Executive. We praise God for these answered prayers!

The other prayer meeting was more cerebal. We were

mostly avid daily news listeners and on the basis of that discussed and decided the best things to pray for a particular situation. It was a good prayer meeting, like the church planting one, but neither had quite the right pattern. These prayer meetings lasted about six and nine months respectively. After this we left prayer meetings alone for some months, being suspicious of merely praying because a church 'ought' to have a prayer meeting. Most of us had been to church prayer meetings that had become lifeless and merely habitual. We decided to wait and see what God would lead us into.

Preparation for prayer

Our primary method of stopping or starting anything is to preach on the subject. We started preaching about prayer because the desire to pray grew in many hearts, including mine. We preached on famous prayers in the Bible—how to pray; how to rise up early to pray; praying the Lord's Prayer; and praying God's names. In the Old Testament a number of different words or a compound of two words are used for God's name eg Jehovah-Jirah which means 'the Lord my provider'. In the example mentioned we would say the name and then pray prayers of thanks and praise for all the things that God had provided for us. We also obtained some audio tapes of Larry Lea's teaching on prayer and, with the additional help of Paul Y Cho's book *Prayer: Key to Revival*, began to see the way forward for us in prayer. Weldon Awai, who has been part of the fellowship from soon after it began, had wisely invested in a multi-system video player when he retired from the Royal Air Force. This meant we could watch Larry Lea videos, which at that time were only playable on American video machines.

Roger Hoffman, one of the founder pastors, had come from, and subsequently returned to, a group of churches in California known as the Open Door Commission. We have had fellowship links with the Commission from the beginning, and Mike Riley, its Chairman, gave us a set of Larry

Lea's videos. Weldon then organised a rota of fellowship groups to go to his house to see the videos. The series has six videos in it, and we encouraged everyone in the fellowship to see all six.

It is important to note that a steady diet of sermons on the 'how to' of faith, on the integrity of God's word, and on relationships and deliverance, produces people or draws like-minded people who want to be involved in serving God in whatever way they can. (From the beginning of the fellowship we have felt that although as people we should try to be all things to all men, nevertheless our preaching, beliefs and worship would not suit everyone—I do not see how they could!)

The people at ODCC were now ready for action. We learned early on that for any new meeting, project or idea to get anywhere there had to be at least one person with the energy, vision and enthusiasm to see it through. An eleventh commandment—'Thou shalt bash on' always applies!

How the prayer meeting developed

On 1st September 1987 we began praying six mornings a week. We prayed from six to seven o'clock Monday to Friday and seven to eight o'clock on Saturday. We prayed through the Lord's Prayer, a clause at a time, each day. The first fifteen to twenty minutes we 'hallowed' or 'honoured' God's name. On a couple of occasions I have compiled and handed out a list of God's Hebrew names in the Bible and let these suggest themes for prayer, eg Jehovah-Shalom which means Jehovah is peace; Jehovah-Rohi which means Jehovah my Shepherd. (This information is available in Nathan Stone's book *Names of God*, Moody, 1944, now in paperback.)

We sing songs about God's greatness, his name, and mighty acts. People praise and thank God in open prayer. During the whole hour people are either praying in tongues or English quietly but audibly (or not so quietly, as the case may be!). Prayers in English are spoken above this like waves rising and falling in a sea of prayer. At six o'clock in the morning we find that constant *verbal* prayer is essential, to focus attention on what is being prayed for and to stay awake! We encourage everyone to pray at once; the audible expressions of prayer and praise in the room lifts people's spirits and urges them on in prayer. When an enthusiastic wave of prayer rises, we clap, say 'Amen' and shout 'Hallelujah' so that we become part of that prayer. During the time of praise we might dance, kneel, lie prostrate, stand, sit or whatever seems appropriate for the prayer. We all respond to the prayers, become a part of them, and give ourselves over to God wholeheartedly because he is *our* Father. Prayer is a passionate affair. Besides the enthusiast who leads, others also start choruses and stir the pray-ers into praying and singing, rather like a general speaking to his troops on the eve of battle.

The leader announces the next phrase in the Lord's Prayer 'Come kingdom of God; be done will of God.' At this point we used to pray—mostly in tongues—while facing first the north, then east, then south and finally west, praying God's kingdom into all those areas. We also prayed for specific people we knew in the direction we faced. That was our pattern for this, the longest section of the prayer schedule, and we maintained it for four months. Now, in this section, we have sheets prepared from *Operation World* by Patrick Johnstone (WEC Publications), missionary magazines and the daily news. We divide the world and pray first for the north—for Great Britain (since we are in the south, our looking north covers most of Great Britain). Subjects suggested by CARE Trust Prayer Sheet, current political events, Christian Conferences or ODCC Crusades, and of course *Revival*, make up the bulk of prayers. Facing east, we then pray for European and Middle Eastern countries. The sheets we pray from have the population, economic condition and political state of the country. This gives us an indication of how to pray. After this we cover any points of special interest and a list of prayer targets. *Operation World* is an excellent, well written and invaluable aid in preparation. Then turning south, we pray for Africa, India and Asia; and finally west—the Americas, the Caribbean, Pacific Isles, Australia and New Zealand.

Finding it a useful guide, we allot the same amount of prayer days to a country as Patrick Johnstone does in *Operation World*. We pray for an average of twelve countries a week. Currently we have prayed for half the nations of the world.

The final five minutes are spent praying for our daily bread. At this time we make specific requests for spiritual and physical needs to be met, and for forgiveness. We pray that this day we will neither give nor receive offences, for victory over temptation, for deliverance and for our spiritual armour. A song of victory usually ends the meeting at seven o'clock.

Lessons learned

Not everyone can attend the prayer meeting due to distance, work or family. Those with a heart to pray do find a way to overcome obstacles and get to the meeting. If work starts early, some come and then go straight to work. Briefcases mingle with cement-covered Doc Marten's and the bulges of expectant mums! Some couples with children alternate their attendance. People are free to come and go when they need to.

At six o'clock in the morning I find praying with eyes closed is best—most of us are not a pretty sight at that time of day! There is a real sense of family and 'We're in this together' at that unearthly hour!

We have learned that a lot of the wrestling and struggling in prayer is actually getting up every morning! People now go to bed earlier, leave fellowship group meetings sooner and probably watch less late-night TV. Real praying affects our lifestyle. It is as if we had not realised that this is the normal—not the fanatical—Christian life. There is a price to be PRAYED! Well, do we want God's name to be honoured, or not? Do we only want to *read* about miracles and mass conversions—or to be part of them?

Praying together has helped many to see that daily prayer is possible. The average number attending is about twenty-two. Enthusiasm comes and goes, but overall, every day is an encouragement, even though hard work. A growing number of people are praying for an hour a day at home, some using copies of the daily prayer sheet.

Guiding principles

Everyone should pray. 'And pray in the Spirit on all occasions with all kinds of prayers' (Eph 6:18, NIV). Praying constantly helps concentration and drives away sleep. Anyone who prays too loudly can be asked to use a little less volume—but not to switch off! I do not know how to pray in English for an hour without praying or singing 'in the Spirit' some of the time (1 Cor 14:14–15). Paul says that tongues are: (a) Speaking to God (1 Cor 14:2a), (b) Edifying (1 Cor 14:4a), (c) For all (1 Cor 14:5a), (d) Used often by himself (1 Cor 14:18), (e) Not to be forbidden (Greek present imperative suggesting on-going nature of prohibition) (1 Cor 14:39a). All this applies equally to speaking or singing in the Spirit (1 Cor 14:15b).

The meeting must have a leader, preferably an enthusiast. The leader should have the ability to encourage, but not dominate prayer. The competency to start a song in the right key is useful, although failure to do so often has the unifying effect of humour—a joke shared. Any sanctimony shrivels speedily at six in the morning!

At times change is endemic in the fellowship; but we believe change is healthy. Change is essential in prayer, whether approach, content, order or whatever because new insights often come with regular prayer. Faith-inspiring innovations are mandatory.

We break our regular pattern of praying for Great Britain and other nations by praying, for example, for a local crusade. I write a special prayer sheet with a list of those responsible for counselling, setting out chairs, the PA system, etc. We also pray for special needs: for example, at a recent crusade that God would help those in what was a predominantly Hindu/Muslim area to have the courage to face

possible alienation from family and friends if they chose to
follow Christ.

*Everyone who prays needs to be physically and vocally
active.* Sitting in silence is the death knell of early morning
prayer. We lift our hands (Ex 17:11–13, Psa 28:2), shout (Psa
32:11, 35:27; 38:11); clap (Psa 47:1, Ez 21:14 & 17, Lam 2:15,
Job 27:23a as a sign of derision or contempt for the evil one);
dance and leap (Psa 149:2 & 3, Acts 3:8), laugh (Psa 126:2–3),
bow or kneel (Psa 95:6). In Acts 4:24 'they raised their voice
with one accord and said . . .'

People at the prayer meeting find an active and vocal
meeting the best at this time of day. The problem of people's
own devotional time if they come to the fellowship's prayer
meeting is not completely solved. Pastorally I know the
struggle that the majority of Christians have in keeping to a
regular time of daily prayer. Since the prayer meeting is
almost always a time of praying for others—which seems to us
most in line with the general example of Jesus' life—then we
believe it represents a big step forward in most people's
devotional life. If we are serious about revival I believe the
time may come when people rise for personal prayer and
meditation on God's word before going to a prayer meeting
or praying through the weekly prayer sheet at home.

Foundations for prayer

Over the years we have built on these foundation stones.
They are the bedrock of our prayer life:
1 Jesus wants us to ask (Jn 15:17) and to receive (Mk 11:24,
   1 Jn 5:14–15). '. . . according to his will' means according
   to his will for asking ie in Jesus' Name and by faith.
2 Pray in Jesus' Name (Jn 14:13–14, 15:16, 16:23–26). This
   means believing that Jesus IS ABLE to do what we pray
   and with his ability we *will* do it.
3 We have a blood covenant with God (Heb 8:6, 12:24,
   13:20), which means we are righteous (in right standing
   with God in Christ) and have access to the throne of grace
   (Heb 4:16).

4   We have authority over the Devil. The Devil is the one
    who steals, kills and destroys (Jn 10:10). We wrestle
    against him (Eph 6:12) *and* overcome him (Col 2:15, Rev
    12:11, Lk 10:19 and 1 Jn 5:4).
5   A great revival is yet to come: (Mt 24:14, Mk 13:10,
    Rom 11:25, Acts 15:12–17, Rom 9:24–26, Eph 2:11–22,
    Rev 7:9–10).

Answered prayer

One of the thrilling aspects of global prayer is witnessing
history made through prayer. We have been amazed and
delighted at the number of answers and the obvious relevance
of a prayer as we have read or heard the news. We pray about
any major world event: that disasters may be reversed,
corrupt dictators overthrown: for example, both Haiti and
the Phillipines have been rid of corrupt dictators recently, and
we feel both were answers to prayer. Meanwhile, the steady
advance of *glasnost* and the consequent improvements in
religious freedom have been matters for intercession and
praise. Five or six people have got just the kinds of jobs they
were seeking as we prayed, sometimes over a period of
several months. With a number of young single people in the
fellowship, we often pray for flats and rooms to become
available and find God is faithful in answering our prayers. A
single-parent family (a mother and three children), who had
had to live with her parents after her marriage break-up, was
provided with a beautiful three-bedroomed council house
within weeks, instead of the expected waiting period of
eighteen months.

New Testament faith and patience is a key, as Hebrews
6:12 illustrates. The Father of the Lord Jesus Christ is the
prayer-answering God. On examination, we find prayers that
have been prayed are definitely answered; the delusion is
thinking *about* praying so much that we think we have
prayed, or worrying and fussing about something and fooling
ourselves into thinking that we have prayed deeply for that
situation.

Things certainly change when we pray, but we do have to invade the realm of the seemingly impossible by faith daily. In recent weeks, we have felt a new excitement and urgency in prayer. Numbers have increased in the prayer meeting and among those who pray at home. We are praying longer for fewer things. We are looking to God to break into our midst as a foretaste of the revival that is to come.

Chapter 5

Portrack Baptist Church

Stockton-on-Tees, Cleveland

Roy Searle

Located in the heart of industrial Teeside, Portrack Baptist Church is the only church situated in the local community, serving an area populated by some 6,000 people. Founded by migrating Welsh steel workers in the late nineteenth century, it was run as a mission of the Stockton Baptist Tabernacle until its independence in 1980, when the fellowship called its first full-time pastor, Roy Searle. In the last eight years the church has experienced renewal and growth that have led to significant changes in its life and ministry. From twenty-seven members in 1980, the church has grown to an active membership of over ninety, becoming a community church, yet one that is now exercising a wider ministry throughout the North East.

The characteristics of the local community are bleak, with many marks of deprivation: unemployment (18% and rising), poor housing, environmental problems, crime at an increasingly high level, many families that have experienced a breakup in relationships, glue-sniffing and alcoholism—and an overwhelming feeling of powerlessness.

A fairly bleak picture by any standards—but one that needs to be seen against the vision that God has given to a church that is bringing a future and a hope to the people whom he is making for his praise and who will declare his glory.

Roy led a hectic life during the writing of this chapter. Having served this church for eight years, he and his wife Shirley moved to Enon Baptist Church in Sunderland, meanwhile producing their fourth child! When Roy is not in the church office, he enjoys tinkering with his (1965) F reg car and is a keen sportsman and supporter of First Division football and Test cricket.

A new creation; the old has gone

Back in the 1960s the area underwent redevelopment, and the old Portrack and Tiley housing estates were razed to the ground and new council housing planned. A densely populated area of terraced back-to-backs was served by some seven churches prior to redevelopment. When the old houses came down, so too did the church buildings, with the exception of the Portrack Mission. While others closed or moved their buildings, the small group associated with the mission resolutely held its ground and determined to stay and reach out to the new community which was to come with redevelopment. Because of this commitment and resolution, the council decided to build the mission a new building on their existing site. Consequently a sanctuary, hall, kitchen and vestry were erected and opened which at the time served the mission's needs more than adequately.

It is only in recent years with the growth of the church that the buildings have shown their limitations. Ironically, an incident which threatened to disrupt the ministry of the church in fact enhanced its work. Plagued at various periods of time by vandalism, the church suffered a particularly harsh blow in 1984 when an arsonist succeeded in gutting the church hall and kitchen; however, the problem became an opportunity, and a new kitchen, hall and suite of rooms were built thus providing much greater resources for the church's ministry in the community.

The worshipping congregation has grown considerably from an evening service of around 30 people in the late 1970s to a morning family worship of around 120 and evening worship which fluctuates between 50 and 80 in attendance on an average Sunday. Gone are the days of one-man ministry as a worship group leads the services, with an emphasis on congregational participation in open worship, praise and prayer. In recent years the fellowship has experienced renewal which has found expression in the church's worship, ministry and mission.

Portrack is a young church with a predominance of young married families and young leadership, a fellowship with all the joy and excitement of new life and growth as well as the problems associated with such experiences. The majority of the fellowship have come to faith in Christ in recent years, and many of their testimonies speak of the power of God in transforming lives by his grace.

The previous emphasis on childrens' and womens' work has changed to reaching out to whole families, which has resulted in an equal proportion of men and women in the church. We work to realise the concept of body ministry with the recognition of the gifts and ministries God brings to his people. Every member is encouraged to perceive and exercise his or her ministry within the body, and nominality is not one of the problems besetting the church at Portrack!

The fellowship's philosophy of ministry revolves around its commitment to renewal, evangelism and social action and is evidenced in the church's programme of ministry and mission. Alongside the pastoral team, church community workers are employed under the Manpower Services Commission Community Programme Scheme who work with volunteers responding to the needs of the children, young people and elderly within the community. An 'Open Door' ministry programme sees the church building open throughout the week for a variety of church and community activities.

From being a church which, in the main, comprised of a

building to which commuting Christians travelled from other areas of Stockton, the emphasis in recent years on the local community has resulted in a greater sense of a community church with the fellowship increasingly drawing people from its 'parish'. This has led to a change in the cultural complexion of the fellowship with a 'working class' feel to the fellowship's life. Visitors to Sunday worship would see this reflected in the congregation's dress, attitude and approach to worship and fellowship with an emphasis on reality and the importance of relationships.

The relationship between evangelism and social action is seen as closely knit: both are partners in the proclamation and demonstration of the gospel. Thus the church's community involvement is seen as integral to the life of the church and its expression of the Good News to people outside of Christ. Evangelism has taken the form of 'lifestyle evangelism' where members are encouraged to reach out into their own neighbourhoods, and growth has come in recent years from friends, neighbours and family coming to faith. The culture is such that very rarely do people come to church; thus the emphasis on evangelism has been on getting out and along-side where people are in their homes and community. A significant number of people in the local community have come to faith through the 'Good News Down The Street'[1] programme of evangelism.

Faithfulness in prayer

In all these ventures prayer has played a significant part. Much of Portrack's ministry has been born of prayer and vision, which have made it a pioneering church in the North East, where God is bringing about a future and a hope to people in the midst of urban deprivation.

In the late seventies the church (known then as 'The Mission') had a programme of activity which revolved around an evening gospel service, Sunday School, Women's Own (meeting, not magazine!) and the mid-week prayer and Bible study meeting. Over the subsequent years the pattern of things was to change considerably as the church grew and developed its ministry. Prayer cells, housegroups and special prayer meetings have replaced the weekly mid-week prayer and Bible study meeting and have brought considerable strength to the prayer life of the church.

Because of the independence of the mission from its mother fellowship, the Stockton Baptist Tabernacle, and because of the calling of a full-time pastor in 1980, the fellowship explored for the first time the idea of housegroups and special prayer meetings in the homes of members. Though the housegroups didn't find full expression until the new pastor arrived, their embryonic forerunners proved of immense spiritual value and impact.

When I arrived in the autumn of 1980 I was deeply conscious of the fellowship's commitment to prayer. The lay pastor prior to my arrival had ably led the church as a mission and with the diaconate of the time had established a degree of commitment among the fellowship that was both heartening and commendable. An active membership of only twenty-seven, in a working-class area, prepared to call a pastor, buy a manse and support the development of the church's ministry—spoke of commitment and faithfulness born of prayer.

Prayer throughout change

Clearly God had brought us together, pastor and fellowship. To be supported and prayed for by every member of the diaconate in the vestry before a Sunday morning service was of great encouragement to a young man in his first pastorate. Here was a people who knew the Lord, acknowledged him and sought his will. Although very traditional in attitudes and approach to things, they nevertheless showed a fair degree of openness to the new developments inevitably associated with my coming.

When local folk began to come into the fellowship, however, their new attitudes and approaches to the Christian life inevitably brought changes. Sadly, some found these difficult

to come to terms with, especially the growing experience of
renewal, and some felt they should leave.

The loss of ten members over a period of eighteen months
between 1983 and 1984 was a body blow to the fellowship and
one which directed much of our time and energies in non-
productive areas of pastoral care. Yet ironically those who
left provided the opportunity for us as a fellowship to see the
Lord raise up new folk, among whom are now members of
the present leadership team. Like the fire which threatened to
hinder the church's ministry yet proved to be in the Lord's
grace a stepping stone to further community involvement, so
the departure of some of those whom the Lord had used to
'prime the pump' led again by God's grace to the fellowship
almost doubling its membership within a year, with further
impact for the gospel in the local community.

Young men will see visions . . .

Fundamental throughout this period of change was the growing conviction of the leadership and membership as to the
vision God had given to the church. This vision first confirmed the call to the pastorate and then grew in intensity
during the early months of my time at Portrack. Before I
accepted the call to the pastorate, I went for a walk around
the estates. As I asked the Lord to share something of his will
for the kingdom in our area, I received a picture of a people
coming alive in Christ, a people through whom the Lord was
going to declare his praise and reveal his glory. Here in
Portrack! I shared the vision in 1981 at the first evening
service of the year and explained its implications. The resultant purpose to the church's ministry and mission became
much clearer, though for some (again, those who were to
leave us), the prospects were uncomfortable. Yet we had
become a people with a vision, a church with a particular
ministry. On the rare occasions that people joined us (for very
few folk transfer into council estate churches!), they were
able to perceive this vision and identify accordingly. My own
conviction in recent years as to the necessity of leadership

imparting vision has been further strengthened by our experience at Portrack. Without vision and purpose the church languishes and is impoverished as it seeks the will of God.

Linked inseparably with this conviction has been the need to plan into a busy life regular periods of 'retreat'. As an activist, I have found that this has required tremendous personal discipline. Yet essential for leadership is surely this need to wait upon the Lord, giving time to seek his will, being in a responsive position to receive his plans so that we might 'know what the Father is doing' and act accordingly in obedience.

Regular 'retreats' were also built into the church's programme so that we could wait upon the Lord. Their value was seen by both leadership and the rest of the fellowship as direction was received and exercised throughout the church's ministry.

Throughout the periods of change, consolidation and growth, we have tried to ensure that prayer has undergirded everything and where we have failed to seek God, resultant difficulties have arisen. We have made conscious efforts over the years to encourage and equip the church in relation to prayer. In the discipleship group that all new members attend, a whole section is given on prayer. Some of the most heart-rending, simple yet profound prayers have come from the lips of those unchurched folk who have come to know the Lord. Devoid of all theological jargon and pious sentiment the real and honest prayers of these folk have humbled me and taught me so much of God's relationship with his people. Theological orthodoxy is no substitute for personal experience!

Praying for each other

Within the housegroups, which form an integral part of the fellowship's life, prayer is again a key component as the groups are encouraged to pray for one another, for the church and for wider issues. A regular series in the Sunday teaching programme looks at various aspects of prayer. During the

services on Sundays people are encouraged to pray, and as a
fellowship we have sought to make praying for one another a
natural, relaxed and spontaneous ministry. Each week a
prayer pointers guide is published for individuals, prayer cells
and housegroups, listing people, situations and specific happenings and areas of ministry for which we seek prayer.
(Nothing that would cause embarrassment or breach of confidentiality is published in the guide.)

Once a month on the first Saturday morning we held a
church prayer meeting which saw members meeting to pray
for the month ahead, for one another and for those in
particular need. During one such meeting a picture was
received which when interpreted and applied led to the
formation of our church prayer cells. Throughout the week,
on every morning, afternoon and evening a prayer cell of two
or three people meets to pray for the life and ministry of the
church. This in itself proved invaluable in many ways: fellowship and ministry, intercession and communication, as well as
a means to call upon immediate prayer support on a daily
basis where appropriate.

The prayer cell structure meant that our ministry throughout the week was covered by people praying. In addition to
this a telephone prayer chain started, which was activated by
a call to anyone on the scheme. He or she in turn would pass
on the prayer request to others in the fellowship. As with the
prayer cells, not only was prayer unleashed, but also an
important means of communication, vital for good relationships, was established.

Leadership and the various groups within the church were
encouraged to see prayer as a priority. Church members'
meetings changed from being business-orientated to focusing
on prayer and the sharing of vision and direction as well. For
the leadership especially, the time factor had become a
struggle in relation to prayer. Necessary sharing of information tended, wrongly maybe, to replace quality prayer time.
The only way we were able to respond more appropriately
was to meet as elders each week for a prayer breakfast. The
temptation to use those times for discussing pressing matters

was not always overcome, but we nevertheless attempted to achieve with a fair degree of success our reason for meeting: to pray together.

The advantages of developing these small groups for prayer was obvious in the way in which the fellowship was mobilised and engaged in prayer. People unable for genuine reasons to get to a mid-week prayer meeting were now a part of the prayer ministry of the church. A depth of sharing and fellowship was experienced as people prayed together for one another and for the fellowship. However what we undoubtedly gained in many respects, we also lost in some ways as the mid-week church prayer meeting went—and with it something important. The Saturday morning meeting has not as yet brought anything comparable in numbers to the old mid-week. The fact that we were not able to persuade some of the older members who previously attended the central prayer meeting to identify with the prayer cell structure is a cause of some regret and questioning.

Concurrent with prayer requests we endeavoured to keep before people the testimonies and situations that arose in answer to prayer, where appropriate during Sunday services and housegroups. People were encouraged to speak of their experiences of God's grace and goodness in ways that made real and visible God's answers to prayer.

Prayer and warfare

The ministry of intercession is one I don't pretend to understand fully. It engages people in spiritual warfare and also provides a perceptiveness born of spending time in prayer with the Lord. It has heartened me to see this ministry of intercession develop spontaneously among individuals within the fellowship, beyond the programmes mentioned already. I remember on one occasion being called upon to minister in a very complex pastoral problem that involved a serious criminal investigation. I remember that God wonderfully equipped and enabled me amid a dreadful situation that if unresolved would have had frightening repercussions for the people involved, and for the fellowship. After some six months of much prayer and various legal proceedings, the matter was resolved, I'm thankful to say. During that period, I had a conversation with someone in the fellowship who exercises a ministry of intercession, who, although unaware of the situation, was nevertheless conscious of the need to uphold in prayer those like myself involved in pastoral support. Little did he know what a difference his prayers had made!

On another occasion I went to talk with another intercessor about a situation that was affecting my future. Before I told her of the matter, she said she knew what I was going to say, for the Lord had revealed it to her during a period of intercession early one morning the week before!

As the church has ventured to move out in faith and obedience to the Lord, it is both fascinating and encouraging to see the Lord raise up intercessors, people who engage in spiritual warfare against principalities and powers. They are few in number, but their ministry and support to the church's ministry will surely prove of eternal significance and worth.

The church's perception and awareness of spiritual warfare has indeed been heightened in recent years. From a position that acknowledged the existence of principalities and powers in theory and belief to one that has led us to combating such powers in ministry—the difference is markedly noticeable. As we have experienced renewal and begun to move out more in ministry, we have been all too aware of the reality of spiritual warfare. Proclaiming and demonstrating the good news of the kingdom inevitably involves an encounter with the powers of darkness.

Confrontations with demonic powers appear to be increasing as in Christ's name we seek to see men and women set free from bondage and brought into the kingdom of light, prayer being an essential part of our spiritual armour and a weapon of warfare. Several in the fellowship can now testify to being delivered from Satan's power as through prayer in the name of Jesus they have received our ministry. It has been remarkable to see the power and authority of Jesus set people free. Growing numbers of people from broken homes, significant numbers who have been involved in the occult or who have been sexually abused, and whose lives are as a result broken and in bondage, have been set free to live in the wholeness and healing Christ brings to men and women.

The growing realisation that God was calling us to penetrate and involve ourselves in the community has led the church to engage in what we have called 'faith walks'. One Sunday evening the congregation was dismissed after the service to walk around the estates, pray against the powers of darkness and affirm the lordship of Christ over the area. We did this quietly and unobtrusively in twos and threes; without drawing attention to ourselves, we engaged in prayer for the community.

The following day, two of our evangelism team had the joy of leading a married couple, Bill and Isa, to faith in Christ in their own home on the estate. What was significant was not only their coming to the Lord but that the area in which they lived had been unpenetrated by the gospel for years. It was an area particularly renowned for occult practice, and very few houses had not faced some form of break-up in relationships.

Our only previous contact of any substance in this particular part of the estate was to respond to a cry for help from a distraught mother whose young son had been behaving oddly following a series of nights with the ouija board at a neighbour's house. Our ministry had then borne little fruit, but, following the faith walk, it now seemed that the light of the gospel was beginning to push back the darkness.

The couple who had come to faith were soon to see members of their own family become Christians, too. Their home became a base for both a 'Good News Down the Street'[1] and for discipleship groups. Irene, one of their relations, came to faith through the housegroups ministries. Going along to the housegroup with her brother and sister-in-law, who were full of the joy of the Lord following their recent conversion, she found herself responding to the group's invitation to pray for those in need. Suffering from

depression, she nevertheless felt warmed by a sensation that
came upon her when they prayed. She returned home conscious of an encounter with the Lord. The next day she awoke
and realised a lightness in her spirit; the depression had lifted,
and she went hot-foot around to the housegroup home,
where she gave her life to Christ at ten to nine in the morning!
Similar testimonies would echo the part prayer has played in
seeing people won for Christ and brought out of darkness into
the light.

Evangelism

Organised programmed methods of evangelism have been
undertaken by the church, although nothing can substitute
lifestyle evangelism where a Christian's life bears witness to
the reality of Christ in their home, neighbourhood and work
environment. Nevertheless programmes such as Evangelism
Explosion, 'Teach and Reach' and 'Good News Down the
Street' have proved to be beneficial both as training programmes for church members and methods by which the
Lord has drawn people to himself.

In each method the importance of prayer was stressed.
With Evangelism Explosion, as teams of three went out on
pre-arranged home visits they would be backed by six prayer
partners who would pray during the period of visitation.
Similarly, on the 'Good News Down the Street' programme,
the whole project was undergirded by prayer. It has been one
of the most encouraging things to observe people come to a
living experience of Christ in their homes through this programme. Another light for Christ is established in the community as people surrender their lives to him and become as
salt and light in their neighbourhood.

On door-to-door visitation, which like the swallow comes
and goes, a key that unlocks many a person's reception of us
has been to ask, 'Is there anything or anyone you would like
us to pray for?' Such a question has led to a number of fruitful contacts and has established some meaningful pastoral
ministry.

Although we have been committed to supporting evangelistic crusades, with two exceptions, these haven't actually featured prominently in the church's mission over recent years. The Sunday evening meeting is no longer a 'Gospel Service' where we play 'spot the unbeliever' and make sure he gets John 3:16 between the eyes! Evangelism has instead developed to one of lifestyle with the emphasis upon witness and outreach into the community rather than purely on church premises.

The two exceptions were, however, encouraging times for the fellowship where valuable lessons were learned for future occasions. In 1984, Billy Graham conducted a series of meetings under the banner of Mission England. Our nearest venue was Sunderland, half an hour's drive north. Appropriate arrangements were made, and we endeavoured to fill a coach for four of the eight nights of the mission taking unbelieving friends. We were heartened to see fifteen folk profess salvation, and ten of those are still going on with the Lord. It was a first experience for many of us of mass evangelism, one that no doubt whetted the appetite of a considerable number of people in the fellowship for further ventures.

A further opportunity came in the November of 1985 with an American Partnership Mission arranged in connection with our Northern Baptist Association. A team of six was to join us for the week's mission. We were blessed since one of our members, John, who had pastored a number of churches in this country and who had also travelled to America, knew the set-up and had already experienced such missions.

The key to the mission was prayerful preparation and maximum membership involvement in the programme. With John's support we did a considerable amount of motivating, preparing and publishing the week. We didn't follow the rules as exactly laid out in the guidelines; consequently, we didn't have a service every night, but rather a series of different meetings over the week, not all overtly evangelistic. Nevertheless, what we were privileged to witness was remarkable. To quote statistics would be inadequate to convey the astonishing things we experienced as the Holy Spirit came upon us.

That the mission started on the Sunday wasn't strictly true as weeks of prayer and planning were an integral part of the programme. However, Sunday morning service witnessed extra chairs and people sitting on the floor and platform, a crowded congregation of people eagerly anticipating what the Lord desired to do among them. I shall never forget the experience of turning around to the American preacher during the song before his sermon and seeing him absolutely broken before the Lord. After a further time of worship, he did eventually stand up and address the congregation. In brokenness and with tears running in streams down his face, he spoke on the love of God, and at the end four people responded and received ministry, but many more lives were touched and moved by the presence and power of God at work among us.

Great numbers were in evidence again at the evening service, and the Spirit was moving in power. At the close of the meeting, various words of knowledge resulted in seven people coming forward to receive ministry, of whom four gave their lives to Christ. The week continued in the same vein with people testifying to new-found faith in Christ, being filled with the Spirit, finding physical and inner healing, and with a number of folk committing themselves to baptism and church membership. The week marked a turning point in the life of the church as we witnessed the Spirit of God at work powerfully among us. We had then a foretaste and glimpse of what the Lord can do among us. The mission certainly signalled a change in the life of the church.

Inevitably, the week witnessed spiritual warfare. One example will illustrate something of our experience. On the first Sunday evening following the service the drummer in the worship group, Bob, had his cymbals stolen as he reloaded his kit back into his car. These were worth at least £600; Bob and Jan, his wife, were sickened, and the theft dealt a blow to the whole church. We recognised where the trouble was coming from and prayed accordingly against the disruptive work of the enemy, who was obviously out to spoil and hinder God's work. Stones at the window during the service and a disturbance in one of the pews had given us sufficient evidence of the enemy's activity. So during the whole week of the mission, the fellowship, among other things, prayed for the return of the cymbals. Our faith and patience was tested to the end. On the final Sunday evening, when we shared around the communion table and testified to the mighty acts of God in salvation and healing, we were nevertheless a little disheartened by the absence of the cymbals. A pan lid on a garden cane was no substitute!

On the Monday morning we duly assembled with our team for their departure. The phonecall came through minutes before our guests climbed aboard their coach. Someone had found the cymbals, intact and undamaged on top of a garage roof! Stockton has never before witnessed half a dozen Americans joined by some twenty or so English folk dancing for joy before the Lord at nine o'clock in the morning on one of its municipal car parks! The week had seemed among many things to remind us of the power of God and the effectiveness of prayer. Our expectancy of the Lord was greatly heightened by the experience.

George and Moyra

During the same year a new organisation was formed with a two-fold purpose to encourage unity among the churches and sharpen the churches' evangelism among the people of Stockton. Its founding members included a couple who had come to Portrack because they identified with the fellowship's vision. Before joining us, George and Moyra had come out of the Methodist church. They had also involved themselves with the local YMCA where they held weekly services on the premises which because of their zeal to share the gospel and reach out to young people saw some very real encouragements. Street kids, punks, skinheads and overseas students were among the group George and Moyra became involved with, serving Christ in pioneering missionary work.

One can imagine the sadness and perplexity they experienced, with Helen, who had joined them, when the local management committee decided to sell the YMCA. A vast complex in the centre of town with accommodation for over ninety people, sports facilities, restaurants and cafes, chapel and lounge areas, it was to be sold to the highest bidder on a commercial basis. What was to become of the young people who stayed there and those who used it as a base to meet, relax and share with friends? Many of these folk were already under pressure: having left home, unemployed, and facing the prospects of a change in government legislation over bed and breakfast accommodation. With a shortage of adequate housing accommodation and the exploitation of many of these youngsters by unscrupulous landlords, the selling of the YMCA was seen to exacerbate the problem. But sell it did, the local council purchasing it eventually in 1987.

But the vision God had revealed to Moyra which led to their first moving to the YMCA remained one of a large centre that would be used for accommodation, recreation, ministry, rehabilitation and training, staffed by the Lord's people and reaching out to the young people of the town. Undaunted by the closure and sale, George, Moyra and Helen, now joined by Christians from a number of the churches in Stockton, formed Stockton for Christ and in faith claimed the building for the Lord.

I well remember leading the 'Repossessing the Land' service in the lounge of the YMCA during the period in which the building was closed and still up for sale. With special permission, seventy of us gathered in the decaying building with no electricity on and no seats to sit on. For two hours we sang and prayed and sought the Lord affirming our conviction that the Lord desired the building for his purpose. Subsequent events with the sale of the building to the council have not diminished that conviction that one day the building will fulfil its divinely appointed purpose. When the council announced its decision to rename the former YMCA as 'Nelson Mandela House', such was the backlash of public opinion that they were forced to change their minds. It is now called Elm House after a former street in the area before redevelopment, but coincidentally 'Elms' is George and Moyra's surname!

Stockton for Christ in the meantime continues to serve the church and kingdom in the town and is pioneering a mission among the 'street kids' at the local Anchorage buildings. Its activity has been well compared with that of a well-known lager, reaching the people other churches cannot reach! Fundamental to the origins, life and growth of Stockton for Christ has been its commitment to prayer. The weekly prayer meeting provides the base for the group's ministry and mission in the town. They have made a significant contribution to the local council of churches bringing both an evangelical voice and a renewal of commitment to mission to that body. As one who has been involved and supportive of their vision, I have been reminded that where God's people humble themselves and seek him, he imparts vision and new life. New ventures, often unpredictable and creative, emerge from a people praying who seek after the Lord.

Long-range prayer

The place of prayer in relation to the fellowship's commitment to world mission has to be seen in the context of how we encourage and seek to stimulate concern for missionary work abroad. The church has currently two couples in training for ministry and missionary work at Bible college and has a supportive interest in seven missionary societies. Each month attention is focused on one of these particular societies. The missionary notice board changes its face accordingly. During October, for example, we usually focus on TEAR Fund. Through various means and activities people are alerted to TEAR Fund's ministry, with opportunities to share, pray and financially support their work. Prayer is given over to the society during the month wherever appropriate.

A variety of methods has been adopted to encourage prayer support for missionary societies. For Regions Beyond Missionary Union (RBMU) individuals are given a particular person or situation to pray for through the month. We are encouraged to put our prayer request in a place that will regularly remind us to pray for our respective missionaries. It has been intriguing and amusing to observe these reminders in various places in members' homes on pastoral visits. Fridge doors, kitchen cupboards, car dashboards, in the toilet above the roll holder are common places, but the most ingenious had to be the one taped to the pool cue! Because of the prayerful interest and support for Terry Waite, the Archbishop's envoy in Lebanon, the church has often prayed and held times of intercession for his release. We have found more value in praying for a particular person than for a situation.

In the church's pastoral ministry considerable changes have taken place in recent years, not least in the implementation of a pastoral assistants team which shares in the pastoral and counselling responsibilities alongside the leadership. After, sometimes during, most services, there will be opportunities for what we refer to as a 'time of ministry', when we give people the opportunity to respond to what God is saying and doing among us. On innumerable occasions such times have required the pastoral assistants and others to be involved in ministering to people. During such periods we simply wait upon God to work as he wills among us, bringing healing, release, direction or the invoking of praise among his people. In prayer we bless the Lord and affirm and acknowledge his authority and reign over us.

During counselling sessions it is not uncommon to move into a time of prayer in which we ask the Lord to come and reveal his purposes for the situation. The value and exercise of the gifts of the Holy Spirit are seen as indispensable both to ministry and mission, with words of knowledge and discernment often unlocking the problem and leading to effective ministry. As well as in our pastoral ministry we have also grown in confidence in our healing ministry.

Grace and frailty

In all the various aspects of the life and ministry of the church prayer has been integral. I believe that failure to seek and acknowledge God results in little of eternal worth. Though there are lamentable weaknesses in our own lives of prayer, by his grace and mercy, God has taken the frail expressions of our love and intercession and responded in measures of blessings beyond our understanding or worth.

No specific technique has been advocated as the way to pray, even though a variety of incentives and opportunities for prayer have been explored and expressed. For in the end prayer is surely to do with relationships rather than ritual: to do with what we are in Christ, as children of God expressing our love for him, calling upon him and affirming his grace and goodness rather than adopting the latest style, form or language of prayer. Honesty must surely be one of the prerequisites to our lives before God and should be reflected in our praying. Be it Fred who ends his prayers, 'Well I think that's about all, Lord, thanks for listening', or Jeff our worship group leader as he leads us in praise and adoration, or Doris who would kneel at her bedside and bless the Lord in tongues—God hears the prayers of his children as they seek him individually and together.

To end let me share with you four prayers vivid in my memory. I recount them not because of their brevity but because of the impact they have made on my own life and that of the fellowship.

Neville, who was wonderfully brought to the Lord during 1984, cried out to God during one evening worship, with tears in his eyes, 'I love you, Lord, and I want you to touch my heart and use my life to glorify you.' In that young man now beats the heart of Jesus with such compassion for people that reaches out to every life he touches with the love of God. He has the heart of a pastor.

Margaret prayed in a song that the Lord gave her, 'I want to praise you, Lord, I want to bless you, Lord, I want to love you, Lord . . . .'—simple words, but the directness and profundity of those words expressed a longing in my own heart and that of the fellowship to know what worship in the Spirit was all about. It was a heart cry from the people of God to know a greater experience of the presence and power of God as we worshipped him.

'*Come Holy Spirit*' was the prayer during evening worship of our renewal weekend, when the power of God came down upon us, and many were brought into a new or deeper experience of the Lord.

And finally the prayer expressed on *Frances*' behalf as she lay in a semi-comatose state in her hospital bed, her life draining from her. I had felt her clasp my hand as I read from Psalm 23. She confirmed her response at the close of the psalm. Following the words 'and your house will be my home for ever', with another clasp of her hand on mine, she said, 'Amen. Yes, Lord.' The first words she'd spoken in days, the last words she was to speak on earth. 'Amen. Yes, Lord.'

Amen!

Note

[1] See *The Church Down Our Street* by Michael Wooderson (MARC: Eastbourne, 1989), in which the author recounts the exciting story of God at work through neighbourhood evangelism.

Chapter 6

Chessington Methodist Church

Chessington, Surrey

Philip Seaton

In St John's Gospel, Nathanael asked Philip, 'Can any good come out of Nazareth?' Similarly, people ask Philip Seaton, 'Can any good come out of Chessington besides the Zoo?' This chapter offers a positive answer, showing how a suburban Methodist church has made an impact in the community. Prayer triplets and carefully thought out local lay witness have led to deeper experiences of God's love and healing through the renewing work of the Holy Spirit.

Philip is married to Pauline, a part-time secretary at a London counselling centre, with four grown children. Before entering full-time Christian ministry he was manager of the meat department in a small family supermarket, then after ordination he served in Darlington, and came to Surrey four years ago. He enjoys exploring the countryside, theatre, film and photography.

When we tell most people that we live in Chessington, their immediate reply is: 'That's where the Zoo is—isn't it! I've been there.' While it is famous for the Zoo, Chessington's history can be traced back to the eleventh century, and it is an area rich in history and personalities. The busy, bustling, sprawling Chessington of today is far different from the rural village it was up until the early 1930s.

At the beginning of the nineteenth century the population was small, and the census of 1821 showed a total of 150 inhabitants. The twentieth century brought with it many changes as in the 1930s much agricultural land was sold for housing development, schools were built and in 1939 the railway linking Chessington with London was opened. The main development came in fact in the immediate post-war years, and along with this came the Methodist church, which started in 1948.

It began with a small group of people meeting in a corrugated Nissen hut which had a distinctive ecclesiastical brick front. A Sunday school also met in the home of one of the church members. From this humble beginning the church premises and congregation have grown, and the membership now totals 180 with a community roll of 500. The church has a large catchment area and is a hub of activity with meetings on the premises every night. These include all the usual church meetings of Sunday school, ladies' meetings, Bible study, guild, youth clubs, and uniformed organisations; plus a play group, mothers and toddlers, a care scheme, arthritis care and a local-authority-sponsored luncheon club for the elderly, which meets weekly. Chessington Methodist Church is a busy suburban church.

Lay Witness 1986

However, in spite of—or perhaps even because of—all its busy-ness, it was felt that something was needed to deepen the spiritual life of the church. So it was that in 1985 the church council decided, after a lot of discussion and prayer, to hold a 'Lay Witness' weekend on 5th–7th October 1986.

The Lay Witness Movement started in America and came to England in October 1976. This has steadily grown over the years, based at Burbage in Leicestershire and administered by Tom and Margaret Moyle. At each Lay Witness weekend a team of 'lay' people (hence the name) tell the stories of what Christ has done and is doing in their lives. It is a low-key movement as they endeavour not to make anyone feel threatened or inferior in any way, but to try to help individuals and the church as a whole to look at themselves and discover how alive and real their faith is.

It was decided to call our weekend 'In Touch with God—Vision and Reality'—which became the 'In Touch' weekend. The guideline the Lay Witness movement recommends is that there must be at least six months' preparation with prayer as the foundation, motivation and covering throughout the whole time. Not an easy task! How do you motivate people to pray who may not be used to praying, who do not always realise the importance or power of prayer, and have little or no experience of praying with others? The only answer, of course, is to pray and ask God to raise up people of prayer. This is exactly what my wife Pauline and I did.

The first real test came when we had to find fourteen people who would accept responsibility for organising the various aspects of the weekend: hospitality, food, transport and prayer. It is never easy to find volunteers, and yet we felt we were not to ask anyone. We prayed that each person God wanted for a particular job would hear his call and volunteer. That is just what happened. One by one, people offered until all fourteen posts were filled, and we were filled with joy as we saw our prayers being answered so wonderfully. We knew that God was beginning a new work among us.

Perhaps the greatest challenge was for someone to encourage people to pray for the event, and we had to resist the temptation to do it ourselves. We were therefore delighted when someone did volunteer to become the prayer secretary and to uphold and draw together all the prayer for this weekend.

I had tried to reintroduce prayer meetings into the life of the church, but apart from a fortnightly 7 am meeting on Thursdays, attended by a small group of loyal members, I had met with little success. The only suggestion we did make was for prayer triplets, the strategy of praying in groups of three for those who are not yet committed Christians, which was conceived and developed by Brian Mills, the Prayer and Revival Secretary of the Evangelical Alliance, for the preparation for Mission England in 1984, when Dr Billy Graham came to England for a nationwide preaching tour at many evangelistic meetings. We introduced this idea in one of the church's monthly newsletters and mentioned it aloud during one of the morning services. As a result, six triplets were gradually formed with people aged between fifteen and seventy. They were then encouraged by Mary Elms, the prayer secretary, who produced prayer cards and newsletters for the groups to guide them in their prayers.

The various triplets began to meet together in each other's homes but were initially all very hesitant and nervous. Eventually, however, they found it helpful to be able to open themselves up to one another and share their problems and concerns. Thus after a short time of praying together in this way members began to discover that not only were their prayers being answered but their own lives were being changed by God.

At first there seemed to be very little enthusiasm or interest among many other church members towards the 'In Touch' weekend, and the going was hard for everyone. Only gradually as the time drew near more folk showed interest, and we are sure that this was the beginning of the answer to our prayers.

During the final week before the weekend itself, on the Wednesday/Thursday, we held a twenty-four-hour prayer vigil supported by just a small number of people, some of whom fasted. In the early hours of Thursday morning as Pauline was praying, God reminded her that he is able to achieve great victories with only a small number of people, as he had shown to Gideon in the Old Testament; so we were to trust him. For all of us who shared in the prayer vigil there was an overwhelming sense of God's presence with us (which continued throughout the whole weekend) so that everyone who came, either as a lay witness or as a participant, became conscious of it too. The vigil concluded with an informal Communion service in the church parlour when about thirty people attended, and we felt God binding us together in his love.

In touch

On Friday afternoon we welcomed the team of seventeen lay witnesses, and a few of us were invited to join their initial preparation meeting, when we were able to learn how they become united as Christ's body. Those who had met before at other weekends were delighted to see each other again. The team leaders David Adams and Stephen Baum welcomed everyone and asked each person to introduce himself or herself and give a brief account of their own situations at home. We all joined in a time of worship and prayer before the team was briefed as to what would be required of them. Some were to be group leaders and others were to be prayer partners, and together they should endeavour to create a relaxed atmosphere which would help the church people to open up and talk about themselves and their faith. It was wonderful too, to see how, even though some of the team had never met each other before, they were able to enjoy fellowship and to pray for each other in a loving way both before the meetings and before they each gave their testimony.

Later, on Friday, we were thrilled to see about a hundred people sit down for the fellowship meal which was followed by praise, and testimonies from some of the team members. We then divided into small discussion groups where we were asked to look at our own spiritual life and to consider how real God is to us. For some this was a very hard task as we had to draw a graph of our spiritual experience and growth over the past years.

On Saturday morning small groups met in people's homes for coffee followed by a time of quiet meditation and sharing. We all came together again for lunch at the church, and one or two witnesses were asked to tell us how God had been working in their lives. The rest of the afternoon was free for everyone to do as they wished before meeting back at the church again for tea, and the evening meeting followed a similar pattern to the Friday evening.

It was especially thrilling to listen to the account of how Christ had rescued and changed the life and marriage of John after he had sunk to the depths of chronic alcoholism, unemployment and degradation. Of course, not all the witnesses had such powerful testimonies to share; nevertheless they were all able to recount what God means to them and how they had been helped or healed by him in some marvellous way. As a result of hearing all these different stories many people were challenged in some way by God's Spirit and felt they wanted to make a response to him. Thus the church was open for quiet personal prayer and counselling, and members of the Lay Witness team were available if anyone needed to talk about their feelings or problems. Tom admitted that he had been forced to see that for him Christianity was only a code of behaviour, but from then on, he wanted God to be real to *him*. After thirty years of churchgoing he now knows God's presence in his life at last!

Sunday began with a church breakfast at 8 am, followed by an informal Communion service where, as we shared the bread and wine, Christ was so real to us and his presence so strongly felt that no one wanted to move. During the morning service both the team leaders shared their testimonies of God's work in their lives. David told us of how dry and lifeless his Christian life had been in 1975 even though he was a Methodist local preacher. One day he was invited to attend a renewal meeting in Leicester when Rev Dr William Davies (Bill Davies), former President of the Methodist Conference, was preaching about the gift of the Holy Spirit and how he can give us power to become Christ's witnesses. As David listened to that message he knew God was speaking to him, and when the invitation for prayer was given he went forward. From then on, his life was changed and is continuing to be changed as God works in him and through him.

At the close of our service the congregation was invited to respond to God's love and power, and there were tears in several people's eyes as the front of the church became filled with people. Truly, we had been 'in touch' with God!

Later, in the evening service, many people recounted what the weekend had meant to them, and it was a real joy to hear the testimonies of our own people. Several people said how much they had enjoyed sharing in the meals together as a church family; others said how blessed they had been in having a team member stay with them in their home; Jane shared how she had been made to think about her Christian life and how she had just been drifting along according to her own plans instead of asking 'What does God want me to do?' Janette admitted that prior to the weekend she had not really known God's presence in her life, but now she had begun a relationship with him that she hadn't even dreamed was possible.

My own disappointment was that not everyone had felt able to share in the weekend. We therefore needed to be careful that their absence did not cause any unnecessary hurts or resentments. I am thankful to say that through continued prayer hurt is being avoided, and we are now seeing the kind of real openness and sharing that is joining us gently together.

The 'In Touch' weekend was only the beginning of a new chapter in the life of the church, and since then God has been working in many people's lives, renewing and changing them by the power of his Holy Spirit. Church members Jack, Barbara and Muriel were challenged to become lay witnesses as a result of the weekend. The triplets have continued to meet and pray. We had prayed for the weekend and had seen our prayers greatly rewarded, but it was even more important that we continue to pray for God's guidance for the future. One of the suggestions that came to me following the 'In Touch' weekend was that the congregation could become more involved in the leading of services in various ways. We gave out a questionnaire to ask people what particular things they would like to do. The response was really encouraging as many people were eager to read the lessons or dramatise them, sing in a group or choir, play their musical instruments, make posters and banners or clay models, write poetry, lead the prayers of intercession or dance with others. We have therefore included all these things but not all in one week or every week, only as the Spirit has led us. We feel it is important to try and keep a balance between the old and the new so that we can all be led on by God together into deeper ways of expressing our worship and love for him.

October 1987

A year later we held a faith lunch to which we invited members of the prayer triplets and also any other interested folk. The purpose of this meeting was to tell each other some of the things we had learned through praying together, and some of the answers we had received. Some people confessed that previously they had never prayed aloud with others as they used to find it difficult and embarrassing; but that they now had been enabled to overcome these barriers. Some admitted that they had been greatly surprised, but delighted, at the way God had actually answered their prayers in such wonderful ways—far more than they expected! One group recounted how they had prayed for someone who had severe cancer who had then been healed. Another group had prayed for a grandmother who was very old and ill; she had been able to die in peace rather than in prolonged suffering. A husband and wife told how their young son had been healed from a severe digestion problem after being on a hypo-allergenic diet of sheep's milk and cheese for years. Now he can eat normal food with no adverse effects, and we all shared the joy of his mother, who no longer had to cook and pack up special but separate foods for meals and parties for her son. A deputy head teacher shared how his triplet had prayed for the comprehensive school where he worked. This had resulted in his finding opportunities to express his faith to other members of the staff; he now meets with some of his colleagues for a weekly prayer meeting at the school. Several people had been prayed for and had now become Christians, and there were others whose faith had been deepened.

We felt that God was telling us that the time had come for

the triplets to be reorganised so that new members could be incorporated. Although several people had moved on to other places (college, new jobs and homes, etc) others were wanting to join a triplet, and we now have about thirty people involved. Some of the groups have four members and others have three, but we believe we have been guided by the Holy Spirit as to which person should be with whom. The majority of the groups meet weekly, but no matter how frequently they do meet, the level of commitment is high and deep. It is not strange either, to hear of a 'prayer breakfast', a 'prayer barbecue', or a 'prayer meal'.

Only a beginning

I believe also that through prayer the worship life of the church is changing. We now have a loyal group who meet regularly to pray and plan together our forthcoming services. Right at the start we made it our policy not to try to include too many different expressions of worship during our morning services but to continue the usual pattern of family worship once a month (when the children are able to take part in the worship through drama, singing, etc) and our monthly morning Communion services. Since we are a Methodist church, visiting preachers do come to lead our worship who have their own way of doing things. However, we offer a list of volunteers who are willing to read the lessons and lead the prayers of intercession. We find that our evening services are therefore more suitable for variation. We have also held three worship workshops when we have come together in an afternoon to prepare for the evening service using all the gifts which God has given us—some of which we were unaware of having. Barbara and Lilian have discovered that they have been inspired to write beautiful poetry; and for Remembrance Sunday Brenda and Derek, with helpers, have designed some appropriate banners. On Palm Sunday this year we presented *Breaking Bread* in our evening service, a new musical setting of the Communion service composed by Paul Field.[1]

From time to time we have healing services with the laying on of hands, in which I have been assisted by several church members. During our worship we may have a time of open prayer, or I may be led to divide the congregation up into small groups of four or five to share their concerns and pray together.

Twice a year the triplets come together to meet as a large group, and on 5th March 1988 we held a Prayer Breakfast to link into the National Day of Prayer and Repentance.

I believe that God has much more that he wants to do in us and among us, and we have a great deal to learn and experience, but we still have people who are hesitant and afraid, and for this reason we are seeking to follow his guidance. We must also be open to receive his love so that we may love one another, and I know that we cannot pray together without feeling a love for those with whom, and for whom, we pray.

As we pray, so we are enabled to step out in faith. At the time of writing this chapter I myself have not been too well and have had to rest. A week ago four of our members came to pray for me and anoint me with oil—something I know they wouldn't have dared to do a year ago! Praise God!

Note

1   *Breaking Bread*, Kingsway, 1988: book by Rob Frost; songbook, cassette and music by Paul Field.

Chapter 7

St Philip & St James, Walderslade

Chatham, Kent

Ken Gardiner

'Pip & Jim's', as it is popularly known, stands not far from the historic naval dockyards of Chatham, in the heart of two post-war council housing estates. Enthusiastically led by Ken Gardiner, Pip & Jim's emphasises commitment not only to church work and prayer but to practical caring and sharing. Housegroups and Prayer and Action groups, as well as a Lydia Fellowship, provide the nucleus for the church's prayer life.

Ordained in mid life, Ken previously worked at the head office of a major insurance company. He has served as vicar of Pip & Jim's since 1970 and with his wife Sheila has three married children and six grandchildren. Like several of the other contributors to this volume, Ken enjoys music and travel.

There is a story about a centipede who was coping with life satisfactorily until someone asked him which leg he put to the ground first. Trying to analyse what, until then, had been a purely subconscious and natural action, threw him off balance and made him a nervous wreck. It is rather like that trying to analyse the prayer life of 'Pip & Jim's'. It tends to throw us off balance because, of course, we are not simply or even principally a praying church. We are I hope a worshipping church, a growing church, a caring church, a missionary church and all sorts of other types of church as well. There is plenty of room for improvement in all these areas, but none would have started or still continue without prayer; so it is difficult to isolate prayer from all the other aspects of the life of the fellowship.

If I could point to a central, regular and well supported prayer meeting as the hub of the church's activity it would be easier; but it isn't like that with us. I suppose that after a while any church will begin to reflect the views, strengths and weaknesses of its leaders, particularly its teachers. I have been the principal pastor here for some nineteen years, so it is inevitable that much of my own experience of God and of prayer should have become part of the woof and the warp of the daily life of our church family.

My spiritual home was a sound, lively, evangelical Anglican Church in the Bible-belt suburbs of South London. In those days all such churches were judged by the strength of their mid-week meeting for Bible study and prayer. If you were keen you attended: I was, I did, and I learned much, sitting at the feet of great Bible teachers. This was the powerhouse of the church. When first I came to this parish there was a similar meeting, and I sought to continue the tradition. For a while it worked well enough, although nothing spectacular seemed to come from it. After a number of months I became unsettled and frustrated. As I am the vicar, the final responsibility for what happens in the church falls on me; and little enough was happening. Naturally, I brought my frustration to God in daily quiet times of prayer and meditation. I realised I was running the parish as I had seen other and wiser men than I run their parishes, even though this parish, set in the middle of two great post-war council housing estates, was utterly different from the one where I had become a Christian in middle-class suburbia.

Finding the plan

As the weeks went by I became convinced that God had a plan for us. Whether it was the same plan as for another parish never crossed my mind; I wanted to discover only what was right for *us*. Although I was the leader I had long been convinced that I was not necessarily the only one to whom God might reveal his plans. Paul's concept of the church as the body of Christ (1 Corinthians 12) makes it clear that no one person has all the gifts needed in a Christian community. So I gathered together a group of people who, I felt, would understand what I hoped to do; shared my thinking with them, and we set about praying that God would show us what he wanted us to be about. Over the years my understanding has clarified, but that was how we began to move forward as a fellowship. I had been profoundly influenced by some words of Christ to the Jews who were persecuting him, 'I tell you the truth, the Son can do nothing by himself; he can do only what he sees his Father doing' (John 5:19).

If Jesus, who was himself God, could do in his humanity only what he saw his Father doing, then how much more important that we also should know what our Father is doing if we were to expect him to bless us. So we began to search for his will rather than follow the advice or experience of others. Do not misunderstand me. I am not saying we ignored the advice of others or their experience, rather that we checked every bright idea with God before assuming it was right for our own parish. Initially we seemed to receive fairly direct guidance. Our little group, waiting before God, received words of knowledge and visions; or perhaps a Bible text would imprint itself on someone's mind which, when we put all these together, pointed us in a particular direction. Although that still happens occasionally, usually the guidance isn't quite so clear nowadays.

I have a theory about that which others may like to test in

their own experience. It seems from Scripture that when God planned to do a particular work in his people he first performed an identical work in the one he had chosen to lead them. Moses spent years in the wilderness alone, before he was sent back to Egypt to lead the people into that same wilderness. Jeremiah had to be broken himself and rebuilt, before God could appoint him to tear down and destroy, to build and to plant (Jeremiah 1:16). I am no Moses or Jeremiah, but I was appointed leader of a group of God's people, and he first taught me a truth which we were later to learn as a fellowship.

Maturing in prayer

Shortly after we arrived my wife and I were debating whether or not we should buy a freezer. At that time they were fairly new in Britain, and few people had them. Were we right to spend so much money? Was it a luxury? We had managed all right for years without it, so did we really need it? For several days I sought the Lord. Some Christians may say I was being too scrupulous on such a matter as that. We are all different, and I was getting myself into quite a stew when in my quiet time one morning I felt the Lord say, 'I am not bothered whether you have the freezer or not. You know enough of me and my ways to decide for yourself whether you should have it. You are no longer a babe, you must begin to make decisions like this in the light of your knowledge of my overall will. You must mature and grow up in me.'

It was like that within the church fellowship. Initially, as I say, we received fairly clear and direct guidance. Although that sometimes happens today, usually it is a matter of praying a thing through and discussing it openly among ourselves. I should explain that we have operated an eldership system for many years now, made up of ordained and lay, paid and unpaid members of the church. The elders meet two or three times a month and the PCC once. As we discuss and pray over decisions we usually come to a common mind. We find a peace deep within our spirit that this is the way to move. Some would quote the words of Isaiah chapter 30 verse 21 about hearing a voice behind you when you turn to the right or to the left saying, 'This is the way, walk in it,' as though we are *always* to expect some such direct guidance; but that is to misunderstand. In Scripture, the way of the Lord is always straight; to turn to right or left is to take a wrong path. When we do that we may well hear a voice within our conscience (ie behind us) saying, '*This* is the way.' To rely only on visions and words of knowledge does not help us to mature as Christians. These may be necessary to inform us of things we could not otherwise know and we need to develop our spiritual ability to receive them, but they by-pass our minds and understanding. This is what Paul is getting at in 1 Corinthians 2:12–16; in that passage he sums up with the statement 'we have the mind of Christ'. We are to mature in Christ until we begin to walk as he walks, love as he loves, think as he thinks. I believe prayer is a two-way activity where we do not simply fling our requests at God but seek to hear him, watch what he is about and then follow what we hear and see.

One evening a month

Do we then no longer have any central prayer meeting for the whole fellowship? We do, one evening a month, although it isn't very well attended; often only about 30 or so come along. First we have a time of worship, singing hymns and spiritual songs to the Lord. Prayer will be interspersed, but always in words of praise and thanksgiving: there is no intercession at that stage. Then there is a short Bible reading and exposition, followed by more singing. We may then have a brief talk introducing a particular subject. Maybe a member of our missionary committee will give us news of one of our link missionaries, or someone will speak about a particular issue shortly facing Parliament which could have a profound effect on the country, for example, abortion or the licensing laws. If there is no speaker, then I scour a number of current Christian newspapers and magazines for brief articles on a variety of subjects. We then break into groups of five or six to pray over different matters which have arisen. If we are using printed articles, someone in each group will read out the particular article he has been given before starting with prayer. It isn't easy to gather everyone together again, because if one group is between prayers, someone in another group is in the middle of a prayer. So the leader asks the musicians to play a chorus quietly; this is the signal for groups to complete their praying and gather together. After a further brief time of singing, we invite people to share needs of themselves or others and particular matters affecting the fellowship as a whole. Then, while we are all together, individuals will pray briefly for each of the matters which have been mentioned.

One morning a week

As well as this monthly meeting we hold an early morning prayer meeting every Saturday from 7–8 am. This is specifically for God's work in our parish. It began in 1986 when I felt a particular need to cry to God for his blessing on what we were seeking to do for him. I let it be known that I would be in church for that period and invited all who would like to to join me. This isn't a large group; apart from one Saturday— allocated nationwide to prayer for a particular matter—the most we have had is twenty. Usually we are about ten.

Here we do not have any plan, but we try to discover what is on God's heart at that time. I'm not sure we always manage to do this, but very often a theme will emerge, and I generally suggest that we stay on that subject for some time before moving on to something else. Who can judge how directly effective any one time of prayer may be? Yet I do believe that much of the blessing we have experienced recently is indeed the result of this regular weekly prayer meeting, small as it may be. A confirmation of this conviction was when one morning one of the group felt led to pray for a particular road in the parish and for the people who lived there. It is a very short road in the heart of the estate where we had three families already within the fellowship. Within three months or so a further two families and another person from that road had joined us—one man's being the most dramatic conversion I have seen for years. Once again it was a case of discovering what the Father is doing and working along with him.

Care, share—and prayer

I believe that the reason why the central church prayer meeting is no longer as popular as it was is the growth of housegroups. When we first began to look for God's will for us as a fellowship, he made it clear that we were to concentrate on building up our relationships. As vicar, I knew most people, but they did not know each other. If I asked one member to contact another for some reason, I would often be told, 'I expect I know her face, vicar, but I can't place the name.' Christ has told us to love one another, and Paul to bear each other's burdens. We cannot possibly do that when we do not know who the others in the fellowship are, let alone what burdens they carry.

Housegroups

We began, therefore, to encourage people to spend time with each other. Time and again I taught that while we cannot create fellowship, we can create the circumstances which will enable fellowship to grow. We arranged many events on a family basis: parish picnics, weekend houseparties, harvest (and other) suppers. We even arranged a parish holiday. However, the main thrust of this family approach was through housegroups. These were more than Bible study groups; they were to be caring and sharing groups. We encouraged the members of each group to enjoy themselves together. At the evening meetings of these groups only the adults could come, and often only one partner because the other was baby-sitting. So we encouraged people to arrange small get-togethers, barbecues, visits to swimming pools and other outings, at times when all the members of each household could be present. As they got to know each other on a deeper basis, so they began to care for each other. That care involved prayer.

So often, it seems to me, Christians pray for each other—and of course that is very important—but we are too busy, too committed to church work, too this or too that, to be able to help each other *practically*. Of course, there are many occasions when we genuinely cannot do anything except pray. Maybe others can give the practical help but do not know how to pray or do not believe in prayer anyway; and we alone are able to offer the necessary prayer. But sometimes I believe we are to be the answers to our own prayers. I well remember a friend telling me that he went to one of the old-time central prayer meetings I was talking about earlier, where the vicar asked, among other matters, for prayer about the need for someone to fill a particular post within the church. In the course of that meeting my friend prayed that the right person would be found and, even as he was praying, realised to his horror that God was calling *him* to it!

It is impossible for anyone in a fellowship of any size to relate deeply to more than a few people; consequently, many relate to none. However, in a housegroup of between eight to twenty people, friendships can be formed. The evening meetings, which are arranged officially on a fortnightly basis, are usually centred on Bible study. But of course people do share any particular joy or burden they have and the others pray, with (if it is appropriate) the laying on of hands for healing, peace, or whatever is lacking. This care, which springs from the basis of coming to know and understand each other, is then manifested in practical ways. No one can care for all, but each can care for some, or at least one. This means that what is often called 'pastoral care' of the fellowship is exercised far more effectively than when it was assumed that, being the vicar, I managed it all. What is more, because people within a group spend sufficient time together to come to know each other in a far deeper way than I can know them, the prayer and the care also reach a deeper level.

Having said that, I must not give the impression that I am

not available to people. Much of my time is taken up with counselling in depth. Very often housegroup leaders suggest to one of their members that he or she should contact me for help in a particular part of their lives. My counselling is always Bible-based, with prayer—I know no other way.

I meet with the housegroup pastors fairly regularly, and from time to time I supply ideas, but usually they are responsible for the content of their meetings. This means, of course, that each group develops in its own way. For some time one group always began its meetings with a review of the matters members had prayed about last time they met. They kept a book of subjects covered, and asked what had happened since. The evening I visited them, every one of six prayers had been answered. They were not major matters, but important to the people concerned. I know very well that prayers are not always answered so swiftly and positively, but it was a wonderful encouragement to pray in faith for the matters which arose that evening after the Bible study.

Another group has set up a prayer-chain so that if anyone is faced with an emergency he or she telephones another member of the group, and within minutes all the others in that group will have been advised and will be praying. The same group has also organised 'prayer triplets'. It isn't easy to get everyone together outside the set housegroup evenings, but groups of three can usually fit in a half hour together some time during the week. Each will bring some particular matter on his heart—usually a non-believing relative or colleague at work, and the three of them will pray and, over the weeks, keep each other informed.

I am convinced it is because of the popularity of these housegroups, with such personal and specific prayers, that the larger gathering, centrally organised and set in the church or hall (as it must be to accommodate the numbers involved) no longer attracts the majority of the fellowship. Although I believe that there is still a place for such a meeting, I do not go along with those who bewail its demise as though it signifies a lack of interest in prayer. In fact, I think far more prayer is being offered and on a far more effective basis. After all, if you have a gathering of a hundred, only one can be praying aloud at a time (unless you break up into groups around the building, as often we do). But if you divide that hundred into eight groups, meeting separately in homes, then eight people can be leading in prayer at the same time and, what is more, everyone else in the group is likely to be able to hear and so join in with understanding—something that does not always happen in a large hall.

I have not mentioned the prayers which go on in individual homes as people have their personal prayer-times. This is because it is impossible to know. I can say only that I am constantly surprised and thrilled when someone new remarks in passing, 'As I was praying the other morning . . . ' or 'When my husband and I were planning our prayers . . . '

As well as the housegroups, some other groups meet. We have two mother and baby fellowships. These are small enough to meet in a home, and several young mothers who find it difficult to get out in the evenings can get together to share news, have a time of Bible study and pray about the things which particularly concern them. Knowing I was to write this chapter I asked one group of women if they could tell me their experiences of answered prayer. One wrote:

> . . . Small insignificant things at first were answered; then things which seemed too big and complicated, how would he solve them? He did amazingly! After two years of solid praying and commitment, then the amazing answers came because, I believe, we were meeting faithfully to honour our Lord in prayer no matter what else came up.

Another said:

> One of the young people for whom we prayed over a period of months has committed his life to the Lord and is coping with day-to-day life much better, witnessing and sharing his faith with others.

Several confirmed what one of them reported:

> In two cases problems in labour seemed inevitable (the doctor said a caesarian would have to be performed). The group prayed both before and—by way of the 'prayer chain'—during the

labours. Both babies were delivered naturally.

Others mentioned praying for babies who would not sleep at night, and for one member of the group who had to feed twenty-five people for a weekend and was tense about it. (She actually enjoyed it!) Everyday things, but these are what our God is interested in, if only we will ask for his help.

Prayer and Action Groups

Recently we have set as one of our goals for the year the establishment of Prayer and Action Groups. The aim is to gather together people who share a particular interest and concern, on an informal basis, who will meet as and when they want to or need to. Our first such group supports the CARE organisation, which publishes literature about social issues and matters due to come before Parliament: issues such as abortion, genetic engineering, the licensing laws. We have a large number of teachers in our fellowship, and we hope to encourage them to meet together to share their particular concerns about education. We also have a number involved in social services and medical care, and it may be that they will meet. As the name implies, the purpose is for both prayer and action. The latter may involve organising petitions, meetings or writing to MPs.

Lydia

Within the parish we have two Lydia groups. Lydia is a world-wide movement involving praying women. Small groups of from three to eight commit themselves to meet regularly for prayer—particularly intercession. Normally there is no agenda and, after personal preparation and a time of worship, the group will sit quietly, waiting before the Lord. After a while each describes what she has found within her mind. For one it may be a particular verse of Scripture that is drawn to her attention. Another may have a mental picture (a vision); yet another may find herself thinking about a person, a country, a government, a subject. Occasionally a particular word comes to mind. As they talk together, it is surprising (although it ought not to be) how often they discover that subjects are duplicated or dovetail together, and then they begin to pray about these things. It sometimes happens, and sufficiently frequently for us to notice, that when some event is featured on the news my wife will say, 'Why, we were praying about that in our Lydia meeting this morning [or yesterday].' For some years our groups have met during the day, so it is only housewives without young children at home who have been free to join. However, we have now set up two evening Lydia groups.

Prayer and parish government

By the law of the Church of England, every Anglican parish must have an electoral roll. This is a list of members entitled to vote at the annual church meeting for the various officers of the parish. Officially all that is necessary is that it shall be available for inspection and contain the names and addresses of each member. In fact, for many years, we have included the telephone numbers as well and divided the list into thirty groups of equal size. We give every family a copy of the list, suggesting that they use it as a prayer list. In this way we pray for every member once a month. It would not be realistic to imagine that everyone does this, but I am sure that several do. Of course, it also helps create a sense of belonging together when every member has a full list of the names, addresses and telephone numbers of all the other members.

The other matter worth mentioning is that when the PCC meets each month, the first half-hour is devoted to a time of worship, mainly singing choruses accompanied on a portable electronic organ and a guitar. At first, having been used to a brief five or ten minutes of open prayer, we wondered if this would cause problems by taking up a quarter of our available discussion time. In fact, it rarely causes such a problem, and somehow the discussion is more relevant; we reach decisions more easily, certainly without rancour.

The community team

About six years ago we took on an extra member of staff, a community worker. The closure of Chatham Dockyard and a nearby oil refinery had caused a great deal of local unemployment. Together with an increase in the number of single-parent families and with the large number of old people in the area, this unemployment meant that there were a number of social problems. The major cases were handled by social services, but many people had difficulty filling in forms and understanding just what benefits were available and when. Our community worker, Bill Cottrell, joined us to set up a team to help. Experienced himself, he recruited a number of women in the fellowship and, with the willing help of social services, trained them in the basics of community help. An office was opened every weekday morning in the church buildings. While the aim was to offer practical help to all who sought it irrespective of creed, we have made no bones about the fact that we are Christians. The office planning meetings include a definite place for prayer and— this is important—all the staff are strongly encouraged to end every interview, whether in the office or at home, with prayer. At first the person who has sought help may be somewhat surprised, but he or she rapidly becomes attracted to the idea. Frequently our staff are asked, 'You won't leave without our prayer, will you?' Sometimes they are told, 'You know, I've been sleeping much better since you prayed with me.' Having been taught to include prayer in their visiting routine, and experiencing the encouraging results, members of our community team find it natural to pray with all sorts of people on all sorts of occasions. For many years I have prayed with people over the telephone when they have contacted me to tell me something. Now several members of the fellowship regard this as normal for them as well.

Asking and answering

For some years now I have believed and taught that God longs to bless us in all sorts of ways, but he waits for us to ask him. Indeed, I am convinced that he does not do anything redemptive until and unless we ask him. He may well reveal his plans, as he did to and through the prophets, but these are stored in heaven, as it were, until we pray, as Christ taught us, 'Your will be done on earth as it is in heaven.' Once again we are back to what I said at the beginning of this chapter, that God has a plan, and our task is to discover that plan and then co-operate by doing whatever we see our Father doing. At such times we really see the answers to our prayers because we are asking for what the Father already wills to give us. We try to bring this belief into our Sunday services, although I must admit it isn't so easy in the morning when we have to regulate the time available to fit in with the young people's teaching classes. However, we have a little more freedom in the evenings. Let me explain what we do.

The service will follow its normal pattern, with the readings and intercessions being taken by different lay people. A large pool of people like to take these, and the quality of the intercessions is excellent. Instead of ploughing through a long list, many intercessors explain at the outset what form the prayers will take and what subject(s) we shall be concentrating upon. Often there will be an opportunity during the service for people to speak about something which has happened to them recently and which gives glory to God. Just occasionally I may ask someone to give a testimony of particular importance that requires all the time available; usually, however, it is an open time for any who wish to come to the front, where we have a microphone. Initially, there was a certain natural trepidation, and I had to prime the pump by asking specific members who I knew had something to say to come forward. Now, however, there is very little problem and we sometimes have to call a halt—asking people to hold back until another time.

Of course, the actual content of the sharing varies considerably. Sometimes there is a rather dramatic healing. As I write I know that one of our members who developed diabetes nine months ago has just been told by the doctor that her pancreas is working normally, and eczema which he said would take months to go has almost cleared overnight. It may be that someone who has been seeking employment or a change of job has a testimony to give. One schoolteacher with special skills told how she had applied for a particular post, but that it went to someone already known to the school. However, at the interview, the head teacher said he knew of another school that urgently required a teacher with her particular expertise. She applied and was offered the post at once; this latter school has a Christian foundation and staff. Often the matter shared is less dramatic. Perhaps something is lost; the person prays about it and is suddenly prompted to look in a particular place where the article has fallen. A car breaks down—right outside a garage. Sometimes the matter appears to be trivial; nevertheless it seems that always someone is helped by what has been said.

I am convinced that much of the growth both in numbers and in the faith of our congregation is due to this opportunity for sharing publicly the answers to prayer. So often in our churches everyone hears the intercessions, but no one hears the results. Consequently no one expects prayers to be answered because they are never told that they are. Unbelievers in the congregation, who may be relatives or friends attending a baptism, hear a testimony from a person who has experienced God's blessing and care in some definite, demonstrable way. The very fact that what has been recounted is down to earth and undramatic may speak to someone far more powerfully than a sensational healing; he or she can relate to it more easily. If God answers someone else's prayers like that, perhaps he will answer mine if I give him a chance. Hearing of answers to prayer in each other's lives is now one of the most exciting events in our services.

In the evening we almost always have a time of silence and waiting. This usually comes at the end of the service when the worship and preaching have had a unifying effect as we have all shared in a common experience over the previous hour.

We *expect* God to share himself with us in some way. That way will vary from service to service. It may be that in the silence of their own thoughts some people will know that the Lord is challenging them to set right something in their lives. Maybe some of the congregation will have mental pictures, visions (they are all very undramatic and normal, no one goes into a trance). One or two may feel that the Lord is revealing some truth; this may be in the form of the actual words conveying the truth, or a general impression of what God is wanting to do or show us; both are equally prophetic. After a time of silence, I invite people to tell what they feel God has been showing or saying to them. Almost always, as various people speak up, a wonderful unity of truth emerges, each revelation confirming and building upon the one before.

Following this, while the majority of the congregation continues in worship, singing spiritual songs (choruses), those who feel it right to do so come forward for ministry and prayer. We do not restrict those who come to minister, indeed we encourage people to join in small groups, but we try to have at least one elder or housegroup pastor within each group. Sometimes the prayer is for assurance or the removal of some hurt, fear or bitterness. Often it is for some form of physical healing, although this may well involve later emotional healing and counselling.

We encourage those who minister to pray with their eyes open (very difficult after the years of schooling they have received to shut their eyes when praying) so that they can watch what is happening to the person to whom they are ministering. Often a reaction will help direct the form of prayer. If it is prayer for healing, we teach people not to ask God to heal, but to thank God that he has given *us* authority to heal and then to come in the name of Christ and command the pain to go, the cause of the pain to be set right, the muscle, ligament, tendon or bone to take up the function for which it was designed. Christ did not ask his Father to heal, he found what his Father was doing and then came with the authority of that knowledge and spoke out what he knew the Father desired in each situation. It isn't easy to teach people to pray with this authority because for so many years they have been taught their unworthiness. Of course, we *are* unworthy but we have been accepted, redeemed and empowered. We must just believe (ie have faith for) that and act accordingly with the authority and power which has been entrusted to us.

As the praying progresses, both with the understanding (in English) and with the spirit (in tongues), we stop and ask the 'patients' what is happening. Sometimes they experience nothing immediately, but often they feel warmth or an improvement in the condition. With this encouragement we continue in prayer, thanking God for what he has done already and claiming the complete healing we believe is his will. On those occasions when a deeper problem is manifested we either take the person through to a counselling room or arrange to see them later when we will have time to talk and pray things through more leisurely. Since this ministry is public, others are encouraged not only to seek such ministry but also to pray for each other. More and more members of our fellowship are prepared to pray in this way, with laying on of hands and with authority in Christ's name, without calling for the clergy or an elder.

Heaven's storehouse

I should be encouraged that so many people are praying in so many different ways on so many different occasions and, of course, I am. However, it only serves to highlight how little we *do* pray and how much more there is available to us from the storehouse of heaven if only we believed and cried to our generous heavenly Father for all he wills us to have—if only we would ask.

Chapter 8

Colne Valley Community Church

Colchester, Essex

Peter Prothero

A small clipping from the Daily Telegraph *of 8/8/88 gives just a hint of the excitement evident at this growing independent church. The headline simply reads 'Churches launch pray-in for a £140,000 miracle', and the article goes on to quote Peter Prothero: 'Christians all over the world, including Korea, America and China, are praying with us.' To find out more, read on!*

Peter studied civil engineering at the University of Manchester Institute of Science and Technology and then went on to a three-year Bible-training programme. He pioneered Cornerstone Print and Design; but then in 1985, with his colleague James Linford, came as overseeing pastor to the Colne Valley Community Church. He and his wife Jacqueline and four children enjoy the varied life of this church, for members are mostly young, with a generous sprinkling of Essex University students from as far afield as the Gulf States, Africa, Israel, Malaysia and China.

The Colne Valley Community Church came into being in 1977, planted by a young American who had a gift for evangelism. By the time I came into full leadership in 1985, along with my colleague, James Linford, numbers that had grown to about 200 had dwindled to 70. How could we lift the morale of the fellowship, and what did God want us to do? These were important questions, especially as so many in the fellowship were leaving. We tried to release them in the right spirit and bless them in their going, but this was still a painful time.

Beginnings

During the early years of the fellowship, we had begun an intensive three-year Bible College training programme, as well as opportunities for Bible study, visitation and outreach. By the time James and I came into the leadership, we were as a fellowship well grounded in the truth of the Bible and yet felt a deep void in our experience. We began therefore to examine our structure, teaching and practice, especially concerning the exercise of spiritual gifts. It was our desire to allow all in the fellowship to express their gifts, to mature in their ministries and to grow in Christ.

I remember one day driving down Hythe Hill in Colchester on my way home. That morning I had been reading about Jesus speaking to the Pharisees with regard to the resurrection, declaring to them that they did not know the Scriptures or the power of God. On this particular day God spoke to me very clearly. It was not an audible voice, but an inner understanding: 'I have taught you my word, and now I'm going to teach you about my power.' I began to get excited. I had no idea what God meant. I didn't share this word with anyone. Like Mary, I just received the words and hid them in my heart.

One of the first items on God's agenda for our fellowship quickly became apparent. Within a few months we were asked to attend a meeting of about thirty local ministers, some of whom were supportive, but some of whom were suspicious of what we were doing and wanted to work out with us whether we were indeed part of the 'main stream' of biblical Christianity in Colchester. This meeting allowed leaders on all sides to express their concern openly, to admit mistakes and express a desire for unity. Although this meeting in itself did not seem to me to be the new beginning that we were hoping for in our fellowship, it did create a great time of reconciliation for many of us.

After the meeting, James learned about the ministry of John Wimber—from Brian, the local Anglican vicar who had chaired the meeting. Although I held back for some time, I did after a few weeks come to share James' enthusiasm for John Wimber's tapes on 'Signs and Wonders'. Here was a man of God teaching on the whole dimension of healing and spiritual gifts in a way that I found palatable. He was not dogmatic but spoke clearly from his experience in the light of the Scriptures. I began to see that this is what God meant when he said he was going to teach me about his power.

Healing prayer

Although we had not been to any Wimber seminars, we began to incorporate some of the teaching of John Wimber, particularly with regard to moving in the spiritual gifts, into the teaching of the fellowship. We also began to pray regularly for the sick, and I believe that this was our introduction to deeper prayer.

The first weekend we did this, I taught a weekend seminar on spiritual warfare. When it came to the last meeting on the Sunday evening, I didn't even want to go. After giving twelve messages, I felt exhausted and that I had no more to offer. I remember turning up half an hour late for the meeting. I pulled James to one side and asked him if he had any idea what God wanted to do that night, and he suggested that we pray for the sick. So with plenty of fear and a high level of unbelief, we invited the sick to come forward for prayer. The first lady had suffered back pains for two years and had even brought a cushion with her to the seminar. We began to invite the Holy Spirit to come in his power to heal.

I had hardly got the words out of my mouth when she turned and said, 'I'm healed!'

'Are you sure?' we said.

She replied, 'I felt a tingling go right through my body and I'm healed.'

I said, 'Do something that would normally make your back hurt.'

She began to bend and stretch and jump. We began to praise and rejoice and glorify the Lord. Although a few were uneasy about what had happened, feeling that we were getting off-centre, the rest of us saw God's hand at work.

As the months went on we began to see more healing. We were beginning to learn about prayer with authority, praying in the name of Jesus, the prayer of agreement of two or three. We incorporated prayer into our whole counselling procedure so that whenever anyone was counselled, there would always be a man and a woman counselling, with another trainee learning, and at least three intercessors in another room praying for the individual being counselled.

Prayer was permeating the warp and woof of our church life. I believe the changes began with healing prayer because we were able to see immediate results. Although we were to learn later that not all answers came so quickly—and to persevere in prayer—we found at first that nothing is more encouraging to further prayer than praying and receiving a positive answer.

The nature of our meetings did not change a lot to begin with. We would have a time of worship; I would teach and preach the word of God. Then we would give an opportunity for people to receive words of knowledge and then say 'Come, Holy Spirit' and pray for the sick. This pattern went on week after week, and week after week we could see people healed: one man who had terminal cancer, people who had epilepsy or crippling arthritis—these are some of the examples of those who were healed. God was beginning to teach us about his power. On Sunday evenings seldom did James and I get away from the church until very late.

We also began to encounter the demonic. This was a particularly difficult transition for me as I had always believed a Christian could not have a demon. Our first encounter was when a young man came to us saying he felt he had some problems but couldn't explain them. We began to pray that the Lord would show us the root of the problem, inviting the Holy Spirit to expose that root and give us some understanding. The young man immediately fell and began to roll on the floor. His face was contorted, and his voice changed. James and I addressed the demon in the name of Jesus and expelled a spirit of pride. After some coughing and a little thrashing around, the young man got up and was perfectly normal.

Experiences such as this made us rethink much of our theology. I had been taught that our practice of ministry and understanding should always be based upon the word of God and not upon experience. While this is true, I had never learned that the men of the Bible wrote the scriptures out of their *experience* of God. Very often we come to the scriptures with a preconceived idea and superimpose on them our own prejudices. Thus we began to see more and more that our world-view was far from biblical but was more Western, rational and intellectual.

A fresh understanding of worship

At the same time that God began to move powerfully in our fellowship with more and more people receiving spiritual gifts, we also began to teach on the importance of worship. Our fellowship is blessed with a number of musicians, so we encouraged all those who could play an instrument to get together for regular practices. We learned all the latest worship choruses and seldom sang any hymns (though we are now reintroducing some into our worship). I led a teaching series on praise and worship and emphasised how they should involve the totality of our being—spirit, soul and body—using the Psalms and David's example when bringing in the Ark. We taught on the intimacy of worship and on different ways of expressing worship: with hands raised; stretched on our faces; with laughter and with shouts—for in the Bible God uses the shout many times to proclaim his victory.

Regarding dance in worship, I remember teaching that we need to give freedom to those in the fellowship who want to dance. With the exception of one or two, however, this just didn't happen. I spoke to the pastor of a nearby fellowship who had some wise counsel: 'Children don't do what you say, they do what you do; and if you want the people to dance, you are going to have to dance yourself.' That was a real blow. I didn't mind other people prancing around, jumping up and down, doing the pogo-stick hop, but I certainly wasn't going to do it myself! It nagged me, however, that I knew there were people who wanted to dance but were held back through self-consciousness. God began to convict me, and I realised that if I wanted them to pray for the sick, I had to pray for the sick. If I wanted them to operate and move out in the spiritual gifts, I had to be willing to do the same. If I wanted them to evangelise and be on the streets, I had to be out there doing it. God gives leadership to the church—to lead. He was just waiting for me to get on with the job!

We began to see in worship that not only were there songs *about* the Lord but that there were songs *to* the Lord. We recognised that it was the songs to the Lord that brought us into a greater sense of intimacy in worship with him. Thus we began to teach the people accordingly. If we are singing a song of declaration and victory, it doesn't really make sense to close our eyes and seem to be enraptured with who the Lord is; it seems more appropriate to do that when we are singing to him and expressing our love for him. So we would often direct the people to look at each other as they sang, 'Don't you know it's time to praise the Lord?' We all felt a little uncomfortable looking at each other at first, but we were singing not only 'with spirit but with the understanding' (1 Cor 14:18). Our worship became more intelligent. The more we worshipped the Lord, the more there was a sense of his presence and his power, and the more we felt encouraged to pray and call upon his name. The fellowship grew; people were healed, many came into the kingdom through conversion because of the signs that had tested the word of God that was preached. We began to see that God was wanting to show us more and to use us more.

We found that we had to change our attitudes towards worship. We came to appreciate that it was not a warm-up to the ministry of the word, but that it was for God alone; but as we gave ourselves to him wholeheartedly in worship, even being willing to express our emotions in a sanctified way, he would visit us. We were not to worship on the basis of how we felt, but on the basis of our love and commitment to Jesus Christ. We were to exercise our *wills* and *choose* to worship; as David said, 'I will praise the Lord.' Worship has since become our highest priority as a fellowship, and out of its intimacy we enter into prayer.

Family matters

As the Holy Spirit has moved through our fellowship, renewing our understanding of prayer, worship and commitment, I have had to re-evaluate my priorities in the light of my family commitments. Just as prayer is a discipline, and time must be scheduled to do it, so I have discovered that the same principle needs to be applied to my family. With a fourth child on the way, we saw the need to have one day a week scheduled, usually a Saturday, when I give myself entirely to my wife and children. Leaders' wives can so often feel that their husbands are married to the church.

I have come to appreciate my wife's prayer ministry and seldom do any counselling at home unless she is present. She has the gift of being able to home in on the real issues. I also seldom make commitments before eight o'clock in the evening, so that my children get the benefit of having my presence at teatime, and I am able to read them a Bible story and tuck them into bed. I don't believe that God calls us to sacrifice our families on the altar of our ministries but that he calls families as a whole to minister together.

Similarly, I seldom accept speaking engagements unless the inviting church is prepared to receive my wife and children as part of the ministry. Whatever commitments and priorities God has challenged us to, at heart I believe he has called us to do it as a family. This will sometimes mean inconvenience and reorganising schedules, but it does mean that we can fulfil the purposes of God together.

We have carried this conviction over into another commitment, too: to a Christian school.

Praying for a school

We opened a Christian school in Colchester, a work pioneered by James Linford. This was the fruit of faithful prayer and research that took three years. Finally we took that step and opened our school with fifteen children. The premises were sadly lacking, but the atmosphere was wonderful; the teachers were all dedicated and the parents were encouraged to pray continually for this venture of faith. As the school grew over the next two years, Her Majesty's Inspectors continued to criticise the facilities we were using. We were desperate for God to provide some property with plenty of grounds for the children to play in and adequate facilities for at least four classrooms. At the close of the summer term in 1987 the HMIs warned us that we would not be allowed to come back to this property that September. We had to find somewhere over the summer break. This led to earnest prayer and seeking the Lord. We visited every estate agent in Colchester; contacted as many people as we could to pray; viewed several properties. We didn't have any money and wondered if we shouldn't just buy a house and convert it but each time we prayed we felt pressed by the Lord to believe he would do something more than that.

We were greatly relieved when in August we did discover a property just outside Colchester with a third of an acre of ground and a beautiful detached house with some room to expand. We began the proceedings to purchase. It cost £145,000. I shared the vision with the fellowship, who didn't seem to get too excited about it, particularly the parents. This house was seen to be on the wrong side of Colchester. Nevertheless we pressed ahead and kept praying. When it was almost time for the school term to begin, the purchase fell through.

We felt devastated. We also felt God had spoken to us clearly about a property in the town that would double up as a church sanctuary and a Christian school. It was up for auction. We shared again with the people and even had some tentative drawings done by an architect for conversion of this old church hall. Everyone got excited, and through our offerings we collected about £15,000 cash. The bank said it would allow us a mortgage of up to £75,000, so we knew we could bid up to £90,000. We went to the auction really believing God was going to come through for us, expecting him to answer our prayers. This was almost the twelfth hour. What a great testimony this would make. We could write a book about it! We went to the auction. The bidding began at £80,000. I remember that before we even had an opportunity to raise our hands it jumped to £90,000 . . . £120,000, and on up to £160,000. I was feeling a little sick by this time. Eventually it was sold for over £210,000.

We felt devastated again. What was God up to! Had we just not heard him at all? We called a special Friday night meeting of the whole church, just to come before God. I spoke on Psalm 50:14: 'Offer to God thanksgiving and pay your vows to the Most High. Call upon me in the day of trouble. I will deliver you and you shall glorify me' (NKJV). We continued to declare our love for God and that we would thank him and trust him to supply the right property in his time.

Until that evening we had deeply felt the pressure of many parents and the responsibility of providing an adequate place for their children. We did not want to see our school fizzle out after two years, nor to let the parents down. At that meeting, then, we simply began to praise the Lord, to offer to him thanksgiving and to ask him to examine our hearts where perhaps we had made promises to him and had not paid our vows. A real spirit of joy fell on the whole congregation. We seemed to fill the place with singing and joy and dancing. I remember the burden of the whole project lifting from my shoulders.

We opened the school once again in the old facilities that we had been using for two years. In faith we wrote to the HMIs telling them that we were currently negotiating a property that we would be in by the new term in January. In the meantime my wife and I viewed a property that looked to us so much like a school that we had to see it. It was way above our budget—£197,000. We looked around it and were impressed. Called Little Ramparts, it stood in four-and-a-half acres of ground, was a single storey and only two miles from the town centre to the north of Colchester. It also overlooked the Colne Valley, which seemed appropriate for us.

I took the other leaders of our fellowship along to see it. As soon as we drove onto the property, two of them began to weep. We all sensed 'This is it!' and asked God for confirmation. He gave us a very specific word, from Leviticus 23:15: 'And you shall count for yourselves from the day *after* the Sabbath, from the day ... *seven Sabbaths shall be completed*' (emphasis mine). We were to go to the estate agent, tell him that we wanted to buy it with cash and that we would have it within fifty days. With legs shaking and stomachs churning we walked into the estate agents. I kept telling myself, 'My father owns the cattle on a thousand hills. I'm not going to be intimidated.'

The agent told us that he had already received five bids for this property, three of whom were investigating planning permission. The agent would only consider ours if we could do an immediate cash purchase. In faith we said we could. We asked how long it would take to complete and were told it would be about seven weeks—exactly forty-nine days which, including the day we had seen the property, made fifty! Again we got excited. We came back to the fellowship and presented the property and the vision to the church. We didn't take any special offerings; we just told the people, 'If you want to be involved in giving to this then come and see us or write to the fellowship.' Within the next four weeks £52,000 came in in cash and with a mortgage from the bank we were able to purchase this property on the exact day that God had told us.

We learned many lessons from this venture in prayer. Many times we are prepared to settle for something less than God's highest.

Praying in the morning

The hardest kind of praying to do is praying for guidance. Many things we do in the Christian life are settled once and for all. We only get baptised once, and then that issue is settled. We only come to Christ and are born again once, and that issue is settled. But guidance is a day-by-day thing. We continually need to hear from God, and the only way to do that is in the place of prayer. Thus we saw the need to be more consecrated and to spend more time before God so that we really could discern his highest will for us.

God taught me very early in our school of prayer that there is no point in asking him to do something or asking for his wisdom on something unless in our hearts we are prepared to respond. Jesus said in John 7:17: 'If any one wants to do his will, he shall know concerning the doctrine, whether it is from God or whether I speak on my own authority.' It was no good Peter asking the Lord to invite him to walk on the water unless he was willing to get out of the boat. Each time, as God has blessed us as a fellowship, we've grown and our level of income has increased; thus we have felt challenged by the Lord to encourage more people into full-time work. Our leadership team has now expanded to four full-time men plus a full-time worship leader and two full-time secretaries.

The early morning prayer meetings at six o'clock every day of the week have an interesting history. In 1986 a missionary couple of fifteen years' experience came to visit us, supposedly for a fortnight, with their tribe of eight children; and within a short while we knew that God was knitting our hearts together. (They were eventually to remain with us permanently.) They began to feel drawn more and more to be a part of the church life here in Colchester. With David's years of experience on the mission field and of seeing the power of God, we felt a degree of security in being able to relate to someone who had maturity and wisdom. He became a sounding board to bounce ideas off.

It wasn't long before I learned that part of David's lifestyle was to get up early in the morning to be praying by six o'clock. He spoke not only about the blessing of doing this but of the great need, as God would thus release more power in the fellowship, enabling us to keep our hearts right before him and to seek the direction and priorities he had for us as a church. We began to see that there was a great temptation to become proud in what we had achieved and not to understand that this was just the beginning of what God wanted to do. The more we looked at the Scriptures the more we began to see the call to seek the Lord in prayer. Often when Jesus was at the height of popularity he would withdraw into a quiet place or to a mountain to pray and we saw clearly from the Scriptures that he didn't make a major decision without spending time in prayer.

So one Tuesday morning we arranged to meet at six o'clock in one of the classrooms of our Christian school. I think there were half a dozen of us the first time. With just a guitar we worshipped the Lord and sang praises to his name. As we worshipped we asked God to lead us in prayer; we didn't just want to come with a shopping list, but we asked him to speak to each one of us and to give us a sense of priority for that day. What could we pray that would be his burden? We waited quietly in silence, perhaps for a minute or two, and then turned to one another and said, 'What did you receive?', 'What impression do you have?' Each of us spoke up, and we discovered that two or three had the same impression. We took this to be the Lord's confirmation and began praying in that direction.

The Lord's presence was wonderful, and we were so

excited that we decided to meet the next day as well. At different times people came to the meeting sick, so after we had worshipped the Lord we would pray for their healing. We saw many healed and this hour before the Lord passed without a sense of drudgery.

It wasn't long before we began to see that God was calling us as a fellowship to be committed to regular early morning prayer. So we announced to the fellowship that every morning of the week, Monday to Saturday, we would be meeting at six o'clock. We encouraged the members of the fellowship to be committed to one early morning prayer meeting per week.

We soon realised that it was important for the prayer meeting to be led. We found that when a group of Christians came together to pray without a definitely appointed leader, the prayers would drift and there would be long periods of empty silence and a lack of direction. We appointed a leader as well as someone to lead worship for every meeting. This maintained the flow and direction of the meetings. If we were not sure what to pray for, we simply asked the Lord to show us and to give us a picture or a scripture, and we spent as long as half an hour or more simply in worship, discovering that true prayer begins with true worship; that we would best 'lift off' in prayer (like a rocket boosted to its destination) through declaration, praise and thanksgiving to God.

Paul says in Philippians 4:6 that all prayer should be with thanksgiving, so we would begin to thank the Lord for what he had done, what he had given us and for the answers to prayer that we had received. We would confess the name of the Lord and character of the Lord. Hebrews 3:1 says that Jesus is the Apostle and High Priest of our confession, and David says in Psalms 34:1: 'His praise shall continually be in my mouth' (NKJV). This commitment to praising and worshipping God was often the breakthrough we needed to enter that real sense of God's presence where we could bring our requests to him. Making that initial breakthrough was not easy. We saw more and more that there would be a need for a worship leader who really did his 'homework'. All of this led to an increased commitment to pray and to have our hearts prepared before the Lord.

Before the Sunday morning service we would meet again, this time at eight o'clock to pray for an hour. Then the musicians would meet from nine o'clock to practise and worship the Lord together. At ten we came back again for another half hour of prayer before the ten thirty morning service. While the musicians were practising from nine till ten, the leaders of the fellowship would get together with some of the housegroup leaders, and we would come before the Lord, enjoying a cup of tea and seeking God's priorities for the following service. More and more we wanted to break away from our preconceived planned programme and remain open to the Holy Spirit to tell us what he wanted to do.

We believed in fellowship, the continual preaching and teaching of God's word, Communion and prayers as outlined in Acts 2:42 but sensed that these elements of church life did not always have to be present at every meeting. Sometimes God showed us that he wanted us just to praise him. I remember the first Sunday night that we did exactly this and praised him for two-and-a-half-hours. I had never experienced anything like it in my life. It wasn't just repetitive chorus singing; it was the Spirit of God lifting us and giving us an energy to praise and declare the name of the Lord. We danced out of the hall through one door, round the street and back into another!

The water tower

During the early days of those morning prayer meetings we felt God speak to us about spiritual warfare. Someone had a vision of a high place where we were able to overlook the whole of Colchester. An old water tower, nicknamed 'Jumbo', was the only place within the town where this was possible. Owned by the Anglian Water Authority, it stood 131 feet tall at the head of the High Street, on the highest point of Colchester. God gave us visions and pictures of water coming out of this tower and going into every home. This seemed to be a picture of the Holy Spirit desiring to flood every home with his presence and with the reality of Jesus Christ.

At first we thought this was purely a symbolic picture, and we continued to pray that God would enable us to enter effectively into spiritual warfare. (Many of the kings in the Old Testament were righteous but failed to take over the high places where idolatrous worship took place.) We knew from Ephesians 6 (verse 12) that the warfare we were involved in was not against flesh and blood 'but against principalities, against powers, against the rulers of darkness of this age, against spiritual hosts of wickedness in the heavenly places'.

More and more we saw that our praying was to be done in the context of warfare. Within two months of that first vision, it was announced publicly that the water tower was to be sold off. It had become redundant, and offers to bid for it were invited. This engendered great excitement; we began to pray fervently that God would take this tower for his kingdom.

Breaking fast together

At the same time a consistent theme in our times of prayer was a desire to see a greater unity among the church leaders in Colchester. I had been particularly burdened for this for well over a year, having experienced some alienation from my brothers who were leaders of other good churches. Being encouraged by my fellow leaders, I wrote to several ministers in and around the town and invited them to come to a prayer breakfast. I felt that God had given me no more agenda than to provide breakfast for them and then to come before him and pray. Paul's pattern whenever he planted a church was to establish elders in every city. If God looked upon Colchester and did not see the denominational barriers or structures that were a problem to us but simply saw the leaders he had appointed, then I felt it was imperative for us as leaders to get together and seek God's face.

After we had finished breakfast, one of the leaders asked what we were doing in Colchester, and I began to share my concern. We spoke particularly about what God had been saying to us about taking the high places and the apparent 'co-incidence' of the tower coming up for sale. We then went into another room and began to worship the Lord. We had hardly sung two songs when the Spirit of God began to move deeply among us and we wept. There was a deep sense of God's grief because of the disunity among the churches, and among their leaders, so we began to call out for his mercy and forgiveness.

The Net-Work Trust

As we did so, God gave one brother a clear picture of a net that had been ripped so that the fish were swimming through all the holes. Another brother had a picture of a net that was being made from the centre outwards. We waited on God and asked him to clarify what he was saying; God drew our attention to a number of portions of Scripture. One was from Luke 5 where the disciples were called by Jesus to launch out for a catch, having spent all night fishing without success. We felt that this was a picture of the church, which had put a lot of energy and money into programmes to reach the lost, but the effectiveness had been minimal. At the end of that fishing trip with Jesus, there was a catch so big that the net broke. We noticed too that in John 21 when Jesus invited the disciples to do a similar thing, there was a great catch but the nets did not break.

God was speaking very clearly to us, and from this we formed the Net-Work Trust. Its two-fold priority is to work together with other church leaders and to restore their relationships with one another. Nets get broken because of use. It is an occupational hazard. We have discovered from experience that leaders in particular get hurt and damaged and out of relationship with one another simply by virtue of the warfare they are in. If it was true for Christians, it was especially true for leaders. God was calling us to be committed to one another in love and relationship, respecting one another's differences but coming together on the basis of our unity and love for Jesus Christ.

Secondly we felt God was saying clearly that it was a net-work of relationships—leaders working together in unity—that would weave the net of Matthew 13 and bring many thousands of 'fish' into the kingdom. It was a time to repent of our angling rods and our boasts of catches—the ones and the twos we had caught so far. God wanted instead to bring our evangelism in line with the book of Acts so that many thousands would come into the kingdom. We saw from Psalm 133 that it is in unity that God commands the blessing, in the place where brethren agree about the lordship of Christ, where people major on the majors and minor on the minors when it comes to doctrinal issues.

We felt that the Jumbo water tower, known to us as the Prayer Tower, was significant in God's economy. It was not to be owned by our church fellowship alone but to be a place of twenty-four-hour prayer and praise for the wider body of Christ. The vision was taken up by the Net-Work leaders to follow the Korean example of investing money in a project committed entirely to prayer. After this inspiring vision the tension was at times almost unbearable as various tenders were made and refused. The tower was finally bought by a fast-growing and successful local development company. This blow led to discouragement and a temporary dimming of the vision. We became introspective and wondered whether we had really heard God right.

During a visit to Colchester a widely travelled and experienced missionary was looking at an architectural drawing of the tower. The Holy Spirit reminded him clearly of the Moravians' prayer tower used for 147 years of prayer, day and night. (This had resulted in over two thousand missionaries being sent around the world.) His experience encouraged some of the leaders to continue pressing on in prayer to see God provide the tower for his own purpose.

On another occasion, at an International Intercessors Conference, we shared the vision with some of the conference leaders. The Spirit of God reassured us in what we were doing as they said it was vital that we trust God to release the tower to us. This brought a renewed commitment to prayer, and we went to see the developer. He showed us his plans for the tower, and we asked if it would be possible for us to pray in it in the meantime. He cordially agreed, and from that high place we began to pray both for the tower itself and for Colchester and the surrounding area.

In the spring of 1988, the developers' plans for a one million-pound office complex, which had already received planning approval, were blocked by a single technicality: because of the number of floors in the building, the fire officer had insisted upon an extra fire escape. This additional financial burden had tipped the balance, and so the developers' plans were abandoned. We offered to buy the tower. Our offer was accepted.

We asked if we could exchange contracts in late September to publicise fully the vision of the tower. In the meantime the vendor received a new bid for the tower, nearly £100,000 more than our agreed price. He said he would honour our sale if we exchanged by the end of the week. An emergency meeting of the Net-Work leaders was called that Wednesday. We had only £400 in the bank and seemed divided about whether we should go ahead or hold out for more time. We prayed and sensed that we should inform our fellowships the next day and provide an opportunity for giving—if the money came in we would exchange contracts, believing God to supply the rest by the completion date four weeks later. By 3 pm that Friday all the deposit money of £15,700 had come in. I took a fast car to London and we exchanged with only two minutes to spare. The next four weeks were the most hair-raising moments of my life!

The Friday before completion, £4,500 was available leaving a balance of £137,000 still to be found. On the following Sunday corporate prayer was again offered, and by the next Tuesday a massive response had reduced this amount to £60,000. The remainder came in the day before completion. Because cheques needed to be cleared at the bank, the actual completion took place in London within a minute of the deadline.

Prayer and praise warfare

We are now in the process of beginning to develop a strategy
for training people in prayer and praise warfare. God has
shown us that if we are to win the battle we must first win it in
the high places. A careful study of the three gospel accounts
of Jesus' transfiguration will show that when he took Peter,
James and John up the mountain, it was specifically to pray
(Luke 9). The Scriptures record that *as he was praying*, he
was transfigured. We had experienced this ourselves—not
that we have all started to radiate, but that God begins to
change us within when we do come into that place of
prayer.

We have also learned from personal experience that fasting
is an important part of the dynamics of prayer. Jesus did not
say 'if you fast', he said 'when you fast'. I am sure that no
Christian leader will be effective until he or she has learned
this discipline. More and more we are including fasting in all
of our major decisions. It is interesting to note that when
Jesus cast the demons out of the Gadarene demoniac they
specifically requested him not to send them out of the region
(Mark 5:10), but Jesus obviously had the level of faith and
authority to do it. Thus we have come to recognise through
prayer warfare that there are principalities and powers over
our town and nation which need to be moved—forces that
need prayer and fasting to be broken. God wants us to banish
the enemy.

Extended prayer meetings led us to initiate a monthly half
night of prayer. This typically begins at eight o'clock with
about forty minutes of worship and the guest speaker will
either teach on prayer or give us information for prayer. One
particular night when we were praying about David Alton's
abortion bill, the statistics about abortion were presented to
us along with other relevant information. We began with
corporate prayer and broke up into smaller groups of four or
five for more intensive prayer. Though we did not see the
breakthrough we hoped for in Britain's legislation, we have
begun to see a significant difference in our own area with a
reduction in the number of abortions.

Giving

Our fellowship has now grown to about three hundred people. As I look back over the last three or four years, I can trace—as well as a growth and commitment to worship and praise—a great increase in the giving of the people. For the most part, people in Britain do not discover the joy in giving. We spoke on this subject for eighteen months at every meeting for between five and ten minutes before the offering. It takes about a year for the penny to drop! Prayer for this giving has been another significant key, with an increased commitment to personal and corporate prayer.

Teaching and learning

The teaching for the fellowship is done through a programme that we have called the Christian Training Centre. These are twelve-week courses that we put on two or three times a year covering such subjects as personal growth, foundation, evangelism and missions, women in ministry and a commitment course. These short-term courses give people a clear objective to aim for and produce a greater level of commitment.

As we continued to pray, we also taught on prayer. I began to examine from Scripture the different kinds of prayers: the prayer of thanksgiving in John 11:41, the prayer of praise in Luke 9:21; the prayer of petition and supplication in Philippians 4:5, 1 Samuel 1:10; the prayer of faith in Mark 11, Matthew 21:22; prayer for healing in James 5:16, Job 42:10; prophetic kinds of prayer according to Acts 13, Acts 14:23; praying in tongues or in the Spirit in 1 Corinthians 14:14; intercessory prayer as in John 17; and the prayer of agreement in Matthew 18. We also began to see the importance of dedicating everything with prayer as was done with the Temple and the Tabernacle—and even with the human spirit, when Jesus was on the cross and committed his spirit into the Father's hands.

Meanwhile God was teaching us—all of us! He taught us that anger and doubt were hindrances to prayer (1 Timothy 2:8), as well as unforgiveness (Matthew 6:14–15). God dealt with us severely on this issue. We came to some meetings where God would show us that people were not reconciled to one another, and the leaders refused to continue until there was repentance and restoration. We would invite the Holy Spirit to come and convict us of wrong things we had said or thought against our brethren and to give us the opportunity for reconciliation. We found that Communion was the ideal place for this. The Scriptures teach us, 'Let a man examine himself and then let him eat.' This has increased the level of harmony within the life of the fellowship, and I believe it has enabled God to trust us with more of his plans. Schism, division and unforgiveness between brethren always hinders our hearing him speak. This principle is so important that Jesus mentions it twice in the Lord's Prayer.

God has also been teaching us about our attitudes in relationships. For many years, because of an emphasis in our fellowship on the finished work, many people were living in unreality and suppressing inner hurts and personal struggles. People were trying to appear spiritual and to say the 'right' things. (There is, of course, a danger of reverting to the opposite extreme of dumping all our problems on people every time they ask us how we feel.) We were finding, however, that God was calling us forward in our relationships until, at the right moments and opportunities, we were willing to disclose hurts, insecurities and fears. As we opened up to one another we were able to pray over these areas and see healing and deliverance.

This intimacy of relationship has greatly strengthened the life of the fellowship, particularly when the Enemy has brought any kind of attack from within to undermine us. We have tried to be honest with each other about our short-comings and sense of inadequacy, and at the same time to pray into one another's lives the sufficiency of Christ and his redemptive work; to ask the Holy Spirit to make that real in areas where we need it. Openhearted prayer in relationships has led to a greater sense of accountability to one another. When I tell someone my problem, I become accountable to him because he can then ask me how I am progressing.

God has also been bringing about a big change in our motivations. The Living Bible says in Proverbs 16, 'You can always prove you are right, but is the Lord convinced?' 'A man's ways seem pure in his own eyes, but the Lord tests the spirit'—as another version puts it. We have found that in our prayer, particularly among the leadership team, we have had to let go many of our own motivations for doing things, and instead we have had to be willing to wait more on the Lord. Just because something is a good idea doesn't mean it is God's. We now gather together every week as leaders and spend an entire day planning, praying and seeking God's wisdom for the care and direction of the flock. The evening of that same day we then spend with the home group leaders and their wives, again worshipping, praying and opening up our hearts to each other. Many of the programmes we have been involved in for years—such as evangelism—we have allowed to die; and yet we have seen more people come to Christ since!

Intercessors

We have an earnest desire for ministry programmes to be initiated by the Holy Spirit and led by him. Our entire counselling ministry, for example, is backed by a group of intercessors who often meet in a different part of the same building where the counselling is in progress. They give themselves to prayer for four or five hours at a time.

We are learning from the Scriptures that Paul had a very special place in his heart for widows. Throughout the Old Testament, God warns Israel to be especially mindful of the widow, the orphan, the stranger and the alien; and throughout Luke's Gospel the widow is featured five times. The first mention is of Anna, the prophetess, who never left the Temple but was given to fasting and prayer. In Luke 18, too, we see the importunate widow whom Jesus uses as an illustration of a believer who is to be steadfast in prayer. One of the qualifications for the widow to be financially supported by the church is that she be somebody given to prayer (1 Timothy

5:1–16). Paul even talks about her praying day and night. These scriptures led us to ask God to bring to us these older women with a heart to serve the Lord Jesus in prayer.

In the world's eyes, old people are redundant, past any usefulness. They are often encouraged to enter old people's homes and are set aside. In the kingdom, however, the opposite appears to be true: as people get older they become more useful. The maturity and wisdom of their years can be channelled into fervent, effective prayer which, according to the Scriptures, is the true and hard work of the kingdom. It is such widows we are praying for to lead the intercession within our fellowship.

Our intercessors amaze us, so accurately have they been able to hear from God. When counselling sessions are going on, they often slip a note under the counsellor's door with specific scriptures, or pictures, or particular events they have sensed the Lord talking to them about, or impressions they have received. Invariably these have been keys that the counsellor has used to unlock the problems of the counsellee. The specifics of these words of knowledge and wisdom have sometimes astounded us with names, places and experiences that nobody ever knew about but that had been revealed in intercession.

Are we living it?

Our strategy for leading the fellowship has been both by teaching and by example. (Nobody within the life of the fellowship is appointed to any position of responsibility until he or she has demonstrated consistent participation in the prayer life of the church.) One of the dangers we have encountered is that because of the subjective nature of pictures, visions or words from the Lord, these things need to be tested. The Bible says (Deut 19:15) 'In the mouth of two or three witnesses let every word be established.'

In the early days of prayer, and because we did not want to grieve or quench the Holy Spirit, I sometimes felt a little intimidated, particularly when there were outspoken people who came across as being very spiritual with impressions from the Lord that we should follow a certain course as a fellowship. If it was the Lord, I didn't want to disobey. If it wasn't, I didn't want to look foolish. We have discovered, however, that when people are in a right relationship with the Lord and with each other, these kinds of impressions from the Lord can be humbly submitted to the leadership and left for them to weigh. Usually when things are from the Lord, people are willing to rest and allow him to do the convicting work of showing the leadership that it is from him.

Strawberry plants

One major change in the infra-structure of the church in the last three years has been the setting up of home groups rather than Bible study groups. For us, although the Bible study groups were for the provision of adequate teaching of the flock, they did not provide the opportunity for small group relationships. It was also difficult to train leaders who could make a Bible study interesting and life-giving. The home groups were given a specific definition: to help the people to learn more about worship and to develop deep and lasting relationships. In this context we encouraged the practice and development of spiritual gifts. We also see this as an ideal opportunity for people to pray for one another, and prayer for the sick is practised too. Each home group is given the goal of multiplying yearly to avoid becoming insular and introspective. They know from the outset that their ultimate goal is to reproduce—strawberry plant fashion.

I am committed to the belief that a church's level of maturity and commitment to prayer will seldom rise above the maturity and commitment of its leadership to prayer. We do not feel that we have arrived in any sense, but like Paul in Philippians 3 we do believe that we are pressing forward in an age where so much else presses in, demanding our time and attention. We need to see the importance that the work of prayer has. We have found that it is not enough just to give one or two exhortations or a number of messages on prayer. It has to be a line upon line and precept upon precept, here a little and there a little. The test of whether or not the people have heard the message is simply this: Are we living it?

Chapter 9

New Life Assembly

Brixton, London

Lovell Bent

In 1985 Revd Lovell Bent moved to Dulwich with a vision of planting churches in London—groups of Christians who would reach out with prayer and caring to the many needy people around them. It was a struggle in the early days, he says. But gradually, as this group expanded into various house-groups, leaders developed and were trained. The prayer life of these housegroups was what sustained the church as it began to plant out into other areas: Dalston, Tottenham, and—most recently—Brixton.

When this chapter was written, New Life, Brixton, was less than a year old but had grown from a nucleus of ten people to a body of forty-five adults and many children. Revd Lovell Bent, the church's pastor, oversees all the New Life Assemblies under the guidance of Philip Mohabir, Chairman of the West Indian Evangelical Alliance. Lovell shares with the WIEA a vision for multiracial churches in which there is a partnership between God's people of whatever race to serve him in the local community.

Lovell Bent works for London Transport when he is not busy with his churches or with his family: Anne, his wife, and two

*teenagers, Faith and Wayne. He and his family live in Herne
Hill.*

Many people must wonder what happens in inner-city areas
such as Toxteth, Handsworth and Brixton after times of
rioting and destruction such as those witnessed by these areas
a few summers ago. When the streets have been cleared of
rioters and debris, what next? This question was asked by
Christians in South London a few years ago who longed to
see God's Kingdom come in Brixton. Revd Lovell Bent was
one who had a sense that God would open Brixton if he
and his colleagues from other New Life Assemblies in
Dulwich, Dalston and Tottenham were to go out in faith
and evangelism. At first, however, it seemed that no doors
would open. Ten people had come out of the other New
Life Assemblies to plant a Brixton church: Lovell's family,
Philip Mohabir's family, and Clarissa Brown and her
family.
    Following the pattern of the other New Life Assemblies,
this 'mustard seed' group began to grow, and its members
prayed for a multi-racial witness to Jesus in Brixton. Someone
suggested that the Brixton Recreation Centre might be a
good place for meetings. Like the rest of the group, Lovell
had his doubts that such a huge non-Christian facility would
offer any space to a church, and at his first approach, the
response was a definite no. Members of the group then
prayed and went back to the Rec. This time the answer was
that the Recreation staff would consider the possibility of
opening one of its social rooms in about three months. As it
turned out, however, the church started using the facility only
one month later. The Recreation Centre provided the fellowship with three small rooms that could be opened into one
large room. In this attractive and comfortable space, the
group began to meet every Sunday morning for worship,
prayer and teaching.

A *church* in a recreation centre?

Despite obvious physical advantages, the rooms occupied by New Life Brixton are not ideal, since many people think buildings rather than people when they talk about 'church'. In the year of New Life Assembly's existence in Brixton, that old view of church has shifted so that members now see church as meaning the people. In this particular church are gathered a great variety of people: Africans from Nigeria, West Indians from Jamaica and Barbados, and English people. (Even two Chinese people come as visitors!) Lovell aims under the guidance of the Holy Spirit to create a multi-racial church that can include single-parent families, single and married folk, teenagers who are seeking God, and many children who come with their parents. There is room, too, for married women whose husbands do not know the Lord. Two stories will serve to illustrate . . .

Deloris

Deloris is a member of the Dulwich branch of New Life Assembly who came to Christ in 1972. The events that led to her conversion make quite a story. She was happily married with children, but her sorrows arose from the fact that her husband was struggling with alcohol. Inevitably, this led to problems both with the children and with money.

During this time, Deloris found comfort by listening to gospel and other religious music. As a child, she had always been encouraged to go to church—as have most adult West Indians—but she had never made a personal commitment to Jesus Christ.

Before Deloris had left Jamaica in 1961, a local pastor had spent some time with her and had encouraged her not to neglect church attendance. He promised that he would not cease to pray for her to become a committed believer. His prayers were indeed answered, for eleven years later, when working in England as a secretary, she made friends at work with Beryl Gardner—a Christian. Beryl invited Deloris to a baptismal service at which she herself would be a candidate. Accepting the invitation, she went to the service.

It was an exciting time for her, and in her heart she entertained a secret desire to be baptised. As the evening unfolded, she became more and more convicted of her sin and began to weep. The candidates were baptised, and as the last one left the pool, the young minister baptising them gave an appeal for any who had come that night not intending to be baptised, but who had met Christ during the service, to come forward to the front and be baptised.

Deloris went forward that Saturday night into the waters of baptism to obey the Lord. This was an answer to prayer, since earlier that week in the quietness of her home she had prayed for God to deliver her from all her problems at home. That deliverance came in the baptismal waters five days later as she surrendered to Christ and 'buried' her old life in the baptismal pool.

Deloris is now a housegroup leader in the Dulwich church. Has her home life changed? Yes—although her husband and children have not yet become Christians, their home is more settled than it ever has been with her husband earning steadily now and the children communicating freely with their parents. (In times past they had run away from home vowing never to come back.) Deloris has found real relief from the depression that had haunted her earlier in her married years. As a community, the New Life Assemblies thank God for prayer and for Jesus.

Sheila and Sarah

Friendships in the fellowship cross racial boundaries in a wonderful way that witnesses to the power of God's Spirit. Sheila is a regular member of the Brixton fellowship and met Lovell through her sister Ceciel, who is a member of the Dulwich group. One day Sheila's husband, Michael, introduced her to a long-lost school friend of his called Paul, and to Paul's wife, Sarah. Though Sarah is not a West Indian, she and Sheila struck up a warm friendship; and at Sheila's invitation, Sarah visited the Brixton church and eventually gave her life to Christ. She now brings her children to church. Her friendship with Sheila proves that God's love transcends racial differences, and the church is praying that Sarah's husband will soon join the rest of the family.

Not just playing games!

As a community placed squarely in the heart of Brixton, the church feels it is called to minister to the many desperate needs of its own area. Among the most severe needs are housing for those within and without the group, and for employment. The church is now praying for what Lovell calls a 'livelihood centre', which would contain a nursery, a canteen and a day-care facility, as well as skills training in such things as typing and sewing.

The church also prays that it will be enabled to reach out to drug addicts—not only to help them overcome their habit, but also to establish a rehabilitation centre. They are praying, too, for the means to set up a half-way house for homeless single mothers. They pray that the Lord will enable them to offer facilities for training, child care and—eventually—employment.

In only a year ... ?

How can such dreams and visions be brought to reality? With its origins in housegroup meetings and other small local gatherings, New Life Assembly has developed a bond of fellowship and caring. Members have a sense of belonging together, a desire to pray and share the word together. As well as worshipping together, they enjoy meeting for occasional social evenings. Outsiders are attracted by the warmth, welcome and togetherness—especially in a society which is broken and not oriented towards *people*. The brokenness of Brixton does not inflict itself on the Afro-Caribbean community alone, but also on white families in the area, so the fellowship is seeking to provide a haven for many who feel cut-off and marginalised in society—whatever their race.

Katherine

Katherine was one person who felt isolated when she first came to England with her husband and settled in London. A West Indian, and a hairdresser by trade, she became a committed Christian in this country. Her husband, however, did not share her faith and lived a life that made Katherine unhappy. She turned to God for help, and many of her friends joined in agreement to pray for them. They spent hours, days, and even a night in prayer and fasting, asking God to be merciful and to save him. The prayers went on even when no change seemed to come.

One day, however—miraculously—Katherine's husband reluctantly accepted an invitation to a service at the church Katherine was attending. There he came under conviction of his sin and gave his life to Christ on the spot! Prayer had brought this man to the Lord and had rescued a marriage. Katherine and her husband are now housegroup leaders in the Dalston church.

Prayer: the basis

At the basis of all the caring, all the evangelism, is prayer. From the very beginning, New Life Assemblies in Dulwich, Dalston, Tottenham and Brixton have given themselves to prayer. In the beginning, prayer groups consisted mainly of elderly folk who were praying alone. There are now several different regular prayer times. At the end of each month, for example, there is a time of fasting and prayer after the Sunday morning meetings. Although this is voluntary, at least 50% of the group attend. In addition, the pattern of housegroup meetings continues. Sunday morning meetings include times of individual prayer, open prayer, and small group prayer. Also, leaders meet every Monday at Lovell's house. At those times, visitors from local Anglican, West-Indian and other

churches join them: Doug Williams from Dulwich, Glen
Thompson from Dalston, and Mrs Daphne Marsh from
Tottenham. This regular pattern of meetings, however, is
pushed aside for urgent times of prayer whenever these are
necessary. In all things, New Life Brixton has found its very
survival depends on prayer.

This enthusiasm and conviction for prayer began at the
grass roots in the housegroups but eventually brought change
throughout the church's pattern of worship. The fellowship
felt that music was essential to the development of its prayer
life and so prayed very specifically for musicians. Prayers
were answered as Lloyd, Josephine, Dorothy, Wayne and
Gwen all came forward with gifts in a variety of musical
instruments such as the saxophone, violin, piano and guitar.
It was also felt that the corporate prayer life of the group
would be greatly enhanced by the development of worship
leaders. Carol Mohabir and Sonia Brown came forward so
that now, in the Sunday morning meeting, music and prayer
interweave and flow together as the Holy Spirit speaks to the
fellowship in the quietness of everyone's heart. As one visitor
once said, 'It's hard to tell where the music ends and prayer
begins,' just as it's sometimes hard to tell where the sea ends
and the sky begins on the horizon.

Prayer also informs the many activities of smaller groupings within the church. Various individuals and groups make
pastoral visits to those in need in Brixton. They work toward
a solution for the problems they encounter and report back to
the church to ask for prayer and advice. A choir group has
grown up from the New Life Assemblies; this leads worship at
celebration times. Recently, for example, the church held a
series of celebrations at Brixton Town Hall. This choir group
also practises regularly and sings in concerts and on tour.
Recently when Lovell went on a mission to Sweden, the choir
accompanied him. The choir has also sung at charity and
fund-raising events to raise money for those with sickle cell
anaemia.

The church supports the choir in prayer and also prays for
the establishment of a youth group in Brixton. As part of its

social ministry, the church commits itself in prayer, too, for its
work among children. During Sunday morning meetings,
responsibilities revolve between different members of the
church. The multi-racial membership of the church is reflected in the mixture of those who give care to the children. In
particular Robin Lucas, an Englishman, Janice Zvimba and
Sonia Brown take a pivotal role.

How shall we tell them?

Committed to reaching out into Brixton, New Life Assembly
is obviously not solely involved in a social ministry, but also in
evangelism. The church is praying for a multi-racial membership of 1,000 members in the Brixton assembly. They are
praying that they will be able to proclaim boldly the Kingdom
of God and support their evangelistic work through prayer
groups which meet faithfully during the week or more before
an evangelistic campaign. Evangelism is also supported by a
back-up prayer team praying individually for those who are
out on the street working door to door, in the underground
station, and in the open-air market. So far there have been
four evangelistic campaigns in Brixton. In Dulwich the housegroups spent three solid months in concentrated prayer for
the establishing of the work in the Brixton area.

All this work is supported by a faithful prayer group
of mainly older women who meet regularly on Mondays at
Mrs Daisy Grant's house to pray for the church leaders, for
those in need, and for all evangelistic work. Meanwhile Doug
Williams of the Dulwich fellowship has conducted several
seminars on prayer which are open to all members of the New
Life Assemblies.

The prayer life of New Life Assembly is not rooted in any
specific tradition. It may take many forms—stillness, singing
(as we have seen), communal and individual prayer. Members of the church see prayer as a calling, as prompted by
the Holy Spirit. New members are encouraged in their
local housegroup to learn to pray quite naturally. Both
in housegroups and in one-to-one counselling sessions,

encouragement and assurance are given to enable the new believer to grow and flourish in a life of prayer.

Any answers?

Perhaps the beginning of many answered prayers in all the New Life Assemblies goes back to when Lovell Bent gave his life to Jesus Christ. At the time, he had a serious speech handicap and longed to communicate his new-found faith to his friends and colleagues.

Lovell had been born the eldest son of a seven-child West Indian family. Prematurely born, he weighed under three pounds. His development was slow as a result, and at two years old he had still not taken his first step. Crawling around the house one day, he discovered a can of kerosene oil and drank some. This tragic accident kept him in a state of unconsciousness for three days with a very low pulse rate and a locked jaw. The local doctor came but could give little encouragement to the family.

As the family gathered on the third day, expecting to have to plan a funeral, Lovell's older sister climbed up on the bed next to her brother and began to call him. He responded! His movements were slight but enough to give the family renewed hope. Lovell then recovered, though he was left with a severe speech impediment. His family took him to several speech specialists but were counselled to accept the condition. Then came Lovell's conversion. A year later, he prayed that the Lord would loose his tongue so that he could use his mouth to give glory to God. After this prayer, he was fully healed and now speaks fluently.

Less dramatic but equally important answers to prayer have been seen throughout the short life of New Life Assembly. Lovell sees the sense of calling in 1985 in itself to be an answer to the prayers of many unknown people in South London in the early 80s. The planting out of one fellowship after another was a further illustration of God's desire to answer when his people pray according to his will.

Prayers for a place to worship have been answered twice in

the last two years. When the Dulwich group began, it had no place of its own, but one member of the group insisted that God had given a vision of a door to which he would provide the key—a door that no one could shut. Later, Lovell drove past a Methodist church in Dulwich whose board showed only a telephone number. Curious, he dialled the number and subsequently went to meet the Revd Clive Pugh, the Methodist minister. In fact the Methodists were about to move to another building, so the Dulwich fellowship was able to use the premises. 'It was prayer that brought us there,' says Lovell, 'and it is prayer that has given us that building.' As already described, the Lord also answered prayer for a place of worship in Brixton.

In all cases, though New Life Assembly has had little or no money to support its work, God has supplied the need. In the beginning, for example, there was no money for a full-time leader. Now Doug Williams is employed full time by the church, and Lovell Bent hopes to give up his job at London Transport within the next year to devote himself to full-time leadership and ministry.

Prayer, the key

The key to prayer is not 'how to pray' but just simply to pray. Lovell encourages members in all the New Life Assemblies to pray in their own way without worrying about others' perception of their prayers. Teaching focuses on showing members that God is not listening to how they pray but to what they say. Lovell teaches that although there are some who are called to be great prayer warriors, we are all called to talk to God.

The Lord's Prayer contains the line 'thy Kingdom come'. New Life Assembly in Brixton has seen the beginning of God's Kingdom coming in Brixton. From the ashes of the riots in Brixton a few years ago has arisen a small body of Christ that reflects in its variety and commitment to its local community the love of the Lord Jesus Christ. New life has come to Dulwich, Dalston, Tottenham and Brixton. Members wonder where the next church planting will be and look forward eagerly to the guidance of the Holy Spirit as they give themselves again and again to God in prayer.

Chapter 10

Stoke Holy Cross and Dunston

Norwich, Norfolk

David Broome

Devoted prayer and a delicious sense of humour characterise this warm chapter from near Norwich. Four miles south of the city, Stoke Holy Cross consists of 1,450 inhabitants, five farms, a school, an evangelical chapel, one shop-cum-post office, a pub, and two Anglican churches. A few local families have remained in the area for generations, but many (including the writer of this chapter) are drawn from the four corners of the country and indeed the earth.

David Broome and his congregation have truly seen the 'God of Surprises' at work: healing, sending angelic visitors and in many other ways. But, as he says himself, they 'have no hot-line to heaven', and have wept with others suffering financial, marital and employment problems without seeing apparent answers to prayer. They have concerned themselves with faith-raising more than fund-raising; David says, 'Cirrhosis of the giver will not be cured by thermometer theology.'

As a young man, David prayed that he would be able to play football for Derby County. God had other ideas and sent him first to the National Coal Board, then to Aden as a medical

*orderly in the RAF, and eventually back to Britain to marry
Monica ('Since I have no degree in theology, I married
one!'). They have three children and enjoy looking after their
garden pond.*

'Twenty minutes a day,' the monk had said. That was The
Rule of Life—the Rule for personal prayer—for ordinands.
The year was 1959, the first of six I spent training for the
priesthood of the Church of England with the Mirfield
Fathers, an Anglican order in West Yorkshire. I am a compulsive talker, but now I found myself gagged before God.
I previously prayed when I was in church or when I was
in special need. At the Community of the Resurrection I
learned to love the trappings of High Church worship: the
bells and smells, the plain chant and the colours—the whole
choreography of catholicism was poetry in motion. Personal
prayer I found much more difficult in spite of many sermons
on spirituality by the brothers. They wanted us to be men of
prayer first and men of letters only after that (which was
useful consolation, as I only got a third class degree). The
Mirfield library contained every spiritual classic that was
worth having, and I wish now that I had read more of them.

Putting on the habit

A monk's robes are called a habit, and even though I never
wore one, I learned from them the habit of daily prayer. This
habit has never left me; it has been the thin red line through
my life ever since. After ten years in holy orders, however,
the mechanical habit was all that I had between myself and
complete unbelief. I am glad that I persisted during those
hard times, because without the daily attempt to meet God, I
would have completely crumbled. I was vicar of a down-town
parish in Leeds which had been described in a book by
Geoffrey Moorhouse as 'the bottom of the social pile, however that pile is constructed'. I often sat in that beautiful

Temple Moore church before a carved oak crucifix with the inscription beneath: 'Pray, love and witness, and never lose heart.' But I had hit the buffers.

In this moment of need I met Jesus in a new and living way. In this I was helped by a spiritual millionaire called Harry Cooke. This quiet and confident man led my wife and myself to the Lord, which is a strange thing to say when you are a Christian leader! I know how Nicodemus felt: 'Are you a master of Israel without knowing these things?' Yes, I needed to be born again. I had resisted all this 'evangelical' talk as I resisted Harry himself. I was jealous that his church was full and mine was empty.

I had asked many others for help, but I can honestly say that this dapper ch p with the Northern Ireland brogue was the first who had really prayed with me. He said that he was not qualified in psychiatry, medicine or social work, but he could pray for me to be filled with the Holy Spirit. He did. And I was! It was like breaking out of the Bermuda Triangle. I was lost and now was found. Prayer, daily offices and Communion had a new reality about them. The Bible became compulsive reading for the first time.

While reading the book of Joel behind the locked doors of the church early one morning, I tried speaking in tongues. I wanted to be alone to try this because, then, as now, I was a little bit diffident about exercising this gift in public. I thought it was best done between consenting adults in private! I love the description of *glossalalia* given by a tough, untutored youth: 'You get so close to God that you begin to talk his language.' This may not satisfy the doubters, but I now know exactly what the young man meant.

I first encountered singing in the Spirit at a convent in Harrogate where two hundred Roman Catholics met once a month under the leadership of a lively sister whom I unkindly nicknamed 'the bionic nun'. This was indeed the music of heaven, and I am not surprised to find that plainsong is a stylisation of the early church's singing in the Spirit. With my Mirfield background, no wonder I liked it.

For me, the new meeting with the Holy Spirit was like

finding a Heineken God who refreshed the parts that had been dry for so long! I know that charismatics make many mistakes and often give the impression that we have a special hot-line to heaven; that is something we must cure. Yes, I found that I had, to some extent, changed one set of problems for another; but these were at least problems of life and not of death. I had gained a new boldness to pray.

Stepping out in prayer

We began to pray about jobs. Five minutes after Michael and I had prayed in a pub near Armley Prison, an old acquaintance came in and offered him a job! At one time, I got so 'high' on job prayers that I felt like the Lord's labour exchange. Four 'unemployables' found jobs after prayer. During one service, I wept to see an unopened wage packet on the offertory plate. This thank offering was the most tangible testimony to our heavenly Father's providence.

The visit of the Fisherfolk to our Leeds church was amazing. When scores of big churches were asking them to come and being turned down, they heard of our church of thirty people and asked to come down to a smaller church 'where the rubber met the road'. After that I was joined by a group of young adults, and it was a joy to have Communion and breakfast at 7 am on Tuesdays. There was joy in all these things, but there was opposition, too, and one man told me openly that he could not wait for me to leave. This hurt, but I told him that only the Lord would shift me.

Such a move was to happen sooner than I expected. After eight years I came to Stoke Holy Cross and Dunston because of what I can only term 'prayer at both ends'. In previous moves I had followed my own instincts, but now it was different. In Leeds, Harry Cooke and I asked God about a move; and here in Norfolk, bless them, there was a small praying group, asking for the right man to be sent as vicar. When they saw who God had sent, some must have reflected that 'God moves in mysterious ways'!

Dear reader, have you ever found yourself to be the answer

to a prayer? I found myself as God's gift to Stoke Holy Cross. Far from being a source of pride, it was a very humbling and big responsibility. We are all, if we think about it, God's gift to someone or somewhere.

House of healing

If I was God's gift to them, then the forty worshippers at Stoke and the ten at Dunston were heaven-sent for me. Their welcome was wonderful. We have never known such kindness and co-operation. The churchwardens have been twenty-two-carat gold—supporting me in everything and often keeping me on the rails with wisdom I did not possess. Without them and the gracious church council who have faithfully followed even when they really didn't know where they were going, nothing that follows would in any way have been possible.

My predecessor had been vicar for twenty-one years. He had left no problems with finance or fabric and had taken brave decisions to introduce a new service of Holy Communion at Stoke, also to install an electric organ. I am grateful for his foresight in these and other matters.

'Not by might, not by power, but by my Spirit, says the Lord of hosts' (Zech 4:6, RSV). This text on the invitation card at my induction was, I told the people, God's manifesto for the parish. To start with, a little scene-shifting at Stoke church was necessary. In this small medieval building, which only holds 120 people, there was not enough room to swing a censer around. (Good job I had left the incense behind at Leeds!) We moved the organ and some pews and stretched a few loyalties by moving the chancel screen to form a vestry. Switching from the sublime to the substantial, we installed a toilet and a kitchen, and rounded it all off with pink carpeting throughout.

A friend, Roger Lacey, made the exquisite new nave altar in oak and cloth of gold. These alterations did not suit everyone, and I knew that the forthcoming church council meeting would be crucial. God spoke to me in the readings at morning prayer on the day of that meeting. The daily office is a blessing to Anglican clergy, and—even though I often say it mechanically and sometimes miss it altogether—I will never let it go because on many days, like this one, it has contained God's message for me, even when I am least expecting it. In the first lesson were the words, 'But now don't be discouraged, any of you. Do the work, for I am with you' (Haggai 2:4). I cannot explain how the musings of a minor Israeli prophet nearly three thousand years ago could have any relevance to a village vicar who was moving the furniture around in his church. It seems too much like Bible Bingo, choosing texts at random out of their context and making a pretext. All I can say is that the words lifted me out of anxiety into calm rejoicing. I stood alone in the church and sang out praise to God. The meeting produced general agreement on all essentials.

Renewal changes lives, not liturgies. If we reordered the church without reordering lives, this would merely be to rearrange the deckchairs on the Titanic. Mission England 1983 started to reorder lives. Each of the 600 dwellings in the parish was canvassed, and we sent a coach every night.

In spite of such efforts, we saw only one convert reach Christian maturity. It would have been worth all the effort just to reach that man, who is now a key part of our worship, but God has always had even more for us. Billy Graham said something that registered with many of our regular congregation who went to hear him: 'If you go to a fire station, that doesn't make you into a fire engine, and if you go to church all your life, that doesn't automatically make you a Christian.' Several of our leaders came to walk more closely with God, especially in the preparatory Christian Life and Witness Classes. Mission England invested these gentle and un demonstrative people with a new boldness. They began to pray and share their faith with one another.

We all gained a new vision of God's healing power with the yearly visits of Fred Smith. This patriarchal ex-policeman conducted services in the same unobtrusive manner he would previously have adopted when giving evidence in court.

There was no sense of sensationalism at all, and yet as that mighty man of God prayed, they came out in streams to give their lives to the Lord. They often fell on the new carpet (good job we had it) and rested serenely in the Spirit. Many were healed—too many to tell.

I remember one lady who came back from the sanctuary holding up her skirt after losing an 8lb growth from her stomach. Many of the wonders trickled back to us after weeks and even months. One lady, the cousin of a bishop, experienced acute pain after Fred had prayed with her. This was because her back was now straight, and her support jacket was 'killing' her. One of our church councillors remarked about those meetings: 'In biblical times, God healed through Jesus—this we read. Recently, we witnessed God's healing power at work through Fred Smith. We were privileged to see it with our own eyes.' The best result of all this was that some local Christians now ventured out into healing and saw that God could answer their prayers as well as the entreaties of Fred Smith.

Peter Adams of Diss Community Church has helped us in many things, and he emphasised that we should all expect to be used by God as we prayed for one another. Although healings here are not in any sense a weekly occurrence, there has been victory over cancer, leukemia, depression, chest complaints, eye complaints, a knee locked for fifteen years, severe stomach and back problems. They have all yielded to prayer from myself and others. Sometimes we only hear of the healings a long time afterwards, and I hope that it is not too heretical to think that if St Luke had waited a while, he might have been able to record the thanksgivings of even more of the ten lepers who were healed! God answers prayer for other things, too; and prayers involving money, marriage, education, employment, in-laws, cars (among other things) have all been answered from time to time.

I have heard also of cases of absent healing, as when Fred Smith prayed for a girl in New Zealand and she was healed. Here is a case, however, of what I can only term 'absent evangelism'. The writer is a civil engineer.

The transformation came about through a series of meetings, although I did not attend one of them! Sue, my wife, decided to support the vicar by attending just one of them, but after the first one she was hooked. She returned brandishing a book called *The Happiest People on Earth*[1] and spoke enthusiastically of people who had given their testimony. My reaction was that it was fine for her, but certainly not for me.

When she went out to a later meeting, I picked up the book and began to read it. This was strange because I do not usually read books unless I have to, but I could not put it down—until Sue came home, when I put it down quickly! When she went out to the next meeting, I started to read again; and as I did so, a strange tingling ran through me, and I was overcome with emotion as I began to accept the truth about Jesus as explained in the book.

I talked about it later with Sue, only to find that on that night several people had prayed that I would accept Jesus into my life. What an encouragement to them that their prayers had been answered in such a direct way—praise the Lord!

No heavenly hot-line

We have no hot-line to heaven, however, and our mistakes and failures remind us of this. We have prayed every Sunday for six years, and on many other occasions too, for two young men—without their condition altering at all. Many have died in spite of our prayers. The wife of a lorry driver who died with cancer had to console me rather than my comforting her. I have also made false claims that someone has been healed, and then they have got worse or died. (Now I see why the Catholic authorities at Lourdes and similar places are so careful when claiming miraculous cures.) Why are some people healed while others are left in their sickness?

'Has God got favourites, David?' said a man whose wife had just died, even though she had been prayed for many times and by many people.

'God has no favourites, and I have no answers' was my reply. I have no idea why some prayers are answered while others seem to lie in the Lord's 'pending' tray for ages. Of one thing I am very sure, though: if we pray, we get some answers;

while if we don't, we get none at all. That's why we carry on praying.

When I feel 'low' because prayer seems to be unanswered, the memory of what I call 'the angel prayer' lifts my spirits. A lad, newly converted, was being drawn to the Jehovah's Witnesses by his family. At that time I was reading a book about angels and, because I am a slave to my latest book, everyone was getting angels for breakfast, dinner and tea. Angels were called in as we prayed for this situation with a group of youth leaders. I prayed that the Lord would send an angel to the lad's family.

God so often takes us at our word. We only learned months afterwards that an angelic visitor had appeared to Dad in his bath and that eventually they had joined a church in their village. The boy did not know about our prayers, and the father certainly did not know. I have never seen an angel myself, but the whole episode rings true because lives were changed. They would be, wouldn't they?

Dreaming dreams

'A great banqueting table has been set before you. It is full of good things, groaning under the weight of the most wonderful food. Rejoice and eat your fill instead of just standing there, picking at the food and scarcely tasting it!' This was an interpretation given after one of the few occasions when anyone in the church has spoken publicly in tongues. It was given by Fred Smith and has been remembered ever since because we are still quite restrained in many ways. God also spoke to us through Tim Lenton at our first parish holiday weekend in 1988 when he said, 'You cannot be worshipping God and criticising people at the same time.' This struck a chord with many of us and sent us to our knees!

God has spoken with prophetic impact in other ways. A retired inspector of schools saw in a dream many young people being baptised, after which the young people's work has slowly picked up. Upper Stoke is separated from the rest of the village by half a mile of open country, and recently a nurse received a picture with Bible texts for that part of the village. It seemed as if walls were being rebuilt. Soon after this, seven new people started to come to the church from one road in that area.

The Lord also used a Mothers' Union banner in the Cathedral to tell us that he had great things in store for Dunston. Fortnightly on Fridays, four of us have met for the last four years for house Communion in a delightful white-walled cottage where the birds sing in summer and a fire roars in winter. We often mention every one of the Dunston's fifty residents in prayer, as well as several who come to worship here from other villages. I am convinced that revival has come to St Remigius' Church because of such persevering prayer. The congregation of over twenty includes all age groups and attitudes. In this delightful medieval church, tucked away in a wood, the totally traditional service has not changed for many years, but the Spirit has moved us on light years. Here there has been healing and salvation. We even had someone answer an altar call in the middle of Matins. This was given by a visiting lay reader while I was away and should, I think, go into the *Guinness Book of Records*.

Recently, however, the Lord showed me a picture of a military aircraft racing along a jungle airstrip. It had not taken off. That's us. We are gathering speed but have not taken off. Many areas remain untouched as yet—fasting, for instance. I am like John Wimber: 'a fat man on my way to heaven'[2] (the similarity ends there!). My feeble attempts are restricted to Lent, Good Friday and other sporadic outbursts. When I am more proficient at abstinence I will preach it with conviction to others and then many doors will open.

Overcoming

'Pray always that impossibilities may be overcome.' This was a word from the Lord that sums up his mighty provision for our Sunday School, which has flourished entirely because of prayer. Stoke Holy Cross parish church is right on the edge of the village and, like many Norfolk churches, it is far away from the centre of population. There are no adjoining buildings for use as Sunday Schools. We think it right that children should have appropriate worship and teaching in a place near the church so that they can join in the last part of the Parish Communion. God must have thought so too because, although he did not move heaven and earth, he moved two Portakabins for us.

These had been in Essex and were moved to the Norwich Union cricket ground just after they had been noticed by one of our people. On the cricket ground, they were used as a temporary pavilion but were then offered to us in beautiful condition for only £200 each. Red tape disappeared amazingly quickly, as permissions from the diocese and planning authorities that would normally have taken six months took—in the case of one legal document—only three days (including postage to Sussex to be signed and returned by a lawyer).

'Pray Always That Impossibilities may be Overcome.' The capitals spell PATIO. This thought from the Lord came to a teacher as we considered the additional expense of rounding off the whole teaching area with a patio. The thought spurred us on, as did another beautiful picture of children dancing, but I have to say that the project also involved a lot of hard work by certain people and the willingness of a generous and far-sighted church council, who agree with me that these children are not tomorrow's church—they are today's.

Even as I write, I am moved by a teacher's story of how a child shared his problems about a family bereavement. It is because of such precious encounters that God wants us to overcome the impossibilities in prayer.

A cynic in the pub asked me how I got the money in, 'Will you put up a thermometer outside the church?' he asked.

'If we put the temperature up, the thermometer can stay down,' was my reply. Cirrhosis of the giver will not be cured by thermometer theology. Hudson Taylor advocated faith-raising not fund-raising. He said, 'God's work done in God's way will not lack supply.' At Stoke Holy Cross, and in Leeds, in two very different situations, I have found this to be true.

Not everyone was happy when we left the plate at the back instead of passing it round. It was thought that 'we might miss a few'. Others are even now unhappy that we no longer have the Gift Day, when people bring donations to church during the course of the day. Financially, though, I have no regrets, though I know that some people who do not attend services used to kneel at the altar rail after giving their gifts. (Any opportunity that we lose for people to kneel before their Lord is worrying to me.)

We have never prayed for money, but our needs have been met, and we have helped to meet the needs of Christ's work in the wider world. Last year our direct giving rose by 57% and our giving to charity has, over the years, risen from nothing to over 10%. The church council has now agreed that we will keep no large surpluses.

Catching a yeti?

Prayer groups are not a panacea for progress. Indeed, we have struggled at times. Over fifty from the church family are in one kind of mid-week meeting or another. Some of these attend meetings run in other villages. The Sunday Gospel is usually read and studied at some point.

There is much love and sharing. My wife writes:

> Our Tuesday group grew from the meeting that existed before we came. It is composed of five ladies over sixty years of age and four between thirty-five and forty-five. One of the plus factors is the guidance and encouragement that older members can give to the others. This mixture of ages is a very positive thing. There have been several answers to prayer, but the loving concern between us is a blessing in itself.

One of the senior members of the group tells us more about some of the answered prayer: 'I asked for prayer for a physically disabled child and also for the grandparents, who were drifting apart. We prayed for several weeks, and I also left the prayer on the altar with Jesus. Our prayers were answered; they are again a loving couple. The baby is not healed, but there is a new love in the whole family.'

The leader of the Friday meeting at Upper Stoke says that everyone can now take part and pray in his or her own words. This group and others know that God does understand language other than the jargon of parsonical prayerspeak. My dream ticket for the church family here is that everyone should be involved in a mid-week meeting of some kind, but for various reasons this has not come about, and in reality I have as much chance of catching a yeti. However, I am encouraged at several informal prayer groups that have sprung up. As I took the draft of this chapter to one house, I stumbled upon three ladies meeting for a few minutes of prayer after going swimming together. Others are increasingly meeting for meals or a drink of coffee, and I know that prayer bonds are formed at such times. Other body-building ventures include Christmas parties with 200 invitations, beach parties, barbecues and visits to the churchwarden's farm to see the new lambs. These maintain closeness in a family that is drawn from a wider area than the village itself. We know that 'the family that prays together stays together'.

'The vicar's lost his place again!'

Silence is golden because it allows God to get a word in edgeways. Quiet periods in worship can also make worshippers nervous—they sometimes think I have lost my place again!

A retired priest who comes occasionally always says that he enjoys the silences. I hope there are other things that help him too. We need more of this silence; we have failed the church by producing liturgies which never use one word where two will do. A young business man has just asked me to consider a contemplative group, and I believe that more contemplation would have stemmed the exodus into transcendental meditation and yoga, which take people out of the world and separate one part of consciousness from another. Christian contemplation, on the other hand, is a great unifier, where soul and body meet again.

Our annual Quiet Day, led by Howard Norton of Quiet

Waters Retreat House, in Bungay, has always given much blessing to the twenty or so people who have come. The services on the Sunday after that have always seemed to have a little bit more glory in them, at least to my mind. I was also encouraged at the number of people who went to a prayer workshop on our Family Holiday Weekend. All this shows the increased interest in personal prayer, as does the evidence of copies of *Every Day With Jesus* in more and more houses, or the well-thumbed *Good News* Bible on the top of the television set in the house of a man for whom prayer, combined with enlightened Christian social work, has really worked wonders. All this shows that more and more people are coming to God in prayer.

Freedom of speech in services is another hope that is slowly being realised. Time is increasingly made for testimonies and individual contributions. On one glorious occasion, people fell over themselves to speak in the intercessions, not in the least restrained by the presence of our archdeacon. One day, we pray that this will be the rule rather than the exception. Meanwhile, the still silent majority are heard through the medium of the prayer basket which is brought up at the start of each service. The slips of paper placed therein are read out later, and have provided some of the most memorable parts of our offering to God.

A praying people

One night, someone asked me to pray with him over a family dispute. Neither of us realised as we prayed that the family was featured in our prayer calendar for the next day. The calendar is a kind of parish prayer wheel on which the name of a different household in the congregation appears each weekday. Each week also, we focus on a street in the village, a local or church organisation, or one of the causes supported from our parish tithe, as well as different countries of the world. Preparation of the calendar every three months—so that everyone has one—is a labour of love but well worth while. It is quite wonderful how often names crop up on the calendar just when we most need to pray for those people. No one will convince me that this is coincidence. Like William Temple, I find that the 'coincidences' surrounding prayer happen far too often for me to believe they are mere chance. The prayer calendar also helps me to be reasonably systematic in visiting the worshipping congregation.

We do not share the peace in the service as some churches do. We ceased doing this in deference to those brothers and sisters who found it too embarrassing. I know full well, though, that the scene I will now describe is, for us, a richer expression of God's *shalom* than the exchange of peace we gave up: picture the scene after a recent service, which is fairly typical. As people chatted over coffee, children dodged here and there, grinding broken biscuits into the carpet as they went. Against this general background were a few groups of two or three, some talking earnestly. In one case there was a supporting arm around a friend who was in tears. At the Communion rail, two men knelt together in prayer.

Comings and goings

Harry Cooke taught me a prayer which I say before each service;

> Lord, bring along to this church those whom you want to be here, and keep away those whose needs are to be met elsewhere.

God is faithful, he has brought people here from different backgrounds and through different routes. One lady came here when she talked to a Christian about buying a house. She did not buy the property—it wasn't even in this village—but, as she says, 'Jesus used an indirect route to lead me back into the Anglican Communion, giving me the extra gift of a dear sister in the Lord. Thank you, Lord.' 'Commit your way unto the Lord, trust in him and he will act' (Psalm 37:5, AV).

Not all of us are card-carrying charismatics; there is a rich mix of peoples and ideas, and this has caused tensions which can only be overcome by love. In our worship, for instance, the would-be arm-wavers keep a low profile out of respect for brothers who think differently. Such sensitivity has avoided any we/they situation, but—even so—a few have left us. In spite of the fact that this hurts us a lot, we have to try to part on good terms and, if at all possible, ensure that no one leaves without a blessing. We know that God is faithful and that their needs will be met elsewhere.

The last word

One of our failings has been in the area of persistent prayer. When no answers arrive, it is all too easy to let things slip off the front page of petition in the same way that newspaper headlines disappear. The opposite fault is to have people on a list for years, and in one case of this we all finished up with no idea of who it was we were praying for or what had happened as a result. If we kept people informed more, then we would be encouraged to pray more.

I am sad that our churches are locked by order of insurers. I know of one woman who never attends church who was in the throes of a divorce. She went to Stoke church for sanctuary after a domestic disagreement, but she found it locked and beat on the doors in frustration. One day we might build up a regular prayer vigil, similar to the lovely Maundy Thursday watch, which would keep the church open for some of the time and provide a prayer chain as well.

The best things in prayer are rightly known only to God. Jesus tells us that 'Your Father, who sees what you do in private, will reward you' (Mt 6:6,GNB). I now know that nothing is worth the effort of doing without prayer. Even the invitation to write this chapter was put out to prayer by people in the parish. Only then did I say yes.

A mural of Bible scenes that was painted on our church hall wall sums it all up: 'We may make our plans, but God has the last word' (Prov 16:1).

Notes

[1]   Ed John and Elizabeth Sherrill, (Hodder & Stoughton: 1977).
[2]   '"I'm just a fat man trying to get to heaven" says the jovial John Wimber . . .' See Edward England's editorial, *Renewal* (Oct/Nov 1985); p 3.

British Church Growth Association

The British Church Growth Association was formed in September 1981 by a widely representative group of Christians committed to church growth either as researchers, teachers, practitioners or consultants. Following the Lausanne Congress on World Evangelisation in 1974, much interest was aroused in Church Growth thinking, which in turn led to the first UK Church Growth Consultation in 1978. Also during the 1970s a number of denominations had taken some church growth thinking and developed it within their own networks. A number of theological colleges and Bible colleges also began to teach church growth theory, particularly in their missiology departments. The Bible Society had begun to develop church growth courses that were being received enthusiastically. Developments in the work of the Evangelical Alliance led to the setting up of a Church Growth Unit and the publication of a *Church Growth Digest.* This unit drew together a number of leaders involved in the church growth field, but it was agreed to widen its impact by the formation of an association which would be even more comprehensive and effective.

Definition

Church Growth investigates the nature, function, structure, health and multiplication of Christian churches as they relate to the effective implementation of Christ's commission to 'Go then to all peoples everywhere and make them my disciples' (Matt 28:19). Church Growth seeks to combine the revealed truths of the Bible with related insights from the contemporary social and behavioural sciences. Although not linked to any one school of church growth it owes much to the formational thinking of Dr Donald McGavran.

Aims

The BCGA aims to help and encourage the Church in Britain to move into growth in every dimension. The facilities and resources of the BCGA are available to researchers, consultants, teachers, practitioners and those just setting out in church growth thinking. The Association endeavours to offer practical help as well as encouraging and initiating Church Growth thinking and research.

Activities

The following are among its activities:
— Producing a quarterly journal particularly geared to the British scene with practical, biblical and theoretical articles of help to the churches as well as offering a forum for the sharing of views.
— Producing a number of occasional in-depth papers on a variety of topics.
— Co-publishing books on Church Growth.
— Running a specialist Church Growth book service offering discounted books to members and producing a catalogue of recommended church growth reading.
— Operating a reference system for information and personnel.
— Organising biennial residential conferences on particular topics of Church Growth relevant to the church in this country eg Church Planting 1983, Conversion 1985, Bridge Building 1987.
— Encouraging, co-ordinating or organising lectures and seminars on particular subjects or with particular speakers which could be of help to the churches.
— Carrying out research in allied fields and building up a research register of work already done or being undertaken in various centres.
— Monitoring church growth at home and overseas.
— Linking in with a European initiative to share insights peculiar to the continent of Europe.
— Encouraging grass-roots involvement through seventeen regional groups.

Government

The Council of the BCGA is made up of fifteen elected members and seven co-opted members who meet three times a year. Although members serve in a personal capacity, the Council aims to be representative of geographical region, denomination and churchmanship, practitioner, researcher and teacher.

The day-to-day running of the Association is carried out by an officer with some secretarial assistance and the active support of members of the Council. The offices are situated in St Mark's Chambers, Kennington Park Road, London SE11 4PW and the telephone number is 01-793-0264. The BCGA is a registered charity, no 28557.

Membership

Membership of the BCGA is open to both individuals and organisations interested in or involved in the theory or practice of Church Growth. On payment of an annual subscription members are entitled to receive the *Church Growth Digest* (the journal of the Association) four times a year, information about activities through the Newsletters, special discounts on conferences and books, membership of the Church Growth Book Service, voting rights to elect members to the Council every two years, links with other researchers, teachers, practitioners, and consultants on a regional or national level as well as help or advice on allied matters.

The current subscription is £8 for individual membership and £17 for organisations or churches.

Further information about the Association and membership is available from the Secretary, British Church Growth Association, St Mark's Chambers Kennington Park Road, London SE11 4PW.